World History

A New Perspective

World History

A New Perspective

Clive Ponting

Chatto & Windus
LONDON

Published by Chatto & Windus 2000

2 4 6 8 10 9 7 5 3 1

Copyright © Clive Ponting 2000

Clive Ponting has asserted his right under the Copyright, Designs
and Patents Act 1988 to be identified as the author of this work

First published in Great Britain in 2000 by
Chatto & Windus
Random House, 20 Vauxhall Bridge Road,
London SW1V 2SA

Random House Australia (Pty) Limited
20 Alfred Street, Milsons Point, Sydney,
New South Wales 2061, Australia

Random House New Zealand Limited
18 Poland Road, Glenfield,
Auckland 10, New Zealand

Random House (Pty) Limited
Endulini, 5A Jubilee Road, Parktown 2193, South Africa

The Random House Group Limited Reg. No. 954009
www.randomhouse.co.uk

A CIP catalogue record for this book
is available from the British Library

ISBN 0-701-16834-X

Papers used by Random House are natural,
recyclable products made from wood grown in sustainable forests;
the manufacturing processes conform to the environmental
regulations of the country of origin

Typeset by SX Composing DTP, Rayleigh, Essex
Printed and bound in Great Britain by
Mackays of Chatham plc, Chatham, Kent

In memory of
Bonnie Hunter Wilkinson
(1926–1997)

Acknowledgement

I would like to thank Maxine Boobyer for drawing the superb collection of maps and charts in this book. Without them the book would be immeasurably poorer.

Contents

xii

Maps

Charts

INTRODUCTION

World History

What is world history? It is not simply a compilation of the histories of the individual states, empires and civilizations that have existed in the world. Such an approach cannot bring out the common themes within these units nor the way in which they have interacted. Neither can it trace the diffusion of knowledge and technologies between the different human communities. World history has to be constructed around common themes and developments. In doing so it needs to take account of the experience of all the different human communities without favouring that of any one group. The fundamental argument of this book is that our way of viewing the history of the world is deeply flawed and biased. Its faults stem from a profound Eurocentrism compounded with a belief in 'western civilization' as the main dynamic force in world history and the embodiment of all that is good and progressive in human societies and ways of thought. Such a view is bound to downplay or dismiss both the role and the importance of other traditions and societies; indeed the experience of the majority of the world's people. This book attempts to provide a more balanced account of human history.

One of the commonest ways of trying to write world history is to structure it around a series of 'civilizations'. One of the first to do so was Oswald Spengler whose major work was translated into English as *The Decline of the West* in 1932. It is mainly a comparison of the 'west' with the Graeco-Roman world and has few other illustrations. Spengler sees civilizations as independent entities free of external influences and with their history largely consisting of artistic and philosophical developments. Each has, from the start, a 'soul' embedded in it which pervades and directs it. The best-known work using this approach is *A Study of History* by Arnold Toynbee, published in twelve volumes over almost thirty years after the early 1930s. Toynbee was very much a product of the European world in the early twentieth century. As a Social Darwinist he argues that civilizations are like organisms. They emerge from a 'challenge and response' in the natural environment and in a struggle for survival go through a common cycle of genesis, growth, breakdown and disintegration. As an elitist he believes that the crucial element in their histories is the 'creative minority'. Others since Toynbee have produced their own systems. Pitirim Sorokin argued in *Social and Cultural Dynamics* that civilizations were 'cultural supersystems' moving in a cyclical process

I

from 'ideational' to 'sensate' and then 'idealistic'. Carroll Quigley writing in the early 1960s thought there were two different types of society – 'parasitic' and 'productive' – each with its own 'instrument of expansion'. More recently David Wilkinson has argued for a 'central civilization' which was created from the merger of Egyptian and Mesopotamian civilizations nearly four thousand years ago, and subsequently incorporated other civilizations until 1850 (when Japan was included) and a single world civilization came into existence. The best of all world histories – *The Rise of the West* by William McNeill – is also essentially 'civilizational' in approach, although it does stress the interactions between these units and the forces that have affected them all.

There are a number of problems in using this approach. Crucially, there is no agreement on what constitutes a civilization or how many there have been. Toynbee started with a list of twenty-three but by the end of his work had accumulated a different list of twenty-eight. Quigley thought there were only sixteen civilizations. Others have suggested nineteen. Thus for some historians Japan is separate from a 'Far Eastern' or Chinese civilization, for others it is not, and in some systems China is differentiated from the rest of Asia. Some identify a separate 'Minoan' civilization on Crete, others see it merely as a precursor to that of ancient Greece. There is no agreement on the existence of a separate Orthodox Christian civilization or on whether there is an Islamic one separate from its heritage of pre-existing civilizations. How groups such as the Hittites and Jews should be treated has never been resolved. About the only area of agreement is that there was a separate 'Egyptian' civilization, although its starting dates vary by over two and a half millennia and its end date by almost a millennium.

An even more fundamental problem in studying world history on the basis of civilizations is that their identification is largely based on certain features of 'high culture' – literary works (especially 'great books'), philosophy, religion and art styles – which are almost entirely the responsibility of a small elite in society (until the last few decades a majority of the world's people were illiterate). Placing the emphasis in world history on 'civilizations' therefore gives far too great an importance to these elements in human history. Closer investigation also reveals that nearly all of these 'civilizations' are made up of very different 'cultures' and languages – as for example in China or western Europe. So although it is obvious that the way in which human societies have evolved in China and in western Europe has produced very different cultures they also contain within themselves almost equally great differences. The idea that civilizations contain 'essences' which are transmitted over time has an element of truth. However, it ignores the fact that, for example, both

China and western Europe in the nineteenth century were fundamentally different in almost every respect from their condition two thousand years earlier – only a small part of a 'civilization' is actually transmitted over long periods of time. The civilizational approach with its emphasis on essentially 'intellectual' features also neglects whole areas of human history, in particular the social, economic, technological, military and strategic, each of which has its own pattern of development. It is therefore not valid to compare a civilization with one which existed several thousand years earlier because of the intervening economic, technological and social developments.

Focusing attention on individual civilizations necessarily tends to treat them as autonomous units evolving according to their own unique dynamics. It therefore ignores two fundamental features of world history. The first is the common economic and technological background to human societies. From this perspective it is far more useful to identify the similarities between human societies rather than their differences in terms of some aspects of high culture. As chapter 6 explains, many of the common rhythms in the histories of the early 'civilizations' identified by Toynbee are no more than the common features of all the early agricultural societies and empires. The second problem is the downplaying of the links between different societies together with the consequent transmission of ideas, religious beliefs and technologies. The only civilizations to develop entirely in isolation were those of the Americas. One of the central elements of world history is the way in which all the different societies have gradually been brought closer together.

Perhaps the commonest way of viewing the history of the world is to see it through the spectacles of 'western civilization'. It is a tradition deeply embedded in European culture and one that owes much to ideas of European supremacy generated in the nineteenth century. It accepts that 'civilization' first emerged in Mesopotamia and Egypt but then rapidly moves on to the more congenial field of the true origins of 'western civilization'. This is believed to be Minoan Crete and Mycenaean Greece as the precursors of 'classical' Greece and Rome. They, particularly the former, are seen as the originators of 'western' ways of thinking, which are 'rational' and 'scientific', and 'western' political traditions, in particular democracy. These attributes were uniquely transmitted to Europe. Although Islam was briefly important, it is the 'rise of Europe' from about 800, at first under the empire of Charlemagne, that produces the driving force of world history. This unique, dynamic and enterprising culture was first demonstrated in the Crusades and, after 1500, in the 'age of exploration' with the associated bringing of the benefits of European civilization to the rest of the world. It is 'western civilization' that was able to produce the 'scientific revolution', the 'industrial revolution', techno-logical progress, capitalism and the unique European political structure of rational, limited government and democracy. In this narrative China, India and the rest of the world have separate, detached histories of little wider importance until they are swept up by an advancing Europe into the 'world civilization' which it created. Europe is therefore seen as the privileged domain of world history, characterized by change and development. As the 'West' it is equivalent to the whole of the 'East' (the rest of Eurasia) which is characterized as being essentially irrational and authoritarian and static and stagnant (until the 'West' arrives). This book rejects such an approach entirely.

The problem of how to deal with western European civilization, in particular in the period after about 1500, is found not just in the 'western civilization' approach but in others also based on 'civilizations' as the key units in world history. Toynbee, having identified Western Christianity as a separate civilization, was then worried by the implications – if it was subject to the 'laws' of history, which he believed he had discovered, then it was doomed to decline. He did not like this prospect and many of the later volumes of his work are little more than musings about how this might be avoided. The global expansion of the 'civilization' which emerged in western Europe undoubtedly changed the way in which the civilizations of the world interacted. Indeed it is at this point, in the middle of the nineteenth century, that William McNeill's book draws to a somewhat unsatisfactory close. His message is, however, clear – history leads up to the 'Rise of the West' and its domination of the world.

At the beginning of the twenty-first century it is far less obvious than when McNeill was writing his book in the 1950s that this is in fact the case. In a remarkable piece of self-criticism written on the twenty-fifth anniversary of the publication of *The Rise of the West*, McNeill admitted that the major weakness of his great work was the discounting of the creation by western Europe after 1500 of an integrated world economy from which it (and its offspring in north America) was the primary beneficiary. In part this is an acceptance of the fact that any approach to world history based primarily on 'civilizations' is bound to downplay the role of economic and social history. It is also a recognition of the work of Immanuel Wallerstein since the early 1970s and his 'world systems' approach. This argues for a fundamental discontinuity in world history around 1500 with the creation by Europe of a world system of capitalism not directly related to any political empire (as previous systems of exploitation had been). In the process it restructured the world into a 'core' of wealthy, industrialized states, a 'periphery' of backward, dependent, agricultural states and a 'semi-periphery' of intermediate status. Some historians have attempted to apply the idea of different types of 'world system' to periods before 1500. They have some validity but have not been fully developed. However, Wallerstein has rejected all of these attempts and insists that the situation after 1500 is unique in world history. The problem with this approach is that it too is deeply Eurocentric. It assumes that western Europe was the only dynamic element in the world and that as early as 1500 it was strong enough to carry out the remaking of the other long-established societies and economies. This book argues that western Europe did not have such power for some considerable time and that it was not until the middle of the eighteenth century that it had even reached a situation of parity with the communities of Asia, in particular India and China.

The idea of western European uniqueness in economic and social terms is not restricted to Wallerstein or his intellectual opponents who argue for a 'European miracle' of property rights, individual enterprise, freedom, wealth creation and accumulation and all the benefits of free market capitalism, limited government and democracy. Marxism too reflects many of the views dominant in nineteenth-century Europe, especially the belief in progress as being at the root of human history. The Marxist view of history, with its fixed stages of primitive communism, slave society, feudalism and capitalism (to be followed by the inevitable triumph of communism), is based entirely on the European experience as understood by the knowledge available in the mid-nineteenth century. It too is irredeemably Eurocentric. To the extent that Marx considered (or knew about) the experience of other societies, it was usually to dismiss it as a form of 'oriental despotism'. Subsequently Marxist historians have attempted to shoehorn the development of all human societies into the model he developed from his view of the European past. Where Marx is important is in his emphasis on the fact that all human societies have been based on exploitation – dominant elites (and states) have appropriated the surpluses produced by the majority for their own ends. Indeed the very concept of 'civilization' is based on the fact that the first farming societies produced a food surplus which could be used to support people – priests, rulers, soldiers and craftsmen – who were not producers and to create more complex, structured and hierarchical societies. (It is in this sense that this book uses the term 'civilization'.) The fact that the food surplus may have been given up voluntarily in the first place to support general community objectives does not alter the fact that it soon became exploitative. At one level all that changed during history was the nature of this surplus – at first it was agricultural but gradually through techno-logical developments, and the greater use of energy sources, new oppor-tunities were opened up – societies became industrial and changed

5

fundamentally. Marx called the latter stages of this process 'capitalism' and saw it as something uniquely European. This book rejects such an approach. Human acquisitiveness, the pursuit of profit and gain through investment, trading and enterprise are common to all societies throughout history. In fact one of the first to develop it on a major scale was China and not Europe. The transition that took place in Europe in the period after about 1600 was not in the nature of these activities but in the shift to fossil-fuel energy sources and the development of new industrial technologies. These simply provided greater opportunities for the forces of acquisitiveness to operate. Other theories, such as Max Weber's views on the essentially Protestant origins of the unique capitalist spirit of Europe, can therefore also be rejected as hopelessly Eurocentric.

How then does this book attempt to deal with these problems? It rejects a Eurocentric perspective in favour of a much wider view of world history which does not favour any one part of the world. It is primarily chronological – it attempts to tell the story of the human community, in every part of the world, through time. The first part, which is the shortest, covers the longest period and deals with the evolution of humans, their diffusion across the world and their life as primarily nomadic gatherers and hunters. The second part deals with the most fundamental transition in the whole of human history – the adoption of farming and the settled communities it produced. It also considers the process by which 'civilization' emerged independently in a number of places across the globe. The last chapter in this part (chapter 5) deals with this process in the Americas and the Pacific and takes the story on until their first contact with the Europeans. It does so because they were isolated, and developed unique, independent civilizations but had, when they encountered the Europeans, only reached the level of social and economic development roughly equivalent to that of Eurasia in about 2000 BCE (where Part Two stops). Parts Three and Four are concerned with the history of Eurasia (the vast area encompassing Asia, Europe and north Africa). Part Three covers the history of the early agricultural empires until about 600 CE. Part Four begins with the fundamental transition brought about by the rise of Islam, considers the huge changes taking place in China about a thousand years ago and then the impact of the Mongols. Part Five once again has a global scope and examines the world balance in the period after the Europeans reached the Americas and made their first direct contacts with the long-established societies of Asia. The final part deals with the emergence of the modern world and considers the massive economic, social and political changes of the last two and a half centuries from the perspective of world history.

There are a number of common themes which run through this

narrative. The first is the way in which the different civilizations which emerged in the world were gradually brought into contact with each other. In Mesopotamia and Egypt this occurred at an early stage. Within a few thousand years contact was made with the Indus valley and then with China. Some of the contacts between the extremities of Eurasia were at first indirect but eventually all were in direct contact with each other. No region in Eurasia was isolated for long. The second theme is therefore the way in which crucial ideas, technologies and religions were transmitted between the different groups. These ultimately proved to be far more important than the unique cultural elements of each civilization. The history of all these regions is therefore interlocked. At times one group was in advance of the others and held certain advantages but in the end no monopoly could be sustained and the new discoveries and inventions passed to other societies. For example, China was particularly productive in the five hundred years or so after about 600 CE. It invented printing, paper, the compass, gunpowder and advanced iron technologies, among others, but these eventually diffused. Similarly, western Europe initiated a number of industrial changes in the hundred years or so after the mid-eighteenth century but these too spread rapidly around the globe. The quicker pace of diffusion was no more than a measure of the growing integration of human societies, another phenomenon found throughout world history.

The third theme is the extension of the 'core' area of civilization. All of the initial civilized societies were surrounded by a less developed area (a 'periphery') which they tended to exploit economically. However, the impact of this exploitation and the contacts it brought with more advanced societies had a decisive impact on elites in the periphery. It drove them to increase their power and develop their own primitive state structures through their ability to control contacts with the more developed areas. The result was the gradual spread of 'civilization'. The process is particularly apparent in the way the early states of Mesopotamia and Egypt influenced the Levant and from there incorporated first Crete, then mainland Greece, then Italy and the Iberian peninsula and finally western Europe into a much wider 'civilized' area. In China civilization gradually extended out of the central river-valley areas northwards and, most important, into the highly productive areas south of the Yangtze which were suitable for intensive wet-field rice production. A similar process was at work about a thousand years ago as large parts of eastern Europe and Russia were incorporated into the 'civilized' area and developed their own primitive states.

The fourth theme is the relationship between the settled societies and the nomadic groups which surrounded them. The former called the latter 'barbarians' and usually portrayed them as ruthless warriors on horseback sweeping down on the cities of the civilized world and destroying them. This is a fundamental misunderstanding. The nomadic societies could not have existed without the settled world and depended on it for many of their products. The reason for the success of the nomads was that for several thousand years they had a technological edge in military terms over the settled communities. The mounted archer, ready to retreat to the steppe when under pressure, was almost impossible to defeat. The settled societies found it easier to buy off the 'barbarians' although they (in particular successive Chinese dynasties) liked to pretend they were culturally superior and that the nomads were paying them 'tribute' rather than the other way round. In practice the nomads quickly learnt that it was better to take the products of the civilized world rather than attack it on a major scale – only a very few did so.

One of the underlying causes of the expansion of the civilized area (which gradually constricted the nomadic world) was the demand for various products found only in the peripheral areas. Trade – its increasing level, the greater number of products involved and the longer distances over which it took place – makes up the fifth major theme. In the very earliest civilization in Mesopotamia we find merchants and traders buying and selling various products in the area of the first cities, in the Levant, down the Gulf as far as Oman, across the Iranian plateau, as far north as Anatolia and eventually in the Indus valley. The fact that some of the products were, at first, mainly luxury items does not reduce the importance of trade in developing contacts and wealth. Bulky items were traded from a fairly early date and poor communications on land did not stop trade by sea and along rivers where such products could be easily moved. Cities dependent on trade emerged at an early stage and nearly all rulers and states accepted that wealthy merchants and cities should be given a large degree of independence. Rulers learnt that it was best simply to tax trade and gain revenue. Trade gradually created the two great 'ocean worlds' of the Mediterranean and the Indian Ocean, with the latter linking together the region from the Gulf, through India and south-east Asia to China. These ocean worlds produced wide networks of trade, technological and religious contacts which were far greater than any individual state or empire. The one major overland route was the 'Silk Road', which eventually linked China and the eastern Mediterranean through central Asia and Iran. It was along all these routes that some of the world's great religions were diffused, partly by traders but also by pilgrims and teachers moving with the merchants. The third ocean world was that of the Atlantic which was created by Europe from the sixteenth century.

The sixth theme is the position of Europe within world history. For most of the last five thousand years or so since the first civilizations emerged, Europe was a peripheral area. Until the last thousand years it hardly had a state structure and economically and socially it was far behind the long-established societies and economies in areas such as Egypt, Mesopotamia, Iran, India and China. For nearly all of world history the richest and most developed societies have been in Asia. Most accounts written from a 'western civilization' perspective ignore these inconvenient facts and then see Europe during the heroic age of 'exploration' as already the most dynamic and prosperous area in the world. This book argues that this is a fundamental misunderstanding. Ever since the opening of trade between the Mediterranean and Indian Ocean worlds it was the 'west' that wanted the products of the 'east'. The problem was that it had little to trade that the 'east' wanted. The result was an endless drain of precious metals to the 'east' to pay for its products – when supplies of bullion ran out trade went into decline. What was different after 1500 was that Europe was able to use the phenomenal sources of wealth it exploited in the Americas gradually to buy its way into the long-established and prosperous trading world of the Indian Ocean. It is a major argument in Part Five that to see Europe as the dominant area of the world from 1500 is a mistake. It could easily impose its will on the Americas because of the very much lower technological development on this isolated continent and the unexpected impact of Eurasian diseases on a population that had no natural immunity. The impact of Europe on the great land empires of the Ottomans, Safavids, Mughals and China was minimal. The most the Europeans could establish were a few trading posts along the coast. The period between 1500 and 1750 is therefore one in which Europe was gradually able to build up its wealth and power to a level comparable to that of the great empires of the 'east'.

This leads on to the seventh major theme – how the modern world of industrialization, rapid technological change, high energy use and urbanized societies was created. For nearly the whole time since the adoption of farming all human societies have been primarily agricultural with about nine out of ten people making a living in this way. However, it was inevitable that the gradual rising wealth derived from trade, the improving infrastructure and the slow pace of technological development would mean that one society would eventually transcend these limits. China very nearly did so in the eleventh and twelfth centuries and only failed because of invasion, first by the Jürchen and then the Mongols. The Islamic world might have done so too – it was far wealthier and more developed than Europe for centuries. But in the end it was Europe that made the transition first. It did so based on the adoption of a vast range of technologies and ideas from the rest of Eurasia (iron furnaces, paper, printing, gunpowder, clockwork, the compass, the stern-post rudder, the stirrup, sophisticated financial and accounting devices, 'Arab' numerals, the concept of zero and even the basic components of the steam engine, which were first developed in China). The working-out of these changes and the industrial advances made after the mid-eighteenth century gave western Europe (and its offshoot in north America) a brief lead over the rest of the world. Even then the western European pattern was not 'adopted' by the rest of the world. The evolution of modern societies and economies was a global process in which the rest of the world did not simply repeat, at a slower pace, the changes made in Europe. Each society worked out the changes in its own way and some were more successful than others because of the constraints under which they operated. However, the impact of Europe was temporary and limited. Countries such as Japan and China were in control of their own destinies and the European impact on them was far less than devotees of the 'western civilization' idea would like to believe.

The underlying threads which run throughout the book are those of unity and diversity. Human societies have had very similar foundations and faced remarkably similar problems as a result. Yet many of the solutions to these problems have been different and every society, empire and state has had its own unique characteristics. However, the contacts between them have diffused ideas and technologies, and each has adopted elements from the rest. Ultimately no human group could develop on its own and only a small part of its cultural and technical heritage could be unique. Every society was constantly affected by the diffusion and rediffusion of ideas. For example this book is written in English, a mainly Germanic language deriving from the impact of the Anglo-Saxons some 1,500 years ago, but also containing very strong elements of French and Latin together with words from almost every other language in the world. It is in an alphabetic script invented by the Phoenicians in the Levant some three thousand years ago and itself derived from a multitude of sources. At the bottom are page numbers in what the Europeans called Arabic notation although they were Indian in origin, as was the idea of positional notation. The book is printed on paper which is a Chinese invention. Until the last decade or so the book would have been printed with movable type based on a Chinese idea, although movable metal type as used in Europe from the fifteenth century was invented in Korea.

Any attempt to write world history (especially from a non-Eurocentric perspective) raises acute problems of terminology. Certain names ought not to be used. The term 'Far East' was developed in the British Foreign Office in the nineteenth century and both Middle East and Near East are similar military terms for various command areas. The latter are particularly unfortunate concepts because they contain two major errors. First, they exclude Greece (as being part of Europe) when for almost the whole of history there has been no dividing line along the current western border of Turkey as marking the beginning of 'Asia'. The eastern Mediterranean, Greece, the Aegean and Anatolia have usually formed a single unit which has nearly always been part of a world centred to the east rather than the west. Second, they include Iran despite the fact that this area was strongly differentiated from the areas to the west (though Iranian empires often controlled these zones) and it had as many contacts eastwards to India and into central Asia as it did westwards. (It was tempting to adopt William McNeill's idea of calling Europe the 'Far West' but this too was rejected.)

A central concept in the book is that of Eurasia as a single historical area. Herodotus (the so-called 'father of history', although that again is a 'western civilization' viewpoint – other historians were writing in China at the same time) did not accept the idea of a separate Asia, Europe and Africa or: 'Why three such names . . . should ever have been given to a tract of land which is in reality one.' The idea that Europe is separate from Asia reflects certain patterns of thought common in the 'west'. However, the existence of Eurasia is a geographical fact and it has had a fundamental impact on history. (The inhabitants of the area did not use the term 'Asia' until recently and it is used in this book reluctantly and only in opposition to the term 'Europe'.) Eurasia is treated as a single continent because Europe is not a continent and India is certainly not a sub-continent, or, if it is, then so is Europe. Logically, Europe is West Asia (especially if India is South Asia) but the use of this term was rejected as too unfamiliar. Also rejected was the use of Eurasia-Africa as too clumsy. Eurasia therefore should be taken as including those areas of Africa which shared the history of the rest of the continent – Egypt and north Africa in particular, but also parts of west Africa once the trans-Saharan camel routes were opened, and east Africa once ships from the Gulf, India and China traded along the coast. The terms used in the book are mainly geographical, such as south-west Asia to include the zone running from Anatolia to Mesopotamia and as far south as Egypt. Where modern names such as Iran have been used they are merely a geographical convenience and do not imply any linkage with modern states.

Chronology also poses major problems. Clearly terms such as 'classical' and 'medieval' cannot be universally used because they apply to a particular 'western' view of history. Use of such periodization in the history of other parts of Eurasia is a severe distortion. This book therefore avoids all such divisions and tries to see the history of the world as one long continuous process. The use of terms such as BC/AD implies acceptance of a western Christian view of world history. Indeed the use of AD (even if we knew when it started) is not even a common Christian viewpoint. The

Byzantine ecclesiastical calendar was based on a creation 5,508 years before the birth of Christ so that the year 800 AD was 6308. The use of – and + was rejected only because the former symbol is too similar to a dash. This book therefore uses BCE (before the common era) and CE (common era), although in dates over the last thousand years or so, where there is no ambiguity, the latter is dropped.

In the transliteration of names the most common 'western' form is used for convenience. Where some terms do not have exact equivalents they are retained in the original language. The transliteration of Chinese is a particular problem. The Wade-Giles system, developed in the late nineteenth century, is retained in place of the modern Pinyin system developed recently in China. So dynastic names are Ch'in not Qin and Sung not Song – Beijing remains as Peking. This is partly a matter of convenience and familiarity. In a few decades time Pinyin will have taken over.

Many scholars have derided the idea of writing world history as bound to lead to vast generalizations at the expense of important detail. However, all history is a matter of generalization and the exclusion of some details – no account can ever be totally comprehensive and all historians select what they think is important. World history may, of necessity, have to concentrate on the wood rather than the trees so that, within a reasonable length, it can consider the major factors that have shaped human history. Concentrating on the trees carries the danger of not seeing the relationships between events, the linkages and diffusions between societies and the unity underlying the diversity.

PART ONE

Ninety-Nine Per Cent of Human History
(to *c*.10,000 BCE)

I

Origins

To begin at the beginning is impossible. The identification of the earliest ancestors of modern humans is fraught with a series of difficulties caused by the patchy fossil record of incomplete skeletons whose dating is problematic. Experts disagree fundamentally over how to organize this record and the relationship between the various skeletons that have been found. Which ones can be grouped into separate species? How are they related? Which ones evolved into modern humans? These are just some of the crucial questions that can be only partially answered.

1.1 Primates

The relationship of humans to the rest of the natural world is, however, clear. They belong to the Primate order of mammals of which there are 185 living species. Primates are divided into two types – anthropoids (apes, monkeys and humans) and prosimians (lemurs and tarsiers). All are highly social animals of the tropics which have hands and feet that can grasp objects through the use of opposable thumbs and great toes (humans are the sole exception to the latter since their feet have developed into plat-forms on which they stand). Primates have nails not claws and their method of moving around is dominated by their hind limbs. They rely mainly on sight rather than smell and have two eyes at the front of their heads to give stereoscopic vision. Their reproductive rate is slow, much lower than most other mammals, they have small families, often only one baby at a time, and they provide very high levels of parental care.

A very distant and insignificant ancestor of all the primates must have lived through the great extinction of the giant reptiles 65 million years ago but the exact lineage of the anthropoids (apes, monkeys and humans) is unclear. They probably have a single ancestor – possibly a creature called *Aegytopithecus* which was about the size of a fox and lived in the Nile valley about 35–30 million years ago. What is certain is that about 25–20 million years ago there was a fundamental division in the anthropoids when the apes (and hence humans) split from the monkeys. Exactly how and where this happened is not known because of a major gap in the fossil record. Several species of early apes have been found including *Proconsul africanus* (a tree-dwelling baboon-sized animal with a mix of ape and monkey characteristics dating to 22–18 million years ago) and *Sivapithecus* (an orang-utan-type creature found in south-west Asia about 12–7 million years ago). These were only two of a number of ape species that flourished over this long period when the apes were slowly increasing in body and brain size and broadening their way of life from fruit-eating in trees to leaf-eating and finding some food from ground-level sources. The next development was that some time between ten and five million years ago the ape family itself split so as to divide gorillas from chimpanzees and hominids (the direct ancestors of humans). Unfortunately no fossils have survived from this period and so exactly what happened is a matter of pure speculation. Although the fossil record of anthropoid evolution is extremely fragmentary modern analysis of the DNA of current anthropoids confirms this general pattern. Humans are very distant from the monkey family, less so from gibbons and orang-utans and close to the African apes. The nearest relatives of humans are chimpanzees, with whom we share 98.4 per cent of DNA nucleotide sequences and 99.6 per cent of amino acid sequences.

1.2 Human Ancestors

The hominid family (of which modern humans are the sole survivors) almost certainly evolved about five million years ago. Over the past seventy-five years a series of fossils has been discovered, but how they should be classified, which ones formed separate species and which evolved into humans are matters of fierce controversy. At first nearly every new fossil that was discovered was classified as a new species but the current tendency is to reduce the number by accepting a greater degree of variability within each species. Even so the picture is still confusing and probably no more than half of the hominid species have so far been discovered. Although one of the earliest discoveries was made in South Africa nearly all the crucial remains come from East Africa and it is unclear whether this has produced a significant bias in the fossil record. However, there is agreement that a number of fundamental changes took place within the hominid family as they adapted to new environments and new ways of finding food, in particular in the more open savannah grasslands rather than the tropical forests. The four key events in the evolution of the hominid family were: living on the ground, the adoption of bipedalism which freed the 'hands' for other tasks, growth in brain size, and the development of culture and its transmission through speech. The first two took place among the early hominids; the remaining two, in particular the last, took much longer.

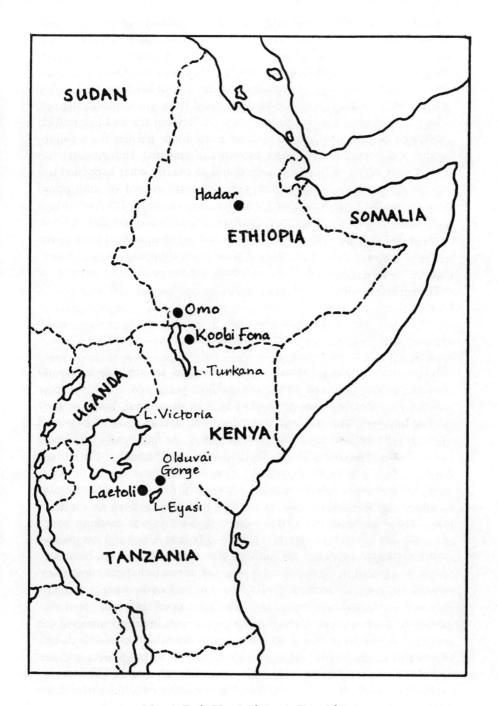

Map 1: Early Hominid sites in East Africa

In the past the evolution of humans was often presented in 'heroic' terms – the evolution through effort of those attributes that enabled them to go on and rule the world. However, we need to remember Stephen Jay Gould's dictum 'No misunderstanding of evolution is more widespread than the assumption that it inevitably leads to a progressive improvement of life.' What happened among the early hominids was a series of chance events, separated by long periods of time, which were not predictable and which had no ultimate purpose. It was not inevitable that modern humans would evolve. Thus bipedalism did not occur so that the hands could be freed to make tools, that was a secondary and unexpected consequence of a development that occurred for other reasons. We should, therefore, see the early hominids not as precursors of humans but as species in their own right which were adapted to particular environments and whose characteristics made them relatively successful. Indeed, the modern tendency is to see these early hominids as less human and more ape-like than earlier interpretations.

The earliest hominids are known as Australopithecines (southern apes). One of the few areas of general agreement is that the earliest known species, from which all other hominids descended, is *Australopithecus afarensis* which existed for around a million years from about 3.7 million years ago. (This is the only known species older than three million years although it is likely that others existed.) The most complete finds (about sixty-five individuals in total) come from the Hadar area in Ethiopia, in particular the skeleton named 'Lucy' by its discoverers Maurice Taieb and Donald Johansen. This fossil, almost half complete, was of a woman about four feet tall and aged between nineteen and twenty-one. This skeleton is roughly contemporary with the finds made further south at Laetoli in northern Tanzania by Mary Leakey. As well as the remains of thirteen hominids she discovered the fossilized footprints of a hominid, judged to be about four feet seven inches tall, which had been walking to a water-hole. These skeletons and footprints confirm that *Australopithecus afarensis* was bipedal though the knees remained bent and the arms were very long, suggesting that the animals still climbed trees. The primary hominid adaptation, millions of years before tools were made, was therefore to begin to walk on the two rear legs. Bipedalism is rare among primates and none other than the hominids do so regularly. It is an extremely risky strategy involving significant muscular and anatomical adaptations, primarily to maintain balance. It probably evolved as a way of adapting to new environments as the climate in East Africa became drier and the amount of open savannah increased. Bipedalism must have evolved as a more efficient way of travelling so as to exploit the varied new food resources available, including possibly scavenging meat. The residual ability to climb trees would have provided shelter against predators. However, we should not over-emphasize the human-like characteristics of these early hominids. Their brains were still chimpanzee-sized, their teeth were intermediate between apes and humans and there was still strong sexual dimorphism (a characteristic notable in apes, far less so in humans) – the males were about thirty per cent taller and almost fifty per cent heavier than the females. Crucially there is no evidence that these animals made tools.

A little later than *Australopithecus afarensis* (about two million years ago) there were a number of hominid species in existence at the same time. One was a so-called 'robust' species which had a large dish-like face with a huge saggital crest above the eyes as a base for massive muscles used in chewing and grinding food. This was probably an adaptation to a particular diet because otherwise this creature was very similar to the more 'gracile' species of which there were certainly three and possibly six different types. The most famous of the latter was *Australopithecus africanus*, first discovered by Raymond Dart in 1925 at Sterkfontein in South Africa. The females of this species were about four feet tall, weighed about sixty pounds and had a brain size only slightly bigger than that of a chimpanzee. The exact relationship of these different species is problematic but one thing is certain – there was no simple 'ladder' up which these animals climbed to produce humans. About the only other certainty is that the 'robust' species did not evolve into modern humans – it died out around one million years ago.

1.3 Early Humans

It seems likely that the genus *Homo*, the direct ancestor of modern humans, emerged around two million years ago. They would have lived alongside the Australopithecines, exploiting much the same environments, and only slowly diverged from them. A fundamental, but unresolved, question is whether there was one or two species of *Homo* living at the same time. The first evidence to be discovered came from Olduvai Gorge, a rift in the Serengeti plain of northern Tanzania exposing an area of old lake bed dating back to about two million years ago. In the early 1960s Richard Leakey discovered a skeleton of a species he called *Homo habilis* because it was associated with the use of tools. The skeleton was very close in type to *Australopithecus africanus*, suggesting a height of little more than three feet. The crucial difference was in the skull which was much less ape-like, had more human-like teeth and a brain size of about 650 cubic centimetres, larger than that of a chimpanzee. It was on this basis that

Leakey decided that this creature was the direct ancestor of humans. However, later discoveries from the Lake Turkana region and the sites of Omo and Koobi Fora, in particular a skull imaginatively named ER-1470, have complicated the picture, pointing to a creature with a much larger brain capacity – about 800 cc – and much taller. Arguments that this was not the same species as *Homo habilis* were reinforced by the discovery in 1986 of a 300-piece skeleton (OH 62) at Olduvai, which suggests that *Homo habilis* was not very human at all. This female seems little different from 'Lucy' even though she lived over a million years later – she was only three feet tall, had very long arms for tree climbing, and sexual dimorphism was still strongly apparent. Only the likely brain size, feet, jaw and teeth suggest a more human-like creature.

Real doubts remain as to whether there really was a species called *Homo habilis*. At least half the specimens claimed for it have been assigned by some experts to other species. If it did exist it had a remarkable variation in brain size too. Also it cannot have existed for very long because the first fossils which are unambiguously of the genus *Homo* have been dated to about 1.6 million years ago. These also come from the Lake Turkana region. At the Koobi Fora site a very well preserved skull (KNM-ER 3733) has been identified as the first known fossil of the direct ancestor of modern humans – *Homo erectus*. The brain size was about 900–1100 cc, about two to three times that of a chimpanzee, and at its upper reaches equal to that of modern humans. It is likely that this human-like creature was about five feet six inches tall and had very good sight. Another fossil from the same area (WT-15000) was of an eleven-year-old boy who had been trampled to death. The skeleton was very modern in structure and the boy was already about five feet four inches tall, far taller than even a mature *Australopithecus*.

Homo erectus was a very stable species that existed for well over a million years before it was replaced by modern humans. Over this period the average brain size increased slowly and the amount of sexual dimorphism decreased – on average the females were only some twelve to fifteen per cent smaller than the males. The significant increase in brain size was almost certainly associated with the first adoption of what are seen as a number of significant 'human' traits – systematic tool making, hunting, 'home sites' or camps and the use of fire. In addition, the adoption of these techniques enabled the ancestors of modern humans to move outside Africa for the first time. Until recently *Homo erectus* had been seen as a relatively simple species to classify and clearly intermediate between the Australopithecines and modern humans, though much closer to the latter than the former. Now some doubts have begun to creep in. In particular these concern the Asian examples, the earliest of which come from the

Mojokerto and Sangiram sites on the Solo river in Indonesia (though not at the ridiculously early date of 1.6 million years ago originally claimed for them). These do seem to be significantly different from the earliest fossil remains found in Europe and both differ from the *Homo erectus* skeletons found in Africa from about 500,000 years ago. Recent theories suggest that it was only the African types that evolved into modern humans – *Homo sapiens*.

1.4 The Origin of Modern Humans

The origin of modern humans, arrogantly named *Homo sapiens*, has been a matter of intense controversy in the last couple of decades. There are two theories and both need to explain the position and history of that caricature caveman – the Neanderthal. For much of the twentieth century discussion about the origin of *Homo sapiens* was dominated by information from Europe – the over 300 Neanderthal skeletons discovered, the very good archaeological sites for the period known as the Upper Palaeolithic (dating from about 30,000 BCE) and the extensive cave art discovered in south-west France and northern Spain. This seemed to be the centre of human advance at this period, a view reinforced by prevailing Eurocentric assumptions. Experts agreed, following Darwin, that the distant origins of humans had to be sought in Africa but that once the early hominids had spread from the continent then all significant advances took place outside Africa. Even though forgeries such as the 'Piltdown Man' were eventually rejected it was still assumed that *Homo sapiens* evolved in Europe, perhaps no more than 40,000 years ago. That position can no longer be sustained.

In the 1980s there were two theories to explain the origins of *Homo sapiens*. The first, put forward by Milford Wolpoff, is known as the 'candelabra' model. This argues that all of the *Homo erectus* populations across Eurasia evolved independently into the archaic forms of *Homo sapiens* and then into fully modern humans. This would mean that the various types of humans across the world (what people a century ago would have called 'races') were long separated from each other, probably for over half a million years. In this theory the Neanderthals of Europe were merely a European variant of archaic *Homo sapiens* which eventually evolved into modern humans. Until recently much of the evidence seemed to support this hypothesis – in particular two skulls from Swanscombe and Steinheim in Europe dated to about 300–200,000 years ago which were judged to have bigger brains than *Homo erectus* and to be the first evidence of a shift towards *Homo sapiens*. Modern analysis suggests that these skulls, together with those from Petralona in Greece (400–300,000 years ago) and Arago in the French Pyrenees (about 200,000 years ago), all demonstrate very distinct archaic features suggesting that these were the ancestors of the Neanderthals and not modern humans. The other major problem with the 'candelabra' model is to explain how the Neanderthals evolved into Homo sapiens. The difficulty arises because two fully Neanderthal individuals have been recovered from the sites of Hahnofersand (near Hamburg) and Saint-Césaire in Charente at dates of 36–31,000 years ago at a time when Homo sapiens lived in western Europe and had already replaced the Neanderthals in south-west Asia.

The second theory, known as the 'Noah's Ark' model, has been proposed by Christopher Stringer and Clive Gamble. It argues that Homo sapiens evolved only once and in one place before spreading across the world and gradually replacing older forms. The original basis for this theory was archaeological work in Africa. This showed that highly developed tools of the type normally associated with European finds dated to about 60,000 years ago were being made in Africa about 140,000 years earlier and that tools associated with the advanced hunters of Europe of some 20,000 years ago were being made in Africa about 60,000 years earlier. In addition the discovery of a male skeleton from Omo Kibish in Ethiopia, dated to about 130,000 years ago, showed that fully modern humans existed much earlier than previously thought. This evidence was reinforced by careful work on a skull recovered from the Qafzeh cave in the Levant. There is no argument that this is fully modern in form and it has now been dated to 90,000 years ago. This means that fully modern Homo sapiens existed in this area for at least 45,000 years alongside more archaic types of humans, including Neanderthals before all of the latter died out. Continued work on fossils from Africa and south-west Asia has now produced a much clearer picture of how Homo sapiens evolved. The earliest forms of Homo sapiens evolved in Africa about 200,000 years ago from the Homo erectus population – at this time they had larger cranial vaults and other more 'modern' anatomical features. By about 100,000 years ago at the latest only very few archaic features remained and some populations of fully modern humans existed in East and South Africa. Modern humans spread out of Africa and by 90,000 years ago at the latest were present in south-west Asia before later spreading into the rest of Asia and Europe.

This picture of a single evolution of Homo sapiens in Africa has been supported by recent work in molecular biology and population genetics. The level of genetic variation in modern humans across the world is very small. It is therefore extremely unlikely that such uniformity could have been produced through the independent evolution of *Homo erectus* into modern humans in Europe, Africa and Asia as proposed in the 'candelabra' model – there could not have been enough interbreeding and exchange of genes to stop significant differences emerging. In the late 1980s work on human mitochondrial DNA, which is only inherited through the maternal line and accumulates mutations faster than nuclear DNA, confirmed this picture. These studies showed that the differences between humans from every part of the world were not only very small but also very recent. Estimates of the rate at which changes in mitochondrial DNA accumulate suggest that all of the differences occurred in the last 200,000 years. This work, combined with that on nuclear DNA and blood group distribution, confirms that there is a clear grouping in humans between Africans on the one hand and Europeans and Asians on the other. The primary split between Africans and non-Africans occurred about 130–100,000 years ago and that between other peoples a little later. Analysis shows that the level of DNA diversity in Africans is greater than the rest of the human population simply because they have had longer to accumulate such changes.

The archaeological and genetic information is therefore in broad agreement about the evolution of modern humans. About 200,000 years ago, possibly a little later, the ancestors of modern humans evolved somewhere in East Africa. By about 100,000 years ago they had evolved into *Homo sapiens* and spread from Africa into south-west Asia where they lived alongside older human forms before gradually replacing them. The fundamental unity of world history is that we are all descended from just one very small group of early humans who emerged in Africa and then spread across the world.

Where does this new picture leave the Neanderthals of Europe? First, we have to recognize that, almost from the first discovery of the partial skeleton in the Feldhofer cave in the Neander valley near Dusseldorf in 1856, the 'Neanderthals' have had a bad press. This stems from the mistaken early reconstructions of what they looked like emphasizing their squat bodies, heavy limbs and huge facial ridges. In practice the Neanderthals were expert hunters, culturally sophisticated and had the same posture and manual abilities as modern humans and a brain capacity that was slightly larger. Where they differed was in having heavier limb bones, greater muscular strength, slightly retreating foreheads and more pronounced eyebrow ridges than modern humans. The clearest development of the 'classic' Neanderthal features occurred among those living in western Europe – skeletons from elsewhere show much greater variability and less extreme features. The roots of the Neanderthals go back to at least 250,000 years ago and they can best be seen as an archaic form of humans confined to Europe and parts of south-west Asia. It is now clear that they did not evolve into modern humans and did not interbreed with *Homo sapiens*. They were gradually replaced by the better adapted humans who evolved in Africa. The two types would have lived in close proximity in many areas for a considerable time and only a marginal advantage for *Homo sapiens* would have allowed them to predominate over time. Computer models suggest that a Neanderthal death rate only two per cent greater than that of *Homo sapiens* would have made them extinct in western Europe within a thousand years. In practice the replacement took much longer than that which suggests that the differences between the two types of humans were very small indeed. Nevertheless by 30,000 years ago the Neanderthals had died out in their last refuge (western Europe) and *Homo sapiens* were the only humans in the world.

1.5 Brains and Language

The most fundamental feature of human evolution across the almost four million years that separates *Australopithecus afarensis* from *Homo sapiens* is the massive and relatively rapid increase in brain size. The facts are easy to ascertain from measuring skulls; the explanation of the changes is much more difficult. The Australopithecines had a brain capacity of about 400–500 cc. This increased by about fifty per cent with *Homo habilis* and had doubled to 850–1000 cc with *Homo erectus*. It increased again to a range of 1100–1400 cc with modern humans. This tripling in brain size in three million years has occurred in no other animals and took place in an order (the primates) that already had proportionately large brains. However, human brains are not just larger than those of the apes – they are much more efficiently organized. There is a reduction in duplication and a freeing of areas to take on extra tasks. This differently structured brain is, some experts believe, already apparent in the Australopithecines, though most would reserve the change to the emergence of *Homo habilis* and *Homo erectus*. Humans also have a unique pattern of development. Their gestation period is roughly the same as the apes yet at birth their brains are already twice as big as apes'. Human brain growth continues for about twelve months after birth, leaving human infants much more helpless and for far longer than apes. The early hominids must therefore have undertaken extended infant care with important consequences for their social organization. The mental distance between humans and the other closely related apes is therefore far greater than even the anatomical differences would suggest.

The most difficult question to answer is why hominid and therefore human brain size increased so rapidly. Earlier theories stressed the pressure from tool making and hunting but these factors are now seen as less important because they almost certainly appeared after the increase in brain size. Studies of the functioning of other primates and their social groups suggest that it was this aspect of their lives that was very important in human evolution. The earliest hominids lived in groups and their ability to function, prosper, interact and reproduce within these groups would have provided a very strong pressure towards the adaptive advantage of greater brain size. In part, this involved the ability to transmit information to new generations. A key mechanism was language – a unique human attribute. The development of language is impossible to detect in the archaeological record. However, the human vocal tract is unique. The larynx is low in the neck, so low that it has a major evolutionary dis-advantage because the air passage has to be closed during swallowing to avoid choking. The advantage stems from the space created above the low larynx which allows the sounds created to be greatly modified to produce speech. In humans the larynx migrates down the neck from about the age of eighteen months and this creates the ability to speak. Luckily the position of the larynx is reflected in the base of the skull and is therefore detectable in the fossil record.

The higher primates, apes in particular, can make a wide range of sounds but these are not sufficient for the complexities of a developed language. The Australopithecines had a similar larynx and could not therefore make any more complex sounds than apes. In *Homo erectus* it seems likely that the larynx had descended to about the level found in an eight-year-old human, making possible at least some primitive language. It is likely that this, together with other abilities linked to greater brain size, enabled these first humans to move out of Africa and exploit much more difficult environments. The anatomy of the Neanderthal skull suggests that they had only a very limited speech potential and therefore a fairly rudimentary language. With the emergence of the earliest groups of *Homo sapiens* a modern form of human larynx is detectable and with it the ability to develop a full-scale language. A larger and better-integrated brain was also essential in order to control and understand speech and develop the complex syntax involved in language.

The development of language would have given the earliest *Homo sapiens* an enormous evolutionary advantage. It would have been apparent at first in social interaction within the group and in activities such as hunt-ing where levels of co-operation could be far higher. Far more important though would be the development of knowledge and culture and the ability to pass this on to other humans, in particular the next generation. It seems likely that the significant advances in human behaviour, the making of ever more complex tools, the development of hunting and gathering strategies and the first indications of art and religious beliefs (which are the subject of the next chapter) were all dependent on the development of speech and language.

2

Gathering and Hunting

The earliest hominids (the ancestors of humans) can be found in the fossil record from almost four million years ago. The first direct ancestors of humans (*Homo erectus*) evolved about one and a half million years ago and modern humans (*Homo sapiens*) about 100,000 years ago. What sort of world did they live in? How did they survive in it? How were they able to expand out of Africa to populate the whole world?

2.1 The World of the Early Humans

During the evolution of the first hominids before about two and a half million years ago the earth's climate was relatively stable and slightly warmer than it is now. However, the slow process of continental drift brought the continents of the northern hemisphere close together in the highest latitudes which resulted in the formation of a large ice cap and induced major fluctuations in temperature from about one and a half million years ago. The exact climatic pattern is difficult to establish before about 700,000 years ago but since then there has been a series of major changes in temperature resulting in at least nine major glacial periods, with intense periods of cold roughly every 90,000 years and with only rare interglacial periods.

A theory to explain these fluctuations in the earth's temperature was put forward by a Yugoslav scientist Milutin Milankovic in the 1920s. He suggested that they were caused by three factors related to the earth's position in space. First, the earth's orbit around the sun is not a circle but an ellipse and the time of the year when it is nearest to the sun varies over a period of 100,000 years. Second, the tilt of the earth's axis changes over a period of about 40,000 years. Third, there is a precession in the earth's axis which varies over a period of 26,000 years. The various combinations of these cycles, Milankovitch argued, would be sufficient to explain the climatic changes. In particular the key was the temperature in the high northern latitudes in summer where the formation of the Arctic allowed snow to accumulate if the summer temperature was not sufficient to melt it – and as the sun's heat was reflected back into space by the bright snow this trend would be reinforced. Milankovitch's work remained purely theoretical until the late 1960s when there was a major expansion in climatic research. This depended on the development of technologies capable of taking cores from deep within the Greenland ice cap and from the seabed, particularly the Pacific, together with the ability to measure the minute differences in the types of oxygen present at different levels within the cores. Analysis of the cores has made it possible to map out a fairly detailed chronology of changing climate and confirm the existence of the various cycles identified by Milankovic.

From about 700,000 years ago there was a steady decrease in temperature leading to an accumulation of giant ice-sheets in the northern hemisphere. The peak of the glaciation came about 525,000 years ago when the amount of water frozen in the ice-sheets was sufficient to lower sea levels to 650 feet below current levels. There was another major glacial period between 180,000 and 128,000 years ago followed by a brief inter-glacial when the climate was warmer than now – hippopotamuses swam in the Thames and lived as far north as Yorkshire. The ice-sheets expanded again from about 113,000 years ago reaching a peak at about 73,000 years ago. A period of very cold but fluctuating temperatures followed before a rapid deterioration of the climate and the peak of the last glacial period 30,000–18,000 years ago. At this time giant ice-sheets extended below St Louis in north America and across much of north-west Europe, with treeless tundra and cold steppe conditions reaching almost as far as the Mediterranean. Sea levels were 425 feet lower than now, the continental shelf of south-east Asia was exposed and the Bering Strait was dry land. The climate began to warm significantly about 11,000 BCE and the ice-sheets retreated rapidly – sea levels rose over 90 feet in the thousand years after 8500 BCE. The Baltic and North Seas were created and Britain became an island about 6000 BCE.

2.2. Hunter or Scavenger?

The earliest hominids evolved in East Africa where the climate was generally equable and fluctuations were not severe although they were still sufficient to cause major changes in vegetation. How did these creatures exploit their environment and find enough food to survive? The first key adaptation was undertaken by tree-living *Australopithecus afarensis* in moving from the normal primate habitat – a forest environment – to being a ground-dwelling creature exploiting the savannah. The only other primate to make this change is the baboon and they are small creatures able to exploit niches in the environment that the large herds of grazing animals on the savannah do not utilize. Yet the earliest hominids were medium-sized and walked upright. At first they probably consumed the standard primate food that they could find – fruit, nuts, leaves and insects. Although their food would have been widely distributed across the savannah these earliest hominids would have used their social organization to spread out to find food and share it when they found it. This would have involved only a slight adaptation of normal primate social organization.

At some stage these creatures began to eat meat – unusual behaviour for primates. This fact has led to intense controversy about the nature of hominid evolution and its impact on humans. The long-held view, which was reinforced by a major conference called 'Man [*sic*] the Hunter' at Chicago in the mid-1960s and popularized by writers like Robert Ardrey in books such as *African Genesis*, was that these early hominids hunted animals and brought the carcasses back to their camps (or 'home bases') where they butchered them, using primitive stone tools. It was argued that the technical and organizational demands of hunting were the driving force behind hominid evolution and a central factor in human behaviour. Some of the earliest known archaeological finds could be interpreted to fit in with this hypothesis. Koobi Fora (dated to about 1.8 million years ago) contained the bones of a dead hippopotamus surrounded by early stone tools. An even more extensive site at Olduvai Gorge (Bed 1) covered over 1,200 square feet and contained masses of animal bones and over 4,000 stone tools. This, argued the excavator Louis Leakey, was a classic campsite for early humans where they lived and slept and brought back the animals they hunted to butcher and eat. All of this activity would suggest a relatively high degree of social activity and integration within the group similar to that of modern hunter-gatherers.

More recent work has suggested a much less flattering picture of these early hominids and that their behaviour was much less 'human'. Studies of modern hunting and gathering groups equipped with bows, poisoned arrows and metal-tipped spears show that they are successful in only about a third of their hunts. The earliest hominids lacked all of these aids and in addition had very small brains and no language to help co-ordinate their activities. Hunting on any significant scale would have been beyond their capabilities. How then should we interpret the earliest sites associated with our ancestors? Work by two archaeologists – Glyn Isaac and Lewis Binford (who re-examined Bed 1 at Olduvai in the early 1980s) – suggests that the earliest hominids were scavengers. The association of animal bones and stone tools does not imply that the animals were hunted by the early hominids. These sites were not camps but carnivore kill sites, or places where the animals died naturally. The early hominids only visited them after the other animals had left, scavenged among the debris and used stone tools to take odd pieces of meat and, in particular, to break open the bones to obtain the marrow. Detailed analysis of the bones showed that few if any had been disarticulated and butchered and in many cases the marks made by the stone tools were on top of the carnivore teeth marks. Among the debris were some hominid bones gnawed by carnivores. Other sites were probably places where the hominids took a few bones back to where they had a pile of tools. These creatures may have made a few shelters but probably the only safe place to sleep was in the trees, which their long arms enabled them to climb easily.

It is clear that the one advantage that the earliest hominids had was the making and use of tools, especially from stone – the first level of human technological development. Many animals use 'tools' – sea otters use rocks to smash open molluscs and chimpanzees use sticks and trimmed blades of grass to get at termites – but none create tools at even the most 'primitive' early hominid levels. Although the earliest known hominid, *Australopithecus afarensis*, walked in a largely upright position, so that the hands were free, no stone tools have been found associated with their remains. It is highly likely, however, that they used 'tools' that were perishable and which therefore have not survived in the archaeological record.

The first known tools, which are given the type name Oldowan, are associated with *Homo habilis* and date to about two million years ago. At first glance they appear crude lumps of rock and little different from the naturally fractured rocks in the same area. However, they are not 'primitive' and making them requires a highly complex understanding of different types of stone and how they fracture. The early techniques to make stone tools have been replicated by archaeologists in the late twentieth century and they needed hours of practice before even the 'crudest' tool could be made. Most of the early tools were made by hard-hammer percussion – hitting two rocks together so that one becomes a 'core' as flakes are detached. However, just hitting the rocks together will not produce tools – the core has to be held at the correct acute angle before flakes can be detached. Other tools were made by less common methods such as using rocks as anvils. Many of the crude-looking lumps of rock with rough edges are in fact the cores from which tools were made and were probably discarded, although some might have been used to smash up bones. It is now clear that the key tools were the flakes which were sharp enough to cut through even elephant hide. These tools gave *Homo habilis* some key advantages over other animals; in particular they could exploit parts of the animals that many carnivores and other scavengers could not reach. The tools demonstrate not just a high level of skill in their construction but also considerable planning – the stone was carried over several miles if necessary, to ensure the best material, tools were made and taken to sites for use and often carried away for re-use. The stone tools were almost certainly used to make better wooden tools such as digging sticks, although these have not survived. The earliest technology shows that the developing brain capacity of the early hominids provided key evolutionary advantages.

2.3 Early Humans

All of the early hominid remains which are older than one million years have been found within 35 degrees of the Equator in East Africa. There were strong reasons why they did not move outside the very limited area in which they evolved for about three million years. These creatures were adapted for using the resources of the savannah and did not have the knowledge and the techniques to live in more difficult conditions where new ways of gaining food were required, especially in winter. It was not until the evolution of the direct ancestor of modern humans (*Homo erectus*) about 1.6 million years ago that the development of a larger brain size could produce better stone technologies, greater knowledge, increased social interaction and probably primitive language. All of these were essential for the spread of the earliest humans out of Africa. With these extra skills small bands of *Homo erectus*, moving from place to place to take advantage of different seasonal foods, could cover some twenty or thirty miles a year and easily move over vast distances within a few generations. The main direction of expansion was towards the north, into the Nile valley, from there to south-west Asia and eventually to south-east Asia within a period of perhaps no more than 100,000 years. The dating of the earliest human sites in Asia is highly controversial. Most experts would reject claims of dates of about 1.5 million years ago (roughly contemporaneous with the evolution of *Homo erectus*) but dates of about 700,000 years ago are generally accepted. The site of Ubeidiya near the confluence of the Jordan and Yarmuk rivers is probably of this period as are the earliest dates in China (Choukoutien near Peking) whereas the Lang Trang Caves in Vietnam can reasonably securely be dated to about 500,000 years ago.

Choukoutien was visited by *Homo erectus* over a period of at least 200,000 years and the caverns contain over 100,000 stone tools, forty human skeletons and the remains of sixty different animal species. The site is also the earliest known for the indisputable human use of fire. The earliest hominids would have lived with the natural fires that regularly spread across the African savannah. At what point they were able to tame them, or create fire themselves, is a matter of considerable dispute. Claims have been made that the traces of fire found at the sites of Swartkrans in South Africa and Chesowanya in Kenya, both dated to about 1.5 million years ago, were made by humans. But although there is a hearth-like arrangement of stones and artefacts at the latter site it seems more likely that the fires were natural. Nevertheless it is clear that by about 700,000 years ago *Homo erectus* was able to make and control fire. This was a significant human advance. It provided protection against predators, enabled more plants to be used as food through cooking to remove poisons and it meant that meat could be cooked rather than eaten raw as all the early hominids had done. By giving warmth at night and in the winter it also made it possible for humans to move into new environments across the globe.

Homo erectus had another key advantage – a much more advanced stone technology than the earlier hominids. Although the older Oldowan-type tools continued to be used a new, very distinctive, set of tools evolved called Acheulian (from the site of St Acheul in northern France where they were first discovered in the nineteenth century). These tools are found across Eurasia and Africa – apart from East Asia where there seems to have been extensive use of bamboo, a highly adaptable material that can be used in numerous different ways, but which is rarely found preserved in archaeological sites. The key stone tool of the Acheulian was the hand-axe. They are found in all sorts of shapes and sizes but, unlike the choppers and scrapers of the Oldowan, they have converging edges meeting at a point. The edges were carefully flaked all round so as to produce two large cutting surfaces as well as a very sharp tip and they therefore provided very effective butchering tools, although they were probably used for a wide variety of tasks. They could also be resharpened before they were thrown away. A hand-axe required a much higher level of skill and strength to make than an Oldowan tool as well as the ability to imagine how it could be formed from a block of stone. Starting from a large stone block it was necessary to use a hammer stone about nine inches long to detach a massive flake which was then shaped by removing flakes from both sides. The last part of the process often involved a 'soft' hammer such as antler or bone to carry out the final shaping. The hand-axe, together with other stone tools such as picks and cleavers, and wooden implements (the earliest recovered date to about 200,000 years ago) used for digging and possibly as spears, provided the basic tool-kit for *Homo erectus* for over a million years. The stone tools became slightly more sophisticated, especially towards the end of the period, with much greater emphasis being placed on the preparation and shaping of the core before any flakes were detached. However, this was a period of considerable technological stability demonstrating that it was well adjusted to the way of life of the earliest humans.

Although *Homo erectus* was able to adapt relatively easily to the tropical and sub-tropical environments of Asia, the settlement of Europe proved very difficult even with a more advanced set of tools and the use of fire. It remained a marginal area of intermittent settlement – the earliest humans did not find it easy to migrate from the south and with a semi-glacial climate for over half the period and full glacial conditions for much of the rest of the time, conditions were generally harsh. Although the area contained a wide selection of animals grazing in large herds they were difficult to exploit and hunting would have been a very high-risk strategy given the level of technology available. Another problem was that in colder periods human groups would have needed to cover a very large territory in order to obtain enough food – as they spread out they were quite likely to lose touch with each other, resulting in difficulties in maintaining their numbers and eventually extinction of some groups. It is likely that the settlement of Europe occurred many times, mainly in the interglacial periods, with the area being abandoned as the climate worsened.

Europe may have been settled from about 700,000 years ago but a more likely date is about 500,000 years ago after the major Elster glaciation. Probably the earliest securely dated site is that of Isernia La Pineta in central Italy at about 500,000 years ago, with a roughly similar date for Boxgrove in southern England. During the better climatic conditions there is evidence that Europe could be a productive environment for *Homo erectus*. The sites of Torralba and Ambrona, north-east of Madrid, have been dated to either 400,000 or 200,000 years ago (there is a dispute about which is correct). They lie in what was then a deep swampy valley along which animals migrated in spring and autumn. The early humans, living in temporary campsites, were able to monitor the movements of the herds and use the natural topography to trap animals in closed valleys and swamps. The Ambrona site contained between thirty and thirty-five dismembered elephant skeletons and the area was littered with hand-axes, cleavers and scrapers. The elephant skulls had been smashed open so that the brains could be eaten.

2.4 Ways of Life

It is clear that *Homo erectus* was capable of a much more sophisticated exploitation of the environment than the early hominids. Their way of life, and that of *Homo sapiens* from about 100,000 years ago, was very close to that of modern hunting and gathering groups. Studies of these groups can therefore provide significant insights into how humans existed before the development of agriculture some 10,000 years ago. They have produced startling results showing that modern gathering and hunting groups have access to a wide range of easily obtained food and plenty of leisure time.

The first studies were carried out on the !Kung-San bushmen of the Kalahari desert in south-west Africa. They were equipped only with digging sticks, simple bows and arrows, ostrich egg-shells as water containers, and clothes made from animal skins. Yet an adult worked on average for just over two days a week and they had a diet that was more than adequate by modern nutritional standards. They lived mainly on a large variety (over 100 different types) of vegetable food although the staple was the mongongo nut. This was available throughout the year, was easy to gather and was highly nutritious – half a pound of mongongo nuts (which could be gathered in half an hour) have the same number of calories as two and a half pounds of rice and the protein of a pound of beef. Both men and women gathered but only the men hunted (the women looked after the children and did domestic work). But hunting was risky and time-consuming and for most of the year provided only a fifth of the diet. The basic social unit was the family but food was shared among the group. During the year the pattern of subsistence shifted depending on what food was available. Sometimes the population split into small groups and at other times when food was plentiful in one spot large groups formed, providing an opportunity for social interaction, marriage, story-telling and other activities. The !Kung saw no reason for agriculture – as one bushman told an anthropologist 'Why should we plant when there are so many mongongo nuts in the world?'

What is remarkable about the study of the !Kung is that they have been marginalized by settled societies and forced to exploit a relatively hostile environment unsuitable for agriculture. Gathering and hunting groups in richer environments live in much the same way but find subsistence even easier to obtain. This would certainly have been the case for the earliest humans. The amount of food such groups utilize is normally only a fraction of that available. Most live by gathering – hunting is much harder work and in the equatorial and tropical areas rarely provides more than a third of the food. Only in the higher latitudes, on the great grasslands and tundras, is the hunting of the large herds of animals important. It is in the Arctic that hunting is overwhelmingly important and the Inuit have required a highly sophisticated technology and a series of major cultural adaptations in order to survive. The ease with which food can be obtained means that gatherers and hunters have large amounts of free time which is used for cultural and social tasks and sleeping. Work is also fairly constant throughout the year unlike agriculture. People have few possessions because they are a hindrance to a mobile way of life and can easily be replaced from readily available materials. Wealth and the means of subsistence do not depend upon the ownership of land – food and raw materials are available for free in the environment.

All gathering and hunting people depend upon an intimate knowledge of the local environment, its seasonal changes and the availability of food in different locations as they move around the territory they exploit. Different strategies can be used at various times – from intensive foraging, through moving frequently to new sites, to semi-permanent camps for several months when food, either vegetable or animal, is available. A few gathering and hunting groups such as those covering the north-west Pacific coast of America even became sedentary. Generally, however, there is a mix of activities through the year and different-sized groups form as subsistence patterns change. The minimum-sized band of a few families usually consists of about twenty-five people but they come together in groups of about 200 people (seven or more bands) as a basic breeding unit with people marrying outside of their band. Larger groups of perhaps 500 people might meet once a year for various social functions.

In general gathering and hunting groups have a well-balanced diet and their health is good. Infant mortality rates are about 200 per thousand (in the 1890s the level in Washington D.C. was 300 per thousand) and life expectancy at birth is about twenty to twenty-five years, about the same as India in the 1920s. Numbers in the band are often controlled through infanticide and abandonment of the old and ill. It was this way of life that was followed for over a million years by early human groups using a relatively low level of technology. It provided a highly stable and well-adapted existence.

2.5 Modern Humans

Until the last couple of decades it was generally agreed that there was a fairly clear division between the technologies used by Neanderthals and those of *Homo sapiens* in the period from about 100,000 years ago. Neanderthals used tools given the type name Mousterian after the rock shelter at Le Moustier in south-west France where they were first discovered. Modern humans made much more sophisticated and smaller tools associated with the complex societies that emerged in southern France and northern Spain at the height of the last ice age, about 20,000 years ago. The radical revision in the picture of the evolution and spread of *Homo sapiens* that has occurred since the 1980s means that this simple division has had to be abandoned. It is now clear that *Homo sapiens*, when they lived for tens of thousands of years alongside Neanderthals and other older human types, made the same sort of tools as those previously

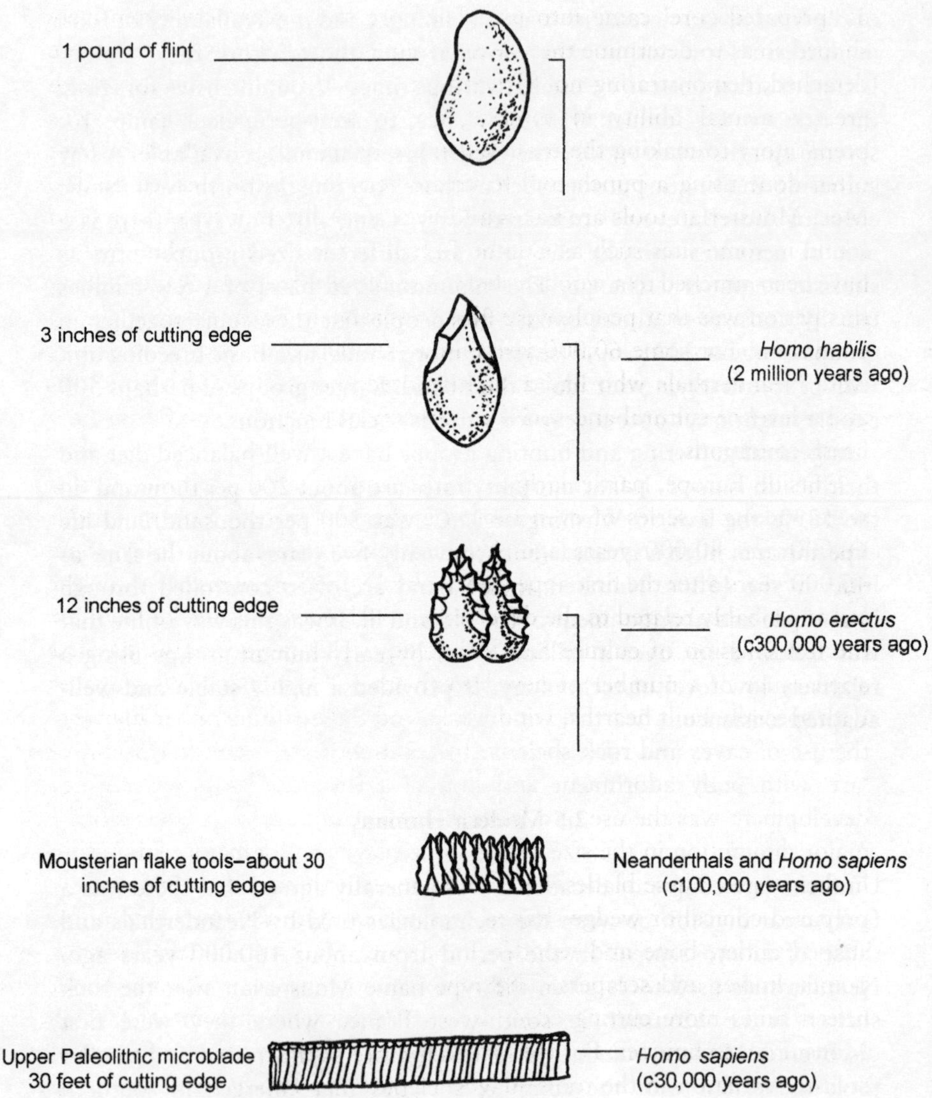

1 pound of flint

3 inches of cutting edge — *Homo habilis*
(2 million years ago)

12 inches of cutting edge — *Homo erectus*
(c300,000 years ago)

Mousterian flake tools–about 30
inches of cutting edge — Neanderthals and *Homo sapiens*
(c100,000 years ago)

Upper Paleolithic microblade
30 feet of cutting edge — *Homo sapiens*
(c30,000 years ago)

Chart 1: Early technology: the increasing efficiency of stone tool production

associated only with the Neanderthals. However, these tools did mark a significant advance on those made by *Homo erectus*. From about 100,000 years ago, at first in Africa and then in south-west Asia, a technique known as 'prepared core' came into use. The core stone was now extensively shaped so as to determine the size and shape of the flakes when they were detached, demonstrating not just greater technical ability but also much greater mental ability in thinking out a number of complex steps preparatory to making the tool. When the flakes were detached this was often done using a punch tool to create very long parallel-sided blades. Most Mousterian tools are flakes and over sixty different types have been found in some sites such as Combe Grenal in the Périgord. Many would have been attached to a wooden shaft. A significant human advance during this period was that people were able to survive in Europe during glacial conditions. For some 60,000 years after 100,000 years ago these groups were Neanderthals who had a sophisticated enough level of technology and a level of cultural and social complexity sufficient to survive in these harsh conditions.

Outside Europe, particularly in the Levant, groups of *Homo sapiens* were making a series of even more significant advances between about 60,000 and 40,000 years ago. Why they occurred at this time (some 40,000 years after the first appearance of fully modern humans) is unclear but is probably related to the development of language as the key tool for the transmission of culture and technology. This period marks the first appearance of a number of new human traits – structured living spaces with specially built hearths, windbreaks and the first huts rather than just the use of caves and rock shelters. In addition there is the first primitive 'art' with body adornment and burial of the dead in graves. A key development was the use of a 'microblade' technology to produce both a major diminution in the size of the stone blades and a major elaboration in their types. These blades were struck in their thousands from carefully prepared conical or wedge-shaped cores. They were then mounted on to shaped antler, bone and wooden handles to act as spear barbs, arrow points, knives and scrapers. This new technology was producing about fifteen times more cutting edges from an equivalent amount of flint as Mousterian techniques. For the first time there appears to be some formal stylistic variation in the tools suggesting that these techniques may have had a cultural and social significance. Analysis of the stone used has shown that some kinds were transported over very large distances and that these special stones were used in different ways from local materials. By about 40,000 years ago tools were being transported over 200 miles and special types of rock and flint were being exchanged between groups. The stones were treated very carefully, and over three-quarters made into tools, compared with less than five per cent of the local flints. These much more sophisticated technologies and more complex levels of social organization first appeared in the Levant just over 50,000 years ago. Then these groups of modern humans began to move into Europe – the first known site is the Bacho Kiro cave in Bulgaria, dated to about 45,000 years ago. The last refuge of the Neanderthals and Mousterian technology was in France, but by about 30,000 years ago these groups had been replaced by *Homo sapiens*. As they adapted to new environments they developed other technologies – spear-throwers, barbed harpoon heads, the bow and arrow, and needles and thread to make more suitable clothing for the harsh world in which they lived.

It was in south-west France and northern Spain during the height of the last ice age, about 20,000 years ago, that a remarkable gathering and hunting way of life developed that is known particularly through its cave art. At this time most of northern Europe, including nearly all of Britain, was covered in a giant ice-sheet hundreds of feet thick. To the south, almost as far as the Mediterranean, there was a wide belt of steppe grassland with some trees in the sheltered valleys. Because this steppe was much further south than that now found in Siberia it had a milder climate (summer temperatures were about 10° C and in winter about freezing), a much richer range of animal species and therefore a wide diversity of resources. In the area of the Dordogne and the Pyrenees conditions were particularly favourable. Twice a year there were huge reindeer migrations – to the east for the summer pastures and to the river valleys in the west for the winter. The rivers were full of salmon and there was a wide range of vegetable foods available including blueberries, raspberries, acorns and hazelnuts. Population density was much higher here than in the rest of Europe and the groups were semi-sedentary, able to exploit the vast herds of reindeer with a high level of efficiency. People lived mainly in south-facing rock shelters, close to water and with good observation points to follow the herds. They probably used hide 'curtains' and even tents within the caves to provide extra shelter. Major sites such as Laugerie Haute and Laugerie Basse in the Dordogne and La Madeleine were probably places where large groups gathered for parts of the year when food was particularly plentiful. There they engaged in their main social activities – marriage, initiation rituals and the exchange of the various exotic goods that have been found, including seashells from northern France and amber from the far north.

It was the ability of the local environment to sustain a large number of people in a semi-sedentary state that resulted in the development of the most sophisticated art known anywhere in the world at any time for gathering and hunting groups. Across south-west Europe there are over

200 caves with various types of art on their walls and over 10,000 sculpted and engraved objects are known. Clearly they all had symbolic importance for the people who made them but attempts over the past century or so to try and understand their significance have met with only limited success. The earliest works date from about 30,000 years ago and consist mainly of animal carvings on ivory, engravings and even a bone flute. The so-called 'Venus' figures, carvings of women with exaggerated breasts, buttocks and hips, which are found from Russia to the Dordogne, date from about 25,000 years ago but were made for only a very short time. They are well known but relatively rare and although they are often thought to be associated with some form of fertility ritual such an interpretation is unlikely since only a few of the figurines are shown as pregnant and the sexual organs are rarely emphasized.

The great cave art, at places such as Lascaux and Altamira, nearly all dates from the height of the ice age around 18,000 years ago, though whether it was done over thousands of years by many people or in short bursts by a just a few is unknown. Some of the animals are painted around natural rock features so as to emphasize movement, but most of the caves appear, at least at first glance, to be a jumbled mass of large and small game animals, human figures, hand impressions and dots and signs. The identification of the animal species is difficult but the commonest is the horse, followed by bison, aurochs (wild cattle), reindeer and red deer. Others such as carnivores, fish and birds are rare and some, such as rodents, are missing altogether. One fact though is certain – the frequency of the types of animals depicted does not bear a direct relationship to the animals actually hunted, which can be discovered from the bones in the caves. Clearly the animal drawings are not simply pictures and have some symbolic meaning. Humans are not depicted with the same care as the animals, though there are stencils and prints of hands and some have argued for a figure known as the 'sorcerer' – a human figure with a supposed 'antler headdress' and 'horse's tail' at the Trois Frères in the Ariège.

The interpretation of this art has resulted in a host of theories. The idea that this was art for art's sake has little support. Neither does the idea that they were simply a form of 'hunting magic', which by showing animals being hunted and killed (and most scenes do not show this) would increase the success rate of the hunt, have much backing. Other theories have divided the caves into different zones and the animals symbolically into either male or female in an overall structured arrangement. The problems with this view are that we do not know the exact structure of the caves some 20,000 years ago since they have certainly changed over that period, and different people have produced radically different divisions of zones within the caves and exactly opposite attributions of the animals to the male and female categories. The various dots and lines do appear to be systematic and to have been added to over time. They may represent some form of reckoning of time, perhaps lunar cycles. Some areas of the caves, especially the darker interiors, were probably involved in some sort of initiation rituals, perhaps involving different clan groups. Studies of modern gathering and hunting groups such as the Australian Aborigines show that they have a highly complex series of beliefs and use art and ritual to structure and give meaning to their existence, partly through the symbolic depiction of the continuity between animals and humans and their social world. It seems likely that the extensive cave art of the last ice age had a similar function.

The environment of south-west Europe at the height of the last ice age was relatively hospitable but elsewhere on the continent conditions were much more difficult. The open plains were covered with snow during the nine-month winter and conditions were always harsh. The ability of human groups to survive in these conditions demonstrates the techno-logical and social advances made over the previous tens of thousands of years. Across central and eastern Europe highly specialized ways of life developed to exploit particular resources. One involved the great reindeer herds that migrated twice a year between their winter grazing grounds on the north German plain, the Hungarian plain or near the Black Sea, to their summer areas of the Jura, south German highlands and the Carpathians, respectively. People either followed the herds throughout the year or intercepted them twice a year on their migration routes. These groups are often depicted as 'reindeer hunters' but in practice this would have been a highly inefficient way of gaining food and likely to achieve little more than causing panic in the herds. It is now clear from a complex series of studies of the location of their seasonal campsites and the animals actually killed that these people were reindeer herders. They followed the herds, corralled them into valleys where they could be observed and manipulated, while some were detached from the main herd and killed at close quarters. Which animals were killed was not a matter of random hunting – over ninety per cent were adult males. This is very close to the proportion found in modern managed reindeer herds and is highly effective since these males are surplus and the size of the herd can be maintained without them. The humans and animals lived closely together although the number of people that could be sustained by this way of life was low.

Other groups were primarily dependent on mammoths for their existence although they also exploited bison and arctic fox, the latter for its fur. The site of Dolni Vestonice overlooking the Dyje river in Moravia was a regular campsite for about 100–120 people and dates to about 25,000 years ago. It is remarkable in a number of ways. Numerous burnt clay figures produced in ovens have been found at the site. They are the earliest fired clay objects in the world by at least 15,000 years. The site also provides the first unequivocal evidence of deliberate human burial, suggesting the existence of at least some primitive religious beliefs. Three bodies were found with ivory pendants around their necks and a fire had been set over their bodies before the grave was filled in. Further east are the two spectacular sites of Kostenki near the river Don and Mezhirich overlooking the Dnieper valley south-east of Kiev. Both date to the height of the last ice age between 22,000 and 18,000 years ago. The former was set in very hostile conditions only some 430 miles south of the massive continental ice-sheet. The main hut at Kostenki covered an area of 420 square feet, the five at Mezhirich were each up to 22 feet across enclosing an area twice that of Kostenki. All were built with foundation walls of mammoth bones which supported a framework of smaller limb bones and vertebrae in a fine 'herring bone' pattern that held up the roof. All had regularly spaced hearths, work areas and deep storage pits in the permafrost to hold meat. The conditions at Kostenki were so harsh that there were underground dwellings.

2.6 The Peopling of the World

The ability of *Homo sapiens* to live in the harshest environments of ice-age Europe was only part of a more general phenomenon – the spread of people across the world. Apart from some islands this was accomplished by the earliest human groups of gatherers and hunters with only fairly primitive technology. *Homo sapiens* evolved in Africa around 150,000 years ago, reached south-west Asia about 100,000 years ago and then spread eastwards, following in the footsteps of *Homo erectus* a million years earlier, to reach south-east Asia about 70–60,000 years ago.

2.6.1 Australia

At the height of the last glaciation, about 20,000 years ago, when sea levels fell dramatically, a vast landmass, now named Sahul, combined Australia, New Guinea and the adjoining islands. At the same time the Malaysian peninsula, Borneo and Sumatra were joined to form 'Sundra'. However, Sahul was never joined to this extended mainland of Eurasia and was always separated by at least sixty miles of ocean from the nearest islands – Timor and Sulawesi. At no time therefore could Australia have been settled without the use of boats. All the evidence now suggests that Australia was settled long before the glacial maximum at a time when the sea distances involved were even greater.

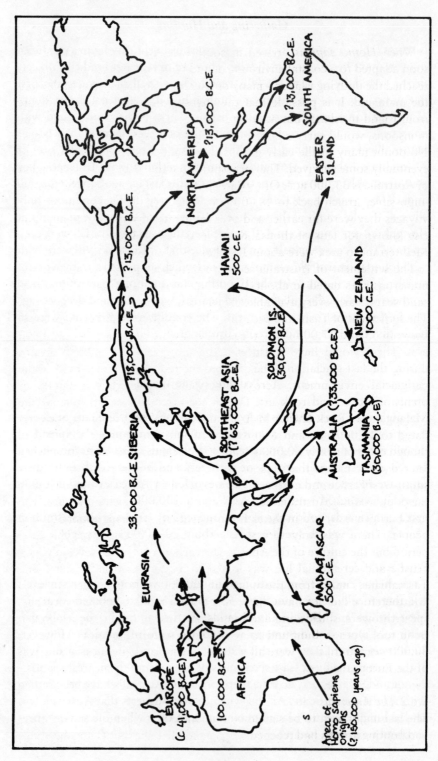

Map 2: The settlement of the world

When *Homo sapiens* arrived in south-east Asia they probably fairly soon adapted to a coastal environment and built boats out of bamboo and reached the outlying islands – many of which would have been visible from the mainland. It is possible that the voyage to Australia was deliberate from island to island, but accidental voyages, drifting downwind on the monsoons, would carry a boat from Timor to Australia in about a week. No doubt many of the early groups that made this voyage died out but eventually some survived. The earliest indisputable date for the settlement of Australia is 33,000 BCE. Other dates put forward, more doubtful but not impossible, stretch back to 48,000 BCE. Whatever the exact date of these voyages they were far earlier and over far greater distances than anything else known for tens of thousands of years – the earliest voyages in the Mediterranean area were about 10,000 BCE.

The settlement of Australia seems to have been very rapid. There are numerous sites dated to about 30,000 BCE and within another ten thousand years nearly every available environmental zone was being exploited. The settlement of Tasmania probably occurred when a land bridge existed between 35 and 27,000 BCE – the earliest dated settlements are at 28,800 BCE. These would have constituted the most southerly human groups during the last glaciation – they hunted the red wallaby that lived in the periglacial environment. Across Australia are numerous examples of prehistoric cave and rock art. Dating these remains is difficult but the Malangangerr Rock Shelter in Arnhem Land is almost certainly correctly dated to 17,000 BCE and Mannahill in South Australia to 14,000 BCE, though dates of nearly 30,000 BCE have been claimed for both. Even at the later dates it means that this art is roughly contemporary with that of south-west France and northern Spain. By about 10,000 BCE it is likely that the population of Australia had reached roughly the level found when the first Europeans arrived in the eighteenth century – perhaps about 300,000 people. There was only very slow technological change over this long period but the culture of the Aborigines reached a very high level in which artistic and ceremonial life was linked to a complex belief system. The Tasmanians, cut off from the mainland, did not develop new technologies and therefore did not have shafted tools with stone heads, boomerangs, spear-throwers, shields and axes. Nevertheless they used their two dozen or so tool types to hunt and forage so as to sustain their way of life for 30,000 years until they were all wiped out within a century of the arrival of the Europeans.

2.6.2 *The Americas*
The last major area to be settled by humans was the Americas. Gathering and hunting groups had reached Siberia and the Lake Baikal area by about

40,000 years ago and moved into the even harsher environment of the far north-east of Eurasia around Kamchatka by about 18,000 BCE. It was these groups that provided the population of the Americas. The level of biological differentiation within the native American population is low and all the groups appear to be closely related to the Siberian populations of the last ice age. The low sea levels at this time meant that there was a single landmass linking Siberia, Alaska and the Aleutians. The area would have been inhospitable (though little worse than Kamchatka), with no large herds of animals. The area could have supported small groups of people. The huge ice-sheets meant that movement south from Alaska would have been almost impossible before about 13,000 BCE. As the climate improved and the ice-sheets retreated, humans followed the animals and moved south.

The dating of the settlement of the Americas is highly controversial. The earliest generally accepted date is 12,500 BCE at the Meadowcroft Rock Shelter, about thirty miles south-west of Pittsburgh. The earliest site in the far south to be securely dated is Monte Verde in southern Chile at 10,500–11,000 BCE. This was a long-term campsite by the side of a stream, with houses, a few hearths and stone tools. Because the site was later covered by a peat bog some wooden items have survived and they can be accurately dated by radiocarbon methods. Much earlier dates have been claimed – for example 45,000 BCE at Boqueiro in Pedro Furada in north-east Brazil but this is a stream-bed site which has shifted continuously and the proposed artefacts are almost certainly not human but naturally fractured rocks. Such dates are substantially out of line with the remaining evidence which suggests that there was no settlement of the Americas before the end of the last ice age.

When the first humans moved south from Alaska they found a vast array of varied and rich habitats that could support them, and the population grew rapidly as it spread out. In this great variety of environments a whole series of different cultures and ways of life evolved. One of the earliest was the so-called 'Clovis' culture which flourished across the Great Plains for a short period between 9200 and 8900 BCE. Highly mobile groups exploited the vast array of animals with big game herds the main source of food supplemented by various vegetable foods. For some decades it was argued that the Clovis groups were probably responsible for what appeared to be a massive extinction of species across north America at the end of the ice age. Thirty-five species became extinct, mainly the large herbivores (mammoth, mastodon, mountain deer, saiga antelope and the giant beaver which was the same size as a black bear) together with the carnivores that preyed on them (sabre-toothed cat, lion, American cheetah and the giant short-faced bear). Such an impact did not seem improbable since examples

of overkill and extinction were well known elsewhere when humans arrived for the first time, particularly on islands. Recent work, however, has cast some doubt over this hypothesis. The mass extinction seems to have been a gradual process, not linked to human hunters, and had probably begun before humans arrived. Increasing doubts about the idea of 'Man the Hunter' and the efficiency of these early hunters have also damaged the theory. (In Europe too there were extinctions at the end of the ice age – mammoth, woolly rhinoceros and the cave bear – but these were the species least hunted by humans.) The impact of the major climatic changes at the end of the ice age was probably crucial, together with the linked changes in vegetation, seasonal temperatures and length of growing season. Together they substantially changed the environment and altered important aspects of animal life such as migration routes. However, it is quite possible that human intervention was important in pushing some species, already suffering from environmental stress, to extinction.
[*Later Americas* 5.1, 5.5]

2.6.3 The Pacific

The last areas of the world to be settled by humans were the remote islands of the Indian Ocean and Pacific, and this was not until about ten thousand years after the settlement of the Americas. It was undertaken not by pure gatherers and hunters but by groups that had a limited amount of agriculture. Madagascar was settled not from Africa but by people sailing from the Indonesian islands about 500 CE. An even more spectacular set of voyages by the Polynesians took place in the Pacific. The voyages to these very remote islands (almost 350 were colonized) are one of the most remarkable parts of human history and were done with no knowledge of geography, no metal tools, no measure of time, no navigation instruments and relied entirely upon observation of natural phenomena and the stars to find directions. The Polynesians sailed and settled across a huge triangle covering an area of over twenty million square miles (almost a quarter of the circumference of the earth) from Hawaii in the north to New Zealand in the south-west and Easter Island in the south-east. Nowhere else in the world has a single cultural group radiated over such a vast area or across such a wide range of different environments. The voyages were not accidental and were undertaken by groups of colonists accompanied by a range of plants and animals. They sailed in large double-hulled canoes (or single-hulled with an outrigger) about seventy feet long with keels carved from solid logs. They were capable of about eight knots and at first the Polynesians sailed from west to east. This may, at first glance, seem odd because it was against the prevailing winds in the Pacific but it allowed for a relatively easy return to

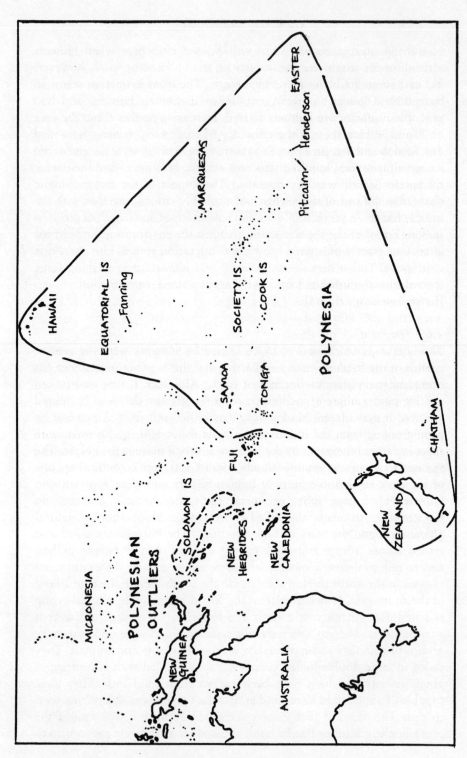

Map 3: The settlement of the Pacific: the Polynesian triangle

base if the voyage proved to be unproductive. Only later were the more difficult north–south voyages attempted.

The key area for the dispersal of the Polynesian people was around coastal New Guinea and the Bismarck Islands where, around 3000–2000 BCE, a very distinctive cultural style known as Lapita evolved. Between 1600 and 500 BCE these groups moved out into Oceania proper and settled Fiji, Samoa and Tonga. From Samoa they reached the Marquesas by 300 CE, possibly several hundred years earlier. The longest west–east voyage, to Easter Island, was accomplished by about 500 CE – it was not navigationally any more difficult than the earlier voyages but it was a much greater test of endurance. The main voyage to the north and Hawaii was undertaken at about the same time and involved sailing north out of the south-east trade winds, across the notorious doldrums and into the north-east trades. The settlers needed to cover a distance of nearly 2,500 miles from the nearest inhabited land of the Marquesas. Even more difficult was the voyage south from the Society Islands. As a result New Zealand was not settled until 800 CE at the earliest and probably not until 1000 CE. Even more remote were the Chatham Islands, over 500 miles downwind from New Zealand, which were only reached about five hundred years ago.

Some of the settlements died out or were abandoned – Fanning, Pitcairn and Henderson islands – but most survived. The islands at the eastern and southern extremities of settlement – Easter Island and New Zealand – required major adaptations for colonization to succeed. The Polynesians came from sub-tropical islands and carried their plants and animals with them but few of them could survive in these very different climates. Instead the settlers had to adopt very new ways of finding food. Yet despite their remoteness the settlers on these islands retained a recognizably Polynesian culture. This was one of the epic achievements in the human settlement of the world.

[*Later Pacific* 5.7]

OVERVIEW I

THE WORLD IN
10,000 BCE

Population: 4 million
Major cities: None

Events:

★   Retreat of major ice-sheets under way, Britain still joined to European continent. No North Sea or Baltic

★   First human groups reach the far south of south America

★   First pottery made by Jomon hunter-gatherers in Japan

★   First small villages in south-west Asia but still using gathering and hunting for food, though some herding of gazelle

★   A few semi-domesticated sheep and goats in Zagros mountains area – people also gathering wild cereals

★   First boats used in the Mediterranean

PART TWO
The Great Transition

3

Crops and Animals

For over a million years humans lived in small, mobile groups gathering their food from the wild and hunting animals. When resources permitted they came together in larger groups and occasionally, when they could rely on particularly rich sources of food, they became semi-sedentary. Then, in a relatively short period of time after the end of the last ice age, about 10,000 BCE, this stable and well-balanced way of life began to change. Across the world humans slowly began to settle in one location and replace gathered plants with ones grown on special plots of land while a few animals were also domesticated. In less than ten thousand years this new way of life had spread around the globe. Gathering and hunting groups survived but they were increasingly pushed into more marginal areas and those that the farmers could not utilize. By the twentieth century only a few groups of such people survived to be studied by anthropologists. The adoption of farming was the most fundamental change in human history and led on to all that we call civilization and recorded human history.

3.1 Why Agriculture?

The crucial question is why this change in a well-adjusted way of life ever took place. The earliest theories suggested that the advantages of agriculture were so obvious that it must have been adopted as soon as human genius, knowledge and invention had progressed far enough. Now such easy answers seem far less plausible. Work with gathering and hunting groups has shown that their life is relatively easy – food is obtained with little effort, it provides a well-balanced and nutritious diet and plenty of time is available for leisure activities. There are also all the problems involved in agriculture to be considered. It requires much more effort than gathering and hunting, especially in the planting and harvesting seasons. Crops have to be stored for much of the year, leading to wastage and the possibility of theft. Although more productive than gathering and hunting, agriculture relies on only a few crops and in a poor season shortages and even famine are much more likely.

Agriculture was adopted not once but on a number of occasions across the world using different crops and animals. The key centres were south-west Asia, China, Mesoamerica, the Andes and the tropical areas of Africa and south-east Asia. (It is much more difficult to understand what happened in the tropics as few plant remains are preserved in archaeological sites because of the humid conditions.) It seems clear therefore that simple explanations will not apply in every case around the globe. For example, one theory put forward a few years ago argued that agriculture was adopted when world population had grown to a level where gathering and hunting groups found it difficult to find new territories to exploit and therefore had no choice but to turn to more intensive ways of gaining their food that involved more effort. This may be a partial explanation of what happened in a relatively densely populated area such as south-west Asia but it seems unlikely to hold good in Mesoamerica where the first signs of agriculture are apparent within only seven thousand years of the first settlement of the American continent.

In the past these fundamental changes have been called a 'Neolithic Revolution' and linked to the invention of pottery and the development of the first small towns. However, human groups can be sedentary without adopting agriculture – for example the native Americans of the Pacific coast of north America who developed highly complex societies based on their exploitation of local marine resources. Other groups have had pottery without agriculture. Indeed the first pottery in the world was produced about 10,000 BCE by the Jomon gatherers and hunters in Japan. (It continued to be made for ten thousand years without any agriculture.) The changes involved in the adoption of agriculture were also very far from revolutionary – no group set out to 'invent' agriculture – the process lasted thousands of years with only very small changes in subsistence and ways of life from one generation to the next. One of the most important aspects of the changes was the 'ratchet effect'. Once groups had adopted changes that resulted in greater food output, population tended to rise making it very difficult to go back to less intensive ways of gaining food.

The most recent work on this complex subject suggests that agriculture should be seen not as a sudden break with the past but as part of a long evolutionary process involving the intensification of the interactions between humans and plants and animals. Gathering and hunting groups modify the environment, to encourage the growth of plants they prefer, using techniques such as controlled burning, the creation of 'irrigated' areas and replanting. It is also clear that groups in Eurasia from about 30,000 years ago were not simply hunters preying randomly on the herds that they came across. Instead they were adopting much more sophisticated and effective strategies of herd management so that they carefully selected the animals they wished to kill. All of these techniques can be seen as stages along a continuum leading to full-scale agriculture. The technology to process nuts and seeds gathered from the wild (grinding stones, pestles and mortars and containers) were all made about twenty thousand years before agriculture developed. Neither did the process stop with the first adoption of agriculture. New plants and animals continued to be domesticated, others were discarded. It took several thousand years after domestication before the 'secondary products revolution' took place – the use of cattle to provide milk and other dairy products. Domesticated varieties were later transported across the world and grown or tended on different continents.

The plants and animals which were domesticated varied across the world depending on what was available in the wild but there were some common characteristics. Probably the first animal to be domesticated was the wolf but not to provide food – the dogs that evolved from the wolf provided companionship, probably helped with hunting and fed from scavenging among the debris left by humans. Humans generally concentrated on domesticating placid, slow-moving animals that ate a wide range of food and already existed in highly social groups with a submissive herd structure – sheep and goats are the obvious examples. Domestication isolated the animals from the wild and gradually led to the selection of characteristics that the farmer thought desirable. Most cultivated seed crops are self-pollinated. This enabled the early farmers to isolate the crop from the wild variety very easily. Wild seed varieties tend to have very rapid seed dispersal but the first farmers would automatically have selected those that stayed on the plant longer. This would quickly (within a few years) further isolate the cultivated varieties, leading eventually to types where the seeds only became detached after threshing, making the plant entirely dependent on humans to reproduce. However, the variety of plants and animals domesticated, together with the different timescales and processes involved across the world, mean that it is best to study the most fundamental change in human history on a regional basis.

3.2 South-West Asia

It was in this area (running from the Levant through south-eastern Turkey to the Zagros mountains in Iran) that agriculture first developed and it is the one that has been most intensively studied. The wild progenitors of all the domesticated crops and animals have been identified, together with the areas where they flourished. A large number of archaeological sites have also provided a mass of information about how different human groups slowly changed the way they found their food. One fundamental fact is that genetic studies of the early plants used in farming strongly suggest that each plant was only domesticated once. Exactly where this happened,

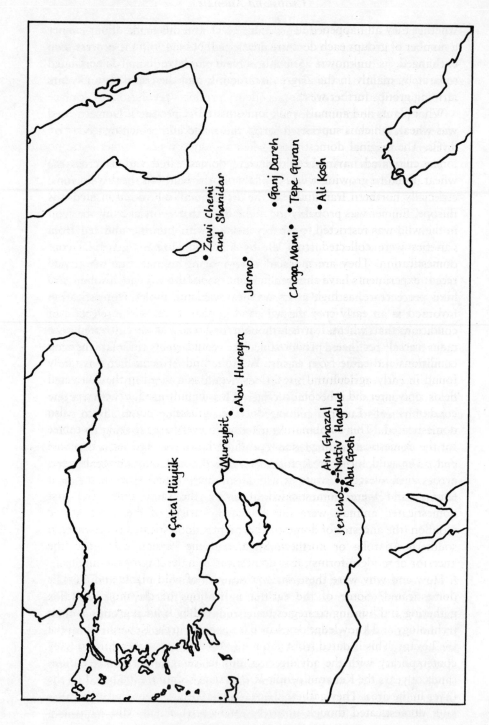

Map 4: South-west Asia: Key sites for the origins of agriculture

whether they all happened in the same place and then spread, or whether a number of groups each domesticated different plants and they were then exchanged, is unknown. Animals appear to have been domesticated separately, mainly in the Zagros mountains, and then spread to existing farming groups further west.

What plants and animals were domesticated? The most important grass was wheat, which is superior to other cereals because of its high nutritive levels. The original domesticated wheats – einkorn and emmer – are no longer cultivated, having been replaced by bread wheat and hard (durum) wheat. Einkorn growing wild is still found widely across south-west Asia, especially northern Iran and Iraq, and it was still cultivated in medieval Europe. Emmer was probably the most important of the early wheats and in the wild was restricted to the Levant and northern Iraq and Iran. Both varieties were collected from the wild for thousands of years before domestication. They are more nutritious than domesticated wheat and recent experiments have shown that yields from the wild could reach 800 kilos per hectare, as high as in medieval England. Barley was much less favoured as an early crop despite the fact that it can withstand harsher conditions than wheat. It was little used for bread but rapidly became the main cereal for beer production. Rye could grow in even harsher conditions and came from eastern Anatolia and Armenia but it is rarely found in early agricultural sites. Oats began as a weed in the cultivated fields, only later did it become a crop – it was mainly used in the temperate conditions of Europe. Alongside the grasses, pulses were also domesticated. (This combination is found in every area that was a centre for the domestication of plants because both are required for a balanced diet.) The wild forms of lentils, peas, broad beans and chickpeas grew across south-west Asia, were gathered from the wild alongside einkorn and emmer, and were domesticated at about the same time. The first domesticated animals were the Armenian variety of the West Asiatic mouflon (the ancestor of domestic sheep), first domesticated somewhere in southern Anatolia or northern Syria, and the Persian wild goat (the ancestor of modern forms), first domesticated in the Zagros mountains.

How and why were these various varieties of wild plants and animals domesticated? Some of the earliest indications of the more complex gathering and hunting strategies being adopted by human groups as their technology and knowledge developed is apparent in the Kebaran culture of the Levant. This is dated from about 18,000 BCE and is therefore roughly contemporary with the advanced groups in ice-age Europe. Over thousands of years the Kebaran people lived a semi-sedentary life based on the caves in the area. They gathered seeds from nearly all the plants that were later domesticated though not very intensively. Their main effort was devoted to the exploitation of the large herds of gazelle in the region. They constitute over four-fifths of the bones recovered from these archaeological sites and their nature suggests that the herds were being manipulated and selectively culled in a way that was very close to full domestication.

The Kebaran culture survived until about 10,000 BCE when the climatic changes associated with the end of the ice age caused significant alterations to the vegetation of the Levant. The gathering and hunting groups in the area adapted to these changes by only small modifications in their earlier ways of finding food. As the climate warmed, plants that had only existed in small refuge areas spread rapidly and widely across the region. In particular the wild grasses – emmer, einkorn and barley – together with oak, almond and pistachio trees (all good food sources) became abundant. A new Natufian culture emerged along the coastal and hill zones from southern Turkey to the Nile valley. It was based on extensive exploitation of the wild grasses and the development of a sophisticated technology to harvest and process the seeds – bone sickles with flint blades, querns, grinding stones, pestles and mortars. In parallel the herding of gazelle continued. The easily available food which could be found in the wild meant that permanent settlements and small villages could be maintained. One of the best studied of these is Abu Hureyra near the Euphrates in Syria. It was a small village of pit dwellings with reed roofs and contained about 300–400 people. They lived harvesting the wild einkorn, rye and barley in the area and killing the large herds of gazelle which arrived in the valley each spring.

A village such as Abu Hureyra shows that agriculture was not a requirement for a settled community provided enough food could be obtained from the local area. There were similar villages across the Levant at this time. This way of life lasted for perhaps two thousand years until it was disrupted by further climatic change. As the earth's climate continued to warm after the ice age the Levant became drier and much closer to a modern Mediterranean climate. As a result the areas where the wild grasses could grow became much smaller, producing a major subsistence crisis for the Natufian groups. The way in which some of them reacted produced agriculture. Villages such as Abu Hureyra were abandoned and some groups probably reverted to a mobile way of life and a full gathering and hunting pattern of subsistence. Others, long adapted to a sedentary style of life and dependence on cereals gathered from areas around the village, gave up the old gathering and hunting way of coping with shortage – mobility. Instead they started to plant wild grasses in land near their village. This enabled them to maintain their existing culture and continue to use all of their seed processing and storage technologies. No doubt it hardly seemed a very momentous step to take.

The first signs of this change are apparent in the villages around the margins of the shrinking lakes of the Jordan valley about 8000 BCE. Overall the transition to agriculture in the Levant took about two thousand years and can be studied at about 150 sites that have been excavated in the area. In the first few hundred years rapid domestication seems to have been confined to a few areas on the edge of the belt of Mediterranean-type vegetation but then spread rapidly. The old idea that the farming communities were 'colonizers', spreading out to take over new agricultural land, has now been abandoned as too redolent of European notions of the early twentieth century about imperialism and 'advanced' societies taking over from those at a lower level. Instead archaeologists now argue for a process of diffusion and adaptation as gathering and hunting groups took over the practices of their farming neighbours while keeping some of their gathering and hunting activities. One of the earliest agricultural sites to be discovered was Jericho, which flourished about 7500 BCE. Beehive-shaped mud-brick huts for about 300 people covered a site of about ten acres surrounded by a huge ditch and a stone wall which had a large circular tower and internal staircase. Clearly this all involved a considerable amount of effort by the inhabitants. The wall and tower were originally thought to be defensive but recent re-examination has shown that their purpose was to divert flood water. As in other villages, the dead were buried within the walls of the houses, usually with the head severed but modelled in painted plaster.

Unfortunately the excavation at Jericho was undertaken long before advanced archaeological techniques were developed to recover remains that could illuminate the earliest phases of agriculture. The site of Netiv Hagdud, some ten miles north of Jericho and dating to 7800–7500 BCE, was excavated in the late 1980s and it provides a very good picture of a village in the intermediate stage between gathering and hunting and agriculture. About twenty to thirty families lived there (it was therefore about half the size of Jericho) and they had a very wide range of foods. From the local spring and shallow lake they took molluscs, snails, crabs, ducks and fish. In the nearby woodland they hunted lizards, rodents, deer, wild pigs and gazelle. They also gathered over fifty species of wild plants, including grasses such as einkorn and emmer, legumes and nuts. In addition, in the easily tilled soil along the side of the lake they had a single domesticated plant – an early form of barley. It was their first step towards agriculture. A much more abrupt transition took place at the village of Abu Hureyra which was reoccupied around 7700 BCE, about three centuries after it was abandoned when the climate changed. The new village of one-storey, mud-brick houses grew to over thirty acres. At first the inhabitants lived much as in the past – herding the gazelle and gathering a wide range of plants from the local area. Then, within no more than a couple of generations, there was a rapid switch to agriculture. The wide range of gathered plants was reduced to half a dozen cultivated species (mainly einkorn and pulses) and the gazelle were abandoned in favour of domesticated sheep and goats.

The switch to sheep and goats in the Levant was almost certainly the result of their introduction from outside following separate developments in the area of the Zagros mountains and the edge of the Mesopotamian plain. This area has been less well studied than the Levant and it is possible that some of the elements in the emergence of agriculture occurred here earlier than they did further west. Certainly it seems that true farming, with its mix of domesticated plants and animals, did develop here first. Gathering and hunting groups in this area were well adapted to making use of the wide range of environments available from the valleys, up through the hills to the mountains. The first stage of the transition to farming can be seen at the sites of Zawi Chemi and Shanidar in the mountains of Kurdistan, dated to about 9000 BCE. These were probably summer camps where goats were kept in a semi-domesticated environment alongside some young sheep and local wild cereals were gathered. At Ganj Dareh near Kermanshah there was another seasonal camp, dated to about 8500 BCE but within five hundred years a small village of rectangular huts had developed. Goats were herded and cereals were cultivated. Further south, on the edge of the Mesopotamian plain, the village of Ali Kosh was settled about 8000 BCE. The inhabitants herded sheep and goats, taking them up into the hills for the summer pastures. Emmer, einkorn, barley and lentils were cultivated from the start and fish and waterfowl were hunted in the nearby marsh. It was from the villages in these areas that the first domesticated animals – sheep and goats – spread westwards and were introduced to the crop growing communities of the Levant.

Further north in Anatolia the early villages such as Hacilar (founded about 6700 BCE) were much simpler than those in the Levant. The inhabitants did not have pottery and used baskets and animal skin containers instead. They cultivated barley and emmer, gathered other grasses from the wild and may have herded sheep and goats though most of the animals were probably still not fully domesticated. Shortly afterwards a major settlement at Çatal Hüyük developed. At its height, about 6000 BCE, it covered 32 acres (about four times the size of Jericho) and had a population of about 5,000. It consisted of sun-dried-brick houses built back to back. Some of the paintings on the walls have been preserved and they depict mainly bulls and women in what appear to be various fertility rituals. Society in this small town with its specialized craftsmen and priests appears to have been markedly less egalitarian than the early farming villages.

Much of the prosperity of Çatal Hüyük seems to have been based on its control of a local source of highly prized obsidian which made very good tools. It is a sign that the various communities across the Levant, Anatolia and the Zagros mountains were in touch with each other along various barter networks. Although most of the developments in agriculture in the region were independent there were clearly exchanges of ideas and techniques. Everywhere by about 6000 BCE fully agricultural economies had emerged. The original cereals became more productive through human selection – the first bread wheats emerged in northern Iran about 6000 BCE when domesticated emmer was crossed with a wild wheat to produce a more adaptable plant. Sheep were also selected to produce wool. Cattle, a much more difficult animal to tame, were probably domesticated between 7000 and 6000 BCE, although it was probably several thousand years before they were selected to produce extra milk and humans began to consume dairy products. Pigs were added to this range of animals – probably for the first time at Çayönü in Anatolia about 6500 BCE. As farming was adopted the population grew slowly – perhaps by about ten per cent a century. The changes would hardly have been noticeable to contemporaries but the long-term consequences were significant. Villages and small towns developed across the region and although the societies seem to have been fairly egalitarian there was a much greater degree of social organization. Each of these communities seems to have had a complex series of rituals, probably involving ancestor worship and especially fertility rituals now that so much of their life depended on the success of the crops they planted and the animals they had domesticated.

3.3 The Spread of Farming from South-West Asia

South-west Asia was the first area in the world where humans came to rely on farming for their existence. From this core region these new techniques spread across a wide area to Europe, southwards to the Nile valley and also eastwards. The last was probably the first area to see the spread of agriculture. By about 6000 BCE in the foothills of the Kopet Dag mountains in north-east Iran and southern Turkmenistan near the Caspian Sea a series of small villages developed (known as the Jeitun culture), the livelihood of which was based on all the domesticated plants and animals of south-west Asia. At Mergarh on the Kachi plain – a major route from central Asia to the Indus valley – by 6000 BCE the inhabitants had shifted from gazelle hunting to domesticated sheep and goats together with crops such as barley and the early wheats. They also used pottery. Within another thousand years people in the northern foothills of the Hindu Kush and on the plain of Bactria were farmers.

3.3.1 Europe

One of the best studied phases in the diffusion of farming is its impact on Europe. The retreat of the ice-sheets and the consequent enormous shifts in vegetation produced a major shock for the gatherers and hunters whose ways of life were well adapted to the ice-age environment. Many animals such as the mammoth and woolly rhino became extinct and were replaced by forest animals such as red and roe deer. No longer able to exploit the large herds of animals, the gatherers and hunters of Europe had to change their ways of life radically. Generally they adopted highly specialized types of subsistence based on very specific resources, in particular from coastal and marine environments. These often involved far more effort in order to obtain and process food but there was little alternative. To cope with these new ways of life they developed highly specialized tools. For example, at Ulkestrup in Denmark (dated to 7500–5700 BCE) people lived on a peat island on a lake, building large huts with wood and bark floors. They fished using canoes with nets, and bone and antler pointed spears. They hunted red deer, wild ox and pigs and trapped birds. In the autumn they gathered hazelnuts and other plant foods. In the winter they hunted elk and other types of game. Clearly the area was productive enough to sustain this permanent settlement. In southern Europe plant foods were more important and some of the inhabitants of Greece and Italy appear to have controlled the herds of red deer and culled them in ways that were very close to domestication.

That farming should spread westwards from Anatolia into the Aegean and south-east Europe is not surprising – their climates were very similar and the type of agriculture developed in south-west Asia could be adopted almost without change. In a few places there does seem to have been colonization by farmers – for example at Knossos on Crete, about 6000 BCE. (Boats had been used in the Mediterranean from at least 10,000 BCE when obsidian from the island of Melos was being traded across the region.) Elsewhere farming was probably adopted as part of a general process of agricultural intensification as knowledge of the new techniques spread from area to area. The first agricultural settlements in Greece at Argissa-Maghula in Thessaly, date to about 6000 BCE and at Nea Nikomedia about five hundred years later. In Italy the first known settlements are on the Tavoliere plain in the south-east of the peninsula and date to about 5000 BCE. At the same time the agricultural 'Karanovo' culture was widespread in the Balkans.

The adoption of farming further west and north in Europe required a series of modifications to the practices that had evolved in south-west Asia. The climate was wetter with year-round rainfall and the growing season was shorter. Planting had to shift from the autumn to the spring, and winter feed was often needed for the animals. Barley and eventually oats therefore became far more important crops. The early farmers had only a limited range of tools – mainly wooden hoes and digging sticks – which could not be used effectively on the heavy soils that predominated in central and north-west Europe. The spread of farming across Europe is associated with the so-called 'Banderkeramik' culture from their very distinctive pottery style. By shortly after 5000 BCE this style and early agriculture had spread up the Danube valley into central Europe, as far west as the Netherlands and as far east as the Vistula. The farmers grew barley, einkorn, emmer and flax, adopted crop rotation and enclosed their animals (cattle, sheep and goats) in hedged fields. The spread of farming must have been anything but a smooth process as many sites failed and were abandoned as people slowly learnt how to adapt to the new conditions. In general they settled on the lightest, most easily cultivated soils, especially gravel river terraces near to medium-sized streams. Gathering and hunting groups often adopted some of the techniques of farming such as using pottery to store gathered wild grains over the winter, but they were slowly confined to the less favourable areas.

The original settlements were small and very widely scattered. As population grew slowly many of these gaps were filled in. From about 4500 BCE many of the settlements became villages with long houses, possibly for extended families, and they were protected by earth enclosures. These early societies were groups of subsistence farmers and seem to have been largely egalitarian – certainly the burials do not seem to reflect any great degree of social differentiation. From about 4000 BCE there appears to be an increasing pace of social change with developing craft specialization, regional trading centres and complex burial rituals. The last were reflected in the megalithic tombs and large burial mounds found particularly in France and Spain.

The level of sophistication of some of these societies can be judged from their ceremonial constructions. At Newgrange, about twenty-five miles north of Dublin, there is a 'passage grave' built about 3300 BCE. The 62-foot-long passage leads to an interior vault which is illuminated on the winter solstice via a special 'roofbox' separate from the main passage. Although usually described as a tomb it is more likely to be a ritual building, constructed by a large community effort, where a few initiates celebrated death and rebirth. Many other sites, especially stone circles, across north-west Europe clearly had a similar ritual function, some also involved burials too. They were not astronomical observatories but rather markers to identify key events in the passage of the sun, moon and perhaps stars across the sky. Some of the most important were the summer and winter solstices and the equinoxes. The other is the complex 18.6-year lunar cycle. All of these alignments can be found at Stonehenge in southern England which was constructed in a series of phases beginning about 2800 BCE. There are over 900 other stone rings in the British Isles and many in France, including the highly complex Carnac set of stones in Brittany. Of the fifty in north-east Scotland surveys have shown that they are all oriented towards the maximum and minimum points of the lunar cycle. [*Later Europe 7.7*]

3.3.2 The Nile valley

Agriculture also spread south from the Levant into the Nile valley, though later than its introduction into south-east Europe. The valley had long been occupied by gathering and hunting groups (the earliest finds date back to about 17,000 BCE) but it was a difficult area to exploit because of the annual flood. From about 6000 BCE the climate in the area seems to have become much drier and some of the gathering and hunting groups moved into the valley. As numbers rose and the area available for exploitation by each group grew smaller the pressure to adopt more intensive techniques increased. People shifted from gathering the wild cereals to cultivating them. Settled communities and villages emerged. The exact dating of the process is not known because this was a period of very low Nile floods and most of the village sites are now underwater. The best available evidence suggests that the first villages emerged after 4300 BCE and that agriculture was fully established 800 years later. [*Later Egypt 4.5*]

3.4 China

The second area of the world to adopt agriculture was China and it did so independently of developments in south-west Asia. In the area of modern China two separate and distinctive types of agriculture emerged based on millet in the north and rice further south. The earliest of the two domestications occurred in the south in the Hupei basin of the middle Yangtze valley and the coastal plain of Hang-chou Bay in the Yangtze delta south of Shanghai. Here, about 6500 BCE, rice was first domesticated. Wild rice is a plant adapted to germinate in dry soil but grow in seasonally flooded shallow water. The exact wild progenitor of the domesticated variety is difficult to identify but it was domesticated by first creating artificial areas in which it could grow and then deliberately planting it in these areas. This could easily be done in the middle and lower Yangtze valley which had vast areas of flooded lakes and lowlands. The companion legume for rice was the soybean. The earliest agricultural societies of Hang-chou Bay also depended on fishing and hunting small birds and animals. Up the river in the Hupei basin the communities were fully agricultural.

In the north where the Yellow (Huang-Ho) river exits from the highlands on to the plains of east China and is joined by the Wei river, agriculture emerged about 5500 BCE. Winters in the area were dry and harsh and the summer rain was unreliable. Farming was therefore based on two drought-resistant crops originally gathered in the highland areas – broomcorn millet and foxtail millet – which have the lowest water requirement of any of the cultivated cereals. Animals were also important – the pig was domesticated by 5500 BCE, independently of its domestication in southwest Asia, and the chicken, for the first time anywhere in the world, by about 5000 BCE. About 500 years later still the water buffalo was used as a draught animal. The wind-blown loess soils in the area were easily worked with the relatively simple tools available – wooden digging sticks and hoes. The first villages in the area (known as the P'ei-li-kang culture) were large with numerous substantial round houses some six feet across and the people living there already had elaborate pottery.

From about 4800 BCE the new, more elaborate, Yang-shao culture spread across the north and similar regional cultures developed in the south. There were very large villages surrounded by deep defensive ditches. The villages had a central plaza around which were arranged family houses, huge storage pits and communal animal pens. Within a few hundred years the level of interaction between these regions seems to have increased in parallel with growing social differentiation within the villages. In the Yangtze delta potters produced highly specialized black, polished ware on a wheel. Prestige goods such as incised turtle shells and jade were being traded over considerable distances. Burials became markedly less egalitarian – in one a young male was buried with over a hundred jade objects and in others human victims accompanied the dead. There are also signs of growing conflict both between areas and also within communities – headless and footless corpses have been found shoved down wells. Religion seems to have become more complex and one of the most distinctive elements of early Chinese civilization – divination by using fire to crack open animal bones – was already being used.

As in south-west Asia agriculture spread from the two core areas of China. Rice may have been domesticated in the southern foothills of the Himalayas, upper Burma and northern Thailand but the latest evidence suggests that it is more likely that it spread westwards from China. It certainly spread south along the river valleys and coastal areas reaching Taiwan about 3500 BCE, East Timor by 2100 BCE and the Philippines about 400 years later. However, it did not reach Japan until about 400 BCE. Wheat and barley reached China, indirectly from south-west Asia via a series of intermediary cultures about 2500 BCE. Sheep and goats arrived a little later but were never very important. The main features of Chinese agriculture had already been set by its own domesticated varieties. [*Later China 7.8*]

3.5 The Americas and Elsewhere

[*Settlement of the Americas 2.6.2*]

3.5.1 Mesoamerica

The third area to domesticate crops was Mesoamerica followed by separate domestications of different plants in both north America and the central Andes. In Mesoamerica the first plants to be cultivated were the gourds – pumpkins and squash, at first as containers, then for their seeds and only finally for their flesh as it became sweet with domestication. This family of plants produced the courgette and marrow and other minor domesticates included tomatoes, avocados and chilli peppers. However, the most important plant was maize followed by its accompanying legume, the common bean. The problem in studying the origins of agriculture in Mesoamerica is that only about half a dozen sites have been excavated.

The ancestor of maize was almost certainly a grass called teosinte which was gathered from the wild and then domesticated in the highland area around Guadalajara in western Mexico about 3500 BCE, perhaps a little earlier. The early cultivators rapidly encountered a problem with maize which did not occur with the wild cereals domesticated in the Old World. For reasons of plant genetics it was difficult to increase the yield of maize by selection and the crossing of varieties. The earliest maize cobs were therefore very different from contemporary maize – they were only about two inches long. At first the cultivated varieties were only a little more productive than those gathered from the wild (they were just easier to harvest). This meant that the transition to agriculture took longer in Mesoamerica than elsewhere and gathering and hunting remained a significant factor for the early groups who cultivated maize. This was certainly the case for the earliest known cultivators in the Tehuacan valley about 2700 BCE where domesticated plants only accounted for about a quarter of the diet. Maize spread across Mesoamerica reaching the valley of Mexico between 2300 and 1500 BCE and the Gulf coast at La Venta

about 1400 BCE. It reached the northern parts of south America about four hundred years later. The common bean was almost certainly domesticated a little later than maize but in the same area. The two plants were needed in combination in order to produce a balanced diet. The first agricultural villages developed in Mesoamerica about 2000 BCE but the pace of development remained slow until maize yields improved.
[*Later Mesoamerica* 5.1]

3.5.2 North America

Domesticated maize spread north from Mexico into the south-west of the United States about 1500 BCE, probably in much the same way as agriculture was adopted in south-west Asia – by a process of diffusion rather than colonization. Here, about 1200 BCE, it was crossed with an indigenous species of teosinte to produce 'maize de ocho' which was better adapted to the shorter growing season of the north. The first villages in the area did not develop until about 300 BCE when maize, together with continued gathering from the wild, formed the basis for the increasingly sophisticated cultures that developed in the area. Maize could not easily be grown further north until new hardier varieties had slowly been bred. It eventually reached eastern north America about 900 CE when it rapidly became an important crop. Work in the last couple of decades has, however, shown that the people of north America did domesticate a small range of plants long before maize arrived from the south. About 2500 BCE a few plants that had long been gathered from the wild were domesticated and grown in small plots along some of the river valleys. These were chenopod (or goosefoot), which continued to be cultivated until about 200 years ago but is now extinct, marsh elder and the sunflower. None of these plants were highly productive and they formed little more than a supplement to the diet of primarily gathering and hunting groups. Settlements and villages remained small for a long period before the arrival of maize, though some spectacular burial mounds were constructed at a number of sites.

3.5.3 The Andes

The plants of north America were of little significance but those domesticated in the central Andes were, like those of Mesoamerica, of major importance. Quinua, which is grown at altitudes above about 5,000 feet, was probably domesticated in southern Peru and Bolivia about 3000 BCE. This process was almost certainly linked to the domestication of the llama and the alpaca which are descended from the wild guanaco and vicuna respectively. Gathering and hunting groups were herding the wild animals from about 7000 BCE since, like sheep and goats, they are docile and relatively easily controlled. Both varieties forage on quinua although the seeds pass through the animals undamaged and therefore grew when their dung was used as fertilizer. Both animal species were fully domesticated by about 3000 BCE and were joined by the only other animal to be domesticated in the area – the guinea pig – at about the same time. (The guinea pig had been a major source of food for gatherers and hunters in the Andes since about 9000 BCE.) Most significant was the domestication of four wild tubers. Three of these (oca, mashua and ullucu) remained confined to the highlands but the fourth – the potato (in a number of varieties) – was also cultivated at lower levels and eventually became one of the world's major food crops. These tubers, which had long been gathered from the wild, were probably first domesticated in the area around Lake Titicaca on the Peru-Bolivia border about 2500 BCE. An intriguing question is why and how potatoes were first eaten and domesticated. Nearly all wild potatoes are potentially toxic and even current cultivated varieties can be fatal when green. Only a few varieties are not poisonous and they may have been identified by their taste, though this would have been a highly dangerous procedure. There is some ethnographic evidence from people in the Andean highlands that clay was eaten at the same time as potatoes in order to reduce their toxicity.

[*Later Peru and the Andes 5.5*]

3.5.4 The rest of the world

The evidence for domestication of plants in other parts of the world is sketchy. Sorghum, currently one of the world's most important cereals was probably first domesticated in the Sudan-Chad area. The exact date is unknown but it must be fairly early because the crop is known in India from about 2000 BCE, having arrived there via the Arabian peninsula. Pearl millet, the most drought-resistant of all cereals, was domesticated near the Sahara and then moved to the Sahel area of West Africa. In Africa these two cereals were combined with local pulses (the cowpea and groundnut) to provide a balanced diet. The African variety of rice (which is distinct from that of Asia) was domesticated about 1500 BCE, somewhere in West Africa. Old World cotton is first found in the Indus valley about 1800 BCE but it is not naturally an Indian plant and probably originated in the Sudan-Nubia area. It is even more difficult to know how and where the major tropical crops were first domesticated since they are almost never preserved in archaeological sites because of the humid climate. Yams, which are found across Africa and south-east Asia, can easily be cultivated by replanting the stalk and this is done by numerous gathering and hunting groups. Taro and breadfruit originated in south-east Asia and spread into Oceania. Manioc and the sweet potato come from tropical south America.

3.6 The Impact of Farming

Across the world in the seven thousand years or so after 10,000 BCE a number of plants and animals were domesticated and most humans abandoned a largely mobile way of life and settled in villages to tend their crops and herds. Gathering and hunting groups had few possessions and the social structure within their small groups was largely egalitarian. A few people might be experts at making particular tools or finding types of food, one or two among the elders might be responsible for the traditions and beliefs of the group and therefore have a special status. Land was not owned and neither were its resources – they were available for whoever chose to take them. Food was shared within the group. All of this changed with farming. The creation of fields for the cultivation of crops and the herding of animals meant that land, together with its products, came to be owned, perhaps at first by the community but very rapidly by individuals. The most fundamental change was that although farming required far greater effort than gathering and hunting it did produce far more food – more than the farmer and his immediate family could consume. This food surplus was the foundation for all later social and political change. It could be used to support people in occupations other than farming – specialist craftsmen, religious functionaries and eventually political and military leaders. The key question is how this surplus was taken from the farmer and by whom. At first it was probably given up voluntarily to support those functions, especially religious, regarded as important by the community. However, even relatively small-scale agricultural societies appear to have developed hierarchies which were often headed by chiefs and clan leaders with authority to redistribute the food surplus. The specialists who were not farmers therefore came to rely on these mechanisms in order to survive. Over a long period of time the methods of food redistribution within society generally appear to have become increasingly coercive.

The adoption of farming had other important consequences. Although some of the dwellings constructed by semi-sedentary gathering and hunting groups could be quite elaborate, once humans settled in one place houses became even more elaborate. Across south-west Asia sun-dried-mud-brick houses (usually with flat roofs) were fairly standard whereas in central and western Europe and China timber houses were the norm. New technologies were also required once mobility was abandoned. After the year's harvest storage was essential, leading to the construction of grain bins and pits. Water was also vital and the making of clay pots, at first by building up rolls of clay and firing it in open fires, developed everywhere (in south-west Asia about 6000 BCE). Most gatherers and hunters used digging sticks and the earliest farmers did the same to plant their crops.

Wooden and stone-bladed hoes capable of breaking up soft soils followed. The farmers also needed tougher working edges – ground and polished stone sickles to harvest crops and axes to clear land. This placed a premium on the best stones, especially obsidian, and networks to trade it over long distances soon emerged.

Although farming enabled humans to produce more food and therefore numbers slowly rose, it also had a number of important drawbacks. The early farmers depended on a much smaller range of plants than gatherers and hunters and were therefore much more vulnerable to crop failures due to poor weather, plant diseases and wastage during storage. In most cases the harvest was only barely sufficient to last through the winter and spring until the new crop was available. A couple of bad harvests in succession could be catastrophic. Storage of food also made it vulnerable to theft and to conflict between different groups. The specialist non-farmers were particularly vulnerable to food shortages and famines, especially if redistribution within society broke down. Having settled in one place these groups of early farmers had, within a few generations, lost the knowledge and techniques to revert to a mobile way of life which enabled gathering and hunting groups to avoid the worst consequences of food shortage. Farmers could also severely damage the local environment. Cutting down trees to create farming land, to build houses and to provide fuel for heating and cooking could have a devastating effect in vulnerable areas. Recent archaeological evidence suggests that some of the earliest farming villages in the Jordan valley had to be abandoned after little more than a thousand years because deforestation led to severe soil erosion and the destruction of farming land.

The adoption of a limited range of crops and animals had important consequences for human diets. It is far from clear that *on average* the amount of food available increased with the adoption of farming. Although total output was larger the population increased as, crucially, did the amount redistributed. The most important consequence though was through a loss of variety, partly because the type of plants domesticated were generally not those highest in nutrients, key vitamins and minerals, but also because storage reduced these levels still further. Domesticated wheat had much less protein than wild einkorn and emmer and also was poor in three key amino acids. Domesticated rice was low in protein and made Vitamin A uptake more difficult. Some of the greatest problems were caused by maize. It was poor in two key amino acids, iron and the vitamin niacin. When it formed a high percentage of the diet it resulted in deficiency diseases – anaemia and pellagra. To some extent the farmers of Mesoamerica were able to compensate for these problems through including beans in their diet and by grinding maize to make tortillas which had lime added during the processing. Farmers also added flavourings to their diets such as chillies in the Americas and onions and garlic in Eurasia, that were high in vitamins. Almost everywhere the level of meat intake fell, except for the more privileged groups in society, and this affected protein and Vitamin B_{12} intake. These general conclusions are reinforced by analysis of the skeletons of some of the earliest farming groups. In southern Europe the first farmers were on average about two inches shorter than their gathering and hunting predecessors. Life expectancy probably declined too.

Of even greater importance was the impact the new way of life had on human disease. The pre-farming gathering and hunting groups had relatively low levels of disease. They would have been vulnerable to some infections and parasites caught from the animals they killed – tapeworms and intestinal infections in particular – and some others such as yaws and malaria (which also infects monkeys and apes). However, the fact that they lived largely in small groups and were highly mobile meant that it was very difficult for diseases to become established and reproduce themselves. As these groups moved out of the tropical and semi-tropical regions their rates of infection probably fell. The adoption of farming and a sedentary life produced, as a secondary consequence, a number of conditions that increased disease levels. The construction of houses, the storage of food and the accumulation of food waste all encouraged vermin, especially insects and rats, to live close to humans. Human waste accumulated and drastically increased the risk of water contamination. Together these factors helped the spread of diseases. Parasites such as hookworm which need to live in the soil for a period found it much easier to infect humans. Cleared land and small amounts of water around houses encouraged mosquitoes and therefore malaria in many areas. Elsewhere ponds and water ditches (especially for irrigation) were a potent breeding ground for the snails that carried schistosomiasis which was known in Egypt by 1200 BCE at the latest and probably even earlier in Mesopotamia.

Most important of all was the fact that humans now lived in much larger communities and much closer to animals. Infectious diseases require a minimum human population so that they can sustain and reproduce themselves and therefore infect new people. Gathering and hunting groups were certainly not big enough to maintain diseases. Only slowly as the population grew, lived in bigger settlements and groups were in contact with each other through trade and exchange networks, could diseases find a big enough human population in which to reproduce. The crucial factor though was the domestication of animals. Humans now lived permanently in close proximity to a range of animals, often even sharing their living space with them, especially in winter. The result was that a number of diseases that were specific to animals were able to mutate and establish themselves in humans – nearly all of the major human diseases are modified animal diseases. Measles is related to rinderpest in cattle (and possibly distemper in dogs), smallpox comes from cowpox, diphtheria also comes from cattle, influenza originated with pigs and chickens and the common cold comes from horses. These new disease patterns did not happen immediately on domestication but took thousands of years to become established as diseases slowly adapted to humans. The consequences for human health and world history were to be fundamental.

Despite the various drawbacks of farming humans learnt to live with them. In practice they had little choice but to do so. Farming was adopted usually in very small incremental steps so that gathering and hunting only slowly declined in importance and ways of life altered gradually. Once the initial steps had been taken it proved impossible to go back. The population rose and was too large to be supported by gathering and hunting and there was probably no longer free land available in the area to make it a feasible option. The knowledge and cultural adaptations of the earlier way of life were rapidly lost. Once engaged in a process of intensifying methods of gaining food the only option was to carry on with that process. The long-term consequences of the changes – the ability to support more specialist non-producers and increasing levels of social coercion – only slowly became apparent.

OVERVIEW 2

THE WORLD IN
5000 BCE

Population: 5 million
Towns: Eridu (4,000), Ubaid (2,000), Ur (2,000)

Events:

★ First villages with temples in Sumer

★ First smelting of copper in Anatolia and Elam

★ First agricultural settlements in Yangtze and Yellow rivers of China – pig and chicken domesticated

★ Earliest farming villages in the Indus valley

★ First agricultural settlements in Italy, the Balkans, Danube valley and Central Europe

★ First proto-writing on seals and tokens in Sumer

4

The Emergence of Civilization

The food surplus produced by the early farming societies meant that they nearly all became more hierarchical and unequal. Chiefs and religious authorities controlled much of the surplus food and redistributed it mainly in accordance with their priorities. As they did so they exercised more control over the people in their community. They also came into conflict with other groups, especially over land and access to water, which led them to intensify their internal control. Societies at this level of development existed everywhere across the world for thousands of years – in much of Europe until the last thousand years, in north America until the destruction of the native American way of life by the Europeans after 1600 CE and in parts of Africa until the late nineteenth century.

4.1 Civilization

In a handful of areas some societies, without any external influence, went much further and became coercive states and created the organizations, institutions and culture which we call civilization. This process occurred at most six times in human history – in Mesopotamia, the Indus valley, China, Mesoamerica and the central Andes. Egypt, the first of the early civilizations to be studied intensively by Europeans, is also usually included in this category for traditional reasons, although there was probably some influence from earlier developments in Mesopotamia. These societies were distinguished by a number of features – they supported an elite of thousands of non-producers (priests, rulers, bureaucrats, craftsmen and warriors) who lived mainly in cities and who exercised power over the rest of the population through forms of taxation and tribute. In the cities there were complexes of public buildings such as temples, palaces and granaries, many of which were on a grand scale. These societies were economically and socially far more complex than the early farming groups and were also strongly territorial. Most developed some form of written script for various forms of record keeping.

These changes were not an automatic process that took place in every society once it had adopted agriculture and it is difficult to isolate the factors that produced civilization. Mesopotamia was the area of the wide, fertile and later irrigated floodplains of the Tigris and Euphrates rivers. In

China developments were concentrated around the Yellow and Yangtze rivers. The Harappan civilization was based in the Indus valley and Egypt depended on the very constricted Nile valley and its annual flood. The early civilizations of Peru were centred in the narrow coastal valleys which were isolated from each other by intervening desert. Yet in Mesoamerica the first civilizations emerged in very inhospitable places such as the Gulf coast and the tropical jungle. Technology seems not to have been central to the changes – significant developments such as the first use of metal generally followed the development of civilization – those of the Americas managed almost entirely without metals. Similarly the growth of the first cities was a consequence not a cause of the changes.

No single cause can explain the complex social, economic and political changes that led to 'civilization'. The productivity of the early farmers, who remained the overwhelming bulk of the population, was very low. Some of the river valleys may have been marginally more productive than other areas but given the techniques available no significant increase in food output by individual farmers was possible. The crucial changes were therefore in the way these societies were organized. The levels of power and authority within them increased dramatically over a period of a few thousand years and this was combined with much greater inequality. As with the development of farming, the most important factors were the 'ratchet' and 'feedback' effects. Once a step was taken it was difficult to reverse, and changes in one area of society had major impacts elsewhere, were magnified and produced more changes in a spiral.

At first the food surplus was probably given voluntarily to support religious activities and for the chief who provided a limited degree of order within society. However, as these societies evolved and became more complex the degree of internal coercion became much greater. Chiefs exercised more authority and new institutions and types of power emerged – economic, ideological, military and political – which were capable of enforcing the redistribution of the surplus to the non-farmers. Societies slowly became less egalitarian as some individuals accumulated more power and wealth than others. Some held more land, others wielded religious, military or political power. A very important part of this process was conflict with other groups (mainly over land) – it reinforced the need for leadership and military power and the internal direction of society. To some extent people could see the benefits from the exercise of power – protection, order and the carrying out of what were regarded as important religious functions. However, after a long process of evolution, these early civilizations were eventually distinguished by the fact that they were states with much more complex levels of internal organization and authority and with a highly unequal distribution of the resources that were available. The amount of power wielded by the elites was such that they were able to ensure the continued extraction of a food surplus from the farmers and impose forced labour on state and religious functions together with service in their primitive armies.

The rest of this chapter considers these changes in Mesopotamia (the most closely studied area), Egypt and the Indus valley. Concluding sections deal with two topics which were common to all three civilizations – developments in technology and the evolution of writing. The next chapter deals with events in the Americas and the Pacific; consideration of developments in China is reserved for chapter 7.

4.2 Mesopotamia: The Origins of Civilization

The valley of the Tigris and Euphrates rivers (Mesopotamia is the name of the Roman province established in the area) was not settled by farmers until about 5700 BCE. The major developments in farming over the previous few thousand years had taken place in the foothills of the mountains surrounding the plain, reflecting the difficult conditions in the wide valley of the twin rivers. The area had long hot summers and harsh, cold winters. There was little water available away from the rivers although the soil was productive when irrigated. It also lacked nearly every key resource: the nearest stone was in the desert west of Eridu, the nearest copper was in Iran and Anatolia and timber was in very short supply – most had to come from the mountains to the north and east and the best (cedar and poplar), which were used in temple construction, had to be transported from the mountains of Lebanon.

4.2.1 The early phases
At first glance therefore this area seems a very unlikely candidate for the first emergence of civilization by about 3000 BCE. On the other hand it was probably the difficult circumstances that demanded a greater degree of social organization from the start of settlement. When the first farmers cultivated the valley they found that rainfall was almost non-existent in the south and the rivers were at their lowest between August and October, when the newly planted crops needed the most water, and at their peak in the spring and early summer (following the melting of the winter snow in the mountains) when the crops had to be protected from flooding. Water control, storage and irrigation were therefore essential. This required not a strong centralized state (that came later) but relatively high levels of co-operation within the farming communities. They appear to have been organized around large kinship groups and the initial settlements were

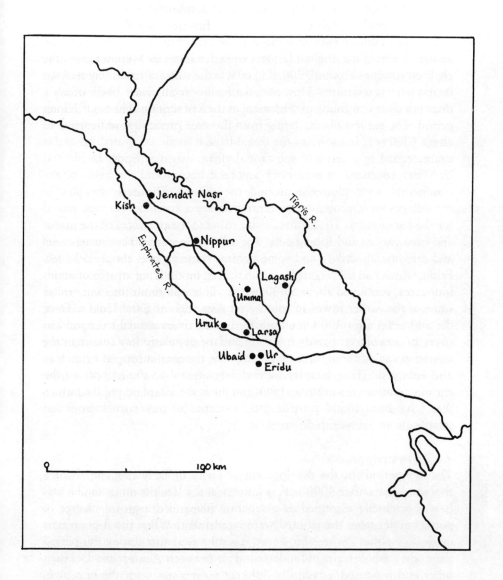

Map 5: The cities of Sumer

therefore fairly large – that at Choga Mani (east of Baghdad), dating to about 5500 BCE, covered an area of about fifteen acres and had a population of about 1,000.

The key developments took place in the far south in the area known as Sumer. Whether the original farmers were the Sumerians (known from the civilized societies around 3000 BCE) or whether the Sumerians entered the region later is unknown. However, the former seems more likely because there is a clear continuity of settlement at the key sites throughout this long period. The earliest phase, dating from the time of the first settlements to about 4000 BCE, is known as the Ubaid from its main excavated site and is characterized by a series of substantial villages such as Eridu, Usaila and Ur. They consisted of mud-brick-and-reed houses and the fields of the community were clustered around the village. The early temples in the villages were probably the centres where a food reserve was stored for the community. The farmers also exploited the resources of the marsh and used canoes and fishing nets. The villages were the focus of religious and ceremonial activity and some became quite large – about 4500 BCE Eridu, which had the largest temple in the region covering an area of about four acres, contained about 5,000 people. This was about the same size as some of the earlier towns in south-west Asia such as Çatal Hüyük. Over the 500 years after 4000 BCE both Eridu and Ur continued to expand to cover an area of over twenty-five acres and the population was maintaining irrigation canals about three miles long. The temple platform at Eridu was also enlarged. These temples were clearly central to the identity of the various communities in Sumer but throughout the Ubaid period the burials that have been found provide little evidence of any significant social stratification and wealth differences.

4.2.2 Uruk

The key period for the development of civilization, lasting for about a thousand years after 4000 BCE, is known as the Uruk from its major site. It was originally identified as a separate phase because of a change of pottery styles from the painted ware typical of the Ubaid to a plain type made on a potter's wheel. However, it is now clear that during this period there was a whole series of fundamental innovations which reinforced each other and produced a radically different society with, for the first time, significant state control. The agricultural surplus from the irrigated land was vital in allowing a range of non-producers to be supported and it was also traded for raw materials from the adjoining areas. The growing specialization within society produced much greater stratification and inequality. As well as religious authorities, secular leaders, armies and warfare developed. The elite lived in the rapidly expanding settlements which became true cities. To help operate and rule this society writing, and with it a class of literate scribes, developed. In parallel the first steps in casting metals were taken.

The nature of these developments can best be traced at Uruk which became the chief city of Sumer. About 3600 BCE a huge temple mound known as a ziggurat was constructed and then steadily expanded. The ceremonial complexes dedicated to the gods Eanna and Anu were built on massive platforms with elaborate approaches and layouts, intricate niches in the walls and columns over six feet in diameter. These columns and the walls were decorated with mosaics made up of small cones painted yellow, black or red. The temples and the other public buildings took up a third of the total area of Uruk which expanded to cover over 600 acres (twice the size of ancient Athens at its peak). The city was surrounded by a wall nearly six miles long. By about 3000 BCE the population was probably nearly 40,000, far in excess of any previous human settlement and more than twice the size of any other city in Sumer. The amount of labour required for all these tasks was substantial and was organized by the temple authorities and the emerging secular ruler of the city. The first primitive writing to manage the various activities of the state appeared about 3400 BCE. Much of the area surrounding Uruk was subject to extensive rather than intensive cultivation by the people of a series of dependent small towns and villages within a radius of about six miles, each with their own small irrigation system. The relationship between these small towns and villages and the city was complex. The deities of the city attracted pilgrimages and offerings (voluntary and forced) from the local population but 'tribute' and 'taxation' (the appropriation of the agricultural surplus) for defence and state projects was enforced through the military and political authority of the city.

4.2.3 The early dynastic

Although the developments at Uruk went further than elsewhere in Sumer, by about 3000 BCE there was a series of city-states across the region, dependent on their local populations for food and surrounded by defensive walls. The period between 3000 and about 2300 BCE is known as the Early Dynastic. Although it is often divided into a series of phases these are derived from stylistic changes in pottery and seals and have little wider significance. It was a period in which the city states fought endless conflicts over the vital resources for life – land and water. For example Lagash conducted a 150-year dispute with Umma over their boundaries in the period around 2500 BCE. A so-called 'Sumerian King List' was written about 1800 BCE but it is largely mythical and although it does contain the names of some real rulers it is impossible to use it to derive any sequence of rulers or patterns of dominance between the city-states. Some of the rulers have the title 'King of Kish' which seems to imply some form of overlordship. (During the dispute with Umma the rulers of Lagash continually appealed to a decision made about 2600 BCE by King Mesalim as 'King of Kish' as though this ought to be binding, but exactly why is unclear.) However, enough evidence has survived from this period to establish in considerable detail how the first civilization in the world functioned.

Until the last few decades it was thought that Sumer consisted of a series of 'temple-states' in which the temples owned all the land, the inhabitants were regarded as temple servants of various ranks and the secular ruler was a deputy of the temple. This is now known to be a major misunderstanding based on a serious misreading in the 1930s of a single archive from the temple of Girsu. The accepted picture of how Sumerian society was organized is now very different. Much of the land was owned by family groups and the 'temple' estates were the property of the city ruler and his family and he was able to distribute them to his followers. The ruler was the protector of the city in the name of the city's god and he maintained the temples and gained status through his relationship with the god. The city ruler carried out key ceremonials in association with the priests and the royal family also held a number of important positions within the temple hierarchy. There was therefore no separation of the religious and secular spheres.

The temple, with its inner room containing a statue of the god made from metal and jewels, involved considerable community effort to build and maintain and its existence was central to the community's identity. (Each city had its own god – Enlil at Nippur, Enki at Eridu and Nanna at Ur.) In theory the temple controlled large tracts of land. Some estates were directly cultivated by peasants who owed a community obligation to work the land. From this land daily deliveries of food were made to support the staff of the temple. However, other land was assigned to office holders within the temple (usually members of the ruling family and other members of the elite) with the amount depending on their status. Many of the temple posts were no more than hereditary sinecures and the estates that went with them became hereditary too. The rest of the temple land was simply rented out to families and individuals. Temples also had extensive workshops employing specialist craftsmen who were fed by the produce brought from the temple estates. These were large commercial enterprises whose production was sold and exchanged through a separate group of merchants.

The palace (*egal* – literally 'great house') was the residence of the ruler or *lugal* ('great man'). In some cities the palace appears to be part of the temple complex (though this does not necessarily imply an original subordination to religious authority) but in others, especially the northern cities, it was a separate building. The palace was the residence of the ruling family and their servants, it had its own workshop and was the centre of administration and the location of the state treasury. Much of the business of the palace related to the *lugal* as a rich, powerful member of the community, its chief judicial officer and important religious functionary but also with the administration of his own extensive estates. There is some evidence that the cities were originally governed by a form of assembly consisting of elders representing the 'wards' of the city, which may themselves have some sort of kinship basis. However, the chief function of the ruler was as a war leader and it is likely that this was the crucial factor in the emergence of secular authority. Rulers may have been temporary war leaders at first (perhaps even elected by the assembly) but it is clear that by about 2600 BCE the office was hereditary and the rulers were effectively monarchs. Their exact title varied from city to city – some were *lugal* and others were *ensi* although the reasons for these differences are not known. Their symbols of authority were similar and have continued ever since – a hat (crown), a stick (sceptre) and a stool (throne).

Warfare was central to the Sumerian city-states. The earliest cylinder seals from the Uruk period (4000 BCE) show battles and prisoners of war. In the Early Dynastic period after about 3000 BCE the so-called Royal Standard of Ur (a wooden object whose function is unknown) and the 'Vulture stelae' of Lagash (dated to about 2450 BCE) show battles and armies, almost certainly made up of conscripts who served as part of their obligation to the state. Infantry were the basis of these armies and they were armed with axes, adzes, large leather shields and spears. They had no swords because neither copper nor bronze was capable of taking a sharp edge but they did have primitive daggers. The ruler had a donkey-drawn chariot with solid wheels. These involved considerable effort both in construction and in training the donkeys. They were largely status symbols because the rulers seem to have fought on foot. Cities were very vulnerable to the occupation of the land on which they depended for food. The siege using battering rams and towers was a central fact of warfare and on capture the city walls were normally destroyed, the male population killed, enslaved or blinded and the women and children enslaved.

4.3 Mesopotamia: Expansion and Conquest

4.3.1 Trade
Because Mesopotamia lacked a whole range of vital raw materials the early

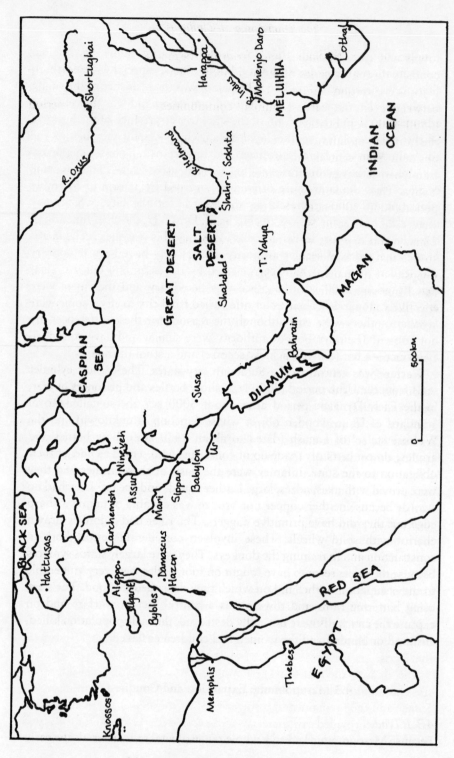

Map 6: Early Mesopotamian trade routes

towns and cities of Sumer had, from the beginning, extensive external contacts through a series of trade networks. These were established long before 'civilization' emerged and they demonstrate the extensive links between even the earliest human communities. In the Ubaid period (5500–4000 BCE) boatloads of grindstones were travelling from Assyria in the northern mountains down the rivers to Sumer, often accompanied by obsidian from central Anatolia. Ubaid pottery is found across southern Iran where it was probably traded for special chlorite bowls made at Tepe Yahya. These trade networks were vastly expanded during the key Uruk period (4000–3000 BCE) when the major social and political developments were taking place in Sumer. To the east, on the Iranian plateau around Elam, metal deposits were being worked and it was probably from this source that the Sumerians learnt how to smelt copper (they had no metal deposits of their own). By 3500 BCE Sumerian influence stretched across the Khuzestan plains of south-west Iran (about seven to ten days' travelling). Uruk-style pottery is found at nearly every settlement, some of which appear to be Sumerian colonies established as a mixture of agricultural and trading cities. One of the most important of their trading links to the east was for the highly prized precious stone lapis lazuli. The nearest source to Sumer was in the mountains of the far north of Afghanistan at Shortughai on the Oxus river (a distance of more than three thousand miles). The stone was brought by caravans to the town of Shahr-i-Sokhta in central Iran where workers reshaped it before it was transported to Elam and eventually Sumer. The cities of Sumer were also trading down the Gulf. The first stop was at 'Dilmun' (usually identified as Bahrain), a centre for trade to 'Magan' (the mountains of Oman). This area provided Sumer with a large quantity of copper in return for textiles, leather and barley. Sumer was also trading to the north, up the valleys of the twin rivers to Syria, the Mediterranean and eastern Anatolia. Some towns in the north of Mesopotamia have considerable deposits of various goods made in Sumer in the Uruk period. Others duplicate all the features of a Sumerian city and its culture, and appear to be trading colonies established by the early Sumerian cities. They are clearly planned and have walls and occupy key positions on the major north–south and east–west trade routes such as those at Carchemish and Habuba Kabira on the great bend of the Euphrates river in north Syria, and further east at Nineveh on the Tigris.

The areas to the east (Susa, Elam and central Iran), to the south down the Gulf, and to the north were peripheral to the major developments in Sumer and they remained at a lower level of social and political organization. They provided raw materials and exotic items essential for the status of the Sumerian religious and political elite. In return Sumer was able to offer mainly textiles and food. There is no doubt that Sumer was the dominant partner in these exchanges and that it enforced its dominance through colonization in key areas and the occasional military expedition. Through their contacts with Sumer some of these peripheral areas also began to develop rapidly. By about 2500 BCE in northern Mesopotamia and Syria there was a series of city-states such as Ashur and Mari developing very rapidly along similar lines to those of Sumer. Some covered an area of over 250 acres and were larger than many of the Sumerian cities. One of the most significant discoveries was only made in the mid-1970s at Ebla in Syria when a previously unknown 'civilization' was found. Over 8,000 tablets were discovered which, as the script was deciphered, illustrated a complex society at much the same level of development as those in Sumer. This was a state headed by a *malikum* (prince or king) and a council of elders, and the city's wealth was based on its extensive trade contacts and its control over the routes into Anatolia.

4.3.2 The first empires

By the late Early Dynastic period (about 2400 BCE) the continual conflict and warfare between the cities of Sumer had produced a growing concentration of power. Lagash incorporated Girsu and Nina and Umma took over Zabala. Uruk and Ur were united under the rule of Lugalkigineddu (one of the first known rulers) and then took over Umma. Eventually about 2350 BCE (possibly a little earlier) Lagalzagesi, the ruler of the three cities of Uruk, Ur and Umma, appears to have expanded his state to control most of Sumer, including Lagash in the north-east, and also extended his influence into northern Mesopotamia and towards the Mediterranean. It was at this point that external influences became dominant within Sumer and the first 'empire' in the world was established.

Sumer was conquered by Sargon, a ruler from the region of Akkad in the Mesopotamian plain north of Nippur. The Akkadian people spoke a Semitic language whereas Sumerian was non-Semitic. The exact relationship between the two peoples in the period before about 2500 BCE is unclear. They appear to have co-existed for a considerable period and some Semitic words appear in even the earliest Sumerian clay tablet records from before 3000 BCE. The exact dating of the empire established by Sargon is controversial – it is usually given as 2340–2159 BCE although later dates of 2300–2100 are possible. The capital city of the empire, Akkad, has not been discovered although it was still inhabited in 300 BCE. Sargon (the name means 'true' or 'legitimate' king – which suggests that he wasn't) seems to have seized power in Kish in a series of court intrigues and to have conquered the surrounding regions, including Sumer, relatively late in his life – he probably died in 2284 BCE.

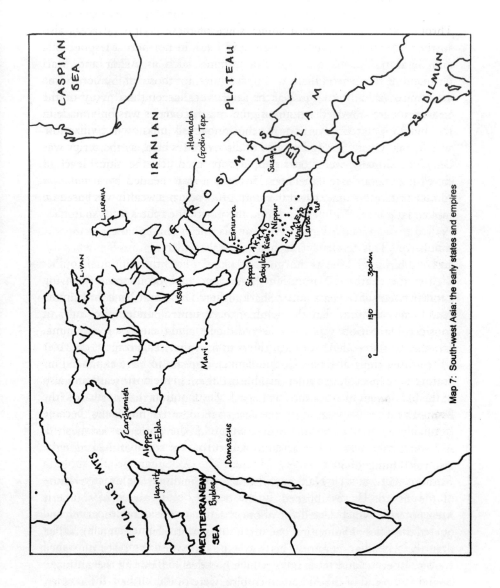

Map 7: South-west Asia: the early states and empires

The empire he founded was successful for over a century under the rule of his two sons Rimush (2284–2275 BCE) and Manishtushu (2275–2260 BCE) and his grandson Naram-Sin (2260–2233 BCE). The empire was probably at its peak under the latter when it had military garrisons in northern Syria and western Iran and Naram-Sin was carrying out campaigns in Anatolia, the Zagros mountains and against Ebla in the east. Throughout this period there was a clear attempt to centralize control of the empire. Akkad took most of the agricultural surplus and weights and measures were standardized among the cities of Sumer for the first time. The king appointed governors for the conquered areas from among not just his immediate family but also other members of the Akkadian elite. Only occasionally were local people appointed. The Semitic language increasingly dominated the area. Sumerian was retained for legal and administrative documents until about 1700 BCE but was in decline as a spoken language. Within the empire the position of the king was further exalted with an increasing emphasis on his role as triumphant warrior and conqueror. This tendency reached its peak under Naram-Sin when he declared himself divine as the 'god of Akkad'.

After the death of Naram-Sin the empire survived in some form for another twenty-five years under Sharkalisharri. However, as later empires found, maintaining even the semblance of centralized empire for any considerable period was extremely difficult given the poor communications and the tendency of local rulers to usurp power. From about 2200 BCE the area controlled by the Akkadian empire shrank back to the region around the capital. Local rulers established themselves in the south in some of the old Sumerian cities such as Lagash, Uruk and further north at Kish. In the Diyala valley region (to the east of modern Baghdad) the Gutians (probably originally nomadic people who had been incorporated into the Akkadian empire as mercenaries) took control. For some of the time they also ruled much of Sumer.

About 2112 BCE Ur-Nammu, who was originally probably a governor of the city of Ur, established a new dynasty and empire in southern Mesopotamia which lasted for about a century. He seems to have conquered the cities of Sumer but overall the area controlled was much smaller than the Akkadian empire. This was a period when the cities of Sumer were prosperous and trade links, which had declined during the confused period at the end of the Akkadian empire, were re-established. It has often been described as a 'Sumerian renaissance' from the earlier domination of Akkad. However, this 'renaissance' was largely confined to literary texts and hymns to the gods – Sumerian was still in decline as a spoken language. In addition the Akkadian inheritance was not rejected, only that of the Gutians. Most royal names were Akkadian, as were personal names and those given to newly founded towns. The rulers continued the Akkadian tradition of naming the years after key events within the royal family – in particular the marriage of the king's daughters to local rulers – always key political events in trying to control an empire. The exact political history of the empire is unclear and even the dates of the rulers are problematic – the second king of the dynasty appears to be Shulgi who promulgated the first known law-code and reigned for about fifty years. A number of texts do survive to give some idea of how the empire was ruled. The king was regarded as divine even while alive and was the subject of elaborate, fawning hymns as part of a court ritual designed to heighten his prestige. Provinces were in the hands of *ensi*, who were probably hereditary, but they were complemented and partly controlled by rival military commanders, *sagin*, from the royal family. Border areas were controlled by a *sukkalmah* or viceroy. Provinces paid taxes of agricultural produce into centrally located centres from which the state supplied temples and its own officials. About 2000 BCE the so-called Third Dynasty of Ur collapsed. Control was lost over much of the empire and eventually another group of ex-nomadic mercenaries similar to the earlier Gutians – the Amorites – took control of most of Sumer.

4.4 Later Mesopotamia

A large number of texts survive from the Third Dynasty of Ur period and they give a reasonably clear picture of the complex society that had emerged in Mesopotamia in the thousand years after the first emergence of 'civilization'. Land remained the basis of society – the overwhelming majority of the population had to produce food in order to support a small number of non-producers. However, access to land was highly unequal. As in the Early Dynastic period nominal temple land was extensive but the idea that they owned all of the land is false – in Lagash the temple held about an eighth of all the irrigated land. Of this temple land some was cultivated directly by temple staff, some was given as fields for the subsistence of temple staff (mainly the elite of society) and the rest was rented out for a share of the crop. The second category of temple land was particularly important because temple posts rapidly became hereditary and it was accepted that the holders of this land could sub-lease it. In practice therefore this land became the hereditary estates of the elite, in particular the royal family, on which they employed a mixture of tenants, share-croppers and labourers. For the majority of the land, extended families and kin-groups, who bought and sold land as a group, became less important after about 3000 BCE. By about 2500 BCE half the known sellers of land were individuals and sales were recorded on tablets complete with field maps to show the ownership and boundaries of the land. This trade in land reinforced existing inequalities and led to the concentration of land-holdings although peasants either owning their own land or cultivating it as tenants survived. However, even before 2000 BCE agricultural wage labourers who owned no land were common. They were employed under contracts setting out the length of time they were to work, their wages (variable for males, females and children) and whether they were paid in silver or in barley. Far more common were the workers on the large palace, temple and elite estates. They were dependent landless labourers who were tied to the estates and were effectively serfs or near slaves, although they did retain a family life. In times of bad harvests whole families sold themselves, sometimes remaining on their land as dependent debt-tenants, sometimes becoming quasi-slaves supported by the people who bought them. Occasionally a ruler issued an edict cancelling debts but these had little long-term impact given the levels of inequality within society.

Apart from the elite of rulers, bureaucrats, scribes and priests there were two significant groups of non-farmers within society – craftsmen and merchants. By about 2000 BCE there was a whole range of specialist craftsmen such as gold-, copper- and silversmiths, carpenters, wood and ivory workers, fine stone workers, rope makers and leather workers. Many were grouped into large units under the control of palace and temple officials. One of the most important industries was textile production (dependent on large flocks of up to 300,000 sheep) in palace factories containing about 6,000 workers (a mix of locals and prisoners of war). One of the problems in analysing the way the Mesopotamian economy was organized is that nearly all the records that survive come from temple and palace archives and these necessarily produce a picture heavily biased towards this 'state' economy. However, even these records show that there were a large number of workers outside this sector – brick makers, shepherds, builders and a range of craftsmen. Some of the workers in the temple and palace workshops may have been dependents but many were employed for wages – although most were paid in barley this reflects the fact that in an early agricultural economy it was the easiest method of payment.

Although the temples and palaces clearly played an important role in redistributing resources through the estates they controlled and the workers they employed, there was also a flourishing commercial sector. Any surplus the peasant had available after meeting his own needs, those of his kin and that appropriated by the state and religious authorities, could be sold to buy other necessities. This is likely to have been small-scale trading because the overwhelming majority of the population had very few possessions. Nevertheless, there are plenty of references to small shops, a 'street of purchases' and a 'gate of exchange'. There was also a considerable group of merchants whose accounts survive from the period around 2000 BCE. They were bound to be partially reliant on the palace and temple workshops to produce goods but it is also clear that they had a major independent role. Trade, in particular foreign trade, was regarded as separate from the palace and temple authorities. Indeed it is difficult to see how it could have been conducted on any other basis. It was the various associations of merchants, later known as *karum*, that negotiated with the palace and organized the extensive trade networks. A major feature of the way they conducted trade was that every product was assigned a value in silver (occasionally copper though this was quite rare after about 3000 BCE). Silver was therefore a standard of account, a medium of exchange and a method of payment, although different goods were normally traded through their nominal silver values. Silver therefore performed all the roles of a currency and provided an accepted medium of exchange over a very wide area. Although there were no silver coins, rings of silver were produced at set values and in such a way that they could be broken down into smaller units. Through this mechanism the merchant-traders, who, as early as 3200 BCE, were scattered in a diaspora along the trade routes, were able to organize the trade in products which were vital for the early Mesopotamian cities.

After the fall of the Third Dynasty of Ur, about 2000 BCE, there was to be no substantial revival in Sumer. The Amorites were in control for some decades and there were short-lived rulers at the cities of Isin and Larsa. About 1900 BCE Sumer came under the control of Babylon, a previously unimportant city of northern Mesopotamia. From this date the centre of civilization was always in the north of the region and eventually the cities of Sumer declined and were abandoned. What were the underlying causes of this decline? The early Sumerian cities all depended on irrigated agriculture but the conditions in Mesopotamia were far from ideal for irrigation. The very high summer temperatures, often up to 40° C, resulted in high rates of evaporation and accumulation of layers of salt near the surface. This was exacerbated by waterlogging caused by very slow rates of drainage in the flat land and the large amounts of silt coming down the twin rivers. The only way to cope with these problems would have been to leave the land fallow for long periods. This was not possible for the Sumerians. The high population levels and the incessant competition for power between the rival cities, often caused by disputes over access to land, meant that every available acre had to be used to grow crops. It was the environmental degradation brought on by irrigation that was a central factor in the slow undermining of the foundations of Sumerian society.

In about 3500 BCE, in the middle of the Uruk period when the fundamental steps towards civilization were taken in Sumer, roughly equal amounts of wheat and barley were grown in the region. However, wheat can only tolerate a level of salt in the soil about half that of barley. The increasing salinity of the soil in Sumer is shown by the decline of wheat production – by 2500 BCE it was only 15 per cent of the total crop and by 1700 BCE it had been abandoned as a crop across the whole region. Even more important was the decline in crop yields. Until about 2400 BCE they were high – at least as high as in medieval Europe. At about this time all the available land was being cultivated and as salt levels rose production fell and some areas were abandoned altogether. Average yields fell by almost a half between 2400–2100 BCE. By 2000 BCE there are contemporary reports of 'the earth turned white' – a clear reference to the impact of salinization. The decline in agricultural output and hence in the size of the food surplus to support the elite of non-producers had a dramatic impact on Sumerian society and the state. The first serious decline in crop yields, about 2400 BCE, is roughly contemporary with the first external conquest of Sumer by Sargon of Akkad. The continued decline over the next centuries is marked by only brief revivals (the Third Dynasty of Ur) and further collapse – the Gutian and Amorite periods. By about 1900 BCE crop yields were only about a third of the level obtained during the Early Dynastic period (c.2900–2400 BCE) when the classic Sumerian city-states first flourished. The agricultural base had been undermined and the region was no longer able to support the infrastructure of a complex state.

[*Later Mesopotamia* 7.1.1]

4.5 Egypt

[*Earlier Egypt* 3.3.2]

4.5.1 Unification
The processes that led to the emergence of civilization began later in the Nile valley than in Mesopotamia but were much more concentrated. Agriculture arrived relatively late and even in about 4000 BCE there were still plenty of only semi-agricultural communities of about a hundred people still heavily dependent on hunting and fishing. There were also villages of about a thousand people with subterranean houses and centralized village granaries. Over the next five hundred years the population rose and settlements spread out to take in most of the relatively narrow band of cultivatable land within the Nile valley. Irrigation works

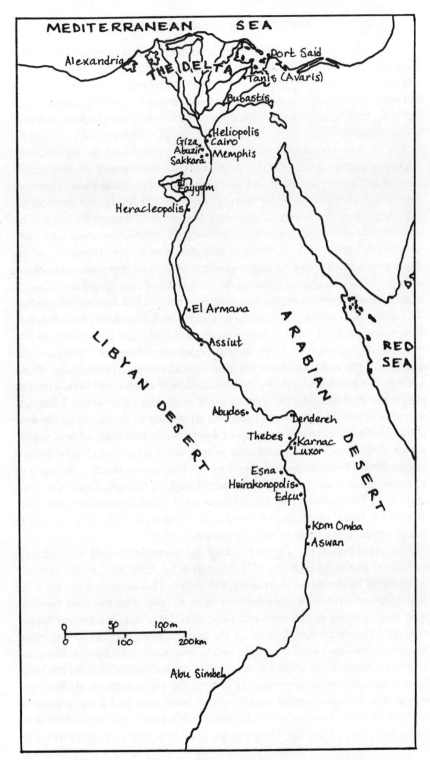

Map 8: The Nile valley: principal sites of Egyptian civilization

were relatively simple in all of the villages which grew wheat and barley in riverside gardens and tended cattle, goats, sheep and pigs. Boats were in use and there was an increasing amount of communication and trade between the villages along the river. There were also the first signs of growing craft specialization and the emergence of 'chiefs' – local rulers of a few villages.

The civilization which emerged in the Nile valley differed from that of Mesopotamia in a number of respects. First, the amount of agricultural land was limited by the level of the annual Nile flood and therefore population densities were far lower than in Sumer. Cities did develop but they tended to be ceremonial centres for the elite rather than the large residential cities of Mesopotamia. Second, the Nile valley was unified at a very early date and separate city-states similar to those found in Mesopotamia did not emerge. Despite long and frequent periods of disunity later in its history, the tradition remained that the great rulers and dynasties of Egypt were characterized by their ability to unify the valley. Third, the Nile valley was narrow and surrounded by desert and therefore Egyptologists have traditionally emphasized the unique nature of the culture, its isolation and the lack of external influences. However, the empires of the valley did have external contacts from an early stage. These were to the south up the Nile, to the east from the delta into Syria and also down the Red Sea. As we shall see in Chapter 7, from about 1500 BCE Egypt was one of a number of empires struggling to dominate south-west Asia. The early external contacts of Egypt were, however, of less significance than those of Mesopotamia where there were less clearly defined geographical boundaries and therefore the region was much more open to external influences. In one fundamental aspect, though, there was little difference between the two areas where the earliest civilizations emerged. Both were based on extensive social and political coercion by a small elite who exploited the mass of the population.

The creation of the Egyptian state seems to be linked to a drastic reduction in the level of the Nile flood around 3300 BCE, which severely affected all of the settlements along the valley. This increased the need for organization within the communities so as to cope with the poor harvests and the need to reallocate land now that large areas were no longer flooded. The chiefs and leaders of the groups along the valley organized these activities and gained prestige and power as a result. People may have seen considerable immediate benefits from community action but the long-term consequences were profound. One of the major settlements in Upper Egypt was Hierakonopolis which, about 3400 BCE, had a population of around 10,000. At some point the town either fused with or took over its main local rival, Nagada. This, a larger unit, was able to cope more easily with the problems of fluctuating food production and it also extended its power to control the trade routes into Lower Egypt. In the period around 3200 BCE (the late pre-dynastic) a number of petty chieftains and leaders along the Nile valley, especially in the upper valley, were engaged in endless conflict with each other and also with various groups trying to move into the valley from Libya and the eastern Sahara as these areas became increasingly arid. Developments in the delta area, which was much more open to influences from both east and west, are unclear – the amount of silt brought down by the Nile and the constant shifts in the position of the river have buried almost all these early sites. The continual warfare between the petty rulers increased the power and status of the chiefs and war leaders. During this period the symbolic regalia and insignia of the later Pharaohs was already in use – a kilt, ostrich feathers, a penis sheath, a red or white crown, a stick and a sceptre. Conventional accounts of this 'pre-dynastic' period end at 3050 BCE with the unification of Egypt under Narmer, a ruler from Hierakonopolis, and the establishment of the First Dynasty of kings.

Exactly what did happen in Egypt at this time is very difficult to understand. The problem stems from the fact that so much of Egyptian history for the 2,500 years after 3000 BCE is still structured by a series of dynasties (twenty-six in total) interrupted by 'intermediate' periods which are distinguished by the fact that the kings did not rule over all of Egypt. This scheme is largely known through the work of Manetho, an Egyptian scholar writing in Greek in the third century BCE. The original does not survive, only citations and summaries in other writers. A similar dynastic scheme is partially preserved in the so-called 'Turin King List' and on a few inscriptions. These schemes are clearly based on a tradition that emerged after 1500 BCE in the 'New Kingdom' period. However, it seems unlikely that much was then known about what had happened over 1,500 years earlier. In these lists kings have only one name yet it is known that the Pharaohs had three names and this seems to have led to confusion and double-counting of some rulers. Conventionally the first king of the First Dynasty was Menes but his exact role is unknown and he may be 'Narmer' under another name. Other information contradicts the 'Manetho' tradition. The 'Palermo stone' inscribed under the Fifth Dynasty (about 2400 BCE), has lost the parts dealing with the first two dynasties, but provides a list of kings before the conventional unification under 'Menes' and suggests that an earlier unified state broke down and that he recreated it. On the other hand the 'Saqqara tablet' (dated to about 1200 BCE) lists all the kings to that date but ignores the initial five kings of the First Dynasty. Why it does so is unknown.

It seems unlikely that the unification of Egypt was a simple and quick process of conquest under a single ruler. There was probably a period of growing political competition in Upper Egypt between a number of small states from which one emerged as victor. It then went on to conquer Lower Egypt where there does not seem to have been such a strong level of political organization. 'Menes' (and/or 'Narmer') was just one of these rulers. However, the idea of the unification of the two parts of Egypt – Upper and Lower – remained central to all the dynasties. It was symbolized by the double crown of the Pharaohs – white for Upper Egypt and red for Lower Egypt. Pharaohs were also 'beloved of the two ladies' – Nekhabet, the vulture goddess of Nekhab near Hierakonopolis, and Wadjet, the cobra goddess of Buto in the Delta. Whether unification was the joining of just two parts of Egypt or whether there were other areas and petty states is unknown. It is, however, clear that the unification of Egypt about 3050 BCE was only part of a much longer process of development. For another thousand years there was a series of regional and local cultures in Egypt and many temples continued to be built in these old styles. It took a considerable time to amalgamate them and impose on them what is now considered to be the quintessentially 'Egyptian' culture. This originated with the court of the Pharaoh and appeared very rapidly around the time of unification. A sophisticated ideology, imagery and ceremonial was built around the divine Pharaoh and the highly distinctive writing system known as hieroglyphic appeared suddenly and fully developed. However, for several centuries this court art and culture was very restricted in scope and concentrated on just a few buildings.

4.5.2 The first dynasties

The Early Dynastic period of the first two dynasties (3050–2700 BCE) was one of transition in which the main features of the Egyptian state were still being elaborated after the very rapid developments in the period from about 3200 BCE. It is impossible to write any coherent history of the period apart from a list of kings which, after the first four rulers, is fairly clear. They ruled all of Egypt, and warfare with the surrounding rulers remained central to the evolution of kingship. The capital was at Memphis, traditionally founded by Menes on land recovered from the Nile. It grew steadily during the period – it was in a key strategic position near the branching of the Nile and it controlled the delta together with the trade routes to the Sinai peninsula which supplied copper and turquoise. The kings continued to be buried in large tombs at Abydos in Upper Egypt. Even at this relatively early stage Egypt had significant external contacts in two main areas. The first was to the south along the Nile to Nubia, a source of raw materials and slaves. More important were the routes to the east across the Sinai into Syria. A series of small 'way-stations' was maintained on routes across the Sinai desert to the major trading settlements and 'colonies' in the southern Levant where an extension of Egyptian influence can be detected from very shortly after unification. From the Levant there were links to Mesopotamia. It was not just goods that travelled along these routes. Some of the art motifs used in Egypt, in particular the winged griffin and two entwined snakes enclosing rosettes, are clearly derived from Mesopotamia and even further east in Elam.

By about 2700 BCE, the conventional start of the 'Old Kingdom' period of the Third to Eighth Dynasties which lasted to about 2200 BCE, a strong, unified and highly complex state had emerged in Egypt. Unfortunately no connected narrative history is possible from the records that survive. The tombs and stelae erected by the rulers shows scenes of constant warfare, together with prisoners of war and booty being brought back from the Sinai and Nubia. A major departure in ceremonial construction came in about 2695 BCE with the 'Step Pyramid' at Sakkara near Memphis. It was the tomb of Djoser who was either the first or second king of the Third Dynasty. The pyramid is part of a large enclosure about 500 yards long and 250 yards wide surrounded by a thick stone wall with external towers and a single entrance. The enclosure also has a series of stone cairns and a platform in front of the pyramid. It was the setting for the stage-managed 'appearance of the king' in the *Sed* festival. The king sat in the two thrones of Upper and Lower Egypt and then strode around the enclosure and cairns to lay symbolical claim to all the land of Egypt and his right to rule its people.

The form of the royal tomb changed in the Fourth Dynasty. It now became a true pyramid with no rectangular enclosure for the *Sed* festival. The pyramid was a symbol of the sun and also of the Pharaoh's relationship with it and the stars rather than the land he ruled. These buildings reached their climax with the Great Pyramid which consists of 2,300,000 blocks of stone weighing on average two and a half tons (some are fifteen tons and none are less than one and a half tons). The top was originally over 480 feet above the ground, although the gold-covered capstone is now missing. All of these Egyptian tombs are filled with astronomical imagery, mainly linked to the transfiguration of the Pharaoh into the stars, in particular the circumpolar stars which never set and were therefore seen as 'immortal'. Although the Great Pyramid has generated a great deal of speculative nonsense, mainly about the mathematics hidden within its proportions, there is no doubt that it contains some deeply symbolic structures. The four sides of its base covering thirteen acres are exactly aligned north–south and east–west. Inside an ascending corridor leads to the steeply inclined Grand Gallery which, made from very hard granite brought from Aswan over 500 miles to the south, is 153 feet long but only seven feet wide, though its ceiling is 28 feet high. There are two shafts in the north and south walls set only a few feet above the floor and extending to the outside. One is oriented towards 'Thuban' (the Egyptian name for the North Star), one of the immortal stars, and the other to Orion (the immortal Osiris). These were not astronomical observatories but symbolized the transformation of the divine Pharaoh after his death. All of these buildings required massive amounts of labour over long periods. Not only was the agricultural surplus appropriated to support the rulers, priests and bureaucrats but the conscription of large amounts of labour for these elite projects, whatever popular support they may have had, demonstrates the power of the early state.

The Egyptian peasantry and state were dependent on the Nile and its annual flood for their survival – after about 2900 BCE there was almost no rain in Egypt south of Memphis. The Nile naturally built levees up to three feet above natural basins which flooded once a year – in mid-August in Upper Egypt, a few weeks later in the north. A normal flood produced about four feet of water in the basins and remained until November (in a bad year some basins would stay dry). An average flood was enough for one crop a year over about two-thirds of the valley surface. In order to improve agriculture it was not necessary to have large-scale irrigation and major radial canals away from the river – a series of low-technology, local schemes was sufficient. What was required was the dredging and deepening of natural overflow channels, the making of ditches to breach low points of the levees, the blocking of overflows to conserve water in the natural basins and the use of buckets to lift water into the fields. With this simple system it was possible to extend the cultivated area beyond the natural flood plain and in a few areas retain enough water to allow a second crop later in the year. The whole rhythm of the Egyptian world was built around the annual Nile flood. The calendar was divided into only three seasons – *Akhet* (inundation), *Peret* (growing) and *Shemu* (drought). The Nile flood was more reliable than that of many rivers but any major failure of the flood, especially if it was repeated for a couple of years, was catastrophic. There would be widespread starvation, death of livestock and pressure to eat the seed required for the next crop. Elite pressure to continue requisitioning food would inevitably lead to social unrest and a political crisis. The Egyptian state was not strong enough to cope with any prolonged crisis.

Many of the phases of Egyptian history are related to changes in the Nile flood. The period around 3200–2800 BCE saw unusually low floods and the social turbulence this caused, and the need for greater organization to cope with the problem, was a significant factor in the emergence of the Egyptian state. The prosperity and stability of the Old Kingdom period from 2700–2200 BCE coincided with a time of generally high and reliable floods. The breakdown of the Old Kingdom and the First Intermediate period from 2180–1991 BCE was almost certainly linked to the catastrophically low floods of the time. During the First Intermediate period the royal buildings and inscriptions associated with the first Pharaohs are strikingly absent but the tombs of the rulers of the small, local kingdoms which emerged are numerous and elaborate. What seems to have happened is that the economic and social dislocation caused by the very low Nile floods resulted in a decreased ability to support the infrastructure of the Egyptian state, a decline in central control and the emergence of local rulers (perhaps from the local governors of the Old Kingdom) who were able to organize some food supply and local protection. Inevitably there was almost continual conflict between these rulers. The outline of the period is confused but there appears to have been a major civil war and social unrest within Egypt for about twenty years after 2180 BCE. Between 2160 and 2040 BCE there was a dynasty centred in an area about sixty miles north of Memphis but it ruled only part of the Nile valley. About 2130 BCE another dynasty emerged at Thebes in Upper Egypt. Sometime between 2040 and 2000 BCE, as the Nile floods began to recover, a ruler called Smatowy ('uniter of the two lands') re-established a single Egyptian kingdom.

[*Later Egypt* **7.1.2**]

4.6 The Indus Valley

The civilization which developed in the Indus valley and the surrounding area about 2300 BCE was the third to develop in the world, yet it is the least known of all the early civilizations. Its script is still undeciphered, so little is known about its internal structure or culture and it declined rapidly after 1750 BCE with very few of its achievements being transmitted to later societies and states. It was the shortest-lived of the early civilizations and its peak of prosperity probably lasted for no more than three centuries after 2300 BCE.

The first evidence for farming in the Indus valley dates to about 6000 BCE. The main crops were wheat and barley – their cultivation almost certainly diffused from the earliest villages in south-west Asia. In addition peas, lentils and dates were grown. A key crop was cotton – the first evidence of its cultivation anywhere in the world. The main domesticated animals were humped cattle, buffalo and pigs, all of which seem to have been domesticated from local herds. Sheep and goats, the key animals of south-west Asia, were of only marginal importance. From about 4000 BCE,

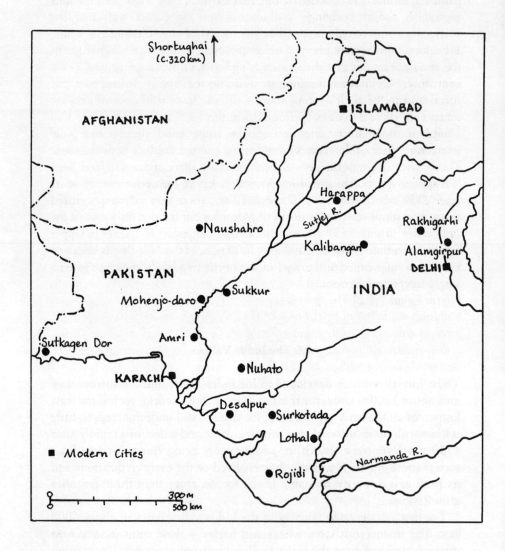

Map 9: The Indus valley civilization

as the population increased, substantial villages built from mud bricks proliferated in the valley and the culture in the region became increasingly uniform. The major problem for these early farmers was that the Indus, fed from the Himalayas, flooded wide areas of the valley between June and September and often changed its course. From about 3000 BCE extensive works were built to contain the flood and to irrigate the surrounding fields. Wheat and barley were planted as the flood receded and were harvested in the spring. The impact of the increasing amount of irrigation and flood control was to increase the food surplus and lead on to a phase of rapid social and political development from about 2600 BCE which, within a century or at the most two, produced a highly complex society.

Little is known about either the process which led to the civilization or its nature. None of the names of the rulers or even of its cities are known. There were two major cities – the sites of Mohenjo-daro in the south and Harappa in the north. At their height they may have had a population of 30-50,000 (about the size of Uruk) but they were the only settlements of this size in the Indus valley – an area of 300,000 square miles. The two cities seem to have had a similar plan. On the western side there was a 'citadel' mound of major public buildings, all of which were oriented north–south. To the east there was a lower city of mainly residential areas. The citadel was surrounded by a brick wall and there may have been one for the whole city. The streets were laid out on a regular plan and the buildings made out of bricks of a uniform size. The whole of the valley had a set of common weights and measures and the art and religious motifs also demonstrate considerable unity. All of these features suggest a high degree of control within the Indus valley society.

The Indus valley civilization was at the centre of a web of widespread trading networks. Gold came from central India, silver from Iran and copper from Rajasthan. A number of trading posts and colonies were also established. Some of these were inland at strategic locations on the passes leading into central Asia. Others were to control access to key resources such as the timber of the Hindu Kush mountains. The wide influence of the civilization is demonstrated by the fact that it maintained a trading colony at Shortughai, the only known source of lapis lazuli, on the Oxus river over 450 miles from the nearest settlement in the Indus valley. There were also links even further north to the far side of the Kopet Dag mountains and the site of Altyn-depe near the Caspian Sea. This was a town of some 7,500 people surrounded by a 35-foot-thick wall, which had a large craft-workers' quarters with fifty pottery kilns, and which regularly traded with the Indus valley. In addition there were settlements to control maritime trade routes such as at Lothal at the head of the Gulf of Cambay and a series of forts along the Makran coast to the west. These forts were important for the trade with Mesopotamia which developed from about 2600 BCE, with ships sailing down the Gulf and then along the Makran coast – the Indus valley was known as 'Meluhha' by the Mesopotamians. The level of trade is demonstrated by the fact that special seals made only in Bahrain have been discovered in the Indus valley and the Indus valley civilization maintained a small colony of interpreters in Mesopotamia, and there was a special village where their merchants stayed.

The Indus valley civilization came to an end very rapidly about 1700 BCE. The reasons for the collapse were complex. As in Mesopotamia irrigation in an unsuitable environment of high temperatures and slow drainage led to salinization of the soil and declining crop yields. In addition the annual flood of the Indus may have been difficult to control. Of far greater importance though was the fact that unlike Mesopotamia where mud bricks were sun-dried, in the Indus valley they were dried in wood-fired ovens. Within a few centuries the valley was denuded of woodland. This would have drastically increased soil erosion and the silting-up of drainage channels and irrigation ditches. It seems that all of these factors led to internal weakness and an inability to sustain the complex society and state that had emerged. The result was external conquest, probably by nomadic groups from the surrounding area. City life and 'civilization' disappeared in the area – there was no recovery as happened in Mesopotamia and Egypt after similar problems. When, almost a millennium later, urban life developed again in India it was centred around the Ganges valley to the south and east. This area remained the core for the various states and empires that emerged in northern India.
[*Later India* 7.3.3]

4.7 Technology

During the emergence of the separate civilizations of Mesopotamia, Egypt and the Indus valley there were a number of developments which affected all three (and many of the peripheral areas too). In particular a number of fundamental technological steps were taken around 3000 BCE at exactly the time when a more complex society and state were emerging in Mesopotamia. There can be little doubt that all of these developments were linked.

Some of the earliest steps were improvements in pottery making. For several thousand years production methods had been relatively crude, with the clay being built up in hand-formed rings and fired directly in the fire. About 4000 BCE the first true pottery kilns were invented, where the pot was separated from the fire by a perforated floor. The kilns were essential to produce true polychrome pots and were built of clay with an outer stone or mud-brick wall. In Mesopotamia they were dome shaped with a vent at the top, in Egypt they were more chimney-like. About 500 years later the first potter's wheel was developed although it was more a turntable which was turned by one hand as the other shaped the pot – the continuously turning wheel was not invented until about 700 BCE. Ovens similar to kilns could also be used to fire mud bricks. In Mesopotamia this technique was restricted to those bricks needed for the most crucial parts of buildings whereas, as we have seen, in the Indus valley mud bricks were fired on an extensive scale. (Egypt retained sun-dried bricks even for royal palaces.) Looms for weaving were in use by about 3500 BCE in both Egypt and Mesopotamia – they were little more than short uprights stuck in the ground with beams along the two sides with the warp threads stretched between them and held in place by weights.

There were also slow changes in agricultural technology. During the early Ubaid period in Mesopotamia clay sickles were used because they were easy to make and there was plenty of raw material available. Just after 3000 BCE they were replaced by flint sickles set into a wooden handle and secured with bitumen (easily available in Mesopotamia through seepage from the underground oil sources). Ploughs – originally little more than forked sticks to scratch the surface of the soil – were made from wood and pulled by humans (as they were for thousands of years in many parts of the world). Few improvements were possible until techniques for harnessing animals had been developed. In Egypt the earliest illustrations show oxen harnessed by the horns. In Mesopotamia onagers (a type of ass) were used. They were controlled by a yoke with a collar to keep it in place which unfortunately also tended to strangle the animal when it pulled. About 3000 BCE in Mesopotamia a major modification was made to the plough. A single pointed piece of wood now formed a share to cut the soil and a sole to push the soil aside thereby forming a deeper and wider furrow. Some ploughs, heavy enough to need two draught animals, had a seed funnel. Although all these ploughs could only cope with light soils they did improve productivity by allowing better planting and easier weeding between well-defined rows.

The harnessing of animals for agricultural work led on to the first artificial land transport in the world. Animal-drawn sledges were known in Mesopotamia from an early date but from about 3500 BCE two-wheeled carts and four-wheeled wagons were in use. These were still very crude and inefficient – the wheels were solid and made from three pieces of wood joined together. They must have broken very easily on rough dirt tracks and probably were of little use outside the cities. Carts were also known in the Indus valley, although pack-oxen tended to be used for longer journeys. In Egypt wheeled vehicles were uncommon – it was relatively easy to move goods (even the heavy stones used in the monumental buildings) along the Nile. On land, sledges pulled by humans using papyrus-reed ropes were the norm – the pyramids were built using huge ramps up which large teams of human workers dragged stones resting on sledges. Little is known about the earliest boats. They must have been used in the Mediterranean by about 10,000 BCE (later than in other parts of the world) because the use of obsidian from the island of Melos can be detected across a wide area of the mainland. Before 3000 BCE ships were sailing down the Gulf from Mesopotamia to Oman and a few centuries later to the Indus valley. The first known wooden boats in Egypt were copies of the early papyrus boats – they had no keel or ribs (and therefore no hold) and everything had to travel on deck where the rowers sat on stools.

Some of the most important technological developments around 3000 BCE were in the use of metals, marking the end of the long human dependence on stone tools. The first contact humans had with metals would have been through use of their pigments – yellow and red ochre (both ores of iron) and malachite (green) and azurite (blue) which are copper ores. These were used for tens of thousands of years before the emergence of settled societies to decorate bodies and for ritual purposes. Copper occurs as a metal in ore deposits and could be hammered into shape, beaten into thin strips and even joined to make rings and small ornaments. These small items (limited in size because the metal only occurs in very small amounts) were made for thousands of years before the first smelting of copper. Exactly where this crucial development took place and how is not known. It is possible that the first copper metal was smelted as part of the process of producing faïence – a synthetic lapis lazuli – by heating stone with copper ore in a crucible at high temperature to produce the blue glass. It seems very unlikely that it happened in Mesopotamia because the area has no copper ore. The most likely places are Anatolia and the Iranian plateau, perhaps as early as 6000–5000 BCE. It was certainly done before the development of pottery kilns which would not have been much help in discovering smelting techniques. Very little equipment was needed – the key was knowledge and understanding. The copper ore was probably mixed with the fuel (charcoal or very dry wood) and left in a shallow pit at white heat for about a day. When the mixture cooled the copper metal would have been at the bottom, although it would have been necessary to chip the glassy slag away. The copper would then have been either hammered or reheated and poured into moulds (already in use to produce mud bricks) – two-piece moulds and closed ones for even more elaborate shapes were developed by about 3300 BCE.

These techniques and the production of metal objects were restricted to a small number of craftsmen. At first mainly small objects were made – beads, pins and hooks. This was partly because the uses of copper were limited – it was difficult to sharpen into an edge and therefore of little use for military and agricultural functions. Copper sickles were used fairly widely in Mesopotamia by 2000 BCE but they were little better than the existing flint type. Also the ores were still in relatively short supply – many items were melted down and the metal reused. However, techniques continued to improve and the use of arsenical ores of copper resulted in a much better product. Around 3000 BCE there was a very rapid increase in the pace of development and within about a century lead, silver, tin and gold were all being used. Indeed gold was hardly used before 3000 BCE yet by 2600 BCE the Mesopotamian craftsmen in the temple and palace workshops were producing immensely sophisticated pieces for the political and religious elite.

The most significant development around 3000 BCE was the discovery that the addition of a small amount of tin ore to the copper ore in the smelting process not only reduced the melting point and made the molten metal easier to cast but produced a much harder end product – bronze. Exactly where this process was first discovered is unknown but again Anatolia (which remained a major producer over a long period) and Iran are the most likely candidates. However, there is a further mystery. Tin ores do not occur near copper ores and are only associated with granite rocks. There are almost no major deposits of tin in the south-west Asia region and the most likely source is in Afghanistan (the only alternatives are northern Portugal, Brittany and Cornwall, whose tin was used extensively much later). The production of bronze therefore depended on the maintenance of very long-distance trade networks. This may well be the reason for the relatively slow adoption of bronze in the thousand years after 3000 BCE. However, high-quality bronze was made in Mesopotamia – the tin content was kept fairly constant at about 8–10 per cent to produce a hard but not brittle metal and the addition of lead made the bronze even more viscous and easy to pour into the complex four-piece moulds which were developed. In Egypt there was little use of bronze before about 2000 BCE but copper, especially the harder arsenical copper, was used extensively.

The major technological development around 2000 BCE was the invention of the goat-skin bellows to raise the temperature of the fire (before only a blowpipe was available). This enabled not just greater quantities of metal to be produced but also the use of the commoner sulphide ores of copper which could be roasted first. Now, instead of adding tinstone to metallic copper, it was reduced to metallic tin first and then the two metals were mixed together and heated. Although this was a much longer process it was much more effective and enabled the proportion of tin to be varied to produce bronze for different purposes. Only with these inventions and modifications could a true 'bronze age' develop. About the same time the first glass was made almost certainly by accident during the production of faïence. The addition of lead (to stop the glass contracting on cooling) also allowed a glaze to be put on an earthenware surface such as bricks, tiles and pottery. However, the use of glass remained very limited for the next thousand years.

The production of the earliest metals relied on very primitive mining techniques. The mines were small and hazardous and therefore usually worked by slaves. There were no ventilation shafts and no pumps available to allow work below the level of the water table. Mining was simply a matter of digging to try and follow the veins of metal and then removing the ore through the use of firesetting and chipping away with stone tools. The introduction of metal tools helped but made no fundamental difference.

[*Later technology* 8.1]

4.8 Writing

The evolution of writing was central to the development of civilization. Although a few such as the Incas managed without writing, it was fundamental to the functioning of the state in most early civilizations. Its purpose was not to represent a language but to store and transmit information. At first this was mainly about trade and administration – literature did not develop for a considerable time and could easily be transmitted orally from generation to generation. The development of writing did not 'cause' civilization – it was developed to meet the needs of the elite in an increasingly complex society and then it reinforced the trends towards greater power and control. Literacy remained restricted to a very small minority until the last hundred years or so, and scripts were often kept deliberately complicated in order to restrict knowledge. This was because writing was central to the power of the state and the ability of it and the elite to control and exploit the majority of people. Only they had access to information; only they were able to take certain decisions and regulate the activities of society. Their monopoly over learning and literacy was also a powerful mechanism for creating a sense of unity among the elite and disseminating their value systems. It is these that we have come to call culture and civilization.

Although all scripts carry out the same functions they have shown

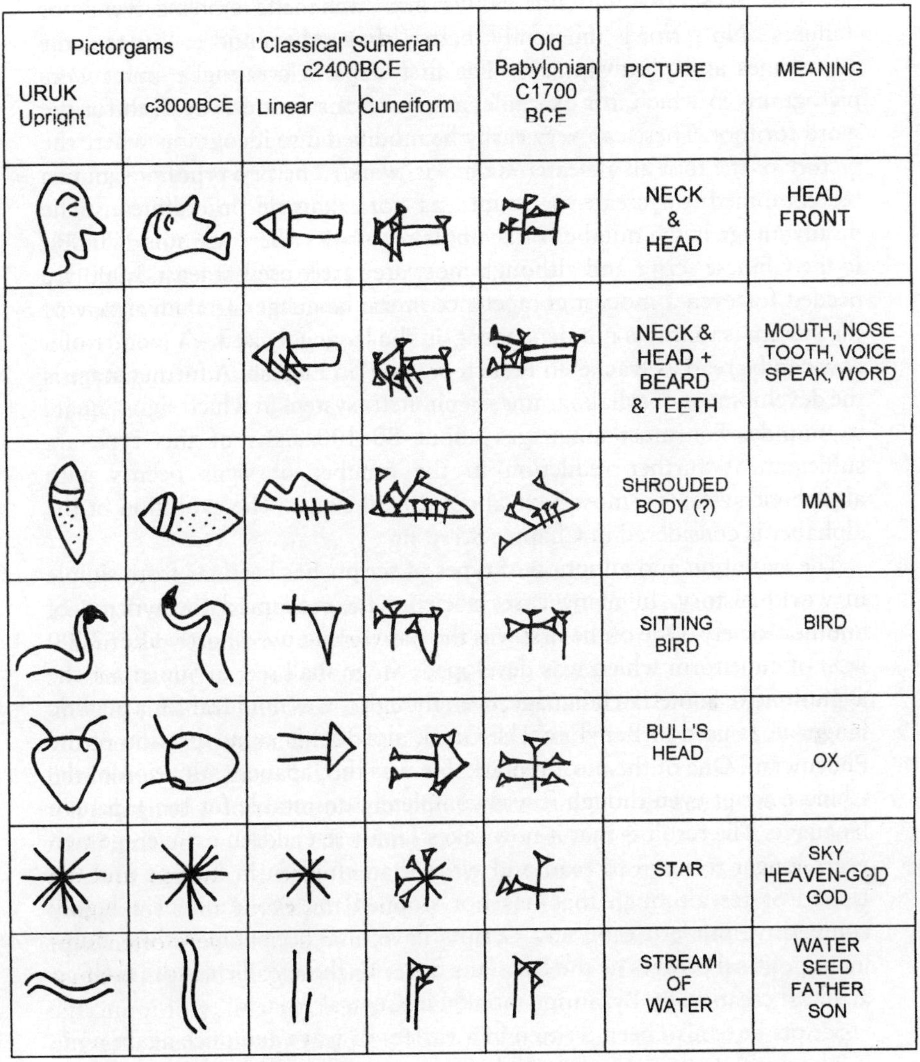

Pictorgams		'Classical' Sumerian c2400BCE		Old Babylonian C1700 BCE	PICTURE	MEANING
URUK Upright	c3000BCE	Linear	Cuneiform			
					NECK & HEAD	HEAD FRONT
					NECK & HEAD + BEARD & TEETH	MOUTH, NOSE TOOTH, VOICE SPEAK, WORD
					SHROUDED BODY (?)	MAN
					SITTING BIRD	BIRD
					BULL'S HEAD	OX
					STAR	SKY HEAVEN-GOD GOD
					STREAM OF WATER	WATER SEED FATHER SON

Chart 2: The evolution of the cuneiform script

remarkable variety in different societies. Until recently it was commonly assumed that scripts evolved through a series of stages before reaching the summit – the alphabet as used in 'western civilization'. It is now clear that there is no such 'ladder' up which writing systems could and should climb and that those that did not evolve into alphabetic systems were not 'failures'. No script is inherently 'better' than others and each has some advantages and disadvantages. The first steps in creating a script were pictograms in which, for example, a picture of a foot can be used for the word for foot. These can very easily be modified into ideograms where the picture of the foot also means 'stand' or 'walk'. The two types of sign can be combined to create a script, as for example in Chinese. The disadvantage is the number of symbols required – there are some 70,000 in the Chinese script and although most are rarely used at least 3,000 are needed for even a modest competence in the language. The advantage of the system is that it is not dependent on the language used – a picture of a cow can be read as 'vache' in French or 'cow' in English. A further stage is the development of syllabograms – a phonetic system in which signs equate to sounds. For most languages about 80–100 signs of this type are sufficient. A further reduction in the number of signs occurs with alphabetic systems – most have about 20–30 signs. (The evolution of the alphabet is considered in Chapter 8.)

The evolution and adoption of types of scripts has been far from simple in world history. In many cases societies have adapted the writing of another society. One of the first was the Babylonian use (shortly after 2000 BCE) of cuneiform which was developed, as we shall see, in Sumer for the agglutinative Sumerian language, even though it was not ideal for a Semitic language as used in Babylon. The Greek alphabet is an adaptation of the Phoenician. One of the most remarkable was the Japanese adoption of the Chinese script even though it was completely unsuitable for the Japanese language. The result is that it now takes Japanese children on average two years longer to learn to read and write than children in Europe and the United States although that has not stopped the evolution of a highly competitive modern economy. Scripts have also been imposed by dominant political powers as the Russians did with the Cyrillic script (itself an artificial creation by Byzantine monks) in Central Asia.

Scripts have also been written in a variety of ways and once again none is inherently 'better'. Modern alphabetic systems as used in 'the West' are written from left to right and from the top to the bottom of the page. All Semitic scripts go in the opposite direction but also from top to bottom of the page – however the manuscript is read in what in western terms is back to front. Chinese (and therefore Japanese) is written in vertical columns from top to bottom but also 'back to front'. The Mayan script of

Mesoamerica was written in pairs of vertical columns. In most pictographic scripts such as Egyptian hieroglyphs the characters 'look' towards the beginning of the line whereas alphabetic signs 'look' towards the end of the line. Early Greek writing was boustrophedon in character – the lines alternated left–right and right–left and the direction of the signs also changed. The division of characters into words and sentences evolved very slowly. Egyptian, cuneiform and Sanskrit do not divide into words and sentences and early medieval European religious manuscripts usually do not do so either. The earliest known divisions occur in the Meroitic script of the Sudan area and the Cypriot; both used dots and strokes rather than gaps.

The earliest known script in the world developed in Mesopotamia. The precursors of writing are found in the Ubaid period (5500–4000 BCE) in two forms – first stamp seals and second, hollow clay balls with seal impressions all over the surface and little clay tokens on the inside, some with impressed numerals on them. The former were presumably used to show ownership but the function of the latter is unknown. The first true writing comes from a series of clay tablets found at the Eanna temple complex at Uruk which date to about 3200 BCE. Their content shows that writing developed to meet the administrative needs of an already complex and hierarchical society. About 85 per cent of the tablets are economic records of the temple administration and deal with the movement of commodities, rations and similar functions. The remainder provide a hierarchical list of occupations starting with the 'king' or 'leader', with fifteen signs for various officials responsible for 'law', 'the city', 'the troops', 'ploughs' and 'barley', signs for religious functionaries and then for a number of occupations such as smith, silversmith, shepherd and herald.

Altogether there are about 2,000 signs on the Eanna tablets most of which are pictographic in form. The signs were easy to inscribe on wet clay tablets but they had a number of disadvantages. The tablets were bulky (some weighed over twelve pounds) and impossible to amend or add to once they had dried. The constraints of writing on clay with a wedge-shaped stylus led to a series of developments in the script. The characters became less pictographic and more abstract as the cuneiform (wedge-shaped) script evolved. The number of signs fell to about 1,000 by 2000 BCE although only a few of these were in regular use. The script was originally written in vertical columns but changed to horizontal and left to right with the characters also turning through ninety degrees. At first the characters conveyed little of the sound of the Sumerian language but this was gradually incorporated. For example, the Sumerian for 'to give' was *sum* for which there was no pictograph. Scribes therefore used the sign for garlic, also *sum*, though it was probably pronounced slightly differently. Following the conquest of Sumer by Sargon of Akkad, the increasing use of Akkadian and the decline of Sumerian, the cuneiform script was adapted for Akkadian. This was done by having three types of sign – syllabic to represent a spoken syllable, ideographic for a word or idea and determinative to tell the reader what type of sign came next. Even more confusing was the fact that some signs had all three functions at different times. Within little more than a thousand years from its first use the relatively simple Sumerian pictograms had evolved into a highly complex script capable of being used for a different language altogether.

As the cuneiform script evolved its use became more widespread. About 2900 BCE it was used at Ur to carve texts on to stone with the details of land purchases. Within another three hundred years it was used for royal inscriptions and religious texts and by 2500 BCE to record slave sales, loan agreements and business records. Three hundred years later the first primitive 'law-code' was written down. The use of writing also spread from Mesopotamia into Elam in Iran and much more directly to Ebla in Syria. The royal palace archive discovered by the Italian expedition in 1975–7 contained 15,000 tablets written in the cuneiform script borrowed from Mesopotamia. The tablets date to about 2500–2300 BCE and are clearly written in a Semitic language. The particular language is unknown, although it is certainly not Akkadian. It has provisionally been named Eblaite.

Whether the development of writing in Mesopotamia influenced events in Egypt is uncertain. It is, however, clear that writing emerged very late in the formation of the Egyptian state and unlike Mesopotamia very few precursors of it have been found. Egyptian writing developed in two types – a monumental script (hieroglyphic) and one suitable for everyday tasks (hieratic). The first short groups of hieroglyphs, strongly pictographic in form, are found at the time of unification and the transition to the First Dynasty. Hieroglyphs remained strongly pictorial and did not evolve in a similar way to cuneiform in Mesopotamia. It is clear that they were created for the rulers and were used in a very restricted way in a few locations – mainly royal tombs. They were designed for the specific purpose of emphasizing the royal-divine functions and have a very limited range of concerns – mainly to show the geographical and administrative units of Egypt in a personified form and the achievements of the Pharaoh and the elite. This was very different from the primarily 'economic' function of the Sumerian script and reflects the very different nature of Egyptian society and the much more centralized state. Only slowly, about the time of the Fourth Dynasty (*c.*2500 BCE), was the script used slightly more widely on the tombs of various office holders and bureaucrats.

Hieroglyphic was much too pictorial for normal writing and in parallel the hieratic script evolved to meet these needs. The first signs that probably evolved into this script can be found on pottery dated to just before 3000 BCE. The script, in which the hieroglyphs were reduced to a few easy strokes of a reed pen, was written on papyri from about 2500 BCE. However, this medium was very expensive and the amount of records kept by the various temple and palace officials seems to be far less than on the cheaper clay tablets of Mesopotamia. Hieratic did develop in some of the same ways as cuneiform – it was a mixed ideographic and syllabic system with determinatives as an aid to reading. However, there was one crucial difference from cuneiform, stemming from the nature of the Egyptian language – only the consonants in each syllable were represented.

The script of the Indus valley is still undeciphered, indeed there is almost no idea of what language it represents. Because it is only known in very short passages using a few signs it seems unlikely that it will ever be understood. Some specialists believe that it may have been created under Mesopotamian influence as part of the extensive trade network between the two societies but there is little hard evidence to support such a conclusion. However, the scribes who wrote the Indus valley script would have been part of the privileged elite just as they were in the other early civilizations. They were performing an essential function for the state and religious authorities in directing and controlling the rest of society. It was a far better life than being a peasant toiling in the fields, forced to give up a large proportion of their harvest, labour on state projects and serve in the army. As two Egyptian papyri comment:

'Be a scribe, it saves you from toil, it protects you from all manner of labour.'

'Be a scribe. Your limbs will be sleek, your hands will grow soft. You will go forth in white clothes, honoured with courtiers saluting you.'

[*Early Chinese script 7.8.2, development of the alphabet 8.7.3*]

OVERVIEW 3

THE WORLD IN
2000 BCE

World Population: 27 million
Regional Population: South-west Asia: 5 million,
China: 5 million, Indus valley: 4 million,
Nile valley: 1 million
Major cities: Lagash (80,000), Memphis (50,000),
Uruk (50,000), Harappa (50,000), Mohenjo-Daro (50,000)

Events:

★ Collapse of Third Dynasty of Ur. Rise of Babylon

★ Reunification of Egypt under Twelfth Dynasty after First
Intermediate period

★ Indus valley civilization at its peak

★ Early Chinese culture – the Shang – beginning to emerge

★ Emergence of the first complex societies on Crete

★ Full-scale production of bronze in south-west Asia and China

★ Development of the chariot in south-west Asia and China

★ First production of glass in south-west Asia

★ Caravanserais established along south-west Asian trade routes

★ Farming villages across Europe

★ Spread of maize cultivation across Mesoamerica. First
agricultural villages in the Americas

★ First cultivated plants in north America

★ Early potatoes domesticated in the Andes

5

Isolation: The Americas and the Pacific

The early civilizations of Mesopotamia, Egypt and the Indus valley were in touch with each other relatively soon after they developed. From about 2000 BCE the states and empires of south-west Asia were in constant interaction and their area of influence spread both westwards into the Mediterranean and eastwards to the states and empires that emerged in Iran and India. In its initial stages the civilization of China remained relatively isolated, but by about 1000 BCE China was also in contact with the states of India and Iran. By 200 BCE at the latest the whole Eurasian world was linked together. It is therefore highly misleading to consider the development of any of these states and societies in isolation except in their very early stages. There was, however, one area of the world where civilization emerged and developed without any contact with Eurasia for thousands of years – the Americas. The Pacific was similarly isolated until its main contact with the Europeans little more than two hundred years ago but although complex societies did develop they did not have the main features of 'civilization'.

The Americas were the last major area of the world to be settled by humans about 12,000 BCE. [2.6.2] It is therefore not surprising that the general pace of development lagged behind that of Eurasia. The adoption of agriculture and the development of the first villages did not occur in Mesoamerica before about 2000–1500 BCE, almost six thousand years later than in south-west Asia. The earliest relatively complex society emerged shortly after 1000 BCE, and the first cities and incipient states date to about the BCE/CE divide. This was a stage of development roughly equivalent to that of the early Sumerian city-states in about 3500 BCE. Thereafter the pace of development was much the same as in Mesopotamia – the military empires of the Toltecs and the Aztec are roughly comparable to the Akkadian empire in Mesopotamia in 2300 BCE. This late start was one of the reasons why the Aztec and Inca empires were so far behind the Europeans and so easily destroyed by them after 1500.

The isolation of the Americas meant that the civilizations which developed there had a number of unique features not found in Eurasia. Agriculture relied on a range of crops not known in Eurasia, in particular, as we have seen, maize, beans and squash. Even more significantly, there were no animals of any consequence that could be domesticated. There were no sheep, goats or pigs and, even more important, no cattle, horses or asses capable of being turned into draught animals. In the Andes the llama and alpaca were domesticated but they could only be used as pack animals. The result was that, although the wheel was known and used on toys, it was impossible to develop land transport, and agriculture had to rely on human power for every activity. As a result water-borne transport was the only alternative to human porters and the movement of basic products such as food was very difficult over more than the shortest distances. Trade was therefore limited mainly to luxury items whereas in Mesopotamia, as early as 2000 BCE, Ur was transporting 72,000 bushels of grain a year to Isin. In addition it was very difficult to sustain armies at any great distance because the soldiers had to carry their own food – this was one of the major limits on the size of the Aztec empire. The other fundamental difference was that the civilizations of the Americas lacked metals of any significance. Only in the central Andes region was metal working developed and even here it remained limited in scope and largely confined to ritual and decorative functions. The consequence was that all the societies of the Americas continued to rely on stone for their tools and weapons.

The different foundations of the civilizations of the Americas and their isolation from Eurasia mean that it is best to consider their history as a single unit, taking the story up to their contact with the Europeans shortly after 1500 CE. There were no links of any importance between the civilizations of Mesoamerica and those of the Andes and the Peruvian coastal region and they can, therefore, be considered separately.

5.1 Early Mesoamerica

[*Contemporaneous Eurasia* 8.3, 8.5.3, 8.8, 8.9, 8.11, 8.12]
The chronological divisions of Mesoamerican history are very different from those of Eurasia. The earliest period (the Formative) dates from the development of the first agricultural villages about 2000 BCE to the emergence of cities and structured states shortly after the BCE/CE divide. At first the number of villages and the population grew only slowly after the development of agriculture because of the breeding problems in increasing the yield of the main food crop, maize. Technological progress was also limited. (The first pottery in the Americas may date to about 3500 BCE on the Pacific coast of Ecuador and perhaps a thousand years later in the valley of Mexico.) The earliest villages traded a few precious stones such as jade, and canoes were in use in the Maya lowlands by about 2200 BCE.

The first complex society and culture emerged about 1200 BCE in the tropical lowlands of the Gulf coast and lasted for about 800 years. It is

Map 10: Mesoamerica

known as Olmec, although that is the name of the people who lived in the area at the time of the Spanish conquest. The actual name of the people of this ancient society is unknown. They were, however, to have a major influence over many features of all subsequent Mesoamerican civilizations. The early developments in this region relied on the fact that it was possible, because of the rich soil and high rainfall (over 120 inches a year), to grow two crops of maize a year, thereby producing a significant agricultural surplus to support the elite. Perhaps the most remarkable surviving features of the Olmec are the colossal carved stone heads over eight feet high with their unusual faces and pronounced thick lips not known in any other American civilization. They are three-dimensional, designed to be viewed from all angles and weigh between 40 and 50 tons. The nearest stone was over eighty miles away and they must have been floated down the rivers to the ceremonial centres. The earliest Olmec site – San Lorenzo – flourished for about 250 years before it was destroyed. Some of the ceremonial heads were tipped into a nearby ravine although others were carefully buried in straight lines. Exactly what happened and why this extensive ceremonial site was abandoned in this way is unknown. Almost immediately it was replaced by the larger island site of La Venta. As well as the large ceremonial heads La Venta had a huge 110-foot-high multi-coloured clay pyramid resting on a base 420 feet long and 240 feet wide. It is not known whether it was a burial mound but there were other long low mounds nearby and all were part of a huge plaza surrounded by seven-foot-tall basalt columns. Nothing is known of what took place at this large ceremonial site. It was destroyed about 400 BCE and the heads were nearly all mutilated. There were also other smaller ceremonial sites in the Olmec area such as Tres Zapotes, about 100 miles to the north-west of La Venta, which had over fifty earthen mounds.

Over the period between 1200–400 BCE Olmec influence spread across much of Mesoamerica, at first to the valley of Oaxaca, later to the valley of Mexico and eventually even to the Pacific coast of Guatemala. Some of these contacts were for trade for elite items such as jade and there were probably a number of Olmec trading colonies in key areas. The Olmec were not a peaceful society and the monuments show numerous scenes of warfare and conquest which may have been an important part of the way in which the elite controlled Olmec society. They were not literate and no fully developed script has been found although some objects appear to be inscribed with hieroglyphs that may be ancestral to some of those later used by the Maya. It does, however, seem clear that the Olmec originated the complex calendar that was common to all subsequent Mesoamerican civilizations. Central to this system was the fact that all Mesoamerican civilizations (again probably derived from the Olmec) used twenty as the base for counting. The Mesoamerican calendar was a combination of two calendars moving in parallel. The first was a solar calendar of eighteen 'months' of twenty days plus five 'dead' days to make the 365-day year. The second was a 'sacred' calendar of twenty day names and the numbers 1 to 13 making a round of 260 days. The reasons for the adoption of this 260-day count are unknown and it does not equate to any obvious astronomical cycle. The two calendars only returned to their exact starting point every fifty-two years. This was a time of immense significance to all the Mesoamerican civilizations because the completion of the cycle could mark the end of the world and the descent of everlasting night as the sun failed to rise. The other major contribution of the Olmecs was the invention (about 500 BCE) of the ball-game which appears to have had a sacred function in all Mesoamerican civilizations. In a large walled court two teams competed to pass a small rubber ball through a 'ring' set high on the walls, probably without using their hands.

After the fall of La Venta about 400 BCE and the end of the Olmec culture there was no major society or state which influenced all of Mesoamerica for about 500 years. The most important sites for this period come from the valley of Oaxaca. From about 500 BCE the site of Monte Alban, set on a series of hills 1,300 feet above the junction of three valleys, came to dominate all the agricultural settlements in the main valley. It was a ceremonial and administrative site for an elite who relied on imports of food, no doubt as tribute, from the surrounding area. There was a series of buildings built around a central plaza and a number of residential compounds and craft production areas. Monte Alban grew rapidly from about 200 BCE when a large defensive wall was built around the site, and at its peak the population was around 20,000. The society, probably Zapotec speaking, dominated the surrounding region and its power was based on warfare and conquest. The site contains some of the earliest hieroglyphic texts (which cannot be read) but they illustrate war and the conquest of towns. Many of the buildings are carved with a series of over 300 peculiar figures known as 'Danzantes'. Most of them show mutilated bodies in odd postures presumably signifying prisoners of war. The site also had ceremonial functions though what they may have been is unknown. One building known as Structure J is oddly aligned compared with all the others at the site. It is probably linked to the heliacal rising of Capella at the time of the first of the two zenith passages of the sun over Monte Alban. It was not therefore an 'observatory' but rather was used to identify a particularly important moment in the calendar.

5.2 Teotihuacan

[*Contemporaneous Eurasia* 9.7, 9.10, 9.11, 9.12, 10.2, 10.3, 10.8, 10.10, 10.11]

Shortly after the BCE/CE divide the first major city and empire emerged in Mesoamerica marking the beginning of the Classic period which lasted until about 900 CE. The site of Teotihuacan in the north-east part of the valley of Mexico covers a vast area and contains numerous residential compounds, temples and two huge pyramids now named after the Sun and the Moon, though these were almost certainly not their original associations. At its peak, about 500 CE, the population was around 100,000 making it one of the largest cities in the world and its influence spread across the whole of Mesoamerica. Yet it is the least understood of all the civilizations of Mesoamerica and nearly all the major questions about its nature remain unanswered. The city appears to have had no real script and only a few hieroglyphic signs have been found. These signs have some similarities to the other systems used in Mesoamerica but there are few indications of the complex calendar employed elsewhere. Who built the city, what language they spoke and what they called their city are unknown. It was clearly a highly stratified society with powerful elite rulers (with a mixture of religious and military functions) but it lacks the dedicatory monuments glorifying the rulers that are found among the Maya a little later and there are no scenes of conquest and capture as at the earlier Monte Alban. The military were clearly important but the city had no defensive wall.

The area was settled about 150 BCE, later than the rest of the valley of Mexico. It developed rapidly thanks to its fertile soil, the use of irrigation and the exploitation of the obsidian deposits in the area. More important was its use as a religious and ritual site. This was centred on the highly modified natural cave which is now beneath the Pyramid of the Sun and which appears to have some form of astronomical alignment indicating a key part of the calendar. The site continued to grow until about 150 CE when the city was rebuilt over a huge area in accordance with a carefully designed but highly artificial plan. It was the most comprehensively planned city of its time anywhere in the world. The main axis is the so-called 'Street of the Dead' – a series of plazas built around twenty-three complexes, each of three temples with a very distinctive style of architecture not seen elsewhere in Mesoamerica. In addition there is a central 'palace' and administrative buildings. The two great pyramids are also along this axis which is oriented exactly 15° 28′ east of north. The main east–west axis is deliberately laid out so as not to be perpendicular to the 'Street of the Dead' but at 16° 30′ south of east. These orientations were difficult to build because they defied the natural topography of the site. That they were carefully chosen is shown by the series of 'pecked crosses' found across the city chipped into floor pavements and rocky outcrops. They consist of a set of concentric circles quartered by two axes which repeat the main alignment of the site. The significance of these two carefully chosen directions is not known although the east–west orientation seems to point to the heliacal rising of the Pleiades on the day of the spring zenith passage of the sun over Teotihuacan, which would have been on 18 May in 150 CE. The city was also divided by a series of walls marking significant internal boundaries.

The nature of Teotihuacan religious beliefs is unclear although there was clearly a very complex symbolism in its art. Many of the temples show a goddess with claws not hands and a headdress made of human hearts – the latter form a common motif across the site. Teotihuacan is the first site at which another distinctive Mesoamerican element can be identified – the temple of the Feathered Serpent (called by the Nahua, Quetzalcoatl) who was a culture hero bringing civilization to humans in much the same way as Prometheus in Greek mythology. During the construction of this temple, which had a long series of serpent heads around it (each weighed four tons without its accompanying collar of petals), there was a series of human sacrifices placed symmetrically at the cardinal directions and in total probably numbering 260 people.

Shortly after the temples were built the population of the valley seems to have been concentrated into the city in what appears to be a highly structured and rigid way. The vast residential area of Teotihuacan consists of about 2,000 one-storey, windowless 'compounds' about sixty yards long and turned in on themselves and their network of courtyards. They all have underfloor drains. Each probably held about sixty people. Because of the street plan they also followed the sacred layout of the city. Such units were unprecedented and never repeated in Mesoamerica. They appear to have been occupied by kinship units and the sizes of the compounds vary according to the group which would have lived in them, their status and occupation. Some areas of the city were reserved for particular occupations – the potters were in the south-west – and there were also sections for 'outsiders', perhaps merchants and traders (those from Oaxaca in the west and from Vera Cruz in the east). Whatever their exact relationship to the ruling elite, these compounds demonstrate an immense power and determination to build a highly structured and ordered society with strong internal discipline.

The main and very rapid phase of construction at Teotihuacan was over within about fifty years, by 200 CE. There was then a period of immense stability lasting perhaps 400 years. The city developed an extensive trade network across Mesoamerica. It imported a number of items – quetzal feathers, jade, copal, rubber and cacao beans – most of which were probably for ceremonial purposes, though the cacao beans may have been a form of currency. In return it exported obsidian, pottery and cloth. Its influence spread over a wide area – the site of Kaminaljuyu, now on the outskirts of Guatemala City, was over 650 miles away yet it was a miniature replica of Teotihuacan. Whether it was a 'colony' of some sort, constructed by a local dependent group or simply a trading post is unknown. Indeed the whole nature of the Teotihuacan 'empire' is equally unclear. Until the last few decades it was thought that Teotihuacan was primarily a theocratic and peaceful society. Recent excavations at the site have shown that the military, identified by a special tassel in their head-dress, were always an important part of the ruling elite. There may have been an empire of conquest but it may equally be only a sphere of cultural and trading influence. Certainly Oaxaca and the site of Monte Alban remained independent of Teotihuacan throughout this period.

The military seem to have become a more important element in Teotihuacan society from about 600 CE but it is unclear whether this is linked to a decline in its influence across Mesoamerica at about this time. All that is known is that in about 750 CE Teotihuacan was destroyed, almost certainly from internal causes since there is no evidence of any external conquest. The destruction of the city was not random. It was concentrated in the central areas and all of the temples along the 'Street of the Dead' were demolished and burnt, not once but over and over again. The old religious images were torn down and thrown away. There was obviously a sustained and systematic destruction of the whole political, social and sacred structure of the city and its society. The city was then abandoned for about fifty years even though all but a handful of the residential compounds were not destroyed. Then, after more than a generation, people began to live again in some of the compounds although they were simply farmers cultivating the surrounding fields and none of the other features of the once great city were re-established.

5.3 The Maya

[*Contemporaneous Eurasia* 10.12, 10.13, 11.1–11.9]

The other major civilization of the Classic period in Mesoamerica is that of the Maya in the lowland tropical jungles across a wide area at the base of the Yucatan peninsula stretching from the Gulf coast to northern Honduras. It flourished alongside Teotihuacan for several centuries but continued after its fall until about 900 CE. It was the most advanced of all the pre-Columbian civilizations of the Americas – it was the only one to create a true script and it also developed the common calendar to a considerably more complex level. The first traces of settlement in the area date to about 2000 BCE. Within about a thousand years there was a fairly uniform style of pottery and contact was made with the early Olmec. Over the centuries villages grew, ceremonial sites were constructed and a ruling elite directed society. Eventually, from the first centuries CE, a series of cities with large temple complexes and public buildings on an extensive scale developed. For many decades of research it was unclear how such a society could have been sustained by what seemed to be the normal method of subsistence in the area – 'slash and burn' or swidden agriculture. In this system a peasant clears a patch of land by burning, plants crops for a few years and then moves on to another plot when the jungle regenerates. With this extensive cultivation system, only relatively low-population densities can be supported and it was clear that there was not enough room between the Mayan cities (often no more than ten miles apart) for the substantial population indicated by their size, if this was how food was grown. However archaeological work since the 1970s, including radar surveys, has shown that the classic Maya practised a highly intensive form of agriculture capable of producing enough food surplus to support an elite. On the hillsides they cleared the jungle and built a complex series of terraces to contain soil erosion. Even more important was the construction of raised fields in swampy areas. Grids of ditches were built and the mud flung up to form a rich soil for the fields. Fish were probably kept in the canals. This system would have required a high degree of maintenance but would have been highly productive for the main crop, maize, which was supplemented by beans, cotton and cacao.

Mayan cities were characterized by the erection of large numbers of carved stone stelae with depictions of humans, inscriptions and a number of dates. It was apparent almost immediately after the Mayan civilization was discovered in the mid-nineteenth century that they had significantly developed the Mesoamerican calendar. Instead of an endless series of fifty-two-year cycles they were incorporated into a much larger structure known as the Long Count. On the now generally accepted correlation with the Christian calendar this began on 11 August 3114 BCE with the creation of the current world order, although why this particular date was selected remains unknown. The Long Count was probably not invented by the Maya – the first known examples come from Stela 2 erected at Chiapa de Corzo in Chiapas state in 36 BCE and from Stela C at Tres Zapotes in the Olmec area in 32 BCE. However, the Maya carried this system to unprecedented lengths. They used as a basis for their calculations the 'year' or *tun* of 360 days. Twenty *tuns* became a *katun* (or 7,200 days) and twenty *katuns* became a *baktun* of 144,000 days or 400 *tuns*. This enabled the Maya to calculate backwards and forwards over vast periods of time – the oldest known date is 400 million years ago on Stela D from Quirigua, erected in 766 CE. The Maya also carried out other sophisticated calculations. As well as working out the lunar cycle they also established the sun eclipse cycle, although they had no way of knowing whether an eclipse would occur in the Maya area. Perhaps the most complex of all their calculations was that involving Venus. They were aware of the planet's 584-day cycle but were also able to match it to both of their calendars so that 65 Venus cycles was known to be equal to 146 cycles of 260 days and 104 cycles of 365 days. However, they also realized that the Venus cycle was not exactly 584 days and therefore inserted a correction over a period of 481 calendar years to leave an average error of fourteen seconds a year. Indirectly the Maya had worked out that the year is equal to 365.2550 days – the most accurate modern calculation suggests a value of 365.2422 days. These were some of the most sophisticated observations and calculations carried out anywhere in the world until the last few centuries.

The obvious importance to the Maya of the astronomical observations and calculations of vast periods of time established an orthodoxy about the nature of Mayan society which lasted until a few decades ago when it was comprehensively undermined. Despite numerous scenes of warfare on the stelae and in murals the Maya were held by archaeologists to have been ruled by a theocracy of priests who spent their time undertaking these complex calculations. This was largely the result of the dominance exercised by the English archaeologist Eric Thompson. In 1954 he wrote 'The hieroglyphic texts of the Classic period deal entirely with the passage of time and astronomical matters . . . they do not appear to treat of individuals at all.' If this interpretation was correct then the Maya were unlike almost any other known society. Thompson also held that the Mayan script was probably untranslatable and, remarkably, not related to any of the languages spoken in the region. His position began to be undermined within a few years of his pronouncement quoted above, and in the last couple of decades large portions of the Maya script have finally been deciphered (using a system Thompson was certain was wrong). The Maya script was extremely complex. It had over 800 signs, though some of these were alternatives with the same meaning, plus a series of special prefixes and suffixes. It was a mixture of ideographic and syllabic with a very strong phonetic element. The gradual establishment of the meaning of some of the key signs, especially the glyphs used for the individual cities, has completely altered our picture of Mayan society. It is now clear that the Maya were divided into petty kingdoms ruled by a militaristic elite who erected the stelae to commemorate themselves, their deeds and their ancestors (real and imagined).

The earliest ceremonial centres and towns in the region emerged by about 50 CE. The next two centuries were a period of increasing conflict, warfare and conquest between the small chiefdoms and states in the Maya lowlands – some grew larger, others were conquered and disappeared. In parallel there was increasing differentiation within Mayan society as the rulers gained greater power to direct the people and established their first dynasties. In the relatively short period between 250–300 CE the pace of change increased markedly. Monumental architecture and the first stelae to praise the achievements of the rulers, complete with Long Count dates and a very complex iconography, were erected across the region. The earliest known stela is number 29 at Tikal which was set up 8 July 292.

One of the most difficult questions to resolve is the exact relationship between Teotihuacan and the early Mayan rulers. The influence of Teotihuacan was so pervasive across Mesoamerica that it is very unlikely that the Maya were isolated from it. The greater organization within the Maya area, and the first development of cities and a ruling warrior elite, coincides with the establishment of the great city of Teotihuacan. It is possible that this was an indigenous reaction to this expansion of influence but on the other hand the Mayan elite may have risen in association with Teotihuacan and ruled the area on its behalf. Part of this influence may have been exercised through the Teotihuacan 'colony' at Kaminaljuyu in the Mayan highlands.Certainly the impact of Teotihuacan can be detected very clearly in the sculpture, ceramics and the iconography used at nearly all the Mayan sites in the period 350–500 CE. It is also possible that some of the early rulers of Tikal were either from Teotihuacan or depended on military support from that city. Stela 31, erected at Tikal in 445 CE, shows Teotihuacan-style warriors surrounding the ruler known as 'Stormy Sky'.

The situation changed radically early in the sixth century. Between 500 and 550 Teotihuacan influence disappeared from the Mayan region, perhaps as a result of growing internal problems. This withdrawal coincided with a marked hiatus in the erection of stelae across all the Mayan cities – there are almost none dated between 534 and 593. This period was followed by the most spectacular phase in Mayan civilization, lasting about two centuries. At Tikal, the largest city, six major temples were built and numerous twin pyramid groups. At other cities similar building projects were under way and everywhere vast numbers of stelae were carved and erected. The exact political structure within the Mayan world is a matter of some dispute. The individual cities were clearly important. So far the 'emblem glyph' (a hieroglyphic sign carved on to the stelae) has been identified for 35 known sites (and three unknown). These were effectively place-names of the capital and the territory it controlled and not the titles of the rulers. Their use coincides with political independence and its abandonment means conquest of some sort. On this basis some of the cities, which never had their own 'emblem glyph', were probably not independent. However, whether the Maya were organized into about eight 'regional' units based on the major cities such as Tikal, Palenque and Copan, or about fifty or so petty kingdoms is unclear. Some conquests can be identified, such as Tikal's of Uaxactun in 378 and Dos Pilas's rule over Seibal for forty years after 735. Most states probably controlled an area of about fifteen miles around their capital though some were clearly much larger – Tikal probably dominated an area containing about 1,500,000 people (equivalent to the total population of contemporary Anglo-Saxon England). Warfare may not have been endemic and was usually confined to the dry season between November and May when enough men could be spared from farming.

During this period the Maya were dominated by a small elite. Although many of the recent discussions have been dominated by the idea of 'dynasties' at the various cities it is not clear how far succession was hereditary. On occasions it certainly was and though descent was generally patrilineal two female rulers are known, both at Palenque – Lady Kanal-Ikal (583–604) and Lady Zak-Kuk (612–615) – though the latter may have been regent for her son. Some of the stelae record royal marriages between different cities. At the same time there was also severe conflict within the elite. A number of the stelae at Tikal were deliberately broken and erased by subsequent rulers and there were major disputes within the royal family at Copan. It is now clear that political power predominated in the Mayan world although there must have been a group of 'priests' capable of making the complex calculations that lay behind the stelae. These monuments were erected, usually on the fifth and twenty-fifth anniversaries of accession, to mark significant dates such as the ruler's birth and key events during his reign. They were probably linked to a special blood-letting ceremony in which a stingray spine and a cord were passed through the tongue of the ruler's wife or his own penis. The splattered blood was then used to conjure up the spirits of the ruler's ancestors – hence the calculation of the mythical genealogies thousands of years into the past.

The peak of Mayan civilization was relatively short-lived. In the years 731–790 more monuments were erected than during any other comparable period. Yet after 800 there was a very rapid decline across the whole region. The last dynastic monuments were erected in 820 at Copan, 879 at Tikal and 889 at Uaxactun. The last Long Count date known anywhere is 909 and the system was not revived by any subsequent Mesoamerican society. The reasons for the collapse of the Maya have long been debated but are still far from clear. One of the crucial factors was clearly the pressure the elite were placing on the rest of society, in particular the relatively fragile subsistence base. As population rose large parts of the area were deforested to create agricultural land, provide timber and fuel and make the vast quantities of lime plaster that coated the ceremonial buildings. The tropical soils of the Maya lowlands are prone to soil erosion and this would not only have damaged fields on the hillsides but also have had a major impact on the very delicate system of raised field farming in the marshy areas. The first signs of growing agricultural problems are apparent during the eighth century when burials show growing infant mortality, deficiency diseases and poor nutrition among the peasants. It seems likely that as the agricultural surplus needed to support the Maya elite declined they increased their demands on the mass of the population. The Mayan state was very weak, with almost no bureaucracy and only limited means available to preserve itself. The spiral of decline was rapid. Growing internal problems and stresses may have led to a 'peasant revolt' and whatever the exact nature of the internal decay this certainly made external conquest, which is apparent at some sites, much easier. Within less than a century Mayan society in the lowlands reverted to a much simpler level, population levels fell, the cities were abandoned and the dynastic monuments were covered by the jungle.

5.4 The Aztecs

[*Contemporaneous Eurasia Chapters 13, 14 & 15*]
The collapse of the Maya around 900 CE marked the end of the 'Classic' period in Mesoamerica. The Post-Classic period (which lasted until the Spanish conquest) was characterized by extensive warfare and militarism, migrations of people and the creation of transient empires. In parallel there was a growing emphasis on human sacrifice which became central to the functioning of these societies. After the demise of Teotihuacan a series of small states flourished briefly in central Mexico – a Mixtec people conquered Cholua in Puebla about 800 CE and moved north into the valley of Mexico, setting up a state based around Xochicalco. More important was the migration of numerous groups from the north of Mexico, beyond the region of settled farming communities, into the main centres.

The most important of these people were the Toltecs who in the early tenth century, led by Topiltzin, established their capital at Tula in the north of the valley of Mexico. By about 1000 CE their empire extended across central Mexico from coast to coast. The massive site at Tula has, unlike Teotihuacan and the Mayan cities, hardly been excavated at all. It

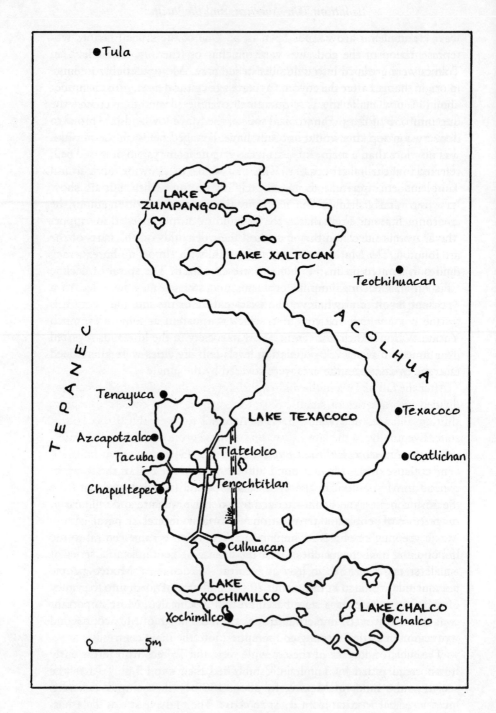

Map 11: The valley of Mexico

was a complex of pyramids, plazas and colonnaded halls in which representation of the gods was rare but that of warriors common. The Toltecs were grouped into a number of military orders, probably totemic in origin, named after the coyote, jaguar and eagle. Their empire collapsed about 1160 when Tula was almost totally destroyed – a huge trench was dug into one of the pyramids and the statues were thrown in. This was done by a group later known as 'Chichimecs' or 'people of the dog'. This was no more than a term of abuse, roughly equivalent to 'barbarian', and referred to the tribal groups of the north of Mexico. Before the fall of Tula, Toltec influence spread into the Yucatan. Major centres such as Chichen Itza were established in the north of the peninsula in very different environmental conditions from the lowland tropical jungle of the classic Maya. At this site a number of the key features of the Post-Classic world are found – *tzompantli*, racks for human skulls, and *chacmools*, reclining figures with a basin in the stomach where human hearts were placed. Chichen Itza declined rapidly after about 1250 and a new capital at Mayapan emerged together with other towns such as Tulum and Cozumel on the coast which controlled the extensive trade around the coast of Yucatan. In Oaxaca too the Classic site of Monte Alban was also abandoned, in about 750–800, and new militaristic centres such as Mitla emerged to dominate the area.

After the fall of Tula in the mid-twelfth century the valley of Mexico was divided into a series of small city-states engaged in an endless round of shifting alliances and wars as they attempted to re-establish the Toltec state. Eventually, in the late 1420s, one of these groups (the Mexica), later called the Aztecs, established control over the whole valley and built an empire that extended across much of central Mexico before the Spanish conquest in 1519–20. The name Aztec is a misnomer and was not used in the period before the Spanish conquest. It was popularized in the early twentieth century and is derived from Aztlan, the legendary home of the Mexica people. They were a small group who entered the valley after the fall of Tula, built the small town of Tenochtitlan on an island in the lake and later established their empire. However, the name Aztec is now so popular that it is almost impossible to avoid using it. Because the creation of the Aztec state took place less than a century before the Spanish conquest many of the oral traditions about what happened survived to be written down by the Europeans. They provide a fascinating insight into the way in which a kin-based society with very limited institutions could be transformed into an empire with an aristocratic elite, highly stratified society and a moderately powerful state structure. It was a process that must have been repeated in its general outline many times in the early civilizations as chieftains, buoyed by success in war, established greater

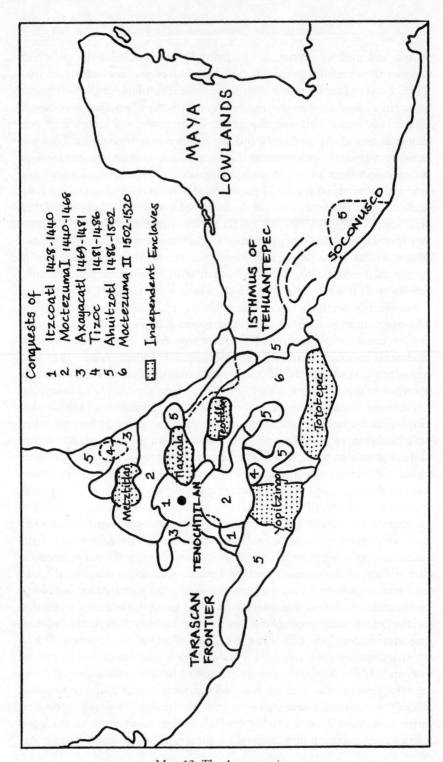

Map 12: The Aztec empire

powers for themselves, set up the primitive institutions of a state and together with the elite created an increasingly unequal society.

The basis of Mexica society in the mid-fourteenth century, shortly after they arrived in the Valley of Mexico, were the fifteen *calpullin*. These were kinship, residential and economic groupings. Each had its own school and temple but land was held by families who could pass it on to the next generation as long as they continued to cultivate it. The *calpullin* were also the basic unit of military organization. Although they were kinship groups there were considerable differences not only between them but also internally and these were passed on from generation to generation. While the leadership of the *calpullin* was in theory open to election, in practice they were hereditary. The first ruler or *tlatoani* of the Mexica was probably an outsider of Toltec descent imposed by the city of Culhuacan in 1370. However, the first three *tlatoani* were little more than war-leaders with very limited powers.

The Mexica were part of the Tepanec group in the west of the valley opposed to the Acolhua confederacy in the east. By the early fifteenth century the Mexica were becoming more powerful within the Tepanec confederation and their relatively obscure god-hero, Huitzilopochtli, had evolved into their patron deity. The key events in the formation of the Aztec state came in 1426–8. The Tepanecs defeated the Acolhua confederacy but when their leader (Tezozomoc) died shortly after the victory, the Mexica seized the opportunity to gain power. They allied with the exiled ruler of Texcoco in the Acolhua confederacy and the small city of Tacuba in their own Tepanec group and, led by the Mexica *tlatoani* Itzcoatl, defeated their rivals. The 'triple alliance' of the three cities took control of the valley although the Mexica dominated the alliance and were the effective rulers.

The Mexica elite took the opportunity of their vastly increased prestige to recast Mexica institutions, entrench their own position and create the outlines of an Aztec state. The process began in 1428 with the burning of all historical and religious texts. Power was concentrated in the *tlatoani* who was advised by a council of four, all of whom came from the royal family and from whom the next *tlatoani* had to be chosen. The key to the creation of a highly unequal society was that the tribute and land resulting from the conquests of 1428 was not divided equally but reserved for the imperial family and its supporting aristocracy. The *calpullin* were marginalized by being restricted to the original Mexica land around the capital Tenochtitlan. Further conquests only reinforced this process as most of the loot and tribute was reserved for the elite. This inequality was formalized by the decrees of Itzcoatl and his successor Moctezuma I. These defined the *pipiltin* (noble) and *macehualtin* (commoner) classes – only the former could practise polygamy and live in two-storey houses, and they were also distinguished by the type of clothes they could wear.

The Aztec drive for expansion during the rest of the fifteenth century derived from two sources. First, the elite's desire for the wealth and power that came from conquest and tribute. Second, the role of Huitzilopochtli who, as part of the restructuring of the late 1420s, had become the state cult and the guarantor of Aztec success. Human sacrifice, which had been on a very small scale before 1428, was now regarded as central in sustaining Huitzilopochtli, the sun, the existing order of the universe and therefore the Aztec people. Conquest provided the necessary prisoners who could be sacrificed by ripping out their hearts whilst they were still alive. The remains of the victims were distributed among the population for eating. Probably about 15,000 people a year were sacrificed, though on major occasions such as the dedication of the Great Temple to Huitzilopochtli in the centre of Tenochtitlan (it was oriented so that the sun rose over the top of the temple at the equinox), about 10,000 were killed during the four-day ceremony.

Some of the drive behind Aztec expansion was economic particularly after the great famine of 1450–4. The fertile Gulf coast was conquered together with the kingdom of Socunusco on the Pacific coast of Guatemala. The need for conquests to find food, tribute and prisoners for sacrifice meant that there was little emphasis on the administration of the empire. The easily conquered areas were taken first but some, such as the highland kingdom of Tlaxcala near the heart of the empire, were left alone because they proved too difficult to conquer. The conquered areas were usually left under the control of local elites once the initial captives were taken and as long as tribute continued to reach Tenochtitlan. Inevitably this led to endless rebellions and reconquests. Internally the capital grew rapidly, as craftsmen and merchants came into the city and the Aztec population grew. The existing gardens and fields built on the lake (the chinampas) proved to be inadequate to support the population and massive reclamation projects were organized. However, by the end of the fifteenth century the Aztec empire was rapidly approaching a crisis. It needed to be consolidated – the initial phase of expansion was largely over and it extended across an area that was already too large to control effectively. Further expansion was blocked by the states in the valley of Oaxaca and in the north and the south there were highly dispersed populations which were very difficult to exploit. But the internal dynamics of the Aztec state meant that any consolidation raised acute problems. The elite relied on the tribute from conquest and, even more important, the Aztec world was deemed to depend on the continuing sacrifice of human victims to Huitzilopochtli. The lack of conquest meant that the supply of victims dried up and even the development of a class of slave-merchants could not supply sufficient numbers.

During the reign of the last Aztec ruler, Moctezuma II (1502–20) these problems became more acute. He spent much of his time reconquering areas which his predecessor Ahuitzotl (1486–1502) was supposed to have conquered. Because further expansion was so difficult Moctezuma attempted to conquer those areas such as Tlaxcala which were near the centre of the empire despite the problems encountered earlier. Campaigns produced little in the way of tribute or captives and therefore only increased internal strains. The attempt to impose rulers and increase central control led to discontent and rebellion. All of these problems produced a fertile environment for the Spanish to exploit when they arrived in 1519.

[*Later Mesoamerica* 16.2, 17.1]

5.5 Early Peru and the Andes

Peru was isolated from Mesoamerica and its pattern of development was largely shaped by geography. Much of the Pacific coastal area is dry, inhospitable desert but it is divided by about forty river valleys which descend from the Andes. Agriculture and irrigation were possible in these valleys but the different civilizations and cultures which emerged were often relatively isolated from each other because of the intervening desert. In the Andes only the high valleys and basins were suitable for agricultural settlement and therefore even in the sixteenth century CE much of the area was still at a tribal level. The main centres where developments did occur were the large basin around Lake Titicaca (on the Peru/Bolivia border) and on the high altiplano where large fields could be created and large flocks of llamas tended.

The first villages developed along the coast after about 2500 BCE, before the invention of pottery and woven textiles in about 1800 BCE. By the latter date the first large ceremonial centres also emerged, especially in the Casma valley on the north coast of Peru. One of the largest was the huge mound at Sechin Alto – it was 250 yards long, 300 yards wide and over 100 feet high. During the 'Early Horizon' period (900–200 BCE) nearly all the coastal valleys were characterized by ceremonial sites with monumental architecture. These were irrigation-based agricultural societies but the authorities within the societies must have wielded considerable power in order to mobilize the large amounts of labour involved in the massive construction works. Warfare was widespread in this period and a very distinctive art and cultural style called Chavin spread from its main centre at the site of Chavin de Huantar across the region. However, it seems unlikely that this represented a military conquest and the imposition of a single culture. The Chavin cultural style probably represents the spread of some form of non-militaristic religious cult across much of coastal Peru.

During this period the utilization of metals began in the central Andes but the impact on society was very limited, their use remaining largely within the elite. The central Andes had a wide range of metal deposits but metal working began not with copper, as in south-west Asia, but with gold, which remained the most important metal. Gold was worked from about 1500 BCE and the first cast and hammered copper goods covered in a thin sheet of gold are found in graves which date to about 900–450 BCE. The elite valued decorative goods made from gold and the craftsmen concentrated upon copper and silver alloys which were very easy to hammer and also copper and gold (the *tumbaga* alloys) which produced a superb gold colour.

About 200 BCE the Chavin style began to die out and for the next 800 years coastal Peru was characterized by regional diversity among the various river valley societies, which were beginning to demonstrate some of the features of early state formation. In the north, where it was possible for cultivation to spread from the rich land of the valleys on to the coastal plain, thereby increasing the agricultural surplus, the Moche culture was dominant. In the south the Nazca culture, associated with the complex of carvings on the desert floor, was the most important. In the far southern highlands of the Andes the religious site of Tiwanaku flourished. The period between 600 and 1000 CE was dominated by the emergence of the first true state and empire in Peru centred on the Ayacucho valley in the central highlands. Before 600 CE the valley contained a number of settlements, all roughly the same size. The rivalry between them as population mounted and the competition for resources became fiercer was won by Wari, which grew into a city covering about 1,000 acres and dominated the valley. Wari had no known script and therefore its social and political structure can only be deduced from the remains of its buildings. They suggest a very strong central authority. The city was divided up by large internal walls into blocked-off compounds where the mass of the population lived in barrack-like accommodation. Some of the buildings in the centre of the city appear to be for administrative functions. From about 700 Wari influence spread beyond the Ayacucho valley. Its distinctive iconography and architectural style can be found at a number of sites along the coastal area (the first time a highland group had dominated this region) but not in the far north or in the southern highlands where Tiwanaku remained independent. Long-distance trade increased and a road system linking the different areas was constructed. The exact nature of the Wari expansion remains controversial. Some experts see it as rather like the Chavin – a spread of religious ideas. Others, based on the evidence of a strong central authority within Wari, believe that military conquest and the establishment of an early empire is more likely.

Wari declined about 1000 CE and from then until the mid-fifteenth century Peru was again characterized by regionally diverse cultures. The most important of these was the Chimu culture in the north centred on the Moche valley and its capital of Chan Chan. For about 400 years after its emergence around 900 CE Chimu seems to have been little different from the earlier Moche culture in the area – an irrigation-based state controlling one of the river valleys and some of the surrounding area. About 1300 there was a particularly severe 'El Nino' event when the offshore Pacific currents altered and produced exceptionally heavy rains which wiped out many of the complex irrigation works. Instead of undertaking the huge task of rebuilding the irrigation system the Chimu state reoriented itself and the elite embarked on a policy of military conquest to obtain the resources it needed. Eventually it quadrupled its zone of control to extend from Tumbes near the current border with Ecuador to near Lima. The degree of control it exercised over this large area was probably limited to exacting tribute and many of the local rulers probably survived. As the Chimu empire expanded so did its capital of Chan Chan which eventually covered an area of over ten square miles. Thirty-four compounds have been identified as residences for the elite together with a mass of small, irregular-shaped rooms jammed together where the bulk of the population lived. However, the most remarkable feature of the city were its ten large compounds – one for each of the rulers after the imperial expansion. Each king had his own palace compound where he ruled the state and where his mummified body would be cared for by part of his family and be worshipped in a complex series of rituals after his death. Probably at least once a year the body was brought out to be the subject of public worship. Some of his entourage or family appear to have been sacrificed either at the time of the ruler's death or afterwards. This practice seems to have deep roots in the early cultures of Peru because it was also practised on an even more elaborate scale by the Inca – the empire that challenged Chimu from the mid-fifteenth century.

5.6 The Inca

[*Contemporaneous Eurasia Chapter 15*]
When the Spanish arrived in Peru in 1532 the Inca empire stretched for over 2,500 miles from the southern frontier of what is now Colombia to

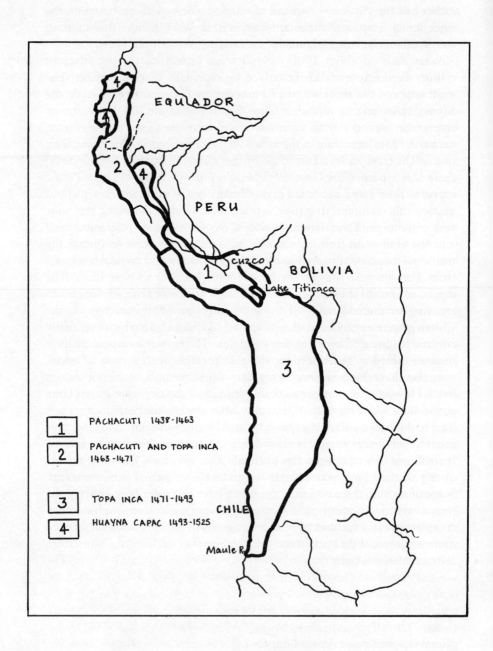

EQUADOR

PERU

Cuzco

BOLIVIA

Lake Titicaca

CHILE

Maule R.

1	PACHACUTI 1438-1463
2	PACHACUTI AND TOPA INCA 1463-1471
3	TOPA INCA 1471-1493
4	HUAYNA CAPAC 1493-1525

Map 13: The Inca empire

the Maule river in central Chile. It was the largest of all the pre-Columbian empires of the Americas and extended over a far greater area than any other similar empire in Eurasia. Like the Aztec empire in Mesoamerica it was a relatively late creation in the century or so before the Spanish conquest.

With the collapse of the Tiwanaku state around 1200 CE the various small states of the altiplano were in almost continuous conflict with each other. About this time in the southern Andes bronze was made for the first time and as well as providing ornaments it was turned into the first metal weapons. The Inca were originally small village farmers from the area around Cuzco who, for a long period, were subservient to the kingdoms of Colla and Lupaca in the Lake Titicaca area. Their early social organization appears to be remarkably close to that of the Mexica in the valley of Mexico and, no doubt, to many other groups around the world at this level of development. The basis of society were the *ayllu* – a kinship group believed to descend from a common ancestor which held the land which individual families cultivated although they also worked together building each other houses. When the Inca empire was created the *ayllu* were supervised by hereditary chiefs known as *curacas* who were able to organize communal labour – whether a similar system applied in early Inca history is unknown. The early political organization of the Inca is equally difficult to discern before about 1400. Authority was probably divided between the *ayllu* leaders and the temporary war-leaders known as *sinchi* who may have become more permanent if they were successful in the endless low-level conflict with other, non-Inca, villages. The early religion of the Inca was complex. From Tiwanaku they adopted the idea of a creator god Viracocha, a sun-god Inti and Illapa the thunder and weather god. However, they were not separate gods (a mistake which derives from Spanish misunderstanding) but different manifestations of a single god. Alongside this worship was the idea of *huaca* which could be a person (a mummified body), a place such as a shrine, or an object such as a statue. *Huaca* were sacred and each *ayllu* was legitimated by, and cared for, a range of *huaca*. This was normally a task entrusted to those in the *ayllu* who were too old to work in the fields.

Inca expansion started under Viracocha in the early fifteenth century. He was the eighth king on the Inca dynastic list but the first about which there is any real knowledge. He was probably the first real king, as opposed to temporary war-leader, and he began the conquest of the area around Cuzco. The major expansion began under Pachakuti (1438–1471) who probably seized power in a military coup in Cuzco when the city was under siege by a coalition of anti-Inca towns. He remade the Inca state in much the same way as the early Aztec rulers after they seized power in the valley of Mexico. By about 1450 the Inca were in control of most of the altiplano and the Lake Titicaca basin. Then they expanded out of the Andean highlands to the coastal areas, moving north between 1463 and 1471 to defeat the Chimu state and then by 1493 the area to the south. By the 1490s the main wave of expansion was over.

To the Inca their empire was known as *Tawantinsuyu* – 'The Land of the Four Quarters'. This title reflected a basic Inca way of viewing the world. The capital Cuzco (which means 'the navel of the earth') was similarly divided, although the 'quarters' were not equal in size – that of the south-west was by far the largest. The city was governed by four *apus*, one for each quarter, as was the empire. Each of the quarters was also related, in a highly complex way, to Inca social organization which was divided into three status groups in the early imperial period. Each of these was represented in the *ceque* – a ritual and social organization. At the centre of Cuzco was the Coricancha or Temple of the Sun. It was regarded as the centre of the empire (and the world) and was carefully oriented to the solstice – sunrise in the summer and sunset in the winter. Other significant siting lines existed from the temple to various towers on the top of the valley so that key dates in the planting calendar could be identified.

The Inca elaborated ancestor worship to an even greater extent than the rival Chimu empire in the north. The bodies of dead kings were mummified and displayed in niches in the Coricancha where they became the most sacred *huacas* of the Inca (it took the Spanish twenty-seven years to track down and destroy all the bodies which had been hidden by the Inca). The dead rulers were treated as though they were still alive and each was 'maintained' by a vast estate worked by an army of servants. As the number of dead rulers increased new land was required to support them and the rising population, especially the elite of non-producers – the *panaqa* who were the kinsmen and descendants of the rulers. The practice of communal labour within the *ayllu* was extended by the Inca state so that each citizen was required to provide labour cultivating land, working on construction projects or serving in the army. By the end of the fifteenth century the Inca empire was, like that of the Aztecs in central Mexico, facing a crisis brought about by its own internal dynamics. Both empires needed more land and people to sustain central features of their societies – either land to support the dead kings or sacrificial victims for Huitzilopochtli. Both were reaching the limits of feasible expansion and control. The Inca were running out of easily acquired land and Huayana Capac spent most of his reign (1493–1525) trying to conquer a relatively small area in modern Ecuador. Even with the well-developed road system and state messengers (which the Inca inherited from their predecessors) it took over ten days for messages to reach Cuzco from the frontiers of the empire. Control of the empire was therefore very difficult, especially as increasingly diverse groups of people were brought within it.

Many of these problems came to a head on the death of Huayana Capac in 1525 when the Inca empire descended into civil war. This was fought between the dead king's two sons – Huascar and Atahualpa. The latter had the weaker claim to the throne because he had not been born from the brother-sister marriage which was designed to ensure a pure royal succession. However, he commanded the loyalty of much of the army. Huascar, who lost the crucial battle in 1532, was less popular because he intended to end one of the key legitimating devices in Inca society which was also the central weakness of the Inca state – the diversion of huge amounts of land to support the dead rulers. As with the Aztecs, when the Spanish arrived in 1532 they found a seriously weakened Inca empire.

5.7 The Pacific

(See Map 3)
As the Polynesian people spread across the Pacific in their series of epic voyages they encountered and settled in a variety of different island worlds and environments. All of them began with a common Polynesian way of life and system of subsistence but this was highly modified by the different circumstances the various groups met. In the homeland of the Polynesians subsistence depended upon cultivation of taro, yam and breadfruit and the keeping of a few animals – pigs, dogs and chickens. (The Polynesians are also unique among human groups in that although they originally had pottery, over time its quality declined sharply and eventually after about 300 CE it was no longer made.) In the new settlements this subsistence pattern had to be adapted to a range of environments ranging from tropical, through temperate to sub-Antarctic. In some cases, for example on the south island of New Zealand, cultivation was abandoned and groups reverted to gathering and hunting. The environmental impact of humans on delicate island environments could be devastating – over thirteen species of the giant flightless moa were driven to extinction on New Zealand, together with about sixteen other bird species. A similarly wide range of extinctions occurred in the Hawaiian islands. Nearly all of the islands the Polynesians settled were isolated from each other and thus provided what is almost a series of separate experiments in the evolution of societies to the chiefdom level and the verge of state creation. Because they were still at this stage when the Europeans began to sail across the Pacific many of the details of that evolution could still be remembered.

To the early Europeans who visited the area the Pacific islands seemed a 'tropical paradise' where both subsistence and life were easy. In practice this was not the case. Regular seasonal droughts were a major problem and famine a very real threat. Storage of food (in pits and through fermentation) and its distribution at crucial times were therefore essential to Polynesian society and this function became one of the major roles of the chiefs. Society was organized on a clan basis where the members were believed to share descent from a common ancestor. However, the clans were sharply divided internally by status and descent. Land was usually held by the clan but cultivated by individual families. Normally, and particularly when a new island was settled, the land was split into segments running from the seashore to the hilltops so that each clan had access to a wide variety of resources. The role of the chief in society was originally to act as an intercessor between the community and its gods and ancestors. Warfare was, however, ubiquitous and deeply engrained. It was normally related to access to land because conquest was usually much easier than undertaking major clearing operations. Successful warriors often usurped the powers of chiefs and subsequently increased their own power by keeping much of the conquered land and using managers to cultivate it on their behalf. Political power was therefore increasingly derived from success in war rather than descent through the chief's family.

The evolution of Polynesian society can best be studied through three examples – Tonga in the heartland of the Polynesian world, Hawaii in the far north and Easter Island in the south-east. Tonga was unique in Polynesia because it maintained an elaborate external voyaging and exchange network both within the scattered islands of the group but also to Fiji in the east and Samoa to the north. The small islands of the Tonga group could each support at most about 10,000 people through intensive dry agriculture (irrigation was not possible). A continuing obsession with genealogies among the people, even after the European invasion, together with archaeological finds, mean that it is possible to reconstruct at least some of its history. Growing stratification within society is apparent about 1000 CE when large ceremonial mounds were built at Mu'a on Tongatapu and at Lapaha. These were centres where two chiefs lived (and were buried) and where they carried out one of their most important functions – the annual tribute ceremonial and redistribution of that tribute among their followers. Until about the fifteenth century the Tu'i Tonga (head chief of the islands) was paramount in both sacred and secular functions. Then the twenty-third chief, Takalaua, was assassinated and the functions divided. The Tu'i Tonga became a purely sacred leader with little real power. The new secular ruler was the *hau* who reorganized the sites of the great ceremonial mounds, built a major dock and extended his powers across most of the archipelago. The new *hau* created a series of sub-chiefs from his own lineage to carry out his administrative decisions. Rule was no longer on a clan basis but instead on a territorial one. By about 1700 there was a very clear distinction between the chiefs and the rest of the people. Commoners were no longer associated with the chiefs on the basis of descent but through their residence on an estate controlled by a chief. Land was no longer held by the clans but by the different grades of chief who allowed the people to cultivate the land in exchange for tribute and labour services. The evolution of very clear status differentiation and inequality, linked to greater power for a very small group, appears to have been repeated on many occasions across the world as the first agricultural societies became more complex. Some went further and changed into full-blown states with even greater inequality and much stronger central power.

Hawaii was settled about 500 CE and unlike Tonga was truly isolated. However, it was a large archipelago with eight major islands and was second in size only to New Zealand in the Polynesian triangle. The fertile soil produced a large food surplus and there was rapid population growth, especially after about 900 CE when large new areas were settled. All of the islands were split into several independent chiefdoms which competed for status and power through warfare, diplomacy and marriage alliances. This level of conflict increased after about 1400 once all the agricultural land was occupied and it was no longer possible for some of the sons of a chief to leave and set up their own area of control with new settlers. The land was farmed intensively and population continued to rise causing further internal strains especially as farming pushed on to very marginal soils and the risk of crop failure and famine increased.

The outcome of these strains was that, in about 1440, on the island of O'ahu individual chiefdoms were replaced by a single ruler who was in effect a petty king. The other islands rapidly went down the same path. Social changes followed from this stronger central political control. The chiefs drew further away from the rest of society and married only into the families of chiefs from the other islands. The chiefs detached themselves from the inherited kinship group and ruled in their own right. Tribute was now made to them and redistributed almost entirely within the chiefly class although they retained a residual responsibility to aid the community in times of famine. Increasingly they owned the land and the bulk of the population worked it as their tenants. Inter-island warfare became more frequent as the chiefs tried to control more territory so they could exact more tribute. Eventually, in 1795, just before the Europeans arrived in force, the Hawaiian islands were conquered and united under a single ruler. Within about 1,300 years Hawaiian society had evolved from a handful of settlers to a primitive kingdom.

Easter Island is one of the most remote inhabited places on earth – 2,000 miles off the coast of south America and over 1,000 miles from even tiny Pitcairn Island. It was settled about 500 CE by a handful of people. They found that the island of only 150 square miles had few natural resources and that hardly any of their sub-tropical crops would grow there – they had to live on a diet of sweet potato and chicken. As the population rose the island divided into clan and kinship groups under a chief in the normal Polynesian way. Each group had its own sacred site or *ahu* – a stone platform for burials, ancestor worship and commemoration of dead chiefs. The ease with which their monotonous but nutritionally adequate diet could be obtained left the islanders with plenty of time for cultural activities which developed to an unprecedented level for Polynesia. One of the ceremonies was the bird-cult at Orongo where remains of forty-seven special houses, numerous platforms and high-relief rock carvings have been found. Some of the rituals involved recitation from the only known Polynesian form of writing called *rongorongo*, which was less a true script and more a series of mnemonic devices. The main effort was devoted to the *ahu* – over 300 were built around the coast of the island. Many of them had astronomical alignments to one of the solstices or the equinox. All had between one and fifteen huge stone statues representing a highly stylized male head and torso carved from the rocks at Rano Raraku quarry using obsidian stone tools. They were about twenty feet high and weighed several tens of tons. Placed on top of the head was a 'topknot' of red stone weighing about ten tons carved at another quarry. Altogether over 600 of these statues are known, many of them incomplete.

The competition between the clans to erect these statues, as the population on the island rose to a peak of about 7,000 around 1550, and the number of clan groups multiplied, was a central feature of Easter Island life. When the settlers arrived the island was heavily forested but the trees were steadily cut down as the population rose in order to provide agricultural land, timber for housing, fuel for heating and cooking and to make the rollers on which the huge statues were dragged across the island. About 1600 there was a major crisis on the island as the timber ran out. The great statues could no longer be transported and erected – a huge number were left abandoned in the quarry. This would have had a fundamental impact on the beliefs of the islanders. Houses could no longer be built and the population had to live in caves or reed huts built from the vegetation that grew around the edges of the lakes in the extinct volcanoes. Canoes could not be built and long voyages could not be made in reed boats – the population was trapped on the island. Deforestation badly affected the soil of the island causing erosion and a drop in crop yields. The chickens became valuable assets and had to be protected in fortified chicken houses.

As the amount of food available fell so did the population. Within a century there were little more than 3,000 people on the island. Social disintegration continued. Warfare between the clans over land and food increased. Slavery became common, as did cannibalism. One of the main aims of warfare became the destruction of the *ahu* of rivals. The great stone statues, which were too large to destroy, were pulled down. When the first Europeans arrived in the early eighteenth century a few of the statues were still standing. A century later they had all been pulled down. The population was left living in extreme poverty with few resources and unable even to remember what their ancestors had achieved before they destroyed the environment of the island and with it their own society.

PART THREE

The Early Empires
(2000 BCE–600 CE)

6

The Early Eurasian World

By about 2000 BCE the first civilizations in Mesopotamia, Egypt and the Indus valley, followed later by China, had evolved into primitive states and empires. For at least another three thousand years world history was characterized by a slow extension of the 'civilized' area across Eurasia, the creation of new states, continuing tension between the settled states and nomadic groups, and the rise and fall of a series of empires. All of these states and empires were constrained by a range of broadly similar factors stemming from the nature of early agricultural societies, the very slow pace of technological change and the limits to effective political authority. They meant that these empires were condemned to be transient affairs and the pattern of their history was broadly similar. Usually after an initial phase of expansion under a dynamic ruler it proved difficult to sustain an effective empire in the face of both internal and external problems. In some cases these problems could be contained, often for several centuries, but ultimately they proved fatal. Not until about 1000 CE in China did any state begin to move beyond the constraints of the early agricultural societies.

6.1 Eurasian Societies

The fundamental problem the early states faced stemmed from the nature of agriculture as it had developed in the period since about 8000 BCE. Although farming was, in return for far greater effort, more productive than gathering and hunting its overall level of productivity was low. The food surplus it could generate was small and therefore these societies could sustain only a very small proportion of the total population in occupations other than farming. Until the last few centuries it was very rare for more than ten per cent of the population to be employed outside agriculture and often the figure was nearer to five per cent. This was a major constraint which severely limited what these societies could achieve. For most of recorded history the experience of the overwhelming majority of humans was that of peasant agriculture and poverty. The bulk of the population lived on the edge of subsistence at the mercy of bad weather and poor harvests. One bad year might not be disastrous, two or more in succession meant almost inevitable famine, starvation and death. Population rose only very slowly and intermittently – there were long periods of stagnation and at times, for short periods, a fall. Population growth was sustained mainly by bringing new land into production, even though it might have a lower level of productivity than that already under cultivation. Technological and productivity improvements were very slow to emerge and had only a limited impact. There was therefore a tendency for the population to rise to the maximum that could be supported on the available land thereby making the impact of poor harvests, warfare and disease even greater. The surplus population that could not be sustained on the land produced large groups of beggars, vagrants, criminals and bandits. Growth in the economy tended to be extensive rather than intensive. The economy might become larger because more people were cultivating more land but there was little fundamental, qualitative change.

The small elite in each society lived detached from the life of the average peasant; often they did not even speak the same language. They survived on the surplus they were able to extract from the peasants in a variety of forms – rent, taxes, tribute and labour service. Many of the peasantry were tied as serfs or debtors to the land. In a few societies extensive slavery provided much of the surplus for the elite. Nearly all of the elite lived in the few major cities across Eurasia. Most empires had a single large city, such as Babylon, Memphis, Alexandria, Chang-an, Rome and Constantinople, which was the location of the ruler's court and administration. The city's population was swollen, often to several hundred thousand people, by the elite, their servants, the craftsmen who provided the goods they wanted and the poor trying to find a living and enough food on which to survive. These large cities were usually located on the coast or navigable rivers, which were the only routes available to transport the large amounts of food needed to feed the population, until the Chinese began the construction of a canal network in the late sixth century CE. In some states the court was largely peripatetic so that it moved around the country to consume the food surplus on the spot – a practice that continued in England until the sixteenth century. These problems reflected the difficulties of transportation and communication faced by all the early states and empires. Apart from a handful of imperial roads built for armies to march along (and messengers to run along) land communication was very poor. Carts were primitive and the difficulties and cost of land transport meant that it was uneconomic, and often impossible, to move bulky goods overland for more than a few tens of miles. Sea transport was equally problematic. Shipping was generally primitive and vulnerable and few ships would sail far out of sight of land. In the Mediterranean, until the last few centuries, voyaging was largely confined to the few calm months in the summer, and across the Indian Ocean, the seas of south-east

Asia and China, shipping was restricted by the seasonality of the monsoon winds.

The overwhelming bulk of the population who lived by subsistence agriculture had very little available to spend on goods other than a few essentials such as tools and household items such as pots. Trade was restricted by the low level of demand and the poor level of communications. Much of the trade that did exist was for the elite (who held most of the disposable income) and was mainly in luxury items because these were usually fairly easy to transport. Land was the main form of wealth and there were few ways for the elite to spend the surplus they accumulated from the peasants except on conspicuous consumption, especially food, clothing and exotic imported items. The number of merchants and craftsmen was therefore limited. To a large extent these groups existed outside the main axis of society between the elite and the peasants. They were usually excluded from the elite and regarded as socially inferior even though their wealth was important to the early states. Over time, as wealth slowly grew, the level of trade increased and it gradually became a more important sector of the economy.

6.2 Eurasian States and Empires

Given these social, economic and communication constraints the early states and empires in Eurasia were bound to be very fragile structures. They had access to very few resources and even these were unstable. There was very little economic and social infrastructure on which they could rely. Nearly all the early states and empires were monarchies, only in a few areas and usually for a relatively short time did a few cities remain independent under a local oligarchy. The monarch often retained important religious, symbolic and ritual functions but there was usually a division of power between him and the religious authorities, although there were plenty of disputes about exactly where that division should be made. Religion was usually of vital importance to the rulers and not just for its legitimizing functions. It was one of the few organizations that existed at more than village and local level, particularly with the rise of salvationist religions such as Christianity and Islam. Often, as in medieval Europe, religious groups provided the only literate element in society and they were therefore vital to the existence of even a primitive state structure.

For most rulers there was a sharp dichotomy in their effective power. Within the court their personal power was often unlimited – their whims were carried out and rivals and ex-favourites alike could be exiled or sent to their deaths at a moment's notice. Politics as such hardly existed – it was mainly a contest between different members of the elite and their families for power, wealth and influence at the ruler's court, or within the elite itself as in republican Rome. In such cases power was inevitably seen in mainly private and personal terms. Outside the court the impersonal power of the ruler across society was very limited. They had no choice but to share power with local elites and somehow hope to control them. These elites were usually strongly entrenched through their landholdings and the local power and patronage this gave them. Often only crude methods of control were available to rulers, such as the holding of family hostages at court. One of the most extensive regimes of this type was in Tokugawa Japan between the early seventeenth century and 1868 when all the local aristocracy had to spend part of the year at the capital Edo and maintain two households, one at Edo and one in their home area.

The functions of these early states and empires were extremely limited. They had only very small bureaucracies to carry out government functions and there was often little distinction made between the activities of the ruler's private household and the state. Their main aim was to collect taxes and maintain an army for external and internal control. Only in a few cases (mainly China) were states able to register the population and land so as to increase their ability to tax – most had little choice but to have very simple taxation systems. Because land was almost the only form of wealth taxes had to be placed on it and levels were usually fixed by province and unit of land because this was all that was practicable. For the peasants the only time they came into contact with 'the state' was during tax collection. This relied on force and would have seemed to the peasants less like taxation in the modern sense and more like the forced requisitioning of the food on which they depended. Usually taxation levels could not be easily altered because the knowledge on which this could be done was not available. The problem was that if population declined the burden of taxation would rise, probably leading to a revolt that the government might not be able to contain. If population rose and a region became wealthier then the government would miss out on vital revenue. Over time taxes usually became increasingly out of line with the real wealth in society. One option for the state was to employ tax-farmers to collect revenue on its behalf. It reflected the lack of a state bureaucracy but did at least provide a generally reliable income to the state. The disadvantage was the amount of money the tax-farmers siphoned off into their own pockets – in eighteenth-century France the state was losing about a quarter of all tax revenues in this way.

Almost no state could provide more than the most minimal internal security. There was no police force and large areas of territory, especially mountains, marshes and regions remote from the capital, were hardly controlled at all. These were the realms of bandits and robbers who attacked travellers and looted villages. If law-breakers were caught punishments were brutal but 'policing' was largely in the hands of local groups and a few landowners. Rulers might occasionally issue edicts on various economic, social and religious matters but they were difficult to enforce and rarely followed. Some states undertook construction work – roads, canals, temples and palaces – but this could only be done by conscripting the local population or using slaves and prisoners of war. A few states were able to relocate whole populations for security reasons – the Assyrian empire adopted this policy on a large scale, moving about four and a half million people during the three hundred years when it was at the peak of its power.

The prime function of the early states and empires remained warfare and the careers of most rulers depended on their success in carrying it out. Often the easiest, and for much of the time the only, way of increasing state revenue was to attack a neighbouring state and either loot its territory or take over agricultural land and its associated peasants so as to gain their agricultural surplus. This increased the ruler's prestige and enabled the elite to be rewarded and therefore, with luck, kept loyal to the ruler. Most state revenue was devoted to maintaining an army. This primary, and often sole, function of the state continued for millennia – in England between 1130 and 1815 over three-quarters of all state revenue was spent on the army and navy.

Because of these general constraints the history of the early states and empires tended to follow a broadly similar pattern which we will see repeated time after time in the succeeding chapters. In the earliest stages states were often able to expand rapidly under the leadership of a single, dynamic leader. Given the general weakness of all states, especially rivals that might be in decline, it was usually possible to conquer considerable areas quickly and, given the small size of most armies, the result of a single battle was often decisive. However, expansion usually came up against strong constraints very quickly. Natural boundaries such as rivers and mountains were often difficult to surmount and the cost, in terms of warfare, and the occupation and administration of any new provinces, had to be balanced against the likely revenue to be obtained especially when communications were poor. In practice the early empires did not have clearly defined 'frontiers'. Instead there were frontier zones where control was limited and fluctuating, subject to local conditions, and often consisted of little more than punitive expeditions to impose order for a while and gain some loot.

The major problems for the early states and empires came after the stage of initial conquest. One of the most important was the succession within the ruling family. All needed a clear, undisputed succession to a male adult ruler to ensure stability. Contested successions between the sons or brothers of a ruler, or the succession of a young son dependent on a regent, were usually sufficient to produce internal weakness and often civil war. Periods of stability producing growth in population, cultivation of new land, increasing tax revenue and greater trade usually coincided with a settled succession over a few generations. However, very few states were able to avoid problems over the succession for longer than this.

In new empires the initial rulers had to solve three linked problems – how to reward their followers, how to control the newly conquered areas and how to maintain an army. The solutions had to be based on a fundamental constraint – land was almost the only asset and form of wealth. The solutions adopted were nearly always the same – the grant of conquered land to individuals within the elite so that they could use it to support a given number of soldiers to be provided to the ruler when required. (This system is called 'feudalism' in European history but it is merely one form of a phenomenon that was common across Eurasia for several millennia.) Usually at first these grants of land were conditional on the provision of soldiers, revokable by the ruler and not hereditary. Occasionally the early rulers were powerful enough to reallocate land when the holder died. However, the common tendency was for these landholdings to become hereditary very quickly. Once this happened the ruler had much less control over the local elites who established their own power bases and could control their own troops. This left the ruler in the position of having to negotiate for support. He needed to control these local elites through the imposition of local and provincial governors who represented the ruler's authority. The problem was that, in the absence of any trained bureaucracy, the ruler had very few people on whom he could rely (and trust) for this task. Empires were, therefore, usually divided into a few large governorships entrusted to members of the ruler's family in the hope that they would have some interest in co-operating to maintain family rule. If there was a strong ruler this system could work but the disadvantage was that it gave members of the royal family strong power bases they could exploit if there was a disputed succession.

If problems over the succession were avoided the early empires could be relatively stable for some time. However, internal problems usually began to accumulate. The elite would become entrenched in their hereditary estates and gain even more power as they increased their landholdings by either buying up land from impoverished peasants or simply appropriating it. Tax systems imposed when the empires were set up gradually lost their effectiveness as they became increasingly out of line with the real distribution of wealth. This problem was exacerbated as the elite increasingly avoided taxes and more land was granted to institutions, especially religious groups, that did not pay taxes. The wealth available to the ruler therefore tended to decline in parallel with the rise of strong provincial elites that were difficult to control because of poor communications. Both trends meant that it was increasingly difficult to sustain an army. Attempts to increase taxation were usually self-defeating and produced only provincial revolts or peasant rebellions, or both. A vicious circle usually emerged – a combination of growing internal weakness, provincial revolts and a disputed succession led to an increasing inability to resist external pressure, loss of territory and therefore revenue, greater weakness and eventually collapse.

The exact nature of that collapse varied from empire to empire. Some such as Teotihuacan and the Maya seem to have suffered total collapse leaving no successor state. Often there was a transition whereby some areas were lost and new institutions and groups emerged elsewhere to continue some of the existing traditions. A prime example of this form of collapse was the Roman empire which disappeared as a political unit in western Europe in the fifth century CE (though much of its culture continued) and a new form of empire emerged in the east which continued, though in a severely attenuated form at the end, for another thousand years. Normally only the very thin and fragile state structure disappeared to be replaced by a new set of rulers. For the bulk of the population – the peasantry – often very little changed. Since they generally had little contact with their rulers the imposition of a new elite of landlords made little fundamental difference. The new rulers might bring some stability after a period of civil war and conquest but it would also mean more effective taxation and requisitioning of their small food surplus.

6.3 The Pattern of Early Eurasian History

Within the history of the rise and fall of the early agricultural empires there were some remarkably consistent patterns and underlying structures which affected different areas. No single political structure was capable of controlling the whole of Eurasia – the distances involved were far too great for anything more than regional empires. Across the vast distances of Eurasia there were three key areas – south-west Asia, India and China – each of which had distinctive traditions and which only gradually came into contact with each other. Within each of the three there was a core area where civilization first emerged – Mesopotamia and Egypt in south-west Asia, the Ganges river plain in India (the Indus valley civilization left almost no impact on later India) and the Yangtze and Yellow rivers in

China. These core areas established links with their peripheral areas which often contained important raw materials. The slow development of trade produced important political developments in the periphery – local rulers controlled this trade and gained power and prestige through their association with the more advanced state. All these factors forced the pace of change so as to produce states in the peripheral areas. 'Civilization' therefore gradually extended into new areas. This process was apparent from the incorporation of Greece and then Italy into the south-west Asian world in the period after about 1500 BCE through to remarkably similar developments in eastern Europe and Russia in the centuries around 1000 CE. Similarly in China the area of 'civilization' gradually extended, especially to the south of the two river plains into areas where highly productive wet-rice agriculture could be practised. The balance within the Chinese state therefore shifted steadily over time. The census taken in 2 CE showed that almost two-thirds of the Chinese population lived in north China, yet by 1200 CE less than a fifth did so. By 1550 CE over two-thirds of the population lived in the south.

In India there was a very clear distinction between three areas – the states and cultures that emerged in the north around the key trade route of the Ganges plain, the Deccan plateau and finally the states of the far south which always tended to be strongly linked to external trade routes joining the Gulf and south-east Asia. No empire ever controlled the whole of modern India and this has led to the common European assumption that Indian history is, therefore, a 'failure'. However, India covers an area as large as modern Europe. Many of its states were far larger than any European state and what is remarkable is that some empires – the Mauryan, Gupta and Mughal – did rule nearly all of the continent. Further north in central Asia states developed around the widely separated oases and their neighbouring cultivatable land. A number of important centres emerged – Bactria and Sogdia on the Oxus and Jaxartes rivers respectively, Fergana further east, Khwarazm on the Oxus delta near the Aral Sea and the Tarim basin oases such as Kashgar. These oases were linked to both Iran and the Indus valley in the west and to China in the east. They were to be central to the development of the trading route between the societies of south-west Asia and China.

In the third core area of Eurasia, south-west Asia, there were three strategic corridors and trade routes for which empires struggled for more than three millennia and where a succession of major cities evolved. The first route was the Nile and Red Sea corridor which linked the Mediterranean to the Indian Ocean trading system. In Egypt three capitals – Memphis, Alexandria and Cairo – controlled this route and were the centres for successive empires. The second route was overland from the

Mediterranean coast of Syria to northern Mesopotamia and from there to two key routes – first down the Gulf leading to the Indian Ocean and, second, the overland routes to central Asia. Babylon, Seleucia and Baghdad were the succession of important cities in Mesopotamia controlling this route. The third key area was from the Aegean through the Dardanelles into the Black Sea and eventually the overland routes to central Asia. Troy was the important early city on this route but thereafter a single site – Byzantium to the Greeks, Constantinople to the late Roman empire and the Ottomans – dominated access. Of these three routes the second was usually by far the most important, not just for its relatively easy communications, but also because it led to both the maritime Gulf route and the overland caravan trails to central Asia.

Not until the early sixteenth century CE did a single empire (the Ottomans) gain more than fleeting control of all three routes. The first empires emerged in the centres of the first two routes – Mesopotamia and the Nile valley – and until the brief period of Assyrian ascendancy in the seventh century BCE no state managed to control both. This was followed by a crucial factor in Eurasian history – the emergence of empires in Iran. They not only provided a link between the world of south-west Asia and India but also changed the balance within the former area. After the first Iranian empire, the Achaemenid, conquered Babylon in 539 BCE there were no further Mesopotamian-based empires and the area was, for a thousand years, usually a frontier region between an Iranian empire and one centred to the west. The Achaemenid empire was the first in south-west Asia to control both the first and second key areas of Egypt and Syria-Mesopotamia and also exercise partial control over the third route through the Black Sea. It collapsed around 330 BCE and for less than a decade the Macedonian Alexander controlled all three routes and as far east as the Indus valley. On his death in 323 BCE his empire rapidly disintegrated and three successor states formed, each controlling one of the key areas. Within two centuries the Roman empire replaced them but although it dominated the Mediterranean, Egypt and the Black Sea route, the area of Syria and Mesopotamia was to be contested for more than 600 years with two further Iranian empires – the Parthian and the Sasanian. The rise of Islam in the seventh century forced the late Roman empire back to controlling just the Black Sea route.

Although geographically part of Eurasia the creation of the Sahara in its modern form between 3000 and 2000 BCE created a semi-isolated world across most of Africa. The North African littoral was part of the Mediterranean world and Egypt remained focused to the north, east and west but only marginally to the south. Its influence spread up the Nile to Nubia but Egyptian culture did not permeate the African continent in the way that that of the Ganges plain did in India. The problem in studying African history is that south of the Sahara the continent remained largely illiterate (though with very strong oral traditions) and therefore no written records of any consequence survive, except those of people who came into contact with the Africans. Africa south of the Sahara had only extremely limited external links. They were restricted largely to sailors from the Red Sea and Gulf areas travelling down the east coast, particularly Arab trading groups after about 700 CE, and in the west the trans-Saharan caravan trade which existed from an early time but did not develop on a major scale until after about 800 CE. Sub-Saharan Africa therefore remained largely isolated from Eurasia and colonization was an internal process in a difficult environment. It was carried out across a multitude of local frontiers as the population slowly grew and farming pushed into new areas. In doing this the farmers faced a number of severe constraints, especially those of disease and poor communications. The tsetse fly and the trypanosomes they carried meant that neither cattle nor pack animals could survive across large areas of the continent south of the desert and savannah regions. Wheeled transport was not really possible and communications, as in most of the Americas, relied on human porters and canoes along the rivers, although many of the latter were only navigable over short stretches. This meant that the agricultural surplus was difficult to move. All of these factors meant that large states did not develop south of the Sahara.

6.4 The Nomadic World

All of the Eurasian civilizations had to cope with a common problem – the nomadic peoples of the complex world of central Asia which formed a huge arc around the area of the settled societies from south-west Asia through India to China. In the early twentieth century it was thought that nomadism was a failed intermediate stage in the transition from gathering and hunting to farming. Now it is appreciated that it is in fact a highly successful adaptation to a particular set of environments and one that depends on the existence of settled societies. The key to the nomadic way of life was the domestication of the horse. This occurred about 3200 BCE, probably somewhere on the plains of southern Ukraine. It enabled people to exploit the extensive but highly seasonal resources of the great grasslands which stretch from the Ukraine across Eurasia to the Lake Baikal area as well as to Mongolia and the far north-east of Manchuria and the Amur river. The herds of the nomads were usually mixed – sheep were the most important, cattle were confined to the wetter areas, camels

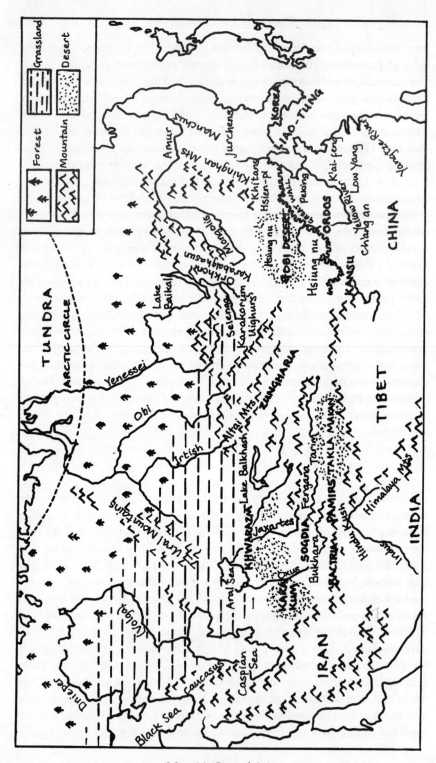

Map 14: Central Asia

(the two-humped 'Bactrian') to the drier. The yak was highly adapted for the high mountains, the dzo (a yak-cow cross) was slightly less specialized. The nomads, who lived in portable houses (*yurt*), herded their animals from area to area according to the seasons – they had no fodder so winter pastures were vital even though the animals usually lost much of their weight on the poor grass. Each group had a recognized area over which they travelled during the year, but there were often conflicts over the best pasture. Occasionally one group would make a conscious decision to move to a new area and this could force a succession of other moves and eventually push some groups into areas which had settled farmers.

The nomads produced little of use to the settled peoples – in the main the horse was the principal item traded. China often had a specialist Horse Trading Office (*Ch'a-ma ssu*) to deal with the nomads and buy the large number of horses they needed for their army. On the other hand the nomads required many items from the settled societies that they did not make themselves – metal tools, food and luxury items such as cloth and silk. Their problem was how to make the settled people trade in such an unbalanced way. The fundamental advantage that the nomads had was their military superiority over the settled civilizations. For thousands of years the nomadic horse-mounted archer was more effective than the infantry of the settled societies. The cavalry of civilized states, though more effective than the infantry, were small in number and could not defeat the nomads. When under attack the nomads simply withdrew into the steppe and dispersed into small bands that were difficult to track down. The best that the settled states could do was build walls to contain the nomads, carry out raids and conduct diplomacy so as to weaken them by encouraging internal divisions. This situation lasted until after the sixteenth century CE. Only then, as the population increased in the settled areas, the farming frontier pushed further into nomadic areas, and gunpowder weapons were adopted, did the settled societies slowly gain the upper hand.

All the settled societies called the nomads 'barbarians' but often had little choice but to come to deals with them. The nomads too rapidly realized that violent attacks, raids on cities and the looting of civilized areas, could be productive only in the short-term. The accepted picture of 'waves of barbarians' sweeping down on settled societies, as is supposed to have happened during the 'fall of the Roman empire', was in fact the exception rather than the rule. The nomads also found that they could not rule settled societies after conquest without becoming sedentary themselves and adopting much of the culture of 'civilization'. This happened not just in western Europe after the decline of the Roman empire, but on numerous occasions in China, including to the Manchus – the last imperial dynasty which ruled from the 1640s until 1911. The normal pattern of relationship between the nomads and the settled societies was essentially symbiotic. There was no distinct frontier between the two. Instead there was a zone where people often shifted from one way of life to another and where nomads occasionally dominated the settled peoples and vice-versa. The threat of force and the general impotence of the settled societies to deal with it was usually enough to induce trade. The Chinese always called this trade 'tribute' by the 'barbarians' which fitted in with their view of their superior status. In practice close analysis of this trade has shown that it was highly asymmetrical and that the balance overwhelmingly favoured the nomads – the Chinese were buying peace along the frontier from groups they could not defeat.

From time to time various peoples came to dominate the nomadic world of the steppe. As with many of the settled empires the initial stages were carried out by a charismatic leader dependent on his own ability and success to hold disparate groups together. These were imperial confederacies which operated in a complex way. At the centre was the leader and his immediate family and court. Within this group there was a high degree of consultation and the succession depended not on an hereditary principle but the choice of the person likely to be the most effective leader. From within this family a series of 'governors' would attempt to control the various tribes in the confederation. At this lower level the existing tribal organization was maintained. The leader of the confederacy often depended on the 'trade' with the settled areas for the goods which he could then distribute among his followers so as to retain his status and their loyalty. Because of this interdependence between the settled and nomadic states they often rose and fell together. The Han empire in China from the second century BCE had its counterpart in the Hsiung-nu confederation on the steppe while the Sui and T'ang (from the late sixth century CE) had to deal with the Turkic empire. These nomadic empires had little incentive to destroy the Chinese state on which they depended – some groups such as the Uighurs even acted to restore order in China and support the existing government. Apart from the Mongols, the conquest of parts of China by these nomadic groups only occurred when the Chinese state was already in decline. The Chinese always liked to believe that during these phases the borrowing was always in one direction – the 'barbarians' adopted Chinese ways and became sinicized. In practice there was almost as much borrowing in the opposite direction, especially in the many frontier areas such as Manchuria where the boundaries between the two worlds were constantly shifting.

6.5 Contacts

Although very distinct cultural traditions emerged in Eurasia, centred around China, India and south-west Asia, none were isolated from external influences or each other. A central feature of Eurasian history is the increasing level of contact between these different groups. These contacts involved trade, the transmission of ideas, especially religion, and the diffusion of technology. At first the level of contact was limited, although from shortly after 3000 BCE Mesopotamia was in touch with both Egypt and the Indus valley. Gradually, as trade grew and communications developed, the amount of contact increased. In some cases merchants travelled along the great trade routes that linked the different areas of Eurasia – the land routes from south-west Asia to India, central Asia and China, the sea routes across the Mediterranean, those from the Gulf and Red Sea to the west coast of India and from India to south-east Asia and the southern coast of China. The journey-times involved in some of these routes meant that it was often easier for merchants to establish permanent colonies in a foreign town. Here, often living in separate quarters, they learnt the local language and ways of life but also spread their own ideas and beliefs. Many people in the local society were attracted to these beliefs because they were associated with the prestige of the foreign community. In particular chiefs and leaders often adopted foreign religions as a way of increasing their status – in south-east Asia many adopted Hinduism and later Islam, and in both West and East Africa Islam was transmitted in the same way. Foreign communities were also central to the widespread adoption of Buddhism in China from the third century CE as it spread from India and central Asia along the trade routes.

Over time, with many up and downs, the links between the different communities of the Eurasian world became stronger. Trade increased not just in terms of its scale but also the wider range of products involved and its greater importance within society. The transmission of ideas, religious beliefs and technology similarly increased. The direct contacts between one end of the Eurasian world and the other, such as those between China and the Mediterranean, remained tenuous and indirect for a long period. The Han and Roman empires were aware of each other's existence but the level of direct contact remained minimal. The diffusion of ideas and the linkages of trade were indirect and took place through the intermediate communities of Eurasia such as those of Iran, India and Central Asia. Such contacts became more direct when the Islamic world, which originated in south-west Asia, came into direct contact with China in the early eighth century CE. As the Eurasian world came closer together we can begin to discern a pattern in the contemporary rise and fall of states and empires – times of prosperity and periods of disturbance and internal problems tended to coincide. The consequences of events in one part of Eurasia were increasingly being felt across the whole vast area.

7

Interaction
(2000–1000 BCE)

About 2000 BCE, with the final decline of Sumer, the area where civilization first developed in Mesopotamia, the rise of Babylon and the recovery
of Egypt from the disintegration of the First Intermediate period, the
various empires of south-west Asia were in much closer touch with each
other than ever before. Over the next millennium (a period often described
as the 'Bronze age') it is possible to detect a common rhythm in the history
of the region. Between 2000 BCE and about 1750 BCE the growth of
Babylon was paralleled by the strength and unity of the Twelfth Dynasty
in Egypt (the Middle Kingdom period). Trade links developed strongly
across south-west Asia and extended into the eastern Mediterranean as the
Aegean area was incorporated and the Minoan civilization developed on
Crete. To the east trade down the Gulf to the Indus valley flourished. This
period was followed by what appears to be a set of common crises in the
250 years after 1750 BCE. Increasing internal problems in Mesopotamia
were paralleled by the decline of Gulf trade and the collapse of the Indus
valley civilization. Egypt was occupied during the Second Intermediate
Period by a group of outsiders known as the 'Hyksos'. In Anatolia the new
kingdom of the Hittites emerged.

Revival followed between 1550 and about 1200 BCE. The period saw the
great imperial conflict between Egypt under the New Kingdom rulers, the
Hittites, a revived Mesopotamia under the Kassites and the developing
kingdom of Assyria in the north. Cyprus developed into a major kingdom
based on the wealth generated by its copper trade, Crete and the Aegean
flourished and the first civilization on the European mainland – the
Mycenaean in southern Greece – emerged. Then, about 1200 BCE, there
was a collapse across a wide area and a 'dark age' lasting several centuries
when records are extremely sparse. The Kassite kingdom collapsed, Egypt
was invaded and defeated, the Mycenaean civilization disappeared as did
the Hittites together with a number of other small kingdoms in the
Anatolian region. Everywhere cities were destroyed. This crisis marked the
end of the 'Bronze age' empires of south-west Asia. Contemporary with
these developments during the second millennium BCE in south-west Asia
was the appearance of the first distinctive Chinese civilization – the Shang.
Exact dating is difficult but the Shang culture, with its very distinctive
bronze technology, emerged shortly after 1800 BCE and lasted to 1027 BCE

(though a date a century earlier for the collapse is also possible). Given the large distance between south-west Asia and China and the very low level of contacts at this time, the collapse of the Shang at about the same time as the great Bronze age empires of south-west Asia is probably no more than a coincidence.

7.1 Expansion and Stability *c*.2000–*c*.1750 BCE

7.1.1 Mesopotamia
[*Earlier Mesopotamia* 4.4]
In the period after the fall of the Third Dynasty of Ur, about 2000 BCE, the southern Mesopotamian region was characterized for almost two centuries by a number of city-states, none of which was able to establish an empire. Many of the rulers of this period have Amorite names but a connected political history of the period is not possible and even the exact order of some of the rulers cannot be established. In the south two cities – Isin and Larsa – fought for supremacy. The rulers of Isin based much of their royal protocol and administrative structure on those of the old dynasty at Ur and devised the so-called 'Sumerian King List' to enhance their legitimacy as the supposed successors of the ancient rulers of the Sumerian city-states. The prosperity of Isin was based on its control of the Gulf trade through Ur, Uruk and Nippur. Once it lost control of Ur it went into decline, although it survived until 1794 BCE, almost a century after Larsa cut off the water supply to most of its agricultural land.

In central Mesopotamia the city of Eshnunna in the Diyala valley was dominant but it was in the north that important new areas and cities were beginning to emerge. One of these was Assur on the Tigris. Very few of the remains of this early period have been excavated since they lie under those of the imperial Assyrian city. The name of the city is probably correct (it is that of its chief god) and a rough list of rulers from about 2000 BCE, when it became independent, can be established. Its development was based on its position on three key trade routes – from the Gulf via Ur, along the Tigris, and the east–west route from Elam to the Levant. The rulers granted tax exemption to the merchants and the city's wealth attracted conquerors – it was eventually conquered by the Amorite, Shamshi-Addad I (1813–1781 BCE). Further west on the Euphrates, on the present Syria/Iraq border, the city of Mari controlled other key trade routes. It was the start of the caravan route through the oasis of Tadmor (the later Palmyra) to Qatna on the Orontes river and the Mediterranean coast at Byblos. It also dominated routes along the Euphrates. It was ruled by an Amorite dynasty and the wealth derived from trade allowed the construction of a vast palace covering over six acres.

The key city from which a new empire was constructed was Babylon. Very little is known about the city itself because the high water table makes excavation below about the seventh century BCE levels almost impossible. Most of its history has to be derived from records at other sites and almost nothing can be established about its rulers from the establishment of the First Dynasty in 1894 BCE until the reign of Sin-muballit (1812–1793 BCE). He is really only known for being the father of the founder of the Babylonian empire – Hammurabi (1792–1749 BCE). At first the latter was the subordinate of Shamshi-Addad of Ashur and Rim-Sin of Larsa and all of his early 'conquests' were made on their behalf. About 1763 BCE he revolted and took power for himself. He defeated Rim-Sin and gained the southern cities of Isin, Uruk, Ur, Nippur and Larsa. In 1761 BCE he conquered Eshnunna in central Mesopotamia and with it controlled the trade from Mesopotamia to the central Iranian plateau. The next year he defeated Mari and gained control of the trade routes to the west and established direct contact with the great trading city of Aleppo. Hammurabi now controlled an extensive empire that dominated Mesopotamia and its associated trade routes – it was the strongest in the region since Sargon founded the Akkadian empire some 600 years earlier. Very little is known about Hammurabi except for his 'law-code' inscribed in the last two years of his reign on a stone stele over seven feet high. It was taken to Susa in the thirteenth century BCE when Babylon was looted by the Elamites and the text is partly destroyed by a later Elamite inscription. From what survives the laws seem to be a very odd and eclectic collection and the prices supposedly set by Hammurabi bear no relation to actual prices on contemporary clay tablets. The stele is probably not a 'law-code' at all but rather another example of the self-praise and list of 'achievements' many rulers set up towards the end of their lives.

7.1.2 Egypt
[*Earlier Egypt* 4.5]
Contemporary with these developments in Mesopotamia was the establishment of the Twelfth Dynasty in Egypt at the end of the First Intermediate phase. The dynasty was long-lasting and ruled from 1991–1785 BCE. It was founded by Ammenemes I – probably a vizier at the court who seized power for himself. He moved the capital and burial site of the Pharaohs to a new city *Itj-towy* or Lisht near Memphis. The stability of the dynasty partly derived from the succession being maintained within a single family and a unique institution in Egyptian history – the designated successor of the current ruler acted as co-ruler. The stability of this period

was marked by a major expansion of Egyptian influence. To the south in Nubia a string of massive fortresses with double walls, watchtowers and an internal gridiron plan were built along the first and second Nile cataracts. Nubia was tightly controlled and the local population forced to labour in the mines producing gold, copper and amethyst. Many Nubians were also recruited as soldiers in the Egyptian army. To the east Egypt developed strong links across the Sinai and into the Levant, building temples, establishing trade routes and exploiting the local mineral resources. Envoys were sent to the rulers as far north as Byblos and southern Anatolia. Occasionally Egyptian armies intervened in the area. These contacts with the Levant also provided strong linkages into the trade routes of south-west Asia that led to Mesopotamia and even further east.

7.2 Crisis c.1750–c.1550 BCE

The crisis in Egypt after the end of the Twelfth Dynasty in 1785 BCE was extensive. The Thirteenth Dynasty period, which probably lasted for about fifty years, was one of confusion – control of all of Egypt was maintained for a while but the 'dynasty' was no more than a multitude of rulers. There was no single family as in the previous dynasty but merely a succession of military, foreign, non-royal or elite rulers who often lasted for a year or less. By about 1750 BCE control of Lower Egypt was probably lost to a number of local rulers. The 'Second Intermediate Period' which followed lasted for about two centuries but was different from the first – there was no civil war but rather a series of external rulers known as the 'Hyksos'. Who these people were is unknown. They probably came from the southern Levant and moved into the area of the Nile delta as central Egyptian control crumbled. The exclusion of the Hyksos from the later lists of legitimate Egyptian rulers is dubious and mainly reflects the propaganda of the succeeding New Kingdom rulers of the reunited Egypt. In practice the Hyksos continued the traditions of the Egyptian kingship – they designated themselves as the 'son of Re', they were served by the Egyptian priests and Egyptians also continued as court officials. A new capital was established at Avaris in the eastern delta. They controlled trade into the southern Levant and, judging by the number of Hyksos finds in Nubia, trade and influence with that area were little different from that under earlier Egyptian rulers. A 'true' line of Egyptian rulers seems to have continued at Thebes but they were almost certainly subordinate to the Hyksos rulers of the delta.

In Mesopotamia Hammurabi's empire proved to be very short-lived. Control of Mari to the west was lost within twenty years and Larsa revolted at the same time. By about 1700 BCE control had also been lost over southern Mesopotamia and the rapidly declining Gulf trade. In 1677 BCE the 'Sealand' dynasty came to control all of the south. The Babylonian empire declined to little more than the area around the city. The final collapse came with the sacking of Babylon by the Hittite king Mursili I in 1595 BCE. About this time in northern Mesopotamia and eastern Anatolia a new kingdom of Mitanni emerged as the other empires weakened and collapsed. Its nature poses a number of questions, few of which can be answered. The language of the state is called 'Hurrian' and although written in cuneiform, bears no relation to any other language of the region. It seems likely that the 'Hurrian' people had always lived in the area because some of their names can be found in Mesopotamian texts dating from as early as about 2200 BCE. The kingdom had two capitals – Washshukanni and Taide – but neither have been located. By about 1500 BCE Mitanni had expanded to include two of the great trading city-states of the Levant, Aleppo and Emar. It remained an important state for several centuries and was strong enough to block Egyptian expansion into the area after 1500 BCE.

Apart from Mitanni another state, more powerful and better known, emerged in the confused period after 1750 BCE – the Hittites in Anatolia. It is unclear how this process took place since there is no information until the kingdom was fully formed about 1650 BCE. It seems likely that a local ruler took control of the old city of Hattusa (the modern Bogazkoy, east of Ankara) and turned it into the capital of a new state. Even a basic chronology of early Hittite history depends on correlations with other areas and the most that can be reliably established is that following an initial period of expansion after 1650 BCE there was a period between about 1595 and 1525 BCE of internal instability and a loss of control over northern Levant. The main source of information about the Hittites comes from the tablets discovered at the capital Hattusa. From this it is clear that the name Hittite is a misnomer given to them by another group the Hatti – the people called themselves *nes* and their language *nesili* (Nesite in modern terms). Their relationship with Mitanni is also unclear – some of the later 'Hittite' kings during the imperial period after about 1400 BCE have Hurrian names and from about a century later the great 'Hittite' ceremonial and cult centre at Yazilikayaya is dominated by 'Hurrian' gods.

7.3 The Indo-Europeans

7.3.1 Language
An even more fundamental problem is the relationship between the Hittites and the various languages of Anatolia because the tablets from

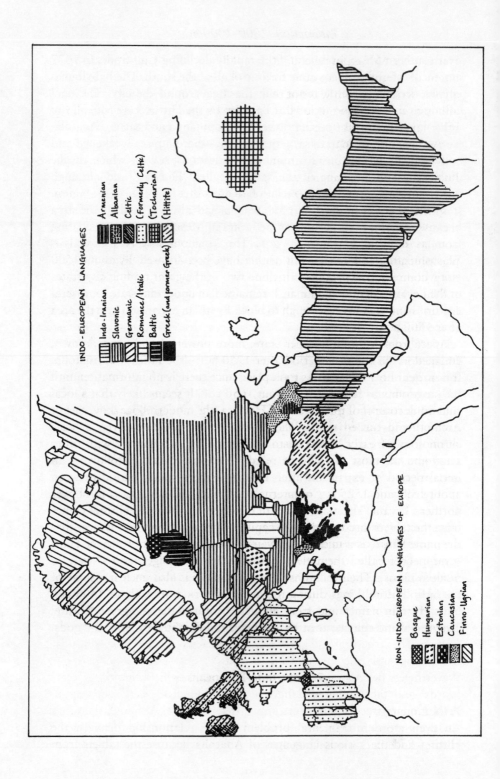

Map 15: The Indo-European languages of Eurasia

Hattusa are written in seven languages, though all of them use an adaptation of Mesopotamian cuneiform. In addition a form of carved hieroglyphic writing (which was not related to Egyptian hieroglyphic) was used although the texts are not in Hittite. The texts that are in 'Hittite', and two other languages of the region (Luwian and Palaic), mark some of the first appearances of a group of languages known as Indo-European which are now spoken by almost half the world's people. The origins of the Indo-Europeans and their languages have been the subject of major controversy for almost two centuries. During this period there has been immense confusion caused by the linking of a variety of very different problems – the divergence and evolution of languages, changes in culture, art style and pottery and the movements of people. However, these are separate phenomena and evidence from one of them cannot necessarily be used to draw conclusions about the others.

When European scholars first became aware of the complexities of Indian history and culture in the late eighteenth century they were immediately struck by the similarities between the dead languages of their 'classical' culture – Greek and Latin – and the similar dead language of India – Sanskrit – and that the latter was also very close to the ancient languages of Iran. It was clear that all these languages were related as part of a major family of languages – Indo-European – with very similar syntax and other structural features. However, they must have been isolated from each other for some time to allow significant divergences to develop. Some of the similarities in Indo-European are striking. In Sanskrit the word for chariot is *ratha* and in Latin the word for wheel is *rota*. The major Hindu gods are clearly identical with those of the Hittites – their names, with their Hittite equivalents in brackets are: Indra (Indara), Varuna (Uruvna), Mitra (Mitira), Naksatras (Nasatiya). Within Indo-European certain relationships are very clear. In Europe the Germanic, Baltic and Slavic languages are more closely related to each other than they are to the Italo-Celtic group. There is no argument that the Romance languages – French, Spanish, Portuguese, Italian and Romanian – are derived from Latin, or that Hindi, Urdu, Bengali, Panjabi, Marathi and Sinti are derived from Sanskrit. Historical linguists have attempted to establish the relationship between the large number of Indo-European languages that are now known. The structural and grammatical similarities within Indo-European are strong and rule out any great mixing with other language types. Nevertheless developments over time, in particular the adoption of 'loan-words' and the mixing of languages (as in English), make any simple 'evolutionary tree' of languages impossible to derive. Although the broad divisions are clear there are almost as many different reconstructions as there are scholars working in the field. Other linguists have attempted to isolate certain common features in all the languages and from this reconstruct the original single language (Proto-Indo-European or PIE) from which all the others are believed to be derived. This is a hazardous procedure in the extreme. Doubts about its reliability were confirmed when it was used to 'reconstruct' Latin from the existing Romance languages and the results could be seen to be wrong. The evolution of languages is a complex matter and apart from some general features it is difficult to establish the exact relationship and evolutionary pattern within the Indo-European family.

7.3.2 History

The historical conclusions that can be drawn from the existence of the Indo-European family of languages are even more uncertain. A large number of the problems stem from the assumptions common in late-nineteenth-century Europe, many of which persisted well into the twentieth century. Changes in 'culture', shown by new styles in burials, weapons, pottery and art, were identified with the arrival of new peoples. Too great an emphasis on the events surrounding the 'fall of the Roman empire' in western Europe in the fifth century CE led to the conclusion that these new people were waves of migrants, forming separate racial and linguistic groups. Racial thinking identified a clear hierarchy within these 'races' with the Germanic peoples, Anglo-Saxons and 'Aryans' in particular at the summit. The advances in civilization, especially 'classical' Greece, had to be identified with these superior people. The Indo-Europeans therefore became waves of nomadic invaders from the steppes of central Asia who overthrew the effete civilizations and peoples of south-west Asia and India. The first of these people were the Hittites who invaded Anatolia about 1750 BCE and established the first 'Indo-European kingdom'. Attempts were made to demonstrate that the Hittites and all the subsequent invaders came from a single 'Indo-European homeland'. It was thought that if the common words within Indo-European could be identified then this would give a good idea of the vocabulary used by the original Indo-Europeans who spoke PIE. It was argued that many of these original or 'ur-words' were related to trees and animals but not crops and vegetables and that this 'proved' that the earliest Indo-Europeans were nomads. In practice there are very few words that have a common root in all Indo-European languages and much of the commonality identified in PIE seems to be entirely random. For example PIE is believed to have a common root for butter but not milk, snow but not rain and feet but not hands. It is also entirely illegitimate to argue that because the Sanskrit word for chariot and the Latin word for wheel are roughly the same then the original Indo-Europeans must have had the chariot.

The problems associated with these lines of argument are well illustrated by two influential theories about the Indo-Europeans. The main proponent of the migration theory of the Indo-Europeans is Marija Gimbutas who has identified them with the 'Kurgan culture' which emerged on the steppes of southern Ukraine and Russia about 4000 BCE. It is associated with distinctive burials in mounds and a particular style of beaker pottery and bronze weapons. This 'culture' is later found across Europe. However, it is not possible to make a simple link between 'culture', language and the migration of people. It is equally possible that this culture represented a distinctive set of religious beliefs which was slowly adopted across Europe without any movement of peoples. On the other hand a small warrior elite may have migrated – but this would be unlikely to have a significant impact on language. As we shall see in the next chapter, the attempt to establish a 'Celtic' world in Europe in the first millennium BCE, with a common culture and set of languages, is similarly fraught with difficulties.

The second theory is associated with Georges Dumézil who has argued that Indo-European languages and societies reflect a tripartite division between priests, warriors and cultivators and that since this division is found in numerous societies across Europe and India this 'proves' they were derived from a common background. This idea is actually incompatible with the idea of nomadic invaders since nomadic groups do not have such a relatively complex division within society. Such a division also reflects a fairly common pattern within societies at a certain level of development and is also apparent in societies that were not Indo-European, such as Japan, and groups who spoke Semitic languages. Neither is there any evidence, as some have suggested, that Indo-European societies are any more patriarchal than others – the early Semitic societies of Mesopotamia for example show the same characteristics.

An alternative to these theories has been developed by the British archaeologist, Colin Renfrew. It is based on the nature of the early Anatolian languages. They show, from the earliest known evidence, about 1700 BCE, a large mixture of non-Indo-European languages such as Hattic, Hurrian, West Semitic, Akkadian, Elamite, Sumerian, Urartian and later Aramaic, as well as the Indo-European Hittite, Luwian and Palaic. It is clear that these 'Anatolian' Indo-European languages are archaic and retain some grammatical forms and constructions that either disappeared very early or were never present in other Indo-European languages. Some linguists have argued that the 'Anatolian' languages therefore split from PIE long before the latter disintegrated and constitute a separate group within a broad 'Hittite–Indo-European group'. It is quite possible that these Anatolian languages have very deep roots in the area and may be one of the languages associated with the first farming groups at small towns such as Çatal

Hüyük. It is therefore possible to suggest that Indo-European originated in Anatolia and spread to Europe with the first farming communities around 5000 BCE. The Indo-European languages then gradually diverged from each other as people settled, integrated with existing groups and slowly split away from each other as new land was colonized. During this phase some of the groups in Europe which did not adopt farming at this time retained their old languages such as Basque and those of the far north of Scotland (which are clearly not Indo-European). (Other languages in Europe such as Hungarian, Finno-Ugrian and Estonian which are not Indo-European were introduced much later.) This theory is compatible with other groups from the vast mix of peoples and languages in the Anatolia-Caucasus-southern Russia area also moving to Europe, although they should not be identified with any specific archaeological 'culture'. There were no waves of Indo-Europeans descending on the civilized world from a 'homeland' on the steppes and bringing with them a peculiar social structure and their unique languages.

7.3.3 India
[*Earlier India* 4.6]
The problems caused by the identification of the Indo-Europeans with conquering warriors from the steppes using chariots and horses to over-throw existing civilizations are well illustrated by the history of India. There is almost no archaeological evidence from the period after the fall of the Indus-valley civilization about 1700 BCE and the early first millennium. The only available sources seem to be the *Rig Veda* or 'Verses of Knowledge' – over a thousand poems to various gods written in Sanskrit. They were not written down until about 600 BCE but are believed to contain an oral tradition dating from a thousand years earlier. They can be supplemented by the *Brahmanas* – commentaries on the *Rig Veda* which exalt the role of the priests or *brahmans*. Much more philosophical and complex are the *Upanishads* – over a hundred texts probably composed about 800 BCE. The *Rig Veda* seems to incorporate a tradition about the conquest of the dark-skinned *dasas* – a word that subsequently meant slave – by a group using chariots, horses and bronze weapons. The conquering groups were organized into tribes headed by a *raja* or king and a group of nobles known as *aryan*. The majority of people were the *vaishyas*, living in a patriarchal society in which only the sons could inherit and carry out religious services for the dead. The conquest of the *dasas* took place in the 'Land of the Seven Rivers', which was probably in the Punjab and the conquering groups do not appear to have been aware of the Ganges.

In the hands of nineteenth-century European scholars these sources were used to create a story of a racially superior group of light-skinned Indo-

European warriors using horses and chariots to sweep down on existing civilizations, destroying them and setting up their own distinctive culture. When the Indus valley civilization was discovered in the early twentieth century it was immediately assumed that it must have been destroyed by this wave of Indo-European invaders – even the date of destruction (about 1700 BCE) seemed to fit this pattern. However, the language of the Indus valley civilization is unknown. There is in fact no reason why it could not be Indo-European and have originated from the early agricultural communities in south-west Asia and Iran. A close reading of the *Rig Veda* shows that there is in fact no mention of invasion, only of battles. The story contained in these texts could equally well refer to the establishment of control over groups of peasants by an aristocratic warrior group (the 'Aryans') that had developed within an existing society and which had its own very clearly defined elite culture and values. In this interpretation the clear links between the Sanskrit of the *Rig Veda* and the Old Iranian of the earliest religious literature – the *Avesta* – derives not from a common Aryan–Indo-European invasion but from similarities within an existing elite culture.

[*Later India* 8.5]

7.4 The Imperial Contest – South-West Asia *c.*1550–*c.*1200 BCE

7.4.1 Hittites, Kassites and Assyrians

From shortly before 1500 BCE there was a general recovery across south-west Asia after the previous two centuries of disruption. The emergence of the Hittite kingdom at this time was only one part of a major restructuring of the south-west Asian world and the beginning of a period of major struggles between the early empires. Hittite expansion began under Tudhaliya I (1430–1410 BCE) who was probably the founder of a new dynasty. At first the main enemy was Mitanni to the south and the Hittites tried to take advantage of any Egyptian victory over Mitanni. However, as Hittite power increased these powers combined against them. Substantial Hittite success did not come until towards the end of the reign of Suppiluliuma I (1370–1330 BCE). He attacked to the east, crossed the Euphrates, sacked the Mitanni capital of Washshukanni and controlled the western half of the kingdom (under a client king Shattiwaza) so that it could act as a buffer against the expansion of Assyria. Suppiluliuma was then able to establish control over northern Syria, including the great trading cities of Aleppo and Carchemish. These victories enabled the next king – Mursili II (1330–1295 BCE) to attack westwards. The Hittite texts reveal that they had two enemies in this area – Arzawa and Ahhiyawa –

though exactly who they were is uncertain. Arzawa was defeated and Hittite control extended to the Aegean. However, Mursili II may have lost control of the capital Hattusa to a group called the 'Gasga' who also remain unidentified. Hittite power was at its peak under the next two rulers – Muwatalli and Hattusili III. They controlled a large area of Anatolia and the Levant and were strong enough to force an agreement and alliance on Egypt. The Hittite empire was successful for some 400 years but it did not develop a strong infrastructure. The Hittite ruler, or 'Great King', at Hattusa was part of a cohesive ruling elite comprising the royal family and aristocracy. He ruled over a range of communities and older political units which retained their own rulers, languages, customs and laws as long as they accepted the ultimate authority of Hattusa. The 'Great King' led the army and was the main priest of all the gods but was not regarded as divine in his own lifetime.

The Hittite destruction of Babylon in 1595 did not lead to their domination of the area. Babylon was instead taken over by the Kassites who ruled the area from 1530 until about 1200 BCE. They probably came from the Zagros mountains but little is known about this long period in Mesopotamia – even constructing a basic list of kings is difficult and Kassite does not appear to be related to any other known language. However, it is clear that this was a period of considerable stability and, judging from the records of other empires, Babylonia was a major imperial state. The whole of Mesopotamia was united after their defeat of the 'Sealand' dynasty in the far south which provided access to the important Gulf trade routes. The Kassites appear to have controlled trade as far south as Bahrain as well as the routes through the Diyala valley into Iran and Central Asia (the source of the highly-prized lapis lazuli). In the far north of Mesopotamia the kingdom of Assyria was small and subordinate to Mitanni until the latter's defeat by the Hittites in about 1340 BCE. This allowed the Assyrians to expand, beginning on a major scale under Adad-nirari I (1307–1275 BCE). He took over the eastern part of the old Mitanni kingdom (the Hittites controlled the west) and pushed south against the Kassites. Control of the northern part of Mesopotamia was achieved under Shalmaneser I (1274–1245 BCE) when Assyria was a powerful state on much the same level as the Hittites and Egyptians. Under his successor Tukulti-Ninurta I (1244–1208 BCE) the Assyrians gained effective control of much of Babylonia and set up their puppet rulers in the capital.

7.4.2 Egypt

The most important developments in south-west Asia during this period took place in Egypt. From about 1550 BCE Egyptian leaders and their armies gradually pushed the Hyksos back into the southern Levant and re-established a unified Egyptian state. Although most Egyptologists tend to stress the conservatism of Egyptian society this was a period of major change within both society and the state. It was marked by the emergence of the military (using the two-wheeled chariot as a major weapon) as a crucial force in what became an imperial society and state based on conquest. During this period (known as the New Kingdom) Egypt was at its wealthiest and most powerful. Internal problems were generally contained and Egyptian control spread from the military camps and fortifications in Nubia as far as central Levant. It was the time when some of the greatest monuments were constructed – Abu Simbel, Karnak, Abydos, western Thebes and el-Amarna. The general chronology of the period is fairly clear, although a detailed political history cannot be written, apart from that based on a few documents. One of these – a treaty with the Hittites made in 1269 BCE (which is known from texts made by both parties) – is perhaps the first known international treaty. In addition there are the so-called 'Amarna Letters' – a series of clay tablets mainly dating to the seventy years after 1400 BCE. They are written in Akkadian, which was still the international language of south-west Asia, and record Egyptian correspondence with the other powers in the region – the Hittites, Cyprus, Babylonia, Mittani, Assyria and, in particular, the local rulers in the Levant whom the Egyptians were attempting to control.

The main restructuring of the Egyptian state took place under Tuthmosis I (1507–1494 BCE) shortly after the final expulsion of the Hyksos. The capital was moved north from Thebes to Memphis, which was better placed to control the key relationships with the states to the east of the Sinai. It was also the centre for military and internal administration. Thebes was retained for religious ceremonies and at the adjacent Karnak the 'valley of the Kings' and 'valley of the Queens' were used for royal burials. In the mid-fifteenth century BCE the Egyptians were conducting campaigns as far east as the Euphrates. Shortly before 1400 BCE, following Amenhopis II's crushing of a major revolt in the Levant, the Egyptians recognized that the feasible limits of their control lay in the centre of that region. Agreements were made with the rulers of Mitanni who were challenging Egypt and under the next Egyptian ruler, Tuthmosis IV, a marriage alliance was concluded.

The last phase of significant Egyptian power was under the Nineteenth Dynasty and in particular Rameses II (1290–1224 BCE). A major effort was made to expand in the Levant but this only ran into opposition from the Hittite empire that was pushing southwards from Anatolia. The battle of Kadesh in 1285 BCE, though lauded as highly successful in the monuments Rameses II erected to himself, was in fact a draw. In the peace treaty with the Hittites in 1269 BCE Rameses again portrays himself as graciously accepting a plea from an inferior. In practice it was a peace of equals that both needed (especially the Egyptians since they were under pressure from groups pushing into Egypt from the desert to the west). In 1256 BCE a Hittite princess married Rameses II and there were no more wars between the two powers. The imperial nature of the Egyptian state was well illustrated by the monuments erected by the rulers. The huge temples and large processional ways were designed to intimidate as well as provide a venue for communal and religious festivities. The carvings and hiero-glyphic texts emphasize military supremacy, the crushing of enemies and the public execution of captives. The divine nature of the ruler, now formally given the title *per'ao* or Pharaoh, meaning 'Great House', was central to its ideology.

The exact nature of the divinity of the Pharaoh and the various Egyptian gods was at the heart of the disputes during the so-called 'Amarna period' and its immediate aftermath lasting from Akhenaten (1364–1347 BCE) to Horemheb (1332–1306 BCE). (Although this was a time of major internal problems there appears to have been no difficulty in maintaining external control of the adjoining areas.) Egyptian religion was never static and it was always developing (and would have continued to do so had it not been swamped by Greek influences from the late fourth century BCE). Its theology, developed by the priests, was built around a fascination with names and words in an attempt to amalgamate two contradictory ideas – the historical multiplicity of gods and a perceived unity of divine power expressed through the power of the sun. The sun-god Ra was therefore given seventy-five names which were also the names of the other gods who were the deities of nature. The human form of the sun-god, Amun-Ra (of Thebes), had a particularly powerful cult. This was also linked to the Egyptian idea of *maat* – which can best be understood as 'truth', 'justice' and the correct order of the universe. *Maat* became a goddess as the daughter of Ra.

This system was overturned by Amenhopis IV when he renamed himself Akhenaten after *aten* – the visible disc of the sun from which numerous rays emanated and ended in a hand. Akhenaten saw the *aten* as the universal creator of all life. This was not new; Amun-Ra at Thebes had often been addressed in the same way. This emphasis on the *aten* can also be seen as the culmination of earlier trends in its emphasis on the power of the sun-god. What was new was the defacing of the images of the other gods, who were no longer regarded as emanations of the sun, the emphasis on the sun-disc without human features and the abolition of a universe populated with a multitude of divine beings. At the same time the resources of the temples of the other gods were reallocated so that they went to the only god Aten. In addition the role of Akhenaten as the sole earthly incarnation of the *aten* was stressed, thereby further emphasizing the merging of god and the Pharaoh. Akhenaten regularly described himself as someone who 'lived on *maat*' – meaning the new truth about the nature of god. He created a completely new city, halfway between Memphis and Thebes, in an area where there were no other temples so that the worship of the *aten* would not be polluted. The city, now known as Amarna, was to be called Akhetaten – the 'horizon of the sun'. Its construction required a huge effort by the state and the workers it mobilized – at its height it probably had a population of about 50,000.

How to interpret this episode is a matter of dispute. On the monuments he erected Akhenaten is usually portrayed with very distinct and distorted features, as were his immediate family. It has been argued that he was suffering from a peculiar, inherited disease. This is unlikely and the carvings are probably a deliberate attempt to portray Akhenaten and his family as non-human and quasi-divine. Certainly Akhenaten and his main wife Nefertiti were invoked as divine and seen as enshrining the essence of *aten* during their lifetime. To many commentators Akhenaten's beliefs seem to be close to monotheism and in the western tradition this is regarded as superior to earlier views and a mark of 'progress' (whether Christianity is monotheistic is a difficult question). In this way Akhenaten could be seen as a precursor of some aspects of Judaism. However, the idea of *aten* was not about any moral teaching – it was the source of life. It was therefore very different from the later (by several hundred years) Jewish beliefs in their god Yahweh who was irascible, intervened in human affairs and gave the Jews an identity separate from all other people.

On Akhenaten's death all of his ideas were rejected, the cult of *aten* was ended and his great city of Amarna was abandoned. He rapidly became simply 'the enemy' and his reign was regarded with horror as an attempt to overthrow the accepted and long-established Egyptian system of beliefs. Exactly why there was such a violent reaction is unknown. What is clear is that it did not extend to Akhenaten's family who continued to rule as part of the Eighteenth Dynasty. He was succeeded by Tutankhamun who was probably his brother and married to one of Akhenaten's daughters. His original name was Tutankhaten and its alteration symbolized the re-establishment of the old order under Amun-Ra. He was succeeded by Ay, probably the father of Akhenaten's main wife Nefertiti. The last ruler of the dynasty, Horemheb who died in 1306 BCE, was married to a daughter of Ay and therefore a sister of Nefertiti.

These internal disturbances over the last fifty years or so of the fourteenth century BCE had little impact on the working of the Egyptian state in the New Kingdom period. Temples and the great burial sites of the Pharaohs, with their large numbers of priests, were maintained by the produce and the workers of a series of estates. For example, Kahun, a town for the maintenance of the pyramid and rites for Senusret II, was laid out to a strict gridiron plan. There were a few large houses with a complex plan where members of the elite lived. The bulk of the population of about 3,000 lived in 220 houses each one-twentieth the size of those of the elite. They were clearly organized into teams or gangs for different occupations and each was entirely dependent on one of the granaries in the elite houses – there was no central granary for the whole city. At other temples the staff were organized into companies; normally there were ten companies and each served at the temple for a month before returning to work in the villages. This was the only way temple and state service could be combined with the need to produce the agricultural surplus on which the elite depended. People working in the temple areas were paid in kind. Scribes measured the initial yield of grain, checked its transport to the granary to ensure there was no theft and checked the weight again on arrival. The grain was turned into bread and beer – the latter was in reality a thick gruel that was not very alcoholic. The scribes did not check the production process in detail but knew how much bread and beer to expect from a given amount of grain. Bread was made in a semi-standard mould and a labourer normally received ten loaves a day and a variable amount of beer. For those higher up the social scale the ration was increased in a series of fixed steps.

On major building projects all the workers, including officials, architects and craftsmen as well as the mass of labourers, were employed directly by the state. The allocation of materials and rations was the responsibility of the scribes who also ensured that the workers performed the set 'work-norm'. Little is known about the details of pyramid and temple construction but each would have involved massive state direction of the population, the establishment of barracks, the quarrying and transport-ation of the stone, the construction of huge ramps which workers could climb to the higher levels and the removal of a vast amount of debris at the end. Some idea of the scale of these activities can be judged from the records of one state project that have survived – an expedition to the quarries at Wadi Hammamat. This involved 18,660 skilled and unskilled workers together with hunters, soldiers, millers, brewers and bakers. They were controlled by eighty officials, twenty 'mayors' from the towns who provided the workers, and eight scribes.

Clearly the state was a major factor in the Egyptian economy but there is plenty of evidence of considerable trade and activity beyond state control. On state and temple projects senior officials could be allocated as many as 500 loaves a day. Since their staff were allocated their food separately, and some of the transactions involved complex fractions that could not have been measured, there must have been a system of credit and a way of exchanging these 'loaves' for other products. How this was done is unknown. Land could be held privately and bought, sold and leased. Private granaries existed and loans could be secured on grain stocks. Grain prices were not fixed by the state despite its strong influence through the amount of production it controlled. (There is plenty of evidence of grain prices rising ten-fold in times of famine despite the stockpiles held by the state.) Many peasants were only on the fringe of trading activity – that remained true of most societies for many millennia. But there is plenty of evidence for barter and trade in a wide variety of products at village level. One papyrus records the purchase of an ox for a jar of fat, two tunics, some scraps of copper and bronze and some vegetable oil. What is important is that this odd mixture of items is taken as equivalent to fifty units of copper and the receipt was issued in terms of silver – which demonstrates the existence of a unit of account with similar functions to money. Indeed there appears to have been a considerable amount of silver in circulation in the economy. Trade up and down the Nile was extensive and there is no evidence that foreign trade was a state monopoly, although the status of merchants was not particularly high.

7.5 The Incorporation of the Aegean

7.5.1 *Crete and Mycenae*

Until about 2000 BCE 'civilization' in the western part of Eurasia was confined to the mainland of south-west Asia in an area stretching from Anatolia and Mesopotamia to Egypt. In the second millennium BCE it spread to the islands of the Aegean, in particular Crete, and eventually to the southern part of mainland Greece at sites such as Mycenae. The problem in dealing with the early history of the Aegean is two-fold. The first is the western obsession with the world of ancient Greece and the 'classics', together with the insistence on treating them as a separate area for study. The societies of the second millennium BCE in the Aegean therefore tend to be interpreted as the forerunners of the world of classical Athens almost a thousand years later rather than being assessed in their own right and as small offshoots of the dominant south-west Asian societies. In particular the role of the Homerian epics in classical studies has led to endless attempts to identify the Mycenaean world with that of the *Iliad* and the *Odyssey*. The second problem is that there is no exact way of dating events in the Aegean at this time. It depends on the correlation of a series of pottery styles which can occasionally be roughly synchronized with Egypt. No dates can therefore be accurate by more than about a century either way.

All of the societies of the Aegean were relatively small-scale and lacked most of the infrastructure found in Egypt and Mesopotamia. Settlements were mainly farming communities, the population of whole regions was probably no more than a few thousand and only a small number of towns had large public areas and some evidence of planning. The number of specialists that could be maintained was much smaller than on the mainland. All of the major advances – the domestication of plants and animals, craft techniques, the use of seals, the development of writing – began on the mainland of Eurasia and drifted westward to the islands. The islands of the Aegean were also under the influence of south-west Asia long before the mainland of Greece. Egyptian influence in the area – largely through trade – was strong. There is little doubt that the Egyptian *Kftiw* is Crete which is shown as paying tribute in the 1470s BCE as the New Kingdom rose to its full power and influence. On the mainland Egypt was trading with the Laurian silver and lead mines near Athens from as early as 1900 BCE and the trade was at its peak about 1400 BCE. It is quite possible that there was Egyptian colonization in this area as there was in the Levant. The Egyptian name for the mainland of Greece can be read as *Tanaya* which is very close to Homer's name *Danaoi*. The common root of these words is *tni* which means 'old' or 'decrepit'. This is clearly linked to Danaos – the person the Greeks believed colonized Argos from Egypt (as in the play by Aeschylus) and who is always shown as being old and decrepit.

It seems likely that from about 2000 BCE the elite on Crete were using their contacts with south-west Asia, in particular Egypt, to enhance their status and create small states centred around Knossos, Phaistos and Mallia. There was competition between these 'mini-states' and a number of guardhouses were built along the roads. At some point many of these early sites were destroyed, possibly in a war won by Knossos which became the dominant settlement on the island. Ever since the excavation of the elaborate site in the early twentieth century by Sir Arthur Evans it has been associated with the ruling kings of Crete and the use of the term 'Palace of Minos' is another example of the influence of classical Greece which may not be warranted. In practice there is very little evidence that the so-called 'palaces' on Crete were residential buildings. There is a complete lack of evidence of a ruling family or king, no characteristic depictions of the ruler in either a military or religious role, no inscriptions glorifying their life and deeds and no tombs or burial buildings. The wall paintings on the buildings, particularly at Knossos, appear to depict various symbolic, religious and ceremonial activities such as the bull-cult (probably derived from Egypt). They lack any depiction of the military or weapons. All of these factors suggest that the buildings formed ceremonial centres for various functions carried out by the elite. In the period after about 1600 BCE the influence of Crete was apparent across the Aegean and on the mainland of Greece but it seems unlikely that there was any political control apart perhaps from the site of Kastri on Kythera, which may have been a colony.

Until the last few years it was thought that the sites on Crete were destroyed following a giant earthquake and eruption (both far greater than that of Krakatoa in the late nineteenth century) on the Cycladean island of Thera in about 1450 BCE. This catastrophe was followed by the conquest of the island by groups from the Greek mainland. Work on ice cores taken from the Greenland ice cap has shown that the eruption in fact took place about 1640–1630 BCE, at least two centuries before the occupation and destruction of the palaces. Although the eruption must have caused considerable problems for Cretan society and the elite they did survive and flourish for about another two centuries before being taken over by Mycenaean groups from the mainland.

The development of these small states on the mainland occurred much later than on Crete and their nature was very different and much closer to some of the early states of south-west Asia. However, this too was a small-scale society – even the major site of Tiryns covered less than twenty acres. The palaces at sites such as Mycenae, Tiryns and Pylos do, however, appear to have been the residences of a ruling military elite with a very small bureaucracy capable of organizing military units and a ration system. The palaces were built on rocky outcrops and surrounded with defensive walls. The rulers were commemorated in elaborate burials in great family vaults. Their prestige came from their success in the small-scale warfare between the petty states of the Greek mainland. Mycenaean groups appear to have conquered Crete about 1450 BCE (there is some evidence in Egyptian sources to support this date). From this time until about 1200 BCE the Mycenaean world was at its peak and part of a much wider trading network across the eastern Mediterranean and south-west Asia. Although Mycenaean culture was fairly uniform across the Aegean and the mainland there is no evidence of any political unity.
[*Later Greece* **8.9**]

7.5.2 Scripts and language
[*Early scripts* **4.8**]
Some further deductions about the world of Crete and Mycenae can be made from their early scripts. On Crete a primitive hieroglyphic was replaced about 1800 BCE by a script known as Linear A. The system was developed locally and the small number of signs suggests that the script

was mainly syllabic but with pictograms for livestock and commodities. It is mainly found on sun-dried clay tablets (in Mesopotamia they were baked), on seals and from a few inscriptions on pots. Only a few words of Linear A can be understood and so the language used by the early inhabitants of Crete remains unknown. One fact though is certain – Linear A is not in any form of Greek; it is more likely that it is written in a Semitic language similar to those of south-west Asia. Linear A lasted until the Mycenaean conquest of Crete. The new rulers then asked the local scribes to modify Linear A so that it would be suitable for their language. At Knossos they produced a script known as Linear B which was then taken back to the mainland and used there. Linear B was deciphered in the 1950s and was discovered to be a very early form of Greek. The origins of the Greek language are complex. It is clearly Indo-European both in form and in much of its vocabulary but there are also non-Indo-European elements in it – words such as *Korinthos* and *Athanai* and *Mukanai* (Mycenae) are derived from an unknown language previously spoken in Greece. Some experts have argued that as many as a third of 'Greek' words may have a Semitic origin. All but a handful of the Linear B texts are purely administrative, dealing with the operation of the court of the ruler, the military and the associated ration system. There is no trace of its use for inscriptions or offerings and no long texts. Indeed Linear B could only work on short administrative texts – anything longer would produce too many alternative readings and because the signs used are derived from Linear A they are not well adapted to the Greek language. Literacy was clearly restricted to a handful of scribes in the ruler's palace and indeed the early form of Greek used may not have been widely spoken in the Mycenaean world. Linear B was not used after the destruction of all the Mycenaean palaces and states about 1150 BCE. When Greece became literate again several hundred years later it used a completely different alphabetic script derived from that used in the Levant. The relationship of the 'proto-Greek' of Linear B to the very clear regional dialects of classical Greece is also completely unclear.

Linear B does give some insight into Mycenaean society with its ruling kings (*wanax*), their palaces (*wanaktoron*), their retainers and the importance of warfare. But how close is it to the world described in Homer? The two epic poems are believed to have been composed about 700 BCE (probably about 500 years after the fall of Mycenae), possibly by two people. The oldest known text is much later (the third century BCE) and is in modernized Ionian-dialect Greek. Some of the details in Homer may be derived from the Mycenaean world, for example the wearing of a helmet covered in plates cut from boars' tusks. The city of Troy (level VIIA) was destroyed about 1250 BCE and although this is often associated

with the 'Trojan war' of the *Iliad* it may be no more than an episode in the widespread destruction across south-west Asia at this time. There is also much in Homer that does not fit the Mycenaean world. Homer's heroes were cremated whereas the Mycenaean rulers were buried in great family vaults. The main titles of the rulers known from Linear B – *hequetas*, *telestas* and *lawagetas* – are all absent in Homer (though the latter would not have scanned). Homer also seems to know little of the geography of western Greece which was the centre of the Mycenaean world. Overall it is clear that Linear B illustrates a very different world from that of Homer and the latter is largely a powerful myth embroidered with a few facts transmitted over the generations from a long lost world.
[*Later Greek alphabet* 8.9.1]

7.5.3 Cyprus

A central part of the eastern Mediterranean world in the second millennium BCE was the island of Cyprus. It was known as the kingdom of *Alashiya* and is mentioned in a wide variety of sources – cuneiform texts, Egyptian and in Linear B. Its wealth and development were based upon its copper resources which were vital for the production of bronze across the whole of south-west Asia and the Aegean. From about 1700 BCE society on the island changed from being one of agricultural villages to one of towns, monumental architecture and a script (based on the Linear A of Crete) for administrative control as trade and growing wealth were used by the elite to create a kingdom. Across the island there have been extensive archaeological finds of copper slag, fragments of furnaces, crucibles and port facilities for the export trade. Most of the copper was exported in a fleet of boats to the great trading cities of the Levant – Ugarit, Byblos, Beirut and Tyre. Copper ingots from Cyprus were used as a standard unit of currency across the Aegean and south-west Asia. Their shape forms the Linear B ideogram for 'ingot' and it also seems to have been the basis for the standardized weights used at both Knossos and the mainland Mycenaean site of Pylos. The rulers of Cyprus saw themselves as the equals of the kings of Egypt and the Hittites but were able to stay neutral in their imperial contest because both sides needed their copper.

7.6 Trade

[*Early trade in Mesopotamia* 4.3.1]
Cyprus flourished as part of a wider trading network that linked the various states and empires of south-west Asia and the Aegean. The main commodities traded were metals and textiles, rare agricultural products

such as oils, spices and aromatics, together with a more limited trade in bulk items such as wool and grain. The main trading centres were the wealthy cities of the Levant coast, Assur on the Tigris in northern Mesopotamia and the cities in southern Mesopotamia which dominated the Gulf trade. Transport by sea was far easier than by land and involved far greater quantities of goods. A letter from the city of Mari, dated to about 1800 BCE, refers to two ships each carrying 1,600 gallons of wine and others carried millstones and bitumen. The recent discovery of a shipwreck off the coast of Turkey shows that the vessel was carrying a complex mix of cargo originating in Egypt, Mesopotamia, the Levant, Cyprus, the Aegean and the European mainland. But there is also plenty of evidence for a substantial and well-organized trade by land involving caravan routes. The earliest caravanserais date to about 2000 BCE when donkeys hauled wagon loads of juniper wood from northern Syria to southern Mesopotamia, suggesting that there were some primitive 'roads'. Although transport costs would have been high by modern standards they clearly were not prohibitive.

The key metal, copper, came from Oman and eastern Anatolia and then from about the middle of the second millennium BCE from Cyprus. The trade from Oman up the Gulf seems to have involved shiploads of about eighteen tons a year and that from Anatolia about a sixth of that amount in the annual caravans. The trade from Cyprus dwarfed both of these suppliers. Egypt traded directly with Cyprus which it knew as part of 'the islands in the midst of the sea'. Tin, the other essential component of bronze, came mainly from surface deposits in Afghanistan by a long overland route across Iran and through Assur in the north and Susa in the south. Central Anatolia was the main source of silver – about a quarter of a ton a year was sent to Mesopotamia – and most gold came from Nubia via Egypt. In order to pay for the metals southern Mesopotamia specialized in high-quality textile production which was exported down the Gulf but also overland to Anatolia. Grain was sent down the Gulf and there was also an extensive trade along the rivers of Mesopotamia and Egypt. Later in the second millennium Mycenaean pottery was traded over a wide area – it has been found in the Cyclades, Dodecanese, Sicily, Cyprus, Malta, eastern Spain as well as at Carchemish and most of the cities of south-west Asia.

How was this trade organized? In answering this question we are lucky that the archives of the merchants trading between Assur in northern Mesopotamia and the central Anatolian city of Kanesh have been discovered. They show a surprisingly 'modern' type of trade. Assur was a small city of about 10,000 people and was a transit centre for international trade – it does not seem to have manufactured anything of significance itself. Trade was in the hands not of the palace or temple but instead was organized by a community of merchants known as the 'harbour'. The main trade was tin (from Afghanistan) and textiles (from southern Mesopotamia) to Anatolia in return for silver and occasionally gold. The tin was obtained through intermediaries in Iran but Assur maintained a trading colony in the southern Mesopotamian city of Sippar to buy textiles. In Kanesh the Assur traders lived in a separate area below the main citadel. (However, without the discovery of the letters it would not have been suspected from the archaeological evidence alone that this was a foreign trading colony, which suggests that trade elsewhere may have been far more extensive than previously thought.) There was clearly a well-organized and reliable trade between the two colonies that was substantial enough for the merchants to maintain a permanent colony over 700 miles from Assur. Large caravans of donkeys transported the goods under a clear set of rules. Taxes were paid at Assur and Kanesh, the Assur merchants were banned from trading in local Anatolian textiles but in return were granted a monopoly of certain luxury items. The trade was organized mainly by family firms who kept family members in the main trading cities. The firms were well aware of fluctuating prices and acceptable profit margins and the letters give instructions on what quantity of goods could be sold at certain prices and the profit levels required. The letters also illustrate how the merchants set up partnerships, invested large amounts of capital (in gold) in their various ventures and how debts could be adjusted in both Assur and Kanesh. Clearly many of the features that characterize later, more sophisticated, trading networks had already evolved.

7.7 The Eurasian Periphery – Europe

[*Earlier Europe* 3.3.1]
Most of mainland Europe was peripheral to the far more advanced south-west Asian and Aegean world. It traded a few highly specialized products such as amber but the overall impact of the early empires and states was minimal. It is also clear that Europe in the second millennium BCE showed a very high level of continuity with the early farming communities which had evolved over the previous couple of millennia. This is particularly true of the so-called 'Kurgan' or 'pit-grave' culture and its associated 'corded ware' pottery and, to a lesser extent, its successor the 'bell beaker' culture. These have often been interpreted as marking waves of Indo-European-speaking nomadic groups sweeping across Europe from the steppes of Russia and the Ukraine and displacing the original farming inhabitants. Most archaeologists would now see these changes as modifications and

intensifications of existing cultures among a largely stable population. The 'pit-grave' culture is distinguished by burials in a grave pit under a mound of earth with a standardized set of grave goods in which the body was dismembered before burial and the grave was oriented to face either east or south. The body was then sprinkled with red ochre. This can best be seen as the spread of a new form of religious belief across Europe which displaced earlier beliefs involving the construction of large communal ceremonial centres.

At this time communities across Europe were very small and isolated. Most villages covered no more than a couple of acres of huts with a population of about a hundred. There were a few hill forts but no areas of specialized production apart from the small number of copper mines. The development of bronze working was slow – communities in the Balkans may have been using copper as early as 5000 BCE (earlier than Mesopotamia) – but although copper deposits were widespread outside northern Europe, tin was only found in a few areas along the Atlantic coast, Bohemia and northern Italy. Even when bronze was adopted in central and southern Europe, Britain and the north were still using only copper. Materials were exchanged over long distances by the early farming peoples and the development of trade and exchange in bronze was no more than an intensification of this process. Between about 2000 and 1500 BCE the population across Europe appears to have risen steadily, probably linked to the use of a heavier plough pulled by horses, which opened up the cultivation of heavier soils in the valleys. In this period the main centre of bronze production was in the Carpathian mountains with its distinguishing 'Otomani' culture which also spread to Moravia and Bohemia. It was characterized by fortified, stone-walled settlements set on hills and provided the main link between the Aegean world and Europe. The increase in bronze production and higher levels of exchange seems to have speeded up social changes caused by the rising population and the expansion of settlements. Equally important was control over other key resources such as salt and the trade in the very small range of high-status items.

Small-scale chiefs and more militarized elites were slowly emerging. Society gradually became more hierarchical and some settlements became more important centres than others. Bronze was increasingly turned into weapons, especially daggers, and warfare between villages was probably common given the number of weapons recovered from the graves of this period. Some of the other changes of the period, previously thought to mark the movement of new peoples, stem from these changes. The warrior elite, who had a few horses, developed their own rituals particularly built around the consumption of alcohol. The 'bell beakers' of western Europe

(where 'corded ware' is unknown) appear to be special vessels associated with these exclusively male rituals. The elite also slowly increased their exploitation of the majority of the population and appropriated the small agricultural surplus they created. Nevertheless the overall level of political organization across Europe was very low. There was little above that of villages and petty chiefs though there was probably the occasional alliance of villages in warfare.
[*Later Europe* 8.12]

7.8 Early China: the Shang

[*Early Chinese agriculture* 3.4]
The process by which the early agricultural villages and communities of the central plain of China around the Wei and Yellow rivers evolved into a complex civilization are largely unknown. There are no written records, as in Mesopotamia, and little archaeological work has been undertaken. About 1800 BCE an almost fully-fledged complex culture and civilization known as the Shang can be identified. Its nature suggests that the process of evolution over the previous millennium or so was remarkably similar to that elsewhere in the world – growing appropriation of the agricultural surplus by an increasingly powerful religious, military and political elite that was capable of mobilizing and directing the rest of society. The emergence of the Shang was part of this long evolution and is marked by a much more complex and dominant elite culture in which bronze working was central. Although these developments took place nearly a thousand years later than in Mesopotamia and Egypt there is little doubt that they were indigenous – there is no trace of any significant external influence. Indeed the technique of bronze working that evolved in China – piece-moulding – was unknown elsewhere in the world. Developments under the Shang, in culture, writing and institutions were the foundations for the later development of the highly distinctive Chinese civilization. The Shang lasted nearly all of the second millennium – they were overthrown in either 1122 or 1027 BCE (both dates have evidence to support them).

7.8.1 Shang society and state
Nearly all of our information about the Shang comes from the site of An-yang which was discovered in 1928. It appears to have been the Shang capital for the first five centuries or so. It is not a city in the conventional sense of the term and was more like a large ceremonial centre. It covered an area over two miles long and a mile wide along the Huan river and contained a series of sites with palaces, temples, graves and residential

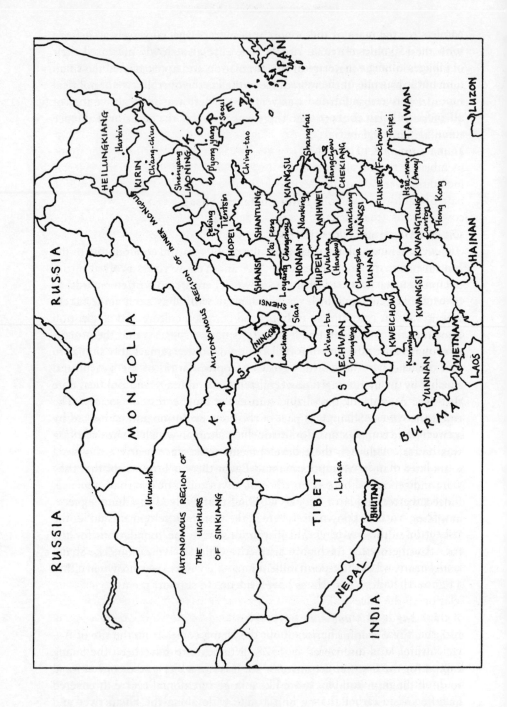

Map 16: China: regions

hamlets for the mass of the population. Over a very wide area stretching for some 150 miles north and south of An-yang was a dependent territory of villages. Shang was certainly not the only 'state' in central China at this time but it was one of the most important. There are references at various times to between eight and thirty-three other states linked by marriage alliances and clan connections. The power of the elite can be judged from some of the royal burials at An-yang containing sacrificial humans and animals. In one of the shaft tombs discovered in 1976 a second-rank member of the royal family was buried with some 400 bronze objects, including over 200 of the highly distinctive ritual drinking vessels and a pair of cauldrons weighing over 300 pounds each, together with 7,000 cowrie shells (the currency unit, brought over long distances from the southern coast) and over 600 rare jade objects. In their religious rituals the elite were at times able to slaughter over 1,000 cattle, although 100–500 at a time were more common.

The organization of the Shang state was a complex mix of clan and other elements. The ruling clan was the Tzu but not all of its members could be king – that was restricted to a royal lineage within the clan. How this was constituted is not clear and the exact ancestry and line of descent is unknown but remote ancestors (real and mythological) were the centre of clan rituals. There were clear rules of succession within the royal lineage which was divided into ten unequal groups (*kan*) for ritual and marriage purposes. A new king could not be from the same *kan* as his predecessor and if there was a change of generation then the succession had to move between the two 'supergroups' into which the ten *kan* were divided. The king had a council to advise him, the most important member of which was a head of a *kan* group from the other supergroup. Successions appear to have been agreed on some occasions, disputed and bloody on others.

All members of the royal clan had religious and administrative functions within the capital and they were central to the Shang institution of the city or *yi*. These were deliberate, planned creations and not natural growths. At the head of each would be a member of the royal family from whom the town took its name. Tablets were set up in the ceremonial hall of the town which set out the position of its head in relation to the ancestral clan and the royal lineage. It is likely that some of these heads of cities may have been local rulers who were co-opted into the royal clan. The head of the city controlled the surrounding agricultural land and owed food and services to the king. How far the king at An-yang was able to control these local rulers is unclear and was, no doubt, highly variable. Indeed it is far from clear that Shang was ever a unified state rather than a loose confederation owing allegiance to a king to whom the other rulers were related either actually or nominally.

The names of over 800 cities are known but their locations and the territories they ruled cannot be identified. The cities were often at war with each other. The mass of the population were organized into units of 100 households known as *tsu*. They had a primarily military function and had to provide 100 soldiers when required – the permanent army only called on some of the *tsu*. Exactly how the *tsu* were constituted is not clear but they were not different clans and they appear to have had very different levels of status.

The Shang ruler combined both secular and religious functions and it was the latter that legitimized the state. The high god *Ti* provided the two elements essential to society and the state – the harvest and military victory. The king's ancestors were able to intercede with him and therefore their worship was essential. Their will was given to the king through divination. As in the pre-Shang period cracks in heated animal bones were used for divination (the societies of south-west Asia usually interpreted the entrails of animals) and the diviners who carried out these functions were some of the most important state officials. What was new in the Shang period was that a question was inscribed on the bone – they were usually about military campaigns, omens for hunting and tribute from subordinate rulers. These bones are the main source for our knowledge about the Shang state.

7.8.2 The Chinese script
[*Early writing in south-west Asia* 4.8]
The questions inscribed on the divination bones provide the first examples of both the Chinese numerical system and the mature Chinese script. The Chinese numerical system was always decimal with signs for one to ten and for one hundred (one for ten thousand was added later). By 1300 BCE at the latest they had also developed a place value system. The Shang bones already show the early Chinese script as fully developed but its evolution over the previous three millennia or so since the primitive forms found on pottery dating to about 5000 BCE cannot be traced because no materials survive. The Chinese script is one of the three completely original scripts in the world – the others being Mesopotamian cuneiform and the Mayan. (Those of Egypt and the Indus valley are probably original but may have been influenced by Mesopotamia.) The Chinese script is, of course, highly adapted to the nature of the Chinese language which is positional – the function of words is determined by their position in a sentence and not as in other languages (especially the Indo-European group) by grammar. Chinese is mainly monosyllabic and because the number of syllables is limited there are a lot of homophones – words having the same pronunciation but different meanings and with different characters in the script.

The Chinese script is based on meaning – each sign is a semantic unit and is not related to pronunciation, as in other scripts. The signs in the Chinese script can be divided into six types. The most basic are the 600 or so that are pictures of objects. The second category is the very limited number of symbolic pictures – a half-moon means evening. The third group is the symbolic compounds in which, for example, the sign for child repeated twice means twins. The fourth category – of inversions – is rare: an example is the child sign upside down to mean childbirth. The fifth category is borrowings and the last is now one of the most important – the sound-indicating signs developed from about the second century BCE. The Chinese script is highly sophisticated and flexible in that combinations of signs (and about 90 per cent of signs are now compounds) can be made to create an almost endless number of new words. The internal structure of the signs has remained constant over the past four millennia although their appearance has changed with the development of new types of writing materials. Chinese is also the only script in the world where the number of signs has increased over time rather than decreased. During the Shang period there were about 2,500 signs, about 100 CE this had risen to just over 9,000, an eleventh-century encyclopedia contains about 24,000 and modern Chinese has around 70,000 characters, although only a few thousand are in common use.

To many westerners the Chinese script, with its multitude of signs, is, compared with an alphabet, an obvious 'failure' – difficult both to learn and write. However, it had one huge advantage over west Eurasian writing systems which profoundly affected Chinese history. The Chinese script was not linked to language and remained unaffected by phonetic changes, dialect variations, different pronunciations and even different linguistic structures. The standardized script imposed under the first unified Chinese state (the Ch'in, shortly before 200 BCE) played a major role in that unification – it enabled people to communicate even though their languages were mutually unintelligible. The indifference of the Chinese script to phonetic change and the evolution of language allowed a massive continuity in culture and knowledge – classical texts dating back to the second century BCE can be read perfectly easily even though it is not known exactly how the language was spoken at that time. China therefore avoided the complex changes that occurred in the Mediterranean and European worlds making, for example, Greek and Latin, the modern Romance languages and English and German mutually unintelligible. It made possible a vast accumulation of knowledge and tradition that was often 'lost' in Europe as languages changed.

[*Later China* 8.2]
[*Derivative Japanese script* 11.7.1]

7.9 Collapse: *c*.1200 BCE

In either 1122 or 1027 BCE the Shang were overthrown by the Chou. This was largely a political event – although the royal administrative records of the Shang were destroyed there was a high degree of economic, social and cultural continuity. Given the relative isolation of China from the west Eurasian world at this time, the fall of the Shang was probably no more than coincidental to the much wider and deeper collapse of states in south-west Asia and the Aegean. The latter event was of far greater significance than the more widely known 'fall' of the western Roman empire around 400 CE. Over a period of forty or fifty years, about 1200 BCE, almost every significant city and palace in the eastern Mediterranean was destroyed and many were never reoccupied. Despite the efforts of some recent archaeologists to rework accepted chronologies, it seems clear that for at least two centuries after 1200 BCE there was a 'Dark Age' across south-west Asia and the Aegean from which almost no records survive, making it impossible to write any coherent history. When, early in the first millennium BCE, the various states and societies began to emerge from this dark age very significant changes had taken place.

In Anatolia every known site has a destruction level dated to about 1200 BCE. The internal problems of the Hittite empire increased markedly after about 1215 BCE, there was external pressure from the developing Assyrian empire to the east and control was lost over most of the territories in western Anatolia. Eventually the capital Hattusa was plundered and burned and with it the Hittite empire disappeared. At Troy on the western coast of Anatolia there are two destruction levels dated to about 1250 BCE and 1190–1180 BCE. On Cyprus the three major cities of Enkomi, Kition and Sinda were sacked, probably twice each. In Syria the trading city of Ugarit was destroyed by fire and not reoccupied. When it was burnt several hundred clay tablets were being baked in an oven and they survived. They record messages to the 'king' asking for 150 ships to be sent as the area was defenceless, troops and ships were in Anatolia and an unnamed 'enemy' was attacking from the sea. In the Levant all the major cities along the route from Syria to Egypt – Ashdod, Ashkelon and Megiddo – were all destroyed. Across mainland Greece and the Aegean every Mycenaean palace was destroyed and nearly all traces of the culture were lost. Although the Cyclades seem to have avoided the worst of the destruction, on Crete it was particularly heavy. The population shifted to highly inaccessible areas in the mountains, such as the site of Karphi over 1,300 feet above the Lasithi plain which itself is nearly 3,000 feet above sea level.

In Mesopotamia there are few signs of destruction but it was clearly a time of major political instability following the end of the Kassite empire after the double invasion by Assyria from the north and Elam from the east. Subsequently none of the small-scale political groupings in the area was able to establish control, and, in the north, although Assyria survived as a state its power was minimal. In Egypt internal problems, especially prolonged struggles over the succession, developed rapidly after the death of Rameses II in 1224 BCE. There appears to have been a gap of some fourteen years between the last Pharaoh of the Nineteenth Dynasty and the accession of Setnakht in 1186 as the first of the Twentieth Dynasty. Egypt's power waned rapidly and control over the Levant was lost around 1135 BCE. Within another decade internal unity had collapsed and at least two separate kingdoms emerged with their capitals at Thebes and at Tanis. The Twentieth Dynasty ended in about 1070 BCE and during the following Third Intermediate period, which lasted until 712 BCE, Egypt was a patchwork of small states before being reunited by an external Sudanese dynasty.

Numerous attempts have been made to explain this widespread upheaval and collapse. Climatic, and therefore agricultural, disruption caused by the major eruption of the Hekla volcano in Iceland in 1159 BCE, which was noticed as far away as China, may have contributed to the problems but cannot have been a primary cause because much of the destruction occurred earlier. There is no doubt that these early empires and states were very fragile structures – deeply divided internally between the elite and the mass of peasants and with little state infrastructure to bind society and the state together. But this had been true for centuries and it is difficult to see why so many should have collapsed over so wide an area and so quickly at this particular time. One of the most widely accepted explanations is of a wave of 'semi-barbarians' known as the 'Sea Peoples' descending on the civilized world. This is another example of the continued domination of late-nineteenth-century ideas emphasizing the importance of migration. In this case it was linked to the 'Dorian invasion' of Greece (to give 'classical' Greece an 'Aryan' foundation) – which, on more detailed examination, has turned out to be a highly doubtful event. The idea that there was even a group called the 'Sea Peoples' is based solely on Egyptian evidence and two inscriptions which have been misinterpreted. They do no more than record battles against the Syrians and their accompanying mercenary contingents from around the Mediterranean world, rather than invasions of groups of Mediterranean 'Sea Peoples' acting on their own.

The most likely explanation of the widespread collapse is a series of fundamental changes in the nature of warfare. All of the states and empires of south-west Asia and the Aegean between 2000 BCE and about 1200 BCE (as well as the Shang in China) depended on the chariot as their main weapon. The chariot was a major technological triumph of the period around 2000 BCE and was developed somewhere in south-west Asia (the Chinese development was separate) and not, as used to be thought, by an external 'barbarian' group. Solid-wheeled carts and wagons pulled by oxen and onagers were developed by about 3000 BCE and some may have been used as prestige items to transport kings and war-leaders to battle – but they were not fighting weapons. The development of the chariot depended on a number of innovations. The domestication of the horse definitely occurred outside the settled civilizations but it is not known where the bridle with bit to control the horse was developed. The lightweight chariot required a light chassis, a leather-mesh platform and the development of heat-bent, spoked wheels which were about ten per cent of the weight of solid wheels. The hub, felloe and spokes were made of three different types of wood, usually elm, oak and ash. The axle was originally centred under the platform but about 1300 BCE was moved to the trailing edge of the platform to give a more balanced ride. Originally there were about four spokes on a wheel but by 1300 BCE in south-west Asia this was increased to six, and three hundred years later in China up to eighteen spokes were being used. About 1700 BCE the chariot was combined with archers using the composite bow (made from wood, horn and sinew and taking several years to construct) which was developed in Anatolia.

The two-man (driver and archer) chariot became the principal weapon of war in south-west Asia and China from about 1700 BCE. The archer could fire almost with impunity at the spear-carrying infantry whose role was reduced to siege warfare and protecting the chariots while they were on the march, in camp and being deployed in long lines before battle. The infantry would accompany the chariots to kill off the wounded. At first only a few chariots (perhaps about 100) were used but, as the number of horses available rose and the chariots' effectiveness as weapons was demonstrated, the early empires increased their numbers. The cost of doing so was large for these early states. The crew needed armour (horse armour was used occasionally) and the amount of land that had to be devoted to growing food for the horses was substantial. A major task for the growing palace bureaucracies was to keep track of these elite units and their provisioning. Numbers grew rapidly in the largest empires – at the battle of Kadesh in 1285 BCE between Egypt and the Hittites each side probably deployed about 3,000 chariots and the infantry were hardly engaged in the battle. The smaller kingdoms such as those of the Mycenaean world could not support more than a few hundred chariots.

About 1200 BCE the early empires which relied on the chariot seem to have had to cope with very rapid changes in the nature of warfare stemming from a number of sources. Infantry acquired better armour in the form of waist-length corselets, leather skirts and the marginally useful bronze greaves. Most important of all was the development of the round shield with integral hand-grip which was vital for hand-to-hand fighting. These changes were combined with two new weapons. First, a short (about three feet long) javelin which was derived from hunting weapons but was very effective against horses. Second, a new type of sword. Until about 1200 BCE swords had sickle-shaped blades suitable for slashing. About 1450 BCE in central Europe 'Naue Type II' was developed (though it took more than a century to reach south-west Asia)– it was long and parallel-bladed with the hilt and blade cast as a single piece. It was therefore strong enough to slash without bending or breaking and could also be used for cut and thrust. All of these changes revolutionized warfare by turning the infantry into an effective weapon that could dominate the chariot. Within a couple of centuries the effective role of the chariot was over and it was reduced once again to a taxi-function of carrying the ruler and a few other members of the elite to battle. In the period around 1200 BCE it seems that the states of south-west Asia and the Aegean were unable to adapt their style of warfare quickly enough. They were defeated by a multitude of different groups from the fringes of the civilized world who had a temporary technological advantage. When the clouds of the 'Dark Age' lifted, in the early first millennium BCE the armies of the new states and empires were dominated by infantry using long swords and round shields. [*Later south-west Asia 8.6*]

8

Expansion
(1000–200 BCE)

Eurasia in the period between 1000 BCE and 200 BCE was characterised by a number of important changes. First, the development and spread of iron making, initially in south-west Asia and then in China using a much more advanced process. Second, by the end of the period a unified state, the largest in the world, had been created in China. Third, the first empire controlling much of India had risen to a peak and declined. Fourth, until 539 BCE south-west Asia was dominated by the Assyrian empire, almost the last empire to be centred on Mesopotamia, the area where civilization had first emerged. It was replaced briefly by a Babylonian empire and then by the first of a series of Iranian empires (the Achaemenid) which was the first to link together the area between the Mediterranean and the far east of Iran. It was defeated by the very short-lived Macedonian empire of Alexander in 330 BCE. Within little more than a decade his empire had divided into three major kingdoms which contested the supremacy of south-west Asia for the next century. Finally, from the beginning of the first millennium BCE the influence of the south-west Asian civilizations also spread westwards across the Mediterranean to incorporate new areas beyond the Aegean. The process began with the Phoenician trading cities and was followed by an expansion from the Greek cities. By the seventh century the Etruscan cities in central Italy developed and they were followed by the city of Rome. The latter slowly established its control over the Italian peninsula and by the end of the period had defeated the former Phoenician colony of Carthage and dominated most of the western Mediterranean. Further north the pace of change in north-west and central Europe was increasing as it came into closer contact with the more advanced states to the south.

8.1 Iron

[*Early technology* **4.7**]
Until about 1000 BCE all Eurasian societies depended on copper and bronze as their main metals – gold and silver were kept for luxury items and occasionally as currencies. Copper and bronze had two main disadvantages – they were relatively soft and they were difficult to sharpen

to an effective cutting edge. The development of iron production was to have a significant impact on both farming and warfare by producing much harder tools and weapons. It is, however, difficult to understand the process by which iron was first made because the techniques involved were radically different from those used for copper and bronze smelting. In south-west Asia the furnaces used in bronze production were not hot enough to produce fluid iron. All that was produced when iron ore was heated was a spongy mass which had to be repeatedly heated and hammered when red hot to eventually produce wrought iron. This required new tools – tongs, anvil and hammer – as well as the development of techniques for forging, shaping and welding red-hot iron, and the ability to control conditions in the furnace.

8.1.1 Iron in south-west Asia and India
Not surprisingly the production of iron was on a very small scale for centuries. It was probably produced accidentally about 2000 BCE and was originally regarded as a precious metal. Techniques for major production were not fully developed for another thousand years. There does not appear to be any single centre where the use of iron was developed and the ideas and techniques involved diffused rapidly between the different societies. The wrought iron that was first produced on a major scale about 1000 BCE was tough and malleable and ideal for agricultural implements, wire, nails, horseshoes and weapons, especially swords. The first tools produced were knives but within a century or so the use of iron in agriculture was widespread – it greatly increased productivity by allowing much easier clearing of land with iron axes and the use of tougher ploughs and hoes. The use of iron also revolutionized other trades such as carpentry and stone working. From south-west Asia the use of iron spread slowly. It reached Egypt shortly after 700 BCE and about the same time the Balkans. In the rest of Europe iron came from the Phoenician traders in the western Mediterranean and there is little evidence of any indigenous production before about 500 BCE, probably because of the relatively low level of organization within society. Indeed the amount of iron used in western Europe did not approach the level of the Mediterranean area for another 1,500 years. From south-west Asia the production of iron also spread eastwards reaching northern India within about a century and the south about five hundred years later. By the third century CE Indian ironworks were making huge pillars almost twenty-five feet high and weighing over six tons. The technological level of the Indian industry was so high that some of its output was exported to the Mediterranean world. In one area the Indian industry was unique – the production of small amounts of crucible steel which was turned into high-quality sword blades

that were prized across Eurasia. The problem they solved was finding a container capable of surviving the very high temperatures involved – about 1400°C. About 300 BCE factories in India also discovered how to use zinc. This process remained unknown in Europe until after 1500 CE when the techniques involved were brought back from India by the Portuguese.

8.1.2 Technological stagnation

The development of iron technology was a major step in human history. However, across south-west Asia and the Mediterranean after about 1000 BCE the general pace of technological change was very slow. No new raw materials were used, no really novel production methods were developed. Instead all the societies of the area seem to have reached a technological plateau in which energy supplies remained limited and changes in techniques were either low-level and incremental or the application of existing techniques to new areas. Only a few new technologies were developed – glassblowing (which needed an iron blowtube) in the Levant and, in about 300 BCE, modifications to the potter's wheel which raised the working head so that the potter could sit and kick the wheel to rotate it, leaving both hands free to mould the clay. The one major advance was the first use of water-power. Water-mills developed somewhere in Greece or Anatolia in the first century BCE – the first reference is to one owned by Mithridates, the king of Pontus, in 65 BCE. The first mills were primitive – they were set horizontally and in the absence of gearing the grinding stone went round at the same speed as the wheel and a very fast stream was needed to enable it to operate. By about the fifth century CE gearing was in use together with the overshot wheel so that water could be kept back in a mill-pond thereby enabling the mill to operate for far longer. The mills were used for grinding wheat and extracting oil from olives.

[*Later technology in west Eurasia* 12.4]

8.1.3 Iron in China and technological advance

The most remarkable development of iron technology and use occurred in China. Some of the techniques involved here were far in advance of the rest of Eurasia and until at least 1800 CE China was the primary iron and steel producing centre in the world. Although the development of iron production in China began about 400 years later than in south-west Asia it was, from the start, based on a very different technology. Instead of producing wrought iron the Chinese moved straight to cast iron (which could be poured into moulds like bronze) almost 2,000 years before the first known European production, in about 1380 CE (and even then the techniques probably diffused from China). This was possible for a number of reasons. The Chinese used good-quality clay to build furnaces capable of sustaining the very high temperatures (at least 1130°C) needed. They also developed the double-action piston bellows for a very regular draught which removed much of the carbon which tended to make cast iron brittle. By the first centuries CE both the piston bellows and the trip hammer, which took the heavy work out of hammering iron, were adapted for water-power. (The first Chinese water-mills are contemporary with those of south-west Asia but only the Chinese adapted them for iron production.) As early as 250 BCE cast iron was being made on an industrial scale – in Szechwan some ironworks employed over a thousand workers and were even producing shaving razors. About 200 CE iron was being cast for statues, huge pillars and pagodas. By 600 CE it was used to make cables for suspension bridges over gaps of up to 300 feet. (Europe did not produce a similar suspension bridge for another 1,100 years – in 1741 the German engineer Fischer von Erlach constructed one based on the knowledge he gained during his visit to China in 1725.)

Because the Chinese had easy access to cast iron as well as wrought iron the production of steel was relatively straightforward. About 400 CE the technique of co-fusion – heating the two types of iron together so as to average their carbon content and produce steel – was developed. This was, in effect, the same principle as the Siemens-Martin open-hearth process finally developed by Europe in the mid-nineteenth century. It is therefore not surprising that as late as 1845 the American steel industry was using Chinese advisers to improve their production techniques. Unlike in south-west Asia and the Mediterranean, the Chinese avoided technological stagnation. The development of iron technology was only part of a more general process of development that was to make China the most advanced economy and society in the world. Almost as important as iron for China was the domestication of the silkworm and the development of a silk industry as early as the fourteenth century BCE. China alone among Eurasian societies had a textile fibre of very long staple (several hundred yards long) and did not have to rely on either flax or cotton with a staple of a few inches that had to be pulled out and spun together. Silk also had a tensile strength far beyond that of any plant fibre. The various techniques involved in silk production remained a closely guarded secret within China for about two thousand years. During this period China was the sole producer of the most prized product made in Eurasia, one that the elite in every society wanted. It was to form the basis of the first major Eurasian trading system.

[*Later technology in China* 12.3]

8.2 China: the Early Chou

[*Earlier China 7.8*]

Chinese tradition, which there is no reason to suppose is fundamentally wrong, was that the state of Chou in Shensi led by King Wu defeated the Shang at the battle of Mu-ye north of the Yellow river, executed the last Shang king (Chou-hsin) and established their own rule and capital at Chou-tsung near Sian in the Wei valley in Shensi. These events occurred in either 1122 or 1027 BCE and were the outcome of what was no more than just another war in a long series of conflicts between the petty states of the Shang period. Chinese tradition was right in seeing this as a significant change in two ways. First, it was the start of a very long process that was to lead, shortly before 200 BCE, to the creation of a single Chinese state. Second, it marked the beginning of a major expansion of Chinese influence outside the core area where the first Chinese cultures developed. From about 1000 BCE Chinese peasants were colonizing areas to the north around Peking, to the north-east in Shantung and also in the plains of the Lower Yangtze. Everywhere as the population grew steadily the number of settlements and towns increased significantly. The history of the Chou can best be divided into three periods. The first until 771 BCE is known as the Western Chou because of the location of the capital in Shensi. The second from 771 to the late fifth century BCE begins with the move of the capital to Ch'eng-chou (near the later capital of Loyang in Honan) and is often called the *Ch'un-Ch'iu* or 'Spring and Autumn period' after the title of the annals of the kingdom of Lu in Shantung. The third lasts until the unification of China under the Ch'in in 221 BCE and is known as the 'Warring States' period.

The exact nature of the Chou state is difficult to interpret. At its apex was the domain of Chou and the unification (as in the Shang) of military and religious functions in the ruler who was given the title of *T'ien-tzu* or 'son of heaven'. The Chou capital was the religious focus of the community and the centre for the veneration of the dead kings. It was an artificial creation laid out to a pre-determined plan in which the macrocosmos and the microcosmos were united in a complex symbolism that is still only partially understood. The city was a square with sides nine *li* long (just under 4,000 yards), each side had three gateways and nine avenues crossed the city in each direction. Each avenue was exactly nine chariot tracks in width. The ruler's palace was in the middle of the city and at its centre was a gnomon which cast no shadow at the summer solstice. As under the Shang each city was named after its ruler who was related in some way (real or artificial) to the Chou king. These families were granted political and religious power over an area called a *feng* from the word for the earth

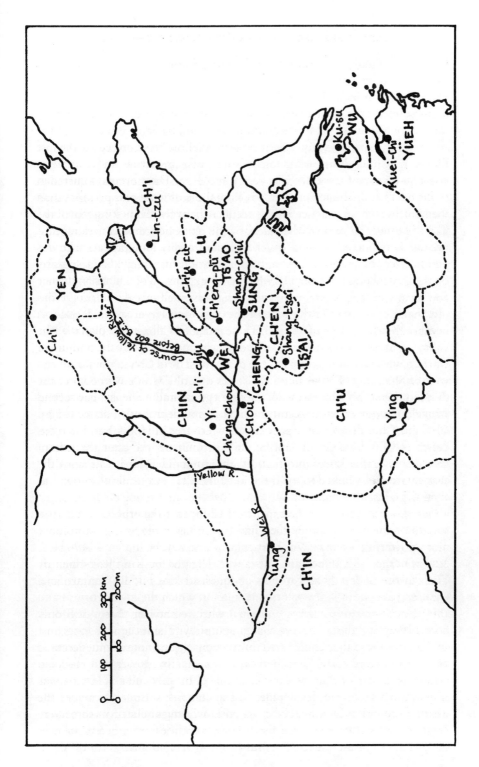

Map 17: China: The states of the 'Spring and Autumn' period (771–403 BCE)

banks which marked its borders. Each ruling family had a custom that the founding father of the city was always venerated and only the first-born son of the principal wife could succeed to both power and the responsibility of ancestor veneration. Secondary branches of the ruling family could only worship the last four generations of ancestors.

It is clear that there was considerable continuity between the Shang and the early Chou. Both were fairly primitive monarchies in which the effective power of the ruler was very limited. Despite nominal adherence to the overall supremacy of the Chou king the multitude of local states and their rulers were in practice independent. At first the Chou king may have had the power to remove the rulers of the cities but these offices rapidly became hereditary – a trend which became steadily more apparent in the period after about 750 BCE. About a dozen powerful principalities emerged on the central plain of China of which Cheng, Sung, Wei, Lu, Ts'ao, Ch'en and Ts'ai were the most important. (Sung was ruled by descendants of the old Shang dynasty.) On the edge of the area even larger states developed because they had room to expand. These included Chin, centred on the Fen valley in Shansi, which increased its power through almost continuous warfare with nomadic groups to the north-west, and Ch'i in the far north-west of Shantung. To the south the rulers of Ch'u, who governed an area that did not speak Chinese, took the title of king and were also part of the struggle for power within central China. Confederations of states led by Ch'i and Chin developed – at first they were free alliances but, after the defeat of Chin by King Chuang of Ch'u in 597 BCE, the stronger powers forced the weaker states into their alliance systems. Further to the south-east, in areas less linked to the original Chinese traditions developed in the central plains, the states of Wu and Yüeh became more powerful after about 600 BCE, mainly at the expense of Ch'u. Like the other states on the fringes of the central valley they had the ability to expand and become more powerful. At first Wu, particularly under King Fu-ch'a (496–473 BCE) was the most important but it was defeated by King Kou-chien of Yüeh in the 460s BCE and lost its conquests in the middle Yangtze and Shantung areas.

Under the strain of almost continual warfare between these kingdoms both society and the state were changing rapidly. The successful states and rulers were those that could move away from the old loose confederation of the Shang and early Chou periods and centralize power and mobilize resources within the areas they controlled. In particular rulers gained resources through the development of agrarian taxation systems which were first found in Lu in the 590s BCE and in Cheng about fifty years later. From the 550s BCE rulers were also issuing law-codes (inscribed on bronze tablets) to increase internal control. However, in many states these developments produced growing internal dissension as some of the major families resisted centralization. In the kingdom of Lu power was seized by three families – the Meng-sun, Shu-sun and Chi-sun. They deprived the ruler, who in theory still derived his legitimacy from the Chou king, of nearly all his power. In Ch'i the T'ien family went further and formally took power for itself. In Chin it was the army leaders who fought for power and eventually partitioned the kingdom into the new states of Han, Wei and Chao.

8.3 China: the Creation of a Centralized State

The partition of Chin in 403 BCE is usually taken as marking the start of the 'Warring States' period. It was an era of accelerating change in the economy, society and the state that culminated in the formation of the first unified Chinese state under the Ch'in in 221 BCE. The contest between the states had seven main participants. The three which emerged from the partition of Chin – Han, Wei and Chao, Ch'i (now governed by the T'ien family), Ch'in in Shensi, Ch'u in the valley of the middle Yangtze and the new kingdom of Yen in the north (the modern province of Hopei) with its capital near the site of Peking. The conflict between these states was shaped by a number of crucial developments. One of the most important was the decline of the military importance of the chariot which had been central to aristocratic power. It was replaced by infantry armies which were first developed by the southern states of Wu and Yüeh where the terrain was unsuitable for chariot warfare. This trend was reinforced by two other changes. First, the development of iron weapons, especially swords. Second, the development of the mounted archer, a technique adopted from the nomads of the steppes, but using a Chinese invention – the automatic crossbow with a sophisticated cocking and trigger device which fed arrows to the firing position and which, more than a thousand years later, was still effective enough to be used for the first gunpowder weapons. By about 300 BCE battles were fought between mass infantry armies under professional commanders who studied the art of war. This alteration in the nature of warfare also produced fundamental social and political changes.The power of the aristocracy and their monopoly over violence and warfare was undercut and the effective states became those which could adapt by controlling and mobilizing their peasantry so as to create a mass army. This was partly possible because the use of iron tools enabled land to be cleared more easily and ploughing to be deeper. The result was that more land could be cultivated by an increasing population which could, if the state was well-organized enough, provide substantial revenue. Rulers came

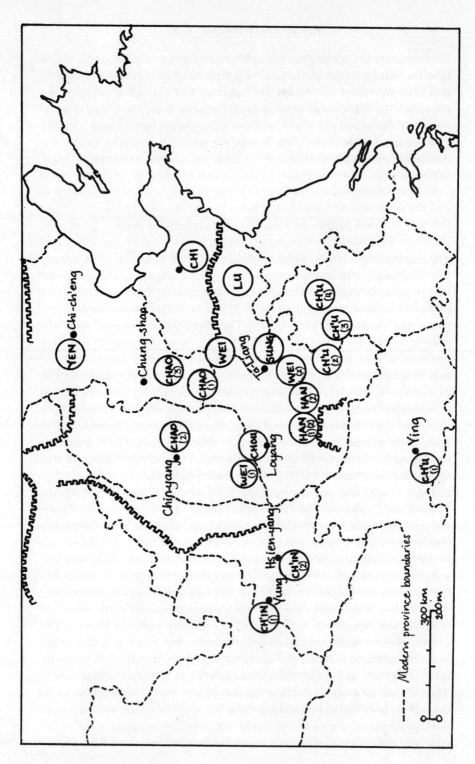

Map 18: China: the 'Warring States' (403–221 BCE)

to rely less on the aristocracy and more on the second rank of landowners who could provide the officials to administer the state both at a local level and from the centre. China became the first area in the world to develop an effective, though still very small, bureaucracy. The old nexus of authority based on a kin and sub-lineage system was replaced by the creation of a 'public realm' in which the authority of the ruler and his local representatives predominated – the old kin system declined in importance and was restricted to the peasant family and its veneration of its ancestors.

Warfare between the states was characterized by brief, shifting alliances and the domination of two major powers – Ch'in and Wei. The states of the central plain, which were unable to expand their settled areas, and therefore their resource base, were gradually absorbed by the expanding peripheral states. The western frontier state of Ch'in, under the professional administrator Shang Yang in the 350s BCE, was the first to adopt the new forms of warfare, taxation and administration. Ch'in was a relatively poor and isolated state that lacked a well-established old aristocracy but was able to expand fairly easily in a frontier area. The population was organized into paramilitary groups of five and ten families which also formed the basis of the taxation system. A new nobility was created but it was based on success in war. A new capital at Hsien-yang was founded in 350 and an internal administrative hierarchy was created. Civil and military functions were separated with the former divided into *hsien* or 'counties' under a *hsien-lung* and the latter into *chün* or 'commanderies' which were groupings of *hsien* headed by a *t'ai-shou*. A system of unified weights and measures was created. Later an official known as the *hsiang* or 'chancellor' emerged as the chief adviser of the ruler.

These changes in the Ch'in state were central to the creation of the Chinese state after 221 BCE following the Ch'in victory over its rivals. In 314 BCE it defeated the nomadic groups on its northern border and was then secure enough to move against the other Chinese states. From 311 BCE it expanded into Szechwan and then Hupei where it defeated Ch'u in 277 BCE. This was followed by a series of wars against the states on its eastern border in the central valley – Han, Wei and Chao. In 249 BCE Ch'in armies defeated the small state of the eastern Chou in Honan and ended in practice, not just in theory, the rule of the old line of the kings of Chou. The foundation of the unified Chinese state took place under Prince Cheng of Ch'in, who gained power in 247 BCE. After a period of consolidation the main conquests were achieved very rapidly in the decade after 231 BCE when the last six remaining independent states were destroyed – Chao (228 BCE), Wei (225 BCE), Ch'u and Han (223 BCE), Yen (222 BCE) and finally Ch'i (221 BCE).

8.4 China: Economy, Society and Ideas

In parallel with these military and political changes there was a series of major social and economic changes. A major expansion in the area of settlement made China not just the largest but also the most populous state in the world when it was unified. The area under cultivation expanded dramatically in the Wei valley, the central plain and the Ch'eng-tu plain in Szechwan. Intensive clearing operations were often sponsored by the state and involved marsh drainage, large-scale irrigation and better water control in the already settled areas. Continuous warfare did not retard, and may even have accelerated, economic and social changes, which meant that from about 300 BCE China had a remarkably 'modern' economy which formed the basis for its later fundamental technological, economic and social advance. Throughout the 'Warring States' period there was free movement of people between the states as new areas were brought under cultivation and new towns grew up. The development of peasant armies broke much of the power of the old warrior aristocracy and all the states had a strong interest in ensuring that they had available enough peasants to man their armies. Although large estates and landlords survived, China developed in a completely different way from south-west Asia, the Mediterranean and Europe. Most land was privately owned and could be freely transferred. By the second century BCE property rights were firmly established. China became a country of free peasants working independently on their own land and with a high degree of mobility. Large landlords did exist but they worked their land mainly with tenants or free labourers. At no time did the Chinese peasants become serfs bound to the land and their owners who could sell them as happened in Europe. In every census the peasants were registered as separate households independently of their landlords. Although slaves did exist they were mainly prisoners of war and criminals and China never developed the large-scale slavery found in 'classical' Greece and Italy. The dominant form of tenancy on the large estates was sharecropping which, from as early as the third century BCE, was regulated by contract. The standard share was 50:50 between the tenant and the landlord and this remained almost constant throughout Chinese history – the landlord gained an extra ten per cent if he supplied the oxen. Many families did not own or rent land but worked as free labourers on the estates of others – from as early as the third century BCE this was on a written contractual basis (within a few centuries there were pre-printed standardized contractual forms for each side to complete).

China was also a free market, cash economy from a very early stage, with a high degree of labour specialization. The peasants were far less self-sufficient than elsewhere in Eurasia and sold their products and participated in a market economy. The peasants paid their taxes in cash not in kind, all goods had prices, workers drafted for labour by the state were paid in cash not in kind, and peasant families recorded their possessions in monetary terms. The first great Chinese historian, Ssu-ma Ch'ien in his *Shih-chi* (*Historical Records*), wrote a description of the Chinese economy and society:

> There must be farmers to produce food, men to extract the wealth of mountains and marshes, artisans to process these things and merchants to circulate them. There is no need to wait for government orders; each man will play his part, doing his best to get what he desires. So cheap goods will go where they fetch more, expensive goods will make men search for cheap ones. When all work willingly at their trades, just as water flows ceaselessly downhill day and night, things will appear unsought and people will produce them without being asked. For clearly this accords with the way and is in keeping with nature.

This was written about 100 BCE, almost two thousand years before Adam Smith, yet provides a very similar description of the working of a market economy in which the metaphor of water flowing plays the same role as Smith's 'invisible hand'.

It was during the period leading up to the creation of the unified Chinese state that many of the defining characteristics of Chinese thought and ideas emerged. For the Chinese these were to be as central as the biblical and classical traditions became for Europe. The problem in assessing this tradition is that 'the West' has come to believe that it can all be encompassed within a single term – 'Confucianism' – and that this tradition was essentially static and highly conservative. Neither of these views can be sustained. China was a highly dynamic society and economy, encompassing a multitude of views and ideas the importance of which varied over time – for several centuries after about 400 CE the inherited tradition was of little importance as China became a Buddhist country and the major centre for its propagation. The origins of 'Confucianism' can be traced back to the Chinese literati of the second century BCE who quoted as their authority an ancient sage K'ung Ch'iu. This was latinized by Jesuit missionaries in the seventeenth century as 'Confucius' from K'ung fu-tzu meaning 'Master K'ung'. K'ung Ch'iu traditionally lived from 551–479 BCE and the very small collection of his sayings – the *Lun-yü* or *Analects* – was only established after his death. In these sayings the main aim of the individual was set out as self-improvement through the accumulation of wisdom and right conduct – virtue was the result of personal effort. There is nothing in this system that is inherently 'conservative'. Neither was it a religion as many Europeans believed – it was an ethical system but without any 'god' to enforce it.

Even more central to Chinese thought was Taoism which is best known through the writings of Chuang Chou (c.370–300 BCE) who wrote most of the *Chuang-tzu*. For Taoists the aim was simplicity (*p'u*), a closeness to the rhythm of natural life, a withdrawal from the world (and in particular public life) and a concentration on direct experience rather than the taught or written world. The only reality was endless transformation. Taoism became widely popular and had a far more profound impact on Chinese thought than the ideas of K'ung Ch'iu. In many respects Taoism was close to some of the teachings of Buddhism (which pre-dated it by several centuries) and later eased the introduction of the latter into China. Some parallels with Buddhism can also be found in the writings of Meng-tzu (later latinized as Mencius) who also lived in the late fourth century BCE. His writings are not particularly profound or original – they largely idealize the past but argue for humanitarian government and that all people have in them moral qualities capable of making them good. These writings had little influence in China until about the tenth century CE when they were incorporated into the prevailing view of the world of educated Chinese.

On a more practical level there were plenty of thinkers who justified the increasing power of the state – they were known as *Fa-chia* or 'legalists'. One of the most important of these authors was Han Fei (c.280–234 BCE). He argued that the ruler had to be absolute, that his subordinates and officials must have their functions defined through objective and binding rules. Law had to be public, certain, the same for all and therefore not subject to variable human judgement. These views had a fundamental impact both on the way the unified Chinese state developed and also on the nature of law. In Chinese law the role of the judge was not, as it eventually became in Europe, to weigh the evidence and decide on the appropriate punishment taking into account a variety of factors. Instead his function was simply to define the crime correctly – once this was done the pre-determined sentence was imposed. For the Chinese state the key was to establish the correct rules and mechanisms, then the character of individuals would be less important.
[*Later China* 9.1]

8.5 The First Indian Empire

[*Earlier India* 7.3.3]
After the collapse of the Indus valley civilization in about 1700 BCE, Indian

history is characterized by a major 'dark age' lasting for over a thousand years. Only the main outline of events can be deduced. Northern India was dominated by the so-called 'Painted Grey Ware' culture found from Rajasthan to the Himalayas in a series of small villages about eight miles apart along the main river valleys. The crucial development was the introduction of iron technology (probably from Iran) and its use in agricultural tools. They enabled settlers to push out into the Ganges valley, clear the heavy jungle and begin to grow rice in the highly fertile ground. This area, the highly productive agriculture it could support, and the food surplus it created, was to form the core area of northern Indian history for more than the next two millennia.

8.5.1 Indian society

One of the most difficult historical problems in this period is to trace the origin of the unique Indian social system misleadingly called 'caste' by the Portuguese in the sixteenth century. The expansion of the agricultural area and the incorporation of new communities added greater complexity to an existing social grouping that distinguished four groups of people – the elite or Brahmans, the Kshatriyas or warriors, the Vaisyas who were the overwhelming peasant majority and the Sudra, the servants and serfs at the bottom. However, a fifth group rapidly emerged below even the Sudra – the Panchamas or outcastes, also called the 'untouchables'. Over time the system became ever more complex as each of the five main groups subdivided. The basis of these divisions was partly occupational (though the fifth group did generally carry out tasks such as leather-working thought to be too polluting for others) but equally important were birth and kin relationships. As the 'civilized' area expanded and new areas, especially in the south, were incorporated, the balance between the different social groups began to vary greatly from area to area so that no simple statement about the Indian social system and its development is possible. Although India appeared to be sharply divided into a multitude of different, partly exclusionary, social groups it is far from clear that the impact of 'caste' was particularly significant or very unusual. Every Eurasian society was divided into very different social groups with small elites of landowners, priests and warriors, a mass of peasants and numerous different occupational categories. Mobility between these groups was very restricted in every society, not just in India.

8.5.2 Buddhism and the Jains

By about 800 BCE the religion of India was becoming increasingly complex and moving away from the simplicities found in most societies across Eurasia. The most orthodox of these departures is found in the group of teachings known as the *Upanishads* (meaning 'to sit in front of'). The aim for the individual was release from suffering and endless rebirth through control of the self. The complex idea of 'karma' (the linking of action and consequences through many rebirths) was elaborated and the chief god of the *Rig Veda* – Brahma – was transformed into Brahman, a universal spirit pervading everything. A more radical departure came with the birth (traditionally in 563 BCE but possibly several centuries later) of Siddhartha Gautama, the son of a ruler of a petty state near Kapilavastu in the Himalayan foothills. He, as the Buddha, founded the first, and most long-lived of all the world's great religions – Buddhism. He taught the universality of suffering, its causes and the method of ending it – what later became known as 'The Noble Eight-fold Path'. The aim of the individual should be to achieve 'nirvana' (literally 'the blowing out') with the end of suffering and endless rebirth. Buddhism was also the first religion to establish both male and female orders (the Sangha) for the followers of the path set out by the Buddha who adopted a life of meditation, chastity, non-violence and poverty. A near contemporary of the Buddha was another Kshatriya prince, Vardhamana Mahavira, who founded the order of monks and lay people who rejected Vedic and Brahmanic authority and became known as the Jainas – followers of 'jina', the conqueror. Mahavira was seen as the last of the twenty-four *tirthankara* or 'ford makers' who showed the way to cross over to the end of suffering. It was a highly ascetic order in which all nature was seen as embodying the cosmic principle and therefore non-violence towards all forms of life was an absolute principle. For lay followers agriculture was therefore impossible and they gravitated into trade and commerce. It was probably this strong asceticism that meant that the Jains never developed the wider appeal of Buddhism.

8.5.3 The Mauryan empire

Buddhism and the Jains emerged in an Indian world that was changing rapidly. Before 500 BCE the first towns were developing in the Ganges plain and northern India was divided into about sixteen small kingdoms. In the western part of the plain the kingdom of Kosala with its capital at Sravasti, which included within its territory the important religious site of Ayodhya, conquered the independent kingdom of Kasi with its capital at Varanasi on the Ganges. In the eastern part of the plain the kingdom of Magadha was the most important. Its capital was at Rajgir and it controlled not just trade along the Ganges, but also the iron and other metal resources of the Barabar hills. It was this combination of a highly productive agriculture and control over trade and metal resources that formed the basis of the power of Magadha. It expanded both eastwards and southwards con-quering the other small states, and by about 400 BCE, under its ruler

Bimbisara, it was the strongest kingdom in northern India and dominated the trade routes along the Ganges and as far as central Asia and the trading city of Taxila.

In about 322 BCE the last Nanda king of Magadha was overthrown by one of his military leaders, Chandragupta, who established a new dynasty. It was the start of a rapid expansion – by 305 BCE the new Mauryan empire controlled most of northern India as far west as the Punjab and the Hindu Kush mountains and was making agreements with the rulers of Iran about their joint frontier. The empire was divided into *janapada* or 'districts', which probably followed existing political divisions and were ruled by Chandragupta's relatives and his generals. A standard coinage was introduced and a land tax. In practice much land was exempt from taxation because it was either held by Buddhist or Jain religious groups or used to encourage settlement in new areas. The power of the central ruler was limited – the area controlled by the new empire was vast and there was little infrastructure to build on – most towns remained self-regulating and quasi-independent. According to tradition Chandragupta abdicated at the peak of his power in 301 BCE and became a Jain monk in south India. He was succeeded by his son Bindusara who ruled until 269 BCE and extended the empire much further to the south.

The best-known ruler of the Mauryan empire is Ashoka (269–232 BCE) because of the edicts and moral instructions he carved on to eighteen cliffs and thirty pillars. These inscriptions are the earliest known examples of Indian writing to be deciphered, although the script is clearly based on much earlier developments that have not survived. Most are in the Brahmi script, the ancestor of modern Hindi, though some are Karoshti, a variant of the south-west Asian Aramaic. In the first ten years of his reign Ashoka expanded the empire to the far south of India. It was the defeat of the kingdom of Kalinga (in modern Orissa) in an extremely bloody war that brought about a fundamental change. Ashoka converted to Buddhism and started a new policy of non-violence which lasted for the rest of his reign. In about 240 BCE he sponsored the third great council of Buddhism. The empire he ruled stretched from near modern Afghanistan to Bangladesh and in the south only three small kingdoms – Kerala, Chola and Pandya – remained independent. Although Ashoka negotiated as an equal with the rulers of the kingdoms to the west in Iran, Egypt and Syria, the degree of internal control he exercised was very limited. Most government remained local and the chief achievement of the Mauryan empire was the long period of internal peace.

The fragility of the Mauryan empire was demonstrated on the death of Ashoka. Disputes over the succession led to civil war, internal disintegration, economic decline and the rapid break-up of the empire into a series of small states as external attacks mounted. The descendants of Ashoka continued to rule in Magadha until 184 BCE when a general, Pushyamitra Shunga, set up a new dynasty which ruled much of central India until 72 BCE.

[*Later India* 9.3]

8.6 South-West Asia: the Supremacy of Assyria

[*Earlier Mesopotamia and Egypt* 7.4 & 7.9]

The first state to emerge from the 'dark age' that lasted, across south-west Asia, for some three hundred years after 1200 BCE was Assyria. It dominated the history of the region from about 900 BCE until 610 BCE and was the first empire to control the whole area between Egypt and Mesopotamia and with it the main trade routes. Its history falls into two phases. Between the late tenth century BCE and 745 BCE its rulers were preoccupied with establishing control over the areas around the Assyrian heartland of upper Mesopotamia. Its imperial phase began in 745 BCE and the period of rapid expansion was largely over within forty years. The empire survived for another century.

Assyrian tradition always stressed the continuity of the state from the original Assyrian kingdom that emerged about 1500 BCE despite the period of decline and internal disruption which was particularly severe in the period around 1050 BCE. There undoubtedly was considerable continuity through this period – Assur was always the central city and royal ceremonial remained unchanged. For a century after about 1000 BCE, once the worst period of weakness was over, effort was devoted to re-establishing control of the area of the old Assyrian kingdom – it was a period of endless wars and campaigns in the northern mountains but was largely complete by the death of Tukulti-Ninurta in 884 BCE. The Assyrian empire has always been portrayed as particularly ruthless but in reality it was little different from any of the other early empires in the region – it certainly depended on conquest and plunder (as did the other empires) but it also operated policies of marriage alliances, supported trade and merchants and in many cases local rulers were left in place after they were defeated.

Major expansion began under Ashurnasirpal II (883–859 BCE) – he conquered parts of the Levant and started the Assyrian tradition of carving massive relief sculptures of royal hunts, campaigns and rituals. He also founded the new capital of Kalhu (later Nimrud). The major Assyrian success was the attack on Babylonia (where a local dynasty had emerged about 900 BCE) under Shamshi-Adad V in 812 BCE. The

Assyrians ravaged the country and left it without any ruler for twelve years although they did not attempt to establish any permanent control. In about 750 BCE Assyria controlled (apart from its historic area including the cities of Assur, Nineveh and Kalhu) the area east of the great bend of the Euphrates, the whole of the north Mesopotamian plain and the foothills of the Zagros mountains to the east. It was still no more than a major kingdom.

The period of rapid imperial expansion began under Tiglath-pileser III (744–727 BCE) who conquered Syria as far south as Damascus and controlled client states up to the Egyptian frontier. The kingdom of Urartu (roughly the modern Armenia), which had been a significant rival for a century, was defeated and its power reduced although it was not conquered. Parts of Babylonia were taken over but it was not until Sargon II in 705 BCE that the whole of Mesopotamia was conquered and incorporated into the empire. Although this was a vital area because of its extensive trade links it proved difficult to control. There were almost continual revolts, even by the puppet kings the Assyrians set up and the whole region had to be reconquered in both 689 and 648 BCE. After about 700 BCE the main thrust of Assyrian expansion was against Egypt which since 712 BCE had been ruled by a Nubian dynasty. Conflict between the two over influence in the Levant led to an Assyrian invasion and capture of Memphis in 671 BCE. As in Mesopotamia control proved very difficult to maintain even after the capture of Thebes. The Assyrians could do no more than set up a client-king, Psammetichus, who in 656 reunited Egypt and established the Saite (Twenty-sixth) dynasty which ruled until 525 BCE. While Assyrian power was strong the Egyptian rulers remained generally subordinate.

Assyrian imperial expansion was based on a major change in military power. The military revolution caused by the demise of the chariot around 1200 BCE was followed through in a fundamental fashion in Assyria. By about 800 BCE the Assyrian army only had about 1,300 chariots but over 50,000 infantry. No state in west Eurasia at this time could support a professional army of this size and therefore it had to be a militia recruited from the mass of peasants. Conquests also increased the power of the king. In the early phases of the Assyrian state it seems likely that there was some of form of elite council that advised the ruler. As the empire grew the king gained more power through his ability to appoint a large number of governors and military commanders and he became increasingly autocratic and absolute. The empire was divided into provinces which were usually called after their chief city. Each had a governor and a palace which was the centre for administration and tax collecting. Many of the cities, which were vital for the revenue the Assyrians derived from taxing trade, remained independent of the local governor and dealt directly with the king. Although a primitive road system was developed communications remained difficult. Effective control therefore relied mainly on the cohesiveness of the small Assyrian ruling minority, which was given land in the conquered areas in order to maintain itself. One policy adopted by the Assyrians, which appears to have been a new departure, was the deportation of various groups around the empire. In part the policy was intended to settle outlying parts of the empire but it also obviously had the effect of terrorizing the population and helping internal control. Although it was not on the scale often asserted it was still substantial and probably affected about four million people.

The collapse of the Assyrian empire was sudden and unexpected. Around 630 BCE it was at the height of its power yet within thirty years it no longer existed and the main cities of the Assyrian heartland – Nimrud, Nineveh and Assur – had all been destroyed. The sources for the collapse are fragmentary and often contradictory and most of the key dates cannot be established with any reliability. The last of the great Assyrian kings, Ashurbanipal, died sometime between 631 and 627 BCE and a bitter internal conflict over the succession followed. This power vacuum enabled Nabopolassar, a Chaldean from the south of Mesopotamia, to set up a kingdom around Babylon, probably in 626 BCE, and establish control over most of Mesopotamia by the end of the decade. By 616 BCE Nabopolassar was strong enough to launch attacks into Assyria and a couple of years later, in alliance with the developing power of the Medes in western Iran, they sacked Assur and in 612 BCE Nineveh. The Assyrians and their Egyptian allies counter-attacked but by 608 BCE Assyrian power had disintegrated and the Assyrians' great cities were in ruins.

The kingdom that Nabopolassar established in Babylonia was short-lived. It was at its height under Nebuchadnezzar II (605–562 BCE) when major battles were fought with Egypt for the control of the Levant (as they had been for a thousand years). The kingdom was relatively wealthy, based on its control over the trade routes down the Gulf and to the east, and the taxation derived from them. Babylon was reconstructed and developed (eventually it covered an area of over three square miles and had a population of over 100,000) and was surrounded by huge double walls and a moat. There was a seven-year civil war over the succession after the death of Nebuchadnezzar out of which Nabodinus established control. His kingdom was destroyed in 539 BCE by the rising Achaemenid empire of Iran [8.8]

8.7 The Phoenicians and the Levant

8.7.1 *The Levant*

In parallel with the rise of Assyria the trading cities of the Levant coast revived after the problems suffered around 1200 BCE. It was the beginning of a period of major expansion and the establishment of a vast trading empire and colonies across the central and western Mediterranean. The states and people involved in this process are usually called Phoenician although that is a Greek name of unknown origin which they themselves never used. They called themselves *can'ani* or Canaanites and their country Canaan. Their history and its significance has largely been ignored and denigrated, especially by classicists who have consistently seen them through the eyes of their later rivals, the Greeks and Romans. They occupied the area of the Levant coastal strip and were organized in small kingdoms built around the prosperous trading cities that had long flourished in the region. Their internal history is far from clear. The main centres were Byblos, Tyre and Sidon of which the last two became increasingly important. These cities remained independent until about 800 BCE when they came under increasing Assyrian influence – they maintained their nominal freedom because the Assyrians wanted the revenue they generated from trade. The independence of Tyre was only formally ended by the Babylonian empire of Nebuchadnezzar II in 564 BCE.

The major period of expansion began around 900 BCE. At first it was probably linked to the trade in metals – into Anatolia, the nearby island of Cyprus for its copper, and increasingly to the west for silver and tin. The first major settlements were in the eastern part of Cyprus around the city of Kition in 820 BCE but the trade to the west required intermediate stopping points on the long voyage. This explains the very early foundation in 814 BCE of what was to become a major city and later the capital of its own empire – Carthage. Settlements in the far west at Lixus in North Africa and Gadir (modern Cadiz) may have been even earlier and were probably linked to attempts to control the trade in tin ore from the Atlantic, especially the Portuguese coast and perhaps even further north to Brittany and Cornwall. Gadir developed into a major trade centre exploiting the inland metal resources especially around the Rio Tinto which was a major mining centre for another thousand years. There were other colonies along the eastern Mediterranean coast of Spain at Malaga, Sexi (modern Almunecar) and Abdera (modern Adra) but these were in sparsely populated areas with few resources and may have been agricultural settlements. Fairly rapidly the Phoenicians filled in the gaps between the western and eastern Mediterranean with more settlements. On Sicily they occupied a large part of the island, including Motya at the western tip,

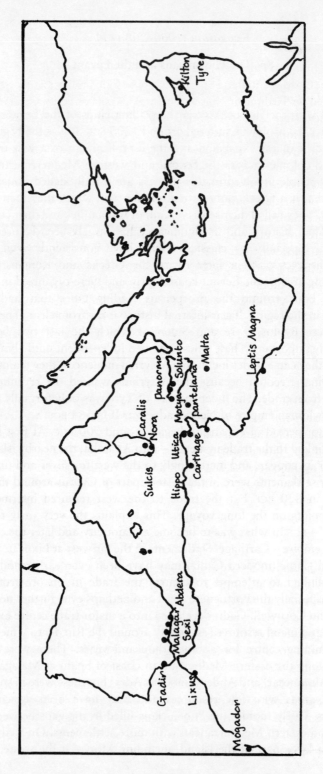

Map 19: Phoenician expansion in the Mediterranean

Panormo (modern Palermo) and Solunto. By 800 BCE they had settlements on Malta, Gozo, Pantelleria and probably Lampedusa. Shortly afterwards they settled on Sardinia at Nora, Sulcis and Caralis (modern Cagliari) from which they were able to control the hinterland, together with more settlements along the Libyan coast – Leptis Magna and Hippo. This trading empire also included the Aegean (as early as 850 BCE the Phoenicians were trading to Rhodes and Crete) as well as parts of mainland Greece. Classical historians are loath to admit any Phoenician influence on the developing states in Greece but the Levantine cities were far longer established and far more influential because they were part of the core area of south-west Asian civilization. There were almost certainly Phoenician settlements in the Aegean and the Greek legend of Kadmos preserved the tradition that Thebes was founded by the Phoenicians.

All of these colonies were part of a trading and settlement empire that dominated the Mediterranean for several centuries. Phoenician boats were still fairly primitive, using square sails together with oars, and their handling would have been heavy. Most sailing was coastal but the island settlements show that they were capable of sailing across open seas, navigating by landmarks and the stars. Voyages were restricted to the summer months (as they were in the Mediterranean until the last few hundred years) and it probably took about three months to sail from Tyre to southern Spain. A return journey could not be completed in one summer season and would therefore take about fifteen or sixteen months with the winter lay-up. Phoenician ships also sailed south from the Straits of Gibraltar to the colony of Mogador, and the voyage even further south to the West African coast would not have been difficult. There is some evidence that in 596–593 BCE Phoenician sailors, sponsored by the Egyptian Pharaoh Nechas, circumnavigated Africa.

8.7.2 Carthage

As the homeland of the Phoenicians fell increasingly under Assyrian and then Babylonian control their colonies became more and more independent. The most important of these was Carthage. It may have been founded by the royal family of Tyre but whatever its exact status it remained subservient to its home city for centuries. An annual embassy was sent to Tyre and offerings, equivalent to ten per cent of Carthage's trading profits, were made at the temple of Melqart, the city god of Tyre. Carthage was not just a trading centre; its wealth and growth (at its height its population was probably over 75,000) depended upon increasing exploitation of its very productive agricultural hinterland. The first step in the creation of a Carthaginian empire was the foundation of its first colony – Ibiza – in 654 BCE. From about 600 BCE it took increasing control of the

Phoenician colonies in the central and western Mediterranean, taking over Sardinia and much of Sicily, as well as southern Spain and North Africa. A key characteristic of Carthage, together with some of its colonies, was the *tophet* or sacred enclosure on the edge of the settlement where human sacrifice, including the burning of children, took place. This tradition, especially the sacrifice of the first-born child, was fairly common in the Levant region but it was only used in exceptional circumstances, whereas in Carthage it became much more frequent. Here it seems to have been a 'privilege' reserved for the kings and the direct descendants of the founders of the city and may have been linked to rituals about its independence. In the two centuries after 400 BCE it seems likely that about 20,000 children were sacrificed. There is some evidence that these were mainly weak children and that the rituals were only a more extreme form of the exposure of the weak practised in the Greek state of Sparta.
[*Later Carthage* 9.5]

8.7.3 The alphabet
[*Earlier scripts* 4.8, 7.5.2 *& China* 7.8.2]
The Phoenician homeland was also important for a fundamental development – the evolution of the alphabet over the period around 1400–900 BCE. A number of key stages have been identified although the exact process involved is not entirely clear. At Serabit el-Khadem in Sinai (the site of turquoise mines) there are about thirty inscriptions dating to around 1400 BCE. Alongside the Egyptian hieroglyphic inscriptions is another script which, although it has been only partially deciphered, is almost certainly in a Semitic language. The script, which in appearance is close to hieroglyphic, has only twenty to thirty signs, suggesting that it is alphabetic. At roughly the same period (possibly two hundred years later) at Ugarit in northern Syria an even more complex situation seems to have existed with five different scripts being used simultaneously – Egyptian hieroglyphic, Akkadian cuneiform, Cypro-Minoan, Hittite hieroglyphic and a Ugaritic 'cuneiform alphabet'. The latter was used to write Ugaritic, a west Semitic language, and the little-known Hurrian. It had thirty signs but they are not derived from Mesopotamian cuneiform originals. It is probably a transitional script between a syllabary and an alphabet. This was a confused situation but it can be deduced that the alphabet arose in an area of strong Egyptian influence and that it was derived from Egyptian hieroglyphic because the latter omitted the vowels. However, the early Ugaritic alphabet did not emerge by the simple process of an individual inventing a consonantal value for each sign. It was only over a period, and without design, that this is how the system eventually developed. What happened at Ugarit was that the scribes added signs for three vowels

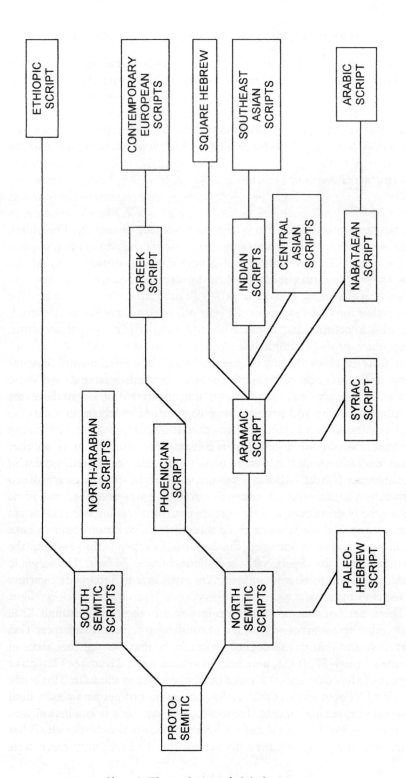

Chart 3: The evolution of alphabetic scripts

(a-i-u) that were needed for their language. A complete alphabet, including all the vowels, can be found at Byblos about 1000 BCE where it is inscribed on the lid of the sarcophagus of King Ahiram and on the walls of his tomb. It is from the Levant that all the alphabetic scripts used in western Eurasia, India and south-east Asia ultimately derive through a process of gradual adaptation into very different languages and evolution into very different scripts.
[*Derivative Greek script* 8.9.1]

8.7.4 Israel

At the same time as the rise of the Assyrian empire and the Phoenician trading cities a few small states emerged in the hills behind the coastal plain of the Levant. They would be of little importance in world history were it not for the fact that parts of their history are recounted in the Old Testament. There are two major problems in dealing with this history. The first is that the Old Testament is a religious not an historical document. It contains anachronisms, duplication and even triplication of incidents, contradictions (for example, the two creation stories of Genesis) and two very different views of Yahweh, the chief god. The earliest possible date for some of the writings is the ninth century but a much later date is more likely – therefore none is contemporary with the emergence of the kingdoms. The second problem is religious. It is widely assumed in the 'western' world that the Old Testament has to be largely true and that any evidence must be fitted into this framework. Most of the archaeological work undertaken in the area is used to try and 'prove' that the Old Testament is correct – thus if a town named in the Old Testament has a destruction level then this is taken as 'proving' it was destroyed by Joshua during the Israelite conquest. In practice there is no reasonable evidence to support any of the assertions about ancient Israelite history before about 1200 BCE and this includes the sojourn in Egypt, the exodus, the wanderings in the desert and the conquest under Joshua. The latter in particular seems to be a seventh-century myth invented to justify the right of Israel to the area.

There were significant changes in this area in the period around 1200 BCE as there were across the whole of south-west Asia. The interpretation that best fits the archaeological evidence is that during the 'time of troubles', 1200–1050 BCE, a number of groups derived from the Caananite culture of the coast set up a series of new villages in the hills. This is the period of 'Judges' in the Old Testament – groups of people fighting both external enemies and among themselves, and sharing a few cult sites such as Shechem, Bethel, Gilgal and Shiloh, although it is far from clear that there was any religious unity between them. The idea that there were 'twelve tribes' is a much later construct. The first king of a unified state was Saul (*c.*1020–1000 BCE) – a military leader who gained control of a small region. He was succeeded by his son Ishbaal who was rapidly overthrown by an alliance between the army commander Abner and David, a small-scale brigand who had once been at Saul's court but who then fought against the first king and his son. David and his son Solomon established a short-lived dynasty over the petty kingdom and created a primitive administrative structure over the hierarchical society which included slaves at the bottom. The narrative in the Old Testament is clearly written to give a particular religious message and is of limited historical value – for example no known temple structure can definitely be dated to this period and the kingdom of Sheba did not exist at this time. David defeated a few of the other small states in the area – Ammon, Moab and Edom but his rule, as with other kings at this time, was largely personal and based on his prestige. The wealth of the kingdom derived from its control over the trade routes between the great trading cities of the coast and the Gulf of Aqaba. By the death of Solomon the kingdom was in decline and sometime in the 920s BCE it split permanently into two – Israel with its capital at Samaria in the north and Judah with its capital at Jerusalem in the south. The biblical narrative was clearly written in the south – hence the idealization of David and the insistence on the view that Israel was always in 'rebellion'. Non-biblical sources for the two petty kingdoms are scanty and mainly restricted to Assyria. Israel (often called Samaria in the Assyrian records) acted as a buffer state between Assyria and Judah and therefore tended to be more unstable. After two centuries of existence it was conquered by Assyria and absorbed into the empire in 721 BCE. Judah became a subject kingdom but retained its nominal independence until, like most of the rest of the Levant, it was incorporated into the Babylonian empire under Nebuchadnezzar II in 587 BCE.

Even a cursory examination of the contemporary evidence shows that the religious situation in the area was far more complex than the relatively simple situation set out in the Old Testament. Archaeological finds at Kuntillet Ajrud in the south of Judah suggest that the chief god, Yahweh, often had a divine consort, and texts from Khirbet el-Kom show that some parts of society saw him as female. Pure monotheism was a much later development and many of the 'foreign' gods excoriated by the Old Testament were, not surprisingly, part of the worship of the area since they derived from a common Levantine culture and represented the much more developed cities of the coast. The complexities of religious beliefs in the area can be judged from the Aramaic text inscribed on the wall of a sanctuary at Deir Alla in Ammon. It tells the story of Balaam (in the Old Testament it is contained in Numbers 22–24) yet none of the deities involved is Israelite.

8.8 The Achaemenid Empire

The empire which emerged in Iran around 560 BCE was in what, until this time, had been a peripheral region to the main core area of south-west Asia. It was the first of the three great Iranian empires which were to dominate the history of western Eurasia for most of the next thousand years. The Achaemenid empire (named after the ruling family) was the largest the world had so far seen and, at its peak shortly before 400 BCE, stretched from the Bosphorus in the west to Egypt, northern India and as far into central Asia as the borders of modern Kazakhstan. It was the first to link all of this vast area together. It was followed by the Parthian empire (c.140 BCE–224 CE) and the Sasanian (224–651 CE). The name Iran derives from the Sasanian name for their homeland – *Eranshahr*. The name Persian is the Greek term for the province of the empire where the speakers of Persian (part of the wider Iranian language group) lived. The problem in interpreting the history of the Achaemenid empire is that the internal sources are meagre (especially after 522 BCE) and much has to be deduced from Greek sources. These are, in the main, only interested in their limited world of the Aegean and are highly unreliable because of their determination to show 'Persians' as cowardly, effete, wealthy, decadent and ruled by women (all the later characteristics of the 'Orient') when the exact opposite was the case, apart from the wealth.

Persia originated in the modern Iranian province of Fars at the south-east end of the Zagros mountains. Little is known of the area before about 700 BCE when it was probably under the control of Elam to the west. In 646 BCE the area was attacked by the Assyrians and a small kingdom broke away to become independent. The Achaemenid empire was, like many others, largely founded by a single conqueror – Cyrus II (the Great) (559–530 BCE). His conquests mark one of the most rapid periods of imperial expansion ever known. He inherited the small Persian kingdom, defeated the neighbouring kingdoms of Susa and the Medes within a decade and then moved westwards. The Anatolian kingdom of Lydia was defeated and its king, Croesus, taken prisoner. Finally, in 539 BCE the king of Babylonia, Nabonidus, was defeated at the battle of Opis and his empire collapsed. Moving eastwards Cyrus extended his power to take control of most of modern Afghanistan and south-central Asia. A new capital – Pasargadae (named after Cyrus' tribe) was built but the centre of the empire was the old capital of the kingdom of the Medes – Ecbatana. By the time of Cyrus' death the only major independent power in western Eurasia was Egypt. His successor Cambyses (530–522 BCE) built a navy, conquered Cyprus and then in 526 BCE led an invasion of Egypt which culminated in the capture of Memphis. The Saite dynasty imposed by the Assyrians was ended.

Exactly what happened on the death of Cambyses is unclear. All that is certain is that Darius I (522–486 BCE), although from the ruling family, was not the legitimate successor and he had to put down a series of revolts. Nevertheless control was rapidly re-established and the Achaemenids never lost their hold on the kingship until their final defeat in 330 BCE. The empire suffered few problems after about 500 BCE and revolts were largely confined to Egypt. The empire was divided into 'satrapies' which tended to increase in number and cover a smaller area as control was intensified. The satraps were always of Persian origin and governed from the main provincial cities and these were linked together by a network of roads with way-stations and garrisons at key points. Administration of the empire below this level was carried out by local elites because there was no viable alternative. Overall, the level of central control was probably higher than in any previous empire. Persians did not pay taxes and could own estates throughout the empire – originally land was granted in return for various forms of military service but fairly rapidly after the establishment of the empire these were remitted to monetary payments and much of the army was composed of mercenaries.

The Achaemenid king was central to the Iranian religion – Zoroastrianism. The exact origin of this religion and its founder – Zarathustra – is largely unknown. The latter almost certainly did exist at some time before the creation of the Achaemenid empire, possibly around 630–550 BCE but these dates could plausibly be about two hundred years earlier. The writings about Zarathustra are contained in the *Avesta* in various verses or poems (*Gathas*) in an archaic style and language and were written over a very long period. Zarathustra probably lived in eastern Iran and was a priest before starting his own teachings. These were based on the essential duality of the world and the endless conflict between good and evil. In the third age of the world, which Zarathustra inaugurated, the balance was tipped in favour of good and the god Ahura, but humans remained free to choose and could, if they wished, help to extirpate evil. Sacred fire played a central part in worship as did the exposure of bodies on death to avoid polluting the earth. Zoroastrianism did not spread to become one of the world's major religions (the Parsees of India are now some of its main adherents) but the influence of its ideas, in particular the duality of good and evil, was profound and affected almost every other religion that emerged in south-west Asia.

By about 500 BCE, within fifty years of its origin, the Achaemenid empire reached its maximum extent with the addition under Darius I of Samos, Thrace and parts of north-west India. Already it faced major problems in controlling the largest empire yet known. In 498 BCE the Greek cities of the Ionian coast rose in revolt and the city of Sardis was burnt. The revolt was put down but Darius was tempted to extend the empire further west to the Greek mainland – he was defeated in 490 BCE at the battle of Marathon. Elsewhere Darius was successful – he ordered the construction of a canal between the Mediterranean and the Red Sea, rebuilt Susa and founded the new dynastic capital of Persepolis. His policies were continued by his successor Xerxes (486–465 BCE). Revolts in Egypt and Mesopotamia were suppressed but an extension of the empire into Greece again failed. Thebes and Thessaly accepted Achaemenid rule, Sparta and Athens did not – in 480 BCE the Greeks won the naval battle at Salamis and the next year the land battle at Plataea. The small forces the Greeks were able to mobilize in their region were just enough to defeat the Achaemenid empire which had overextended itself in the far west. Over the next couple of decades the empire lost territory to the Greeks in Thrace, the islands of the Aegean and along the Anatolian coast.

Xerxes and his heir were murdered in 465 BCE – Artaxerxes took the throne and ruled for the next forty years. An Egyptian revolt supported by the Greeks was put down and a Greek invasion of Cyprus failed. The outbreak of the Peloponnesian war between Sparta and Athens in 431 BCE gave the Achaemenids much greater room to manoeuvre in the Aegean and after the Athenian defeat in Sicily in 413 BCE full control over the Ionian cities was re-established (the Greeks finally accepted this in 386 BCE). Control over Egypt was lost in 399 BCE and not regained for more than fifty years. Although there was a series of internal problems and palace coups around 338 BCE the Achaemenid empire still seemed strong – yet within ten years it had ceased to exist after its conquest by the Macedonian, Alexander.

8.9 Greece

When, around 900 BCE, Greece emerged from the 'dark ages' that followed the Mycenaean collapse about three hundred years earlier most of the old world had been lost. One factor however was unchanged – the area remained peripheral to the centres of south-west Asian civilization and it was economically and culturally dependent on the more advanced areas for several centuries. Much of what is seen as distinctively 'Greek civilization' – city-states, colonization and trading across the Aegean and the Mediterranean – was initiated by the Phoenicians and it was through contact with south-west Asia that many of the characteristics of later Greek civilization were first developed.

8.9.1 The Greek alphabet
[*Earlier script in the region 7.5.2*]

One of the most important transmissions along this route was the Phoenician alphabet. All of the evidence shows that this was the origin of the Greek alphabet (all trace of the completely different Linear B script of the Mycenaeans was lost after 1200 BCE). The old Greek word for 'letters' was 'Phoenician objects' – *phoinikeia*. The Greek letter shapes were adapted from the Phoenician and the order of the alphabets was essentially the same. The names of the Greek letters have no meaning but come from Phoenician words which do. Thus *alpha* comes from *aleph* meaning ox, *beta* from *beth* meaning house, and *gamma* from *gimel* meaning throwing stick. The only significant difference in Greek was the addition of vowels (not really needed in Semitic languages) but this had been done several centuries earlier in the Levant for other languages. There are also a significant number of Semitic 'loan words' in Greek, particularly in areas such as the shapes of pottery, clothing, fishing and sailing terms. The Greek alphabet was devised about 850–800 BCE, possibly by a single person involved in the trade between Greece and the Levant; whether they were Greek or Phoenician is unknown. It was followed by a sudden burst of record keeping in Greece – Olympic victors from 776 BCE, Athenian magistrates from 683 BCE and for the first law-codes from about a decade later. For centuries literacy was confined to a very small elite and it was not until after 500 BCE that there was a major shift away from the earlier uses of writing which until then, across Eurasia, had largely been confined to royal inscriptions, trading accounts, law-codes and religious hymns. The first known examples of drama (Euripides and Sophocles) and critical history (Herodotus and Thucydides) are found in the Greek world after 500 BCE. They were followed, a little later, by some of the earliest thinking about politics and society (Plato and Aristotle) although the legalists in China (who share many similarities with the Greek writers) date to much the same period.

8.9.2 Early Greece
The penetration of south-west Asian culture into Greece occurred through two main places. The first, Al-Mina, was a port on the coast of Syria near the mouth of the Orontes river. It flourished for about five hundred years after 800 BCE and although classical scholars like to see it as a Greek colony it is more likely to have been a Phoenician port which traded with Greece and had some Greek traders resident there. The second was the city of Corinth, especially in the period after 725 BCE (called by classical historians the 'orientalizing' phase). Pottery decoration here (and a little later in Athens) became heavily influenced by south-west Asian ideas with

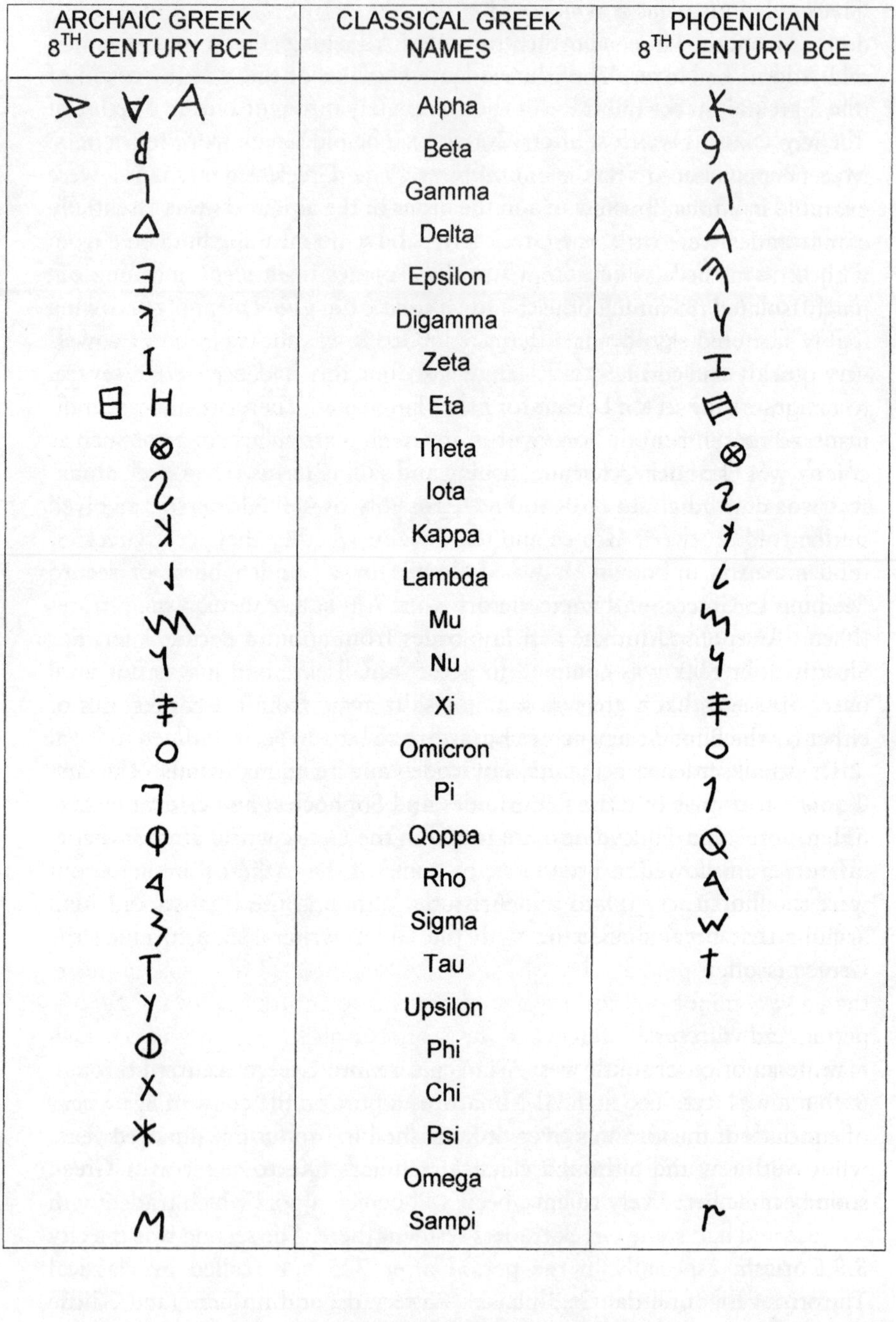

ARCHAIC GREEK 8TH CENTURY BCE	CLASSICAL GREEK NAMES	PHOENICIAN 8TH CENTURY BCE
Ɐ Ɐ A	Alpha	𐤊
𐤁	Beta	𐤂
𐤂	Gamma	𐤂
△	Delta	△
Ǝ	Epsilon	⋟
𐤓	Digamma	𐤙
𐤉	Zeta	I
𐤇 H	Eta	𐤇
⊗	Theta	⊗
𐤆	Iota	𐤆
𐤊	Kappa	𐤊
𐤋	Lambda	𐤋
Ⱳ	Mu	𐤌
𐤍	Nu	𐤍
‡	Xi	‡
O	Omicron	O
𐤐	Pi	𐤐
Φ	Qoppa	Q
𐤓	Rho	𐤓
𐤔	Sigma	W
T	Tau	𐤕
Y	Upsilon	
Φ	Phi	
X	Chi	
✳	Psi	
	Omega	
M	Sampi	𐤓

Chart 4: The Greek and Phoenician alphabets

the use of lotus flowers, palmettes and the so-called 'tree of life'. Some Greek religious ideas travelled along the same route – the cult of Adonis derived from the Phoenician fertility cult of Astarte who became Aphrodite and Adonis her lover. The general systemization of the Greek gods also relied greatly on the more developed mythologies of south-west Asia.

There was clearly considerable continuity in population from Mycenaean Greece to the new world that emerged around 900 BCE, as for example in Attica, but few, if any, institutions survived. At first the small communities were little more than groupings of people around a temple with little in the way of a common framework. They were bound to be partly isolated from each other by the fact that the fertile soil in Greece was highly scattered. As populations rose a shortage of suitable land developed very quickly and certainly not long after 800 BCE. This forced some groups to emigrate and set up colonies which were, as with the Phoenicians, not just trading centres but also agricultural settlements. By 750 BCE the first colony was established outside the Aegean – Pithekoussai on Ischia off the west coast of Italy. This was followed by Syracuse in Sicily (733 BCE) and settlements on the Italian mainland (Taranto), in Thrace, at Byzantium (660 BCE) and in North Africa – Cyrene about 630 BCE. In the western Mediterranean colonies were established at Massalia (Marseilles), Nicaea (Nice), Antipolis (Antibes) and Emporion (Ampurias in northern Spain). Shortly after 600 BCE the main thrust of the colonization movement was over – it seems likely that most of the best sites had already been taken either by the Phoenicians or by the Greeks themselves.

The small settlements in Greece slowly evolved into mini-states of which Corinth was probably the first to develop. They too were affected by the military revolution around 1200 BCE with its emphasis on primarily infantry armies equipped with shields, spears and swords. In Greece these were the 'hoplites' – it was the elite who could afford such weapons and armour that became the citizens of the new states. Although 'classical' Greece is often portrayed as the home of 'democracy' this was no more than a very minor political form confined to a handful of states for a short period and with little influence on subsequent political developments. The main form of government as the various states formed in the century after 650 BCE was 'tyranny' – the Greek word for the small monarchies typical of much of Eurasia. Originally they may have been semi-popular rulers who overthrew the oligarchies that controlled much of Greece but they soon became hereditary rulers.

8.9.3 Sparta
The strongest of all the Greek states was Sparta and it dominated Greek history until the rise of Macedon in the mid-fourth century. It developed

about 800 BCE through the amalgamation of four villages under the rule of two 'kings' from the Eurypartid and Agiad families. It expanded through conquest and the crucial event was the war with Messenia (*c*.735–715 BCE), the conquest of this fertile area and the formation of the peculiar Spartan state that survived unchanged for over three centuries. In many ways it was, apart from the unusual kingship, a typical 'hoplite state' in which all male citizens had a vote in an assembly, although power lay with the *Gerousia* or council of twenty-eight elders aged over sixty. The nature of the Spartan state was defined by its overriding military priorities. These were set by the fact that the conquered peasants of Messenia were treated as state slaves or helots, forced to wear dog-skin hats and could be killed with impunity by any Spartan. Weak Spartan males were exposed at birth, there was a strict military education from the age of seven and all adult males were allocated to communal dining groups. All of this was designed to emphasize the overriding priority of the maintenance of the Spartan state. The Spartan system at the time, and subsequently, appealed to those who placed the state above the individual. Both Plato and Aristotle admired the system – they just wanted a wider aim in education than the emphasis on military courage – and the former's *Republic* is little more than a slightly critical endorsement of Spartan institutions. Although Sparta was a strong, military state its ability to intervene in wider Greek affairs was limited by the need to keep much of its army at home in order to suppress the helots and deter any invasion which might spark a revolt. (The first successful invasion in 370–369 BCE did just this and led to the loss of Messenia and the effective end of the Spartan system.)

8.9.4 Athens

The Greek state that is often set in opposition to the Spartan system is Athens, although to identify it as 'democratic' is a major over-simplification. In the late 590s BCE a 'reform' under Solon ended the old aristocratic monopoly of office-holding but substituted instead a class-based system in which the bottom group was excluded altogether and the chief offices could only be held by the top group. The reforms were largely ineffective and from 546–510 BCE Athens was ruled by the 'tyranny' of the Peisistratid family. This was ended by Athenian exiles supported by Sparta. In the fighting between different aristocratic factions that followed the group led by Kleisthenes came out on top and carried out a series of reforms to benefit themselves.They ended the old 'tribes' and created ten artificial units for the whole of Attica as the basis for military organization and election to the *Boule* or Council of 500 that was the effective government of the city. During the century from 510 BCE Athens changed from subservience to Sparta to the creation of a short-lived empire. Athens created its own myths around success against the 'Persians' at Marathon in 490 BCE and at Salamis a decade later, even though it was Sparta which had led Greek resistance to the Achaemenid attack in 480–479 BCE. A naval alliance – the 'Delian League' was forged, probably in 477 BCE, but within twenty-five years it had become an Athenian empire, following the removal of the treasury of the League from Delos to Athens in 454 BCE. It was the wealth from this treasury and the silver mines at Laurion which funded the reconstruction of the city, especially the building of the Parthenon and Propylaia. Athens broke with Sparta in 462 BCE and its challenge to Spartan supremacy led to the Peloponnesian war in which Athens was overwhelmingly defeated by the end of the fifth century.

In theory Athens was a democracy of its male citizens. The *ekklesia* or assembly held ultimate authority and for some decisions such as ostracism a quorum of 6,000 was required. Payment for attendance was introduced in the 390s. In practice most citizens did not attend – the hill where it met (the Pnyx) could not hold more than a fifth of the citizens and most decisions were taken by the small number who could attend – it is highly unlikely that those living outside the city could participate regularly. Day-to-day authority was held by the *Boule* or council of 500 which dominated the assembly by deciding what it could discuss and by implementing its decisions. It was chosen by lot from males over thirty and a person could only serve twice. This might seem democratic (and certainly was far more so than the *Gerousia* of Sparta) but in practice few people put themselves forward to be chosen and debates were dominated by a small political elite who had the wealth, time and education in rhetoric and public speaking to participate in political affairs and take the considerable risks involved in a political career. Apart from two brief interludes of oligarchic rule between 411–410 BCE and 404–403 BCE the system survived until 322 BCE when the Macedonians set up a property qualification for voting which excluded two-thirds of the citizens.

However, Athens was far less democratic than it seemed on the surface. Only about one in six of the adult population had any political rights. All women were excluded and the privileges of male citizenship were increasingly tightly defined. Originally this was given to all the descendants of Athenian men registered in one of the 'tribes' or *demes* created by Kleisthenes in 510 BCE. In 450–451 BCE this was tightened by Pericles to require descent through both male and female line so that citizenship became sealed off and confined to a self-perpetuating group. This left the metics (non-citizen residents of Athens) who, as a group, were at least as large as the number of male citizens, outside the system. They had to pay a special tax (citizens were normally exempt), had to serve in the army (they made up a quarter of the total) but could not own houses or have any

political rights. However, the fundamental fact about Athenian democracy was that it rested upon slavery – though not in the same way as the helots in Sparta. Indeed Athens was the first of the few slave societies that have existed in world history. Most of the other societies in south-west Asia since the emergence of civilization in Mesopotamia had slaves but their total numbers were small and they were not central to the functioning of the society and economy. In Athens there were about 100,000 slaves and they made up a third of the population – as high a proportion as the southern states of the United States in 1860 CE. Slaves were found in every area of society – the police force in Athens for the century after 477 BCE was provided by a corps of state-owned slaves from the Black Sea area, the state-owned silver mines at Laurion, on which the wealth of Athens largely depended, were operated by slave labour. What was unusual in Athens was the scale of slavery, given that there was a shortage of land, a surplus of free labour and a lack of the large estates that have typified slave labour systems. Most of the slaves must have worked on the small farms of the majority of Athenian citizens who presumably did not wish to undertake this work. If they had time to participate in the semi-democratic politics of Athens they could do so because of the slaves they employed in every area of life. Most slaves came through a well-organized slave trade rather than enslavement of defeated enemies – the Greeks spent most of their time fighting each other rather than external enemies. The Greeks, with their strongly held views about their own superiority to all other peoples, especially 'barbarians', were quite happy with this system. Aristotle was a strong believer in the 'natural' state of slavery that benefited both the master and the slave. As he put it in his *Politics*: 'By nature some are free, others slaves, and . . . for these it is both right and expedient that they should serve as slaves.'
[*Later Roman slavery* 9.6]

8.10 The Macedonian Empire

Both the Greek city states and the Achaemenid empire were destroyed by the Macedonian empire which developed very quickly after 350 BCE but disintegrated equally quickly. In many ways its history was similar to the emergence of the Achaemenid empire under Cyrus the Great two hundred years earlier – a series of rapid conquests by a group previously on the periphery of the 'civilized' world of south-east Asia – but the Macedonians did not develop the institutions and structure that enabled the empire to survive in a unified form.

8.10.1 Alexander

Macedonia, in the far north of the Greek world, first emerged as a subordinate kingdom recognizing the authority of the Achaemenids. It became a major power under Philip in the 340s BCE. In 338 BCE he defeated most of the Greek states (including Athens, Boetia and Corinth) at the battle of Chaeronea. The next year a league of the mainland states, dominated by Macedonia, was created and declared war on the Achaemenids. The only state of any significance to stand outside was Sparta. Philip was assassinated in mysterious circumstances in 336 BCE and power passed to his son Alexander who, after defeating a revolt by Thebes, took control of Greece and its forces. At first the war he fought could be seen as a reversal of the events over 150 years earlier as the Greek cities of Anatolia were 'freed' from Achaemenid control. (In practice the cities had been largely self-governing and after Alexander's conquest transferred their tribute to him in place of the Achaemenid king.) The war became one of conquest after the battle of Issus (333 BCE) as Alexander crossed into the central provinces of the Achaemenid empire. In 332 BCE Tyre was captured and the next year Egypt was conquered (there may have been some sympathy here for the overthrow of Achaemenid rule). A new capital, Alexandria, was established. Darius III, the Achaemenid king, fought well but Alexander was both a good and a lucky general and victory at the battle of Guagamela in 331 BCE enabled the Macedonians to enter Persepolis, the capital of the empire. Darius died the next year and the Achaemenid empire came to an end.

From this point Alexander's megalomanic tendencies became stronger. He demanded absolute loyalty and believed both his own propaganda about his divinity and his paranoia about plots. He was interested in little apart from conquest and personal glory. In the three years after the death of Darius he campaigned mainly in the far east of the Achaemenid empire – he crossed the Hindu Kush, reached the Jaxartes river, put down revolts in Sogdiana and Bactria and campaigned in the Indus valley. The idea that he reached 'the end of the known world' is merely a Greek conceit – the area may have been new to the Greeks but had been part of the Achaemenid empire for two centuries and Alexander knew little of India and nothing of China. His conquests in the Indus valley were rapidly lost after his return westwards in 326 BCE. The last three years of his life were spent trying to keep control of his vast, sprawling empire which, for the seven or so years it lasted, was the largest known in world history up to that time. The empire had little administrative structure – financial and military affairs were in the hands of Macedonians (not Greeks) but usually local rulers and governors were left in place after the conquest. The centre of the empire, for strategic and financial reasons, was Mesopotamia, which was far richer than the Greek provinces to the west. It was here in Babylon that Alexander died in 323 BCE.

8.10.2 The Hellenistic kingdoms

For the next twenty years Alexander's generals fought over the division of the spoils. For a couple of years it seemed as though Perdiccas, Alexander's head of cavalry, might be able to secure a compromise that would have kept a united empire but he was murdered by his rivals in 320 BCE. A complex series of struggles ensued with endless shifting alliances and jockeying for position mainly focused around the attempt of Antigonus, the satrap of Phrygia, to control the whole empire. He was defeated in 301 BCE by a coalition of his rivals at the battle of Ipsus. This confirmed the division of the empire among the generals who had been giving themselves royal titles for the previous five years. The new kingdoms that emerged were recognizable as the successors to the states that had existed before Alexander. Ptolemy gained control of Egypt (and took Alexander's body to Alexandria). Iran, Mesopotamia and northern Syria fell to Seleucus, and Lysimachus controlled most of Anatolia and Thrace. Much of the almost continual fighting between the successor states after 301 BCE was for control of the old heartland of Macedonia and Greece. It was held by the son of Antigonus, then by the king of Egypt before it was invaded by nomadic groups from the north and finally Antigonus Gonatus, the grandson of Antigonus was able to establish a kingdom.

The strongest of the successor kingdoms was probably that of Egypt which could depend on the long-established institutions of the area. The old sphere of influence into the Levant and southern Syria was re-established, Cyprus was conquered for a period in the 290s BCE and, in alliance with Rhodes, control was exercised over trade in the Aegean region. The revenues derived from trade were vital to pay both for mercenaries and the Egyptian troops that came to dominate the army. The centre of the kingdom was the new, cosmopolitan capital of Alexandria. However, the financial pressure and ever increasing taxation resulting from almost continual warfare produced growing internal problems and peasant revolts. Following a civil war upper Egypt broke away under Nubian rulers between 207–186 BCE and even in lower Egypt effective government collapsed. For the next century the Egyptian state was weak and ineffective. The history of the Seleucid state is one of almost constant decline from its peak about 300 BCE. In the east Bactria broke away around 250 BCE following the revolt of the satrap Diodotus, although it had been largely independent for decades. The Bactrians crossed the Hindu Kush and set up their own kingdom of Gandhara in north-west India. Across Iran power steadily passed to the Parthians and most of Anatolia was lost in 188 BCE. After further losses the Seleucids were left ruling just a small area of northern Syria.

For classical historians the great achievement of Alexander and his successors in the Hellenistic kingdoms has always been seen as the spread of a superior Greek culture eastwards. For example at Ali Khanum on the Oxus river (now the northern frontier of Afghanistan) there are the remains of a Greek gymnasium and a pillar inscribed with 140 moral maxims copied from a similar pillar at Delphi. Greek spread as the language of government (to a large extent replacing Aramaic which had been the *lingua franca* of the Achaemenid empire), although in Egypt administration was always bilingual. Until about 250 BCE there was also a wave of Greek colonization across the various Hellenistic states and the establishment of a number of new Greek cities. However, any dissemination of Greek culture (which was not 'superior' to, merely different from, those long-established in areas such as Egypt, Mesopotamia, Iran and north-west India) was largely incidental to the main purpose of empire – exploitation, loot and the accumulation of wealth for the ruling Macedonian elite through military control, taxation and heavy labour for the local population. Any homogeneity across the Hellenistic world was confined to the small Macedonian and Greek elite. The Greeks were convinced of their own superiority, idealized themselves in art and literature and despised all other traditions to the point of active hostility. The spread of Greek institutions such as gymnasia, temples and theatres was largely restricted to the Greek enclaves as a 'colonial' culture, cut off from the local population. As in most colonial situations the culture of the ruling elite was taken up mainly by those who hoped to advance within the new system. At the same time there was also a flow of ideas from India and Iran westwards to the Mediterranean. This began perhaps as early as Alexander's own encounter with Indian ascetics of the Jain and Buddhist traditions at the great trading city of Taxila at the junction of the Central Asian and Indian trade routes.

8.11 The Incorporation of Italy

8.11.1 *The Etruscans*

Until after 1000 BCE Italy was hardly affected by developments in southwest Asia and the Aegean. It was gradually incorporated into this world through the activities of first Phoenician and then Greek traders. Most is known about the interaction between them and the local population on the west coast of Italy in Etruria, north of Rome. It appears to be another example of the impact of external trade in forcing the pace of development

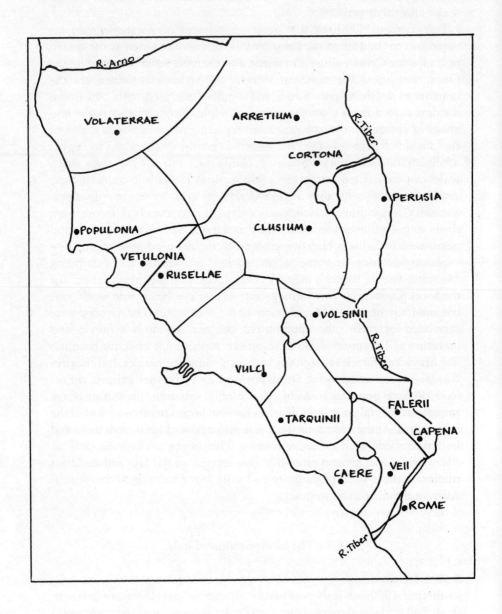

Map 20: The Etruscan cities

of local groups into small states by entrenching and developing the power of the elites that controlled trade and contacts with the more advanced traders. Around 1000 BCE a widespread culture known as 'Villanovan' encompassed the iron-using agricultural villages across a wide area of Italy as far south as Salerno. In the period, from about 800–700 BCE, in Etruria a more developed culture known as Etruscan evolved as trade increased and villages developed into small towns, especially in the coastal areas and places such as Vulci, Volaterrae, Veii, Tarquinii and Rusellae. Much of the wealth of the region derived from its metal resources – some of the few in the Italian peninsula. The people of the area called themselves 'Rasenna' not Etruscans, which was a name given to them later. Their origins are unclear and their script has not been fully deciphered. They may have spoken a non-Indo-European language which some experts have argued originated in Anatolia. However, the development of Etruscan culture seems to be entirely indigenous with very strong continuity through the transition from Villanovan.

The Etruscans were organized, like the Phoenicians and Greeks, in city-states which, like the former, were ruled by kings or *lauchme*. The symbols of sovereignty for the rulers were, as later in Rome, an axe and a bundle of rods (*fasces*). From about 600 BCE the kings appear to have been replaced by a ruling oligarchy – the Roman tradition of the expulsion of Tarquinius in 510 BCE would, if true, be part of this process. The Etruscan cities seem to have been organized into a league of twelve (though the names of cities are unknown) which had a common shrine and some common institutions including a *zilath mechl rasnal* or 'magistrate of the people of Rasenna'. The league seems to have been mainly religious in function and common military action was rarely undertaken. Etruscan culture is known largely through their tombs and odd writings about them from their enemies, in particular Rome. Their influence spread widely across Italy – by 500 BCE it stretched from the Po valley in the north to Campania in the south although the exact nature of this common culture and whether it represented some form of 'empire' is unknown.

8.11.2 Early Rome

Rome developed as part of this Etruscan world. Small agricultural villages on the main hills of Rome – Palatine, Esquiline and Quirinal – date to about 700 BCE and about a century later settlers moved into the valleys and began draining the area of the later Forum. Rome was then ruled by Etruscan kings and this period was one of rapid growth and the construction of the first public buildings. Much of the early Roman culture was Etruscan: the triad of Capitoline gods – Jupiter, Juno and Minerva –

was Etruscan in origin. At some point around 500 BCE the Etruscan ruler was expelled and a local oligarchy took control.

The political system of Rome bore some similarities to that of a Greek city-state but 'democracy' was even more limited than in Athens and the ruling elite kept a firm grip on power. The Greek state which Rome most closely resembled was not Athens but militaristic Sparta. The basis of the early state was the agricultural freeholder or *assiduus* who was distinguished from the *proletarius* or landless labourer. Until 107 BCE service as a legionary was both a right and a duty of the *assiduus*. Voting in the assembly – the *comita centuriata* – was by army unit in which the wealthier and better armed voted first. No debate was possible in the assembly – it could only approve or disapprove proposals put by the Senate. The latter body was composed of the elite patricians who had to pass a strict property qualification. It was from this elite that the two annual governing magistrates or consuls were drawn, together with other lesser office holders. The very restricted nature of the elite led to considerable conflict with a rising element of wealthy landowners – the plebeians. The conflict was finally resolved in 342 BCE by establishing a slightly wider governing elite – the plebeians gained their own assembly and two magistrates, the tribunes, who had a power of veto over the actions of the consuls. Political conflict within the governing elite was fierce and occasionally involved the wider assembly but there was a strong consensus about the ultimate rationale and aim of the Roman state – it was organized on a military basis for expansion and the acquisition of loot.

After 500 BCE the Romans fought battles every year in a series of petty wars to establish their control over the immediate area around the city, which was concluded with the capture of Veii in 396 BCE. Over the next sixty years Rome pushed southwards but it was not until victory at the battle of Sentinum in 295 BCE that Roman hegemony in Italy south of the Po valley was established. Within the immediate area of Rome some communities were incorporated as citizens but after 295 BCE the largest group of people in Italy were the 'allies'. They were bound to Rome after military defeat and required to provide military forces and although they were not citizens they stood to gain some of the benefits from further conquest. In the 290s BCE Rome was still a very small state with an overwhelming majority of subsistence peasants, no professional army, a very limited superstructure of government by a semi-amateur elite and no permanent bureaucracy. There was little or no coinage and trade levels were still low. It was a local power and still on the fringes of the Eurasian world.

[*Later Rome* 9.5]

8.12 The Eurasian Periphery: Central and Western Europe

[*Earlier Europe* 3.3.1]

The rest of Europe remained at an even lower level of social, economic and political organization than the Italian peninsula. The introduction of iron tools and weapons from about 750 BCE only amplified the slowly developing trends towards greater organization and hierarchy within a society of agricultural villages and a few metal-producing centres. The elite of warriors and chiefs were buried in barrows together with their weapons and a few primitive wagons. Some of the hill forts became the residences of this elite. Their power increased still further after about 600 BCE as they controlled the growing trade with the Mediterranean. This was mainly through northern Italy and the Greek trading colony at Marseilles which dominated the routes up the Rhone valley. A key centre was the site of the Heuneburg on the upper Danube – it covered a triangular promontory 600 yards long and 200 yards wide at its base and was surrounded by a defensive wall of unbaked bricks set on a stone base. It was clearly the residence of a local chief and his warrior elite who grew wealthy and gained power through their control over the trade routes to the south and their access to the prestige goods obtained from the Mediterranean.

About 500–450 BCE, for reasons that are unclear, there was a major change in the societies across central and western Europe, a decline in existing centres and a disruption to trade with the south. It is characterized by the emergence of a new cultural style known as La Tène and is often linked to 'the Celts'. The question of who 'the Celts' may have been and the link between culture and language has become immensely confused and not made any simpler by the attribution of the term 'Celtic' to cultures, and even the Christian church, that flourished in the area over a thousand years later after 500 CE. All of these features cannot be lumped together under a single name. There is no evidence that the people who lived across western and central Europe ever called themselves Celts. The name probably derives from the Greek colony at Marseilles who called one of the local tribes *Keltoi* and then, with their usual combination of arrogance and superiority, applied it to all the people of the 'barbarian' hinterland. Later the term was applied to whoever the Romans chose to call Celts. But even here there was confusion – Caesar only reports a third of Gaul as being Celtic and the Romans did not regard Britain and Ireland as 'Celtic'. A Celtic language group existed within the Indo-European family but only survived in areas not reached by the Romans (as in Ireland) or only lightly affected by them such as Britain. However, there is no simple equation between the Celtic-speaking areas and the La Tène art style. There is little La Tène art from Iberia, even in the Celtic-speaking areas, and some of the best examples of the style come from Denmark where a Germanic language was spoken. The idea of the Celts has, like that of the Indo-Europeans, been inextricably linked to the idea of migrations from the east. However, there is little evidence to support this theory either. Given the lack of evidence for the languages spoken across Europe before this time, these 'Celtic' groups may be no more than the original farming communities gradually differentiating their languages over a very long period of time. Migrations probably played little part in their history apart from on a small scale such as the movement into northern Italy around 400 BCE.

From about 450 BCE a series of very different societies emerged across Europe. In the zone nearest to the Mediterranean development was most rapid under the pressure of trade and later Roman expansion. By the first century BCE in Gaul there were *oppida* (Caesar's term) or fortified hilltop towns for the residence of the elite who controlled societies on the verge of becoming organized states. In Czechoslovakia major 'industrial' villages such as Msecke Zehrovice developed. There were also major trade centres such as Manching in Bavaria which had a defensive wall over four miles long built out of timber held together with over 400 tons of iron nails. All of these features required much greater social organization than had ever been seen before in Europe north of the Alps. On the other hand in many of the upland areas, such as the Pennines in Britain, society was little more than a collection of very poor scattered farming villages which were a world away from the developed societies of Eurasia in China, India and south-west Asia.

OVERVIEW 4

THE WORLD IN
500 BCE

World Population: 100 million
Regional Population: China: 30 million, India 25 million,
Greece 3 million
Major Cities: Babylon (250,000), Ecbatana (200,000),
Loyang (150,000), Athens (150,000), Sravasti (150,000),
Memphis (100,000), Carthage (50,000)

Events:

★ Polynesians settle Fiji, Samoa and Tonga

★ China divided into numerous states – 'Spring and Autumn period'

★ North India divided into numerous small kingdoms

★ Achaemenid empire ruling from Bosphorus to Egypt, Mesopotamia, Iran, north-west India and Centra Asia

★ Carthaginian empire dominant in central and western Mediterranean

★ Small states in Greece, Greek colonies in Mediterranean

★ Etruscan cities in central Italy, Rome independent

★ Height of Olmec civilization on Gulf coast of Mesoamerica. Emergence of Monte Alban in Oaxaca

★ Ceremonial centres in coastal valleys of Peru

★ La Tène culture emerging in central and western Europe

★ Emergence of Buddhism and the Jains in northern India

★ First production of cast iron in China

★ Metal goods (gold and copper) made in Peru

★ Iron working in west Africa

9

The Linking of the Eurasian World
(200 BCE–200 CE)

Until about 200 BCE the empires and states at opposite ends of the Eurasian continent in south-west Asia and China had developed almost entirely in isolation from each other. Mesopotamia had traded with the Indus valley and the empires of Iran had contacts with the north-west of India. After Alexander the Mediterranean world was dimly aware of the Mauryan empire in India. China seems to have had no contacts with India let alone the areas further to the west. The only other possible contacts, which would have been very limited and indirect, would have been via the scattered nomadic peoples of central Asia. No significant technologies, trade or ideas travelled between the far ends of Eurasia. That situation began to change after about 200 BCE. The crucial factor was the development of the unified Chinese state under the Ch'in and then the Han. This initiated a westwards expansion by China into central Asia which eventually brought it into contact with the Parthian empire in Iran and the smaller Kushan kingdom in Bactria and north-west India. In parallel with these developments the expansion of Rome eastwards to the frontiers of the Parthian empire in Mesopotamia provided the final link in the chain which stretched from China to the Mediterranean. For the first time in world history the various parts of Eurasia were joined together. At first the links were tentative but in the four hundred years after 200 BCE a substantial trade network was established. The various Eurasian societies were still largely independent of each other but the links between them were never entirely broken thereafter.

9.1 China: The Creation of the Unified State

[*Earlier China 8.2–8.4*]
The creation of a unified Chinese state in 221 BCE was the result, as we have seen in the last chapter, of the success of Ch'in in defeating all of its rival warring states. Prince Cheng of Ch'in took the title of *huang-ti* ('august sovereign'), which became the normal title of subsequent emperors, and a new name – Ch'ih-shih Huang-ti. He applied to the whole of China the policies adopted by the Ch'in state over the previous century during its rise to power. Under the direction of his main adviser, the legalist Li Ssu, China

232

was divided into thirty-six and then forty-eight *chün* or 'commanderies' with subsidiary *hsien* or 'prefectures'. The Chinese script was standardized, a single currency was introduced (a copper coin with a square hole in the middle which survived until the twentieth century), weights and measures were unified and even the gauge of cart-wheels was standardized. At the same time the internal walls of the old kingdoms were demolished, construction of a network of roads and canals was begun and a defensive wall against the nomadic Hsiung-nu was extended in the north and north-west frontier areas. Control of the old provincial aristocracy was achieved by forcing 120,000 families to live in the capital. These were revolutionary changes and the growing criticism of the new state was reflected in the decision, taken in 213 BCE, to burn all writings not about medicine, agriculture and divination – luckily it was not fully implemented or we would have even less information about early Chinese history. Whilst much of the reconstruction of the state was still under way the Ch'in emperor died in 210 BCE. (The underground army of 'terracotta warriors' discovered in the 1970s were the protectors of his tomb.) He was succeeded by his son but China rapidly disintegrated into civil war. In this chaotic period Liu Pang, a minor Ch'in official not from the old aristocracy, eliminated his rivals and by 202 BCE was in control of China. He was the founder of the Han dynasty which, with only one interruption, was to survive for almost four hundred years. It was this long period of dynastic stability that made possible the development of many of the distinctive elements of the Chinese state which became far more centralized and effective in maintaining its power than any other in Eurasia at this time.

Under the Han the reputation of the Ch'in was blackened but in practice the Han state was built on exactly the same foundations. The *chün* and *hsien* were maintained together with the division of the central government into military, civil and inspectorate functions. Given the long independent histories and diverse experiences of the different Chinese states it is not surprising that the full development of a unified state, which was still in its early stages under the Ch'in, took many decades. Initially Liu Pang could do no more than adopt the device used by many of the early Eurasian rulers – twenty of his immediate kinsmen were made rulers of some of the old kingdoms in the hope that they would remain loyal. They were supervised by imperial commissioners but it was not until the defeat (in 154 BCE) of the rebellion of the seven kingdoms led by the princes of Wu and Ch'u that full central control was established. This was reinforced by a legal change made in 127 BCE which ended primogeniture among the subordinate princes and forced the sharing of land and titles among all legitimate sons. Within little more than a generation the last remains of the old kingdoms had disappeared.

The creation of internal peace and stability in the decades after 200 BCE led to a steady rise in population and a further increase in the cultivated area. Gradually the state was able to exercise greater control over the population. Between 192 and 190 BCE over 150,000 peasants were conscripted to build the walls of the newly created capital, Ch'ang-an. An accurate census was carried out which laid the basis for the most sophisticated taxation system anywhere in Eurasia. Every peasant family had to pay four taxes. The first was a land tax paid at the very low level of one-thirtieth of the notional crop – it had to be notional because the bureaucracy could only assess acreage and not the actual crop yield across an area as large as China. The second was a poll tax paid by men and women with a special rate for children over seven. The third was a property tax instituted in 142 BCE and levied at 1.2 per cent on all property (not just the peasants) and all trading profits. Lastly the peasants could pay a tax to exempt themselves from military and corvée duty. The scale of the monetary economy in China, and the fact that the peasants were not constrained within a subsistence system as they were in most of the rest of Eurasia, is shown by the fact that, apart from the land tax, all of these taxes had to be paid in cash.

9.2 Han Expansion and the Hsiung-nu

The development of the Hsiung-nu empire of the steppes in parallel with the rise of the Han is the first example of a phenomenon that became common in Eurasian history. Although the Hsiung-nu (an Altaic-speaking group) had dominated the steppes of central Asia for a couple of centuries and caused problems for the Chinese along the frontier, they could only establish their empire by exploiting a sedentary state and this could not be done on an extensive scale until the rise of the Han. Control over the products obtained from the Chinese enabled the leader of the Hsiung-nu confederation to bolster and maintain his power by distributing these high-status goods to his followers. The Hsiung-nu empire was founded by Motu (c.209–174 BCE) and further expanded by his son Lao-shang (his Chinese name) into the oases of central Asia. This pushed another nomadic group – the Yüeh-chih – further west to the borders of India and the Parthian empire. The newly established Han empire (with a population probably fifty times that of the nomads) tried to secure victory over the Hsiung-nu but were themselves defeated in 201–200 BCE. The nomads with their archers on horseback and the ability to retreat into the steppes, always retained military superiority over the sedentary states. The Chinese retreated south of the partially constructed Great Wall and bought peace

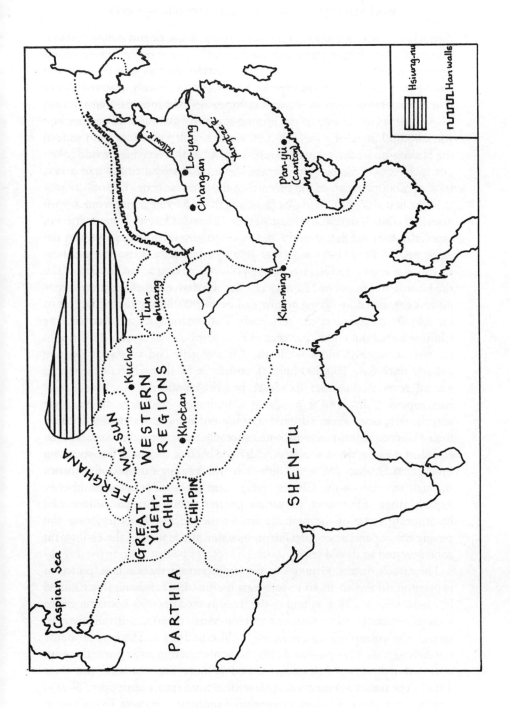

Map 21: Central and East Eurasia under the early Han

through a policy of appeasement – marriage alliances and paying tribute. The Han, like all later Chinese dynasties, were convinced of their cultural superiority and always described the 'barbarians' as subordinate and paying 'tribute' to their empire. An analysis of the goods involved shows that it was almost entirely a one-way 'trade' in favour of the 'barbarians'. The annual Han subsidy to the Hsiung-nu in the early second century BCE was 200,000 litres of wine, 100,000 yards of silk as well as grain to feed the Hsiung-nu leader's court. In return the Chinese received the odd token gift such as two camels. On average the subsidies paid to the barbarians took up about a tenth of the revenue of the Chinese state.

In the first sixty years after its founding the Han state concentrated upon asserting control over the largest state in Eurasia. Once this was achieved, especially after the defeat of the 'seven kingdoms' rebellion in 154 BCE, the emperor Wu Ti (141–87 BCE) was able to adopt an expansionary policy. In 133 BCE it was decided to end the policy of paying an annual tribute to the Hsiung-nu. Between 127 and 119 BCE a massive attack on the Hsiung-nu was organized involving an army of over 100,000 (by far the largest so far mobilized anywhere in the world). The outcome was a disaster. The Chinese lost about eighty per cent of their army and although the Hsiung-nu were contained for a while the Chinese still had to pay a massive subsidy (including 100,000 horses), costing in total nearly half the state's annual revenue, in order to secure peace. A policy of war had nearly bankrupted China and a policy of containment and subsidy was, not surprisingly, once again adopted. Hsiung-nu strength was maintained by their ability to sustain an undisputed succession for almost 150 years. That ended in 59 BCE when the empire divided after a civil war between two brothers – Hu-han-yeh and Chih-chih (the Hsiung-nu are only known through the names the Chinese gave them). The Chinese were able to exploit these differences to create greater room for manoeuvre and incorporate some of the nomads within the empire. But they were still paying tribute and after a decline in its value at the time of the civil war it soon reverted to its old levels.

The attack on the Hsiung-nu was only part of the Chinese policy of expansion. In the north and north-east the first Han *chün* was established in Manchuria in 128 BCE, and in the three years after 109 BCE most of the Korean peninsula was conquered and the north, together with the western coast, were controlled for the next four hundred years. The frontier in the north-west was also pushed back. To settle these new regions the Han operated a system of state-sponsored colonization. In 127 BCE over 100,000 peasants were settled in Mongolia. Seven years later over 700,000 victims of massive flooding in western Shantung were sent to Shensi. In 102 BCE 180,000 soldiers and peasants were settled in the north-western provinces. These frontier areas were always difficult to control and there was no simple boundary which marked the division between the settled and nomadic worlds. The Great Wall did not mark a fixed and distinct frontier and there was a wide area where the two worlds mixed and the balance between them constantly shifted. Defence against the nomads was never simply military – it involved a complex mixture of diplomacy, commerce, settlement, assimilation and some military force. In 166 BCE the Chinese established a complex system of signalling by flags and smoke to relay information about activities in the frontier region. The military garrisons (which controlled movement through a passport system) were the first line of defence followed by farmer-soldiers in military-agricultural settlements – the only method available at that time to support a large frontier army.

Expansion to the south was much easier because the Chinese only encountered relatively unorganized tribal peoples and a few weak kingdoms that did not have the military superiority of the nomadic groups. The movement of the Chinese people south of the Yangtze, which was in full flow under the Han, was one of the most fundamental forces in Chinese history. It was not simply a matter of military conquest but also the slow movement of people south to open new land along the frontier of cultivation. This movement assimilated different tribal groups that have now been lost without trace and shifted the whole balance of the Chinese state to the south by incorporating one of the richest and most fertile areas in China with an entirely different type of agriculture – wet-field rice cultivation. This process also involved the military defeat of a number of kingdoms. It began in 110 BCE with the destruction of the kingdom of Yüeh of Min (in modern Fukien). At the same time Han troops reached Canton and the Red river delta of Vietnam and established control in the area (Chinese traders had reached Da-nang even further south several centuries earlier). Northern Vietnam always proved a difficult area for the Chinese to control because of the huge distances involved, the very poor communications and the ease with which a revolt could be started. Further west the kingdom of Tien, which was very wealthy because it controlled the river crossings on the route between the upper Yangtze and Burma, was conquered in 109 BCE. The king was allowed to continue to rule until a revolt in 87–74 BCE. During this period expeditions against the K'un-ming tribes of western Yunnan extended Chinese control to near the current frontier of Burma. Some decades later the Shan kingdom of northern Burma was paying tribute to the Han.

[*Later China* 9.7.1 *and Central Asian trade* 9.8]

9.3 India

[*Earlier India* 8.5]

After the collapse of the Mauryan empire and throughout the period between 200 BCE and 200 CE, India was politically fragmented. Only the most general political history can be established and the proposed dates of the various kingdoms vary by as much as two centuries. Most is known about the kingdoms of north-west India because they were in touch both with Iran in the west and China to the east. The kingdom of Bactria, which became fully independent of the Seleucids by 250 BCE at the latest, was ruled by a small Macedonian elite who, despite their isolation, maintained their Greek culture for about another century. At the beginning of the second century BCE they extended their control southwards over the Punjab, ruling from their capital Sagala (modern Sialkot). The last king of the dynasty is known as Menander to the Greeks but Milinda to the Indians. About 150 BCE he abandoned Greek culture altogether and converted to Buddhism and the text known as 'The Questions of King Milinda' now provides one of the standard introductions to Buddhism. The kingdom was destroyed by nomads moving out of central Asia. Subsequently a group from the Bactrian kingdom moved from the Kabul valley to Taxila and established the small kingdom of Gandhara which derived its wealth from its control over the key trade routes from the Ganges valley and India to central Asia. It is often seen by 'classical' historians as 'Greek' but it was in fact a major centre for Buddhist art, and the area where the Mahayana tradition within Buddhism developed. It was the influence of the Gandhara kingdom that helped disseminate these teachings further westwards into south-west Asia. The last of the Bactrian rulers in Gandhara (Hermaeus) was killed about 50 BCE during an attack from the north by Scythian nomads and simultaneously from the west by the Parthian empire of Iran.

The most important of all the north-west Indian kingdoms was the Kushan. Its origins and even its dates are very unclear. It was probably a kingdom of the Yüeh-chih who were driven westwards by the Hsiung-nu as the latter came under pressure from the Han empire. The Kushans (or Yüeh-chih) were probably the most easterly of the Indo-European speakers – a language now called 'Tocharian' (Tukhara in contemporary Indian accounts). The most important of its rulers was Kanishka but he has been variously dated to 58 BCE, 78 CE and 128 CE – it is impossible at the moment to resolve these conflicting dates but one towards the end of this two-hundred year period seems more probable. The capital of the kingdom was Purushapura (modern Peshawar) and its control stretched over an area covering Bactria, Kashmir, Sind, the Punjab and as far east as Delhi.

How the kingdom was organized is unknown as is its history. Like Gandhara its wealth derived from its control of all the key trade routes from northern India, especially the Ganges valley, through Taxila and Bactria into central Asia and eastwards to China. The area it controlled was a key part of the networks established across Eurasia. It was also a crucial area for the mingling of the different cultures and ideas of Eurasia. High-quality standardized gold and silver coins were issued by the Kushan rulers – many use Greek script but also show Iranian, Sumerian and Indian gods as well as the Buddha. Within the kingdom Buddhism was dominant and most of the literary works that survive are Buddhist but written in Sanskrit. It was the location for the Fourth Great Council of Buddhism and played a key part in the later transmission of Buddhism along the central Asian trade routes to China. The Kushan kingdom survived for three hundred years until about 240 CE when it was conquered by the rising Iranian empire of the Sasanians.
[*Later India 10.10*]

9.4 The Parthian Empire

Very little is known about the Parthian empire which ruled Iran and much of Mesopotamia for almost five hundred years between 247 BCE and 226 CE because almost no official documents have survived. The empire is called Parthian by western sources but Arsacid by eastern texts after the founder of the empire, Arsaces – what the people themselves called their empire is unknown. However, the empire played a key role in Eurasian history. It was the main intermediary between the Roman and Han empires and the key trading partner that linked the two together although it discouraged direct contact. The 'Parthians' are first known under the Achaemenid empire living in the eastern Iranian province of Khurasan. They were probably part of the Seleucid kingdom of the Macedonians but as that kingdom concentrated more and more on affairs in its western regions control over this area was lost. The Parthian state emerged in the area between the Seleucids and the kingdom of Bactria and appears to have been founded by Arsaces in 247 BCE (at least that is the date from which the Parthians saw their own history as beginning). For more than fifty years it was no more than a small kingdom gradually pushing westwards in almost continual wars with the Seleucids who did not recognize it as an independent state until 209 BCE. The real foundation of the empire dates to Mithridates I who took the throne in about 170 BCE. He expanded the kingdom south-westwards towards the Iranian heartland, moving the capital from Nisa to Hekatompylos, occupying Media and in 141 BCE

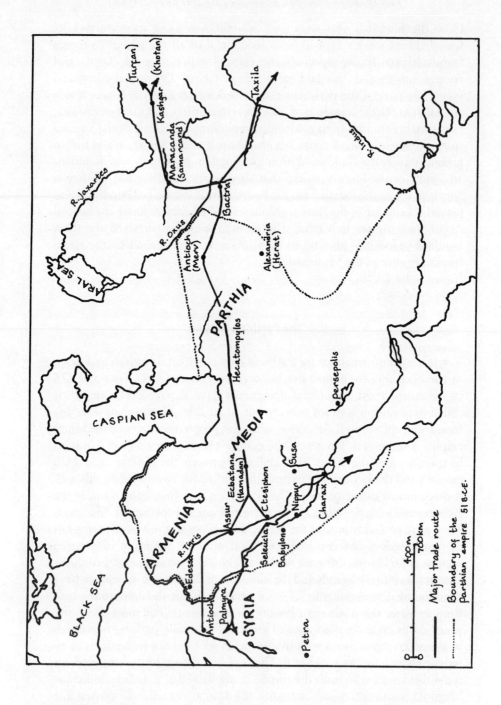

Map 22: The Parthian empire

Seleucia, the Seleucid capital in central Mesopotamia. By the time of his death in 138 BCE the Parthian empire stretched from the Tigris and Euphrates in the west to the borders of Bactria in the east. It took another two decades to stabilize the empire against attacks in the west from the last Seleucids and the east from the Yüeh-chih. The last phase of expansion was northwards from Mesopotamia into Armenia.

In 92 BCE the Parthians first came into contact with the Romans who were expanding eastwards towards Mesopotamia. It was the start of a conflict which lasted for over 600 years, continuing under the successors to the Parthians, the Sasanians. No decisive battle was ever fought, though the heavy defeat inflicted on the Romans at the battle of Carrhae in 53 BCE perhaps came nearest to this outcome. Neither side had the power to inflict a decisive strategic defeat on the other – even the Roman capture of the new Parthian capital of Ctesiphon (just across the Tigris from Seleucia) on three occasions (116, 164 and 198 CE) proved to be no more than temporary successes. For centuries there was a series of intermittent campaigns, usually in Mesopotamia but occasionally in Armenia, which involved considerable effort but changed almost nothing. In the east the Parthians faced the Kushan kingdom, again with little decisive outcome despite the attempt by the Romans to form an alliance with the latter.

Over time the focus of the Parthian empire shifted westwards to the rich area of Mesopotamia from which it was able to dominate the east–west trade routes – hence the construction of the new capital of Ctesiphon. The internal government of the Parthian empire is far from clear, but there does seem to have been a lack of any strong central government. The Arsacid family always retained the kingship but there were numerous internal disputes over the succession. The empire seems to have been divided into a series of 'kingdoms' such as Armenia and Greater Media ruled by members of the aristocracy – Fars province was possibly ruled by the Achaemenid family. The other chief aristocratic families were the Suren, Karen, Gew and Mihran who maintained extensive and expensive courts in their own provinces and provided most of the army, which was commanded by the Arsacid king. Initially the official language of the empire was Greek because the Parthians took over the remaining Seleucid bureaucracy. Aramaic (the language of the Achaemenid empire) remained important in the west and Parthian did not become an official language until the last few decades of the empire, around 200 CE. The religion of the empire was very mixed. Zoroastrianism was important but was not the state religion of Iran until the Sasanians. Greek beliefs were largely confined to the Greek community. Buddhism was very important as it diffused westwards from the Kushan kingdom.

[*Later Iran 10.13*]

9.5 Roman Expansion

[*Earlier Rome 8.11.2, Carthage 8.7.2 & Greece 8.10*]

The establishment of domination over most of the Italian peninsula following the battle of Sentinum in 295 BCE posed major problems for the Roman state. For the previous two centuries Rome had, except in the most abnormal circumstances, made war every year – the dynamic of military conquest and expansion was built into the state. (The idea that Rome was essentially 'defensive' and 'forced' to make annexations derives from Roman apologetics at the time which were repeated by nearly all classical historians until recently.) A Roman political career was built upon success in war during the tenure of senatorial office. This gave prestige and, in the best cases, the award of a 'triumph' for the successful general. Inevitably the tendency was for all office holders to favour war. The whole ethos of the Roman state was militaristic and a higher percentage of the population was continuously under arms than in any other pre-industrial state – about two-thirds of young males served for an average of seven years in the army. On the battlefield the Romans appear to have been far more violent and less lenient than their contemporaries – the deliberate slaughter of all the population of a town that refused to surrender was normal. It is hardly surprising that Rome continued a policy of conquest and expansion after gaining control of Italy.

The first Roman involvement with the world outside Italy came with the war with Pyrrhus, the ruler of Epirus, who dared to support the city of Tarentum against Rome. He was defeated at the battle of Beneventum in 275 BCE. Having gained full control of southern Italy Rome next challenged the control Carthage exercised over Sicily. The war continued until 241 BCE when Carthage agreed to give up Sicily and pay an indemnity. Three years later the Romans conquered Sardinia and Corsica. They were only a regional power but beginning to rise at the expense of Carthage which still controlled much of Spain and the western Mediterranean as well as North Africa. There were strong trading links between the two powers but continued Roman expansion into Spain led to the second war between the two powers. In 218 BCE the Carthaginian general Hannibal invaded Italy and gained some support from the Roman allies in the peninsula. He was successful in a series of battles leading up to the major Roman defeat at Cannae in 216 BCE. However, most of the allies remained loyal and Hannibal was unable to inflict a decisive defeat and break Roman power. Slowly Rome was able to rebuild its strength by mobilizing even more of its population. The decisive Carthaginian defeat in Europe was at the battle of the river Metaurus in north-east Italy in 207 BCE. The Romans were then able to mount an expedition to North Africa which inflicted the final and decisive defeat on Carthage at the battle of Zama in 202 BCE.

It was the support of some of the Greek kingdoms, especially Philip V of Macedon, for Carthage which determined Rome to become deeply involved in the east. In 197 BCE Philip was defeated at the battle of Cynoscephalae and the Romans issued a disingenuous declaration about the freedom of the Greeks. A further war with Macedonia over influence within Greece began in 171 BCE and Perseus, the son of Philip V was defeated at the battle of Pydna in 168 BCE. The kingdom of Macedonia was abolished and split into four parts while strong action was also taken against the Greek cities such as Rhodes which had supported Macedon. Rome was now the strongest power in the Mediterranean region. It effectively dominated Greece and began to extend its influence in Anatolia and the eastern Mediterranean. In the west there were problems in controlling Spain once it was taken from Carthage. There were two revolts in 197 and 154 BCE – the first led to a twenty-year war and in the second, although the Romans were defeated at Numantia in 137 BCE, they totally destroyed the city four years later. The last major problem was how to deal with Carthage when it finished paying off the fifty-year indemnity set at the end of the war in 201 BCE. The Romans had long decided upon a policy of war to stop any revival of Carthaginian power. In 146 BCE Carthage was easily defeated and the city utterly destroyed and North Africa was annexed. Rome now controlled almost the whole of the Mediterranean.

9.6 Roman Society

Continual war and conquest had a major impact on Rome. Both society and the state came to rely on the money, plunder, land and slaves that it produced. The conquest of Sicily, Sardinia and Corsica around 240 BCE was on a different basis from those on the Italian mainland. The newly conquered areas did not become allies – they were required to pay tribute in cash. By about 200 BCE three-quarters of all Roman state revenue came from abroad, and over the next 150 years mainly from the conquest of the wealthy areas in the eastern Mediterranean. Overall these revenues increased six-fold. This extra wealth, together with the more immediate gains from loot and plunder during the campaigns, brought about a series of fundamental changes in society and placed a huge strain on the very fragile Roman institutions which had developed when it was a small agricultural state.

Although some of the booty gained during war was distributed to the soldiers the overwhelming majority of it went to the wealthy governing elite. This vastly increased their wealth and created huge estates. The value of this land was augmented by the abolition in 167 BCE of all taxes on Italian land – overseas tribute more than compensated for this loss of revenue. As land became more valuable more small peasants were dispossessed and public land was appropriated by the elite. The inevitable consequence was the decline of the group which had been the backbone of the early Roman state – the peasant *assiduus* who owned his own land. The size of the citizen body and those required to undertake military service therefore declined in parallel. As those that remained were required to serve longer it was even easier for the elite to take their land during their absence. In 107 BCE, mainly because of the manpower shortages, those without property were enrolled in the army. Although not entirely without precedent this was a significant departure and the new soldiers expected to be given land when they were finally disbanded. In 82 BCE when Sulla disbanded twenty-three of his legions he had to resettle nearly 100,000 troops – in total by about 25 BCE around 250,000 soldiers were given land. This could only be done at the expense of the peasant land that remained. In practice the distribution made little long-term difference – most of the soldiers lost their land quickly to the elite either through sale or the use of force. The best estimate is that between 90 BCE and the end of the century about half the peasant families of Italy (over 1.5 million people) were thrown off their land. Many drifted into the swelling city of Rome whose population may have reached about 500,000. They were unable to feed themselves, and the state bought a degree of internal peace through the distribution of cheap, and then free, food from 58 BCE – it took up a sixth of the state's revenues but no doubt it seemed to the elite a small price to pay. The problem for the elite was to gain access to the new wealth. There were still only two senators a year who had access to the greatest loot and plunder. Once control over the Mediterranean region was achieved the number of conquests and campaigns declined. Control of public offices (especially the provincial governorships) therefore became the main source of wealth through corruption, the sale of the right to gather taxes, and extortion. As the rewards of a political career increased competition and rivalry became even greater – greed, ambition and the killing of rivals became central features of 'politics'. Roman institutions could not cope and the state slid into civil war.

A fundamental impact of conquest and expansion was that Italy became a slave society like Athens [8.9.4], but on an even bigger scale. Rome had slaves from the beginning (a tax was placed on manumissions as early as 357 BCE) but it was not a slave society until about 250 BCE. From this time war provided a steady supply of slaves to work the large estates of the elite. The possession of a vast retinue of slaves became a sign of wealth and distinction among the elite. It was one of the few forms of wealth available in Roman society – by early in the first century CE Italy had about two million slaves and they made up a third of the total population. Slavery on this scale required a continuing and massive supply of slaves, especially through war. On the capture of a city the population might be sold by the commander to slave traders or distributed among the troops who probably would also sell most of them very quickly. Breeding of slaves was important and on the fall of Carthage in 146 BCE 25,000 women were sold into slavery. In 67 CE when the future emperor Vespasian captured Tiberias in Galilee, 1,200 of the weak and infirm were murdered, 6,000 men were deported to work on the Corinth canal and the remaining population of 30,000 were sold into slavery. In 198 CE when Septimus Severus captured the Parthian capital of Ctesiphon the population of about 100,000 were all sold into slavery. (There are plenty of examples, such as that of the Cantabri in Spain in 22 BCE, where the population committed mass suicide rather than see the Romans ruthlessly divide up their families and sell them into slavery.) However, warfare was not enough to sustain the slave population of Italy which, because of their short life expectancy, would have needed at least 250,000 new slaves every year simply to maintain numbers. (This compares with a European slave trade to the Americas of about 80,000 a year when it was at its height in the late eighteenth century.) Most slaves therefore came through a well-developed slave trade from across the peripheral regions of the Mediterranean – northern Europe, the Black Sea area and Africa.

The experiences of the slaves were very different. Most worked in large gangs on agricultural estates. Those who went to the mines (especially in Spain where there was a slave workforce of over 40,000) could expect to be worked to death very quickly, whereas those who were household slaves to the elite might have a much easier life. Although a few slave owners may have been relatively humane, manumission was possible and there were a few wealthy ex-slaves, the system ultimately rested on violence, force and the total power of the owner whose property the slave became. Slaves could be sold and families (which were not legally recognized) broken up. Many slaves wore metal collars which were inscribed with instructions on how to return them if they ran away. An inscription discovered at Puteoli reveals that a company of undertakers offered a torture and execution service for owners with a series of options such as flogging and crucifixion for set rates. The state naturally supported the slave owners. In 61 CE the prefect of Rome, Pedanius Secundus, was murdered by one of his slaves over a personal grievance. The ancestral custom of the Romans was, in these circumstances, to execute all the slaves living under the same roof which, in this case, involved over 400 people including women and children. The Senate debated the issue and decided not to change the law, troops put down some riots and the executions were carried out. Some slaves did manage to escape to the wilder areas where the state had little power but slave revolts were limited, local and short-lived. There were three in Italy and Sicily between 140 and 70 BCE – the most important of them was the last led by Spartacus. It was put down after a long military campaign and concluded with 6,000 slaves being crucified along the road between Capua and Rome. This sort of punishment was not unusual or confined to slaves in the Roman world – Augustus crucified the same number of soldiers from the defeated army of his rival Pompeius. It is perhaps significant that no major figure among the Roman elite ever suggested the abolition of slavery even though some thought it was against nature and the spiritual equality of humans. Such debates remained philosophical rather than practical.

9.7 Internal Crisis: the Han and Roman Empires

In the century or so after about 90 BCE both the Han and Roman empires passed through an internal crisis. However, neither saw any significant loss of territory and both emerged from the period with a new system of government and entered long periods of prosperity and stability which lasted until the late second century CE. Exactly why these two distant empires followed roughly similar political trajectories at this stage is unclear. It is probably no more than coincidence but it is possible that disturbances in one area began to affect other parts of Eurasia as connections between different parts of the continent deepened.

9.7.1 China
The problems in China began with the death of the emperor Wu Ti in 87 BCE after a long reign of over fifty years. With no adult heir he was succeeded by General Huo Kuang as regent. During the twenty years until his death in 68 BCE the general exercised what was in effect a personal and family dictatorship. All of his relatives were executed two years after his death as the Han dynasty regained effective control. However, there were continuing dynastic problems, endless court intrigue, rule by powerful empresses and weak child rulers. The inevitable result was a steady lessening of control by the central government. These problems were compounded by growing social problems caused by the increasing population (land shortage and a concentration of land into great estates controlled by the elite) and those caused by increasing wealth in the hands of merchants and manufacturers as the non-agricultural sector of the economy

expanded. In 9 CE the Han dynasty was overthrown by Wang Mang who established the new Hsin dynasty. The problem he faced was how to secure control in circumstances where the government was already weak and social dislocation was difficult to contain. In order to remove some of the causes of social tension Wang Mang attempted to nationalize and then redistribute the landed estates on a more egalitarian basis. He found that the government did not have the power to enforce such a policy. Currency manipulation worsened many of the problems and extensive floods in the Yellow river basin led to more peasant revolts. In the forty years after 22 BCE there were over twenty known major peasant uprisings across China. The most extensive of these was the last – the *ch'ih-mei* or 'red eyebrows' from the way they painted their faces. One of their demands was for a restoration of the Han. This was achieved in 25 CE under Kuang Wu Ti, a major landowner near Nanyang with no more than vague claims to Han descent. Based on the militia he created to guard his own estate he gradually secured control of his local area, expanded the army, put down regional rebellions, suppressed the peasant revolts and declared himself emperor of a restored Han dynasty.

9.7.2 Rome

The crisis in the Roman empire began with quarrels within the elite. In 133 BCE Tiberius Gracchus, one of the tribunes, argued for restrictions on the holding of public land (which was being taken over by the elite), and the redistribution of surplus land, including the legacy of Attalus III of Pergamum, who had made the Roman people his heir, to the landless peasants. This was an argument about how the spoils of empire and conquest should be distributed. Gracchus was murdered by his opponents in the elite. Ten years later his brother Gaius proposed making the people of Italy, who increasingly provided the bulk of the Roman armies, Roman citizens. He was killed when his revolt failed. Even greater problems occurred in 91–88 BCE when the Italian allies revolted and began a civil war to demand citizenship. The Romans conceded the principle very quickly. At the same time Mithridates VI of Pontus in Anatolia invaded the Roman province of Asia. An ambitious member of the elite, L. Cornelius Sulla, insisted on being given command of the forces in the east, marched on Rome, removed his opponents from power, killed some and outlawed others. It was the first time a general had used his forces against the Roman government – it was to be the first of many such instances over the following decades.

When Sulla returned victorious from the east in 83 BCE a brief civil war led to mass slaughter and the establishment of Sulla as dictator – his power was illegal and rested on nothing more than brute force. Opponents were once again either killed or proscribed, the Senate was packed with his supporters, the rights of the tribunes were restricted and the Italian cities which had opposed him were deprived of their citizenship, fined and had their land confiscated and given to Sulla's veterans. After his death in 78 BCE the situation worsened. The oligarchy had no method for governing what was now an extensive empire – there was no effective bureaucracy as in China and government was a purely private affair for whoever held a particular office. There was little choice but to give wide powers to special commanders, at first in Spain and then in the east. Here Pompeius was effectively independent – he annexed the remains of the kingdom of Mithridates and then the Seleucids without any reference to the Senate. Similarly between 58–50 BCE Caesar conquered Transalpine Gaul without any reference to the Senate. In 57 BCE Pompeius was given command over the grain supply for Rome, the first time such individual power had been given in a civil matter. The old institutions of Rome had disintegrated under the pressure of war and empire. As the rewards of political success in terms of power, wealth and loot grew greater so did the penalties for failure – death, proscription and confiscation of all assets. As the stakes of the political game rose actions became more extreme. Commanders and provincial governors could not afford to give up their power bases for fear of what their opponents would do to them.

The decisive event came in 49 BCE when Caesar crossed the boundary of his command – the river Rubicon – and marched on Rome to secure power, fearful of what his opponents would do when his period of office ended. He began a civil war which lasted for almost twenty years. The increasing power of a few military commanders is shown by the fact that when Sulla marched on Rome in 88 BCE only one of his officers followed – when Caesar did so only one did not follow him and he was already a supporter of his rival Pompeius. Caesar defeated his rivals and by 44 BCE was effectively king. He was assassinated and in 43 BCE a triumvirate was formed by his followers – Lepidus, Marcus Antonius and Octavius (the heir to Caesar's huge wealth when he was posthumously adopted in Caesar's will). It was hardly a government since they divided the empire among themselves. They defeated Brutus and Cassius, the murderers of Caesar, at the battle of Philippi in 42 BCE and then continued the civil war among themselves. It ended in 31 BCE at the battle of Actium when Marcus Antonius and his lover Cleopatra the queen of Egypt, were defeated and Octavius became sole ruler. The triumph of Octavius marked the end of the old Roman system and the triumph of a new despotism. Although the outward forms of republican government were retained, effective power was concentrated in the hands of the new ruler who was, in effect and soon in practice, emperor. Many among the wealthy were quite happy with the new system as long as it provided stability. For over two centuries it did so apart from one brief civil war.

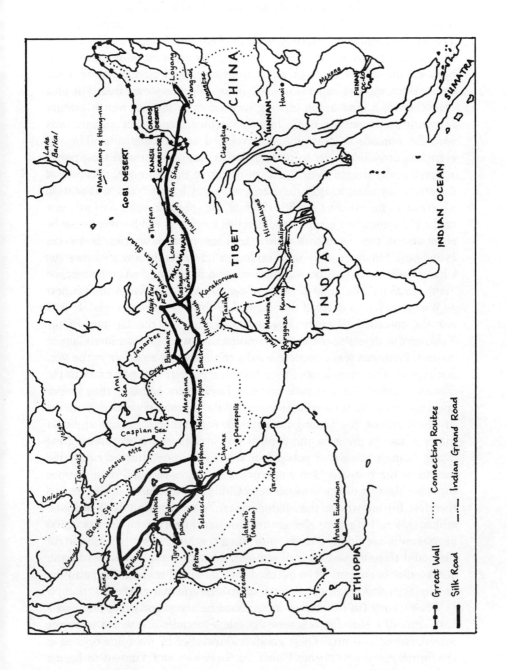

Map 23: Eurasian connections in the Roman–Han period

9.8 Eurasian Connections: the Silk Road

The internal problems affecting both the Han and Roman empires in the first century BCE had little impact on the growing number of connections between the different states and empires of Eurasia. Crucial to these connections was the expansion of Chinese influence westwards. The area controlled by China began moving westwards in the late fourth century BCE with the expansion of Ch'in into Szechwan, and trade and contacts with the nomads of central Asia developed at the same time. The key events occurred in the late second century as part of the new Chinese policy adopted under the emperor Wu Ti of defeating the Hsiung-nu. As part of the search for allies against them an emissary, Chang Ch'ien, was sent on a mission to the far west in 139–126 BCE. He spent ten years as a prisoner of the Hsiung-nu but escaped and reached Ferghana and Bactria where he encountered the Yüeh-chih who had been pushed westwards by the Hsiung-nu. However, they were no longer interested in a war of revenge. Chang Ch'ien was sent on a second mission in 115 BCE when he reached Ferghana, Sogdiana and the oases of central Asia (known to the Chinese as Wu-sun). Wu Ti decided that control of this area was essential. In 101 BCE the so-called 'Western Regions', extending to the far side of the Taklamakan desert near the Pamir mountains, were taken under Chinese control, Ferghana was conquered and a tributary system set up in the Wu-sun region. The oasis states in the last area preferred to pay taxes to the Chinese rather than tribute to the Hsiung-nu because the former encouraged the trade on which so much of their wealth depended. With the divisions among the Hsiung-nu after 59 BCE the Han became the only major power in the area and control was maintained. It wavered during Wang Mang's seizure of power but was easily re-established under the second of the restored Han emperors. The routes through these regions provided the first direct links between China and the Parthian empire and therefore further west to the Mediterranean. They made up the 'Silk Road' which was to be a vital element in Eurasian history for the next 1,500 years. It was not simply a trade route but a conduit along which important ideas and technologies were disseminated between the different societies across the continent. It was used not just by traders but also by missionaries and religious pilgrims, craftsmen and many others.

When Chang Ch'ien arrived in Ferghana he was surprised to find that a vast array of Chinese goods were on sale, especially silk which was only manufactured in China. These goods had travelled by the route opened in the fourth century BCE from China via Szechwan and Yunnan to Burma and eastern India. From there they had been traded along the Indian Grand Road (built under the Mauryan empire) up the Ganges valley to the great

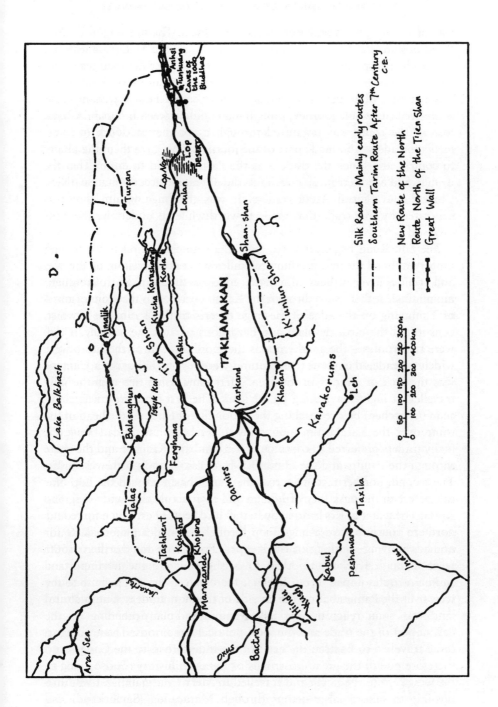

Map 24: The 'Silk Road' in Central Asia

trading city of Taxila and then into Central Asia. The opening of the Silk Road provided a direct route not just to Iran and the Mediterranean but also to the prosperous states of north-west India. The Silk Road was not a natural route – it was over 5,000 miles long across an inhospitable landscape, much of it desert with only a few oases. Few merchants ever completed the whole journey, though many did between India and China. Instead the route was organized through a complex network of intermediate traders who made part of the journey. This gave them the ability to control and block the trade – as the Parthians did to ensure that the Roman and Mediterranean merchants did not make direct contact with the Chinese and central Asian traders. It was the huge wealth that was generated by this trade that made it worthwhile to undertake the risks involved.

The Silk Road began at Ch'ang-an (the Chinese capital until the first century CE) and the first five hundred miles was easy travelling up the Wei and Yellow river valleys along the edge of the Nan Shan (southern mountains). It then went through the Kansu corridor to the frontier town of Tunhuang on the edge of the huge deserts of the Tarim basin which constituted the most desolate and hazardous part of the journey. There were two routes – the southern was the more difficult as the oases were widely spread and daytime temperatures were very high, but the advantage was the lack of bandits in the area. Merchants using this route usually travelled at night, navigating by the stars. The first main stop was Shan-shan (Cherchen) before reaching the major city of Khotan, the head of the route over the Karakorum mountains to Kashmir and India. However, many traders preferred to continue to Yarkand and Kashgar and the route through the Pamirs and the Hindu Kush to Taxila and north-west India. The second, northern, route across the Tarim basin crossed the Lop Nor salt desert to the oasis city of Loulan and then across the sandy desert to Korla. The water at Korla dried up in the third century CE which forced the northern route to take a huge loop through Turfan, a major centre for nomads moving south from the steppes. From here the northern route went through Kucha and Aksu to Kashgar where the northern and southern routes joined. From Kashgar there was a very steep climb to the west over the Pamirs but on the far side of the mountains rich agricultural land was soon reached. The Silk Road now split depending on the destination of the trade and the local political conditions. Those going to India travelled to Bactria, the head of the Indian road to the Ganges and therefore one of the great crossroads of Eurasian history. Those going to the west kept to the north and travelled to Merv (Margiana) – it was also possible to take a large detour through Maracanda (Samarkand) and Bukhara to reach Merv. From Merv the route to the west crossed the

Iranian plateau following the Elburz mountains in order to have regular water supplies. The route then followed a string of walled cities – Hekatompylos, Rhagae and Ecbatana – to central Mesopotamia (Babylon, Seleucia, Ctesiphon or Baghdad depending on the period). From here well-established and flourishing routes led to Aleppo, Antioch and the Mediterranean or, less frequently, to Palmyra and Petra.

The trade along this tortuous route was profitable because of the massive demand, and therefore very high prices in south-west Asia and the Mediterranean, for silk – the luxury item that all of the elite wanted but whose production secrets were closely guarded by the Chinese. Silk was even used as a currency along the road. But it was not just silk that the Romans in particular wanted – the other key item was cast iron, acknowledged by Pliny to be the best the Romans knew. Although knowledge of Chinese techniques spread westwards to the Hsiung-nu about 75 BCE, to the Wu-sun oases about forty years later and to Ferghana in the first century CE, it did not for now spread any further west. (The western parts of Eurasia remained in ignorance about how to make cast iron for more than another thousand years.) The problem with the Silk Road, as with all trade between the two ends of Eurasia (as we shall see in the next section) was that the west produced little or nothing that India and China wanted. The profits were made from the east-to-west trade.

9.9 Eurasian Connections: the Maritime Routes

Routes between Egypt and the bottom of the Red Sea probably date to the early second millennium BCE. They usually combined ship and caravan travel because of the difficulty of sailing up the Red Sea against the prevailing winds. Traders from Egypt normally ended their journeys at the straits of Bab el-Mandeb where local and Indian traders sailed across the Arabian sea to north-west India. This pattern of trade lasted until about 100 BCE when Mediterranean traders opened direct links with western India. Classical historians often assert that Roman traders 'discovered' the monsoons – in fact local traders had sailed with these winds for thousands of years before the Mediterranean traders became familiar with them. It was the demand among the Mediterranean elite for the products of the east – pepper, Indian and Chinese cloth and, of course, silk – that made this trade profitable.

The normal route was across the Mediterranean to Egypt, down the Nile and by caravan to the trading ports such as Berenice at the top of the Red Sea. The ships sailed in convoys (sometimes as many as 120 ships in a season) to the Arabian sea and across on the summer monsoon to the west

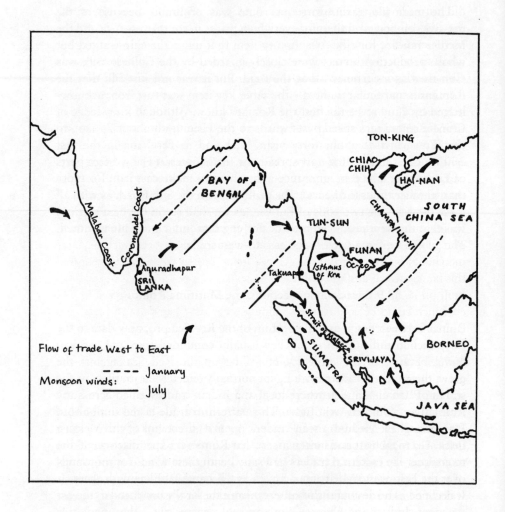

Map 25: Maritime trade of south-east Asia

coast of India. At first the main port for Mediterranean traders was Barygaza near the mouth of the Indus but later voyages were made almost directly eastwards across the Indian Ocean to ports further south. There were over sixteen major ports along this coast where traders from different communities could meet and conclude their bargains. They provided the key link in the east–west maritime trade routes. Mediterranean merchants did not normally travel further east than south India and the trade across the Bay of Bengal and into south-east Asia was dominated by Indian merchants. The long-established routes in this area involved sailing to the north of the Kra isthmus to ports such as Takuapa. By the third century CE Chinese visitors reported that there were over 500 Iranian and Sogdian merchants and their families permanently resident here together with huge numbers of Indians and Hindu priests. Indian traders (and a handful from the Mediterranean) sailed past the Malay peninsula to the islands of south-east Asia which they knew as Suvarnadvipa – 'Golden Island'. By about 200 CE the ships sailing eastwards from India were over 200 feet long, carried about 300 tons of cargo together with 200 people, and towed a smaller vessel in case of accidents.

At the Kra isthmus goods were carried on a short land journey before sailing on to southern Vietnam and the developing area of Funan with its port of Oc-èo. Funan developed as the key interchange between the Malay merchants operating from the Kra isthmus, Indian traders who ventured this far eastwards and the Chinese merchants sailing south. Its influence was built on its highly productive wet-rice agriculture in the hinterland of Oc-èo which could be sold to the visiting merchants. Originally the area was controlled by strong local chiefs who were able to gain prestige and power from their control over the trade and their adoption of external customs and religion such as Hinduism. Around 100 CE, as the wealth from trade grew, the area became a petty kingdom under a ruler known to the Chinese as Hun P'an-huang. A century later the area was controlled by a military leader, Fan Shih-man, who was elected after the death of the son of Hun P'an-huang. He created a small empire by taking control of the Mekong delta area to the east and increasing the food surplus. Expeditions were sent to conquer the eastern coast of the Malay peninsula and gain more control over the east–west trade routes. This was the zenith of Funan's prosperity. It declined as trade routes shifted away from the Kra isthmus and to the all-sea route through the straits of Malacca and via Java to China. China only bothered to send two missions to Funan after the third century CE and the area seems to have been taken over by a strongly Indianized group of rulers from the Malay peninsula. From Funan trade was in Chinese hands along the coast of Vietnam via Chiao-chih (Tongkin), the centre of the pearl trade, to the developing southern ports of China, in particular Canton.

As with the Silk Road, merchants on the east–west maritime routes rarely made a complete voyage along the whole route. Chinese ships seem to have reached the Bay of Bengal by the fourth century BCE and certainly reached India by the first century BCE. They probably sailed on to the Red Sea and the Horn of Africa and certainly a group of Chinese merchants reached the ports of Mesopotamia in 360 CE. Indian traders did sail as far as China on occasions and envoys from some of the minor Indian kingdoms travelled along this route to the Han court in 159–61 CE. An Indian delegation was also sent to Octavius in Rome late in the first century BCE. The Roman and Han empires were aware of each other. China was aware of the rough nature of the Roman empire but always saw it as a maritime country – *Hai-hsi Kuo*, 'the country west of the sea'. The Romans saw China as a land empire but had little idea of the distances involved. Augustus had a map of the world set up in Rome which showed China (which he hoped to conquer) to the east of the Rhine but by only three times the width of Gaul. There were a few direct contacts. In 36 BCE the Chinese general Ch'en T'ang captured about 150 Roman legionaries somewhere in central Asia – they were probably deserters who had gone over to the Parthians and been sent to the far east of that empire. They were taken even further east and settled in Chang-i province in the far north-west of the Han empire. This was only a small incident but it illustrates the range of contacts across Eurasia as societies came closer together. Some Roman merchants did reach the Han court along the maritime route in 166 CE. The Chinese believed them to be (or they passed themselves off as) emissaries of the emperor 'An-tun' (Antoninus Pius) who had in fact died five years earlier. They had little to offer the Han emperor – only rhino horns and turtle shells which were not Roman and which they had gained on their travels.

The experience of these merchants was symptomatic of the problems in the east–west trade. The Mediterranean traders had little to offer which the merchants of the far wealthier societies in India and China wanted – the best available was coral and glass. However, the societies in the west of Eurasia had a very strong demand for the products of the 'east' – spices, silk, iron, cloth, ivory, indigo, onyx and exotic animal skins. Since the 'west' had so little to offer the only way that trade could be sustained was to buy these goods for hard currency – gold and silver. Classical and later European historians often describe the trade as the 'export' of bullion from the Mediterranean and Europe. In fact it was no more than the poorer area of Eurasia using the only assets it had – precious metals – to buy the products the elite desperately wanted from the richer region. This highly unbalanced 'trade' continued in the same pattern until the nineteenth century CE. During the first century CE Pliny suggested that the Roman empire sent over 55 million gold coins to India to sustain trade. In the trading cities along the Indian coast they were cut and pierced, strung up, weighed and turned into bullion – if they were debased they were not accepted.

[*Later South-east Asia 11.7.2; later Indian Ocean trade 12.2.1*]

9.10 Han China: Prosperity and Stability

The restoration of the Han in 25 CE led to a long period of stability and prosperity, especially under the first three emperors until the end of the first century CE. The new regime was built around the big landed families of the central plain, especially Honan, which had supported Kuang Wu Ti in his campaigns against the peasant rebellions and the emperor Wang Mang. The capital was transferred eastwards to Loyang on the Yellow river. Internally China was peaceful and this was reflected in the increasing wealth and importance of the manufacturing and merchant communities. Overseas trade in south-east Asia and westwards to the rest of Eurasia was at a peak. Population grew quickly in some areas such as the southern part of the central plain and in Szechwan and Hunan. The labour force of landless labourers for the great estates therefore increased. However, peasant problems were contained and there were no major revolts until 108 CE.

The situation on the northern and north-western frontiers with the nomads was generally quiet too. The split in the Hsiung-nu gave the Chinese much greater flexibility although there was a considerable degree of caution too – Kuang Wu Ti rejected the idea of attacking the northern Hsiung-nu as too expensive and too difficult. The most important change of policy was the slow drift of the southern Hsiung-nu confederacy within the Han empire as less effort was made to control areas on the fringes of the empire. In many ways this policy strengthened the Han state. By the end of the first century there were about 250,000 Hsiung-nu settled as labourers on the great estates or deployed as soldiers in the Chinese army to control the 'barbarians' who were still outside the empire (the same policy was adopted later by the Romans). However, much of the tributary system remained in place with the Chinese still making annual payments to the Hsiung-nu and being forced to entertain at vast expense about 500 of the Hsiung-nu aristocracy at the Han court. There was a brief Hsiung-nu incursion in 89–90 CE but conditions in the 'western regions', which were extended to include Ferghana and the old Wu-sun area, remained stable and trade along the Silk Road prospered.

It is often argued that after the death of the emperor Ho Ti in 105 CE

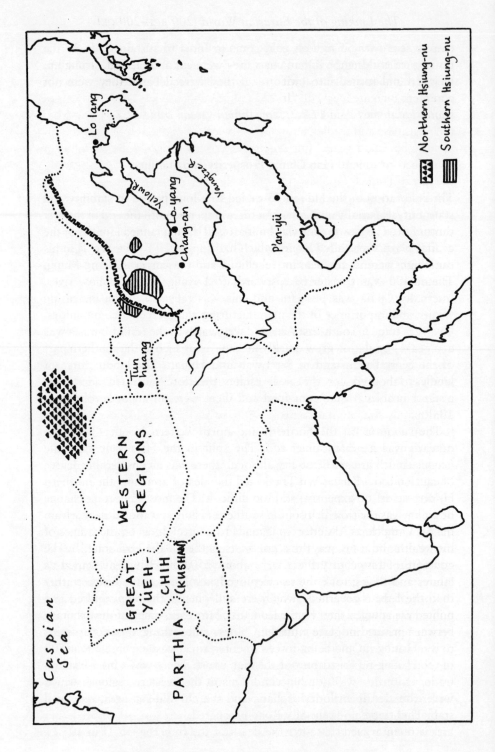

Map 26: Central and East Eurasia under the later Han

there was growing instability in the Han. It is true that the succession of a number of child emperors allowed the power of two groups – the great landed families associated with the imperial family and the eunuchs at court – to increase markedly. In 135 CE the eunuchs were allowed to adopt sons so that they could pass on the huge wealth they were gaining from their business and trading activities. However, these developments do not seem to have had a great impact outside court circles and the government continued to function effectively. The eunuchs dominated the court and the great landed families the countryside. Trade and manufacturing continued to prosper and China remained not just the largest Eurasian state but also the wealthiest. Problems were accumulating, particularly through the growing population placing increasing pressure on the available land which led to peasant discontent as exploitation increased, but these were contained. It was not until the major crisis beginning around 170 CE that the Han empire suffered any major problems.

9.11 The Roman Empire: Prosperity and Stability

The new system instituted by Octavius (renamed Augustus) after his victory in the civil war in 31 BCE rested on military power. He maintained a standing army (from 9 CE a force of 25 legions was standard) which was used mainly for internal control and to stop any rivals gaining power. It took up about half of all state revenues but only a small number of external campaigns were undertaken and these were mainly to keep the army occupied. Augustus created a praetorian guard for his own protection in Rome. Rome had never had a real bureaucracy – senators and other office holders relied on their private resources in order to run state business, hence the ease with which state money could be siphoned off into private hands. Little changed under Augustus. His household was vast because of his wealth and it became the court which undertook the minimal level of government found in the Roman empire. It administered the emperor's estates and slaves, took the revenues from the provinces which he rather than the Senate governed, invented taxes when they were required and minted coins when they were needed. As before, no distinction was made between private and state money. In the provinces the level of government power was low. Outside Italy the provinces had to pay tribute to Rome in the form of a combination of land and poll taxes together with taxes on trade. Once this was done locals were largely left to govern themselves under the overall authority of a Roman governor and his minute personal staff. There were no external attacks on the empire of any consequence and little attempt was made to extend the empire any further. The areas on the fringes of the empire were very poor and could add little to the empire to offset the costs of an expensive garrison. Britain was conquered under Claudius in 43 CE (the northern frontier was normally roughly along the current England–Scotland border; it was briefly extended further north but given up) and Dacia was incorporated in 106. In some areas such as Judea and Armenia there were client-kings but they were effectively part of the empire. The main area where intermittent warfare continued was in Mesopotamia against the Parthians. It was incorporated as a province under Trajan in 115–17 but given up by his successor Hadrian.

In general the imperial succession caused few problems – it passed at first through the family of Augustus. Some, such as Tiberius and Nero, were hardly great assets to the empire but although this might matter to the elite and the court it made little impact on the bulk of the population. On the death of Nero there was a civil war in 68-9 CE (the 'year of the three emperors') which was resolved when an army commander Vespasian took power. His Flavian dynasty lasted until the death of Domitian in 96 CE. During the next century the succession was usually managed by the formal adoption of an heir by the emperor although this was often little more than a fig-leaf for the seizure of power. The second century CE continued the period of stability and prosperity. It was this that led Edward Gibbon to write:

> If a man were called to fix the period in the history of the world during which the condition of the human race was most happy and prosperous, he would, without hesitation, name that which elapsed from the death of Domitian [96] to the accession of Commodus [180].

His views were inevitably limited by a partial view of Eurasian history and too influenced by the position of the Roman elite. Nevertheless they reflected a very real period of internal peace and external stability across the Roman empire from Britain to the Levant at a time when stability elsewhere in Eurasia allowed long-distance trade to flourish.

Over the first two centuries CE the nature of the Roman empire slowly changed and the special position of Rome and Italy was lost. At the time of Augustus most of the empire was inhabited by people who were not Roman citizens. This privilege was slowly extended to a number of cities until in 212 the emperor Caracalla made an almost universal grant of citizenship. From the end of the first century emperors were largely of provincial origin and not from the Roman elite. Trajan (98–117), Hadrian (117–38) and Marcus Aurelius (161–80) were from Spain, and Antoninus Pius (138–161) was from a Gallic family. There was also a gradual influx of provincials into Italy where they slowly infiltrated both the senatorial and equestrian orders. Provincials from the Latin-speaking western provinces were admitted to the senate in the first century CE and Greek speakers from the east afterwards. By 200 the majority in both these 'Roman' orders were provincial in origin although until the end of the second century only Italians normally commanded legions. The whole character of the empire was slowly changing – it was no longer a 'Roman' empire but a Mediterranean one. It was in the eastern Mediterranean that the wealth of the empire was concentrated and access was gained to the Eurasian trade routes. Europe north of the Alps remained mainly tribal, poor and undeveloped with only a few, very small towns, and a thin veneer of 'Roman' civilization. It contributed little to the empire and the elite had no concept of any cultural unity with this region – that was reserved for the Greek-speaking eastern part of the empire.

9.12 The Beginnings of the Eurasian Crisis

Towards the end of the second century there were signs that the long period of stability across Eurasia was drawing to an end. The problems began in China as the agrarian crisis, which had been brewing for some time as population rose to the limits the cultivated land could support, was brought to a head by the disastrous floods (mainly caused by extensive deforestation upstream) along the Yellow river in the 170s. The loss of land, the disruption and the outbreak of disease produced widespread peasant rebellions. The most important was that of the *Huang-chin* or 'Yellow Turbans' led by Chang Chiao and his two brothers. They drew on Taoist tradition and the sect of *T'ai P'ing* or 'Great Peace' to create a messianic, salvationist creed which was partly linked to an attempt to cure the diseases which became rampant. Although for much of the time the movement was engaged in religious observance it had over 360,000 followers under arms. There was a similar but separate movement in Szechwan led by Chang Ling. These peasant rebellions spread rapidly despite the death of the three Chang brothers soon after the foundation of the 'Yellow Turbans'. By 188 the revolt had spread into Shensi, Hopei, Liaotung and Shansi. The authority of the emperor became increasingly nominal as the army took more and more power in the attempt to put down the 'Yellow Turban' rebellion. The last Han emperor, Hsien Ti, was put on the throne by the army commander Tung Cho in 189. The next year his troops sacked the capital Loyang and destroyed both the imperial library and the Han archives. In 192 Tung Cho was assassinated. Although the Han dynasty was not formally abolished until 220 it had no effective power after 190. China descended into anarchy as rival army commanders tried to put down the peasant rebellions and fought each other to establish their own kingdoms. The unified Chinese state disintegrated. It was not to be re-established for almost four hundred years.

The problems within the Han empire and the instability it caused along the Eurasian trade routes probably spread westwards into the Parthian empire. From early in the third century there were widespread revolts in the eastern provinces nearest to central Asia. The rebellions were led by Ardashir who founded the new Sasanian empire. The last Parthian king, Artabanus V, was killed in battle with the Sasanians in either 224 or 226. Within a decade the last Parthian resistance in the mountains of Iran was over. By the mid-third century the Kushan state had also disintegrated. Further west in the Roman empire there were clear signs of growing problems too. Although Gibbon dated the beginning of the decline of the empire to the accession of Marcus Aurelius' natural son Commodus in 190, this is too early a date. Although Commodus had all the defects of earlier emperors such as Tiberius and Nero his reign lasted for only three years. He was replaced by Septimus Severus, the first of a new dynasty of army rulers from Libya who based their power on their control of the powerful Danubian army of ten legions plus auxiliaries. Under the first two rulers of the Severan dynasty – Septimus Severus and his son Caracalla – the period of general stability continued. It was not until the accession of the weaker Elagabalus (218–22) and Severus Alexander (222–35) that the serious problems began. This may have been linked to the spread of problems and trade disruption westwards from the Parthian empire in the 220s. By the next decade the Roman empire entered a period of near anarchy very similar to that which affected China after the 190s. Across Eurasia the long period of stability which had lasted for almost four hundred years with only limited interruptions was over.

[*Later China 10.2, later Roman empire 10.3*]

OVERVIEW 5

THE WORLD IN
150 CE

World Population: 180 million
Regional Population: China: 60 million,
Roman empire: 45 million, India: 40 million,
Africa: 16 million, Americas: 15 million
Major cities: Loyang (500,000), Rome (500,000),
Alexandria (400,000), Seleucia (300,000),
Ch'ang-an (250,000), Antioch (150,000),
Teotihuacan (50,000)

Events:

★ Peak of Han prosperity. China controlling an area as far west as the major central Asian cities

★ Kushan empire flourishing in north-west India

★ Parthian empire in Mesopotamia and Iran

★ Roman empire at its peak – stretching from Britain and the Rhine, across Mediterranean to the Levant

★ Construction of Teotihuacan in its main elaborate form

★ Moche, Nazca and Tiwanaku cultures in Peru

★ Hun P'an-huang kingdom in Funan on India-China trade route

★ Silk Road flourishing

★ Spread of Buddhism from India to central Asia and China

★ First water mills in use across Eurasia

★ First use of paper in China

★ Compass in use in China

★ Metal goods (gold and copper) made in Peru

Crisis
(200–600 CE)

In the four hundred years after 200 the Eurasian world entered a general crisis. China was disunited and in the north 'barbarians' from central Asia infiltrated the borders and set up their own kingdoms. Despite this disunity the influence of Chinese culture spread more widely, and Korea and in particular Japan were incorporated into the wider Eurasian world. In the far west of Eurasia the Roman empire slowly lost control of its western provinces. As in China, 'barbarians' set up their kingdoms, although they remained, to varying degrees, influenced by Roman imperial traditions. Unlike the Han the Roman empire survived by refocusing itself in the richer eastern half of the empire and remaking its institutions. In the process it gradually lost most of what made it a 'Roman' empire and it became a new state. Its main opponent was the Sasanian empire of Iran, the successor to the Parthians, which continued the conflict over the Mesopotamian region. The Sasanian empire was a relatively stable state that escaped many of the problems that affected China and the Roman empire, although it too went through a period of major weakness in the fourth and fifth centuries. Further east, in north-west India, the Kushan state disappeared by about 250 at the latest. North and central India saw the rise and fall of the Gupta empire in the two hundred years after 320. Despite these major disruptions this period in Eurasia was of immense long-term significance to world history because it saw the spread of two of the world's great religions – Buddhism and Christianity.

10.1 Disease

[*Earlier disease patterns 3.6*]
The linking together of the Eurasian world between 200 BCE and 200 CE not only established trading and cultural links which were not lost during the crisis of 200-600 CE (in many respects they were intensified) but it had another dramatic impact – the spread of disease. It is this factor which helps explain some of the underlying problems and the internal collapses that affected Eurasia in this period. As we have seen, the adoption of farming, the rise of sedentary societies and the growth of towns and then cities drastically affected the impact of disease on humans. They were

exposed to new diseases that spread from the animals they domesticated and were also affected by those caused by humans living closely together with inadequate water supplies and sanitation. However, at first the diseases that affected humans were different in the different parts of Eurasia that were still largely isolated from each other. In each area there were outbreaks of disease but the population gradually acquired immunity to the ones to which they were exposed. The linking together of Eurasia meant that as traders and pilgrims moved across the continent, along the Silk Road and via the maritime routes, they spread diseases to which people had not been exposed before. The effects were devastating.

One of the major problems in the history of disease is identifying the diseases which spread across Eurasia. Contemporary accounts are often generalized and unhelpful in their description of the symptoms and the problem is made more difficult by the fact that the first impact of these new diseases was usually far greater, and the symptoms far worse, than they became after people acquired some immunity. However, it does seem clear that despite some major disease outbreaks, for example at Athens in 430 BCE at a crucial point in the Peloponnesian war, the population of south-west Asia and the Mediterranean did not originally suffer from either smallpox or measles. These diseases arrived in two distinct outbreaks, though it is difficult to identify which was which. Between 165 and 180 CE there was a devastating epidemic across the Roman empire which spread from soldiers fighting in Mesopotamia, the focus of trade routes from central Asia and China. The second outbreak was in 251–66. China also suffered a major epidemic beginning in 161–2 among the army in the north-western provinces which suggests that it was probably the same disease as that which affected the Roman empire at this time and that it too spread along the Eurasian trade routes. A little later, between 310 and 322, nearly all of China was affected by two major epidemics in which perhaps a third of the population died in many areas.

One disease which can be identified with some certainty – bubonic plague – produced the first Eurasian-wide epidemic. Its impact was remarkably similar to that of a better-known later outbreak (the 'Black Death' about eight hundred years later 15.1). In both probably about a third of the population died. It almost certainly originated somewhere in north-east India, the only likely centre where the black rat which spread the disease could have been infected. From here it travelled by ship to the Mediterranean, reaching Constantinople in 542. The impact was devastating – at its peak the disease killed over 10,000 people a day in the city. It spread around the Mediterranean but appears not to have reached north-west Europe because the trade linkages with this area were very low. (The new disease that did reach north-west Europe at this time was leprosy.) The bubonic plague also travelled eastwards reaching Kwantung in China in 610 on ships which came from south-east Asia and India. It arrived in China for a second time in 762–806, again in the coastal provinces, brought by ships from India. Between a third and a half of the people in the area died. It reached Japan in 808 where reports again speak of half the population dying. The impact of the spread of all these diseases across Eurasia was fundamental. Overall, between 200 and 1000 CE the population of the world only increased from 220 million to 265 million, the slowest rate of growth since the development of agriculture. This largely reflected the problem societies faced as they adapted to the new disease balance produced by the linking together of Eurasia.

10.2 China: Disintegration c.200–c.430

[Earlier China 9.10, 9.12]
The Han dynasty was formally ended in 220 but long before then it had no effective power and China had begun to disintegrate into a series of small kingdoms as rival military commanders and the main aristocratic families battled for control. Early in the third century it seemed that one family, the Ts'ao, might be able to re-establish a unified dynasty. By 219 they had united the north and pushed south to try and conquer the Yangtze valley. They were defeated at the battle of the Red Cliff on the Yangtze in Hupei and as a result China was divided into three kingdoms. In the south the two allies against the Ts'ao founded their own kingdoms. Liu Pei established the Han dynasty of Szechwan which survived until 263 and Sun Ch'üan founded the Wu dynasty, with its capital at Nanking after 229, which lasted until 280. In the north the Ts'ao family set up the Wei dynasty, at the old capital Loyang, and ruled there until 265. It was a strongly military state. Much of the army was provided by 'barbarian' auxiliaries but the leading families which commanded the armies became a highly exclusive ruling elite, marrying only among themselves. It was these families which eventually undermined the Wei state. The army commander Ssu-ma Yen, who had defeated the Han of Szechwan in 263, returned to Loyang and seized power himself.

Ssu-ma Yen established the new dynasty of the Western Chin which also had its capital at Loyang. After it conquered the Wu at Nanking in 280 it might be argued that China was reunified. In practice little or no central government power could be exercised and much of the south of the country was outside Chin control. However, it was in the north, the very centre of Western Chin power (and the old core region of Chinese civilization) that total disintegration occurred first. It was caused by civil war within the new imperial family, famine, disease and the movement of more than one million refugees further south. It opened the way for an influx of nomadic groups from the steppes. In 316 the old capital of Loyang was abandoned and largely dismantled. The Chin dynasty moved south and established itself as the Eastern Chin at Nanking. However, it still did not control all of southern China – a separate dynasty of the Ch'eng Han ruled at Ch'engtu in Szechwan until 347 when it was annexed by the Chin. This gave the trading communities of southern China access to the trade routes leading to central Asia and did allow some recovery of trade and prosperity. In the north the period from 304 to 439 is known as the 'Sixteen Kingdoms of the Five Barbarians' which gives an accurate indication of the level of political fragmentation in the area. It was a period of huge confusion with small kingdoms, constantly shifting capitals and competing 'barbarian' armies (some from outside the old Han empire, some from inside). The multitude of kingdoms liked to see themselves as heirs to the Chinese tradition and often took their names from the states of the 'Warring States' period over six hundred years earlier. The Chinese elite who remained in the north retreated within their estates, fortified them and set up their own armies.

Over the more than two centuries between the end of the Han dynasty and the 430s some defining themes do emerge out of the general disintegration and considerable social and political chaos. In the north the move of large numbers of nomadic people within the old boundaries of the Han empire and their conversion into peasant farmers was a continuation of the policies followed towards the Hsiung-nu since the restoration of the Han in 25 CE. The multiplicity of states that emerged all continued the policy of trying to maintain control of the border regions from central Asia to Korea. In the former area expeditions and embassies were still sent westwards and although the level of 'Chinese' authority was variable it did extend into the Tarim basin and the Silk Road remained open. Korea was under Chinese control until early in the fourth century. In the south of China the movement of large numbers of people from the north (especially from the early fourth century) was also part of a long-established process. Slowly areas south of the Yangtze, especially around Canton, were settled by Chinese immigrants and the original inhabitants were either killed, assimilated and sinicized, or pushed into the remote mountains. Trade with south-east Asia and India continued – embassies were sent, contact was established with the developing kingdoms on the south-east coast of Vietnam and an expedition was also sent against Taiwan. Szechwan remained relatively isolated, autonomous and wealthy because of its rich soils, mineral resources and control over the trade routes to Yunnan and central Asia. The main problem for the rulers of Szechwan was that its only access eastwards was down the Yangtze valley and this tended to produce endless conflict with the states in the latter area.

10.3 The Roman Empire: Disintegration and Reconstruction 235–337

[Earlier Roman empire 9.11, 9.12]
The murder of Alexander Severus, the last Severan emperor, in 235 marked the beginning of a period of internal anarchy within the Roman empire and external weakness which lasted for fifty years. However, unlike the Han, the empire survived and was reconstructed in the late third century, leading to another period of relative stability until the mid-fourth century. Between 235 and the accession of Diocletian in 284 no line of emperors was established and most lasted only a few months. The various provincial armies put forward their own nominees, often their commanders, but just as readily murdered them a few months later. The role and influence of the Senate declined sharply and never recovered. During this period Rome lost its position as the main imperial residence and centre of the empire and never regained it. Each contestant for the imperial throne increased the size of the army he controlled and the system for paying the army rapidly broke down as central government almost ceased to exist. These problems were linked to the shortage of gold and silver caused by the fact that so much had been sent to India and China to pay for the goods the elite wanted. The silver currency was so debased that it became almost worthless. The various armies were no longer paid in cash and taxes were collected as food so that the military could be fed. Externally the empire was weak. In 251 the emperor Decius suffered a heavy defeat at the hands of the Goths and there were numerous incursions of nomadic and tribal groups both north of the Alps and in the Balkans. In the east there was almost continuous warfare with the Sasanian empire which had replaced the Parthians. Under Shapur they captured Antioch and a number of other cities in the Levant in 256. Four years later they inflicted the greatest humiliation the Romans had suffered for centuries – not only was the Roman army defeated but the emperor Valerian was captured and held as a prisoner.

After 284 the Roman empire entered a period of major reconstruction lasting for fifty years under Diocletian and Constantine. It laid the foundations for what was in effect a new state – the Later Roman empire – which had little in common with the system that had developed over the previous three centuries. Although control over the western provinces of the empire was gradually lost from the late fourth century this new structure survived in the east for almost four hundred years until the rise of Islam. It was not the result of any far-sighted plan but merely a series of ad-hoc decisions that happened to produce a moderately successful new imperial system. A central problem, as in all the early empires, was the imperial succession. Diocletian attempted to solve the problem by having two emperors (nominally for the east and west of the empire) each with their designated successors. The system worked for two decades mainly because of the prestige that accrued to Diocletian following his success in ending the turmoil of the previous fifty years. When he retired in 305 there was a five-year civil war before Constantine won the battle of the Milvian Bridge and entered Rome. But he too had a co-emperor in the east, Licinius, and it was not until the latter was defeated in 324 that Constantine became sole emperor. On his death in 337 the empire was partitioned among his three sons and another civil war ensued. In the end the problem of succession was insoluble – the brief period of stability after 284 resulted from a series of chance events.

In the last resort imperial power was based on the military. Diocletian undertook a restructuring of the army which determined many of the other policies he adopted. More legions were created but they were smaller in size. The army was also split into two – a field army and frontier forces. Its total size is difficult to estimate but it may have been about 400,000 and it was a major social and economic burden. Diocletian had little choice but to recognize the collapse of the monetary economy and the continued need to support the army in kind. This was done through a land tax assessed on agricultural output but based on what the army required. It was paid locally to the army because it was impossible to move food over any significant distance. In practice the elite secured significant exemptions and the burden of the tax fell almost entirely on the peasantry. The overriding aim of the government was to ensure the continuing flow of taxes in the form of food so as to maintain the army. One way to do this was to try and tie the peasantry to their existing estates. This policy simply reflected a growing social trend – the increasing power of landlords over their tenants and the creation of a new social group, the *coloni*, a type of serf tied to the land and required to work on the landlord's estate. Diocletian tried to make all occupations, not just the peasants, hereditary but no government, let alone one as weak as that of the late Roman empire, could enforce such a policy and it remained no more than theoretical. Equally theoretical was Diocletian's edict on prices of 301 which was designed to cope with continuing inflation.

One area where the government could take effective action was in the creation of separate military and civil governors for each province. In parallel a new set of provinces was created, all much smaller than their predecessors. For example, Britain was now divided into four provinces rather than one and the Iberian peninsula was divided into five provinces. It was symptomatic of the fact that effective government control could only be exercised over a very limited area. The special status of Italy was finally abolished and the land tax imposed in its eleven provinces. This reflected the declining importance of the old centres of the empire, in particular Rome. New centres emerged such as Nicomedia near the Bosphorus (Diocletian's main residence until his retirement), Thessalonica, Milan and Aquileia. Constantine carried this one stage further with dedication and rebuilding of Byzantium as Constantinople after 330. This city, with its superb natural harbour and key strategic site astride the trade routes to the Black Sea, became his main residence for the last seven years of his life. At first this probably seemed no more than another example of a policy common among earlier emperors of founding a city or using an existing one as a new imperial administrative centre. There was one important difference – not only did Constantine open up the Senate so that it became an empire-wide order but he created a second Senate in Constantinople. It was a further symbol of the decline in the position of Rome and Italy and the fact that this was no longer a 'Roman' empire except in name and ideology. Constantinople did not become a major imperial capital until the late fourth century but then it was to remain one for another 1,500 years.

10.4 The Spread of Buddhism

The turmoil across Eurasia after 200 CE did not impede, and may even have encouraged, the spread of two of the world's great religions – Buddhism and Christianity. In the first five hundred years or so of its existence Buddhism was largely confined to India. It spread from India in the early centuries CE and was transformed in Tibet, central Asia and China – in the latter area it adapted to Chinese traditions in much the same way that Christianity did within the Roman empire. China became effectively a Buddhist state for over six hundred years after about 400 and it was central to the further diffusion of Buddhism into Korea and Japan. The expansion of Buddhism was a far more extensive phenomenon than the contemporaneous diffusion of Christianity within the Roman empire and represented the most complex cultural exchange within Eurasia up to this time.

By the last couple of centuries BCE Buddhism in India was becoming more institutionalized through the development of the *sangha* or monastic orders and the rise of monasteries, many of which owned substantial amounts of property. It also attracted growing numbers of wealthy lay followers, especially among merchants who helped spread Buddhist ideas along their trade routes. In parallel new elements emerged within Buddhism. The original doctrine (the *Theravada* tradition) stressed the asceticism of the *sangha* and the importance of individual enlightenment through meditation. It was supplemented by the development of the *Mahayana* or 'greater vehicle' school. The latter stressed the idea of the *Bodhisattva* or enlightened being who rejected the attainment of *nirvana* and accepted continued rebirth until all beings obtained enlightenment. These developments were linked to the increased complexity of Indian Buddhist philosophy, especially the *Prajnaparamita* or 'perfection of wisdom' school and its ideas about the universal void and essential emptiness of all phenomena. In addition other schools developed a tradition, which became particularly important in Tibet later, stressing the more mystical and devotional aspects of Buddhism and the semi-divinity of the Buddha. The increasing variety of the various Buddhist traditions widened its appeal considerably.

The most important area for the development of these new ideas was north-west India and the Kushan empire. From here Buddhism spread along the trade routes, especially the Silk Road. It certainly moved westwards into the Parthian empire and probably some knowledge of it travelled even further west towards the Mediterranean. It is difficult to judge the impact of Buddhism on the development of Christian ideas but as the sole religion in the world at this time to have a highly developed monastic system its impact on the later development of Christian monasticism was fundamental. Far more important was its spread eastwards to China. The first translators of texts into Chinese were the Parthians, Sogdians and the people of the oases states of central Asia, not the Indians. The first references to Buddhism in China date to 65 CE in northern Kiangsu. At first it seems to have been confined to foreign traders who reached northern China along the Silk Road and then to those groups associated with them. Shortly after 300 it also spread along the maritime trade routes into southern China. At first the impact was confined to *Theravada* meditational practices but soon there were an increasing number of translations of the *Mahayana* philosophical texts.

The great expansion of Buddhism among the Chinese began in the late fourth century and its growth very quickly became phenomenal once it established a Chinese base and was no longer seen as a foreign import. Buddhism could adapt easily into the Chinese tradition, especially Taoism, which had elements which could be seen as sharing common features with Buddhism. Ideas about fate and destiny could be equated with Buddhist ideas about *karma*. Many Buddhist moral teachings and practices such as meditation were also compatible with existing Chinese ideas. Two of the main importers, translators and developers of Indian works were Hui-yüan (334–417) in the Yangtze area and Kumarajiva (350–413) in northern China. Monastic orders were rapidly established and pilgrims travelled along the trade routes by land and sea to India especially once the complexity, subtlety and diversity of Buddhism and the need to return to the authentic Indian texts were appreciated. Numerous accounts by these pilgrims exist but perhaps the most famous is that of Fa-hsien. He left Chang-an in 399 and travelled along the Silk Road to north-west India and then down the Ganges valley, where he visited the numerous Buddhist sites. He went by ship to Sri Lanka, Sumatra and Java before returning to China in 414. His *Fo-kuo-chi* ('Report on the Buddhist kingdoms') has been preserved in its entirety. It and the accounts of similar Chinese pilgrims over the succeeding centuries provide the only major source of information for the history of India at this time. In total, over 1,700 Buddhist texts were translated into Chinese by huge teams of translators who established standardized Chinese terms for the highly complex Indian philosophical concepts. In the four centuries after 515 fifteen biblio-graphical catalogues of the translations were produced. These works, together with the *Theravada* texts in the Pali language of Sri Lanka, now form the major source for numerous Buddhist texts. They made a funda-mental and enduring impact on the Chinese conception of the world which was reinforced by the fact that it was not just Buddhist texts that reached China. Almost as important were the Indian works on mathematics, astronomy and medicine which had a similar impact on other areas of Chinese thinking and knowledge.

The rapidly growing popularity of Buddhism had a major impact on Chinese society. A census in northern China taken in 477 showed that there were 6,478 registered monasteries with over 77,000 monks. By 534 there were over 30,000 monasteries with about two million monks. The first royal monasteries were established by the Northern Wei dynasty of the Tabgatch in 476 at P'ing-ch'eng. Later their capital, Loyang, became the most important Buddhist centre in Asia. By 534 there were over 1,300 monasteries and the largest (the Yung-ming) with a nine-storey stupa was the tallest building in the city. It contained over 3,000 foreign monks and had over 1,000 rooms for visiting foreign pilgrims. New forms of Buddhist art were developed, in particular the *Ch'ien-fo-tung* or rock art caves. The first were the 1,000 Buddha complex near Ten-huang on the Silk Road which was begun in 366 and from here the practice spread rapidly across northern China and Szechwan. Equally popular were wall paintings, of which few now survive. Monasteries became the centres of cultural and artistic life but the problem for the state was the impact they had on society and the economy. Buddhist institutions insisted on complete independence from the state. The *sangha* were exempt from secular law and obligations to the state such as military service. The property of the monasteries was inalienable and increased at a phenomenal rate because of the massive upsurge of belief. This posed two major problems – finding enough soldiers to man the army and dealing with the decline in tax revenue as the estates of the monasteries increased. A government department – *Chien-fu-ts'ao* ('Office of Supervising Merit-Creating Affairs') was established by the Northern Wei, staffed by Buddhist monks and its chief became the supervisor of all monks. The aim was to try and create a mechanism to restrict the number of people becoming monks – quotas were even set for each area. In general, such was the support for Buddhism, not just at a popular level but also among the aristocracy and the royal families, that the effectiveness of these controls was very limited.

10.5 Paganism

Christianity in the Roman empire encountered a very different world and spread in a very different way from Buddhism in China. The problem in analysing what happened is that nearly all the sources for the story are Christian and they inevitably give a very biased account. There is, for example, no evidence to substantiate the claim, often made by Christian historians, that there was a decline in paganism in the first centuries CE or that there was a 'spiritual gap' waiting to be filled by Christianity. It is impossible to make detailed statements about either what people believed or the supposed rise and fall of particular beliefs – the evidence available is much too limited and the most important aspects of personal beliefs are unknowable. It was certainly not automatic that Christianity would succeed and replace long-accepted beliefs – Hinduism (in many respects very like south-west Asian and Mediterranean paganism) survived in India and so did long-held ideas in China. Neither did Christianity become so well entrenched that it could not be swept away very rapidly by the spread of Islam in the seventh century in the very areas where Christianity had long been strongest. By about 800 Christianity had been pushed back into the peripheral areas of western Eurasia.

In the first centuries CE paganism had great internal vitality and was at the heart of the social life of the Roman empire. It encapsulated long-established custom and beliefs and was maintained and supported because people believed that it was right and because they thought it benefited them. Religion was at the heart of social life from the yearly round of great public ceremonials, to feasting and drinking, to the most basic pre-occupations of life such as health, success and having children. Offerings were made to whichever god was believed to control that aspect of life in much the same way as was done later to the saints in Christianity. Paganism was not a totally shapeless profusion of gods – some were much more important than others, some were particularly strong locally and others performed important social functions. By far the most important, judging by the number of inscriptions, were Zeus in the east and Jupiter in the west (outside Africa). Gods were often seen as having multiple forms such as the mother of the gods, represented as Cybele, Bellona, Astarte and Ma according to each particular area and its accepted beliefs. There was no problem about having more than one god represented in one place of worship. These places varied in function from the great healing sites such as the Asclepion at Epidaurus, which was rather like the modern Lourdes, to those restricted to the followers and initiates of particular gods such as Cybele or participators in the Eleusinian mysteries. In general the Mediterranean world was not influenced by the Iberian, Celtic or Germanic gods that the Romans encountered when they conquered areas north of the Alps, although Epona, the Gallic god of horses, was popular among the charioteers and circus people of Rome. Each emperor usually had one particular god or cult that he favoured. Hadrian completed the temple of Zeus in Athens and Elagabalus in the early third century built a temple in Rome for the Syrian god he worshipped. But there was no attempt to enforce a particular set of beliefs and cults could rise and decline depending on their popularity. The beliefs of the few philosophers among the elite – the Stoics, Epicureans and the kind of philosophy found in the *Meditations* of the emperor Marcus Aurelius, bore no relation to those of the mass of the population.

Some beliefs and cults went beyond worship of particular gods for the benefits they might bring and had a more complex view of the place of the individual in the universe through ideas about the soul, afterlife and rebirth. These religions are often described as 'oriental cults' although it is difficult to see exactly what was 'oriental' about them. Use of such terminology rests upon long-established European views of the world in which 'the orient' is seen as irrational and mysterious and influencing the 'rational' and 'scientific' mind of the Greeks and Romans (and hence Europeans). There had long been a transmission of beliefs from the eastern Mediterranean to the west through Greece and Italy. For example, it is difficult to believe that Pythagoras and his supporters who argued for the transmigration of souls and rebirth were not influenced by similar Indian ideas. The most significant of all of these beliefs in the early centuries CE was Mithraism. It is often thought to be 'Persian' in origin although there is no evidence to support such an assertion – in fact no place of origin can be traced and it appears for the first time shortly before 100 CE already widely spread across the western Roman empire and in Rome (especially Ostia). It was very effective at gaining converts but little is known about its beliefs and structure because no writings survive and everything has to be interpreted from the chapels and their carvings. There were no public ceremonies and worship was in groups of about fifty meeting in small chapels and crypts. It seems clear that Mithras was a saviour god who, through ritual slaughter of a bull, saved the world and became identified with *Sol Invictus* – the 'Invincible Sun'. Some of the inscriptions on the walls of the chapels include the phrase: 'And us you have saved by shedding the eternal blood'. Mithras had two helpers, Cautes and Cautoprates, whose statues usually flanked the chapel entrance – they represented the rising and setting sun respectively and Mithras the midday sun. The worshippers purified themselves in baths before entering the chapel and then followed a period of preaching and instruction before a sacred meal of consecrated bread and water in memory of Mithras. Believers went through seven stages of initiation, advance and purification which were linked to the planets, the moon and the sun – indeed the representations of the stars on the roofs of many of the chapels provide an accurate picture of the night sky in the second and third centuries CE.

Another religion emerged a couple of centuries after Mithraism – Manichaeism. Its founder, Mani (216–76), was from a Zoroastrian family in Mesopotamia. He saw all existing faiths (including Christianity) as limited and only for a particular people whereas his own, which was strongly dualist and saw the world as a conflict between good and evil (clearly derived from Zoroastrianism), was universal. It had a wide appeal, being intellectually coherent in explaining the problem of evil and giving the hope of individual salvation. It was ascetic with a clear moral code and produced a strong community spirit among its followers. By the late third century it had spread widely, mainly through merchants, across the Mediterranean, through the Sasanian empire and into north-west India. It always faced strong persecution from both Zoroastrianism (which viewed it as a heresy) and later Christianity. The spread of Islam effectively eliminated it in south-west Asia but it survived in central Asia and spread into China where it was transformed by incorporating elements of Taoism and Buddhism.

10.6 Early Christianity

'Paganism' was highly tolerant and accepted all beliefs. Until the early centuries CE monotheism was merely a Jewish peculiarity. The problem in considering the evolution of monotheistic beliefs – Judaism, its offshoot

Christianity and the closely related Islam – is that because much of the world now follows the latter two beliefs, they are usually seen as an 'advance' of human understanding. However, from a wider perspective they can also be seen as lacking the philosophical subtleties of Buddhism and Taoism. In addition, monotheism poses a number of acute problems which are not faced by other religions and which have never been wholly resolved. In particular, if God is omnipotent why is there evil and suffering in the world? Christianity was also to be plagued by endless disputes over the exact relationship between God and his son, made even more difficult by the introduction of a third element, the Holy Ghost. Overall, the worst, most vicious and long-lasting disputes, wars and persecutions in world history have occurred within this family of religions.

All that can reliably be said about Christian origins is that by the late first century CE what had begun as a Jewish sect had spread beyond the Jewish community, mainly under the influence of the teachings of Paul who, as is clear from the Christian texts, radically reshaped earlier beliefs about Jesus, his status and his teachings. By the early second century Christianity was of little importance within the Roman empire – it was merely a minor cult which passed largely unnoticed. Yet within three centuries it was to be the official state religion with profound consequences for later history. How did this come about? It seems fairly clear that until the early fourth century very little changed. The Christians seem to have been a small, introverted community who rarely married outside their group and who avoided attention as far as possible. According to a letter from the bishop of Rome in 251 it seems as though there might have been about 150 Christian ministers in the city (a third of them were exorcists) and a total congregation of about 1,500, perhaps a few more. This was a minuscule proportion of the population of a city of about 500,000 inhabitants. Yet this was one of the main centres of Christianity, suggesting that strength elsewhere was far less and in most places non-existent. The two main histories of the third century do not even mention the Christians, the only sources are those preserved by the Church itself. Most of the people in the empire probably had little idea about what the Christians believed.

The problem in dealing with the history of Christianity is that all the sources come from within the Church so that everything is shown in the best possible light and anything detrimental is omitted. These sources set out coherent and powerful arguments for the large body of highly complex theology within Christianity and converts are shown as rapidly accepting these ideas, changing their lives and becoming part of a devout spiritual community. In practice theology was only for a very small minority of the elite, there is little evidence of preaching and most Christian literature seems to have been aimed at the already converted. It is unlikely that doctrine was a major element in conversion except for a very small number. The most important element for most converts was exorcism, the driving out of 'spirits' and 'devils', together with miracles, cures and prophesying, all of which could be taken as demonstrating the power of Jesus, his followers and a God who was antagonistic to all other beliefs. The Church also made much of its persecution by the state, although it is difficult to see why this and the associated creation of martyrs should make converts. In practice the persecutions were very infrequent, limited and ineffective. The Roman state simply did not have the power to enforce beliefs. In 303 Diocletian issued an edict to destroy Christian churches and scriptures and although this lasted in theory until 311 its impact was very limited. It was later exaggerated by the Christians in order to magnify the impact of Constantine.

10.7 Constantine and the Established Church

The key event for Christianity came in 312 with the 'conversion' of Constantine on the night before the battle of the Milvian Bridge which secured his position as emperor. He is supposed in some accounts (but not all) to have had a dream (for pagans a key means of revelation) linking his success to Christianity. The problem in dealing with the events of his reign are that the sources, especially the main church history by Eusebius, are flagrantly biased in favour of Constantine because of his role in ensuring the ultimate success of Christianity. Indeed it is very difficult to believe that Christianity would have triumphed without the support of Constantine and the later emperors. Even then progress was very slow. In the early fourth century Christianity was still a very small, minority religion – the army remained strongly tolerant and non-Christian until the end of the fourth century and two-thirds of Constantine's own government was not Christian. By the early fifth century even in the eastern, most Christianized part of the empire, about half the holders of public office were still not Christians. Not until well into the fifth century did Roman society become Christian. The old Roman elite, now largely isolated from the imperial court which was at Milan even when the emperor chose to visit Italy (which he rarely did), remained the last bastion of paganism. Not until the fifth century were the cities more Christian than pagan and the country-side, especially in remote and backward areas such as Sardinia and Britain, remained overwhelmingly pagan. Even Constantine himself retained many pagan attributes. Until 321 his coins were still inscribed with the symbols of Apollo and the sun. Although the christogram was used after 324 this seems to have had little meaning and became essentially an imperial symbol which was even used on the coins of the pretender Marnetius who was not a Christian. Constantine still allowed pagan temples such as that at Hispellum in Italy to be built and dedicated to the imperial family into the 330s.

Constantine did what emperors had done in the past – favoured his own religious beliefs. He began in 313 with the edict of Milan which granted toleration to all religions, although such a move only benefited Christianity. However, he did not engage in any mass conversion attempt either voluntary or by force – such an idea was still unknown. He could, however, lead by example through the dedication of churches, gifts of land, the granting of exemption from taxation and the looting of temples to provide resources for the church. Because he was emperor his actions had a disproportionate impact and convinced many, especially in the elite, that conversion and support for the church was the route to success. Constantine remained a brutal and violent ruler in the Roman tradition. Although it is possible to trace some Christian impact on his legislation, such as the removal of the penalties on celibacy, little changed in other areas. The church was allowed to hold slaves and did so on its estates; the only change was that slaves themselves were not to be branded on the forehead (elsewhere was still acceptable). A slave nurse who abducted a girl for marriage was to be killed by having molten lead poured down her throat. Wives could now only obtain a divorce (which had been easy in Roman society) and retain their dowry if their husband was a murderer or sorcerer.

One key element of Constantine's policy, which was to have a profound effect on all the subsequent history of the church, was that he saw himself not just as its patron but as its governor. Even more important was the fact that the leaders of the church willingly accepted this role, no doubt in gratitude for the privileged position he gave them. Christianity, unlike contemporary Buddhism in China and most other religions, became a state church dependent on state favours. The new position of the church had a fundamental impact on its beliefs. Until the fourth century Christianity contained, like most religions, a variety of beliefs and saw no reason to insist that only one was 'correct'. That changed under Constantine who insisted, as did many leaders of the church, that only one doctrine could be tolerated. The result was that Christianity became deeply and venomously divided between different doctrines. Most centred around the very difficult theology of the Trinity and the nature of free will and original sin. A particular problem was the nature of Christ – was he only divine (monophytism), or was he not divine (Arianism) or did he have two separate natures (Nestorianism), or was he a complex mixture of the two (which was the one finally adopted)? The attempt to define 'correct' belief and a 'creed' created 'heresies'. The adherents of the latter were no more than the minority who lost the debate within the church councils called by the emperor, starting with that at Nicaea in 325. At the same time the church was also split by schisms such as the Donatist in North Africa and conflict between the increasingly powerful bishoprics in the main cities of the empire – Rome, Antioch, Jerusalem, Alexandria and Constantinople. At the same time the desire within the church for acceptance and influence meant that many elements of paganism were incorporated into Christian beliefs such as the festivals of Easter and Christmas and the growing role of the saints.

One reason for the success of Christianity was the long reign of Constantine (twenty-five years) and the fact that his family and all subsequent emperors were also Christians apart from Julian who, in his short reign in the early 360s, had no time to affect events and did little apart from removing the tax privileges of the church). Over the course of the fourth century imperial policy was to favour Christianity and it gained more and more privileges, power and wealth. Money flowed to the church through donations, tax exemption and loot from temples. More and more functions and ceremonials within society were taken over by the church. Bishops became increasingly powerful local leaders, particularly in the west of the empire as imperial administration weakened. Slowly and steadily the number of its adherents increased. A few such as Augustine were converted by intellectual arguments but most were not. Some of the conversions were probably insincere and based on the increasingly clear evidence that Christian belief was the route to success. As before there seems to have been little discussion of the subtleties of doctrine and much more reliance on miracles, healing and exorcism. Some converts had little choice – slaves had to follow the beliefs of their masters which could be enforced through beatings (which were endorsed by the church). Landowners could even lose their estates if they allowed, even unwittingly, their use for prohibited (i.e. non-Christian) worship. Violence and physical coercion, supported by parts of the army, were used against pagans and heretics. In 386 bishop Marcellus used soldiers to destroy the great temple of Zeus at Apamea in Syria. Six years later the local bishop led a mob in Alexandria to destroy the Serapaeum (the temple of Serapis) which was described by Ammianus as 'next to the Capitol . . . the most magnificent building in the world'. In 407 an imperial edict ordered that: 'If any images stand even now in the temples and shrines . . . they shall be torn from their foundations . . . Altars shall be destroyed in all places.' As Christian influence increased so did the anti-Jewish policy of the state. Christians who converted to Judaism lost all their property. In addition Jews were banned from imperial administration, from acting as advocates and in 438 were barred from all state honours.

One aspect of the rise of Christianity was the emergence of ascetics and monasteries. This began in the mid-fourth century in Egypt and spread into the Levant – by the early fifth century there were over sixty monasteries in the latter area. Many individuals became celibate after conversion. Some of the ideas behind this movement almost certainly came from further east where they had developed almost a thousand years earlier and therefore outside a specifically Christian context. At this stage the monasteries were not organized into the great religious orders that became common several centuries later in Europe. They were wealthy and privileged and often confined to members of the elite – there is little evidence of much giving to the poor despite the huge transfer of wealth to the church. By the fifth century the church was deeply embedded into the structure of the late Roman empire and had acquired considerable wealth and power. The majority of the population were now Christian, at least to some extent. The church, which remained highly intolerant of other beliefs, increasingly used its power to enforce its beliefs and regulate social activities to an extent that would have been unimaginable a few centuries earlier.

10.8 Revival in China

From about the mid-fifth century, at the time when the Roman empire had become mainly Christian and Buddhism had spread widely in China, there are clear signs of a recovery in China from the chaos of the previous two hundred and fifty years. In the south of the country reviving trade with central Asia and by sea into south-east Asia brought increasing wealth. Power was in the hands of a dominant aristocratic elite composed of the descendants of those who had moved south in the period after 300 and the indigenous rich landlords of the Yangtze valley and the coasts of Hangchou Bay. They were able to exempt themselves from taxation and government requisitions and controlled their own private armies which, in aggregate, were more powerful than those controlled by the state. Late in the fifth century they were able to impose a legal ban on marriages between the aristocracy and those they regarded as 'commoners'. These groups held the real power at the court of the weak dynasties that ruled southern China until well into the sixth century. The Sung dynasty (420–79) was founded by Liu Yü, an army leader in the battles against the northern dynasties. He overthrew the Eastern Chin who had ruled the area since the great migration from the north. The Sung were reasonably stable until the 450s but were themselves overthrown by a military revolt which founded the

Ch'i dynasty (479–502). Attempts to control the power of the aristocracy led to another military revolt and the establishment of the Liang dynasty (502–57). The long reign (almost fifty years) of its founder Wu produced some stability but it was increasingly unable to control the activities of freelance military groups which were little better than bandits preying on the peasantry. The Liang dynasty lost control of Szechwan in 553 and the south descended into a brutal civil war in which many of the aristocracy were killed. Out of that conflict emerged the Ch'en dynasty (557–89) but it remained weak and ineffective, unable to deploy any significant military force.

The most important events for the future history of China took place in the north. After the chaos of the 'Sixteen kingdoms of the Five Barbarians' the area was reunified by the Northern Wei dynasty. This was founded by a former nomadic people, the Tabgatch (called Toba by the Chinese). They were granted land in northern Shansi in 315 and by the end of the fourth century they had established a kingdom with its capital at Ta-t'ung which expanded into Hopei and Honan and by 439 had unified most of northern China. The Tabgatch formed the nomadic aristocracy which held most of the land in the kingdom although the administration was still carried out by Chinese. The bulk of the peasantry were also Chinese and were subject to strong organization. Groups of five families formed *lin* or 'neighbour-hoods', five *lin* made up a *li* or 'village' and five *li* constituted a *tang* or 'commune'. These formed the basis for military units and the leaders at each level were responsible to the central government. As new areas were controlled the government moved peasants around to begin cultivating the land and creating tax revenue – between 386 and 409 over 450,000 people were moved to the area around Ta-t'ung. The Tabgatch were soon acting as a normal Chinese power, attacking the nomads to the north and north-west. In 429 there was a major campaign against the *Juan-juan* (an abusive Chinese name meaning 'wriggling worms') who may have been the Avars who invaded Europe about two centuries later.

As the Tabgatch settled and established their state some of the old aristocracy drifted back to the steppes to continue their nomadic life. Those who remained steadily adopted Chinese culture. Early in the fifth century the Chinese penal code was adopted but the main changes came under Hsiao Wen Ti (471–99) who adopted the Chinese dynastic name of Yüan. In 480 Chinese imperial rituals replaced nomadic ones and three years later intermarriage between the Tabgatch and the Chinese was not only allowed but positively encouraged. In 494 the capital of Ta-t'ung was abandoned and the imperial court moved to the old Chinese capital of Loyang (abandoned in 315) and began rebuilding it. In the same year the Tabgatch language was prohibited at court in favour of Chinese and in 495 the Tabgatch elite were ordered to adopt Chinese names. The Tabgatch were still a powerful state in the early sixth century but they then suffered a rapid and total collapse. A revolt in 523 by the 'barbarian' groups guarding the steppe frontier set off a vicious civil war which lasted until 534. Eventually Loyang was captured and all the members of the royal family together with their courtiers were killed. The empire was divided up among the military who had won the civil war.

General Kao Huan established the Eastern Wei dynasty at Yeh in southern Hopei. He was a traditionalist who was hostile to Chinese influences and he remained close to the Tabgatch warrior elite who dominated the state. General Yü Wen T'ai set up the Western Wei at the old imperial site of Ch'ang-an and depended on many of the sinicized elite of the previous Northern Wei dynasty. The Western Wei were able to deploy more strength and influence in central Asia than any Chinese dynasty for over three hundred years. Embassies were sent from Sasanian Iran in 553, 558 and 578 and the various kingdoms in central Asia (Sogdiana, Bukhara and Khotan) sent missions to Ch'ang-an in 560, 564, 567 and 574. The main strength of the state was the peasant militia army created in 550 which gave it a decisive military superiority over its rivals and it was from Ch'ang-an that China was to be reunified by the end of the sixth century. Yü Wen T'ai died in 556 and was succeeded by his son (who founded the nominally new dynasty of Chou) and he destroyed the Eastern Wei (now called Ch'i) in 577. Despite this success at reunifying the north under a single dynasty there was a revolt led by a member of the royal family, Yang Chien, in 581. He seized power and set up the Sui dynasty. In 589 the Sui easily conquered the weak southern state of the Ch'en at Nanking and reunified China for the first time in almost four hundred years.

The tradition among Chinese historians writing their carefully structured and patterned dynastic histories, which have been followed to a large extent by many western historians of China, has been to emphasize the continuities of Chinese history, the strength of Chinese culture and the desire of the 'barbarians' to become sinicized as rapidly as possible. However, it is clear that the long period of disunity in the four hundred years after the Han brought about major changes in Chinese culture, society and the state. Fundamental to the changes was the impact of Buddhism, especially under the Tabgatch. For at least five hundred years after the early fifth century China was a Buddhist state with a predominantly Buddhist culture and this was a profound discontinuity with the earlier Chinese empire under the Han. Even after the decline of Buddhism much of its influence remained and China could not and did not return to its old culture. Similarly although the 'barbarians' who settled within the borders

of the old Han state eventually adopted many Chinese cultural and administrative traits this was not a one-way process. China was profoundly altered by the settlement of former nomads as peasants and the incorporation of the nomadic elites. The result was that a new cultural, social and political synthesis emerged. Many of the great families who dominated the Sui and T'ang state in China until the early tenth century, with names such as Yü-wen, Mu-jung, Ling-hu and Yü-ch'ih are clearly derived from the Turkish and Hsien-pi nomads of the steppes. The T'ang rulers themselves, who adopted the Chinese name of Li, were in fact half Turkish in origin.
[*Later China 11.5*]

10.9 The Incorporation of the East Eurasian Periphery

In parallel with the disunity of China between the fall of the Han around 200 CE and the establishment of the Sui in 589 there was a major expansion of Chinese influence mainly linked to the spread of Buddhism. The result was that by the early fourth century the first primitive states had emerged in Korea and by the sixth century there were the first signs that Japan was moving in the same direction.

10.9.1 Korea
Korea had long been a frontier area for the Han and other northern Chinese states. Varying degrees of control were exercised and slowly local Korean rulers emerged within the provinces created by the Han. They were dependent on the Chinese for their status and their rule was largely based on kinship (as was Korean society as a whole), with power passing from brother to brother within the ruling clans before moving to the next generation. Following the end of the Han and the growing chaos in northern China, especially after the fall of the Wei in 265, the Chinese gradually lost control of Korea, enabling local rulers to set up their own states. From the early fourth century there were three major states in the Korean peninsula – Silla and Paekche in the south and Koguryo in the north. The last became the most powerful not just because it was closest to Chinese influence but because it had room to expand northwards into Manchuria. Although Koguryo was defeated by Paekche in 371 it recovered quickly and expanded rapidly under Kwanggaet'o (391–413) and during the long reign of Changsu (413–91). The capital was moved from the mountains to P'yongyang and throughout the fifth century Koguryo was a major empire stretching from the north of Manchuria to the south of the peninsula. It maintained this position through much of the sixth century despite the

expansion of the kingdom of Silla (always the most backward of the Korean states) along the eastern side of the peninsula. All three states were still fairly primitive – they were dominated by a few aristocratic land-owning families who commanded most of the armies, and the level of central control was low. Culturally the most important development was the spread of Buddhism from China. Koguryo officially became Buddhist in 366, Paekche in 384 and the more remote Silla in the mid-fifth century. It seems likely that writing (in the form of the Chinese script) spread into Korea with the Buddhist monks although it was highly unsuitable for the very different Korean language. As Buddhism established itself Korea became a centre for its further diffusion to Japan.
[*Later Korea 13.6.1*]

10.9.2 Japan

The geography of Japan helps to explain some of the fundamental factors behind its unique history. As a group of islands over a hundred miles from the Eurasian mainland it was remote from all the complex changes occurring in China. Even after the fourth century CE when Chinese culture was an overwhelming influence for centuries, the history of Japan remained dominated by internal factors. The islands were never invaded and only once before 1945 was there even a threat of invasion – under the Mongols in the late thirteenth century. However, although Japan was a large country (bigger than modern Germany) only a fifth of the land was suitable for agriculture and there was also a lack of important minerals. These problems were largely offset by the fact that areas suitable for agriculture could grow wet-rice intensively thereby producing a large food surplus. Economic, social and political development remained confined to the few areas of intensive agriculture – the south-west part of the main island of Honshu (the region around Osaka, Kyoto and Kobe) and the eastern extension around modern Tokyo (formerly Edo).

In Japan sedentary societies with pottery (the Jomon culture) were well-established for about ten thousand years before the development of agriculture around 300 BCE. The 'Jomon' were probably a number of different peoples, possibly even speaking different languages, who shared a common culture based on gathering, hunting and fishing, especially for tuna. It is possible that a few crops were grown from about 1000 BCE. Wet-rice agriculture almost certainly arrived with the intrusion of the 'Yayoi' culture (named from its type site near Tokyo). These were clearly new people who were anatomically distinct from the 'Jomon' although their exact origin is unknown. They used iron tools and dominated south-west Japan by about 100 BCE and then gradually moved east and north adapting their agriculture to the changing conditions and shifting to millet, barley

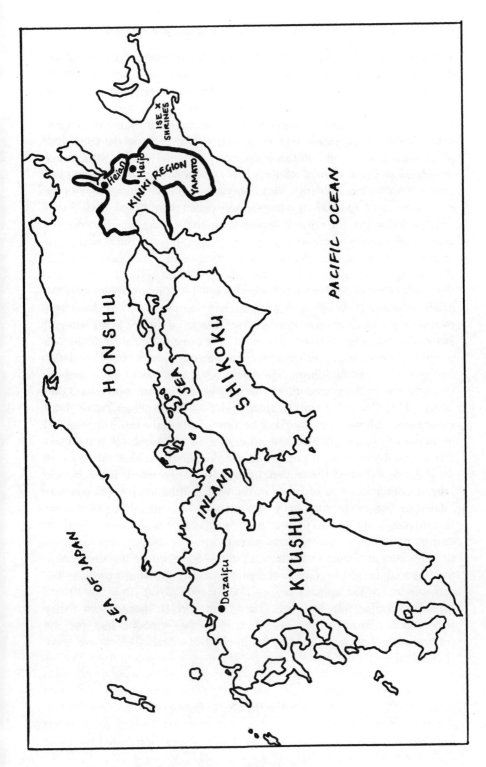

Map 27: Early Japan

and wheat in the drier areas of north-east Honshu. Based on the developing food surplus in the south-west the first chiefdoms and small states began to emerge. The leaders, identified by their tattoos, were buried in large stone burial chambers and earth mounds some 500 yards long and 120 feet high which are found across the Kinki region of southern Honshu. Much of the culture seems to be close to that of the Silla in the south-east of the Korean peninsula, the area nearest to Japan. These small Japanese chiefdoms and states (there were probably about a hundred of them) were intermittently in touch with China. They seem to have sent envoys to the Han court in 57 and 107 CE – the Chinese called them *Wa* or 'dwarf'.

The core of the emerging Japanese state and culture was the Yamato region in the centre of the wet-rice-growing area. It was from here that the islands of Shikoku and Kyushu were conquered. The Yamato rulers claimed a general supremacy over the other chieftains of the area who were the heads of tribal or clan units known as *uji*. The Yamato rulers were the heads of one of these *uji*, whose superiority was probably based on their relation with the chief ceremonial centre – the set of shrines to the sun-god at Ise. The traditional Japanese religion only came to be called 'Shinto' (a word of Chinese origin meaning 'way of the gods') much later in order to distinguish it from Buddhism. The Yamato sun cult was supreme and the other cults were integrated into a carefully graded system with over 3,000 levels. These were mainly nature cults – ex-emperors were later incorporated although they did not become divine in the sense understood in western Eurasia. 'Shinto' had no organized philosophical system but instead emphasized ritual purity and simple worship. The Yamato rulers were the founders of the imperial family of Japan which is by far the longest continuous line of rulers in the world, although their power was limited or non-existent for many centuries and the actual line of descent was extremely complex. The pace of Japan was slow and even by the sixth century there was no effective centralized state. The claim to supremacy by the emperors at Yamato was increasingly undermined by disputes within the imperial family over the succession and the growing power of the commanders of the military units – the *Otomo* ('Great Attendants') and *Monobe* (Corporation of Arms). The imperial 'rulers' became what they remained for most of Japanese history – the symbolic line for the transmission of authority which was in practice exercised elsewhere. [*Later Japan 11.7.1*]

10.10 India: the Gupta Empire

Like the earlier Mauryan empire, the Guptas, who dominated northern

India between about 320 and 550, were based in the state of Magadha in the eastern Ganges plain. This was always a powerful state because of its control over important mineral resources, especially iron, and its ability to dominate the key trade routes along the valley, especially those to north-west India and therefore into central Asia. The founder of the Gupta dynasty was Chandra Gupta (no relation to the founder of the Mauryan empire who had the same name, and it was a Hindu not a Buddhist empire). He took power in Pataliputra in 320 and extended his area of control through a marriage alliance with the Lichavi family which ruled the state of Vaishali, north of the Ganges. The main expansion and the establishment of the empire took place under his son Samudra (330–c.375). He conquered both the Punjab to the west and Bengal to the east and also brought Kashmir in the north and much of the Deccan plateau to the south under his control. He probably had some form of indirect rule over, and obtained tribute from, the kingdoms in the south of India and possibly even the Buddhist kingdom in central Sri Lanka. Under his successor Chandra Gupta II, who ruled until 415, the Gupta empire was at its peak, especially after control over the ports of western India (and therefore trade with the Gulf and Red Sea) was obtained in 409.

Very little is known about the internal structure of the Gupta empire but it is very unlikely that there was any strong central government. Control was exercised through local rulers who accepted the general overlordship of the Gupta emperor and paid some of their taxes to him as tribute. Detailed central control was impossible and neither was there a strong bureaucracy in the Gupta capital. The period of prosperity and general internal peace lasted until the mid-fifth century when growing external pressure, especially from the movement of nomadic groups south from central Asia, caused acute problems. Skanda Gupta (455–67) spent most of his reign campaigning in north-west India against the nomads who were probably groups of Huns (the same people who were causing major problems in western Europe at the same time). The growing expense of the warfare, the strain this placed on imperial resources and the increasing demand for taxes and tribute only led to internal revolts which could not be controlled. The Gupta empire went into rapid decline after 467, although the exact chain of events is unknown. By the 490s the Huns were in control of the Punjab and then they took over Kashmir and much of the Gangetic plain (the heartland of the empire) by 515.

From the early sixth century northern India was fragmented into more than fifty states. In the west, around the Kathiawar peninsula, the kingdom of Valabhi was ruled by the Maukhari dynasty. In Rajasthan the kingdom of the Gurjaras was centred on the capital Jodhpur. In the east there were separate states in Bengal, Assam, Orissa and Nepal. Some unity was eventually brought by Harsha Vardhana, the ruler of Thanesar north of Delhi in the early seventh century. He expanded his kingdom across northern India along the Ganges valley and established a new capital at Kanauj which became one of the most flourishing cities in eastern Eurasia. Southern India was almost entirely isolated from this world and saw a much more diffuse system of political control without the development of even the relatively weak states of northern India. The majority of the peasant population lived in villages around the drainage basins of the major rivers where, based on the communal construction of tanks and reservoirs, irrigation agriculture was highly productive. In the more isolated upland and forest regions of southern India most of the people still depended on gathering and hunting. Over both these groups different warrior elites – the Pallavas in Kanchipuram and the Pandyas and Cholas in Tanjore – exercised varying degrees of control. The warriors were little more than raiders and plunderers. They were, however, content to allow considerable freedom to the large number of merchants in the ports of both the west and east coasts who were at the centre of the maritime routes that linked Eurasia and from whom the warriors could derive some of their wealth. Similar warrior groups were important on the relatively barren Deccan plateau where they descended on the towns of the Andhura coast to gain loot. About 550 the Chalukyas took control of the south-west Deccan and under Pulakeshin II in the early seventh century they extended their rule as far as Elephanta island off Bombay. The Chalukyas defeated both Harsha Vardhana in the north and the Pallavas to the south. In 752 they were overthrown by one of their subordinates who founded the Rashtrakuta dynasty based at Ellora near Aurangabad. It was under the second king of the Rashtrakutas, Krishna II (756–75), that the huge rock-cut temple, larger than the Parthenon, depicting Shiva's paradise was constructed.

[*Later India 13.9*]

10.11 The Crisis of the Late Roman Empire

By the time that China was beginning to emerge from the worst of the chaos following the demise of the Han dynasty, and the Gupta empire dominated much of India, the Roman empire was entering a period of major crisis. The stabilization under Diocletian and Constantine solved some of the internal problems but fundamental weaknesses remained. The first problem was the perennial issue of the imperial succession. On the death of Constantine in 337 his three sons partitioned the empire and fought a long civil war. By 350 Constantius II, the only survivor, became sole emperor. However, he had no heir, and Julian, one of the sons of a half-brother of Constantine, revolted and took power on the death of Constantius in 361. He reigned for only two years and his mysterious death, possibly the result of a Christian conspiracy because of his support for paganism, brought the house of Constantine to an end. The next emperors, Jovian and Valentinian, were chosen by the army and the latter revived the practice of having a co-emperor (Valens) although the empire was not formally divided. That did happen in 395 when, on the death of Theodosius, the empire was split between his two sons – Honorius in the west and Arcadius in the east. This formal division continued until the deposition of the last emperor in the west in 476. Throughout this period there was no way of ensuring the imperial succession and it was decided through a complex mixture of descent, marriage, court factions and, most important of all, the support of the army.

The second major problem was supporting an adequate army. In a largely subsistence economy the army had to be fed from local resources and along the frontiers most soldiers (as on the Chinese frontier) were soldier-peasants supporting themselves. But as the tax base decreased and the ability of the central government to raise revenue declined so did the ability to recruit and pay mercenaries. The size of the Roman army fell significantly, probably from about 150,000 in the early empire to less than half that size by the late fourth century. In the last resort size mattered – the Romans had no technological or military advantage over their opponents. Equally important the Romans, like the Chinese, came to rely on increasing numbers of 'barbarian' mercenaries. This might not be a problem as long as the central government was strong enough to control them but as it weakened so the independence of the 'barbarian' military leaders increased.

The third problem flowed from the disputes over the succession, a weakening central government and an increasingly ineffective army – a growing inability to defend the frontiers of the empire. Until the late fourth century control had been maintained over all the provinces of the empire except Dacia which was acquired late and was difficult to defend – it was lost in the mid-third century. The first signs of major problems came in the 370s following Julian's disastrous defeat in Mesopotamia at the hands of the Sasanians in 363. A Germanic tribal people, the Goths, were being pushed westwards by the Huns and in 376 they were allowed to settle across a wide area of the Balkans and Thrace, largely because the imperial authorities had little choice. Two years later they rebelled and at the battle of Adrianople the emperor Valens was killed. A final settlement was reached in 382 when the Goths became military auxiliaries and received an annual subsidy from the imperial government.

Although the problem of the Goths had been contained the method adopted illustrated the final factor in the problems faced by the empire. In the last resort the empire in the east was well enough organized, strong enough and, even more important, rich enough, to control and, if necessary, buy off the 'barbarians'. The acute problems therefore came in the west where the empire was weak, faced the main pressure from the 'barbarians' and was too poor to buy peace. The major collapse of the empire occurred here from the early fifth century. It marked a drawing back of the area controlled by the 'civilized' states away from the west Eurasian periphery which had been incorporated over the previous thousand years, and a concentration on the old core region in the east of the Mediterranean. The problems began in 406 with a crossing of the Rhine by a variety of Germanic tribes, although their impact at this stage was limited. The next year an imperial claimant, Constantine III, began a revolt in Britain. He took the legions he controlled with him to the continent to try and enforce his claim to the throne and Roman troops did not return. The 'Roman' armies in the west were already under a 'barbarian' commander – Stilicho – who held more power than the emperor (there were similar 'barbarian' commanders in the east but they were kept under control). The Goths in the Balkans divided, and the Ostrogoths under Alaric moved west. In 410 they sacked Rome and the next year the last 'Roman' legions left Iberia. In 418 the other part of the Goths, the Visigoths, began to settle in southern Gaul and later moved into Spain. In 428 the 'Roman' armies fought their last campaign along the Rhine. As control over the western provinces weakened the imperial government, which had moved from Milan to the more inaccessible Ravenna, could do little more than try and play off one group of 'barbarians' against another. In 432 nearly all the troops in North Africa were withdrawn to take part in the civil war raging in Italy.

The number of 'barbarian' invaders remained small. By 439 less than 80,000 Vandals had taken over the whole of North Africa. By 455 under Gaiseric they had taken control of Corsica, Sardinia and the Balearics and also sacked Rome. The old capital had only narrowly avoided that fate a couple of years earlier when the Huns under Attila, who had been bought off by the eastern government in the early 440s with payments of 6,000 pounds of gold a year, moved westwards when the new emperor Marcian stopped the subsidy. Only the death of Attila and an internal war over the succession spared the western empire further destruction. From 457 effective power in the west lay with the Germanic commander of the imperial armies – Ricimer. On his death in 472 the role was taken over by the last 'master of the soldiers', Odoacer. In 476 he deposed the last emperor in the west, who had the suitably diminutive name of Romulus

Augustulus, and took the title of king, under the nominal authority of the eastern emperor. Although often seen as marking the 'fall of the Roman empire', the events of 476 were of little more than symbolic importance and mainly important for the east which became the sole inheritor of the Roman tradition.

Even after 476 much of the old Roman tradition survived in the west. In 490 Theodoric, the leader of the Ostrogoths, who had been held captive in Constantinople in the 460s and twice been 'master of the soldiers', took power in Italy. In 493 he captured Ravenna where Odoacer was killed. Theodoric was steeped in the Roman tradition. He restarted both the free distribution of grain and the circuses in Rome and the elite largely survived – the Senate still functioned and the western consulship continued until 541 when it was ended by the eastern emperor. In 505 Theodoric took control of Pannonia to create a defensive barrier to the north-east and three years later took over Provence. In Gaul there was a more complex series of events. Various groups tried to establish their supremacy – the Visigoths in the south, the Burgundians in the Rhône valley, a group led by Gundobad, a former commander of the Roman armies, and the Franks. This last group did not sweep into Gaul in a 'barbarian invasion' but took over power in the north under Childeric I who was, like Gundobad, a former commander of the remaining imperial armies. The Franks established their supremacy in Gaul under Childeric's son Clovis following their victory in 507 at the battle of Vouillé (near Poitiers) over the Visigothic kingdom centred on Toulouse.

Until the middle of the sixth century, despite the emergence of new kingdoms headed by 'barbarians', there was still considerable continuity with the old empire. Indeed it is best to see the whole period between 400 and 550 in western Europe not as one of a violent wave of barbarian invaders but as a slow, steady erosion of imperial power. Germanic people had been moving into the empire for centuries and in the process absorbing much of the Roman culture and altering their own way of life. The strength of the Roman armies and government declined, more Germanic people moved within the borders of the empire and their leaders took control of the 'imperial' armies. Eventually they established their own kingdoms but these still owed much to Roman tradition and often paid at least nominal allegiance to the eastern emperor. The elite survived, many now in the Christian church, and Roman law continued alongside Germanic law. The emperors in the east adopted a pragmatic policy – they could not impose a western emperor but they did not regard the new kingdoms as permanent and simply reached the best accommodation they could.

The mass of the peasantry survived but their status was changing across the whole of the empire long before the final collapse in the west. Slavery

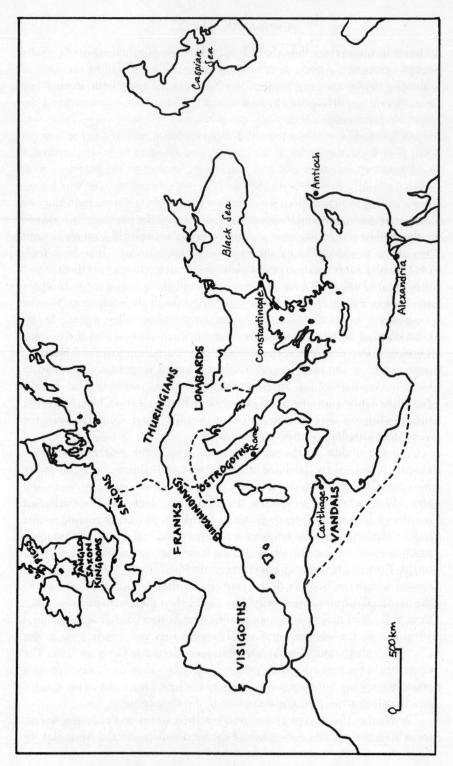

Map 28: The 'barbarians' in the western empire c.525 CE

declined in importance but the status of the former slaves and the free peasants merged together to create an entirely new class of unfree serfs who were tied to the land (exactly the development that did not occur in China where the free peasantry remained the main rural group). At the height of the Roman empire large-scale slavery was mainly confined to Italy. Elsewhere the free tenants survived and were free either to leave when their leases (normally five years under Roman law) expired or they could renew them on an annual basis. A group known as *coloni*, or serfs tied to the land, existed but they were on a relatively small scale. The main change came after Diocletian as a result of the tax system he introduced in a desperate attempt to find enough money to support the army. Peasants were inscribed on tax registers and tied to the land on a hereditary basis. The peasant freeholder was tied to his village but the leaseholder was tied to his specific plot. The former may not have noticed much difference in status because villages probably did not enforce controls very strongly. The latter group certainly did, especially as the legal controls over them strengthened. In 332 Constantine allowed landowners to chain *coloni* whom they suspected of wanting to leave. In 365 *coloni* were stopped from alienating their property without their landlord's consent, and in the 370s the government allowed landlords rather than the state tax collectors to levy taxes on the *coloni*. At the bottom of this social group were the *adscripticii* who were effectively slaves since they could be sold by the landlord with the land to which they were tied. Slaves were 'raised' into this group by the late fourth century when legislation prohibited the sale of slaves except with the land which they worked. By the late fifth century slaves and *adscripticii* were not eligible for military service because they were not regarded as being free. *Coloni* were personally free but in practice tied to the land. The exact proportion of peasants in each of these groups varied from area to area. In some places, particularly Egypt, free peasants on short leases did survive but in areas such as Italy, which had long been dominated by large estates, the unfree serfs predominated. These developments were of critical importance to later European history. The unfree peasantry, the serfs, became the dominant part of the rural population in most areas of the continent for a thousand years.

10.12 The Revival of the Eastern Roman Empire

In the eastern empire the government structure established under Diocletian and Constantine survived largely intact until the mid-seventh century. The empire remained powerful and wealthy and its rulers always considered that its authority should extend to the western provinces. The problem was

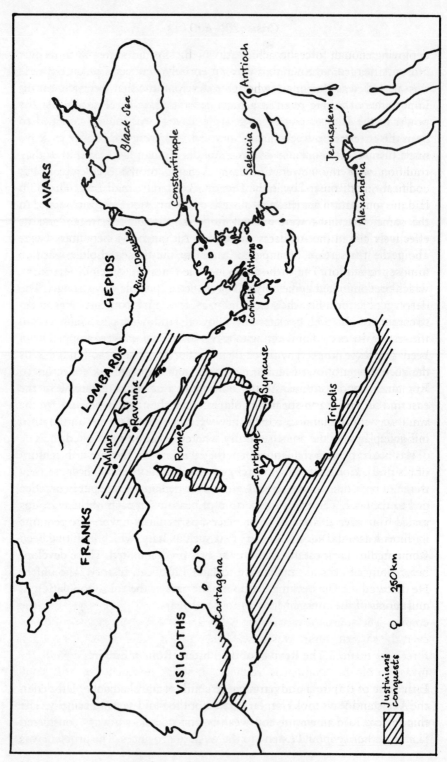

Map 29: The 'reconquest' under Justinian

deploying enough forces to achieve this – the expedition in 468 to recover North Africa from the Vandals was a spectacular failure. The key figure in this period was Justinian who provides yet another example of the importance of a long reign in achieving the stability necessary to deploy power in the early empires. Justinian was emperor from 527–65 but had been the effective power behind the throne from 518 under the rule of his uncle Justin I. His reign also demonstrates the moulding together of Roman tradition with the newer Christian elements of the late empire. His codification of Roman law in the *Digest* (533) and *Codex Iustinianus* (534) laid the foundation for the legal systems of many later European states. At the same time laws were passed forbidding pagans to teach and he effectively closed the Academy in Athens. Although his reconquests were about the reassertion of imperial authority they were also designed to impose the authority of orthodoxy over the heresies, especially Arianism, which predominated in the barbarian kingdoms. Justinian's legacy was also deeply ambiguous. He was successful in reconquering North Africa but the consequence was the imposition of a Greek-speaking administration (as in the rest of the east) in an area which, under the earlier empire, had always been Latin-speaking. The attempt to reconquer Italy led to a highly destructive twenty-year war that eliminated most of what was left of the old Roman elite and institutions. At the end many senatorial families left for the east and set up a Latin-speaking colony in Constantinople. The cost of the wars was enormous and combined with the impact of the outbreak of bubonic plague in the 540s, seriously weakened the empire.

It is unclear whether Justinian envisaged a major reconquest at the start of his reign. North Africa was easily regained from the Vandals in 533 but that had been long-standing policy, partly because of the importance of its grain production. In 536 Justinian's commander Belisarius regained Sicily and in 540 entered Rome. The problem was that forces were also required in the east against the Sasanians and only 5,000 men could be left to defend Rome against a force of 20,000 Ostrogoths. Rome fell to them twice before larger forces under the eunuch Narses could be spared in the 550s. He defeated the Gothic king Totila at the battle of Busta Gallorum in 552 and most of war-ravaged Italy was secured, at least temporarily, for the empire. The southern coastal fringe of Spain was also controlled. However, the eastern empire was so weakened that it could not deploy enough forces to maintain control of either Italy or the Balkans. In 568 the invasion of the Lombards reduced imperial authority to the small Exarchate of Ravenna and parts of the south of the peninsula. In the 580s the Avars and Slavs took over large parts of the Balkans. It was finally clear that the old Roman empire could not be restored.

[*Later Roman empire 11.4*]

10.13 The Roman-Sasanian Contest

[Earlier Iran 9.4]
The major problem for the eastern Roman empire, especially under Justinian and his successors, was that it had to fight a two-front war. The most powerful enemy it faced was the Sasanian empire of Iran and therefore the forces that could be spared for the west were usually very limited. The contest between the two empires seriously weakened both of them without achieving a decisive outcome.

The Sasanian empire, the last of three great Iranian empires, was founded by Ardashir who overthrew the Parthians in 224, although warfare against the remaining Parthians continued for more than a decade. The Sasanians took over most of the old Parthian empire except for Armenia and in the mid-third century under Shapur (who also defeated the Romans and captured the emperor Valerian) they were able to take advantage of the break-up of the Kushan empire to extend their control into parts of central Asia including Bactria. From the late third century after the death of Shapur (probably in 272) there appears to have been a long period of stability. Control was secured over northern Mesopotamia after the defeat of the Romans under Julian in 363. The frontier with the Romans thereafter was largely stable and intermittent hostilities were centred around a few fortified cities, sieges and buying off opponents. At this time the Sasanian army appears to have been on a levy basis with the aristocracy supplying the cavalry and the peasantry the infantry.

The peak of the Sasanian empire occurred under Khusro I (known as Chosroes in the west) who ruled from 531 to 579. The basis of his power was the imposition, for the first time, of an effective land tax which provided enough money for the emperor to create a standing army under his own control. This broke the power of the local aristocracy, increased central power and enabled the king to rule through a wider group of local landowners than the small aristocracy that had controlled the earlier army. With the Romans engaged in the west the Sasanians were able to capture Antioch, the second city of the eastern empire, in 540. The war with the Romans continued until 561 when the latter secured peace by paying a large subsidy. The Sasanians also had enough power simultaneously to deploy forces in the east of the empire and in 558 extend their authority as far as the Oxus river.

After the death of Khusro I there was a disputed succession and Khusro II (591–628) was only put on the throne against the pretender Vahram Chobin with the help of the Roman emperor Maurice. In return the Romans were given a number of frontier cities. The Sasanian opportunity came with the execution of the emperor Maurice by the usurper Phocas in

602 and the ensuing chaos within the empire. The Sasanians captured Antioch, Alexandria and the now holy city of Jerusalem. The Roman revival came under the emperor Heraclius who gained power in 610. From 622, after the recapture of the chief cities of the empire, he waged war in Mesopotamia, leaving Constantinople to defend itself against a joint siege by the Sasanians and the Avars. The Roman capture of Ctesiphon was followed by a military revolt and the death of Khusro II in 628. In the next four years there were five Sasanian emperors. The problem was that the eastern Roman empire, although victorious, was as weakened by the almost thirty years of continuous warfare as its rival. Neither was in a position to withstand the upsurge of the Islamic Arab armies from Arabia in the 630s. It was the rapid victories of these armies that were to radically transform the Eurasian world.

OVERVIEW 6

THE WORLD IN
600 CE

World Population: 200 million
Regional Population: China: 50 million, India: 50 million,
Rest of Asia: 40 million, Europe: 25 million
Major cities: Constantinople (500,000), Ch'ang-an
(500,000), Loyang (400,000), Ctesiphon (300,000),
Alexandria (200,000), Teotihuacan (100,000), Kanauj
(100,000), Tikal (50,000), Rome (50,000)

Events:

★ First settlement of Madagascar
★ Polynesians settle Hawaii and Easter Island
★ China reunified under the Sui
★ Sasanian empire ruling Mesopotamia, Iran and as far east as the Oxus river
★ East Roman empire ruling Anatolia, Levant, Egypt, North Africa, Greece and parts of Balkans
★ 'Barbarian kingdoms' across western Europe
★ Teotihuacan influence beginning to decline across Mesoamerica
★ Emergence of major Mayan city-states
★ Rice cultivation across southern Japan – early states emerging
★ Trans-Saharan caravan routes open
★ 1,200-mile-long Grand Canal built in China
★ Iron cables for suspension bridges in China
★ Horse collar used in China
★ Stirrup widely used in China, Central Asia and India
★ Paper used in Korea and Japan
★ Camel replacing wheeled transport in North Africa, Egypt, Levant, Mesopotamia and Iran
★ Secret of silk production taken from China to Levant
★ Heavy plough used in Europe
★ Buddhism at the height of its influence in China

PART FOUR
The Great Empires
(600–1500)

11

The Rise of Islam
(600–1000)

The rise of Islam marked a fundamental transition in Eurasian history. Within little more than a hundred years from its creation it formed an empire and a social and cultural unit on a scale never seen before in the world. No other religion in world history spread so far and so fast. It stretched from Spain across the southern Mediterranean to south-west Asia, Iran and on into central Asia and India. It was the first great empire to unite what had previously been widely different and separate cultures and the first to link within one system the Mediterranean and Indian Ocean worlds. Eventually the world of Islam incorporated south-east Asia, the eastern coast of Africa and large parts of West Africa. Islam was, together with China, the leading civilization in the world for more than a thousand years and included many of the world's great cities and some of its most productive agriculture.

The expansion of Islam created an extensive world linked together by a single currency, the dinar, and an international language, Arabic. The new religion, for more than a thousand years the greatest and most influential of the world's monotheistic religions, created a relatively open social structure for believers. The Islamic world consisted of highly cosmopolitan trading empires and independent merchant elites in the great cities linked together by sea and caravan routes from the extremities of the empire at Cordoba and Samarkand to the centre at Damascus, Baghdad and later Cairo. In many ways the expansion of Islam under the Arabs was another example of the impact of nomadic groups from the periphery on the settled communities of the 'civilized' states. After the rapid conquests the Arab elite was absorbed by existing cultures, although the settled societies were themselves transformed by the impact of the new religion. What emerged was a new syncretic civilization in south-west Asia and Iran. In the former area Islam was the true inheritor of Hellenism, especially Plato and Aristotle together with Euclid, Archimedes, Ptolemy and Galen. It was the main mechanism for the later transmission of this knowledge to western Europe. In Iran a new Iranian-Arabic synthesis emerged and Islam's contacts with India provided the primary route along which Indian achievements, particularly in mathematics, travelled westwards to the Islamic world and eventually western Europe.

In parallel with the rise of Islam in the early seventh century there was a major revival in China under the Sui and T'ang dynasties. Not only was there significant internal economic development but it was also a time of major military expansion, especially into central Asia where Chinese control was both more extensive and deeper than under the Han. By the middle of the eighth century the two great expansionist forces in Eurasia – Islam and China – collided in central Asia. It was the first time in world history that an empire based in south-west Asia and the Mediterranean came into direct contact (and conflict) with the great state at the eastern end of the Eurasian continent. During this imperial contest these two powers also had to contend with two major central Asian empires – the Turkic and the Tibetan. In parallel with these developments, on the fringes of Eurasia early states were emerging in Japan and in western Europe.

In the four centuries after 600 a broad rhythm of events can be distinguished across Eurasia. The great empires and states experienced a major upswing of expansion and internal stability in the 150 years or so after 600. A period of major instability began in the 750s (starting around the time of the battle of Talas between Islam and China in 751). Internal problems within the Islamic and Chinese worlds multiplied and were apparent in the transition to the Abbasid empire in Islam and the decline of the T'ang. The speed of decline increased and by the tenth century China was again divided and the Abbasids no longer controlled a unified Islamic world. In addition the central Asian empires of the Turks and Tibetans collapsed and the limited recovery in western Europe around 800 ended with further invasions by groups from the periphery.

11.1 Early Islam

The sudden irruption of the Arabs from the Arabian peninsula in the 630s was totally unexpected. The area had always been marginal because of its aridity – there was some agriculture in southern Arabia, Oman and a few scattered oases but in most of the peninsula nomadic groups, herding camels in the inner desert and sheep and goats on the fringes, predominated. There had been a few small kingdoms in the Yemen and also in the north around the trading cities of Petra (the Nabataean capital until 106 CE when it was conquered by the Romans) and Palmyra. The Roman and Sasanian empires had exercised a vague authority over the area at different times but the interior remained at a tribal level. The nomads here were poor and very different from those of central Asia – Arabia was a backwater not a cultural crossroads. The most significant development in the sixth century was the rise of Mecca as a caravan and trading city controlling the north–south trade routes. This was the result of the decline of the cities further north, especially Palmyra, and an increase in piracy in the Red Sea which diverted trade inland. Mecca was also a pilgrimage city with its shrine of the Kaaba. The city and the adjoining area was controlled by the Quraysh tribe which was created in the early sixth century. It had no chief but was ruled by an assembly of clan leaders and was characterized by the threat (and use) of blood feuds between the different clans. It was into this world that Muhammad emerged as a religious prophet in the early seventh century.

The problem in assessing early Islamic history and the life of Muhammad is that almost nothing can be known except through the orthodox history created in the 690s by the Umayyad caliph Abd al-Malik. In a massive editing process a single powerful tradition was created. (About the only text known that dates before 800 is the text of the Quran which says almost nothing about Muhammad. The standard biography is a ninth-century edition by Ibn Hisham of a work by Ibn Ishaq who died in 767.) Muhammad was born about 570 in Mecca and began preaching in his early forties shortly after his first religious revelation. He had no more than a hundred or so followers and was opposed by the Quraysh. In 622 he left Mecca for Yathrib (later known as Medina) where, as part of an old tradition, he was invited, as a religious leader, to head the community and stop the feuding between the local clans. He was probably invited because the large Jewish community in the city was sympathetic to Muhammad's rigid monotheism. Shortly after his arrival Muhammad drew up a constitution for Medina which created both a community (the *umma*) and a state in what had been a stateless environment. More important was the elaboration of his religious message which was collected in the Quran, the revelation to Muhammad by the angel Gabriel. The final text of the Quran was agreed under the caliph Uthman (644–56) and although there are some variants there is little doubt that it is the authentic teaching of Muhammad and that it does not suffer from the textual problems of transmission that affect the New Testament. (In addition there is the *hadith* – Muhammad's utterances which are not part of the divinely inspired Quran.) At Medina Muhammad elaborated the five pillars of Islam: *salat* (ritual prayer), *zakat* (almsgiving), *hajj* (pilgrimage), *shahada* (the obligation to bear witness to the faith) and the observance of the fast of Ramadan. Islam shares large parts of the Judaeo-Christian inheritance. The Quran recognizes Adam as a common ancestor of all humans, and other prophets and figures such as Abraham and Moses and even Jesus, although the latter is a merely human prophet who is not crucified. There is also little doubt that early Islam was very close to Judaism in its monotheism, moral code, religious observances and in the important role of the prophet sent to the chosen people. It is also close to Christianity with its emphasis on the judgement of each individual at the end of the world. At first Muslims prayed facing Jerusalem not Mecca and the importance of Jerusalem (and its conquest) may have continued for longer than the Islamic tradition now allows – if it did it would make sense of some of the early Arab military campaigns.

Despite the close relationship with Judaism in early Islam, Muhammad broke with the Jews in Medina in 624 and they were either expelled or enslaved. At the same time Muhammad was under pressure from the Quraysh of Mecca and in 625 low-level warfare and raids on the caravan traffic began. In 630 Muhammad conquered Mecca, purified the Kaaba and turned it into a monotheist sanctuary. By the time of his death two years later most of the Arab tribes of the Arabian peninsula (who had a common identity but no state structure) had been incorporated into the new Islamic *umma*. Over the next few decades they were to undergo one of the most remarkable and intensive transformations in world history. Instead of their ancestral paganism they became monotheists and the main protagonists of a major new world religion. From being desert nomads they settled in the long-established civilized regions. Their old tribal structure disappeared as a new state evolved. Instead of living in poverty they became immensely wealthy. In place of their old provincialism they moved to being at the centre of the Eurasian world. It is therefore hardly surprising that all of the changes placed immense strain on the Arabs. The fundamental problem was that Muhammad created not just a religious community but also a political one. His successors had to find a way of legitimizing the new Muslim state in the conquered areas based on the very limited guidance that Muhammad had given them. They had to define the role of the Arab conquering elite and its relationship with the over-whelming majority of people in the new empire. Within little more than a century they had fought three civil wars over the various issues involved and the Islamic world had fractured irretrievably.

11.2 The Expansion of Islam

The dominating factor in the early history of Islam after the death of Muhammad in 632 was a series of conquests whose scale was unparalleled in world history. In the first few years there were raids into Syria and Mesopotamia against the east Roman empire and the Sasanians. Initially the Arabs were unsuccessful and it seems unlikely that they (and therefore Islam) would have been successful without the mutual exhaustion of the two empires following the decades of incessant warfare between them. Renewed Arab attacks in the late 630s were successful. In 636 Damascus

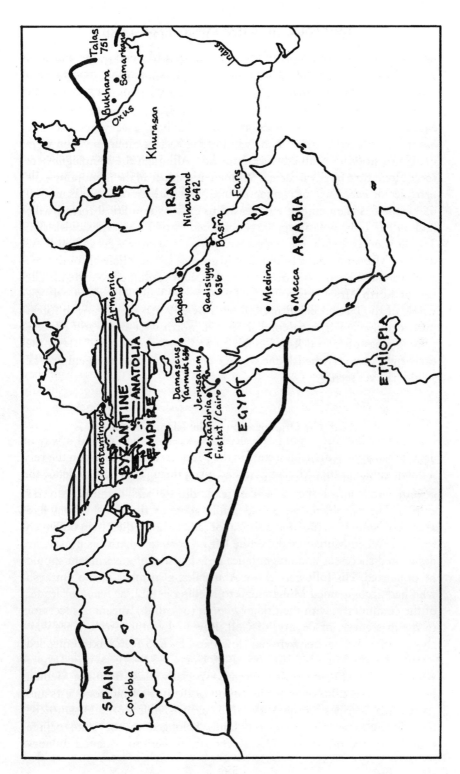

Map 30: The establishment of Islam

was captured and the next year, after the battle of Yarmuk, the East Roman empire was in full retreat – it lost Jerusalem in 638 and the rest of Syria by 641. In the same year as the battle of Yarmuk (637) the Arabs defeated the Sasanians at the battle of Qadisiya and captured most of Mesopotamia, including the capital of Ctesiphon. Five years later the Sasanians lost the battle of Nihawand in the Zagros mountains and were unable to stop the Arab advance into Iran. Although the campaigns here took a long time finally to defeat Sasanian resistance in the mountains – the province of Fars was not conquered until 649 and remote Khurasan until 654 – the Sasanian empire had ceased to exist as a political force by the mid-640s. To the west Egypt was conquered by 643 when Alexandria fell. Tripoli was reached in the same year. Within just over a decade after the death of Muhammad the Islamic world controlled the whole of south-west Asia, Iran and Egypt, and from this core area it continued to expand. The rest of North Africa was conquered between 643 and 711 and nearly the whole of the Iberian peninsula followed by 759. To the east Arab forces pushed out from Iran to control Sind in north-west India and the key trading cities of central Asia – Bukhara and Samarkand – by 713. By the early eighth century the Islamic world encompassed the largest empire the world had yet seen.

11.3 The Organization of the Islamic World

11.3.1 The early caliphate

As with all expansionist empires the problem the Arabs faced was how to govern and control such a widespread, diffuse and culturally diverse empire. Their problems were made more acute by the fact that they had almost no state structure and political organization of their own on which to build. When Muhammad died he left no sons to inherit his power, no designated successor and no guidance on what sort of government should be organized. His followers chose Abu Bakr, a member of the Quraysh who had accompanied Muhammad to Medina in 622, as *imam* or leader of the community, with the title of *khalifa* (or caliph), meaning successor to the messenger, or deputy, of God. Revolts by other Arab tribes who chose their own leaders were put down and by 633 Abu Bakr controlled Arabia. He died in 634. His successor, Umar (634–44), favoured those who had been closest to Muhammad, especially those from the Medina period. He was caliph during the period of the most rapid conquests and established the rules for the Arabs in the early Islamic world. He enforced the decision that the conquered lands belonged to the state or the community and not to individuals. The Arabs were to remain a military elite, living in garrisons and supported by the income from the conquered lands. They were forbidden to engage in agriculture. These decisions ensured that the Arabs were not quickly absorbed by the conquered peoples. However, some method had to be found to control and govern the Arabs themselves. Artificial tribes were created from 638 and their chiefs, who commanded them in war and were responsible for them in peace, were appointed by the caliph and formed the *ashraf* or governing aristocracy. The caliphs, like other rulers in the early empires, had little institutional structure on which they could rely. Their family was all they could fall back on and the four governors of the empire were all kinsmen of the caliph. The consequence was that there was little distinction between public and private spheres in either administration, finance or the exercise of power.

The level of destruction during the conquests was very low and Arab policy was based on disturbing the existing population as little as possible. For most of the population – the peasants – there was probably little change in their lives, they simply paid their taxes to a different government. There were a series of treaties with cities and provinces which usually gave a large degree of autonomy in local affairs with the local elites remaining in power in return for tribute. Existing policies were continued – the old Roman grain levy on Egypt was simply transferred from Constantinople to Mecca and Medina and then Baghdad. The religious settlement was crucial. Islam was a tolerant religion from the start – Muhammad had allowed Jews and Christians to retain their religion in return for payment of a tax. That policy was continued after the conquests. No attempt was made to convert non-believers – belief in Islam defined the new rulers and it was seen as a mark of Arab superiority. Conversion only raised the difficult issue of status and reduced government revenue.

11.3.2 The Umayyads and the first and second civil wars

The third caliph Uthman was a Meccan aristocrat who favoured the Umayyad clan and other Meccans who had not been among the original companions of Muhammad. It was the first sign of a reassertion of older, pre-Islamic, power structures. At the same time wealth and power within the Islamic world were increasingly found outside Arabia, making Medina inappropriate as a capital. The strains within the Arab world came to a head with the murder of Uthman by Arab soldiers in 656. The result was a five-year civil war and struggle for power that not only decided who governed the Islamic world but also led to a fundamental split that was profoundly to affect Islam. There were a number of claimants to power in 656. Ali, the cousin and son-in-law of Muhammad based his claim mainly on his religious devotion to Muhammad. He quickly eliminated Talha and al-Zubayr who were Meccan aristocrats supported by Aisha, the youngest widow of Muhammad. The other claimant was Muawiya the governor of Syria, a late convert to Islam but from the same Umayyad family as the murdered Uthman. The battle of Siffin in 657 between the forces of Ali and Muawiya was a draw. It was followed by disputes within the group supporting Ali during which some known as Kharijis (secessionists) left. Ali was murdered in 661 by some Kharijis and Muawiya became generally recognized as caliph. He was the first to have no personal links with Muhammad.

The first civil war of 656–61 produced a fundamental split within Islam. The Shiites (from *shia* or party) held Ali to have been designated by Muhammad as his successor. From this point of view the first three caliphs were invalid and only Ali and his descendants could rightfully hold the office of caliph which was primarily religious in nature. The Kharijis endorsed the legitimacy of the first two caliphs but held that Uthman, Ali and all later caliphs were in error. They argued that the caliphate should not descend in either the Umayyad family or that of Ali but should instead pass to whoever was elected on grounds of their own qualities. The remaining groups (later known as Sunni), who were the majority, eventually coalesced around a view that did not take sides in the first civil war. Instead they came to hold the position that the caliph was only the political guardian of the Islamic community and that spiritual leadership could be found at any time from within the scholars of the Islamic world.

The victory of Muawiya in the first civil war confirmed the Meccan aristocracy and the Umayyad family in particular as holders of the caliphate. This new structure was reinforced by the shift of the capital from Medina to Damascus, the centre of Umayyad power. Muawiya had to cope with factionalism within the Arab elite, particularly between the Medina and Mecca groups, as well as the growing religious divisions. He survived largely through the support of the Arab tribes based in Syria and the loyalty of his kinsmen who were the effective government of the empire in the provinces. The emergence of the Umayyads as an imperial family was confirmed by Muawiya's decision to nominate his son Yazid as his successor as caliph. This was a deeply divisive decision because the office of caliph was supposed to be elected and the Umayyad were seen by many in the Arab elite as opportunist late converts. The result was a second civil war from 680 until 692. It began with the revolt of al-Husayn, the son of Ali. He and his family were murdered at Karbala, creating the greatest martyr of the Shiites. The main anti-Umayyad force was led by Ibn al-Zubayr, the son of the protagonist in the first civil war, who argued that the Islamic world should be ruled from Mecca. After the early death of Yazid in 683, Marwan I (a Umayyad) was elected as caliph by the Qudaa

– the main tribal supporters of the family. He controlled Syria and Egypt. It was not until 692 that his son, Abd al-Malik, defeated and killed al-Zubayr (who controlled most of Mesopotamia) and gained power over the whole Islamic world. The Umayyads had confirmed their position as caliphs, but by force (including bombarding the holy city of Mecca) and not by agreement. They were to rule until the 740s.

11.3.3 Umayyad society

The world that the Umayyads governed was changing rapidly as the old institutions established at the time of the conquests broke down. The idea of the Arabs as a ruling military elite, separate from the bulk of the population and defined by their religion could not be sustained. Now that internal and external peace was largely secured Arabs left the army and took up civilian occupations. In Mesopotamia and Iran many became large landowners. The Arab clan system was also breaking down as society became more complex and Arabs and non-Arabs gradually integrated. A key factor was a change in the way the army was recruited. Although tribal loyalties remained strong they no longer formed the basic units of the army which moved towards a regimental system. The main army was increasingly recruited from Syria with local militias (both Arab and non-Arab) for local defence. Gradually the army became the main instrument of internal control and provincial governors were drawn from it rather than being chosen simply on the basis that they were the kinsmen of the caliph. This led to an unstable situation as the civilian caliph attempted to control the army and with it the government of the empire. This instability was exacerbated by the shift in the centre of gravity of the Islamic world from Syria to Mesopotamia combined with the most significant social change – the growing pace of conversion. At first this was largely restricted to slaves in Arab households and people close to the Arab community but gradually new groups, especially among the old Sasanian governing elite, became Muslim. The process had to be controlled because it undermined the very basis of the Arab empire – it was the non-believers who paid the taxes. As Arabs and Muslims became landowners it was impossible for the state to exempt them from taxation but taxing them undermined the regime established during the conquests. All of these changes in the decades following the 690s meant that the state was changing from being essentially Arab in character to a wider Islamic basis.

Although the position of the Arabic elite altered fundamentally, Arabic spread rapidly as the language of administration, literature and religion in the Islamic world. It became the main spoken language of Egypt, Syria and Mesopotamia and its use spread faster than conversion to Islam. Other languages such as Coptic in Egypt and Aramaic in Syria and Mesopotamia survived but became less and less important. However, the administrative system in both Egypt and Syria remained much the same as under the East Roman empire and an Islamic basis of government was only established very slowly. The situation was different in Iran. In the western part the Arab settlers became bilingual but further east they abandoned Arabic and adopted Persian, which the conquests spread further east into Transoxania where it replaced Sogdian. This was the start of a very important process – the creation of a new Iranian-Arab-Islamic synthesis that incorporated many of the older Iranian traditions.

11.4 The Creation of the Byzantine State

[Earlier Roman empire 10.12]
The very rapid rise of Islam had a fundamental impact on the East Roman empire which, unlike the Sasanian empire, survived, albeit in a very different form. Within a few decades imperial control of Syria, the Levant, Egypt and North Africa was ended. This involved the loss of a large proportion of the empire's population, some of its wealthiest cities and trade routes (and the revenue they generated) as well as the crucial grain supply from Egypt which sustained the population of Constantinople. The empire was pushed away from the central core of south-west Asia and rapidly declined from its position as a major empire to being no more than an important regional state. The rhythms of its history were now largely determined by those of the great Islamic empire – when the latter was strong it was weak and vice-versa. The need to concentrate the military forces of the empire against Islam in the east resulted in the loss of more territory in the Balkans to the Slavs and Avars. The empire was only able to keep control of the major cities on the periphery of the Balkans – Athens, Patras, Corinth, Thessalonica and the fortresses in Thrace such as Adrianople. These conquests were very near to Constantinople and the empire had to keep control of Thrace which now produced much of the food needed by Constantinople. Its major asset was its control over the trade route through the Bosphorus to the Black Sea.

It is the huge loss of territory that marks the real transition from the Eastern Roman empire to the Byzantine state. However, the population did not call themselves Byzantines (derived from the name of the original Greek colony on the site of Constantinople) despite the dominance of the Greek language and culture. They claimed to be *Romaioi* (Romans) and Christians (the two were effectively synonymous). They were acutely conscious of their descent from the Romans, the continuity of their history and especially of the significance of the capital as the second Rome.

However, the internal changes made after the rise of Islam produced a radically different state from that constructed by Diocletian and Constantine which had survived in the east until the mid-seventh century. Although Byzantine history is often seen as one of 'decline' the state survived for eight centuries after its reconstruction. It was a major regional power for many centuries although in a severely attenuated form after the conquest by the western Christians in 1204. In addition its cultural impact was far wider than its area of direct political control, spreading across much of the Balkans and into eastern Europe and Russia.

Within twenty years of the death of Muhammad the East Roman empire controlled little more than Anatolia, which now became the core of the new Byzantine state. The huge loss of population, land and revenue together with decades of continuous war (and internal conflict), led to a major simplification of society. The agricultural surplus was no longer available to support a major infrastructure and many cities declined leaving Constantinople as the only real city in the state. The Byzantine empire became a military state organized so as to produce an army and governed by the military (who often decided who should be emperor). The old landowning class largely disappeared during the turmoil of the seventh century and the Senate became a collection of senior office holders. The old division between civil and military power (the basis of the late Roman empire constructed by Diocletian) was abolished and power was centralized. This structure was first introduced in Italy after the loss of most of the peninsula to the Lombards in the 560s and was probably extended in the Levant under Heraclius during his reconquests from the Sasanians. From the 650s the remains of the empire were divided into military districts (*themes*) under a *strategos* responsible for all government – the civil governor was his deputy not equal. The government no longer had the revenue to support the old mercenary army and therefore had to change to a different system. Soldiers in each *theme* were given an inalienable grant of land and exemption from most taxation and in return, on a hereditary basis, they had to provide the bulk of the army. The basis of the state therefore became the peasant-soldiers of Anatolia – the power of the old landowners was broken and the *coloni* or serfs of the late Roman empire were replaced by these free peasants who owed a military obligation to the state. Although the old landowning class largely disappeared there was an inevitable tendency over time for the military governors and provincial elite to gain more power and more control over the peasant-soldiers. For centuries, however, the Byzantine state remained strong enough to keep these developments in check. Even if some of the revenues from an estate were conceded to a local landowner the state drew up a *praktikon* or a register of peasant obligations and had enough power to revise it continually. Landlords did not become fully independent. It was not until well into the ninth century that a new class of peasant – the *paroikoi* who held land from the landlords in some form of dependency – began to come into existence.

The Islamic civil war of 656–61 gave the Byzantine state a breathing space after the losses of the 630s and 640s, but it then faced a major crisis for the rest of the seventh century. Most important were the sieges of Constantinople in 660, 668 and 674–8 which were followed by the loss of the whole of the lower Danube region to the Bulgars after 681. A decade later Islamic forces gained control of Armenia – the only consolation was the agreement with the Arabs that neither side would place forces on Cyprus and that they would share the tax revenue (the deal lasted for three centuries). After 695 the Byzantine state was racked by civil war and a succession of weak or powerless rulers. In 705 the mutilated Justinian II (he had had his nose cut off in the 695 revolt) re-entered Constantinople, but only with Bulgar support and he had to pay them tribute. It was not until 717, when the *strategos* of Anatolia seized power as Leo III, that a settled dynasty was established.

Almost immediately the state was further divided by a deepening religious controversy. A fundamental tenet of Islam was the total opposition to any representation of either God or people (including Muhammad). This was to have a huge impact on eastern Christianity through two movements – the Paulicians and the iconoclasts. The former were close to the Nestorians in their belief that Jesus was human and that God only later conferred on him a share in his divinity. They also supported a position known as aphthartodocetism – that Jesus's body was divine and therefore the crucifixion was an illusion. Iconoclasm was more central to the eastern church and deeply rooted in the peasant armies of Anatolia and the secular clergy – the main opponents of the movement were the monks. It was given official sanction by Leo III in 726 and despite popular opposition in the city a decree was issued in 730 ordering the destruction of all religious images. Leo III died in 741 and after a brief civil war within the army was succeeded by his son Constantine V, a radical iconoclast. His temporary success against Islam in the late 740s seemed to lend support to his religious views and in 754 a church council declared that the veneration of images was contrary to the doctrines of the church and subject to anathema. (Only subsequently was this not recognized as a valid council.)

After the death of Constantine V in 775 the Byzantine state entered a period of major instability lasting for almost a century. At first power was held by Constantine's widow Irene who, at the Council of Nicaea in 787, ended support for iconoclasm. (This caused the Paulicians to abandon the church, adopt a fully Manichaeist position on the duality of the world and

establish their own state on the upper Euphrates with the support of the caliphate.) Further rebellions led to the deposition and blinding of Irene's son Constantine VI and her own deposition in 802. During renewed Arab and Bulgar attacks the emperor Nicephorous was killed (his skull was used as a goblet by King Krum of the Bulgars). Leo V, a mild iconoclast, was murdered in 820 by a supporter of icons and the next year a military-peasant revolt in Anatolia could only be put down with Bulgar help. Decades of losses to Islam (especially in Sicily), court intrigues, weak emperors and regents followed until the 860s.
[*Later Byzantine empire 11.10.4*]

11.5 China: the Sui and the T'ang – Revival and Expansion

[*Earlier China 10.8*]
The reunification of China under the Sui dynasty in the late sixth century was the culmination of a long process over the previous century or more, beginning with the 'barbarian' Tabgatch, during which the various kingdoms in the north had been reduced to a single state. The final conquest of the weak Ch'en state at Nanking in 589 did not therefore mark any sharp division with the past. Both the Sui, and their successors the T'ang, were, in their institutions, ruling elites and cultures, part of the synthesis of Han Chinese and 'barbarian' elements that had taken place, particularly in the north of the country, over the previous centuries. The reunification of China did, however, lead to a period of rapid external expansion during the seventh century and a major economic revival within the Chinese state.

Although China was reunified under the Sui they, like the Ch'in, the first dynasty to unify the country in the third century BCE, reigned for only a short period before being overthrown. The first Sui emperor, General Yang Chien, was succeeded by his son Yang in 605 but the internal strains caused by warfare, particularly against the Korean states, led to growing peasant revolts and eventually to an aristocratic revolt. In 617 Li Yüan, the general responsible for defence against the nomads along the frontier in Shansi, allied with the Turkic tribes, captured the capital Ch'ang-an and founded the T'ang dynasty. It took until 626 for Li Yüan to crush his various rivals, pacify and control the country. He was then able to embark on a policy of expansion.

11.5.1 Expansion
The period from 626 until 683 marks the greatest period of military expansion in Chinese history. In 630, in alliance with the Uighur Turks,

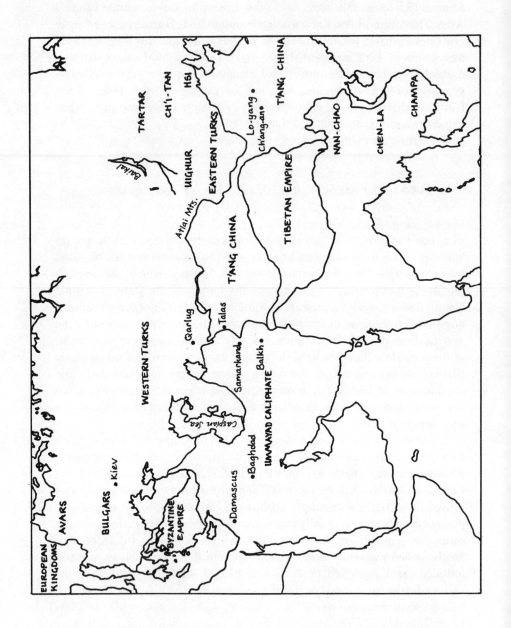

Map 31: Eurasia in the early eighth century CE

the eastern Turks were defeated in a major battle south of Lake Baikal in Siberia. This opened the way for Chinese expansion westwards into central Asia. The kingdom of Kao-ch'ang (founded by Chinese colonists some centuries earlier), which controlled the route to the Tarim basin, was incorporated. As T'ang troops pushed west they not only re-established control over the Silk Road but also conquered areas which six hundred years earlier had only recognized a very general Han overlordship. What had been the 'western regions' and the oasis states of central Asia now became part of the Chinese state. Prefectures were established in Transoxania, on the borders of Iran at Bukhara (An), at Tashkent (Shih) and at Samarkand (Kang). In 648 China was powerful enough to settle the succession to the throne in the northern Indian state of Magadha. Nevertheless these remained difficult areas to control because of the vast size of the Chinese state – the garrison at Kashgar (Su-lo) was over 3,000 miles from the capital Chang-an. In the north-east the Sui had been unable to defeat the Korean kingdom of Koguryo and their heavy defeat at the battle of the Salsu river in 612 was one of the factors behind their eventual overthrow. The T'ang invasion of Korea in 645 was largely successful and, in alliance with the small Korean state of Silla in the south of the peninsula, Koguryo was conquered and incorporated into China in 660. The Chinese dominated Korea and established their own administrative system in Silla and the dependent kingdom of P'o-hai (Parhae to the Koreans) in the north of the peninsula. In the far south Chinese influence extended to southern Vietnam where the kingdoms of Champa and Chen-la recognized their overlordship. Within fifty years Chinese power had been extended on an unprecedented scale from the eastern border of Iran to Korea, Manchuria and Mongolia and as far south as the Mekong delta in Vietnam.

11.5.2 Economy and society
This phenomenal expansion rested upon the construction, mainly by the two Sui emperors, of a strong economic and administrative base. A crucial factor was the continuing shift in the balance of the Chinese population to the south of the country. In 606 about a fifth of all households were in the south. Yet within 150 years the proportion had doubled. This area was by far the most productive agriculturally and was based on wet-rice farming which, in some areas, could produce two crops a year. Although the agricultural surplus was largely in the south the administrative centre of China was in the north around the capital of Ch'ang-an and the old capital Loyang. In addition the army had to be deployed against the main threats along the northern and north-western frontiers. It was impossible to move vast quantities of bulk food overland given the primitive transport system. The Sui solved this problem, which was fundamental to all pre-industrial

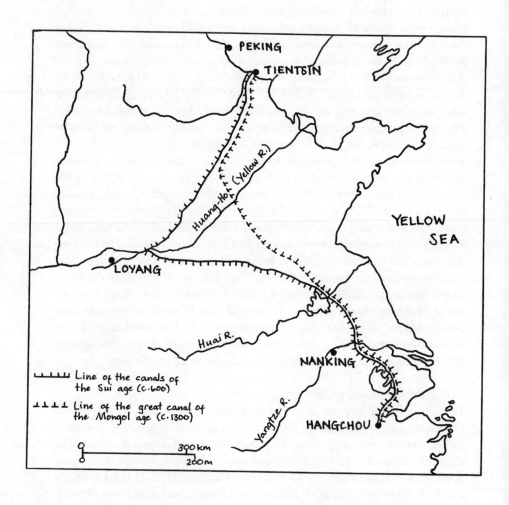

PEKING

TIENTSIN

Huang-Ho (Yellow R.)

YELLOW
SEA

LOYANG

Huai R.

NANKING

⊥⊥⊥⊥ Line of the canals of
the Sui age (c.600)

⊥⊥⊥⊥ Line of the great canal of
the Mongol age (c.1300)

Yangtze R.

HANGCHOU

300 km
200 m

Map 32: China: the Grand Canal

societies, by the construction of the greatest feat of human engineering in world history up to that time. Between 587 and 608 a network of canals and navigable rivers was constructed linking the valleys of the Yellow and Wei rivers with the lower Yangtze and then from Loyang northwards towards Peking. (The only problem was in moving up the Yellow river, against the current, to the capital Ch'ang-an, and here much of the transport had to be by road.) The centrepiece of the whole project was the Grand Canal from Hangchou to near Loyang and then north to Tientsin. It was built by over five million conscripted peasants guarded by 50,000 police – possibly as many as half the workers died. The canal was 1,200 miles long, and over forty yards wide. It had an imperial road alongside it, with way-stations and relay posts. Huge granaries were constructed to hold the transported grain – the largest had a capacity of 33 million bushels. By the early eighth century over 120,000 tons of rice a year was being transported from the south to the capital.

Such a vast quantity of food was required because by about 700 Ch'ang-an was the largest city in the world with a population approaching one million (Rome, the largest city in Christian Europe, had about 50,000 people). It was rebuilt on a massive scale by the Sui. The walls of the capital stretched for six miles from east to west and five miles north to south. The city was laid out on a regular, rectangular plan of fourteen avenues running north–south and eleven from east to west. Some of the avenues were 150 yards wide and they marked off 110 walled sections within the city. In addition there were two huge market places connected to the canals, each of them covering an area greater than the whole of medieval London. At the centre was the walled area (covering about three square miles) of the imperial city. Here the most complex and efficient government in Eurasia tried to administer the vast, sprawling Chinese state. The *Shang-shu-sheng* or 'department of state affairs' consisted of six ministries – for public administration, finance, army, justice, public works and rights. The *Men-hsia-sheng* or imperial chancellery checked and issued imperial decrees. The *Chung-shu-sheng* or grand secretariat produced all official texts. All of these bodies were controlled by the Council of State, consisting of the emperor, the civil servant heads of the six great ministries, and key figures at the imperial court. In addition there was the *Yü-shih-t'ai* or court of censors, which considered public complaints about the government and inspected all government institutions. The *Ta-li-ssu* was the high court of justice which decided all complex legal cases and only it could impose the death penalty. The first complete Chinese legal code of over 500 articles was issued by the T'ang in 624 although it was based on the partial codes drawn up by the Western Chin in 268 and the Northern Chou in 564. At a provincial level the old Chinese system of *chou* or prefectures continued.

All of these bodies were staffed by bureaucrats recruited through an examination system which, although it existed under the Han, was not formalized until 669.

The agrarian basis of the T'ang state was a remarkable system for maintaining the free peasants. It was based on the system which originated under the Northern Wei in 486 and provided for a distribution of plots of land for the lifetime of the recipient only. The Northern Wei had used this for reclaimed land but from 624 the T'ang expanded it to cover all land and linked it to the tax system created five years earlier. Big estates were divided into individual plots which were held until either death or the age of sixty. For adult male peasants the plot was, on average, just under three acres. The system was not, however, egalitarian – the old, ill, widows and monks got less; members of the administrative hierarchy received between eight and eight hundred acres according to grade and an imperial prince even more. These large plots were then sub-divided for the peasantry to work. The exact area given to each peasant also varied according to the intensity of agriculture – in the mulberry-tree areas used to produce silkworms and in the hemp-growing areas they were generally smaller. Such a system required a highly efficient bureaucracy to carry out an exact census of the population and survey the productivity of the land. The government also had to have enough power to enforce this redistribution of land. It used to be thought that the T'ang system was largely theoretical but documents recently discovered in central Asia show that it did function and land was re-allocated from generation to generation, although whether this was done to a similar extent in the highly productive rice-growing regions is less clear. The ability of the government to enforce the system meant that there was no advantage to landlords in creating a class of serfs as in Europe – instead they simply rented out the land to the peasants. This agricultural system was linked to taxation which was assessed not on land or via the landlord but on the individual peasant, again reinforcing the factors favouring a free peasantry. The peasant was liable for three taxes – *tsu* on cereals, *tiao* on silk and hemp, and *yung* – labour for the state. The problem with the taxation system was that the level of exemptions for the aristocracy, bureaucracy and religious institutions meant that the bulk of the burden fell on the peasantry.

One of the reasons why the T'ang were concerned to maintain a free peasantry was that they formed the backbone of the army. The system was based on that created by the Northern Chou who had militia units defending the frontier. The T'ang extended this form of organization to the whole empire and mobilized the peasants as required. However, the military leaders came from the old nomadic aristocracy and they provided the cavalry. They, and not the civil service bureaucracy, were the governing

elite of the empire. The T'ang period saw a major increase in the importance of the cavalry who were archers using the crossbow, in imitation of
the great nomadic empires. The horses used were originally captured from
the Turks but from about 650 there were state stud farms with over
700,000 horses which provided the basis of the army and the expansion of
T'ang control. At first these horses were the small Mongolian type from the
steppes but they were crossed with those from central Asia and Tibet. Arab
horses were obtained as gifts in 703. The problem for the government was
maintaining the supply of horses and therefore the effectiveness of the
army, particularly from the late seventh century.

The late seventh and early eighth centuries were a time of some internal
problems for the T'ang. The government was dominated by Wu Chao, the
ex-concubine of two T'ang emperors – T'ai-tsung (626–49) and Kao-tsung
(649–83). After their death Wu Chao became the first and only female
emperor in Chinese history and the only member of the Chou dynasty. She
moved the capital to Loyang, executed large numbers of the elite but
received considerable support from the Buddhist institutions which she
favoured. She was able to retain power until her death in 705 when the
T'ang were restored. Under the emperor Hsüan-tsung (712–56) the T'ang
were able to maintain the system created over a century earlier although it
came under increasing strain. In 721–4 the census registers were reworked
in order to bring the tax and landholding bases of the empire back into
alignment. But there were growing problems in maintaining the militia
system and the power of the armies commanded by the generals increased.
However, until the mid-eighth century, when the external pressures caused
by the imperial contest in central Asia grew greater, the T'ang were able to
sustain the system and China remained powerful, prosperous, united and
internally at peace.

11.5.3 Beliefs
[Early Buddhism in China 10.4]
Throughout the period of the Sui and the T'ang China remained a
Buddhist state. It had a key role in the evolution of east Eurasian Buddhism
– the Chinese schools of Buddhism which developed at this time provided
the mainstream of Buddhism in Japan. Buddhism was central to Chinese
society and civilization and was the basis of its influence in Korea and
Japan. By the mid-seventh century China had 185 teams of translators
working on the great Indian Buddhist texts and numerous pilgrims made
the journey to India. Hsüan-tsung, who was fluent in Sanskrit, travelled
overland and brought back the texts of the highly sophisticated and
complex Vijnanavada philosophical school which were later to have a
major impact on Japan. Others included the Korean monk Hui-ch'ao, who

travelled by sea to India and came back through central Asia in 729 and Wu-k'ung, who made the same journey leaving in 751 and returning in 790. China was influenced by the development in India during the seventh century of Tantric Buddhism which travelled along the sea routes to Sri Lanka and south-east Asia and then to central Asia and Tibet. The first Indian practitioners reached China in 716 and the major texts were translated in the 750s. China was also important for the development of two new traditions of Buddhism. The Pure Land school was a highly simplified form of Buddhism in which adherents were devoted to the Buddha Amitabha and made a constantly repeated vow to be reborn in his pure land. More important was the development in the eighth century of the Ch'an (Pure Light) which in Japan was known as the Zen school. It was iconoclastic, hostile to tradition and rejected the process of long training in favour of sudden illumination through the use of paradoxes.

China was also open to a wide range of influences, especially along the main central Asian trade routes. There were large foreign colonies in all the major cities and Ch'ang-an in particular was highly cosmopolitan. The first Zoroastrian temple was set up in the capital in 631 and others followed in all the major cities. Manichaeism was authorized to be taught from 694. Another external influence was Nestorian Christianity, although the way in which it lost nearly all of its Christian content under the powerful influence of Buddhism illustrates the complexities of cultural transmission in Eurasia. Nestorius was the patriarch of Constantinople in the early fifth century who argued for the two natures of Christ. He was declared a heretic and was excommunicated. The Nestorian church developed strongly in the Sasanian empire because its adherents were so hostile to the East Roman empire where they were persecuted. It was tolerated under Islam and spread eastwards along the trade routes. The missionary Alopen was received by the T'ang emperor T'ai-tsung in 635 and three years later was allowed to teach – the emperor declared: 'This teaching is helpful to all creatures and beneficial to all men. So let it have free course throughout the empire.' In China it was known as *po-ssu ching-chiao* (the religion of the sacred texts of Iran) but it remained an alien community with converts largely confined to the Sogdian merchants. It was still recognizably Christian as the stele erected at the Nestorian church in Ch'ang-an in 781 with a bilingual text in Syriac and Chinese demonstrates (when the Jesuit missionaries discovered it in the seventeenth century it caused them great mystification). However, the Chinese, with their Taoist and Buddhist background, could not comprehend the concepts involved in Christianity even though the church adopted Buddhist terms by calling its texts sutras and Christian saints Buddhas. Eventually it lost its Christian basis as is illustrated by bishop Cyriacus, the head of the church in Ch'ang-an in the early eighth century. His 'Sutra on Mysterious Rest and Joy' contains no recognizable Christian doctrine and instead Jesus teaches the Buddhist ideas of the avoidance of striving and desire and the importance of non-action.

In the south of China Islam arrived with the traders from India and south-east Asia. It was strong in Canton (Khanfu to the Arabs) which had both Sunni and Shia mosques.

11.6 The Imperial Contest in Central Asia

11.6.1 The Turks

The rise of the Sui and the T'ang and the reunification of China led to a similar process to that under the Han and the parallel rise of the Hsiung-nu empire on the steppes. A nomadic empire, the Turkic (Türk means 'forceful' or 'strong') known to the Chinese as the T'u-chüeh, rose at the same time as a revived China. The Turkic empire is the first of the steppe empires to have its own records and though what has survived is extremely fragmentary it does make it possible to get away from a purely Chinese interpretation of events. The Turks emerged as an independent nomadic group in the mid-sixth century under their leader Bumin when, in alliance with the Western Wei dynasty, they destroyed the Juan-juan nomadic empire in 552. The Turks split almost immediately on Bumin's death but the eastern part expanded rapidly under Muqan (553–72), conquered the other steppe people and created a state which reached the borders of China just as it was reunified under the Sui. The Turkic empire remained divided into western and eastern halves for the next century. The Chinese naturally tried to encourage these divisions and in 630 the T'ang were able to defeat the eastern Turks. The western part of the empire remained peaceful and the leaders seem to have been mainly interested in propagating Buddhism. Turkic society was organized into 'tents' (an extended family), clans and tribes. Political power rested at the tribal level but the number of clans (which did not have to be related to each other) in a tribe depended on the qualities of the leader. Similarly, the number of tribes in the state depended on the leader. Unlike the earlier steppe empires such as the Hsiung-nu the Turkic empire had a moderately developed political structure. They were led by the *qaghan* who had to be a member of the tribe which founded or restored the empire and he ruled in conjunction with a deputy, the *yabghu*, who may have been his brother. As with all the steppe empires there were no rules for the succession – power passed to whoever in the ruling family seemed the most suitable. The wealth of the Turks depended on their ability to tax trade along the Silk Road. At first their main aim was to cut out the Sasanians and deal with the East Roman empire direct – they sent emissaries to Constantinople in 567–8 – but they found it difficult to sustain this policy, especially after the rise of Islam. Their raids on China were less about gaining loot than insisting that the Chinese pay a 'subsidy' in the form of silk which they could trade to the west. The normal Chinese subsidy was 100,000 rolls of silk a year.

11.6.2 The Tibetan empire

The Tibetan empire (the people called themselves *Bod-pa*) emerged as an organized state from a loose tribal grouping in the early seventh century. The Yarlung dynasty was founded by Slon-btsan rlung-nam (570–620) but the construction of a state was not complete until the rule of his son Srong-brtsan sgam-po in the 640s. The process was very typical of state formation in a peripheral region and took place under the pressure of Chinese expansion from the east and was based on some control over the central Asian trade routes. The Gupta script of Kashmir was adopted and modified for Tibetan. Buddhism also came from India but it faced strong competition from the existing Bon religion (which was largely animistic) and did not formally become the state religion until 779. Tibet itself was divided into three (later four) *ru* or 'banners' which had military governors. The conquered regions outside the core area of Tibet were very difficult to control. They became state property under the emperor but over such vast and remote areas he had little option other than to appoint military governors who attempted to control the local rulers who in theory recognized Tibetan overlordship. The Tibetan rulers were often weak, especially in the late seventh century, and dominated by factions at court and within the military aristocracy. The Tibetan empire was therefore a weak structure even by the standards of the early Eurasian empires.

11.6.3 The imperial contest

The contest between the four great empires – Chinese, Turkic, Tibetan and Arab – began in the early eighth century. The Chinese had military garrisons as far west as Kashgar and the Tibetans dominated the area to the south. The Turkic empire to the north was restored after 683 following the revolt of Qutluq Elterish, the defeat of the Chinese and the reunification of the empire. The Arab armies arrived from the west in 712–13 when they conquered Transoxania, Bukhara and Samarkand. In 715 the Chinese general Lu Hsiu-ching reconquered Ferghana and for the first time in world history the empires at the opposite ends of Eurasia came into direct military contact with each other. For the rest of the eighth century these four empires competed to control the vast area of central Asia. There was a rough balance between the forces that the two distant empires (the Arab and Chinese) and the local but less well-organized Turks and Tibetans could deploy in the area and there followed a series of shifting alliances between them. The Tibetans were allied with the Turks in the 720s and late in the decade they attacked the Arabs and supported Khusro, a descendant of the last Sasanian ruler in Iran, during his revolt against the Arabs. There was constant border warfare between the Chinese and the Tibetans but the latter were able to keep control of the Pamirs and therefore the trade routes into India. The Turks, under pressure not just from the Arabs to the west but other groups on the steppe such as the Tölös and Turgash, collapsed in the 730s. They were replaced by the rising power of the Uighurs (part of the Tölös group) who took over the eastern Turk capital of Qara-Balghasun and established a steppe empire which ruled from the Altai mountains to Lake Baikal.

The Arabs tried to form an alliance with the Tibetans against the Chinese and sent emissaries to Lhasa, the Tibetan capital, in 732 and 744. However, the Tibetans were weak at this period as Chinese power across the Tarim basin and into Ferghana reached its zenith. From the mid-740s the main contest was between the Arabs and the Chinese as the latter pushed further west towards Samarkand and the Oxus river. It was resolved by the battle of Talas in 751, one of the most significant in Eurasian history. The Arab armies inflicted a decisive defeat on the Chinese army commanded by the Korean general Kao Hsien-chih. It marked the beginning of major internal problems and external weakness for T'ang China. However, the Arabs were not able to take advantage of this Chinese weakness to push further east because of the power of their nominal allies the Tibetans. The latter rose to the peak of their power under Khri-srong lde-brtsan (755–97) and cut off the Chinese from direct contact with the Arabs. By 756 the Tibetans controlled the key oasis city of Turfan, moved eastwards and in 762 captured the Chinese capital Ch'ang-an. The war continued for another twenty years until a peace treaty in 783 confirmed Tibetan rule over most of the former 'western regions' of China as far as the Kansu corridor in the east and in the south-east the Tibetans also controlled large parts of Szechwan. The power of Tibet was also felt south of the Himalayas. The Buddhist king of Magadha and Bengal – Dharmapala (760–815) – recognized Tibetan overlordship and Muslim writers referred to the Bay of Bengal as the 'Tibetan Sea'. The problem for the Tibetans was that they had to keep forces in the west against a possible Arab attack and therefore they had limited power to deploy against the Chinese. Another invasion of China was defeated in 789 but they were victorious over a joint Chinese and Uighur attack two years later at the battle of Pei-t'ing and kept control of the Tarim basin and the key east–west trade routes for another fifty years. Although the Arab armies were unable to take advantage of their victory at the battle of Talas to push eastwards their victory did have two very important long-term consequences. First, it confirmed Arab and therefore Islamic control of much of central Asia – the great trading cities of Samarkand and Bukhara were to be part of the Islamic rather than the Chinese world and subsequently Islamic influence did seep eastwards along the trade routes. Second, over the course of the next century, the Turkic tribes of the steppes were converted to Islam and they too were gradually drawn into the Islamic world to the west rather than the Chinese world to the east. Within a couple of centuries the Turkic tribes were moving westwards where they were to have a fundamental impact on the Islamic world which was to last until the twentieth century. [*13.7.2*]

11.7 The Eurasian Periphery: Japan and South-East Asia

11.7.1 Japan
[*Earlier Japan 10.9.2, Chinese script 7.8.2*]
During the sixth century the first true state began to emerge in Japan under the early emperors. However, as with many peripheral states, it was the influence of the dominant cultural and political power in the area – China – that was vital in shaping the early Japanese state with the local elite taking over Chinese institutions and ideas as a way of increasing their own prestige and power. Even before reunification under the Sui, Chinese influence was widespread in Japan, although much, especially Buddhism, was transmitted via Korea – the first Buddhist images and sutras came from the Korean state of Paekche in 538. It did not become the official religion until 587 following the conversion of the emperor together with the head of one of the most important clans, the Soga, who dominated the court until the mid-seventh century.

There were two great waves of Chinese influence in Japan during the early and mid-seventh century. During this time there were sixteen official missions to China, Buddhist pilgrims moved freely between the two countries and all of the Buddhist schools that were to predominate in Japan were offshoots of Chinese schools of the T'ang period. The Chinese also slowly dropped the abusive term *Wa* (or 'dwarf') for the Japanese and the country became 'Nippon' (the source of the sun) or in its Chinese form *Jih-pen* (Japan). The process of adopting Chinese models began with the calendar in 604. Then the country was divided up using the Chinese system into 66 provinces and 592 districts and at a lower level into units of three villages each with the peasants organized into groups of five families who were mutually responsible for their behaviour and taxes. The provinces were divided into 'circuits' reflecting the routes central officials took as they inspected local government. The names for the islands of Japan derive from these early administrative divisions – Kyushu is 'Nine Provinces' and Shikoku is 'Four Countries'. In the centre the emperor became *Tenno* or 'Heavenly Emperor' – a very Chinese title – and the new court ceremonial was adapted from the Chinese. Japan had a Grand Council of State with eight ministries – the six of the T'ang plus two for court administration. However, it did not have a bureaucracy chosen by examination – offices were reserved for the aristocratic elite and rapidly became hereditary. The central government gradually extended its control and replaced the old *uji* (clan) system. It imposed taxes on agricultural produce and textiles, a corvée (which could be commuted to food) and military service. In 701 the Taiho law-code, the first in Japan and closely modelled on Chinese examples, was published. In 646 an imperial edict abolished all existing landholdings and instituted the T'ang equal-allotment scheme based on a census of the country. It is, however, unclear how far the government was able to impose and regulate such a complex system. The Japanese government may have been modelled on that of China but it had far less power because of the lack of an effective economic and social infra-structure in Japan – there was still no currency and only one major city. That city, Nara in Yamato, became the Japanese capital after 710 – before then the imperial rulers lived on their own estates. The city had a grid plan modelled on that of Ch'ang-an but had no city walls because there were no external enemies. Much of the western half was never built but the capital was surrounded by a large number of Buddhist monasteries. Nara remained the capital until 794 when a new city, Heian, also laid out on the Ch'ang-an grid plan but lacking city walls, was constructed. Following a slight shift in site it became Kyoto, the capital until 1185 and always a key city in Japan (the current city still has the original eighth-century street numbers). Kyoto grew into a major city with a population of about 200,000 (far larger than any in Europe – Paris had about 25,000 people at this time).

Japan's isolation meant that it had no external enemies and it was a time of internal peace – after a revolt in 764 there was no further rebellion for more than five centuries. Population grew steadily but there was still plenty of agricultural land available to avoid any peasant discontent. In the eighth century southern Kyushu was incorporated into the state and in northern Honshu the power of the Ainu people (who may have been descendants of the original 'Jomon' hunter-gatherers) was broken and settlement extended into this area. However, although the power of the *uji* or clans was broken the power of the central government declined steadily. It did not have the ability to control the local landowners and the equal-plot system broke down as large estates developed. Control over local tax registers was taken over by the landowners and they were able to gain more and more tax exemptions. Peasants tended to put themselves under the control of the landlords because although they became semi-serfs they avoided having to pay taxes to the government. As the central government's tax revenues declined so did its power. By the tenth century most peasants and the agricultural land were controlled by the large estates and the government's tax revenue was minimal. The power of the emperors was always limited but fell further into decline during the ninth century. Women were removed from the imperial succession – between 592 and 770 they provided nearly half the emperors, after this date only two. The emperors came to be dominated by the Fujiwara family which owned huge estates and controlled nearly all government offices between 857 and 1160. (They dominated the court until the nineteenth century and regents were always chosen from one of five chief branches of the family.)

During the four centuries or so after the emergence of the Japanese state the Chinese script was adapted to the Japanese language. The outcome was probably the least efficient script anywhere in the world. At first the Japanese elite used Chinese and key Buddhist texts were read and written in Chinese. Gradually as contacts with China declined in the eighth century the Japanese needed to devise a script for their own language. The Chinese script was totally unsuited for the completely different Japanese language which, unlike Chinese, is polysyllabic and highly inflected – the Chinese script could not indicate the essential inflected endings of verbs and adjectives or even provide a one-to-one correlation of words. The problem was that the Japanese were isolated, dominated culturally by the Chinese and therefore had little alternative but to adapt the Chinese script – a syllabic or alphabetic script would have been far preferable (the latter would have required only fourteen characters for tenth-century Japanese) but none was available to them. By the tenth century three different writing systems had developed in Japan. Chinese characters were retained for the large number of Chinese words incorporated into Japanese and for texts in Chinese (or rather the Japanese version of Chinese because this script was unintelligible to the Chinese). Second were the *kana* (a semi-phonetic script) for poems and some prose. Third was a combination of the Chinese characters (for nouns, the roots of verbs and adjectives) and the *kana* (mainly for inflexions and post positions). However, even with this complicated system the pronunciation and even the meaning of a character could be unclear and only determined by context. It was this third system which evolved into modern Japanese.

[*Later Japan 13.6.2*]

11.7.2 South-east Asia
[*Earlier South-east Asia 9.9*]

South-east Asia was not isolated like Japan. It was at the centre of the Eurasian trade routes which linked the Indian Ocean world with China. It was therefore very open to influences spreading from both India and China. The revenue which could be derived from trade and the prestige gained from contacts with the more advanced cultures and religions enabled the elites of the region to increase their power and establish small states. We have already seen this process at work in the Kra isthmus and southern Vietnam in the early centuries CE when the east–west trade routes passed through this area. From the fifth century the trade routes shifted to the Straits of Malacca and led to the rise of states in Sumatra and Java. They were centred on the ports which were the main stopping points where traders from India and China met. Some, in particular the Arab merchants, made the complete journey to China but they too needed to stop over to await the right winds. The 'states' that emerged remained very weak and the ruler controlled little more than the area around the port city. He used the wealth from the taxes on trade to buy the support of the inland chiefs who in return provided food and accepted some general subordination to the coastal ruler.

The first, and most important, state to emerge in the area was Srivijaya, centred around Palembang on the south-east coast of Sumatra. It dominated the trade routes from the late seventh century until the early eleventh century. The ruler was able to suppress piracy in the area and therefore attract trade to the thirteen or so ports that he controlled. The main task of the royal administration was to supervise the markets and ensure that measures were correct and coins not debased. Originally the Srivijaya rulers embraced Hinduism, especially the cults of Siva and Vishnu, attracted by its emphasis on social order. However, from the late seventh century there was a major spread of Mahayana Buddhism across mainland and island south-east Asia. One Chinese pilgrim spent the 670s at Srivijaya on his way back from India and found over 1,000 Buddhist monks in the city. Most of western Java was under Srivijaya influence but further east the Saliendra rulers of central Java set up their own petty states in the Mataram area, calling themselves 'maharaja' to increase their prestige. A series of major temples, such as those at Borobudur, were built across the region and acted as focal points for integrating the local population. This system lasted until the sacking of Srivijaya by seamen from the southern Indian kingdom of the Cholas in 1025. South-east Sumatra never recovered and domination of the east–west sea routes passed to the states of central and east Java.

[*Later South-east Asia 12.2.1*]

11.8 The Eurasian Periphery: Western Europe

In the three centuries after the decline of the Roman empire in the fifth century western Europe was divided into a series of small, very weak kingdoms. The population was low and thinly scattered in isolated, almost entirely self-sufficient villages in a largely wooded landscape. There were a few towns but most of them were little larger than the villages. There was barely any trade except on a very local basis. Communications were poor and the resources available to the monarchs were minimal and state power was largely non-existent. Overall, the level of economic and political development probably remained as low as that of Japan. The areas east of the Rhine were still at the same tribal level as when the Romans encountered them in the first century BCE.

11.8.1 Iberia and Britain

The Iberian peninsula was taken over by the Visigoths by the 470s but the state was weak and divided and lost the south-east coastal area to the East Roman reconquest between the 550s and 620. Reccared (586–601) was seen by the church chroniclers as the most important king because he converted from Arianism to orthodoxy and the church, concentrated around the capital Toledo, therefore supported him and his successors. During the seventh century there was an almost complete breakdown in the succession to the throne amidst constant in-fighting among the royal family. The kingdom was crumbling and easily destroyed by the Arab invasion in the early eighth century – Toledo was captured in 711 and within a decade nearly all of the peninsula was under Arab control. Only a handful of Christian communities (they were hardly states) survived in the most remote northern and western mountains.

Britain was always a very poor and marginal province in the Roman empire. The exact chronology after the withdrawal of the legions in 407 is unclear. The country was divided among a large number of small, antagonistic kingdoms ruled by Romano-British, Anglo-Saxon and mixed families although there was some continuity from the Roman period and a few of the towns such as Cirencester continued to be occupied for a while. The Anglo-Saxon groups had been brought in as mercenaries and remained to set up their own kingdoms but the idea that there was a mass immigration pushing the 'Celts' to the west is not supported by any archaeological evidence. By the late sixth century a few larger, more coherent kingdoms such as Northumbria and Kent had emerged but the most important development was the rise of Mercia in the centre of the country out of a multitude of small kingdoms and chiefdoms. Through various forms of hegemony and confederations it came to dominate the southern part of the island, especially under Offa (757–96).

11.8.2 Italy

In Italy the reconquest under Justinian not only devastated the country but was also unsustainable. The Lombards were probably invited into the north of the country by the remaining Roman authorities as frontier defence forces. In the four years after 568 they occupied much of the north, established their capital at Milan and left just a few imperial enclaves such as Ravenna. The Lombards were portrayed as particularly barbarous by the church chroniclers but this was mainly because the church was still tied to the empire and opposed to the Lombard rulers because they tolerated Arianism and allowed it to flourish (there were even Arian churches in Rome). The Lombards were an elite living off the taxes on the peasants established in the Roman and Ostrogothic periods. The peninsula was divided into largely independent duchies and the Lombard area slowly expanded as Byzantine power declined. The Lombard kingdom was relatively successful and survived for over 150 years. The slow decline of Byzantine power in Italy increased that of the church in Rome. The Christian church was still regarded as a single entity and the councils held in the east under the emperor were held to be valid in the west. In 653 the emperor was still powerful enough to bring Pope Martin I to Constantinople to stand trial. Slowly differences between the western and eastern churches grew greater. Language barriers increased, there were continuing doctrinal disputes, especially over iconoclasm, and the secular power of the papacy increased as that of Byzantium waned. At the same time the church was the only institution whose authority spread, however vaguely, across the different west European kingdoms and it provided almost the only literate element in society. It also became more powerful through the development of monasteries. From the sixth century they became more tightly organized under a series of rules (those of Benedict became the most famous) which set up absolutist and totalitarian societies under the rule of the abbot. Gregory I (590–604) was the first pope to have been a monk. These institutions began to spread Christianity to areas which had been either outside or on the fringes of the Roman empire, beginning with Ireland and western Scotland and moving into the Low Countries and Frisia. The Roman church sent its own mission to Britain in 597 although the Irish church had been influential in the area for some time.

11.8.3 The Frankish kingdom and empire

An area intermediate between Italy, where the Roman tradition and influence remained strong for some centuries, and Britain, where the veneer of Romanization disappeared fairly quickly, was the former province of Gaul. Frankish settlement was largely confined to the northeast – in the south, which was more closely linked to the Mediterranean world, there was greater continuity and many of the old Roman elite and the peasantry survived. Gaul was a vast area which had contained numerous tribal groupings before the Romans and it was to remain divided for almost another thousand years – the idea that it was a proto-France in the making is a major misunderstanding. Frankish control over much of Gaul was established under Clovis but on his death in 511 the kingdom was divided among his four sons – they did not rule territorially defined units and each held land scattered across the region. The Franks conquered the Burgundian kingdom in 534 and control over Provence was obtained two years later. As the sons of Clovis died the kingdom was slowly reunited but immediately divided again on the death of the last – Chlotar I – in 561. It was reunited again under Chlotar II in 613 but divided once again in 638 on the death of Dagobert I. The power of the government in the various kingdoms seems to have been as strong as anywhere else in western Europe – it issued charters and had some control over local government through the appointment of the *dux* (duke) and *comes* (count) (interestingly both retained their Latin titles).

From the 660s the Frankish kings (the Merovingians) lost power and were increasingly dominated by various aristocratic factions. In Austrasia (the east of the Frankish kingdom) the monarchs came under the control of the Arnulfings (later known as Carolingians) who were the hereditary mayors of the palace. They held effective power from the early eighth century and under Charles (later known as Martel – 'the hammer') they defeated the Neustrians (the west of the Frankish kingdom), the Saxon tribes to the east, and in 733 a small Arab raiding party near Poitiers. This did not 'save' Europe from Arab control (Islam never tried to extend its control north of the Pyrenees) but it did give Austrasia control of Aquitaine, and by the end of the decade it also controlled Burgundy and Provence. In 743 another Merovingian, Childeric III, was put on the throne but with the consent of the Frankish aristocracy the Carolingians then decided to take the throne themselves. In 750–51 a mission was sent to Rome to secure the acquiescence of the pope and in 751 Pippin III (the son of Charles Martel) was crowned as king. He was formally anointed by Pope Stephen II when the latter visited France in 754. This was the beginning of a long alliance between the Carolingians and the papacy based on the fact that each side needed the other. For the kings the church legitimized their very dubious claim to the throne and for the papacy the Carolingians provided support against both the Lombards and the emperor in Constantinople.

Map 33: The Carolingian empire

On the death of Pippin III in 768 the kingdom was again split between his two sons; Charles (later 'the Great' or Charlemagne) took Austrasia and parts of Neustria, and Carloman ruled most of the new conquests. Only the death of the latter in 771 reunited the kingdom. Charles spent much of his time campaigning in the east against the Saxons who were difficult to defeat because they had no central organization above that of chiefs and no towns that could be conquered. By about 785 control was extended as far east as the Elbe and the people were forcibly converted to Christianity. (By 794 control was also secured over Bavaria.) In 774 the Lombards were defeated and their kingdom annexed. Despite the fact that Charles came from a different people and spoke a different language he took the title 'King of the Lombards' (a very alien concept to contemporaries). The most important events of the reign took place in Rome following the election of Leo III to the papacy in 795. The papacy was little more than a valuable prize in the struggles between the elite families of Rome for wealth and power. In the spring of 799 Leo, under attack from his rivals, fled to the Franks and was re-established by their armies in the summer of 800. In December Charles went to Rome to hold a council of enquiry into the conduct of the pope. On 23 December it conveniently decided it had no power to judge the pope who merely took an oath of innocence. Two days later the pope crowned Charles emperor.

The creation of an emperor in the west was not the consequence of Charles's conquests but merely the outcome of a series of events in Rome. However, the event was to have major long-term consequences and shape much of western Europe's political history for many centuries. Nobody at the time knew what the event really meant or what its impact was to be. The use of a crown was new (it was not to be used in Byzantium for more than a century) but most of the ceremonial was derived from dimly known Roman precedents. Stephen II had made Pippin III 'Patrician of the Romans' and after the events of 799–800 Leo had little alternative but to go further in order to cement the alliance between the papacy and the Frankish kingdom. The protagonists could argue that their actions were necessary because, after the death of Constantine VI in 797, the imperial throne in Constantinople was held by a woman, Irene. However, the events in Rome were not accepted by the empire in the east, although nothing could be done until the reign of Michael I (811–13). Then in a treaty with Charles the latter was only recognized as 'Imperator Francorum'. Charles himself left Rome in 801 and never returned though from that year he gave himself the highly inaccurate title of 'Emperor governing the Roman Empire'.

The empire created by Charles was very typical of all early empires. It was almost entirely dependent on its creator and had a very weak institutional base because the economic and social infrastructure could not support anything more complex. There was no effective internal administration – local control was delegated to counts who were 'supervised' by someone from the court occasionally being sent out to see what was happening. The counts took an oath of loyalty to Charles and that was almost the sole mechanism for holding the empire together, apart from the loot derived from conquest. Each count needed only one notary to deal with the small number of official documents which were prepared by the clerics of the royal chapel who were the 'administrators' of the empire. Charles, like most early European rulers, was illiterate and although he tried to learn to read and write late in life he failed. Perhaps Charles's major achievement was the revision of the 'Lex Salica' – the law-code of the Franks – and the creation of similar codes for subject peoples although this was done mainly in order to distinguish them from the ruling Franks. The inherent weaknesses of the empire – its dependence on the prestige of its creator largely derived from his conquests, the difficulty of controlling such a widespread and diverse territory and the permanent problem of the imperial succession – were to become apparent very rapidly after the death of Charles in 814.

11.9 Eurasian problems

In the period between about 600 and 750 the history of Eurasia was characterized by a general upswing in terms of a significant recovery from the problems that had marked the previous four centuries since the fall of the Han, the end of the Parthian empire and the beginning of serious internal problems within the Roman empire. The two key factors were the rise and rapid expansion of Islam to create the largest empire the world had yet seen and the reunification, expansion and prosperity of China under the Sui and T'ang. In central Asia the Turkic and Tibetan empires were powerful. Even the Byzantine state, which experienced a very significant reduction in its power, was able to restructure itself and survive. On the fringes of Eurasia the first state emerged in Japan, and in western Europe there was some greater political organization with the creation of the brief Frankish empire under Charlemagne.

However, from about 750 there were growing signs of problems across Eurasia. For more than two centuries most states experienced internal difficulties and an increasing inability to retain control over their extensive territories. The Islamic empire fragmented with the distant provinces becoming independent, the T'ang dynasty declined and from about 900 China was again divided among competing kingdoms. The Tibetan empire

OVERVIEW 7

THE WORLD IN
750 CE

World Population: 220 million
Regional Population: India: 60 million, China: 50 million,
Rest of Asia: 40 million, Europe: 25 million
Major cities: Ch'ang-an (1,000,000), Baghdad (500,000),
Constantinople (300,000), Loyang (250,000), Kyoto
(200,000), Alexandria (200,000), Cordoba (160,000),
Tikal (75,000), Rome (50,000), Paris (20,000)

Events:

★ Islamic empire dominant from Spain to North Africa, Egypt, the Levant, Mesopotamia, Iran and north-west India. Umayyad caliphate overthrown, replaced by Abbasids
★ Expansion of Chinese empire under T'ang at its peak
★ Islamic and Chinese empires in conflict in Central Asia, together with Uighur and Tibetan empires. Battle of Talas (751)
★ Emerging Japanese state
★ Byzantine empire weak and racked by disputes over iconoclasm
★ Petty kingdoms in western Europe. Carolingians take power in Frankish kingdom
★ Teotihuacan systematically destroyed by internal revolt – final collapse of empire
★ Mayan civilization at its height
★ Monte Alban in Oaxaca abandoned
★ Wari 'empire' in Peru
★ Early states in West Africa – Kanem, Ghana and Gao
★ Islamic penetration of East African coast
★ Ethiopian kingdom in Wollo
★ First wood block printing in China, Korea and Japan
★ Paper manufacturing established in Islamic world
★ First use of stirrup in western Europe

disintegrated, the primitive Japanese state found it increasingly difficult to maintain internal control and in western Europe the Frankish empire collapsed and the region experienced instability and a new wave of invasions.

The marked downswing across Eurasia began in 744 when Syrian soldiers killed the Umayyad caliph, al-Walid II, and inaugurated the third Islamic civil war in less than a century. Although the Syrian rebels were defeated by Marwan, the Umayyad governor of Jazira (Armenia-Azerbaijan), he was then defeated by a Shiite uprising in the Iranian province of Khurasan. Although Islam was divided in the late 740s it was the success of its armies at the battle of Talas (751) against the T'ang that inaugurated the period of increasing instability in China. The battle was followed by the rebellion of General An Lu-shan and his capture of the capital. Although the revolt was eventually put down Chinese power was in decline and control over the outlying parts of the empire was steadily lost.

11.10 Islam: the Abbasid Empire

The fundamental problem for the Abbasids, once they had secured control over the key central areas of the Islamic world, was to devise a coherent rationale for their rule. This they never managed to achieve. Although they claimed the caliphate they were in practice a dynastic empire that happened to rule the Islamic world. In establishing their rule they widened the ruling elite beyond that of the Arabs who had dominated Islam during its first century. The Syrian imperial troops of the Umayyads were replaced by the Khurasanis who had led the revolt and they provided both the garrisons at key points and most of the military governors. The main Abbasid base was Iran (the Abbasids spoke Persian) and they imported many practices of the Sasanian empire into Islamic administration. They also relied on many Nestorian Christians as administrators and the chief court official – the Wazir – came from the Barmakid family who were Buddhists from Balkh in central Asia. The capital of the caliphate was shifted from Damascus to Mesopotamia, where the new city of Baghdad (very close to the old sites of Seleucia and Ctesiphon) was built under the caliph al-Mansur (754–75). It rapidly became the largest city in the world outside China, with a highly cosmopolitan population drawn from all over the Islamic world and grew to almost 900,000 people within a century of its foundation.

The Abbasids had to govern an Islamic empire even though most Islamic scholars rejected their claims to the caliphate. The result was almost continuous religious conflict. Some of the problems stemmed from the way in which Islamic scholars (the *ulama*) interpreted Islamic law (the *shari'a*) in accordance with Arab tribal law as it existed under Muhammad and the first two caliphs. This was an impossible basis on which to rule a vast empire as the Umayyads had appreciated within little more than three decades of Muhammad's death. Increasingly even Sunni scholars came to reject the caliphate, especially since the Abbasids had no real claim to it, as no more than a necessary evil to provide a government in the Islamic world. The caliphate might gain some merit from supporting Islam but that was to be defined by the *ulama*. The Shiites also rejected the Abbasids despite the origins of the revolt in the Shiite heritage and the occasional Abbasid support for them. The Shiites narrowed the priestly lineage within Muhammad's family to just two descendants of Ali (Hasan and Husayn). In response the Abbasids tried to create a wider view of Islam through the concept of *shuubiyya* – the idea that Islam was compatible with any culture, including those of the non-Arab world such as Iran. This was rejected by the *ulama* as incompatible with Muhammad's ideas. The early ninth-century caliph Al-Mamun attempted to enlist Shiite support and chose their eighth imam, Ali al-Rida, as his heir. After a major revolt in Mesopotamia he was forced to abandon the plan although he then tried to claim the authority of the Shiite imam for himself. In 833 he instituted an inquisition (*mihna*) against the *ulama* which continued into the reign of al-Mutawakkil (847–61). The attack failed because, unlike Christianity, the *ulama* did not form an organized church which could be suppressed – their leadership was individual and came from below from those who accepted their religious authority. Eventually the Abbasids drifted closer to the Sunnis who were at least prepared to accept the existence of their caliphate.

11.10.1 Iberia

The Abbasids never controlled all of the old Umayyad empire. In 756 Abd al-Rahman ibn Muawiya, who had escaped the Abbasid slaughter of the rest of the Umayyad family, took control of the Islamic province of al-Andalus (Iberia) and founded the dynasty which was to rule there until 1031. The Iberian peninsula had long benefited economically from being incorporated into the wider Islamic world. The wealth that was generated was sufficient to support a standing mercenary army (mainly Berbers from north Africa). The old Visigothic estates, largely worked by slaves, broke up and most of the population became tenant farmers creating an agricultural surplus which was sold across the Islamic world. Under the Umayyads there was growing prosperity and the capital at Cordoba had a population of about 160,000 by 900 when it was by far the largest city in western Europe. It was probably at its height under Abd al-Rahman III (912–61) who declared himself caliph and helped establish the library which had over 400,000 volumes. The great mosque (later incorporated into the cathedral) was built under al-Hakam (961–76). Iberia under Islamic rule was a tolerant world and the Jewish community saw a marked improvement in its condition from the persecution under the Christian church and the Visigoths. The bulk of the population became *Mozarabs* – they adopted large parts of Muslim culture such as ways of dress and diet but remained Christians. Elsewhere in the Islamic world the Abbasids slowly lost control as factionalism and religious conflict in the capital and the court mounted. In 789 Morocco seceded under the Alid dynasty of the Idrisids. In 800 the Abbasid caliph, Harun al-Rashid, granted autonomy, and effective independence, to the governor of the rest of north Africa who created the Aghlabid dynasty. In 821 al-Mamun recognized the new dynasty of Tahirids ruling in Khurasan.

11.10.2 Military slavery

In the areas they did control the Abbasids were responsible for creating an institution which was unique to the Islamic world and which had a profound affect on later Islamic history – military slavery. At first glance it might seem very strange to arm slaves – it was the one thing the Athenian, Roman and later European slave empires avoided at all costs. It had its origins (as far as they can be traced) in the breakdown of the original Muslim ideal of the elite Arab army separate from the conquered society. As the army settled and integrated into society, more people converted to Islam. As more of the world was conquered the Islamic empires faced a serious problem because Islamic law prohibited fighting other members of the community. The recruitment of slave soldiers from the marginal areas along the frontiers of the Islamic world solved some of these problems and had some advantages compared with the use of mercenaries. The slaves were recruited earlier in life, lacked a family and could therefore be educated and moulded so as to have the correct values. They were owned by the state or ruler and became the elite troops. However, the problem was that they often only had any loyalty to the generation of rulers that recruited them. The first slave soldiers were recruited under the Abbasid al-Mutasim (833–42) from among the Turks of central Asia. Nearly all subsequent Islamic dynasties came to rely on slave soldiers and they reached their apogee under the Mamluks who ruled Egypt between 1250 and 1517. They were a 'dynasty' of slave soldiers who became rulers and themselves recruited more army slaves who eventually became the new generation of rulers.

11.10.3 The Fatimids and disintegration

The final disintegration of the Abbasid empire began when Turkish slave soldiers murdered the caliph al-Mutawakkil in 861. A period of increasing anarchy followed. A second-generation slave soldier, Ibn Tulun, seized power in Egypt and the Abbasids did not regain control of the area until 905. Between 869 and 883 there was a series of huge slave revolts among the Africans who had been brought to southern Mesopotamia to work on the sugar estates and remove salt from the degraded landscape so that more areas could be brought back into cultivation. One of the strongest anti-Abbasid forces in the Islamic world was the growing radical Shiite movement – Ismailism. This broke with and redefined the whole Shiite tradition through its messianic belief in a new form of Islam, based on the inner meaning of the Quran – it was devoid of law and ritual and depended on a spiritual revelation through a hierarchy of initiation. It clearly embraced some pre-Islamic beliefs and Sunni scholars refused to regard it as Islamic. As a political movement Ismailism controlled north Africa from 909 and conquered Egypt in 969 where it established a new capital at Fustat (Cairo). There they created a major cult of Ali with tombs and pilgrimage sites. From a secular perspective it was little more than a conquest regime based on Berber tribal forces and Turkish and Sudanese slave regiments. Much of the administration was carried on by Jewish and Christian officials as before under the Abbasids and the ruler adopted Byzantine ritual and elaborated it still further. The Fatimids controlled southern Syria and Damascus for a century after 978 but in Egypt the regime broke down from 1021 in internal warfare and religious schism.

Even before the Fatimids conquered Egypt in the 960s the Abbasid caliphate was effectively over. From the early tenth century their control over even the core of the empire in Mesopotamia was minimal and in 945 the region was conquered by Iranian mercenaries, the Buyids, who established their own regime and turned the caliph into a puppet. From one perspective the decline of the Abbasid empire can be seen as a process by which local landowners, the military and provincial rulers took power and set up their own smaller states opposed to central control from Baghdad. However, this 'decline' can also be seen as the almost inevitable development of diversity within the Islamic world because a single, extensive empire was unsustainable. That diversity remained almost entirely political – the extensive trading network across the whole Islamic world was little changed by the collapse of the Abbasids and the essential cultural and religious unity of the Islamic world remained intact.

[Later Islamic world 13.7]

11.10.4 The Byzantine world

The decline of the Abbasids from the 860s was almost exactly paralleled by a rise in Byzantine power – as in the past the rhythms of Byzantine history were the opposite of those in the Islamic world. In 864 the Bulgars were defeated and forcibly converted. It was to be the start of a long process of Christianization in the Balkans and the spread of Byzantine cultural influence. Three years later in a court coup the son of a Macedonian peasant became, as Basil I, the first emperor of the Macedonian dynasty which was to rule for two centuries. The reign of this dynasty coincided with the peak of Byzantine power although it still remained limited. Malta was lost in 870 and although Bari was recaptured three years later and advances made in Anatolia, the last strongholds on Sicily were lost in 902. As Abbasid power declined in the 930s and 940s gains were made in eastern Anatolia and northern Syria. In the 960s Aleppo and Crete were captured and control of the latter significantly reduced Muslim raids into the Aegean. Four Armenian kingdoms were annexed, Taron in 968, Taiq in 1000, Vaspurakan in 1021 and Ani in 1045, although the latter was soon lost. Nevertheless despite the internal problems of the Islamic world the Byzantines did not have the power to make more than marginal changes in the balance of power. They were more successful in the Balkans and eastern Europe. In 989 Vladimir of Kiev was converted and the petty princedom he established became a spiritual and cultural dependency of Byzantium. More important was victory at the battle of the Struma river in 1014 when the main Bulgarian army was defeated and over 15,000 prisoners were blinded. Four years later the Bulgarian state was destroyed and incorporated into Byzantium. The main problem for the Byzantine rulers was the strengthening of the position of the military aristocracy in Anatolia, the expansion of their estates and their increasing ability to turn the soldier-peasants into serfs. Not only did this lower tax revenues it also undermined the very foundations of the Byzantine state as it had been constructed in the mid-seventh century and had serious implications for the future.

11.11 East Eurasian Problems: China, Tibet and the Uighurs

The defeat by the Arabs at the battle of Talas in 751 marked the beginning of serious problems for the T'ang empire. It was followed almost immediately by the revolt of General An Lu-shan. He came from a mixed Sogdian and Turkic background and controlled the armies of the Peking, Shansi and Shantung areas. In 755 he captured the capital and although he died in 757 the rebellion continued under another military leader, Shih

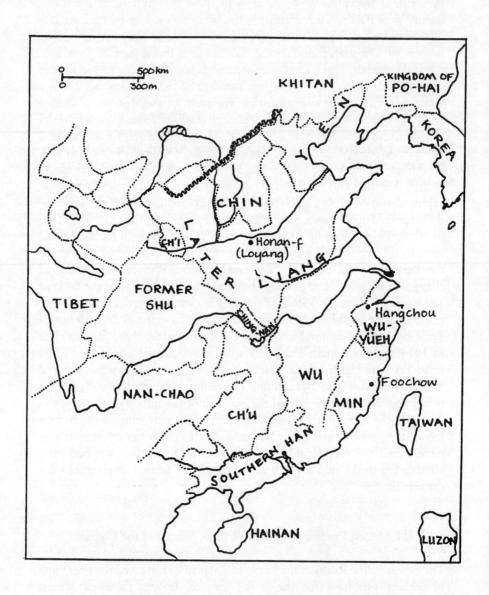

Map 34: China in the tenth century: the 'Five Dynasties'

Ssu-ming, and was only suppressed with Tibetan and Uighur assistance. From the 750s the Chinese were also steadily losing areas they had controlled for centuries. Within forty years they had retreated from almost all of central Asia where Islam, the Tibetans and the Uighurs now predominated. In Korea the Silla kingdom became effectively independent under its strongest ruler, Kyongdok (742–65). However, the widespread aristocratic and peasant rebellions later in the eighth century led to a decline in power and the collapse of the Silla kingdom within a century. In the south from the 750s the Nan-chao kingdom expanded in an area of very mixed Chinese, Indian and Tibetan influences. By 827 it dominated the Red river area, defeated the Chinese in the 860s and occupied Szechwan. From 902 it was known as the Ta-li kingdom and it survived until the thirteenth century. In 939 Vietnam shook off all control from southern China and subsequently was nearly always independent of China.

The Uighurs dominated the east-central steppe from their capital of Qara-Balghasun. They generally supported the Chinese and helped to put down the An Lu-shan rebellion. They did so because they relied on China for tribute. The Chinese had to pay forty pieces of silk for each Uighur horse (eight times the rate paid earlier to the Turks) and were consistently given the worst horses. In 765 the T'ang had to pay the Uighurs a special subsidy of 100,000 pieces of silk to make them leave the capital. Within a century the Chinese were paying fifty pieces of silk per horse and 500,000 pieces of silk a year. As with the other central Asian empires the Uighurs needed stability so they could derive revenue from trade along the Silk Road. They were close to the Sogdian traders to the west and from them adopted Manichaeism in the 760s, and the Sogdian script. The Uighurs rapidly became a settled people, exploiting the extensive central Asian trade networks. They developed a sophisticated legal system which included the ability to sue for damages on breach of contract – an essential provision for their traders.

Increasing sedentariness probably weakened the military power of the Uighurs, as did internal disputes over the succession which resulted in a civil war after 832. Within two decades the Uighur empire was defeated by the Qirghiz (a Turkic tribe from the Otüken region) and split into three kingdoms – Kan-chou, Sha-chou and, the most important, Qocho, centred around the oasis trading city of Turfan. In the mid-ninth century the Uighurs converted to Mahayana Buddhism. They survived as independent kingdoms because neither the Tibetans nor the Chinese were strong enough to defeat them. The early ninth century saw an expansion of Tibetan power as the T'ang and Uighurs weakened and they were even able to besiege distant Samarkand. In 822 they secured a peace treaty with the Chinese, recognizing Tibetan independence – the text was inscribed on an obelisk which stood in Lhasa until 1959. Tibetan power was short-lived and collapsed in the 840s following an aristocratic revolt (partly directed against the Buddhist monasteries) and the murder of the king, ghang-dar-ma, who left no heir. Anarchy ensued. Buddhism was reintroduced into Tibet in the early tenth century by dGongs-pa rab-gsal, based in the monastery of Amdo. It was here that the oldest school of Tibetan Buddhism – rNying-ma-pa – was established. Politically Tibet remained divided into a series of small kingdoms.

The collapse of the Uighurs in the 830s removed one of the major supports of the T'ang dynasty. However, it was already suffering from a number of problems common to all pre-industrial empires as they declined – factionalism and weakness at the centre, growing external threats that were difficult to defeat, and an increasing inability to maintain internal control, especially over provincial administrators and the local military commissioners (*chieh-tu-shih*). By the 870s the breakdown of the T'ang 'equitable field system' was producing escalating peasant discontent as local elites seized the land. Large groups of bandits and robbers roamed the countryside and within a decade some of them were over 600,000 strong. In 881–3 they captured the capital Ch'ang-an, government troops re-captured it, sacked it and then lost it again to the peasant looters. The emperors left Ch'ang-an, now in ruins, and Loyang also lost many of its residents. From the mid-880s the emperors held little real power although the T'ang dynasty did not formally come to an end until 907. The empire broke up and the military commissioners who had from the late ninth century been nominating their successors without any interference from the centre, now set up their own kingdoms. During the tenth century China was divided under the 'Five Dynasties' – the kingdoms which controlled the major regions of China, the Shu in northern Szechwan, the Southern Han around Canton, the Min in Fukien, the Ch'u in Hunan and the Wu-Yüeh in Chekiang.

The disintegration of the late ninth and tenth centuries although short-lived (China was reunited by 979) had a number of major consequences. Much of the old aristocracy of the north, who were descended from the nomadic groups who had settled in China and set up their own dynasties after the fall of the Han, disappeared in the fighting. As a military elite they also lost power as more and more of the armies under the military commissioners became full-time conscript armies. Although this was a period of political fragmentation it was also a period of rapidly rising prosperity within China, which laid the foundations for the extraordinary achievements of the next three centuries under the Sung. In the Yangtze area growing agricultural productivity through the use of improved irrigation techniques and new higher-yielding varieties of rice saw a rapid rise in wealth and increasing trade. Control over the routes to central Asia was no longer in Chinese hands and merchants and traders turned towards the sea routes and the southern coastal cities. Here the first signs of the commercial revolution of the next centuries was already apparent and overall the government was able to shift the tax base from agriculture and land to commerce and trade.

From the early ninth century there was also a major cultural change in China characterized by a growing hostility to foreign influences and pressure to return to what were seen as pre-Buddhist Chinese traditions. This trend was partly political and stemmed from the destruction caused by the An Lu-shan rebellion – he and his troops were seen (largely correctly) as non-Chinese – and from the intensifying pressure from the Tibetans and the Uighurs in central Asia, especially their control over the horse trade. As early as 760 there were attacks on foreign merchants in Yangchow. At the same time there was growing resentment aimed at the power and wealth of the Buddhist monasteries at a time when Buddhism was weakening because it was cut off from central Asia. Many of the Chinese in the south of the country, especially the cultural elite, resented what they saw as the power of the non-Chinese elites in the north and propagated what they believed to be a revitalized Chinese traditionalism – or 'neo-Confucianism'. In practice this was far removed from the ideas developed a thousand years earlier under the Han. In the 840s religions of 'Iranian' origin – Zoroastrianism, Manichaeism and Nestorian Christianity – were forbidden. Between 842 and 845 a series of measures was taken against Buddhism. Monasteries were purged of 'unsuitable' monks and the private possessions of monks were confiscated (the latter could be justified on Buddhist grounds). In addition 4,600 monasteries were either closed or demolished, 260,000 men and women from the *sangha* were forced to return to secular life and more of the estates were taxed. These anti-Buddhist decrees were probably not fully applied except in the capital and were eased after the 840s. Buddhism, especially the Ch'an school, continued to flourish in many provinces but overall the decrees of the 840s accelerated a process already under way – a steady decline in the importance of Buddhism within Chinese society and state. [*Later China 13.1*]

11.12 West Eurasian Problems: Disintegration and Invasion

Charlemagne had intended, in accordance with Frankish tradition, to divide his empire among his three sons. Only the early death of two of them meant that Louis (the Pious) was the sole successor. He crowned himself emperor just before his father's death but the key moment came two years later in 816 when he was re-crowned by Pope Stephen IV at Reims. It effectively established a precedent that the emperor had to be crowned by the pope in order to be legitimate and was to be a major source of problems for centuries. Until about 830 Louis was able to maintain the limited control his father had exercised over the empire but problems then mounted rapidly. Without the loot from conquest there was little to cement the loyalty of the elite and the growing number of revolts were escalated by coups and plots within the royal family and disputes between Louis's three sons over the inheritance. Louis died in 840 and three years later at Verdun his sons finally agreed how to divide up the empire. Lothar, who had been designated by the pope as successor to the imperial title since 823, took the central territories including the Italian peninsula. Charles (the Bald) took the west and Louis (the German) took the east. The latter two had combined against Lothar and the oaths they took in 842 at Strasbourg are the first known examples of the early French Romance and Old High German languages. However, the territories they ruled had nothing to do with nations and languages – they were just areas of personal rule agreed upon for family reasons. For most of the rest of the ninth century there was almost continuous fighting between the three kingdoms over territory and the imperial title. By the 880s the royal lines were dying out – in 884 Charles the Fat was theoretically the sole ruler of the empire but he no longer had any real power and anyway was mad. When he died four years later the empire broke up permanently.

As central authority collapsed such power as the state possessed passed to the local counts who soon became hereditary rulers. By 911 the Carolingian line in the east Frankish kingdom was extinct and although there were some Carolingian rulers elected in west Francia in the tenth century the last, Louis V, died in 987. The last royal coins were minted in the ninth century and the few coins that were minted in the tenth century came under the authority of bishops and local rulers. By the tenth century the Frankish empire had disintegrated into a series of local powers – Flanders, Normandy, Burgundy, Aquitaine, Bavaria, Gascony and numerous smaller units. The history of the tenth century is largely about their family disputes, marriage alliances and links to what remained of the royal line. This disintegration is often characterized as 'feudalism' but this term covers no more than a specific west European form of a common phenomenon in all pre-industrial empires and states. Land was the chief source of wealth and the only way an army could be sustained was by granting land to support the warriors. As central control weakened there

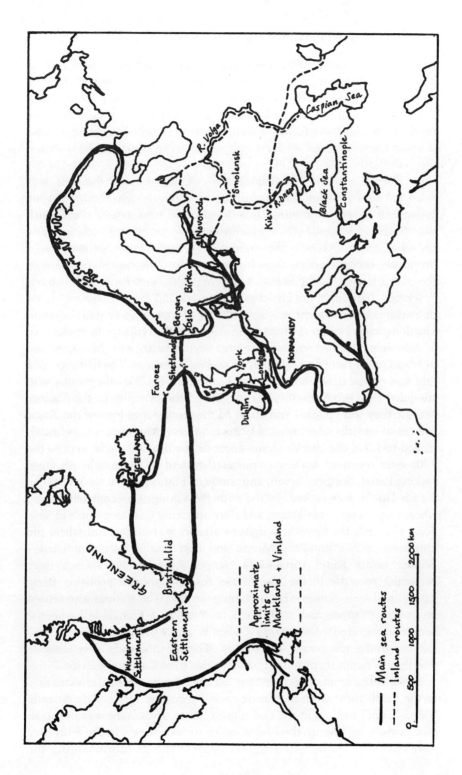

Map 35: The Viking world

was always the danger that the land granted by the ruler would become hereditary. The inevitable consequence was that even more power and land would accumulate in the hands of the local military elite. All that was distinctive about European 'feudalism' was the degree of breakdown in the ninth and tenth centuries, the amount of power (especially legal) that local landlords achieved and the large proportion of serfs tied to the land and their landlords.

As central authority declined across western Europe the area was subjected to a growing number of invasions which only accelerated the collapse of government authority as local rulers took action to deal with the attacks. The result was a vicious circle of crumbling authority and declining order. At first the main threat came from Scandinavia, a previously very peripheral area. It had come into increasing contact with the rest of Europe as the Frankish empire pushed into Frisia and as trade developed, particularly at Hedeby in Denmark and Birka on the east coast of Sweden. Development was very typical of a peripheral area – a weak kingdom emerged in Denmark in the eighth century but most of Scandinavia remained politically unorganized. Exactly why the population of Scandinavia turned to widespread raiding is unclear. The first recorded raid was on the island monastery of Lindisfarne in 793 – the monks who compiled the chronicles always exaggerated the brutality of the Vikings because they were pagans and attacked the monasteries (one of the major sources of wealth) whereas local Christian rulers, who were just as brutal, tended to leave the church alone. Some of the heaviest raids were in the 840s over much of northern France (they had to be bought off from sacking Paris), northern Spain, and southern France, and at the end of the decade Dublin was sacked. By the 850s the Vikings also controlled Kiev, where they set up a small state, and were attacking Constantinople in 860. From the 860s the heaviest weight of attacks was in England where the kingdoms of Northumbria, Mercia and East Anglia were eliminated – Wessex under King Alfred only escaped because the Vikings were beginning to settle in the east of the country (though probably fairly lightly) and their armies were becoming smaller. The Vikings also settled in northern France and in 911 the ruler of west Francia, Charles the Simple, recognized a fait accompli when he made the Viking leader Rollo the ruler of the new area of 'Normandy'. The advantage of this system was that these Vikings then resisted further raids from their compatriots.

The disintegration across western Europe became even more extensive. In the south there were increasing raids by Islamic forces. The Balearic Islands were captured in the mid-ninth century at the same time as Arab groups were moving up the Rhône valley to take slaves. In the 840s they were raiding in southern Italy and the papal territories further north – the papacy was even forced to turn to the eastern emperor for support. A more important threat came from the east and the Hungarians. The exact origin of these people is unclear since they seem to be referred to under a variety of names, although never by the name they called themselves – Magyar. Hungarian is a Finno-Ugrian language (with some Turkish elements) and is unrelated to the Indo-European languages that dominate Europe. They probably migrated from the middle Volga region, where they were known as 'Onogurs', under pressure from another nomadic group, the Pechenegs. They crossed the Carpathians in the 880s and by the 890s were raiding over the Alps into Italy. In the first two decades of the tenth century they raided widely across east Francia, in particular in Thuringia, Saxony and Alemannia. They were not defeated decisively until 955, after which they began to settle in the area of the Hungarian plain. The result of internal weakness and external attack was that in the tenth century western Europe remained a very poor, backward and barely organized region on the periphery of the Eurasian world.

[*Later Europe 13.12*]

OVERVIEW 8

THE WORLD IN
1000 CE

World Population: 265 million
Regional Population: India: 80 million, China: 65 million,
Rest of Asia: 40 million, Africa: 35 million,
Europe: 35 million (France: 6 million, Germany: 3 million,
Italy 5 million)
Major cities: K'ai-feng (450,000), Hangchou (450,000),
Constantinople (300,000), Sian (300,000), Cairo (200,000),
Kyoto (200,000), Baghdad (150,000), Canton (150,000),
Seville (125,000), Isfahan (110,000), Samarkand (70,000),
Venice (35,000), Milan (45,000), London (30,000)

Events:

★   Polynesians settle New Zealand

★   China reunified under Sung dynasty

★   Khitan empire in north China, Mongolia and Manchuria

★   Koryo kingdom in Korea

★   Ghaznavids ruling Iran, Afghanistan and Indus valley

★   Srivijaya dominating trade in south-east Asia

★   Umayyad caliphate in Spain

★   Very slow political recovery in western Europe from tenth-century invasions. Small kingdoms in England and northern Spain, weak Ottonian empire, weak Capetian rulers around Paris

★   Polish Catholic church established under Piast dynasty. Establishment of Hungarian kingdom. Conversion of Scandinavia to Christianity under way. Viking rulers of Rus converted to eastern church

★   Islam reaching West Africa

★   Kingdom of Ife in forest region of West Africa

★   Chinese trading on East African coast

★   Mapungubwe in Zimbabwe

★   Toltec empire in central Mexico

★   Chimu state in northern Peru

★   Large ceremonial centres on Tonga

★   Vikings reach north America from Greenland

★   First gunpowder weapons in China

★   Paper money in China

★   Paper first used in Islamic Spain

★   First tidal mill at Basra, increasing use of water-mills in western Europe and windmills in Islamic world

★   Horse collar used in Europe

★   Maize cultivation reaches north-east America

12

The Later Eurasian World

By 1000 CE the Eurasian world had begun to change significantly in many respects from the conditions found under the early agricultural empires which had existed across the continent for about the previous three millennia. The pace of change had been very slow but overall the world's population had risen from about 30 million in 2000 BCE to 50 million a thousand years later. The boom brought about by the introduction of iron tools and the ability to cultivate more land had doubled the population by 500 BCE and doubled it again to about 200 million by the first century CE. Then a long period of relative stagnation set in – little more land could be cultivated, technology was largely static and the spread of disease brought about by the linking together of the Eurasian continent severely restricted population growth. By 1000 CE the world's population had only grown to about 250 million.

Eurasian societies remained overwhelmingly agricultural with about nine out of ten people directly dependent on agriculture for their existence as either free peasants, landless labourers or serfs. Many of the remainder were indirectly dependent because they were employed in the processing of agricultural produce – milling, tanning, brewing and textile production. Economic growth was, when it occurred, primarily extensive – more people meant that more land could be cultivated – but the fundamental constraints within society were little altered. Some wealth could be generated from trade but demand remained low as long as the peasantry were primarily subsistence producers. Very slowly, with many interruptions, the amount of trade expanded and the number of products traded, and the distances over which they travelled, grew. This produced new sources of wealth within society and gradually these had a multiplier effect by building up demand and trade still further. The result was that over many centuries societies became a little wealthier and the sources of wealth widened. These changes went further and faster in the areas of Eurasia which had the most productive agriculture capable of supporting a larger infrastructure of trade and production. They were particularly noticeable in three areas: China, which had a monetary economy and highly developed trading system from about the second century BCE; India with its highly productive agriculture and trading cities (especially in the south); and in much of the Islamic world. In parallel with these changes the pace of technological development began to increase in the last few centuries of the first millennium CE, further widening the possibilities open to society.

By about 1000 China was the first society in Eurasia to begin to break free from some of the major constraints that had affected earlier societies.There were fundamental transformations in the economy affecting agriculture, industrial production, trade and finance which also had repercussions for the state, its taxation system and the wealth it could command. These are considered in detail in the next chapter. This chapter deals with the broader Eurasian world, very roughly in the period of the great empires from 600–1500. It traces some of the constraints that still restricted major changes in the economy and society, but also looks at the growing trading networks across Eurasia, the increasing number of cities that drew their wealth from trade and the acceleration of technological change, largely originating in China.

12.1 Farming and Ways of Life

Apart from a few areas of Eurasia – the irrigated rice production of the Yangtze valley using high-yielding varieties, parts of India, Mesopotamia and Egypt – agricultural productivity was poor. Yields were low, especially in Europe where on average they were little better than twice the amount of seed planted (modern agriculture produces about a thirty-fold increase). Wine yields were about a seventh of current levels. In Europe the shortage of animals caused by the difficulty of finding enough winter food (animals were often so weak by the spring that they had to be carried into the fields to eat the new grass) meant that manure was also in very short supply. Some thirteenth-century texts from the Paris region do no more than suggest that land ought to be manured at least every ten years. Because the animals were badly fed their output was very low too – a fourteenth-century English cow produced about a sixth of the milk and a third of the meat of a modern animal.

The overwhelming mass of the population was at the mercy of bad harvests caused by adverse weather, destruction by pests and warfare. These problems were made more acute by the amount of peasant produce taken by landlords or the state in taxation. In Japan the peasants produced rice but this largely went to the landlords and the state and they had to exist on millet and wild grasses. In Europe most peasants were forced to give up about a third of their gross output and rarely had any surplus for sale. In Russia, where the winter might last for over 200 days, the peasants needed vast amounts of fodder to keep their few animals alive, and obtaining food from the forests, like the gathering and hunting peoples of the past, remained very important. In a few areas around the towns and cities of Eurasia a more commercial agriculture was possible because a market existed – even a small peasant plot could be profitable in these circumstances. Famine was an ever present danger – in eleventh century France there were twenty-six general famines affecting the whole country. In many cases it was not just that food was short and the poor could not buy it – there was an absolute shortage of food. In 1315–17 there was a particularly bad series of harvests across western Europe and in August 1316 when King Edward II arrived in St Albans even he found it impossible to buy food because there was none available.

The bulk of the peasants were poor with almost no possessions. In Japan the peasants wore hemp – it was the only material available. In Europe towns were almost entirely constructed from wood before the seventeenth century and peasants had mud and earth huts with no windows and lived with their animals to keep warm. As late as 1560 in Pescara a quarter of the population was living in a shanty-town consisting of holes in the earth. Household furniture was only common in a rich society such as China. Public baths were mainly found in Islamic countries and only China had an effective system for removing human and animal waste from the cities. In Siena at the end of the thirteenth century the town council employed a sow and four piglets to eat the refuse in the Piazza del Campo. In Europe most people survived on a very monotonous diet of bread, gruel, slops and soup, and rice made up almost the entire diet in China, south-east Asia and parts of India. Meat and fish were rarities normally only consumed by the rich except at certain festivals and celebrations during the year. It is therefore hardly surprising that the health and life expectancy of individuals was low. In the Levant in the early Islamic period the average age of death was the same as it had been about 9000 BCE. In Scandinavia around 1200 CE the average life-span was about eighteen years and half of all individuals died as children. At the age of fifteen people might expect to live until they were thirty-four. A detailed study of over a hundred cemeteries north of the Alps dating to between 1000 and 1200 CE shows that, apart from the very high infant mortality rates, a third of males and a quarter of females died between fourteen and twenty (mainly from malaria, smallpox, dysentery and tuberculosis). Overall less than a quarter of the population survived until they were over forty. A few people, especially among the elite who ate better and did little manual work, could live long lives – Popes Lucius III and Celestine III in the late twelfth century died in their nineties. The result was that Eurasia had a very different population structure from modern societies. Only about five per cent of the population were aged over sixty-five and children were the main class of dependents. Even so many could not be cared for and infanticide was common. In Europe about one in ten of all those born were abandoned and cast off as foundlings.

12.1.1 The diffusion of new crops

The rise of Islam and the creation of a world with a shared culture stretching from the western Mediterranean to south-east Asia and into Africa produced the first major transformation in the world's agriculture. It broke down many of the cultural barriers to the transmission of ideas and ended the long-standing barrier between the Mediterranean world and that of the Indian Ocean. The outcome was the first substantial spreading of crops since the development of farming some ten thousand years earlier. The new crops not only widened the subsistence base and slightly reduced the impact of crop failure but also produced greater variety in the diet. The main centre for the diffusion of the new crops was India where a number of plants from south-east Asia had been brought back by traders and cultivated for many centuries. When the Islamic traders reached India they brought a number of plants to Iran and Mesopotamia where they were adapted to new conditions before many of them were moved further west into the Mediterranean region.

The major crops involved were the cereals. Sorghum reached India from Africa but was brought to south-west Asia in the tenth century and to Spain a century later. Rice was almost unknown in south-west Asia before the rise of Islam but it was then brought from India and spread rapidly into every climatically suitable area. The hard wheat varieties were probably first grown in Ethiopia but were then taken from the Red Sea area across the whole of the Mediterranean region by the Arabs. Even more important was sugar cane. Its origins probably lie in south-east Asia from where it spread to China by the first century CE and also westwards to India and eventually Iran. The great expansion of cultivation came under Islam when it was introduced into Mesopotamia and spread to the Levant and the eastern islands of the Mediterranean, especially Cyprus, by the tenth century. It also spread down the East African coast as far as Zanzibar. The taste for sugar was universal but it required large amounts of hard labour to process the sugar cane. It was the European demand for sugar that later became one of the decisive forces in world history. (The spread of sugar cane cultivation under European control, first in the Mediterranean then in the Atlantic islands and finally in the Americas, was the basis for the largest slave empires known in the world.) Almost as important was the spread of old-world cotton. This was first grown in north-west India by the Indus valley civilization but took a long time to spread because of its strict climatic requirements – it had only reached parts of the Gulf, Nubia and south-east Asia by the last century BCE. The most important change was the development of a much hardier variety around the central Asian oases and the trading city of Turfan in the eighth century. Within two hundred years it was grown across the whole Islamic world, creating a new textile industry as knowledge of how to spin cotton spread rapidly.

A number of other less central but still important crops were also diffused. Some of the most significant were the citrus trees which were difficult to cultivate because they had to be kept true by grafting. They originated in a very small area of Assam and north Burma but were developed into different varieties in China, India and the Malay peninsula. Only one variety (the citron) had reached south-west Asia before Islam but by the tenth century the sour orange, lemon and lime were all brought from north-west India to the Mediterranean. The banana originated in Burma and south-east Asia and reached India and China by the fourth century BCE. Under Islam it was taken westwards and spread along the north African coast to reach Spain and also along the east African coast to reach Zanzibar by the tenth century. Spinach and aubergine both originated in India and reached China and Iran by the seventh century – under Islam they spread rapidly westwards reaching Spain by the tenth century at the latest. Other crops could not be adapted to grow in the Mediterranean and only spread into parts of the Islamic world. The coconut palm reached India from Malaya by the sixth century BCE but took a long time to travel further westwards because of the difficulty of adapting it to even slightly harsher climates. It was probably grown in east Africa by the tenth century but not in the Gulf (Oman and Dhofar) until the fourteenth century. The mango also travelled from India and was grown in Oman by the ninth century and slightly later in east Africa.

The spread of these new crops from the Islamic world to Christian Europe was much slower. It occurred through the two main areas for the transmission of Islamic knowledge and technology – Spain and Sicily. In the thirteenth century sorghum and hard wheat reached Italy (the latter producing that classic of Italian cuisine – pasta) followed in the fourteenth century by oranges and lemons and a century later by rice (grown on huge estates in the Po valley). The reasons for this much slower diffusion northwards were neither climatic nor the absence of irrigation techniques but simply a lack of agricultural innovation in southern Europe. In the Islamic world the new crops produced an agricultural revolution by allowing more intensive cropping, better rotations and an expansion of the cultivated area. In some of the most fertile areas it was even possible to grow three crops a year – in Cyprus a cotton crop could be grown between two crops of wheat and in the best irrigated areas of Mesopotamia and the Yangtze valley in China two crops of rice were possible. Agricultural risks were lowered by the wider range of crops and the rise in incomes they produced supported a general rise in economic development. It was the

agricultural base that helped to sustain the Islamic world as one of the two richest areas in the world (the other was China).
[*Later diffusion of crops and animals 16.3*]

12.2 Islam at the Centre of Eurasian Trade

The rise of Islam not only transformed the structure of Eurasia politically but also economically. Although China and the Mediterranean had been linked together through the Silk Road and the maritime routes from the last centuries BCE, the linkages had been mainly indirect. The Parthian and later Sasanian empires in Iran had successfully excluded the merchants of the Levant and the Mediterranean from direct contact with China along the central Asian routes. The maritime links via the Indian Ocean routes were similarly divided up into the hands of a succession of traders. Islam fundamentally altered this situation by producing an economic zone and area of influence on a scale never seen before. Although it was concentrated around its core (and richest region) of the Levant and Mesopotamia it was an open trading system that linked together nearly every part of Eurasia. In the east it stretched through the Indian Ocean (including the east coast of Africa) to south-east Asia and therefore to China, which was also reached along the central Asian overland routes. In the south it extended down the Nile to the Sudan but also along the trans-Saharan caravan routes to west and central Africa. To the west it included not only north-west Europe but also the routes along the Atlantic coasts. In the north it drew in the trade routes along the great Russian rivers.

The basis of the trading structure were the wealthy cities at the centre of the Islamic world – Damascus, Cairo and, increasingly, Baghdad, which within a few decades after its foundation by the Abbasids became the largest city in the world outside China. At first it was a circular town arranged around the palace and mosque with a series of concentric walls with houses in between. Its wealth, partly deriving from the presence of the court, swelled the population and the suburbs sprawled outwards. At its height it covered an area five times as large as Constantinople and had a population of about 900,000. A typical 'town' in England at this period such as Leicester had a population of 1,300. The centrality of the Islamic world was reflected in the domination of its currencies in Eurasian trade. Until the end of the seventh century the old Byzantine and Sasanian coins remained in circulation. Then, based on its access to the gold produced in west Africa and transported across the Sahara, Islam produced its own currency. The gold coin was the *dinar* and the silver coin the *dirhem* – the latter tended to dominate further east but the dinar was the main unit of

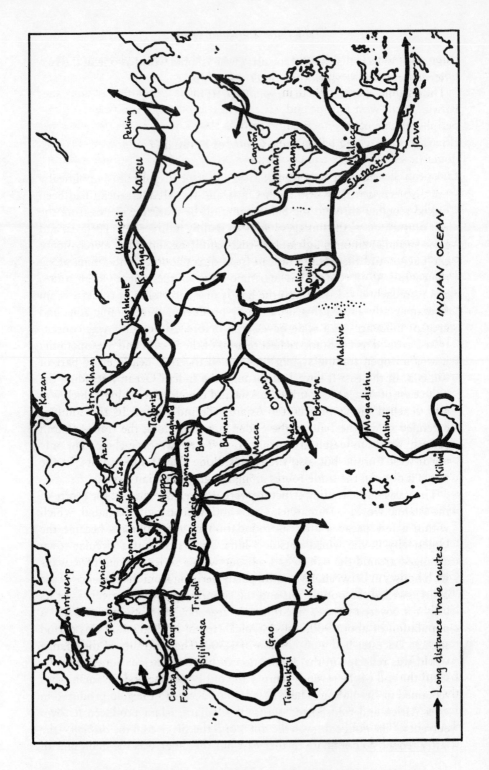

Map 36: Islam at the centre of Eurasia: trade routes 600–1500 CE

value in trade. The Byzantines did produce their own gold coin – the *nomisma* – but its circulation was limited.

The Islamic world pulled in products from its peripheral regions in Russia, north-west Europe and Africa. These products were typical of the periphery. One of the most important was slaves, which were used on the extensive sugar plantations in southern Mesopotamia, in the mines and as domestic labour. They came from three main areas. Central and eastern European slaves were transported through Verdun (a major castration centre), Arles and Venice or via the Black Sea. Those from central Asia travelled via Samarkand (another castration centre) and Bukhara. Slaves also came from all over Africa – across the Sahara to north Africa and Egypt, from Ethiopia and Sudan to Egypt and from the east African coast to Aden, Socotra and then to the Gulf. Also important in the trade of the European periphery were amber, furs and especially timber, which was in short supply in the Islamic world – it was needed for shipbuilding, in sugar production and to make charcoal. The main focus of Islamic trade though was to the other prosperous and developed areas of Eurasia – India and China. Trade along these routes was gradually transformed from being primarily one of luxuries to being dominated by major staple cargoes travelling to wherever the demand was greatest. Trade in one luxury product declined – raw silk from China. At some time in either the late sixth or early seventh centuries a Nestorian monk smuggled some silkworms out of China. He also took with him the secret of how to cultivate them and spin the silk. In Damascus and Aleppo Islamic producers turned the region into the supplier of raw silk to the whole area, including the Byzantines. But, although raw silk was manufactured in south-west Asia, high-quality manufactured silk from China (still the best in Eurasia) remained one of the major traded items.

The trade of the Islamic world was on a large scale – as many as 8,000 merchants were travelling along the north African coast either by boat or by caravan every year. It was dominated by a number of different groups. One of the most important were the Jewish groups, especially the 'Radhanites' (the derivation of the term is unclear). They probably existed before the rise of Islam but they had much greater freedom than under the anti-Semitic policies of the Christian kingdoms. They ousted many of the 'Syri' merchants (mainly Nestorian and Jacobite Christians and the Armenians who largely controlled the trade between Islam and Byzantium). They took increasing control of long-distance trade which they were to dominate until the eleventh century. They were centred in Egypt, especially Cairo, which controlled much of the trade down the Red Sea to India (probably more important under Islam than the routes down the Gulf) and the trade to southern Europe, in particular Italy. Copper, lead and textiles were traded to India in return for spices, dyes and foodstuffs. The eleventh- and twelfth-century documents of these traders were discovered in the late nineteenth century in the *Geniza* or storeroom of a Cairo synagogue where they had been thrown for safe-keeping. They provide a detailed insight into how trade was organized under Islam. Most of the trade was undertaken by small traders who formed partnerships for specific ventures. Business was largely conducted on credit with payment not due for two months. The money used was not usually individual coins but sealed boxes authenticated by either the government, merchant or bankers. There were money changers for foreign currency across Cairo. However, much of the trade did not involve cash. Banks issued promissory notes, credit facilities, 'orders to pay' (cheques) and bills of exchange and they therefore also developed the accounting techniques to keep track of these transactions. (The Islamic prohibition on usury was easily circumvented and Muslim bankers were engaged in all aspects of this trade.) One of the other major trading groups was the Kharijites of north Africa who were effectively independent of the Abbasid caliphate from the late 750s. They founded the great caravan city of Sijilmasa which was the centre of the trade routes across the Sahara to the Sahel and the Sudan which brought back gold and slaves to the Islamic world.

12.2.1 *The Indian Ocean world*

The Indian Ocean world was far more cosmopolitan and the Islamic traders formed only one element in its complex trading networks. No one power dominated and none made any attempt to use force to gain trade advantages or control routes. Many of the convoys which sailed across the oceans were composed of traders from a wide variety of groups and locations – they travelled together because of the hazards involved in long-distance sailing. Islamic merchants did, however, travel further than most of their predecessors even though a full round trip to China took at least eighteen months because of the seasonal wind patterns. Ships gathered at the mouth of the Gulf and the Red Sea in September and crossed the Indian Ocean, tacking against the north-east monsoon, to reach the southern ports of India. Then they crossed the Bay of Bengal on the south-west monsoon in December to catch the southerly monsoon in the South China Sea to reach Canton in April and May. The return ships left Canton in the autumn to catch the northerly monsoon, followed by the early north-east monsoon in the Indian Ocean so as to be back in the Gulf and the Red Sea by about May. The first direct Islamic embassy reached China in 660 and within a few decades there were large communities of Islamic traders in most of the southern Chinese ports. This trade was not simply one-way – Chinese merchants not only dominated the trade to Java and Sumatra but

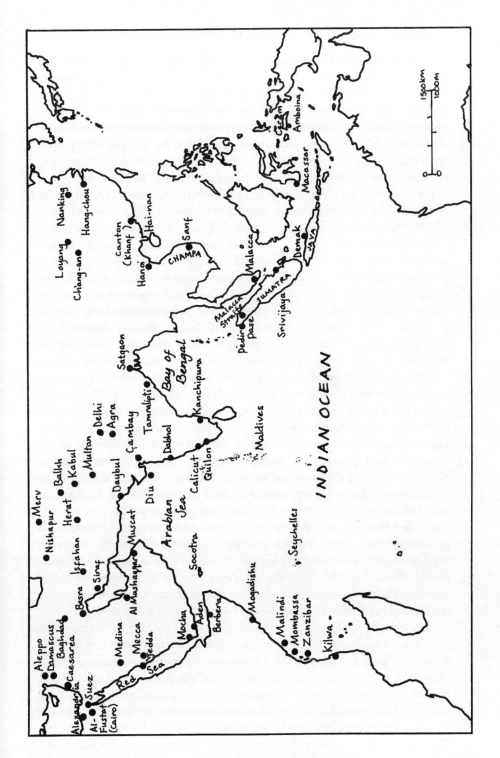

Map 37: The Indian Ocean world 600–1500 CE

they often went westwards into the Indian Ocean. As early as the fifth century Chinese ships were common in the Gulf and at Aden and by the eighth century they were trading on a significant scale along the east African coast. The Chinese prisoners taken by the Islamic armies at the battle of Talas in 751 were brought back to Mesopotamia where they were able to return home on a Chinese junk which left the Gulf in 762. Indeed the great Arab geographer al-Muqaddasi writing in the late tenth century saw the whole Arab world as being based around the 'Sea of China'.

The intermediate cities along the east–west trade routes were, as in the past, central to the efficient functioning of the trade. They provided ports of call, places where supplies could be obtained and markets where goods could be exchanged. Some of the most important were along the Indian coast, on Sri Lanka, the Maldives and those in south-east Asia (Sumatra, Java and southern Vietnam). The most important were those of India. The major Indian states were land-based and were usually quite content for the coastal trading cities to be independent and prosperous as long as they provided some revenue in return. Overall India remained highly prosperous because of its strong agricultural base and the ability of its industries to meet nearly all domestic demand. It was therefore able to export specialized products in demand elsewhere – especially manufactured cottons and silks together with dyes and metalwork. The level of imports was much lower and the long-established drain of gold and silver eastwards, established under the Roman empire, continued. The Gujarat area had long been in contact with the Gulf because it was possible to sail along the coast between the two at almost any time of the year without having to wait for the monsoon seasons. The principal port was Cambay which had a substantial community of Arab traders from the Gulf region but also traded itself over a wide region, especially down the east African coast. By about the twelfth century the trade of this area had shifted from luxuries to basic products such as textiles (especially cottons), weapons, semi-processed raw materials plus silk, horses, grains, sugar, salt and dried foods. Further south along the Malabar coast Calicut was the most important port following the decline of Quilon. It was the major link in the trade from the Red Sea and the main port of call for Chinese junks when they sailed into the Indian Ocean. Local merchants traded to Sumatra and Java and, in addition, by the late fifteenth century there were over 15,000 Muslim traders at Calicut. The Chola state in south-east India was also important to the east–west trade and strongly supported the local Tamil traders and their various corporations. At various times the Chola controlled Sri Lanka and the Maldives and even raided as far east as Sumatra where they destroyed the commercial predominance of Srivijaya. The key to much of the trade was the high-quality textile production of the area which was the basis of the wealth of the merchant class of Kanchipuram.

12.2.2 European trade

Europe was at the far western end of the Eurasian trading world and the type of trade, its level and the sophistication (or lack of it) in the financial mechanisms reflected this peripheral status for many centuries. On the whole Europe continued to produce raw materials – wine, wool, timber, fish and furs – and only slowly did it begin to produce more manufactured goods. Even then it made little that the Islamic world needed and faced continuing problems in paying for the products it wanted from eastern trade because of the massive trade imbalance. Europe was brought into the Eurasian trade network from the south through ports such as Amalfi and Bari in the eleventh century. The most important development in this period was the slow expansion of European trade into new areas in the north – around Flanders (the cloth industry was largely supplied with English wool for centuries), Scandinavia, the Baltic and Russia. North–south trade within Europe was small enough to be accommodated by the slow, expensive overland trade through the fairs of Champagne at towns such as Troyes and Provins and even these were no more than regional fairs until the Italian merchants arrived in the late twelfth century. Trading voyages from the Mediterranean to northern Europe were not made on any scale before the late thirteenth century because the ships were unable to cope with the hazards of the Atlantic unlike the ships of Islam, India and China which regularly undertook long ocean voyages.

From the eleventh to the fourteenth centuries European trade was dominated by the towns of northern Italy. Venice was one of the most important, exploiting its links with the Byzantines to establish control over the Adriatic before financing a coalition of west European 'crusaders' to sack Constantinople in 1204. Its main rivals were Pisa and then Genoa which, by the mid-thirteenth century, dominated trade into the Black Sea. Most of the trade of these cities was inland to the manufacturing towns of Lombardy, in particular Milan. In northern Europe as Germanic settlement expanded eastwards a trading network emerged in the Baltic with voyages during the summer between towns such as Lübeck, Rostock, Stettin and Riga. The trade relied on primary products from the forests of the east – furs and timber – and was organized through the Hanseatic League which was dominated by a few large towns (most of its towns had less than a thousand inhabitants). It was not until the fifteenth century that the German cities came under growing competition from those of Flanders and Holland as trade shifted towards the supply of grain (mainly rye) to feed the cities of the latter area.

Although the level of European trade was far greater by the fifteenth century than it had been five hundred years earlier it was still very small by Eurasian standards. Even in 1400 Venice had just twenty merchant galleys, of which about five made a voyage to the Levant in the summer, Genoa sent about the same number and the Catalan trading city of Barcelona slightly less. In total the amount of cargo brought back was around 4,000 tons, about the same as one small modern freighter. The level of commercial sophistication was also low. The fairs of Champagne were designed so that nearly all the transactions were done through barter. This was vital because Europe lacked gold and silver to use as currency. The main gold coinage was either the Islamic dinar or the Byzantine *nomisma*. Even with the growth of trade no new gold coinage was struck until the Genoese *genovivo* in 1252, followed fairly rapidly by the Florentine *florin* and the Venetian *ducat*. In general the volume of coins issued was very low and silver currency rarely circulated outside the immediate area where it was minted. The fundamental problem was that Europe produced very little gold or silver before the opening of the central European mines in the late fifteenth century and most of what it had went to the east to pay for goods from the Islamic world. In the mid-fourteenth century the mints in France had to stop production because there was no silver available. Debasement of the currency was therefore inevitable. Between 1250 and 1500 the number of grammes of silver in 240 pennies fell from 80 to 22 in France and from 70 to 9 in Milan. Because of their contacts with the Islamic world merchants in Italy slowly adopted some of the latter's more sophisticated commercial practices. Bills of exchange were first used in Italy in about 1300 and became common in long-distance trade within fifty years. In the north the trade of the Hanseatic towns still mainly relied on barter and credit was very rare. Double-entry bookkeeping was unusual outside Italy and not used on any scale in the north until the sixteenth century. Loans were made despite the objections of the church authorities (as in Islam) but the risks were high. When Edward III of England simply refused to pay his debts in 1341 the result was the bankruptcy of the Peruzzi and Bardi families of Florence within five years.

12.2.3 The trading world
By the fifteenth century Europe was still a marginal area within the Eurasian world. However, it did share some of the characteristics of the increasingly integrated trading world which was now operating at a far higher level than a thousand years earlier as trade expanded in both variety and volume. Around major cities in areas such as southern coastal China, Bengal, the Nile, northern Italy and Flanders agriculture was largely commercialized to meet the demands of urban markets and peasants paid their rents in cash

rather than kind. In remoter areas subsistence agriculture still prevailed. Commercial and industrial development was similar in many areas – for example the specialized textile production in Flanders and Kanchipuram in southern India. However, there is little doubt that the level of industrialization and commercialization was far greater in China and India than in Europe – about a tenth of the population of China was urban, the same proportion as Britain in 1800. Everywhere semi-independent (or independent) trading cities such as Venice, Aden, Calicut and Malacca existed as the focus of trading networks. These cities were, especially outside Europe, cosmopolitan with traders from many different groups conducting business. By the fifteenth century Malacca was trading with the Mediterranean, inner Asia, east Africa, India, China, Japan and all of south-east Asia, and eighty-four different languages were spoken in the city. Rulers were generally content to encourage these cities because the wealth they generated provided a major source of revenue. The state played a variety of roles – in Venice it built boats and then hired them out to merchants, China sometimes did the same but generally it allowed merchants to take their own risks. Over time political risks changed, trade patterns shifted, new routes were opened and old ones declined and so the prosperity of the different cities rose and fell. Nevertheless, the level of trade across Eurasia was increasing in size and the trading networks were, very slowly, becoming more closely integrated. The result was that events in one region and the disruptions they caused were more and more being transmitted across the system to affect every area.

12.3 Science and Technology: China

In the same way as Eurasia was increasingly linked together by a complex web of trading relationships so no area could maintain a monopoly over scientific and technological change – this too spread, as the Chinese found to their cost with silk production. Nevertheless there is no doubt that until the seventeenth century China and, to a lesser extent, Islam were the areas of the greatest knowledge, inventiveness and technical advance in Eurasia. Such an assertion may seem at variance with the standard 'western civiliz-ation' perspective which sees the development of the 'scientific method' and 'rationality' as the sole prerogative of classical Greece and eventually 'the West'. In such accounts 'the east' is seen as essentially unscientific and stagnant. This is part of a general tendency absurdly to overvalue the culture of ancient Greece and devalue all other traditions. There is no doubt that Greece was important in some areas – for example Euclidean geometry was far in advance of that anywhere else in Eurasia. (China,

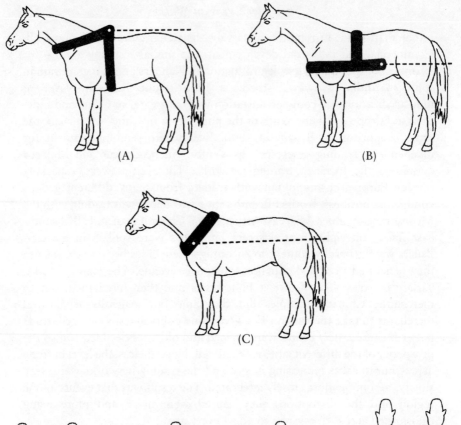
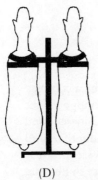

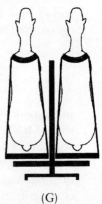

(A) ancient throat-and-girth harness
(B) modern breast-strap harness
(C) modern collar harness
(D) top view of throat harness
(E) top view of breast-strap harness
(F) top view of collar harness
(G) top view of collar harness showing use of whippletree to attach two animals to a wagon

Chart 5: Types of horse harnessing

together with much of Islam, was far stronger in algebra). However, the Greeks were equally capable of fundamental misunderstandings such as the crystalline celestial spheres of Ptolemaic astronomy (which lasted in Europe until the late sixteenth century) or, in optics, the belief that rays of light came from the eye rather than the object. It was certainly the case that Chinese work rejected the mechanical, reductionist view that came to predominate in Europe in favour of an organic materialism; a more holistic view in which phenomena were interrelated through a cosmic pattern which could be discovered. The Chinese therefore tended to favour field theories and action at a distance rather than atomism and mechanical interaction. This did not make measurement and classification difficult and Chinese 'scientists' were equally capable of making sophisticated instruments such as the seismograph (in use by 130 CE) and the decimally graduated sliding callipers developed at the same time.

One area where the Chinese were far in advance of any other area was astronomy. The earliest solar eclipse observation was made in 1361 BCE about 300 years after the first recording of comets (the so-called 'Halley's comet' was identified in 467 BCE) and by 635 CE Chinese observers knew that the tails of comets always pointed away from the sun. Systematic sunspot records were kept from 28 BCE – about 1,500 years before the arguments in renaissance Europe about who 'discovered' the phenomenon. Even more important were the records of novae and supernovae (still used by modern astronomers) including the earliest known in 1400 BCE and the one which created the Crab nebula in 1054 CE, which is only known because of Chinese and Japanese records. As early as the eighth century CE Chinese scientists were making expeditions to Java and other islands to survey the constellations of the southern hemisphere. Chinese scientists were giving star positions by degrees as early as 350 BCE. Modern astronomy uses Chinese equatorial mounting and co-ordinates rather than the altazimuth system of Islam or the ecliptic co-ordinates of the Greeks. These are based on the work of Tycho Brae in the late sixteenth century who gained his knowledge from Arab texts derived from the scientific mission to China led by the Muslim astronomer Jamal al-Din in the thirteenth century. Equally important was the Chinese measurement of time. They adapted the water clocks known in Egypt and Mesopotamia through the development of the escapement mechanism which is central to all modern clocks and watches. This was first done by the Buddhist monk I-Hsing in 725 CE, six centuries before similar devices were used in Europe. However, Chinese clocks remained hydro-mechanical rather than the more advanced, purely mechanical clocks developed in Europe in the fourteenth century.

The strength of Chinese science and technology was in producing practical solutions to problems and therefore significant changes to the economy and society. One of the first was the development of an effective way of harnessing horses so that they could pull loads. Horses were first controlled through a throat and girth harness derived from those used for oxen, cows and buffalo. It worked on the yoke principle which was effective on the latter animals because it pulled against the vertebrae joining the neck to the body. However, on horses it produced the main point of traction on the throat with the yoke exerting pressure on the windpipe as the horse applied more effort. This choking of the animal made horses unsuitable for pulling heavy weights as in ploughing and they could only be used for light work such as chariots. An effective harness required the pulling point to be low, along the sides of the animal. However, this required a different vehicle design – the animals had to be attached not to a central pole but to two side shafts which involved a so-called 'whipple-tree' design to provide manoeuvrability. These problems were first solved in China with the evolution of the breast-strap harness, together with the two-shaft vehicle, which with a back strap held up the shafts and ensured that the horse pulled horizontally with its chest. This system enabled horses to pull heavy loads, in particular ploughs that could break up heavy soil. It was developed in the third century BCE but was not known in Europe until at least 600 CE. The second development was the modern horse collar – a padded frame around the neck with the shafts attached at shoulder level so that the horse pulled with its shoulders not its chest – a far superior method for very heavy loads. It was used in China about 500 CE but not for another five hundred years in Europe.

China also developed a wide range of other inventions such as the wheelbarrow in the third century CE which did not reach Europe for a thousand years. The highly advanced iron industry producing cast iron (not made in Europe until the fourteenth century at the earliest) enabled the construction of iron-chain suspension bridges from the sixth century CE (the first in Europe was in the 1740s) and in 610 a segmental arch bridge – the first in Europe was the Ponte Vecchio in Florence built in 1345. As late as 1675 the Russians were using Chinese experts to advise them on bridge building. Deep-drilling for salt and natural gas began in Szechwan with high-quality steel used for drilling bits reaching down to 2,000 feet below the surface. Long bamboo tubes with valves were used to bring up the brine – the same method as used in the first American oil-wells in the nineteenth century. Water power was developed at about the same time as the rest of Eurasia (the first century CE) but was used mainly for operating the double-action piston bellows in the iron and steel industry rather than grinding cereals. The crank was first used for rotary fan winnowing machines in the first centuries CE but was not known in Europe for more than seven hundred years. By about 1200 the Chinese had combined the crank, connecting rod and piston-rod with water power to produce the 'blowing engine' for blast furnaces and forges (it had all the components for motion in a steam engine but worked in reverse). Water power was also widely applied to the textile industry, especially silk production which, because of the very long, high-tensile silk thread, was well suited to the use of machines. By 1090 China had the silk winding machine which produced two types of motion from the same source: the cocoons were kept in a hot water bath, the fibres were guided through rings and laid down on a great reel; it also had an early form of flyer and a ramping arm to lay down the silk evenly. At the same time the spinning wheel was mechanized and a driving belt developed to power three spindles simultaneously.

Some of the most significant Chinese developments were in seafaring and navigation. Chinese ships were completely different in design from those of the rest of Eurasia. The *chhuan* or 'junk' was essentially a rectangular box developed from the prehistoric bamboo raft. It had a segmental construction with the hold divided by transverse bulkheads to provide watertight compartments – a practice adopted by European ships in the nineteenth century when shipbuilders became acquainted with Chinese techniques. Ships built in this way could be far larger than those using other methods and the square-ended transom stern also allowed the use of the stern-post rudder from the first century BCE (not known in Europe until over a thousand years later in 1180 CE). The first fore-and-aft sails were developed in the third century CE and enabled ships to sail well to windward – something which the square-sailed ships of Europe could not do. The efficiency of the Chinese sailing ship meant that China never had the multi-oared slave-rowed galleys of the Mediterranean, which lasted until the late sixteenth century. What the Chinese did have were treadmill-operated paddle-wheel boats used in naval warfare on rivers and lakes. By the twelfth century these boats had up to twenty-three wheels – eleven-a-side and one at the stern. Chinese navigation depended upon understanding magnetism and the construction of very accurate charts. The study of magnetism was purely Chinese in origin and grew out of the Taoist interest in divination. The earliest compasses (known as 'floating fish' by Muslims) used iron model fish to point north and south. They were not magnetized by being rubbed on a lodestone but by being heated to red-hot temperatures whilst being held in a north–south position. The first certain reference to magnetic pointers dates to 83 CE but they were probably in use some time before this. The first known examples in Europe date to the late twelfth century, the same time as the adoption from China of the stern-post rudder. At least two centuries before then the Chinese knew that the north magnetic pole moved and was not the same as true north. For some time the Europeans tried to fiddle their compasses so that magnetic and true north coincided. The knowledge of magnetism enabled the Chinese to construct maps with accurate co-ordinates from the fourth century CE. By the fifteenth century Chinese maps for sailors showed routes and compass bearings complete with timings and the points at which direction should be changed.

12.4 Science and Technology: Islam and Europe

Islam was the principal inheritor of the Greek tradition in science and the development of scientific thought played a significant role in Islamic culture. This was partly through the translation of large numbers of manuscripts into Arabic and the accumulation of vast stores of knowledge at institutions such as the *Bayt al-Hikma* (the House of Wisdom) built in Baghdad in 813 and similar institutions under the Fatimids in Egypt. Even more important was the spread of Islam eastwards and the access this gave to the knowledge accumulated in India. In mathematics Islamic scholars adopted the Indian system of reckoning (though using Arabic numerals) and the Indian concept of zero (which had earlier spread to China). By 875 al-Khuwarizmi had laid the foundations of algebra (hence the name algorithm) and by the early twelfth century Umar Khayyam (better known to modern westerners as the poet Omar Khayyam) was already classifying equations in the third degree (x^3) into twenty-five categories. In astronomy the main impetus came from the Indian treatise *Siddhanta*, which was translated in Baghdad in 771, and other works known in the ninth century. However, the main limitation was still the domination of the Greek astronomy of Ptolemy. Even more important was the work of Ibn al-Haytham on optics which finally corrected the Greek mistake about the direction in which light rays travelled.

In technology the world of Islam made a number of significant advances. Although the ships were not as sophisticated as the Chinese 'junk' they were far in advance of those of Europe. They were 'carvel' built – planks were laid edge to edge not overlapped as in the 'clinker' built vessels of northern Europe. The main feature of the rig was the lateen sail, attached to a heavy spar suspended at an angle to the mast, that enabled the ship to sail much closer to the wind than the square rig used in Europe. Both of these techniques were later adopted by European shipbuilders and sailors. Huge shipyards and ports were built across the Islamic world – by the tenth century Tunis had an anchorage for over 200 vessels – and accurate charts for sailing to India and beyond, with hazards and tides marked, were being produced. All three types of water-mill – undershot

(Vetruvian), overshot and horizontal – were in use by the ninth century and the first tidal mills were operational at Basra in the eleventh century (about a hundred years before the first known example in Europe). In military warfare the Islamic world developed special techniques of incendiary warfare at first using petroleum and pitch mixtures with troops protected with special fireproof clothing. In 673 a Syrian architect from Baalbeck, Callinicus, defected to the Byzantines taking some of the secrets with him. This became the so-called 'Greek fire' – a name that was given by western Europeans but not used by the Byzantines who knew where the secret had originated. Islamic forces continued to develop new technologies in this area with more advanced recipes using saltpetre and distilled petroleum (the Islamic world had very advanced distillation techniques) and a form of 'flamethrower' – *zarraya* – in which a bronze piston pump forced the ignited fluid through a nozzle.

The most remarkable development across nearly all of the Islamic world was the replacement of wheeled vehicles by the camel. The one-humped camel was probably first domesticated about 1500 BCE, somewhere in the Arabian peninsula, though they were not common for another five hundred years. For many centuries they were kept for their milk until the development, shortly before 100 BCE, of the north Arabian saddle – an inverted V-frame over the hump (with a pad for a seat) so that the weight was distributed over the ribs not the hump. When it was used as a pack saddle loads were tied to each side. This was another example of an invention by nomadic people which had a profound effect on settled societies. Until about the third century CE wheeled traffic and paved roads were common across the whole area from north Africa to Iran but the camel had a number of significant advantages. It was far cheaper to maintain than an ox, mule or horse and did not suffer from the harnessing problems of the latter two. Only limited loads could be pulled by these animals and carts were far more expensive and much more difficult to maintain than the relatively small amount of equipment needed for a camel. A camel could travel twice as far in a day, did not need roads and one person could control about six camels when they were tied together. The abandonment of the primitive wheeled transport and the appalling 'roads', often no more than rutted tracks, which predominated before the nineteenth century, was therefore a major step forward. Infrastructure investment could then be concentrated on bridges and caravanserai rather than trying to maintain roads. Wheeled transport was retained in some areas such as Anatolia where it was more efficient. However, the use of the camel extended widely and rapidly across what became the centre of the Islamic world because of its large number of advantages. It spread westwards into north Africa where a unique saddle was developed for riding in front of the hump – it was more efficient for riding but not for loads – and was fundamental in developing the trans-Sahara caravan trade. Further east, the two-humped camel was domesticated in Iran or Afghanistan, possibly a little earlier than the one-humped variety. It spread westwards as far as Mesopotamia and also east to India and was the basis of caravan traffic along the Silk Road under the Parthian and Sasanian empires. Hybrids of the two types were even more efficient and could carry heavier loads but were very difficult to maintain in breeding. The one-humped camel spread eastwards with the rise of Islam and the two-humped or Bactrian variety was soon rarely used west of the Oxus river.

Islam was the main route for the diffusion of knowledge and technology to Christian Europe. It was through this route that Europe became acquainted with Greek science, Aristotle and numerous crucial tech-nologies, together with developments such as 'Arabic numerals' (in fact Indian), the concept of zero, double-entry bookkeeping and various forms of mercantile credit. The impact of Islam can be seen from the Arabic derivation of numerous key words – muslin, mohair, damask, arsenal, admiral, alcohol, alkali, sugar, syrup, sherbet, saffron and (of paper) ream (from *rismah*). In Spain key words for central technologies were derived from Arabic – *tahona* (mill), *acena* (water-wheel) and *acequia* (irrigation canal). It was Spain (especially Toledo) and Sicily, the two areas where Islamic and north European culture most closely mingled, that were the key to the transmission of this knowledge. The Europeans only became aware of Aristotle through the work of Ibn Sina (known to Europe as Avicenna) and the commentary of Ibn Rushd (known as Averröes). It was central to the development of all European thought, in particular for individuals such as Aquinas. In addition the Islamic institutions of learning were the model for the development of the university, and the division of the curriculum and the methods of teaching were largely identical.

European backwardness was shown by the fact that hardly any metal was used between about 400 and 1000 and even after this levels of utilization were low. One major development was the use of the heavy plough with a combination of vertical coulter to cut the sod in the line of the furrow, a horizontal ploughshare and an angled mould-board to turn over the loose earth. It was much heavier and more difficult to pull through the soil and needed a team of eight oxen. No peasant could afford to maintain that many animals and so they had to be kept as a team and hired out. The development of the horse-collar led to a slow conversion to horse-pulled teams after about 1100. The heavy plough had no intrinsic advantages over the lighter plough except that it was better suited to the heavy soils of north-west Europe – elsewhere farmers could manage with the much cheaper and easier to use and maintain scratch plough pulled by two oxen. Europe was also the last area of Eurasia to adopt the foot-stirrup for horse-riding. It was probably developed by nomadic groups somewhere in central Asia and was known in India in the third century CE, reaching China along the Silk Road where by 477 it had developed so as to enclose the whole foot. It took two centuries to travel westwards and was known in Iran by 694. Its first use in Europe was by the Frankish armies in the 730s. The advantage of the stirrup was that it made the rider much more difficult to knock-off the horse but the idea that as a result it produced European 'feudalism' is naive technological determinism. It did not do so in the rest of Eurasia and 'feudalism' was the result of the particular social and economic conditions in Europe in the ninth century and after. The use of iron horseshoes also spread from central Asia to China, Islam, Byzantium and finally western Europe by about the tenth century.

Europe slowly adopted new technologies. One of the most important was the water-mill – there were 5,624 in England in 1086 but many were hardly used because it was so difficult to transport grain over any distance. The use of water-mills slowly extended – to making mash for beer in France from the mid-ninth century and stamp-mills for hemp and fulling cloth by the eleventh and twelfth centuries, but the mechanization of forges was much slower. In the Islamic world windmills developed from about the tenth century but they had vertical axles. In Europe a unique development was the horizontal axle windmill probably first used in England in the twelfth century – by the thirteenth century there were over 120 such windmills around Ypres. Most important of all was the adoption by Europe of technologies used elsewhere in Eurasia, often a thousand years earlier. Many came from Islam. The ogive arch (which was central to Gothic architecture) came from the Islamic world via Amalfi. European glass making, especially that of Venice, came from the Levant in the late thirteenth century. Similarly the translation in 1277 in Toledo of an Arabic text on time-keeping, including the idea of the weight-driven clock with a mercury escapement, which had been used in Arabic Spain since the eleventh century, was vital for the development of European time-keeping devices. Other technologies came from China. The magnetic compass and the stern-post rudder were in use by the late twelfth century but the late fourteenth century was crucial for the adoption of a number of Chinese techniques from cast iron to segmental arched bridges. By the fifteenth century therefore Europe was beginning to catch up with the developments in technology across the rest of Eurasia.

12.5 Paper, Printing and Gunpowder

Three of the most important Chinese technological developments, which were to have a major impact on world history, were paper, printing and gunpowder. They were developed in China between the first and ninth centuries but took a long time to diffuse westwards, first to the Islamic world and finally to Christian Europe.

12.5.1 Paper

Before the invention of paper societies were restricted to a few materials for writing, all of which had significant disadvantages – stone engraving (almost impossible to move), bark (very fragile), clay tablets (heavy), papyrus (fragile) and parchment or vellum. Although the latter was more durable and had a better surface than paper it could take the skins from more than two hundred animals to make a single book and monasteries in Europe often had to stop book production because they ran out of suitable animal skins.

Paper was developed in China about 105 CE under the supervision of a Han court official. The earliest type comprised a mixture of raw fibres (especially mulberry bark, laurel and grass) and rags. The fibres were soaked for a hundred days, any outer bark was removed and the pulp mixed with lime, boiled for eight days and repeatedly washed. It was then strained, pounded into a soft dough, bleached, washed and starched. To make paper a frame was dipped into the vat containing this mixture, drained and dried on a heated wall. Techniques gradually improved and within a hundred years the use of paper was extensive in China. Unlike silk no attempt was made to keep its production methods a secret and it spread rapidly into central Asia. By the seventh century it had reached Korea and Japan and a little later India. Samarkand was making paper from about 650 as Chinese influence under the T'ang reached its maximum westerly extent. It was the conquest of the area by Islamic troops, particularly after the battle of Talas in 751, that resulted in the transmission of paper technology westwards. Islamic troops took captured Chinese workmen to Baghdad and there in 793 they established a paper-mill. Paper rapidly replaced parchment across the Islamic world and also the specialist use of papyrus in Egypt. It spread across north Africa to reach Islamic Spain by the tenth century. The major problem the Islamic paper-makers faced was the lack of suitable tree bark and therefore the proportion of rags was increased which reduced the quality of the paper. Europe was slow to adopt the use of paper. Both Roger II in Sicily in 1145 and Frederick II in Germany in 1221 banned its use in official documents. The first paper-mill in Christian Europe was established in Italy in 1276 – the technology came

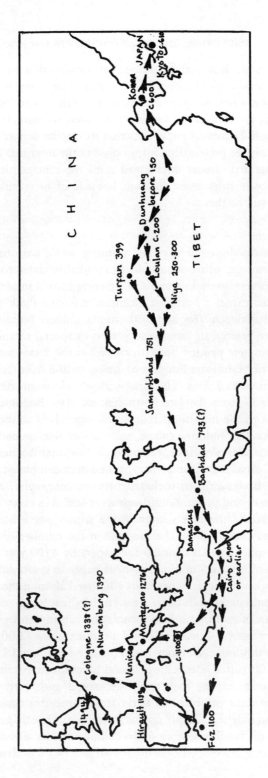

Map 38: The spread of paper from China

from the Islamic world and Europe had no idea that the invention was actually Chinese and dated back over a thousand years. France, Italy and Germany began making paper in the fourteenth century but England did not have a paper-mill until 1495 and the Dutch not until 1586. One of the problems with European paper was that its quality was very low because of the even higher proportion of rags used in the mixture. The production process remained almost unchanged until the nineteenth century when wood pulp was substituted for rags because of increasing demand and quality fell still further.

12.5.2 *Printing*

Without the development of paper, printing would have been impossible. The first printing, using wood-blocks, probably dates to about 700 in China. Two very early examples of printing also come from Korea and Japan. In the former a Buddhist incantation from Pulguk-sa temple dates to 751 and between 764 and 770 over a million Buddhist *dharani* or sayings were printed in Japan and placed in special temples and stupas. The first complete printed book to survive is the *Diamond Sutra* (one of the classics of Mahayana Buddhism) dating to 868 from Tunhuang on the Silk Road in central Asia. The large-scale development of block-printing came in China from the late tenth century. The Buddhists (despite the persecutions of the mid-ninth century) produced six different editions of the *Tripitaka*, the Buddhist canon, and each edition needed about 80,000 wood-blocks. The government-sponsored National Academy printed the 'Confucian' classics and the Taoists printed their complete canon too. Very rapidly the books printed included history, geography, medicine, philosophy, poetry and prose. Bookshops were found in every city and China was undoubtedly the first society in the world where literacy extended beyond a very small elite. The increase in the number of books printed produced a phenomenal demand for paper. By 1100 just one prefecture (Hsin-an) sent over 1.5 million sheets of paper in seven different varieties to the capital every year. Paper-mills employed about a thousand workers each and could make rolls of paper up to fifty feet long.

Wood-blocks required a long process of carving and preparation but were very effective – printers could produce about 2,000 double-page sheets every day and each block could be used for about 15,000 prints and another 10,000 after re-touching. Wood-blocks were particularly suitable for the Chinese script, they could be stored and were well suited to producing regular printings of fairly small runs at a time. The printers developed an indelible lampblack ink, known incorrectly as 'Indian ink' in Europe. By the twelfth century multi-colour printing was common. In the 1040s Pi Sheng developed ceramic movable type. Wooden movable type proved more difficult but about 1300 many of the problems were solved by Wang Chen and the type was stored in compartments on a revolving table about seven feet in diameter. By 1322 Ma Ch'eng-te was using over 100,000 movable characters. It was the sheer number of characters required in Chinese that restricted the use of movable type and made wood-block printing much more efficient.

The spread of printing westwards from China is much more difficult to trace than the use of paper. The Uighurs were printing books in the ninth century using their alphabet derived from the Sogdian (but with titles and page numbers in Chinese) using Chinese wooden blocks. From here its use probably spread to the Mongols and it was only under the Mongol empire that printing spread westwards. It was being used in Iran in 1294 and around this time in Germany too. Religious prints and block books were known in Europe fairly widely by the early fourteenth century, some six hundred years after eastern Eurasia. The techniques were identical with those used in China. The crucial development in printing was the use of movable metal type. This was first done in Korea in 1403 where the government set up a Bureau of Type Casting in the Office of Publications. The techniques used to make the metal type were adapted from coin casting and were required because of the very high demand for books and the increasing size of print runs. The increasing speed of technological diffusion across Eurasia is shown from the fact that Johann Gutenberg, wrongly credited by Europeans as the 'inventor' of printing, was experimenting with similar movable type (which was very suitable for alphabetic writing systems) by the late 1440s in Strasbourg and Mainz. In 1455 he produced an edition of the Bible, the first book to be printed with movable type in Europe.

12.5.3 Gunpowder

The development of printing was to have as big an impact on Europe by the sixteenth century as it did in China six hundred years earlier. It was also at this time that Europe was coming to terms with the impact of another equally important Chinese invention – gunpowder. It was first developed about the same time as wood-block printing in the ninth century when the Taoist alchemists first noted down the dangers of mixing together the ingredients of gunpowder – charcoal, saltpetre (potassium nitrate) and sulphur. By 919 *huo yao* or the 'fire drug' was used as an igniter in a flamethrower. By about 950 the Chinese had perfected the 'fire-lance' – a portable flamethrower in which the rocket composition was not allowed to fly loose. True explosives developed as experiments showed what happened as the amount of saltpetre in the mixture was increased. By about 1000 primitive bombs and grenades were being built with thicker and thicker casings and in 1044 the exact formula for gunpowder was first written down (it was not known in Europe until 1327). In the late twelfth century multiple rocket launchers were in use with two stage rockets which automatically released a rain of arrows when over the target. Most important was the development of increasingly tougher tubes (hardened paper, bronze and finally cast iron) from which projectiles could be fired. By 1120 barrel guns were used as flamethrowers and about 1280 the first true gun, in which the projectile filled the barrel, was developed and used against the Mongols.

All of these developments took place entirely within China and before any knowledge of gunpowder weapons had reached to other parts of Eurasia. The technology of gunpowder spread rapidly westwards after the late thirteenth century, probably under the Mongols, reaching the Islamic world well before Christian Europe. It seems likely that Islamic forces were throwing primitive explosive grenades during the siege of Acre in 1291. The first primitive cannon were used by the Mamluks in Egypt and reached north Africa and Spain by the early fourteenth century. It was from here that knowledge of gunpowder weapons reached western Europe. Their use is first recorded at the battle of Crécy in 1346, but the development of effective weapons was much faster in the Islamic world than Europe. By the siege of Constantinople in 1453 the Ottoman forces were using pairs of guns that needed seventy oxen to move them and over a thousand men (it was often easier to cast them on the spot than try to move them). They were made from bronze and had a bore of almost three feet and fired a ball weighing over 300 pounds. The impact of these new weapons was to be most dramatic in an unstable Europe divided into numerous petty states and racked by almost continuous warfare. In China their impact was to be far less destabilizing.

[*Later impact of gunpowder on Eurasia 18.1*]

13

The Age of China
(1000–c.1250)

By the tenth century China was by far the most developed region of Eurasia. Its economy and society were based upon a free peasantry and a highly productive agriculture, especially in the south. The development of high-yielding varieties of rice, gravity- and machine-fed irrigation systems and machinery such as the seed drill meant that two crops a year and a substantial food surplus were produced. The majority of peasants were no longer subsistence producers but were active participants in a monetary economy through selling their produce. Much of the agricultural surplus was moved along the Grand Canal to the great cities which were the largest in the world. China was also the most urbanized country in the world. Technologically it was the leading region of Eurasia and had a monopoly in many key areas – cast-iron production, piston bellows, suspension-bridge construction, the compass and printing. The impact of the latter was dramatic as knowledge spread widely through society. The wealth of China was unmatched even in the Islamic world and the level of internal and external trade was higher than elsewhere in Eurasia. The cumulative impact of all these developments was crucial and China was on the verge of even more fundamental changes. It was to become the first society in Eurasia to escape from many of the constraints of the early agricultural societies.

Although China was disunited for much of the tenth century, the impact of the confused political situation was far less than during the chaos following the collapse of the Han around 200, and seems to have had little effect on the economy. The period of disunity after the T'ang was also very short. In 951 General Kuo Wei founded the Chou dynasty at K'ai-feng and united nearly all of northern China. His reign was short and in 960 an army coup installed General Chao K'uang-yin as ruler. He was the founder of the Sung dynasty which was to rule China until the late thirteenth century. Within twenty years, in one of the most remarkable series of military campaigns in Eurasian history, he unified an area seven times as large as modern France. The pace of change can be seen from his destruction of the rival tenth-century dynasties. In 963 the kingdom of Ch'u in the middle Yangtze was conquered, followed two years later by the Later Shu in Szechwan. In 971 the Southern Han of Kwantung were eliminated followed four years later by the Chiang-nan of Anhwei, Kiangsi and

Hunan. In 978 the Wu-yüeh of Kiangsu and Chekiang were conquered and the last, the Northern Han (a Turkish kingdom) of Shansi, were defeated in 979. However, unlike the Han and the T'ang, the Sung did not continue to expand outwards to control central Asia and the northern steppes. The Sung were contained by the Khitan empire to the north, the remnants of the Tibetan empire to the west and in the south-west by the Ta-li kingdom (the successor to the Nan-chao). In 968 Vietnam was unified and independent and from 1009 the Ly dynasty, which ruled until 1225, was strong enough to attack southern China.

Within a little over a century after the founding of the dynasty the Sung were defeated by the Jürchen, a sinicized nomadic people from Manchuria. They lost the northern half of China, including the capital K'ai-feng, in 1127. They then ruled as the Southern Sung from Hangchou until 1279 when they were conquered by the Mongols. For these reasons the Chinese official historians, who tried to force all history into a consistent dynastic pattern and were particularly obsessed by China's relations with the 'barbarians', always classified the Sung as a weak dynasty, incapable of maintaining the Chinese tradition. Work by modern historians, particularly over the last thirty years, has completely transformed this view of the Sung. They are now seen as ruling over an immensely wealthy country with a dynamic and technologically creative economy. It is now clear that China in this period was on the edge of the economic and social changes that occurred in Europe some six hundred years later and which led to the so-called 'commercial revolution' and the 'industrial revolution'. The remaining question is why China just failed to make this transition.

13.1 Sung China and its Neighbours

The institutions of the Sung state were established under the second emperor, T'ai-tsung (976–97) once the reconquest was over. They provided for a strong bureaucracy and a centralized state on a scale not seen before in China (or elsewhere in the world). At the apex of the government was the Council of State which had between five and nine members – it was chaired by the emperor but he only had a casting vote. Attached to it was the Court of Academicians who drew up official documents. The general administrative structure was simpler than under the T'ang with only three major departments – Economy and Finance (which dealt with taxation, the budget, state monopolies and the census), the Army department and the Secretariat, which handled justice and personnel. There were three separate offices for dealing with complaints from the public and their staff had immunity even from the emperor. The examination system for the selection of civil servants was at its height. There were three levels of competition – in the prefectures, in the capital supervised by the imperial secretariat and in the palace under the emperor. Objectivity was obtained through the anonymous marking of scripts although much still depended on patronage and recommendation. The system could only operate because of the existence of an educated, literate elite (mathematics and astronomy were also a central part of the exams) on a scale unknown in Europe until the last few centuries. The formal central bureaucracy in China amounted to about 25,000 civil servants, with about twenty times as many working in the provinces. This was at a time when the states of Europe were administered, to the extent that they had an effective government, by a handful of clerics in the royal household.

A central part of Sung policy concerned the army, its financing and the maintenance of civilian control. The size of the army expanded rapidly from about 375,000 in 975 to over 1,250,000 by the middle of the eleventh century. Of this total about 300,000 were deployed around the capital, the same number on the northern frontier against the Khitan, and over 400,000 along the north-western frontier. The army was no longer recruited under the dispersed regional militia system of the T'ang but consisted mainly of professional mercenaries. Any one of these armies would have bankrupted the Chinese state at the time of the Han and an army on this massive scale (the largest then seen in the world and larger than any in Europe until the nineteenth century) could only be financed because of the immense wealth of China and the efficiency of the taxation system. Even so there were conflicts within the government about the cost of the system. Reformers such as Wang An-shih battled with more conservative figures such as Ssu-ma Kuang in an attempt to reduce the size of the army which was difficult to recruit and maintain. The army was also technologically advanced with a growing range of gunpowder weapons, incendiary devices and rockets. Given their very large army and its high level of technology, the inevitable question is why the Sung were relatively unsuccessful militarily. The main reason was their inability to maintain a technological edge – knowledge about the new weapons drifted quickly across the borders and was used by the strong states which surrounded China to make their own weapons.

The most important of these states was that of the Khitan who emerged under A-pao-chi in the early tenth century during the collapse of the T'ang. The Khitan capital was at Peking, although confusingly they called it Nanking, or 'southern capital', (Peking means 'northern capital'). They were at the height of their power in the early eleventh century and were another example of the rise of a nomadic empire in parallel with that of a reviving China. The Khitan empire covered most of Manchuria, eastern

Mongolia, northern Shansi and the Peking area. They also dominated the steppe area and were in contact with the declining Abbasid caliphate in Baghdad with whom they made a marriage alliance. The strength of the empire can be judged from the fact that 'Khitai' became the name for China in the Persian, west Turkish and east Slavonic languages and for Europeans (for example Marco Polo) northern China was 'Cathay'. The Khitan inflicted a major defeat in 1004 on the Sung, who had to pay a large annual tribute of 100,000 ounces of silver and 200,000 rolls of silk, which was raised further in 1042. The Khitan had a central role in trading relations not just with the north but also with central Asia. They also changed rapidly from being a nomadic people to one with agriculture, fortified towns, iron foundries and weaving factories, all adopted from the Chinese. The Khitan empire was in decline by the late eleventh century and it was finally defeated by the Jürchen in 1125. Many Khitan went westwards and joined the Uighurs in Sinkiang where by 1133 the kingdom of Karakhitan ('the black Khitan'), with its capital at Balasaghun, controlled many of the central Asian oasis cities as far west as Kashgar and Samarkand. The ruling elite remained strongly sinicized but there was also a very strong Buddhist and Nestorian culture. The state survived until 1218 when it was conquered by the Mongols.

Along the north-western frontier of China an even more complex state emerged in the early eleventh century when the Tangut conquered the two key trading cities of Wuwei and Chang-yeh and in 1038 established the Western Hsia empire. It was ruled by a Tangut (nomadic) elite but comprised a mixture of Tibetan, Uighur, Turkic, Chinese and the Hsien-pei (the descendants of the Tabgatch who had ruled northern China five hundred years earlier). It contained both nomadic and sedentary groups but its wealth depended upon the exploitation of the trade routes between China and central Asia. The Tangut forced the Sung to make peace in 1044 and to pay an annual tribute of 72,000 ounces of silver, 135,000 rolls of silk and 30,000 pounds of tea. A Sung attack in 1081 failed and they had to continue paying tribute. The culture of the Western Hsia was a complex mixture of various traditions. A vast amount of Buddhist literature in Tangut is known but it is derived not from the Tibetan tradition but from the Chinese. The Western Hsia empire survived until 1227 when it too was destroyed by the Mongols.

The nomadic empire with the greatest impact on the Sung was the Jürchen, the ancestors of the people who founded the 'Manchu' empire which ruled in China from the 1640s until 1911. They were unknown as a people until more than a century after the establishment of the Sung and were probably primarily horse breeders on the edge of the Chinese world. By 1115 their empire, which was established by Aguta, ruled much of

Manchuria from its capital north-east of Harbin. In 1120 it was allied with the Sung, but the collapse of the Khitan in the mid-1120s provided an opportunity for rapid expansion. By 1126 they occupied much of northern China (far beyond the limits of the Khitan empire) and in the next year they captured the Sung capital of K'ai-feng and forced the dynasty to move to southern China. Raids into the south continued and the Chinese emperor Hui-tsung was even taken prisoner. A peace treaty in 1142 established the frontier between the two states as the Huai river and forced the Sung to pay an annual tribute. Two decades of hostile co-existence and frontier warfare followed until a succession crisis within the Jürchen elite weakened the state considerably. However, the Jürchen continued to rule a large empire across northern China, Manchuria and Mongolia. The capital was moved to Peking after 1153 and the administration was in the hands of former Sung officials who had joined the new rulers. The empire was sinicized from the start – indeed it was, like many in the past, simply another empire ruling a large part of China through the Chinese administrative class. By the late twelfth century Shih-tsung (1161–89) found it impossible to revive Jürchen traditions, or place a ban on intermarriage or stop the decline of the language. However, official texts continued to be drafted in Jürchen before they were translated into Chinese. The Jürchen empire survived until the rise of the Mongols – it lost much of its territory by 1216 and was finally conquered in the late 1220s.

13.2 Sung Agriculture

The strength of the Sung agricultural economy lay in the south of the country and was the consequence of the large-scale migration of the Chinese population to the south over the preceding centuries. It was also based upon a series of developments, individually often of relatively minor importance but cumulatively crucial. An independent peasantry with secure tenancies and a relatively free market in land were the vital foundations on which much else rested. This position, which had developed even before the Han and been reinforced under the T'ang, was further strengthened by an imperial decree of 1153. This made clear that no tenant could be included with the sale of land (thus making serfdom as it existed in Europe impossible) and no new owner could abrogate the right of a tenant to till the land. Tenants were therefore given a permanent right to the land but they also had the right to sell the tenancy and even keep the future right to repurchase it. Landlords therefore had to exist almost entirely from the monetary rents from their land. In addition, a series of technological changes accumulated over a long period. By the third century

CE in north China the scratch plough was modified to one capable of turning over a sod to make a furrow. This was further improved in the eighth century with an adaptable ploughshare and mould-board made of iron so that the depth of the furrow could be altered. In wet-field rice farming, as practised in the south, it needed only a single ox or water-buffalo to pull it, not the large team required in Europe. In the north, the dry farming area, this plough was adapted to cut four furrows at a time and combined with a seed drill where the seeds were mixed with organic manure in the hopper. In the south improved water-control technologies – pumps for massive land reclamation in polders, wheel-and-bucket systems and machine-controlled irrigation – increased productivity and brought new areas into cultivation. Overall the area cultivated under the Sung probably doubled. Special early-ripening rice was introduced from Vietnam and by the twelfth century forty-three varieties of rice were being cultivated, each adapted to different soils, climates and ripening times. Information about new agricultural techniques spread rapidly through the wood-block printing of numerous farming manuals.

The move of the government to the south after 1127 only intensified these trends. By dividing China it stopped the transfer of much of the rice surplus in the south to the capital in the north (as had taken place for most of the previous five hundred years). The increased surplus in the south enabled even more people to be supported outside agriculture. With rising wealth and a growing population in the cities Chinese agriculture became more and more specialized and commercial. Different provinces and regions concentrated on the production of particular items – timber for shipbuilding and construction, sugar, paper, hemp, mulberry trees and silk – and around the cities market gardening to meet urban demand flourished. With greater specialization more people bought food in the markets, thereby enhancing the level of commercialization within agriculture still further. The trade in agricultural products rose rapidly based upon the developing internal communications network along the rivers and canals – there were over 30,000 miles of canals and improved, navigable rivers in China. There is no doubt that by the eleventh and twelfth centuries Chinese agriculture was by far the most advanced in the world.

13.3 Sung Industry

The general technological sophistication within China combined with growing wealth, urbanization and rising demand, especially from the army for weapons, produced the beginnings of an 'industrial revolution'. Iron production (almost entirely cast iron, which was still unknown in Europe) rose from about 13,000 tons a year in 806 to 125,000 tons by 1076 when it was growing at over 3 per cent a year. This level of output compares with English production of 76,000 tons in 1788 on the eve of what is conventionally described as the 'industrial revolution'. Increasingly, this iron was made in large factories requiring major capital investment – the ironworks at Likuo in Kiangsu employed over 3,600 workers. Huge new mines were opened in the south of the country and by 1100 every source of iron ore known in twentieth-century China was already being exploited. The capital for these enterprises was provided by the wealthy elite, many of whom derived their income from agriculture. As the output of iron grew ten-fold the price fell rapidly – by about four-fifths in the eleventh century alone (a larger fall than in England between 1600 and 1825) – thereby increasing demand still further. Greater production and demand meant that by the late eleventh century the main production area in northern Kiangsu was running out of wood to make charcoal to fire the furnaces (as happened in England in the eighteenth century). Chinese iron producers took the same steps as occurred seven centuries later in England, with the use of coke in blast furnaces – a process certainly being used by 1046 and probably from as early as the ninth century. In addition other new techniques were developed including the forging of cast iron under a cold blast for partial decarbonization – in effect the same as the Bessemer process 'invented' in mid-nineteenth century Europe. In parallel with the rise in iron production other metal output grew too – by the end of the eleventh century China was producing 93,000 tons of copper a year, 65,000 tons of lead and nearly 50,000 tons of tin. Much of the demand for this increased metal output came from armaments production to sustain the vast armies of the Sung. In the late eleventh century two arms-production works alone employed over 8,000 workers and made 32,000 swords and suits of armour a year. Another special bow-and-arrow works made over 16 million bows, arrows and steel arrowheads every year. By 1160 central arms production was over 3.2 million weapons a year (production in provincial factories was additional to this figure). Technological change was not confined to the metal-production industries. Equally important were the textile industries. The silk-winding machine worked by a treadle which was in use by 1090, was adapted to the much more difficult hemp thread. About a century later an even more complex mechanical spinning machine for hemp, driven by water-power and using 32 spindles on each machine, was operational. These were very similar to the textile machines that were introduced in late eighteenth-century England.

13.4 Sung Trade and Finance

The involvement of much of the peasantry and countryside in a commercialized agriculture was only part of an immense growth in trade, both internal and external. Unlike the other early agricultural empires China developed a national market in agricultural products. It was not simply the movement of rice from the south to the northern cities along the Grand Canal but the establishment of a national rice market controlled by profit-making merchants and brokers at every level and with shops selling rice in all the major cities. This market was followed by the development of similar ones for fruit, sugar, timber, paper, silk and other specialized products. There was a network of markets stretching from the villages to the cities and from the provinces and regions to the whole of China. Probably as much as a third of total farm output was sold and traded rather than being consumed directly by the peasants or their landlords. These markets were linked together by a large community of traders, merchants, brokers, transport agents and shopkeepers and depended on an efficient storage and transport system. The latter was still almost entirely dependent on rivers, canals and coastal trade. The fleets of vessels required for this trade were vast. As early as the eighth century Liu Yen, the commissioner for salt and iron under the T'ang, had over 2,000 boats built for service on the Yangtze alone. Each could carry about ten tons of cargo and in total they were equivalent to a third of the total British merchant fleet a thousand years later. When Marco Polo visited China in the late thirteenth century (after a period of very destructive warfare) he found over 5,000 ships afloat on the Yangtze at the one port of I-ching and learnt that there were similarly vast numbers in the other 200 ports. He commented on the Yangtze that 'In the amount of shipping it carries and the total volume and value of traffic, it exceeds all the rivers of the Christians put together and their seas into the bargain' – and Marco Polo came from the greatest port in Christian Europe.

Seaborne trade was even more important. Under the T'ang China had been mainly involved in the trade through central Asia and only to a lesser extent in south-east Asia and the Indian Ocean routes. Under the Sung, with access to central Asia largely blocked, particularly after the Jürchen conquest of the north, Chinese traders turned increasingly to the oceans and came to dominate the trade routes to a far greater extent than in the past. This was partly because of the development of the ocean-going 'junk' in the tenth century (using the well-developed rudder, compass and accurate charts). These ships were vast with between four and six masts, twelve large sails and four decks. They could carry either a thousand men or very large cargoes. The records of the voyages are no longer those of the

Buddhist pilgrims to India, as in the early centuries CE, but of the merchants themselves and their visits to Borneo, Java, India and the Red Sea. Some such as the *Chu-fan-chih* (*Accounts of Foreign Countries*) by Chao Ju-kua of 1225 even contain some details about the Mediterranean world. The great trading junks were not just owned by the merchants whose goods they carried – they were owned by monasteries, civil and military officials, landowners and even groups of peasants. There were permanent and temporary partnerships, intermediaries and investment managers and ships could also be chartered. Equally important was a separation of investment and management – the former could be as part of a wide range of investors in part of a cargo, or for a complete cargo or ship. The carriage of cargoes was regulated by contract and model contracts were rapidly developed, standardized and printed. A new group of shipping brokers also emerged.

These developments in internal and external trade were only part of a growing commercialization of society. Just as merchants created mechanisms to allow investments in trading voyages and industrial production, so new methods of dealing with a vastly increased level of trade emerged. Even earlier than the Islamic world Chinese institutions developed a variety of mechanisms for financial transactions – credit systems among merchants, cheques, promissory notes, bills of exchange and money-changing offices in the main cities and ports. As the volume of trade rose the volume of currency produced by the government grew. The Sung introduced a standard copper coin in 960 and the volume of coins in circulation rose eleven-fold in just over a century. However, even this was not sufficient for the developing Chinese economy. It was in this area that the invention of printing was to prove crucial with the introduction of paper currency (something which was not widespread in Europe for another eight hundred years). The first state-printed paper money in the world was issued in Szechwan in 1024 – within a century it was a major form of currency across China. By 1161 the Sung were issuing ten million notes a year and within another half-century paper currency had largely replaced coins.

As the nature of the Chinese economy changed the state had to adapt too. In about 1000 the yield from taxes on commerce was already roughly equal to that from all the agricultural taxes combined. Within a century agricultural taxes were only a small fraction of state revenue. The most important element became customs duties on internal and external trade, which were levied at between ten and forty per cent depending on the goods. By 1077 there were 2,000 customs houses to collect the levies on internal trade and by 1205 the number had increased to about 10,000. The sheer scale of the developing trade within China (and externally too) can be seen from the fact that customs revenue grew 130-fold in the two centuries after the Sung dynasty came to power. By the late twelfth century all taxes, apart from the revenue derived from the government's salt monopoly, were paid in paper currency. Just how much revenue did the government obtain? Calculations about the total size of the Sung economy are very difficult to make because even though China had the largest and most efficient bureaucracy in the world the statistics to make the necessary calculations are scarce. The best estimates suggest that the Sung government was collecting somewhere between ten and fifteen per cent of China's wealth as tax revenue. This is an extraordinarily high proportion but shows how the Sung were able to support such a vast army and buy peace with its neighbours. The enlarged revenue was also used to fund a range of public welfare institutions – orphanages, hospices, dispensaries, cemeteries and granaries. As a comparison, in Europe until the late nineteenth century no state took more than about five per cent of wealth as taxation because their functions were so limited and the state infrastructure was so weak.

13.5 Sung Society

The rapid growth and commercialization of the Sung economy had profound effects on Chinese society. At the top the position of the aristocracy changed fundamentally. They were no longer primarily military, relying on their estates and the peasants who worked them to man the army units they commanded. The army became largely mercenary and the aristocracy came to rely on cash rents from the peasants as their main source of wealth. Once they did so they could move to the towns and employ stewards to run their estates. Increasingly their wealth came from loans at interest to their peasants and from investing in other areas of the economy – overseas trade, shipping and industry. They could spend their wealth in the towns on the proliferating range of goods available. Rapid economic growth and greater wealth undoubtedly increased inequality within Chinese society as the main gains were concentrated in a relatively small proportion of the population. Although overall there was a reduction in tax privileges and exemptions under the Sung, the burden of taxation still fell primarily on the peasants who remained the overwhelming majority of the population. Although the burden may have shifted from direct taxes on land and corvée labour for the state, the peasants, increasingly integrated into a monetary economy, had to pay the bulk of the duties on trade through the growing prices of the goods they bought. Greater commercial farming strengthened the pressure on the peasants as they shifted from the greater security of subsistence farming, and peasant revolts remained common throughout the Sung period. Social mobility did however broaden as the opportunities available in an expanding and diversifying economy grew and new sources of wealth developed. Commercially generated wealth became increasingly vital in gaining access to education and status and merchants married into the aristocracy. Overall, the picture of Chinese society at this time is remarkably similar to that of Europe in the seventeenth and eighteenth centuries.

Perhaps the most significant development in Sung society was the very rapid growth of cities to a level not reached elsewhere in the world until the nineteenth century. The most important city until the twelfth century was K'ai-feng, a capital during the Five Dynasties period in the tenth century and, more important, under the early Sung. The first city wall was built in 781 but new walls were needed in 954 because of rapid growth. Unlike most earlier bloated capital cities, which depended on the wealth generated by a small elite and the loot from conquered territories, K'ai-feng was a commercial and trading city. Rules to keep trading within particular areas of the city broke down rapidly and in 1063 the curfew was abolished, allowing entertainment areas to mushroom across the city. The total population in 1100 was probably around 500,000 making it the biggest city in the world following the decline of Baghdad after the fall of the Abbasids – the largest city in Christian Europe was probably Venice at about a tenth of the population of K'ai-feng. Just one borough of the Sung capital ('Left Number Two' in the north-east corner of the city) had a population greater than the whole of Paris.

In 1100 the population of the great southern city of Hangchou was probably only slightly smaller than that of K'ai-feng and its wealth was built on overseas trade. With the loss of K'ai-feng to the Jürchen in 1127 and the move of the capital to the south, the population of Hangchou grew rapidly. By 1200 it had probably risen to over two million – about ten times as big as any other city in the world (the population of London at this time was 40,000 at most). This figure may seem extraordinarily high but evidence from overseas travellers – Marco Polo and Ibn Batuta – who both visited the city after it had begun to decline, is remarkably consistent. They both state that the main street had ten market places evenly spaced at four-mile intervals and that it took more than a day to walk the length of the main street. Probably about 800,000 people lived within the city walls but the suburbs spread for miles beyond the walls so that it was probably about twenty-five miles from one side of the urban area to the other. It was undoubtedly the largest city in the world before nineteenth-century London. Overall it seems likely that about one in five of the population under the southern Sung lived in cities – other cities such as Canton and Nanking had about 200,000 people and were each as large as any of the other great cities in the world at this time, such as Cairo and Constantinople. Equally important was the rise of market towns in every part of southern China as local trade expanded and was more closely integrated into a developing national economy. This level of urbanization was not found anywhere else in the world until early nineteenth-century Europe.

By the eleventh century Buddhism was in a steep decline and after more than six centuries at the centre of Chinese culture, it no longer had a significant influence over the elite. It was replaced by a broad naturalistic rationalism, a spirit of curiosity, enquiry and experiment very similar to that of eighteenth-century Europe. It was founded on the vast expansion of knowledge brought about by the development of printing, a large book trade, the decline of Buddhist monasteries and the rise of private schools and libraries as the major sources of knowledge. By the early eleventh century the four great Sung classics were completed and printed. They were the *Wen-yüan ying-hua*, a major literary anthology, the *T'ai-p'ing yü-lan*, an encyclopaedia in 1,000 chapters, the *T'ai-p'ing kuang-chi*, a collection of strange stories in 500 chapters and the *Ts'e-fu yüan-kuei*, a series of political texts and essays in 1,000 chapters. There was also a vast output of privately produced books covering areas such as horticulture, archaeology (the bronzes of the Shang period), records of over 2,000 historical inscriptions and architecture and an illustrated geography of the Sung empire in 1,566 chapters. One of the most important was the *Tzu-chih t'ung chien* (*The Complete Mirror for the Illustration of Government*) by Ssu-ma Kuang which was a history of China from 403 BCE to 959 CE and included thirty chapters which were critical assessments of the sources used in its composition.

The overall picture of Sung China shows a dynamic society and economy which was, in many ways, similar to that of western Europe some six or seven hundred years later. The total population was about 115 million in 1200 (more than twice the level only four hundred years earlier) and it contained about a third of the world's people. It had the most prosperous agriculture, innovative technology, a growing industrial base and a highly developed commercial sector. It had already moved significantly beyond the constraints found in early agricultural societies and was probably on the verge of the complex series of transitions made in western Europe in the eighteenth and early nineteenth centuries that finally broke the bonds of pre-industrial societies. Why did China not take these last steps? The answers are complex but are mainly related to the impact of external invasion. The conquest of the north by the Jürchen isolated the southern Sung from much of the iron industry. The phenomenal growth in the Southern Sung period after 1127 was then cut short by the devastating impact of the Mongol invasion and conquest. The high level of destruction, and China's full incorporation into a foreign empire for the only time in its history, had a devastating impact on continued economic growth and technological advance. By 1300 the population of China had fallen by more than a quarter compared with the level a century earlier and it fell further in the fourteenth century under the impact of plague and disease. By the time the Ming came to power and expelled the Mongols in the 1360s the main task was recovery from the devastation of the previous 150 years.

[*Later China 14.5.1*]

13.6 The East Eurasian Periphery: Korea, Japan and the Khmer

13.6.1 Korea
[*Earlier Korea 10.9.1*]

Although Sung China was the most developed power in Eurasia its impact outside China was limited mainly to its trading contacts with south-east Asia. Korea, though still deeply influenced by Chinese culture, remained a Buddhist state even after Buddhism's decline in China. However, unlike its position under the Han and the T'ang, Korea remained politically independent of China during the Sung period because the Khitan and Jürchen empires were a major barrier to any expansion of Chinese power. The result was that a new kingdom of Koryo emerged in north-east Korea around 920 and gradually expanded to control most of the peninsula. Under King Kwangjong in the mid-tenth century there was a major effort to create some centralized administration through the adoption of the Chinese examination system for the civil service and the creation of a centralized, professional army. A full administrative structure was not in place until the mid-eleventh century when Korea was divided into eight provinces, five military commands (plus two border regions) and was governed through three cities – Pyongyang in the west, Seoul in the south and Kyongju in the east. The king tried to keep control through the granting of land for civil and military service but, as was usually the case in the early states, the land rapidly became the personal property of the aristocracy. On their estates more and more of the population became slaves – at its peak this affected about a third of the population, making Korea the largest slave society in the world at this time. As power passed from the very limited central government, Korea became more and more unstable. The military attempted a coup in 1014, a major revolt in 1170 set up a new king, Myongjong, and there were peasant revolts throughout the 1170s. Myongjong was overthrown by General Ch'oe Ch'ung-hon in a military coup in 1196 and Korea was then subject to military rule. [*Later Korea 15.5.1*]

13.6.2 Japan
[*Earlier Japan 11.7.1*]

In Japan, which was politically isolated and increasingly culturally independent of China, the period between the tenth and thirteenth centuries saw the emergence of a unique system of government which, in its essentials, was to survive until the 1860s. These changes were based upon a number of economic, social and political developments over the previous centuries. Most important was the development of agricultural estates (*shoen*) dependent on irrigated rice farming and the creation of a number of social groups on the estates. At the bottom were the small number of slaves and serfs followed by the hired labourers, free peasants and then the managers and owners at the top. All received a different percentage of the estates' output according to legal rights (*shiki*), usually specified in written documents or occasionally enshrined in customary law. These *shiki* could be inherited (by women as well as men) and divided (there was no system of primogeniture). A person could hold more than one type of *shiki* on different estates. The result was a complex social structure in which a person could be subordinate on one estate but superior on another. However, the most important group was the owners who lived on an estate – many were ex-court officials or descendants from the imperial line who had established their own areas of control. Military changes reinforced the effect of the rise of *shoen*. In 792 the conscripted central army controlled by the imperial administration at Kyoto was abandoned and military force became the prerogative of the local aristocracy. Military groupings were built around the owners of the main estates and the most successful leaders were able to recruit extra followers – *samurai* – who were rewarded with land and bound to the leader by loyalty rather than any contractual and legal commitment. In many respects the situation in Japan was similar to that in contemporary western Europe as the Carolingian empire collapsed. There were however two crucial differences. First, Japan was not subject to external invasion. Second, the authority of the emperor, in name if not in practice, was retained. Although Japan was dominated by a series of petty local rulers there was no evolution of separate monarchies and most of the struggles within the aristocracy were about control of the imperial line and the right to rule in its name.

By the late tenth century Japan was subject to almost continual warfare between the different local military groups. Some such as the Seiwa Genji in the Kanto area were highly successful and expanded their control into

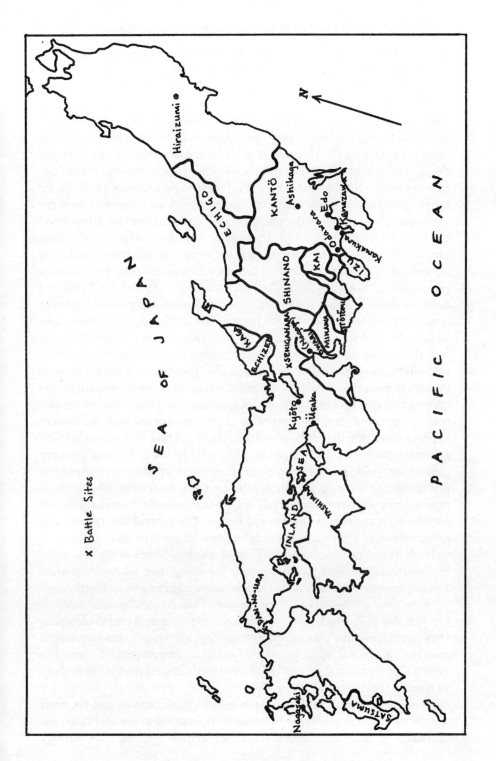

Map 39: Japan under the early Shogunate

northern Honshu as the last part of the process of incorporating this area into Japan. Local groups allied with different factions at the imperial court and with different Buddhist monasteries which now had their own armed followers to protect them. The main supporters of the imperial court and especially the numerous retired emperors (few ever reigned until their death) were the Ise Heike who controlled most of the area around the Inland Sea. During the Hogen war of 1156 and the Heiji war of 1159–60 the Ise Heike gained military control over the imperial city of Kyoto but they controlled little outside this area. Following a revolt in 1180 the Ise Heike groups fled Kyoto, taking the emperor with them, but were eventually defeated (and the emperor was drowned) at the great naval battle of Dan-no-ura in 1185 after major war had swept across all of Japan. The outcome of the civil war was that groups from the Kanto region, led by Yoritomo, came to control much of the country and other provincial warrior units recognized his supremacy. He took land from his defeated rivals and gave it to his followers but not directly – nominally the land was granted by the imperial government in Kyoto, which continued to function and was supported by revenue from its own land. Yoritomo was able to obtain a degree of central control over the local landowners through the appointment of stewards or *jito*. They were supported by their own *shiki* from the estate they managed – they were not appointed by the owners and their position rapidly became hereditary. The role of the *jito* was to provide a minimal level of local government through the correct apportionment of the *shiki* of the estates, by acting as local judge and collecting the *hyoromai* or rice tax which was levied at a rate of two per cent of the yield. In each province one *jito* was appointed as *shugo*, or protector, and his role was to control and administer the other *jito*. In practice this structure was largely theoretical outside the main areas of settlement in the Kanto and around Kyoto. The control Yoritomo could exercise west of Kyoto and in northern Honshu was limited.

The base of Yoritomo's personal power was Kamakura in the Kanto and his household became the foundation for the power he could exercise across Japan. It became a centre for the administration of justice through the *Monchujo* or 'Board of Enquiry' and in 1232 it issued a written code – the Joei Code – which became the accepted customary law of Japan. However, Yoritomo was effectively running a private government with only the theoretical approval of the imperial authorities in Kyoto. The system was formalized in 1192 when Yoritomo was appointed as *Seii-tai-shogun* or 'Barbarian-Quelling Generalissimo'. This was an old title for imperial military leaders dating back to the eighth century and the wars against the Ainu in northern Honshu. Its revival led to the establishment of what, at least in theory, could be seen as an imperial military

government. The title of shogun became traditional for the military rulers of the various families who ruled Japan until 1868. The civil government, almost entirely powerless, was the imperial *bakufu* at Kyoto. By the end of the twelfth century the Kamakura shogunate (named after its capital) was established. Its rule was based largely on the personal loyalty of the family retainers spread across the country as *jito* carrying out local government and remitting the rice tax to Kamakura. The problem was that Yoritomo had killed all his rivals in the family leaving only his two very young sons to succeed him on his death in 1199. A prolonged struggle among the followers of Yoritomo eventually led to the triumph of the Hojo family. They were able to put Hojo *jito* into more estates and set up various boards to control what remained of the imperial government. The rule of the Hojo family lasted into the fourteenth century.
[*Later Japan 15.5.2*]

13.6.3 The Khmer
In mainland south-east Asia the development of irrigation systems and wet-rice agriculture led to a major agricultural surplus and emerging states. But unlike Japan they were, because of their position on the east–west trade routes, much more open to external influence, from India and Islam as well as China. As a result they always obtained a significant part of their revenue from taxes on trade. Most important was the development of the Khmer state. It was based on small-scale but highly effective irrigation capable of producing two rice crops a year and a large surplus. The evolution of a complex society was very typical of events in a peripheral region under the impact of external influence. From about the sixth century the food surplus was increasingly appropriated by the chiefs (the leaders of the clans) who were becoming more powerful through their association with the Indian traders of the coast who provided access to elite goods. Gradually the chiefs took over more and more Indian religious rituals, identified themselves with the Hindu pantheon, increased their status and power and took on some of the attributes of kings. By the end of the ninth century under Indravarman I the first major public buildings and temples were being erected. At the bottom of this increasingly stratified and exploitative society were the *khnums* – prisoners of war – and their descendants who were in effect slaves working in gangs in the fields. In theory the temples were the main agents for integrating Khmer society – they owned the land and redistributed the agricultural surplus – but in practice power lay with the elite and the rulers. Land was given to the temples but it continued to be owned by elite families and only the rights to some produce and labour went to the temples. In addition, the temples themselves were controlled by the elite and so they were able to

control food redistribution. The role of the ruler was to regulate the complex system of land endowments, how much of the food production the elite could control and therefore the relative power of different groups.

The power of the elite and the rulers expanded as they controlled more and more of the agricultural surplus and could direct more and more peasant labour. However, a full state structure did not emerge. Huge temple complexes, dams, moats and roads were built – all oriented either north–south or east–west as part of a symbolic representation of the heavenly order on earth. The great temples at Angkor Wat were built under Suryavarman II in the early twelfth century in honour of his symbolic union with Vishnu. The eclecticism of the rulers was demonstrated by the construction of the Angkor Thom temples under Jayavarman VII later in the twelfth century – they were Buddhist temples for Bodhisattva Lokesvara, although they also incorporated temples for Shiva and Vishnu. The accounts of some of the temples show the scale on which they operated. In the late twelfth century the Ta Prohm temple had 12,640 people living within the walls of the temple, including 18 high priests, 2,740 officiants and 2,632 assistants (of whom 615 were dancers, 439 were hermits and 970 were students). It was supported by its own estates worked by slaves and temple serfs who provided over 2,500 tons of rice a year. The total population of the Khmer area was probably about 300,000 still mainly scattered in over 13,000 villages. There were no major towns, only the temple complexes. The Khmer 'state' expanded its influence into northern Thailand and the Kra isthmus as early as the eleventh century and was linked not just to the trade centres on the Vietnamese coast but also to the Islamic trading port of Takuapa on the west Malay coast and to the Chola merchants of southern India. It was under pressure from the Buddhist kingdom of Pagan in Burma and usually allied with the Sri Lankan rulers of Polonnaruwa against Pagan. The Khmer 'state' survived into the thirteenth century when it was attacked by the Mongols. It collapsed shortly afterwards mainly as a result of peasant revolt and conflict within the elite.

13.7 The Islamic World: Political Fragmentation

[*Earlier Islam 11.10*]

The collapse of the Abbasid caliphate during the ninth century and the conquest of Mesopotamia by the Buyids marked the final disintegration of the political unity of the Islamic world which had begun as early as the 750s when Umayyad rulers refused to accept the Abbasid victory in the civil war and set up their own government over much of the Iberian peninsula. This process should not be viewed as part of a general 'decline' of Islam but rather as the end of the early Islamic empire when some unified control was exercised over an area that was so large that it was almost impossible to govern it as a single political unit. Islam was to remain, like Christian Europe, politically divided but a culturally highly distinct region of the world. In the two centuries after 1000 Islam became more politically divided than ever before. Overall, apart from the brief interlude of the crusader states in the Levant and the loss of much of the Iberian peninsula, Islam not only retained control of its existing territory but continued to expand its influence politically and culturally.

13.7.1 The Islamic world in the eleventh century

In the west of the Islamic world the Umayyad dynasty was in decline and in 1031, after the sack of Cordoba by Berber nomads from North Africa, the state broke up into miniature 'kingdoms'. This weakness allowed the small Christian states of northern Spain to expand and in 1086 the old Islamic capital of Toledo was lost. The consequence was an Islamic revival under which the Almoravids ('volunteers for holy war'), a highly disciplined military-religious group (rather like the later Christian military orders) from north Africa, were called in as rulers. They were replaced in the 1150s by a roughly similar group, the Almohads, who took control of Morocco and southern Spain. The Fatimids of Egypt were able to maintain their control of western Arabia and Syria as far north as Damascus. As nominally Shia Muslims they were the enemies of the caliphate in Mesopotamia but the latter was relatively powerless and the Buyids, the military rulers of the area, were also in decline. In the late tenth century they lost control of the old heartland of the Abbasids, Khurasan in northern Iran, to a group of slave soldiers, the Ghaznavids, who founded a new dynasty under Alptigin. At their height in the early eleventh century they ruled over most of Iran, Khurasan, Afghanistan and the Indus valley. They also exercised a loose control over much of Transoxania as far as Samarkand and the Jaxartes river. Ghaznavid rule in Iran was based mainly on a reassertion of Sasanian traditions rather than purely Islamic ones and marks yet another step in the long process of reassertion by the strong Iranian tradition. In 1025 the Ghaznavid ruler Mahmud invited some Seljuq Turks to serve as mercenaries in Khurasan. They rebelled in 1036 and began a process that saw the growing domination of the Islamic heartland by the Turks (a process which lasted until 1918).

13.7.2 The impact of the Turks
[*Earlier Turkish history 11.6.1*]

In 751 the Qarluq Turks had fought with Muslim and Tibetan forces at the

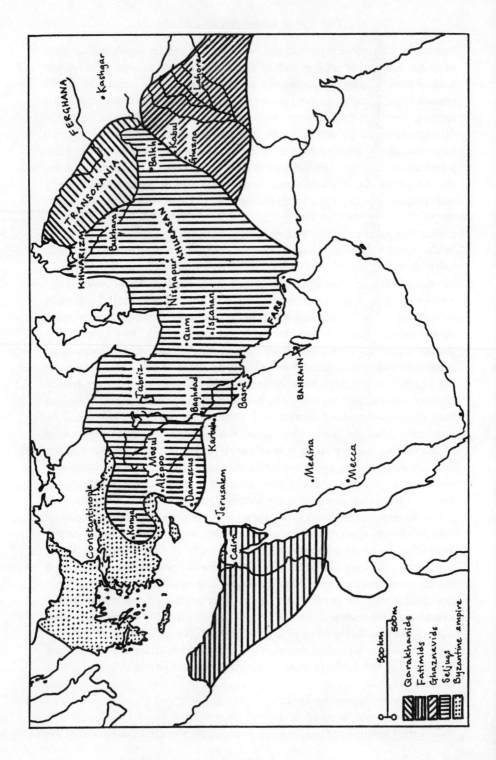

Map 40: The rise of the Seljuq Turks

battle of Talas and had therefore been opposed by the Chinese and Uighurs. Over the next century they were pushed further west under Uighur and Tibetan pressure. On the edge of the Muslim world they converted to Islam in the late ninth century and in the mid-tenth century a weak Qaraqanid state emerged in the area of Transoxania under nominal Ghaznavid control. In the north of the area the Seljuqs, the paramount Oghuz Turkish clan, rose to power and it was this group that moved into Khurasan in 1025. After their rebellion they captured Nishapur in 1038 and defeated the Ghaznavids in 1040 (they were pushed back into Afghanistan and the northern Indus valley). The Seljuks continued to move westwards and took control of the whole of Iran. (For the next nine centuries Iran was to be ruled by either a Turkish or Mongol elite). The Seljuqs were Sunni Muslims and their rise provided an effective counter to the power of the Shia Fatimids in Egypt and Syria. This was recognized in 1050 when the caliph gave the Seljuq leader, Tughril Beg, the title of Sultan, the first regular use of this name. In 1055 the Seljuqs drove the Buyids from Baghdad and took control of the caliphate, although they preferred to rule from Nishapur and then Isfahan. Like the Ghaznavids they relied mainly on Iranian bureaucrats and traditions of rule rather than purely Islamic elements. The Seljuq empire was theoretically united until the death of Malik Shah in 1092 but at no time was there any real central control and Seljuq military leaders established their rule over whatever fertile lands they could seize. By the 1060s the Fatimids lost control of Syria and Damascus but, even more important, the Seljuqs were in conflict with the Byzantine empire.

By the mid-eleventh century the Byzantine revival under the Macedonian dynasty was long over and its power was weakening as it lost control over the military aristocracy which governed much of Anatolia. In 1054 there was a final schism in the Christian church between east and west over a number of issues – the celibacy of the secular clergy, the use of leavened or unleavened bread for the Eucharist, papal supremacy and the introduction of the 'filioque' clause (concerning the position of the Holy Ghost) into the creed. In 1056 the Comneni family, one of the leaders of the military aristocracy in Anatolia, revolted. The emperor, Romanus Diogenes, tried a counter-attack against the Seljuqs and advanced to near Lake Van. At the battle of Manzikert in 1071 Byzantine forces were totally defeated by the Seljuqs under Alp Arslan and the emperor was captured. The outcome was the loss of almost the whole of Anatolia to the Seljuqs who set up two new dynasties – a Seljuq one at Konya and the Danishmenids in central and eastern Anatolia. For the Byzantines the loss of Anatolia, the heartland of the empire for four hundred years and the source of their military strength, was a near fatal blow. Although the state survived it never recovered its former strength. In the immediate aftermath of Manzikert there was civil war and numerous revolts followed by a seizure of power by the Comneni family in 1081. Unable to deploy significant military forces they had to try and buy help. In 1082 Venice was given unrestricted trading rights throughout the empire in return for help against the Normans who were taking over imperial possessions in southern Italy and Sicily.

The division of the Seljuq 'empire' into a multitude of small territories by the late eleventh century (the result of the continuation of nomadic inheritance practices in a sedentary state) provided an opportunity for the states of western Europe. Called in to aid the Byzantines, the First Crusade of 1096 was of little direct help to the empire (the amount of looting was a serious problem). However, the capture of Antioch (1097) and Jerusalem (1099) (the latter from the Fatimids) and the establishment of the Kingdom of Jerusalem did provide a major respite for the Byzantines. The impact of the crusade on the Islamic world was very limited – Syria and the Levant were already highly fragmented and the new, relatively small, crusader state made little difference. Although Aleppo was recaptured in 1128 an effective Islamic response was not forthcoming until the 1140s. It was led by Zengi, the *atabeg* (governor) of Mosul, supported by a largely Kurdish army. Edessa was recaptured in 1144 and three years later the siege of Damascus by the Second Crusade was defeated. The Fatimids in Egypt were replaced by Zengi's son Nur al-Din ruling from Damascus. On his death in 1174 a Kurd from the Ayyubid clan, Saladin, a local military ruler in Egypt, occupied Damascus and Syria, defeated the western Christians at the battle of Hattin in 1187, and recaptured Jerusalem. This created a unified Ayyubid state which continued to rule Egypt and Syria until 1250. It defeated the attempt of the Third Crusade to recapture Jerusalem (1189–92) and also defeated other Christian attacks on Egypt in 1197, 1217, 1229 and 1249. Only the port of Acre survived as a tiny Christian enclave until 1291.

13.7.3 The Islamic world in the late twelfth century

The Seljuqs ruling in Mesopotamia and Iran took little interest in events in the Levant. They concentrated their efforts on trying to keep control in the east but were ultimately unsuccessful. In 1148 the Khwarazm-shahs led by the Turkish general Atsiz took control of Transoxania and in 1193 conquered Khurasan. By the early thirteenth century they ruled an empire stretching from western Iran to parts of Afghanistan and north-west India. By about 1200 the core of the Islamic world was even more divided than it had been two hundred years earlier. It consisted of at least nine separate states or empires. The Ayyubids ruled Egypt and Syria, the Seljuqs controlled most of Anatolia, the Zengids parts of northern Mesopotamia and eastern Syria and the remnants of the Abbasids southern Mesopotamia. A multitude of local rulers controlled the Caucasus area, the Hazaraspids were effectively independent governors of Luristan as were the Salghurids in the province of Fars.The Khwarazm-shahs controlled much of eastern Iran and as far as the Oxus river, although the Ghurids dominated the southern part of this area.

13.8 The Unity of Islam

The period between 1000 and the early thirteenth century was very different from that of the early caliphate, the Umayyads and the Abbasids. The first period set the main outlines of Islam and the societies it created. The subsequent period was one of increasing differentiation within the existing framework. With the decline of the Abbasid caliphate, Baghdad was no longer the single city which dominated the Islamic world. Instead there was a multitude of centres – Samarkand, Bukhara, Nishapur, Isfahan, Cairo and Fez. Even more important was the continuing evolution of religious differences and the rise of sectarian communities.

The Shia communities changed as the immediate divine guidance of the imamate was lost by the mid-tenth century. Instead its religious and cultural heritage was codified as the *Hadith* mainly under al-Kulayni – the imam came to be redefined in semi-gnostic terms as an emanation of God and the bearer of direct knowledge of the supreme truths of religion. A pattern of religious ritual emerged – the cursing of Muawiya, a public mourning of the death of Husayn at Karbala, a day of celebration for Muhammad's supposed adoption of Ali as his successor, and pilgrimages to the chief Shia tombs of Ali at Najaf, Husayn at Karbala and Ali al-Rida at Mashhad. Shia communities were in continuous opposition to nearly all Islamic political regimes but expected salvation through living in accordance with the *Hadith* and absorption in the martyrdom of Shia leaders and the mystical elements of the imamate.

In the Sunni tradition the decline of the caliphate, with its obviously solely political function following the institution of the Abbasids, led to the emergence of religious leadership separate from the caliphate. This was based on independent scholarly groups whose authority came from acceptance of their insight. By the eleventh century the schools that developed around different teachers, as students moved from one to another, became formalized as *madrasa* – colleges for the study of Islamic law with permanent endowments of land or rent from land. The movement probably started in Khurasan but spread rapidly under the Seljuqs as a way of organizing religious and legal instruction. It was the rise of the Seljuqs, who were uncompromisingly Sunni and anti-Shia, that saw a strong revival of the Sunni tradition after the increasing strength of Shiism especially under the Fatimids. For the Seljuqs religious and political opposition to the Fatimids went together. It was reinforced by strong state support for Sunni activity and institutions.

In parallel with the two main traditions in Islam, by the tenth century another grouping emerged. It was more individual and less organized but of major long-term importance. Sufism was a highly personal, devotional and mystic form of Islam which incorporated much from Indian traditions especially meditational techniques and the idea of the *guru*, developed in both Hinduism and Buddhism. Different semi-monastic schools developed at centres (*khanaqa*) around various Sufi leaders. By the end of the eleventh century some *khanaqa* were the tombs of the great Sufi masters and became places of pilgrimage. Sufi students became disciples living in total obedience to the masters they chose. Initiation into Sufism became more elaborate and religious brotherhoods or *tariqat* emerged among the different Sufi traditions. These became particularly important in frontier areas linked to the *ghazi* commitment to holy war in the cause of Islam.

Even under the Abbasids Islam tended to remain a religion of the elite and strong Christian and Zoroastrian communities remained across the Islamic world. Large-scale conversion to Islam was part of the general religious ferment within Islam from the tenth century. In little more than a century only a few non-Islamic communities remained – mainly the small Christian communities of northern Mesopotamia and Syria. The political changes, especially rule by external elites (mainly ex-nomads), even though they were Muslims, created a growing separation of the Islamic community from the political world, especially in the Sunni tradition. Existing elites in society tended to turn away from politics and dominate through their position as the religious leaders of the community and as patrons for those wanting favours and advancement. Other communities such as the merchants also had a very strong social base separate from the political world. The religious traditions of Islam therefore cut across the various political units and provided a mechanism for binding people into a wider community that still existed across the whole of the centre of Eurasia from north Africa to India and beyond. Despite the political divisions Islam continued to expand – across India, into west Africa and along the coast of east Africa. The next three sections consider this expansion, taking the story, in these areas which did not feel the effects of the Mongol empire, into the fifteenth century in order to provide a more coherent narrative.

13.9 The Expansion of Islam: India

[*Earlier India 10.10*]

Following the fall of the Gupta empire in the sixth century India remained politically fragmented. Islam had an impact from its first era of expansion when in 711–13 Arab forces reached Sind. Expansion from this area was slow and northern India remained subject to endemic warfare between rival dynasties – the Palas of Bengal, the Rashtrakutas of the western Deccan plateau and the Pratiharas in the north and west who were largely able to contain Muslim forces. The main impact of Islam on India did not come until the post-Abbasid military regimes emerged in eastern Iran and Afghanistan. In 1030, just as they were losing control of their core territory to the Seljuqs, the Ghaznavids captured Lahore and continued to rule the northern part of the Indus valley and Afghanistan. They were replaced in the twelfth century by the Ghurids who began the conquest of north-west India by capturing Peshawar, Lahore and Delhi. In 1206 one of their generals, Qutb al-Din Aybeg, declared himself independent and founded the Aybeg dynasty, the first of the 'Delhi Sultanates' that were to rule much of India until 1526.

The three centuries of the sultanates can be seen as a single period of Indian history because despite the five dynasties that ruled each came from within the same Afghan-Turkish elite. Each of the dynasties tried to centralize power but without any real success – the Sultan remained no more than the most important of a large number of local Muslim and Hindu rulers but with some claims to a more general overlordship and collection of tribute. In some areas, particularly Rajasthan, the level of control by the sultanate was very low. The Aybeg dynasty ruled until 1290 over most of northern India and the Indus valley. The major expansion of the sultanate came under Ala al-Din Khalji (1296–1316) when the Gujarat, much of the Deccan and parts of southern India were brought under nominal control and recognized the overlordship of the sultanate. The Khalji dynasty collapsed almost immediately after the death of its founder and was replaced by the Tughluq dynasty which ruled from 1320–1413. They tried to find some balance to the powerful Muslim families that held effective power in many areas. These families were the rulers of Bengal, Kashmir, Gujarat, Jawnpur, Malwa and two dynasties – the Bahmanids and the Faruqis – dominated the Deccan. Turkish warriors were brought in to form a new elite and non-Muslims were appointed to both the civil government and the military. Construction of Hindu temples was allowed but the Sultans were all strongly Sunni and imposed a poll tax on non-Muslims and strengthened the position of Sharia law. From the mid-fourteenth century the Delhi sultanates were in decline. There were

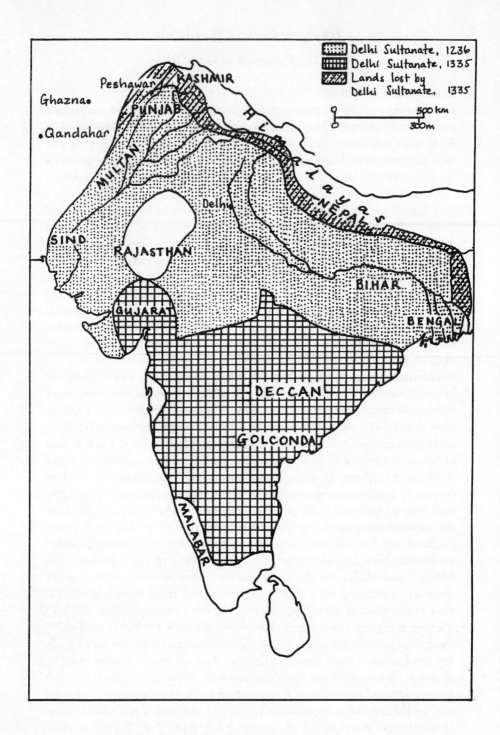

Map 41: The Delhi Sultanates

growing local revolts, especially in the Deccan, and more autonomous and fully independent Hindu kingdoms emerged. In the south the Vijayanagar military state expanded from the northern edge of the Tamil region. In theory it was the defender of the Hindus but its wars were almost entirely against the other Hindu states of the south – the Hoysala state of Karnataka and the Reddi kingdom of Kondavidu – rather than the sultanate in the north. After the 1350s it established an empire in the south which was to last for two centuries. The last dynasties of the sultanate (Sayyid in 1414–51 and Lodi until 1526) continued to rule from Delhi but they remained very weak.

All of the Delhi dynasties faced huge problems in attempting to rule the vast area of India with its cultural, religious and political complexity. At first they were aggressively Muslim and made little attempt to incorporate Hindu rulers into the elite, even though their concept of kingship, largely derived from the Iranian tradition with its emphasis on loyalty to the ruler and the importance of hierarchy, was attractive to Hindu rulers and tended to validate Hindu society. The new elite were very like the Arabs in early Islam – hostile to conversion and content to rule as a military elite with their own special religion. Only slowly did a new cosmopolitan mixture of Indian, Muslim and Iranian elements begin to emerge. A new synthesis of languages and literatures developed – Muslim poets began writing in a new literary Bengali language using Arabic and Persian loan words, about Hindu gods and myths. Islam was strong where Hinduism was weak, especially among some of the tribal groups of gatherers and hunters who adopted Islam when they became farmers, and in urban areas where some of the rigidities of Hindu rural society were less apparent. Overall, however, despite the large number of Muslim religious teachers moving to India and the patronage and support they received from the state, the level of conversion was low – no more than about a fifth or a quarter of the population. Most Muslims were concentrated in the Indus valley, north-west India, Bengal, Assam and some parts of the Deccan. Generally, local Hindu political and religious structures survived intact and, with the decline of Buddhism, India remained an overwhelmingly Hindu area. One area where Islam did have a significant impact was Sufism. This was largely because Sufism itself absorbed much from the Indian tradition, especially its metaphysical elements, Hindu and Buddhist training techniques and the master–disciple relationship. On the whole, the sultanate period was one of great prosperity in India – it was central to much of the east–west Eurasian trade, its trading cities flourished, agriculture was highly productive and internal trade grew significantly. India was, after China, the richest area of Eurasia.

[*Later India 18.5*]

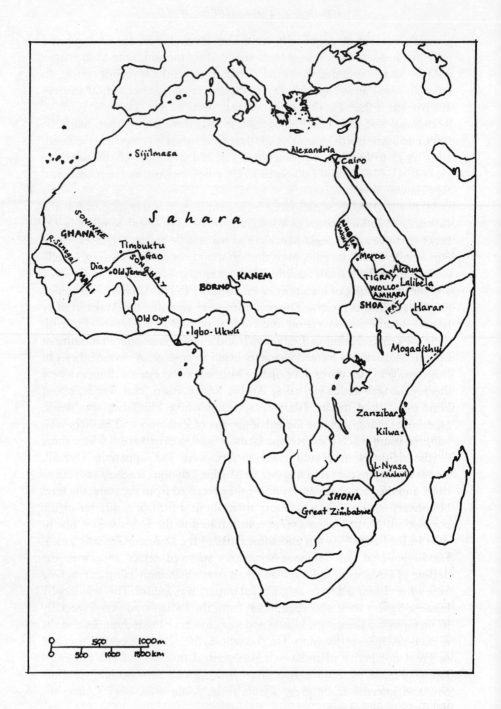

Map 42: Early Africa

13.10 The Expansion of Islam: West Africa

West Africa contained a number of different environmental areas and each had significant problems which retarded the growth of an agricultural surplus and therefore state formation. In the north in the dry savanna along the southern fringes of the Sahara the main crops were millet and fonio (a very small grain), further south it was possible to grow sorghum. Rice was grown in a few areas and east of the Ivory Coast, with two rainfall peaks a year, highly productive yams were cultivated. The equatorial forest contained little to eat or hunt, it was difficult to penetrate and even more difficult to clear. Most of it was unoccupied or left to pygmy groups. Iron technology spread from the north about 500 BCE but many of the techniques used were highly original. Instead of cast and wrought iron local producers made high-carbon steel directly in a smelting furnace with a shaft up to twenty feet high with preheating of the bellows-driven air. The history of the region was dominated by the internal frontier – the gradual clearing of land from the forest by a multitude of village communities. By early in the first millennium CE it had reached the point at which the various villages and their territories were beginning to coalesce and larger political units were beginning to form. However, the agricultural surplus was small and the low population levels and the easy availability of land to clear meant that it was always possible to avoid political control by moving away to colonize new areas. The village remained central to West African life and in many areas there was little organization above that of the *kafu* – the political chief of a group of villages. The 'states' that did emerge were very weak and directly controlled only a very small core area – the surrounding villages and *kafu* were vaguely associated with the core area, although often they had little idea who claimed to rule over them.

The key to many developments was the emergence of the trans-Saharan caravan trade based on two important commodities. In west Africa salt was essential for the diet and one of the main constituents of trade (the Hausa language has over fifty words for different types of salt). The salt was dug from the dried lakes of the Sahara by large gangs of slaves and moved south – in return gold and slaves moved northwards. The development of the caravan trade depended upon the introduction of the camel into north Africa around 300–400 CE which made it relatively easy to move from oasis to oasis, where date palms (which needed high temperatures and irrigation water) could be grown. Caravans, often containing 10,000 or more animals stretching for fifteen miles across the desert, took about a couple of months to travel between north and west Africa. They left the north in September and returned in the spring.

However, the camels could not travel far beyond the edge of the desert because the climate became too humid. The result was the development of trading towns along the fringes of the Sahara where the caravans stopped and traders from the south brought their goods. South of these towns trade was generally controlled by local merchants although a number of Muslim traders did reach the coast of west Africa.

The first of the trading towns was Old Jene, in modern Mali, dating to the fifth century (though little excavation has taken place to find other sites of this period). It was a substantial town (its walls were over a mile long), and it controlled about sixty villages in the immediate area. However, the main developments did not occur until after the penetration of Islamic traders across the Sahara and the impact of the demand of the Islamic world for slaves and gold. As in many other peripheral areas this increased the pace of social and political development and led to the formation of three kingdoms in west Africa in the period 700–900. Around Lake Chad the kingdom of Kanem (and its successor Borno) lacked gold and therefore concentrated on the supply of slaves. Both were loose confederations of mainly pastoral people ruled by a small warrior elite. In the west, Ghana was a kingdom of the Soninke people centred not in the modern state of Ghana but in eastern Mauretania. It was at the far end of the trade route from Tahert through Sijilmasa and it controlled the export of gold from the Bambuk field in Senegambia although not the production of the gold itself. Its chief town has not been identified. The main rival of Ghana was Gao, a kingdom of the Songhay people stretching along the Niger river further to the east. It too was at the end of a route from Tahert which brought in salt, which was used as a currency in Gao. Islam was spread south by the Kharijite traders and it was the local traders who adopted it first, the farmers last. The ruler of Gao converted to Islam about 1000, followed by Kanem a century later. Ghana adopted Sunni Islam via the Almoravids of north Africa in 1070.

The kingdom of Ghana was destroyed about 1240 after a long period of decline. It was followed by the establishment of the Mali 'empire'.The rise of Mali in the thirteenth century was linked to military changes – the decline in importance of the infantry and the rise of cavalry as the use of horses spread from Egypt. However, their use remained confined to the savanna and to a small elite because of their price – in the 1450s a horse sold for the same price as fourteen slaves. Mali was the main trade rival of Gao until the latter was defeated shortly after the return of the Mali ruler Mansa Musa from a pilgrimage to Mecca in 1324. The great trade centre of Mali was Timbuktu which, in the fourteenth century, was one of the major cities in the Islamic world with its own university. At its height in the early fifteenth century Mali 'controlled' the area from the lower

Senegambia in the west to Gao in the east and from the fringes of the Sahara in the north to the Niger in the south. It even imported highly prized white slaves from the eastern Mediterranean. However, in 1433 it lost Timbuktu to Tuareg nomads and shortly afterwards Songhay regained its independence under Sonni Ali Ber. These developments in the savanna region were followed at an even slower pace in the forest areas further south in west Africa – many regions still remained stateless in the late fifteenth century. The first 'state' – Ife – emerged in about 1000 on the forest edge, based on its control of a small goldfield, but by the fifteenth century only Benin, which specialized in producing very high-quality bronzes, was of any significance.

[*Later West Africa 17.8*]

13.11 The Expansion of Islam: East Africa

Unlike west Africa, where the environment produced a series of east-to-west climatic belts that separated nomads and cultivators, the climate and terrain of east Africa produced a complex mix of environments. Colonization and settlement of the land was just as much a central feature of history here as in the west. By about 400 CE Bantu-speaking cultivators using iron tools had spread across much of east and southern Africa but the farming frontier was patchy and population distribution was very uneven and at a very low level. East Africa was very different from the west in that the coastal area always formed part of the Indian Ocean world and traders from the Red Sea and the Gulf regularly voyaged southwards down the coast. Around 400 CE Iranian pottery was traded for fifty miles into the interior of Tanzania and as far south as Chibuene in Mozambique. The first known trace of Islam is from the small wooden mosque (it could hold less than ten people) built at Lamu on the Kenyan coast in the eighth century. A century later Chinese traders were also active along the coast. The main period of expansion began in the ninth century when traders from the Gulf established settlements, bringing their own bricks and pottery with them. Trading ports grew up at Gezira (south of Mogadishu), Unguja Ukuu on Zanzibar and at Chibuene. They exported ivory to India and China, mangrove poles, gold and about a thousand slaves a year to the Gulf. Many of the slaves worked in the sugar plantations in the south of Mesopotamia but some became soldiers and one in the fifteenth century even seized the throne of Bengal.

There was a major acceleration in Islamic trade from about 1000. Eight trading ports built new stone mosques, Chinese imports to Africa rose ten-fold under the early Sung, and a Muslim dynasty was established at

Kilwa in southern Tanzania in about 1070. It lasted for two centuries until it was overthrown by the Mahdali dynasty who probably came from the Yemen. Kilwa developed into a major port with a population of about 20,000, trading inland and across the Indian Ocean to India, especially Gujarat. A local language, Swahili, developed although at this time it was largely free of Arabic words. Unlike the traders from north Africa who travelled across the Sahara the Islamic traders of east Africa rarely seem to have penetrated far inland – they were content for local merchants to bring products down to the ports. Internal trade was at a low level except for the development of gold working and the emergence of the first towns inland on the plateau between the Limpopo and the Zambesi in Zimbabwe. The first settlement was around Mapungubwe around 1000, a small trading post where the local chief and the elite lived on the top of the hill above the peasant farming villages. It declined after two centuries and was replaced by Great Zimbabwe in the rich grazing country north of the Limpopo. This was the most significant settlement of the African iron age with a hilltop palace, a massive walled enclosure and, from the late thirteenth century, huge granite walls. It was the residence of a local dynasty that controlled the gold trade to Kilwa on the coast. It probably sent over a ton of gold every year for shipment to the Gulf and India. It declined in the fifteenth century following over-grazing in the area and the exhaustion of the gold supplies.

13.11.1 Christian Ethiopia

In the inland and mountainous areas of the southern Nile Christianity survived the impact of Islam. The kingdom of Aksum, which was linked to the Red Sea trade routes through the export of ivory, adopted Christianity in 333 under King Ezanaa. It derived its tradition from Alexandria and was therefore monophysite in theology and the church remained dominated by monks of the Egyptian Coptic church into the twentieth century. The state religion only spread very slowly among the people as the scriptures were translated into Ge'ez (a Semitic language common at Aksum) using a script derived from South Arabian. The Aksum kingdom was heavily disrupted by the Roman-Sasanian wars and then by the rise of Islam. By the early seventh century a process was under way which continued until the twentieth century – the slow drift of the kingdom southwards. As the Aksumite and local Cushitic cultures merged they created a new Ethiopian kingdom centred not in Aksum and Tigray but in Wollo. The shift southwards not only involved the conquest of better land but also opened the trade routes to the Red Sea, especially at Zeila. The Ethiopian kingdom sent slaves, gold and ivory to the Islamic traders on the coast for export to the Gulf and India. Islam penetrated along these trade routes, as it did in west and east Africa, first to the Somali peoples and then even further inland where by the late twelfth century there were small Islamic kingdoms in Ifat and eastern Shoa.

However, Ethiopia remained largely isolated from all external influences. It therefore produced its own unique form of Christianity. In 1137 a local prince seized the throne and established the Zagwe dynasty, which ruled until 1270. Under these rulers the great rock cut churches of Lalibela were built, laid out as a model of the city of Zion around a stream (the Jordan) and a hill (Calvary). The church developed strong monastic institutions in which the Bible and Judaic practices were central. They had the same dietary restrictions as Jews, a holy ark and a belief in themselves as the chosen nation, symbolized by St George and the archangels battling against Islam. The secular priests were normally married peasants whose posts were hereditary – the monks were closer to the normal Christian pattern.

As Ethiopia continued to expand southwards, local forces in Shoa overthrew the monarchy and set up their own dynasty. Their first king, Yikunno Amlak, grandly claimed descent from Solomon but his grandson Amda Siyon (1314–44) was the conqueror of the whole Islamic area of the Ifat and northwards into the old homeland of Aksum. It was during his reign that the remaining Jewish traditions in Ethiopia produced the separate Falasha community. Ethiopia was the first literate African kingdom so that some records remain and an outline history is possible. In general it was, like the Islamic kingdoms, a peasant colonizing society with only very weak central institutions – the king was merely the first among a group of local rulers – the state did not have a capital until the mid-fifteenth century and even that was abandoned after twenty years. By then the monarchy hardly existed.

13.12 The West Eurasian Periphery: Europe – Recovery, Expansion, Definition

[Earlier Europe 11.12]
The collapse of the Carolingian empire and the Viking and Hungarian invasions produced disintegration in western Europe. It became an area with hardly any organized states – rule was mainly local by whichever landlord could gain some of the very small agricultural surplus from his serfs, control some military resources and provide a limited degree of order. The population of the whole of Europe was low – about 35 million (roughly the same as at the height of the Roman empire eight hundred years earlier) – and scattered among a series of villages largely isolated

from each other by vast tracks of forest and uncultivated land. Towns, in so far as they existed, were small – the largest, Rome and Paris – had perhaps 25–40,000 inhabitants, but most had a thousand or so. Trade was at very low levels – largely the export of slaves and primary products to the Islamic world.

13.12.1 Recovery and expansion

The three centuries after 1000 saw a remarkable expansion of Europe. The population more than doubled to about 80 million by 1300 and the cultivated area expanded enormously as new farming communities were established. At first much of the expansion was within the settled area of western Europe as land around the existing villages was brought into cultivation. Fairly rapidly this was transformed into a colonization movement, especially in central and eastern Europe, as settlers established new villages and towns. However, growth was extensive rather than intensive – there were more people but they were nearly all peasants living at much the same level as their ancestors. There was no radical transformation in the economy, although towards the end of the period Europe was beginning to adopt some of the technologies developed centuries earlier in China and the Islamic world. In parallel with this growth, some organized but relatively weak political units were beginning to emerge across Europe out of the chaos of the preceding centuries. In addition, for the first time in world history, events in northern Europe began to have an impact on the more prosperous and developed areas around the Mediterranean.

The timing of the recovery varied from area to area. It began first in regions such as Burgundy which were relatively remote from the invasions of the ninth and tenth centuries and by 1080 most of the Ile-de-France had been cleared of forest as had much of southern England. By about 1200 most of the best soils of western Europe had been cleared and settlements were pushing into the more marginal land – sandy or clay soils, high ground and heathlands. As the land filled up the excess population in some areas, especially Germany, pushed eastwards into regions that were barely organized politically, where the farmers were still practising swidden (slash and burn) agriculture in the forests and where new settlements could be established fairly easily. In the early tenth century Germans settled the area between the Elbe and Saale rivers. The Hungarian invasions held up further movement until the twelfth century although Vienna was founded in 1018. Then settlers moved into Holstein, Mecklenburg and Brandenburg. The process was well organized as land agents divided up the land, provided equipment for the settlers and developed villages and towns, often to standardized designs. By the late twelfth century settlements reached Livonia and Courland, followed by Riga (1201) and East

Prussia (1231). By the mid-thirteenth century, when the best lands had been occupied, the movement eastwards began to weaken. The overall result was to produce not a clear-cut frontier between Germanic colonizers and indigenous groups but a complex mix of settlements and peoples that was to plague European history into the late twentieth century.

The great expansion of European settlement took place at a time when the climate was very favourable – temperatures in the centuries around 900–1200 were, on average, about one centigrade degree warmer than today. The tree line in central Europe was about 500 feet higher, vines grew in England as far north as the Severn and farming was possible on Dartmoor as high as 1,300 feet. One of the most important impacts that this warmer climate had was in the expansion of Viking settlement across the northern Atlantic. Vikings from south-west Norway settled Iceland about 870 – it became a mainly pastoral society with a population at its height in 1100 of about 60,000, nominally under the King of Norway but in practice with its own *Althing* or assembly. From here in 982 Erik the Red sailed westwards and discovered Greenland. He returned there four years later in a convoy of fourteen ships with settlers. This was a much more marginal area than Iceland and the Viking population probably never exceeded 3,000. About 1200 they came across people they called *Skraeling* who were Inuit groups still moving north-eastwards to colonize new lands as they had been doing since the settlement of the Americas more than ten thousand years earlier. In about 1000 Leif, the son of Erik the Red, was the first European to reach the mainland of the Americas when he sailed further westwards from Greenland, reached the coast of Labrador, which he called Markland, and then travelled further south to the coast of Newfoundland which he called Vinland. The Vikings later settled at L'Anse aux Meadows and there was a large community on Belle Isle. It seems unlikely that these settlements survived for long – they were probably eliminated by native American groups. However, the Vikings continued to sail from Greenland to Markland for furs and timber into the fourteenth century.

European expansion was not just agricultural. Among the aristocratic elite, some younger sons, excluded by an increasingly dominant system of primogeniture, sought their own land and territories to rule. For example some of the ex-Viking settlers in northern France, under Robert Guiscard, operating originally as mercenaries, conquered their own lands around Bari and then across much of southern Italy in the late eleventh century. Within a few decades they were kings of Sicily, one of the richest and most cosmopolitan areas of the Mediterranean with its mix of Byzantine, Islamic and northern European traditions. In England, after the conquest in 1066, the Normans moved into Wales and Ireland to exploit and rule new territories. A few decades later similar military groups were able to gain temporary control over parts of the Levant and establish the Kingdom of Jerusalem. In general though, Christian Europe still lacked significant power – it could advance into the poorly organized areas such as Wales, Ireland, central and eastern Europe, but elsewhere it could do little more than take advantage of temporary weaknesses as Byzantine and Fatimid power declined in southern Italy, Sicily and the Levant. In the latter area once Islam had reorganized, the crusader states were quickly defeated.

13.12.2 Iberia
[Earlier Iberia 11.10.1]

These limitations were particularly apparent in the Iberian peninsula. The first details about the small semi-Christian 'states' ruled by local lords that survived in the remote, poor and mountainous country of the Asturias that Islam did not think it worth conquering, date to the late eighth century. Early in the tenth century their capital was established at Leon but it was not until the end of the century that the rulers laid claim to a title. In 1077 Alfonso VI was crowned as 'king of Leon' although he grandly claimed to be *'totius hispaniae imperator'*. He was, however, able to take advantage of Islamic weakness and division following the collapse of the Umayyad caliphate in Cordoba. In 1064 Christian forces took Coimbra in what became Portugal, but more important was the conquest of the old capital Toledo in 1085. An Islamic revival under the Almoravids from north Africa led to the loss of Lisbon and Valencia. By the early twelfth century although the Christians still held Toledo it was a frontier town. The Christian kingdoms remained small and deeply divided. The largest was Leon-Castile. A small Portuguese kingdom existed by the early twelfth century, as did Navarre and Aragon (a small mountain kingdom until it united with various local rulers in Catalonia in the first three decades of the twelfth century). Although the kingdoms expanded south into Islamic territory and made gains in the 1140s (Lisbon was taken in 1147) some were only temporary (Almeria was lost in 1157) and the pace of conquest was still dictated by the strength of Islam. It was not until 1212 that the Christian kingdoms, under papal pressure, agreed on a joint campaign against Islam and won the decisive battle of Las Navas de Tolosa in that year. The Almohads (who had replaced the Almoravids in the 1150s) withdrew to north Africa and Islamic resistance crumbled. The key was the conquest of Cadiz and Seville in 1248, after which Islamic control was restricted to the south-east of the peninsula around Granada. However, Muslims were still a large proportion of the population across Iberia – as high as 75 per cent in the Valencia region. This posed enormous problems for the aggressively Christian kingdoms that had expanded from the north.

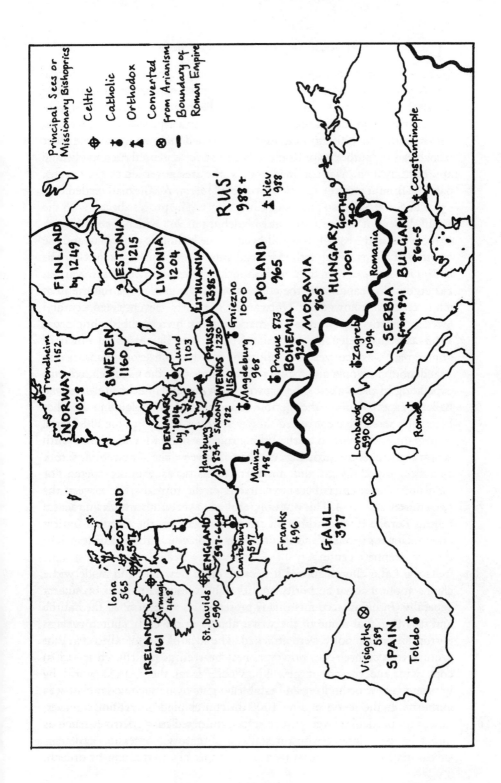

Map 43: The conversion of Europe

13.12.3 The expansion of Christianity

It was not just in the Iberian peninsula that the expansion of settlement meant the spread of Christianity. The three centuries or so after 1000 were particularly important in the process of defining a separate, Latin, western Christendom. In 900 Latin Christianity (defined in terms of churches that recognized the authority of Rome and the papacy and used rites and liturgy approved by them) was confined to Italy, the area governed by the Franks, parts of Britain and the northern fringe of Iberia. As German settlements expanded in the east so did Latin Christianity. The process began with the establishment of the bishopric at Magdeburg in 968 which directed much of the work in the east. It was followed by the bishopric of Poznan and the creation of a separate church in Poland with the archbishopric of Gniezno in 1000. The next year the first bishopric was established in Hungary at Esztergom. In Scandinavia the conversion of Denmark began in the mid-tenth century followed by Norway in the early eleventh century and Sweden shortly afterwards. Denmark had its own archbishopric from 1103 as did Sweden (at Uppsala) from 1164. By this time much of Pomerania was converted, followed in the thirteenth century by Brandenburg, Livonia and Estonia. At the same time the Greek church was expanding in the wake of the growth of Byzantine influence through the Balkans especially after the forcible conversion of the Bulgars in the mid-860s. The Serbs were converted shortly afterwards, followed in 988 by the principalities established by the Viking rulers around Kiev. By the eleventh century there were growing conflicts between the Latin and Greek churches, especially in the northern Balkans, as they competed for influence. The conflicts became worse after the formal split between the two churches in 1054. This division resulted in yet another fault line across central Europe (though different from that between the German settlers and indigenous groups) and this too was to plague European history into the late twentieth century.

As the Latin church spread it became more powerful and made wider claims about its own authority and its right to impose policies on society generally. In many accounts this is presented as a 'reform' of the church and it is true that some of the worst abuses in the early church such as corruption and simony were attacked. The idea of the so-called 'twelfth-century renaissance' can, however, best be seen as the church trying to cope with the spread of new knowledge from the Islamic world by imposing a new orthodoxy and establishing its own much wider claims to authority. In the centuries after 1000 the church made increasing claims to power (in particular over secular rulers), initiated new doctrines (such as infant baptism, intercession for souls in purgatory, confession and transubstantiation), created new institutions (especially new monastic orders), defined beliefs, revitalized the idea of 'heresy' and gradually enlisted the secular rulers in creating a persecuting and intolerant society in western Europe that was to continue for centuries and form a strong element in the European heritage. There were plenty of models in early Christianity under the emperors after Constantine and in the early church thinkers such as Augustine for the use of forcible conversion and persecution. However, after the initial disputes over doctrine within the newly established church (which produced the 'heresies' of the Arians, the monophysites, the Nestorians, the Pelasgians and others) there was a long period of relative calm within the church. It was the claims made by the church as Europe revived that produced a new intolerance.

One area where there were plenty of early examples to support the policies of the church was anti-Semitism. Following the establishment of Christianity Jews lost the earlier Roman privilege that allowed their own form of worship to continue, and were forbidden to marry Christians, acquire Christian slaves or build new synagogues. In 694 the council of Toledo in the Visigothic kingdom reduced all Jews south of the Pyrenees to the status of slaves. (It was hardly surprising therefore that the Jews of Iberia welcomed the greater tolerance of Islam.) However in general the Jews were tolerated if not welcomed and integrated – they were more cosmopolitan, literate and had contacts outside the narrow Christian world of western Europe. Growing anti-Semitism can be detected during the eleventh century – a 'tradition' arose in the towns of south-west France of striking a Jew in the face outside church on Easter Sunday, although in places this could be commuted to a special tax. It reached a first peak with the religious fanaticism associated with the First Crusade of 1096. The first walled ghetto was created by Bishop Rudiger of Speyer in 1084 and various anti-Semitic atrocities were associated with the crusading armies in Rouen, Worms, Mainz, Cologne and across Germany to Prague.

During the twelfth century these measures were taken further and Jews were depicted as the enemy of the Christian community. Legally they lacked the right to hold land and transmit property by inheritance and they were not protected by the courts – they were defined as the serfs of the king who could confiscate their property at will and become their heir. The temptation for the often bankrupt rulers and indebted elite of western Europe was obvious. Philip II of France was particularly anti-Semitic – Jews were expelled from the royal lands in 1181 (and in the next year from the whole of France) but only after they had made forced 'loans' to the king and seen most of their property confiscated. In England the monarchy was slightly wealthier but on the coronation of Richard I on 3 September 1189 at least thirty Jews in London were burnt to death and the pogroms spread across England leading to the massacre of over 150 Jews in York the next year. The church defined its position at the Lateran council in 1215. Jews were to wear a distinctive dress, they were not eligible for any public office and if they converted to Christianity they were not to observe any of their former rituals. They were beyond the pale of Christian civilization. Edward I of England expelled them from his territories in Gascony in 1288–9 and two years later from England.

The Jews, as a separate community, were relatively easy for the church to define. However, it also sought to create new definitions of 'heresy'. These were useful for branding opponents of the greater power and wealth of the church such as the Waldensians, many Franciscans and the 'Brethren of the Free Spirit', who argued, from within the church, for a return to the early Christian ideals of poverty. It was also useful for dealing with other beliefs such as those of the Cathars who had their own churches, bishops and rituals which appealed to the poor and powerless and probably provided a more direct religious experience than the established church. By the late twelfth century the Cathars were strong in Languedoc, Provence, Lombardy and Tuscany. The response of the church was, once again, established at the Lateran council of 1215 – secular rulers were to take every step to extirpate heresy on pain of the church withdrawing their power and handing their lands to good Christians. A crusade, not against Islam, but the Cathars of the south of France was proclaimed, with the added incentive that all the lands of the heretics would be confiscated and handed to those who took part in the crusade. The church established an inquisition to enquire into individual beliefs, which was used not just against the Cathars but also Jews, lapsed converts and others who disagreed with the church. Heretics were handed over to the secular power for punishment.

It was not just Jews and 'heretics' who were persecuted by the church but also other groups in society. Leprosy emerged as a disease in Europe in the sixth century but does not appear to have been widespread until the eleventh century. In 1179 the Lateran council defined how lepers should be treated. The diagnosis of leprosy was equivalent to proclaiming a person as dead – the leper was made to stand in an open grave as a priest said the ritual for the dead and usually some earth was thrown over the leper's head as a symbol. Lepers were excluded from the community by expulsion or confinement, lost all their rights over their property, could not attend church or be buried in a Christian cemetery. They were forbidden to walk the streets of London in 1200 and those of Paris two years later. In France under Philip V they were regularly tortured by the inquisition to admit poisoning the wells, hundreds were burnt and the revenues of the lazar houses were confiscated. Another group increasingly condemned from the twelfth century were male homosexuals. They were first formally condemned by the church in 1179 and the main civil law-codes established death as the punishment. From the thirteenth century female prostitutes were treated in the same way as Jews, although the church authorities decided that they would not be polluted if they accepted alms and gifts from them.

13.13 Europe: the Emergence of Kingdoms

In western Europe the expansion of population and settlement from the late tenth century was mirrored by the gradual emergence of larger political units and kingdoms out of the chaotic conditions of the previous couple of centuries. One of the earliest was in England where the kingdom of Wessex, which had managed to escape the worst of the Viking invasions, expanded during the tenth century, incorporating the areas of Viking settlement, until it established its rule over most of England.

13.13.1 The 'empire'

More significant were developments in the eastern part of the old Frankish empire. On the extinction of the Carolingian line following the death of Louis the Child in 911, the nobles chose the Franconian duke Conrad as their ruler. Before his death in 919 he recommended Henry of Saxony ('Henry the Fowler') as his successor – he was the founder of the Saxon (or Ottonian) dynasty which ruled until 1024. In the nineteenth century (and later) this was seen as the foundation of the first 'German' empire. However, this is a misleading concept. The empire did not see itself as 'German', the territories the emperors nominally ruled were in some areas much wider than modern Germany and in others much smaller. In practice it was an attempt to recreate the 'Roman' empire that was briefly in existence under Charlemagne. At first the kings had very little power over and above that which came from their position as rulers of their own principalities. That was partly changed by Otto I (936–73) mainly as a consequence of the prestige he gained from his decisive victory over the Hungarians at the battle of Lech in 955, and his intervention in Italy where he became 'King of the Lombards'. In 962 Otto was crowned emperor by the pope. As with Charlemagne, it was the result of a trade-off between the two sides – Otto gained increased status, the pope had the land grants made by the Carolingians confirmed. As in the past the 'empire' was an artificial creation and the respective powers of pope and emperor were to cause major disputes for centuries. To these problems were added the fundamental weakness of the empire – the emperor's lack of effective internal power. The lands he controlled were small and scattered and did

Map 44: The western empire in the tenth century

not provide either the revenue or the power base for government – the territorial princes had more concentrated power in the areas they controlled and were more powerful than the emperor when there were disputes over the imperial succession and when the papacy intervened in politics. The empire was even weaker than most early agricultural states. It was unclear whether the monarchy was hereditary or elective and if the latter who were the electors. The empire had no capital and the emperor travelled through his 'realm' but only between his own estates and those of a few bishoprics and monasteries he controlled. This was the only way he and his court could gain access to the small food surplus.

The only moderately strong emperor was Frederick of Swabia, the founder of the Hohenstaufen dynasty (named after their castle of Stauf). As so often in the early states this was mainly because of his long reign from 1150 until his death on the Third Crusade in 1190. He was able to take advantage of a weakened papacy but his major problem was trying to find an effective basis for imperial rule in Italy between the different interests of empire, papacy and the Lombard League of important towns. Soon after his death there was a major alteration in the balance of power when his son Henry VI inherited the throne of Sicily. The joint resources of the two areas threatened to make the empire overwhelmingly dominant in Italy and Henry was therefore opposed by both the papacy and the German princes who also opposed his attempt to make the imperial title hereditary. Whether it would have been possible to govern an empire spread from northern Germany to Sicily is doubtful but Henry's death in 1197 leaving his three-year-old son, Frederick, as heir effectively ended the project. Imperial power in Germany and Sicily disintegrated and although Frederick was crowned as emperor he spent most of his time in the richer and more cosmopolitan Sicily, rarely visiting Germany. On his death in 1250 (he was buried in his Arab robes in Palermo cathedral) the Hohenstaufen dynasty effectively came to an end. His last legitimate heir (his grandson Conradin) was executed by Charles of Anjou, who had taken the throne of Sicily in 1266, and this ended any possibility of a hereditary imperial title. In 1272 Count Rudolf of Habsburg was elected as emperor but the 'empire' existed in little more than name. For the next century there was a succession of emperors from different families but effective power lay with the mass of local rulers both secular and clerical.
[*Later 'empire' 15.9.1*]

13.13.2 'France' and the Angevins
In the west Frankish kingdom the disintegration of power continued for longer than in the east. It was not until 987 when Hugh Capet was elected

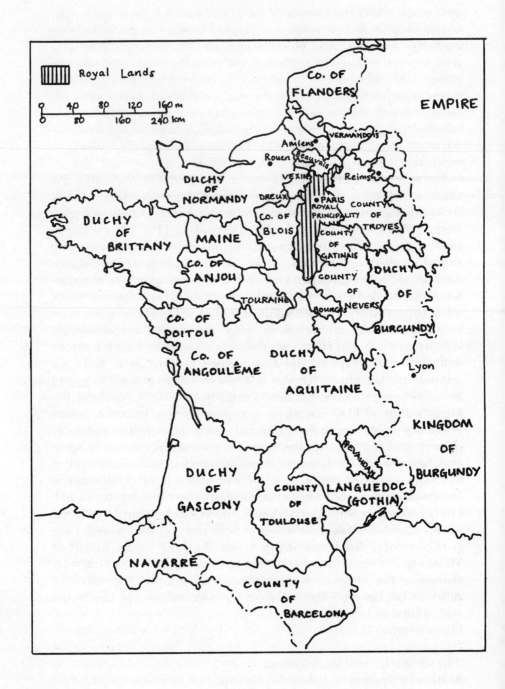

Map 45: 'France' in the mid-eleventh century

as king and united what was left of the earlier royal lands with his own duchy, that the recovery began. His accession to the throne is often portrayed as the emergence of 'France' and the beginning of its history as royal control was slowly expanded over the succeeding centuries. In practice there was no idea in the tenth century, and for a very long time thereafter, what the area of the old west Frankish kingdom should be called. 'Francia' was no more than the area from about the Loire to the borders of Lotharingia (which stretched to west of Verdun) and there was no concept of it being inhabited by a single people. Hugh Capet was not crowned as King of 'France' but as King of the Gauls, the Bretons, the Normans, the Aquitanians, the Goths, the Spanish and the Gascons, all of whom he did not control. During the tenth century provincial rulers had established their areas of control and men like William V of Aquitaine and Odo of Blois were fighting for inheritances in Italy, Burgundy and Lotharingia. In all of these struggles the crown was largely irrelevant, although nobody disputed its right to exist. The early Capetian rulers controlled little more than the royal lands centred around Paris and even here their authority was limited. The one great advantage of the Capetians (unlike the emperors in 'Germany') was that they produced a secure line of succession with long reigns – in the two centuries after 1060 there were only six kings. As so often in these early kingdoms long reigns and an untroubled succession meant a steady increase in power.

In the eleventh and twelfth centuries the Capetians were not the most powerful rulers in the area of 'France'. In the early eleventh century the strongest of all the local principalities was Normandy. Expansion under William from the mid-1040s reached its height with the enforcement of his claim to the English throne in 1066. From then until 1204 (except for short periods in 1087-96, 1100-06 and 1144-54) England and Normandy had a joint ruler although England tended to be the more powerful element. The Norman ruler was more powerful than the Capetian king and in 1109 Henry I refused to pay homage for Normandy on the grounds that he too was a king. The balance of power tipped even further against the Capetians in 1154 when Henry II became king of England and ruler of Normandy, Maine and Anjou. On his marriage to Eleanor of Aquitaine (who had been divorced by the Capetian Louis VII) he gained her vast inheritance. Once again the territories of a single ruler had been created by a mixture of aristocratic marriage alliances and chance. The 'Angevin empire' stretched from the borders of Scotland to the Pyrenees and was the most extensive political unit in twelfth-century western Europe. But it was too large to rule effectively and the increasing military demands, made worse by Richard I's expenses on the Third Crusade, reached a climax in the reign of John, leading to growing internal problems.

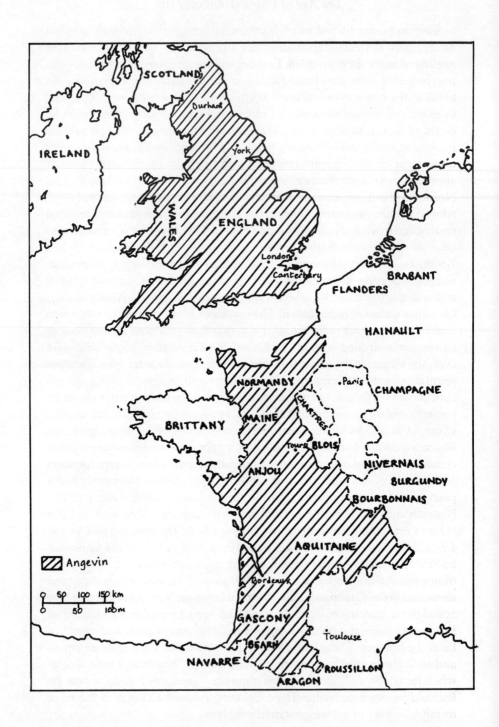

Map 46: The Angevin empire

Angevin power helped to revive the position of the Capetians as other rulers rallied to them in an attempt to contain the Angevins. Until the early twelfth century the Capetians had not even been able to exercise much power within their own royal lands, let alone outside them. The position of the king improved slowly through control over the appointment of some bishops, the issuing of coinage, the economic recovery (which was pronounced in the Ile-de-France), the right to summon an army from the provincial rulers and increasing visits outside the royal lands. It was not until the reign of Philip II (1180–1223) that significant gains were made and the Angevin empire was demolished. He conquered Anjou, Poitou, Normandy and Brittany and after the battle of Bouvines in 1214 his control in the north was largely unchallenged. The new lands provided a vast increase in royal wealth and power and administration could be based on the relatively efficient systems established by the Normans and Angevins. The situation in the south was very different. The English kings retained extensive territories in Gascony and it was only with the support of the papacy and the declaration of the Albigensian crusade against the Cathars that the monarchy could challenge the very powerful Counts of Toulouse. The extra wealth from the conquest of Languedoc, which was effectively controlled from the 1240s, further increased royal power. However, the Capetians were now trying to control a range of heterogeneous territories with different institutions, histories and languages. Central control was therefore very limited and the various regions retained considerable autonomy even under the strongest of the Capetian kings, Philip IV ('the Fair'), between 1285 and 1314. Just how much the Capetians owed to an undisputed succession and a series of long reigns was demonstrated when the line became extinct on the death of Charles IV in 1328. It was the beginning of a long period of internal disintegration, competing royal claims and long civil and external wars.
[*Later France and England 15.9.2*]

13.13.3 Central and eastern Europe
Further east in Europe monarchies emerged in what had been for thousands of years very marginal and peripheral areas but which were now slowly becoming an organized part of the Eurasian world. To the north, in Scandinavia states formed in Denmark, Norway and Sweden. In central Europe, as German settlers pushed east, kingdoms in Bohemia and then Poland developed. In the latter Mieszko I founded the Piast dynasty in 963 and took the crucial decision that was to affect the rest of Polish history when he adopted the Latin rather than the Greek form of Christianity. Poland (the name derived from *Polska*, the Polish word for a field or open terrain) always looked westwards towards the empire. After their defeat by

Otto I in 955 the Hungarians settled on the great plains in central Europe and an organized state began to emerge under the Arpad ruler Geza, in the late eleventh century. Like the Poles he looked westwards for support from the emperor and Latin Christianity. In 1000 Geza's son Vajk adopted the name Istvan (Stephen) and was crowned with a crown donated by the pope and with the support of the emperor Otto III. Hungary conquered Croatia and Dalmatia in 1089 although the port cities on the Adriatic coast were lost to Venice in 1102. Later in the twelfth century control was extended into Bosnia when Hungary became a major power in the northern Balkans and central Europe. However, on the death of Bella III in 1196 the kingdom collapsed into civil war and by the mid-thirteenth century the Hungarian monarchy was merely a shadow of its great past.

Further east an even weaker series of states emerged in what is now Ukraine, Belorussia and western Russia. During the ninth century Vikings called *Rus* established control in the territories of various eastern Slav tribes, built a few primitive towns (Kiev, Novgorod and Smolensk) and established trade routes down the great rivers to the Black Sea and Constantinople. These settlements coalesced into a primitive state at the same time as other peripheral states such as Poland and Hungary emerged and as the Khazar empire (ruled by a Jewish elite) declined on the southern steppes. It was the links with Byzantium that were to give the Rus state its defining characteristics. During the tenth century Greek Christianity penetrated the region and its adoption, probably in 988, by the Rus ruler was, as elsewhere, a central part of the process of the formation of an organized state. The culture of the state was defined by the Greek church, it used the Cyrillic alphabet (developed in the ninth century by St Cyril and St Methodius) and church texts were written in a language known as Old Church Slavonic in which Slavic words were cast in a Byzantine style. The area ruled by the Rus was unorganized and at a very low economic level. Most of the products traded were forest products – furs, honey and beeswax – together with slaves. Not until 1050 did the main city Novgorod have a stone cathedral and that was the only non-wooden building in the town for another century. Communications were poor and it was very difficult to control any unified state given the disputes within the royal family. There was a brief period with a single ruler, Iaroslav (1036–54), but the Rus then disintegrated into a loose confederation of princedoms. These were concentrated around the main towns and acknowledged the nominal supremacy of the ruler at Kiev but allowed him little or no effective power. By the late twelfth century Kiev was in decline – Novgorod became the chief city as it incorporated new territories and developed as the principal trading town linking the Baltic with the great river routes to the south. There were about a dozen separate principalities

at this time linked by little more than a common elite culture derived from the princely family and the church centred on Kiev.
[*Later eastern Europe 14.5.3*]

13.13.4 The destruction of the Byzantine empire

The rise of new powers in the Balkans, especially Hungary, together with the trading city of Venice and the Norman kingdom in southern Italy and Sicily meant that it was Byzantium rather than Islam that felt the impact of the expansion of western Europe. The loss of most of Anatolia after the battle of Manzikert in 1071 was not compensated by any increase in power in the west. Here the Byzantines had to make deals with Venice and then Pisa giving them trading rights in return for assistance. The divisions in the Islamic world of the Levant in the early twelfth century gave the Byzantines a little more room for manoeuvre and they captured Antioch before losing it and regaining it in 1159. However, the revival of Seljuq power led to the catastrophic defeat at the battle of Myriokephalon in 1176 which was almost as bad as that at Manzikert a century earlier. Most of the Balkans was controlled by the Hungarians and the Serbs; in 1185 Thessalonika fell to the Normans and in 1191 Cyprus was taken by members of the Third Crusade under Richard I of England. The Byzantines were also at war with their old supporters, Venice. The effective end of the empire came in the early thirteenth century when the members of the 'Fourth Crusade', supposed to be attacking Islam, ran out of money and their creditors, the Venetians, diverted them to Constantinople. The city was captured and looted in 1204 and the empire was divided up among the crusaders. Baldwin of Flanders was crowned as emperor, the Venetians took Crete, Euboea and other Greek islands, the Marquis of Montferrat became King of Thessalonika, Othon de la Roche took Athens and Boetia and Geoffroi de Villehardouin ruled the Peloponnese. The Byzantine empire, the effective successor to the east Roman empire, was reduced to a few remote territories at Trebizond, in the Epirus and around Nicaea.

OVERVIEW 9

THE WORLD IN
1200

World Population: 360 million
Regional Population: China: 115 million, India: 85 million,
Rest of Asia: 50 million, Europe: 60 million
Major cities: Hangchou (2,500,000), Fez (250,000),
Cairo (250,000), Constantinople (200,000),
Canton (200,000), Nanking (200,000),
Polonnaruwa (140,000), Baghdad (100,000),
Damascus (100,000), Paris (100,000), London (40,000)

Events:

★   Sung ruling south China from Hangchou

★   Jürchen ruling north China and Manchuria from Peking

★   Karakhitan controlling most of central Asia

★   Emergence of Chinggis-khan as Mongol leader

★   Kamakura shogunate in Japan

★   Khmer state in Cambodia

★   Kwarazm-shahs ruling Transoxania, Khurasan, Afghanistan and
north-west India

The Age of China (1000–c.1250)

★ Establishment of Delhi sultanates in north India

★ Ayyubid state in Egypt and Levant – Acre last remaining crusader possession

★ Decline of Byzantine empire – Seljuqs ruling Anatolia. Fourth Crusade captures Constantinople (1204)

★ Christian kingdoms in Portugal and central and northern Spain

★ Hohenstaufen empire in Germany, Italy and Sicily disintegrating

★ Angevin empire controlling England, parts of Ireland and Wales, Normandy and much of western 'France'. Capetians in central 'France', independent rulers in south

★ Civil war in Hungarian kingdom

★ Collapse of Toltec empire in central Mexico. Chichen Itza in Yucatan at its height

★ Collapse of Tiwanaku state in Andes

★ Kilwa major Islamic centre in East Africa

★ Ethiopian kingdom under Zagwe dynasty – rock cut churches at Lalibea

★ Great Zimbabwe major trading centre

★ Multi-colour printing in China

★ European ships adopt Chinese stern-post rudder and compass

★ Horizontal axled windmill in western Europe

★ First bronze and metal weapons in Andes

14

The Mongol Empire
(1200–1350)

The Mongol empire emerged out of a power vacuum on the central Asian steppes. It followed the collapse of the Turkic and Uighur empires and the successful conquest of northern China by the Jürchen from Manchuria in the 1120s. For several decades there was anarchy but by the end of the twelfth century the Jürchen were conducting campaigns on the steppe against the Mongol tribes controlling the region. However, almost nothing is known of the Mongols' early history. Once they do appear, their history is usually treated as a sensationalist story of conquest, plunder, looting and destruction lacking any motivation or coherence. This is a major distortion – the Mongols created the largest empire ever to exist in Eurasia. At its height it stretched from Hungary in the west to Korea and China in the east and from the steppes in the north to the Levant, Iran and Burma in the south. It was the first and only steppe empire to control all of its neighbouring sedentary states. Only a few areas of Eurasia escaped the direct impact of the Mongols – western Europe, Egypt, India and south-east Asia. Most of the history of Eurasia in the hundred and fifty years after 1200 can only be understood through the impact of the Mongols.

14.1 Chinggis-khan

The rise of the Mongols is synonymous with the rise of Temujin – later known as Chinggis-khan. His father was Yesugei, a leader of the Borjigid clan, who was killed, sometime in the mid-twelfth century, in a battle with the Tatar tribes. Temujin inherited his position as the war-leader of various Mongol clans and tribal federations. By the end of the twelfth century he had established his position as a major Mongol leader but the key to his dominant position was the Baljuna Covenant made in 1203 between Temujin and nineteen of his followers, all of whom became his main lieutenants during the conquests. Three years later at a *quriltai*, or gathering of the Mongols at the Onon river, Temujin was chosen as leader and given the title 'Chinggis-khan'. Its exact meaning is unclear but is probably either 'Supreme Ruler over the Oceans' or 'Emperor of Emperors'.

Having established his supremacy among the Mongols, Chinggis-khan's first aim was the conquest of the Jürchen-ruled areas of northern China.

The only practicable route with food, water and supplies was to follow the Silk Road through the Kansu corridor but that area was controlled by the Tangut elite of the Western Hsia. After a series of attacks they accepted Mongol overlordship and stopped paying tribute to the Jürchen. In the years 1211–13 there was frontier warfare with the Jürchen leading to the capture of their capital (near modern Peking) in 1214. The Jürchen moved further south but were beginning to be squeezed between the Mongols and the Southern Sung. Already military units were defecting to the Mongols, together with numerous Chinese officials (both civilian and military). By 1216 the Mongols controlled much of north-east China but were finding it very difficult to inflict a decisive defeat on the Jürchen. By the early 1220s little progress had been made.

Chinggis-khan was not leading the army in north China, nearly half of which was made up of Jürchen troops. He spent most of his time further west. A Mongol trade mission sent to the Khwarazm Turkish rulers of Transoxania and Khurasan was killed in 1218 and in response a punitive expedition was mounted – it quickly turned into a series of major conquests. Mongol troops attacked Transoxania in 1219, captured the great trading cities of Bukhara and Samarkand the next year and destroyed the Khwarazm state with little difficulty. They decided to push on further west along the well-established trade routes. The Oxus river was crossed in 1221 and the town of Balkh utterly destroyed (the modern city is on a new site and the ancient city has never been found). It was followed by a two-pronged attack on Iran led by Chinggis-khan and his youngest son Tolui. The latter conquered Khurasan and Chinggis-khan captured the town of Merv, killed the entire population (probably about 100,000 people), and did the same after Nishapur revolted against Mongol control. The conquest of Iran was finally completed after the Mongol victory at the battle of Kalabagh in 1222. There is little doubt that warfare and slaughter on this scale were unusual even by the standards of the time. The population losses across Transoxania and eastern Iran were huge. They were made worse by the deliberate destruction of the delicate *qanat* system of underground water channels, which had been laboriously constructed over centuries, and which ran for miles across the countryside supplying the water essential not just for irrigation but for all farming. The impact on food production was quick and devastating and was felt immediately in the cities which could no longer live on the food surplus of the countryside. People starved and the population fell rapidly after the Mongol conquest.

By the early 1220s the Mongols were attacking across a vast area – units were conducting raids into the Caucasus and some forces were near Novgorod. At the same time, on his return from Iran, Chinggis-khan took the decision to construct a Mongol capital, Qaraqorum, although no permanent buildings were finished until after his death. He also decided to destroy both the Tangut and Jürchen states following a Tangut revolt in 1224. He achieved the former but not the latter before his death in August 1227. At this point the Mongol empire was only slightly bigger than many previous steppe empires – the Tangut were defeated and Iran conquered but even the conquest of the Jürchen in northern China was not complete.

14.2 Ogodei and Guyuk

On his death Chinggis-khan's empire was divided up among his four sons. Jochi, the eldest, took the Qipchaq steppe and the area that led towards the principalities of the Rus. Chaghatai took the area around Samarkand, Transoxania and modern Turkestan. The youngest son Tolui, under the normal Mongol inheritance system, took Chinggis-khan's ancestral territory on the steppe. Ogodei, the third son, was designated as supreme ruler, although he was not formally chosen as such until a *quriltai* of the Mongols in 1229. It was Ogodei who ensured that the Mongol conquests under his father were not ephemeral and began the construction of a major empire. He was decisive in determining Mongol strategy but only took part in one campaign – in Honan and the Wei river valley against the Jürchen who had retaken territory from the Mongols during the confused period after the death of Chinggis-khan.

Ogodei's first decision was to complete the conquests envisaged by Chinggis-khan, in particular the elimination of the Jürchen. This was achieved, with the tacit assistance of the Southern Sung, in a major campaign lasting for four years after 1231. It ended with the abdication and suicide of the last Jürchen emperor. In Iran a former Khwarezm leader, Jalal al-Din, was trying to rebuild a Turkic empire although he was simultaneously under pressure from the Seljuqs in the west. In 1228 he massacred all the Mongol prisoners held at his capital of Isfahan. He was unable to resist the inevitable Mongol retaliation and fled westwards. Khurasan was put under direct Mongol rule and their troops were operating as far west as Georgia and Armenia by the early 1230s. By 1234 Ogodei's immediate aims had been met and a *quriltai* was called to resolve future strategy. When it met on the banks of the Orkhon river near Qaraqorum, it decided to conquer the Korean peninsula (Mongol troops had been operating in the area since 1231), move westwards into the territories of the Rus and conquer the Southern Sung. The first aim was achieved in 1236 but the campaigns against the Southern Sung ended in stalemate – the Mongols could do little more than raid into Szechwan. Mongol efforts were therefore concentrated in the west under the leadership of Guyuk and Mongke, both future emperors. The attacks began in the Volga region in 1235 and within two years Voronezh and Ryazan were captured, together with the then very minor city of Moscow, followed in early 1238 by the major cities of Vladimir and Novgorod. After the fall of Kiev in 1240 the Mongols controlled all of the principalities of the Rus. In the early spring of 1241 a three-pronged attack was launched on the weak Hungarian kingdom. It was rapidly conquered. The Mongols moved further west and in April 1241 at the battle of Leignitz an army of German and Polish knights under the command of Duke Henry I of Silesia was utterly routed. It seemed inevitable that the Mongols would continue their campaigns by assaulting western Europe. Given the weaknesses and divisions among the kingdoms in the area there seems little reason to doubt that any Mongol attack would have been successful. The German states and those even further west survived only because of divisions within the Mongol leadership over what strategy to follow, the withdrawal of some troops and then the unexpected death of Ogodei in December 1241 (the result of excessive drinking). Ogodei left no designated successor and the Mongol world was thrown into confusion. Guyuk was eventually chosen as leader at a *quriltai* in 1246 but civil war followed and continued even after his death in 1248. A new leader was not chosen until the election of Mongke in 1251. Even then there was still dissent within the Mongol elite until Mongke eliminated all his rivals.

14.3 The Empire at its Peak

On his accession in 1251 Mongke inherited an ailing Mongol empire, yet by his death in 1258 it was on the verge of becoming the greatest empire the world had seen. The Mongol empire adopted a system common among all the early empires which lacked an effective infrastructure – power was placed in the hands of various members of the ruling family in the hope that they would be loyal. Under Ogodei the Qipchaq Horde (often incorrectly called the 'Golden Horde') had been semi-independent under the control of Jochi and then his second son Batu who ruled until 1255 when he was succeeded by his brother Berke. In the period after the conquests of the early 1240s it established a system that lasted for two hundred years. It controlled the various rulers of the Rus who all recognized Mongol overlordship, received their authority from the Mongol ruler at his capital of Sarai near the Caspian Sea, paid tribute to him and governed on his behalf. To the south Mongke appointed his brother Hulegu as leader of the Mongols at Samarkand with the title of Il-khan or 'viceroy', a title that continued to be used by the Mongol rulers of Iran. His

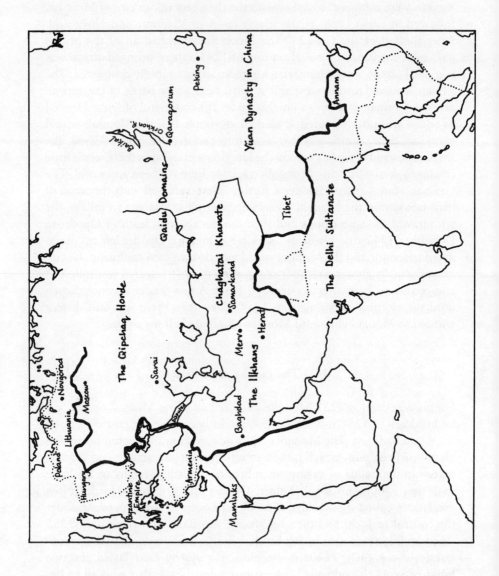

Map 47: The Mongol empire in the late thirteenth century

first task was to complete the conquests in the west. Some attempt was made to build support among Muslims by attacks on the Ismaili sect in their remote, fortified, mountainous regions – most Muslims regarded them as heretics. Then the attacks shifted to Mesopotamia where in February 1258 the former capital of Islam, Baghdad, was captured. The looting, which lasted for a week, destroyed much of the city, killed many of its population (still over 100,000 despite a decline from its peak during the early Abbasid period) and devastated the surrounding countryside. As in many areas of Iran a few decades earlier, a large proportion of the irrigation systems was destroyed resulting in permanent damage to the infrastructure. The last Abbasid caliph, who had long lost any effective power, was killed. Mongol forces then moved west and destroyed Aleppo. Damascus surrendered in early March 1260 and by the summer the Mongol armies had reached Gaza. It was only then that Hulegu heard that his brother Mongke had died in China almost two years earlier.

Hulegu travelled east leaving only small Mongol forces behind. They faced the Mamluks, slave soldiers who, led by one of their officers, Aybeg, had overthrown the Ayyubid rulers in Egypt in 1250 and set up their own state. This was the high point of the Islamic slave army system – all of the elite, including the ruler, were either slaves or ex-slaves and the military commands were restricted to foreigners (usually Turkish or Circassian) who were purchased as slaves and rose through the system. No native of Egypt or Syria was allowed to be a military commander and in theory not even the sons of slaves and rulers could command. In 1260 they rejected Mongol demands for their surrender and at the battle of Ain Jalat defeated (or at least drew with) the weak forces left behind by Hulegu. The Mamluks survived and continued to rule Egypt and most of Syria until 1517.

Mongke had died during a massive three-pronged attack on the Southern Sung which began in 1258. In 1260 his brother, Qubilai, whom Mongke had appointed as Il-khan in northern China, declared himself as the Mongol leader, although he continued to rule from his base in China. Many historians have argued that the Mongol empire effectively ceased to exist at this date and that Qubilai was no more than an emperor ruling over China. That was not how the Mongols saw it at the time. In Iran Hulegu recognized Qubilai's authority and the latter confirmed Hulegu's son, Abaqa as ruler in 1265 and formally enthroned him as Il-khan in 1270. In 1267 the successor to Berke as head of the Qipchaq Horde, Mongke Temur, also accepted Quibilai's ultimate authority. It was under Qubilai that the Mongols completed the conquest of China and brought their empire to its peak.

The final attack on the Southern Sung was a major undertaking, even using the resources of northern China, and it was not completed until the late 1270s. The decisive battle of Ting-chia was won in 1275 but even then the Mongols still had to win a naval battle against a Sung fleet of over 2,000 vessels. The capital Hangchou was captured in 1276 but the war continued for another three years across southern China until final victory was achieved. In 1279 Quibilai proclaimed himself the first emperor of the new Yüan dynasty. With the resources of the whole of China now at their disposal the Mongols envisaged further major campaigns. By the early 1280s they were fighting in northern Burma and the Irrawady valley as well as in Vietnam against the Champa and the Khmer kingdoms. Naval raids using fleets of over 1,000 ships were made on Sumatra and Java. In Tibet, under the threat of invasion, there was a greater degree of internal coherence than at any time since the collapse of the Tibetan empire in the mid-ninth century. A council of local rulers chose the head abbot of the Sa-skya monastery, Kun-dga rgyal-mtshan, as negotiator. In 1247 the Mongols accepted him as the ruler of Tibet and, in return for the imposition of Mongol officials to collect an annual tribute, the invasion was called off. It was the beginning of the peculiar Tibetan system mixing religious and secular power which was to continue into the twentieth century. However, even the Mongols were reaching the limits of feasible expansion – no Chinese dynasty had ever controlled Tibet, Burma, Sumatra and Java, and even holding Vietnam was proving difficult against well-organized guerrilla warfare and eventually it had to be abandoned. In 1281 it was decided to attack Japan, another area which had never been controlled from China. A massive armada of 4,400 ships and an invasion force of over 45,000 troops, together with their horses, was assembled. The fleet was destroyed in a typhoon – to the Japanese it was a *kamikaze* ('divine wind') which saved them from probable destruction. It marked the end of the period of Mongol conquests and the beginning of a phase of consolidation and an attempt to govern the largest empire ever created in Eurasia.

14.4 Ruling the Empire

Qubilai remained the head of the Mongol empire but he increasingly centred his rule on China which was by far the richest of all the areas the Mongols controlled. For a long period the Mongols retained both their nomadic life and its customs. Even in the late thirteenth century many continued to live at Qaraqorum and vast wagon convoys, which took over four months for the round trip, were bringing over half a million bushels of grain a year from China to feed the population. Nevertheless Mongol life and institutions began to change. One of the most important was the emergence of a powerful princely house headed by the sons of Chinggis-khan and their families. In the past the rulers on the steppe had been those who were thought to have the right military qualities. Now the descendants of Chinggis-khan largely monopolized power. In parallel with this trend a new elite emerged based not, as in the past, on the clans and various groupings of them, but on the role individuals had played in the conquests, and their status was passed on to their families. The compensation for the remaining Mongols was that the status of all of them increased as they became the conquering elite across Eurasia. The main Mongol institution remained the army (indeed it was Mongol society because all adult males were members) and social mobility in the Mongol world still largely depended on military prowess. The new unit created by Chinggis-khan in 1203 was the *keshik* or imperial bodyguard which was slowly expanded during the thirteenth century and until 1312 only Mongols could become members.

At first the administrative functions carried out by the Mongols were minimal but this had to change as the empire expanded. Their problem was that they had neither the experience, nor the necessary numbers, to govern such a vast empire. However, the Mongol elite remained reluctant to share power, dilute their own influence and increase the likelihood that they would be absorbed into the world of their sedentary neighbours. The resolution of these conflicting pressures was to be a major theme of Mongol history for decades. A crucial role in the process was played by the Khitan who were the first major people that the Mongols conquered. From them the Mongols took many ideas, vocabulary and institutions as they attempted to construct an administration, especially after the capture of the Jürchen capital Chung-tu. The crucial figure in this early phase was Yeh-lü Ch'u-ts'ai, a sinicized Khitan who had joined the court of Chinggis-khan in 1218. He adopted the Sung system of finance, which was still operating under the Jürchen, and brought in more officials from both the Jürchen and the Sung. However, his attempts to introduce the full Chinese model of government alienated too many Mongols and he lost power in 1236. The primary aim of Mongol government in this early phase was the raising of money. After the conquest of an area a tax of one-tenth was usually imposed on all possessions. Then customs duties (the *tamgha*) were set up, followed by the traditional form of regular nomadic tribute – the *alban* – and the more infrequent levy or *qubchiri*. These were maintained for some decades, often under different names, in every part of the empire and only slowly were they adapted and incorporated into the taxation systems in place before the conquest. The first sign that the Mongols were moving towards a more coherent form of administration was the complete census of the empire initiated in 1252 by Mongke. It took until the end of the decade to complete such a vast undertaking but when it was finished only adult males in religious institutions had been exempted.

In administering such a vast empire the Mongols faced two particular problems. The first was that though local government could be conducted in local languages the decrees of the central government had to be issued in a large number of languages if they were to be understood – Persian, Uighur, Chinese, Tibetan, Tangut, Arabic and Mongol itself. All of these required very different scripts and so large teams of translators and scribes had to be maintained in the capital. Each of the main sedentary peoples also had their own separate administrative departments. Even so coherence across such a sprawling empire was very difficult to ensure. This reflected the second problem – the difficulty of communication. We have already seen how it took nearly two years for important news – the death of Mongke in China – to reach his brother Hulegu campaigning in Mesopotamia and Syria. Even military campaigns were difficult to organize. Under Mongke the conquests for each year were decided at an assembly of army leaders in January and this rigid timetable and plan were then adhered to so that the armies were at least co-ordinated to some extent. This was essential given the size of the forces involved – the final conquest of Iran involved over 75,000 troops together with siege equipment, horses and flocks of sheep and goats to feed the army. It was the need to stick to a pre-determined timetable that explains why some cities were simply ignored and by-passed by the Mongol armies during the conquests. The Mongols therefore needed an efficient system of communication within the empire. It was created by Ogodei in 1234 and was similar to the systems created by other pre-industrial empires although its extent was far greater. A series of post-stages were created at distances of a day's journey – about every twenty-five to thirty miles along the main routes of the empire. Quicker couriers and runners might between them carry a message over a distance of perhaps 200 miles in a day. The stage-posts were maintained by the army who provided men, horses and fodder, in their turn supported by the local population who had to feed both the humans and the animals – there was supposed to be a regular system to assess the burden but in practice it was largely arbitrary and depended on what the troops could force the people to provide. Authorization to use the system came from the possession of a *paiza* or tablet of either wood, silver or gold. This was supposed to be restricted to government business but important merchants were able to use the system. The whole system was known to the Mongols as *yam* which suggests that it was adopted from the Chinese via the Khitan – the Chinese word for a stage on a journey is *chan*.

It was along these various routes that a large number of people travelled from east to west and vice-versa. The idea that this was encouraged by a 'Mongol peace' is a little fanciful but contacts across Eurasia at this time, as before, were substantial. The Mongol attack on Baghdad in 1258 was commanded by a Chinese general because of Chinese experience of siege warfare. Subsequently a number of Chinese engineers worked on the Mesopotamian irrigation systems. Chinese administrators also travelled across the Mongol empire, especially to Iran, on various missions. In 1275 a Chinese Nestorian monk, Rabban Bar Sauma (not his Chinese name), began an extraordinary journey. He travelled along the Silk Road, on through Iran to Palestine to visit Christian sites. In 1287–9 he visited Constantinople and Rome and travelled on to France where he met both Edward III of England in Gascony and Philip IV in Paris before his death in 1294. The Christian interest in the Mongols began in the 1220s when they were seen as a force created by God, under the command of King David (Chinggis-khan), to attack the infidel Muslims. They were soon disillusioned after the attacks on eastern and central Europe around 1240 when the pope's call for a crusade was ignored. Nevertheless interest in the Mongols revived because they were not Muslims (Europe's greatest enemy). The Mongols did not have a structured religion (it was more a shamanistic form of animism) but, partly because of the multitude of religions within the empire, they were highly tolerant. Within the Mongol court the main influences were Nestorian Christianity (still strong in central Asia) and Ch'an Buddhism. The vague ideas propagated in western Europe about alliances against Islam and the Mamluks in Egypt came to nothing. A mission to Qaraqorum in 1245–7 was dismissed by Guyuk and the European rulers told to submit and pay tribute. The Flemish Franciscan Wilhelm van Ruysbroeck reached the Mongol court in 1253 but he had no impact.

Other travellers, monks and religious figures also moved around the Mongol-dominated Eurasian world. The most famous of the western travellers was Marco Polo who claimed to have left Venice in 1271 and travelled along the old-established trade routes through Mesopotamia, Iran and central Asia to reach China in 1275. He stayed for seventeen years before travelling home along the Indian Ocean trading routes via Sumatra, Sri Lanka and India, reaching Venice again in 1295. Odoric of Pordenone did this journey in reverse between 1315 and 1330. Other merchants and their families from the Italian cities also reached China – a tombstone in Yangchou records the death in 1342 of Catherine de Viglione who probably came from Genoa. Another Franciscan, Giovanni di Monte Corvino, travelled by the sea routes to China where he was technically archbishop of Peking although his flock was minute. He died in Peking in 1328. Perhaps the greatest of all the travellers across Eurasia at this time was the historian Ibn-Batuta who was able to take advantage of the cultural and economic connections within the extensive Islamic world. He left Tangier in 1325 for the pilgrimage to Mecca. From there he travelled on to Mesopotamia before sailing down the Gulf to India, the Maldives and Sri Lanka before reaching China. Like Marco Polo he stayed for many years before sailing back via India to the Gulf and the land journey through Syria and Egypt. He reached Fez in 1349. The next year he visited the Islamic state of Granada before leaving in 1351 to cross the Sahara and spend two years in the Islamic kingdom of Mali. During his quarter of a century of travelling he covered 73,000 miles and visited the equivalent of forty-four modern countries.

14.5 The Break-up of the Empire

Although Qubilai was the supreme ruler of the Mongol world, he concentrated on his role as emperor of China. Inevitably the sheer difficulty of ruling the Mongol empire meant that it split into increasingly autonomous units controlled by descendants of Chinggis-khan. By the time Qubilai died in 1294 and was succeeded by his grandson Temur, his theoretical supremacy was no longer of any importance. In general the process of division was peaceful – the only internal conflict was between the Il-khans of Iran and the Qipchaq Horde in the early 1260s over the boundary between them (it was won by the Il-khans).

14.5.1 China
In China Qubilai had to deal with the fundamental consequences of almost fifty years of continuous warfare – the population fell by more than a quarter from 115 million to 85 million over the course of the thirteenth century. This, together with the high levels of destruction in the cities and countryside, was a catastrophic blow to the agricultural base and infrastructure which had been built up in the previous centuries and which had reached such a peak under the Sung. Nearly all of these achievements, which seemed to push China to the edge of major economic and social change, were thrown into reverse. The first priority was therefore to rebuild the agricultural base – the process was directed by a new institution, the *Ta-ssu-nung-ssu* or 'Great Office of Agricultural Affairs'. But progress was slow and the disintegration of the economic infrastructure compared with the sophisticated system in use under the Sung can be judged from the fact that, although a paper currency was re-introduced in 1260, the land tax was now paid in grain and the household tax was paid by direct peasant labour. Only the poll tax was paid in cash.

There was some revival in trade, especially along the Silk Road now that this was all under Mongol political control rather than under the different central Asian empires as it had been during the Sung dynasty. Trade into south-east Asia and the Indian Ocean remained at the same high levels as it had been under the Sung, as is demonstrated by the number of travellers finding easy access to these routes. The rice trade between the south and the north of China was restored to the levels of the early Sung before the Jürchen conquest of the north stopped transport along the Grand Canal. However, the bulk of this trade now went by sea, even after the restoration of the canal and its extension to the new Mongol capital of Peking in the far north of the country between 1279 and 1294.

An equally difficult problem was how to administer China and how much reliance to place on the old Chinese administrative elite. Qubilai attempted to modify the established system so as to ensure Mongol predominance. The examination system, which had fallen into disuse after 1238 because of the disruption caused by the war with the Mongols, was not restored until 1315. Even then quotas were employed for different groups and the Mongols reserved a quarter of all appointments for themselves. In central administration the *Chung-shu sheng* or 'Central Secretariat', which had been established by Yeh-lü Ch'u-ts'ai under Ogodei and then filled largely by Chinese personnel, was turned into the main government institution. However, it was headed by the Mongol heir-apparent and all the top personnel were non-Chinese. It was complemented by the *Shu-mi yüan* or 'Bureau of State Affairs' which dealt with military affairs (very broadly defined) and reported directly to the emperor. An idea of its functions can be gathered by its two subordinate bureaus for surveillance and pacification. The old Chinese institution of the 'Censorate' or *Yü-tai shih* was turned into a department which openly supervised local government and carried out secret surveillance of the Chinese parts of the central government. China was divided into twelve provinces and each replicated the structure of the central government with all the main appointments made by the emperor and with the top posts reserved for non-Chinese. However, the 'Censorate' only had three provincial divisions. This was designed to try and increase the level of central control. It became a strongly held Chinese belief in subsequent centuries that the Mongols (like the other 'barbarians' who ruled China) had become increasingly attracted to Chinese life and culture and became 'sinicized'. Although many of the Mongol elite did begin to lose touch with the world of the steppe, generally they did not adopt Chinese ways. They did not learn Chinese but continued to dominate the Chinese in the higher levels of government. The Mongols remained a separate governing elite. Similarly there does not seem to have been any great 'anti-Mongol' feeling across China – most of the peasant revolts had their roots in the same rural discontent found under most Chinese dynasties.

The Mongols remained highly tolerant in religious matters although they did not favour indigenous Chinese Taoist beliefs. Between 1255 and 1258 Qubilai encouraged a series of debates between Taoists and Tibetan Buddhist representatives. He came down in favour of the latter and condemned Taoism. Buddhism became the favoured religion again – it was exempted from taxation and began to acquire major estates and wealth. Qubilai confirmed the position of the Sa-skya abbot in Tibet and its head, 'Phags-pa, became his spiritual adviser. He also headed the government Office of Buddhist Affairs; there were separate organizations for the other religions (Christianity, Islam and Taoism were grouped together). [*Later China 14.6 & 15.2*]

14.5.2 Iran and Mesopotamia

The second most important area ruled by the Mongols was Iran and Mesopotamia under the Il-khans. When Hulegu died in 1265 he was succeeded by his son Abaqa who was formally recognized as Il-khan by Qubilai and enthroned in 1270. This was the last occasion such a procedure was used. Under Abaqa the Mongols remained a ruling, alien elite in the sophisticated and long-established Iranian Islamic world. The population saw them as heathen outsiders and submission to their rule was largely based on the very real fear of slaughter and destruction (as shown again in the suppression of the revolt in Khurasan in 1270), high levels of taxation and the imposition of strong military rule. In 1281 the Mamluks in Egypt defeated a badly led Mongol attack and after the death of Abaqa the Ilkhanate descended into civil war which only worsened the already high level of destruction resulting from the conquest. The most significant event in the history of the Ilkhanate was the accession to power of Ghazan in 1295. Until then the Mongol rulers, particularly Ghazan's predecessor Arghun, had been, like their compatriots, tolerant in matters of religion and had even tended to favour Buddhism and Christianity. However, Ghazan converted to Islam and in 1297 made a highly symbolic public rejection of the steppe heritage when he exchanged the broad-brimmed Mongol hat for the traditional Iranian headgear. With the fervour of the convert, Ghazan ordered the destruction of all non-Muslim religious buildings. It was during his reign that the Mongols made the transition which they did not make in China – the Ilkhanate became a Muslim state (as Iran had been for six centuries) ruled by converted Mongols. Ghazan was also successful militarily – by 1300 Aleppo and Damascus were recaptured from the Mamluks and control over Syria was established. No attempt was made to push further into Egypt. Ghazan died in 1304 and

was succeeded by his half-brother who took the name of Oljeitu ('the fortunate'). He ruled for fourteen years in peaceful conditions and secured a reconciliation with the Qipchaq Horde.
[*Later Iran 18.3*]

14.5.3 The Qipchaq

The Qipchaq ruled over the territories of the Rus as far as Ukraine but, because the area was so poor, they were not attracted to settle in the region and remained centred around their capital at Sarai near the Caspian Sea. The Qipchaq were primarily a steppe empire that happened to rule over some sedentary people in the far western part of their territory. The taxation system they adopted reflected this position and it was therefore very different from that used by the Mongols in the wealthy regions of China and Iran. It retained its largely pastoral basis in which the nomadic population of whatever origin paid taxes based on the size of their herd. They paid far less than the conquered, settled population of the Rus, where taxation levels were proportionately as high as elsewhere in the Mongol empire. The main function of the local rulers of the Rus was to collect this taxation and tribute and send it to the Mongols at Sarai. At first the local princes were tightly controlled in their administration by Mongol *baskaki* who carried out most of the important functions. It was only as the local princes proved their trustworthiness that they were allowed to act as agents of the Mongols. This meant that the Mongols had a direct interest in the succession within the Rus states. In the past this was usually decided by conflict within the ruling family. Now the disputes were arbitrated by the administration in Sarai and it was their approval that was crucial if one of the princes was to be recognized as ruler. The local rulers such as the Nevskii family in Novgorod therefore actively sought Mongol approval and governed on their behalf. Even under the series of relatively weak Qipchaq rulers between 1280 and 1313 the Rus princes, divided among themselves and largely powerless, were unable to take advantage of the situation to establish a greater degree of independence.

The power of the Qipchaq revived under Oz-beg (1313–40). He re-established firm control over the western territories. In 1328 he imposed a settlement on the Rus princes who for several decades had been arguing over who should be their nominal head and take the title of Grand Prince of Vladimir. Oz-beg gave the title to Ivan of the Daniilovichi dynasty of Moscow. They had no claim to the title and were therefore highly dependent on the Qipchaq to retain their position. It was his decision which began the process by which the very small and primitive state of Moscow started its long rise to pre-eminence among the principalities of the Rus. In 1339 the city of Smolensk was sacked for not paying tribute

and Mongol raids once again penetrated deep into Hungary, eastern Galicia and Prussia. Under Oz-beg's successor, Jani-beg (1342–57) the power of the Qipchaq was sustained and expanded further with the conquest of Azerbaijan.
[*Later history 15.10.3*]

14.5.4 The Chaghatai khanate

The least-known part of the Mongol empire is the Chaghatai khanate which covered much of Transoxania and Turkestan (it had no fixed and firm frontiers) and had the cities of Bukhara and Samarkand at its core. It was founded by Chaghatai, the second son of Chinggis-khan, and was the only true steppe part of the Mongol empire and the only one which rejected most of the traditions of sedentary life – it even sacked its own two main cities in order to provide loot for the army. It had no real capital but the main rallying point for the nomads was Almaligh on the Ili river. The bulk of the area over which it ruled was inhabited by nomadic Turkic people who had migrated there several centuries earlier. The result was that the Mongol minority were gradually absorbed into the Turkic majority and a new language, Chaghatai Turkish, developed. What little is known about the internal history of the khanate comes from external sources. Although established in the 1220s the rulers of the khanate accepted the supremacy of the Mongol leaders from Ogodei to Qubilai and full autonomy did not come until the tenth ruler, Du'a (1282–1307). Islam, which was strong in Transoxania, was, as in the Il-khan and Qipchaq areas, adopted as the state religion in preference to the Buddhism which was still strong in Turkestan. The conversion took place at some time during the rule of Tarmashirin (1326–34). After his death the khanate was divided into two and it was from this area that the last of the great nomadic conquerors – Temur – emerged in the late fourteenth century.
[*Later central Asia 15.6*]

14.6 The End of Mongol Rule

Although the Mongol empire gradually split into autonomous units in the last quarter of the thirteenth century, the descendants of Chinggis-khan continued to rule over all of the vast territories of the empire until the 1330s. The first area which experienced a breakdown was the Ilkhanate of Iran and Mesopotamia. After the death of Oljeitu in 1316 there was a long period of internal dissension over the succession among the Mongol elite which resulted in growing weakness in the central government and an increasing inability to keep control over the strong provincial governors and rulers. The Ilkhanate finally collapsed in 1335 and over the next couple of years it was partitioned among a number of different local dynasties. The Sarbardars ruled in Khurasan, the Jalayirs controlled the central region around Baghdad and Tabriz, the Muzaffarids took the province of Fars and the Karts the area around Herat. These rulers survived until the 1380s and the conquests of Temur.

The beginnings of the end of Mongol rule in China can be dated to roughly the same period. After the death in 1307 of Qubilai's heir and grandson, Temur (no relation to the later nomadic ruler), there were growing problems and disputes over the imperial succession. These were at first contained but disputes between the various factions within the Mongol court broke into the open in 1328. A 'coup' by Qipcaq el-Temur and Merkid Bayan led to the growing dependence of the emperor on these two leaders who did not come from the family of Chinggis-khan. At the same time from the early fourteenth century there were growing peasant rebellions across China caused by food shortages, famines and rising prices. They were made worse by extensive flooding along the Yellow river after 1327. These peasant risings were also linked to various religious revolts, in particular Buddhist messianic movements which believed in the coming of the future Buddha, Maitreya (Mi-le to the Chinese). By 1340 there were large-scale revolts across Honan, Hunan, Kwantung and Szechwan. In 1344 a vast area of land downstream of K'ai-feng was flooded as the dykes collapsed. It took more than five years to repair the breaches and agricultural land and villages were lost across a wide area. This was probably the immediate cause of the outbreak of the major insurrection of the *Hung-chin* or 'Red Turbans' in 1351. By that time the last Mongol emperor, Toghon Temur, who had come to the throne in 1333, was beginning to lose control of large areas of the country – Szechwan was already effectively independent under a separate Mongol ruler. By the late 1350s all control over vast areas of southern China and across the lower Yangtze valley was lost. A few years later the peasant rebels moved north and in 1368 took the Mongol capital, Peking. The Mongols abandoned it without a fight and, although some stayed behind in China, most of the leadership returned to the steppe. Some established a new Northern Yüan dynasty which was to be a major threat to the new rulers of China for several decades.

Further west the Chaghatai khanate divided in the 1330s and new nomadic leaders emerged later in the fourteenth century. The one area where the Mongols did continue to rule was on the Qipchaq steppe and the territories of the Rus. Despite internal weaknesses the Qipchaq revived in the 1380s after a coup by Toqtamish, the leader of a minor Mongol group within the horde. The Rus refused to pay tribute and in 1382 Toqtamish invaded, captured Moscow, looted it and burnt it to the ground. The Qipchaq survived the impact of Temur in the late fourteenth century and Moscow remained subservient to them. It was not until after 1410 that the Mongol rulers began to lose influence in their far western territories. Then in the 1430s the Qipchaq split into three separate units – the khanates of Crimea, Astrakhan and Kazan – some of which were to survive for another three centuries.

15

Recovery
(1350–1500)

15.1 Famine and Plague

[Earlier Eurasian disease patterns 10.1]

The peasant discontent and rebellions which spread across China in the mid-fourteenth century and led to the collapse of Mongol rule by 1368, were only one symptom of growing problems within Eurasia. Although China, together with Iran and Mesopotamia, had suffered from the very high level of destruction during the Mongol invasions, elsewhere in Eurasia, particularly in Europe, there were more fundamental problems. These were caused by the rising population reaching levels that could not be sustained by the still relatively primitive agricultural base. By 1300 the population of Europe was about 80 million compared with only 35 million three hundred years earlier. To some extent this increase was the result of bringing new areas into cultivation but by the end of the thirteenth century that process was reaching its limits given the available technology. Across Europe crop yields were beginning to fall. Many parts of Europe were overcrowded – the population of areas such as northern Italy, Flanders, Brabant and around Paris was probably as high as in the early nineteenth century although the level of agricultural productivity was far lower. The situation was made worse by a deteriorating climate. The optimum conditions of the twelfth century soon disappeared after 1200 and the impact of the worsening climate can be traced across Europe. The Viking settlements in Greenland were marginal even when the climate was mild. As the hay-growing season steadily shortened, crops declined and it was difficult to keep cattle alive during the winter. As the climate deteriorated the Inuit moved south and destroyed the settlement at Godthaab around 1350. Pack-ice now remained in the seas around Greenland throughout the summer and contact with the rest of Europe was lost after 1408. The eastern settlement at Julianehaab died out under Inuit attack sometime in the fifteenth century. Iceland too became a much more marginal society – wheat growing died out (only a one-degree centigrade drop in average temperatures was enough to shorten the growing season by a third) and the population fell rapidly. The uplands of southern Scotland reverted to pasture from arable and vine-growing died out in England after 1400.

The general climatic deterioration posed major problems. The crisis in

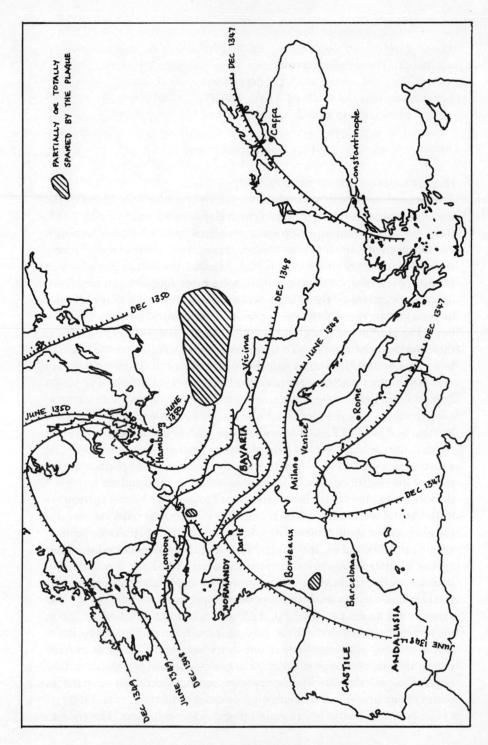

Map 48: The spread of the 'Black Death' in Europe

Europe became apparent during the catastrophic events of 1315–17 when a large part of the population was already living on the margins of subsistence. The weather throughout 1315 was dreadful. It was wet in every season, the spring sowing failed in most areas because of water-logged fields, ploughs stuck in the mud and the hay crop was neither ripe nor dry when cut and stored. Overall the harvest was about half normal levels and of very low quality. By early 1316 food across Europe was already in short supply and the seed for the next planting was being eaten. That year was also very wet and harvests were again at about half normal levels. The second successive poor harvest produced a major crisis – wheat prices tripled, and in places of real shortage rose eight-fold. The poor could not buy food and in some places there was an absolute shortage – there was simply no food available. The poor were dying in huge numbers, bands of starving peasants swarmed across the countryside and many turned to robbery to find food or money. The food that was available was of very low quality – bread contained pigeon and pig droppings and animals that had died of disease were eaten, causing outbreaks of disease among humans. There are widespread reports of cannibalism from Britain to the Baltic; in Ireland in 1318 bodies were dug up from graves to provide food and in Silesia the bodies of executed criminals were eaten. Lack of fodder and numerous diseases killed over two-thirds of the sheep in some areas and in the four years after 1319 about two-thirds of Europe's oxen died. Although the weather was less bad and harvests improved it took many years for Europe to recover. As it did so it was, like the rest of Eurasia, hit by a major outbreak of disease – the so-called 'Black Death'.

There are no reports of bubonic plague in Eurasia after its last occurrence in Europe in 757. However, it did not die out and remained endemic among some rodents. It seems to have re-emerged, probably in Yunnan, sometime in the early fourteenth century. The efficiency and depth of the Eurasian trading links is demonstrated by the way the disease spread along the trade routes. The first major outbreak of plague occurred in China in 1331 and in 1338 it reached the Nestorian traders at Issyk Kul in central Asia. It reached the Genoan trading colony of Caffa in the Crimea in 1346 (possibly brought by the Mongol armies besieging the city). From there the plague reached Constantinople, Sicily, Egypt and southern France by the end of 1347 and northern France and southern England during the next year. Then it travelled north, reaching even Greenland and then back eastwards reaching Moscow by December 1350. It was spread by rats and infected humans who were trying to flee outbreaks of the disease. In its pneumonic form, when it was spread by direct contact between humans through coughing and sneezing, the plague was almost one hundred per cent lethal. If transmitted by fleas from

447

infected rats it probably killed just under two-thirds of those who were infected. The impact of the plague in Europe, Egypt and the Levant between 1346 and 1350 was terrible and far worse than in China. (It also spread to India and Africa but so little information is available that it is impossible to assess its impact.) In Europe and parts of south-west Asia probably about a third of the population died, in some places it was much higher and only a few remote areas escaped. Not surprisingly, it also produced disintegration within society as families were destroyed and villages were abandoned.

The plague was not a single occurrence. Over the rest of the fourteenth century there were continuing regular outbreaks across Eurasia – it was particularly bad in Europe in the 1360s and 1370s. It took almost a century and several generations, for the population to acquire some degree of immunity and for the virulence of plague outbreaks to decline. However, it remained a dreadful fact of life for centuries in Europe. Between 1347 and 1536 there was, on average, a major outbreak somewhere in Europe every eleven years and even over the next century and a half this average only fell to one every fifteen years. In the six years after 1596 about half the population of northern Spain died during one outbreak. During the seventeenth century about two million people died of the plague in France. The last occurrence of the plague in England was that of 1665 which was concentrated in London – it came from Amsterdam and at its height about 6,000 people a week were dying. The last outbreak in western Europe was in Marseilles in 1720–21 but it remained endemic in south-west Asia and Egypt for far longer.

The major impact of the plague, famine and a deteriorating climate across Eurasia was concentrated in the fourteenth century. The world's population, which had risen by over a third from 265 million in 1000 to about 360 million in 1200, did not rise over the next two centuries and probably fell back slightly. This was the result not just of the plague but also of the impact of the Mongol invasions (particularly in Iran and Mesopotamia) and almost a century of continuous warfare in China which reduced the population by a third from its peak of 115 million to 85 million by 1300. There was no recovery in China in the fourteenth century – indeed the population probably fell again significantly under the impact of the plague and was not back even to the level of 1300 by the end of the century. Overall the population of Asia in 1400 was probably no higher than it had been in 1100. In Europe the population peak came shortly after 1300 at about 80 million. Under the impact of very poor harvests, excess population, famine and then the plague, it fell by at least a quarter over the century as a whole, producing a total of no more than 60 million in 1400. For those who survived this catastrophic century, especially the generations after about 1350, there were significant improvements. Overall there was a shortage of labour compared with the amount of land available and the conditions of the peasantry, especially in the rents they had to pay, improved significantly. In addition there was less pressure on food supplies. There was no fundamental change in either the economy or society – it remained overwhelmingly dominated by agriculture – but there was some amelioration in the conditions of most of the population of Eurasia.

15.2 China: the Rise of the Ming

[Earlier China 14.5.1]
The mass peasant uprisings and religious millenarian movements that increasingly affected China from the later 1320s reached a peak after the mid-1340s and resulted in the end of Mongol rule. They produced a new group of leaders who had no links with the old elites. They came from some of the poorest groups in Chinese society and were leading what, by modern standards, would be described as revolutionary movements. The social and political turmoil led to the construction of a very different Chinese state after the Mongols left in 1368. Along the central and southern coasts the uprisings were led by Fang Kuo-chen who came from a family of fishermen and salt traders. By the late 1350s he controlled a fleet of over a thousand ships that was capturing and looting numerous port cities. Most of the lower Yangtze valley and the old Sung capital of Hangchou was controlled by Chang Shih-ch'eng who came from a family of canal boatmen. The most important of all the leaders was Chu Yüan-chang who in 1368 was to become the emperor Hung-wu, the founder of the Ming ('brightness') dynasty. Chu's choice of the unusual dynastic name of Ming may well be associated with his earlier religious beliefs, in particular the influence of Manichaeism. The revolutionary peasant uprisings of the mid-fourteenth century are often portrayed by Chinese historians as a nationalist uprising against the hated Mongols. However, there appears to have been very little anti-Mongol feeling in these primarily social revolts and Chu himself used many Mongols in his armies and rewarded them with titles.

Chu Yüan-chang is one of the central figures of Chinese history. He established a pattern of government that was to last for generations and led a remarkable recovery within China and a major expansion of its influence. He was born in 1328, the grandson of a Kiangsu goldwasher. His father was an itinerant farm labourer in Anhwei and his mother was the daughter of a master sorcerer. During the great famine of 1344, after the Yellow river burst its banks, he became a Buddhist monk. By 1348 he was the leader of a small group of peasant rebels in north-eastern Anhwei. He then joined the *Hung-chin* or 'Red Turbans' and became their leader in the area. As the revolt spread he led the peasants who captured Nanking in 1359 and within four years they controlled most of central China. Between 1365 and 1367 he eliminated most of his rival rebel leaders and in 1368 took the Mongol capital of Peking. In a little more than a decade Ming control was extended over the whole of China and beyond, including Szechwan (1371), the Kansu corridor (1372), Yunnan (1382) and eventually Korea (1392).

The overwhelming priority for the new Ming government was to rebuild China's agricultural base which had been devastated by the fighting of the thirteenth century, floods, plague and more than two decades of peasant uprisings and civil war. The sheer scale of what they were able to achieve demonstrates not only the depth of the Chinese infrastructure which had survived these disturbances but also the strength of the Chinese system of government. To encourage land reclamation population transfers were organized and immigrants were given new land and granted tax exemptions. As the programme got under way in the early 1370s about 200,000 acres a year were reclaimed but within a few years this had risen to over two million acres a year. Central to the programme was the planting of new trees and forests – in 1391 fifty million trees were planted around Nanking and five years later eighty-four million fruit trees were planted in Honan and Hupei provinces. In total about a billion trees were planted across China in the late fourteenth century. In addition some 40,000 reservoirs were either built or repaired to support irrigation schemes. By 1381–2 the Ming government was able to conduct a full census, revise it a decade later and survey the entire country in 1387.

Chu and his advisers believed that they were restoring the classic government pattern of the T'ang and the Sung. However, they had little choice but to incorporate some Mongol practices used over the previous century or more and they also made their own innovations. The result was a very different style of government, and one which was to set the pattern for Chinese government until the mid-nineteenth century. Chu was suspicious of both the people who had risen to power with him and the educated elite who made up most of the Chinese administration. He tried to bring in more administrators from less privileged social groups and immediately on taking power set up a national university at Nanking to train a new generation of bureaucrats. However, patronage remained the key to selection and advance within the system. Chu suppressed the old Central Secretariat, which had held the key to power under the Mongols, and took direct control of the six main ministries. These were the three chief departments of finance, public works and the army together with justice, public administration and rites. He also took control of military strategy through a co-ordinating board. Within little more than a decade the new emperor found that it was impossible for him to take all the key decisions – the scope and complexity of Chinese government (especially when compared with the very limited capabilities of most Eurasian governments at this time) was such that this was beyond the capabilities of any one person. In 1382 a major reorganization took place. A special staff of five 'grand secretaries' was created to act closely with the emperor and on his behalf. Chu still distrusted most of the administration and in parallel created the *chin-i-wei* ('The Guards with Brocade Uniforms'), a sort of primitive spying system to keep control of government officials. (Their powers were reduced significantly in 1387.) Overall the new system of government concentrated much greater power in the hands of the emperor than ever before. It also established the use of secret committees and special advisers operating only for the emperor as opposed to the more structured bureaucratic system that existed earlier.

Chu died in 1398 after overseeing the re-establishment of Chinese government and economic and social recovery. His successor attempted to restrict the power of the imperial princes who were, in the fashion of most pre-industrial empires, the governors of the main provinces. This led to the rebellion of one of his uncles, Chu Ti, who commanded the armies of the Peking region. He captured Nanking in 1402, took power as the emperor Yung-lo, and ruled until 1424. His reign, which was built on the widespread recovery in the last three decades of the fourteenth century, was to witness one of the most remarkable periods in Chinese history.

15.3 China and the Surrounding World

Chinese expansion began under Chu Yüan-chang and continued under Yung-lo. In the north the Mongol kingdom set up after the loss of China collapsed. The two main nomadic groups to the north of China were now the Oirats in the north-west and the Tatars in the north-east. (The latter are usually wrongly called Tartars by Europeans – the Tartars of later Russian history were of a different Turkish origin.) In the first decade of the fifteenth century Chinese armies advanced further north than ever before and in 1410 at the battle of the river Onon, north-east of Ulan Bator in Mongolia, the nomadic groups were heavily defeated. Mongolia was occupied by the Chinese as far north as the Amur river. Four years earlier a Chinese army over 200,000-strong intervened in Vietnam, defeated local forces and ended the rule of the long-established Tran dynasty. The Red river area and much of central Vietnam was annexed. However, as in the

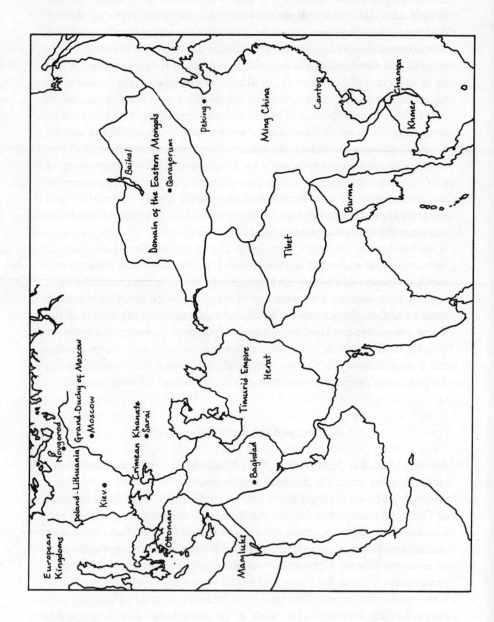

Map 49: Eurasia in the early fifteenth century

past, it proved too difficult for any Chinese dynasty to maintain control of this area. In 1418 a revolt led by Le Loi drove out the Chinese within a decade and set up the new Vietnamese dynasty of the Le. Chinese diplomatic missions were also sent westwards into central Asia, reaching Transoxania in 1413, 1416 and 1420 although there was no attempt to recreate the extensive control the Chinese had exercised in the area under the T'ang before 750. One of the palace eunuchs, Hou Hsien, was perhaps the most extensive Chinese traveller in the area. He visited Tibet and India in 1403–6, Nepal in 1413, Bengal in 1415 and 1420 (travelling on the second occasion by sea) and Tibet again in 1427. The re-establishment of a strong dynasty in China also led to numerous diplomatic and trade missions from the surrounding area. In the year after Chu took power (1369) there were missions from Korea, Japan, Vietnam and Champa. In the next two years they were followed by ones from the remains of the Khmer kingdom, Thailand and Malaya. In 1390 representatives from the Coromandel coast of India arrived. In 1408 the king of Borneo died in Nanking, he had lived there with his family and court for several years. In the same year and again in 1441 representatives from the Mamluks of Egypt arrived in China.

Even more remarkable were the voyages that the Chinese undertook across south-east Asia and the Indian Ocean as far as the coast of Africa. These are often portrayed as 'voyages of exploration' but, as we have seen in previous chapters, the Chinese had long been trading and sailing across the Indian Ocean. They were, in particular, very familiar with the east African coast where they bought ivory, rhino horn, pearls and various spices and aromatics. The earliest Chinese coin hoards found on the east African coast date to 620 and huge quantities of tenth-century porcelain have been found at sites along the Tanzanian coast. A ninth-century Chinese book contains details of Berbera, and the *Hsin T'ang Shu*, which dates to 1060, has details of the port of Malindi and the rest of the Kenyan coast. A book of 1178 describes Madagascar at length. A Chinese map which dates to 1402 (and Korean ones too) show southern Africa pointing in the right direction – the Europeans still thought it pointed east. The Chinese also knew a considerable amount about the area from their contacts with the large number of Islamic traders who frequented the ports of southern China. The fifteenth-century voyages were therefore not an exploration of an unknown world but journeys along well-frequented and long-established routes that had for thousands of years been part of a single trading network. They were the re-establishment of old contacts now that China had recovered from a period of internal turmoil.

The great voyages were under the command of Cheng Ho (1371–1433), a eunuch, ambassador and formally 'Admiral of the Triple Treasure'. He came from a Muslim family in Yunnan. His father had made the pilgrimage to Mecca so he would have been well aware of the trading and pilgrimage routes to south-east Asia and across the Indian Ocean. Between 1405 and 1433 he made seven voyages in large fleets of over sixty massive sea-going junks of about 1,500 tons, each capable of carrying about 500 men as well as cargo. (The European ships which reached the Indian Ocean about a century later were of about 300 tons and the total Chinese navy consisted of about 6,500 ships by this date.) The first three voyages in 1405–11 were to Java, Thailand, Sri Lanka together with Calicut and Cochin on the Indian coast. In 1415 he sailed to Sumatra and then directly across the Indian Ocean to Aden before visiting Ormuz, the Gulf and the Maldive Islands. The final three voyages were to east Africa, especially Mogadishu, Mozambique and the Straits of Madagascar. It was on one of these voyages that two giraffes were sent from Malindi to China ahead of the returning convoy.

These voyages were very different from those of the Europeans in the early sixteenth century. There was no attempt to conquer the people the Chinese met nor to convert them – the latter idea was unknown to the Chinese who themselves practised a variety of religions. Nor was there any attempt to impose Chinese culture, values and domination, still less enslave the people they met. The Chinese were already well aware of the people they were to visit as is shown by events on Sri Lanka when the fleet arrived in 1409. A stele commemorating the event was erected with inscriptions in three languages – Chinese, Tamil and Persian. Gifts were also brought from the emperor for all the three religions on the island. They were made to Buddhism, in particular the famous Temple of the Tooth at Kandy, to the Tamil god Devundara Deviyo and to various Islamic mosques. In total the gifts amounted to 1,000 pieces of gold, 5,000 pieces of silver and 100 rolls of silk together with other items. On the return to China the results of the voyages were published on a large scale. The three most famous books were the *Treatise on the Barbarian Kingdoms of the Western Oceans* (1434), *The Marvels Discovered by the Boat Bound for the Galaxy* (1436) and *The Marvels of the Oceans* (1451). By the time the last book was published the main voyages were long over but, having re-established contacts, Chinese traders continued to sail across south-east Asia and the Indian Ocean.

[*Compare with early European expansion 15.11 & 17.1*]

15.4 China: Stability

From the 1430s the main attention of the Chinese government was turned not to south-east Asia (an unproblematic trading area) but to the northern frontier. This was the consequence of two factors. In 1421 Peking became the capital, replacing Nanking which had held that position since 1368, although the final transfer of all government functions was not completed until 1450. Peking (or cities in this area) had been the capital under the Khitan, Jürchen and Mongols but this was the first time a Chinese dynasty had had its capital so far north and so far from the rich agricultural and trading areas of the Yangtze and the south. The move was made possible by further work on the Grand Canal following its restoration and extension to Peking under the Mongols. In 1411–15 a series of large, deep-water locks were completed which meant that even the largest vessels could now use the canal throughout the year, thereby reducing the need for coastal voyages. However, the major problem with making Peking the capital was that it was almost a frontier city and remained vulnerable to invasions by nomadic peoples from the steppe. This became a real worry with the increasing incursions by the Oirats, who had been reunified under Essen Khan in the 1440s. Between 1449 and 1457 they even held the emperor Cheng-t'ung prisoner and the Chinese were forced to ransom him. The Chinese response was to withdraw inside the Great Walls built between 1403 and 1435 along the approximate line of the sixth-century fortifications. A new 'inner' Great Wall was built in the 1440s and extended between 1465 and 1487. In places there were double and even triple walls and overall they stretched for 3,000 miles (it is these walls that tourists currently see near Peking). From the mid-fifteenth century the Chinese made little attempt to advance northwards but were content to defend the frontier.

In its early years the Ming dynasty established military colonies in the main frontier areas – around Peking and in the south-west (Yunnan and Kweichow) – as well as immediately around the first capital Nanking and along the Grand Canal (to ensure the security of this vital supply line). In each ten-man unit three were soldiers and seven were farmers supplying the food to maintain the fighting men. Such a system was not new and had been adopted by other governments as one of the few ways of supporting military units in remote frontier areas given the difficulty of moving large amounts of food by land. At first the obligations of the units were hereditary, again the only way of maintaining units in the furthest reaches of the empire. Not unexpectedly, the system began to break down by the mid-fifteenth century. The descendants of the original 'army families' began to desert to more congenial occupations and the lands used to support the colonies were increasingly taken over by local landlords, even though this was technically illegal. As the wealth of China increased, the agricultural foundations were rebuilt and trade recovered, it was possible to shift to a more sophisticated system for sustaining the army. The government did not favour creating local militias, suspecting that they would become the leaders of revolts. Instead tax revenue had risen sufficiently to pay for a major mercenary army. The army estates in the north of the country were taken over by merchants. They rented the land to peasants and then sold their produce to the soldiers.

These changes were only possible because of the wider changes in the Chinese economy which reinforced its position as by far the wealthiest in Eurasia. Until the late fourteenth century and during the major period of recovery, the Ming had to revert to the old system of government taxes being paid in kind. Gradually a fully monetary economy was rebuilt. In 1394 copper coins were redeemed for the new paper currency then being issued and in 1403 the government decreed that gold and silver were not to be used in business transactions, only paper currency. The civil service was also paid in paper money. However, the government was not as prudent as the Sung and printed too many notes. The resulting inflation produced a crash in the value of the paper currency from the mid-fifteenth century and its increasing replacement by a silver currency. This took place first in the main commercial areas – the lower Yangtze valley and the trading cities of the southern coast. It was gradually adopted for all transactions – for provincial taxes to the central government in 1465, the salt tax in 1475 and in 1485–6 it was decreed that all craftsmen and peasants could avoid corvée duties by paying the tax in silver. This system once again demonstrates the fact that the Chinese economy was fully monetarized with the peasants selling their produce rather than giving it up in kind. By the late fifteenth century China had a silver-based economy.

During the fifteenth century the nature of Chinese government also changed. It became much less centralized after 1430 as the provincial 'grand co-ordinators' became effectively responsible for all aspects of administration. At the centre the 'grand secretaries' created by the first Ming emperor in 1382 became increasingly powerful – they were given formal administrative posts from 1424 and two years later a formal 'Grand Secretariat' (effectively the same as that suppressed in 1368) was recreated and consisted of the heads of the six main ministries, the five chief military men and the head of the censorate. The original Ming idea of the emperor personally supervising every aspect of government was not restored and much of the old bureaucratic structure was recreated. Equally important though was the rise of the power of the eunuchs within government. By the early fifteenth century they had command of the emperor's personal guard, management of the imperial workshops and control of tribute payments. In the 1420s a new secret service the *tung-ch'ang* ('Eastern Esplanade') under eunuch control replaced the older

Brocaded Guards. In general the eunuchs tended to be drawn from the north of the country and not from the old southern elite who still supplied most of the administrators through the examination system. By the last quarter of the fifteenth century the emperor was increasingly dominated by the eunuchs within the imperial court.

The distinguishing characteristic of China until the late sixteenth century was the high degree of stability and prosperity across the country. Although there were peasant revolts these were on a relatively small scale and easily contained. The population continued to grow – doubling from about 80 million in 1400 to 160 million in 1600 – far faster than the world average. Even so the pressure on land and food supplies from a population at least a third higher than its previous peak in 1200 seems to have been contained through slow increases in productivity and bringing still more land into cultivation. Internal and external trade was at a high level despite a formal ban on the latter which was not lifted until 1567. In a monetarized economy the wealthy landlords could live on their rents in the great cities – Peking had a population of 672,000 in 1500 and was by far the largest city in the world. In addition there were other major cities so that four of the seven largest in the world were in China – Hangchou (375,000), Nanking (285,000) and Canton (250,000) – even though they were smaller than under the Sung. (There were only two European cities in the top twenty in the world in 1500 – the larger was Paris at 225,000, whereas London had just 50,000). At the same time industrial production recovered – by the mid-fifteenth century all the state craftsmen established under the early Ming during the period of recovery had moved to private employment. More and more peasants were taking up part-time industrial employment, especially in textile manufacturing, during the seasons when the requirements of agricultural labour were at their lowest, thereby increasing still further their involvement in the monetary economy. There is no doubt that by the sixteenth century China was by far the richest and most developed economy and society in Eurasia.
[*Later China 17.15.3 & 19.2*]

15.5 Korea, Japan and South-East Asia

15.5.1 Korea
[*Earlier Korea 13.6.1*]
Korea was under Mongol control until their rule in China collapsed. On the establishment of the Ming it was briefly semi-independent until the Chinese re-established their dominance following the coup by the Korean military leader Yi Song-gye against the old Koryo dynasty in 1388. The

foreign policy of the new Yi dynasty was described as *sadae* or 'serving the great' – three tribute missions a year were sent to China. Numerous institutions were also adopted from the Ming. The examination system produced an administrative class or *yangban* which came to dominate the state. Gunpowder weapons, especially cannon and rockets, were taken from the Chinese and a new government department, the Superintendency for Gunpowder Weapons, set up. In 1401 a paper currency modelled on that of the Chinese was introduced. In 1400 all the old aristocratic units were incorporated into the central army which had a professional elite and was made up of conscripts. A full land survey of the kingdom was carried out in 1390, the old aristocratic families were dispossessed, the followers of Yi Song-gye were given land around the capital and the rest was taken as state land. However, this system could not be sustained. It broke down during the fifteenth century as more land passed into private hands and as it was given to support army units, government institutions and Buddhist monasteries and temples. As the wealth of Korea increased, officials were paid cash salaries after 1566 rather than being given land. There were also two crucial developments within Korea under the early Yi dynasty. The first was the earliest use anywhere in the world of movable metal type in printing. The second was the development of the Korean script. In the early centuries CE Korea had, like Japan later, adopted the Chinese script even though, again like Japan, it was unsuitable for the polysyllabic and agglutinative Korean language. In the late seventh century a syllabic script of thirty-six signs was developed from the original Chinese signs but the system soon became confused as more signs were added. A few decades after the introduction of movable-type printing the system was reformed under King Sejong and a new popular script was introduced in 1446. It had eleven vowels and seventeen consonants but did not replace Chinese completely – like the Japanese system, but in a much less complicated way, it was used to clarify the ambiguities that were endemic in the old script.

15.5.2 Japan
[*Earlier Japan 13.6.2*]
The hundred miles of ocean which separated Japan from the Eurasian mainland again ensured that its history was individual and its development almost entirely governed by internal factors. It had avoided attack by the Mongols in 1274 and again in 1281 when the *kamikaze* or 'divine wind' (a typhoon) destroyed the invasion fleet. However, the cost of anti-invasion preparations and the building of fortifications was large and caused major difficulties for the Kamakura shogunate government. Internally it was divided and many of the other military families had little or no loyalty to the Hojo family which had taken power in the 1230s. The

hereditary warrior class was also expanding (there was no primogeniture) but the amount of land to support them did not increase proportionately – they had growing debts and they became increasingly poor. Overall the powers of the shogunate at Kamakura were limited and central government was weak.

The decisive factor in the early fourteenth century was the split in the imperial line at Kyoto and the attempt by various factions to increase power at the expense of the shogunate. In 1331 a revolt by Go-Daigo, from one of the imperial lines, led to the Genko civil war which spread across most of Japan. In 1333 a Kamakura general, Ashikaga Takauji, was sent to capture Go-Daigo. But he was anti-Hojo, changed sides and supported Go-Daigo. For the next three years Go-Daigo tried to re-establish full imperial government (the Kemmu restoration) but ultimately lost after Ashikaga defeated his rivals in the Kanto area, captured Kyoto and then seized Go-Daigo in 1336. Almost immediately Go-Daigo escaped and set up a weak imperial government at Yoshino. For more than fifty years there were two rival imperial lines in Japan around which various military factions manoeuvred for power and influence. The period ended in 1392 when the Yoshino line gave up the struggle and returned to Kyoto.

After his capture of Kyoto, Ashikaga used the imperial line he controlled to set up his position as shogun from 1338 and inaugurate the line of shoguns that survived until 1573. However, the government system and the power it wielded was very different from the original shogunate established at Kamakura some 150 years earlier. Although there was little challenge to the Ashikaga family and their title of shogun, their power was very limited across Japan. In theory they appointed the local and provincial governors but in practice they only ratified the position of the powerful local lords and major estate holders. These local lords, later known as daimyo, were the key figures who, over the next two centuries, slowly accumulated more and more power as they made and re-made various alliances. They brought in more followers and warriors and gradually established a system where family loyalty was uppermost and in which only one son (chosen or adopted, rather than through primogeniture) was to inherit (women were excluded from inheritance). Society was dominated by this warrior elite with its special chivalric code of bravery, loyalty and honour. The last was enshrined in the practice of suicide through disembowelling on defeat known as *seppuku* (the western term 'harakiri' is a vulgar Japanese term meaning 'belly-slitting'). Within the central government at Kyoto the military (represented by the shogunate) gained power over almost every area. Because the government of the shogun was now in Kyoto rather than Kamakura a key post of *kanrei* or 'manager' emerged at Kamakura where most of the Ashikaga family estates were located and where economic power was centred. This was held by a member of the Ashikaga family until 1439 when, after a failed revolt, it was given to the Uesugi family. The shogunate was able to keep the peace until 1467 when growing conflicts between the daimyo spilled over into more than a century of almost continuous warfare.

Despite the relative turbulence of Japanese political development at this time, economically it was a period of growing wealth and prosperity. Agriculture was highly productive using the same high-yielding varieties of rice as in China, together with sophisticated irrigation systems and large quantities of fertilizers. Probably about two-thirds of the land was covered by *shöen* or estates owned by the nobility together with *zaichi-ryoshu* or local overlords who were mainly the military elite. However, the peasants in the villages gained significant levels of autonomy – they rather than the proprietor adjudicated on crimes committed in the village – and major peasant revolts and protests in 1428 and 1441 secured the abrogation of all debts. Increasingly the peasants shifted from being self-sufficient and paying their taxes and dues in kind (usually to Kyoto-based landlords) to much greater involvement in the money economy as trade and wealth spread through society. From the eleventh century Japan traded with Korea and China in its own ships and in 1404, after the third Ashikaga shogun Yoshimitsu had entered into a formal tributary relationship with the Ming, trade was regulated through a formal treaty. Japan sold copper, sulphur, timber and specialist swords (37,000 a year by the 1480s) to China. In return large quantities of Chinese currency flooded into the country. A money economy was created and merchants soon created credit mechanisms, money-transfer systems and loans at interest through the bankers or *doso* ('storehouse men'). Merchants were able to cope with local power centres and formed *za*, roughly similar to the European guilds, to negotiate with rulers and gain exemption from local taxes. Merchants became autonomous units within the major trading cities. In the west ports trading with the mainland grew – Hakata (now part of Fukuoka) and Sakai (later part of Osaka) and inland fortress towns had large markets.

From the thirteenth century Buddhism grew rapidly in Japan and acquired its own unique characteristics as it evolved from its Chinese progenitors. Most of the warrior elite were Buddhists but there was not the confusion between chivalry and religion which emerged among similar groups in Europe – in Japan the two concepts were kept very separate. In 1175 the *Jodo* sect arrived in Japan with its belief in the paradise of the Buddha Amida and rebirth there through simply and sincerely repeating the name of Buddha. The Buddhist court at Kyoto ruled against it as being non-Buddhist, which indeed it was because it discarded nearly all of the Buddha's teachings. Nevertheless it became highly popular. From 1222 the

Nichiren sect developed. It shared many characteristics with the Pure Land school but placed its emphasis on the Lotus Sutra and had a much stronger Japanese element. By far the most influential, especially at Kyoto during the Ashikaga shogunate, was Zen which was introduced by monks who had been to China in the twelfth century – the *Rinzai* sect was formalized in 1191 and the *Soto* in 1227. Despite their differences they both stressed character, discipline and the rejection of scholasticism together with an emphasis on the role of the guru and the direct experience of enlightenment. The later could be obtained through *zazen* (sitting in meditation) and the use of *koan* – insoluble intellectual problems designed to produce sudden enlightenment.
[*Later Japan 18.6*]

15.5.3 South-east Asia
[*Earlier South-east Asia 12.2.1*]
Unlike Japan, south-east Asia remained at the centre of the ocean trade routes and the key link between the Indian Ocean and the seas dominated by China. The important development in the late thirteenth century, after the Mongol raids were over, was the accession of Ketarajasa to the throne of Majapahit in central Java in 1294. Under his rule much greater internal control was achieved, with taxes paid direct to the central state rather than via local rulers. There was, for almost the first time in south-east Asia, a direct link between the agricultural surplus generated in the increasingly commercialized wet-rice production areas and control over the trading ports along the coast. Majapahit also extended its control over Sumatra, parts of Borneo and the Malay peninsula so as to create the most extensive trading empire seen in the area. Most of its wealth derived from fairly light taxation on the international trade which passed through its various ports. Trade with China was particularly important as merchants came to buy the wide variety of spices available and as a result large amounts of bullion flowed into the Majapahit state. When Marco Polo arrived there on his way home from China he thought it was the wealthiest place on earth – far richer than Europe.

Ultimately the Majapahit rulers could not keep control over the whole of the empire. In 1402 Prince Paramesvara, a fugitive from south-east Sumatra, conquered the small city of Malacca which dominated the more northerly trade route through the Straits of Malacca. During the course of the fifteenth century it was to become the dominant trading city of the region. It was part of a new development under which a single city port could thrive as an independent state because of the wealth it could generate from trade – it no longer needed to incorporate the inland areas as long as it could ensure the continued flow of products and food. In parallel with

Malacca other states such as Aceh and Johore became important, but they too relied on major food imports – rice, salt, dried fish and pepper – to sustain their inhabitants. The more goods that could be encouraged to flow through their cities the greater their role in the crucial international trade and the cities were therefore engaged in an intense commercial rivalry. Across the whole of south-east Asia trade was already at a very high level – the same level as in the eighteenth century when it was dominated by the Europeans. Malacca was typical of all these cities. It originated in military conquest but rapidly changed to a policy of political neutrality and low taxes to encourage trade. In this it was highly successful – by 1500 it had traders from over sixty different countries and cities across the Indian Ocean and Asian trading network from Cairo to China, Okinawa in the Ryukyu islands, India and every area of south-east Asia. Each of these communities had separate residential areas within the city and each was entitled to autonomy and freedom from control from the local ruler – that was the price he was willing to pay for the revenue trade generated. The largest group at Malacca were the Gujarati traders from the main centre of Indian trade.

The period from the late thirteenth century saw a growing impact from Islam in south-east Asia although few details about how this occurred are known. Many of the elite had earlier been influenced by Hinduism and Buddhism as they spread along the trade routes from India – it was part of the process by which these areas were incorporated into the wider world. The main influences in the dissemination of Islam appear to have been the merchants trading from Arabia, the Gulf and India who settled in the ports, often married into local families and spread a religion that appealed to those local rulers who were opposed to the existing Hindu elites. In addition there were Islamic missionaries from Gujarat, Bengal and Arabia, especially Sufis, who turned Islam into a highly popular religion across the region and not just one for the elite. A few indications of the spread of Islam can be found. In 1282 the Hindu Malay ruler of Samudra in northern Sumatra had Muslim advisers and when Ibn-Batuta called there in 1345–6 during his various journeys he found a large group of Islamic scholars. In 1292 Marco Polo also reported a large Muslim community at Pasai not far from Samudra. The rulers of Malacca converted to Islam in the early fifteenth century and this formed a base for its further spread. In 1474 the Malay rulers of Pahang, Kedah and Patani all converted and Islam also spread to the coastal communities of Java such as Tuban and from there to the interior. In 1498 the Moluccas converted followed by the coastal towns of Borneo and from there Islam spread to the Philippines.

The whole area of south-east Asia was fully incorporated into the vast trading world that linked the Islamic heartland, India and China. Ibn-

Majid, who wrote a handbook for mariners in the late fifteenth century, before any Europeans had reached the area, set out the sailing times and monsoons from the Gulf and Red Sea through to China. He also included details not only of all the East African coast but also of how to round the Cape of Good Hope, and sail up the west coast of Africa to reach the Mediterranean from the Atlantic.
[*Later Indian Ocean world 17.10–17.13*]

15.6 Temur

[*Earlier central Asia 14.5.4*]
Temur, or as he is often known Timur-i-lang (from the Persian for Temur the lame), was the last of the great nomadic conquerors to affect the sedentary societies of Eurasia. His career and aims were deeply influenced by the earlier achievements of the Mongols and their ability to rule over the surrounding settled societies. He was, however, far less successful than his predecessors, though the level of destruction he caused was often as great as during the Mongol conquests. He was born some time around 1330 near Samarkand and he emerged from being part of the leading family of the Barlas clan to head a tribal confederacy within the Ulus Chaghatai, one of the successor 'states' to the Mongol Chaghatai khanate after it broke up in 1334. His career followed the standard pattern for a charismatic military leader on the steppe within a highly fractured political structure with almost no central government.

By 1370 he gained power over the Ulus Chaghatai, a mixed pastoral and settled zone around Transoxania and northern and eastern Afghanistan. The rest of Temur's life until his death in 1405 was to be one of almost ceaseless campaigning. He replaced many of the old tribal leaders with his own appointees but only exercised the most minimal control over them. Ultimately his power depended on his ability to provide his followers with loot. This helps to explain why so many of his campaigns went over old ground and why there was little attempt to create a government for the areas nominally under his control. In 1380–1 he campaigned in Khurasan before moving to western Iran. In the late 1380s he concentrated on Iran and the Caucasus (he nominally conquered Georgia) before turning on the Qipchaq Horde to the north. In 1393 he repeated the Mongol conquest of Baghdad and the next year he was attacking Moscow. Four years later he attacked Delhi. In the first years of the fifteenth century he recaptured Baghdad, reconquered Georgia and also took Damascus and Aleppo. The destruction, massacres and looting on these campaigns was extensive and halted the recovery from the Mongol invasions over a century earlier. In

1404 he set off to conquer Ming China but died early the next year. Temur's army was a motley collection of Muslims, Christians, Turks, Tajiks, Arabs, Georgians and Indians. In the areas that were 'conquered' local rulers were left in place as long as they transferred tax revenues to Temur – they often contributed troops to the campaigns but they were never admitted to the nomadic elite around Temur.

Not surprisingly the 'empire' of Temur split immediately on his death and the struggle for power, which was again highly destructive, lasted until about 1420 when all attempts to reunite the disparate territories was abandoned. Ulugh-beg established control over Transoxania and the major cities of Samarkand and Bukhara and produced another variant of the Iranian-Islamic synthesis which had been under way for eight hundred years. It was a wealthy kingdom, gaining its revenues from the central Asian trade networks and using them to construct numerous impressive buildings in the main cities, especially mosques. More marginal areas such as Azerbaijan, Fars and the Caucasus, split away under local rulers. The other major successor state was that in Khurasan and the adjacent regions with its capital at Herat. For forty years after 1407 it was headed by Shah Rukh who developed a strict Islamic regime.

[*Later central Asia 18.4*]

15.7 The Rise and Defeat of the Ottomans

As the Mongols expanded in the thirteenth century a number of Turkic peoples drifted westwards and settled in western Anatolia in an area of disputed land between the Byzantines and the Seljuqs. The Ottomans were one of these groups and of little or no importance until the mid-fourteenth century. However, within little more than a century they had captured Constantinople and ended the state that was the last, very distant, successor of the Roman empire. They also controlled most of the Balkans and had extended Islam further into Europe than ever before. By the early sixteenth century they also controlled south-west Asia and Egypt and were extending their power across the Mediterranean.

By the time the Ottomans moved into Anatolia the Byzantines had revived from the nadir of 1204 when Constantinople was captured and looted by the crusaders directed by Venice and the empire was partitioned between them. The most successful of the small Byzantine successor states was that centred around Nicaea. Gradually, in conflict with its rivals such as the state of Epirus in Greece, it extended its control until in 1261 the old capital was regained by the emperor Michael VIII Palaeologus, in alliance with Genoa, the main rival of Venice. However, the revived Byzantine state controlled little, even compared with the weak late-twelfth-century empire. Most of Greece was still under rulers from western Europe, the Greek islands were nearly all controlled by Venice, Cyprus was ruled by a French dynasty and in the northern Balkans Serbia and Bulgaria were independent. It was also relatively easy for a number of local *ghazi* leaders such as the Ottomans to found little 'states' in Anatolia between 1260 and 1320 on land taken from the Byzantines in a *gaza* or 'holy war'. From the start the duty to spread Islam was central to the Ottomans, although they did not see this as involving massive wars of destruction. As a frontier society the Ottoman state was cosmopolitan and contained large numbers of Christians from the beginning. It was highly tolerant, even by Islamic standards, and the aim of expansion was simply to subdue and control the 'infidel' and bring them within the wider Islamic world. Institutionally the Ottomans incorporated many of the existing Seljuq government practices and the towns remained largely self-governing.

By 1320 the Ottomans had expanded as far as Bursa. Over the next two decades the Byzantines were plagued by incessant civil war leading by 1339 to the loss of nearly all their territory in Anatolia to the Ottomans. The Byzantines decided to concentrate on defending Thrace where most of the estates of the emperor John Cantacuzenus were located – by this time the emperors were no more than one member of the small ruling aristocracy. This allowed the Ottomans under their leader, Orhan, to make a decisive move by annexing the small principality of Karesi on the eastern side of the Dardanelles in 1345. The next year Orhan allied with John V Cantacuzenus, a claimant to the Byzantine throne, and married his daughter Theodora. In 1352 Orhan's son Suleyman was aiding John, now emperor, in his battles against the Serbs and Bulgarians. During the campaign he took the fortress of Tzympe on Gallipoli, refused to give it up, took more key points and moved large numbers of troops and later settlers from Karesi on to the western side of the Dardanelles. From this base the Ottomans were able to expand into the Balkans.

The main period of Ottoman expansion came under Murad after 1360. They met little concerted opposition from the weak and divided Christian states. The key was the capture of Adrianople in Thrace in 1369 which opened up relatively easy routes into the Balkans. Three years later the Dobrudja and Bulgaria were conquered, to the west the Albanian coast was reached by 1385 and two years later Thessalonika was taken. From here it was possible to move north through the passes. The key victory was at the battle of Kosovo in 1389 when the Serb armies were utterly defeated and nearly all of the Balkans taken. The kingdom of Serbia was finally reduced to vassal status in 1396 after feeble crusading forces were defeated at the battle of Nicopolis. The Byzantines were left as a small rump state just able to defend the city of Constantinople, but they were an Ottoman dependency. Ottoman military effectiveness was, in a common Islamic pattern, based on their slave army first formed from prisoners of war after the capture of Adrianople. They were known as *yeniçeri* or 'janissaries' to the Europeans. The difference in the Ottoman army was that slave soldiers were recruited from the non-Muslim population within the empire rather than from outside (as in all other examples). This policy was known as *devsirme* or 'rotation' because it was applied to the provinces in succession. Most soldiers came from the frontier areas and only the sultan not the local commanders was allowed to recruit in this way. The Ottoman military levy was probably no worse than the feudal and other levies on the peasant population made by the previous Christian rulers. Indeed Ottoman rule tended to increase the power of the state and brought a greater degree of order into a world where earlier feudal disintegration and the power of local lords over the peasants had reached high levels. To this extent it probably benefited the peasants by reducing over-exploitation and setting taxes and levies at sustainable levels. Slowly Ottoman and other Muslim settlers moved into the Balkans from Anatolia establishing their own farming colonies. The Ottoman state was highly tolerant and non-believers only had to pay a poll tax – by the seventeenth century many state offices were specifically reserved for Christians (a formalization of existing practices). Local elites were generally incorporated and many became part of the Ottoman army and provided their own soldiers to fight alongside the elite *yaniçeri*.

The Ottomans also expanded eastwards across Anatolia where they came into contact with the principalities of Eretna (with its capital at Sivas) and Karaman, which included Konya the old Seljuq capital. The latter was defeated in 1387 by an Ottoman army largely composed of Serbian and Christian troops. By the end of the 1390s most of these small states were conquered and the Ottomans ruled an empire which stretched from the Danube to the Euphrates. At this point the Ottomans came up against Temur and his army of nomadic warriors. In 1402 they were decisively defeated at the battle of Ankara where their ruler, Sultan Bayezid, was taken prisoner. In Anatolia local rulers were re-established under Temur's control, the remainder of the Ottoman territories were divided up among Bayezid's sons who then struggled for control over the empire and in the Balkans local rulers tried to re-establish their independence. It seemed that the most likely outcome of the defeat would be the disintegration of the Ottoman state.

OVERVIEW 10

THE WORLD IN
1400

World Population: 350 million
Regional Population: India: 100 million, China: 80 million,
Rest of Asia: 85 million, Europe: 60 million (France
11 million, Italy 7 million, Germany 6.5 million, England
2.5 million), Africa: 40 million
Major cities: Nanking (475,000), Cairo (450,000),
Vijayanagar (350,000), Hangchou (300,000),
Peking (300,000), Canton (300,000), Paris (275,000),
Kyoto (200,000), Milan (125,000), Venice (100,000),
Samarkand (100,000), Damascus (100,000),
Baghdad (100,000), London (45,000), Chan-Chan (45,000)

Events:

★   Chinese recovery under Ming largely complete – expansion into
Mongolia and Korea. Start of voyages to south-east Asia, Indian
Ocean, Gulf and East Africa

★   Ashikaga shogunate in Japan

★   Malacca established – replacing Majapahit at centre of south-
east Asian trade routes

★   'Empire' of Temur at its height. Emergence of Safavid movement
in Iran

★   Delhi sultanates in decline in north India

★   Vijayanagar state in south India

★   Mamluks ruling Egypt and Levant

★   Ottomans controlling most of Balkans and Anatolia. Rump Byzantine state around Constantinople

★   City states of Italy prosperous

★   'Great Schism' in papacy

★   Hiatus in 'Hundred Years War' between England and France

★   Islamic control in Iberia restricted to Andalucia

★   Poland-Lithuania major kingdom in eastern Europe

★   Mongols still dominant over Rus

★   Contact lost with Viking settlements in Greenland

★   Small city-states in valley of Mexico, including 'Aztecs' at Tenochtitlan

★   Chimu empire in north and central Peru

★   First Inca conquests in Andes

★   Empire of Mali dominant in west Africa – centred on Timbuktu

★   Benin state in forest region of west Africa

★   Paper currency restored in China and Korea

★   Movable wooden type used in China

★   Movable metal type developed in Korea

★   First production of cast iron in Europe

★   First manufacture of paper in France, Germany and Italy

15.8 Ottoman Revival and Expansion

In the twenty years after the battle of Ankara the Ottoman world was divided by internal conflicts and constantly shifting alliances between the different groups in the Balkans and Anatolia. Much of the latter area still owed allegiance to Temur's son Shahrukh and even the Byzantines were able to gather enough strength to recapture the key city of Thessalonika. It was not until 1423 that Murad was able to gain sole power among the Ottomans and start to rebuild the state – a process that was to take almost thirty years. At first he made peace in Anatolia to avoid the problems of a two-front war which was always a major danger for the Ottomans. By 1430 Thessalonika was recaptured from the Byzantines and a major conflict began with the Hungarian kingdom for control of the Balkans. In 1439 the Ottomans regained Serbia although it was almost immediately lost again as a major military effort had to be made to keep control of Anatolia in the east. Effective control of the Balkans was achieved by victory over the Hungarians at the battle of Varna in 1444. By this date the Ottomans had almost restored their position to that of 1402 and were about to make their most spectacular gains.

By the 1430s the Byzantines had lost most of their military strength and controlled only the city of Constantinople and that largely because the Ottomans were still too busy elsewhere. Their last hope was to enlist western European support in an anti-Islamic crusade and that depended on a reunion of the churches which had been separated for the last four hundred years. After long negotiations that objective was finally achieved, largely on Latin terms, at the Council of Ferrara and Florence in 1439. It did not, however, bring any military support – western Europe was too weak and too preoccupied with its own problems. The end of the old East Roman empire followed the accession of Sultan Mehmed II in 1451. He was able to assemble an army that outnumbered the defenders of Constantinople by ten to one. The attackers also had effective cannon able to create breaches in the walls that had been impregnable for a thousand years. In 1453 Constantinople was captured. The Byzantine empire was finally at an end although two minor units survived. The Greek province of Morea, with its capital of Mistra near Sparta, was already an Ottoman vassal state and it was finally absorbed and conquered in 1460. A year later the last outpost at Trebizond fell to the Ottomans. Constantinople was rebuilt and repopulated after the long Byzantine decline and turned into the capital city of a major empire. The Topkapi palace and the great imperial mosque were built together with the huge covered market. Within a century and a half the population had risen to about 700,000 making it the second largest city in the world. The Greek colloquial name for the city was adopted in Turkish as Istanbul but in official usage, documents and coins the city remained Kustantiniyye until 1920. The Ottomans borrowed much from the remains of the Byzantine administration and always called their conquered territory in south-eastern Europe *Rum-li* or 'Rome-land' and the Sultan was addressed as *Qaysar-i-Rum* or 'Caesar of Rome' by his fellow Muslim rulers.

After the capture of Constantinople Ottoman expansion continued. In 1454 the Ottoman fleet (the lack of one had been a major early weakness) operated in the Black Sea and the Genoese colonies there recognized Ottoman suzerainty. In the north the Danube became the frontier after the siege of Belgrade failed in 1456. The remaining small independent units in the Balkans were mopped up – Serbia (1459), Morea (1460), Bosnia (1463) and northern Albania (1464–79). In Anatolia the principality of Karaman was finally reconquered in 1468. From this point the Ottomans began to pose a significant threat to the western European powers in the Mediterranean. In 1479 Scutari was captured from Venice and control established along much of the eastern Adriatic. In 1480 Ottoman forces landed on the Italian peninsula and captured Otranto. The pope prepared to flee to France in the face of this Islamic assault. However, in 1481 the period of Ottoman expansion came to a temporary end. Mehmet II died, Otranto was lost and a *yeniçeri* revolt took time to put down. The last two decades of the fifteenth century were a period of consolidation following the spectacular recovery and advance over the previous fifty years.
[*Later Ottoman history 17.15.1 & 18.2*]

15.9 Europe: Fragmentation in the West

In Europe the agricultural problems of the early fourteenth century and the devastating impact of the Black Death combined to produce a major crisis. Overall the population fell by a third, farming declined and the taxation base for the primitive states was undermined, leaving them much weaker and less able to cope with the problems they faced. Europe was still the most backward area of Eurasia (the east even more than the west) and the recovery from the mid-fourteenth century catastrophe took longer here than elsewhere, even though the area avoided the devastating impact of the Mongol invasions and the campaigns of Temur. Europe remained highly divided politically although for the elite, especially in the west, there was a fairly uniform culture built around the Latin church. Where political authority fragmented it was possible for small, independent communities to emerge. Often, as in the rest of Eurasia, these were trading cities where the rulers relied on the revenue from this source to sustain them. They were no less divided than the larger political units – class conflicts were often acute and disputes between the leading families were endemic. Overall the period between 1350 and 1450 was one of considerable weakness for all the monarchies of Europe (together with the papacy) and only in the last half of the fifteenth century were there significant signs of recovery.

15.9.1 The 'empire'
[Earlier history of the 'empire' 13.13.1]
The most fragmented of all the areas of Europe was the territory of the empire – very roughly Germany and Austria with some of the surrounding areas. There was a mass of small states in the west, the most developed region, whereas the east had the larger units of the Duchies of Bavaria and Austria and the Mark of Brandenburg and Prussia (controlled by the Teutonic Order of Knights and their Grand Master). Following the extinction of the Hohenstaufens in the late thirteenth century the imperial title was retained but it was even more meaningless than in the past. There was no question of the empire becoming a coherent and effective political unit – real power lay elsewhere and the title gave little more than a general claim to overlordship. It was accepted that the emperor had to be crowned by the pope and this could provide a justification for intervention in Italy, although the level of imperial control there was always even lower than in Germany. The emperor was elected by the four Rhineland powers – the archbishops of Mainz, Cologne and Trier together with the Count Palatine; and three from the east – the Elector of Saxony, the Margrave of Brandenburg and the King of Bohemia.

For much of the fourteenth century the choice for the electors was real. The main conflict was between three aristocratic houses – the Luxemburgs, the Habsburgs and the Wittelsbachs. The first originated in the Duchy that gave the house its name but for most of the fourteenth century they were also kings of Bohemia. The Habsburgs came from Switzerland where in 1315 they were defeated by the small peasant cantons which formed the Swiss confederation (Uri, Schwyz and Unterwalden) at the battle of Morganten. That defeat ensured the survival of the confederation which, in the middle of the century, was joined by the towns of Lucerne, Zurich and Bern. The Habsburgs increasingly concentrated their attentions on their territories in Austria. The Wittelsbachs were Dukes of Bavaria and Count Palatine but were relatively weak because of internal divisions within the family. The history of the fourteenth century is confused, of little long-term significance, and mainly revolves around the use of the imperial title to try and increase family power. There were only two significant emperors. The first was Lewis the Bavarian (1314–47), a Wittelsbach who defeated his Habsburg rivals at the battle of Mühldorf in

1322. Lewis was a major enemy of the pope, especially in Italy, and managed to add Brandenburg and Tirol to his family holdings during his time as emperor. He was succeeded by Charles IV, a Luxemburg who had been allied with the pope against Lewis in the early 1340s and who abandoned the imperial interest in Italy. He spent most of his time strengthening family holdings in the east. The most important event of his reign was the Golden Bull of 1356 which regulated and froze the imperial electoral system and provided for the succession of his son Wenceslas.

By the end of the fourteenth century the three great aristocratic families were increasingly weakened by continued division of the family inheritance. It effectively ended the power of the Wittelsbachs for centuries, the Luxemburg lands were divided into three on the death of Charles IV in 1378, as were the Habsburg lands in 1395. Political authority across the empire was in decline – the league of Swabian towns carved out their own area of authority, in the Czech lands the Hussite revolutionary and 'heretic' armies were in control and there was a peasant revolt in the Swiss confederation. Imperial power was almost non-existent and Sigismund, who became emperor in 1410, found it far more profitable to concentrate on his other role as king of Hungary. The most significant long-term development came on his death in 1437. Duke Albert of Austria (the emperor Albert II) was elected. He was a Habsburg and although at first he had little control even over the family lands, the imperial title was to remain in the family. Over the next century the Habsburgs were to become the chief dynastic power in Europe.

15.9.2 England and France
[*Earlier history 13.13.2*]

To the west the interaction between the English and French monarchies produced a period of immense instability and conflict which was not resolved until the 1450s (the so-called 'Hundred Years War'). The initial problem stemmed from the extinction of the line of Capetian kings and the accession of Philip VI as the first Valois king of France in 1328. The English monarchs made a claim to the French throne, though they were basing this on descent through the female line which had never been accepted in the French monarchy. However, it was sufficient, together with disputes over Gascony (a leftover of the Angevin empire held as a fief of the French monarch since 1259), to provide a fig-leaf for English intervention and campaigns of looting. 'France', to the extent that it existed at all, was very far from being a cohesive unit and only the long-held royal lands built up under the Capetians provided a solid base. Control of the south, even outside Gascony, was still limited and in the north the Counts of Flanders were effectively independent and controlled the increasingly prosperous trading towns such as Bruges. The main French ally was the old enemy of the English, Scotland, but its power was weak given the low level of development in the kingdom. England was far less rich than France but had a stronger, more centralized, monarchy that was capable of mobilizing its resources fairly effectively for limited campaigns. It was well capable of taking advantage of French weakness.

The English tried to ally with Flanders but with little success except in the early 1340s, though in 1346 they were, after success at the battle of Crécy, able to take Calais and hold it for the next two centuries. The first nadir in French fortunes came in 1356 after the battle of Poitiers when the French king was captured, government disintegrated and much of France was affected by roving bands of peasants pillaging the countryside and towns, just like the English troops. The latter did not have the strength to inflict a decisive defeat on the French and from 1364, following the accession of Charles V, a major French recovery took place. Control was reasserted and Charles was able to find enough tax revenue to create a standing army some 6,000 strong (about one-hundredth of the size of the contemporary Ming army in China). After Charles's death in 1380 there was little fighting for another quarter of a century until Henry V of England revived the claim to the French throne. The French royal family was increasingly divided by the growing insanity of Charles VI and English victory at the battle of Agincourt in 1415 brought about the second nadir of French fortunes. English campaigns of looting across northern France led to the reassertion of control over Normandy by 1419 and the capture of Paris in tacit alliance with the Duke of Burgundy. The early death of Henry V in 1422 (the same year as Charles VI died) and the succession of his infant son as Henry VI led to increasing English weakness. The French revival began in 1429 under the charismatic religious fanatic, Joan of Arc, but it was not until 1444 that the English were confined to their old territories of Normandy and Gascony. The English were finally expelled in 1453 and for the first time the French monarchy under Charles VII ruled over a territory whose extent bore some relation to that of modern France. At the same time England suffered from civil war ('The Wars of the Roses') which was not ended until the accession of the first of the new Tudor dynasty, Henry VII, in 1485.

15.9.3 *Italy and the papacy*

The Italian peninsula was also highly fragmented. The largest political unit, though it was highly fragile, was the kingdom of Naples which, after the mid-thirteenth century, was ruled by the Anjou family. They also ruled in Provence but not in Sicily though they claimed that title – the island was ruled by the Aragonese royal family. Further north were the papal territories, and the rest of Italy was a patchwork of cities and principalities. All of the states were small, though relatively wealthy by European standards because of the revenues derived from trade. Their small populations meant that the rulers spent their resources on recruiting mercenary armies (the *condottieri*) who were difficult to control and quite likely to turn on their employers if they were not paid or did not gain sufficient loot from the constant warfare. By 1320 most of the cities no longer had republican governments of the main merchant families but had drifted towards either rule by a single family or a closely controlled oligarchy. Milan was dominated by the Visconti family, Ferrara by the Este and Verona by the Della Scala. Venice was slightly different – it was an oligarchy controlled by the Great Council but new families were not admitted to the ruling group after 1297. The Doge (or Duke) was effectively an elected monarch. Siena's government did survive in a broadly republican form, as did Genoa's but the latter was highly unstable and lost its independence to the rising power of Milan in the late fourteenth century. Florence remained a republican commune from the 1340s until the rise of the Medici family a century later.

From the early fourteenth century until the mid-fifteenth century the papacy was divided and weak. In 1309 the French monarchy seized control of the papacy and maintained it during the so-called 'Avignon captivity', which lasted until 1377. Although the popes were away from Rome the period saw the rise of an increasingly elaborate papal court, growing wealth and increasing involvement in political manoeuvring, though carefully disguised behind a religious façade. There was a succession of French popes as the French clergy and secular authorities manipulated the election process. By the time Gregory XI died in 1378 the pope had returned to Rome but the election of Urban VI immediately led to the 'Great Schism' with a rival, Clement VII, established at Avignon by 1379. The existence of two popes divided western Europe largely along secular lines into pro- and anti-French groups. The weakness of the papacy and the division within the Latin church led to the rise of the 'conciliar movement' – the claim that church councils (which had decided doctrine in the fourth and fifth centuries) should be the ultimate authority. The main result of the council which met at Pisa in 1409 was to elect a third pope. The situation was finally resolved at the council of Constance (1414–18) which not only ended the split but also condemned and burnt John Hus, the leader of the Hussite religious reformers in Bohemia. Martin V (1417–31) returned to Rome but the struggles of the previous decades had significantly altered the nature of the papacy. It was now largely based upon the secular power provided by the papal territories in Italy and for the next four centuries the papacy played a major part in the complex power struggles in the peninsula.

15.9.4 Iberia
[*Earlier history 13.12.2*]

The Iberian peninsula was badly fragmented once the major period of the reconquest of Islamic areas was over, by the mid-thirteenth century. For the next two and a half centuries the 'reconquista' was at a very low level and amounted to little more than some desultory border conflicts. The Islamic kingdom of Granada was highly prosperous, although more Muslims lived outside its borders than within it – those who lived in the Christian kingdoms were kept in a legally separate category (like the Jews) and subject to increasing discrimination. For much of the period after the mid-thirteenth century the strongest of the Christian states was Aragon. It was blocked from expanding to the south by the territory of Castile around Valencia and therefore turned away from Iberia and concentrated on its Mediterranean empire and trading network. Following its takeover of Sicily after the 'Sicilian Vespers' of 1282 its empire included Sardinia and Corsica and from 1343 the Balearic Islands. In the complex power struggles of the period Aragon was opposed by the papacy, the house of Anjou, at times by the French monarchy and constantly by its main commercial rival Genoa. The tiny kingdom of Navarre survived the frequent plans of Castile and Aragon to partition it and from the late fourteenth century seemed more likely, because of marriage alliances, to finish up as part of the French kingdom. The Portuguese kingdom was very weak with constant divisions within the royal house (a problem that affected the other Iberian kingdoms too) and the formal papal suzerainty produced frequent interference from either Rome or Avignon. The largest of the kingdoms was Castile in central Spain. It slowly drew closer to Aragon after the extinction of the male line of the old Aragonese royal house on the death of Martin I in 1410. That policy reached its height in 1469 with the marriage of Ferdinand of Aragon and Isabel of Castile (the heir to the crown). From 1479 they ruled both kingdoms jointly but there was no question of creating a single Spanish kingdom. Aragon and Castile remained separate and retained their own unique institutions.

15.10 Europe: the Kingdoms in the East

The history of eastern Europe from about 1300 was, in some ways, the opposite of that of the west. Instead of fragmentation there was the emergence of kingdoms such as Hungary and Poland-Lithuania controlling large territorial areas. However, they remained relatively weak. Further east, Moscow became the dominant power among the Rus as the power of the Qipchaq Horde faded with its tripartite division in the 1430s.

15.10.1 Poland-Lithuania

Poland was reunited under a Piast duke in 1320 and for the next fifty years the kingdom was at peace with the Teutonic Knights (who had expanded eastwards to control large areas around the Baltic by the late thirteenth century) and Bohemia. Poland expanded eastwards as the power of the Qipchaq Horde declined in the far west of its territories and the Rus principalities remained weak and divided. Poland took Galicia (including the city of Lwow) and Volhynia – by 1370 it had tripled its size. The death of Kazimiercz III in 1370 ended the Piast dynasty and he was succeeded by his nephew Louis of Anjou (who was also Lajos I of Hungary). In order to buy off the opposition he made large land grants and extended the privileges of the nobility, clergy and towns under the Statute of Kosice in 1374. When he died in 1382 he left no successor. The growing power of the nobility was demonstrated when, after an interregnum, the daughter of Louis, Jadwiga, was crowned Queen but her fiancé, Wilhelm von Habsburg, was driven out of Poland – he was unacceptable because of the threat of a union with the Habsburg territories. Instead Jadwiga was forced to marry Jogaila, the Grand Duke of Lithuania who was then elected as King Jagiello of Poland. The two states were united to form the largest kingdom in Europe. (Lithuania was still mainly pagan and as the price of union Jagiello converted to the Latin Catholic church.)

The fifteenth century saw the continuing growth of Polish-Lithuanian power. An army of Poles, Lithuanians, Czechs, Ruthenes and Wallachians inflicted a total defeat on the Teutonic Knights at the battle of Grünwald (near Tannenberg) in 1410. Half the knights were killed (including the Grand Master) and the other half (about 14,000 men) were taken prisoner. The order was left with most of its land until 1454 when Gdansk, Elblag and Torun sought Polish protection. A fourteen-year war followed in which the Poles and Lithuanians were ultimately successful. In 1466 the lands of the order were divided. West Prussia became an autonomous province within Poland whereas East Prussia and Livonia remained under Teutonic control though subject to Polish sovereignty. Gdansk was returned to Poland and rapidly became the major port for the export of Polish products, mainly grain, to the Netherlands. In the east Lithuania dominated most of the old lands of the Rus.

[Later Poland-Lithuania 18.10.1]

15.10.2 Hungary

Hungary was, like Poland-Lithuania (to which it was united for a very short time in the 1440s), potentially a very large kingdom, but, even more than its neighbour, it suffered from an unstable and weak dynastic line; and it also had to cope with the growing power of the Ottomans, who were ultimately to bring about its demise. However, on two occasions Hungary nearly became a central part of what could have been major empires in eastern Europe. Hungary recovered only slowly from the Mongol invasions and in the late thirteenth century the central state collapsed as the aristocracy seized more and more power. For seven years after the death in 1301 of the last Arpad king, Andras III, there was no ruler. Eventually the church and the lower nobility forced the election of Charles of Anjou (the son of the King of Naples who was related by marriage to the Arpads) as Karoly I in 1308. During his long reign until 1342 he was able to rebuild the position of the monarchy, take back much of the land the aristocracy had appropriated, and increase royal revenues through taxes on the growing mining of gold and silver. His successor, Lajos I (1342–82), spent most of his resources on three major efforts to seize the throne of Naples. He did, however, manage to re-establish Hungarian hegemony in Croatia, Slovenia and Dalmatia. Although he became king of Poland in 1370 he saw no advantages in a union of the two kingdoms.

On the death of Lajos there was a major power struggle in Hungary. The king of Naples seized the throne but was murdered, and the nobility supported Sigismund of Luxemburg who became King Zygmunt in 1387. He took the imperial title in 1410 and a decade later became king of Bohemia. Potentially this could have been the foundation of a major kingdom. However, most of his time was devoted to the increasing problems of Bohemia where the Hussite movement and rebellion was at its peak around 1415. After his death in 1437 there was again chaos in Hungary for three years until the Jagiellon king of Poland-Lithuania, Wladyslaw III, was chosen as King Ulaszlo of Hungary. Again this could have formed the basis for a major empire across much of central and eastern Europe. However, it only lasted for four years as the kingdom faced the reviving power of the Ottomans. Ulaszlo died at the battle of Varna in 1444. He was replaced by Janos Hunyadi, a warlord from Transylvania, who was elected as regent on behalf of the Habsburgs. However, on his death in 1458 his son Matyas was chosen as king. Instead of attacking the powerful Ottomans he turned westwards and in 1470 took Bohemia. Eventually Bohemia was partitioned – Matyas Hunyadi took Moravia and Silesia, followed in 1485 by eastern Austria, where he made Vienna his capital. On his death in 1490 control over Vienna and eastern Austria was lost. The Hungarian nobility were, like their counterparts in Poland a century earlier, desperate to avoid being incorporated into the Habsburg territories. They therefore offered the kingdom to Wladyslaw, the Jagiellon ruler of Bohemia, who became Ulazslo II.

15.10.3 The rise of Moscow
[*Earlier history* **14.5.3**]

In the territories of the Rus to the east of Poland-Lithuania, the Qipchaq Horde at Sarai on the Volga near the Caspian Sea was the dominant power until the 1430s. Then it split into the three khanates of Kazan, Crimea and Astrakhan which gave the petty states in the west a little more room for manoeuvre. The rulers of Moscow (who controlled little more than the city itself) had been invested by the Mongols with the title Grand Prince of Vladimir which gave notional supremacy over the other Rus states. Moscow and its rulers, the Daniilovichi dynasty, were so weak that they had to rely on Mongol patronage and support to maintain this position. The rulers had to pay tribute and make regular visits to Sarai to pay homage and, as a by-product, boost their prestige among the Rus. Nevertheless it was the start of a long, and often interrupted process, by which the state of Moscow slowly expanded. The status of Moscow was also increased when the head of the Greek Orthodox church in the Rus (the Metropolitan) moved his residence from Kiev to Vladimir in 1299 and to Moscow in 1325. The church had been under Mongol protection since 1257 (it was exempt from taxation), had maintained a bishop at Sarai after 1261, and prayed for the health of the Mongol khan. The main impact of the church was, because of its background, to disseminate Byzantine culture within Moscow.

In secular matters the Mongols remained the dominant influence (something which nationalist Russian historians have always been determined to play down). Moscow, like the other principalities, adopted the Mongol method of fighting on horseback but even more important was the use of Mongol administrative practices. These were adopted because the princes had to administer their realms on behalf of the Mongols. The Russian title for a civilian governor, *daruga*, and a military governor, *baskak*, are clearly derived from the Mongol *daruya* and the Turkish *basqaq* – the latter name was taken over by the Mongols in the western parts of the empire. In origin these were the Mongol officials who were the overseers of the Rus principalities in the early fourteenth century. They were subsequently replaced by Rus appointees as the Mongols began to trust the local princes to be loyal and continue to pay tribute. The Moscow system of social status and military rank known as *Mestnichestvo*, which continued into the nineteenth century, was derived from the Mongol system. Mongol punishments were also incorporated in the law-codes of the Rus.

Moscow was divided by civil war between the early 1430s and the mid-1440s but there was then a marked recovery as Mongol control faded. This left Moscow freer to reach an accommodation with the rising power of Poland-Lithuania in the west. In 1449 Vasilii II of Moscow made a treaty with Casimir IV on their mutual borders and spheres of influence. It gave Moscow the dominant position in Novgorod and Pskov and the territories of the north-east, and left Poland-Lithuania in control of all the western lands of the Rus (modern Ukraine and Belorussia) as far east as Smolensk. The rulers of Moscow still sent tribute to the Crimean khanate but when Ivan III took the throne in 1462 he was the first to do so without the explicit consent of the Mongols. In parallel the church was seeking to boost the position of the Moscow rulers and becoming anti-Mongol as the influence of the latter waned. It sought to emphasize the links with the Byzantines, especially after the fall of Constantinople in 1453. It even began to put forward the absurd claim that Moscow was the 'third Rome'. However, the principality remained a very backward area. The peasants were largely self-sufficient, apart from the need for salt, and lived in widely separated communities practising 'slash and burn' farming in the forests that covered most of the landscape. The population took a long time to recover from the Black Death and the constant recurrence of the plague for the rest of the fourteenth century. There were less than thirty towns in the whole principality in the late fifteenth century and most of these had only a couple of thousand people living in them.

[*Later Moscow 18.10.2*]
[*Later European dynastic conflicts 18.9*]

15.11 Into the Atlantic

From the perspective of world history one of the most important developments in fifteenth-century Europe was its expansion into the Atlantic. This was primarily undertaken by the Portuguese long after the 'reconquista' was completed in Portugal in 1249, but following the establishment of the new monarchy in 1395 under João I. His son Henrique, who took the throne in 1419, was also master of the military order of Avis, and one of the main supporters of this expansion. (He was first called 'Henry the Navigator' by an English historian in the nineteenth century, although he went to North Africa just three times during his long reign which lasted until his death in 1460.) The Portuguese voyages were not part of some long-range plan to circumvent Islamic control of the eastern Mediterranean and the routes into the Indian Ocean. Still less were they the result of some nebulous 'spirit of discovery' or mystical European expansionary dynamic. They took place over a long period of time, step by step as immediate, easy profits could be seen. Financial considerations were always dominant and the first stages were usually sponsored by a small group and only once the potential for profit was demonstrated did the monarch come in with support.

The expansion began just before Henrique became king, with the capture of Ceuta on the North African coast in 1415. However, Portugal could not succeed against the Islamic rulers of Morocco – it had a population one-sixth of the size and was far less wealthy. What the Portuguese could try to do was outflank the Moroccans and their control over the lucrative trans-Saharan trade routes so as to gain direct access to the gold of west Africa. Although the Portuguese developed the three-masted caravel (with the lateen rig used in the Islamic world for several centuries), the problem they faced was the currents off the African coast. The Canary current along the Saharan coast ran constantly from north to south which meant that for Mediterranean sailors, who had little or no experience of sailing far from land, Cape Bojador (just south of the Canaries) was the point of no return. The Islamic sailors who circum-navigated Africa in a clockwise direction avoided the problem by sailing further out to sea. It was not until the Portuguese slowly learnt how to exploit the islands of the Canaries, Madeira and the Azores to return home that they could do the same. The first Portuguese sailor to round Cape Bojador and return was Gil Eannes in 1434. However, it was to be more than fifty years before the first European sailor reached the Cape of Good Hope at the southern point of Africa and another ten after that before it was rounded by Vasco da Gama in 1498.

The key to the voyages was therefore the Atlantic islands. It was here that the nature and impact of European expansion across the Atlantic in the succeeding centuries was first demonstrated in microcosm. The earliest islands to be exploited were the Canaries which were discovered by the Europeans in the early fourteenth century. From as early as the 1380s they were subject to raids for slaves by the Portuguese, French and Aragonese. The seven islands of the group were inhabited by Guanches – about 80,000 people who were close to the Berbers and had settled the islands in the first centuries CE, bringing with them their crops and domesticated animals (goats, pigs and dogs but not cattle and horses). The Guanches hold the dubious distinction of being the first people to be driven to extinction by the Europeans. The Europeans (mainly Castilians) conquered the islands one by one (the last was Tenerife in 1496) using force to take over the land, selling the inhabitants as slaves and bringing in European crops and animals – in particular they set up sugar plantations. The last of the Guanches died in the 1540s. The other Atlantic islands were uninhabited and were settled shortly after the Canaries – Madeira in 1425, the Azores between 1427 and 1450 and the Cape Verde Islands in the 1450s.

Sugar was the key to the exploitation of all of these islands except the Azores where the climate was too cool. The European acquaintance with sugar (one of the important crops diffused across the Islamic world) began in the early twelfth century when, after the First Crusade, the Venetians took over some of the villages around Tyre and turned them into estates to export sugar to Europe. At first it was a very minor commodity though important because Europe had no other sweetener apart from honey. The crucial problem with sugar production was that it was highly labour-intensive in both growing and processing. Because of the huge weight and bulk of the raw cane it was very costly to transport, especially by land, and therefore each estate had to have its own factory. There the cane had to be crushed to extract the juices, which were boiled to concentrate them, in a series of back-breaking and intensive operations lasting many hours. Few people would do this work willingly. However, once it had been processed and concentrated the sugar had a very high value for its bulk and could be traded over long distances by ship at a considerable profit. The industry only began on a major scale after the loss of the Levant to a resurgent Islam and the shift of production to Cyprus under a mixture of crusader aristo-crats and Venetian merchants. The local population on Cyprus spent most of their time growing their own food and few would work on the sugar estates. The owners therefore brought in slaves from the Black Sea area (and a few from Africa) to do most of the work. The level of demand and production was low and therefore so was the trade in slaves – no more than about a thousand people a year. It was little greater when sugar production began in Sicily.

In the Atlantic islands, once the initial exploitation of the timber and raw materials was over, it rapidly became clear that sugar production would be the most profitable way of using the new territories. The problem was the heavy labour involved – the Europeans refused to work as more than supervisors. The solution was to bring in slaves from Africa. The crucial developments in this trade began in the 1440s as the Portuguese began to trade regularly along the west African coast, paying tribute to the local rulers for the privilege. In these activities the Europeans brought with them a collection of attitudes – a long-established dislike of black skin colour, views of their own superiority (partly derived from the Bible), a hatred of Islam as the religion against which Europe had defined itself, together with a crusading and missionary belief in the superiority of Christianity. From 1442 the pope recognized the Portuguese voyages, the settlement of the islands and the trade along the African coast as a crusade – and King Henrique was appointed head of a new 'Order of Christ'. Enslavement of the Africans was morally justified according to the pope because it was part of the process of bringing Christianity to them. Similarly it was acceptable to buy slaves from the Muslims because the profits would be reinvested in the crusade, although weapons should not be offered as payment because that would only strengthen the infidel. The first captives were taken to Portugal but in 1455 they were used to build the Portuguese fort at Arguin on the African coast and again in 1480–82 at El Mina.

The bringing together of two of the main elements of the European Atlantic world occurred when the slaves were taken to the islands to work on the sugar plantations. Sugar production began on Madeira in 1455. Most of the capital to set up the mills came from Genoa and the technical advisers came from Sicily. Its position in the Atlantic meant that it could easily export the sugar to northern Europe and this provided the incentive for Genoese and Flemish merchants, both determined to break the Venetian domination of the eastern Mediterranean trade, to develop this new area. By 1480 Antwerp had some seventy ships engaged in the Madeira sugar trade, with the refining and distribution concentrated in Antwerp. By the 1490s Madeira had overtaken Cyprus as a producer of sugar. In the 1480s the Portuguese government set up the *Casa dos Escravos* to organize the slave traffic from Africa to the islands and Portugal. Merchants bought the rights to buy and sell slaves in particular areas and the government took thirty per cent of the profits. Soon there were large public auctions of slaves in Lisbon (where they already made up about a tenth of the population). Africans were preferred to Moriscos and Muslims and many were also sold on to Castile to work in the sugar plantations that developed around Valencia. The total slave population of all the Atlantic islands was about 10,000 at any one time. Even this limited number required a total trade in about 140,000 slaves between the 1440s and the end of the fifteenth century.

Even before the discovery of the Americas the outlines of the Atlantic world the Europeans were to construct were already visible. Its essential characteristics were the conquest and elimination of the indigenous people, the trade in slaves from Africa and the development of commercial plantations to supply goods to Europe. Over the next few centuries this system was to be replicated on a gigantic scale.

PART FIVE
The World Balance
(1500–1750)

OVERVIEW 11

THE WORLD IN
1500

World Population: 440 million
Regional Population: China: 110 million, India: 90 million,
Rest of Asia: 50 million, Europe: 80 million, Africa:
40 million, Americas: 70 million (Mexico: 20 million,
Inca empire: 11 million)
Major cities: Peking (672,000), Vijayanagar (500,000),
Cairo (450,000), Hangchou (375,000),
Constantinople (350,000), Nanking (285,000),
Canton (250,000), Paris (250,000), Tenochtitlan (80,000),
London (50,000), Cuzco (50,000)

Events:

★ Ming dynasty at the height of its power in China

★ Collapse of Ashikaga shogunate in Japan – autonomous daimyo control most of country

★ Malacca at height of prosperity at focus of south-east Asia trade routes

★ Uzbek empire in central Asia

★ Mughal invasions of north India, Delhi sultanates on point of collapse

★ First European ships reach India

★ Safavid empire in Iran

★ Ottoman empire controlling Anatolia and most of Balkans

★ Stronger states in England, Spain and France. Emergence of the Habsburg empire

★ Jagiellon family ruling Poland-Lithuania, Hungary and Bohemia

★ Slow expansion of Moscow under way

★ Conquest of Canaries complete. First Spanish settlements in Caribbean

★ Aztec empire at its height in central Mexico

★ Inca empire at its height in Peru and Bolivia

★ Polynesians settle Chatham Islands

★ First kings ruling Hawaii. Easter Island civilization at its peak

★ Early printing in Europe

★ First production of paper in England

16

The Columbian World

On the evening of 11 October 1492 Christopher Columbus, a Genoese from a long-established merchant family, on board his ship *Santa Maria* in the western Atlantic, thought he saw a light in the distance. A few hours later Rodrigo de Triana, the lookout on the *Pinta*, sighted land and on 12 October a party from the expedition stepped ashore. They were in the Greater Antilles in the Caribbean, although they thought they were in Asia, and Columbus was to die still believing he had 'discovered' the eastern coast of Eurasia. They were not the first Europeans to reach the Americas – the Vikings had done so about five hundred years earlier and established a few short-lived settlements. This voyage, which in many ways was little more than a pushing westwards from the base of the Azores established in the fifteenth century, was to have a profound impact on world history. The long isolation of the Americas was brought to an end and they were slowly incorporated into the world created in Eurasia over the previous millennia. Eurasia, especially Europe, was affected by the discovery of new people, ideas, cultures and crops but the greatest impact was felt in the Americas. The terms on which the Americas were brought into the wider world were dictated by the Europeans.

16.1 The Rise of Europe

The 'discovery' of the Americas profoundly changed the position of Europe which until then had been highly marginal within Eurasia. It provided the Europeans with an opportunity to create an Atlantic commercial world from which they could derive large profits and power. Gradually over the next three centuries they were able to build on this position so that by the nineteenth century they became the dominant area of the world. The attitudes the Europeans brought with them (already demonstrated in the Atlantic islands earlier in the fifteenth century) were very different from those of the Chinese as they sailed around the Indian Ocean less than a century earlier. Columbus observed of the Arawak people he met on his first voyage: 'They invite you to share anything they possess and show as much love as if their hearts went with it . . . How easy it would be to convert these people – and to make them work for us.' Altogether Columbus made four voyages across the Atlantic between 1492 and 1506 as, guided by the native Caribs, his ships explored parts of the West Indies, the central American coast and the northern coast of south America. The first settlement, Isabella, was established on Hispaniola in 1494. Columbus was followed by other sailors. In June 1497 John Cabot sailed from Bristol to find Asia but instead arrived in Newfoundland and the next year sailed down the coast as far as Delaware. In 1497 Amerigo Vespucci (who was to give his name to the American continent) skirted the southern coast of north America.

It was in early 1498 that the Portuguese Vasco da Gama rounded the Cape of Good Hope and sailed up the east coast of Africa. At the port of Malindi he met a Muslim Indian pilot, Ahmed Ibn-Majid, who was equipped with maps of the Indian Ocean, sophisticated navigational instruments (he laughed at the ones da Gama showed him), as well as a deep knowledge of sailing in the area. He agreed to guide the Portuguese along the well-established trade routes to the port of Calicut where they arrived on 18 May 1498. It was the first time Europeans had directly encountered the wealth of the long-established trading routes in this part of Eurasia and their impact here was to be much more limited than in the Atlantic world. Although it took more than two centuries before Europe was familiar with all the rest of the world this linking together of all the world's oceans was something which no other society in the world had ever achieved before. In 1519–22 the small flotilla of ships led by Ferdinand Magellan made the first complete voyage around the globe – he did not complete the journey himself because he was killed by some of the inhabitants of the Philippines. The first successful west-to-east crossing of the Pacific by the Europeans took place in 1565. In the seventeenth century the Dutch learnt how to use the westerlies of the 'Roaring Forties' to avoid the monsoon areas of the Indian Ocean and sail directly from southern Africa to the islands of south-east Asia. The occasional mistake meant that they reached the west coast of Australia. But it was not until the mid-eighteenth century and the voyages of James Cook that the Europeans knew very much about the east coast of Australia, New Zealand and Polynesia.

Overall the impact of Europe on the rest of the world in the two hundred and fifty years after 1500 was slow and limited. By 1750 the Europeans only controlled the eastern coast of north America, much of central and south America, a few coastal forts and trading posts along the African coast together with the very small settlement at the Cape, a handful of forts and trading posts across the Indian Ocean world and some islands in south-east Asia. In parallel Russian expansion across Siberia had reached the Pacific coast. The great empires and states of Eurasia, in particular China, Japan, India, Iran, and the Ottomans, which were built upon long-established traditions and the vast wealth accumulated over centuries, were little affected by Europe in the period between 1500 and 1750. Their histories and development continued according to their own dynamics and internal forces. Where Europe did have a major and catastrophic impact was in the Americas. Here they encountered peoples who, because of the late settlement of the continent after the end of the last ice age and the later start in the development of agriculture, were at a stage of development roughly equivalent to that found in Mesopotamia and Egypt about 2000 BCE. They did not even have metal weapons with which to face the primitive gunpowder weapons of the Europeans. They were also unfamiliar with the horse and mounted warriors. Most important of all, they had no immunity to the diseases the Europeans brought with them. In these circumstances the ruthlessness and violence of the Europeans were only an additional factor in their success.

Within four hundred years of the first voyages to the Americas Europe was the dominant region of the world. For a long time Europeans have sought to explain to themselves the reasons for their success. Ideas of racial superiority, a special restless and questing European character and divine guidance are now less fashionable and in their place many have tried to substitute the idea that there was a 'European miracle' which uniquely privileged this one part of the world. These explanations are built around what is seen as a particular European inheritance of internal geographical advantages, a collection of small states rather than a single large empire, a different type of family structure, private property, enforceable contracts, free markets, the accumulation of wealth, emerging capitalism and a rational scientific mind. In practice, as the previous chapters have illustrated, there was little that distinguished Europe from the rest of Eurasia in 1492 except its relative backwardness. European agriculture remained at a low level of productivity and its levels of trade and wealth were far below that of the rest of Eurasia. Free markets, legally enforceable contracts, private property and large accumulations of wealth among merchants had been common in China for more than a thousand years and were found in much of the rest of Eurasia. The European trading cities were also not unique – similar independent entities were found across Eurasia and were often far more cosmopolitan. Europe was very far from being the technologically creative area of Eurasia apart from its development of the vertical windmill and the mechanical clock. What it had done in the period after about 1000 was absorb the technological developments made elsewhere, especially in China – cast iron, paper, printing and gunpowder. Neither did Europe have any advantage in sailing technology. Again it had absorbed Chinese developments (the stern-post rudder and the compass) and those of the Islamic world (the lateen sail) but its ships were still only about a quarter of the size of the Chinese ocean-going junk. The sailors of the Islamic world, India and China were sailing just as far as the Europeans and often with a greater degree of proficiency. Although western Europe had, by luck, avoided the impact of the Mongol invasions, it was still far less wealthy than the rest of Eurasia. That is hardly surprising because as late as 1000 it was a very peripheral and marginal area of Eurasia with a low population, poor agriculture, few towns, very little trade and a very limited level of political development. It grew significantly in the next five hundred years but still had a long way to go.

The one great advantage that Europe did have was a geographical accident. Its location on the far western edge of Eurasia meant that it was the region able to voyage to the Americas and find societies at a far lower level of development. It was the wealth that was plundered from the Americas – at first the gold and silver and then what derived from the slave plantations – that enabled Europe to catch up with the rest of Eurasia. This wealth was then used by western Europe to buy its way into the Asian trading system and secure further advantages. By about 1750 Europe was at roughly the same level of wealth and development as the rest of Eurasia and in a position to begin to assert itself at the expense of the longer established societies, particularly in India, and to develop other sparsely inhabited regions of the world – north and south America, Australia and New Zealand. At the same time it was also about to make the fundamental transition away from the type of agricultural and commercial societies that had dominated previous Eurasian history. It was this transition which the Chinese had just failed to make some six hundred years earlier under the Sung. From the perspective of the rest of Eurasia the impact of Europe could be seen as just another example of a common historical phenomenon – a peripheral society descending violently on the wealthy and long-established societies causing significant short-term disruption. Some of the societies in Eurasia succumbed to this pressure but others found ways, as in the past, of adjusting to the new situation, absorbing the new elements and creating a new synthesis.

16.2 The Columbian World: Disease

[*Earlier disease patterns 10.1 & 15.1*]
As we have seen, the extensive contacts (primarily trading networks) within Eurasia had spread diseases across the whole continent. At first they were highly virulent, as the terrible disease outbreaks between 200 and 700 CE and again during the Black Death demonstrated. Gradually, however, people acquired a degree of immunity and the diseases lost some of their

potency as they became endemic in the population. The people of the Americas were in a very different position. All the evidence suggests that they were far healthier than the European population around 1500. Because of their lack of domesticated animals (the main source of human diseases) they had avoided the impact of the diseases which spread with the adoption of agriculture. One thing is certain – they had never been exposed to the diseases of Eurasia and had no immunity to them. The impact of the arrival of the Europeans was therefore catastrophic. It was not just their technological superiority that was decisive; far more important was the potent but unintentional weapon of disease. The Europeans did not find a wilderness to colonize in the Americas though within a century of their arrival they had created one.

The first disease to strike the Americas was smallpox, which began in the Antilles in 1519. That it had not arrived more rapidly after Columbus's voyages was merely because of chance – the long voyage and the lack of carriers of the disease on the ships. It spread first to Yucatan and then played a crucial role in the capture of the Aztec capital Tenochtitlan by Hernando Cortés and his handful of soldiers. After entering the capital they were driven out and had to retreat to Tlaxcala and regroup. As they did so a two-month epidemic raged in Tenochtitlan. It killed huge numbers, including many of the Aztec leaders such as Cuitlahuac who had taken over after the death of Moctezuma and was trying to organize resistance to the invaders. It was a demoralized wreck of a society that was then unable to resist the renewed Spanish assault. Smallpox reached Peru before Pizarro and his band of adventurers and had begun to devastate the Incas, already badly divided by the civil war among the leadership. Although the Aztec and the Incas faced a technologically superior enemy they had the advantage of far greater numbers and they might have been able to survive at least the initial impact of a small number of Europeans but for the effect of disease. It caused massive disruption in society – there were so many dead that the survivors were unable to bury them all and the bodies rotted in the streets. Almost every family would have lost someone and those that did survive would usually have been pock-marked or blind. Even more disturbing, the invaders would have been largely immune to the dreadful attacks of the disease, giving them a semi-divine status. It is hardly surprising therefore that the local inhabitants were unable to offer effective resistance to the invaders. However, it was not just smallpox that devastated the native American population. Its impact was reinforced by the arrival of other diseases – measles in 1530–31, followed by typhus in 1546 (the latter was relatively new in Europe too having first developed in the 1490s). The last new diseases to arrive in the Americas both came from Africa and probably travelled along with the slaves transported by the

Europeans. Malaria was endemic in the Amazon area by the 1650s and yellow fever arrived in Yucatan and Cuba in 1648 when the specialized *Aedes aegypti* mosquito travelled in the water casks on the ships.

The overall impact of the diseases the Europeans took to the Americas depends on estimates of the population of the area around 1500 and these are highly contentious. (There are generally agreed figures for the area about a century after the European conquest.) In the early twentieth century very low estimates were standard partly because European and American scholars did not believe the native Americans could have had very sophisticated societies and partly because they wanted to play down the scale of the destruction. Some of the very high estimates produced a few decades ago have now been scaled down but the consensus among experts still shows the dreadful scale of human destruction. The population of central Mexico (effectively the area of the Aztec empire) was about 20 million in 1500, equivalent to a quarter of the total European population and twice as many as the whole of Italy and four times as many as in Britain. Within a century the population of the area had fallen to a little over one million. In the Andes area (the Inca empire) the population fell from about 11 million in 1500 to less than a million by 1600. The native population of the Caribbean, which was probably about 6 million in 1500, was almost entirely exterminated. Nearly all of the population loss was caused by disease although enslavement and work in the mines and on the plantations later in the sixteenth century played a part. The total population of the Americas was probably about 70 million in 1500 out of a total world population of about 425 million – by 1600 it was about 8 million out of 545 million (in the mid-sixteenth century the population of the Americas may have hit a low of about 4 million). Although a population collapse by about 90 per cent may seem unbelievable it is consistent with other evidence of the effects of disease on groups with no resistance. How many people actually died? It is hard to estimate but it is unlikely that it was much less than about 100 million. Death on this scale was the greatest any society had to bear in human history – and the few who survived faced an immense cultural shock as their whole way of life disappeared as their communities died around them and what was left was destroyed by the European invaders.

The transmission of diseases between Europe and the Americas was almost certainly not just in one direction. The first outbreak of syphilis in Europe is unusual among diseases in that it can be dated precisely to the early 1490s. The first cases seem to have been in Barcelona in 1493 and it was then spread, as with so many other diseases, by armies. In 1494 Charles VIII of France invaded Italy to claim the throne of Naples and his soldiers carried the disease with them. The invasion failed and Charles retreated back to France and the disbanded army spread the disease still further. It reached England and the Low Countries in 1496 and Hungary and Russia in 1499. By then it had already spread along the Eurasian trade routes in the reverse direction to the bubonic plague ('Black Death') in the 1330s and 1340s. The speed at which it travelled shows how much more closely integrated Eurasia had become. By 1498 it was in Egypt and India and by 1505 it arrived in Canton and spread to Japan. Every society saw it as a 'foreign disease' and the names chosen are related to how it spread. To the English and Italians it was the 'French disease'. The French called it the 'Naples disease' and to the Poles it was the 'German disease'. The Indians called it 'the disease of the Franks' and to the Chinese it was the 'ulcer of Canton' after the port where it first arrived. The Japanese called it both the 'T'ang disease' and the 'Portuguese disease'.

The crucial question is therefore whether the disease was brought back by the sailors on Columbus's voyages. Certainly contemporaries were absolutely convinced that this was how the disease arrived in Europe. That opinion is reinforced by the fact that there is no unequivocal description of syphilis in Eurasia before the early 1490s. There is also some evidence of syphilitic damage in pre-Columbian American skeletons. There is little doubt that syphilis was a new disease in the 1490s because of its extreme virulence – it would not have had a similar impact in the population of the Americas because they would, like the Europeans with smallpox and measles, have acquired a considerable degree of immunity over time. The alternative explanation is that syphilis is derived from the closely related tropical disease yaws (known as *bejel* in south-east Asia) which is also one of the treponematoses diseases. For this to be the case yaws would have had to change its nature suddenly around 1490 so that not only did it adapt to being transmitted venereally but also became much more virulent. The timing may therefore be entirely coincidental with the voyages of Columbus. However, it seems far more likely that syphilis was the price that the whole of Eurasia had to pay for the European 'discovery' of the Americas. (It is even possible that yaws and all the treponematoses diseases came from the Americas and spread to the tropics – certainly the Sri Lankans were convinced they only caught yaws from the Europeans.)

The initial impact of syphilis in the early sixteenth century was terrifying in a population with no resistance to the virulent new disease. Its severity was in decline by the 1540s as it became endemic – by the seventeenth century it was a dangerous infection but far less violent in the symptoms it produced. However, there remained no known cure until the twentieth century. There were two popular remedies. The first, mercury, was effective in significantly slowing the pace of the disease but had the major disadvantage of being poisonous when taken in any quantity. The second, guaiacum, was made from the wood of a tree found in the West Indies. It was not toxic like mercury but even by the 1530s it was generally reckoned to be ineffective. However, the lack of any alternative treatments meant that it remained in the British Pharmacopoeia of approved drugs until 1932.

16.3 The Columbian World: Animals and Crops

[*Earlier diffusion of crops 12.1.1*]
Eurasia and the Americas developed independently economically, socially and politically and had different sets of diseases. In addition, the separation of the continents millions of years earlier meant that the animals and plants the earliest human communities had available to domesticate were entirely different too. The Americas, apart from having the llamas and alpacas of the Andes, lacked animals suitable for use in farming and transportation (both as draught and pack animals). Their domesticated crops were also unique. The creation of the Islamic world in the seventh century produced the first major diffusion of crops within Eurasia. The Columbian world after 1500 produced the second, and greatest, diffusion of crops and animals – on this occasion across the globe. It had a profound effect on every society – widening the range of crops that could be grown, enabling new areas to be cultivated and increasing the productivity of existing farmland. The spread and adoption of new crops and animals took several centuries but the long-term effect was to lay the foundations for the unprecedented worldwide growth in population from about 1700. (It also led to the creation of what are now seen as 'traditional' cuisines. For example, the two central items of Italian food – pasta and tomatoes – were both introduced in the last six hundred years, one from the Islamic world and one from the Americas. The chilli pepper of Indian cooking is also an introduction from the Americas.)

The first animals were taken to the Americas on Columbus's second voyage in 1493. He carried almost the complete range of European domesticated animals – horses, dogs, pigs, cattle, chicken, sheep and goats. The animal that made the greatest impression was the horse. The native Americans had never seen an animal of such a size, let alone a mounted warrior and their impact was, not surprisingly, frightening. Horses also, together with the mule, formed the basis of Spanish colonial society. They provided the main means of communication and a major element missing from pre-Columbian society – a pack animal for transporting goods across terrain where there were no roads. They became a vital part of the economy in many areas, in particular the raising of cattle on the plains of south America which would have been impossible without horses to control the herds. Horses went wild very quickly – in the north once they were bred on the better grasslands of the Mexican highlands and in the south when they spread from Peru across the Andes to the pampas. Vast herds of horses grazed here even before the Spanish arrived at Buenos Aires in the 1580s. In the north they spread to the Great Plains of north America and changed the way of life for many native American peoples as some adapted to horse-riding and exploiting the vast herds of buffalo. Horses also enabled the native peoples to resist the Europeans better and to fight each other in new ways.

Cattle raising rapidly became one of the principal activities of Spanish America and was central to colonial expansion across the great American grasslands. By 1587 over 100,000 hides a year were being exported from Mexico to Spain. Oxen also allowed the plough to be used for the first time in the Americas – without draught animals the native Americans did not move beyond the digging stick. Sheep and goats took longer to adapt and it was not until the 1580s that their numbers increased rapidly after they were herded on the Mexican highlands. The European animals were the first in the Americas to turn grass into meat, milk and wool (the latter two were completely new products for the peoples of central America).

The first areas conquered by the Europeans were not suitable for European crops and apart from a few vegetables they nearly all failed in the semi-tropical islands of the Caribbean. The first successful import was in 1516 – the banana from the Canaries (the Europeans had obtained this crop from the Islamic world). Sugar was first cultivated on a significant scale until the 1530s on Hispaniola. European temperate crops could not thrive until the Mexican highlands and then Peru were conquered – maize remained the major crop. Vines did not grow well in Mexico and the first major American production had to await their introduction into Peru in the 1550s and later to Chile. Olive trees were introduced into Peru and Chile a decade later. By the end of the sixteenth century all the main European food plants and animals were being cultivated and herded in the Americas.

Even more important than the European crops taken to the Americas were the plants which travelled in the opposite direction. They did not stay in western Europe but spread rapidly across the whole of Eurasia and Africa. (Animals from the Americas were of little importance apart from the turkey.) The crops were of two main types – those that became staples in world agriculture such as maize, potatoes, sweet potatoes, beans and manioc – and those that added variety to the diet: tomatoes, chillis, pumpkins, squashes, papaya, avocado, and the pineapple. The most important of all of these was maize, now one of the two major crops in the world. It spread first outside Europe – it was being cultivated in west Africa by 1550, in Mesopotamia by 1574 and in China just before the end of the sixteenth century. By then it had also been adopted in Egypt and the Levant. Maize was only grown relatively late in Europe because of the harsher climate in the sixteenth and seventeenth centuries which significantly reduced the number of areas where it could be cultivated. The first areas were in the south (it was probably grown on a very limited scale in Portugal in the sixteenth century) but the crop was not adopted on a major scale in Europe until the nineteenth century. The American crop which had the greatest impact in Europe was the potato, although it was mainly confined to Ireland and Germany before the late eighteenth century. It was seen as the food of the very poor but it did mean that it was possible, in the right climatic areas, for peasants to survive on little land. In Ireland about one and a half acres of potatoes, together with some milk, was enough to support a family for a year. The population of the island rose from 3.2 million in 1754 to 8.2 million ninety years later despite the fact that nearly 2 million people emigrated. Overdependence on this single crop caused a disaster in the mid-1840s when the potato blight and subsequent famine struck.

The region of Eurasia which adopted American crops quickest and on the largest scale was China. By the mid-sixteenth century peanuts, maize and the sweet potato were grown extensively. The latter was particularly important because it could be grown on land not used for other crops. In parallel maize rapidly became the staple crop of the uplands of south-west China, followed a little later by northern China. In China maize was grown for human food whereas in Europe it was usually a fodder crop. The impact of the American crops helped make China the area of the world with the fastest-growing population in the eighteenth century and they transformed its agricultural output – in the early seventeenth century rice made up about seventy per cent of China's food production but by the twentieth century it had fallen to less than half this figure. Japan adopted the sweet potato from China in the late seventeenth century but was growing the potato even earlier than China in the early seventeenth century. In Africa, apart from maize, the most important of the American crops was manioc (and its processed product tapioca) which was introduced into the Congo and Angola regions by the Portuguese in the mid-sixteenth century.

There were two other American crops which were to have a significant impact on world history. The first, cacao, was highly prized in pre-Columbian societies and the beans were even used as currency. It was adopted slowly in Europe and the drinking of chocolate did not become fashionable for some centuries. The second was tobacco. The Europeans adopted the habit of smoking from the native Americans they met and it spread widely across Europe in the early seventeenth century. At first it was mainly smoked in small pipes or used as snuff, only later were cigarettes and cigars developed. Tobacco became a major crop in north America and by the nineteenth century a major world industry was involved in making and selling tobacco. It was not until the mid-twentieth century that the amount of human suffering the habit and the industry caused began to be appreciated but by then a large part of the world's population were addicted to the drug.

17

The Early World Economy:
The Atlantic and Indian Oceans

Between 1500 and 1750 the relationship between Europe and the rest of the world was formed by two very different ocean worlds – those of the Atlantic and of the Indian Oceans. In the former the Europeans encountered technologically less advanced societies that were, accidentally, devastated by Eurasian diseases. The Europeans were able relatively quickly to develop their power and create a society and economy from which they were almost the sole beneficiaries. The Americas became the major source of wealth that began to transform western Europe. In the Indian Ocean the Europeans encountered societies that were as technologically advanced as themselves (if not more so) and far wealthier. The economies, societies and political systems of this world were built on long-established and stable foundations and the Europeans could make little impact. Indeed the nature of European trade with the area demonstrates that it was still relatively backward in Eurasian terms. The key factor as far as the western Europeans were concerned was the bringing together of the two oceans. It was the wealth that they could extract from the Atlantic world which enabled them to penetrate the Indian Ocean world and begin to improve their position. The significant impact of Europe on the other societies of Eurasia did not occur until after 1750.

17.1 The Early Spanish Empire

The 'new world', about which Columbus reported on his return from the Caribbean, immediately posed critical questions about the policies to be adopted there. How should the people be treated? What rights did the 'discoverers' have? If these areas were to be conquered what was the aim of the conquest? In answering these questions the Spanish and the church authorities, who together took the initial decisions, drew upon the traditions which had developed in Spain and the rest of Europe over the preceding centuries. The kingdoms which originally colonized the Americas (Spain and Portugal) had their roots in a long tradition of religious intolerance, persecution, territorial expansion and stigmatization of 'infidels' and 'pagans'. The church reinforced these attitudes with a biblical justification of conquest – the natives would be invited to submit (whether they understood what was required was immaterial), if they did not do so then they could legitimately be exterminated or enslaved. This form of

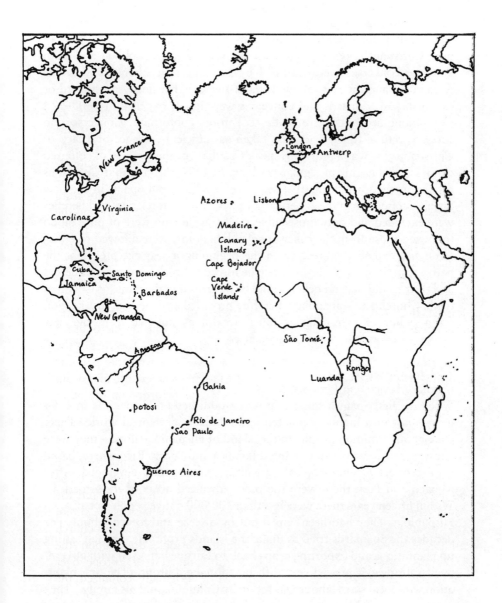

Map 50: The Atlantic world

justification was very close to that of a 'holy war' which the kingdoms believed they had been fighting for the previous centuries during the 'reconquista' against Islam. In fifteenth-century Spain there was a wave of anti-Muslim, anti-Jewish and anti-'converso' ideas and legislation. In 1449 pure Christian blood was made a condition for office-holding and from 1480 the 'conversos' were dealt with by the inquisition. About 2,000 people were burnt and the rest (about 100,000) were either fined, imprisoned or expelled. (All Moriscos and conversos were finally expelled in 1608–12.) Continuous attempts were made to enforce conformity. Converso and Morisco refusal to eat pork was taken as sufficient evidence of a lack of Christianity, as was a refusal to speak Castilian, or the wearing of coloured clothes and engaging in regular washing. In 1492, the year that Columbus arrived in the Caribbean, all Jews were expelled from Spain. In the new Spanish conquests in the Americas all Jews, Moors, foreigners and heretics were excluded and only those subjects of Castile who were of pure blood (not even those from the other Spanish kingdoms) were allowed to enter, settle and exploit the area. From the beginning it was accepted that the native Americans could legitimately be forced to work for their conquerors and their traditions and beliefs could be destroyed in the name of Christian truth. Church and state policy therefore provided a convenient justification for a policy of extracting as much wealth as possible from the new conquests regardless of the consequences.

17.1.1 Expansion
[Earlier Mexico and Peru 5.4 & 5.6]

When the first Spanish settlement was established on Hispaniola in 1494 it was part of a highly populated and relatively developed world. There were about 4 million people on the island of Hispaniola alone – they were Arawak people who also inhabited Jamaica and Puerto Rico where, based on a productive semi-tropical agriculture, small states developed. After Mexico and Peru these were the most advanced areas of the Americas. Within fifteen years there were less than 100,000 native people left alive on Hispaniola. They had been wiped out by disease and forced labour. For decades the Spaniards tried to make the islands profitable through setting up plantations and exporting crops back to Europe but, even with government subsidies, it proved very difficult to make a profit. (The first plantation with local slave labour was set up by Columbus and his family.) They searched for gold but little could be found. The Caribbean was also very difficult to exploit – the local people, especially the Kulinago, Carib and Arawak people to the south and east of Hispaniola, long resisted the Spanish and were able to defeat their ships at sea as late as the seventeenth century. They were only finally overwhelmed by the sheer weight of numbers. As the population of the islands began to die the Spanish turned to slave-raiding expeditions further and further afield until they reached the mainland – between 1515 and 1542 over 200,000 people were taken from the coast of Nicaragua alone – but the slaves died so fast that this was not enough.

Mexico was conquered by Hernando Cortés in a freelance expedition organized from Cuba. He landed at Vera Cruz and, exploiting the discontent within the Aztec empire and the impact of disease, he was able to conquer the area. He was followed after 1524 by other freebooters – Guzman, who conquered western Mexico (New Galicia), de Alvarado in Guatemala and Pizarro in Peru. By the 1530s much of central America and Peru was under nominal Spanish control, although resistance from the native Americans continued for centuries among the 'Chichimecs' of northern Mexico, the Araucanians of Chile and the peoples of Brazil. In many ways the history of the Americas until the nineteenth century (and in places like the Amazon until the present day) was one of the gradual extension of European settlement, the subjugation of the native population (as late as the 1780s there was an Inca rising against the Spanish) and the pushing of these people into ever more remote regions. As a Brazilian government spokesman put it in the 1980s: 'When we are certain that every corner of the Amazon is inhabited by genuine Brazilians and not by the Indians, only then will we be able to say that the Amazon is ours.'

17.1.2 Exploitation

The organization of these new Spanish territories proved to be very difficult. There was hardly any government and the authorities were capable of little more than dividing up the 'empire' so as to provide a framework for individual exploitation. Natives who resisted were sold into slavery and the rest were divided up into *encomiendas*. These gave jurisdiction over groups of native subjects (though in theory not their land) and the owners could force them to work on estates, in the mines or on public works. The level of exploitation was so high that most died within a couple of years. By the early 1540s there was a crisis in Spanish America. The natives were dying so fast from disease and exploitation that the *encomienda* system could not be sustained. Some Christian missionaries objected to the system but three of the missionary orders argued for its retention. In 1542 both slavery and the *encomienda* were in theory abolished. The former continued – the Araucanians in southern Chile were used as slaves until the 1680s and the Apache, Navajo and Shoshoni in the north of Mexico until the nineteenth century. The latter was replaced by full Spanish ownership of land and the continued requirement for the native peasants to labour for their new Spanish masters.

During the conquest of the Aztec and Inca empires most of the readily available precious metals from the great religious and secular treasures of the empires were collected together, melted down and sent back to Spain. The temples and other major buildings were destroyed and the people forcibly converted. Cathedrals were built on the ruins of the principal temples. Once the initial plunder was obtained it took time to find other sources of wealth. It was the discovery in 1545 of the silver deposits at Potosi, over 12,000 feet up in the Andes of Bolivia, that transformed the wealth the Spanish could gain from the Americas. At their height in the 1580s the mines were producing more than 300 tons of silver a year. To achieve this output the local population was subject to forced labour – the workers had to stay underground for a week at a time and process the ore using highly toxic mercury; not surprisingly the death rate was high. The population of Potosi was about 160,000 (nearly all of whom were forced labourers) making it one of the largest cities in the world – bigger than Paris, Rome, Madrid, Seville and London. The level of exploitation did not stop with the forced labour. The miners needed clothing and food and this was taken as tribute from the local villages and then sold by the Spanish to the miners. Making the clothes involved another 10,000 forced labourers working as weavers in Quito and elsewhere. Local communities also had to pay the salaries of the Spanish officials who organized the forced labour and that of the priest who tried to convert them. Under this level of exploitation the local population was nearly wiped out in a few decades. By the end of the sixteenth century the Spanish were forcing huge caravans of slaves to walk from Buenos Aires over the Andes to Potosi while in the north they moved them from the Caribbean into New Granada (Colombia) to work the placer mines.

By the end of the sixteenth century the Atlantic economy was still hardly developed. The initial conquests had been made and the loot and plunder from the Inca and Aztec empires, together with the silver and gold produced by the forced labour of the inhabitants who survived the impact of the Eurasian diseases, had been shipped to Europe. (By 1640 about 17,000 tons of silver and 200 tons of gold had been sent to Europe.) Elsewhere in the Americas the Portuguese had a foothold in Brazil as did the Spanish around the estuary of the River Plate. The other west European nations were hardly involved at all – the French had sailed up the St Lawrence river in the north and they, together with the English and the Dutch, were carrying out state-licensed piracy against Spanish and Portuguese ships hoping to gain some of the spoils. It was far from clear how the Atlantic economy would be developed.

17.2 Atlantic Slavery

For most of the sixteenth century the Spanish managed to exploit their empire without the large-scale use of imported slaves – it was easier to use the natives. In 1550 there were about 15,000 slaves in Spanish America and by the end of the century a total of about 50,000 slaves had been imported (that is the official figure but the large contraband trade probably doubled that number). Even so it was still less than the level of Spanish immigration. The slaves were mainly used on public works, especially the Cuban shipyards and arsenals, and made up about half the Cuban population by 1610. From the early seventeenth century they were taken in increasing numbers to the mainland, especially Mexico and Peru, to replace the natives who had died out – by 1636 half the population of Lima were either slaves or their descendants.

Before 1500 Europe was not a large slave-owning community, although there had been a trade in slaves for centuries (the word for slave in all west European languages refers to the Slav people who were sold in the Mediterranean). Christianity accepted slavery from the start – in the late Roman empire Christians were allowed to hold Christian slaves and the church itself was a large-scale owner of slaves on its estates. The development of Protestantism in the sixteenth century, with its emphasis on the need to respect private property and subordination to the secular ruler, did not change these attitudes. Indeed Luther even urged Christian slaves not to leave their Ottoman owners. These views were combined with long-established European attitudes that regarded blackness and Africans as abnormal. On a religious basis they were identified with Noah's son Ham who was cursed. In addition they were either infidels or pagans and therefore slavery, if it resulted in their conversion, was even more justified. Slavery was also believed to be the only way of making Africans work for benefit of their superiors. All of these attitudes were combined with a belief in the supremacy of a white skin. In 1601 Elizabeth I ordered the expulsion of all blacks from England and in 1753 the Scottish philosopher David Hume proclaimed: 'There never was a civilized nation of any other complexion but white.' Ultimately though it was the development of the plantation system and the profits it produced that created slavery – long-established racial and religious views only provided a justification for the extreme exploitation of the Africans. Land could be taken from the natives in the Americas relatively easily, the problem was the labour supply as the population died out. Even the people at the bottom of European society who were prepared to go to the Americas as indentured labour (their passage was paid by their employer in return for several years' work) were reluctant to work in the conditions found in plantations. They preferred to work in small units and, as another disadvantage, wanted their own land at the end of their contract. They also tended to die from tropical diseases, especially in the Caribbean. They were difficult to replace, often not suitable for hard labour and as whites there were limits to how far they could be exploited. In the end they also had to be freed.

During the seventeenth century the Europeans gradually decided that the large-scale import of African slaves was the answer to these problems. The plantation system as it developed in the Atlantic world had a number of peculiar features. Nearly all the labour was provided by slaves yet the population of slaves (and owners) was not self-sustaining outside north America. It therefore required a large-scale trade in slaves to keep it operating. Although the plantations depended on slavery they were examples of large-scale capitalist agriculture requiring large amounts of investment to establish and run, particularly in sugar production. They were also designed to export nearly all their production. The various aspects of the Atlantic economy as it developed from the early seventeenth century were linked together by African slavery, the exploitation this required, and the profits the Europeans made from it. The average life-expectancy of a slave in the Caribbean, even a young, healthy male, was about seven years. In the 1690s such a slave could be bought for about £20 which was the value of the sugar each slave produced every year. After allowing for other expenses, and the high death rate, this still left a huge profit for the owner. The failure of the slaves to reproduce themselves made little difference.

European societies were rough and brutal. The conditions of those at the bottom, especially convicts, 'vagrants' and the 'idle poor' were terrible and the Irish peasants in the 1840s were probably in a worse economic state than many slaves in the preceding centuries. But there were fundamental differences between the way these people were treated and the conditions of the slaves. For example, the slave ships on the passage between Africa and the Americas packed in four times as many Africans as there were European convicts on similar ships. These differences reflected European perceptions of how Africans could be treated. Slaves were different from even the most brutalized of workers in European societies because they lost all basic human rights – not just to freedom but also to family and children (the fact that some slave families existed is not relevant because they depended on the will of the owner and could be, and often were, broken up for profit). Africans became property as the English Solicitor-General's official opinion in 1677 confirmed: 'negroes ought to be esteemed goods and commodities'. In the last (and often far from last) resort, slavery depended upon violence. There was a delicate line for owners to tread between making slaves work and keeping them alive. Basic to the system was the lash and flogging with even more draconian punishments kept in reserve. The legal system supported the owners and gave them freedom – killing a slave was not a crime in the English colonies because it was held that no owner would willingly destroy his own property. For rebellion the punishment was to nail each limb to the ground and burn the hands and feet and then the limbs, so as to produce a very slow and agonizing death. Lesser 'crimes' resulted in castration, cutting off half a foot with an axe or whipping followed by pepper and salt being rubbed into the skin. These brutal punishments were viewed as necessary by the owners for reasons of security. This reflected the fact that on some of the Caribbean islands four out of five of the population were slaves – a proportion which was unprecedented in world history.

When slaves arrived in the Americas they were highly demoralized after enslavement and the horrors of the passage from Africa. They were then renamed so as to complete their disorientation. Nearly three-quarters of them went to work on sugar plantations where they were subject to the further shock of the work regime with its discipline, hierarchy and effort. The Europeans created a myth that the Africans were uniquely suited to hard labour in a tropical climate even though most of the slaves did not come from tropical areas and had been brought up in societies where women did most of the agricultural work. Indeed in much of the Caribbean about two-thirds of the field workers were women. They also had to face the very common threat of sexual assault from their owners and the expectation that they would produce slave children thereby increasing the owners' profits still further. However, the slave system could not survive purely through the threat of violence. There had to be some prospect of both promotion and easier conditions as an overseer or house-hold slave, a family life (even with the ever-present threat that it would be broken up), a small plot of land, Sundays free and some community life with the other slaves.

Despite a minimal amelioration of harsh conditions, resistance at all levels was common – refusal to work hard, petty theft and sabotage. Outright rebellion was rare because it was so difficult to organize and because the owners based their organization on the assumption that revolt was always likely. Only once did it succeed on a major scale – Haiti in the 1790s – and the revolts in Virginia in 1800 and under Nat Turner in 1831 were the exceptions rather than the rule. The other main revolts in the Caribbean came in the early nineteenth century – Barbados in 1816, Demerara in 1823 and Jamaica in 1831–2. After each of them several hundred slaves were executed. The European powers realized their mutual interest in keeping the slaves under control and during the colonial warfare of the seventeenth and eighteenth centuries they were always very careful to avoid inciting slave revolts. The only alternative for the slaves was to run away. This was almost impossible on the islands of the Caribbean and in north America there was strong legislation, and an effective system, for returning runaways. Nevertheless areas controlled by ex-slaves did exist, even in some of the remote areas on West Indian islands such as Jamaica. The most extensive was Palmares in Pernambuco between 1672 and 1694. Its capital was at Macaco (the current Brazilian city of Uniao) and its territory stretched for 130 miles along the coast and for a hundred miles inland. It needed a major army campaign over several years to put it down.

17.3 Brazil: Slavery and Plantations

It was in Brazil under the Portuguese that the characteristic features of the Atlantic economy – plantations, slaves and the trade with Africa – were developed on a major scale in the early seventeenth century. During the long history of Atlantic slavery the majority of African slaves went to Brazil and it was also the last state in the area to abolish slavery in 1888. The Portuguese empire was essentially commercial from the beginning, although until the 1580s Brazil played only a very minor part. It had no precious metals readily available and ships called there mainly for the brazil wood which produced a good red dye. There were about three million native Americans in the region but they were thinly spread and therefore avoided some of the worst impact of European diseases. At first it was fairly easy to get the natives to trade for European goods but they soon had all the goods they wanted. A small colony was established at Bahia in 1549 but the superb natural harbour at Rio de Janeiro was first settled by the French (it was taken from them by the Portuguese in the 1550s). It was only at this stage that concessions, including the right to native labour (like the Spanish *encomienda* system), were given out by the government to various adventurers. Plantations were set up to grow sugar and they flourished because in north-east Brazil the soil and climate was ideal and there were plenty of streams and rivers to provide water-power for the sugar mills. Production on the Atlantic islands was already in decline as soil fertility fell and as early as 1580 Brazil was producing three times as much sugar as Madeira and São Tomé combined. Production was based on extensive native slavery – there were probably about 50,000 such slaves by 1570. One of the main owners was the Jesuit estates and they also hired out their slaves to other producers. Every settler bought slaves to avoid doing manual labour as one early commentator on the colony noted:

The first thing they try to obtain is slaves to work the farms. Anyone who succeeds in obtaining two pairs or half a dozen of them has the means to sustain his family in a respectable way, even though he may have no other earthly possessions. For one fishes for him, another hunts and the rest cultivate and till his fields.

By the end of the sixteenth century the native slaves outnumbered the European settlers by about three to one.

It was only as the supply of native slaves began to dry up that the Portuguese turned to Africa to replace them. The voyage from Africa was short and Portugal dominated trade along the Angolan and Congo coasts opposite Brazil. One of the first groups to buy African slaves was the Jesuits but by 1600 there were still only about 15,000 in the colony – far less than the number of local slaves. By 1630 the number had quadrupled to over 60,000 and the annual trade was about 10,000 a year. About half that number were sent to Spanish America so that the total Atlantic trade at this time was about 15,000 slaves a year. The profits were large – slaves could be sold in Brazil for about ten times the value of goods traded for them along the African coast. (This was partly because the limited trade in slaves at this time kept prices fairly low in Africa.) The slaves were required for the sugar plantations as the trade boomed. By the early seventeenth century Brazil was exporting about 20,000 tons of sugar a year (about four-fifths of Europe's consumption) and the colony had become the centrepiece of the Portuguese empire, contributing about 40 per cent of the state's revenue. Portuguese traders had already established a triangular trade – goods for slaves in Africa, slaves sold in Brazil and sugar taken back to Europe. By the first decades of the seventeenth century about half the population of Brazil were slaves and they formed the essential labour force on which the prosperity of the colony depended (in the Spanish Americas slaves were still only about two per cent of the population).

17.4 The Dutch and the French

The wealth of both the Spanish and Portuguese empires attracted the other European powers, especially the Dutch, who were fighting for independence from Spain. At first most of the effort was put into raiding the great silver and treasure fleets that sailed from Havana to Cadiz but the key development was the foundation of the West India Company in 1621 which, like the East India Company founded in 1602 and similar English companies, combined both state and commercial policy aims. The Dutch wanted to harm Spanish trade (Portugal was ruled by Spain at the time) and gain profits for themselves. Brazil and its sugar were therefore prime targets. (The West India Company took theological advice on the morality of slave trading – the Dutch Calvinists came down against it.) In the early 1630s the Dutch captured Pernambuco province. Their abstention from the slave trade did not last long. They began by selling rather than freeing slaves they captured from Portuguese and Spanish ships. Then in 1637 they captured El Mina, the main Portuguese trading post for slaves on the African coast, and began importing about 2,000 slaves a year into their part of Brazil. In 1640 Portugal became independent from Spain and five years later there was a revolt in Pernambuco against Dutch rule. Very few Dutch settlers had moved to Brazil and little effort was made to retain the colony, which passed back under Portuguese control in 1654. The Portuguese restored their slave trade on independence from Spain and by the late seventeenth century there were about 100,000 slaves in the colony compared with about 60,000 in the middle of the century. About three-quarters of them were employed in sugar production.

The French were involved in the West Indian islands from the early seventeenth century but colonization was at a low level. In the 1640s there were about 7,000 settlers on Martinique, Guadeloupe and the neighbouring islands, and the majority of them were indentured labourers. Most of the slaves were imported by the Dutch and the English who also controlled the sugar trade to France until the French founded their own company in the 1660s. By then half the population of the islands were slaves as sugar production increased. The main expansion came after the 1690s when Saint-Domingue was taken from Spain – by the early eighteenth century there were about 50,000 slaves on the islands. In 1685 Louis XIV drew up the 'Code Noir' for the colonies. All Jews were to be expelled as 'declared enemies' of Christians. Slavery was recognized subject to a single condition – the slaves were to be baptized and instructed in Catholicism. Some protection for the slaves was included in the code but there was no mechanism provided to enforce these provisions. At this time the level of slavery in the French colonies was about the same as Brazil in the late sixteenth century. The next hundred years was to witness a phenomenal growth.

17.5 Early English Slavery

The early English contacts with the Americas were, like the Dutch, largely restricted to piracy and looting under men like Drake and Hawkins. The first colony in Virginia suffered from competition with similar projects in Ireland and the failure of the local natives to play the part assigned to them by the English – peasants prepared to grow food and provide cheap labour for the settlers. No gold was found and the settlers only survived because the natives were prepared to give food. In return the English declared perpetual war on them so that they could seize their land. It was not until the 1620s that the Virginia Company stumbled across a formula that enabled the colony to survive. Land was allocated free to those who paid for their own voyage; those who came as indentured servants could buy land when they were freed. Between 1640 and the end of the century over 100,000 indentured servants went to the colonies in north America. (The majority of European emigrants who went to the American colonies before 1783 were indentured labourers not free workers.) Tobacco formed the main and most profitable crop for export back to Europe but the number of slaves remained low – there were only 2,000 in Virginia in 1670.

The colonies on the American mainland developed slowly unlike Barbados which was first settled in 1624 – it was chosen because it was upwind in relation to the rest of the Caribbean and therefore difficult for Spain, the main power in the region, to attack. The colony originally grew tobacco but remained poor and undeveloped – in 1638 the population totalled 6,000 including 2,000 indentured servants brought from England at a cost of £12 for five years' labour, and 200 African slaves who cost about £25 each. It was the introduction of sugar cultivation (learnt from the Dutch) which transformed the small island of less than 150 square miles and demonstrated the potential of the plantation system. In 1638 no sugar was grown, yet by 1645 plantations covered half the island and were soon producing two-thirds of the sugar consumed in England, the main market in Europe. Setting up the plantations required large amounts of capital because no crop was harvested for eighteen months. The mill-owners therefore tended to buy out the smallholders and set up their own estates. At first the indentured labourers worked alongside the slaves but fairly rapidly whites came to hold supervisory roles only – it was easier to control the slaves than discontented white servants who had to be treated much more leniently.

From the early 1640s Barbados grew phenomenally. Within a decade there were 20,000 slaves (mainly brought in by the Dutch as prices dropped because they could not sell them in Brazil) and less than half that number of indentured servants. By the mid-1650s the island was exporting as much sugar as the whole of Brazil. By the 1680s there were over 50,000 slaves in the colony (about three-quarters of the total population), with the overwhelming majority working on large estates of over a hundred acres in gangs of more than a hundred slaves. The slaves worked for eighteen hours a day as the mills operated round the clock during the six- to seven-month harvesting season. Not surprisingly mortality rates were very high.

It was by far the largest English colony in the Americas – much bigger than Virginia and Massachusetts on the mainland. Sugar production also began on Jamaica and over 85,000 slaves were taken to the island in the last half of the seventeenth century.

From the 1660s the English began to trade in slaves on a major scale. In 1663 the Company of Royal Adventurers to Africa (whose major subscribers were King Charles II and the royal family) was given a monopoly over the supply of slaves to all the English colonies in the Americas. It was replaced in 1672 by a new monopoly, the Royal African Company, which had a wider group of subscribers from within the royal family and the London merchant community. In the forty years after it was set up it bought about 125,000 slaves in Africa. After about 1690 the company found it more and more difficult to sustain its monopoly as independent merchants tried to gain their share of the huge profits to be made out of the slave trade.

17.6 The Eighteenth-Century Plantation Economies

17.6.1 The West Indies

The eighteenth century was the great age of the sugar plantations. By the middle of the century sugar overtook grain as the most valuable commodity in European trade – it made up a fifth of all European imports and by the last decades of the century four-fifths of the sugar came from the British and French colonies in the West Indies. Over the course of the century the French colonies were the most successful, especially Saint-Domingue, where better irrigation, water-power and machinery, together with concentration on newer types of sugar, increased profits. The French also diversified more into coffee and indigo production. A glittering, wealthy society grew up on the islands among the slave owners and merchants. On Saint-Domingue there was a theatre for 1,500 which put on Mozart's *Marriage of Figaro* only a few weeks after its première in Paris. In the British colonies Jamaica clearly had the greatest potential – the small island of Barbados was reaching its maximum output, although profits were increased by making the more valuable white sugar. Before about 1740 Jamaica suffered from poor external and internal security but then grew rapidly as a few landlords created vast estates worked by gangs of around 500 slaves. Across the British West Indies the expansion of sugar production seemed to be never-ending as demand in Europe continued to grow. Sugar consumption in Britain rose five-fold in just sixty years after 1710 and by the middle of the eighteenth century over half of Britain's overseas trade was made up of just sugar and tobacco.

The wealth that was generated in the West Indies depended on the slaves who arrived in ever-increasing numbers. In the 1690s there were 27,000 slaves in the French colonies and 95,000 in the British islands. A century later these figures had risen to 675,000 and 480,000 respectively – a ten-fold increase. Death rates were phenomenally high. Between 1712 and 1734 over 75,000 slaves were imported into Barbados yet the slave population rose by only 4,000. On average one slave child was born for every six slaves who died and therefore the owners relied on importation rather than the breeding of slaves. Their crude calculation was that raising a child to working age (young as that was) would cost about £40 (allowing for lost work from the mother and child mortality) whereas a new slave could be bought for about £25.
[*The slave revolt on Haiti 21.6*]

17.6.2 North America
The eighteenth century also witnessed a major expansion of slavery in the English colonies of north America. Between 1700 and 1770 the slave population rose from about 50,000 to over 500,000. By the latter date the three major slave plantation crops – tobacco, indigo and rice – made up more than three-quarters of all exports from these colonies to Britain. Early in the eighteenth century there were still native slaves – over 1,400 in South Carolina (about ten per cent of the total population) but they were soon replaced by Africans. The majority of the population of north America were small-scale farmers growing the same sort of crops as farmers in Britain. There was therefore little demand for their products (any excess demand in Britain could be met from Ireland). The farm surplus of north America was therefore sold in the West Indies (to both British and French colonies) to provide food for the slaves – nearly all the land on the islands was devoted to growing sugar. Alongside these small farmers were the tobacco plantations which, on average, were as big as a sugar plantation but used fewer slaves because the labour demands of the crop were lower. The plantations moved further inland every seven years or so because tobacco rapidly exhausted the soil. In the half-century from 1710 tobacco production (primarily in Maryland and Virginia) tripled as the region had a near monopoly over European imports. An even higher rate of growth occurred further south in Georgia and south Carolina, where the rice and indigo plantations expanded rapidly. These two colonies exported just 12,000 pounds of rice in 1698 yet by 1770 this figure had risen to 83 million pounds.

The mainland system of slavery was very different from that in the West Indies and death rates were much lower for a number of reasons. The pattern of work was not so heavy, in particular it lacked the all-night processing of sugar, and the climate was better. Many of the slaves in north America were bought from the West Indies already 'seasoned' to plantation work and the new climate, rather than being imported direct from Africa. In addition, more females were engaged in household work than in the West Indies. The result was that slaves lived longer, tended to form family units, reproduced themselves, created more slaves and reduced the need for imports. Almost two-thirds of north American slaves were in Maryland and Virginia but even here they made up only about a third of the population, far lower than the four-fifths which was common on the West Indian islands. In the mainland colonies to the north numbers were very low, no more than about five per cent of the population. This was largely because there were no plantation crops that could be grown in the more temperate climate – most slaves were either domestics or worked in the towns. Nevertheless in all of the British colonies in the Americas the state recognized and supported slavery even though no such status was accepted in Britain itself.

17.6.3 Brazil

In Brazil slavery was revitalized by the re-establishment of Portuguese control over the whole colony in the 1650s and by the discovery of gold in southern Brazil in the 1690s. By the 1720s gold output was about ten tons a year and it was worth almost as much as sugar exports which were suffering from severe competition from West Indies production. Many of the slaves were native Americans. There was a long struggle between the settlers and the Jesuits, who set up 'missions' (sugar plantations and cattle ranches) where the natives were forcibly converted, over who should control the remaining natives. Vast slaving expeditions were made into the interior, some of which were organized by the Jesuits who then branded the natives and forced them to work on the 'missions'. One of these expeditions paid for the rebuilding of the cathedral of São Luis in 1718. During the gold rush after the 1690s many of the natives of the north-east were enslaved by the gold prospectors. However, as in the past, the natives could not supply nearly as much labour as the European settlers wanted and slave imports rose to record levels – by 1750 there were over 500,000 slaves in Brazil and they made up about a third of the population (about the same proportion as in the southern colonies on the north American mainland). Where Brazil differed from the British colonies was that manumission of slaves was relatively common and they were even able to join the army.

17.6.4 The Spanish empire

In the Spanish colonies the extraction of gold and silver was still the

dominant factor in the eighteenth century. The Andean mines were still worked almost entirely by native labour and only a few thousand slaves were used to supplement them. On the mainland only Venezuela had large, slave-worked plantations exporting cacao and indigo. The one classic plantation economy in the Spanish empire was on Cuba where sugar and tobacco were produced. Here about a quarter of the population were slaves. The right to supply slaves to the Spanish empire was gained by Britain as part of the Treaty of Utrecht in 1713 and the free entry of slaves into the empire was not allowed until 1787. This significantly held back the growth of plantations and therefore production. Even the smaller European powers had their own slave empires during the eighteenth century. On the Danish islands of St Thomas and Sainte Croix there were about 20,000 slaves at any one time. They were nearly all engaged in sugar production which prospered when the other colonies in the Caribbean were affected by the wars between the major European powers.
[*Independence of Latin America 21.7*]

17.7 The Slave Trade

The maintenance of the European slave empires in the Americas required a major trade in slaves from Africa. It was the most complex international trade developed by European merchants in the three centuries after 1500 and was global in scope. It involved Indian textile manufacturers, European manufacturers (especially of iron goods and firearms), African traders, European shippers, plantation owners, plus credit and banking agencies. Every maritime power in Europe was involved. Although it entailed a massive waste of human life and immense suffering it was, from a purely commercial point of view, incredibly successful. It was the most dynamic sector of a number of west European economies and central to the overall growth and growing prosperity of the region.

Over the last three decades a highly accurate census of the slave trade has been carried out by historians and they show that the slave trade reached its height in the eighteenth century. In the first century of the European conquest of the Americas up to 1600, 370,000 slaves were taken to the continent. In the next hundred years this rose to 1,870,000. In the eighteenth century 6,130,000 slaves were taken from Africa to the Americas. The result was that the total slave population in the Americas rose from about 330,000 in 1700 to over 3 million a century later. In this period the trade had passed beyond the control of regulated state monopolies and was in the hands of a mass of private merchants. During the eighteenth century the British dominated the trade and carried over forty per cent of the slaves (2.5 million people), the Portuguese were the second major shipper with just under a third (1.8 million) and the French took about a fifth of the total (1.2 million). Out of the total of about 6 million slaves a third went to Brazil, just under a quarter to each of the British and French West Indies and only a little over five per cent to the north American mainland. About two-thirds of the total transported were males (a higher percentage than in the preceding centuries) and almost a quarter were children.

The largest single cost for the slave merchants was the price of the slaves on the African coast. They could not control this price which was set by the Africans – it tended to rise and was very carefully determined by the quality of the goods the Europeans had to offer. In the hundred years after 1670 the average price of a male slave in Africa rose from £3 to £15 and the price they could be sold for in the Americas therefore rose as well, from £17 to £35 and to nearly £50 by the end of the eighteenth century. These prices meant that profits were large – the annual rate of profit for British slave traders in the eighteenth century was just under ten per cent a year, the same as that derived from a slave plantation in the West Indies and three times the amount that could be gained from investing in land. The major cost for the slavers was the goods they had to buy for trade along the African coast. Certain goods were essential – from Europe iron, firearms (by the end of the eighteenth century the British were sending 300,000 guns a year to Africa), cloth and paper and, from the American plantations, rum and tobacco. Most important were the products Europe could buy in Asia, in particular spices and textiles. The latter were vital because until the end of the eighteenth century Indian textiles were of a far higher quality than those made in Europe and the Africans would not accept the inferior product. The two major importers of Indian textiles, Liverpool and Nantes, were also two of the biggest slaving ports. For the French, Indian textiles were just under sixty per cent of the value of the goods they traded to buy slaves (European textiles were five per cent) and for the English they were the largest single item taken to Africa – they were still a third of the total even after the significant development of the English industry from the 1750s.

The next major cost for the slavers was the passage from Africa to the Americas. It was their need to make a profit which caused the terrible conditions on these voyages. Costs were high because slave ships carried twice the normal crew for security reasons – the danger of revolt was always highest at the beginning when the slaves finally realized they were being taken away from Africa. The death toll on the slave ships was horrendous – about fifteen to twenty per cent of all those taken from Africa. On the shorter trips direct from Africa to Brazil this figure might be lower but on the long journey from Angola to north America it approached a third of all those on board. The slaves were tightly packed head-to-toe and chained. They were normally kept below deck for the voyage where the poor diet, lack of water, seasickness and diarrhoea produced unbelievable conditions. In the seventeenth century the smell of the ships even when over the horizon alerted the population of New Amsterdam (now New York) to their arrival. The slavers accepted these conditions because if the slaves had been given even the same amount of space as a European emigrant they would only have landed half as many slaves and their profits would have disappeared. Mortality on the voyages fell slightly during the eighteenth century from the normal rate of one in five as the slavers increased the amount of food and water, used specially designed ships and in some cases even gave out lemon juice to guard against scurvy and inoculated against smallpox. However, death rates at the very lowest levels (one in twenty) were still about five times as high as on European convict ships. They were the result of the severe over-crowding which Europeans thought acceptable for Africans but not for their own criminals.

The slave traders could bear the small extra cost of a few improvements because of the very high profits and the volume of the trade which was about 80,000 slaves a year in the last two decades of the eighteenth century. With the trade at this level it is not surprising that it was the key to the populating of the Americas. In the three hundred years or so before 1820 well over three times as many Africans were taken across the Atlantic as European emigrants – 8.4 million compared with 2.4 million. Yet in 1820 the population of the Americas was half white and half black. That is a measure of the mortality on the American slave plantations.
[*The nineteenth-century Atlantic economy 21.8*]

17.8 Africa in the Atlantic Economy

Like the Americas large parts of western Africa, especially the regions south of Cameroon, were largely isolated from Eurasian history until the late fifteenth century. The arrival of the Portuguese changed that situation but the impression made by the early Europeans was very limited. The African chiefdoms and states had coastal navies with ships carrying about a hundred men which, although they found it difficult to board the high-sided Portuguese vessels, were well capable of offering considerable resistance to the handful of European ships in the area. Portuguese attempts to land in Senegambia and near the island of Gorée were defeated in 1446 and 1447. Later in 1535 the Portuguese tried to conquer the

Bissagos islands off the Guinea coast but failed utterly. The Africans therefore kept the coastal trade under their own control and the Portuguese (and later other European states) found it easier to send 'presents' and 'tribute' to local leaders and conclude treaties allowing them to trade. The rulers usually insisted on 'special' prices for their own purchases and if they were granted were happy for general trade to be opened. Attempts to raid along the coast only ruined trade as both the Castilians and the English found to their cost. A few forts and trading posts were established but even these were difficult to sustain in the tropics. (Detailed records kept by the British Royal African Company show that for every ten soldiers sent to west Africa between 1695 and 1722 six died in the first year, two more died between years two and seven and only one man lived to be discharged in Britain.) Only one very small colony was established for several centuries. In 1579 the Portuguese trading post in Angola was expanded into a coastal colony after a trade dispute. Even this could only be done in alliance with the rival Kongo ruler who provided nearly all the troops.

The trade that evolved along the African coast was largely dictated by the Africans. They only wanted a certain range of products from the Europeans because they manufactured most of the essentials themselves. (The idea that Africans sold slaves in return for a few beads and trinkets was a myth put about by the Europeans.) By the late seventeenth century about 150 tons of iron was exported every year to Senegambia but this was only about ten per cent of the total used in the region – the rest was produced locally and in many cases was of a higher quality than the European product. In the early seventeenth century the eastern Kongo region was exporting over 100,000 yards of cloth a year – this was the same amount as total Dutch exports and from roughly the same size of population. The Gold Coast area imported about 20,000 yards of cloth a year (both European and Indian) but this was two per cent of total local consumption. European goods were refused or sent back if the quality was low or they were not what was wanted. Africa was also exporting to Europe – during the eighteenth century a million mats were sent from Senegambia to Britain.

Central to the trade with Africa, and the main reason for its existence, was the purchase of slaves. Slavery had long existed in Africa and partly derived from the unusual absence of landed property and from a social system under which people, not land, were owned and taxed. Peasants had the right to farm the land and to its produce but did not have the right to sell the land. 'Nobles' had titles but not private estates with rents as in Europe. Instead they had state revenue assigned to them by the ruler (often wrongly titled a king by the Europeans) who did not own the land himself (another European misconception). Slaves and people therefore provided the main route to wealth because they could be used to farm land (which was available to whoever cultivated it) and their produce could be appropriated by the elite. War was the main source of slaves and the slave trade was entirely in African hands until the final sale on the coast. However, although African elites benefited from the wealth this trade generated, the only reason for its existence was the European demand for Africans to work on the American plantations.

Until the mid-seventeenth century the effect of Europe was to widen and deepen considerably the existing African demand for slaves. Many areas resisted the European demand for slaves – Benin in the 1550s and the Kongo at the end of the sixteenth century, and in the latter area the trade did not start on any scale for another hundred years. Some groups such as the Kru in modern Liberia resisted so strongly that the Europeans stopped trying to enslave them, and others such as the Baga of modern Guinea and the Jola to the south of Senegal refused to participate in the trade. Over the centuries the main slaving areas moved south along the African coast – by the early nineteenth century they were concentrated in the Bight of Biafra, Angola and Mozambique on the east coast. Two factors radically transformed the situation in Africa. First, the huge increase in the European demand for slaves from the early eighteenth century and second the sale by the Europeans of the flintlock rather than the matchlock musket from the middle of the seventeenth century. European gunpowder weapons made little impact on Africa for more than a century after 1500 (crude early artillery were almost useless against earth fortifications) but the flintlock had twice the rate of fire and half the failure rate of its predecessor and a number of African military empires were created with it. They were often created by quite small groups who were able to entrench their positions and become major suppliers of slaves to the Europeans.

In the early eighteenth century the Bambara kingdom on the upper Niger river expanded and became a major supplier of slaves through Senegambia during the first three decades of the century. When the supply dried up the slave traders moved elsewhere. At the same time Oyo, the dominant Yoruba kingdom of south-west Nigeria, conquered Dahomey in order to gain access to the sea and become a major supplier of slaves. The expanded kingdom lasted for about a century until it collapsed under the strain of trying to control such a large empire. By the early nineteenth century the Yoruba were, for the first time, sold as slaves themselves and they soon became one of the main sources for the nineteenth-century trade. New states also emerged based on the wealth the elites could gain from the trade. In the early eighteenth century this was particularly apparent among the Akan people of the Gold Coast (modern Ghana). By 1701 the most powerful state was Asante which derived its wealth from the productive agriculture around the capital Kumasi (which had about 15,000 people) and its control over the slave trade routes. By the early nineteenth century it was one of the wealthiest and largest states in Africa. In Angola a number of trading states derived their wealth from the trade with the Portuguese – Matamba and Kasanje and, later in the eighteenth century, Lunda inland to the east. Everywhere the trade and its profits were controlled by a small elite. In the main they were the rulers and rich merchants together with the middlemen on the coast such as the Afro-Portuguese in Senegambia and upper Guinea and the Ijaw traders of the Niger delta.

What was the overall impact of the slave trade on Africa? In total about 12 million people were bought by the Europeans and taken to the Americas as slaves. However, even this very high figure is not an accurate measure. The best estimates suggest that about four out of ten of the people originally enslaved died before they even reached the ships, or were kept as slaves in Africa (this was particularly true for females who were prized as slaves in Africa whereas the Europeans preferred males). This suggests that the European trade in 12 million slaves involved the enslavement of some 20 million people. The slave trade was also concentrated in particular areas. During the seventeenth and eighteenth centuries most slaves came from regions less than a hundred miles from the coast and it was not until the nineteenth century that the trade expanded over much greater distances, in some cases as much as five hundred miles. In the main slaving regions such as Angola and the Bight of Benin there is little doubt that the scale of the slave trade caused a decline in population. In the surrounding regions it was large enough to stop any population increase for a couple of centuries or more and this was at the time when the population of the rest of the world was increasing rapidly.
[*Later Africa 21.19*]

17.9 Gold and Silver

When Vasco da Gama, guided by his Muslim pilot, arrived at Calicut in May 1498 he was granted an audience with the ruler. He laid out the goods brought from Europe – striped cloths, scarlet hoods, hats, strings of corals (bought en route), hand washbasins, sugar, oil and honey. The ruler and his court merely laughed at this collection – the goods were far inferior to the ones the Indians either made or obtained from the Indian Ocean trading networks. They refused to take any and insisted on the payment of gold and silver for the goods the Portuguese wanted. The Portuguese faced the same problem as the Romans 1,500 years earlier – Asia was the wealthiest part of the world and wanted little from 'the west' whereas the countries of Europe wanted the products of 'the east'. The only way they could be bought was by paying hard cash in the form of gold and silver. Under the Romans and again after the establishment of the wealthy Islamic empire there was a steady drain of the two precious metals from west to east until supplies began to run out. It was the European domination of the Atlantic world that gave them access to gold and silver in previously undreamt-of quantities and this enabled them to buy their way into the Asian trading system. The gold and silver of the Americas was the link between the Atlantic and Indian Ocean trading systems.

Europe produced very little gold or silver itself – about 100,000 kilograms a year at its peak in the 1530s but falling to a third of this level by the early seventeenth century. Gold was obtained from west Africa at the rate of about 20,000 kilos a year, though just over twice this level at the peak of the trade in the early seventeenth century. These quantities were small compared with the huge wealth obtained from the plunder of the Aztec and Inca empires and, even more important, the forced labour of the natives in the Potosi silver mines. In the three centuries after 1500 about 85 per cent of the world's silver production and 70 per cent of the gold output came from the Americas and was under European control. On average the Spanish were officially shipping about 330,000 kilos of silver every year to Europe across the Atlantic. In addition, from the middle of the sixteenth century silver was shipped from Acapulco across the Pacific to Manila at the rate of about 150,000 kilos a year – the contraband trade probably doubled this figure.

Europe retained little of this vast silver output – Spain itself had a copper-based currency. Most of it went to India and China to buy goods and a large proportion also went to the Levant and the Ottoman empire to purchase goods there. Much of the silver was shipped through Amsterdam and London in unopened boxes and then by sea to India. The key role of the silver in European trade can be judged from the fact that the profits of the Dutch East India Company fluctuated according to their access to American silver because this dictated how much they could buy in Asia. How much silver and gold went to Asia? Exact figures are difficult to calculate but during the seventeenth century the total was about 28 million kg (about 28,000 tons) of silver. Almost all of the silver imported into India became currency – the total amount in circulation tripled in the seventeenth century and there is little evidence of any significant inflation because the currency was needed in a rapidly expanding economy. However, the prime beneficiary of American silver was China, the richest country in the world. Chinese silver production was low (about 1,000 kg a year). Japan was a very important supplier until the late sixteenth century at about 125,000 kg a year, largely to buy Chinese silk. (Japan was originally known to the Europeans as the 'silver islands'.) The major impact came from American silver, particularly after it was shipped directly across the Pacific. From the mid-sixteenth century the Chinese government was able to commute all its land taxes, labour obligations and levies into silver payments as the metal flooded into the country. By the 1640s the Chinese treasury was gaining 750,000 kg of silver every year. (The total amount of American silver shipped to China in the seventeenth century was equivalent to the Chinese state revenue for twenty-three years.) The level of wealth in China can be seen from the fact that in the seventeenth century it was estimated that even a 'poor' cloth merchant in Shanghai had a capital (not turnover) of about five tons of silver and the richest families had hoards of several hundred tons of silver.

17.10 Europe and Asia: the Portuguese

[Earlier Indian Ocean trade 12.2.1, 12.2.3 & 15.5.3]
The nature of the European impact on the Indian Ocean world was made clear from the first major expedition of thirteen ships under Alvares Cabral which left Lisbon in March 1500. When it arrived at Calicut it bombarded the town for two days to try and force the ruler to expel Muslim traders. For more than a thousand years the Indian Ocean trading world had been almost entirely peaceful and cosmopolitan with different communities co-operating together for profit. Ships in the Indian Ocean were normally unarmed and sailed together so as to avoid pirates and provide assistance during bad weather. The Portuguese could have operated peacefully in this world, though they would have been at a disadvantage because of the poor quality of their goods. Instead they, like the other European states, chose violence as a way of entering the established trading world and securing advantages. They also adopted what was to become a common European way of operating – commercial companies were licensed by the state at home, usually given a monopoly, and acted like a state abroad.

The main phase of Portuguese expansion lasted for the first fifteen years of the sixteenth century when they used force to seize major ports across the Indian Ocean trade routes. At first they were not successful – they lost the first encounter with a joint Mamluk and Gujarati fleet in 1508, although in the next year they were victorious in a battle off the port of Diu. The first success came with the capture of Goa in 1510. The next year the key trading city of Malacca was secured. (The expelled ruler founded the Sultanate of Johor on the Malay peninsula and allied with the Srivijayan state at Palembang – the place of origin of the Malacca rulers in

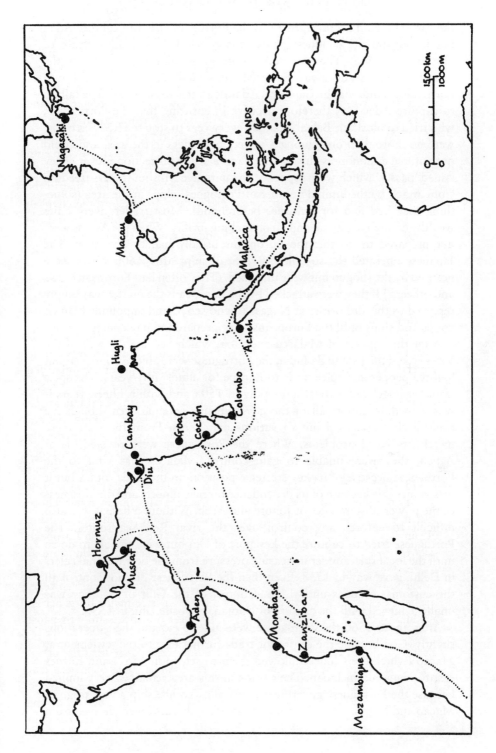

Map 51: Portugal and Asia: the sixteenth century

the early fifteenth century.) In 1513 the Portuguese tried to capture Aden but failed and the conquest phase was concluded with the capture of Hormuz in 1515. The overriding Portuguese aim was to divert the lucrative spice trade away from Mamluk and Venetian control into Portuguese hands via the Cape and Atlantic routes to Antwerp. The failure to capture Aden was therefore decisive in ensuring that the Portuguese, who tried to blockade Bab al-Mandeb every year to stop the Red Sea trade, were no more than one among a variety of traders in the area and could not enforce a monopoly. Instead they ran a crude protection racket. They issued 'passes' which were supposed to guarantee Muslim traders freedom from attack by the limited number of Portuguese ships in the area (something they had had for centuries beforehand). Most traders were quite wealthy enough to pay up and go on making profits. When the Asians were not prepared to do this the Europeans usually had to give way. The Japanese operated the so-called 'Red Seal' ships after 1600 which were licensed by the shogun but were unarmed. (They often had European crews and officers.) If they were attacked by the Europeans the matter was simply reported to the authorities at Nagasaki who seized and impounded Dutch goods and ships until the Europeans were prepared to pay compensation.

After the capture of Malacca and Goa, which became the seat of the Viceroy and the Estado da India, the Portuguese were able to control about half the pepper and spice trade to Europe for almost fifty years. The spice trade was declared a royal monopoly in 1505 and within fifteen years it was providing almost all of the government's revenue even though the trade itself was leased out to various merchants. From the start these merchants faced problems. Where the Portuguese were resisted, as at Acheh, they were unable to gain control. Malacca was vital to the Portuguese because of its key strategic position on the trade routes but it was vulnerable because of its dependence on rice imports and the closeness of the powerful sultanates of Johore and Aceh. Without a base it was also difficult to enforce any control over the rival Red Sea routes. The Portuguese tried to capture the key port of Diu but were unable to do so until the local ruler, under increasing pressure from the new Mughal rulers in Delhi, gave way in 1538. Even then the Portuguese did not control all the customs revenues until 1555. Control of the Gulf of Cambay was finally achieved with the capture of Daman, opposite Diu, in 1559.

After about 1560 the Portuguese were able to expand their operations slightly. Goa became the centre for trade further east to the settlement at Macao (which the Chinese allowed them to set up in 1557) and further east to Nagasaki in Japan. Their trade in this area remained very limited because the Portuguese government only allowed one ship a year to go to Macao and Nagasaki. Most of the profits from this area were derived from a small involvement in the China–Japan trade – taking silver from Japan in return for Chinese silk. The trade into Bengal was always profitable but the Portuguese were not allowed to settle there until Hugli was established in 1580; they were expelled by the Mughals in 1632. After the initial period of violence in the first decades of the sixteenth century they were not seen as much of a threat and no power bothered to build a navy to oppose them. In general their impact was limited and a majority of their profits increasingly came from their involvement in intra-Asian trade rather than the shipment of goods to Europe. After about 1560 they were beginning to lose their position. The sultanate of Acheh had maintained its own routes for the spice trade to the Red Sea and this trade was reviving strongly in the latter half of the sixteenth century under encouragement from the Ottomans in Egypt. In return the Ottomans supplied Acheh with high-quality military equipment with which to resist the Portuguese. Portugal was unable to stop the diversion of increasing amounts of trade from their own routes to the long-established routes via the Red Sea and Egypt. Their predominance in the trade between the Indian Ocean area and Europe was therefore very short-lived.

17.11 Europe and Asia: the Dutch

The first major challenge from Europe to the Portuguese position came from the Dutch. They had been at war with Spain (which controlled Portugal) since the 1560s and this gave them as great a sense of religious righteousness as the Iberian communities gained from the *reconquista*. In 1602 the Dutch government set up the Vereenigde Oost-Indische Compagnie (VOC), or East India Company, to stop conflicts among Dutch merchants over control of the trade. It was effectively the Dutch state (which was dominated by the merchants) in another form – the VOC was even given the right to make war and peace. From 1605 the main battles were with the Portuguese as a carry-over of the war in Europe and military costs took up more than a third of the VOC's initial capital in the seven years to 1612. (These high costs were sustainable because of the trade monopoly the company held at home and the large profits which could be derived from it.) In 1605 Amboina in the Moluccas was captured but the Dutch had little success after this. In 1606 they failed to take Malacca and in 1607–8 they twice failed to capture Mozambique, the key port on the route to the western coast of India. The main Dutch innovation was to take greater direct control over the spice islands through conquest. In 1620–1 they captured Banda (the source of nutmeg) after a difficult campaign. The Bandanese fleet was faster and could outmanoeuvre the Dutch and the

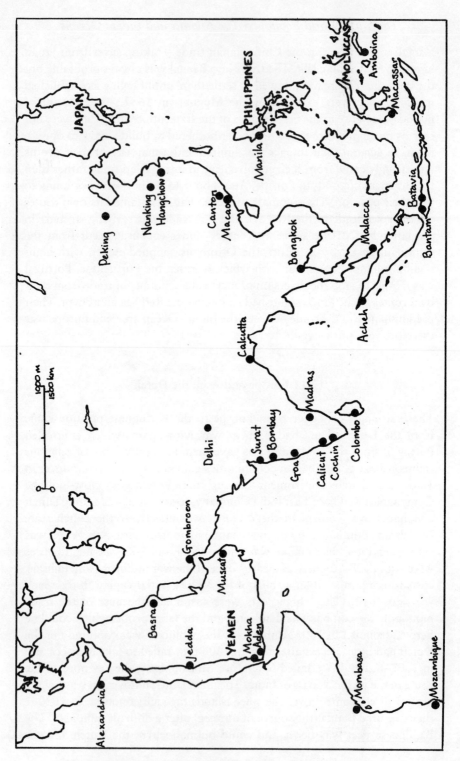

Map 52: Europe and Asia: the seventeenth and eighteenth centuries

town had to be starved into submission through cutting off its rice supply. On its capture the directorate of the VOC called for extermination of the population. About 2,500 people were killed and another 3,000 transported. The Dutch took over the local spice-growing estates and moved in slave labour to work them.

The real assault on the Portuguese did not take place until the mid-seventeenth century. In 1641 the Dutch finally captured the key city of Malacca followed in 1656 by Colombo on Sri Lanka and in 1663 Cochin on the west coast of India. The main centre for the Dutch in south-east Asia was Batavia on Java from which the important sources of spices such as Banda and Macassar in the Celebes could be controlled. This enabled the Dutch to exert almost total control over the trade in a number of key spices – cloves, nutmeg, mace and cinnamon – as they had enough power to force the local rulers to sell only to them. However, they very quickly realized that such policies would not work with the great land powers such as China and India, nor with the powerful Japanese. In 1622 the Dutch destroyed over eighty junks off the coast of China in an attempt to force an opening of trade. The Chinese refused to bow to the threats. The Dutch were stopped from trading with China until 1727 when they were finally allowed to go to the port of Canton. Chinese merchants from Fukien did go to Java but they kept the trade in their own hands and dictated their own terms.

The Dutch were very keen to trade with Japan and were prepared to accept almost any humiliation in order to ensure its continuance. The Japanese saw the Dutch as a useful counterweight to the Portuguese who traded through the port of Nagasaki from the 1540s. After the Portuguese were excluded the Dutch were forced to withdraw to the small island of Deshima just off the coast. The island measured 82 paces by 236 and was linked to the mainland by a causeway guarded by a fortified gatehouse. The Dutch were spied on by their Japanese servants and controlled by a 150-strong official interpreter corps. Just one ship a year was allowed to call and its officers were usually 'beaten with sticks as if they were dogs'. They were allowed to visit the mainland once a year in order to pay homage to the shogun. The Dutch stayed for more than two centuries because the trade was so profitable even though half the ships that made the voyage were lost and the cost of maintaining the dozen or so men at Deshima was as expensive as the 500-man garrison at Batavia. At first the Dutch traded silver from Japan to China but after the ban on silver exports in 1668 they concentrated on silk, porcelain and lacquerware, which they traded for Indian cotton and Bengal raw silk. The VOC told its agents in Deshima in 1650 they had to bear the conditions and were 'to look to the wishes of that bold, haughty and exacting nation, in order to please them in everything'. The nature of Dutch trade with the Japanese shows that, like the Portuguese, they found the greatest profit in becoming part of the Asian trading network rather than taking a few products back to Europe.

17.12 Europe and Asia: the English

In the sixteenth century England was still relatively poor compared with the rest of Europe and over four-fifths of its exports were cloth. (The quality was very crude and when English merchants tried to sell this cloth in Japan in the early seventeenth century, the Japanese, used to high-quality Chinese materials, refused to trade.) The first breakthrough came in 1581 when the Ottomans allowed the English to trade in the Greek islands and at Aleppo, which was the terminus of the overland trade routes from the east. The East India Company (EIC), set up in 1600, was, as with other European ventures in Asia, a monopoly. It paid no duties for four years and, crucially, was allowed to export gold and silver so that it could buy products in the east. At first it was not very successful because it did not have the power to challenge either the Portuguese or the Dutch. It abandoned trying to trade with the Japanese in the early 1620s and its main breakthrough came in the Gulf. In alliance with the Safavids in Iran the EIC captured Hormuz from the Portuguese and gradually became the main European trader in the region. The EIC still had to pay off the government – James I got £10,000, his favourite Buckingham the same and Buckingham's wife £2,000 – in total the company had to pay over about half the profits from the capture of Hormuz.

The position of the EIC improved slowly during the seventeenth century. In 1639 it was granted a concession by the local Indian ruler to trade at the small fishing village of Madras. A much bigger gain came in 1661 when the Portuguese provided Bombay as the marriage dowry for the Infanta Catherine's wedding to Charles II. The city was given to the EIC in 1668 but only after the company had made 'loans' to the king of £10,000 (1662), £50,000 (1666) and £70,000 (1667). That it could do so on this scale merely illustrates the profits that could be made in the trade with Asia. In 1698 a rival company was allowed to operate after it 'loaned' the government £2 million. The two companies were merged in 1709 with a new capital sum of £3 million which again had to be 'loaned' to the government while the company operated on borrowed money. By then the EIC had lost an ill-judged war with the Mughals in 1690–1 but in the peace treaty was given the right to trade at the obscure village of Calcutta – the Dutch traded at the nearby Hugli. The EIC was under growing French pressure following the establishment of Pondicherry near Madras in 1674 and Chandernagore, upstream of Calcutta. The British kept ahead of the French (their trade volume was about four times higher) and increasingly became the main European country trading with India.

Until 1718 the Dutch VOC dominated the tea trade, buying green tea brought by Chinese junks to Batavia. During a Chinese–Dutch trade dispute the British were able to build on the right to trade at Canton which had been given to them by the Chinese in 1710. The conditions imposed by the Chinese were strict – the British were only allowed to buy tea, raw silk and porcelain and they had to pay for it in silver. They had to surrender all arms and munitions before entering the harbour and no traders were allowed to reside there. The EIC used its position to dominate the trade to Europe in black tea which was becoming increasingly popular and replacing the green tea which the Dutch largely controlled. The Chinese insistence that goods could only be bought for silver was typical of the overwhelming majority of the EIC's trade – in the 1680s almost 90 per cent of the goods they took from England consisted of silver (from the Americas). The other major item of trade was Indian cotton and textiles. In the 1620s the EIC was importing about 250,000 lengths of Indian cotton every year. By the 1680s this figure had risen to nearly 2 million lengths a year and in some years it was double this level. Some was re-exported to Africa to buy slaves but the majority was sold in Britain because of its very high quality. In 1676 the English textile industry adopted Indian techniques for calico printing but still could not withstand the competition. English broadcloths were not wanted in India – they were of such poor quality that they were used as coverings for elephants. The English industry only began to expand after 1722 when the home market was closed to Indian textiles (they could only be re-exported). This was a classic case of import substitution against a more efficient competitor and it formed the basis for the massive expansion of English textile production in the eighteenth century which is usually seen as the beginnings of the 'industrial revolution'.

17.13 Asia and the Europeans

It is necessary to keep the size of the European presence in Asia in perspective. During the sixteenth century the Portuguese were the only European state to trade with the region and until the 1630s they sent on average just seven ships a year to the east. A third of these were lost, only four a year made the return journey and the rest stayed to trade in Asia. Until 1665 the Dutch did not send more than nine ships a year to the east with a total tonnage of about 3,750 tons. At the peak of Dutch trade in 1735 they sent thirty ships of about 20,000 tons total. Not until after 1750 did the average size of European ships in the Asian trade rise above 1,000 tons (still smaller than a Chinese junk of the twelfth century). The scale of European trade can be compared with that of the Ottoman capital Constantinople which had, on average, 4,300 ships a year calling at the port in the early sixteenth century. In the 1570s the customs revenue of the rulers of Gujarat alone was over three times the value of all the Portuguese trade in Asia. The number of Europeans in Asia was minuscule. In the sixteenth century the Portuguese had about 10,000 people in the whole area between the Gulf and Nagasaki. In 1700 the English had 114 people resident at Madras, about 700 in Bombay and 1,200 in Calcutta.

The linked trading world of the Indian Ocean, India, south-east Asia and China was based on a huge internal market (over two-thirds of the world's population lived in Asia in 1700 compared with a fifth in Europe), highly commercialized economies and trading patterns which had been established for more than a millennium. The rhythms of trade were still dictated by the seasonal winds and ports and trading cities rose and declined in importance from a variety of factors just as they had in the past. Surat replaced Cambay in Gujarat, especially after the Mughals gained control of the overland routes to Delhi in 1573. Bandar Abbas (Gombroon) took over from Hormuz after the Portuguese capture of the latter and from 1722 the civil war in Iran increased the importance of Basra. Mokha on the Red Sea prospered with the development of the coffee trade to Europe. In the early seventeenth century Malacca declined and was replaced by Banten (Bantam to the Europeans) in north-west Java where large communities of Indian and Chinese traders gathered. It was conquered by the Dutch in 1682 and trade was forced to Batavia. The ports and trading forts controlled by the Europeans also waxed and waned – Goa declined as Batavia, Madras and Calcutta became more important.

This Indian Ocean trading world had always been highly cosmopolitan and it remained so after the arrival of the Europeans – they were just another trading community. From the start the Europeans were forced (and some chose) to become part of this wider world. In 1499 two Portuguese deserted Vasco da Gama and chose to serve Indian rulers for higher wages. In 1503 two gunfounders moved from Milan to Calicut and two years later Venetian technicians began work at Malabar. The Portuguese were very much in a minority. Even in their headquarters of Goa they were outnumbered by Asian traders (especially Hindus, Nestorians, Armenians and Jains) without whose help they would have been unable to tap into the long-established local trading networks. By the mid-sixteenth century in the Portuguese controlled towns along the west coast of India they were outnumbered three to one by the Gujarati population. At Hormuz in 1600 four out of ten of the population were Muslim, nearly a third Hindu (mainly from Gujarat) and less than a fifth were Portuguese. Europeans also became part of the Asian world far outside the areas they directly controlled – there were numerous Portuguese in Burma and in the late seventeenth century the King of Thailand had a Greek adviser called Constantine Phaulcon. Asians often hired or owned European ships and also hired European officers and crews to man them. The Europeans had to rely on locals to help them find their way in the complex Asian trading world. In the eighteenth century European ships normally called at the great trading port of Surat rather than British-controlled Bombay because the former had a much better banking structure and the facilities to provide loans and other forms of credit. In Bengal a group known as 'banian' supplied the capital and became the partner of EIC officials who wanted to enter trade on their own account. Both gained because the goods were duty free. This system became even more sophisticated with the establishment of 'agency houses' in the eighteenth century. They traded on behalf of the Europeans (in return for a major share of the profits) and by the end of the century were responsible for more English trade than the EIC, even though the latter still had a formal monopoly.

The overwhelming majority of trade across the Indian Ocean and southeast Asia was not in European hands. Both China and Japan were strong enough to dictate the terms on which trade could be conducted and largely excluded the Europeans. European historians often assert that Japan was 'closed' to external trade after 1640, apart from the one ship a year that the Dutch were allowed to send to Nagasaki. In fact Japan had an extensive foreign trade – in the 1680s over a hundred ships a year were trading between Japan and China. In the seventeenth century there was a major revival in Indian trade with the Gulf and an exodus of Hindu merchants, mainly from Gujarat, all over the area. Merchants from the Coromandel coast controlled the trade to Thailand where they were able to undercut European merchants and trade Indian textiles for various precious stones and other exotic goods. The competition was so fierce that the Europeans withdrew all their trading factories from the area before the end of the seventeenth century. There was also a major increase in the trade between Thailand and China with Chinese merchants selling porcelain and silk in exchange for teak and rice. By the early eighteenth century Bangkok was the largest centre in Asia for the construction of junks. The Europeans also came to rely on Asian shipbuilding. This was partly because of the very high-quality teak, which lasted far longer than European woods (even oak), and the growing shortage of suitable wood in Europe. The ships which brought Chinese goods to Europe in the eighteenth century were nearly all built in India.

The Europeans found it most profitable to be part of the complex intra-Asian trading network simply because the scale of the trade was so large. In the late seventeenth century the Dutch were carrying large quantities of tin from Sumatra to China where the demand was greatest. Nearly half the camphor they bought in Japan was taken to India and four-fifths of the copper from Japan was sold in India. The complexity of the system can be judged from the fact that on the north Javan coast sugar was produced under VOC control on estates owned by the local Javanese aristocracy using Chinese indentured labour. The market for the sugar was not in Europe but Safavid Iran. For many of their requirements the Dutch relied on Indian iron and weapons output. In the 1660s they were taking to Batavia from India over 115,000 pounds of nails, 188,000 pounds of cannonballs, 189,000 pounds of iron bars and about 5 tons of steel a year.

Overall the European impact on Asia was very limited and far from revolutionary in the two and half centuries after 1500. European shipping was small scale and not very efficient. Use of the route via the Cape of Good Hope did not lower costs by enough to alter the long-established trade through the Red Sea and Egypt to Venice which was operating as in the past from the 1530s. Indeed it is not even clear that shipping costs via the Cape were lower than the old overland caravan routes. What this route did provide was a supplement that slowly increased the level of trade between Europe and the rest of Eurasia. It was part of the long process of the growing integration of trade across Eurasia that had been developing for several millennia. It also helped the Europeans develop their commercial and credit networks to the level of those already existing in China and India.

17.14 The Old Eurasian Trade Routes

[Early 'Silk Road' 9.8]
The full effects of the new trade routes took several centuries to emerge. Older trade routes therefore survived remarkably well. The long-established trans-Saharan routes did lose out in direct competition with the sea routes to Europe. But that trade had always been fairly small and for the trade to north Africa, especially high-value products such as gold, the camel caravans continued to flourish. Taking the gold to the coast and then by sea held no significant advantages. The trade in slaves continued to grow (though it was minuscule compared with the European trade across the Atlantic) and the Europeans were almost entirely excluded from the Mediterranean slave markets. New items also entered the trade such as gum, hides and ivory. This trans-Sahara trade was largely isolated from

European competition by the forests to the south of the savanna and the strong cultural links with north Africa which the Europeans could not penetrate.This position did not change until the nineteenth century.

The longest-established of all the great Eurasian trading systems was the Silk Road linking south-west Asia with China. A trip along its full length might take eighteen months in the sixteenth century but that was little slower than the ocean routes to China after allowance was made for the waits necessary to catch the monsoon winds. All the evidence shows that the route continued to flourish well into the seventeenth century. From the mid-fifteenth century the Silk Road was dominated by strong and stable empires – the Ottoman and the Ming at either end, the successor states to the empire of Temur in central Asia and the Safavids of Iran from the early sixteenth century. From the 1450s merchants from Mecca were regularly in China and those from Egypt only slightly less often. The trade between the Ottoman empire and China was on a large scale, especially highly prized Ming porcelain. Some factories in China specialized in the trade to the west and two of the largest collections of Ming ware in the world are now in Istanbul and Iran. Only during the seventeenth century did the old Silk Road begin to lose its importance. Political instability, especially in central Asia, played a part and by the time in the eighteenth century when China had established its political control further west than at any time since the T'ang over a thousand years earlier, the route was suffering from severe competition. This came from the growing trade through south-east Asia and the Indian Ocean and also, late in the century, the development of Russian routes.

New land routes were also developing in south-west Asia. In this area Armenian merchants played a central role. During the sixteenth century they controlled the routes from Constantinople to Aleppo and across Mesopotamia into Iran. By the end of the century they were also well established in Gujarat. The overland caravan route from Aleppo to India continued to flourish and was not seriously disrupted until the opening of the Suez canal in the late nineteenth century. The Armenians became strongly linked to the Safavid empire in Iran and set up trade links which avoided the Ottomans such as those using the Caspian and Volga routes to Moscow. Their communities spread out across the Eurasian trade routes from Antwerp and London in the west to India and as far east as Manila. The Armenians also specialized in the route from China to India via Lhasa and the links between their scattered communities meant that they could provide a banking service which stretched across nearly the whole of Eurasia. The complexities of the Eurasian world, the closeness of the connections between the different communities and the linkages between different areas is illustrated by the fact that in the 1730s the Royal African

Company in London hired Melchior de Jaspas, an Arabic-speaking Armenian, to deal with the Muslim traders in the Gambia who provided the slaves for the Atlantic trade on which the company depended for its wealth. He stayed in the Gambia for several years and, like so many other Europeans, died there.

17.15 Eurasian Economies: the Ottomans, India and China

17.15.1 The Ottomans
[Ottoman political history 18.2]
The empire of the Ottomans was central to the developing world economy from the early sixteenth century. After 1517 it was one of the handful of empires in Eurasian history to control the three key trade routes of south-west Asia – through the Bosphorus to the Black Sea, from the Levant to Mesopotamia and the overland routes to central Asia and China and that from Egypt down the Red Sea to Aden and India. Other complementary routes developed from Damascus through Bursa to Lvov and the states of eastern Europe and that up the Danube; both were far more important for the spice trade than the route between Egypt and Venice. The Ottoman empire was also the centre for the supply of silk, for its large internal market and also for Europe. Until about 1650 the trade was centred on Bursa but it then moved to Smyrna (modern Izmir). The Ottoman empire had strong merchant communities in the major cities such as Constantinople, Aleppo and Cairo. They were hardly taxed by the Ottoman government which allowed them as much freedom, if not more, than European governments. The Ottomans had a major navy which was capable of protecting the trade routes, especially those bringing grain from Egypt to the capital. The navy was also used to support Ottoman merchants – as in its attack on the Portuguese at Diu in 1538, which was part of the successful attempt to re-build the spice trade through Egypt. Control of this part of the Indian Ocean, especially Mokha and the port of Aden, also secured the developing coffee trade. The resources available within the Ottoman empire were substantial – in the early seventeenth century the government was able to commission 118 ships belonging to a consortium of 56 shipowners to make 658 voyages a year to bring grain from the Black Sea to the capital.

17.15.2 India
[Political history 18.5]
The Ottoman empire was a major land and naval power. The Mughal empire in India was overwhelmingly land-based, deriving its wealth

primarily from the highly productive agriculture. Merchants were left to trade freely – they had little state support but in return they paid hardly any taxes. Many among the Mughal elite and the ruling family were closely involved in trade, especially through the great port cities and had their own fleets of ships which dominated the trade of Bengal. This area was also one of the major silk-producing areas of the world – by the end of the seventeenth century it was supplying most of India and the Dutch were taking it to Japan because of its high quality. Further south in the sultanates of Bijapur and Golconda (not conquered by the Mughals until the 1680s) the long-established and very close links between the rulers and the trading cities and large merchant class continued. These cities were, as in the past, closely tied into the Asian trading network and the rulers derived most of their revenue from trade.

As in most of Eurasia much of India's industrial production took place in the countryside as peasants sought ways of supplementing their incomes during the periods when agricultural work was slack. Areas specialized in particular products such as silk, cotton, salt and saltpetre manufacture. The Kasimbazar area supplied a total of 2.2 million pounds of silk a year. Three European trading companies employed over 1,600 silk weavers but even so only took about half of the total production – the rest was sold locally or through Indian merchants. By the 1640s Masulipatam and Varanasi each had over 7,000 cotton weavers producing for both the home market and export to Europe and Africa. Indian cottons were probably the highest quality in Eurasia. Another area where India produced very high-quality materials was steel. Until the early nineteenth century probably only Sweden could produce goods of similar quality.

17.15.3 China
[*Political history 15.4*]
By the sixteenth century China had long recovered from the effects of the Mongol invasion and the Black Death. The large and prosperous economy developed under the Ming was, as in the past, based on a highly productive agriculture which was still improving. Yields rose by 60 per cent between the late fourteenth century and 1600 and were well above even the best achieved in eighteenth-century Europe, twice those of France and probably close to the maximum possible in a pre-industrial system. The area cultivated was also continuing to expand – the Chinese population doubled between 1400 and 1700. In many areas a highly specialized and commercial agriculture existed, much of it oriented towards the export trade. This was particularly the case in Fukien, Kiangsi and Anhwei where large areas were either leased by or under the control of tea firms. In other areas nearly three-quarters of the land was used for growing cotton with the

peasants dependent on buying their food on the market. Other areas specialized in tobacco and sugar-cane production.

These developments were all part of a highly commercial economy which was stimulated by the massive inflow of silver from the Americas. By the seventeenth century China had returned to a paper currency, though most of it was issued by private rather than state banks. The main centre for private banking was in Shansi where major firms were founded in the eighteenth century – the eight largest had over thirty branches across China and by the early nineteenth century were expanding into Japan too. As wealth increased, investment in commerce and industry grew far faster than that in land, and large commercial families, such as the eighteenth-century salt merchants and the Co-Hong foreign trade merchants in Canton, controlled huge concentrations of capital. The political power of the merchants was increasing and many cities were effectively run by guilds and confederations of merchants, as in Europe and India. As cities continued to grow they were integrated in a huge internal market where much of Chinese trade took place – cotton cloth was traded over distances of eight hundred miles. In Europe, with its fragmented political structure, trade over these distances would have counted as exports. Even so, export duties provided half of China's state revenue by the late sixteenth century. There was also a major cotton trade to the north, in particular Manchuria, where large underground factories developed because of the very dry air in the region. In the late seventeenth century there were over 3,500 ships moving from the south to the north every year each carrying between twenty and forty tons of cargo. The scale of cotton production was such that large imports of raw cotton were required. By the late eighteenth century China was importing over 27 million pounds of cotton every year from India – twice the amount that Britain was importing from the United States in 1800 as the 'industrial revolution' took off.

In parallel with these developments there were significant technological improvements – such as five-colour printing and sophisticated silk and cotton looms which required at least three people to operate. An elite of skilled workers and craftsmen existed alongside the unskilled factory workers as industrial production expanded rapidly. Some places specialized in particular types of production – porcelain at Ching-te-chen, cotton weaving at Sung-chiang and luxury silks at Soochow. Kiangsi specialized in paper production – by the end of the sixteenth century there were over thirty factories employing more than 30,000 workers. Similarly in the iron and steel industry, which was concentrated in Hupei, Shensi and Szechwan, there were complexes of six or seven furnaces each employing between two and three thousand men. Hemp, silk and cotton production were equally concentrated and the merchants organized the production and sale of cloth involving over 4,000 weavers and several times that number of spinners. The different areas of China could afford to specialize in certain types of production because of the well-developed internal communications network. This was certainly as good as pre-railway Europe and, in terms of the amount of navigable rivers and canals, probably a great deal better.

17.16 Eurasia in *c.*1750

The control the west European powers (in particular Britain, France and the Dutch) exercised over the Atlantic economy through their technical (and disease) supremacy over the native peoples of the Americas meant they were able to generate substantial wealth from it. It came in the form of gold and silver, the direct profits from the slave trade and especially from the products the slaves grew (sugar, tobacco, indigo and rice). It transformed the position of western Europe in Eurasia. There is little doubt that in 1500 when Columbus arrived in the Americas and the Portuguese reached the Indian Ocean, Europe was still far behind the long-established societies of the rest of Eurasia. The wealth derived from the Americas directly increased the wealth of a few countries in western Europe and helped in the development of their commercial and banking systems and provided capital which could be invested to develop their economies. Even more crucially it provided assets by which they could penetrate the sophisticated trading world of Asia. The products Europe could make or supply were of little interest to the great powers of India and China that already made a wider range of higher-quality products. The Europeans had no technical or military superiority over these states and could deploy little power in the region, certainly not enough to conquer the great land empires. Without the gold and silver of the Americas, Europe would not have been able to buy the products of Asia, make money and gradually infiltrate and gain some of the wealth that could be derived from the trade of the area.

Estimates of wealth in the mid-to-late eighteenth century demonstrate that Europe used the period between 1500 and about 1750 to catch up with the wealthier areas of Eurasia, in particular China and India. Although the figures are necessarily tentative they are broadly consistent and show a very clear trend. By the mid-eighteenth century all the various states and empires of Eurasia had roughly the same level of wealth in terms of gross national product per head. (China and India were still far bigger economies than any in Europe because of their sheer size in terms of land area, natural resources and population.) In 1750 the average citizen of

China was probably marginally wealthier than an inhabitant of western Europe (by about ten per cent). India was at about the same level as western Europe, perhaps a little less wealthy on average. Japan was slightly poorer than the other major states in Eurasia, its average wealth was probably about a fifth less than western Europe. In 1500 less than one in twenty Europeans lived in large towns and there were only a handful of cities on the continent. By the late eighteenth century about nine out of ten Europeans still lived in the countryside and were dependent on agriculture as they had been in the past. In 1800 the urban population of Europe was still marginally lower as a proportion of the total than in China and the largest cities in the world were still outside Europe – Peking and Canton were larger than London, and Hangchou, Edo and Constantinople were all larger than Paris. The European landed aristocracy were still the dominant social and political class and they controlled most of the surplus produced by the peasants. Industrial production was still, as in the rest of Eurasia, undertaken by skilled workers in small units or working at home. The transportation infrastructure was still poor. However, the first dim signs were appearing of the huge economic growth and technological innovation that were to occur in the nineteenth century and which were to transform Europe's position in the world.

18

The Gunpowder Empires and States

18.1 The Impact of Gunpowder on Eurasia

The development of gunpowder weapons was an entirely Chinese achievement. Over the three centuries or so before 1280 they created not only the explosive mixture but also metal-barrelled guns, rocket projectiles and cannon to make effective weapons. This new technology spread rapidly westwards and the first very primitive weapons were being used in Europe by the mid-fourteenth century. However, they were not adopted on a large scale for another century because the earliest weapons, made by trying to weld iron together, burst too easily. Only when bell-casting techniques using bronze and brass were used could effective weapons be made. The first states to make major use of gunpowder weapons were in the Islamic world. In 1453 the Ottomans successfully used 62 massive siege guns against the walls of Constantinople. Three years later at the siege of Belgrade they were able to deploy nearly 200 guns. In India cannon were first used in the north in the 1440s and in the Deccan thirty years later. Some of these early guns were so heavy that they could only be transported by water and occasionally they were even cast on the spot. It was not until the late fifteenth century that effective semi-mobile guns were made. Europe first made a cast-iron cannon, which reduced costs by as much as ninety per cent, in 1543. The problem was the lack of capacity to make such weapons and brass and bronze weapons therefore remained common well into the seventeenth century (the French did not adopt an all-iron gun policy until the 1660s). In parallel with the adoption of gunpowder artillery weapons the first infantry weapon, the arquebus, was developed in Europe in the early sixteenth century with the first primitive musket following in the 1550s.

In China the effect of gunpowder weapons was not disruptive because they were first adopted on a major scale under the Ming when there was a high level of internal stability and only limited external conflict. After the initial development of these weapons the lack of warfare meant that China lagged behind the Islamic world until the early sixteenth century when large siege guns were adopted from the Ottomans after a diplomatic mission to China in 1520. Then the pace of change was swift. By 1564 the Chinese were using iron cannonballs on the northern frontier and in the 1570s the Great Wall was given a system of 'pill boxes' for use by musketeers, and mobile artillery were also deployed. Where the Chinese were far in advance of the rest of Eurasia was in the development of fortifications because they had had much longer to work out how to deal with the new gunpowder weapons. Whole towns and cities were fortified with massive walls up to fifteen yards thick which were able to withstand almost any bombardment. In 1840 a 74-gun British warship equipped with 32-pounder guns carried out a two-hour bombardment of Canton but the commander had to report that it had 'no effect whatever'. In 1860 when the British General Knollys arrived in Peking he was staggered to find walls around the city which were fifty feet high, fifty feet wide and paved on top for traffic.

Further west in Eurasia the impact of gunpowder weapons was much more destabilizing. The great Ottoman revival from the 1420s, its capture of Constantinople and control over most of the Balkans by the 1480s, was largely built upon its success in the use of the new weapons. In India the rise of the Mughal empire in the early sixteenth century was similarly based on their adoption of matchlock muskets (some thirty years before Europe) and field cannon. In Japan gunpowder weapons played a major role in the reunification of the country in the late sixteenth century. The most significant impact was however in a Europe already divided into numerous small states and racked by dynastic conflict which was made worse, later in the sixteenth century, by religious divisions. The new weapons produced a military revolution that had a fundamental effect not just within armies but on the very nature of the European state and its subsequent evolution.

Europe was still a marginal area of Eurasia in the sixteenth century. China, the largest state in the world, with a population of 160 million in 1600, was, under the Ming, highly prosperous and stable with few external problems, and its history, which has already been covered [15.4 & 17.15.3], is not considered here. The sixteenth century in Eurasia was dominated by the rise of two major empires – the Safavid in Iran and the Mughal in India. In parallel the expansion of the Ottomans continued and they reached the peak of their power. These three, together with the smaller Uzbek state, formed the four great 'Turkic' states in which the ruling families all spoke related Turkic languages. All four were closely linked (not always harmoniously) and were at the centre of the Islamic world which still dominated all the central regions of Eurasia and formed a major trading network. In the mid-sixteenth century these four empires had a population of about 135 million which was more than two and a half times that of Europe.

18.2 The Ottoman Empire

[Earlier Ottoman history 15.8]
The Ottoman territories formed the last of the great empires to dominate the original heartland of civilization in south-west Asia. It was the only empire which united that area with the Mediterranean and the Balkans. In the Mediterranean it expanded Islamic power back to a level not seen for more than five centuries. It controlled the three great trade routes of south-west Asia (through the Bosphorus to the Black Sea, from the Levant to Mesopotamia and the land routes to central Asia, and the route down the Red Sea to the Indian Ocean) together with the three main cereal-exporting regions (Mesopotamia, Egypt and the Black Sea region). For three hundred years after the 1470s the Black Sea and the Sea of Azov were Ottoman lakes. Although from the late eighteenth century it lost ground in Europe, it retained control of south-west Asia (apart from Egypt) until 1918 and was not formally abolished until 1923. Although, like the Byzantine empire, its history is often seen as one of terminal decay from the mid-sixteenth century, it was highly successful for centuries and it was still expanding its area of control in the eighteenth century. The first major losses of territory did not occur until the late eighteenth century (over five hundred years after the empire's creation).

18.2.1 Expansion
After the rapid expansion of Ottoman power through the Balkans following the capture of Constantinople in 1453 there was a period of consolidation in the 1480s and 1490s. The first signs of renewed expansion came in the war with Venice in 1499–1502 during which the two fortresses of Modon and Coron in southern Greece were captured once their walls had been battered down by Ottoman artillery. The major turning point came with the deposition of Bayezid II by his son Selim in 1512. Two years later at the battle of Chaldiran near Lake Van the Safavids of Iran were defeated, the Ottomans expanded into the far east of Anatolia and blocked any Safavid push further westwards. Selim then moved south to attack the Mamluks, capturing the key trading city of Aleppo in 1516. The next year at the battle of Reydaniyya the Mamluks were finally defeated and the Ottomans took control of Egypt. The Sherif of Mecca also recognized Ottoman supremacy and their rule extended over Arabia and the holy city. The attacks on the Mamluks and control of Arabia reinforced the Ottoman position (central to all Turkic policy since the Seljuqs) of strong Sunni orthodoxy against their rivals the Safavids. Expansion through the Levant and into Egypt also altered the balance within the Ottoman empire – it was now much more strongly Muslim and the Christians in the Balkans

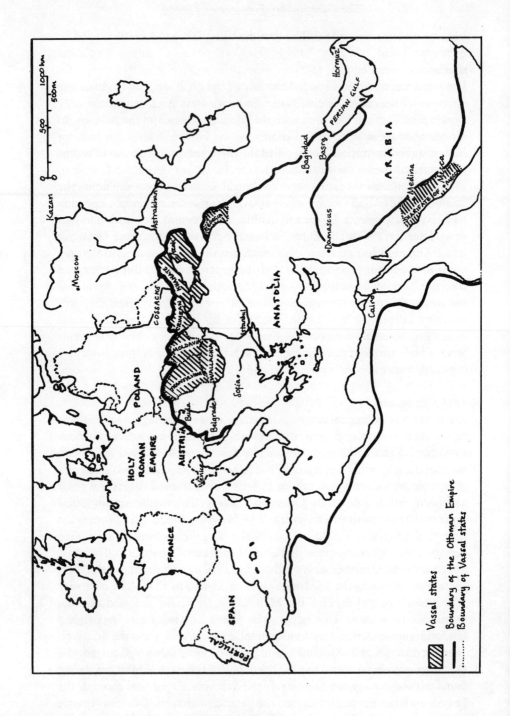

Map 53: The Ottoman empire in the mid-sixteenth century

became a very small minority. Selim died in 1520 and was succeeded by Suleyman I who ruled until 1566. (He is often known in Europe as 'the magnificent' though his real title was 'law-giver'.) He resumed the Ottoman thrust through the Balkans and in 1521 Belgrade was finally captured (followed by the island of Rhodes in the Mediterranean in the next year). Victory at the battle of Mohacs in 1526 effectively ended Hungary as an independent kingdom – within three years the Ottomans had installed a puppet ruler in Budapest who accepted an Ottoman garrison and paid an annual tribute.

The Ottomans were now near the height of their power. Their empire stretched from Algiers in the west to Azerbaijan in the east, from Budapest to Basra and from the Crimea to Mokha and Aden at the end of the Red Sea. Fleets were maintained in the western Mediterranean, the Black Sea and the eastern Indian Ocean and battles were fought as far apart as the coast of Gujarat in western India and at Algiers. In the 1580s the Ottoman navy was carrying out raids on Mozambique. The Ottoman empire was the principal Mediterranean power controlling three-quarters of the shoreline. It was central to the manoeuvrings of the western European powers throughout the sixteenth century and was the most powerful state with which they all had to deal. Many of them spent a considerable amount of time and effort trying to enlist the Ottomans as allies. Much of the history of western Europe in this period makes more sense when viewed from an Ottoman perspective than from that of the petty states on the western frontier of the empire. In general the Ottomans were opposed to the chief European power – the Habsburgs – and supported the minor powers who opposed them such as France, England and the small German states.

During the Italian wars of the early sixteenth century all the participants were worried about another Ottoman invasion of the peninsula and a repeat of the capture of Otranto in 1480. It was from the 1530s that the Ottomans played a decisive role in Europe. In 1533 a subsidy of 100,000 gold pieces was paid to Francis I of France to support him and to help build an alliance of German princes and the English against the Habsburgs. The subsidy was repeated in 1535 and the French were allowed to trade in the Ottoman empire – in return Ottoman traders were allowed into southern France. In 1538 Venice agreed to a join a Habsburg–papal alliance against the Ottomans. It lost the naval war in the Adriatic and when it was forced to make peace in 1540 had to pay a major indemnity and lose the fortresses of Nauplion and Monemvasia in southern Greece. In 1555 the Ottomans provided the crucial official backing to a private loan by Joseph Nasi, a Jewish tax-farmer in the Ottoman empire, which kept the French monarchy solvent. Although support for the Protestant German princes against the Habsburgs was partly a matter of realpolitik the Ottomans were keenly interested in the development of Protestantism which they saw as in some ways similar to Islam, especially in its iconoclasm. Calvinism was tolerated in Hungary and Transylvania and spread widely. The only major set back the Ottomans faced in the mid-sixteenth century was in 1565 when they failed to capture the island of Malta from the Knights they had driven from Rhodes forty years earlier. Although their defeat at the naval battle of Lepanto in 1571 was seen as a great victory by Christian Europe it did not change the strategic situation in the Mediterranean. The Ottoman navy was quickly rebuilt and the Spanish were unable to stop them taking Tunis.

18.2.2 The nature of the empire

The Ottoman empire was formally known as the 'domains and rule of the House of Osman', and was a dynastic empire (like its great rival the Habsburgs in Europe), ruling a collection of different territories. It was a highly tolerant empire that incorporated, without major problems, the three main monotheistic religions together with a multitude of different groups and languages with their complex histories and inter-relationships. Tens of thousands of Jews expelled by the Christian states of Spain, Portugal and Italy settled in the empire. Moriscos from Andalucia settled in Constantinople after they were expelled in the mid-sixteenth century. Old Believers from Russia were, a little later, allowed to settle in Anatolia and escape persecution at home. The conquest of the Balkans and the incorporation of large Christian populations, which unlike those of south-west Asia had no experience of Muslim rule, posed the main problem. Toleration – and in rural areas, where the bulk of the population lived, a lack of interference with local customs – together with local government which removed most of the worst abuses of the previous Christian land-lords and petty rulers, produced stability. The Ottomans even retained the tax on pig slaughtering despite Islamic prohibitions on the practice. In Hungary the major landlords fled westwards to the Habsburg-controlled areas but they still claimed dues from their serfs in the Ottoman empire and the authorities allowed the payments to continue. Settlers moved in from Anatolia and by the early sixteenth century about a fifth of the population of the Balkans were Muslims. Of these more than a third were Christian converts and in areas such as Bosnia (where the Bogomils had always been strong) conversion to Islam was at a very high level.

The sultan was central to the Ottoman system for much of the sixteenth century but the problem of the succession remained because of the retention of the old nomadic custom of choosing the best successor rather than the oldest son. The advantage was that it usually avoided having a weak ruler but the disadvantage was the increased divisions, usually only resolved by the slaughter of the losers. However, by the early seventeenth century, a more bureaucratic system of government developed in which the personal qualities and role of the sultan were far less important. The empire was governed through an imperial council not the ruler's household as in so many European states. Viziers carried out important military and administrative tasks and were supplemented by provincial and district governors, state judges for imperial law (which covered all the subjects of the empire – the Muslims also had *sharia* law), and a large number of administrators. Under the *dirlik* system local governors and officials were not assigned lands of their own but merely the revenues from certain lands whilst they held office. In towns shares of customs duties and trade taxes were assigned to support local government. Governors also had to provide troops out of the revenues which they were assigned. The income of the sultan and the imperial government came from mines, forests and the trade revenues of the major cities such as Constantinople and Aleppo. The sultan also maintained the army elite and all of the navy from his revenues. By the end of the sixteenth century central control of the provinces was increasing, especially in the Levant, Egypt and the areas conquered from the Safavids. The Ottoman government was probably about as efficient as any of the pre-industrial societies given the severe limitations under which they all operated.

The Ottoman political system was inclusive and tolerant with numerous jobs reserved for the Christian minority. Although most of the rest of Europe expected the Christian population to rise up in revolt against the 'Ottoman yoke', those within the empire took a very different view of their 'oppressors'. There was no significant resistance of any kind until the nineteenth century. Indeed many European Christians actively sought out employment within the Ottoman empire. One of the most powerful Ottoman eunuchs in the late sixteenth century was Hasan Aga – who was in fact Samson Rowlie from Great Yarmouth; one of his many tasks was to deal with the English merchants who were allowed to trade in part of the empire. In Algiers the state executioner Abd-es-Salaam was a former butcher from Exeter called Absalom. One of the most important Ottoman generals was a Campbell from Scotland who converted to Islam and joined the 'Janissaries'. In 1606 the English consul in Egypt, Benjamin Bishop, converted to Islam. Later in the seventeenth century Charles II sent a Captain Hamilton to ransom some Englishmen who had been enslaved in north Africa. The mission was a total failure – the slaves had risen through the government hierarchy, were far wealthier than they would have been in England and had married local women. They all refused to return. [*Later history 19.3*]

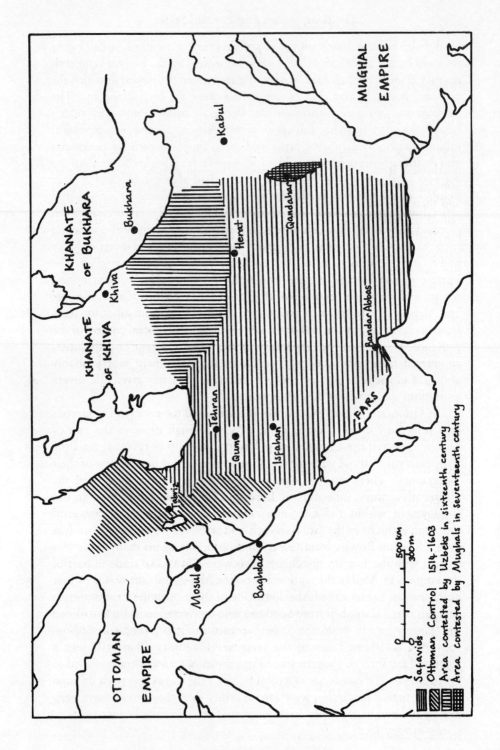

Map 54: The Safavid empire

18.3 Safavid Iran

[*Earlier Iran 15.6*]

A series of mystical and popular religious movements such as the Kubrawi, Hurufiya and Sarbadar emerged in Iran from the thirteenth century. The most important was the Safavid movement founded by Safi al-Din (1252–1334), a religious teacher from a Kurdish family of Ardabil in north-west Iran. All of these movements formed part of a resurgence of popular Islam opposed to the external military rulers of Iran (the Mongols and their successors). Remarkably they were to lead to the establishment, out of the Safavid movement, of a dynasty that ruled Iran for over two hundred years between 1501 and 1722. The crucial transformation of the Safavids came with Sadr al-Din the son of their founder who was head of the movement until his death in 1391. He claimed direct descent from Muhammad and turned the Safavid movement into a hierarchical and propertied order – the head or *murshid* became a hereditary not elected office. He demanded total obedience from his followers and was supported by his agents, the *khalifas*. In the early fifteenth century the Safavids became a political force in north-west Iran and eastern Anatolia as the empire established by Temur broke up amid severe internal power struggles. They also turned on the small Christian communities in Georgia and Trebizond and then on other Islamic states – their religious ideology provided the justification for what were, in essence, political struggles. They gained most of their support from groups excluded by the existing elites especially the *Qizilbash*, the military leaders who took their name from their red headgear. During the fifteenth century the religious beliefs of the Safavids became more elaborate – from a mainly Sunni base their faith became a mix of Shia and Sufi beliefs. It also incorporated a wide variety of other ideas ranging from Buddhism to Zoroastrianism but in general it was aggressively Shia and anti-Sunni. The culmination of this process came under Isma'il, who became leader in 1487 – he proclaimed himself the hidden imam and the reincarnation of Ali.

In 1501 Isma'il occupied Tabriz in north-east Iran and declared himself Shah. During the rest of the decade he established his control over the whole of Iran. It was a period that effectively set the modern borders of Iran – the Ottomans controlled Anatolia and the Shaybanid empire took control of Transoxania to the east. The major problems for the Safavids were to create some central political structure in Iran (none had existed for more than a century), rebuild the economic and social infrastructure (in many respects it was still suffering from the effects of the Mongol invasion two and a half centuries earlier) and control the *Qizilbash* military leaders who had actually conquered Iran on behalf of the Safavids. The *Qizilbash* organized themselves as chieftains with subject clans, villages and towns and enforced their right to control armies and take a share of tax revenues. Urban merchants were generally successful in keeping themselves as a separate group. In addition the Safavids had to deal with numerous secret religious societies and constant rebellions. For much of the sixteenth century the power of the early Shahs was therefore very limited. Only slowly were they able to develop the institutions of central government and establish some control. The key institution was the 'viceroy' or *wakil*, the commander of the armies in a region and head of the religious order. He was supported by a *wazir* as head of the civilian administration and an *amir*, as military commander. The Shah also began, in the long-established Islamic tradition, to recruit slave armies as a way of reducing the power of the *Qizilbash*.

The peak of central control and leadership came under Shah Abbas (1588–1629). The slave armies (consisting mainly of Georgian and Armenian converts) became the foundation of the regime and were re-equipped with musketry and artillery to match the effective armies of the Ottomans. The new army also provided the opportunity to weaken the power of the main elite army leaders and in local administration to favour lower social groups who depended on the Shah for their rise to power. Shah Abbas also imported Chinese craftsmen to rebuild silk, carpet and porcelain production. In conjunction with English merchants the new port of Bandar Abbas was established after the expulsion of the Portuguese from Hormuz. Although Dutch and French merchants were important in Iranian trade it came to be dominated by the English by the end of the seventeenth century. The main achievement of Shah Abbas was to supervise the construction of a new capital, Isfahan, which came to symbolize the new regime. By 1666 it had 162 mosques, 48 colleges, 182 caravanserais and 273 public baths. In the longer-term perspective of Safavid rule, the reign of Shah Abbas can be seen as a relatively brief interlude of greater central control in a regime characterized by the power of local groups and the general weakness of central government.

From the early seventeenth century a growing problem for the Safavids was the increasing lack of control which the regime could exercise over the Shia *ulama* who were increasingly replacing the religious authority of the dynasty. Safavid ideas were founded on absolutist claims derived from the control Sufi masters exercised over their pupils. Under the Safavids this became the idea of the *murshid-i kamil* or 'perfect master', the adherence to a strict code of conduct (*sufigare*) with disobedience leading to expulsion from the Safavid order and even execution. These Safavid ideas suffered a severe blow with their defeat by the orthodox Sunni Ottomans at the battle of Chaldiran in 1514 and the loss of most of the territories which the movement had controlled since its emergence. The Safavids therefore dropped most of their messianic claims and shifted to using Shiism to support the regime, even though the majority of the population of the empire were Sunni. The *ulama* were organized into a state-controlled bureaucracy and land, endowments and immunity from taxation were given to the new Shia establishments and families. The new religious elite therefore became part of the landowning aristocracy. Shiism imposed a wave of persecution against both Sufi leaders and Sunni institutions without parallel in Islam. Tombs were destroyed, the first three caliphs insulted, the pilgrimage to Mecca downgraded in favour of that to Karbala. Under Shah Abbas the great Shia shrines at Mashhad and Qum were rebuilt and given major property endowments to support themselves. These efforts continued until the late seventeenth century when the head of the Shia *ulama*, Muhammad Baqir al-Majlisi, completed the suppression of Sunni groups and expelled the last Sufis from Isfahan. It was these religious differences within Islam that lay at the root of the deep and continuing conflict between the Ottomans and the Safavids. The latter, with their puritanical belief in a single truth that could save people, caused as many problems for Islam as Luther and the Protestants did for Christianity.

[*Later Iran 19.9*]

18.4 The Uzbek Empire

[*Earlier central Asia 15.6*]
Further east the Uzbek empire was founded by Shaybani Khan Uzbek who ruled from 1500 to 1510 – he was a genuine descendant of Chinggis-khan although most of his followers were of Turkic descent. He and his successors destroyed the last vestiges of the states established by the successors of Temur and ruled the area as leaders of a coalition of clans. The chief city, religious centre and capital was Bukhara although there was an independent dynasty at Khiva after 1512. The Uzbeks remained isolated from the other major states of the area, although they were intermittently at war with the Safavids over Khurasan and with the Indian states over the Hindu Kush. Both the Bukhara and Khiva khanates survived as independent states until the 1860s. Further east in the Tarim basin the last of the Chaghatai khans (also the direct descendants of Chinggis) ruled in the Kashgar area until 1678 when the various cities became independent for almost a century.

[*Later central Asia 21.11*]

18.5 The Mughal empire

[Earlier India 13.9]
The establishment of the Mughal empire was a classic example of the impact of the new gunpowder weapons. In the early sixteenth century Babur, a Chaghatai Turkish ruler descended from the Timurids, led a number of invasions of northern India from Kabul. He was finally successful in 1526 at the battle of Panipat near Delhi when the last of the rulers of the Delhi sultanates, Sultan Ibrahim Lodi, was defeated. The use of matchlock muskets and cannon by Babur's army against the cavalry of their rivals proved to be decisive. A year later Babur defeated the Rajput confederacy of Hindu rulers in Rajasthan when, once again, the new weapons proved to be crucial. Babur established a new capital at Agra and by the time of his death in 1530 had extended his rule over an area stretching from Kabul across the Punjab to Delhi and as far east as Bihar. As with many conquest empires, few central institutions and little effective control had been established. Babur's successor Humayun proved ineffective at maintaining the empire. By 1540 he was in exile in Kabul and most of northern India was ruled by a rival Afghan leader, Sher Shah. The latter died in 1545 and his empire also broke up. By 1555 Humayun had reconquered Delhi but he died the next year and rule passed to his twelve-year-old son Akbar. At this point, given the weaknesses inherent in the Mughal position, it seemed very unlikely that the recent reconquests could be retained let alone extended.

The true creation of the Mughal empire was the work of Akbar during his long reign until 1605. By 1560 he controlled the key area stretching from Lahore in the west to Delhi, Agra and the great agricultural and trading wealth of the Ganges plain. The Hindu rulers of Rajasthan were incorporated and expansion south-westwards into Gujarat, following the capture of Ahmadabad in 1572, gave access to the Indian Ocean and the wealth of the great trading cities. Expansion eastwards took longer but by the 1580s Bihar and Bengal were controlled. In 1585 the capital was moved to Lahore so that the ultimately successful campaigns in Kashmir and Sind could be controlled more easily. In the last decade or so of his reign Akbar concentrated on the partially successful conquest of the Deccan, a complex area comprising five Muslim sultanates, who were hostile to the successors of Temur, and the Hindu Marathas who had long opposed all the Muslim kingdoms. By the early seventeenth century the Mughal empire dominated India, ruling a vast area from Baluchistan in the west to Assam in the east and from Kashmir in the north to the Deccan plateau in the south.

As well as extending the empire Akbar was able to establish a stable system of internal rule that led to a high level of internal peace and security in India which lasted for some 150 years from the mid-sixteenth century. The Mughal empire became a complex mixture of the Islamic-Iranian tradition, deriving from the Turkic and Mongol background of the rulers, and existing Indian cultures. Akbar's first aim was to reduce the power of the thirty or so high-ranking Turkish and Uzbek military leaders who had returned to India in the late 1540s with Humayun. He brought in new groups, especially from Iran but also Hindu and Muslim Indians who had largely been excluded by the rulers of the Delhi sultanates. Central rule came from the emperor and his four ministers together with the governors for each province and their ministers. Given the size of the empire it was inevitable that central power was limited and shared with local landlords and military commanders, hence Akbar's emphasis (which was shared by his successors) on widening this elite as much as possible and introducing more people who were dependent on the emperor. Ultimately Mughal rule depended on force and the possession of effective gunpowder weapons, especially cannon. They conquered the forts of the rulers of Rajasthan and new cities such as Allahabad (the former Prayag) at the junction of the Ganges and Yamuna rivers, Lahore and Agra all had heavy fortresses defended by cannon.

Mughal rule was also based on the prosperity of India. This was partly derived from the huge influx of gold and silver from the Americas as the Europeans bought the products that India made and traded. The population of Agra in 1600 was about 500,000, making it the third largest city in the world and cities such as Lahore with a population of about 350,000 were about twice the size of London. Equally important was the highly productive agriculture. By 1600 Mughal India was one of the wealthiest empires in the world – Akbar's revenue was twenty-five times that of James I of England. Its strength was based on an increasing ability to control the local landlords and gain access to this potential revenue for the state. Rural areas were largely controlled by local chiefs, *zamindars* to the Mughals, who often had their own infantry forces, and imposed their taxes on the peasantry (in the form of food and labour services) which were used to maintain their own estates and provide for their military forces. Gradually the Mughals were able to incorporate them into the structure of the empire by turning them into a semi-official class who passed on some of their revenue to the state, although the level of control over them always remained limited. From the early 1580s the Mughals were able to carry out a full survey of the empire using the new standard weights and measures to establish yields and new revenue assessments, although these were always closely linked to past yields and prices. Under the *zabt* system state revenues had to be paid in cash (a sign of the level of monetarization within the economy) – these demands were set out in writing and had to be accepted in writing by the zamindars. In return there was a determination of the zamindars' rights and they obtained an official patent from the provincial revenue officer, gave a bond for their performance and gained permission for inheritance by a single heir. After five years of satisfactory performance, control over the system was allowed to revert to the local elites as long as they continued to pass on the right amount of revenue – a sign (as with other pre-industrial empires) of the limited effectiveness of the Mughal state and the difficulty of keeping revenue assessments in line with real wealth.

The Mughals were, like their predecessors in the Delhi sultanates, Muslim rulers. This was symbolized by the construction between 1571 and 1585 of the new city of Fatehpur Sikri near Agra – the latter remained the administrative capital but the new complex, the residence for the court, was an Islamic city dominated by its mosque. However, Akbar became less enthusiastic about Islam later in his reign and encouraged religious debates and in consequence came into increasing conflict with the *ulama*. In 1578 he instituted a new policy of investigating the land grants (all of which were tax exempt) given to Islamic institutions and taking back those he judged not to be justified. In addition similar privileges were given to other religions if they were judged to be suitable. He also encouraged non-orthodox Islamic groups such as the Mahdawis, a messianic group who believed that the Mahdi or Muhammad would return after a thousand years (1592 in the Christian calendar). In 1579 Akbar took the momentous step of abolishing one of the fundamentals of Islamic rule – the tax on non-Muslims. Perhaps not surprisingly there was an Islamic revolt in 1579–80 which was forcibly put down. Akbar was attempting to establish a less Islamic basis for the Mughal empire in a situation where the majority of its subjects were not Muslims. He had not been able to do this by the time of his death in 1605 but had he done so the subsequent history of India might have been very different.

[*Later India 19.13*]

18.6 Japan: Civil War and Reunification

[*Earlier Japan 15.5.2*]

By the mid-fifteenth century the Ashikaga shogunate, established over a century earlier, was in severe decline. In 1467 the Onin war between different factions began over a disputed succession to the shogunate. Within six years the leaders of both factions were dead but the war continued until 1477 and total exhaustion on both sides. By then the remaining

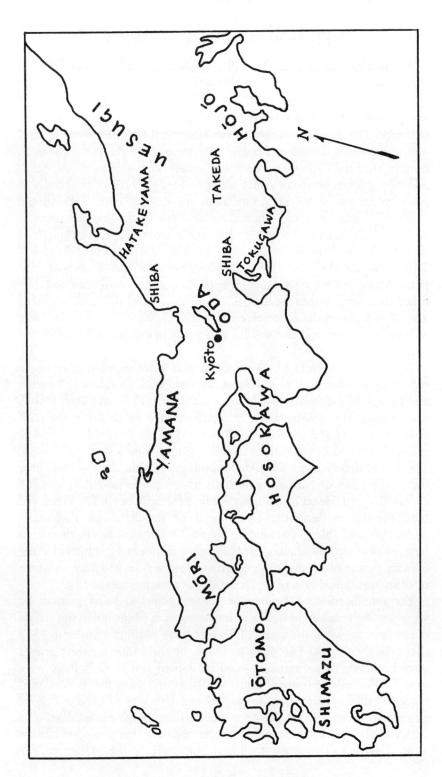

Map 55: Japan in the fifteenth and sixteenth centuries

authority of the shogunate had disappeared and with it any effective central government in Japan. For the next century there was almost continuous warfare but it had almost nothing to do with the shogunate. It was a series of struggles between local lords (*daimyo*) for power and influence. The *daimyo* emerged in the late fourteenth century as central power began to decline and were fully formed by the early sixteenth century after the Onin war. These local rulers were able to impose taxes and labour levies on the peasants who provided the bulk of the armies as pikemen became more important than the cavalry elite. The *daimyo* solidified their estates and retained revenue due to the imperial court at Kyoto, which therefore became increasingly impoverished. The capitals of these local units were the 'castle towns' built around the forts of the rulers. These were also the centres for trade where the *daimyo* could impose their taxes. More and more the *daimyo* were issuing their own laws and they called their lands *kokka* ('states' or 'countries'). When the first Europeans arrived in Japan in the sixteenth century they thought they were the same as European states and had no idea of the role of either the shogun or the emperor.

The continuous warfare between the *daimyo* saw the end of many of the old ruling families such as the Shiba, Hatakeyama, Hosokawa, Yamana and Uesugi. In their place new families such as the Hojo and Mori rose to prominence. The disintegration of Japan reached its height in the mid-sixteenth century and was followed by a period when three military leaders gradually created a more unified state and gained control over the *daimyo*. The first of these leaders was Oda Nobunaga, a minor *daimyo* from near the modern city of Nagoya, who built up his power and then in 1568 captured Kyoto. He set up a puppet Ashikaga shogun but in 1573 removed him, thereby marking the formal end of the Ashikaga shogunate. Nobunaga was able to consolidate his position around Kyoto through a long series of attritional wars, the building of castles and a reduction in the military power of the great monasteries. However, he had little influence in either western or eastern Japan before his assassination in 1582.

The reunification of Japan was mainly achieved using gunpowder weapons. Although some had been imported from China it was the arrival of the Portuguese on the island of Tanegashima south of Kyushu in 1543 that brought the first European weapons. By the 1550s Japanese armies were beginning to use muskets (made in Japan) and in 1575 there were over 3,000 musketeers at the battle of Nagashino using the 'volley' technique in ranks so as to increase the rate of fire (it was adopted in Europe about two decades later). To cope with artillery huge castles developed with complex bastions and outlying forts (Odawara the stronghold of the Hojo *daimyo* had over twenty forts) but, unlike those of Europe, the castles were elegant seven-storey buildings. By the 1580s massive armies of over 300,000 men were involved in the great battles to reunify Japan.

The Europeans brought not only gunpowder weapons but also missionaries – the first, Francis Xavier, arrived in 1549. Many of the *daimyo* encouraged trade and contacts with the Portuguese as a way of improving their own position and wealth. In 1562 the small Omura *daimyo* converted to Christianity and in 1571 established Nagasaki as the main port of call for the Portuguese. By the late sixteenth century there were probably about 300,000 Christians in Japan out of a total population of about 12 million. The disintegration of central authority in Japan was therefore a fortuitous benefit for the Portuguese and the missionaries. Once central authority was re-established the Europeans found it much more difficult to make an impression on Japan.

That reunification was achieved by Hideyoshi, a foot soldier from a poor family who had risen through the ranks by ability to become Nobunaga's main general. On the latter's assassination in 1582 Hideyoshi was quickly victorious in the struggle for power and within three years he controlled most of central Japan. With an army of over 250,000 he conquered Kyushu and defeated the Hojo at the long siege of Odawara – it was finally starved into submission in 1590. By the early 1590s Japan was effectively reunited under Hideyoshi who, like his mentor Nobunaga, did not claim the position of shogun but remained, at least in theory, no more than the emperor's chief minister at Kyoto. However, he had enough authority to carry out a land survey of the whole of Japan, establish a currency and conduct foreign relations. In 1587 the Christian missionaries were formally expelled and although many remained their activities were tightly circumscribed until the expulsion decree was strictly enforced in 1597. Hideyoshi also had the power to launch a massive invasion of Korea in 1592 with an army of over 160,000 men. It was ultimately unsuccessful as was a second attempt in 1597 with a slightly smaller army. These were the only attempts by Japan to extend its rule outside the home islands before the late nineteenth century. These campaigns also placed a major strain on Ming China and the first signs of internal breakdown within China date to this period. Hideyoshi died in 1598 and the regency for his five-year-old son Hideyori collapsed in civil war within two years. The victor in that war was Tokugawa Ieyasu who had begun his career as a local ruler in Mikawa province in eastern Japan. He was an ally of Nobunaga and a major figure in Hideyoshi's regime and once in control of the whole of Japan in 1603 he, unlike his immediate predecessors, took the title of shogun. Thereafter Japan was always a unified state with a strong central government.

During the late sixteenth century, as Japan was reunified, important social and economic changes were taking place. The *daimyo* were

originally local military magnates leading their dependent warriors (*samurai*) in battle so as to expand their domains. However, during the sixteenth century they were forced to rationalize their landholdings as the old estate or *shoen* system collapsed – peasant landlords became more common and the *daimyo* had to become administrators carrying out local land surveys in order to establish their own tax base. Rural communities were increasingly organized in self-governing villages (*mura*) with secure tenure, and the *daimyo* could only rely on rents from their lands. In addition the *samurai* were gradually separated from their land and moved into the castle towns of the *daimyo* and were paid (in rice) for their services. Although the *daimyo* were not abolished with the re-establishment of the shogunate and effective central government they were incorporated into the new system. As internal warfare ended, the basis of power in Japan changed from military to political. The *samurai* might be high-status warriors but increasingly their functions became ceremonial – there were no wars to fight either internally or externally. The *daimyo* became political administrators acting on behalf of the central government and using legal and bureaucratic methods to govern their own domains. Their power now came from the local offices, created by the imperial government, which they held and which they could usually pass on to their heirs. During the sixteenth century the *daimyo* had been able to tax trade effectively through control over the castle towns and their markets. However, because the Japanese trade system was always organized on a national basis there were limits to their power and the merchant communities remained close to the imperial authorities. Hideyoshi had enough power to restrict *daimyo* control over commerce and ensure that a national market became part of the rebuilding of a unified Japanese state.
[*Later Japan 19.8*]

18.7 Europe: Reality and 'Renaissance'

18.7.1 Reality
In 1500 the population of Europe reached the same level as in 1300 (about 80 million) and the recovery from the disasters of the fourteenth century (especially famine and recurrent plague) was largely complete. Over the course of the sixteenth century it grew by about a quarter to around 100 million in 1600 (still only about 60 per cent of that of China). The major problem was that there was no significant increase in agricultural productivity through the introduction of new techniques and crops. The population rise during the fifteenth century was largely achieved by bringing into cultivation the land that was abandoned in the mid-fourteenth century.

From the early sixteenth century there was little new land available to accommodate the continuing rise in the population. From the 1550s therefore there was a growing number of very marginal peasants and landless labourers with the latter creating falling wages. By 1600 the purchasing power of male labourers was about half what it had been in 1550 and very little of that decline was the result of inflation caused by the flood of American gold and silver (as we have seen most of that was sent to India and China). The position of the overwhelming majority of the population was worsened still further by growing landlord exactions. In addition state taxes rose substantially during the sixteenth century in most areas of Europe. Only in a few anomalous regions such as the Low Countries, around London and a few towns in northern Italy, did growing commercialization, the supply of crops for the urban population and greater investment give the peasants a stronger position.

Until about the 1550s industrial output grew as the rising population produced a small upturn in demand, the state increased military expenditure and transportation costs fell marginally. From the 1550s output fell except in a few areas such as the Netherlands and the English woollen trade. Industrial production was still largely dependent on agriculture and its products and was, like the rest of Eurasia, mainly carried out in small-scale units dominated by craftsmen. Output was varied by opening or closing these units rather than through any fundamental change in production techniques. Also important was rural industry where the peasants were dependent on the merchants who sold or leased them raw materials which they turned into finished products. It was a system very suitable for poorly organized markets with low demand and enabled the merchants to vary output easily, although all of the burden then fell on the part-time peasant workers.

The agricultural and industrial systems in Europe reflected and also helped to produce a society with extreme inequality where the mass of the people lived in great poverty. The overwhelming priority for most people was to find enough food to stay alive. For the peasants it depended on the size of the crop (largely determined by the weather) and how much of the crop their landlords demanded. The rest of the people had to spend at least four-fifths of their income on food and in a bad year of poor harvests and rising prices even that was not sufficient. Food expenditure left little for other necessities. Clothing was therefore rare and very important – the rules of the hospital in Perugia in 1582 stated that the clothes of the dead 'should not be usurped but should be given to lawful inheritors' and in many cities people fought over the clothes of those who died of the plague. Even less was available to spend on housing – in Turin in 1630 people were living 65 to a house and at the same time in Florence the figure was even higher at 70–100 to a house. The average peasant had a mud or thatch hut with no windows, a hole in the roof to let out the smoke from the fire, and they shared their living quarters with their animals so as to keep warm. The low level of productivity meant that all had to work including the children and the old. Even the rich had very little on which their wealth could be spent apart from a small range of luxuries, excessive food, ostentatious clothing (most states had laws restricting the wearing of certain prestige clothes to the aristocracy), large houses and an excessive number of servants.

About one in ten of the European population was rich, about half were very poor and the rest were beggars or near beggars. Even in England (one of the richest countries in Europe) in the late seventeenth century (when conditions had improved compared with those a century earlier) it was estimated that a quarter of the population were paupers suffering from continuous poverty and underemployment and with no reserves for even the most minor problem. In France in the same period paupers probably made up about forty per cent of the population. A detailed survey of the village of Navalmoral just south of Toledo in the 1580s gives a clear picture of Europe in the sixteenth century. It had a population of 243 families making a total of about 1,000 people. Of these just 22 families owned half of the land, there were 60 families of peasants, 28 families had no land but grazed some livestock, 95 families were landless labourers, there were 21 widows living alone with no visible means of support and 17 families did not even have a place to live. The rich needed the poor as a source of labour (in most towns about a quarter of the population were servants) but in times of shortage, employment and charity would decline (even church charity could decline if no tithes were paid). When this happened people had no option but to wander the countryside searching for food or charity and taking to theft when there was no alternative. The rich and the state authorities had a constant fear of the poor, especially armed bands and the vagrants and beggars who often made up a quarter of the population in the large cities. They were either driven away or set to work in conditions of near slavery in workhouses.

18.7.2 'Renaissance'
This picture puts into perspective the idea of the 'Renaissance' as a defining characteristic of late fifteenth- and sixteenth-century Europe. The concept of the 'Renaissance' was largely created by members of the leisured and 'cultivated' elite of nineteenth-century Europe such as Jacob Burckhardt and Walter Pater. They were great believers in the civilizing role of 'the arts' and admired what they saw as the creativity and individualism of Italy enshrined in men such as Michelangelo, Leonardo and Botticelli, who were

'modern men' leading Europe from the 'Dark Ages' to its true position at the summit of world culture. For them the Renaissance was about the revival of classical architecture, Latin and its literary genres, together with the construction of what became the central features of a 'humanist' education – the classics, grammar, rhetoric, poetry, ethics and history. This was linked to an imitation of ancient Greece and, more particularly Rome and its history – or rather the Roman view of its own history enshrined in writers such as Livy and Tacitus.

Over the last century historians have begun to paint a very different picture of the 'Renaissance'. It certainly was not a universal phenomenon across Eurasia and in nearly every respect it was no more than Europe beginning to catch up with other longer-established cultures and societies. For example the classical texts treasured in fifteenth-century Italy had been known in the Islamic world since the seventh century. There had been other 'renaissances' before, for example in the twelfth century when Europe gained access to Aristotle through translations of Arabic texts. The 'Renaissance' was also much closer to the culture and ideas of preceding centuries and far less modern than it was thought to be in the nineteenth century. Almost every characteristic once attributed to the 'Renaissance' can be found earlier in Europe and also in other cultures. Where it was important was in beginning to define a particular European view of the world, in particular that western Europe was the heir to the traditions of Greece and Rome. On the other hand it was in the sixteenth century that Europe began to abandon some of the notions about the world that it had inherited from ancient Greece. This was particularly noticeable in astronomy with Copernicus, Kepler, Tycho Brahe and Galileo abandoning the Ptolemaic system (against stiff resistance from powerful elements in European society such as the church) and moving towards a more 'modern' system. (China had never suffered from the Ptolemaic ideas and therefore never needed to make such changes.) Even so most of these astronomers were mystics, astrologers and obsessed with magic (as was Sir Isaac Newton a century later). Although it is often claimed that these and other scientific advances in the sixteenth and seventeenth centuries were the foundations for Europe's later industrial advance this was not the case. Most of these discoveries had little 'practical' use and technological change depended, as in the past, on a series of adaptations and small-scale changes by craftsmen and industrialists who had little or no formal scientific training. It was not until well into the nineteenth century (in particular the discovery of electricity and magnetism) that scientific advances led to major industrial advances.

18.8 Europe: Religious Divisions

In the sixteenth century, and for some time thereafter, Europe was to be rent by religious divisions on a scale never experienced before. Five hundred years earlier the western and eastern churches had drifted apart but now the western church was to be divided and religious intolerance and persecution reached new levels. Although the sixteenth century was marked by the rise of 'Protestantism' (itself covering a wide variety of beliefs), for most of western and central Europe it was a period which saw the reassertion of the power of the church and a greater and largely successful determination to enforce what was to be believed.

The demand for reform in the church was not new in the early sixteenth century. The English cleric John Wyclif who died in 1384 rejected the idea of transubstantiation, argued for clerical marriage and a vernacular Bible and also favoured the idea of predestination. The Czech John Huss attacked church corruption and the practice of reserving the wine for the priests at communion. He was given an imperial safe conduct to argue his case at the Council of Constance but once in the hands of the church authorities was condemned and burnt as a heretic in 1415. The crucial question is therefore why the 'reformation' only came in the early sixteenth century. The condition of the church was probably no worse at this time than it had been in previous centuries. Similarly it is unlikely that (as used to be argued) the 'Renaissance' had any very strong influence. After all two of the strongest defenders of the status quo, Erasmus and Sir Thomas More, were both deeply influenced by the 'humanist' ideas of the 'Renaissance'. Printing may have helped spread some of the ideas more quickly but this new technology did not itself produce the religious changes and new ideas.

The protests by Martin Luther began around the renewed sale of indulgences (giving remittance of past sins) by the pope in 1517 in order to pay for the rebuilding of St Peter's. Luther developed his ideas further in his 95 Theses (which were probably not nailed to the door of the church) and the emerging doctrine of justification by faith. He almost certainly would not have survived but for the support of some of the petty German secular rulers, in particular Frederick of Saxony, and the considerable freedom they had within the empire. In 1520 Luther refused to recant and instead published the *Address to the Christian Nobility of the German Nation* and *On the Freedom of the Christian Man*. The next year he was given an imperial safe conduct by Charles V to the Diet of Worms. Unlike John Huss, Luther was lucky in that the safe conduct was honoured despite his condemnation as a heretic.

Luther was not the only critic of the church. In three cities other leaders

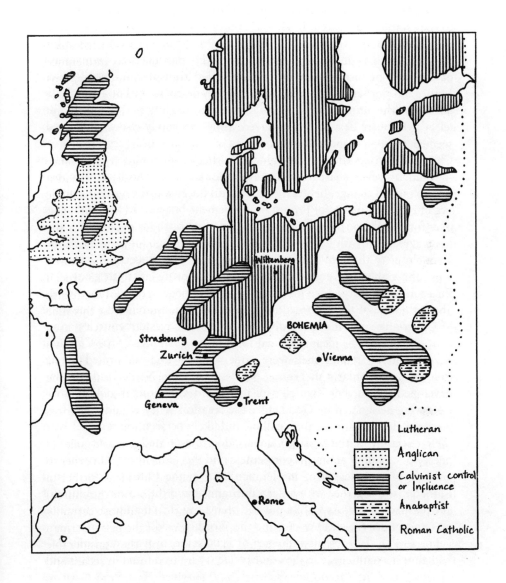

Map 56: European religious divisions in the mid-sixteenth century

played a key role in establishing Protestantism as an institutional and political alternative to Catholicism. The problem was that they could not agree on doctrine, which resulted in a diffuse and badly divided alternative to the established church. In Zurich Huldrich Zwingli was not only more important for the future development of Protestantism than Luther but also reached his conclusions independently. He produced his own variant of the idea of justification by faith, rejected transubstantiation (which Luther did not) and hardened the idea of predestination. For Zwingli the latter was the ultimate sign of God's sovereignty. However, the idea of an 'elect' who were destined to be saved while everybody else was damned, seemed to many, including Luther, to go against the very essence of Christian ideas. Although Zwingli and Luther could not agree on doctrine they did, however, share the same respect for secular authority and opposition to radical change. In Strasbourg Martin Bucer was the head of a highly organized and successful Protestant movement but he had little influence over future religious developments. He usually, for the sake of unity, came to an agreement with Luther over doctrine even though his personal beliefs were closer to those of Zwingli. There was never a 'Bucerism'. Instead it was John Calvin in Geneva who, although achieving less in that city than Bucer in Strasbourg, gave his name to a movement, created a mythology about the role of the reformed religion in Geneva, established a new type of Christianity and made the divisions within the western church permanent. He set out his ideas in a final form in the *Institutes of the Christian Religion* in 1559 and they were later adapted and elaborated by his followers, particularly in France, Scotland and the Netherlands. Calvin developed still further Zwingli's ideas on predestination, arguing that the elect were designated by God before the creation. They would know they were the elect because of their calling and likely persecution together with their rejection of the world. Calvin's doctrines rested on a frightening degree of certainty about his correctness and this led, almost inevitably, to an even greater degree of intolerance than in the Catholic church and Lutheranism, together with a deep puritanism and the close regulation of every aspect of life. As Calvin put it, 'what I say is so manifestly true that no one can deny it without denying the Word of God'.

For several decades the influence of Protestantism was very limited. It had almost no influence in the countryside where traditional beliefs (many of which had little to do with Christianity) survived. The main successes came in the towns although even here Calvin was driven out of Geneva in 1538 and Bucer from Strasbourg in 1549. The new beliefs tended to be restricted to a small group of enthusiastic self-perpetuating converts convinced of their own righteousness and correctness. During the sixteenth century in Württemberg, out of a total of 511 'reformed' pastors over two-thirds were the sons of pastors. Even in the Netherlands where Calvinism had a major impact probably less than one in ten of the population in the 1580s was part of the 'reformed' church. The main strength of Protestantism was less its beliefs than the political support it could generate. Lutheranism survived because it was supported by the rulers of Saxony, Hesse and Württemberg, whose alliance was formalized at the Diet of Speyer in 1529. These rulers had to balance the risks involved in defying both the emperor (whose authority was limited) and the papacy against the very obvious benefits from secularizing church property (especially the monasteries) and the huge increase in wealth and power this could bring a ruler. England produced its own unique solution. In 1521 Henry VIII was made 'Defender of the Faith' by the pope for his defence of the seven sacraments against Luther. When the pope refused to grant him a divorce from his first wife Catherine of Aragon Henry imposed state control of the church, stopped appeals to Rome and created a 'Church of England'. It was not a 'reformed' church and Henry remained no more than a schismatic Catholic. However, control over the church and the dissolution of the monasteries later in the 1530s provided a massive increase in wealth for the monarchy and its supporters (it was soon squandered). Although Protestant ideas infiltrated the church in England the more extreme Calvinists did not become dominant.

As in England, it was usually the wishes of the ruler which determined the beliefs of his subjects. Protestantism was imposed by princely decree in Denmark and roughly similar processes were at work in Sweden and Norway. Calvinism too depended on state support as in the Palatinate and Hungary. Only in France and the Netherlands did Calvinism become associated with resistance to the ruler and in the latter it was soon backed by the new regime after the revolt against Spain. The vagaries of belief and the role of the ruler in sixteenth-century Europe are well illustrated by events in the Rhine Palatinate. It changed from Catholicism to Lutheranism in 1544, to Calvinism in 1559, back to Lutheranism in 1576 and back to Calvinism again in 1583. It was this 'confessional absolutism' – the determination of religious belief by secular rulers, rather than the process of individual conversion – that typified Europe. The outcome was that Protestantism reached the peak of its influence in the 1590s when perhaps as many as half of the European population were in theory subscribers to the new beliefs. By the mid-seventeenth century this proportion had fallen back to about a fifth as Catholicism re-established itself in the Habsburg lands, Bavaria and France. At the same time Protestantism remained bitterly divided.

The Catholic revival is often seen as a 'Counter-Reformation', although in practice it was a largely internally generated reform based upon a number of earlier developments. It too created a level of intolerance which matched that of the most extreme Protestants. The revival had a very strong Spanish influence, although there was no simple harmony of interests between the Habsburgs and the Spanish monarchs on the one hand and the papacy on the other. One of the most important developments was the creation of the Jesuit order whose main aims were conversion, teaching and the extermination of heresy. It was very different from the old monastic orders which were turned inwards towards the spiritual life of the individual and the monastic community. The new order was recognized by the pope in 1540 partly because of its absolute support for the papacy. The Jesuits were also part of a growing Catholic puritanism which came to predominate in Spain. It was in Spain that the Holy Office (or Inquisition), which had been directed against Muslims and Jews, turned to a more general attack on non-Catholics. At first it was used against odd sects such as the Illuminists and Erasmians but from the 1550s it concentrated on the Protestants. In 1542 the Roman Inquisition, established in the thirteenth century, was revived. Mass burnings and *autos-da-fé* ('acts of faith') were carried out, spreading into Portugal in 1547 and across the Americas – the first in Lima was in 1570 with Mexico City following a year later. Between 1550 and 1800 the Inquisition held about 150,000 trials and about 3,000 people were killed. Far more important was the fear which it generated and its other punishments – torture, imprisonment (at the cost of the accused), confiscation of goods, public humiliation and perpetual infamy. In the case of the latter the penitent's gown which the 'guilty' always had to wear in public was displayed in the local church after death and when the gown finally rotted the surviving relatives had to replace it. As the 1578 handbook of the Inquisition put it, 'The ultimate end of the trial and condemnation to death is not to save the soul of the accused, but to maintain public order and to terrorize the people.' The imposition of belief was therefore as strict as in any Calvinist state but it did ensure that Spain, Portugal and Italy remained almost exclusively Catholic and that it also dominated France. Catholic doctrine was also re-asserted. The Council of Trent (which met intermittently between 1543 and 1563) was not a challenge to papal authority as the councils of the early fifteenth century had been. However, it was part of a more general process of reforming the papacy from the very high levels of corruption found in the late fifteenth and early sixteenth centuries. The Council produced a clear statement of belief (though it was little more than a restatement of accepted doctrine) but that was the one thing that Protestantism could not do.

The religious divisions and intolerance within Europe were not confined to the Catholic–Protestant split. Jews were expelled from many areas, both

Catholic and Protestant – Spain (1492), Portugal (1497), Saxony (1537), Brunswick (1543), Hanover and Lüneberg (1553), the Papal state (1569), Brandenburg (1573), the Palatinate (1575), Silesia (1582) and in Venice the ghetto was formally established. In the 1530s the first Protestant was killed for his beliefs by other Protestants on the orders of Zwingli. Both Catholics and Protestants were equally opposed to the so-called 'Anabaptists'. They were not an organized group with a single set of beliefs and the term was used by their opponents for almost any group opposed to organized religion and it was often used interchangeably with 'heretic'. These groups generally supported individual religious experience against the imposition of belief by the state and often were socially revolutionary too. They were a prime example of what could happen once a successful attack on the established religion had been made – many saw no reason to stop where Luther did or accept the rigidities of Calvinism. The Protestants turned on the 'Anabaptists' after the events in Münster in 1534–5. The 'Anabaptists' gained control of the town council in 1534 and under Jan of Leyden started implementing their religious and social ideas about the new community, including polygamy. They had very little support and the town was captured by Philip of Hesse, a Protestant prince and syphilitic, to whom Luther had conveniently given permission to be a bigamist. Jan and the other leaders were bound in iron cages to stakes outside the cathedral. Their tongues were ripped out with red-hot pincers and they were then tortured to death.

Established religions and states found it equally difficult to deal with popular beliefs. Even for the educated elite there was no real difference between 'science' and 'magic' until well into the eighteenth century, as is shown in the careers of men like Kepler (a fortune-teller) and Newton. Even the papacy was strongly influenced by Hermetic ideas. Popular beliefs were a complex mixture of Christianity (usually only partially understood) and other ideas in which 'magic' permeated every aspect of life. However, it was the specific Christian idea of the Devil that helped in the con-struction of a new crime – 'witchcraft'. It first appeared in the Dominican inquisition in the 1480s but was later common to both Catholics and Protestants. As Calvin put it 'God expressly commands that all witches and enchantresses shall be put to death and this law of God is a universal law.' Jean Bodin, one of the major legal thinkers of the sixteenth century, called for the burning not only of all witches but also of those who did not believe that witchcraft was a great threat to the world. The elite certainly believed that there were vast numbers of witches. Henri Boguet, who closely studied 'demonology', decided that there were 1,800,000 witches across Europe all of whom were engaged in a well-organized conspiracy against Christian religion and society. The practice of 'magic' certainly did exist at every level of European society but the idea of 'devil-worship' is much more problematic and there is no evidence for its existence apart from in confessions obtained under torture.

The idea of 'witchcraft' was therefore in the minds of those who believed in this vast conspiracy, made accusations and persecuted the unfortunate. The accusations followed a fairly standard catalogue of ideas – a pact with the devil (sometimes involving sex) and responsibility for everything which had gone wrong in society. The result was a major outbreak of intolerance and persecution across Europe. In the three centuries after 1450 over 100,000 people (mostly women) were prosecuted for witchcraft, practising magic and worshipping the devil. Of these about 60,000 were killed, usually by being burnt. About half of the prosecutions were in Germany and the peak of the persecution came in the late sixteenth and early seventeenth centuries. Witch-hunting was usually concentrated into very short periods of frantic activity and mass hysteria as people, church and secular leaders turned on those believed to be engaged in this vast conspiracy against them and their society. Witches were usually burnt in large groups of more than twenty but sometimes the persecutions were on an even more intensive basis. In Eichstätt 274 people were burned to death in a single year and in 1589 at Quedlinburg 133 people were burned in a single day. After the mid-seventeenth century the witch-hunting and persecution died away although why this happened is unclear.

18.9 Europe: Dynastic Conflict

The growing religious divisions within Europe in the sixteenth century only served to heighten the existing dynastic conflicts. The result was to make Europe the most unstable region of Eurasia in the sixteenth century where the continuous warfare and high level of religious intolerance and persecution stood in stark contrast to the relative stability and peace in the great empires of the Ottomans and the Ming. The politics of Europe was characterized not by 'nation-states' but by the dynastic interests of the ruling and aristocratic families and the assertion of often obscure claims dating back centuries. In this respect sixteenth-century Europe was no different from the Europe of the fourteenth and fifteenth centuries with the conflicts between the Habsburgs, Luxemburgs and Wittelsbachs for the imperial title, or the assertion of the English claim to the French throne in the 1330s which led to the 'Hundred Years War'. As in other pre-industrial states, the maintenance of a secure succession was vital to dynastic success. The Ottoman sultan might kill all his brothers to secure the title but Philip II of Spain plotted to kill his mad son Don Carlos. In England the need for

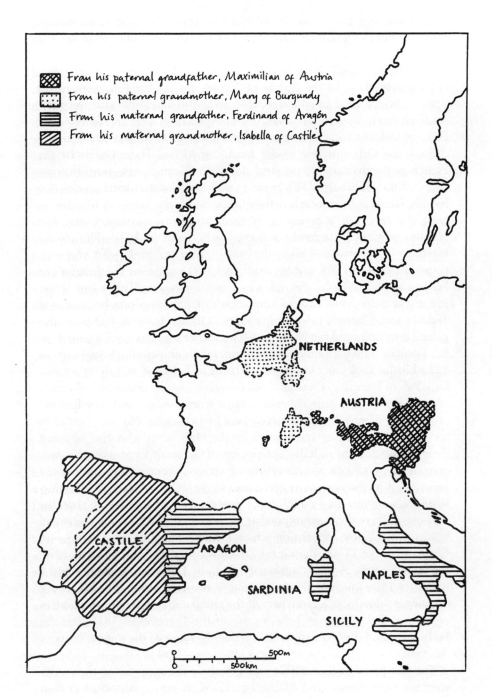

From his paternal grandfather, Maximilian of Austria
From his paternal grandmother, Mary of Burgundy
From his maternal grandfather, Ferdinand of Aragón
From his maternal grandmother, Isabella of Castile

NETHERLANDS

AUSTRIA

CASTILE

ARAGON

NAPLES

SARDINIA

SICILY

500m

500km

Map 57: The Habsburg inheritance of Charles V

a male heir was central to Henry VIII's succession of marriages and his daughter Elizabeth had her rival Mary of Scotland executed to secure the throne.

In 1494 the French king, Charles VIII, decided to revive the 200-year-old Angevin claim to the throne of Naples against the Aragonese royal house. This required an invasion across over 400 miles of hostile territory, made no strategic sense and was, not unexpectedly, a failure. In 1499 the Duke of Orleans became king as Louis XII and he added another dynastic claim – the Orleanist one to the Duchy of Milan. These claims by the French monarchy ran into the rival claims (and actual possessions in some cases) of the Habsburgs. The growing and extensive territories controlled by this family, which reached their peak under the emperor Charles V, were the result of a series of dynastic accidents and marriages. The Habsburgs gained Burgundy and the Netherlands in 1477. The crucial marriage was between Philip, the son of Maximilian I (who was also emperor between 1508 and his death in 1519) and Juana the daughter of Ferdinand and Isabella, the rulers of Castile, Aragon, Naples and Sicily. Juana was the first monarch to unite these different kingdoms but was mad and her son, Charles, ruled in her name. On the death of Philip he also gained Burgundy and the Netherlands and, after a massive bribe funded by the German banking family of the Fuggers, the imperial title in 1519. In 1526 he also took the old Habsburg lands of Bohemia and the truncated kingdom of Hungary. Charles V ruled a rambling and disparate collection of territories whose only coherence came from the fact that they had the same ruler. Nevertheless the developing French monarchy was bound to see itself as potentially surrounded by the Habsburgs who also opposed their dynastic claims in Italy. The princes in Germany were, as in the past, generally opposed to any assertion of imperial control and the papacy (because of its own extensive territories in the centre of Italy) was equally suspicious of increasing Habsburg power. The problem was that the Habsburgs were the most important supporters of the Catholic cause and it was this religious dimension which dictated much of their policy – in Germany in the 1540s, during the Dutch revolt after 1566 and even with the launch of the Armada against England in 1588. For a century and a half after 1500 much of European history revolved around the Habsburg attempts to dominate a large part of the continent and the opposition this provoked. It was not until the Treaty of the Pyrenees in 1659 that the Habsburgs and the Spanish monarchy finally accepted the impossibility of this task.

The first phase of the conflict was in Italy in the early sixteenth century over the rival French and Habsburg claims. It was a period of endless warfare, invasions by both sides, huge casualties, increasing devastation, shifting alliances between the small states of the peninsula and the lack of a decisive victory. Charles V seemed to have achieved the latter at the battle of Pavia in 1525 when Francis I of France was captured. The price of his release was the treaty of Madrid the next year when Francis was forced to give up the French royal family's claims to Naples, Milan and Genoa. The pope then conveniently dispensed Francis from his undertakings so that he could lead an alliance against the Habsburgs. The result was the sack of Rome in 1527 by the imperial armies under Charles. After this a long stalemate ensued. It was not resolved until after both Francis and Charles were no longer on the throne. The treaty of Cateau-Cambrésis of 1559 ended the first phase of the struggle. After sixty-five years of conflict the French royal family kept nothing in Italy except the insignificant Marquisate of Saluzzo, although it did retain Metz, Toul and Verdun on its eastern border.

The problem for the Habsburgs was that the conflict with the French monarchy was only one of the many they faced. They saw one of their central roles, deriving from the imperial title, as being the defenders of Christianity against the superior power of the Ottomans in the Mediterranean. In the same way they also felt they had to defend Catholicism against the Lutherans in Germany. In the late 1540s, following his success at the battle of Mühlberg against the Protestant League of Schmalkalden, Charles V seemed to be on the verge of success and forcing an end to the schism within the church. Then he lost the backing of some of the princes who had supported him (partially the result of French influence) and by 1552 he had given up the attempt to enforce religious uniformity. The peace of Augsburg in 1555 accepted that religion would follow the dictates of the secular ruler and reflected the fact that for centuries the emperor had lacked effective power compared with the German princes. The settlement did ensure that Germany had half a century of religious peace although this was made easier by the fact that no settlement with the religiously extreme Calvinists was required. By the mid-1550s the Habsburgs were on the verge of bankruptcy (it became actual in 1557). Even though they controlled about a quarter of Europe's population, including some of its richest areas (especially the Low Countries), and had access to the wealth of the Americas, they were unable to devise and implement an effective policy to control such a wide and disparate area. This was too great a task for a pre-industrial dynastic empire with a limited infrastructure. In 1555 Charles V abdicated. Like so many dynastic rulers he split up the territories he ruled. On his abdication he passed the imperial title to his brother Ferdinand I (1555–64), and in Spain power passed to his son Philip II (1556–98). Thereafter the Habsburgs were effectively split in two with different rulers in Vienna and Madrid.

At the same time the French monarchy collapsed after the death of Henry II in 1559 and the succession of the fifteen-year-old Francis II. The monarchy disintegrated into factionalism under the powerful influence of Catherine de Medici and the various aristocratic and royal houses which were also divided by religion. Navarre was Protestant and Guise was Catholic, the Montmorency were originally Catholic but then changed sides. For the rest of the sixteenth century there were eight civil wars and an almost total breakdown of the French state. Many of the problems were caused by the increasing strength of the Calvinists. The Catholics feared that they would seize power in much the same way as they had done in Scotland in 1559 when Mary of Guise, who was regent for her daughter Mary was removed from power. In 1560 the 'conspiracy of Amboise', which aimed to kill the Duke of Guise, kidnap the young king and seize power, was defeated. In 1572 the Catholics struck first in the 'massacre' of St Bartholomew when about 2,000 Protestants were killed in Paris. The conflict continued until 1591 when Henry of Navarre, originally a Protestant, became king and effectively made Catholicism the state religion. In 1598 the Edict of Nantes granted toleration for other Christians. The outcome was that Henry was assassinated by a Jesuit in 1610 for being tolerant and therefore not a true Catholic. The internal French disputes gave the Habsburgs greater scope for action but they found it impossible to mobilize enough power to put down the revolt in the Netherlands. In the late 1580s and early 1590s it seemed possible that they might achieve their aims with the launch of the Armada against England and the Netherlands and with a Spanish army later marching on Paris. However, their situation rapidly deteriorated and in 1598 they were forced to make peace with France, followed by one with England in 1604 and a long truce with the Dutch in 1609.

The next series of major wars to affect Europe began in 1618 with the revolt of the Protestant estates of Bohemia against their Catholic Habsburg ruler, Ferdinand II (emperor between 1619 and 1637). Initial Habsburg successes were soon countered by increasing external involvement – the Dutch in 1621, after the expiry of their truce with Spain, and the Danish kingdom in 1626. Nevertheless by the late 1620s the imperial armies under Wallenstein seemed to be on the verge of success. This only drew in other powers to try and stop a Habsburg victory beginning with the Swedish king Gustavus Adolphus in 1630. Direct Spanish involvement in 1634 predictably led to direct French intervention a year later. A Spanish invasion of France failed and revolts in Portugal and Catalonia in the 1640s only weakened the Habsburg position still further. Both sides were nearing exhaustion but the problem was finding a settlement that was acceptable to all. The war ended in a confused fashion, starting with a

Spanish-Dutch peace in 1648 (depriving the French of a major ally) and a more general German settlement at the peace of Westphalia. The struggle then remained as a purely French and Spanish one until the peace of 1659 from which the French gained Artois and Rousillon. The Habsburgs failed to impose their domination on Europe. However, it was an impossible task given the variety of territories over which they ruled, the privileges and separate identities each territory was able to insist on retaining, and the complexities of the strategic problems facing the Habsburgs. Most of the burdens fell on Castile which lacked the strong commercial and agricultural base to support them. By the late seventeenth century Spain was in relative decline, economically, socially and politically.

18.10 Eastern Europe

18.10.1 Poland-Lithuania
[*Earlier Poland-Lithuania 15.10.1*]
In the early sixteenth century the family of the Jagiellon kings of Poland-Lithuania also provided the kings of Hungary and Bohemia. Together they ruled about a third of the European continent. Although this was merely a dynastic union of very different territories, the family seemed to be more powerful than their rivals the Habsburgs. However, the death of the childless Ulaszlo II at the battle of Mohacs against the Ottomans in 1526 saw the latter two titles pass to the Habsburgs, although they controlled little of Hungary until the 1680s. Nevertheless the Jagiellon kings of Poland and Lithuania still ruled over the largest state in Europe. It was closely linked to the world of western Europe mainly through the wealth derived from the export of grain to the Low Countries through the port of Gdansk. The monarchy was as strong as those in western Europe – it owned about a sixth of the land in the country, controlled the small bureaucracy and commanded the army.

It was far from inevitable that the state would disintegrate into the internal weakness that was to characterize it in the eighteenth century and lead to its partition. Nevertheless there were internal problems (as in most European states at this time). The union of Poland and Lithuania was only through the crowns, and the aristocracy in each country feared domination by the other. The situation was worsened in the 1560s by the imminent death of the childless Zygmunt II and the need to select a new dynasty at a time when the state was under external threat from the rising power of Moscow, and, to a lesser extent, Sweden. Nevertheless the state was quite capable of taking decisive action. In 1569 the Sejm (parliament) and Senate of Poland met jointly with their opposite numbers in Lithuania and agreed the pact of Lublin. Under it they agreed to meet jointly at a new capital (the small town of Warsaw) and create a 'Commonwealth' with a single currency and no internal customs barriers. The Lithuanian provinces of Ukraine, including Podladsie, Volhynia and Kiev were transferred to Poland. In 1572 Zygmunt died and the next year the Sejm met to choose a successor. It rejected (as in the past) the Habsburgs, together with Johann III of Sweden and Ivan IV of Moscow who were both suspected (correctly) of wanting to dismember the kingdom. Instead they chose a Valois – Henry the brother of the French king, Charles IX. However he, and all subsequent rulers, had to accept the 'Acta Henriciana' which required the monarch to retain the elective principle, convoke the Sejm every two years, maintain religious toleration and obtain Sejm approval for new taxes, declarations of war and the imposition of military service on the nobility. If the king broke the agreement the nobility had the right to resist. These provisions did restrict the power of the monarch but not to such an extent that it was impossible for a state as strong as many others in Europe to evolve.

The provision in the 1573 agreement about religious toleration was important because Poland-Lithuania had contained a variety of beliefs even before the Reformation and had avoided the worst excesses of intolerance of the rest of Europe. Four out of ten of the population were Orthodox Christians and there were also Lutherans (especially among the German-speaking population), Calvinists, Menonites, Anabaptists and Unitarians as well as a substantial Jewish population. By the last quarter of the sixteenth century Catholics made up less than forty per cent of the population and the imposition of a single religious belief would have been very difficult. The religious divisions were increased still further in the 1590s with the creation of the Uniate church. It maintained Orthodox rites and customs (especially the married clergy) but owed allegiance to the papacy. The aim behind its creation was primarily political – to weaken the allegiance of the orthodox population in the eastern part of the country to Moscow, the main rival of Poland-Lithuania. However, large factions in both the Catholic and Orthodox churches refused to accept the new body, thereby deepening the religious divide.

These divisions did not seriously weaken the kingdom. In 1575 Henry left Poland, which he hated, to become king of France. He was replaced by Stefan Bathory, the Prince of Transylvania and the only other non-Habsburg, Swedish and Muscovite candidate in 1573. Under Bathory, Poland-Lithuania developed as a strong state – crown revenues were doubled, a large, well-equipped army was created and Moscow was decisively defeated. When Bathory died in 1586 the Habsburgs were again rejected but there was little alternative to the selection of Sigismund Vasa (the heir to the Swedish throne) who became Zygmunt III in 1587.

Zygmunt was mainly interested in gaining the throne of Sweden and unsuccessfully tried to cede the Polish crown to the Habsburgs in 1589. When he was rejected as king of Sweden on the death of his father in 1592 the chance of a union of the two states passed and Zygmunt had little choice but to concentrate on his own kingdom. He was strongly Catholic (one of the reasons he was rejected in Sweden) but largely avoided involvement in the Thirty Years War (there were conflicts with Sweden over influence within the Baltic area). When he died in 1632 he was succeeded by his son Wladyslaw IV who was in his turn succeeded by his brother in 1648. Despite the formally elective system Poland was, after 1587, a dynastic state like the rest of Europe.

[*Later Poland-Lithuania 19.5.2*]

18.10.2 Moscow
[*Earlier Moscow 15.10.3*]

Further to the east the late fifteenth century witnessed the major expansion of Moscow. Under Ivan III (1462–1505) and Vasilii III (1505–33) the area controlled by Moscow tripled. At first this involved the area immediately around Moscow with the conquest of Yaroslavl and Rostov followed by Novgorod in 1478, Tver in 1485 and Pskov in 1510. The last independent Rus principality, Riazan, was taken in 1520. There was also some expansion westwards against Lithuania with the capture of Viazma in 1494 but little progress could be made against the stronger state and the peace treaty of 1522 settled the western border of Moscow for the rest of the century. From 1489 the rulers of Moscow used the title of 'tsar' and in the 1490s they also began using the symbol of the double-headed eagle in imitation of the Habsburgs. Despite these claims to a higher status the rulers of Moscow were only petty monarchs ruling a backward area on the edge of the European world. Government was still largely on a household basis with little bureaucracy or use of written records. Control over a vast area with very poor communications was bound to be weak. There was little internal unity – Novgorod retained its own currency – and administrators sent out from Moscow were able to carve out their own spheres of influence and levels of corruption were high. The main force behind the construction of a stronger state was the creation of an army controlled by the monarch and based on gunpowder weapons. The first such weapons were used late in the fifteenth century and Italian technicians were imported to supervise their manufacture. However, the pace of development was slow and no fundamental changes occurred until the mid-sixteenth century.

The most important ruler of Moscow in the sixteenth century was Ivan IV (1533–84), also known as 'the Terrible'. He was central to the

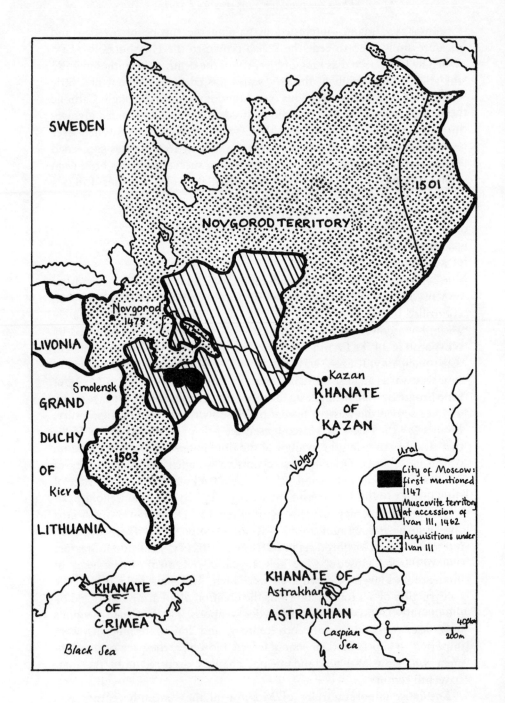

SWEDEN

1501

NOVGOROD TERRITORY

Novgorod
1478

LIVONIA

Smolensk

GRAND

DUCHY

OF

Kiev

LITHUANIA

1503

Kazan

KHANATE
OF
KAZAN

Volga

Ural

City of Moscow:
first mentioned
1147

Muscovite territory
at accession of
Ivan III, 1462

Acquisitions under
Ivan III

KHANATE
OF
CRIMEA

Black Sea

KHANATE OF
Astrakhan
ASTRAKHAN

Caspian
Sea

400km

200m

Map 58: The growth of Moscow

construction of a more developed state and the continued expansion of Moscow but he was also largely responsible for its internal disintegration at the end of the century. He suffered from a severe deformity of the spine and to counter the pain he took large quantities of alcohol and other drugs which only increased his existing paranoid tendencies. He inherited the throne as a child and was not crowned tsar (he was the first ruler to go through this form of coronation) until 1547 after a period of intense factional struggle between different aristocratic groups. The growing power of the state was demonstrated in 1550 when the first units of musketeers paid centrally by the state in cash were established. With territorial expansion to the west blocked by Lithuania, Moscow turned southwards to its nearest neighbour, the Khanate of Kazan. Even after the division of the ex-Mongol territories Moscow's relations with the khanates was close – they controlled the main trade route to the south (important for the supply of slaves to the Ottomans) and at times of weakness Moscow was still paying 'tribute', though they preferred to call the items 'presents'. Following intermittent warfare throughout the 1540s Ivan was responsible for the major campaign which captured Kazan in 1552. This was a major change in the balance of power and the first ever success for the ex-Rus states against their conquerors of the thirteenth century. Moscow now controlled the Volga trade route to the Black Sea and the conquest of Kazan opened the way to further expansion eastwards. Nevertheless the military power of Moscow was still very limited and plans to attack the much stronger Khanate of the Crimea had to be abandoned. Instead in 1558 Ivan turned westwards to attack Livonia, the remaining territory of the Teutonic Knights; however Moscow was blocked by the rival powers of Poland-Lithuania, Denmark and Sweden. The war continued but no real gains were made before a final truce with the other Baltic powers in the early 1580s.

The cost of this war was one of the primary reasons for the growing internal problems of the Moscow state. Even more important were Ivan's own policies. He faced growing opposition from within his own family, from within the main aristocratic families, the *boyars* who formed the ruler's council, and from the increasing number of exiles in Lithuania. The result was the setting up in 1564–5 of the *oprichnina* – a separate state administration directly under the tsar which administered large parts of the country, while the *boyar* council (nominally responsible to Ivan) ruled the rest. The exact purpose behind the creation of the *oprichnina* is unclear but it was probably a peculiar way of trying to deal with the power of the main aristocratic families and reflected Ivan's own paranoia. The new elite of the *oprichnina* owed total loyalty to Ivan and helped carry out a growing but incoherent policy of forced exile and execution of whole families of real and supposed enemies, all of which was dictated by Ivan's whims. From 1567 torture and murder (including that of Ivan's choice as head of the church) became even more common as the number of actual and unsubstantiated plots increased. In 1570 a major terror campaign was carried out in Novgorod. Officially about 2,000 people were killed; in practice the total was far higher and the town was effectively looted. The *oprichnina* was wound up in 1572 but the atmosphere it created remained. Long before Ivan's death in 1584 Moscow was disintegrating internally. [*Later Moscow 19.5.1*]

18.11 The Military Revolution

The constant dynastic conflict across Europe, made worse by the growing religious divisions, and heightened by the impact of gunpowder weapons, produced a military revolution within Europe. The demands this made on the still relatively primitive European monarchies of the early sixteenth century brought about, for those that were able to adapt, a further revolution in the nature of the state. Armies in the late fifteenth century still mainly consisted of archers (who could fire about ten arrows per minute with some accuracy up to about 200 yards), cavalry and some pikemen. In addition armies might have a few artillery pieces. The development of the latter brought about major changes in defensive technology – fortress walls became lower and thicker with bastions and covering artillery. Defensive works spread over large areas. Costs rose substantially but the new defensive systems worked and towns became very difficult to capture even with long sieges, the digging of tunnels and counter-tunnels and the use of vast armies. The result was that very few battles were ever decisive. The first infantry gunpowder weapon in Europe was the arquebus, developed in the early sixteenth century – it took several minutes to reload and was accurate up to about half the distance of an archer but it was effective because little training was required. It was the full development of the musket by the 1550s (the first were used by the Spanish armies in Italy) that brought about a major revolution. It could penetrate plate armour at a distance of a hundred yards and the older weapons such as the broad-sword, halberd and crossbow, which had been in decline for decades, finally disappeared (even the English gave up their traditional longbow in the 1560s). Pikemen were far less effective but were retained to protect the musketeers because of the latter's low rate of fire. The solution was the development in the 1590s of volley fire by long ranks of musketeers. However, this required much greater training, drill and discipline with units having to have much greater cohesion. By the 1620s the Swedish army had six ranks of musketeers who were so well drilled that they could keep up continuous fire. Rifled guns existed but their rate of fire was even slower and their use was therefore restricted to snipers. By the early seventeenth century the first field artillery pieces were developed – the Swedes could deploy eighty such guns in the 1630s.

The result of these technological changes was to produce a rapid increase in the size of European armies. In the late fifteenth century the armies of Charles VIII in Italy (and his Spanish opponents) were no bigger than about 20,000 and were minuscule compared with the great armies the Sung had controlled in China some six hundred years earlier. Within a century the Spanish army had increased roughly ten-fold to about 200,000 and by the 1630s an army of 150,000 was normal for any major military power. By the end of the seventeenth century the French army was about 400,000-strong and the decline in Spanish power was well illustrated by the fact that it could only support an army of about 50,000. Even medium-sized powers such as the Dutch and the Swedes had armies of over 100,000 by the late seventeenth century. At first the technological changes had their impact in the main areas of conflict – Italy, France, Spain and the Low Countries. England, hardly threatened by invasion, had few modern fortifications and a much smaller army – in some battles during the civil war of the 1640s such as Naseby no field artillery were used.

There were also major changes in naval technology with the evolution, over the two centuries after 1450, of the heavily armed sailing ship. By the early sixteenth century gunpowder weapons were in use at sea with muzzle-loading bronze guns firing a sixty-pound iron ball. By the end of the century the galleon had been developed and the first fleet for long-range operations on the high seas was produced by the Dutch in the early seventeenth century to attack the Spanish. It was equipped with the first frigates of 300 tons each with 40 guns – by the mid-seventeenth century the Dutch had a fleet of 157 warships. By the end of the seventeenth century the major European navies were capable of operating in the Caribbean, Indian Ocean and the Pacific and attacking each other thousands of miles from their bases. (Even more advanced ships were being developed in Asia. In the 1590s the Koreans produced the 'turtle ship', a form of early ironclad. It was over 100 feet long and encased in hexagonal metal plates so that it could not be boarded or holed. It had twelve gun ports on each side with 22 loopholes for small-arms fire, flame-throwers and toxic smoke generators. They were crucial in the defeat of the Japanese invasion in the 1590s.)

These growing armies and navies required substantial support. In the 1440s the French artillery units used 20,000 pounds of powder a year – two hundred years later they used 500,000 pounds of powder. Infantry weapons needed to be made in workshops and iron and metal production had to increase. Arsenals and dockyards had to be constructed. Armies had to be recruited and paid in some form or other. Military expenditure came to take up nearly all of the state's revenue – in the rich Ottoman empire the army and navy took up almost two-thirds of government revenue. Even states such as England that avoided involvement in the major European wars could still be bankrupted. The war with Scotland and France (which was only fought intermittently between 1542 and 1550) cost about £450,000 a year yet the total state revenue was only £200,000 a year. The war was financed by selling off the monastic lands Henry VIII had confiscated (two-thirds of the total had been sold by 1547), increasing taxes, imposing forced loans, confiscating assets and running up a debt of £500,000. The situation was far worse in Spain which had to bear the bulk of the cost of Habsburg policies. When Philip II took the throne in 1556 he found that all the state's revenue for the next five years was already pledged to pay outstanding loans and interest. The Spanish monarchy was bankrupt and was so again in 1575, 1596, 1607, 1627, 1647 and 1653. The money loaned to the monarchy was effectively confiscated but it was always able to raise more capital by simply refusing to pay any interest on existing loans until extra money was forthcoming.

Most states lacked the bureaucratic infrastructure to manage and deploy large armies and their recruitment remained problematic. Armies were mainly composed of those who joined because it was the only alternative to immediate starvation. In many places local magistrates were given a quota of criminals to find for the army. Armies were therefore collections of ill-disciplined, heterogeneous and constantly changing units held together mainly by the prospect of loot. Desertion rates were very high and on average armies lost a quarter of their strength every year to disease, desertion and warfare – the strength of the Spanish army in Flanders fell from 60,000 in June 1576 to 11,000 by November. Between 1572 and 1609 the Spanish army in the Low Countries mutinied no less than forty-five times. Unable to organize their own forces, most states by the early seventeenth century relied on contractors to do it for them – at the height of the European war in the 1630s over 400 such people were involved. Some such as Wallenstein were maintaining whole armies on behalf of the emperor and could become very wealthy if they were successful. Only Sweden under Gustavus Adolphus had a system of conscription but the cost it imposed on the country was terrible. In the two decades after 1620 the parish of Bygdeå was forced to provide 230 men for the army. All but fifteen of them died in service and five of the survivors were crippled – the male population of the parish fell by almost a half. Troops were paid very little and supplying them was difficult given their size and the poor state of

European communications. A garrison of 3,000 in a city was often as large as the town itself and an army of even 30,000 was larger than most cities in Europe. These problems were made worse by the fodder required for the horses, and by the huge numbers of camp followers which could double the size of an army. In 1646 two Bavarian regiments had 960 troops but were accompanied by 416 women and children and 310 servants. Armies obtained their food as a form of 'protection money' from the villages through which they passed (having rapidly found this was more efficient than looting). In the worst areas of fighting villages had to buy off both sides and face the threat of the diseases spread by the armies. Those on the main communication routes suffered as the armies passed and repassed. Even though the Ottoman army had a well-developed logistic system it always marched along the same main routes through Anatolia. During the 1579 campaign against the Safavids it was forced to take new routes because all the villages along its normal path had been abandoned.

18.12 The Rise of the European State

The pressures brought about by the military revolution and the consequent need to finance and support large armies and navies were fundamental in the growth of the European state. (A similar process can be identified in the 'Warring States' period in China in the three centuries before the emergence of the Han empire, about 200 BCE. The significant difference in Europe between 1500 and 1945 was that despite numerous attempts no single state was able to defeat the others and unify the whole area.) There has been a tendency to take a rather 'mystical' view of the rise of the European states. They are believed to incorporate and embody pre-existing 'nations' which emerged as part of an inexorable process of advance once the 'universal empire' and the 'universal church' were in decline after about 1300. These states, it is believed, came to be characterized by representative or at least semi-democratic government, limited and controlled state power, the rule of law, the preservation of individual and local liberties and privileges followed by the gradual creation and extension of political rights to all citizens. These features, it is often argued, were essential preconditions to the rise of Europe and crucial for the development of industrialization and 'capitalism' and therefore mark the path which other societies and states have to follow in order to become 'modern'. In every respect these ideas bear little relation to the processes involved in the creation of the European state. Four crucial factors were involved. First, the consolidation of political units into a well-defined and continuous territory. Second, the increasing centralization of power through the removal of local 'privileges' and the imposition of more taxes. Third, war-making externally and the increasing monopoly over coercive power internally. Finally, the creation of a state structure, bureaucracy and codes of law superior to other institutions in society.

There had never been a 'universal empire' in Europe – Charlemagne's empire (which covered only a small part of Europe) was so fleeting as to be almost unnoticeable and the successors who claimed the title of emperor had little real power. The papacy made grandiose claims but could not enforce them against secular rulers and, fairly rapidly, became merely a power in the Italian peninsula. Neither were there 'nation-states' in Europe – nearly all European political units were composite states built around particular ruling families and dynasties. Many units were divided by large tracts of hostile land such as those of the Habsburgs. Others were divided by the sea such as England and Ireland or England and the territories it held on the continent until the mid-sixteenth century. Others were con-tiguous but retained strong separate identities such as Piedmont and Savoy and Poland and Lithuania. Often all that united these areas was the fact that they were ruled by the same monarch. In the early sixteenth century there were only a few large political units in Europe such as Castile, France and England which had relatively strong administrations and a very limited sense of collective identity among the elite. Dynastic ambition, derived from long-standing ideas about family and patrimony among the European aristocracy, cut across these few strong units and tended to dilute their limited effectiveness. The religious divisions of the sixteenth century added to the problems of the composite states. It made it difficult to impose uniformity and attempts to do so usually only caused greater problems as the Habsburgs and Spain found in the Netherlands and the English in Ireland. In Castile, England and the Netherlands, religion did help create a strong and very aggressive sense of mission; the idea that they were part of a divine plan. This was heightened by the creation of empire which was Castilian within a still very poorly defined 'Spain', and English within a 'United Kingdom' which did not exist before 1800 at the earliest.

Most of the European states in the early sixteenth century were very weak internally and made up of a multitude of different communities, jurisdictions and autonomous areas. The United Provinces was created in 1579 by a federal union between Utrecht and seven other north Netherlands provinces and always had a very limited central structure. In France the independent possessions of the Bourbons – Béarn, Navarre, Armagnac, Vendôme and Rodez – were only incorporated on the accession of Henry IV in 1589. Scotland and England were 'united' in 1603 on the accession of James VI of Scotland as James I of England but each retained an entirely separate identity until the Act of Union of 1707. Even then although the Scottish parliament disappeared, a separate legal, religious and educational structure was retained. In Spain the parliament of Aragon had much greater powers than that of Castile and the attempt to alter this was one of the main reasons behind the Aragonese revolt in 1591. England with its 'common law' was unusual in having a fairly uniform legal system – in 1600 France still had over 700 separate law-codes and the Low Countries had roughly the same number. Even within the territories of a single family such as the Habsburgs there were until 1618 separate rulers with their own courts for Lower, Upper and Inner Austria, Tyrol and Bohemia. Administrative and legal unity, as in the absorption of Wales by England in the 1530s and the creation of Savoy from scratch after 1559, was unusual in the European pattern. Other divisions within the composite states derived from language. In Spain, Basque and Catalan were central to the creation of separate identities as were Breton and Occitan in France. In Wales, although it might be incorporated legally and administratively into England, the different language remained a determining factor in local identity. Elsewhere, remote areas, for example Cornwall in England, had little to do with central government and in Poland and Lithuania many of the remote areas were still pagan. This was partly a reflection of the fact that communications were still very poor – a major problem for the Habsburgs was that it took a minimum of two weeks for a letter to travel from Madrid to either Brussels or Milan and often a lot longer.

A major part of state building in Europe was the removal of these local units and identities and rights. Everywhere in the sixteenth and seventeenth centuries (except in the Swiss cantons) local assemblies lost power to the expanding central state. Other units that had some claims to sovereignty and a separate identity such as free cities, principalities, bishoprics and local jurisdictions were gradually absorbed into a developing single structure. The process was not a peaceful one and met resistance in many areas. In Spain not only Aragon but also Catalonia revolted and Portugal broke away to become independent again. Eventually in the early eighteenth century Aragon lost nearly all its privileges but Catalonia retained considerable autonomy. Even in a relatively small and integrated state such as England there were constant local revolts in the late fifteenth and early sixteenth centuries as the power of the central state extended. They occurred in 1489 in Yorkshire, Cornwall in 1497, the northern counties in 1536 (the 'Pilgrimage of Grace' following the dissolution of the monasteries), the western counties in 1547, followed by Kett's rebellion in 1549 and Wyatt's rebellion in 1553.

In addition rulers enforced a new system under which they held a monopoly over the use of violence within the state. Europe in the fifteenth century was characterized, as it had been for centuries, by powerful aristocratic groups and landowners possessing their own military forces and well-defended castles (in much the same pattern as in Japan). They normally recognized the authority of the monarch and would fight along-side him. However, they also retained their own power bases and could equally well rebel. With only minimal revenues the monarch often had no more resources than the leading members of the aristocracy. Rulers therefore found it difficult to recruit a professional or mercenary army although they were becoming commoner in Europe from the thirteenth century, especially in the richer areas such as Italy. From the sixteenth century rulers gradually eliminated alternative power bases within society and established their sole claim to the use of force. Armies came to be recruited by the state through pay, rather than some 'feudal' obligation, and castles were either rendered obsolete by gunpowder weapons or demolished. These changes were largely completed in England by the end of the sixteenth century and on an increasing scale in France from the 1620s although the process was not complete until the 1660s. Even so the actual level of control and government within a state was still minimal. Despite torture, public executions and draconian law-codes large areas, especially parts of the major cities and remote regions, were hardly governed at all and highwaymen and bandits were rife.

As military costs rose monarchs had to seek greater control and impose taxes if they were to be successful and survive. These pressures were directly related to the relationship between rulers and assemblies of the nobility and other interests in the state. These 'estates' or 'parliaments' developed in a number of areas in Europe in the centuries before 1500 but were generally eclipsed by the growth of the state and strong rulers in the succeeding centuries. The assemblies represented the powerful (the aris-tocracy) and other important communities (the church and the towns) and defended their privileges and those of the local communities. The early and primitive states in Europe had very limited powers of coercion and so monarchs had to rely on some degree of consent in raising the revenue they needed. In return for agreement to taxes these groups might be able to negotiate additional privileges and exemptions. Increasingly from the fifteenth century rulers began to circumvent these institutions by imposing special taxes for limited purposes (usually military), making them permanent and expanding taxes that did not require approval. Once this had been done the estates and parliaments did not need to meet and the independence and power of the monarchy therefore expanded. The major problem for rulers was to balance their desire for revenue to fund their ambitions against the possibility that increasing taxation might produce revolt. The only real exception to the general trend was England where there was a redistribution of power within the elite and by the end of the seventeenth century the monarch ruled in conjunction with the landed (and increasingly commercial) elite. It made little difference to the policies of the state.

The idea that any of these early European states were in some way 'representative' is an illusion. The estates and parliaments that did survive only represented a very small proportion of the population and a few special interest groups who were able to secure advantages and privileges for themselves. Even the remaining 'free' cities were run by very small cliques of the elite (usually the main merchant families). In Genoa 700 men (and their families) controlled the city. In Nuremberg power was restricted by law to 43 families (about 200 people at most) out of a total population of 20,000 in the city and another 20,000 in the immediate area. These families then chose the seven elders who took all decisions. In 1525 when they decided to support Luther the whole city was forced to follow suit. Seville was even more restrictive – a 'consulate' of no more than five wealthy merchants was in control and could take decisions in their own private interests whenever they wanted. In London in the early seventeenth century about 200 wealthy merchants effectively controlled the city. In the Netherlands the ruling elite was at most 10,000 out of a total population of over two million.

As the military requirements of the state increased administration had to change. Across most of Europe monarchical government had been largely personal and administration, such as it was, a function of officials in the king's household. Usually there was little control over local administration or the legal system which usually varied from area to area. Once again England was unusual (largely because of its size) in that from as early as the mid-twelfth century the monarch had been able to impose a central legal administration through his own travelling judges, and local landlords were incorporated into the system as justices of the peace. From the early sixteenth century it became increasingly clear that the demands of the military revolution required a more complex administration and the development of a primitive bureaucratic system to provide for the army and its munitions as well as operating the developing taxation systems. Most west European states went through a major reorganization in the 1530s and 1540s (typified by the role of Thomas Cromwell in England under Henry VIII) as the first phase of changes were implemented. Slowly administration became more institutionalized – the number of state employees in France (excluding the military) rose from 12,000 in 1505 to over 80,000 by the 1660s. There were still huge areas of waste and extravagance through bribes, sinecures, corruption and theft made worse through the farming of taxes and the creation of monopolies, but the overall trend was clear.

European rulers had to change too. They had to shift from being military leaders emphasizing courtly behaviour (such as fencing and dancing) to becoming administrators deciding state policy. Many found the transition too difficult and many were incapable – Frederick William I of Brandenburg (1640–88), the so-called 'Great Elector' was educationally subnormal and at the age of nine could still not count to ten or recite the alphabet. Many therefore came to rely on the 'favourite' in the court who was able to dictate policy through his influence over the king. In the early seventeenth century France was dominated by Cardinal Richelieu (1624–42) and his successor Mazarin (1643–61). In Spain, Olivares (1622–42) and in England Buckingham (1618-28) had similar roles. Even highly educated rulers such as Gustavus Adolphus of Sweden delegated full powers to his chief minister, Oxenstierna. All of these men were able to use their position to build up huge networks of power and corruption within the state. It was not until the late seventeenth century that primitive ministerial systems began to emerge in a number of countries with the allocation of specific government functions to a group of men who held the confidence of the monarch.

The rulers of Europe did not undertake these far-reaching changes, institute fundamental alterations in the nature of the state and take the risks involved in demanding more taxes, imposing greater central control and fighting their fellow rulers in order to create the 'nation-state'. They did so in order to increase their own power and glory. The rest was a side-effect. At the end of the process when stronger states had evolved national identities were formed around these new units. The borders that emerged in Europe as a result of this process were arbitrary and long subject to change. They did not reflect any inherent 'national' identities. The eastern border of France constantly changed until 1918, Belgium was an artificial creation of the nineteenth century, Ireland was at times part of Britain and at times independent, and Bavaria joined Germany (a construct of the mid-nineteenth century) rather than Austria in 1871. Even then most of the peasants had little sense of identity with the state in which they lived. As late as the 1870s a survey showed that the majority of peasants in France did not see themselves as 'French' and the government embarked on a major campaign to create a 'French identity' and allegiance to the state.

Overall very few west European states were successful in coping with this new world. In 1500 there were over 500 independent political entities in Europe but by 1900 there were about twenty-five. Even major independent states such as Bohemia, Scotland, Naples and Burgundy disappeared, as well as a host of petty principalities and independent cities and bishoprics. There was no simple recipe for success. Access to the wealth generated outside Europe was important but not crucial. Spain and

Portugal did not develop into strong states and from the mid-seventeenth century were in relative decline compared with their European rivals. The Netherlands had access to considerable wealth from trade and although it retained a very strong and distinct identity, it did not develop strong state institutions. Revenue from trade was important in some areas. Tolls on shipping passing through the Sound were vital for the development of the Danish state, and taxes on wool exports to the Low Countries were a crucial source of revenue for the English monarchy. For a while highly commercial city-states such as those of northern Italy could use their wealth to buy military force through the use of mercenaries. However, as commercial wealth together with that looted from the Americas spread through Europe, other states could do the same. Some states were created without this base. In Brandenburg-Prussia and Moscow-Russia the lack of a strong commercial base meant that brute force played a greater role in the creation of the state. Accidents of geography such as the relatively protected positions of England and Sweden were important and the constant warfare in Germany, especially in the early seventeenth century made the building of states more difficult – the most successful was Brandenburg-Prussia on the eastern periphery. As in other pre-industrial states a stable dynasty and relatively able rulers were important. Again the exception was England which changed its royal family four times between 1600 and 1714 and had a civil war and a republic. It survived these internal problems because of its isolated position and the difficulty of external intervention.

The construction of states in Europe was therefore a very expensive process. It involved almost continuous warfare across the continent bringing with it death and suffering on a massive scale. Many people and societies lost their independence and with it their rights and privileges. It was also expensive in terms of extra taxation and the confiscation of resources needed to support armies and bureaucracies, together with the greater internal coercion this involved. It also brought some benefits – a degree of internal order and a coherent legal and judicial system. It laid the foundations for the later European state as it developed in the nineteenth century – greater power, internal coercion through police forces and conscription matched by slowly developing economic and social justice, although the latter was usually resisted by the privileged elite.

From the wider perspective of world history the process of state formation in Europe was of crucial long-term significance. When Europe came to dominate the world other areas were forced into the same mould. States such as China, Japan and the Ottoman empire had to take on the characteristics of European states (for example by creating foreign ministries) in order to function within the world that Europe created.

When the European overseas empires collapsed in the mid-twentieth century, together with the Soviet empire at the end of the century, over a hundred new states were created on the European model although most of them lacked the necessary infrastructure and therefore were very weak.

19

The Seventeenth-Century Crisis and After

Since the linking together of the Eurasian world in the last two centuries BCE there had been three crises which affected the continent as a whole. The first was long-drawn-out and lasted from the late second century CE until the sixth century and saw the collapse of the Han empire in China, the decline of the Roman empire in the west and the end of the Parthian empire in Iran. The second was more short-lived and was concentrated in the period between 750 and the mid-tenth century and was characterized by the break-up of the Islamic empire after the Abbasid seizure of power, the decline of the T'ang in China and the end of the very brief recovery in western Europe. The third in the mid-fourteenth century was linked to the spread of the 'Black Death' across Eurasia. It followed over-population and famine in Europe and saw the collapse of Mongol rule in China and the civil wars which led to the establishment of the Ming. The fourth crisis to affect Eurasia as a whole was that of the 'seventeenth century', although it lasted from about 1560 to 1660. The Ottoman and Mughal empires escaped the worst of the problems and Japan, still relatively isolated, was almost unscathed. China was badly disrupted – the 300-year-old Ming empire collapsed in the mid-seventeenth century and was replaced by the Manchu or Ch'ing empire which survived until the end of imperial China in 1911. The region of Eurasia which was by far the worst affected by the 'seventeenth-century crisis' was Europe, where the period between about 1560 and 1660 was characterized by war, civil war, famine and numerous peasant revolts.

19.1 The Nature of the Crisis

The problem for all states across Eurasia by the mid-sixteenth century was the rapidly rising population. A full recovery from the plagues of the fourteenth century had been made by about 1500 in Europe, a little earlier elsewhere. Population continued to grow and the old problem of the balance between population and the ability of the agricultural base to support increasing numbers once again became apparent, just as it had around 1300. Agricultural productivity levels had risen but the improvements were limited and the extra numbers that could be supported were small. The period between 1400 (when the worst of the plagues were over) and 1600 witnessed the fastest rise in population that the world had so far seen. It rose by over a half from about 350 million to almost 550 million. In some areas the rise was even greater. The population of Europe rose by two-thirds from 60 million to 100 million and the population of China doubled to 160 million. Inevitably this meant that the limits of the cultivatable land were reached, average yields began to stabilize and then fall, the land available to the average peasant grew smaller and the amount of food available per person declined. More and more people were living on the edge of malnutrition and starvation. For example, in Anatolia, the agricultural heartland of the Ottoman empire, the population rose by 70 per cent between 1500 and 1570 but the cultivated acreage rose by only 20 per cent. In China the average amount of land per head fell by a third between 1480 and 1600 – it was only the introduction of new crops from the Americas such as maize and sweet potatoes that enabled the increasing number of people to be fed at all.

These problems were made far worse by a climatic deterioration across Eurasia, although its effects were concentrated in Europe. The period of warm climate between about 900 and 1200 was followed by a slow decline of average temperatures which by the mid-sixteenth century brought on the 'Little Ice Age' which lasted, in Europe, until the mid-nineteenth century. Average temperatures were about 1°C lower than the average for the twentieth century. This might seem only a slight variation but it was sufficient to reduce the growing season by about a month and lower the height at which crops could be grown by around 600 feet. After 1580 glaciers across Europe advanced in many places by over a mile and did not begin to retreat until the 1850s. Between 1564 and 1814 the Thames froze in the winter at least twenty times as did the Rhône three times between 1590 and 1603. Even the Guadalquivir at Seville froze in the winter of 1602–3. At Marseilles the sea froze in 1595 and in 1684 there was pack-ice off the coast of England. In the 1580s the Denmark Strait between Iceland and Greenland was regularly blocked by pack-ice even in summer. Short periods of very severe weather also occurred with catastrophic effects. Between 1599 and 1603 a series of very cold mistral winds destroyed many of the olive groves in Provence and heavy frosts around Valencia killed the fruit trees. Similar effects were felt elsewhere. Heavy frosts in the thirty years after 1646 ended orange growing in Kwangsi province in China and drought in the late sixteenth century led to the abandonment of the new Mughal capital at Fatephur Sikri near Agra. The careful records kept in Japan of the time when the cherry trees blossomed show dates becoming later and later during this period. Agriculture in Japan was more vulnerable to climatic problems in the early seventeenth century because of the shift of rice cultivation from the south and west to the more marginal north and east. The 1630s were characterized by very cool summers which reduced the growing season in the north, together with floods and droughts elsewhere. The result was the terrible Kan'ei famine when large numbers of peasants died and grain prices in the cities reached unprecedented levels.

There was no simple relationship between temperature, rainfall and the size of the crop because the impact of these factors depended on how they were distributed across the seasons – very cold winters could be beneficial in killing pests. Nevertheless the effect of the deteriorating climate can be seen in many areas. It was undoubtedly responsible for the great European famine of 1594–7 when four bad harvests in succession meant that across a large area people were reduced to eating cats and dogs and there was widespread cannibalism. The impact of harvest failure on the people of Europe is illustrated in graphic and terrible detail by the parish register of Orslosa in western Sweden. In the early summer of 1596 it seemed that the crop would at last be good but in June there were heavy rains and floods:

> . . . the water went over the fields and pastures, so that the grass and corn were ruined . . . In the winter the cattle fell ill from the rotten hay and straw which was taken out of the water . . . It went the same way with the cows and the calves, and the dogs which ate their dead bodies also died. The soil was sick for three years, so that it could bear no harvest . . . Even those who had good farms turned their young people away, and many even their own children, because they were not able to watch the misery of them starving to death . . . Afterwards the parents left their house . . . going whither they were able, till they lay dead of hunger and starvation . . . People ground and chopped many unsuitable things into bread; such as mash, chaff, bark, buds, nettles, leaves, hay, straw, peatmoss, nut-shells, pea-stalks, etc. This made people so weak and their bodies so swollen that innumerable people died. Many widows, too, were found dead on the ground with red hummock grass, seeds which grew in the fields, and other kinds of grass in their mouths . . . Children starved to death at their mothers' breasts, for they had nothing to give them suck. Many people, men and women, young and old, were compelled in their hunger to take to stealing . . . other inflictions came and also the bloody flux [dysentery] which put people in such a plight that countless died of it.

The greatest impact of the poor climate undoubtedly came in Scandinavia where many regions became extremely marginal for growing crops. This was apparent in the terrible famine in Finland in 1696–7 when about a third of the population died. Further south major adjustments had to be made. In England there was a shift towards spring rather than autumn sown crops in order to avoid the damage caused by the harsh winters. In the Netherlands, buckwheat, which is hardy and has a short growing season, although it was hardly grown in Europe before 1550, became an increasingly important crop. Major problems were caused by the wet winters leading to waterlogged soils and poor arable yields. Cold, late springs also produced a vicious circle by reducing grass growth, lowering milk output and leading to the slaughter of cattle if the smaller hay crop was insufficient to see the animals through the winter until the grass grew again.

The rising population, cultivation of more marginal land, lower average yields and a deteriorating climate produced an agricultural crisis. Between 1500 and 1650 average grain prices in Europe, the Ottoman empire and China rose over five-fold. (This was not the result of any inflation caused by the influx of silver from the Americas because the same effects can be seen in England where the amount of silver in circulation only rose by a third over the period.) These trends were exacerbated by the marginal condition of most peasants. In the Beauvaisis in France in the seventeenth century the average peasant had to give up a fifth of his output in rent and similar proportions in tithes and taxes. In addition another fifth was required to meet expenses and provide seed for the next crop. If the farmer was a tenant he might have about a third of his output available as food, perhaps slightly under a half if he owned his land. In these conditions about three-quarters of the farms in the region were too small to support a family and any crop failure, or even a poor harvest, could be catastrophic.

The peasant had almost no means of escape from this situation except starvation, revolt or migration (mainly to the towns). (Emigration to the colonies was not really an option at this stage because most, especially those in the Americas, were so underdeveloped. Nevertheless many people did sell themselves as indentured servants.) Revolts were common, as were large groups of 'bandits' (often no more than groups of peasants trying to stay alive) but most went to the towns where opportunities for begging were greater. The number of beggars in London rose twelve-fold between 1520 and 1600 even though the total population only quadrupled. The government faced the problem of controlling these people who were seen as 'dangerous' and the limited amount of charity available was spent on the 'deserving' or 'respectable' poor. The rest were harshly treated and either expelled (a limited, short-term solution) or consigned to 'workhouses' (the first in London was built in 1552). They took the poor off the streets and provided employers with cheap labour but the conditions for the inmates were terrible and dehumanizing.

19.2 The Crisis in China: the fall of the Ming

China experienced a long period of internal stability between about 1400 and 1550 when the power of the Ming was at its height. From the mid-sixteenth century there were growing problems. Along the northern border there was a reassertion of Mongol power. It began with the unification of the various tribes in Mongolia under Dayan Khan in the early sixteenth century but reached its peak under his son Altan Khan who ruled for the fifty years after 1532. In the 1540s the Mongols made incursions into Shansi province and the Peking area – they took over 200,000 prisoners together with a million cattle and horses in just one month in 1542. By 1550 they were besieging Peking and forced the reopening of the horse trade. In 1552 they conquered northern Shansi and then occupied the old capital of Qaraqorum. After defeating the Kirghiz and the Kazakhs they moved on to control much of Tibet by the 1570s. By the time a peace treaty was signed with the Ming the Mongols controlled much of central Asia. In the south there was growing piracy which the Chinese blamed on the Japanese although the largest groups were controlled by Wang Chih, a Chinese merchant from Anhwei who was also trading across south-east Asia.

The major problems were, however, internal. Many stemmed from the nature of the land tax which accounted for two-thirds of the government's revenue. The quotas for each area had been set in 1385 under the early Ming. As population rose and its distribution changed and as new areas were brought into cultivation the government faced a problem familiar to other pre-industrial empires – how to bring the tax into line with the actual distribution of wealth. Even the relatively powerful Chinese government found it impossible to defeat the influence of the powerful local landlords who were able to avoid any fundamental re-assessment of the tax burden. This had major consequences. Although the army at a local level had land to support the soldier-peasant communities, it also relied on local taxes to support it. Population growth, a general shortage of food and the mal-distribution of the tax burden meant that much of the army could no longer be fed or supported. The soldiers deserted and many units were only at a tenth of the theoretical strength agreed in the late fourteenth century. To some extent these problems were circumvented by the recruitment of mercenaries by the central government – as in Europe they were usually recruited from those who found army service the only alternative to starvation. However, the government was badly affected by the growing expense of the mercenary army – costs rose eight-fold in the sixteenth century as numbers on the northern frontier increased and a greater number of costly gunpowder weapons were required.

Until the early 1590s revenue was just about adequate to cover expenditure. Then, for a few years, the government was able to draw on the huge reserves accumulated from trade and the influx of silver from the Americas. However, they were not sufficient to fund the long and very expensive war in Korea in 1593-8 caused by the Japanese invasion led by Hideyoshi. Although the eventual outcome was a Chinese victory, the state was beginning to run out of money. The attempt to impose new taxes and raise existing ones only produced a growing number of internal revolts both in the countryside and the cities. In the 1620s the Ming government, finding it difficult to fund the mercenary army, imposed conscription in many border regions but that only led to revolts in Yunnan, Szechwan and Kweichow. The government was characterized by increasing conflict between the administrators, court favourites and the eunuchs, growing corruption and numerous plots against the emperor. In the north-western provinces there was a Muslim revolt largely triggered by dislocation to the central Asian trade routes. The poor weather played a major part too. In 1627-8 droughts and bad harvests in northern Shensi created large bands of peasants, joined by deserters and soldiers discharged because they could not be paid, who roamed the countryside and sacked the cities. In the early 1630s these groups became bigger as rural distress increased and other provinces such as Hopei, Honan and Anhwei were affected. The government and the army could not mobilize enough power to suppress these rebellions. By the early 1640s the Ming were on the verge of total collapse. In northern China the rebel leaders, especially Li Tzu-ch'eng (a former shepherd and worker in the government postal relay service), were looking to replace the Ming as they controlled more and more areas and created their own administration. In February 1644 at his capital Hsi-an (the renamed Ch'ang-an) Li Tzu-ch'eng proclaimed the new Ta Shun dynasty. Two months later his armies entered Peking and the last Ming emperor, Ch'ung-chen, strangled himself. In September 1644 a former soldier, Chang Hsien-chung, who controlled Szechwan, set up 'The Great Kingdom of the West'.

China appeared to be heading towards another period of disunity or the imposition of a new revolutionary regime as under the Ming some three hundred years earlier. But, instead, China was conquered by another group of nomadic people from the steppes – the Manchu. They were Jürchen and descendants of the rulers of the empire which had taken northern China from the Sung and controlled it between 1115 and 1234 before succumbing to the Mongol conquest. They were allied to the Chinese in 1589 and fought alongside them in the campaign against the Japanese in Korea in the 1590s. The slow decline of Ming power provided the opportunity for them to establish control over an area to the north-east of China with a mix of Chinese people and various ex-nomadic but now sedentary peoples. The Jürchen aristocracy modelled their military units on Chinese customs and made full use of the extensive range of gunpowder weapons developed by the Chinese. These units were called *ch'i* or 'banners' and were distinguished by the colour of their flags. They were created in 1601 and divided into Inner Banners (composed of Jürchen and their direct descendants) and the Outer Banners (composed of auxiliaries). For almost two hundred years they remained the most formidable military force in eastern Eurasia. The Jürchen empire expanded under Nurhaci – they captured Liaoyang in 1621 and made Mukden their capital in 1625. By this time they were dependent on bilingual Chinese administrators who acted as intermediaries with the Chinese elite in the areas the Jürchen controlled and they held most of the key positions in the administration, often on a hereditary basis. Many were given the privilege of enrolling in the Inner Banners as *pao-i*, 'people of the house'.

The major period of Jürchen expansion came under Abahai (1627–43). In 1635 they adopted the name of Manchu and a year later changed their dynastic name from the historic Chin to Ta-ch'ing (meaning 'great Ch'ing'). They found expansion southwards relatively easy as Ming power disintegrated. By 1638 they controlled the whole of Korea, Manchuria followed and by 1644 they also ruled the Amur region. In 1644 they defeated the rebel leader Li Tzu-ch'eng and occupied Peking. Control over northern China was achieved fairly easily in the next few years. By 1647 the Manchus reached Canton in the south but here they encountered stronger Chinese units. These were led by various members of the Ming dynasty who were trying to keep control of this rich area and rebuild the dynasty in much the same way as the Southern Sung had done in the 1120s. In 1647 Yung-li was proclaimed the new Ming emperor – he recaptured Canton and controlled much of southern China. However, in 1648 he was forced to withdraw to Yunnan where internal disputes, especially among the Ming generals, resulted in ineffective resistance to the Manchus. Nevertheless it was not until 1661 that Yung-li was captured in north-east Burma and killed. The successful conquest of the south only posed more problems for the Manchu leadership especially in controlling the generals (some of whom had defected from the Ming) who had made the conquests. Wu San-kuei, who had defeated Yung-li, controlled Yunnan, Kweichow, Hunan, Shensi and Kansu. He revolted in 1673 and with the support of other military leaders and governors in southern China founded the Chou empire which lasted until 1681. By the mid-1670s it seemed on the point of reconquering northern China and ending Manchu rule. Some of his supporters began to defect but it was the death of Wu in

1678 that led to the end of the rebellion and the full establishment of Manchu control over the south by the early 1680s.

The Manchu also had to face a massive revival of piracy off the southern coast under a major supporter of the Ming, Cheng Ch'eng-kung (known to Europeans as Coxinga). Cheng was able to mobilize a navy of over 2,000 ships and an army of more than 100,000 men by the mid-1650s. His power only began to decline following the failure to capture Nanking in 1659. By 1661 he had been driven to Taiwan where he defeated and expelled the Dutch. He sent envoys to Manila in the Philippines where the Spanish only had a tiny garrison of 600 men. The Spanish governor decided to withdraw to Mindanao, but not before ordering the massacre of all Chinese residents – at least 6,000 were killed in Manila and about 30,000 across the Philippines. The Spanish were only saved by the death of Cheng in 1662. Taiwan was not recaptured by the Dutch but was eventually conquered by the Manchu in 1683. By this date Manchu rule was firmly established over China and the long period of internal troubles was at an end. The 1680s marked the beginning of a period of great internal stability and prosperity in China which lasted until the mid-nineteenth century.

19.3 The Crisis in the Ottoman Empire

Like the Ming the Ottomans found that they were seriously affected by population growth and the bringing of new land into cultivation. Usually the new land was not taxed because it was not part of the existing land register and therefore the tax base became increasingly out of line with the real economy. In addition as population rose, landholdings tended to become smaller and the number of landless labourers rose. Rural discontent increased as a result. These problems were magnified because of the military landholding system. As in nearly all pre-industrial states, provincial lands were divided into estates (*timar*) of various sizes in order to support the cavalry. Unusually the income of the military from the *timar* was fixed in cash terms but was collected in kind. As grain prices rose dramatically during the sixteenth century the actual amount of food obtained for the fixed cash rent fell rapidly. The inevitable result was that the cavalry could no longer afford to support themselves and most simply gave up their estates. The number of *timar* cavalry declined from 87,000 in 1560 to 8,000 seventy years later. When the estates were given up they reverted to the state but then were taken over by court favourites and other powerful groups and were removed from the taxation register. The basis of the Ottoman army therefore had to be changed by expanding the imperial *yaniçeri* ('janissaries') and *sipahis* and by the recruitment of the increasing number of landless peasants as musketeers. The central army increased in size five-fold in just over a century after 1530. However, the problem for the Ottomans was that this army had to be paid for and its pay had to keep pace (at least to some extent) with rising prices. Even after allowing for the major increase in trade revenues (those derived from the spice trade from south-east Asia quadrupled in the century after 1480) the eroding land-tax base meant that the large budget surplus of the 1520s had disappeared by the 1580s and a major deficit appeared in the seventeenth century.

Major tax rises were imposed in the 1590s and almost immediately produced peasant revolts. The so-called *celali* revolts, composed (as in the contemporary revolts in China) of deserters, unpaid mercenaries, discontented peasants, landless labourers and even local landlords, spread rapidly. Between 1599 and 1607 they engulfed most of Anatolia and Syria. In the latter area the Druze leader Fahreddin Ma'n led a revolt which lasted until 1635. Rivalries within the army between the imperial units and local commanders led to further rebellions and the *yaniçeri* revolt in Constantinople in 1589 was particularly serious. It marked the beginning of a much more active role for the new, larger full-time army in Ottoman politics – they were deeply involved in the plot which led to the murder of the sultan, Osman II, in 1622. At this time the Ottomans were also engaged in a major war with the Safavids which lasted, with a brief interval of peace, from 1603 until 1639. The Safavids reconquered Azerbaijan at the start of the war and captured Baghdad and Mosul in 1624, slaughtering a large part of the Sunni population in the cities. The Ottoman attempt to retake Baghdad failed in 1626 and again in 1630, but the Ottomans were finally successful in 1638, and the next year the treaty of Kasr-i Sirin brought a long peace between the two rival Islamic empires.

The perennial danger for the Ottomans was having to fight a two-front war with the Safavids in the east and the Habsburgs to the west. At this period the Habsburgs were mainly preoccupied with wars against their European rivals and after the war of 1593–1606 they agreed a peace treaty with the Ottomans at Zsitra-Torok and paid a 'tribute' of 200,000 florins. The peace was renewed several times until 1663. The Ottoman empire survived the seventeenth century crisis relatively unscathed. Although affected by many of the same problems as the Ming, they were able to defeat their main rivals the Safavids, and the west European powers posed little threat. In these circumstances the internal problems could be contained even when another sultan, Ibrahim I, was assassinated in 1648. The suppression of Abaza Hasan Pasha's revolt in 1658 marked the end of the period of instability. The wealth and internal strength of the empire ensured that it had only lost the province of Azerbaijan and retained all its other territories. By the mid-seventeenth century the Ottoman empire was still one of the three major powers in Eurasia.

19.4 The Crisis in Western Europe

The seventeenth-century crisis was particularly acute in western Europe for a number of reasons. Although population growth was not as rapid as in China, the impact of the deteriorating climate was much greater and the agricultural crisis was therefore on a larger scale. The instability in Europe caused by dynastic rivalries and religious divisions was heightened by the impact of the military revolution. (In the seventeenth century Europe was almost constantly at war – there were only four years of peace.) It was the increasing and revolutionary demands of the state on society that tipped the balance towards further instability. In order to finance the new, larger armies equipped with gunpowder weapons taxes had to be increased and the burden this imposed on a largely agricultural economy where the mass of peasants already existed on the very margins of subsistence was too great. Various groups from the peasants to local and regional communities (usually defending their privileges and autonomy) eventually tried to resist these new demands. This resistance was not 'revolutionary' – that is an inappropriate term derived from nineteenth- and twentieth-century usage. The revolts were in fact 'reactionary' – a defence of existing institutions and privileges against the demands of the state. The crisis was worsened by the fact that the rulers and their courts were often culturally isolated from the rest of society (even the landowning elite) and, in some instances, these divisions were worsened by religious differences.

Peasant discontent produced revolts across the continent often on a massive scale. For example, in Aquitaine, which had a population of about 1½ million, there were over 250 revolts in the twenty-five years after 1635. In Provence the situation was equally bad. In just over a century between 1596 and 1715 there were 374 revolts among a population of 600,000. In the main these revolts were not against landlords and the church (though this played a part) but against the state and its tax demands. For peasants who might have only a third of their crop available to live on extra taxes simply could not be afforded. In the Bordeaux area the *taille* (a general tax) was constant between 1610 and 1632 but had quadrupled by 1648 to pay for the war against Spain and the Habsburg emperor in Germany. These tax demands were central to the outbreak of revolt in the 1640s and the almost total breakdown of the French state in the Fronde of 1648–53. In many cases these peasant revolts were heightened by regional revolts in defence of privilege. This was particularly the case in Spain where the demands of almost constant war – with the Dutch, with France from the mid-1630s and in Italy (with Savoy and Mantua) – proved too much for a state which did not have a highly productive agricultural base and where many key trading items were in decline (exports of wool fell 40 per cent in the period 1612–70). The full-scale crisis came in the 1640s with the revolt in Catalonia (which lasted until 1652) and that in Portugal which led to the successful reassertion of its independence (not recognized by Spain until 1668). In addition the Spanish monarchy had to cope with revolutions in Naples and Palermo in the late 1640s.

The interaction of financial demands, local resistance and religious differences was found in England in the early seventeenth century – a country which was hardly involved in any of the highly destructive European wars in the first half of the century and where the impact of the military revolution was limited. Nevertheless the monarchy was unable to solve its financial crisis, control the different elements within what was a classic 'composite' monarchy or contain the religious differences both within England and between the different units of the British monarchy, in particular those between England and the largely Catholic Ireland and the predominantly Calvinist Scotland. In the first decades of the seventeenth century the monarchy faced a fiscal crisis following the earlier sale of its main assets (the lands confiscated by Henry VIII on the dissolution of the monasteries in the late 1530s) and, as in so many other countries of Eurasia, land-tax assessments became increasingly out of line with the real wealth of the country. The sale of land and honours, together with the granting of monopolies and other chartered privileges, had largely been exhausted as a source of revenue by the 1620s. The problem for the monarchy was that the landed elite (and other vested interests) which dominated Parliament had been able to retain a stronger degree of control over government revenue than in most other European states and were able to resist demands for new taxes.

In the 1630s Charles I tried to adopt a solution common in other European monarchies – raising taxes outside parliamentary control thereby shifting towards greater independent power for the ruler. An attempt was made vastly to extend an old naval tax – ship money – into a regular land tax which was beyond the control of parliament. By the late 1630s it seemed that the attempt might be successful even though the financial position of the monarchy remained weak (existing debt was taking up half of all revenue). However, the monarchy was brought down by a regional revolt in Scotland in 1637, mainly over religious policy, followed by a revolt in Ireland. Attempts to suppress these outbreaks were unsuccessful and a bankrupt monarchy had to summon the English parliament. It was the Scottish army in northern England and its support for parliament (partly on religious grounds) which ensured that Charles I was ultimately unsuccessful. Attempts at reaching a settlement between king and parliament in 1640–2 failed over a mixture of religious differences, the incompatible demands of both sides and mutual distrust. Civil war followed, leading to the execution of Charles in 1649 – seemingly the most radical outcome of any of the western European crises of the seventeenth century. In practice the new parliamentary army under Cromwell took control and suppressed the few signs of genuine radical discontent with the existing social and economic order. It was difficult to devise a new stable system of rule and shortly after the death of Cromwell the monarchy was restored in 1660. The return of the monarchy in Britain produced a situation which was unusual in Europe. The monarch governed in association with the landed elite, a situation which was reinforced in 1688–9 when control over taxation was conceded to Parliament.

Elsewhere in Europe the outcome of the seventeenth-century crisis and the associated military revolution was to entrench the power of the monarch. He was generally able to secure additional revenue and raise taxes without any overt method of obtaining consent and govern without the involvement of the assemblies and estates. In France the Estates-General had been relatively weak from the fifteenth century and did not meet after the early seventeenth century until 1789. In Bavaria the power of the estates was broken by 1648. Over the next decade or so the rulers of Brandenburg-Prussia gained the power to support a standing army independent of the estates, and the same happened in Hesse-Cassel. In Denmark the financial crisis following the Northern War with Sweden led to the creation of an absolute monarchy. In Sweden itself the position of the monarch was immeasurably strengthened by the end of the seventeenth century. In Spain the estates of Aragon lost most of their privileges. From the late seventeenth century western Europe was, with the exceptions of Britain, the Netherlands and the Swiss cantons, largely ruled by monarchs who had almost absolute powers.

19.5 The Crisis in Eastern Europe

19.5.1 Moscow
[Earlier Moscow 18.10.2]

In eastern Europe the seventeenth century crisis was felt first in Moscow. It suffered many of the same problems as the rest of Europe but in an even more acute form. Population grew and in a very marginal area climatic deterioration was devastating. The major crop failure and famine of

1601–2 led to a widespread peasant revolt. These problems were exacerbated by the military revolution, the introduction of musketeers, and the long wars against Kazan and Poland-Lithuania which led to increased government expenditure. Taxes were raised – in Novgorod they rose in real terms eight-fold in the course of the sixteenth century – which only intensified peasant discontent. The government tried to impose a system of joint tax responsibility on the peasant communities but many simply moved away and settled in new areas beyond government control.The situation was made worse by internal divisions within the governing elite, the paranoid policies of Ivan IV and the lack of a clear succession. Ivan IV was succeeded by Fedor, a weak ruler dominated by his brother-in-law Boris Godunov. When Fedor died in 1598 the ruling line of Moscow princes was extinct. Boris seized power but few regarded him as a legitimate ruler.

Between 1598 and 1613 Moscow disintegrated into almost total anarchy with no tsar after the death of Boris in 1605 – he was followed by a series of pretenders and others who tried to claim the throne but none could establish any control. Peasant revolts were made worse by outside intervention as both Poland-Lithuania and Sweden took advantage of the collapse of one of their main rivals. By 1610 the situation was so desperate that some of the *boyar* aristocracy even offered the throne to Prince Wladyslaw of Poland who, as a strong Catholic, was anathema to the Orthodox church and many other members of the governing elite. Polish troops held Moscow and continued to do so until 1612. In 1611 the Poles captured Smolensk and the Swedes Novgorod. It seemed quite possible that Moscow would cease to exist and be partitioned between its enemies, with perhaps a semi-anarchical rump in the areas the other states did not want. The main resistance to the Poles was led, on religious grounds, by the Patriarch of Moscow, and eventually a quasi-national assembly made up of the aristocracy, the church and a few representatives of the towns, was summoned. In February 1613 it elected Mikhail Romanov as tsar. The new ruling line, whose legitimacy was regarded as extremely dubious for many years, was to rule until 1917. For some decades after 1613 although the Romanovs established control within the territories of Moscow they were weak and so was the state. There was continual peasant unrest, especially in the south, and there was no question of making any conquests at the expense of the Islamic rulers to the south and east (even Smolensk was not recovered until 1634).

19.5.2 Poland-Lithuania
[Earlier Poland-Lithuania 18.10.1]
Poland-Lithuania avoided involvement in the worst of the wars of the early

seventeenth century, apart from its invasion and occupation of Moscow). The military revolution had had little impact, the cavalry still dominated the army and the pressure for strong state development did not occur on any scale. Cavalry were cheap to maintain and only about a fifth of the state budget was spent on the army (in most European states the proportion was normally over four-fifths). Poland did, however, have a fairly strong navy which was capable of defeating that of Sweden in 1627. In addition the Sejm was powerful (more so even than the English parliament) – it maintained control over taxation. The major crisis in Poland-Lithuania came in the middle of the century. In the early 1640s there were devastating raids by cavalry from the Crimean khanate, followed in 1648 by a Cossack rebellion in the south, more raids from the Crimea and a major peasant uprising in the Ukraine supported by Moscow. In that year Wladyslaw IV died and was succeeded by his younger brother Jan Kazimiercz. In 1655 a Swedish invasion of Pomerania led to the sacking of Warsaw, Crakow and a number of other cities. As the problems mounted the population turned on the Jewish inhabitants and in the first half of the 1650s about 100,000 were either killed or fled into exile. The remainder retreated into ghettos. Altogether probably a quarter of the Polish population either died or were killed between 1648 and 1660. Poland also lost control over Brandenburg-Prussia whose ruler took the opportunity provided by these internal problems to declare himself independent. (In 1701 his successor finally decided he now merited the title of king.) In 1668 Kazimiercz gave up the struggle and abdicated, ending the line of Vasa kings who had ruled Poland since 1587. The situation in Poland seemed no worse than any other European state and recovery from the problems of the seventeenth century crisis seemed to be under way. In fact Poland-Lithuania was about to enter a period of unprecedented decline leading to its partition and disappearance as a state within little more than a century [19.11.2].

19.5.3 Serfdom

It was in the sixteenth and seventeenth centuries that the social history of eastern Europe began to diverge strongly from that of the west. In both areas the impact of the Black Death and subsequent plagues had been to improve the position of the peasants because landlords faced a labour shortage. Existing demands for labour on the landlords' estates could not be enforced and were increasingly commuted into money rents (a situation that had prevailed in China for almost two thousand years). Slowly, growing commercialization of the economy made these changes sustainable. After 1500 these trends continued in western Europe and landlords came to rely on money rents rather than peasant labour as the primary means of benefiting from their tenants. Other forms of dues gradually became less important, though France to some extent went against this general trend. However, in parts of central, and all of eastern Europe, the trend from the late fifteenth century was in the opposite direction. Serfdom was reimposed, peasant holdings were expropriated and taken over by the landlords, peasants were legally tied to the land they cultivated, the labour services they owed to their landlords were intensified and the rights and jurisdiction the landlords could exercise over them were increased. The reasons for these differences were complex. In eastern Europe there was still a shortage of labour compared with the amount of land that could be cultivated (population densities were much lower than in western Europe). Landlords therefore found it difficult to control the peasants through rents when land was available (which it increasingly was not in western Europe) and when the level of monetarization in the economy was much lower than in western Europe. Legal controls through serfdom gave the landlords the power they wanted, forced the peasants to cultivate the landlord's land and enabled him to sell the surplus produce. It was this latter factor that was different from the situation a few centuries earlier. Agriculture on the estates of the landlords was highly commercialized because of the growing export of grain to western Europe. In the hundred years after 1460 Polish-Lithuanian exports of rye rose sixteen-fold and eventually accounted for a third of total production. In Hungary 55,000 cattle a year were moved west and made up over 90 per cent of Hungary's total exports. The reimposition of serfdom was also possible because the aristocracy either controlled, or in some cases monopolized, the parliaments and estates and could use their political power to reinforce their economic and social predominance. Serfdom was legally established in Bohemia (1487), Poland (1495), Hungary (1514), Prussia (1526), Silesia and Brandenburg (1528), Upper Austria (1539) and Livonia (1561).

In Moscow the monetary economy was even less developed than elsewhere in eastern Europe. In the early sixteenth century about 10 per cent of the population were *kholopy*, effectively slaves, although only a few were employed in agriculture. The bulk of the population were legally free peasants who cultivated their landlords' land and in return owed either *barshchina* (labour service) or *obrok* (rent in cash or kind) – the commonest was rent in kind because of the lack of money. In 1497 the government decreed that peasants could only move during two weeks in November (after the harvest) and on payment of an exit fee. However, labour was still short and some landlords were prepared to pay the fee on behalf of the peasant in order to obtain the labour they needed. It was the political, economic and social collapse of Moscow in the late sixteenth century that finally instituted full legal serfdom. In the chaos peasants fled their land and villages (over four-fifths of the land in the Moscow district was uncultivated in the 1580s), setting up settlements in newly cleared areas. The landlords, short of labour, obtained a government decree in 1581 which banned peasant movement in parts of the country during a 'forbidden year'. Most years became 'forbidden years' and in 1592 the decree was widened to apply to the whole country. During the anarchy that prevailed in the early seventeenth century control over the peasantry was difficult to enforce although from 1603 the existing decree was reissued every year and therefore every one became a 'forbidden year'. With the re-establishment of a government after 1613 the decree could be enforced and serfdom fully imposed. Finally, in 1649, these provisions were formally incorporated into the law-code and all serfs were bound to their place of residence and to their landlord – even if they escaped no absence, however long, could remove that obligation.

From the early seventeenth century the population of Moscow (and later Russia) was increasingly polarized into the elite nobles and landlords on the one hand, and a mass of serfs on the other, as distinctions within the peasantry tended to disappear. By the eighteenth century about half the population were privately owned serfs and another quarter were owned by the church. Serfdom was strongest in the best agricultural areas where the landlords could use them to produce an agricultural surplus they could sell – in the northern forest regions and Siberia privately owned serfs were rare. The status of the serfs declined and they rapidly became indistinguishable from slaves. Landlords could move serfs wherever they wanted on their various estates and as early as the 1660s they were buying and selling serfs without any accompanying land (others were won or lost at cards). They had become personal property – the landlord could punish them as he wanted and they even required a pass to leave the estate. The only right that serfs had, which slaves usually did not, was that they could be conscripted into the army. Until 1793 this was for life but it was then reduced to just twenty-five years, if any soldier was lucky enough to live that long.

19.6 Recovery

Across Eurasia in the years around 1660 most of the major states and empires began to recover from almost a century of disruption. In China the Ch'ing re-established central control after the disintegration which brought about the end of the Ming and inaugurated a period of almost unprecedented stability and increasing wealth. In the Ottoman empire the suppression of the revolt by Abaza Hasan Pasha in 1658 began a period of stability dominated by the Köprülü family who were the grand viziers until the end of the seventeenth century. In India the Mughal empire was still strong, and in Japan the Tokugawa shogunate ruled an internally and externally peaceful society with an economy which was growing steadily. In Europe the initial impact of the military revolution was over and most states had found ways of raising the revenue they needed to pay for their armies and navies. Population growth slowed (overall in the seventeenth century it increased by only 12 per cent, less than half the rate in the sixteenth century) and this enabled the steadily rising agricultural productivity to create a slightly better balance between the number of people and the amount of food available. Commercial wealth was growing, especially as the increasing amount of plantation agriculture in the Americas benefited European states, in particular England and France. These trends were reflected in a greater degree of internal stability within the states of Europe. The religious disputes of the previous century and a half were less virulent as a division into Protestant and Catholic states stabilized. Europe was usually at war but they were far less destructive wars than those since 1500. The monarchy was restored in England and in France Louis XIV instituted a period of strong rule. Across Europe monarchs and princes ruled with almost no internal opposition.

19.7 China: Stability and Prosperity

When the Ch'ing seized power in northern China they still saw themselves as an alien elite ruling over the Chinese. Mixed marriages were banned, cities such as Peking were segregated (the Manchu city was in the northern part) and like the Chin empire six hundred years earlier they imposed the wearing of the *pien-tzu* or pigtail (a nomadic custom dating back to the Tabgatch in the fourth century) despite the numerous revolts this produced among the Chinese. Immediately after the conquest a series of *ch'üan* or enclave estates for the Manchu were created on confiscated land. The labour force to work these estates came from prisoners of war and landless peasants kept in conditions of near slavery. The Ch'ing rapidly discovered that the system was highly inefficient and unworkable – the *ch'üan* were given up, the peasants regained their land and in 1685 the Manchu 'banners' were forbidden to confiscate any more land. In practice the Manchu very rapidly adopted Chinese institutions – as early as 1646 the examination system was restarted to produce a new group of administrators loyal to the Ch'ing. By the end of the seventeenth century there was very little antagonism between the Manchu and the Chinese as stability and prosperity returned.

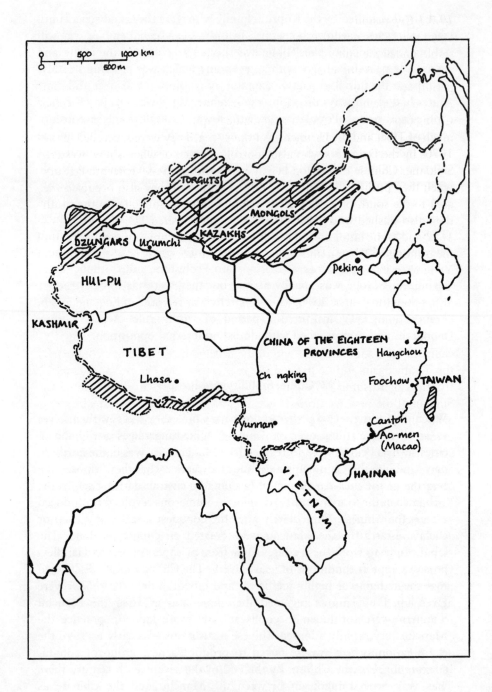

Map 59: The Ch'ing empire in 1760

19.7.1 Expansion

From the 1680s until the end of the eighteenth century China was highly stable under the rule of just three long-lived Ch'ing emperors: K'ang-hsi (1661–1722), Yung-cheng (1723–36) and Ch'ien-lung (1736–96). The period saw a major expansion of Chinese control and influence into central Asia on a scale not seen since the T'ang a thousand years earlier. When the Ch'ing took power in China the nomadic empire of the Koshots controlled much of Tibet and the Urumchi-Kokonor area. They were succeeded in the 1670s by the Dzungars who also controlled much of what is now western Sinkiang. Chinese expansion began at the end of the seventeenth century when they pushed the Dzungars further west and they also occupied the area to the south of Lake Baikal, including all of Mongolia. In the south they also pushed into Tibet. The Dalai Lama visited Peking as early as 1652 and in the latter part of the century Peking became a major centre for the printing of Tibetan and Mongol Buddhist works. In 1732 the emperor Yung-cheng converted his palace in the city (the Yung-ho-kung) into a Tibetan Buddhist temple. In 1751 Tibet was made a Chinese protectorate although with a high degree of autonomy. Chinese influence also pushed over the Himalayas into Nepal and Bhutan. The final assault on the Dzungars came when they were largely exterminated in the military campaign of 1756–7. By the end of the decade the Chinese had conquered the Tarim Basin and controlled the area as far west as Kokand and the frontiers of Kashmir. These territories were incorporated into China as Sinkiang ('the new territories'), although they remained governed by the army. In the early 1760s the Chinese empire reached its greatest ever extent. It controlled an area a third bigger than that of modern China – it stretched from Kashmir and Kokand in the west to Taiwan in the east and from Mongolia in the north to the Tonkin area of Vietnam in the south. Over the next forty years very little of this territory was lost – revolts in Kansu in central Asia and on Taiwan were put down in the 1780s, Yunnan and much of northern Burma recognized Chinese sovereignty in the early 1770s and in 1791 the Chinese army was conducting punishment raids in Nepal. Only in the late 1780s, as Vietnamese piracy increased, did the Chinese armies withdraw from northern Vietnam (an area the Chinese had never been able to control easily) and a new Nguyen dynasty took power and changed the name of the country from *Dai Viet* ('Great Land of Viet') to Vietnam ('Viet of the South').

19.7.2 Economy and society
[*Contemporaneous European economy 20.3–20.5*]
There was internal stability in China – the only peasant revolts were in the frontier regions and the most densely populated area of the Lower Yangtze

valley was peaceful. This led to the most rapid population growth so far seen in world history. In 1650 when the Ch'ing took power the population of China was about 140 million and by the end of the century it had recovered from the effects of the collapse of the Ming to reach about 160 million (the same as in 1600). In the eighteenth century the population more than doubled to over 330 million. China was by far the largest state in the world – the whole of Europe had about 180 million people in 1800, England and Wales less than 10 million. Population growth on this scale could not have been sustained without a highly productive agriculture. The amount of land cultivated in China probably doubled in the period between 1650 and 1800 as new lands in Sinkiang, Kweichow, Yunnan and Kwangsi in particular were colonized. Productivity continued to improve too and here the increasing cultivation of crops from the Americas such as maize and sweet potatoes was very important.

Agriculture also benefited from two other factors. First, the level of government taxation was very low – in the early eighteenth century it was already at the lowest levels known in Chinese history. In 1711 it was fixed in absolute terms and the vast growth in output in the eighteenth century was therefore untaxed. Second, large landlords were in a very small minority (even the imperial estates accounted for less than one per cent of the cultivated land) and production was in the hands of peasant families who had security of tenure. Agriculture was highly commercialized with large amounts of rural wage labour. In the Lower Yangtze valley tea plantations covered much of the area. About four-fifths of the population was dependent on grain which they bought in the market rather than produced and consumed themselves. Some peasants were so wealthy that they could buy private education for their children. Although the grain trade was highly commercialized the government tried to even out market fluctuations through the state-owned or -controlled granaries. Major granaries were financed directly by the state and outside the major cities there were community and charity granaries financed by taxes on landlords and merchants. In total the state held about 10 per cent of the total grain production. Stocks were either sold to reduce prices, loaned to peasants for short-term relief, or used to alleviate any famine. Because of the well-developed internal communications network, principally of canals, the government had the ability to move stocks around the country to where they were needed. No European country had such a sophisticated system.

Government taxation probably took no more than 5 per cent of China's wealth every year. Yet the government had a massive surplus because of the huge wealth generated by the Chinese economy. Direct state intervention in the economy was very low – there were no restrictions on foreign trade by Chinese merchants and even the few remaining monopolies such as that on salt were run by merchants. These merchants were some of the wealthiest people in China and made very large profits from distributing about 400,000 tons of salt across the country every year. Chinese merchants controlled tea production and its increasing export to Europe, mainly through the English East India Company at Canton. (Tea exports increased 28-fold in the eighteenth century but even then still accounted for little more than a tenth of Chinese production – the rest went to the internal market.) An increasingly commercial economy also relied on the import of large quantities of rice from across south-east Asia. This trade involved thousands of junks, each of over 1,000 tons and with a crew of nearly 200, and Chinese merchants spread out across the region to organize the trade. By the end of the eighteenth century there were over 200,000 in Borneo alone running a mini-Chinese state ('the Lanfang Company') which survived until 1884.

In both 1700 and 1800 Peking was the largest city in the world with a population of about one million, and Canton, with over 800,000 people in 1800, was larger than any city in Europe apart from London. Industrial production per head was at least as high as in Europe and was based on a high degree of specialization for the large and growing internal market, particularly in the cities. By 1700 the cotton goods industry of Sung-chiang (south-west of Shanghai) employed on a permanent basis over 200,000 people and a large number of casual workers. The industrial and merchant families of China were tightly organized around a mixture of family and share partnerships, exactly the same as in Europe. They also formed 'lodges' – informal associations for mutual assistance in accommodation, storage of goods and financial assistance. Under the Ming they were based on particular trades and places of origin but they spread rapidly across China in the eighteenth century. Many of the cities, as in Europe, were governed by groups of wealthy merchants and industrialists. These groups were supported by highly developed banking institutions for deposits, loans, transfer of funds between different parts of China and the issuing of promissory notes and banknotes. Equally important was the development of partnership law, mortgages on land and the very complex system of contract law needed to regulate so many commercial dealings. As in Europe an increasingly mobile and prosperous society with a growing economy brought with it social strains. China too had long-established hereditary status groups of landlords, administrators and court officials with inherited wealth who felt threatened by the growing power of the new groups who looked for, and often obtained, considerable amounts of upwards social mobility bought with their wealth.

It was only towards the end of the eighteenth century that there were the first signs of some of the problems which were to plague China on a growing scale in the next century. By the 1780s the rate of population growth was probably reaching the limits which even the productive Chinese agriculture could support. When growth continued into the early nineteenth century (the population rose more slowly but still by a quarter between 1800 and 1850) the situation became critical. Already by the 1790s some areas of the country were beginning to experience rural discontent. Peasant revolts became commoner and secret societies such as the *Pai-lien-chiao* (White Lotus), which had played a major role in the mid-fourteenth century during the expulsion of the Mongols and three hundred years later during the collapse of the Ming, reappeared. The government still had plenty of power and money to put down these revolts but they were a harbinger of what was to come.

[*Later China 21.12*]

19.8 Japan Under the Tokugawa

[*Earlier Japan 18.6*]

The Tokugawa shogunate established in 1603 was strong enough to cope with the seventeenth-century crisis as it affected Japan. It was at a low level and largely restricted to the agricultural problems of the 1630s, the consequent high rice prices and the Shimabara revolt of 1637-8 which they helped cause. With no threat of external intervention these problems could be contained. On taking power Tokugawa Ieyasu followed a cautious policy as his power was consolidated. He kept the central part of Japan and the capital of Kyoto under the control of his immediate family. The emperors lived in Kyoto but Ieyasu kept his capital at his old base of Edo (modern Tokyo) – a small fishing village given to him by Hideyoshi in 1590. Most of the major *daimyo* survived, even those of his main enemies the Mori and Shimazu, but his followers were also rewarded with large amounts of land. Hideyoshi's heir (the main threat to the Tokugawa) was defeated in 1615 and his castle of Osaka captured. Ieyasu officially resigned as shogun in 1605 and handed power to his son so as to avoid a succession dispute, although in practice he retained power until his death in 1616.

Because of Ieyasu's caution the main institutions of the Tokugawa shogunate were created by his son Hidetada (who died in 1623) and his successor Iemitsu who ruled until 1651. The Tokugawa administration (the *bakufu*) ruled the family lands directly. They included about a third of the population of Japan and most of the major cities including Edo, Kyoto, Osaka and Nagasaki. The power this gave the Tokugawa is demonstrated by the fact that they controlled a rice yield seven times bigger than that of the next largest *daimyo*, the Maeda of Kanazawa. It was on this foundation that they could impose their power over the other *daimyo* who were divided into three categories. The *shimpan* (related han) were members of the Tokugawa family who did not normally become shogun. These collateral Tokugawa, especially those of the 'Three Houses' (*sanke*) were the descendants of the seventh, eighth and ninth sons of Ieyasu who controlled key areas of Japan and provided the shogun on three occasions. The *fudai* were the *daimyo* who had recognized Ieyasu before his campaign to take power in 1600 and were therefore regarded as being in a special position. The third category was the *tozama* (or 'outer *daimyo*') which contained most of the largest lords (except the Maeda). These were people who had opposed Ieyasu in various ways and were therefore treated with suspicion. They included the Mori of western Honshu and the Shimazu of Satsuma in southern Kyushu, who were to play a major role in the final overthrow of the Tokugawa in the mid-nineteenth century. Under the Tokugawa the number and power of the *tozama* declined as they were punished for various infractions of the law (real or invented) and their lands and rights given to the more trustworthy *fudai*.

The *daimyo* kept their retainers (the *samurai*) but both rapidly lost their military function, in particular the latter became officials within the *daimyo* administration. This reflected the fact that the *daimyo* themselves, originally military lords, were transformed into local administrators controlled by shogunal law. They did not pay taxes to the shogun (he had enough revenues from his own lands). However, they did make very carefully graded annual 'gifts' of tribute and were also required to bear the cost of local government in their areas and finance some military expenses. In total the *daimyo* had greater economic and military strength than the shogun but they were divided and very closely controlled. All were involved in a complex set of marriage alliances with the Tokugawa and they were not allowed to communicate directly with each other, only through the government in Edo. They could not expand their military forces or build castles without shogunal approval and the Tokugawa had enough strength to enforce this ruling. The main control over the *daimyo* was the highly regulated *sankin-kotai* system. From 1634 each *daimyo* was forced to provide hostages who resided at Edo. In addition they had to live there themselves in attendance on the shogun for half the year and maintain a second, very expensive, residence in Edo. The longer Japan experienced internal peace the less relevant the old military capabilities of the *daimyo* became.

Central to the creation of the strong Tokugawa state was its strict control over external relations and the ending of the system whereby the local *daimyo* could make their own decisions. Contact with foreigners now required the approval of the Edo government. The Tokugawa saw themselves as the equals of the Chinese government (partly because Japan had never been invaded by 'barbarians') and refused to accept their allotted place in the Chinese system of diplomacy and political hierarchy in the region. The Japanese were strong enough to dictate the terms of their involvement with foreigners, avoided the effects of the disruptions following the collapse of the Ming and then benefited from the long period of stability throughout the eighteenth century. Because of the very strong anti-Christian ethos of the Tokugawa (Christianity was largely eliminated as a religion in Japan by the 1630s) the Dutch were confined to the island of Deshima off Nagasaki and kept in humiliating conditions. The level of foreign trade was high and the *daimyo* of Tsushima, Satsuma and Matsumae traded, using Japanese ships, under the general authority of the Edo government and became very wealthy as a consequence. The main trade routes were through Korea and the Ryukyu Islands (in particular Okinawa) with China. The Chinese bought large quantities of silver and, later in the seventeenth century, copper – over 5,000 tons a year was being exported from Japan. The trade through Korea was large enough to take up nearly 10 per cent of the silver minted each year in Japan. Japan was not therefore cut off from the outside world – it was strong enough to decide the terms of its involvement and remain free of war.

[*Later Japan 21.15*]

19.9 The Ottoman and Safavid Empires

From the late 1650s the Ottoman empire was under the domination of the Köprülü family, who were effectively hereditary grand viziers and held numerous other key offices. This was part of a process, similar to that under way in western Europe, leading to the creation of a developed military-political bureaucracy to manage state affairs thereby ensuring the long-term survival of the empire. Extensive, high-quality records were kept which were at least as good as those of the European monarchies. In local administration there was a growing decentralization of power and increasing flexibility as the central government came to rely, as did European governments, on the local landowners to carry out political, administrative and legal functions. These powerful local groups developed their own networks of patronage and corruption as did their counterparts in Europe. It was under this developing system that the Ottoman empire reached its greatest territorial extent. Most of the island of Crete, which lay near the route of the grain ships from Egypt to Constantinople, was captured from

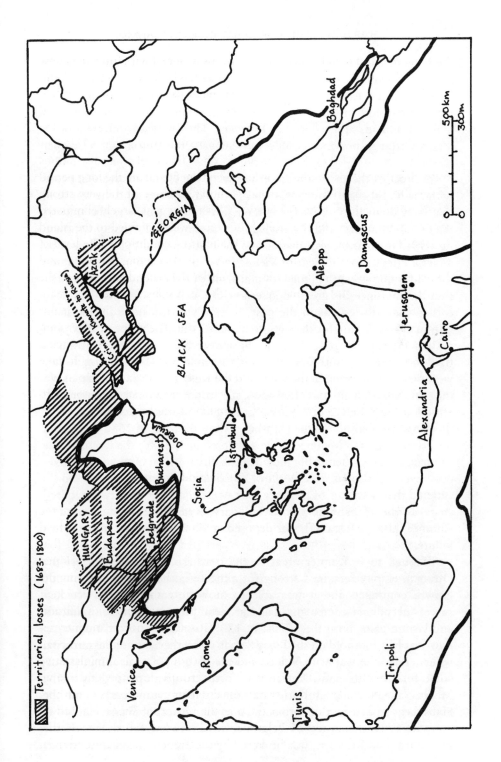

Map 60: The Ottoman empire 1660–1800

the Venetians in 1645–6, although the key port of Candia (Iraklion) withstood a siege until 1669. The Ottomans now controlled all of the eastern Mediterranean. Around the northern shores of the Black Sea the southward expansion of Poland into the Ukraine and the conflict with the Cossack nomads dragged in the Ottomans. The result was the creation of a new Ottoman province – Podolya – between the Dniester and Dnieper rivers.

For most of the early seventeenth century the Ottomans were at peace with the Habsburgs. However, their internal difficulties (and the war with the Safavids in Iran) meant that their level of control over the frontier region of Hungary and Transylvania was limited. Reviving Ottoman power led to an unsuccessful attack on the Habsburgs in 1663 followed by a major effort with the siege of Vienna in 1683. This action demonstrated the continuing strength of the Ottomans and that there had been no significant decline since the great conquests in the Balkans some two centuries earlier. Nevertheless, as in the past, Vienna was too far from the main Ottoman power base for the siege to be successful. The shape of European diplomacy had changed little from the sixteenth century – the Habsburgs tried to recreate an anti-Ottoman alliance based on Venice although they were now able to bring in the Poles and the Russians. The Ottomans, as in the past, had the tacit, and often open, support of the French who were still anti-Habsburg. Venice briefly reconquered the Morea and Athens but lost them again and although the Habsburgs took Belgrade in 1688 they could not retain it. Sultan Mehmed IV was deposed in 1687 for the failure of the campaign against Vienna but it made little difference to Ottoman effectiveness. Eventually in 1699 the peace of Karlowitz was agreed. The Ottomans suffered their first loss of territory (bar Azerbaijan) for over two hundred years as the Habsburgs gained Hungary, Transylvania and Belgrade. Another sultan, Mustafa II, was deposed in 1703 largely as a result of this failure.

Although these frontier areas in the northern Balkans were lost the Ottoman empire remained strong for almost another century. Economic growth continued and it was able to mobilize resources and conduct successful military campaigns. The European powers made no significant and lasting gains until the 1770s. In 1709 Russia was forced to give up Azov, its first foothold on the Black Sea. In 1718 the peace of Passarowitz, which ended the war with Venice and the Habsburgs, was a mixed outcome for the Ottomans. Venice was forced to give up its gains in the Mediterranean made at Karlowitz some twenty years earlier but the Habsburgs gained part of Serbia and a small portion of Wallachia. However, in 1739 the peace of Belgrade, which ended the war with the Habsburgs and Russians, was brokered by the French, the historic friends of the Ottomans. The outcome was that the Habsburgs had to give up all the gains they had made in 1718 and return to the position as at the end of the seventeenth century. For the next thirty years there was peace in the Balkans and the Ottomans maintained the essentials of the position they had constructed over three hundred years earlier.

The Ottomans had, since the early sixteenth century, faced a difficult strategic problem and the threat of a two-front war with the Europeans in the west and the Safavids in Iran. That problem was resolved in the early eighteenth century with the collapse of Safavid power in Iran. After the peace made with the Ottomans in 1639 both the Safavid army and the central administration were in decline – control over local lords had always been patchy and now the central government in Isfahan became even less effective. Local chieftains became semi-independent and there was a general revival among the tribal groups in Afghanistan and central Asia (a phenomenon which affected the Mughals in India too). Eventually the Ghalzai Afghans of Kandahar, led by Mir Wais, captured Isfahan in 1722. Immediately the Ottomans (in agreement with the Russians) attacked. In 1724 they took Armenia and part of Azerbaijan and the Russians took the Caspian provinces of Jilan, Mazandaran and Astarabad. The Ottomans no longer faced a significant threat in the east. The semi-anarchy in Iran continued and in 1736 the last powerless Safavid ruler was deposed by Nadir Shah Afshar, a chieftain of Chaghatai (Mongol) descent who was allied with various Afghan and Turkic elements. He also invaded India in 1739 but was assassinated in 1747 whereupon the coalition he ruled quickly fell apart. He was succeeded in Iran by Karim Khan, the leader of a coalition of settled Zand tribal groups in western Iran. He ruled, nominally as *vakil* or lieutenant of the vacant Safavid throne, until 1779. The Zand were then defeated by the Qajars, descendants of the original Turkish governors of Mazandaran and Astarabad under the Safavids. They went on to control the whole of Iran by 1810 and founded the dynasty which was to rule until 1924. Other Islamic rulers in the region were also augmenting their power. In 1650 Sultan Ibn Saif of Oman took the Portuguese fort of Muscat – the captured Portuguese vessels were formed into his fleet which, by the end of the seventeenth century, consisted of 24 large ships with a 74-gun vessel and two 60-gun frigates. In 1698 the Oman dynasty captured the Portuguese trading centre of Fort Jesus at Mombasa on the Kenyan coast.

The collapse of the Safavids brought about fundamental religious changes. Nadir Shah Afshar was a Sunni and began the process of down-playing the Shiia elements. For the leaders of the latter this was quite acceptable as they freed themselves from the Safavid religious claims, became more autonomous as the *ulama* withdrew from the state and,

within a century, became the chief opponents of the Iranian regime. The Zand and the Qajars were more tolerant than the Safavids and their rule saw a major revival of Sufism, especially the Nurbakshi sect which came from India under Shah Masum Ali in 1785. The religious changes in Iran were paralleled by an even more important movement in the Ottoman provinces of Arabia. The new purist and ascetic Islamic movement – the Wahhabi (named after its main teacher Ibn Abd al-Wahhab) – spread under the protection of a local Bedouin leader Ibn Saud in the early eighteenth century. (There were similar movements in the Yemen opposed to Hindu and other non-Muslim traders in the region.) The Wahhabi put pressure on the Ottomans across the region, reaching Egypt in the 1770s, but did not achieve major success until their takeover of Medina and Mecca in 1806. The changes in Arabia were symptomatic of a gradual loss of Ottoman control over a number of provinces in the late eighteenth century as different regional identities asserted themselves. In Egypt the Mamluk slave soldiers from the Christian provinces in south-east Europe and also the Sudan had always been a dominant elite. By the late eighteenth century under Ali Bey they, rather than the Ottoman governor, provided the effective government of the province, building their strength on the strong trade revenues. The provincial elite in Syria were increasingly defining themselves as Arabs (a dubious claim) or on a religious basis (Sunni, Shia or Alawite) rather than as Ottomans. Around the port of Acre the local ruler Dahir-al-Umar dominated the region and controlled the export of cotton cloth to France – compared with him the Ottoman governors in Sidon and Damascus had very little power. The Ottomans in Constantinople were able to depose Dahir in 1775 but his replacement, Ahmed Jezzar Pasha, a Bosnian, proved to be equally independent and built up his own province. All of these problems were symptomatic of those which were to affect the Ottoman empire on an increasing scale from the end of the eighteenth century.
[*Later Ottoman history 21.10*]

19.10 European Conflicts

[*Earlier European dynastic struggles 18.9*]
From the mid-seventeenth century Europe was far more stable than it had been in the previous century although a series of wars continued from the 1660s until 1815 with very few interruptions. The intense religious disputes generated by the Reformation had abated and none of the wars of the period were centred around the Protestant-Catholic division. Instead they were a continuation of the earlier dynastic conflicts as the emerging

OVERVIEW 12

THE WORLD IN
1700

World Population: 610 million
Regional Population: China: 160 million, India: 160 million,
Rest of Asia: 95 million (Japan: 26 million),
Europe: 120 million (France: 22 million,
Germany: 13 million, Spain: 8 million, England: 6 million),
Africa: 60 million, Americas: 12 million)
Major cities: Constantinople (700,000), Peking (700,000),
Isfahan (600,000), London (550,000), Paris (550,000),
Edo (550,000), Delhi (500,000), Ahmedabad (350,000),
Osaka (350,000), Kyoto (350,000), Cairo (350,000),
Canton (300,000), Nanking (300,000),
Hangchou (300,000), Naples (200,000)

Events:

★ China prosperous and stable under Ch'ing dynasty. Major
expansion under way – control of Mongolia and parts of
Sinkiang. Blocking of Russian expansion in Amur river area

★ Japan stable with external and internal peace under Tokugawa

★ Dutch control of Batavia and most of Spice Islands

★ Mughal empire at its greatest extent

★ A few British settlements in India – Bombay, Madras and Calcutta

★ Ottomans ruling from Balkans through Anatolia, Levant and Egypt to North Africa. First loss of territory to Habsburgs in Hungary and Transylvania plus Belgrade

★ Safavids in Iran in steep decline

★ Omanis ruling much of coastal east Africa from Mombasa

★ Decline of Spain, Dutch republic and Sweden. France dominant European land power

★ Russian control of Siberia as far as Pacific coast, founding of St Petersburg, expansion of Russian power in Baltic. Major decline of Poland

★ Rise of England as maritime and colonial power

★ Small European settlements in north America confined to eastern coastal areas

★ European slave plantations in Brazil and the Caribbean. Rapidly rising slave trade from Africa

European states fought for relative advantage. There were few decisive wars but overall the period saw a relative decline of Spain, the Netherlands and Sweden, the collapse and elimination of Poland and the failure of France (both under the monarchy and, after the revolution of 1789 and the early 1790s, Napoleon) to achieve a position of more than temporary predominance. The main beneficiaries were the peripheral powers to the west and the east – Britain and Russia. The other growing power was the new kingdom of Prussia, whilst Austria and the Ottomans were largely able to retain their positions. Although the pattern of alliances between these states constantly shifted, especially in the mid-1750s, they were largely defined, from the 1690s, by the opposition of Britain and France.

By the 1660s the initial impact of the military revolution and gunpowder weapons had been absorbed and there were no fundamental technical changes until after 1815. Muskets now fired faster (three ranks were sufficient to keep up continuous fire from well-trained troops) but there was no command for 'take aim' – the infantry simply fired straight ahead because the weapons had no sights. Although warfare in Europe was prolonged – there were major wars between 1689–97, 1702–14, 1739–48, 1756–63, 1778–83 and 1793–1815 – the level of destruction was far less than in the century before 1660. Within the military the main changes were the differentiation and specialization of the infantry, cavalry and artillery. They were increasingly enlisted on a long-term, mercenary basis (though often through forced recruitment) and the mobilization of a mass army did not take place until 1792 under the revolutionary government in France. Even then it was limited – by 1799 substitutes were allowed, many of the conscripts came from the conquered territories and by 1812, when Napoleon invaded Russia, the majority of his army did not even speak French. The military problem was to co-ordinate the activities of all these units. This proved to be very difficult for armies of more than about 50,000 because communications were poor, maps of the countryside were often non-existent, and once the units spread out they could not be controlled. The first step towards solving the problem was the invention of the division – a self-contained unit of about 12,000 men containing all the elements of an army and therefore capable of acting independently. The French first experimented with the idea in the 1740s but did not adopt it fully until the late 1780s, just before the revolution.

Armies continued to grow in size – by the early eighteenth century the French army was over 400,000-strong, the largest ever seen in Europe. By 1812 that part of the French army which invaded Russia numbered over 600,000 men and they were accompanied by almost 1,150 field guns (light field artillery capable of keeping up with the infantry, drawn by only three horses and handled by eight men, which had been developed in the 1760s).

Armies of this size operated on a front over 300 miles wide and were large enough to capture fortresses and towns. Fortifications, which still dominated the warfare of the late seventeenth and early eighteenth centuries, declined in importance and only occasionally were defensive lines such as those of Torres Vedras in the Peninsular War effective. The supply of weapons for the European armies was not usually a problem because of the growing European industrial base – the main difficulty remained finding enough food for the men and enough fodder for the horses. Navies also grew in size – in 1789 all the fleets of the European powers did not amount to more than about 450 warships. By 1815 the British Royal Navy had over 1,000 ships manned by over 140,000 men.

The cost of warfare was still high, especially for the smaller states where the rulers tried to gain power and prestige beyond the capabilities of the state. The new state of Prussia maintained an army of 150,000 in the late 1750s and over 200,000 thirty years later. This made it about the fourth largest in Europe even though Prussia was only the thirteenth most populous state. A successful infrastructure could be built up – Prussia manufactured 15,000 muskets a year and 560,000 pounds of powder, produced standardized uniforms and maintained food stores sufficient for 60,000 men for two years. However, the human cost of the policies of the Prussian state was enormous. A quarter of young males were conscripted (about a third of the army were foreign mercenaries) and 180,000 died in the war of 1756–63. That was a casualty rate of fourteen out of fifteen enlisted men, and 300,000 civilians were also killed. Ninety per cent of the state's revenue was spent on war and the currency was debased. Prussia could only continue fighting for two reasons – massive subsidies from the British and wartime plunder. The cost of war was so great that army officers were not allowed to marry because the state could not afford to pay widows' pensions.

The major changes in warfare in this period were organizational. In the late seventeenth century the state took more control over the military and their supply instead of leaving this task to contractors. It was yet another stage in the growth of the state and its increasing ability to control and direct resources. The supply of the army was placed under civilians and the army and navy were paid by the state. (There were still plenty of opportunities for corruption and the looting of public money as the British commander of the early eighteenth century, Marlborough, demonstrated.) It was financial power which became increasingly important, especially as most of the wars were fought between coalitions. No state could fund the continually growing costs of war from taxation – they still lacked the administrative infrastructure to tax on a wide basis and were still concerned about their ability to control the social discontent that accompanied rising taxes. Europe did not have large amounts of bullion – the gold and silver produced in the Americas was still going to India and China. Growing trade did, however, produce increasing commercial wealth and European states were able to tap into these resources. In particular they developed banking and credit financing methods to sustain the debts the cost of warfare produced and the interest they had to pay on these sums. The most successful state in mobilizing these resources was Britain and it was this success that lay behind much of its growing power and influence during the eighteenth century. However, sophisticated credit mechanisms were not enough on their own. The Dutch, who were by far the most commercial state in Europe in the late seventeenth century, led the development of these mechanisms (not surprisingly because the Dutch state was largely controlled by the merchants and bankers), but found that they could not, in the long run, compensate for other strategic weaknesses.

The states of Europe responded in different ways to these different military, administrative and financial challenges. Spain was a declining power in the late seventeenth century with a weak economic base and its army in 1700 was half the size of that of the 1650s. Although it controlled the largest of the European colonial empires its effective strength was low. The Dutch were one of the strongest powers in the late seventeenth century and twice defeated the English in a naval war. The most difficult problem they faced was that they were vulnerable to a land war, especially a French invasion from the south. This required a large army – 100,000 strong by the late seventeenth century compared with 20,000 in the war of independence with Spain a century earlier – and the construction of an elaborate system of expensive fortifications in the border regions. The assistance provided by England under its Dutch ruler William III after 1689, enabled the Dutch to survive but they had to bear the brunt of the costs of the war with France which lasted until 1697. Increasingly it was the British who benefited from conducting a naval and colonial war outside Europe, and the Dutch saw their commercial strength decline relative to that of Britain and France during the eighteenth century. Neutrality in the 1750s and 1780s did not improve the position because by then Britain was the superior sea power and able to block Dutch trade. The Dutch finally succumbed to a French invasion in the early 1790s.

France under Louis XIV was the main power in the late seventeenth century. The size of the army increased ten-fold in the fifty years after 1660 but it still found it difficult to achieve its aims. Geographical barriers in the south (the Pyrenees and the Alps) made expansion into Spain and Italy difficult and the main thrust was therefore to the north-east against the Habsburgs in Flanders and the Dutch further north. The area was heavily fortified and no decisive military victory could be secured but the mere threat of one was usually enough to bring in the British to oppose the French. Expansion eastwards was equally problematic and an alliance with either Austria or Prussia inevitably meant the opposition of the other. The fundamental problem for the French monarchy was that although it was probably the single strongest power in Europe it was also a growing colonial power in the West Indies, much of Canada, and also in India. It did not have the resources to conduct both a land war in Europe and a colonial war against the British. The result was that it usually lost the latter. On the one occasion when it did not have to fight in both spheres simultaneously – the American War of Independence – it was able to win the naval battle against the British. The Habsburgs in Austria continued to rule over a very disparate collection of territories. They had to deal with a variety of problems – the Ottoman empire in the Balkans, the long-term threat that Russia would gain from expansion at the expense of the Ottomans and the general hostility of Prussia especially after they took Silesia in 1740. Nevertheless the Habsburg rulers of Austria were generally successful – the empire expanded enormously in the nineteenth century and the monarchy survived until 1918. Prussia became a major power in the early eighteenth century mainly because of the decline of Sweden and Poland and the weakness of Austria following the disputes over the Habsburg succession. However, it remained relatively weak until 1815 and heavily dependent on British subsidies.

19.11 The Peripheral Powers of Europe: Britain and Russia

The powers which gained the most from the European conflicts of the eighteenth century were in the far west – Britain – and the far east of the region – Russia. Both were less directly involved in the land wars of Europe and were able to concentrate most of their effort elsewhere. The former secured a massive extension of its colonial empire (despite the loss of much of north America) and the latter expanded first across Siberia to the Pacific and then westwards further into Europe.

19.11.1 Britain
The kingdom of England was transformed into Britain in the two decades after the 1680s when it became largely secure in its islands with the final conquest of Ireland and the union with Scotland of 1707 – both removed opportunities for other European opponents to exploit. Although primarily a maritime power Britain felt it could not allow the opposite shores of the continent (from which an invasion could be mounted) to be dominated by a single strong power. Nevertheless its military operations

on the continent were usually limited, even under Marlborough in the early eighteenth century and Wellington a hundred years later. The British believed at the time, based in part on the importance of the navy and the existence of a relatively small army, that they were different from the rest of Europe because they were not militaristic and only had a weak central state. An historical tradition grew up to confirm this view. In practice Britain after 1660 was as much a military state as the rest of Europe, the only difference was that it was expressed in a slightly different form.

In the century after 1680 the size of the navy doubled and the army increased by 50 per cent. Although the reluctance to support a standing army in peacetime remained, in war the British army was large – in the early eighteenth century it was twice the size of that of Spain. The navy was usually either the largest or one of the largest in Europe. The advantage of a strong navy was that the gains it enabled the British to make overseas reinforced its commercial position. Britain was involved in war for eighty-seven years in the period between 1692 and 1815, a record which matched that of any other European state. During this period the state developed a strong machinery to support this effort, particularly in the Admiralty with its range of dockyards but also in arms manufacture. Both had a major impact on the economy. Military spending took up about three-quarters of all government expenditure in the eighteenth century and state expenditure quadrupled in this period. Overall military expenditure was, on average, taking up about ten per cent of national wealth every year (a far greater proportion than in the twentieth century). However, much of the British effort was financial – either buying mercenaries (especially Hessians from Germany) or funding its allies to undertake the bulk of the land war on the continent while it secured the overseas spoils. By 1813 Britain was subsidizing armies of over 450,000 on the continent against Napoleon while its own army amounted to 140,000 men.

Part of the cost of war was paid for from taxation, which was as high as in any European power – between 1660 and 1815 British taxes rose eighteen-fold in real terms. Even this level of taxation was not enough to pay for the military effort. The government was spending more than it received in taxation by about £2 million a year in the 1680s but this rose to over £8 million a century later and even higher by the early nineteenth century. The government's military expenditure was funded by running up a huge debt in the developing London banking and capital market through the Bank of England which was set up by the government in 1694. The British national debt did not exist in 1689, was £16 million in the late 1690s and nearly £250 million by the 1780s. Financing this growing debt took up over half the government's revenue. The way in which this was done reinforced the power of the dominant landowning and commercial elite who, through Parliament, had a stronger say over state policy than in other European states. (About one in seven Members of Parliament were military and naval men and the system of representation also over-represented the dockyard and naval towns.) Taxes on land and commercial wealth were very light or non-existent. Instead the burden of taxation fell overwhelmingly as excise duties on products such as tea and alcohol which were mainly paid by the poor. Tax revenue was thus recycled into payments on the government debt held by the elite who therefore received the interest payments and benefited from the military and naval policies of the state which they directed. As long as the government's credit was maintained the system could continue.

19.11.2 Russia
[Earlier Moscow 19.5.1]

In the far east of Europe the conquest of the khanates of Kazan and Astrakhan by Moscow in the mid-sixteenth century opened up major new areas for settlement in the south towards the Black Sea – by the early eighteenth century a quarter of the Russian population was living in the region. Even more important it opened a route for expansion eastwards into Siberia and parts of the steppe controlled by the nomadic peoples. This was a fundamental change in the balance of Eurasian history. Ever since the early thirteenth century the peoples of the area now controlled by Moscow had been dominated by the Qipchaq Horde and its successors. From the 1550s Moscow began to expand at the expense of the nomads. It was to be a long process, not completed until the late nineteenth century when the Russians finally secured control of central Asia, but it marked the final victory of the settled communities over the nomadic peoples of Eurasia.

The main force behind the eastward drive was the search for furs. For centuries the principalities of the Rus had based their wealth on the sale of furs to western Europe – in the early fifteenth century Novgorod alone was exporting about 500,000 skins a year. However, the killing of so many animals and the gradual clearance of the forests to provide agricultural land, meant that fur animals were almost extinct west of the Urals by the sixteenth century. Fur traders crossed the Urals into Siberia on a major scale in the early 1580s and found vast numbers of animals. They pushed along the shallow Siberian rivers, building fortified stockades at the key points along the routes. They reached Tomsk in 1604, Krasnoyarsk in 1628, Yakutsk near Lake Baikal in 1652 and Okhotsk on the Pacific coast in 1647. The Russians therefore reached the Pacific coast long before they had territories on the Baltic and Black Sea coasts. The movement east-wards across Siberia was very similar to the westward movement across

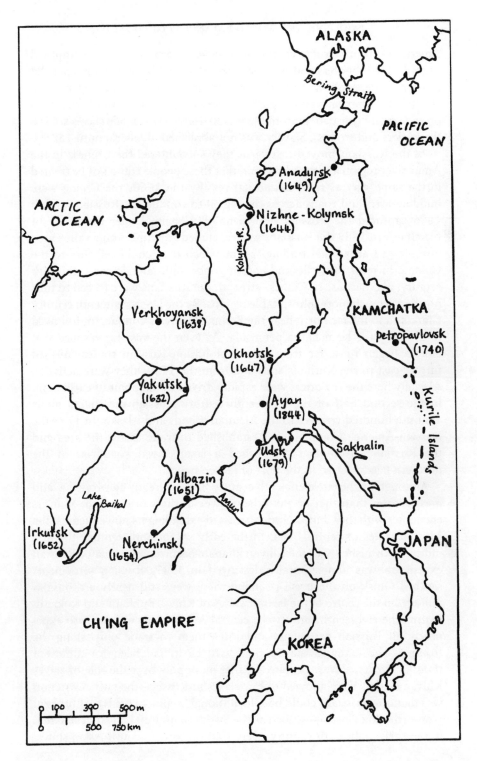

Map 61: The eastward expansion of Russia

America in the nineteenth century – both were frontier societies composed of traders, freebooters and fugitives and both were lawless. Only later did peasant settlers follow. In both areas the indigenous people felt the full effects of the expansionary push. In Siberia the tribes were forced to provide *yasak* (fur tribute from the males) and *yasyr* (female slaves sold to the settlers and troops). Slavery was not abolished in Siberia until 1825.

As the Russians moved eastwards they encountered the Chinese in the Amur river region and rapidly found that these people could not be treated in the same way as the Siberian natives. By the 1660s the Ch'ing were building forts and roads across the region to contain the Russians and in 1685 captured the Russian settlement of Albazin. Under the treaty of Nerchinsk in 1689 the Russians were excluded from the Amur valley area but allowed an annual trading fair at which they could sell furs to the Chinese in return for silk and cotton goods and, later in the eighteenth century, tea. Because of Chinese strength the Russians were forced to turn north into much more inhospitable regions. By the late seventeenth century Chukotka in the far north near the Bering Strait was conquered, followed in 1707 by the Kamchatka peninsula. As even the vast fur resources of Siberia began to suffer from over-exploitation Russian traders pushed further east to the Kurile Islands and from the 1740s they were active in Alaska where the sea otters were rapidly driven to the point of extinction. In the second half of the eighteenth century Russian merchants made almost a hundred voyages to the Aleutian islands and Alaska. In 1799 the Russian-America Company was established to trade across the area and the Russian government established a small naval squadron in the northern Pacific based at the port of Petropavlosk.

Although by the late eighteenth century Russia already controlled a land mass greater than that of any other power in the world it had, as in its encounter with the Chinese, little success in extending its power against the Muslim states of central Asia. In the early seventeenth century the first military skirmishes with the Khivan khanate occurred but a major Russian expedition was almost totally destroyed in 1717. Russian settlements reached Omsk on the Irtish river but these were still nearly a thousand miles from the centre of the Islamic states of Khiva, Bukhara and Kokand. During the eighteenth century the central Asian states were able to expel nearly all Russian merchants and force them to trade only along the frontier. The main Russian export was, as it had been for almost a thousand years, slaves. Despite a tsarist monopoly over the sale of slaves Khivan traders were allowed to buy slaves in Russia – the only restriction was that no Christians could be sold, although in practice this was broken. Non-orthodox Christians, such as the Swedes captured by Peter the Great in the early eighteenth century, were sold on to the central Asian states.

Map 62: The westward expansion of Russia

Over the course of the eighteenth century the majority of Russian diplomatic missions to Bukhara and the other capitals were solely to ransom Russian slaves.

In parallel with the great eastward expansion of Russia there was a drive to the west once Moscow had recovered from the disasters of the early seventeenth century. It was under the rule of Peter the Great (1689-1725) that the principality of Moscow was converted into the state of Russia – it was symbolized by the construction (largely accomplished by slave labourers) of the new capital of St Petersburg. The expansion was far from straightforward. In the 1690s Denmark, Poland and Russia agreed to combine against the dominant Baltic power, Sweden. The latter (with tacit English and Dutch naval support) was quickly victorious – Denmark left the coalition in 1700, Russia was defeated at the battle of Narva and the Swedes overran Poland and Saxony. The triumph was only short-lived and the Russians inflicted an almost total defeat on the Swedes at the battle of Poltava in 1709. When peace was finally agreed in 1721 Sweden lost the whole of its Baltic empire and Russia gained eastern Karelia, Estonia and Livonia, thereby establishing itself as a major Baltic power. The main thrust of Russian westward expansion was, however, against Poland. In 1697, with strong Russian support, August II of Saxony was chosen as King of Poland. After the defeat by the Swedes he was put back on the throne by the Russians and thereafter Poland remained what the Russians wanted – a weak power on their western border. The Polish army was limited in size to 20,000 men and the power of the elite in the Sejm ensured that few effective decisions were taken (it was at this time that the use of the notorious single vote veto was extensive but it was a symptom rather than a cause of the decline).

In 1734 August III of Saxony was placed on the Polish throne, again largely under Russian influence. However, he spent just two years out of the next thirty in the country. Nevertheless, despite its weakness Poland continued to survive and stayed out of the European wars. In 1770 it was still a larger state than either Spain or France, though far less powerful than the latter. Strategically its position was very weak since it had to face the rapidly growing power of Prussia, Russia and Habsburg Austria. In 1772 the three major powers agreed on a first partition – Poland lost a third of its territory including Minsk and eastern Belorussia to the Russians. The threat of internal reforms in Poland, which might lead to the creation of a more effective state, resulted in a Russian invasion in 1792 and a second partition involving Prussia as well. Russia gained most of Lithuania. Rebellions led by Tadeusz Kosciuszko were put down. In 1795 the third and final partition of Poland took place. Russia gained almost two-thirds of the rump of Poland (including Volhynia) and Prussia gained about a fifth which was enough to almost double its population. The long-established Polish state, once one of the most powerful in Europe, had ceased to exist. The westward expansion of Russia had reached a new peak but was to continue until 1815.

[*Later Russian expansion 21.11*]

19.12 The European War 1792–1815

Despite the long and almost continual wars across the European continent between 1660 and 1815 things changed surprisingly little. States might make temporary gains (as France did under Napoleon) or suffer serious setbacks (as Prussia did at the height of the Seven Years War) but in 1815 France was in roughly the same position as in the late seventeenth century, Austria remained strong and Prussia gained but not as much as the two peripheral powers of Britain and Russia.

The nearest approach to a decisive outcome to the European struggles came with the longest of all wars which continued (with one minor break) from 1792 until 1815. The near bankruptcy of the French state in the late 1780s, mainly caused by the expense of the war for American independence, led to the summoning of the Estates-General for the first time in over 150 years. Within a couple of years France was embroiled in a revolution which seemed, at first glance, to weaken its power significantly. It was partly the increasing radicalism of the revolution which led to the outbreak of war in 1792. The coalition against France (Prussia, Austria, Russia and Britain) produced the most one-sided of all the eighteenth-century wars. However, France was not defeated. Instead it emerged victorious through its own internal strength and the divisions within the coalition. The French carried out a major mobilization to produce an army of over 650,000 men which, using the reforms instituted in the 1780s, proved to be highly effective. After repelling the initial coalition assault it embarked on a policy of expansion which had little to do with the aims of the revolution and much more to do with older French strategic aspirations. The three powers in eastern Europe were too involved in the final partition of Poland to mount any effective opposition. By 1795 Flanders and the Dutch republic were conquered, Prussia and the other small German states reverted to neutrality and Spain changed sides to support the French. In 1796 Sardinia-Piedmont was crushed by the rising commander Napoleon Bonaparte and at the peace of Campo Formio in 1797 the Austrians were largely driven out of Italy. That left Britain isolated, facing the high cost of the war and the naval mutinies at Spithead and the Nore in 1797. The British could still defeat the Spanish and Dutch fleets and make colonial gains but it could not break the French on land. The strategic stalemate which characterized much of the war until 1815 had arrived.

French setbacks in 1798 (the failure of the expedition to Ireland and the defeat of the Egyptian expedition at the naval battle of Aboukir Bay) tempted Russia, Austria, the Ottomans, Portugal and Naples into a new coalition against France. In two years it achieved nothing. Britain fought on but with little success. The peace of Amiens in 1802 was no more than a breathing space and the war resumed in the next year when the British refused to hand over Malta. France was now dominated by Napoleon as an effective dictator. He had himself crowned emperor in 1805, bringing about the formal end of the 'Holy Roman Empire' created in tenth-century Germany. The career of Napoleon was, in many ways, remarkably similar to that of other pre-industrial conquerors in Eurasia over the previous four thousand years. A policy of military expansion was paid for by the loot of conquest. As long as that expansion continued the system was successful. He found it difficult to establish any effective basis for his rule (which was difficult anyway because of the poor communications) and like similar rulers relied on family members and his main military supporters to govern the empire on his behalf. However, there were significant 'modern' elements in his rule because he could rely on the much greater power of the European state by the late eighteenth century resulting from the impact of the military revolution and growing commercial and industrial wealth.

The European war was continuous from 1803. Britain could maintain naval supremacy, confirmed by the battle of Trafalgar in 1805, but could not defeat Napoleon on land where within two years he dominated Europe. In 1805 the Austrians and Russians suffered a major defeat at the battles of Ulm and Austerlitz and Prussia was totally defeated at the battle of Jena in 1806. The next year the Russians were weakened enough after the battle of Friedland to accept a deal that left Napoleon and France as the overwhelmingly dominant European power. In south and west Germany the Confederation of the Rhine was dominated by France and all of western Poland was in the French-controlled Grand Duchy of Warsaw. After 1806 Prussia had to pay an indemnity equivalent to half the normal tax revenue of the French government. Austria too had to pay an indemnity and half of the revenue from the kingdom of Italy went to France. All the European land powers were part of the highly successful system under which British trade was excluded from the continent by the Berlin and Milan decrees of 1806–7.

The apogee of French power passed with the growing revolt in Spain after 1809 – over 350,000 French troops could not suppress it and it provided the opportunity for small British forces to intervene on the

Map 63: Europe at the height of Napoleon's power 1810

continent. Russia withdrew from the French economic system in 1810 and the French invasion of Russia in 1812 produced, after startling initial success, a disaster as the army was forced to retreat after burning Moscow. Over 400,000 troops were lost. This tempted the other European powers to take British subsidies to join the war. Nevertheless until his major defeat at the battle of Leipzig in October 1813 it seemed possible that Napoleon could defeat one of the three powers (Russia, Austria and Prussia) separately and break the coalition against him. Instead he was forced to retreat into France and abdicate in April 1814. Within a year he escaped from Elba and seized power in France. He was finally defeated by the British and Prussian armies at Waterloo in June 1815.

The Vienna settlement which ended the war produced a relatively stable system in Europe which no power could dominate. France was surrounded by a kingdom of the United Netherlands (modern Belgium and the Netherlands) in the north-east and a greatly expanded Sardinia-Piedmont in the south-east. Prussia gained significantly and although its territories were concentrated in the east it now had scattered possessions as far west as the Rhine. However, it did not gain Saxony because of Austrian objections. Russia continued to hold most of Poland – Austria was compensated by being given much of northern Italy. Outside Europe there was no balance of power – Britain was overwhelmingly predominant. Apart from the creation of an independent Belgium in 1830 the settlement constructed at Vienna lasted for about fifty years until the creation of an Italian kingdom and the unification of Germany under Prussia.

19.13 The Mughal Empire

[*Earlier India 18.5*]

19.13.1 The empire at its height

The Mughal empire was largely the creation of Akbar in the late sixteenth century. In 1600 it was one of the most powerful states in the world. Under Jahangir (1606–27) the empire was stable (the revolt by his heir Khurram was put down in 1622) and the frontiers were secure. Expansion southwards into the Deccan continued. Under his successor Shah Jahan (1628–58) the empire was probably at its peak and was little affected by the seventeenth-century crisis that was so damaging in the rest of Eurasia. In the north an attempt to expand beyond Afghanistan into central Asia was a failure – the lines of communication were simply too long to mount an effective campaign, and in the north-west the Safavids were a major barrier to expansion. The only major gain in the region was the defeat of

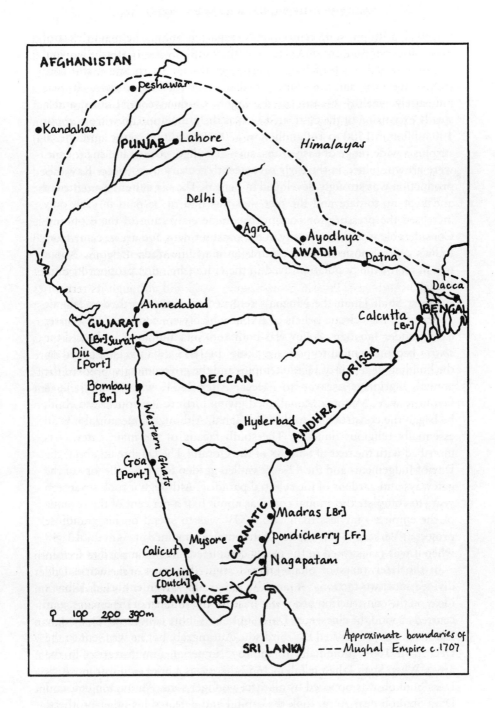

Map 64: The later Mughal empire

Garhwal, a Rajput state centred on Srinagar, in 1656. The main thrust of expansion therefore continued to be in the south. By the 1650s the Mughal empire covered much of India apart from the far south and it still controlled the original homeland of the Mughals, Afghanistan. It was immensely wealthy because of the highly productive agriculture and a steady expansion of the cultivated area as the population grew from about 100 million in 1500 to 160 million in 1700. In addition to the agricultural surplus a wide range of cash crops, such as indigo, cotton and sugar cane, were grown, joined in the early seventeenth century by tobacco. Raw-silk production was strongly developed in Bengal. The tax system was efficient and kept up-to-date and the fact that this had to be paid in cash only increased the pressure for continued commercialization of the economy. Considerable wealth, especially in the coastal towns and areas, came from India's central position on the Eurasian maritime trade network. About one in ten of the population lived in the cities (the same proportion as in Europe).

Under Shah Jahan the Mughals returned to a more orthodox Islamic policy after the eclectic beliefs of Akbar which were continued to a lesser extent under Jahangir. Policy was both anti-Shia and anti-Hindu and the *sharia* became central to policy making. In 1633 a ban was imposed on the building or repair of Hindu temples and the government sponsored the annual pilgrimage caravan to Mecca. After 1631, when Shah Jahan's favourite wife, Mumtaz Mahal, died giving birth to her fourteenth child, he began the construction of the Taj Mahal. Although a memorial it is an essentially religious building. The south façade of the main gateway is inscribed with the text of Sura 89 of the Quran ('The Daybreak' about the Day of Judgement) and the 42-acre walled garden forms an allegory of the gateways and gardens of the celestial paradise. Although it took seventeen years to complete the annual cost was about half a per cent of the revenue of the empire – far less than Louis XIV was to spend on his grandiose project at Versailles. The capital of the empire remained at Agra until 1648 when it was transferred to the newly completed Shahjahanabad at Delhi.

In the later years of Shah Jahan's reign the court was increasingly divided into two factions. A more liberal group, which endorsed Akbar's ideas on the construction of a wider base for the support of the empire, was centred around the eldest son, Dara Shukoh. A more conservative, strongly Islamic group, supported the third son, Aurangzeb, but he was sent to the Deccan in 1644 (nominally to improve imperial administration in the area). When Shah Jahan fell ill in 1657 there was a brief civil war in which Dara Shukoh was opposed by all three younger sons. Aurangzeb defeated Dara Shukoh near Agra, took the capital and defeated his other brothers. By 1661, after Dara Shukoh was killed, Aurangzeb was in undisputed control of the empire. Under his rule the empire had a strongly pro-Islamic policy. A number of Hindu temples, especially at Varanasi, were pulled down and taxes imposed on pilgrims to Hindu temples and shrines. In 1665 Hindu traders had to pay twice as much in internal customs duties than Muslim merchants (although tax rates were still very low). The graduated property tax (the *jiziya*), which had been abolished by Akbar exactly a century earlier, was reimposed in 1679. In theory all Hindus were dismissed from government office but this decree was not carried out. The new Sikh religion was attacked and its leader executed for blasphemy.

The first signs of growing problems within the empire came in the late seventeenth century although at this time they were easily suppressed and the Mughal empire reached its greatest territorial extent. In the hilly areas of the western Deccan south of Bombay, the Maratha state was emerging under its founder Shivaji who in 1674 was crowned as an independent Hindu monarch. The Marathas were to be central to Indian history for the next 150 years. On Shivaji's death in 1680 the Marathas were joined in a general anti-Mughal revolt by the Rajput nobles in Rajasthan and by Aurangzeb's son Akbar. This forced Aurangzeb to shift the focus of the empire to the south away from the rich Ganges plain and concentrate on controlling the difficult country of the Deccan. The two autonomous states in the area, Bijapur and Golconda were conquered in 1686–7 and fully incorporated into the empire. Akbar escaped to the old enemy of the Mughals, the Safavids, but in 1688 the Maratha ruler was captured. In total four new provinces were added to the empire which reached its greatest ever extent – only the very far south of India remained outside its control. However, these conquests did not bring stability and Aurangzeb was forced to stay in the Deccan through the 1690s, attempting to suppress the Marathas in the south-western coastal areas. This long campaign and war of attrition wore down the Mughal army and also meant that less attention was paid to the rest of the empire – there was a major revolt in Bengal in 1696–7.

19.13.2 The collapse of the empire

When Aurangzeb died in 1707 the Mughal empire was still a strong state but over the next fifty years it broke down. The immediate cause was Aurangzeb's decision to divide the empire between his three sons. The predictable civil war rapidly ensued followed by a Sikh revolt and a revival of the Marathas. In 1712 the death of the victor in the civil war, Bahadur Shah, produced another internal conflict leading to a palace coup in 1713 when a large part of the ruling family and their elite associates were killed. In 1719 palace officials deposed, blinded and then killed the emperor Farrukhsiyar and chose a new prince as a puppet ruler. In 1739 Delhi was sacked by Nadir Shah Afshar, the Chaghatai leader who had already deposed the last of the Safavid rulers in Iran. There were further invasions of northern India from Afghanistan in 1747 and 1759-61.

The breakdown of Mughal rule did not affect the economic and social base in India. It was followed by the emergence of a new political system with relatively strong regional states as local landlords and rulers (increasingly wealthy from the stability the Mughals had produced) detached themselves from central rule and created their own states based on the revenues which had originally been passed to the central government. There was no attempt to remove the emperor and no other ruler tried to claim the title (even the British maintained the nominal imperial system until 1858). Across India new regional powers emerged. One of the first was the Hindu Marathas whose independence was recognized by the Mughals in 1718. As they gradually extended their area of control they seemed on the verge of reuniting India by the late 1750s. However, they were defeated by the Afghans under Ahmed Shah Abdali at the battle of Panipat in 1761. Nevertheless in 1784 the Mughal emperor submitted to the 'protection' of the main Maratha leader, Mahadji Scindia, who became the 'Regent Plenipotentiary' of the empire. In Awadh new Shiite rulers, opposed to the strongly Sunni Mughals, took control. In southern Mysore under Haidar Ali (1761-82) and Tipu Sultan (1782-99) effective local rulers carved out their own kingdoms as did local rulers in Hyderabad and Bengal. By the 1790s the Sikhs in Punjab and the Talpur Emirs in Sind had also established their own areas of rule.

The breakdown of Mughal rule created a situation of fundamental long-term significance in world history. By the 1750s the British, who had defeated the French to become the main European power in India, were able to exploit the situation to create their own areas of rule and slowly build an Indian empire of their own. This process would have been far more difficult, perhaps impossible, without the prior decline in central Mughal power. Until the 1750s none of the European powers had been able to do more than create a few trading posts and forts around the coast of India and their armies were small and ineffective. Now, exploiting the internal divisions of India, the British were able in the course of the next hundred years to dominate India and use it as a base to expand further in Asia.

[*Later India 21.3*]

19.14 The World Balance *c.*1750

During the two and half centuries since Columbus the world balance had changed very little. The Europeans had easily conquered the Aztec and Inca empires and established their control over central and south America. In north America the small European colonies were still confined to the eastern seaboard and had still not crossed the Appalachians on any scale. The European impact on the Ottomans (apart from the small Habsburg recovery in the late seventeenth century) was minimal – all of the southern and eastern shores of the Mediterranean were still under Islamic control. The end of Safavid rule in Iran did not affect Europe and in India their settlements were still confined to a few coastal cities. The European impression on China, the largest and most powerful state in the world, and on Japan was even smaller. In south-east Asia the Dutch controlled some of the islands. Nowhere had European armies fought any of the great Eurasian states (the Ottomans, the Mughals and China) outside Europe – their only victories had been against the indigenous peoples of the Americas. In Africa, apart from the small colony at the Cape, the Europeans were confined to a handful of trading posts and forts. Australia, New Zealand and the rest of the Pacific had still not been settled by Europeans. What had changed between 1500 and 1750 was that the wealth of Europe had increased significantly. This was based largely on the profits made from the exploitation of the Americas, the vast slave plantations of the Atlantic economy and the opportunity this gave for the Europeans to participate in the great Asian trading systems. By the mid-eighteenth century the long economic backwardness of Europe was over and it was, for the first time, as wealthy as the longer-established Eurasian societies of India and China. The foundations had been laid for the most fundamental economic, social and political changes in Eurasian history.

PART SIX

The Creation of the Modern World
(1750–2000)

The Origins of the Modern Economy and Society
(*c.*1750–*c.*1900)

20.1 The Transformation

Until the mid-eighteenth century every economy and society in the world was overwhelmingly agricultural with small commercial, industrial and service sectors. Overall, about nine out of ten of the population were dependent on agriculture, a proportion which had changed little over the previous several millennia. During the two hundred and fifty years after 1750 the world changed radically. Farming became far more productive to the extent that in the main industrialized countries less than one in twenty (in some cases only one in fifty) of the population were employed in agriculture. This massive reduction in the number of farmers occurred in parallel with an unprecedented increase in the world's population – it grew over six-fold between 1750 and 2000. The variety and volume of industrial production increased even more – world industrial output by the last part of the twentieth century was, every year, about ninety times greater than in 1750. In parallel, the consumption of raw materials increased and there was a fundamental transformation in the amount of energy available to societies. The consequence of these changes was that the levels of pollution caused by industrial production and energy consumption also grew dramatically. These economic changes also produced profound social changes. By the early twentieth century about three-quarters of the population in the most industrialized societies lived in cities compared with about 10 per cent only a century earlier. By the end of the twentieth century, for the first time in world history, the majority of the world's population lived in cities. More people were employed not just in industry but also in the service sector. This applied not just to banking, trade and commerce but also to government bureaucracies, education and health care. People became better educated and by the end of the twentieth century, for the first time, a majority of the world's population was literate.

Although these changes began in Europe, in particular Britain, their significance was global. At first this was reflected in the demand for raw materials (such as American cotton and Chilean copper) and more food (from Latin America and Australasia), but industrialization spread rapidly. This process was no different from the earlier spread of ideas and technologies across Eurasia, especially from China westwards. All that was different now was that the speed of change was much greater because communication was much easier. Early industrialization was noticeable in the United States and Japan by the mid-nineteenth century. The United States made dramatic progress in the second half of the nineteenth century because of its large internal market and extensive resource base. Developments in Japan were slower but very significant by the second half of the twentieth century. By that time numerous other societies across the globe were industrializing.

The pace of change was very slow at first. Between 1750 and 1850 world industrial output did not even double and slow growth was characteristic of Britain, the leading (and, for a time, sole) industrial power. Between 1860 and 1913 the rate of change increased dramatically with world industrial output quadrupling as powers such as the United States and Germany industrialized rapidly. In the twentieth century world industrial output rose about thirty-five fold with most of the increase concentrated in the period after 1950. By the 1990s the world economy was growing at such a rate that every two years it added output equivalent to the *total* world output in 1900.

20.2 The Problem

How did the world's economies and societies escape from the predominance of the agricultural base that had characterized world history for about ten thousand years? The earliest farmers could produce a small farming surplus which was taken from them to support a small group of non-producers – priests, warriors, rulers, bureaucrats and a few craftsmen who not only made products for the elite but also exchanged or sold a few of their products to the farmers. The number of non-producers who could be supported was largely determined by the productivity of farming (more might be forcibly taken from the farmers in the short term but this could not be a long-term solution). The productivity of agriculture increased very slowly through a series of small changes – more sophisticated irrigation, better tools made out of iron, improved ploughs, the breeding of more productive varieties of crops, better crop rotations and the diffusion of new crops at first within Eurasia (as for example within the Islamic empire soon after its creation) and then from the Americas to Eurasia from the sixteenth century onwards. Population rose and new areas were brought into cultivation but they were often less productive than the main agricultural areas. As a result the overall agricultural surplus might go up slightly but without a fundamental change in techniques. The problem was that the cultivation of more marginal areas tended to increase vulnerability to climatic changes, crop diseases and bad harvests. At times, for example in Europe in about 1300, the population rose to a level which was seriously out-of-line with the ability of the agricultural base to support these numbers, resulting in large-scale famine.

A rising population increased the market for the goods made by craftsmen but the mass of peasant producers never had enough disposable income to create a major market for goods. The elite, though relatively rich, were too small to be a significant market except for a few luxury items. Trade was however crucial in generating extra wealth. Very slowly, with many ups and downs, the quantity and variety of goods traded increased, as did the distances over which trade was possible. This very slowly increased the wealth of societies. In parallel the accumulation of technological changes over many centuries – new energy sources such as water and wind power and the invention of new products such as cast iron, silk and paper created new markets and new possibilities. Most important of all, the diffusion of ideas and technologies across Eurasia meant that each society did not have to discover every process for itself and so change became cumulative and its pace accelerated.

Escape from these constraints and the development of an increasingly industrial economy required a number of factors to come together and interact in the right way. Technology – the creation of new processes and products – was of central importance. But it needed the prior accumulation of wealth to provide the capital with which to develop the new machines and techniques and to create a market where their products could be sold. The new products needed a labour force to make them in circumstances where most people were already needed in farming to provide enough food. Increasing agricultural productivity was therefore essential but only if societies avoided the trap where a rising population consumed the extra agricultural surplus without leaving enough to sustain a growing industrial workforce. More people living in poverty would not provide a market for new products – that required increasing wealth and disposable income. Given the need for the gradual accumulation of a number of new techniques and the difficulty of finding the right balance, over a long period of time, between all the complex factors involved, it is perhaps hardly surprising that all Eurasian societies found that a fundamental shift away from a predominantly agricultural society was very difficult to achieve.

It is clear that China under the Sung in the eleventh and twelfth centuries came very close to achieving this breakthrough. It had a highly productive agriculture, a commercialized economy, a number of key technological advances were made and industrial production was rising rapidly. Ultimately the transition was not made because of the invasion of the north by the Jürchen followed by the conquest of the whole country by the

Mongols in the thirteenth century. Why were Britain and then western Europe able to make that transition between the mid-eighteenth and mid-nineteenth centuries? In the past it was often argued that the changes were the result of a unique European questing and dynamic spirit perhaps, as Max Weber argued early in the twentieth century, deriving from a supposed Protestant ethic of hard work, enterprise and self-improvement. Explanations favoured in the second half of the twentieth century have tended to be built around institutional factors and ideas about free market economies, limited government, sanctity of contract, the free accumulation of wealth and social stability through the development of a complex civil society. All of these arguments are still based on a supposed European exceptionalism that ignores the experience of the rest of Eurasia. The societies and economies elsewhere across the continent were equally enterprising, dedicated to the accumulation of wealth and technologically dynamic. China had a free peasantry deeply embedded in a highly commercial economy at least 1,500 years before Europe, with sanctity of contract, technological innovation and the accumulation of wealth on a massive scale. As we have seen China and India were wealthier than Europe until at least the middle of the eighteenth century and levels of industrial output per head were as high if not higher. A more convincing explanation of the ultimate success of first Britain and then western Europe lies in the way they were able to exploit their unique position in the world to overcome the constraints inherent in pre-industrial economies and societies.

20.3 Europe: Food and People

[*Contemporaneous China 19.7.2*]
In many respects the eighteenth century was an unpropitious time for a fundamental economic advance. Everywhere across the world the population was rising rapidly. In China it more than doubled from 160 million to 330 million. Growth in Europe was slower with a fifty per cent rise from 120 million to 180 million, although some areas grew much faster – the population of Russia more than doubled. Early in the nineteenth century the world's population passed the one billion mark. The reasons for this rapid growth are far from clear – there were no significant medical improvements and the most likely explanation is the long internal peace in China combined with the worldwide impact of the more productive crops diffused from the Americas. Similar spurts of growth had occurred in the past (though not on this scale) and they had resulted in growing impoverishment, excess labour in the countryside and eventually an overall shortage of food – not the circumstances in which escape from pre-industrial constraints seemed likely.

In the past it used to be argued that it was European agriculture, particularly that in Britain, which laid the foundations for growing industrialization. This, it was believed, was achieved through improvements in productivity over the century or so before 1750. This was combined with the forcible release of surplus labour in the countryside, following the enclosure of land by the landlords, so as to create a labour force for an expanding industrial base. The growing prosperity in the countryside provided a market for the goods made in the developing industrial sector producing a virtuous circle of growth and increasing wealth. It is now clear that this explanation is much too simplistic and only partially correct. In the century before 1750 there is little doubt that English agriculture became more commercial (in the same way as that of the Netherlands slightly earlier) so as to be one of the most productive in Europe. Output grew about twice as fast as population through a succession of cumulative small-scale improvements – the adoption of new crops, the use of better rotations and new machinery. Most of the changes came from small farmers, not the 'improving landlords' such as 'Turnip' Townshend and Jethro Tull who claimed the credit. The major contribution of the landlords was enclosure – the seizure of over seven million acres of communal land and its conversion into private property as the number of large estates grew – by the 1790s over a quarter of all the land in England was held in estates of over 3,000 acres. Many landlords did adopt new techniques although the productivity of the remaining 'open-field' areas also increased rapidly as they adapted to increasing commercial pressures. The problem was that landlords generally only ploughed back about a tenth of their farm revenues into improvements, the rest was spent on their own prestige consumption. The impact of all these changes should not be exaggerated – in 1800 English wheat yields were still about the same as those in the rest of north-west Europe and in 1750 yields in East Anglia were no different from those achieved some five hundred years earlier.

Although important developments took place before 1750 the contribution of English agriculture during the crucial period of early industrialization in the century after 1750 was poor and it may even have been a negative factor. Between 1760 and 1800 agricultural output rose at half the rate of population growth, suggesting that the economy would eventually be caught in the same trap that had affected pre-industrial economies in the past. English agriculture was unable to cope with the doubling of the population in the first half of the nineteenth century. The effects of the failure of agricultural output to keep pace with population growth were quickly apparent as in the late eighteenth century food prices rose and reduced the amount people had to spend on other goods. In the agricultural areas (where the mass of the population lived) rising numbers caused real wages to fall, further reducing demand for industrial products. Despite extra profits and wealth for the landlords from rising prices they did not generally invest in industry, preferring to spend the money on immediate consumption. In fact there may even have been a net inflow of capital into agriculture as wealthy merchants bought up landed estates in order to achieve social respectability. The number of agricultural workers in England continued to rise until after 1850 (although it fell in relative terms) and there was little movement of agricultural workers into industry. The mobility of labour across the country was low, industry developed in locations far from the main areas of commercial agriculture and farm workers lacked the skills needed in industry and usually preferred to live in the countryside. The result of the rapid rise in the rural population was therefore growing impoverishment and the creation of a mass of paupers – by the 1830s the average rural worker in Britain was as poor as they had been for several centuries.

How then did the English economy escape from the trap of not having enough food to support the rising population, let alone an increasing proportion of the workforce engaged in industrial production? It did so by importing food from its nearest colony – Ireland. The final establishment of English political control over the island of Ireland in the late seventeenth century led to the creation of a series of large estates owned by largely absentee English landlords. The Irish population grew rapidly in the eighteenth century as the impoverished peasantry came to rely on the highly productive potato as their main (and often only) crop – other food was exported to England. By the end of the eighteenth century Ireland was supplying about half of Britain's imports of grain, butter and meat. Even more important this amounted to a sixth of total consumption and provided the crucial supplement to the failure of English agriculture to meet the demands of the rising population. The phenomenal rise in the British population in the early nineteenth century and the beginnings of substantial industrialization could not have been sustained without imports of food from Ireland. By the 1830s imports from Ireland had more than quintupled, supplying four-fifths of British food imports. In total between 1815 and 1846 Britain imported food worth about a third of its agricultural output – it was enough to sustain industrial development until sources of food from outside Europe became available.

Elsewhere in Europe the situation was worse. In France the population rose by about six million between 1720 and 1790 yet there is no evidence of any increase in domestic grain production and productivity levels were lower than in England. During the eighteenth century grain prices rose faster than wages and about 40 per cent of the population (as many as 70 per cent in some regions) were living in conditions of long-term malnutrition because they ate less than 1,800 calories a day and most of that came from poor-quality grains. Conditions were as bad as during the great boom in European population around 1300. Not until after 1825 did the average amount of food eaten per person in France reach the levels found in India in the late twentieth century. The European countryside was still dominated by large estates – in 1800 half of all the land was still owned by the church, the nobility and urban corporations. The sale of church land during the French revolution (as with the sale of ex-monastic land in England in the 1540s) only benefited substantial landowners or very wealthy tenants because it was sold to the highest bidder. In some areas the situation was even worse – in southern Spain at the end of the eighteenth century three-quarters of the population was made up of landless labourers and their families.

By 1800 it was only in Britain, France, the Low Countries, the Alps and west and central Germany that landlords lived on peasant rents rather than by directly exploiting the peasants through different forms of serfdom. The remains of serfdom were abolished in France in 1793 and by French-occupying armies in Savoy (1792), Naples (1806) and Spain (1808). Serfdom was largely abolished in Prussia between 1806 and 1811 (although not fully until 1848) but in such a way that the peasants hardly benefited. Hereditary servitude and labour services disappeared but the jurisdiction and police powers of the landlords were retained and the peasants had to compensate their landlords by surrendering some of their land. In 1816 conditions were made tougher so that only those few peasants who owned their own plough team could emancipate themselves. On the whole, the large estates remained, the peasants had no alternative but to work on them and the number of landless labourers rose. They did so substantially in the Baltic provinces after 1816 because the serfs were emancipated but received no land. Elsewhere, especially in Austria and the Danubian area, the work expected of the serfs was increasing in the nineteenth century. Serfdom was not abolished in Austria until 1848, in Hungary five years later and in Russia in 1861. The last European country to abolish serfdom was Romania in 1864.

20.4 Technology

[Earlier technology 12.3–12.4]
During the period between the mid-eighteenth century and the late nineteenth century there were two waves of technological advance which began to transform the British economy and then those of western Europe and the United States. The first wave lasted until about 1830 and was

characterized by the greater mechanization of textile production, increases in iron production and the slow development of the steam engine. However, no single invention could transform the whole of an economy and the pace of change within the British economy and the rate of growth was very slow until the decades after 1850. The new textile machines had a very limited application – it was developments in the iron and steel industry that were the most important. In the early eighteenth century coke was used to smelt iron, something the Chinese had been doing for almost a thousand years. However, it was not until 1784, when Henry Cort developed the puddling and rolling process to refine pig iron into bar iron in a reverberatory furnace fired by coal, that significant increases in output were possible. Equally important was the slow development of the steam engine from the first basic use of pistons and valve gear by the Chinese to the steam pump developed by Thomas Newcomen in 1712 to raise water from deep mine shafts. It had only a limited range of applications and was no more than one per cent fuel efficient. That was improved by James Watt in the late eighteenth century when he separated the condenser from the piston cylinder so that the latter could be kept hot, and improved the gearing to produce a double-acting engine. Most of these engines were also used in mines and were still less than five per cent fuel efficient. It was not until Watt's patent expired in 1800 that Richard Trevithick was able to develop a smaller, more efficient engine working at a pressure of ten atmospheres. Nevertheless until the mid-nineteenth century steam engines remained no more efficient than water power.

The one area where steam engines did make an impact was in the development of railways. Until the late 1820s these were largely horse-drawn and confined to mines and other industrial enterprises. The major problem was to develop iron rails capable of taking the weight of a steam locomotive and its loads. Once this had been done railways developed rapidly and provided a boost to economic growth through the demand they created for resources and the goods and people they could move. Although iron rails were vital for the development of railways major changes in production processes and the extensive use of steel did not occur until the mid-nineteenth century. In 1857 Henry Bessemer patented his production method in which steel was refined by blowing air through the molten ore making large-scale production and the regulation of the chemical content of the steel possible. This process had been used outside Europe for centuries but not on a large industrial scale. The Siemens-Martin process of open-hearth production was developed primarily on the European continent using the rich phosphorous iron ores available there. Steam power was applied even earlier to shipping. One of the first steam-driven vessels was Robert Fulton's *Clermont* on the Hudson river in New

York in 1807, followed by Henry Bell's *Comet* on the Clyde in 1811. Within a decade they were found across Europe – steamboats crossed the English Channel in 1821 and were in use on the Rhine in 1824 and on the Danube between Vienna and Pest in 1831. In the 1830s engines developing 320 horsepower were produced and steam-driven paddle-wheelers (though with sails) were crossing the Atlantic in fourteen days by 1839. By the 1840s propellers and iron-hulled ships were in use, followed in the late 1850s by 1,600-horsepower engines on Brunel's giant 680-feet-long *Great Eastern.*

None of these industrial advances relied on developments in European scientific knowledge. They were made by engineers, workers and crafts-men who were skilled in particular trades and who used their knowledge to develop new techniques and make improvements in order to solve practical problems. The first new technology which did rely on science was that of electricity and magnetism. In 1821 Michael Faraday developed the first electric motor and a decade later the dynamo. However, it was several decades before this new technology could be applied on a major scale following a series of inventions in generating and distributing systems together with those to produce lighting, heating and power from electri-city. Its main use before the late nineteenth century was in communications with the development of the telegraph and the first submarine cable (laid between Britain and France in 1851). It was not until 1875 that the first large-scale lighting application was made at the Gare du Nord in Paris and not until 1884 that the first electric trams were running in Glasgow and Frankfurt. The full potential of electricity did not begin to be applied until the twentieth century.

[*Later technology 20.10, 21.2 & 23.3*]

20.5 Energy

Even more fundamental than these technological changes from the mid-eighteenth century was the radical transformation in the amount of energy available to societies and the sources from which it came. Until the eighteenth century all the societies of the world had suffered from an acute energy shortage. Nearly all of the energy that was available came from human and animal power and even the latter was severely restricted by harnessing problems. For thousands of years it was vast amounts of human toil and effort, with its cost in terms of early death, injury and suffering, that were the foundation of every society. The power of the rulers and the elite was demonstrated by their ability to mobilize this effort for their own ends whether in monumental constructions or working on their agricultural estates. Humans ate less food than animals and until the nineteenth century provided the main energy input into farming through clearing land, building terraces and irrigation systems, sowing, weeding and digging. As late as 1806 one French agricultural writer could still advocate abandoning the plough and returning to digging fields by hand which although slower, was cheaper and more thorough. Humans also provided the power in industry – the Great Crane in the market place at Bruges, regarded as the technological marvel of the fifteenth century, was powered by a human treadmill. In the nineteenth century prisons in Britain operated a treadmill which could be hired by local industrialists. Everywhere people acted as porters for goods and also to transport other people (usually from the elite) in palanquins carried by four or six people (common in Asia), the sedan chair carried by two people (common in Europe) and the rickshaw. The main constraint on using animal power, apart from harnessing problems, was the amount of feed they required – a horse needed about four or five acres of land and because of the limited productivity of agriculture it was often difficult to give up this much land when humans hardly had enough to eat. Oxen needed slightly less land and they remained the main draught animal – in eighteenth century Europe there were about 24 million oxen compared with little more than half that number of horses. Horses were also important in industry as sources of power (hence the use of the term 'horsepower' to measure power generation) and were used extensively in mining, brewing and to power some of the earliest textile machines.

Water power developed in Eurasia around the BCE/CE divide. Its use grew slowly and was followed, about a thousand years later, by wind power. Water power provided the major source of industrial power for centuries and continued to do so until well into the nineteenth century. Textile industries and many of the early factories were located along rivers as the use of water power expanded – in the United States until the 1880s steam power was usually only used where it was essential to locate an industry away from a river. The scale of operations possible with water power can be judged from the Mastodon Mill on the Mohawk river which took water in 102-inch diameter pipes to turbines that generated 1,200 horsepower and drove two miles of shafting, turning ten miles of belts, 70,000 spindles and 1,500 looms, producing 60,000 yards of cotton a day. As late as 1900 Nuremberg still had 180 operational water-mills. In areas where water power was not available wind power could be developed on a major scale – in the sixteenth century the Netherlands had over 8,000 windmills to power saws, dress leather, roll copper plates, throw silk and for fulling cloth.

The main source of fuel for all societies until the nineteenth century was wood. It was easily available (often free) and burned well when dried – the problem was that it was also needed for a wide variety of other uses such as houses, fortifications, bridge construction, industrial machinery and containers and in shipbuilding. In the form of charcoal it was the primary fuel for industries such as iron smelting, brewing, glass making and brick production. Forests were also cleared to create agricultural land from the time of the very first farming settlements in south-west Asia. The wide variety of uses for wood meant that slowly over the centuries timber became scarcer and in China it was a constraint on industrialization as early as the twelfth century. In Europe the major clearance of the forests began with the great expansion of settlement as population rose after 1000 CE. As industry developed it began to consume prodigious quantities of wood. An average small iron furnace used up about 250 acres of woodland every year but other processes were even more destructive. In the mid-seventeenth century Russian potash production was using up a total of three million tons of wood a year and in the Kama region, where there were over 1,200 salt works, all the local forests had been felled and wood had to be transported from over 200 miles away to fuel the boilers.

A timber shortage was first noticed in Europe in specialized areas such as shipbuilding. In the early sixteenth century Venice ran out of timber with which to make ships and had to import wood and often finished hulls from its colonies along the Dalmatian coast. Portugal too was short of wood and relied on ships made from Brazilian and Indian hardwoods which were constructed in Bahia and Goa. In the 1580s when Philip II of Spain built the armada to sail against England and the Dutch he had to import timber from Poland. In England itself shortages were first noticed in the mid-seventeenth century and reliance had to be placed on imports from Scandinavia and the Baltic region (in 1756 Britain bought the right to export 600,000 trees a year from Russia) and the American colonies of New Hampshire and then Maine. As early as 1696 warships for the Royal Navy were built in New Hampshire because of the shortage of wood in Britain. The shortage of timber for shipbuilding was only a symptom of a major energy crisis affecting the whole of Europe. Local sources of wood and charcoal were becoming exhausted – given the poor state of communications and the costs involved it was impossible to move supplies very far. As early as 1560 the iron foundries of Slovakia were forced to cut back production as charcoal supplies began to dry up. Thirty years later the bakers of Montpellier in the south of France had to cut down bushes to heat their ovens because there was no timber left around the town. In the 1720s the salt evaporation works at Wieliczka in Poland had to close because all the local wood was exhausted. In 1717 a newly constructed iron furnace in Wales could not begin production for four years until it had accumulated enough stocks of charcoal and even then it only had enough fuel to operate for thirty-six weeks before it was forced to close. In most areas of Britain blast furnaces could only operate in short bursts of activity every few years.

The response to this increasing energy shortage was a switch to what was widely regarded as an inferior fuel – coal. As wood prices rose, first the poor, and later even the rich, were forced to use coal as *Stow's Annals* for 1631 in England commented: 'There is so great a scarcity of wood throughout the whole kingdom . . . the inhabitants in general are constrained to make their fires of sea-coal or pit-coal, even in the chambers of honorable personages.' In 1550 English coal production was about 210,000 tons but by 1630 it had risen to 1.5 million tons. By 1700 London was reliant on imports of over 550,000 tons of coal a year brought by sea from Newcastle (a fifteen-fold increase since 1550). Although people might prefer wood they could burn coal in existing fires and stoves and some industries such as smithing, brewing and soap-boiling could easily change over to the new fuel. However, the impurities in coal ruled out its use in most industries until new processes had been developed. Coal was used in glass production after 1610 and in brick making a decade later. By the 1640s coke was used to dry malt and four decades later to smelt lead, copper and tin. The last major industry to be adapted was iron smelting during the eighteenth century.

The gradual adoption of coal as a fuel was not just a substitution of one energy source for another. It was a fundamental shift in the type of energy available to human societies. Until the use of coal only renewable sources of energy were used – human, animal, water, wind and timber (although the last was usually used in a non-renewable way). Now for the first time humans slowly became dependent on the vast, but ultimately non-renewable, fossil fuel resources stored beneath the earth's surface. As wood prices rose, deeper coal mines became profitable and also practicable as increasingly efficient steam-driven pumps began to operate. Although much early industry depended on water power it was the growing use of coal that characterized European industrialization in the nineteenth century. The growth in coal production was staggering. In 1800 world output was about 15 million tons, by 1860 it had reached 132 million tons and by the end of the nineteenth century it was just over 700 million tons (a forty-six-fold increase). (Yet the industry changed little in terms of technology over the century – it remained almost totally reliant on human labour in difficult and extremely dangerous conditions.) In the last two years of the nineteenth century the world used more coal than it did in the whole of the eighteenth century. From a negligible contribution, coal came to account for about 90 per cent of the world's greatly expanded energy consumption. The new rates of energy consumption and industrialization could not have been sustained with wood – in 1900 the world's coal consumption was equivalent to destroying and transporting a forest three times the size of Britain every year. There were not enough forests in the world to sustain production on this scale for long and the problems which would have been involved in transporting such large quantities of wood around the world were probably insurmountable.

The impact of coal in the nineteenth century could be found everywhere. It not only powered the railways it was also one of the main sources of their freight traffic. It transformed the world's shipping which, until the nineteenth century, had depended on either human or wind power. The amount of steam-powered shipping in the world rose from just 32,000 tons in 1831 to over three million tons in the mid-1870s. An important by-product of rising coal consumption was the use of waste gases to provide the first non-natural source of lighting. Until the nineteenth century people relied on candles from animal fat in their homes (only the wealthy could afford the non-putrid-smelling candles made from whale spermacetti) and most towns were dark at night, though London did have a few streets lit by whale-oil lamps. Town gas (derived from coal) was first used to light a factory in Salford in 1807 and the first districts in London were lit by gas supplied from a central plant through underground mains in 1814–16. By 1823 gas-lighting systems had been built in fifty-two towns and it was soon adopted in Boston, New York (which relied on coal imported from Britain) and Berlin. Gradually over the course of the century the domestic use of gas for lighting and cooking spread, at least to those who could afford the high installation costs.

20.6 The British Experience

Britain was the first country to industrialize. What took place in the century or so after about 1750 is usually described as an 'industrial revolution' – a term first used in 1884 by Arnold Toynbee, a social reformer not an historian. Although this term is now indelibly associated with Britain at this time it is a serious misnomer. New technologies had been developed over a long period of human history and most of the new ones adopted in the century after 1750 built upon a multitude of earlier inventions. Even though the amount of technological change in the late eighteenth and early nineteenth centuries was probably unprecedented, these changes should be seen as part of a much longer process leading to the even more fundamental technological developments of the late nineteenth and twentieth centuries as the pace of change continued to accelerate. Concentrating on the changes in a few industrial sectors such as textile production over a few decades also tends to downplay the other fundamental changes under way that were to produce radically different human societies – the shift in energy sources, the increasing availability of energy, urbanization, the rise of service industries, the growth of an industrial workforce and the changing role of the state. Recent historical investigation has shown that the overall rate of growth during the so-called 'industrial revolution' in Britain was actually very slow and many sectors of the economy were hardly altered. Between 1760 and 1800 the British economy grew at about one per cent a year and the rate did not increase to about two per cent a year until the 1820s. Rapid growth at about three per cent a year did not come until the 1830s and for a few years in the 1840s, largely as a result of railway investment and development. Growth rates fell again after about 1850. This slow growth meant that, because of the rapidly rising population, average wealth per head hardly grew at all until after about 1830.

In the classic accounts of the 'industrial revolution' great emphasis is placed upon the role of the textile industry, the invention of new machinery and the development of factories. All of these factors need to be kept in perspective. In the early eighteenth century in Britain (as in the rest of Eurasia) textile production was largely a rural phenomenon – peasants combined it with their agricultural work, often keeping a machine in an upstairs room, relying on a merchant to supply raw materials and buy the end product, working on piece-rates and largely setting their own pace of work. Many of the developments in the eighteenth century were, not surprisingly, attuned to this production system. The first stocking frame was designed to fit into peasant cottages and Kay's flying shuttle of 1733 was intended to augment the productivity of handlooms. The machines which are usually seen as the archetypal cotton factory machines – Hargreaves's spinning jenny (1764), Arkwright's water frame (1769) and Crompton's mule (1779) – were all initially placed in the dwellings of domestic workers. The factories that did develop were often at first little more than concentrations of workers using domestic scale machines – the gains to the owners came from the greater work discipline they could impose. Hand production continued alongside factory production for decades – in the cotton industry steam-powered spinning in factories existed alongside handloom weaving because of the technical problems involved in the latter area and the desire of the owners and merchants to spread their risks and exploit cheap labour in weaving. Although the power loom was invented in 1787 it did not start displacing cotton handlooms on a major scale until the mid-1820s and was not a significant force in the woollen industry until the 1830s. Factories therefore remained small – although the number of mills in Yorkshire tripled to over 600 between 1800 and 1835 most only employed a handful of workers (the average was less than fifty) and they were often sub-let into small units. Even by 1851 only 10 per cent of the mills employed more than 200 people. In the 1840s the cotton industry was still only responsible for a tenth of Britain's industrial output and it employed less than five per cent of the non-agricultural labour force.

Despite these limitations the cotton industry accounted for half of all the productivity growth in Britain between 1760 and 1830. However, it remained atypical – it was a partially modern industry embedded within a very traditional industrial structure. Other industries such as paper production, soap and candle making began to switch to factory production in the early nineteenth century but they grew very slowly. Most industrial workers were still employed in low-technology industries which saw little change apart from the continued accumulation of a multitude of small improvements. In the Midlands metal industries' increasing demand produced a multiplication of small workshops employing a relatively skilled workforce of craftsmen. The changes in the textile industry were probably not even the most important within British industry – in the long term the rise of coal production (where there were almost no technical improvements), iron and later steel making, the development of engineering industries and, after about 1830 the development of railways, were far more important. For example, in 1800 Britain made 200,000 tons of iron and it cost on average £6.30 a ton. In 1870 5,500,000 tons were produced and the average price had fallen to £2.60 a ton.

In this complex economy development was very uneven – some sectors were very dynamic, others stagnated or went into decline (the Weald in Kent contained half of England's blast furnaces in 1600 but by the mid-nineteenth century the industry had largely disappeared). Until at least the mid-nineteenth century internal communication networks were still under-developed and for many products national markets hardly existed, especially for labour and capital, and therefore wage rates varied greatly across the country. Despite the opening of the London Stock Exchange in 1802 regional capital markets were hardly linked to London before the 1840s. However, regional specialization did develop – the cotton industry tended to concentrate in southern Lancashire and wool production in West Yorkshire. The Midlands concentrated on metal and hardware but the location of the coalfields increasingly determined the location of heavy industry such as iron and steel manufacture and shipbuilding.

Even by the mid-nineteenth century Britain had only begun the process of industrialization and the census taken in 1851 shows just how slow the process of change had been. The two largest occupational categories recorded in the census were agriculture and domestic service (indeed agricultural employment was at its peak). The number of workers in the building trade outnumbered those in cotton manufacturing. There were more shoe makers than coalminers and more blacksmiths than workers in the iron and steel industry. Nevertheless because Britain was the first country to become primarily industrial, its position in the world had been transformed. Its share of world manufacturing output rose from about two per cent in 1760 to 10 per cent in 1830 and reached a peak of 20 per cent in 1860. It produced over half the world's iron, accounted for half the world's coal use and consumed a similar amount of its raw cotton production. It controlled a fifth of the world's trade and two-fifths of the trade in manufactured goods.

20.7 Why Britain?

Explanations of initial industrialization in Britain, by both liberal and Marxist historians, have emphasized internal factors. A common argument is that the development of a commercialized agriculture in the period after about 1650 led to a virtuous circle of rising agricultural productivity, an expanding home economy produced by a rising population and growing wealth, growing urbanization and technological improvements, all of which led to industrialization. On the other hand major doubts must remain about whether any pre-industrial society could generate enough capital and bring about (over several decades) the particular balance of economic and social forces needed to ensure industrialization purely from its own resources. It seems far more likely that external factors played a significant role – in particular the position of Europe, and in particular Britain, within the Atlantic economy [17.1–17.9]. There can be no question that Europe generated large amounts of wealth from this area – the looting of the resources of the Americas (especially gold and silver), the production of goods for Africa, the direct profits from the slave trade and, most important of all, the wealth generated by slave labour on the plantations of the Americas. By the second half of the eighteenth century Britain was the dominant force within this Atlantic economy. The idea that these factors played a significant role in British industrialization was first raised by the Caribbean historian Eric Williams in his book *Capitalism and Slavery*. When it was published over fifty years ago its arguments were dismissed, not always for good reasons (many were related to a refusal to accept his criticisms of Britain's past). Historical work in the last couple of decades has shown that, with some modifications, his thesis has much to commend it.

Explanations of the role of the Atlantic economy, and in particular slavery, in industrialization concentrate on three key areas – the profits and capital generated, the market provided for British industrial output, and the supply of raw materials to British industry. There is no doubt that the Atlantic trade built around slavery was immensely profitable to Britain. The average profit rate just from the direct trade in slaves was about 10 per cent a year (even higher in the 1790s). In total the profits from the Atlantic slave economy amounted to about £4 million a year. To put this figure in perspective it was over five times the amount that the English landlords gained from their Irish estates and ten times the profits of the East India Company. Clearly not all of this money was invested in British industry or on the economic infrastructure such as canals – much was spent on consumption or buying landed estates (though that is a form of investment). Nevertheless, over the course of the eighteenth century much was invested into canals, roads, docks, mines, agricultural drainage and other types of improvements to the economy which aided industrialization. Overall the profits from slavery in the mid-eighteenth century were equivalent to the total amount of capital formation in the British economy. This therefore provided a substantial increase in the resources available in Britain. If only a third or a quarter of the total profits were invested into industry they would have provided a crucial extra increment of resources. That they had this impact is likely for two reasons – the timing of investment and its regional nature. The key period for investment in the British economy was between the 1760s and 1790s when it almost doubled as a proportion of Britain's national wealth. This period coincides with the greatest boom in the Atlantic economy when both the profits on the slave trade and those from the plantations tripled. The major market for English cotton production was Africa and the Americas and this was organized mainly through the chief port of the slave trade, Liverpool. At a time when national markets were undeveloped, especially those for raising capital and finding investments, the local networks in Lancashire were very important. The very close connections between the merchants in the slave trade and the local cotton manufacturers provided a direct link for the investment of slave trade profits into one of the key industries in the expanding economy.

The links between profits from slavery and investment in industry are difficult to trace in detail but it seems likely that there was a direct relationship between the two. However, the way in which the slave-based Atlantic economy provided a market for British industry is indisputable. The English cotton textile industry began to develop in the early eighteenth century once the competition from high-quality Indian goods brought back by the East India Company was removed through protective legislation. However, production stagnated because of low growth in the

British economy and the steady level of exports to Europe. It was Africa and the Americas which provided the major opportunity for cotton exports. A central feature of the Atlantic slave economy was the sale of goods in Africa to buy slaves and the provision of clothes and goods for the slave workers in the Americas. By the 1770s exports to these regions had risen seven-fold since the beginning of the century, were as large as those to the whole of Europe and six times bigger than those to Asia. By the 1790s exports of cotton goods were growing at over 17 per cent a year and exports made up four-fifths of the total growth in demand. The biggest single market was Africa, Brazil and Cuba and 98 per cent of exported English cotton check goods went to either Africa or the American plantations. The picture is little changed when all industries are considered. Exports were the most dynamic part of the eighteenth-century economy and provided the key element of extra demand that could make investment in new machinery worthwhile. Industrial exports rose by over 150 per cent between 1700 and 1770 but the British market only increased by 14 per cent. Of these exports the Atlantic area accounted for 15 per cent of the total in 1700 but over 70 per cent by 1770. The American and African trade took over 80 per cent of nail exports and only slightly less for wrought-iron exports. The Atlantic slave economy was therefore a key part of the British economy and one where Britain faced little competition and certainly far less than in the highly competitive markets of Asia. It provided a major market for exports and was the most dynamic market available whether for the iron and cotton goods traded in Africa for the slaves or for the clothes the slaves in the Americas wore or the tools they used on the plantations.

In the third area, the supply of raw cotton to the developing British industry, the link to the slave economy is direct and on a large scale. The vast expansion of cotton production could not have taken place without a similar increase in cotton supplies. This was particularly important because British cotton goods could not compete with high-quality Indian goods – their advantage came from being of no more than reasonable quality but cheap and available in quantity. The Atlantic economy provided access to an almost unlimited supply of land in the Americas and a large supply of forced labour to keep production costs to a minimum. In 1790 the United States produced just 1.5 million pounds of cotton. The invention of the cotton gin by Eli Whitney in 1791 improved processing and by 1800 production reached 35 million pounds before increasing to 160 million pounds by 1820. During that period the price of raw cotton fell by two-thirds. In the 1820s the American slave plantations were providing three-quarters of Britain's raw cotton imports and they were therefore the basis for the success of the British industry. As cotton growing spread westwards into new areas such as Alabama, Mississippi and Texas, American production increased to 2.3 billion pounds by 1860 when it accounted for two-thirds of world production and about 90 per cent of Britain's imports of raw cotton. The slave economy of the south of the United States and the mechanized cotton industry of Britain were inextricably linked together.

20.8 The European Experience

Industrialization was not a primarily British phenomenon which every other country, especially those in western Europe, imitated. From the perspective of world history the phenomenon of industrialization should be seen as at first a regional one in western Europe but, in an only slightly longer timescale, it was global in scope – by the 1860s industrialization was under way in the United States and Japan. In the twentieth century an increasing number of societies made the same transition. In none of these economies was it a matter of 'imitating' Britain – that was simply not possible. Britain had a number of special factors (especially easy access to coal and the wealth derived from the Atlantic economy) which meant that it industrialized first, though only by a few decades. In Britain the cotton industry was always far more important than elsewhere in Europe (as late as 1910 Britain still consumed more raw cotton than Germany, France and Italy combined). In other areas, especially the chemical sector which developed after about 1860, Britain was always behind the rest of Europe, in particular Germany. Everywhere each economy developed according to its own dynamic and with its own type of industrialization depending on the natural resources available and its successful industries. New technologies gave the initiating country a short-term advantage but they diffused rapidly just as they had throughout Eurasian history. However, diffusion gave the countries industrializing later immediate access to the most up-to-date technology. This meant that for some decades they had less outdated factories and machinery to replace and therefore had an initial spurt of very rapid growth.

The second country in Europe (and therefore the world) to industrialize was Belgium. Like Britain this area (Belgium was not an independent country until 1830) began to industrialize in the eighteenth century. A coal mine near Liège was using a Newcomen steam pump by 1720, less than a decade after it was first used in Britain. It was the coal industry, particularly in the Limburg region, that provided the foundation for Belgian industry. Heavy industry, especially metallurgical, provided a much bigger share of early industrial output than in Britain, although from the 1790s cotton spinning expanded, using British machinery, and took over much of the European market in the early nineteenth century. Belgium, as an even smaller country than Britain, became intensively industrialized. In Germany large areas, especially in the east and Bavaria were hardly touched by early industrialization. On the other hand Saxony had an important industrial sector by the 1840s with a large cotton industry, though this was almost entirely water-powered. It was the main coal-producing areas – the Ruhr and Silesia – which saw the highest levels of industrialization and the development of heavy industries. The main spurt of German industrialization did not come until after the 1860s but progress was then very rapid indeed.

France is often seen as an aberration in European terms and a relative 'failure' in the nineteenth century. However, instead of following the British and Belgian models of industrialization it produced its own distinctive (and less socially destructive) model. The key factors in French industrialization were the very low population growth rate (less than half that of elsewhere in Europe) and the shortage (and high cost) of coal. By 1900 coal production per capita in France was a third of that in Belgium and Germany and only a seventh of that in Britain, even though the reserves that did exist were more intensively exploited than anywhere else in Europe. Because of the relative lack of coal heavy industry was less important in France than the rest of Europe and industry did not become as concentrated as in some areas of Europe such as the Scottish, Welsh and Durham coalfields in Britain and the Ruhr in Germany. Urbanization was therefore also relatively low and small firms tended to predominate in the geographically dispersed industrial sector. Nevertheless growth rates were high – about two per cent a year before 1860, slightly higher thereafter. By the end of the nineteenth century France was one of the richest countries in Europe.

The experience of France was very typical of those countries (such as Switzerland, Denmark, Norway, Sweden and the Netherlands) which lacked large reserves of coal and therefore tended to industrialize relatively late in the nineteenth century. By the last part of the nineteenth century all (apart from Denmark which was rich through the export of almost two-thirds of its agricultural output) were major industrial powers – indeed the highest growth rate in wealth per head in Europe between 1860 and 1913 was in Sweden. Norway concentrated on shipping and the Dutch on the processing of raw material imports. Switzerland, which appeared to lack every fundamental requirement for an industrial economy, concentrated on producing a highly trained workforce specializing in high-quality production and by the end of the nineteenth century it also had the second largest organic chemical industry in the world. Elsewhere in Europe industrialization tended to be a highly regional phenomenon. In Austria-Hungary economic growth and industrial development was concentrated in two areas – Bohemia and Moravia (which accounted for nearly two-thirds of industrial output) and central Austria (the other third). Elsewhere communications were difficult and agriculture still predominated. The north-west of Italy was relatively industrialized (at least at the levels typical of France and Austria) but elsewhere, particularly in the south the country was still rural and undeveloped. Similarly in Spain industrial development was concentrated in Catalonia and the Basque country around Bilbao (a major iron and steel producer) whereas the north-west and south of the country were similar to southern Italy.

20.9 The American Experience

American industrialization followed a unique pattern produced by its own very special position. In 1800 the United States was a relatively rich country based on the export of raw materials (the plantation crops in the south and timber from the north) and its close involvement in the Atlantic slave economy. Its merchants were importing just under forty per cent of all the slaves taken to the Americas, were vital to the sugar, molasses and rum trades and were also supplying the plantations of the West Indies with a number of manufactured goods. About half of New England's ships were involved in the trade to the West Indies. The United States remained a small, almost entirely agricultural, country with a population of just over 5 million confined to the east of the Appalachians. By the end of the nineteenth century it had a population of 77 million and was the largest industrial power in the world, making a third of the world's manufactured output (even so, 40 per cent of the population still worked on farms). Remarkably this massive industrial expansion took place in parallel with a huge extension of the agricultural area and the settlement of most of the continent.

Although there was much technological borrowing from Europe (especially in the cotton textile industry) early American industrialization was dominated by wood and water power. The great forests had not been cleared, as in Europe, and they provided an easy source of cheap energy. In 1850 wood still accounted for over 90 per cent of the United States' fuel supplies and half of the nation's iron output was produced using charcoal – the Hopewell furnace in Pennsylvania was consuming over 750 acres of timber every year. Stoves and boilers were built to use wood and steamboats on the great rivers such as the Mississippi were wood-fired as were most railway locomotives (unlike in Britain where they were coke- or coal-fired from the start because of the shortage of wood). As late as 1870 wood still constituted three-quarters of the fuel supply for industry and transport. Not until the mid-1880s did coal become the principal source of energy in the United States. The other major source of power for industry, particularly textile production, was water.

As in Britain industrial development was closely tied to cotton manufacturing (it was the largest industry in 1860) and it too depended on the slave economy of the southern states. The early development of textile manufacture in New England was financed by the leading merchants such as the Browns of Massachusetts and the Lowells of Boston who had made their money from the slave trade. The industry was also dependent on raw cotton from the south – by 1860 it was using about 430 million pounds a year, roughly a third of the amount that was exported to Britain. Most of US industry was in the northern states although in the 1850s about 10 per cent of the total output came from the south, much of it produced by the 200,000 industrial slaves (most were hired out by local plantation owners). In the first half of the nineteenth century growth in the United States was slow – only a little over one per cent a year. As in Britain (and much of Europe) early industrialization did not increase the rate of growth. The period of rapid industrial expansion in the United States did not come until after the end of the civil war in 1865. Then expansion was at a phenomenal rate. Industrial production increased five-fold by 1900, creating a major industrial belt in New England, the mid-Atlantic states and the mid-west. Production diversified into every area from iron and steel to heavy engineering, shipbuilding and the newly developing chemicals sector.

20.10 Communications

Industrialization in Europe and the United States could not have taken place without major improvements in the economic infrastructure. Until the eighteenth century Europe was probably behind China in the development of its communication network. Roads were poor, canals were little developed which meant that coastal shipping and navigable rivers were the main means of transport. The eighteenth century was characterized by the extensive development of a canal network which made it possible, almost for the first time, to move bulk goods over long distances. A few railways developed but they were horse-drawn and confined to short freight lines around collieries and in some industrial districts. It was the slow evolution of a variety of technologies in the first three decades of the nineteenth century which made railways possible. Efficient steam power capable of pulling loads required the development of better boilers, pistons and gearing as well as rails capable of taking such heavy loads. Even after the first passenger-carrying and steam-driven railways opened in Britain (the Stockton and Darlington in 1825 and the Liverpool and Manchester in 1830) continuous development was still required to produce more powerful locomotives capable of travelling at speed. In parallel, other technologies such as signalling and communications via the telegraph had to be developed.

Railways grew rapidly after 1830 and changed from being short lines of a few miles to large trunk routes joining major cities. By the early 1840s the major cities of Britain were either linked to London or the construction of lines was under way. In 1844 the first trunk route on the continent, from Antwerp to Cologne was opened and by 1850 the railway network stretched as far east as Warsaw. Perhaps their most important function was to help create and then integrate markets at a national level and allow some areas to specialize in the production of particular items. They were especially important in moving bulk items quickly, for example coal. Road transport hardly changed during the nineteenth century and remained far more expensive than railways. Railways were not necessarily cheaper than canals (except in Britain) but they were faster. (In Belgium, Germany and France the canal network continued to expand even after 1850.) As the railway network grew – there were just under 2,000 miles in Europe in 1840 but 225,000 miles by the early twentieth century – costs fell dramatically. In the 1890s freight rates were about half the level of the 1840s. This reduced costs in the economy but even more important were the vast quantities of raw materials, manufactured goods and food which travelled by rail by the end of the century. They simply could not have been moved in any other way and without railways European economies could not have operated at the level they did. In 1845 just 7 per cent of Belgium's freight traffic moved by rail. In 1910 over three-quarters of a vastly increased total did so. Almost as important was the amount of passenger travel (overall it provided about half the railway's receipts) for both business and pleasure and the phenomenal impact this made on people's lives and society in general.

Railways were a major factor creating demand for industrial products in the economy. They needed coal and also high-quality iron, and, from the middle of the century, steel rails. Locomotives had to be built and repaired either in the works constructed by the companies, often in towns such as Crewe and Swindon which were entirely based on the railway, or by private companies. The building of lines took up vast amounts of labour, especially since they were constructed with only minimal machinery, and once built they created a wide range of new, often highly skilled jobs.

Except in Britain and Belgium, most countries depended for some time on imported rails and locomotives – in the 1850s the Spanish railway's demand for rails was equivalent to twice the total output of the country's tiny iron industry. Railways also had a major effect on agriculture by enabling animals to be moved rapidly across the country for slaughter instead of moving them on foot and also in creating new markets for perishable products such as butter and milk. In 1861 just 4 per cent of the milk sold in London travelled by rail but thirty years later the proportion, of a vastly increased market, had risen to over 80 per cent. Railways were particularly important for countries such as Mexico, Spain, Russia and parts of France where river and canal communications were poor. However, they could not create an industrial economy on their own – their greatest impact therefore came in the relatively sophisticated and developed economies such as Britain, Belgium and later Germany, where railways helped existing industries develop still further. Railway development in the United States was very rapid. By 1840 it already had more miles of track than Britain. The first transcontinental line was completed in the 1860s and by the end of the century there were almost 170,000 miles of track. As in most European countries industrial development began before the construction of railways and they subsequently helped to increase growth and reduce costs. However, in the United States the economic and industrial impact of the railways was probably less than in Europe. They were not even the primary users of iron – during the nineteenth century more went into nails than locomotives and track.

The development of railways did not bring about the demise of horse-drawn travel (apart from the stagecoach). By generating more traffic, both passenger and freight, railways increased the demand for horses and their numbers reached a peak in both Europe and the United States at the end of the nineteenth century. This trend was particularly apparent in Britain which had one of the densest railway networks in the world. In 1810 there were about 15,000 privately owned carriages, rising to 40,000 by 1840 and 120,000 by 1870. The number of horses kept in towns for both private and business traffic rose from 350,000 in 1830 to 1,200,000 by 1900. Public transport depended on horses – in 1902 London had 3,700 horse-drawn omnibuses (each using two horses and needing about ten horses a day to maintain the service), 7,500 hansom cabs and 3,900 hackney coaches. Railway companies also used large numbers of horses to distribute goods from their stations and goods depots. In 1913 nearly 90 per cent of London's goods traffic was still horse-drawn, with the railway companies using over 6,000 animals and the coal merchants about 8,000. Overall Britain had about 3½ million horses and they ate about four million tons of oats and hay a year. This took up a vast amount of agricultural land and required a huge effort to distribute around the country. The United States faced the same problems. In 1900 it had close to 30 million horses (200,000 of them were in New York) and horse feed took up around 90 million acres of cropland which was about a quarter of the total. This was probably about the maximum that the agricultural system could support without affecting human food supplies and in Britain could only be sustained because of the import of large quantities of food. [*Communications beyond Europe 21.2*]

20.11 Industrialization and Society

Over the course of the nineteenth century industrialization brought about a profound transformation in the societies of much of Europe and in the United States. For the first time in human history the majority of people were not directly employed in agriculture – the transition came in Britain in the 1850s, a few decades later in much of the rest of Europe. By the early twentieth century only about a third of the French population and a quarter of the German were directly dependent on farming and the relative backwardness of Italy can be judged from the fact that sixty per cent of the population were still engaged in agriculture. More and more people came to live in cities, the range of occupations increased markedly and, on average, across the century as a whole people became wealthier. However, these changes were very far from being painless. Some people lost their livelihoods – for example, the 500,000 handloom weavers in Britain – and for many decades people lived in dreadful conditions in the new industrial cities and were subject to a much lower quality of life. Improvements eventually came but they took a very long time to emerge.

20.11.1 Poverty, wealth and health
[*Earlier Europe 18.7.1*]
The conditions experienced during the early stages of industrialization in Britain have been the subject of bitter historical debate over the last few decades although a consensus is beginning to emerge. Between about 1760 and the 1820s it is extremely unlikely that even on average there was any improvement in living standards. A few people may have benefited but the overwhelming majority did not. Rising population (which was rapid after about 1800) meant lower incomes, rising food prices and therefore increasing poverty. Real wages for males certainly fell until at least 1810 and for females the fall lasted much longer. There was so much cheap labour available that it probably slowed down the rate of mechanization

and technological innovation. Few workers had reserves of money or possessions they could pawn in hard times when unemployment in some trades could reach three-quarters of the workforce. In the 1840s about a tenth of the population in England were still classified as paupers. At times this proportion rose dramatically – in the depression of the early 1840s in the Lancashire town of Clitheroe it was estimated that 2,300 people out of a total population of 6,700 were paupers. The figures available for life expectancy, infant mortality and the decline in average height all suggest that there was a fall in nutritional standards and the general standard of living. It is also important to take into account more intangible aspects of the quality of life during early industrialization. The workers in factories were subject to a regime of strict time and labour discipline which was the very opposite of the relative freedom and ability to set their own pace of work when self-employed in the countryside. In addition they did not have their peasant holding to fall back on when times were hard. Conditions were often even worse for women and children who predominated in the factory workforce (and many other occupations such as mining too). In 1816 children aged under eighteen made up half the workforce in the cotton factories. In the Yorkshire woollen mills in 1835 women and juveniles under twenty-one made up nearly 80 per cent of the workforce.

20.11.2 The rise of cities

One of the most fundamental changes brought about by industrialization was urbanization. Until the nineteenth century most cities in the world were parasitic on the rest of the economy – they sucked in people and food but contributed very little in return. They were places of consumption, often built around the ruler's court and its large numbers of hangers-on, the elite and their servants. Industrialization changed this pattern and turned cities into one of the major contributors to the economy in terms of industrial output and later through the provision of financial and commercial services. In 1800 about 90 per cent of the European population lived in the countryside and even in Britain and the Netherlands, the most urbanized areas, the proportion was still 80 per cent. The pace of change was slow even in Britain – in the early 1850s 60 per cent of the British population was still rural. Yet by 1900 three-quarters of the British population lived in towns and cities and one in five lived in London. However, these proportions do not reflect the overall rise in population – the total numbers living in British cities rose from 2 million in 1800 to almost 30 million in 1900. In 1750 London was the only city in England with a population of more than 50,000 – a century later there were twenty-nine such towns. Some grew very rapidly as industry developed – the population of Manchester increased from 27,000 in 1770 to 180,000 only sixty years later.

The conditions people found in these cities were appalling. In 1833 about 20,000 people in Manchester (almost a tenth of the population) were living in cellars. There was an almost total lack of sanitation in all the cities. One of the worst areas was the 'Potteries' of north Kensington in London, an eight-acre area originally dug out to provide brick clay for the surrounding suburbs and then left to collect all the sewage from the neighbourhood. It was full of open sewers and stagnant lakes (one covered over an acre). In the early 1850s about a thousand people lived there together with more than 3,000 pigs which fed off the refuse. But London was in a generally disgusting state as John Phillips, the engineer to the Metropolitan Commission of Sewers, reported in 1847:

> There are . . . thousands of houses in the metropolis which have no drainage whatever, and the greater part of them have stinking overflowing cesspools. And there are hundreds of streets, courts and alleys that have no sewers . . . I have visited very many places where filth was lying scattered about the rooms, vaults, cellar areas and yards, so thick and so deep that it was hardly possible to move for it.

Other towns were just as bad. Friedrich Engels toured Manchester in the 1840s during his investigations into the conditions of the workers in Britain. He described one area of the town where 200 people shared a single privy: 'In one of these courts, right at the entrance where the covered passage ends is a privy without a door. This privy is so dirty that the inhabitants can only enter or leave the court by wading through puddles of stale urine and excrement.' He also stood on the Ducie bridge over the river Irk and described the scene below:

> At the bottom the Irk flows or rather stagnates . . . [it] receives as well the contents of the adjacent sewers and privies. Below Ducie Bridge, on the left, one looks into piles of rubbish, the refuse, filth and decaying matter of the courts on the steep left bank of the river. [It] . . . is a narrow, coal-black stinking river full of filth and garbage which it deposits on the lower-lying right bank. In dry weather, an extended series of the most revolting blackish green pools of slime remain standing on this bank, out of whose depths bubbles of miasmatic gases constantly rise and give forth a stench that is unbearable even on the bridge forty or fifty feet above the level of the water.

Attempts to improve the situation often only made matters worse. The invention of the water closet and the construction of sewers (it was legal to connect water closets to surface streams in England after 1815 and compulsory after 1847) simply ensured that the rivers were turned into open sewers containing slowly decomposing waste products. In London the sewers emptied into the river Fleet which carried their contents to the Thames, where the rubbish was left to float up and down on the tide in the centre of the city. In hot weather the smell spread over the whole city. In 1858, during what was called 'The Great Stink', the stench was so bad that sittings of the House of Commons had to be abandoned.

In these conditions it is hardly surprising that diseases were endemic and spread easily and rapidly. Long-established diseases such as typhoid were rampant and tuberculosis became a major threat in the overcrowded and poor living conditions of the industrial cities. Even more of a problem was the spread of a new disease – cholera – in a pattern which closely resembled that of the bubonic plague (the 'Black Death') some five centuries earlier. Cholera had long been endemic in India and regularly spread along the pilgrimage routes from the Ganges, occasionally even reaching China. The Bengal outbreak of 1826 spread the disease to the eastern Mediterranean, from there to Russian troops fighting the Ottomans and they took it back to Poland and the Baltic by 1831. Within a year it had spread to Britain, the main cities of Europe, the United States and most of the Islamic world. In the insanitary conditions of European and American cities it spread like wildfire among a population that had no resistance. There were repeated epidemics for decades as scientists and doctors argued over the way the disease was spread. Only slowly did improvements to sanitation and water supply systems stop the disease. The last great cholera epidemic in Britain was in 1866 followed by France in 1884 and Germany in 1892 (in the latter outbreak 8,600 people died in Hamburg alone). The impact of disease, poor food and the conditions in the industrial cities meant that mortality rates in England rose between 1810 and the middle of the century and only then began a slow decline. In 1840, almost six out of ten working-class children in Manchester died before the age of five (almost twice the rate of rural areas).

It was only from the mid-nineteenth century that conditions for the majority of the population in Britain began slowly to improve. The state intervened to restrict some of the worst abuses of the industrial system – at first the amount of child and female labour and then the hours worked by males. As the overall level of wealth began to increase some of the benefits reached the industrial workforce, especially the skilled workers. Real wages improved from the 1850s until the end of the nineteenth century when they began to stagnate. Gradually a half-day holiday on Saturday afternoons became common and with more money available spectator sports such as professional football became increasing attractions by the 1880s. There can be no doubt that by the late nineteenth century the average real wealth per head had increased significantly compared with the conditions a century earlier. People found it easier to afford not just the basic necessities such as food, clothing and housing but they might, if they were lucky, have some money left over for a few 'luxuries', even a short (usually unpaid) holiday. Society continued to change in other ways as new types of jobs could be afforded, for example teachers and doctors. Indeed the nineteenth century was characterized by the expansion of 'professions' from the varieties of engineers to lawyers, accountants and academics, all with their own regulatory bodies and institutions as civil society became ever more complex.

Huge inequalities remained in the industrial societies and many people lived in acute poverty, especially if they worked in trades with little security of employment such as dockers or those very vulnerable to economic fluctuations. A period of unemployment, injury at work or ill-health could still be devastating. In 1889 it was estimated that a third of the population of London lived below the poverty line and were 'at all times more or less in want'. Similar surveys in other cities confirmed this picture. The poorest sections of the community ate about half as much food as the richest and their state of health was still poor. In 1899 when 11,000 Manchester men tried to enlist in the army for the Boer war only 1,000 were fit enough to be accepted. Diseases such as scurvy, rickets and anaemia, all caused by defective nutrition, were common. Housing was still a major problem. In the British census of 1901 for conditions to qualify as 'overcrowded' there had to be a household of at least two adults and four children living in two rooms without their own water supply and sanitation. Even on this very restrictive definition almost one in ten of the British population suffered from such conditions. In the areas of the greatest deprivation the figure was far higher – over a third of the population in some London boroughs such as Finsbury, over half the population of Glasgow and two-thirds of Dundee.

As industrialization gathered pace in western Europe and the United States, cities grew and conditions similar to those in Britain were experienced everywhere. In Europe new manufacturing towns emerged across a wide area, in Belgium, north-east France and the Ruhr area in Germany. Industrialization also produced large, formless, urban conglomerations caused by the expansion and joining up of what had once been a series of independent communities. In Britain this was first noticed by the mid-nineteenth century in the Black Country of the West Midlands and the Five Towns of the Potteries in Staffordshire. One of the most extreme forms of this sort of development came in the Ruhr after the start of deep coalmining and the building of a railway network in the 1840s and 1850s. A mass of immigrants created the labour force and the villages of the area grew in an unplanned fashion until, eventually, they joined together in an industrial and urban sprawl spreading over tens of miles, eventually incorporating eleven cities and four districts. By 1871 the population of the region was just below 1 million, by 1910 it was 3½ million. In the United States urbanization was equally rapid. In 1830 there were still only twenty-three towns with a population greater than 10,000 and only two big cities – New York (200,000) and Philadelphia (160,000). As immigrants flooded in from Europe cities grew, the urban population doubled every decade to reach 6 million by 1860. By 1910 there were fifty cities with more than 100,000 inhabitants. Conditions in these cities were as bad as in Europe. The infant mortality rate in New York doubled between 1810 and 1870. In the late nineteenth century the legal requirement for new tenement blocks (the old ones were far worse) was that they should have one lavatory for every twenty inhabitants and one water tap for each block.

As the size of cities increased dramatically with industrialization they changed their nature, especially under the influence of the railways. In pre-industrial societies the centres of cities were where people worked and lived (even the wealthy). In the nineteenth century they began to expand and sprawl across the landscape even as population densities in the centre rose and huge slums such as Covent Garden and Holborn in London developed. Local market gardens and fields were destroyed and separate villages and towns, such as Charlottenburg and Spandau in Berlin, were incorporated into the new cities. Most growth was entirely unplanned and the result of speculative development leading to the creation of suburbs – places where people lived but did not work. They were the consequence of the new public transport systems particularly the railways. In London the steady building of new lines from the 1840s led to the growth of new, largely residential suburbs such as Camberwell, Hornsey, Kilburn, Fulham and Ealing. Residents of the first suburbs in the United States were transported by a horse-drawn street railway introduced in New York in 1832 and adopted by eight other cities before 1860. In New York after 1869 there was an ambitious system of elevated railways which enabled people to live even further from the city centre. Even more important was the development of the underground railway. The first was built in London in 1863 (using steam engines) but deep lines and an extensive system had to await electrification. Other cities followed suit a little later – Boston in 1897 (there were over 50 million passengers in the first year on a tiny network), Paris in 1900, Berlin in 1902 and New York in 1904. These developments had two consequences. The heart of the major cities became the hub of financial and commercial rather than industrial activity and the population fell rapidly – in the 1850s the City of London had about 130,000 residents but this fell to almost none within a few decades as offices took over. Second, the majority of the population came to live in the suburbs at even greater distances from the city, especially in the United States where land was generally cheap. In 1850 the edge of the city of Boston was two miles from the business centre. In 1900, following the development of mass transport systems, the city extended ten miles from the centre. The only major exception to this pattern was Paris which had a very poor suburban railway network.

The urbanization of Europe and north America was a fundamental change in world history. Until the nineteenth century all the major cities of the world had been outside Europe. Even in 1800 Peking and Edo were as large as London. By 1850 London was the largest city in the world with a population of 2.3 million (about the same as Hangchou at the height of the Sung in the twelfth century). Peking was still second, ahead of Paris. Canton, Hangchou and Constantinople were still larger than New York. By 1900 the six largest cities in the world were either in Europe or the United States. London was by far the largest at 6.5 million followed by New York (4.2 million), Paris (3.3 million) and Berlin (2.4 million). The only city outside this area in the top twelve was Tokyo with 1.5 million inhabitants. Peking was now smaller than Manchester, Birmingham and Philadelphia and little bigger than Glasgow and Boston.
[*Later urbanization 23.5*]

20.11.3 Pollution

The increase in industrial production, its concentration in a few areas, and the rapid development of coal as the principal source of energy inevitably led to a major increase in pollution. (During the nineteenth century world coal consumption increased forty-six fold and iron production rose sixty-fold.) The consequences of the shift to coal burning in Britain in the early seventeenth century were apparent very quickly. As early as 1608 visitors to Sheffield were warned that they would be 'half choked with town smoke' and in 1725 a writer in Newcastle commented that 'the perpetual clouds of smoke hovering in the air make everything look as black as London'. In the nineteenth century the problem worsened in every city as numbers rose and coal became almost the only form of domestic heating and cooking. By 1880 there were 600,000 homes in inner London with 3½ million fireplaces. London fog (or smogs) became increasingly common, unpleasant and a major health hazard. During the middle decades of the century the number of foggy days in the year tripled and death rates rose sharply. In December 1873 there were about 500 deaths caused by the severe fog and in February 1880 over 2,000 people died in three weeks.

This pattern was repeated remorselessly every year for decades as smoke pollution worsened.

Increasing industrialization not only increased smoke and sulphur dioxide pollution in the atmosphere but rapidly widened the number of pollutants. By the nineteenth century across Europe and north America there were areas of concentrated pollution and environmental degradation – ruined landscapes of chimneys belching smoke and poisonous gases, huge slag heaps of waste materials, rivers full of a cocktail of industrial wastes and surrounding areas where the vegetation was destroyed. As early as 1750 the population of Burslem in the Potteries were described as groping their way through the dense smoke that covered the town. In the Monongahela valley near Pittsburgh there were 14,000 smokestacks pouring out fumes into the atmosphere. The amount of chemicals in the atmosphere altered its composition over wide areas and turned it acid so that it destroyed buildings and further ruined rivers and lakes. The phenomenon of acid rain was first identified in Manchester in the 1850s and explained in detail by Robert Smith in his book *Acid and Rain*, published in 1872.

The vast increase in the number of horses in the nineteenth century produced dreadful conditions in the industrial cities. Streets were covered in horse droppings and urine and even the armies of crossing sweepers could not make the streets bearable, especially when it rained. In 1830 animals dumped about three million tons of manure on the streets of British towns and most of it was just piled up into rotting, stinking heaps. By 1900 the volume of manure had more than tripled. Many of the horses dropped dead on the streets from overwork – in 1900 New York was removing 15,000 horse corpses a year from its streets.

[*Later pollution 23.8*]

20.12 Government and Society

[*Earlier European states 18.12*]

These fundamental changes in the economies and societies of the industrializing countries and the immense stresses they created had a profound impact on governments. Until well into the nineteenth century the governments of Europe were very limited in their functions apart from provision for war. They had changed little from the pre-industrial model. Apart from the odd exception of Switzerland they were monarchies in which the ruler was advised by a small group of aristocrats who drew their wealth from their large landholdings. In a few countries such as Britain the decision-taking elite was slightly wider but was still almost entirely made up of a self-perpetuating landowning oligarchy. At a local level justice and administration were still largely in the hands of the same elite apart from in the towns where the merchant elite dominated.

The growth of cities, the shift of population away from the countryside and the emergence of new sources of wealth seriously disrupted the pattern that had survived for many centuries, making it much more difficult for elites to retain control and maintain their old methods of governing. In general they were able to keep much of their dominance by slowly incorporating the new industrial and commercial groups. The major problem was the growth of an industrial working class in the cities which posed acute problems of order and control which could not be solved within the traditional framework. Although the industrial workers were badly divided by differences between the skilled and the larger number of unskilled they still represented a very different group in society from any that had ever existed before. They were working in larger units, were more dependent on the fluctuations of the market and were therefore far more insecure than rural labourers in the past. They also bore the brunt of the terrible conditions produced by early industrialization. Over several decades they created a new working-class culture and institutions. However, they found it very difficult to alter their conditions given their lack of power and the determination of the existing elites to keep control. Considering the conditions many people faced in the industrializing countries perhaps the only surprising aspect of European history in the nineteenth century is that there was no major social revolution.

The social tensions brought about by industrialization were first felt in Britain. The semi-revolutionary movements of the years of the war against France between the early 1790s and 1815 owed something to the egalitarian rhetoric of the revolution in France but far more to the conditions developing in the industrial towns. At the same time there was 'Luddism' – the breaking of newly installed machines which took away the jobs of workers such as the handloom weavers. In the acute distress and discontent caused by the economic depression which followed the end of the war the government responded through the use of spies and *agents provocateurs*, the suspension of habeas corpus and military repression (even during the war the government kept more troops in Britain than were fighting in the Peninsular War against Napoleon). Trade unions and workers' organizations were banned under the Combination Acts. Demands for social and political reform reached their height with the Chartist movement which was at its strongest in the late 1830s and early 1840s when economic conditions were particularly bad.

A major part of the British government's response to the massive social and economic changes under way was to take much greater power to control individuals, especially the working class, the poor and vagrants. The 1834 Poor Law established workhouses as the only places where 'relief' could be granted – they were designed to be harsh places (families were split up) in order to discourage people from using them. Control was exercised through the creation of new institutions such as the police (first developed in Paris in the eighteenth century) from the 1820s in London and in the mid-1830s it was made compulsory to establish them in every major city. The crowding together of so many people in the cities led to a redefinition of 'crime' and a growing fear of what the elite called the 'dangerous classes'. Criminal prosecutions rose four and a half times faster than did the population between 1800 and 1840. New definitions of criminal behaviour and political crime were developed through harsher laws, particularly in defence of property, which produced further criminalization of the poor. Offenders were seen as threatening not just their victims but 'society' as a whole. The use of the death penalty increased but, more important, the role of prisons changed. Originally they were places where people awaiting trial or sentence were briefly incarcerated in dreadful conditions. From the 1820s they were increasingly 'reformed' to turn them into places of strict discipline where the emphasis was on altering 'character' rather than merely imposing bodily punishment. Criminals were to be controlled, managed and altered so that on release they could take their place as useful members of the new industrial society.

Across Europe governments found that, very slowly, they had to take on new functions as society and the economy became more complex. At first these related to regulation of the worst features of the new industrial system – the employment of women and children, the hours worked by men and the payment of workers in 'truck' (tokens only redeemable in company shops). In the large cities some measures had to be taken to provide water and sanitation or there would be a complete breakdown and the threat of disease which would affect the 'respectable' as well as the poor. The railways were one of the first industries to be regulated. On the European continent governments played a key role in planning and, in some cases, even operating the system. Much of the driving force behind this development was an appreciation of the strategic importance of the railways in moving large numbers of troops quickly and many systems were built with these priorities in mind. In Britain there was only minimal control over the building of new lines and large-scale duplication was the result. Even so the government found it had to undertake at least minimal regulation of the railway companies and develop expert inspectors to provide for public safety. In the United States the government was even more closely involved. The first company, the Baltimore and Ohio, was given a statutory monopoly and exemption from taxation. State investment in the railways was common (by 1860 Massachusetts had invested $8 million in eight different companies). The most important assistance given by the state was land – between 1850 and 1880 the federal government gave railway companies 180 million acres of public land to help the construction of lines, especially the transcontinental routes.

In the latter part of the nineteenth century some governments began to go a little further in their intervention in the economy and society. Schemes to compensate workers for industrial injuries were either created or imposed on employers. A few states began wider schemes of welfare provision – small pensions on a non-contributory basis, help in finding jobs and forms of unemployment pay. The motivation behind these schemes was usually one of integrating the working class into the existing social and political structure by ameliorating their conditions and reducing the incentive to revolt. A key factor throughout the nineteenth century was the development of education systems and the rising level of literacy throughout European society. By the middle of the century probably a majority of the population in countries such as Sweden, Prussia, England, France and Austria (and the whites in the United States) were literate – a remarkable departure in world history. Only in countries such as Italy, Spain and Russia were literacy rates low (about 10–25 per cent of the population), a level typical of all pre-industrial societies. Some governments such as that of Prussia took a strong interest in education and produced an effective state system from the middle of the century; in Britain, though, even primary education did not become compulsory until 1870. Almost everywhere the provision of education was bedevilled by religious controversy and arguments about the role the churches should and could play. By the end of the nineteenth century literacy rates in western Europe were usually around nine out of ten of the population (but less than half this figure in Italy and Spain). However, secondary education for the bulk of the population was often not compulsory; where it did exist it usually only extended to the age of fourteen and the chances of a child from outside the elite receiving higher education were minimal.

Nevertheless, by the end of the nineteenth century the economies and societies of western Europe and north America had been radically transformed compared with the situation only a century earlier. No human society had ever experienced such a rapid pace of change before. Europe, especially the west, changed from being overwhelmingly rural and agricultural to being industrial and urban. The peasants and the landlord elite were no longer the dominant forces in society. The industrial working class was in most cases the largest group in society but society itself had become far more complex, with industrialists, managers, merchants, bankers and the professions all wielding considerable power and influence. Every member of society was wealthier than their predecessors at the beginning of the century and the range of goods they had available to buy was much greater. However, huge inequalities and massive poverty remained. The process of change did not end in 1900, indeed it became faster and more radical. New technologies were developed and brought about a whole succession of further transformations in the economy and society at an unprecedented speed.

21

Europe and the World
(*c.*1750–*c.*1900)

The transformation of Europe in the nineteenth century was not restricted to industrialization and urbanization. Between 1750 and 1900, partly based on these internal economic changes, it came to dominate the rest of the world. In 1750 the position of Europe within the wider world was only marginally changed from the situation in the early sixteenth century. Europe effectively dominated the Americas but in Africa and, more particularly, Asia it still had only a few toeholds in the form of trading stations and forts. Its influence over the great land empires of the Ottomans and the Ch'ing in China was minimal. However, by 1900 Europe, and its offshoots, dominated all of the Americas and Australasia; the British were paramount in India, the Ottomans had lost most of their territories in Europe and the southern shore of the Mediterranean, Africa was almost completely partitioned by the European powers and China was under severe pressure. Only Japan escaped and kept almost total control over its destiny. In 1800 Britain ruled, outside the British Isles, 20 million people. In 1900 this had risen to 400 million (a quarter of the world's population). In 1800 Europe, together with its immediate offshoots, controlled about a third of the world's land surface: in 1900 over four-fifths. It was the most rapid transformation and extension of power in world history.

21.1 Eurasian Views

21.1.1. *Europe*
As the societies and cultures of Eurasia became ever more closely involved with each other after 1750 (a massive intensification of one of the major trends of world history) they regarded each other with mutual incomprehension. It was this period that was vital in the construction of Europe's conception of its role and position in the world. Europe had always tended to define itself against the more advanced and stronger Islamic world that predominated in the Mediterranean and south-west Asia (and the Balkans for much of the time). Originally Europe defined itself as part of 'Christendom' even though Christendom was badly divided after 1054 (and even more so from the sixteenth century) and did not coincide with Europe (the Christian Byzantines controlled Anatolia until 1071 and the

Muslim Ottomans controlled much of Europe for centuries). Nevertheless the idea of 'Christendom' was important until the late seventeenth century, especially in opposition to the nearest of the great Eurasian empires (that of the Ottomans), and it remained significant for the Habsburgs for much longer. The last European treaty to refer to the *respublica Christiana* was the treaty of Utrecht in 1714.

From the early eighteenth century Europe increasingly came to see itself as a special region, embodying unique characteristics which were superior to those of the rest of the world. In addition to its longstanding anti-Islamic views and its conviction that it was racially superior to the blacks it was enslaving in Africa and the Americas, the European elite developed new concepts. In particular they came to believe in 'progress' – the ultimate perfectibility of humans and their ability to master nature and improve society. Europe was naturally the bringer of progress. They also created the idea of 'civilization' and the gradation of other societies in comparison to the European ideal. China was usually placed towards the top of this list although the Europeans knew almost nothing about its history, politics, society and economy. Some interest was taken by the British in Indian society and culture but it soon passed, as did the great interest in Egyptology following the French expedition to Egypt in the late 1790s. Islamic society came to have a special place – it was seen as decaying, exotic and corrupt, in other words 'oriental' and the exact opposite of everything that Europe stood for. At the bottom of the pile were the Africans, native Americans and other tribal people – ideas about the 'noble savage' did not stop the Europeans treating these people as barely human. The nature of world history was gradually rewritten as the idea of European civilization (later 'western' civilization) became its central force. Europe, it was asserted, embodied Greek thought, Roman law and government, Christianity and a 'Germanic' folk culture of liberty and democracy (the latter therefore made 'Anglo-Saxons' or Aryans superior to all other human races). In practice none of the first three were specifically 'European' and the last was a unique European concept of how to divide up the people of the world into very different categories with inherent (and inheritable) characteristics. It was these ideas that became increasingly important in the nineteenth century as a defining concept in European superiority. The history of Greece and Rome was appropriated as a specifically European inheritance – they became the 'classics' and central to the education of the European elite in the nineteenth century (and later). Such ideas played a central role in enlisting support for the Greek revolt against the Ottomans in the 1820s and for the idea of 'Turkey in Europe', as though it was illegitimate for the Ottomans to be part of the European world (which they had been for the previous five centuries).

Europe developed an immense self-confidence about itself and its institutions as being the summit of human history. Its growing wealth and power reinforced these views and were regarded as merely the just reward for its 'dynamism', 'progress' and its economic organization based on the market and capitalism. Its institutions were also more advanced. Europe was superior because it was divided into 'nation-states' not large despotic empires. The European states were roughly equal, held together through their common interests ('the concert of Europe') and the 'balance of power'. This was the model that should be applied elsewhere in the world. Europe was also the home of 'liberty' as opposed to despotism. This 'liberty' was always defined so as to be equivalent to the European state which was seen as rational, bureaucratic, limited and defending individual property. Any idea that it might include the interests of the peasants and workers was usually excluded. Many of the various aspects of European thought came together in Montesquieu's *The Spirit of the Laws*. Islam, he argued, was conducive to fatalism and despotism and the climate in Asia only reinforced these weaknesses. Europe was law, morality, aristocracy, monarchy and the liberty these brought. The Ottomans enshrined servitude, partly because they lacked (or rather Montesquieu believed they lacked) an aristocracy and private property. Others were convinced that Christianity was obviously superior to all other religions and therefore had to be propagated across the world to eliminate 'superstition' and Islam. This persuasion can be traced in Britain through the foundation of the Society for the Propagation of Christian Knowledge (1698), the Society for the Propagation of the Gospel in Foreign Parts (1701), the Baptist Missionary Society (1792), the Church Missionary Society (1799) and the British and Foreign Bible Society (1804). It was these and similar institutions in other countries which were dedicated to missionary activity across the world as part of the 'civilizing' work of Europe.

21.1.2 Islam

In 1800 Islam remained the dominant religion of Eurasia and politically it still controlled south-east Europe, the southern shore of the Mediterranean, south-west Asia, Iran, central Asia, much of India, the east African coast and much of south-east Asia. Until the eighteenth century it had little concept of Europe as a cultural entity which it saw as an area of little interest (it was merely one of the lands over which Muslims did not rule) and from which the long-established and superior civilization of Islam had little or nothing to learn. The Christian lands were always seen as divided into two – *Rum* or Rome, the orthodox world, and the Franks, *Firangistan*, a place of iniquity which lacked civilization. In the nineteenth century the impact of Europe was to make the Islamic world question many of its inherited values and assumptions. However, it was also a period of religious vitality in Islam with a growing appreciation of the need for Islamic action and significant internal reform both religious and political which did not depend on European models. These movements, which spread (as with similar ideas in the past) along the trade and pilgrimage routes, were characterized by an attack on dubious traditions and were all to some extent, anti-Sufi. The puritanical Wahhabi movement, allied with the Saud family, controlled Arabia by the early nineteenth century. In 1803 three pilgrims on their return from Mecca founded the Padri movement in Indonesia which was strongly influenced by Wahhabi ideas. In 1821 the Faraizi reform movement in Bengal was founded by Hajji Shariat Allah after his return from Mecca. In 1852 Hajji Umar Tamil founded a new Islamic state in Timbuktu and upper Senegal after his return from a seven-year stay in Arabia. (It was not finally defeated by the French until 1893.) In 1856 Muhammad Ali left Mecca and founded the Sanusi order at Jaghbub in Libya. His reformist message spread peacefully through the Sufi lodges across the western and central Sahara region. In 1881 Muhammad Ahmad declared himself the Mahdi and led a holy war against Egyptian influence in Sudan. The Mahdist state survived until it was destroyed by the British after the battle of Omdurman in 1898. Three years earlier Muhammad Abd Allah Hasan returned from Mecca to preach a reformist message in Somalia. For more than twenty years he fought a holy war (very successfully at first) against lax Muslims, Ethiopians and the British – the latter libelled him as the 'mad Mullah'.

21.1.3 India
During the eighteenth century the various communities in India came into much closer contact with Europeans, especially the British. To strict Hindus the Europeans (this term together with British and English were used interchangeably) were *mlechchha* ('unclean foreigners'), *gurundas* ('cow-killers') or *lal bandar* ('red monkeys'). In general among the intelligentsia (not just those collaborating with British rule) there was, over the course of the nineteenth century, a gradual acceptance of European superiority in technological and military areas. The one significant exception was religion – there was an almost total incomprehension of Christianity, in particular its intolerance, sectarianism and narrow vision. Nearly all Indians found Christianity highly irrational and could not accept the obvious failure of the British and other European powers to live up to their proclaimed beliefs. They also resented European criticism of the 'caste' system because they could see no real difference between it and the highly developed class and status systems of the Europeans. The Europeans were equally incomprehensible to the Chinese and Japanese but they paid

far less attention to these foreigners than did the Indians because they were not ruled by them.

21.2 Technology

From the early nineteenth century Europe was clearly the leading region of Eurasia in terms of technology. This was important not just because of the transformation it wrought in the European economies and societies but because it was a vital tool in the establishment of European control over much of the world. Until this technological superiority was available Europe had only been able to dominate the much less advanced areas of the world – the Americas and then Australasia. Europe had no military superiority over the great empires of Eurasia (they too had gunpowder weapons) and its lack of numbers, and the difficulty of supporting troops at vast distances across the globe, meant that Europe did not fight any of the great Eurasian powers outside Europe before 1750. Even then its superiority was very limited until the development of new weapons and technologies in the mid-nineteenth century. It was the breech-loading rifle, breech-loading artillery and the rapid firing Maxim gun which tipped the balance in Europe's favour. European armies occasionally lost if they were very heavily outnumbered (as the British did to the Zulus at Rorke's Drift) but normally 'battles' were little more than organized slaughter – at Omdurman in 1898 over 11,000 Africans were killed but only 140 British troops.

The first important development was the steam-powered gunboat which made rapid travel upstream along the rivers of Africa and Asia possible. They were first used along the Irrawaddy river during the British war against the Burmese kingdom in 1824–6. Large-scale use did not begin until the 1830s and the first assaults on China. Although useful, gunboats could not be decisive until the Europeans found a way of dealing with the tropical diseases, especially malaria, which for centuries had effectively precluded their settlement in Africa and much of Asia. On average, half the troops Britain sent to the small colony of Sierra Leone between 1819 and 1836 died, nearly all the rest were invalided out and only one in fifty was still fit for further service. In some years death rates approached eighty per cent and the Royal African Corps was composed of military criminals who exchanged their sentence for service in Africa. The bark of the cinchona tree from the Andes was used against malaria from the seventeenth century, although why it worked was unknown. Quinine was first extracted from the bark by two chemists in the 1820s and by the end of the decade was manufactured in large quantities. It was first used as a cure for the milder *vivax* malaria but by the 1840s it was being used in large doses as a prophylactic before infection against the much more virulent *falciparum* malaria. European death rates from malaria fell more than five-fold. The British and the Dutch also started growing the tree in Asia to provide their own supplies. It was now possible for Europeans to live in the tropics with at least a reasonable chance that they might survive.

One of the most important of all developments in the nineteenth century was a revolution in the speed of communications. Internally railways allowed people to travel across most countries within a day but even more important for the development of European control were the changes in sailing times. Until the 1830s the Europeans, like their predecessors in the sixteenth century and the Arab and Roman sailors two millennia earlier, were dependent on the monsoon winds for communications with Asia, particularly India. A message from Britain to India took about five to eight months to arrive, depending on the time of year. Because of the monsoons a response would not arrive back in Britain until almost two years had elapsed. Railways and steamships shortened this time dramatically. In the 1850s it was possible to cross the Channel by steamboat, take the train across France, travel to Alexandria by steamer and on to Cairo by train and then by camel to Suez before taking the steamer to Bombay. The journey took about thirty days and the return the same – about a tenth of the previous time. The opening of the Suez canal in 1869 cut the all-sea journey time from Britain to Bombay in half (and to Singapore by a third) – in its first year it was used by 486 ships with a total tonnage of 436,000 tons; in 1900 3,441 ships with a tonnage of 9.7 million tons passed through the canal.

This method of communication, like all of those so far in human history, depended on the physical transmission of messages, and their speed depended upon how fast humans could travel, by foot, on horseback, by railway or by ship. This linkage was broken by the fundamental revolution of the 1830s. It followed the discovery of electricity, the development of the telegraph and ways of transmitting messages such as the Morse code. Now, for the first time, messages and information could be sent far faster than humans could travel. Initially telegraph wires were confined to land (the British government required the railways to provide routes alongside their tracks) and it took time and the development of a number of technologies before reliable submarine cables could be laid. Although cross-Channel and transatlantic cables were laid they did not last and it was not until the 1860s that most of the technical difficulties were solved. Britain was linked to India by cable in 1865, although it was another five years before the system worked reliably. A message could then be sent in five hours and a response received within the day. Improvements in message-sending technology, allowing two-way traffic and multiple messages, meant that by 1895 two million telegrams a year were being exchanged between Britain and India. A decade earlier the British had established a submarine cable network linking the whole world and previously remote and disregarded islands such as Ascension Island and St Helena in the Atlantic became key places on the global network. Other countries built their own networks – by 1900 there were seven cables linking France and Algeria, and the United States had links across the Pacific using remote bases such as Guam and Midway.

As the world was linked together in a communications network for the first time in world history the Europeans imposed their own standardized time. This was a relatively new development even internally. Until the mid-nineteenth century each town and city kept its own time – there was no problem because communications were so slow people did not notice the difference. However, railways found that they could not operate on this basis and had to impose a single time in their timetables. In Britain they chose that based on the observatory at Greenwich, although it was normally known as 'railway time'. Gradually the whole country adopted a single time. The same process was at work once communications were possible around the globe – the way in which it was done was controlled by the Europeans. They chose Greenwich Mean Time as the base and then divided the world into hourly time-zones for every fifteen degrees of longitude. This meant that at some point two adjacent places would be twenty-four hours apart and the Europeans naturally decided that this inconvenience (the International Date Line) would be placed in the Pacific (dividing island chains) rather than in the Atlantic dividing Europe and the Americas.

21.3 The Establishment of British Power in India and South-east Asia 1750–1818

[*Earlier India 19.13*]

The first major impact of Europe upon Asia came in India in the mid-eighteenth century. It followed the break-up of the Mughal empire after the death of Aurangzeb in 1707 and the emergence of a number of local and regional kingdoms owing only nominal allegiance to the weak Mughal ruler in Delhi. In the early 1750s the British defeated the French in a series of petty conflicts (each side had forces of about a thousand men) leaving the latter controlling only Pondicherry. British power remained over-whelmingly maritime and was based on the control of a few coastal trading cities. The British hardly had an army in the area and they realized that

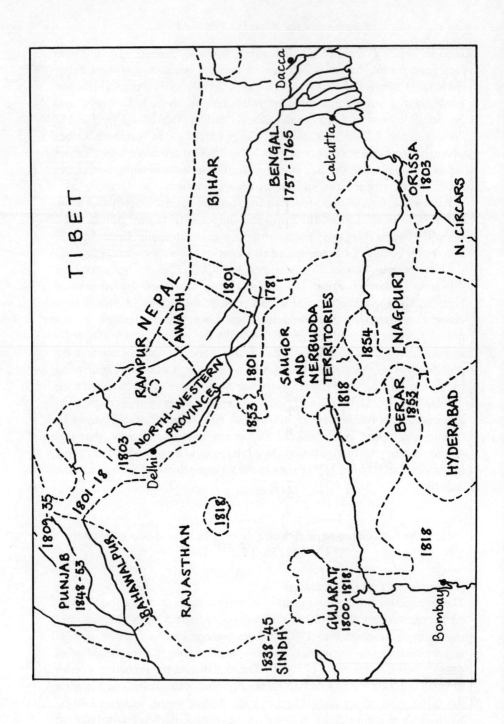

Map 65: British expansion in north India

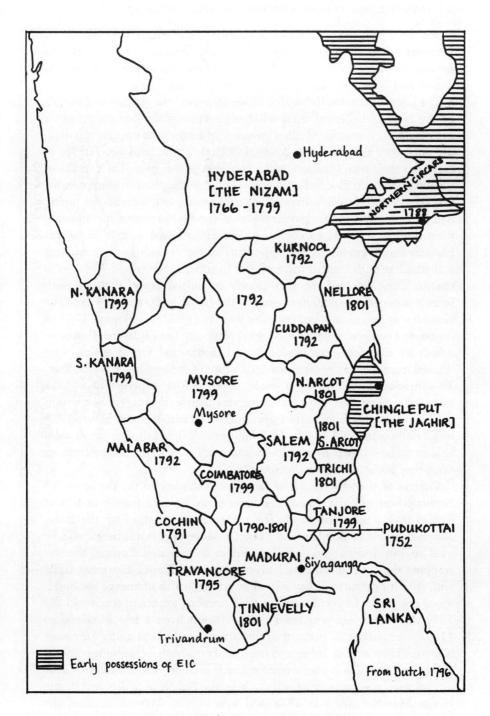

Map 66: British expansion in south India

they did not have the power to attack a unified and strong Mughal empire. Eventual British domination was only possible because they were able to exploit the internal divisions of India to control one area and then use its wealth and manpower to increase their power over the rest of India.

The key events came in the late 1750s following the capture of Calcutta by the Nawab of Bengal, Siraj-ud-Daulah. He was the descendant of an early eighteenth-century Mughal governor of Bengal and the family had, in the same way as many other Mughal officials at the time, been trying to carve out their own kingdom and establish a power base. The capture of Calcutta, the main East India Company (EIC) trading base in eastern India, was part of the Nawab's attempts to gain money and increase his power and he demanded higher payments from the EIC in return for allowing their trading activities to continue. The EIC refused to give in to this blackmail and, exploiting the opponents of the Nawab in the area, sent Robert Clive with a small force of 900 European troops and 2,000 local troops. They defeated the very poorly organized army of the Nawab (which was perhaps 30,000 strong) at the battle of Plassey in 1757. The Nawab was executed, a puppet ruler was set up but it took until 1765 to negotiate a settlement with the Mughal emperor. The EIC were allowed to collect all the state revenues of Bengal, Bihar and Orissa which were derived from the very prosperous agriculture of the area and paid in silver. This produced wealth on a scale never before experienced by the Europeans. Even after allowing for the very high level of corruption within the EIC, its profits from customs revenue alone rose from nil before 1757 to £2 million in 1764 and to £7.5 million in 1769. British officials were able to trade on their own account and since they were exempt from all taxes they accumulated vast fortunes.

Control of the vast wealth of Bengal was the key to the expansion of British power in India. Indian resources could be used for the benefit of Britain in a number of ways. The tax revenues propped up the ailing administrations in Bombay and Madras. More important, they could be used to buy Indian goods to be sold in Britain and Europe, thereby stopping the drain of gold and silver which had limited European trade with Asia for centuries. They also allowed the British to finance the build-up of one of the largest European-style standing armies in the world. By 1782 the British army in India had increased from a few thousand to 115,000 and about 90 per cent of this army were Indians under European control. (They were called sepoys from the Persian *sipahi* meaning soldier.) However, the EIC was over-extending itself in its greed and was often near to bankruptcy as some of its wars failed – the British were defeated by the Hindu Maratha rulers in 1779 and a year later Mysore attacked the Madras area, leading to a long conflict. The government in London intervened in order to impose some administrative framework and stop some of the worst excesses of corruption. The 1783 India Act and the Charter Act of 1793 created a Governor-General in Calcutta and a Board of Control in London to administer British-controlled India even though the EIC continued. By the early 1790s India was contributing £500,000 a year to the British treasury.

British expansion in India was a deliberate policy designed to widen the tax base and find new ways of paying for an increasingly expensive army. In many cases pressure ('blackmail') was put on local rulers to accept British 'protection' through the stationing of British armies and 'tribute' to help pay for the army. Many did so voluntarily but the pressure from the British for more 'tribute' and tax revenue from their 'allies' only increased the strains felt by the local rulers. Many could not survive and were taken over by the British. India slowly became a patchwork of areas directly controlled by the British and ones where subordinate local rulers were left in place subject to strict British supervision. British expansion was opposed by three major Indian states – Mysore, the Marathas and the Sikhs. These states were becoming much better organized, adopting European techniques in their armies (using European 'advisers', especially from France) and were capable of deploying major forces which the British found difficult to overcome. Although Mysore was defeated in 1792, leading to the cession of considerable territory in southern India around Madras and in the west, it was not until Richard Wellesley was Governor-General (1798–1805) that a well-organized British offensive was mounted. Wellesley and his advisers had a much clearer concept of imperial expansion and European supremacy and were prepared to put them into effect. Stronger control was taken over states in alliance with Britain – Awadh (known to the British as Oudh) was annexed and a coup was organized in the major state of Hyderabad to ensure British supremacy. In the second war against the Marathas (1803–5) the British had to deploy over 50,000 troops before they were successful – they captured Delhi and established control over the Mughal court although the emperor was allowed to remain in place. The price of success was high – the EIC debt tripled between 1798 and 1806. The Marathas were not finally defeated until the third war of 1817 when the British had to deploy an army of over 120,000 with more than 300 guns. By 1818 British domination of India was largely secure, although large areas were still outside their influence. They now controlled unparalleled wealth – in 1820 British revenues from India were seven times higher than in 1770.

India formed a base, and provided the military manpower, for a further expansion of British control. Britain began to move into south-east Asia in 1786 when the EIC gained Penang as a base for trade and operations in the area. The war against Napoleon enabled the British to control Java and Sumatra between 1811 and 1816 when the kingdom at Jogjakarta was destroyed. The islands were returned to the Dutch after the war but Sri Lanka was not. Here the British were able to use Indian troops to defeat the strong inland kingdom of Kandy in 1818 and take effective control of the whole island. The next year Singapore was founded as the great rival to Malacca and the Javan ports. It was the start of a strong alliance between Britain and the Chinese merchants in the area which formed the basis for a major expansion of British trade across the region. In 1824–6 and again in 1852 the Indian army was used to conquer large parts of Burma in order to control the timber trade.

21.4 Britain and India: 1818–77

From 1818 the British established a moderately stable, though fragile system in India. Large parts of the country were ruled directly and elsewhere the British insisted on their 'paramountcy' and political control – Indian states were not allowed bilateral relations. They were regulated through the residency system of British 'advisers' together with very tight control over their finances and the contributions they had to make to fund the Indian army and the British administration. Within this system rulers were allowed considerable local autonomy, especially within their courts and over ceremonial occasions. For some time the frontiers of British India remained insecure, especially in the north-west. Sindh was not conquered until 1839–42 but the Sikh rulers who controlled the Punjab were powerful, controlled a very effective army (commanded by French soldiers after 1822) and had their own gun foundry (also run by a Frenchman). In the first Sikh war of 1845 the British only deployed forces roughly the same size as the Sikhs and did not secure a decisive victory until a major display of force was mounted in 1848. Attempts to conquer Afghanistan in the late 1830s and early 1840s were a disaster. Nevertheless, by the late 1840s the frontiers of India were more secure than they had been for decades.

21.4.1 Britain and the Indian economy
The primary motivation of EIC and British rule remained trade and wealth. This was immediately apparent in the late eighteenth century in Awadh as British penetration increased as the Nawab was unable to meet the growing demands the British placed upon him for 'subsidy' and revenue to maintain the army. EIC officials and traders began to remake the economy of Awadh so that it produced the goods the British wanted – primarily cotton and indigo for export. The reason for this was that in

1784 the British duty on imported tea was reduced from 120 per cent to 12½ per cent in order to provide extra revenue for the EIC. Demand rose rapidly but the EIC still had to find a way of paying for the tea it bought in China and gold and silver was still in short supply. Raw cotton exports were a vital element – exports from Calcutta to China (largely from Awadh) rose from 15 bales in 1800 to 60,000 within five years. (The indigo went to Britain.) But this was not enough to pay for the amount of tea required and the British started exporting opium to China. By 1820 it was providing a sixth of the revenue of the Indian government. The British, and the EIC in particular, had managed to produce what was, for them, a 'virtuous circle'. Indian land tax revenues were used to pay for the army which controlled India and which could also be used to expand British power across Asia. (Within four years of taking control of the Bombay territories in 1818 the British doubled the land tax.) Increasing control of trade also brought in more revenue which kept profits high for the investors in the EIC (dividends were usually over 10 per cent a year). The wealth of India not only paid the British to rule the area but left a substantial surplus too.

British control over the Indian economy was also vital. In the early nineteenth century the Indian textile industry still produced much higher-quality goods than that of Britain. Wage differentials were not great – British workers were probably only paid about a third more than their Indian counterparts – and therefore the mechanization of the British industry was vital in creating a price advantage. What the government could do was ensure that British industry had free access to the Indian market through a refusal to impose any tariffs to protect the Indian industry. In 1813 Britain exported about one million yards of cotton fabric worth about £100,000 to India. By 1890 two billion yards of cotton were exported worth about £20 million. Although British cotton did not penetrate into every Indian village this was a massive takeover of the Indian market and contributed significantly to the de-industrialization of India in the nineteenth century. It reflected the strength of the Lancashire textile industry lobby and its influence over a large number of marginal seats in Parliament. After 1870 there was a fundamental reversal of the character of Eurasian trade which had lasted for two thousand years. Instead of Europe buying more goods in Asia than it could sell, British control over the Indian economy enabled it to sell more than it bought. The British trade surplus with India became central to its economy and helped pay for a substantial part of its trade deficit with the rest of the world. Britain also benefited from the Indian economy in other ways. Much of the small modern industry in the country, such as the jute mills, were British-owned and the profits were repatriated to Britain. The first railways were built in India in 1853 – a line twenty-four miles long inland from Bombay. By 1902 there were 26,000 miles of track in the country, more than in the rest of Asia and three times the amount in Africa. However, many of these lines were built with an Indian government (i.e. British government) guarantee. Dividends for the British investors were guaranteed at about 5 per cent a year. If they fell below this level the investors were still paid dividends, but by the government from the taxes it imposed on India. It was a good one-way bet for British investors.

21.4.2 The Great Rebellion and after

Although Britain was the paramount power in India by 1850 its rule still had a fragile base. British, as opposed to British-officered Indian forces, were still small, the number of administrators were even smaller and they were poorly organized in what was still, to a large extent, a framework set by the EIC. Revolts against British rule were common in the early nineteenth century. They affected both the Madras and Bengal armies, zamindars and local landlords protesting about rising land taxation, peasants protesting about the same policies and various nomadic and tribal peoples. Many of the rural 'revolts' under the Mughals had been about a refusal to pay taxes but the British treated this as a civil rather than a military matter. Nevertheless the penalties were stiff and usually involved forfeiture of landholdings. British attempts to extend their control and impose taxation in areas which had been beyond effective Mughal control also created resentment, as did the imposition of local rulers who were prepared to accede to British demands. There was a whole series of disturbances across India in the first half of the nineteenth century but the British were able to keep them local and regional and deploy their power so as to dominate these areas and stop the revolt spreading. There was a general dislike of the British but a lack of common action against them.

What was different about the Great Rebellion in 1857 was its scale, the wide range of groups involved and the threat it posed to British control of the Ganges plain, always the key area for the control of northern India. The problems began in the army with the passing of the General Enlistment Act of 1856 under which Indian troops had to affirm their willingness to serve overseas (part of the British determination to use the resources of India for their own imperial ends). To strict Hindus this raised the possibility of pollution. The introduction of the new Lee-Enfield rifle, which required the biting of the cartridge, and which the Indian troops believed was covered in cow grease, was only the last spark which ignited the mutiny in some army regiments. The mutiny spread quickly but the British seemed to be keeping it under control until it widened into a more general revolt. The key was the involvement of the Mughal emperor,

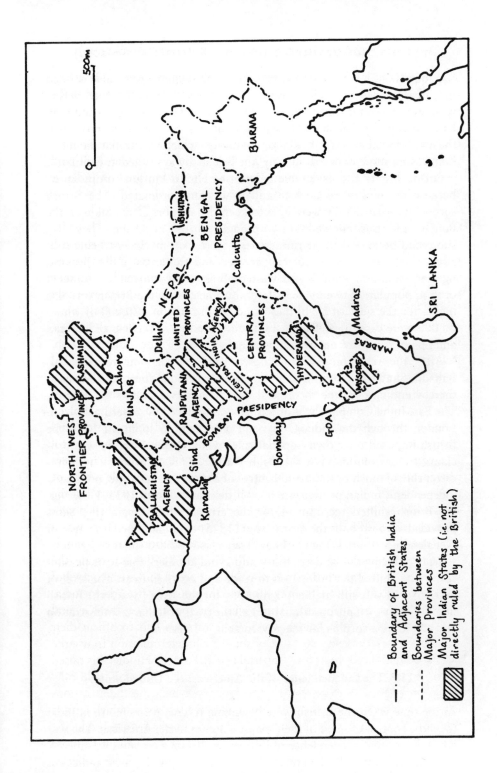

Map 67: India in 1900

Bahadur Shah, which not only gave the revolt legitimacy but also divided the areas where the British were able to keep control. There was a widespread peasant revolt, often supported by the landlords who had been badly affected by British taxation policies. It was the scale of the revolt and the involvement of numerous different groups which meant that the rebellion was far more than the 'mutiny' the British always called it. Ultimately it failed, despite a considerable amount of Hindu-Muslim co-operation, because its aims were unclear and it was uncoordinated. The British succeeded because they were able to keep the support of the Sikhs in the Punjab and this allowed a two-pronged thrust at Delhi. They also succeeded because of their ruthlessness. Stories of 'mutineers' being shot alive from cannon were not exaggerated and the areas of the heaviest fighting (southern Awadh and western Bihar) still showed a significant drop in population twenty years later. But the cost to the British was also high – for the siege of Delhi they required an army of 120,000 of whom 40,000 were casualties. The financial cost in terms of the loss of land tax and opium trade revenue was substantial.

After the rebellion was put down British India was restructured. Bahadur Shah was put on trial and the Mughal empire formally abolished, thereby ending even the theoretical British subservience to the Mughals. The East India Company was abolished and replaced by government from London through the India Office and a Viceroy in India. In 1877 the British imposed their own imperial ruler when Queen Victoria was proclaimed Queen-Empress at the Delhi Durbar. This government system – direct rule of much of India and control of almost 600 separate, nominally independent, Indian princes remained little changed until 1935. However, the British shifted recruitment for the army to the Punjab (the Sikhs provided almost half the army after 1875) and increased the use of Nepalese mercenaries, the Gurkhas. They also modified the tax system by sharply reducing the land tax to try and avoid another large-scale peasant revolt and shifted the burden on to trade and other sources. The level of taxes overall was still high enough to pay for the army (which the British used for their own purposes), to meet all the costs of Indian administration and still leave a surplus for the government in London.

21.5 The Independence of the Americas: the United States

At the time when the British were beginning to create an empire in India they lost control of most of their major colonies in the Americas. The war which led to the independence of thirteen of Britain's colonies was merely the first in a wave of rebellions and was followed by the most radical of them all, the slave revolt on Saint-Domingue (later Haiti) and then by the independence of the Spanish and Portuguese colonies in central and south America. By 1830 the European states had lost control of nearly all the Americas – they were left with a few islands in the Caribbean where the sugar economies were beginning to decay, and the thinly populated area of Canada. Although this might have seemed a major loss of European power in practice it was not. The native population had either been exterminated or reduced to powerlessness and the people who now ruled the Americas were the descendants of the Europeans and shared nearly all their views. They continued to provide a major area for European migration and eventually a significant source of food. They remained closely integrated into the European world.

The British colonies spread along the eastern seaboard of the American mainland had long depended on British help against attack from both the native Americans and the other European colonial powers, in particular the French. British success in the Seven Years War of 1756–63 removed the latter threat. The subsequent British attempt to impose taxes on the American colonies (the Stamp Act and the duties on tea) may have been ineptly handled but were a reasonable attempt to make the colonies contribute towards the costs of their defence. However, the British could deploy little effective power at a distance of some 3,000 miles and the political crisis was allowed to deteriorate into open rebellion, leading to the Declaration of Independence in 1776. In the war that followed the British found that the colonies were invulnerable to the main British weapon, sea power (especially when they had the support of the French navy), and the little military power the British could deploy at this distance was largely ineffective, even if they could have established how to 'win' such a war. By 1783 the British gave up and recognized the independence of the colonies – it was not a major blow because none of their European rivals gained substantially. Perhaps the most remarkable aspect of the war was that large parts remained loyal, not just within the thirteen colonies where the war was often a civil conflict (though without any significant social revolution), but more importantly in Canada. This was partly an accident – the failure of supply for the rebel army when it began operations against Quebec and a particularly harsh winter – but also because the British had carefully cultivated the French settlers in the recently conquered colonies. In 1774 the Quebec Act had recognized the Catholic church in the colony and allowed Catholics to hold office, something which was not allowed in Britain for another fifty years.

In many ways the Declaration of Independence, the war and the recognition of independence were not the most important developments in the United States. The significant departure came with the creation of a federal state and constitution in 1787–90 to replace the very weak Articles of Confederation agreed between the thirteen colonies in 1781. The United States was different from the European states not just because it had a constitution but because it lacked an entrenched aristocratic elite and inherited structures of power. However, it was very far from being a democratic state, even putting on one side the large slave population (which was to grow enormously over the next seventy years). Only the House of Representatives was widely elected, while the other elements in the constitution were designed to hamper and contain any democratic element. The powerful Senate had two members for each state regardless of population and they were indirectly elected. The President was also indirectly elected and the independent judicial arm of the federal government was powerful. As with so many other newly independent states later in the nineteenth and twentieth centuries, the military leader in the war for independence, George Washington, became the first president. Nevertheless when Washington stepped down in 1797 and handed power, after some form of election, to another member of the revolutionary elite, John Adams, it was the first 'democratic' handover of power in the world.

Even though the new state was very far from being unified (the individual states retained significant powers) it was far stronger than the earlier thirteen colonies. Its population grew steadily and settlement pushed westwards over the Appalachians into the lands up to the Mississippi. It became even stronger (at least in theory) after the purchase of the huge, but almost entirely unsettled, Louisiana territory from France in 1803. This was followed by the acquisition of Florida from Spain in 1821 and then Texas, which had declared itself independent of Mexico. The attack on Mexico itself in 1848 secured the area as far as the Pacific coast (though the British ensured that Canada pushed westwards in parallel so that the United States did not expand northwards). By 1850 the United States had become a massive continental power controlling a vast territory and resources once they could be exploited. The expansion of American power was not primarily at the expense of the European powers – it was the native Americans who were the losers. They had already suffered as the earliest colonists expanded from the first small settlements buying and then expropriating the land they wanted and either pushing the native peoples westwards (putting more pressure on the other tribes) or confining them to reservations on the worst land the settlers did not want. In the early nineteenth century even enforced land sales (at nominal prices) did not clear as much land as the settlers wanted, especially in the south as cotton production expanded. Forced removal was agreed by Congress, even for the Cherokees who had a settled and prosperous way of life with their own schools and newspapers. The US army forced 90,000 native people westwards, of whom a third died as a result of conditions on the march. The process was repeated time after time with different tribal groups in different parts of the country as the pressure for more land mounted – between 1829 and 1866 the Winnebagos were forcibly moved westwards six times and the population fell by a half. By 1844 there were less than 30,000 native people living in the eastern United States and most of those were in a very remote area around Lake Superior. In a series of brutal wars in the 1860s and 1870s the tribes on the Great Plains were defeated and removed from all the best land. They were settled in 'reservations' but were moved again if the settlers wanted that land. By 1900 there were no more than 150,000 native people alive in the United States (in 1500 the population had been over five million).

21.6 The Independence of the Americas: the Slave Revolt

The slave revolt which began in the French colony of Saint-Domingue in 1791 was the most violent attack on the plantation and slave system ever made. By 1804 the colony was independent as the state of Haiti – it was the first European colony with a non-European population to become independent. In the 1780s Saint-Domingue was the most prosperous of all the French West Indian colonies with a population of 40,000 whites, 28,000 free coloured people and 452,000 slaves. The number of slaves was rising and their conditions deteriorating equally rapidly as the demand for sugar rose. The problems began with the summoning of the Estates-General in France to solve the financial problems of the state largely stemming from the war against Britain in support of the American colonies. The *grands blancs*, mainly the plantation owners, elected their own representatives and sent them uninvited to Paris where, although they had not been members of the seventeenth-century assembly, they were still accepted. On Saint-Domingue the elite set up their own assemblies (one for each province and one for the colony as a whole) but excluded most other whites – only those who owned more than twenty slaves could vote. They were opposed by the *petits blancs* who by the summer of 1790 seemed to be in control of the colony. Both groups of whites claimed to represent the 'revolution' but in practice only represented themselves. The coloured community revolted in autumn 1790 but were suppressed. They achieved formal equality with the whites in May 1791 following agitation in France.

It was the divisions within the white community and the conflict with the coloured groups which provided the opportunity for the one event the European slave owners in the Americas always feared – a major slave revolt. It began in the northern province in August 1791 when over 200 estates were burned and more than 1,000 whites killed. The result was near anarchy and a four-sided civil war between the two white factions, the coloureds and the slaves. In 1793 British forces from Jamaica and Spanish forces from the east of the island intervened. Commissioners (or governors) sent from France tried, as revolutionaries, to ally with the *petits blancs* but the *grands blancs* attempted a coup and the commissioners started arming over 12,000 slaves to oppose them. In 1794 the National Assembly in France abolished slavery and on the island there was a growing alliance between the commissioners from France and the ex-slaves against the elite whites. The main leader of the slaves was Toussaint L'Ouverture and at first he was nominally allied with the remnants of French rule. He defeated both the British and Spanish forces by 1798, then the coloured groups and finally the Governor-General sent out from France. By 1801 Toussaint was in control, although the French only recognized him as 'Governor' of what they still regarded as a colony. Their attempt at reconquest in 1803 was only partially successful, although Toussaint L'Ouverture was captured and sent to France. The remnants of French power were driven out by Toussaint's two deputies, Jean-Jacques Desallines and Henri Christophe, who declared Haiti to be an independent state at the beginning of 1804. It was to be a country run by the ex-slaves. The constitution adopted in the next year declared that all people, of whatever colour, were to be known as *noirs*, although no white person was allowed to own property. In 1816 it was agreed that any African could become a citizen after residence of one year. The problems the new state faced were overwhelming. The sugar market collapsed, it was ignored by the European states and left to sink into extreme poverty. In the circumstances it was hardly surprising that no stable government could be sustained and Haiti slipped into factionalism and near anarchy.

21.7 The Independence of the Americas: Latin America

The revolt in the Spanish colonies in the Americas began in 1810 and was a consequence of Napoleon's invasion of Spain – nominally the first revolts were in favour of Ferdinand VII as the legitimate king of Spain. In practice the revolt was, as in the British colonies earlier, led by the local elite for their own purposes. However, the outcome was very different for a number of reasons. First, the elite feared the native majority in the Spanish colonies where European settlement had never been on the scale of the colonies further north. Second, there were far greater differences within the Spanish colonies than even those between the north and south of the United States. Third, and perhaps most important of all, was the

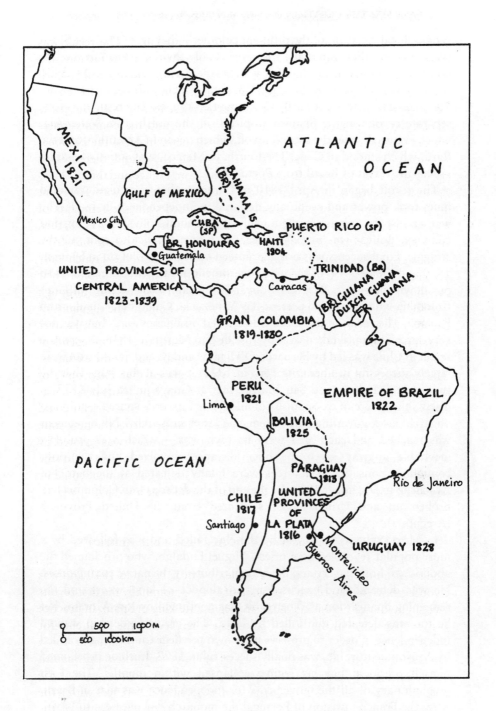

Map 68: The independence of Latin America

geographical isolation of the different colonies – they were closer to Spain than to each other. Internally they were badly divided – even in the late nineteenth century in Colombia it was cheaper to bring goods to Medellin from London than from the capital Bogotá, which, although it was only 200 miles away, was cut off by two mountain ranges. The result was four separate revolts in the Spanish empire – in the north from Venezuela, which eventually met the second revolt, which began in Argentina, and the third, which started in Chile. The fourth, in Mexico, was entirely separate as was the revolt of Brazil from Portugal.

The revolt began in April 1810 in Caracas when a creole-dominated junta took power and eventually declared its independence in 1811. The war against the Spanish in the north, led by Simón Bolívar, was long and complex. Bolívar was in exile twice and returned twice to continue the struggle. Final success was not guaranteed until the revolution in Spain in 1820 and the decision of the new government not to send more troops to put down the revolt. By 1821 Bolívar had established the state of Gran Colombia which included present-day Venezuela, Colombia, Ecuador and Panama. The revolt in the south was centred on Buenos Aires but was not very successful until taken over by José de San Martín in 1816. A separate revolt in Chile was led by Bernardo O'Higgins and he and San Martín were largely successful in liberating Peru in 1821. It was at this stage that the two leaders, Bolívar and San Martín, met at Guayaquil in July 1822 to discuss the future of ex-Spanish colonies. The former favoured republican oligarchy as a governmental system, the latter monarchy. No agreement was reached and each area went its own way – which was probably inevitable anyway given the huge distances involved and the poor communications. Spanish forces were finally defeated at the battle of Ayacucho in December 1824. By the end of the decade Gran Colombia had broken up and Uruguay had separated from the United Provinces (Argentina).

In Mexico the initial revolt by the elite failed and was followed by a more popular revolt led by a priest, Miguel Hidalgo, who proclaimed the abolition of both slavery and the annual tribute by the native communities. He was defeated and executed by an alliance of landowners and the remaining Spanish forces. The revolt was continued by José Morelos but he too was defeated and killed by 1815. The creole leadership wanted independence in order to preserve their own privileges and their revolt, led by Agustín de Iturbide, was finally successful in 1822. Iturbide proclaimed himself president but his regime collapsed within months. The least revolutionary of all the movements for independence was that in Brazil. After the French invasion of Portugal the monarch fled overseas to Brazil. When the monarchy was restored in Portugal in 1815 the kingdom of

Brazil was made co-equal with the home country. The final split came after the revolt in Portugal in 1820 when one of the Portuguese royal family became emperor of Brazil.

21.8 The Atlantic Economy in the Nineteenth Century

[*Earlier Atlantic economy 17.1–17.9*]
The creation of independent states in the Americas did not (apart from Haiti) fundamentally alter the nature of the Atlantic economy. Slavery remained central to the economies, particularly in the southern United States, Brazil and Cuba and the slave trade continued. The United States was based on slavery from the start. Most of the 'Founding Fathers', including Washington, Jefferson and, in total, eight of the first twelve presidents were slave owners. The Virginia Declaration of Rights made at Williamsburg on 6 May 1776 proclaimed 'all men are by nature equally free and independent, and have certain inherent rights . . . namely, the enjoyment of life and liberty'. The Declaration of Independence attacked British 'tyranny' and stated: 'We hold these truths to be self-evident, that all men are created equal, that they are endowed by their Creator with certain unalienable Rights, that among these are Life, Liberty and the pursuit of happiness.' But these proclamations made by the American leaders in defence of their own 'liberty' and 'freedom' ring very hollow because they excluded all 700,000 slaves and the small number of free blacks who, judging from the wording, were regarded as less than human. The drafting of the new federal constitution in 1787 required a number of compromises and although direct mention of slavery was avoided through the use of euphemisms such as 'other persons' it was given a special status by treating slaves as being worth only three-fifths of a free person. There was also to be no ban on slave imports before 1808, and more slaves were imported in this period than in any other two decades in American history.

The first seventy years of United States history was to be dominated by the problem of slavery. As cotton production for the growing British market expanded dramatically the number of slaves rose from about 700,000 in 1790 to over 4 million by 1860. Slavery also spread into nine new states and halfway across the continent to the western border of Texas. After 1830 there were more slaves in the United States than all the rest of the Americas combined. Slaves made up about a third of the population in the southern states but after the ban on further imports in 1808 the slave population grew through internal reproduction. Although the treatment of the slaves was less harsh than in the West Indies the conditions they endured were terrible, especially because of the breeding of slaves and the breaking-up of slave families as cotton production moved westwards into new land. By the late 1850s Alabama, Mississippi, Louisiana and Georgia produced four-fifths of the American cotton crop and the old slave states in the east concentrated on raising slaves. Between 1790 and 1860 about one million slaves were moved westwards in this internal slave trade (about seven out of ten of these slaves were sold rather than moving west with their owners). The result was that a third of slave marriages were forcibly broken up and half of all slave children were separated from at least one of their parents.

The differences between the northern and southern states became more apparent from the early nineteenth century. In the northern states, where slave numbers had always been small, and where there were no great economic interests involved in the retention of slavery, abolition became increasingly common in the late eighteenth century. The Vermont constitution of 1777 prohibited slavery, and elsewhere slaves were gradually freed, though slave children often had to remain in slavery until they were aged twenty-eight in order to give their owners some economic return. The last northern state to abolish slavery was New Jersey in 1804 and by 1810 about three-quarters of the northern blacks were free (but subject to massive discrimination). However, as cotton production expanded and the slave trade was prohibited, few slaves in the south were freed and many states, starting with South Carolina in 1800, prohibited manumission without specific legislative authority. The export of cotton to Britain became central to the Atlantic economy and slavery became the basis of the wealth of the south. In the twenty years before 1860 the economy of the southern states grew faster than those of the north and overall they were as prosperous as any of the states of western Europe apart from Britain. However, slavery produced two serious problems: industrialization and urbanization were retarded and the distribution of wealth was highly uneven. Only one in four white families actually owned slaves, though most had some stake in the slave economy, and the average wealth of the slave owners was fourteen times greater than the rest of the population. Nevertheless, even the poorest whites subscribed to the increasingly important racial justification for slavery – ideas of white supremacy were often all that they had to distinguish them from the equally poor black slaves.

The major political problem for the newly created United States as it expanded across the continent was how to divide up the new territories between slave and free. New land was needed if cotton production (which depended on slavery) was to flourish yet could the new state withstand the strains caused by an expansion of slavery? In 1803 slavery was prohibited in the Northwest Territory (modern Ohio, Indiana, Illinois, Michigan and

Wisconsin) but under the 'Missouri compromise' of 1820 an east–west line was drawn across the country with slavery allowed to the south of it. The huge territories taken from Mexico in 1848 nearly caused a breakdown in this agreement, especially since much of the opposition to the spread of slavery arose from a desire to exclude all blacks from the new territories so as to keep them as a white preserve. By 1860 slavery was flourishing in the south and there was no sign of its imminent demise. However, the southern states, convinced that the election of Abraham Lincoln as president heralded abolition, became the only slave owners in the Americas to fight to preserve slavery. It was a serious misjudgement because this decision and the civil war it provoked provided an opportunity for legal abolition.

The campaign to abolish the slave trade and slavery itself became more prominent in Britain in the late eighteenth century (before then it had been confined mainly to the Quakers). It has often been seen as a moral crusade, partly stemming from enlightenment ideas of human equality, and as acting against Britain's economic interests and therefore a matter for self-congratulation (even though Britain had done more than any other state to create the Atlantic slave economies). However, it is far from clear why ideas traditionally associated with the Enlightenment should have become important at this stage (after all the state which probably owed most to these ideas, the United States, witnessed a huge expansion of slavery in the nineteenth century). It is also far from clear that it was against Britain's economic interests to abolish the slave trade in the early nineteenth century. The Atlantic economy of the eighteenth century was changing rapidly. The sugar islands of the West Indies were in decline and American independence disrupted many of the trade patterns from which British merchants drew their profits. In addition exports to Africa and the Americas were becoming less important as industrialization increased and new markets were created elsewhere. Equally important was the fact that the idea of emancipation was constructed in a very particular way. 'Freedom' became the opposite of 'slavery' which affected black people in other countries and was characterized by a system under which people became property. In Britain however there were 'free institutions' (despite the fact that only a tiny minority had any political rights) and people were 'free' to sell their labour on the market. This was seen not only as morally acceptable but as a positive good because it reinforced free-market capitalism. Defined in this way emancipation was far less threatening to privileged groups in Britain.

By 1810 Britain, the United States, the Netherlands and Denmark had all abolished the slave trade. This had the paradoxical effect of increasing the value of all the existing slaves in the Americas and creating a large contraband trade. Having been the major trader in slaves in the eighteenth century the British, particularly after 1815, became morally self-righteous and switched to trying to suppress the trade. In practice what they did was interfere in the trade carried on by other countries but to little overall effect. In the nineteenth century the British seized about 1,600 slave ships and freed about 150,000 Africans. However, in total over three million slaves were taken to the Americas after 1807, mainly to Brazil and Cuba, and this level was over twice that of the seventeenth century, though less than during the height of the trade in the eighteenth century when it was dominated by Britain. Profits from the slave trade rose during the nineteenth century as prices fell in Africa but increased in the Americas. The slaves freed by the British warships were given no choice over what happened to them – most were taken to Freetown in the new colony of Sierra Leone established in the 1790s. It was a dumping ground for poor blacks expelled from London, the few loyalist Africans who supported the British during the American war of independence and for the freed slaves. The British did little to interfere in the growing slave trade from Africa to the Islamic world – this probably involved about three million people in the nineteenth century (as many as were taken to the Americas) and by 1870 there were as many slaves in Islamic Africa as in Brazil and Cuba.

The abolition of the slave trade did not end slavery – after 1807 Britain still had over 600,000 slaves in the West Indies. Although the demand for sugar in Europe was still rising (average consumption in Britain rose from four pounds per head per year in 1700 to eighteen pounds in 1800, thirty-six pounds by 1850 and over one hundred pounds by the twentieth century), the soil of the West Indian islands was becoming exhausted and production was beginning to shift elsewhere. Slavery was abolished in the British islands between 1833 and 1838 but only with substantial compensation for the slave owners – £20 million (worth about £1 billion today), which was the full value of the slaves. This was highly convenient for the slave owners as their profits fell. The plantation owners still employed the ex-slaves as workers but the cost of decline fell on the latter rather than the owners who no longer had to look after their large capital investment in slaves. Abolition occurred in the French and Danish colonies in 1848 and the Dutch in 1863. This left the three major slave economies of the United States, Cuba and Brazil. The American civil war which began in 1861 was nominally about unity and the right of secession, but in practice it was about the future of slavery. Lincoln had to proceed with caution for two reasons. First, the strength of the Democrats in the northern states who were ambivalent about the war and fighting to abolish slavery. Second, the position of the border slave states which had not joined the Confederacy (if they, especially Maryland, did so they would tip the balance against the north and leave the federal capital, Washington, surrounded by Confederate territory). There was no slave revolt in the south though there was growing non-cooperation as the northern armies advanced and over 180,000 blacks (half of them from the south) fought in the Union forces. Lincoln eventually felt strong enough to issue the Emancipation Proclamation in January 1863 as a war measure – it affected only those slaves still in the rebel-held areas, not those in Union-controlled territory. Slavery was not formally abolished until the passage of the Thirteenth Amendment in 1865 when the south was defeated. Because of the war slavery was abolished without compensation. After the war a limited attempt was made to reconstruct the southern states but it was flawed and not carried through with any great vigour. In the end the blacks were left with the same political and civil rights as whites (the Fourteenth and Fifteenth Amendments) but little was done to enforce these rights. By the mid-1870s white control in the southern states had been largely re-established and the economy was little altered. The blacks remained an underclass of share-croppers subject to massive discrimination in every aspect of life.

During the nineteenth century the Spanish colony of Cuba became the major cane-sugar producer in the world and as early as 1850 had more miles of railway than any other country in Latin America. Sugar production (and therefore the slaves) were concentrated in the west of the island with a rising population of small white farmers growing coffee and tobacco in the east. In 1868 (following a revolution in Spain) there was a ten-year war for independence – the Spanish government was allied with the great planters in the west and was opposed to any freeing of the slaves. However, they were worried that the Americans (now converted to the anti-slavery cause), the British and the French might intervene and side with the rebels. Legislation was therefore passed in Spain to free the slave children (equivalent to very long-term abolition). However, the Spanish colonial authorities refused to support it and this forced the rebels in the east of the island to side with the slaves. It started a process of slow individual emancipation by slave owners. It was not until 1880 that the Spanish government set up a transitional 'apprenticeship' scheme for the slaves which was to last until 1888. However, a major fall in the sugar price brought forward eventual freedom by making slavery uneconomic for the owners. In 1886 the remaining 30,000 or so slaves were freed. Brazil, the last slave state in the Americas, initially benefited from the ending of British duties on the import of sugar in 1846 but then lost out to the more efficient Cuban industry. Increasingly the developing coffee plantations in São Paulo, Rio and Minas Gerais, with their expanding export trade to Europe and north America, became more important than the sugar estates. The slave owners in the sugar-growing north-east region found it more profitable to sell their slaves to the south rather than use them to grow sugar. Even so in the 1850s Brazil was still importing about 37,000 slaves a year to work on the new coffee plantations. Much of the opposition to slavery in Brazil came from racist views about the need for more whites in the country and the likelihood of attracting more immigration from Europe if slavery was abolished. This was linked to the fact that the coffee growers in the frontier areas found that as production expanded even the large-scale import of slaves could not meet their demand for labour. Legislation in the 1870s provided that the children of slaves would become free when they reached the age of twenty-one (as in Cuba it was hardly revolutionary but it did provide for the eventual end of slavery). In practice slavery disintegrated during the 1880s and by 1888, when it was formally abolished, there were only about 100,000 slaves left in São Paulo. Slavery, which had been central to the Atlantic economy for over three centuries, was finally ended.

21.9 Europe: People and Food

[Earlier European agriculture 20.3]
As we have seen in the previous chapter European, and in particular British, agriculture only just coped with the rapidly rising population in the early nineteenth century as industrialization increased. (Britain depended on food imports from Ireland for much of the first half of the nineteenth century.) The population of the whole of Europe rose from 180 million in 1800 to nearly 400 million by 1900. The extra people could not have been fed (let alone their diet improved), and more people employed in the industrial and service sectors of the economy, without a number of very important changes stemming from Europe's increasing influence over the rest of the world. Europe started to import large quantities of food from the rest of the world and export large numbers of surplus people to relieve its own population problem. These solutions were not available to other regions of Eurasia which had similar rises in population and this significantly affected their ability to compete with Europe.

The newly independent states of the Americas (apart from Haiti) remained part of the European world. The close cultural and language ties of the European states with their former colonies did not disappear and as expanding countries they provided ideal places for emigration from an increasingly crowded Europe. New areas were opened up too. The British settlement of Australia in the late 1780s, originally as a dumping ground for the convicts they could no longer send to the American colonies, gradually expanded. By the 1830s the colony of South Australia was created specifically to cater for emigration. The inhabitants of Australia (the Aborigines) who had lived there for some 30,000 years were treated as only semi-human. All their land was declared a possession of the British and in 1805 it was decided that since they could not understand European law they did not need to be put on trial and could face immediate settler 'justice'. As European settlement expanded the Aborigines tried to resist but the conflict was hopelessly one-sided – about 2,000 Europeans were killed along the frontier but over 20,000 natives. The survivors, often ruined by disease and alcohol, were driven into the areas the settlers did not want. The most extreme fate befell the 5,000 or so inhabitants of Tasmania. A series of atrocities reduced the population to about 2,000 by 1830 when the British Governor decided to remove them altogether from the settled areas. A giant sweep across the island was organized and by 1834 all of the natives had been expelled to Flinders Island in the Bass Strait. There, thoroughly disoriented, particularly by the attempts of the evangelical Christian missionaries to make them give up their tribal customs and wear European clothes, their numbers fell rapidly. By 1843 only 43 were left alive. The last lonely and neglected survivor of all the Tasmanian Aborigines died in 1876. New Zealand was also opened for settlement (it was the first British colony to be entirely settled with free labour) but the Polynesian Maoris were much stronger than the Aborigines on Australia. The British were able to secure most of the land but had to come to an agreement with the Maoris under which many of their traditions and much of their culture were preserved under a degree of semi-autonomy.

The Americas, north and south, Australasia and the small colonies developing in southern Africa at the Cape and in Natal, provided the main areas where emigrants from Europe settled. By 1800 few Europeans had emigrated – the population of south America was about 500,000 and there were 5 million in north America (both these figures include natural population growth), Australia had 10,000 Europeans, New Zealand none. Even before the late 1840s emigration rates remained low – about 100,000 a year at most. Nevertheless, between 1800 and 1914 the net migration from Europe was about 50 million people, equivalent to a quarter of the total population of Europe in 1820. Most left because of the poor living conditions in Europe and in the hope that they might be able to make a better life in a new country. Population movement on this scale was unprecedented in world history and represented a major gain to the European economies and societies in terms of not having to feed and accommodate all these extra people (and their descendants). Over half of the emigrants went to the United States with most coming from Britain, in particular Ireland. After the terrible famine of 1846–9 over 1½ million people left

Ireland and just under one million left Germany at the same time. By the late nineteenth century about one million people a year were leaving Europe; a third came from Italy, one of the poorest countries in western Europe, where there was a large surplus of labour in the countryside.

These people left to live in countries with which they had strong connections, where they would find climates roughly similar to those of Europe and where they could grow many of the same crops. The result was a major increase in the cultivated area in the world – in the sixty years after 1860 over one billion acres of new land was brought into cultivation, mainly in the United States, Canada, Argentina and Australia. However, this land could not have provided extra food for Europe without a number of other developments. First, it required the opening up of the interior of these continents through railway construction so that crops and animals could be moved to the ports. Most of this infrastructure was provided by European investment – by the early twentieth century the British owned all the railways in Argentina. Second, changes in ocean shipping were needed, in particular the introduction of large steamships, which dramatically reduced sailing times, increased the cargoes that could be carried and lowered costs. After the early 1870s, following the opening of the first transcontinental railway in the United States and improvements in shipping, freight rates between the central United States and Britain fell by over half in twenty years. The price of US wheat in Britain fell by 40 per cent and exports tripled. Other technologies, in particular freezing and chilling, further transformed the world food trade. The first chilled compartments were used to transport American beef to Britain in 1870 but it was the development of the first refrigerated ship, the *Frigorifique*, which was used between Buenos Aires and France in 1877, which brought about major changes. The trade from Latin America grew rapidly, followed by the first freezer ship from Australia to Britain in 1879 and from New Zealand in 1882. All of these countries came to rely on the export of meat, hides and wool. By the 1890s the first butter and cheese were being transported from New Zealand to Britain. In 1901 the first bananas were imported into Britain from Jamaica.

The result of these changes was a vast increase in the amount of food traded in the world (though nearly all of it went to Europe). In 1850 world exports of food were no more than 4 million tons; by the 1880s they had increased to 18 million tons and by 1914 had reached 40 million tons. It was in this area that the nineteenth century marked a major change in world history. Until then most communities had been almost entirely self-sufficient in food, and the movement of bulky items by land was prohibitively expensive over more than short distances. There had been some trade in bulk food items such as the grain supplies for Rome and

Constantinople, those within China along the Grand Canal and from the Baltic to the Low Countries, but overwhelmingly the food trade had been in high-value, luxury items. Before the mid-nineteenth century Europe's food imports were almost entirely spices, sugar, coffee, tea and cocoa. Then imports shifted to bulk items that formed the basis of the diet – grains, meat and dairy products. By the first decade of the twentieth century Britain was importing 80 per cent of its wheat consumption, 65 per cent of its fruit and 40 per cent of its meat. This enabled Britain to have less than 10 per cent of its workforce engaged in agriculture. Without these imports (and the emigration of large numbers of people) the pace of industrialization could not have been so fast in Europe, and Britain in particular. The countries that exported the food (and other raw materials) to Europe, such as Australia, Canada, New Zealand and Argentina, became very prosperous and were some of the wealthiest in the world. By 1900 the gross domestic product (GDP) per head in Argentina was as high as that of Italy and twice that of Japan.

21.10 The Ottoman Empire

[*Earlier Ottoman history 19.9*]
From the mid-eighteenth century the British were able, over the next hundred years, to take advantage of the break-up of the Mughal empire to establish their predominance in India. Although the other great Islamic empire, that of the Ottomans, was much nearer the centres of European power it was able to offer far stronger resistance to European expansion and managed to survive until 1918. In the mid-eighteenth century, apart from the border provinces of Hungary and Transylvania, which were lost to the Habsburgs at the end of the seventeenth century, the empire was still as extensive as in the sixteenth century. During the late eighteenth century the main threat to the Ottomans came not from the Habsburgs in the Balkans but from the Russians along the coast of the Black Sea. Russian settlement had been pushing southwards for some centuries but it was the Russian-Ottoman war of 1768–74 which separated the khanate of Crimea from the Ottomans and led to the recognition of a vague Russian claim to the protection of Orthodox Christians within the Ottoman empire. The Crimea was annexed by Russia in 1783 and the settlements at Sevastopol and Simferopol were established a year later. Further west the Ottomans agreed to a Russian border on the Dniester river in 1792 and Odessa was founded in 1794.

The territories taken by the Russians were in the far north of the empire and were hardly central to Ottoman concerns. The major problem the

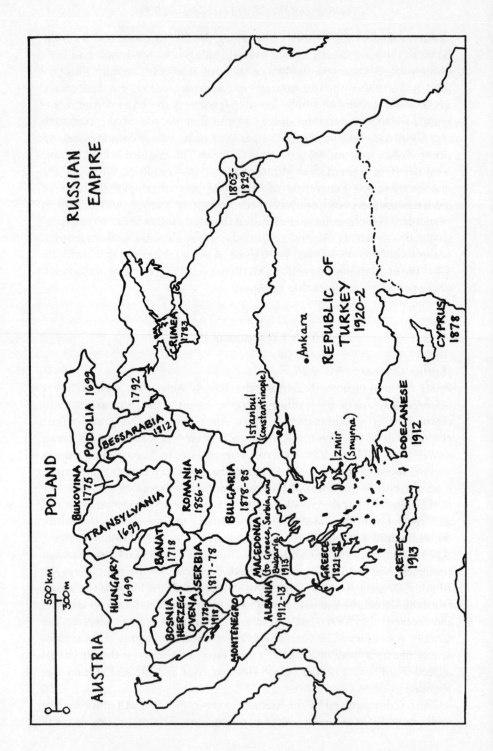

Map 69: The Ottoman empire: territorial losses 1699–1913

empire faced at the beginning of the nineteenth century was a lack of central control and the emergence of semi-autonomous rulers in many provinces. Algeria and Tunisia were controlled by dynasties that had emerged from the army garrisons. Libya was under the hereditary governors of the Qaramanli family. Egypt was controlled by various Mamluk factions and the Baghdad and Basra area was ruled by Georgian Mamluks. Arabia was largely independent. The Ottoman government was quite happy to deal with local elites and select governors acceptable to them, as long as they paid taxes to Constantinople and guarded the border. Taxes were, in any case, very low – less than 2 per cent of the total wealth of the empire. Trade continued without any government interference and much social and economic power was held by groups who were separate from the government. The empire also retained considerable strength. Although the French expedition to Egypt under Napoleon was successful against the Mamluks, it was heavily defeated by the Ottomans at the battle of Acre in 1799 and eventually forced to surrender.

The history of the Ottoman empire in the nineteenth century has largely been written from a European perspective (especially the diplomatic papers of the European powers) and is therefore heavily biased. This narrative becomes the story of the 'Sick Man of Europe' and how the European powers were forced to deal with the 'Eastern Question'. In this story it is an unspoken assumption that liberalism and nationalism (as enshrined in European ambitions) are 'progressive' and therefore inevitable. On the other hand the Ottomans (as with all of Islam) are portrayed as static, unmodern and decaying. This Ottoman 'failure' provides the justification for the dismemberment of the empire in the nineteenth century and its final partition by Britain and France after 1918.

The nineteenth-century history of the Ottoman empire is in fact characterized by major internal reform as it adapted to growing European pressure. The process began under Selim III (1789–1807) although at this stage the opposition of two major groups – the *ulema* and the *yaniçeri* ('janissaries') – long in decline and now corrupt and ineffective made any major changes difficult. Permanent embassies were established in the major European capitals and some military reform undertaken, especially through the imposition of conscription in 1802 to provide new regiments. This threat to *yaniçeri* power led to their deposition of the sultan. Nevertheless major reforms were achieved under Mahmud II (1808–39). The *yaniçeri* were abolished in 1826, followed by the old *timar* system for the recruitment of the army. This led the way to the creation of a European-style army which by the 1840s was over 300,000 strong, as large as any of those in Christian Europe. The new army took up most of the state's resources (as the military still did in the rest of Europe). Even in

1828 the Ottomans were able to put up stiff resistance to the Russians and the new army was to be equally effective against the Russians in the 1870s. Army reform was followed by the creation of government ministries on the European model and a more effective tax system. The major period of reform began in the late 1840s with the creation of a Ministry of Education and the removal of education policy from the *ulema*. In 1864 a uniform system of local government was created, with local councils formed from the elected representatives of a variety of local groups. Legal reform was more difficult because of the role of the Islamic *shari'a*. In 1850 a commercial code was promulgated and provided for mixed tribunals of Ottoman and European judges using European procedures for cases involving Europeans. This system was later extended to the criminal law and Christian testimony against Muslims was also allowed. In 1858 a new criminal code, based on the French model, created state courts under a Ministry of Justice. Civil law reform proved to be more difficult but by the 1870s a compromise between the religious and secular systems was achieved. In many ways these administrative reforms were very similar to those being carried out by the European powers as they grappled with the new demands placed upon them.

Government reform meant that the nineteenth century saw a major rise in the power of the Ottoman state and its increasing control over local groups which, for some time, had been semi-autonomous. In some areas, such as central Arabia, Yemen, inland Oman, the Zagros and Kurdish mountains, the remote parts of Sudan and Libya and among the Druze of Lebanon, this greater interference was resisted. However, the outcome was usually to reinforce the power of the government as military force was successfully used to control these local groups. In most areas stronger central government was welcomed (apart from the introduction of conscription), especially if it led to control over local, arbitrary rulers. The major problem for the Ottomans came in the Balkans and here resistance to greater government power was increasingly expressed in religious and national terms, especially by the elites who were largely excluded from government (hence the attraction of having their own). In the past when Ottoman government was at a low level of effectiveness this exclusion from power did not really matter but once extra functions were undertaken it did. Much of the conflict in the Balkans was a revolt against local rulers and the failure of the Ottomans to control them, and against Ottoman power if they were controlled. Only later was it seen as both a religious and a secular struggle involving national identity built around a real and a mythical past. It was not until the 1820s that these problems became significant, at first in Greece. The problem for the European powers was less the opposition of the Balkan population to Ottoman rule (which was usually at a low level) than the impact these struggles might have on the major European powers and their interests. It was for this reason that the European powers struggled to find acceptable bases for a series of settlements – about the only consistent feature was the opposition of all the other powers to Russian claims.

The Greek revolt of the early 1820s raised romantic ideas and illusions in Europe about a largely imaginary 'classical' past and a Greece once again struggling for 'freedom' as it had in the past against the Achaemenids. The revolt was a failure until Russian and British intervention at the end of the decade which was followed by the establishment of a very small Greek kingdom in the Peloponnese and parts of central Greece – its total population was less than one million. The history of Greece for the next century was one of huge ambitions in a revanchist struggle against the Ottomans. As the Greek prime minister, Ioannis Kolettis, put it in 1844: 'The Kingdom of Greece is not Greece; it is only the smallest and poorest part of Greece. Greece includes every place where Greek history or the Greek race was present.' Elsewhere in the Balkans Ottoman power remained largely intact. In Serbia the Ottomans had encouraged the rebels against the local rulers and the area gained full autonomy in 1830. The principalities of Moldavia and Wallachia had long been semi-autonomous under orthodox Christian governors and were open to Russian influence, especially after they established control up to the frontier of Moldavia in 1792. Russian forces occupied the principalities on eight occasions between 1711 and 1853 but were removed every time – the Ottomans were highly reliant on grain surplus produced here to feed Constantinople, especially after the loss of the Crimea. After the settlement at the end of the war with Russia in 1829 Ottoman control in the area was only nominal – the governors were appointed for life (and were in effect chosen by Russia), taxes were fixed and the fortresses on the left bank of the Danube were evacuated. After the Crimean war Russian control was lessened and the choice of governors was internationalized. Even after unification of the principalities in 1859–61 nominal Ottoman control was retained.

This was the extent of Ottoman losses in Europe before the 1870s. Elsewhere Algeria was conquered by France in 1830, but the Ottomans had exercised no real control for a long time. More important was the loss of Egypt. In 1805 Muhammad Ali, one of the leaders of the Ottoman army which had reconquered Egypt from the French, seized power. He controlled an army of about 200,000 (mainly African slaves and Egyptian peasants conscripted for life) and embarked on a policy of increasing cotton production to meet the rapidly growing demand in Europe, in particular Britain. However, his expansionary policies ran into British opposition in the 1830s and he was forced to cut back the army to a size of only 18,000 and abolish Egyptian industrial monopolies – by 1849 there were only two factories left in the whole of Egypt as the market was swamped by British goods. Nevertheless, the Egyptian state in the mid-nineteenth century was remarkably strong in some areas. Wealth came from a vast expansion in cotton production (it increased ten-fold in the four decades after the 1840s) and this helped to pay for a state-run immunization scheme against smallpox. By 1850 over 2,500 barber-vaccinators were immunizing 80,000 children a year and helping to set up a provincial health service. As a result the population rose from 4½ million in 1846 to 10 million by the end of the century. The problem was that the increase in population and the expansion of cotton production meant that grain had to be imported after 1864. This, together with growing external control over Egypt's trade, led to bankruptcy and the setting up of a European commission to control the state's finances in 1876. When this did not work the British and French forcibly intervened in 1882 and the former took effective control of the country. A year earlier the French had taken over Tunisia.

The major crisis for the Ottomans came in the mid-1870s. It began with a revolt in Bosnia-Herzegovina and Bulgaria and was followed by the involvement of the small independent kingdoms of Serbia and Montenegro. (The Ottoman garrison had finally been removed from Serbia in 1867 and the small, isolated mountain kingdom of Montenegro had been effectively independent for centuries.) Both states wanted different parts of Bosnia-Herzegovina but were defeated by the Ottomans, who put down the revolt with considerable brutality. The Balkan states were rescued by Russian intervention and the subsequent treaty of San Stefano imposed a settlement which met Russian objectives. However, it was not acceptable to the other European powers who, at the Congress of Berlin in 1878, agreed on a different solution. An expanded Serbia became fully independent as did Romania. Bosnia-Herzegovina was placed under Austro-Hungarian protection. The large Bulgaria created by the Russians at San Stefano was reduced by giving the southern part back to the Ottomans (the autonomous eastern Rumelia created in 1878 was united with Bulgaria in 1886). Britain awarded itself Cyprus for its role in the settlement of the Balkan crisis.

The Congress of Berlin left Macedonia as the last major area of Europe under Ottoman control. The complex population pattern and the variety of different claims from the newly independent Balkan states meant that it was very difficult to find any solution for this area. It was these rivalries between the Balkan states rather than the future of the Ottoman empire which were to bedevil the history of the area for more than a century. The rival claims of the Christian states, based on their different perceptions of history and ethnic identities, were incompatible and irresolvable. The rivalries they produced within the wider European state system were also destabilizing. The annexation of Bosnia-Herzegovina by Austria-Hungary in 1908 was accommodated by the main European powers but it ensured the growing hostility of Serbia. In 1912–13 the Balkan powers agreed on a joint attack on the Ottomans which was successful. They then fell out over division of the spoils. The main loser in the second war was Bulgaria (a large part of the Dobruja with a Bulgar population went to Romania) although a division of Macedonia between Serbia, Greece and Bulgaria was eventually agreed. (The Ottomans regained eastern Thrace during this second war.) The Balkan wars left Albania, where nearly three-quarters of the population were Muslim, and where the only 'nationalist' movement was largely anti-Bulgarian and anti-Montenegran rather than anti-Ottoman, as the last area to be resolved. An international conference agreed to create only a 'small' Albania, excluding the Serbian province of Kosovo where the population were overwhelmingly Albanian. At the same time as the Balkan wars the Ottomans were also under pressure elsewhere. They lost Crete (which went to Greece) and both Libya and the Dodecanese islands to Italy.

Under the immense pressure placed on the Ottomans in the late 1870s the internal reform process came to a halt and the tentative 1878 constitution (based on that of Belgium) never came into effect. The nature of the Ottoman empire was also significantly altered. The loss of control over the large Christian populations of the Balkans meant that it became much more Islamic in nature and this became a strong unifying element. There was greater emphasis on the role of the sultan as caliph and head of the Islamic community. As most of the outlying areas of the empire, especially in north Africa and Egypt were lost the state also became more Turkish in nature and this identity began to replace the cosmopolitanism of the Ottoman empire at its height. The perceived weakness of the Ottomans in the face of European expansion led to the formation of the 'Young Turk' movement by Ibrahim Temo (who was an Albanian) in 1889. In 1908, acting through the Committee of Union and Progress, the Young Turks staged a military coup which forced the sultan to restore the relatively liberal constitution of the 1870s. Power lay with the increasingly efficient army, which was retrained by a German military mission, and local elites. Despite the defeats in the Balkan wars and at the hands of Italy, internal reform continued. Its effectiveness was demonstrated when Turkey entered the war on the German and Austro-Hungarian side in 1914. The British were humiliated when they attempted to land at Gallipoli and again during an incompetent campaign in Mesopotamia. It was not until 1918 that the

British were victorious in an attack from Egypt into the Levant. Never-theless by the end of 1918 Britain and France were in a position finally to carve up the remains of the Ottoman empire among themselves – Britain gained most and left the French with just Syria and the Lebanon. The Ottoman empire was one of the most long-lasting of all the great empires in south-west Asia – it survived and expanded for more than four hundred years from the mid-fourteenth century and it took more than a century and a half for the European powers to dismember it.

21.11 Russian Expansion

[*Earlier Russian expansion 19.11.2*]
By the late eighteenth century Russian expansion had reached the Pacific, the Baltic and the Black Sea. In the west Poland was partitioned and Finland was brought under formal control in 1809 as a Grand Duchy, although it retained its own army, legal system, currency, taxation, religion (Lutheran) and even a tariff against Russian goods. After 1815 westward expansion was blocked by the other European powers (in particular Prussia and Austria) and any extension of influence into the Balkans was also opposed. Russian expansion in the early nineteenth century was therefore largely directed at the Caucasus region. It proved difficult to establish control over these remote mountainous areas of small kingdoms (mainly Christian and with long histories) and different ethnic groups (who usually opposed each other violently). The process was long drawn-out and although nominally completed in the 1850s effective control took decades longer to establish. The first area to be annexed was Georgia in 1804, followed in the next year by Azerbaijan and then the Chechen area of Ossetia in 1806. Armenia was not conquered until 1828. From these areas control was gradually extended into the more remote and mountainous regions where opposition was often greatest – Chechnia was not annexed until 1859 and the most remote areas of Abkhazia were not reached until 1864.

By the 1830s the Russians were also beginning to push into central Asia and the area of the three khanates of Khiva, Bukhara and Khokand which had emerged in the fifteenth century after the collapse of Temur's empire. Khiva was the smallest of the three and in decline in the early nineteenth century while Khokand was expanding at the expense of Bukhara. In 1839–40 the Russians, still largely confined behind the Ural and Irtish rivers in the far north of Kazakhstan, launched a major attack on Khiva, almost 800 miles away. The expedition had to retreat before it had covered even half the distance. Over the next couple of decades the Russians moved

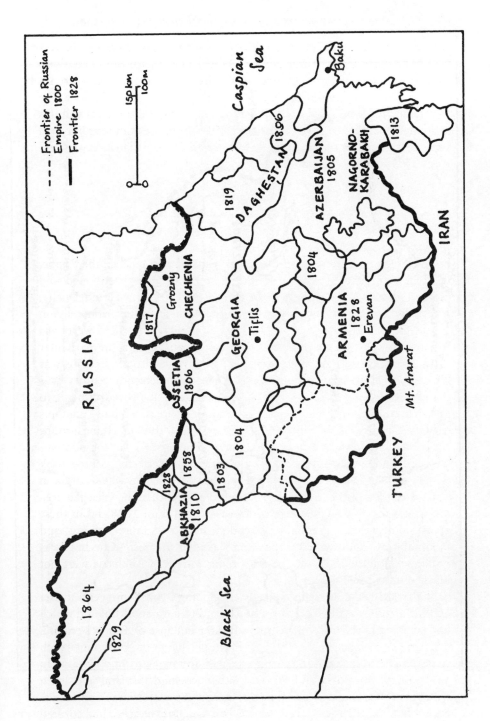

Map 70: Russian expansion in the Caucasus

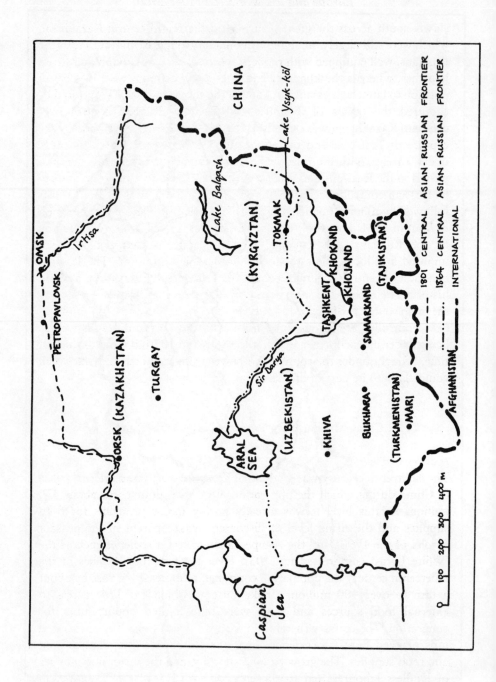

Map 71: Russian expansion in Central Asia

slowly south across the great plains of northern and central Kazakhstan which were still largely inhabited by nomadic groups. By the late 1850s the Russians, well equipped with modern weapons such as cannon and steam launches, whereas the khanates had only a few cannon, were in a better position to launch an assault. In 1860 in the eastern area of Kyrgyztan they captured the towns of Tokmak and Pishpek. Russian control over southern Kazakhstan was established by 1864, followed a year later by the capture of Tashkent and the annexation of the area in 1866. In 1868, under a treaty with the ruler of Bukhara, the major town of Samarkand passed to the Russians and trade was opened. Khiva was now surrounded by Russian-controlled territory but was not captured until 1873. This was followed by a move further south into Turkmenistan and the annexation of Mari in 1884. The whole of central Asia was treated as a colonial region by the Russians – it remained largely Islamic, conscription was not imposed and local rulers retained considerable autonomy. The Russian conquest of central Asia marked another fundamental transition in world history. The region had long been crucial in Eurasian history – it was on the main route ('the Silk Road') between Mesopotamia and China and had been controlled at various times from both the west and east as well as being under independent states. In the 1860s and 1870s it was, for the first time, brought under the control of a power from the north and one which could claim to be part of the European world.

21.12 China: the Early Stages of the Nineteenth-Century Crisis

[Earlier China 19.7]
The eighteenth century was a period of great prosperity and internal peace in China during which the population more than doubled to about 330 million. At this level it was already posing major problems for food supplies and the rising level of discontent was apparent in the peasant revolts of the 1790s and the reappearance of secret societies such as the 'White Lotus' (suppressed in 1803). Over the first four decades of the nineteenth century the population continued to increase – it rose by about a fifth to over 400 million. Unlike Europe, China had little access to external food sources and there were only limited opportunities for emigration. The country therefore once again faced the problem that had long plagued Eurasian societies – a mismatch between population, land and food supplies. The growing land shortage and the increasing number of landless labourers led to the creation in 1811 of the *T'ien-li-chao* (Society of the Celestial Order), effectively a reincarnation of the White Lotus society. Peasant revolts spread across Honan, Hupei and Shantung

and were not put down until 1814. By the 1830s there were, for the first time, revolts in southern China where the *San-ho-hui* (Triad) secret society took root. There were also revolts in the frontier provinces and some loss of control in these regions. In 1807 the Tibetans in Kokonor revolted and in 1825-8 the Muslim communities of the Kashgar and Yarkand region became semi-independent, as did the Yao people of Kweichow in the early 1830s. However, this level of discontent was not serious and China remained a rich, powerful and flourishing state. In the 1830s there were still few signs of the disaster that was to strike within a couple of decades.

The early nineteenth century saw the beginning of the European impact on China. In 1793 the first British mission to China arrived in Peking with 'presents' worth about £15,000 – the Chinese regarded them as 'tribute from the Kingdom of England'. The aim of the mission was to open up trade but the Chinese refused on the grounds that 'our celestial empire possesses all things in prolific abundance'. This was true – the Chinese made all the products that Europe did and usually to a higher standard. The British East India Company (EIC) tried to interest the Chinese merchants at Canton in English woollens and cottons but they refused to buy them because the Chinese industry could meet internal demand (even for a market of around 400 million people) and their products were judged to be better. The problem for the EIC was the growing European demand for tea – in 1720 the Chinese exported about 13,000 tons, a century later the figure had risen to 360,000 tons. Even though the EIC had access to the growing revenues from Indian taxation it was not enough to pay for all the Chinese goods wanted in Europe when so few European goods were in demand in China (this was the same problem that had dominated west–east trade for two millennia). In order to generate more money the EIC moved into the opium trade. Opium was not grown on any scale in China and when the Portuguese had tried to develop the trade through Fukien the Chinese banned it in 1731. The Portuguese were reduced to smuggling in a couple of hundred cases of the drug each year. From the 1760s, after it took Bengal, the EIC had increasing control over opium growing in India. They tried to export it to China but the Chinese issued formal bans on the opium trade in 1796, 1813 and 1814 – by then the EIC were smuggling about 5,000 cases a year into China. In 1816 the EIC decided to develop the opium trade systematically – by 1830 it was smuggling in about 20,000 cases every year and within a decade this figure had doubled. The sale of opium in China became the principal source of revenue for the British empire in India and one of the major supports for their rule.

The British decision to force opium upon the Chinese for the money that could be gained from the trade had a major impact on Chinese society not just in terms of the human suffering it produced but also because of the growing corruption produced by the smuggling. During the late 1830s the Chinese government debated how to respond to the growing crisis. Eventually the prohibitionists led by Lin Tse-hsü won and he was sent to Canton in 1839 where he seized 20,000 cases of illegal opium and ordered the British merchants to leave the city. The British government decided to back their merchants, the EIC and the opium trade. In 1840 the British were reduced to pirate raids along the south China coast until reinforcements arrived the next year. The British fleet then attacked a number of forts, sailed up the Yangtze to Nanking and troops attacked Canton. The Chinese agreed to negotiate but the treaty of Nanking of 1842 was to have more fundamental consequences than the Chinese imagined. Under it they ceded the island of Hong Kong, paid an 'indemnity' of 21 million silver dollars (even though the British had started the war) and were forced to open Amoy, Shanghai and Ning-po to trade, in addition to Canton where the monopoly held by a group of Chinese merchants was to be abolished. The next year the British also demanded and obtained extraterritorial status so that they were not subject to Chinese law. In many ways this was the same policy as that followed by the Portuguese in the sixteenth century – the use of force to gain trade advantages. The immediate result was that the British could now legally ship vast quantities of opium into China – in 1850 they traded 70,000 cases and by the 1870s over 100,000 cases a year (a twenty-fold increase in half a century).

21.13 China: the Nineteenth-Century Crisis – Internal Revolt

British actions during the 'Opium War' were a portent of what was to come later in the century but in the 1840s the opening of a few ports to British goods (when, apart from opium, they still had little to trade) had only a limited effect on China. The real crisis that China faced was an internal one and the great revolts which devastated the country between 1850 and the late 1870s were the outcome of the slowly mounting crisis of the early nineteenth century. The first major rebellion began in the south of the country and was led by Hung Hsiu-ch'üan who came from the minority Hakka immigrants into the area. He grew up in a poor family in eastern Kwangtung, received a good education (as many of the poor in China did) but failed the official exams. He was influenced by the earliest Christian missionaries who had penetrated the area and he decided he was the Messiah who would redeem China. This has led many 'western' historians to see the rebellion as essentially 'Christian' in nature but that is a major misunderstanding. Many peasant leaders in the past had claimed to be some form of Messiah, often the future Buddha, Maitreya, and the movement led by Hung was much more deeply influenced by Chinese traditions. It was originally called the *Pai-shang-ti-hui* ('Association of the Worshippers of God') and gained about 30,000 supporters in two years. It soon became known as the *T'ai P'ing* or 'Great Peace' and took its name from the aim of the 'Yellow Turban' peasant revolt of the late second century CE at the time of the collapse of the Han dynasty. It was also rapidly integrated with the numerous secret societies which flourished in south China. Full-scale rebellion began in the eastern Kwangsi village of Chin-t'ien-ts'un in 1850. The peasants took over the great estates and redistributed the land to those able to cultivate it – a conscious imitation of the T'ang equal-distribution system of the seventh century. The movement was egalitarian – there was no individual property or trade allowed – and each individual was looked after by the community. It was nationalist to the extent that the pigtail was abandoned as a sign of revolt against the Manchu but also puritanical (luxuries and gambling were banned) and feminist – women had equality in land apportionment and they also formed separate female armies. As in previous revolts the secret societies had deep roots, including hereditary membership in the peasant communities, and were able to take over local administration and provide their own alternative government very quickly. The revolt was not an unstructured mass movement across rural China but a well-organized and well-led peasant rebellion with very clear aims.

In 1851 Hung Hsiu'chüan founded the Kingdom of the Great Peace and declared himself *t'ien-wang* or 'king of heaven'. By 1852 the *T'ai P'ing* movement controlled north-east Kwangsi, south-west Hunan and had begun to advance into the middle Yangtze valley. In 1853 they captured Nanking which became *t'ien-ching*, 'capital of heaven' and remained the capital until 1864. From here the movement was able to conquer the lower Yangtze valley, cut the Imperial Canal and stop the grain supplies to Peking. The *T'ai P'ing* armies moved north and west but failed to capture Peking and were forced to retreat. Nevertheless government troops were defeated and with the *T'ai P'ing* controlling large parts of the country the government lost a considerable part of its revenue. The chaos was made worse by one of the greatest disasters ever to strike China. In 1855 there were major floods along the Yellow river, largely as a result of the extensive deforestation in the early nineteenth century as more land was brought into cultivation to feed the rapidly rising population. The river drastically changed its course so that it reached the sea to the north of the Shantung peninsula rather than in the south (a distance equivalent to that between London and Newcastle). Extensive flooding continued for years until the new river course was stabilized by the late 1860s. However, from the late 1850s the imperial government began to recover, largely as a result of initiatives at the local and regional level funded by rich merchants. Internally the *T'ai P'ing* were suffering from increased dissension and from 1862 the European powers, worried by a possible threat by the *T'ai P'ing* to their interests in Shanghai (in fact the rebels had been very careful not to alienate the Europeans), decided to back the imperial government. By 1864 imperial forces were able to recapture Nanking and Hung committed suicide. The rebels continued fighting in Fukien until 1866 and some groups then migrated south into Vietnam where, as the 'Black Flags', they led the resistance to the French invasion of the country.

The *T'ai P'ing* rebellion was only the most important of a whole series of revolts across China. The Nien rebellion in the north started later but lasted longer. It seems to have been based around the 'White Lotus' society but its links with the *T'ai P'ing* were limited and there was no effective co-ordination. It was equally revolutionary and anti-Manchu but lacked the wider ideological content of the *T'ai P'ing*. It began in 1851 along the borders of Shantung, Anhwei, Kiangsu and Honan and became large scale and very serious for the government after the great floods of 1855. The government achieved almost no success against the rebels until after 1864 and as late as 1867 the Nien were still able to march on Peking. The rebellion was finally defeated by troops freed by the suppression of the *T'ai P'ing* revolt in the south. In the frontier regions there were also numerous rebellions by non-Chinese peoples. The 1854 revolt in Kweichow lasted until 1872. It was followed a year later by a revolt in Yunnan. In the far north-west there was a major Muslim rebellion after 1862, partly in opposition to the growing Chinese migration into the area. It was not until after 1868 that the imperial government was able to embark on the slow re-conquest of the north-west and it was accompanied by large-scale massacres and destruction. It was largely completed by 1872 although Sinkiang was not fully under control until 1878.

The huge rebellions which spread across China in the 1850s were a fundamental blow in terms of the wealth and infrastructure destroyed and the number of lives lost. The probable death toll in the *T'ai P'ing* rebellion was between 20 and 30 million. In Yunnan probably about half the population was killed during the suppression of the revolt and the proportion in the north-western provinces and Sinkiang is unlikely to have been much lower. The death toll in Shensi and Kansu was probably about 5 million with the same number killed in Kweichow. In the late 1870s about 13 million people died in the great famine which affected northern China. Warfare affected some of the richest provinces in the country for years at a time. The rebellions also nearly brought the imperial government to its knees and in the process the Chinese state was transformed. The reconquest and reconstruction took place under the emperor T'ung-chih (1862–75) and the effort involved and the new institutions created demonstrate yet again the immense vitality of Chinese society. The immediate impact of the severe population loss was to reduce the pressure on land and therefore the level of rural discontent. Agrarian reconstruction was the first priority of the government and this meant that the tax burden had to fall mainly on trade and industry. In the late 1850s a new tax, the *li-chin*, was imposed on all internal trade at a variable rate of 2–20 per cent (it was retained until 1930). The problem was that this was bound to reduce trade and increase the pressure for provincial self-sufficiency. The tax on grain remained unchanged and the reform of the external customs in 1863 meant that this source now provided about a third of the government's revenue. The extra revenue was needed to pay for major reforms in the army. The old 'banners' inherited from the Manchu system of the seventeenth century proved to be unable to cope with the rebellions. New armies, commanded by new leaders, were created at a provincial level in order to put down the rebellions and these went on to form the new national army. It was through these immense internal efforts that the Chinese government was able to restore control over most of the country by about 1870.

21.14 China: External Pressure

The European powers, together with the United States, were able to take advantage of the weakness of the Chinese government in the late 1850s and early 1860s to extract far-reaching privileges for themselves. Whether they would have been able to do so (or so easily) without the great rebellions of the 1850s remains extremely doubtful. (Once the Chinese government recovered its strength by the early 1870s the Europeans stopped making excessive demands and concessions were not granted.) In 1856 the Chinese authorities stopped the British ship *Arrow* which was smuggling extra opium. Once again the British government backed the opium trade and took military action – Canton was besieged and the forts around Tientsin in the north were attacked. When the Chinese agreed to negotiate they were forced to accept the treaty of Tientsin (1858). Under its terms ten new cities were opened up to foreigners, consulates were established in Peking and an indemnity had to be paid. The most important provision was that Christian missionaries were to have the right to settle freely anywhere in China and own land and property. The Chinese continued fighting and their successful resistance prompted a full-scale British and

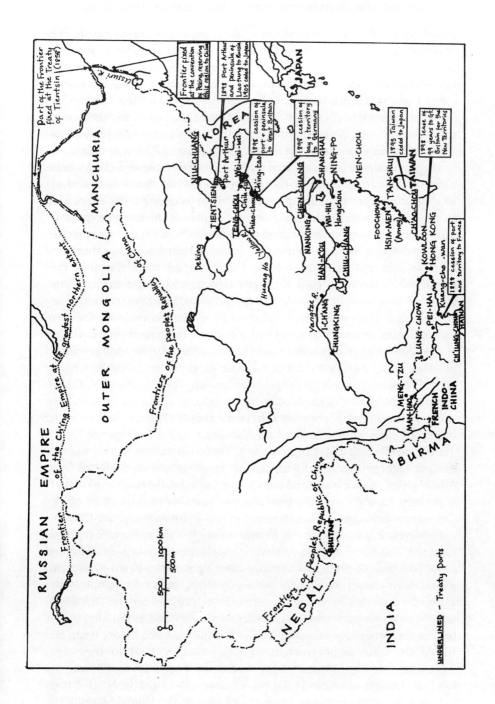

Map 72: China: the external impact in the nineteenth century

Labels within the map:

RUSSIAN EMPIRE

Ussuri R.

Part of the Frontier fixed at the Treaty of Tientsin (1858)

Frontier fixed at the convention at Peking, restoring this region to China

1898 Port Arthur and peninsula of Liao-tung to Russia; 1905 ceded to Japan

MANCHURIA

Frontier of the Ching Empire at its greatest northern extent

OUTER MONGOLIA

Frontiers of the People's Republic of China

KOREA

JAPAN

NIU-CHUANG

Port Arthur Wei-hai-wei

1898 cession of port + peninsula to Great Britain

TIENTSIEN

TENG-CHOU Chih-fu

Chiao-chou Ching-tao

1898 cession of bay + territory to Germany

SHANGHAI NING-PO

WEN-CHOU

CHEN-CHIANG

WU-HU Hangchou

Peking

NANKING

HAN-KOU

Huang Ho (Yellow R.)

CHIU-CHIANG

TAN-SHUI TAIWAN

1895 Taiwan ceded to Japan

FOOCHOW

HSIA-MEN (Amoy)

CHIA-O-CHOU

1898 lease of 99 years to Gt Britain for the New Territories

Yangtze R.

I-CHANG

CHUNGKING

Frontiers of People's Republic of China

LIUNG-CHOW

KOWLON HONG KONG

PEI-HAI

Kuang-cho-wan

1899 cession of port and territory to France

NEPAL

BHUTAN

INDIA

MENG-TZU

MAN-HAO

FRENCH INDO-CHINA

BURMA

CHIUNG-CHOW HAINAN

1000 km

500 m

500

0

UNDERLINED — Treaty Ports

French attack which led to the capture of Peking in 1860 when the Summer Palace was burned to the ground. The Chinese were forced to make more concessions in addition to paying yet another indemnity. Tientsin was opened to foreigners and the peninsula of Chiu-lung (Kowloon) opposite Hong Kong was ceded to Britain. Foreign fleets were to have the freedom to sail on Chinese rivers and, most important of all, European textiles were to be exempt from Chinese customs duties. In 1863 the Chinese were also forced to grant a large international concession at Shanghai.

The various privileges exacted by the European powers (and similar rights had to be granted to the Americans and Russians too) severely weakened an already badly disrupted Chinese economy. The exemption from customs duties meant that European (especially British) textiles could be dumped cheaply on the Chinese market to help pay for Chinese goods. A few western merchants began to live in the treaty ports but they were very isolated and saw little of the Chinese apart from the ones they employed as servants. They were generally arrogant and superior and, although they took little interest in the profoundly different culture they encountered, they were influential in forming the predominant 'western' view of China as static, decaying and corrupt. A far greater problem as far as the Chinese were concerned were the activities, attitudes and privileged position of the missionaries. For example in 1870 the Sisters of Charity started offering rewards to people who brought them orphans. A French consul, faced by a delegation led by the main local magistrate who came to protest at this practice, opened fire on the crowd. The crowd then killed twenty foreigners and destroyed the Catholic mission. In response French gunboats sailed up the Yangtze, the Chinese authorities were forced to execute eighteen people nominated as 'suspects', demote all the local officials, pay an indemnity and send a humiliating embassy of expiation. It is perhaps hardly surprising that hostility towards foreigners, especially Christian missionaries, was increasing in late-nineteenth-century China.

However, it is important not to over-emphasize the effect of Europe on China. A number of trading concessions in the ports backed up by limited naval power could not fundamentally affect a great land-based power with a reasonably strong government and a very strong cultural tradition. What European intervention did was make it more difficult for the Chinese to adapt to the pressure they were under (internally and externally) and it limited their room for manoeuvre. The Europeans gained more trade and forced the Chinese government to forgo revenue vital to their own reconstruction. The indemnities imposed had the same effect. Without the internal disruption of the 1850s the Chinese would probably have been able to react to the growing effect of Europe and the United States in the same way as Japan and gain time to adapt in their own way. They lost this vital breathing space and were therefore forced to make concessions. Nevertheless the impact of the external powers was contained until the 1890s. By the early 1860s, as the imperial government regained control of much of the country, a major industrial modernization process was under way, which, not surprisingly, concentrated at first on the armaments industries. In 1865–7 major shipyards and arsenals were completed at Shanghai which, by the end of the decade, were some of the largest in the world. In 1866 new naval shipyards for steam-powered warships were completed at Ma-wei near Foochow and the first gunboats were launched in 1868. By the mid-1870s naval cadets were being trained in Britain, France and Germany and by 1887 the Chinese were able to open their own naval academy at Canton, alongside a new armaments facility. By 1888 the Chinese Northern fleet was fully operational (construction had begun in 1880).

Elsewhere in the economy the new elites which had emerged from the chaos of the 1850s were leading the process of adopting new technologies, setting up new enterprises and constructing a more modern infrastructure. (They were from the conventionally trained bureaucratic elite so often derided as being hopelessly steeped in an outmoded tradition.) The new enterprises included the Chinese Steamship Company (1872), the K'ai-p'ing Mining Company (and railway) of 1878 and the Shanghai Electrical Company of 1882. In 1880 Tientsin had its own telegraph company and by the next year Shanghai and Tientsin were linked by telegraph. In 1894 a massive iron-and-steel complex was completed at Han-yang, two years ahead of that at Yawata in Japan. In the early 1890s there is little doubt that China was at least as technologically advanced as Japan (possibly even a little ahead) and the level of capital investment was about the same. By the early 1890s therefore China seemed to have recovered well from the mid-century disasters. The external pressure from the European powers had been contained once the government was back in control from the mid-1860s and industrial development was well under way. Then disaster struck again, this time at the hands of Japan.
[*Later China 21.18 & 24.3*]

21.15 Japan Under the Later Tokugawa

[*Earlier Japan 19.8*]
The general view of Japanese history until the last couple of decades was that its phenomenal modern development only began with the end of the Tokugawa shogunate and the 'Meiji restoration' of 1868. This brought about an 'opening' to the west, the adoption of 'western' technology and

'modernization'. It is now clear that the real foundations for Japan's modern history are to be discovered in the period of the Tokugawa shogunate between the early seventeenth century and the mid-nineteenth century. Tokugawa rule was firmly established by the 1630s and thereafter there was internal peace – the only incidents in the next two centuries were two attempted coups by minor *samurai* in 1651–2, which were easily put down, and an Ainu revolt on Hokkaido in 1669 which was equally easily suppressed. Externally there was, as for nearly all of Japan's history, no threat and what the Europeans saw as 'isolation' was no more than a determination to control very closely the terms under which foreigners could operate in Japan. As we have seen Japan was integrated into the regional power structure and trade with China was on a large scale.

The key to Japanese development during this long period of peace and stability, when political history is of almost no importance, was the relationship between the agricultural base and population growth. The cultivated area probably doubled between 1600 and 1850. The highly productive paddy-field rice production was further improved through the introduction of new techniques and the new American crops enabled land unsuitable for rice growing to be cultivated. Agriculture was built on a very strong peasant base of family farms and was becoming increasingly commercialized. The government rice tax did not increase over seventeenth-century levels and a large part of the agricultural surplus therefore stayed with the peasants, improved their diet, and increased their income through sale of the surplus. The population of Japan was large – 26 million in 1700 when it was higher than France, twice the size of Spain and five times as big as England and Wales. Growth was relatively steady despite three major famines – Kyoho (1730s), Temmei (1780s) and Tempo (1830s). Population growth was regulated in the same way as in Europe – a relatively high age of marriage combined with abortion and infanticide (the latter was common in Europe but more disguised). Overall therefore the Japanese achieved a balance between food output and population growth at least as favourable as that in Europe, if not more so. From 1600 to about 1850 food production doubled but the population only rose by a half, producing increasing prosperity.

Equally important was the growing urbanization of Japan. Before 1600 there were only about thirty settlements in the country with a population of more than 5,000. By the early nineteenth century this figure had risen to over 160. Edo, the Tokugawa capital, grew phenomenally from being a small fishing port to a city with a population of about one million by 1800, making it about as large as London and one of the three largest in the world. By the early nineteenth century about four million Japanese lived in the cities, which was as high a proportion as anywhere in Europe (including Britain and the Netherlands) and much higher than countries such as Spain and Italy. The growth of cities reflected the increasing commercialization and industrialization of society. This was based on the creation of a unified system of weights, measures and coinage under the early Tokugawa and the trade in food to the castle towns to feed the resident *samurai* as they became officials rather than warriors. At first trade and commerce were concentrated around the major cities of Osaka and Edo. In the Kinai region around Osaka there was a rich fertile plain with a highly commercialized agriculture attuned to the growing urban market. There were also good ports for trade and a rapidly growing industry processing agricultural products. Developments around Osaka were followed fairly quickly by similar changes around Edo and they then expanded into other regions, particular as industry (especially textile production) spread into rural areas in exactly the same way as in much of Europe. Regional specialization in both agriculture and industry developed as the internal communications system improved. Greater commercialization led on to the development of banking institutions – the *junin ryogaeya* or 'big ten' money exchangers of Osaka and Edo – from the early eighteenth century. They issued their own bills of exchange and promissory notes and had extensive credit networks and money-transmission systems across the country. The rice market was highly commercialized with dealers, spot and future prices, special warehousing firms and agents in all the main ports. The slow population growth meant that labour was usually in relatively short supply especially as peasants moved into the towns to take up new occupations. In the countryside the shortage of labour meant better terms and rising wages for the peasants. The result was the development of a full-scale labour market, a high degree of mobility and a variety of different labour contracts for varying periods.

The Japanese economy and society had managed to move into a 'virtuous circle' of rising prosperity in very much the same way as parts of Europe in the seventeenth and eighteenth centuries. The pace of change may have been slightly slower than in Europe – perhaps because the internal and external peace produced a less competitive atmosphere, although it also avoided some of the unnecessary costs of the almost continual warfare in Europe. The continued rise in the standard of living meant that by the 1850s it was probably comparable to that of Britain and the United States. Life expectancy was the same as in western Europe and the average diet in Japan was far superior to that of the working class in Britain (which was largely based on white bread, margarine and tea). Japanese houses were generally better too – they were wooden structures with sliding doors to allow sun and air inside and although very susceptible to fire were well adapted to survive earthquakes. Because houses were usually only one storey high, urban densities were far lower than in Europe and the United States. When British sanitary engineers visited Japan in the 1870s they thought urban water supplies were of a far higher standard than those in London. Because there were no horses the streets were reasonably clean and 'night soil' was removed under a well-organized system. It was these developments in the period leading up to the 1850s which meant that Japan was not far behind developments in Europe and the United States. They also laid the essential foundations for the very rapid changes in the second half of the nineteenth century.

21.16 Japan and the Outside World

In the early nineteenth century the Japanese government was still able to dictate the terms on which dealings with the European powers took place. When a Russian envoy landed at Nagasaki in 1804 in an attempt to open trade he was rebuffed. The Dutch were still confined to Deshima island off Nagasaki and only allowed to make a four-yearly visit to Edo to give 'presents' or tribute to the shogun. Japan was culturally confident, prosperous, highly literate and took an increasing interest in things European – a translation office was set up in 1811 for French, English and Russian works and the Dutch were included after 1840. European ships were still driven away – in 1825 a government decree strengthened the policy of *sako ku* (translated as either 'isolation' or 'self-reliance') and in 1837 the US ship *Morrison* was fired on by coastal defence batteries. The Japanese were well aware of the outcome of the 'Opium War' in China and realized that their security had always relied, to some extent, on a strong China. In 1844 the Dutch king sent a message warning that it would be difficult to maintain the policy of isolation for much longer as European and American power in the area grew.

By the late 1840s numerous 'western' groups such as businessmen, missionaries and diplomats, were convinced that the methods applied against China, especially the use of force, would be equally successful in 'opening up' Japan for the penetration of their particular interests. In this period the British played a relatively minor role (unlike their role in China) and the lead was taken by the United States which had become a Pacific power after the annexation of California following the successful war with Mexico in 1848. American whalers had been in the Pacific for some time but now the emphasis was on opening up trade with both Japan and China. In 1851 a US mission under Commander Perry was despatched and after sailing across the Atlantic and Indian Oceans it arrived in Edo Bay on

8 July 1853. The Americans were determined to force the opening of contacts and not on Japanese terms as at Nagasaki. It was the beginning of a roughly fifteen-year period when considerable external pressure was placed on Japan (for almost the first time in its history) and the Tokugawa government found it increasingly difficult to deal with the problems this created.

In March 1854, after long negotiations, the Japanese agreed to the essentials of what the Americans wanted. Shimoda and Hakodate were opened to American ships (but as ports of call, not for trade) and a US consul was to reside in the former city. Six months later the British obtained similar concessions. The Japanese realized they needed to make concessions while they built up their strength (by adopting the latest European technology) but were able to steer a course between outright resistance leading to military intervention and conceding fundamental points which reduced their ability to keep control of the process. The British and French attack on China in 1857–60 clearly illustrated the dangers of getting the balance wrong and what would happen if Japan were to become internally divided. In 1857 the Dutch negotiated a more liberal regime at Deshima but without securing any fundamental changes. The major departure came with the 1858 trade treaty with the United States negotiated by the consul in Shimoda, Townsend Harris. Under its provisions the US was to be free to trade (including in Edo and Osaka) and more ports were to be opened. It also secured diplomatic representation in Edo and extra-territorial jurisdiction. The Japanese secured a ban on the opium trade. Similar treaties rapidly followed with the British, Russians, French and Dutch (who finally secured an end to their humiliating conditions at Deshima). The problem for the Japanese government in the early 1860s was implementing these treaties. They put Japan in roughly the same position as China in the 1840s, though the level of European and American settlement in the ports was much lower and largely confined to Yokohama and Kobe. Popular opposition to these settlements led to sixteen foreigners being killed between 1859 and 1867. On each occasion indemnities were imposed and for ten years the British kept a small infantry force at Yokohama. In 1866 a general tariff convention forced the Japanese to maintain a low level of duties (generally at about 5 per cent). In parallel the Japanese began to take steps to adapt to the new conditions – the Institute of Barbarian Books (established in 1811) was renamed the Institute of Western Books in 1862 and the next year it became the Development Office and an important mechanism for disseminating new information.

21.17 Japan: the Reaction to External Pressure

The decisions taken by the Tokugawa shogunate in dealing with the external pressure placed on Japan, though successful in keeping a high degree of Japanese autonomy and avoiding the fate of China, created acute internal political conflict. For the first time in two and a half centuries the continuation of the shogunate was called into question and those groups long opposed to the Tokugawa became much more vociferous. They were able to build on the fears raised by the European and American demands and the acute awareness that the future of the Japanese state and its long-established cultural identity were at stake. Many felt that too much had been conceded already. Internal law was largely a *daimyo* responsibility and it was far from clear that the shogunate had the power to grant extra-territoriality to the 'western' states and it certainly did not have the power to enforce it. The Tokugawa found that they were unable to stop a gradual decline in support among the *daimyo* and the increasing importance of the imperial court at Kyoto. The *daimyo* of Choshu and Satsuma (always opponents of the Tokugawa) revolted and, in alliance with the imperial court, posed as 'imperial forces'. The Tokugawa forces were unable to defeat the revolt in 1866 and the emperor demanded the resignation of the last Tokugawa shogun (Tokugawa Yoshinobu) which was forthcoming in 1867. The 'imperial' army then captured Edo (which was renamed Tokyo in 1868) and by 1869 had established control over the whole country.

The events of the mid and late 1860s are often portrayed as a restoration leading to 'Meiji' ('enlightened rule'). In practice there was no 'restoration' but rather the working-out of a new political order in which the only certainty was the end of the Tokugawa shogunate. It was far from clear that a new stable order would emerge from what was no more than a coup by two *daimyo* from the south-west of the country who distrusted each other almost as much as they opposed the Tokugawa. Satsuma and Choshu were quickly joined by the Tosa and Saga *daimyo* and all four were able to build on the support of the boy emperor Mutsuhito. The most important initial problem was how to incorporate the *samurai*, who owed loyalty to the *daimyo*, into the newly emerging 'national' system built around the emperor. In 1869 the *samurai* system was abolished in Satsuma, Choshu and Tosa and the *daimyo* became governors of their provinces. Similar changes followed in the other areas of Japan. Both Satsuma and Choshu favoured increasing centralization as a way of ridding themselves of the very high costs of maintaining their armies and carrying out local administration. In 1871 the first phase of reconstruction came to an end when the *daimyo* were formally abolished, all the lords were recalled to Tokyo, and new units of local government were created with governors appointed by the central government. This phase ended in 1877 after the rebellion by *samurai* in Satsuma was easily suppressed. All *samurai* were now pensioned off and the stipends they received were changed into interest-bearing state bonds. The wearing of swords was prohibited.

The period after the creation of a national government in the late 1860s was characterized by Japan acquiring all the ingredients of what the Europeans saw as a modern state. National unification came before it was achieved in Italy and Germany and followed much the same path. It involved the creation of a centralized administration, the imposition of conscription to create effective military power and the development of a national education system in exactly the same way as the European powers were doing. (The Japanese national school system was created at almost exactly the same time as that in Britain and rapidly became more effective.) However, none of these changes would have been possible without the infrastructure created during the Tokugawa period. In 1872–3 a delegation of forty-eight prominent Japanese toured the United States and Europe to decide what institutions and policies to adopt. Priority was given to building up military strength as a way of fending off further external demands and keeping the pace and nature of change under Japanese control. Institutional development was slower but generally similar to the semi-authoritarian model found in Germany. A Council of State (*Dajokan*) was created but it was relatively powerless – real power lay with the imperial advisers. In 1876 a powerless 'senate' (*genroin*) was created. In 1881 an imperial decree created a national assembly but it was not to meet until 1890. In 1884 a new aristocracy was created from the aristocrats at the imperial court, the main landowners and senior civil servants which in 1890 formed the upper house of the new national assembly. There were provisions to allow wealthy merchants and industrialists to join once they were judged suitable. In 1885 a system of cabinet government was instituted.

Even more important was the increasing pace of technical innovation. This too was based on developments under the Tokugawa. By the late 1860s industry already accounted for about a third of national wealth and without this base of knowledge, skill and the infrastructure, the developments in the late nineteenth century would have been impossible. For example in 1842 James Nasmyth patented the steam hammer in Britain. By 1860 there was a working steam engine and hammer in Nagasaki – the Japanese had never seen such a machine: they constructed it from the plans in a book. The pace of change in the iron-and-steel industry was remarkable. In the 1850s the reverberatory furnace was in use, followed by puddling and the hot-power bellows by the early 1870s. Both of these came about a century after their first use in Europe. By the 1890s the Siemens-Martin open-hearth process was in operation; this was less than thirty years after its development in Europe. By 1909 the Dobashi steelworks was using the Stassano electric arc process only a decade after it was introduced in Europe.

All of these developments had a major impact on Japanese national power. The avoidance of the internal disintegration that affected China ensured that Japan was never put under severe external pressure and was able to dictate the pace and nature of its development free of significant interference. Japan was also able to assert its power. In the early 1870s it demanded revision of the 'unequal' tariff treaties, though it was not taken seriously at this time. In 1875 a new frontier agreement was made with Russia. This revised the 1855 treaty which had split the Kurile Islands between the two powers and provided for joint ownership of Sakhalin. In 1875 Sakhalin became Russian but the Kuriles became Japanese. The next year Japan, using a provoked naval incident, forced the opening of Korean ports and obtained extra-territorial status for its citizens. It was the start of a process of replacing Chinese with Japanese influence which was to lead to Korea becoming a Japanese protectorate in 1905 and a full colony in 1910. In 1879 the Ryukyu kingdom (Okinawa) was incorporated into Japan as a province. In 1899 Japan was successful in regaining a large degree of autonomy over its tariffs (they were increased to about 20 per cent) and in 1911 total control was achieved.

21.18 Asia in the Late Nineteenth Century

By the late nineteenth century European powers had established control over considerable parts of Asia. The British ruled India and Burma, most of Malaya and northern Borneo. The French had, in the second half of the century, gained control over what became Indochina – Vietnam, Cambodia and Laos – whereas Thailand (Siam) remained nominally independent. In 1898 after the Spanish-American war the United States took over the Philippines. Along the coast of China there were a number of 'treaty ports' which were open to European and American trade. Major changes had also taken place in the far north. Russian expansion into the Amur river area, which the Chinese had blocked in the eighteenth century, resumed as China disintegrated in the 1850s. The Russians took over a large area along the coast as far south as the Korean frontier. Vladivostok was founded in 1860 and rapidly became the main Russian settlement on the Pacific coast. In 1860, as a reward for Russian 'mediation' with Britain and France after their occupation of Peking, the

Map 73: Asia at the end of the nineteenth century

Chinese had to accept a huge loss of territory as far south as the borders of Manchuria.

However, it is important not to exaggerate the degree of European and American influence over Asia at this time. Even a relatively weak state such as Korea was able to burn American merchant ships in Pyongyang harbour in 1866 in order to enforce a no-trade policy and they also forced the withdrawal of a punitive expedition sent in 1871. The existence of a few treaty ports along the Chinese coast did not mean that the Europeans had any great control over Chinese policy or could influence events across the second largest country in the world. Most of Asia remained far beyond European control and even the limited influence exercised in China was not found in Japan or Korea. Britain, the largest naval power in the world, had only limited power in the region. A fully independent China Station was established at Hong Kong in 1844 – it had thirty-five ships by the late 1860s. Within a decade the number had fallen to only twenty and they were operational for less than fifty days a year. External economic power was also very limited. In the 1890s over half of all the European firms operating in the region were found in just three cities – Hong Kong (a British colony), Shanghai (which had a large international concession) and Yokahama. Britain was the largest overseas investor in the world in the late nineteenth century but its total investment in Japan amounted to just £10 million. There was one European firm operating in Tokyo, one in Osaka and two in Peking. In the Japanese ports where trading concessions operated there were only 6,000 European residents. Internal trade was in Japanese hands and European and American groups were confined to the ports and a small part of the export-import trade.

The main disruption in the region was initiated not by the European powers but by Japan. The 1894–5 Sino-Japanese war, mainly over Korea, led to a substantial Japanese victory. Under the Treaty of Shimonoseki the Japanese annexed Taiwan and the Pescadores and imposed an indemnity equivalent to three times the annual revenue of the Chinese government (by 1897 Japanese reserves were so large that they were able to adopt the gold standard). The European powers forced the Japanese to give up some of their gains on the mainland but this was only the prelude to their own demands designed to take advantage of Chinese weakness (as in the late 1850s and early 1860s). In 1897 Germany annexed the Ch'ing-tao and Chiao-chou areas in Shantung followed in the next year by British annexation of the Wei-hai-wei peninsula and port in Shantung and the lease on the 'New Territories' opposite Hong Kong. Also in 1898 the Russians took over the south of the Liaotung peninsula and the port of Lü-shun (Port Arthur). The Japanese gained more concessions in Hupei, Tientsin and Foochow. The French took their share of the spoils by annexing the port and region of Kuang-chou-wan in the far south near Indochina. In 1899 the Americans sent the 'Open Door' note to the other major powers arguing for equal access to China. This was not a defence of China since it admitted the validity of the existing concessions. It was merely an attempt to secure American interests in a situation where they had few concessions themselves.

Most important of all was the reaction in China to these events. It took the form of a nationalist revival and a widespread movement against European influence, in particular the Christian missions and the Chinese who had converted to Christianity. A new movement – the 'Boxers' – heavily influenced by the earlier secret societies, spread across the country taking different forms in different areas. Recruits were attracted through public exhibitions of 'boxing', in reality a series of invulnerability rituals which involved spirit possession, followed by initiation into the secret society and adherence to its strict rules (there were separate organizations for women). The 'Boxers' were both anti-western and pro-Ch'ing as was shown in their songs:

> We are only afraid of being like India, unable to defend our land;
> We are only afraid of being like Annam, of having no hope of reviving,
> We Chinese have no part in this China of ours . . .
> When at last all the Foreign Devils
> Are expelled to the very last man,
> The Great Ch'ing, united, together
> Will bring peace to our land.

It was the punitive measures taken by the European powers (together with surreptitious support from the imperial court) which caused the movement to spread rapidly in early 1900. By March 1900 the Boxers controlled the Tientsin region and by mid-June they controlled Peking. In Tientsin troops from the European legations, trying to rescue Chinese Christians, killed over forty Boxers and seized the Chinese forts. In Peking the government asked all the foreign embassies to leave. On 20 June the German minister was murdered, the Europeans retreated into the legation area and the Chinese declared war. About 470 foreigners and 3,000 Chinese Christians were besieged for fifty-five days, although the fighting was hardly intense – the Chinese only fired 4,000 shells in the entire period and more of the besiegers than the besieged died. Across China about 200 missionaries and over 30,000 Chinese Christians were killed.

All the European states and Japan regarded this as a clear challenge by inferiors to their position in China and, sinking their differences, agreed on a joint expedition. Germany took a strong lead with the Emperor Wilhelm II declaring:

> Peking should be razed to the ground. Show no mercy! Take no prisoners! A thousand years ago [*sic*], the Huns of King Attila made a name for themselves which is still considered formidable in history and legend. Thus may you impose the name of Germany in China for a thousand years, in such a way that no Chinese will ever dare to look askance at a German again.

In early August 1900 a 20,000-strong 'western' force (over half of the troops were Japanese) set out from Tientsin and, after two minor skirmishes, lifted the siege in Peking. Despite the lack of resistance the passage of these troops was marked by the wholesale rape and slaughter of the local population, and the destruction of villages. Peking itself was sacked and looted, and thousands more Chinese killed. The Russians committed similar atrocities as they took advantage of the situation to gain control of much of Manchuria. Once the fighting stopped the revenge the European powers took on China had an even greater impact. They secured a massive indemnity by taking over all the revenues from the Chinese customs and the salt tax. Examinations to the civil service were stopped for five years to try and ensure no Boxers were recruited. The Chinese were prohibited from importing arms for two years, the legation area in Peking was expanded – no Chinese could live there, it was guarded by foreign troops – and all Chinese forts in the city were to be destroyed. These conditions were humiliating (and designed to be so) but it was the indemnity which ruined the Chinese state. It took away its major sources of revenue and ensured that it would not be able to continue the process of internal reform and emerge in control of its destiny in the way that Japan had done. Even though the European powers (and increasingly Japan) managed to cripple China partially they still did not control the country, its politics or economy. Chinese history in the first half of the twentieth century was largely shaped by the desire to escape from the restraints placed on the country by outsiders.

21.19 Africa

[*Earlier Africa 17.8*]
For over three hundred years after 1500 direct European control of Africa was restricted to a few forts and trading posts together with the small settlement at the Cape. The major problem the continent faced, especially

south of the Sahara, was the very low population level – Africa had only about 100 million people in 1900. This, together with the difficult communications and the disease patterns, meant that the social and economic base for the construction of large political structures did not exist. When the European impact did come in the late nineteenth century it therefore quickly overwhelmed the existing organizations. It was the first time in world history that Africa, outside the northern areas along the Mediterranean, had been ruled by external powers.

In west Africa the impact of the slave trade diminished over the course of the nineteenth century and slowly other items were traded to Europe, in particular palm oil. The British controlled the area around the Gambia river and also Sierra Leone (for freed slaves), together with settlements on the 'Gold Coast' and further east at Lagos. The Portuguese held a few islands and Luanda on the mainland, the French were at St Louis-du-Sénégal and Libreville (founded in 1849). Liberia was established by the United States in 1822 as a dumping ground for the free blacks it did not want living in America – it became fully independent in 1847. As late as the early 1870s, when the British moved inland from the Gold Coast to attack the kingdom of Asante, destroying the capital Kumasi, they retreated back to the coast in order to avoid taking on inland commitments. The main power in the region in this period was the caliphate of Sokoto – a loose alliance of about thirty 'states' established in 1817 which were governed by Islamic law and recognized the general authority of the ruler in Sokoto. It was the last great slave-holding state in the world. Further east, troops from Egypt pushed south into the Sudan but it was soon taken over by the British (nominally it remained an Anglo-Egyptian territory).

In southern Africa there was almost constant warfare in the early nineteenth century among the Nguni speakers which resulted in the dominance of a minor chief among the Mthethwa, Shaka, the founder of the Zulu kingdom. Although he was assassinated in 1828 the kingdom, dominated by the military, survived as a major regional power. Equally important was the creation of the Swazi kingdom to the north and west of the Zulu and the kingdom of the Ndebele in south-west Zimbabwe where, having fled north from the Zulus, they ruled over the local Shona people from the 1840s. The main pressure on these kingdoms came from the south after the British took over the Dutch colony at the Cape in 1806. The slave population of the colony reached a peak of over 40,000 people in 1838, just before abolition. Even after this date the black labourers remained only semi-free and strict segregation was started by the British in the eastern Cape from 1828. These events were too much for many of the poor whites, especially those of mainly Dutch descent (the Afrikaners). They moved northwards into the Orange river area and by the 1840s to

Transvaal in order to avoid what they saw as 'racial equality'. They became effectively independent but remained very small states – even by 1870 there were still only 45,000 whites in the Orange Free State and the Transvaal. Further east the British colony of Natal grew slowly (the Zulus remained a major threat for decades) and there were no major developments in southern Africa until the discovery of the huge diamond mines at Kimberley in 1867. The revenue generated was enough to pay for self-government by the small white community in the Cape. The British tried to bring the two northern Boer republics under control in the late 1870s but failed. In the 1890s the growing mineral wealth in Transvaal encouraged the British to take more drastic action. They managed to provoke a war although it took three years before Boer resistance was overcome. The republics were eventually incorporated into the white-controlled Union of South Africa created in 1910.

In east Africa there was a significant change in the early nineteenth century following the expulsion of the Portuguese and the establishment of Omani rule. They took control of Kilwa in 1785 and Zanzibar in 1800 and had governors in all the coastal ports under the authority of the sultan in Zanzibar. Trade routes into the interior for ivory and slaves were opened up. About 50,000 slaves a year were sent to the Gulf and Mesopotamia and there were about 100,000 slaves on the island of Zanzibar (about half the population) mainly growing cloves for the European market. In the interior some states rejected outside contact – by 1878 Rwanda had only allowed one Arab trader to enter the country – but elsewhere, especially around the Great Lakes, external influences were very important. The old kingdom of Buganda fractured under the pressure and trade was beginning to transform economies – cattle were being driven about 600 miles to the coast for sale and caravans taking slaves and ivory in the same direction also brought new products from the coast. As in the past the kingdom of Ethiopia was largely exempt from these influences. Between about 1750 and 1850 it hardly existed as an organized political unit – it was dominated by local warlords. It was reunited in the early 1870s under Yohannes IV and he and his successor, Menelik (who ruled until 1913), turned it into a major regional power. A new capital was built at Addis Ababa, reflecting the continued southward drift of settlement that had been under way for 1,500 years. In 1896 Ethiopia was strong enough to repel an Italian assault and won a decisive victory at the battle of Adowa. It also became an imperial power in its own right. Between 1880 and 1900 Ethiopia tripled in size and took control of Tigré, parts of Somalia, the Ogaden and Eritrea where it ruled over very different groups of people from those who had formed the old core of the kingdom.

The partition of Africa between the European powers reflected internal

European pressures rather than any factors within Africa itself. Until the 1870s the coastal forts and trading stations of the European powers had their own zones of influence along the trade routes to the interior. Only a few areas had been formally demarcated and apart from the Cape area (which was climatically suitable for European settlement) these were along the southern shore of the Mediterranean – an area of direct importance to the European states. France took Algeria in 1830 and Tunisia in 1881, the British were predominant in Egypt (though the French did not accept this until 1904). The partition of Africa south of the Sahara was the result of a general fear among the European powers that if they did not establish their own recognized zones of control then a rival would do so. Much of the demarcation was agreed at Berlin in 1885–6 (the Americans attended the conference so as to ensure they could trade in key areas). The French gained much of west Africa but with the British expanding the Gold Coast and Nigeria. Southern Africa was largely British as was much of east Africa. The Germans obtained their first major colonies – the Cameroons, South-West Africa and East Africa (later Tanganikya). The Portuguese expanded their empire enormously with the acquisition of Angola and Mozambique. The Belgian monarch was given the Congo as his own private possession and it did not pass to Belgium until 1908 after two decades of gross mismanagement, the looting of resources and barbaric treatment of the population. (About eight million Africans died in the Congo during his rule.)

The diplomats drew lines on a map to create colonies which completely ignored realities on the ground, divided up people of similar groups and brought together those who were very different. In Africa maps meant little and colonial rule still had to be established – it involved decades of warfare. Between 1871 and the outbreak of the First World War the only French, British, German and Portuguese military activity was in colonial wars. Even so control was still limited. In 1900 the last major Asante revolt was put down in west Africa but only three years earlier the British had been forced to give up most of the interior of Somalia and confine their influence to the coastal strip (a position not reversed until 1920). In Morocco in 1911 the French still only controlled the eastern and Atlantic areas and it took another three years to conquer Fez and the Atlas mountains. In 1909 the Spanish were defeated when they tried to extend their control out of their coastal enclaves. Although the Italians took Libya from the Ottomans in 1912 they controlled little more than the coastal strip.

Even when conquest and 'pacification' (a favourite European term) were complete the European powers faced a major problem – they were both powerful and weak at the same time. They were powerful because

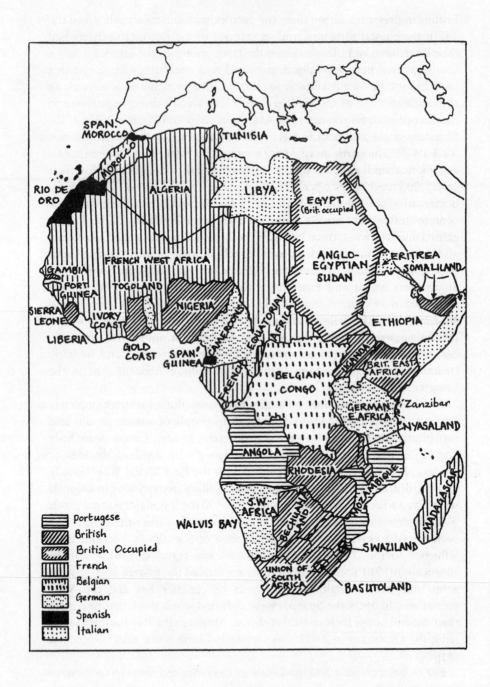

Map 74: Africa in the early twentieth century

ultimately they could mobilize overwhelming military strength, but they were weak because normally in any colony they only had limited military force available and a thinly dispersed administration. In Nigeria the British had 4,000 soldiers and a police force of the same size but in these units all but 75 officers were African. In Northern Rhodesia (Zambia) – an area as big as Britain, Germany, Denmark, Switzerland and the Benelux countries combined – the British relied on just one badly equipped battalion of 750 Africans under 19 British officers and 8 NCOs. In the early twentieth century French forces in west Africa (which had a population of 16 million people scattered over an area fourteen times the size of France) consisted of 2,700 French officers with 230 interpreters, 6,000 armed African *gardes civiles*, 14,000 African troops and one all-French battalion. European administration was equally thin on the ground: in 1909 the British had five District Officers to govern half a million people in the Asante region of the Gold Coast. Outside a few countries such as Algeria, South Africa, Kenya and Southern Rhodesia European settlement was almost non-existent. In 1914 there were just ninety-six Europeans (including missionaries) living in Rwanda. In order to govern these colonies the Europeans therefore had to rely on groups of collaborators who would rule on their behalf at a local level. In a few cases such as Buganda in Uganda, local rulers were left with an almost free hand. In northern Nigeria the Fulani governments of the urban-centred Hausa states, with their established bureaucracies, law courts, fiscal and legal records and educated, literate elite, were easily assimilated into the imperial structure. Elsewhere this was more difficult and often important locals were appointed as paid 'chiefs' to rule over artificially created 'tribes'.

21.20 The World Balance at the End of the Nineteenth Century

The industrialization of Europe and the United States in the nineteenth century radically changed the balance of economic and political power in the world. In the mid-eighteenth century the level of industrial production per head in Europe, China and India was roughly similar and the United States was at about half this level. By the end of the nineteenth century the world economy was dominated by a handful of economies in western Europe (Britain, Germany and France) and the United States which produced over three-quarters of the world's industrial output. Increasing European political power enabled it to remake the economies of those parts of the world it controlled. It did so by removing tariffs so as to allow easy penetration of European goods and by concentrating on the production of raw materials and food to supply European industries and population. In 1830 the states outside Europe still produced two-thirds of the world's industrial output and even in 1860 China's total industrial output was the same as Britain's. Yet by the end of the century British industrial production per head was over forty times the Chinese level. This was not simply a matter of Europe and the United States forging ahead while the rest of the world remained static. Under European pressure the rest of the world actually deindustrialized in the nineteenth century. By 1900 per capita industrial production in countries such as India and China was at about a third of its level in the mid-eighteenth century.

By the end of the nineteenth century the world economic balance was very different from that of the mid-eighteenth century. From a rough equality between Europe, India and China it had changed into three very unequal parts – the core, the semi-periphery and the periphery. The core industrialized countries of north-west Europe and the United States had only an eighth of the world's population yet produced the overwhelming majority of the world's industrial output, about three-quarters of the world's trade and an even greater proportion of its foreign investment. The semi-periphery was made up of three types of state. The first was in south and eastern Europe – Russia, Spain, Portugal, Italy, Austria-Hungary and the Balkan states. They were still largely agricultural, less wealthy and developed than the core states though often important militarily. Some, like Russia and Italy, appeared to be developing into economies and societies more like the core states, while others, such as Spain and Portugal, appeared to be in decline. The second type of state was found outside Europe – the settlement colonies of Canada, Australia, New Zealand and parts of Latin America such as Argentina, Uruguay and Chile. These were relatively prosperous societies with economies built on the export of primary products, in particular food, to the core states. The third type of state in the semi-periphery had just one member – Japan. It had escaped European political control and embarked on a process of industrialization (and the creation of a modern state structure). It was still a largely rural nation (industrial output per head was still one-fifteenth of the level of the United States) but it was an important regional power capable of challenging and defeating the European powers as Russia found to its cost in 1904–5.

The rest of the world made up the economic periphery. Only two major states had escaped European control – the Ottoman empire and China – but both faced huge internal problems which external pressure only exacerbated. Nevertheless both were in a much stronger position than India and Africa because their political destiny was still in their own hands. Economic development in the colonies was in the hands of the European powers and they concentrated on developing primary production and only constructed a limited infrastructure of railways and roads to bring these products to the ports for shipment to Europe and north America. Although slavery had been formally abolished in the European empires (though not in practice in much of Portuguese Africa) it had been replaced by other, similar, forms of labour. Within the colonies forced labour was common and was supplemented by indentured labour in a large number of areas. As the old sugar colonies in the West Indies declined new production areas such as Mauritius, Natal, Fiji and Queensland were opened up. These plantations, and those growing other tropical products for the European market, were worked by labourers shipped across the world. They were held in conditions of near slavery for up to ten years and although supposedly entitled to a return journey home that rarely materialized. In the second half of the nineteenth century over 450,000 indentured labourers went from India to the British West Indies, others went to Natal, Mauritius and Fiji (where they became a majority of the population). Others went to Malaya to work in the tin industry or to Sri Lanka to work on the tea plantations. In Queensland workers from the Pacific islands were moved in, on Hawaii and in Peru they came from China and Japan. The Dutch transferred large numbers of people from Java to Surinam.

The economic restructuring of the world went hand in hand with growing European (and American) political power. By the end of the nineteenth century about half the world's population (700 million people) was subject to alien rule. There were two worldwide empires – the British and the French. By far the largest was the British, which controlled about 350 million people. It stretched from the decaying sugar-producing islands of the West Indies through much of Africa and nearly all of India to the trading colonies of Singapore and Hong Kong in Asia. It also included the white-settled and self-governing colonies of Canada, Australia, New Zealand and South Africa. The French empire had just over 50 million people. Central to the empire was the large bloc of colonies in west and equatorial Africa together with Algeria, Tunisia and Morocco in the north. The other important area was Indochina but the small islands of the Pacific and the West Indies were marginal. The third largest empire was the Dutch (35 million people) in which the islands of the Dutch East Indies were of overwhelming importance (the rest was the poor sugar-producing colony of Surinam and a few minor islands). The Dutch empire was the only major empire not to expand in the nineteenth century. Nearly all of the Portuguese empire had been acquired since 1884 – Angola and Mozambique were added to the islands of São Tomé, Cape Verde and the old Indian possessions of Goa and Diu. Portugal's neighbour Spain lost most of its empire at the end of the nineteenth century (Cuba, the Philippines and other Pacific islands) and was left with Rio Oro and a few other insignificant parts of Africa (in total it controlled less than one million people). The German empire was created after the mid-1880s, but its territories – Tanganyika, south-west Africa, Cameroon and Togoland in Africa and some island possessions in the Pacific – were of little value. The most rapidly expanding empire was that of the United States, although it always liked to pretend that it was not an imperial power. Until 1898 all the huge territories acquired by the United States had (bar the naval base on Midway Island) been on the American continent and its inhabitants had been promised citizenship and eventual incorporation into the union. That changed after the 'splendid little war' against Spain in 1898 when it acquired an empire at a cost of just 385 men killed. Cuba was allowed independence under strict American supervision. Puerto Rico, Guam and the Philippines were taken over but with no promise about future statehood. Hawaii was annexed and incorporated in order to stop any Japanese takeover. In 1903 the United States took over the Panama Canal Zone after it organized a coup to detach Panama from Colombia. The main non-European empire was that of Japan which controlled about 16 million people in Taiwan and Korea.

By 1900 the world had been utterly transformed from its pattern in 1750 and the European powers were at the peak of their influence. However, the forces which were to destroy much of that influence within little more than half a century were already at work.

OVERVIEW 13

THE WORLD IN
1900

World Population: 1,625 million
Regional Population: China: 475 million,
Europe: 390 million, India, 290 million,
Rest of Asia: 200 million, Africa: 110 million,
North America: 80 million
Major cities: London (6.5 million), New York (4.2 million),
Paris (3.3 million), Berlin (2.4 million), Chicago (1.7
million), Vienna (1.6 million), Tokyo (1.5 million),
St Petersburg (1.4 million), Philadelphia (1.4 million),
Manchester (1.25 million), Birmingham (1.25 million),
Moscow (1.1 million), Peking (1.1 million),
Calcutta (1 million), Glasgow (1 million)

Events:

★   Asia outside Japan, China and Korea, dominated by European powers

★   Early industrialization well under way in Japan. Expansion to control Korea and Taiwan

★   Nationalist movement in China – the 'Boxers' – defeated by Europeans and Japanese. China weak – most government revenue taken by external powers, major trading and legal concessions

★   India controlled by Britain

★   Ottoman empire controlling Macedonia, Thrace, Anatolia, the Levant, Arabia and Mesopotamia

★   Weak Qajar dynasty in Iran

★   Africa, apart from Liberia and Ethiopia, partitioned by the European powers

★   Latin America independent but states generally weak and internally divided

★   World economy dominated by the industrialized powers of western Europe and the United States

★   World industrial production three times the level of 1750

★   World use of coal forty-six times greater than in 1800

★   New industries developing – chemicals, electrical and vehicles

★   First steps in development of radio

★   First flight by a Zeppelin

22

The European Civil Wars
(1815–1945)

From the perspective of world history the European state system as it had developed by the nineteenth century was abnormal. Most of the world had always been ruled by large empires incorporating many different people. When well organized and prosperous they were able to maintain internal peace and security over large areas. Europe (outside the Ottoman-controlled areas) was never in this position. Instead the area was divided into several hundred (later many less than this) intensely competitive political units. Despite the mythology (largely created in the nineteenth century) of the European 'nation-state' the identity of 'nations' tended to follow the creation of states rather than the reverse.

The period after the defeat of Napoleon in 1815 was unusually peaceful in Europe. Before 1860 there were only two relatively minor wars – the Crimean (1854–6) and the Franco-Austrian (1859). The latter led to the unification of Italy but it was the wars of the 1860s which produced German unification that were the most destabilizing in the long term because of their impact on all the other European powers. It now became much clearer just how dysfunctional the European state system could become. The extension of the system into the Balkans in the late nineteenth century increased instability because of the irreconcilable claims made by the variety of peoples in the area, each of which believed in their separate identity and therefore their right to a state of their own. Combined with the technological changes in warfare in the second half of the nineteenth century these problems led to the most destructive war in world history until that time. The 1914–18 war in Europe was hardly a world war, although it did eventually involve both Japan and the United States. It was the destruction of the Russian, Austro-Hungarian and German empires towards the end of that war which led to the even more destabilizing extension of the state system into the rest of central and eastern Europe. Europe did not recover from the 1914–18 war before the second round of the civil war began in 1939. This was partly because defeat in the 1914–18 war produced in Germany the movement that brought together nearly all the worst aspects of Europe's past – Nazism. By 1941 this second Europe-wide conflict had developed into a true world conflict which was the most catastrophic war in human history. It resulted in immense destruction and probably the most barbaric act in world history – the deliberate murder of about six million Jews, around half of them in specially constructed death camps. It was a terrible demonstration of the power of the European state and the ideology it could incorporate. Nevertheless the total defeat of Germany in 1945 marked a major break in European history. The continent was now dominated by one external power, the United States, and one which had always been on the European periphery, Russia (later the Soviet Union). The brief period of European ascendancy in the world was over – it had been ended by the region's internal conflicts.

22.1 European Stability 1815–70

The settlement agreed at Vienna in 1815 resulted in a number of complex balances. The long-established dynastic empire of the Habsburgs had the greatest interest in maintaining the settlement and had a central role in it. They were a major check on their old enemy, France, especially in Italy and also on Russia in the Balkans. The German Confederation carefully pre-served the Austrian role and in addition the medium-sized states of Bavaria, Saxony and Hanover (who had their own armies and foreign policy) helped balance Prussia and worked against any German 'nationalism'. There was no elected German parliament – the Federal Diet at Frankfurt consisted of the representatives of thirty-nine governments, including Austria and Prussia who were both partly outside the Confederation. Prussia came to dominate the free trade area (Zollverein) which developed from the 1830s because Austria excluded itself but the latter remained dominant (especially in the Federal Diet) until the 1850s. Generally the Habsburgs, Prussia and Russia could act together in, for example, putting down an outbreak of 'liberalism' in Naples in 1821 or ensuring that they all kept control over the old Polish territories. France was still strong (it remained larger than Prussia) but had no support for any adjustment of the 1815 settlement. Nevertheless it recovered relatively quickly from its defeat, especially outside Europe in the Levant and by taking Algeria in 1830. By the early 1850s it was a major power as it demonstrated in the Crimean war and in that against Austria. Britain remained a maritime power. It regarded the European balance as broadly satisfactory and concentrated on imperial expansion, which was relatively easy. Spending on the army and the navy was much lower than in the eighteenth century and this meant that fighting even a limited war such as that in the Crimea strained resources and the relatively weak state structure to the limits. That war also strained Russia to the limits and beyond. Although it had the largest army in Europe its infrastructure was poor – there were no railways south of Moscow. This meant that the

British and French could send troops to the Crimea quicker than the Russians. By 1856 Russia was on the verge of bankruptcy and sued for peace.

The French defeat of the Habsburgs in 1859 at the battles of Magenta and Solferino led to the unification of Italy under the kingdom of Piedmont-Sardinia. In 1859–60 it took over Lombardy, Parma, Modena and Tuscany and, more reluctantly, the whole of southern Italy after Garibaldi defeated and overthrew the kingdom of the Two Sicilies. This left Venezia (under Austrian rule) and the Papal States in central Italy, outside the new kingdom. (France took Nice and Savoy as a reward for its assistance.) This was only the beginning of the creation of an Italian national identity (and even a single language) from the multitude of different communities on the peninsula, a process that was still incomplete by the end of the twentieth century. In Germany, as in Italy, the process of unification was not one involving any 'national' uprising but rather of domination by a single state, in this case Prussia. It was achieved through a series of wars. The first against Denmark over the disputed territory of Schleswig-Holstein was of little significance. The second in 1866 against Austria and its allies Saxony, Hanover and the north German states was of fundamental importance. The rapid Prussian victory at the battle of Sadowa, and the settlement which followed, forced the withdrawal of Austria from what were now seen as 'German' affairs. A new North German Confederation, dominated by Prussia was created – it included Saxony, Thuringia, Darmstadt, Mecklenburg and Oldenburg. Even more important, other states such as Hanover, Nassau and Hesse-Cassel were incorporated into Prussia. The decision by Louis Napoleon (Napoleon III), the emperor of France, to provoke a war with Prussia in 1870 turned out to be catastrophic for the French, who were rapidly defeated. Victory enabled Prussia to push through a unification of Germany (including Bavaria and the other south German states). In addition the French provinces of Alsace and Lorraine were annexed. A new German empire was declared in 1871 with the Prussian monarch as Kaiser. It claimed to be the 'Second Reich' – the first being that of the Ottonian monarchs a thousand years earlier. These claims were unfounded and this was the first time in European history that there had been a large, strong state in the centre of Europe. Its effects were to be highly destabilizing.

Between 1815 and 1870 Europe was highly stable internally with political power remaining almost entirely in the hands of the existing elites. The social disruptions brought about by industrialization (which outside Britain were very limited before the 1850s) were contained. In Britain itself there were only very limited changes. The extensive legal discrimination against Catholics was lifted in 1828 and four years later the electoral system was reformed to increase its legitimacy by cementing landlord control in rural areas and bringing in a small number of new interest groups from the developing cities. The total electorate remained small and the only radical challenge to the system, the Chartist movement, was contained despite the extensive support it gained in the economic crisis of the late 1830s and early 1840s. In the new state of Belgium the total electorate was only 46,000 and in France, even after the 'semi-liberal' revolution of 1830 when Charles X was deposed and replaced by Louis-Philippe, an electorate of just 250,000 chose the deputies in the National Assembly but the latter had to come from an even more restricted group of 56,000. These three states in western Europe were constitutional but oligarchic and there was no pretence that they were 'democratic' or making any effort to move in that direction. In central and eastern Europe the government of states such as Prussia, Austria and Russia, where the pace of economic change was much slower, remained aristocratic, bureaucratic and, to a very large extent, arbitrary.

In general, governments found that in any crisis, or threatened crisis, a few concessions were enough to rally any discontented elements in the elite and propertied classes and avoid any more radical changes. This was illustrated by the 'failed revolutions' across Europe in 1848. Here the liberals, with their ideas of a constitutional and, to some extent, representative government subject to the rule of law, combined with a 'free press', had little in common with the more radical groups who had some support among the still relatively small industrial working class. The first major revolt came in Paris in late February 1848, followed a couple of weeks later by one in Vienna in which the long-serving Metternich was finally dismissed for advocating military repression. The old order was restored very quickly, starting in Naples in May. At the beginning of December Franz Joseph took the Habsburg throne – he was to rule until 1918. In the same month Louis Napoleon took three-quarters of the vote in the elections for the president in France. The National Assembly was controlled by royalists and conservatives, education was made the responsibility of the Catholic church, censorship was increased and in early 1850 the semi-democratic system came to an end when 3 million people were deprived of the right to vote. By 1851 Louis Napoleon was a largely autocratic ruler and took the title of Napoleon III. In Prussia the old system was restored in 1849–50. Despite the major changes in the map of Europe between 1859 and 1871 there was only one revolution – it took place, as so often, in a state defeated in war. In France, as the Napoleonic system collapsed, groups struggled for power, eventually setting up the Third Republic. However, they did not control Paris which was under siege by the Prussians. Here radical groups gained power and set up a Commune. It was savagely put down once the

French army regained the city. Elsewhere there were few changes. In Britain the right to vote was extended in 1867 when the electorate was doubled, though even then it was still only about two million. In Italy the stiff tax and literacy tests restricted the electorate to just half a million.

22.2 The European Balance 1871–1914

The impact of the unification of Italy and Germany on the European power structure was at first contained. Italy was not a major power and Germany, under the direction of Bismarck, was able to postpone the impact of its increasing strength. France, determined to regain Alsace-Lorraine, was hostile but the other powers were content to accept the 1871 settlement. Internally Europe remained deeply conservative and elites were able to retain their entrenched positions. Apart from France and Switzerland (and Portugal after 1910), Europe was monarchical. In some countries such as Britain the power of the monarch was circumscribed though still important; elsewhere, in particular Germany, Austria-Hungary and Russia, it was central to the political system. Everywhere the nobility and the aristocracy were closely associated with the monarch and were important politically through their domination of the upper houses of parliament. None of the European states was fully democratic. Everywhere the majority of decisions were taken within increasingly complex state bureaucracies or in courts of law. Huge power was also exercised by institutions such as the church. It was only in the last couple of decades of the nineteenth century that parties representing (or claiming to represent) the industrial working class began to have any influence over politics and even then it remained very small.

In the late nineteenth century European states came to take even greater control over their citizens. This was partly the result of accumulating changes in military technology producing a new type of warfare. Three changes in the 1850s and 1860s were particularly important. The principle of the rifle had been understood since the development of gunpowder weapons but without breech-loading their rate of fire was so slow that they were usually only used by snipers. In 1849 Captain Minié of the French army invented a soft-headed bullet which could be dropped down the barrel. This gave a reasonable rate of fire and much greater accuracy and these weapons were quickly adopted across Europe. By the late 1850s they were combined with the second major change – the machine production of weapons. This was first used in the Springfield arsenal in the United States in the 1820s but was not adopted quickly because it was very wasteful of materials compared with individual assembly. The two great advantages were the large numbers of weapons that could be made and the production of standardized, interchangeable parts. It was adopted in Europe at the British arms factory at Enfield in 1859 and machines were soon capable of producing 200,000 Minié bullets a day. Machine production also allowed the development of lightweight breech-loading artillery (used in the Franco-Prussian war of 1870–1). These were followed by breech-loading rifles with a rapid rate of fire and which could be reloaded while lying down. The problem was their shorter range and lack of accuracy compared with the Minié rifle – they therefore required much greater tactical discipline and control of forces through better trained officers and NCOs.

These technological changes meant that it was now possible for the European states to equip forces on a much greater scale than in the past. However, they could only be afforded by conscripting young men and paying them a pittance. The larger armies also required a reserve structure where ex-conscripts could be forced to continue their military training. Both of these tasks required a strong bureaucracy capable of mobilizing large numbers of people. Every young male therefore came to feel the power of the state very directly. Prussia was one of the first states to move in this direction. It imposed a three-year period of conscription with no exemptions granted. This was followed by four years' service in the reserves and then service in the Landwehr. This meant that Prussia could mobilize the equivalent of seven years' intake into the army and leave a well-trained Landwehr to guard its home territory. Mobilization of the population on this scale was only possible because of two other developments. First the electric telegraph allowed centralized command structures capable of controlling huge numbers. Second, the developing railway systems of Europe allowed large armies to be moved rapidly as long as complex mobilization schedules were planned carefully in advance. Railways also allowed these armies to be supplied with munitions and food, although horses were still essential to move supplies from the railhead. Armies remained dominated by an aristocratic leadership but they were increasingly dependent on technological developments and the growing industrial base of the European powers.

By the time that these changes had been incorporated into European military structures there were growing signs that the European balance was under pressure from an increasingly powerful Germany. German unification and industrialization came relatively late in European terms and therefore it posed difficult problems for the existing powers in accommodating its demands. Germany was a highly successful industrial power – its industrial production was greater than that of Britain by the early twentieth century and it dominated the newly developing chemical industry. However, by the time it asserted its claim to an imperial status equal to that of the other major European powers there were few areas of the world left to be taken over and the German empire remained restricted to relatively poor areas which the other powers had not wanted. Although thwarted overseas Germany was also opposed in Europe because any increase in its power here would be even more destabilizing because it threatened the status quo which benefited the other powers. German rhetoric and attitudes, based as they were on the common European mixture of social Darwinism, racism, militarism and imperialism, were no different from those of the other powers. By the late 1890s Europe was divided into two – the Dual Alliance of France and Russia and the Triple Alliance of Germany, Austria-Hungary and Italy. There was a rough balance between them. Russian manpower compensated for the fundamental French weakness – its very slow rate of population growth, which made it difficult to sustain an army capable of matching that of Germany. Russia could, because of its vast population, maintain armed forces of nearly 1.2 million men (more than twice those of Germany), but the infrastructure to support them in terms of munitions output and railways was always limited. In the Triple Alliance Austria-Hungary was only a minor asset to Germany, and Italy was a semi-industrialized country which was militarily weak, as the Ethiopians demonstrated in 1896. Italy's position in the alliance was anomalous, given its disputes with Austria-Hungary over territory in the Alps and Dalmatia, its long coastline, French naval supremacy and its dependence on Britain for over four-fifths of its coal. By the end of the nineteenth century most strategists and diplomats did not expect Italy to join its nominal allies in any European war.

Britain, the European power most detached from the continent's power structure, faced the most fundamental strategic problems in the late nineteenth and early twentieth centuries. It was the nearest to being a 'world power' although its industrial supremacy was over by the 1870s as other states, first the United States and then Germany, overtook it. The expansion of the empire in the late nineteenth century was, to a large extent, a sign of weakness – a determination to deny areas to its rivals which only increased liabilities rather than strength. Britain as a status quo power could not benefit from any likely redistribution of power in the world. The main aim of British policy makers was therefore to try and preserve Britain's position for as long as possible in the face of a series of economic, military and strategic developments which threatened to undermine it. As the major naval power in the world the British were adversely affected both by the increasing importance of railways, which enabled the continental powers to move troops more quickly by land than the British could by sea, and by the rise of powers outside Europe. The most important of these was the United States. In the 1880s the US navy was smaller than that of Chile, but a six-fold increase, which meant that by 1904 the Americans were building fourteen battleships and thirteen cruisers simultaneously, turned it into the third largest in the world. Britain had to recognize effective American supremacy in the western hemisphere. Even more difficult problems were posed by the rise of Japan as a major regional power. This made the vulnerability of Britain's empire in the area (the trading colonies of Singapore and Hong Kong and the white dominions of Australia and New Zealand) all too apparent. Britain therefore sought an alliance with Japan in 1902. For the next twenty years that alliance, which protected the empire in the Pacific, south-east Asia and Oceania, was to be a cornerstone of British policy. The alliance with Japan also helped in dealing with the central British strategic problem – the defence of the large Indian empire acquired since the 1750s against a possible Russian threat. This stemmed from the extension of Russian power into central Asia and the building of railways towards Afghanistan and the Indian frontier. Although the logistical difficulties involved in any attack were immense the British felt they could not discount them. The alliance with Japan provided some support (as their defeat of the Russians in 1904–5 demonstrated) but the British felt that they also had to come to an agreement with Russia and this meant that they first had to reach a settlement with Russia's ally France over their numerous colonial disputes. Although once these agreements were made by 1907 the British had stabilized their strategic situation they did so at a major cost: they were forced to take sides (at least implicitly) in the alliance system which divided Europe. This tendency was reinforced by the German decision to demonstrate its status by building an ocean-going navy, though optimized for action in the North Sea. The British were bound to see this as a direct threat.

In parallel with these strategic changes, developments in technology were bringing even more changes to the nature of warfare and forcing states to adapt at an ever-increasing pace. As early as 1870 the French were using the first primitive machine-gun, capable of firing about 150 rounds a minute. It was the development of the Maxim gun in 1884 that produced a highly effective weapon, rapidly adopted and modified by all the armies of the world. When combined with an invention originally developed to control cattle on the plains of north America – barbed wire – it gave overwhelming superiority to the defence in any battle. At sea explosive shells had ended the supremacy of wooden ships by the 1860s. In the first decade of the twentieth century a further step-jump in technology produced the all-big-gun battleship with heavy armour using special steels, oil-fired turbine engines and mechanical computers for range-finding and gun-laying. At the same time the first submarines were developed and the introduction of the diesel engine changed their role from defensive to offensive weapons as their operational range increased to 5,000 miles. Exactly how these weapons would be used in war was unclear.

A major new area of warfare was in the air. The first flight by unpowered balloon came in the late eighteenth century but it was the development of relatively lightweight but powerful internal combustion engines which brought revolutionary change. The first Zeppelin airship flew in 1900 and although Germany had eight machines operational by 1914 they had little idea how to use such relatively clumsy weapons. The first powered flight by the Wright brothers took place in December 1903 and by 1914 Britain, France and Germany each had several hundred military aircraft operational. Their main use seemed likely to be reconnaissance but the Italians had already gained the dubious distinction of being the first power to bomb civilians when their planes dropped grenades on a Libyan town in October 1911 during the war against the Ottomans. Equally important were developments in the field of communications which affected all areas of warfare. Following on from the electric telegraph, telephone networks were available by the end of the nineteenth century and in 1897 Marconi took out a patent for radio (in 1901 he transmitted the first signals across the Atlantic). Civilian development of the new technology was slow but the military adopted it very quickly. By 1914 the British had equipped 435 ships with radio and built thirty shore stations to communicate with them. This made it much easier to control fleets at a distance but also provided opponents with an opportunity to intercept the radio signals.

It is too simplistic to see Europe in the early twentieth century as divided into two heavily armed camps engaged in a major arms race and waiting for war to break out. There were rivalries but the major diplomatic crises – Morocco in 1905–6 and 1911, the Austro-Hungarian annexation of Bosnia-Herzegovina in 1907 and the Balkan wars of 1912–13 – were successfully resolved. Spending on arms was at normal peacetime levels – about 2 or 3 per cent of national income. Germany was not uniquely militaristic. Between 1890 and 1914 it spent just over 3 per cent of its GDP on defence; this was less than Britain, and it spent twice as much on social welfare programmes. However, after 1912 all the major powers were increasingly prepared to consider a war, which they expected to be relatively short, as a possible solution to the problems they faced. In particular the German government felt that the strategic balance was becoming increasingly unfavourable as they faced a probable two-front war. They believed that the construction of new railways by the Russians (particularly westwards into Poland) would speed up their relatively slow mobilization schedule and ruin German war plans by making it impossible for them to defeat France quickly (as they had in 1870) before turning east to face the Russians. Growing Social Democratic strength (demonstrated in the 1912 Reichstag elections) convinced many in the German elite that war might be the only way to maintain the existing social and political order, by creating an atmosphere in which the working class would rally to support the nation.

During the diplomatic crisis in July 1914 that followed the assassination of the heir to the Austro-Hungarian throne by Serb nationalists, the German government encouraged its allies in Vienna to make extreme demands and showed little concern about the risk of a general European war. If the primary responsibility for the outbreak of war rests with the German and Austro-Hungarian governments, neither the Russian nor French governments showed much desire to avoid conflict. The outbreak of a European war in the first days of August 1914 left the British in a quandary. A German victory would leave them dangerously isolated, but on the other hand if France and Russia defeated Germany while the British remained neutral, they would have alienated the two powers which posed the greatest threat to their empire. In the end the German invasion of neutral Belgium (part of their war plans for years) provided a suitable justification for British entry into the fray. The war widened within a month when Turkey joined in on the German side; as expected, Italy stayed neutral until the spring of 1915. Then it joined Britain, France and Russia, after being bribed with the prospect of major gains at the end of the war.

22.3 The First European Civil War 1914–18

The outbreak of war in August 1914 demonstrated the immense power of the European state over its citizens. Any ideas the socialists had of workers' solidarity rapidly disappeared as mobilization schedules and chauvinism took hold. Everywhere the young male population was conscripted into the army and moved to the front by rail in a highly complex operation meticulously planned years in advance. In two weeks the French mobilized 3.7 million men and moved them on over 7,000 special trains to the eastern frontier with Germany. In Austria-Hungary, although the mobilization orders had to be issued in fifteen languages, all the various minorities fought for the empire. However, the war did not turn out to be the short conflict that most strategists expected. The mass armies which had been mobilized necessitated the creation of a war economy to keep them supplied, which in turn meant greater state direction of all aspects of the economy and society and the mobilization of the 'home front' in order to secure victory. This had two further effects. First, this huge national effort meant that war aims had to become more extensive and the compromises which followed exhaustion in the wars of the eighteenth century were now ruled out. Second, mobilization of the economy turned civilians into targets. From the outbreak of the war the British blockade of Germany was deliberately targeted at civilians and was designed to break their morale through starvation. The Germans responded by using their submarines to sink unarmed merchant ships without warning in an effort to break Britain's supply lines. (The British were particularly vulnerable to this form of warfare because of their dependence on external supplies of food, which had developed in the late nineteenth century.) The bombing of people by aeroplanes and airships began in December 1914 when the French attacked German towns. The Germans responded in kind and by the end of the war both sides had developed long-range four-engined heavy bombers specifically designed to bomb cities and kill civilians.

At first the war was characterized by fairly rapid movement but after the failure of the initial German attack on France through Belgium a front line stretching from the Swiss frontier to the Belgian coast stabilized, and increasingly complex trench systems and static warfare became the norm. Only in the east, where the front was over 750 miles wide, did relatively fluid warfare, with cavalry still playing an important role, prevail, although the huge distances involved meant that decisive battles were rare. On the western front the defence held the upper hand through the combination of trenches, barbed wire and machine-guns. These made any substantial breakthrough almost impossible and it was difficult to co-ordinate attacks because telephone cables were easily broken and portable radios had not been developed. The war was dominated by large-scale artillery bombardments, which caused the majority of casualties but were unable to break down defences. Sustained trench warfare was only possible because of medical advances. As late as the Boer war the British were still losing five times as many men to disease as enemy action. In the 1904–5 war with Russia the Japanese demonstrated the importance of inoculation and sanitary measures in the static warfare around Port Arthur. They cut losses from disease to a quarter of those from enemy action. By 1912 the identification of the role of the body louse in spreading typhus was identified and the building of large delousing stations stopped what would otherwise have been even greater losses in trench warfare.

Developments in technology were unable to break the strategic and tactical deadlock. The combination of existing technologies – the internal combustion engine, armour and the caterpillar track – produced the tank but despite the hopes placed in them they did not prove decisive; they were slow (in theory four miles an hour, but on the battlefield less than a mile an hour) and their reliability was poor. Chemical warfare was also indecisive. The Germans first used chlorine gas against the Russians at the

753

end of January 1915, but after an initial shock its impact was limited. Gas masks and respirators meant that even when new gases were used (sixty-three different types by 1918) none was decisive although they were used on a massive scale – on occasions over 40,000 gas shells were fired in a single night before an attack. Aircraft were also problematic weapons although their uses widened rapidly. At first crews fought with revolvers, rifles and steel arrows, and supremacy fluctuated from side to side as new designs and technological improvements were introduced. The use of bombers was not decisive: the bomb-loads they could carry were too small.

The war was prolonged by the rough balance between the two sides, by the nature of coalition warfare and by the ability of both sides to mobilize their economies and societies. Neither side could outproduce the other and despite heavy losses every state was able to mobilize more men into the front line. The British adopted their usual role of providing financial support to their allies which kept the latter fighting into 1917. Then the British began to run out of resources, especially to pay for the munitions they were buying in the United States. They were only saved from bankruptcy by US entry into the war in April 1917. That was a highly significant moment – it was the first time that the United States had participated in a European conflict and was the first sign of a gradual shift in the balance of power between Europe and the United States. It was still not a world war – Japan had quickly mopped up the German possessions in China and the Pacific and its colonies in Africa had been captured by the British and French – but all the significant fighting was in Europe. In early 1918 Germany achieved a near total victory on the eastern front and imposed a draconian peace on the new revolutionary socialist government in Moscow. The troops freed were moved to the west and the spring offensive in 1918, when the German forces showed great tactical skill in finding ways of defeating the trench system that had defied the Allies for three years, almost split the British and French armies and almost brought victory. However, no decisive breakthrough was achieved and by the summer the Allied armies were beginning to push the German forces back. The end of the war came unexpectedly in the autumn of 1918. The Turks were defeated in Palestine and Syria, an Allied offensive from Salonika broke the Austro-Hungarian army in the Balkans and although the fighting on the western front was still far from the German border, eventual failure seemed likely. Domestically the pressure of the blockade and starvation was beginning to tell. The war was finally ended following mutinies, political collapse and revolution in Vienna and then Berlin.

The losses in the war were the heaviest then known in human history. Apart from the defeat of Germany and Austria-Hungary it was difficult to see what had been achieved. The war aims had been greater than ever before but so had the level of death and destruction. In total over 8 million servicemen were killed and 21 million were wounded. By far the greatest losses were borne by France. They mobilized nearly 8 million men and more than six out of ten were either killed or wounded. The British, as in previous wars, mobilized the smallest percentage of the male population of any of the major combatants and bore the lowest percentage of losses. Even greater than the total military losses were the roughly 10 million civilian deaths, principally from starvation and disease. The political map of Europe was changed beyond recognition by the impact of the war. The monarchies of Russia, Austria-Hungary and Germany were swept away in revolution. By the autumn of 1918 Russia had disintegrated into civil war and lost much of the territory it had gained in eastern Europe since the seventeenth century. The Habsburg empire, which had survived since the fourteenth century and for more than four hundred years had been one of the dominant powers in Europe, disappeared. Further east the Ottoman empire, which had also survived since the fourteenth century and had been one of the great world powers, finally disintegrated. In many respects Europe never recovered from the 1914–18 war. The settlement at the end of the conflict could not address all the problems the war had created. In many respects it made the situation even worse. It turned out to be no more than an interval in the European civil war which was to be resumed with even more devastating consequences within twenty years.

22.4 Revolution

Europe was badly battered not just by the civil war between its states but also by the threat (and reality) of internal social and economic revolution. The industrialized economies and societies of western Europe were characterized by large-scale inequality. Many people, not just Marxists, socialists and revolutionaries, believed that the long-term survival of such societies was doubtful – the poor and exploited were bound to revolt against their conditions and try to establish a more just and egalitarian society. In practice these societies proved to be highly stable for a number of reasons. First, industrial workers, who in theory should have been the most radical group because of the scale on which they were exploited, never constituted a majority in any society. Second, these workers were divided among themselves. There were strong differences of interest between the skilled and the unskilled and many industrial communities were introverted and isolated from each other. Third, most workers were mainly interested in specific improvements to their wages and working conditions. Such improvements were achieved, partly under trade union pressure, and governments also slowly constructed social welfare programmes. These gave the workers a stake, albeit very small, in the continuation of the existing society. The industrial societies of Europe in the twentieth century were therefore characterized by a lack of revolution.

The nearest approach to revolution came in 1918-19 in Germany and Austria after their defeat in the war. In Germany in October 1918 the military leadership resigned as the old German elite tried to wash its hands of responsibility for national defeat and leave the thankless task of negotiating an end to the war to others. On 9 November a new Social Democratic government took power in Berlin and mutinies in the armed forces and the formation of workers' and soldiers' councils seemed to mark the onset of social revolution. From the beginning the new government co-operated with the army authorities. This was essential if Germany was to meet the armistice condition that the army be withdrawn to German territory within a few weeks. In return the army offered support in keeping order. The workers' and soldiers' councils were kept in moderate SPD hands (except briefly in Munich) and attempted coups from both the left and the right were defeated. Most of the old imperial institutions – the army, the civil service and the judiciary – survived the 1918–19 transition intact. The discipline and organization of the Social Democrats and the strong roots they had developed in the working class over the period since the 1870s ensured that there was little support for revolutionary groups on the left and that the disintegration of power did not go far enough to give them any opportunities to exploit. The main threat to the new democracy came, as events in the 1920s and early 1930s were to prove, from groups on the right never reconciled to either defeat or the very limited changes of 1918–19.

The revolution that did occur took place in a country where Marxist theory suggested it was impossible – semi-industrialized Russia. The central political problem in Russia was the reassertion of traditional tsarist autocracy from the 1880s in a situation where an increasingly sophisti-cated civil society, partly produced by economic development, was denied any civil rights or any meaningful participation apart from the almost powerless local councils, the *zemstvos*. The internal problems in Russia were made worse by its determination to act as a major power in both Europe and Asia. The humiliating defeat by Japan in the war of 1904–5 (the first inflicted on a European country by an Asian state) sparked a revolution which the government was only just able to suppress. In order to buy off the moderate liberal groups the government offered to implement changes which would have created a constitutional monarchy. Once order was restored it reneged on these promises and none of Russia's fundamental problems had been addressed by the outbreak of war in 1914;

they had merely been contained. It was the pressures of the war, in particular the major defeats in the autumn of 1916, combined with economic dislocation, rising food prices and repression which produced a crisis in Petrograd (as St Petersburg had been renamed) in January 1917. Demonstrations and strikes led to the formation of a soviet (workers' and soldiers' council) and within a week the military leadership, fearing that the troops would not act to repress the workers, recommended abdication to the tsar. In an incredibly short period, and with little resistance, the autocracy which had always characterized Muscovy and Russia, together with the Romanov dynasty which had ruled since the early seventeenth century, disintegrated. A provisional government under Prince Lvov was formed which, in conjunction with the soviet, held power in the capital. However, across the country as the old autocracy collapsed, the absence of strong local institutions led to the seizure of power by local soviets reflecting the interests of soldiers, peasants and workers. A largely peasant army wanted peace and land, but the government decided to stay in the war and postpone the question of land reform until after a Constituent Assembly met to write a new constitution. Inevitably the peasants took control of events, seized the estates and divided them up. The government lacked an army to suppress them. Its decision to launch a major offensive in June 1917 was a disastrous failure. Increasingly, replacement of the provisional government, probably by a transfer of power to the soviets, seemed the only way of achieving the objectives of the peasants, soldiers and workers. The small revolutionary parties, in particular the Bolsheviks, had to adapt to these demands. The membership of the Bolshevik party increased from about 10,000 in February to over 200,000 in October. The central organization had almost no control over this process and the party was very far from Lenin's idea (developed at the beginning of the century) of a small, tightly knit group of dedicated revolutionaries. Eventually Lenin was successful in arguing for a seizure of power in the name of the Petrograd soviet where the Bolsheviks held a majority. A handful of troops was enough to disperse the provisional government and the Bolsheviks took power.

In the immediate aftermath of their coup the Bolsheviks had a fragile hold on power in Petrograd, Moscow and some other places where they controlled the local soviets. They were clearly a minority in the country though a powerful one. Their lack of support was reflected in the elections to the Constituent Assembly, which Bolshevik troops dispersed as soon as it met. Their ability to stay in power depended on the complex political and social situation as the Russian empire disintegrated and the 'white' armies fought both to sustain the empire and to remove the Bolsheviks from power. The result was a bitter four-year-long civil war between a multitude of forces. The Bolsheviks were gradually able to build a 4-million-strong Red Army and defeat the principal 'white' armies under Admiral Kolchak in Siberia and General Denikin in the south-west. The 'white' leaders were ill co-ordinated, unable to deliver a decisive blow against the Bolsheviks and weakened by their determination to restore tsarism and the landed estates, which alienated the peasants, and by their aim of restoring the Russian empire, which meant they could not build alliances with the nationalist groups.

The victory of the Bolsheviks in Russia had a fundamental impact. In the short term it immeasurably added to the problems faced by the Allied leaders as they tried to construct a peace settlement at Versailles. Intervention in the civil war by the main Allied states (Britain, France, the United States and Japan) on the side of the 'whites' failed. For a while it seemed that revolution might spread from Russia to the rest of Europe – a Bolshevik regime under Béla Kun controlled Hungary for a period, Germany seemed on the verge of revolution and in 1920 the Red Army swept westwards as far as Warsaw. This only increased the determination of the Allies to isolate Russia (it became the Soviet Union in the early 1920s) from the rest of Europe. The establishment of the revolutionary regime in the Soviet Union also created a new factor to complicate still further the civil war between the European powers. To the old-established European elites the victory of the Bolsheviks represented their worst nightmare – social and economic revolution. Fear of communism became a central part of European politics for decades and affected the balance power because of the almost total isolation of the Soviet Union. Outside Europe the Soviet Union became a model for other groups trying to overthrow powerful elites or colonial rulers. When it began to industrialize on a large scale after 1928 it was seen as a model of how to achieve this without depending on the existing industrial powers of Europe and north America. After 1945 opposition to the Soviet Union and its allies by the United States and its allies was a central feature of world politics for almost five decades.

22.5 The Versailles Settlement

The Allied leaders who gathered at Versailles at the end of 1918 faced a daunting series of problems in attempting to create a new order out of the wreckage of the Austro-Hungarian, Russian, German and Ottoman empires which had dominated Europe for centuries. They also had to deal with a defeated Germany and balance their own very different interests. In practice they had minimal control over events and little information about the complexity of the ethnic map of central and eastern Europe. Allied rhetoric about self-determination, combined with the idealism of President Wilson (enshrined in his Fourteen Points), proved difficult to apply in practice and often conflicted with overriding strategic and political requirements. The idea of creating 'nation-states' in eastern Europe (based on a false premise about western European history) came up against the realities of the ethnic map which had emerged from the movements of peoples dating back to the expansion of European settlement in the tenth century. These considerations also had to be balanced against the strategic requirement to contain both Germany and revolutionary Russia. If every nationality were allowed to exercise a 'right' to self-determination then there would be chaos, with a patchwork of politically and economically unviable mini-states. The problem with the solution adopted at Versailles was that in the last resort it was, not unexpectedly, a victors' peace. Instead of 'nation-states' a series of mini-empires was created in which previously important minorities became dominant nationalities and other states such as Poland and Romania were either re-created or expanded. The frontiers established were to a large extent arbitrary and little account was taken of local opinion, except for a few instances in which plebiscites were held. The problems created at Versailles were to dog European history for the rest of the twentieth century.

The creation of Czechoslovakia was never put to a vote and the major economic and social differences between the industrialized Czech area of Moravia and Bohemia and rural Slovakia were not resolved. The decision by the Allies to include the Sudetenland with its majority German population, to give the new state defensible frontiers, only increased the minority problem. In what became in effect a Czech empire the Czechs were a minority in the country they ruled. Even more problematic was the new state of Yugoslavia, which contained numerous nationalities, several religions, eight different legal systems and two alphabets for the basic language. It had even less legitimacy than Czechoslovakia. In December 1918 the Allies recognized a 'Kingdom of the Serbs, Croats and Slovenes' embracing pre-war Serbia and Montenegro and a large group of territories taken from the Austro-Hungarian empire. All its frontiers were in dispute but they were seen as a reward to Serbia for its efforts in the war when it lost over a million people (a quarter of its population). Yugoslavia became a Serbian empire with the continuation of the old Serb monarchy, the retention of Belgrade as the capital and the invention of a fake Serbo-Croat identity. The Croats, the largest minority, demanded a federal solution but this was rejected. Although the re-creation of Poland involved minority problems (about a third of the population was non-Polish) the major issue was the state's new frontiers. The creation of a corridor to the sea at

Gdansk (Danzig) split Germany into two parts. In the east the Poles (as a result of victory in the Russo-Polish war) established their control over territory 200 miles beyond the border agreed by the Allies (the so-called 'Curzon line'). The population in this area was never reconciled to Polish rule or the dominant Catholic church. In the Balkans the rewards went to Romania for joining the Allies in 1916. It took over Transylvania and Bukovina from Hungary, and Bessarabia from Russia with the result that about a third of the population were minorities and only the borders with Czechoslovakia and Poland were uncontentious. Two states – Bulgaria and Hungary – were clear losers from this settlement.

Equally problematic was the division of the Ottoman empire. Nearly all of it was split between Britain and France through the creation of client states under puppet Arab rulers imported for the purpose. After considerable argument between the two Allies, Britain dominated Iraq, Palestine and Jordan together with a vaguer protectorate over the Arabian peninsula. France gained Syria and Lebanon. An Armenian state was rejected even though about 1.7 million Armenians had been killed by the Turks during the war in the first of the twentieth century's genocides. A Kurdish state was also refused. The Allies originally planned to truncate Turkey drastically with Greece receiving most of the benefits. They found that they could not sustain this decision against the growing strength of a Turkish nationalist movement under Mustafa Kemal which expelled Greek forces from Anatolia. In the early 1920s the Allies finally accepted that Turkey would control the historic heartland of Anatolia as well as part of Thrace. The most controversial decision, and one which created immense problems and untold suffering for the rest of the twentieth century, was over Palestine. Zionism made the most extreme claim of any national movement through its demand for the 'restoration' of a Jewish state in Palestine, even though none had existed there for almost two thousand years. In the site for this new state only eight per cent of the population was Jewish. Zionism became a form of European colonialism in its refusal to recognize that the existing population had any rights. This attitude was compounded by the declaration made by the British government in 1917 (the 'Balfour Declaration'). It was a document typical of European attitudes to the rest of the world – a promise made by Britain to an outside group about a territory it did not control and without any consideration of the wishes of the existing population. Britain said it would 'favour the establishment in Palestine of a national home for the Jewish people'. Exactly what this meant was unclear – although it was stated that nothing would be done that would prejudice the civil and religious rights of the existing population, that promise carefully excluded their political rights. In private the British were much clearer about their objectives. In 1919 Balfour told the

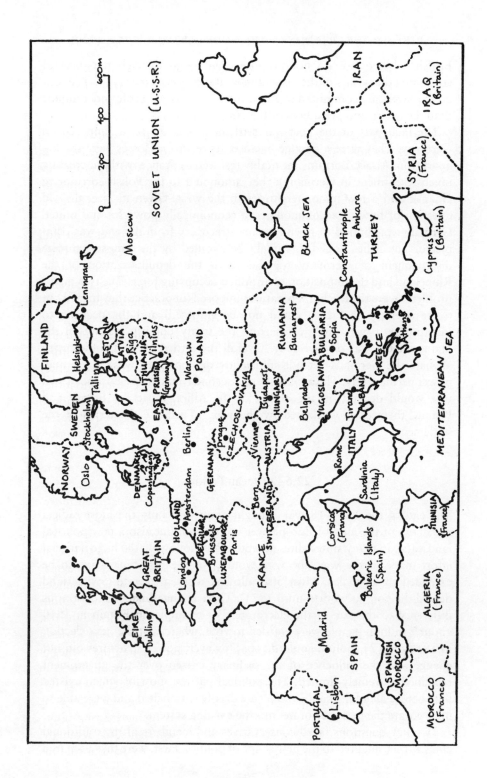

Map 75: Europe 1919–1938

British cabinet: 'we do not propose even to go through the form of consulting the wishes of the present inhabitants of the country . . . The four great powers are committed to Zionism . . . [it is] of far profounder import than the desire and prejudices of the 700,000 Arabs.'

The final part of the post-war settlement was the terms imposed on Germany. They were a strange balance. Its territorial losses were small – apart from Alsace-Lorraine inevitably restored to France (without creating much resentment in Germany), they amounted to the Polish corridor to Gdansk and a few minor territories in the west. Given its size, the old question of how to accommodate an economically powerful and united Germany was bound to re-emerge once recovery from the war was completed. The Allies hoped this might be avoided by the almost complete disarmament of Germany together with the demilitarization of the Rhineland and the imposition of an Allied occupying force. The two major problems were the level of reparations imposed (in practice they turned out to be so large that they could not be enforced) and the decision to incorporate a 'war guilt' clause into the treaty unfairly placing all the blame for the war on Germany. Overall the settlement was sufficient to alienate the Germans yet not sufficiently draconian to weaken German power permanently. The avoidance of a second round in the European civil war would depend on the ability of the Allies, especially France and Britain, themselves weakened by the war, to enforce the terms of the settlement.

22.6 European Politics

The end of the 1914–18 war brought about not only the most radical reshaping of the map of Europe ever undertaken but also a new political landscape. In many states elites accepted that, following the huge national effort made in the war, the vote would, for the first time, have to be extended to all males. Most also allowed women to vote (Switzerland denied the vote to women until 1971). These changes made an enormous difference to the size of the electorate. For example, in Britain in 1910 about 7 million people were entitled to vote, whereas at the next election in 1918 over 21 million could do so. However, power structures did not change and the influence of the ordinary citizen over the government remained extremely limited. The political parties, most of which existed long before all adults could vote, were deeply entrenched and were able to incorporate the new electorate into the existing system.

Two key questions faced conservatives and members of the traditional elites as they adapted to the new shape of politics. First, were they prepared to work within the framework of liberal democracy and constitutional rules? Second, how would they react to what they saw as threats to their position, property and status from increasing taxation and an ill-defined 'socialism'? Both of these questions were made more acute by the existence of revolutionary communism in the Soviet Union and the threat, real or imagined, that this 'virus' might be transmitted to other countries. In the immediate aftermath of the war and the economic dislocation this brought about almost any demands by the workers and trade unions seemed to the elite and governing groups to presage revolution. It was a period of repression in most of the industrialized countries. In practice the fear of revolution in the industrialized countries was largely imaginary. By the early 1920s European politics was stabilized on a strongly conservative basis. In many cases the old nineteenth-century liberal parties either split (as in Britain) or went into decline as many of their supporters moved towards more conservative parties. The socialist parties found it very difficult to achieve success in this political environment. The growth in electoral support, which seemed so strong in the early decades of the century, slowed and nowhere did it reach over half the vote despite the fact that this was the time when the working class was at its largest as a proportion of European societies. The socialist parties found that if they participated in parliamentary politics they had to accept the rules (written and unwritten) of that game, including forgoing the alternative of mass industrial action. In many cases they found that proportional represen-tation was introduced in parallel with an extension of the electorate in order to ensure that they could not obtain a majority. Overall, therefore, the socialist parties made little impression on European politics. Although they achieved power it was usually as members of a coalition (France in 1936) or as a minority government (Britain in 1924 and 1929–31). Only in Sweden did they become a majority government after 1932. All of them had to cope with the economic difficulties of the 1920s and 1930s when it was unclear how socialist remedies, such as common ownership, would ameliorate these problems. Most socialist governments turned out to be highly conventional in their economic policies and they introduced only a few limited social reforms which were little different from those which other reforming parties supported.

Most European states in the immediate post-war period were demo-cratic. However, far more typical of European politics in the 1920s and 1930s than socialism was the steady rise of authoritarian dictatorships of various military and right-wing groups. In Portugal a military coup in 1926 brought António de Oliveira Salazar, a deeply conservative, Catholic economist, into power. By 1932 he was effective dictator and the regime survived, even after his death, until 1974. In neighbouring Spain a military junta under General Miguel Primo de Rivera took power in 1923 and lasted until 1930. This was followed by the fall of the monarchy, the establishment of the Second Republic in 1931 and a period of political instability. The army coup in July 1936 against a Popular Front government failed and led to a bitter civil war until early 1939. The leader of the coup, General Franco, became head of state and incorporated numerous right-wing groups into an authoritarian regime which ruled until his death in 1975. In Greece a royal, bureaucratic dictatorship under General Metaxas was set up in 1936. In Romania King Carol was able to set up his own dictatorship under the ultra-nationalist Orthodox patriarch, Miron Cristea, in 1937. In Bulgaria a series of authoritarian governments in the 1920s was followed by a royal dictatorship under Tsar Boris in 1935. Given its divisions Yugoslavia was bound to be highly fractured and unstable and from the late 1920s was governed by a centralized royal dictatorship. In Hungary a royal dictatorship was not an option because the Allies refused to allow a Habsburg restoration. From the early 1920s the country was run by a deeply conservative, aristocratic, landholding elite under a regent, Admiral Miklos Horthy (the last commander of the Austro-Hungarian navy). Austria was democratic in the 1920s though bitterly divided between the socialists and the conservative, rural Christian Social Union. In March 1933 a CSU-dominated government took power to rule by decree, a Fatherland Front was established and in early 1934 the socialists were banned. In Poland an unstable political system was overthrown in 1926 by a coup led by the military leader in the war with Russia, General Pilsudski. Under various guises the regime survived until Pilsudski's death in 1935 and was followed by an authoritarian, nationalist, military-dominated regime. The three Baltic republics, which became independent during the collapse of the Russian empire, were originally all highly democratic. All suffered from extreme political instability and succumbed to coups led by heroes from the battles for independence with the support of various right-wing and military groups. By the late 1930s the number of democracies left in Europe was in single figures (Britain, France, the Benelux countries, Norway, Sweden, Denmark and Ireland).

22.7 Fascism and Nazism

After 1918 a new element in the European civil war emerged. It was shaped by economic instability, military defeat (or denial of what were seen as the legitimate spoils of victory) and the threat to the established social and economic order from the Bolshevik victory in Russia. Although in Britain and France the existing political, social and economic relations seemed to be broadly confirmed by victory, elsewhere elites rejected liberal democracy and drifted towards authoritarian solutions as a way of protecting their position. In Italy and then Germany (and much later in a highly derivative form across Europe) new political movements emerged which capitalized on numerous discontents. Despite their very real differences they were broadly described as fascist and although limited in scope came to dominate much of European politics in the inter-war decades.

Fascism was the only major ideological innovation to emerge in the twentieth century. Fascist parties were not found before 1914 and their late arrival partly explains why so many of their ideas were defined in opposition to others. Fascism was anti-liberal, anti-democratic, anti-communist and in many respects anti-conservative. It advocated a new, national, organic, authoritarian state, a rebirth or 'cleansing' of the nation and broadly corporatist economic solutions which owed something to socialism. It developed a political style based on symbolism, mass meetings, a party militia stressing youth and masculinity, and charismatic leadership. Although fascism is usually portrayed as an aberration in European ideology (which emphasized progress and the rational construction of a better world through either liberal democracy or Marxism) this is not the case. Fascism was deeply rooted in the European tradition and combined elements that formed part of the mainstream of European ideas. From revolutionary France it took the idea of mass mobilization and from nineteenth-century history the centrality of nationalism. These were combined with social Darwinism, with its emphasis on struggle and the 'survival of the fittest', eugenics with its aim of creating better people, the growing importance of military values, the belief that war was a positive force, revolutionary socialism – fascist leaders such as Mussolini, Déat and Mosley came from the left of politics – and also anti-Semitism. One of its appeals was to those who felt marginalized and powerless in the face of the impersonal economic forces increasingly dominating industrialized societies. In practice fascism had a limited effect. Established liberal democratic regimes in western Europe did not break down and where authoritarian and military governments were successful they did not allow fascism to succeed. Fascism only gained power in two countries – Italy and Germany – where parliamentary systems were under strain. In Italy the transition to a full liberal democracy was still incomplete in 1918 and there was widespread discontent over the failure to make major gains from the decision to join the Allies in 1915. In Germany the Weimar republic lacked a firm base in society and the trauma of defeat and revolution in 1918 produced a highly unstable political situation. However, even in these two countries the fascists did not gain power through civil war or a coup – state institutions remained strong enough to resist. Nor was it possible to take power through elections – the 38 per cent of the vote obtained by the Nazis in 1932 was their high point in truly democratic elections. The route to power was through coalitions with other conservative groups and then exploiting opportunities to seize power.

Fascism first appeared in Italy in 1919, although at that stage it bore little resemblance to what later became typical of the doctrine. It was developed by Benito Mussolini who, before the war, had been a leader of the radical socialist party. The failure of working-class solidarity in 1914 convinced him that nationalism was the strongest force. In developing his ideas he drew on a multitude of sources. From the revolutionary syndicalists he adopted the idea of direct action, the use of violence and the mobilization of the masses. From the 'Futurists' he took their belief in the positive effects of violence and the idealization of the new. From the nationalists such as D'Annunzio and De Ambris he took their corporatism and the symbols of the new movement – the legionaries and *fasces* (recalling Rome), the use of blackshirts and the so-called 'Roman salute', which had been invented for a 1914 film. The 1919 programme of the party was radical and socialist but one by one these elements were dropped. The fascists only gained 15 per cent of the vote in the 1921 elections but Mussolini eventually took power in October 1922 in a coalition government chosen by the king. Later mythology, designed to fit in with the fascist idea of 'action', emphasized the so-called 'March on Rome'. In fact there was no march and Mussolini travelled from Milan by train.

Mussolini's position was weak and only slowly, by the end of the 1920s, had an authoritarian dictatorship been constructed through rigged elections, the collapse of the socialist and Catholic trade unions, an increasing emphasis on corporatism and the transformation of the Fascist party into a wider state party. In practice, despite the grandiose rhetoric about the new system (described as *totalitario*), a semi-pluralistic structure survived. King Victor Emmanuel III was still head of state (he finally dismissed Mussolini in 1943), industry and the armed forces remained largely autonomous and the police were a state not a party function. The fascist government was not particularly oppressive and no more unpopular than most governments. Despite the reality of a generally conservative, nationalist and authoritarian government in a condition of near torpor, Italy was portrayed, and seen in some quarters, as a dynamic state with a philosophy for the future and as a role model for other aspiring dictators.

The Nazi movement in Germany, despite the similarities in style and form, was very different from Italian fascism. Nazism was exclusive and racial – anti-Semitism was central to its 'philosophy' which it was not in fascism (in 1938 there were 10,000 Jewish members of the Italian party).

Unlike Mussolini, Adolf Hitler had no political background when in early 1919 he was sent by the army to monitor a minor right-wing political party in Munich. Eventually he became a fringe politician and leader of the National Socialist German Workers' Party (NSDAP). Its programme bore a strong resemblance to the early fascist party in Italy with its combination of socialism and nationalism. However, it drew little support despite the post-war chaos, the fear of left-wing revolution, French occupation of the Ruhr and the unprecedented hyperinflation. Other right-wing groups had more support among the old elite, the military and nationalist organizations. The attempt to recreate the 'March on Rome' through the Beer Hall Putsch in Munich in November 1923 ended in humiliating failure within hours. Hitler was sent to jail. Here he set out his world view in *Mein Kampf* – it emphasized a racial nationalism, based on a crude social Darwinist view of the world, and a popular anti-Semitism which he had learnt during his time in Vienna before 1914. Although Hitler was dominant within the movement its ideology was confused and it remained unimportant and on the fringes of politics – it gained less than 3 per cent of the vote in the 1928 elections.

The prospects for the Nazi party were transformed by the economic depression after 1929 and the steady collapse of the Weimar political system. Its emphasis on action and national revival was attractive in a situation where the democratic system had failed to develop deep roots and most Germans, who were never reconciled to the Versailles peace terms, especially the 'war guilt' clause, wanted a political and military status commensurate with German economic power. The Nazis gained support rapidly as the depression began to bite. From just under 20 per cent of the vote in 1930, their share rose to a peak of nearly 40 per cent in July 1932 before falling back to 33 per cent in the November 1932 elections. However, they remained excluded from power, distrusted by the nationalist politicians and senior army officers. The key to Nazi success was not electoral support but manoeuvrings within the political and military elite as the constitution was suspended and the government ruled by decree. It was at the moment when Nazi fortunes were on the wane in the winter of 1932–3 that these groups decided that Hitler, as the leader of the largest political force in Germany, would have to be brought into government. On 30 January 1933 Hitler became chancellor in a coalition made up overwhelmingly of established conservative forces – they believed they could keep Hitler under control and that the Nazis would provide no more than a popular element in the government.

Hitler was able to attain almost complete power within three months. He convinced his coalition partners to call an election and the burning down of the Reichstag by a lone communist gave the excuse for a security clampdown. Even so, and despite propaganda about a newly revived Germany, the Nazis received just under 44 per cent of the vote (and took a smaller proportion of the seats than the Social Democrats in 1919). They could only obtain a majority with the support of the nationalist DNVP for an Enabling Bill to give full powers to the government – it was supported by all the other political groups (except the Social Democrats) including the Catholic Zentrum. By July all political parties apart from the Nazis had either been banned or had dissolved themselves. The Nazis dominated the government but continued to rule in conjunction with existing institutions, especially the army, which was appeased by rearmament and the destruction of the leadership of the party militia (the SA) in June 1934. Two months later Hitler assumed the joint office of chancellor and president as Führer.

22.8 Communism

In Russia the civil war of 1917–22 marked a profound discontinuity between the essentially popular revolution of 1917 and the highly authoritarian state structure built upon a highly disciplined Bolshevik party. A standing army with strict discipline was rebuilt, workers' control of industry was replaced by the control of state managers, political opposition was suppressed, censorship imposed and the soviets weakened or suspended. By the time victory in the civil war was secured it was apparent that there would be no European revolution and the Bolshevik leaders would have to survive on their own. They rejected any openness in favour of retaining power and reinterpreted their Marxist ideology in order to justify what they were doing. The symbolic moment came in February 1921 with the rebellion at the Kronstadt naval base near Petrograd – it called for the restoration of soviet power and freedom for competing political parties. The rebellion was ruthlessly suppressed and the party moved even further along the road to dictatorship. The highly authoritarian political system was partly designed to ensure that the old pre-revolutionary society was not recreated in the much more liberal economic system the party had been forced to introduce in early 1921. The 'war communism' of the civil war period, which was little more than a euphemism for forced requisitioning, was replaced by the New Economic Policy which allowed private ownership of small-scale industry, limited profit making and the renting and sale of land by peasants. The economy recovered quickly from the disasters of the civil war – by the late 1920s output was back to 1913 levels. The political situation became highly fluid after December 1922 following Lenin's stroke and eventual death in early

1924. For several years in the second half of the 1920s the Bolshevik leaders – Kamenev, Zinoviev, Stalin, Bukharin and Trotsky – manoeuvred for position and argued about the direction the revolution should take. The fundamental problem was the semi-industrialized Soviet economy and the difficulty of finding the capital necessary for industrialization in a situation where, because of its ideological isolation and the opposition of the capitalist states, the government could not rely on foreign capital investment. The social and economic restructuring involved could not be pain free – the only question (as in all countries going through this process) was who should bear the cost. The basis of Soviet policy after 1928 was forced industrialization through a series of Five-Year Plans. At first the *kulaks* (supposedly wealthy peasants) were dispossessed and deported. Then land was taken from the peasants through collectivization – they were forced to work in communes and the state decided how much food would be taken leaving the peasants to survive on the remainder. Industrialization on a major scale resulted in high social mobility and rapid urbanization. The Bolsheviks were no longer Lenin's vanguard party of dedicated revolutionaries (although they retained that mythology), but a bureaucratic party trying to control a potentially revolutionary social situation and undertake economic planning on a scale no state had ever attempted before. Internal discipline was essential but under Stalin (who dominated the leadership after 1928) other long-established tendencies in the revolutionary movement came to the fore.

On seizing power and during the civil war the Bolsheviks developed a policy of 'revolutionary terror' and police repression. The Soviet security police went through many guises (Cheka, GPU, OGPU, NKVD, KGB) but remained essentially the same. As Lenin told a fellow revolutionary, 'You do not imagine that we shall be victorious without applying the most cruel revolutionary terror?' The shooting of hostages and other 'counter-revolutionaries' started within a few months of the revolution and in April 1919 compulsory labour mobilization was introduced and forced labour camps were introduced. The biggest single cause of death under the Soviet government followed the collectivization of agriculture. About 5 million people ('rich *kulaks*') were deported to Siberia and either taken to labour camps or dumped in the countryside and told to build a new village – about 1 million died. In the five years after 1929 about 20 million family farms were replaced by 240,000 collective farms. The peasants slaughtered their animals rather than hand them over, any hoarding of food or eating of 'state property' was punishable by ten years in jail. Mass famine, especially in the Ukraine, was the result. In 1933 the population of the Soviet Union actually fell by nearly 6 million which, after allowing for births, suggests that the collectivization of agriculture resulted in about 8 million deaths. From the mid-1930s a more widespread terror spread through Soviet society. It was concentrated in two key areas. First, the Bolshevik leadership. At the 1939 Party Congress only 59 of the 2,000 delegates who had attended the previous Congress in 1934 still survived and 98 of the 149 members of the 1934 Central Committee had been eliminated, as had all Stalin's rivals – Kamenev, Bukharin and Zinoviev. Second, the leadership of the Red Army was largely destroyed. In June 1937 Marshal Tukachevsky, a hero of the civil war, was arrested and shot. By the end of the process three out of five marshals of the Soviet Union, sixty out of sixty-seven corps commanders and three-quarters of the divisional commanders were either dead or in forced labour camps. For the ordinary citizen the process was much more random. There was little or no rationale as to who was arrested and any suspicion, denunciation, false confession or event from the past could lead either to death or, more likely, a long sentence in a forced labour camp – in effect they became state-owned slaves.

Exactly how many people passed through the extensive network of about 500 forced labour camps (the Gulags) and how many died is a matter of acute historical debate. In the last few years the very high figures that were current during the Cold War have been revised downwards substantially, though the toll in human life remains huge. On average about 10 per cent of those arrested, in total about 1 million people, were shot before they reached the camps. At its height the population of the Gulags was about 4 million people. The death rate in the camps was about ten per cent a year; higher in the terrible north Siberian camps of Kolyma and in 1941-3 when food rations were cut and work norms increased. Overall these figures suggest that between the mid-1930s and the early 1950s about 8 million people passed through the camp system and of those about 4 million died. Together with those shot, this would give a minimum death toll at the height of the Soviet system of terror and forced labour of about 5 million people. To this has to be added the 8 million who died during collectivization, deaths during deportations and deaths before the mid-1930s giving an overall death toll of about 17 million people. The outcome of the 1917 revolution was a terrifying illustration of the power of the European state as it had developed by the twentieth century and the impact of the European ideologies developed in the nineteenth century.

22.9 The European Balance 1919–39

The internal stresses within European society after the 1914–18 war – dictatorship, fascism, Nazism and communism – only added to the problems caused by the unusual post-war international power balance. The Soviet Union was forced back further to the east than the Russian frontiers had been since the eighteenth century following the loss of eastern Poland, parts of Belorussia and all of the Baltic states. For ideological reasons it was shunned by the other states. In central and eastern Europe, Germany, which still largely retained its 1914 boundaries, faced only a series of weak states, each of them internally divided over nationality questions. The United States, whose economic and potential military strength had been so vital to eventual Allied success, withdrew from European political affairs after its failure to ratify the Versailles treaty.

The structure of world power after 1919 was therefore anomalous, with the two strongest powers standing aside. This meant that the responsibility for maintaining the post-war settlement fell on France and Britain. Both were gravely weakened – French manpower losses were the highest in the war and it remained potentially vulnerable because the German population was still a third larger. Now, instead of Russia (as before 1914), it had only weak allies to the east of Germany. Britain was left with even greater problems, despite the expansion of the empire in the old Ottoman territories which brought it to its greatest-ever extent. The British had both huge debts to the Americans and a national debt which had risen eleven-fold during the war. In 1919 the government decided that they could not afford to compete with the United States in a naval race and, for the first time in two centuries, conceded naval supremacy to another power. Three years later an even more fundamental decision was taken, which determined British strategy for the next two decades. At the Washington naval conference Japan was allowed a fleet three-fifths the size of those of the United States and Britain. This was enough to give the Japanese local superiority in the Pacific. The problem was that the Americans insisted that the British should end their twenty-year-old alliance with Japan. In the past Japan had effectively protected British possessions in Asia and Australasia, now they had to be treated as potentially hostile. Plans were drawn up so that in a crisis most of the Royal Navy could be sent to a major new base to be constructed at Singapore. However, it was far from clear that Britain would ever be able to send nearly the whole of its fleet to the far side of the globe, especially if it faced a simultaneous crisis in Europe.

These problems remained latent until the early 1930s when the Japanese invaded Manchuria and Hitler gained power. Then the British faced an insoluble problem. They were, as in the past, a status-quo power trying to protect an empire which covered a quarter of the globe even though they were only a small European power which accounted for less than 10 per cent of the world's industrial output. Potentially they faced two strong enemies – Germany and Japan – in different parts of the world without the resources to meet more than one adequately. They could do little else than begin rearmament (directed primarily against Germany), try to postpone any conflict for as long as possible and hope to find a diplomatic solution. In the mid-1930s the situation was made worse by the actions of Italy. Mussolini was tempted to substitute a more adventurous foreign policy for domestic deadlock as a way of continuing an activist image. In 1935 he decided to revive imperial Roman glory and avenge the 1896 defeat at Adowa by attacking Ethiopia. The attack ran foul of the League of Nations, established as part of the Versailles settlement. The British and French could not decide whether to appease Mussolini and so keep him as an ally, or use the League to invoke sanctions and end the aggression. They finished up applying neither policy properly. Their botched diplomacy and Mussolini's success drew Italy into alliance with Germany. The British now had to plan for another potentially hostile power across their lines of communication between Europe and the Pacific.

As all the European powers rearmed (the Soviet Union to a greater extent than all the others) a new burst of technological development occurred which largely determined the weapons that would be used in the 1939–45 war. The most fundamental changes came in air warfare. In the early 1930s fighters were still very like their predecessors in 1918 – lightly armed, fabric-covered biplanes capable of about 200 mph. By the late 1930s they had been replaced by aluminium monoplanes with multiple machine-guns or cannons, cockpit armour, self-sealing fuel tanks and very powerful engines capable of top speeds of about 400 mph. At the beginning of the 1930s it was universally assumed that no effective defence could be mounted against bombers because no adequate warning of an attack was possible. The problem was solved in the mid-1930s by Britain and Germany through the development of radar (the use of radio waves to locate attacking aircraft). Once radar stations were linked to ground-control centres and these by radio to aircraft, it was possible to guide the fighters on to the attacking bombers. In land warfare more efficient engines meant that tanks were radically transformed – they became heavier, carried more armour and bigger guns. At sea the battleship was gradually giving way to the aircraft carrier as the main capital ship and the introduction of sonar (location by sound waves) gave a minimal capability to detect submerged submarines.

As rearmament progressed the British found that no diplomatic agreement which preserved Britain's position and status could be made with the expansionist powers of Germany, Japan and Italy. Hitler was able to exploit the undeniable grievances of Germany over the Versailles settlement to redraw the boundaries of Europe – sending forces into the demilitarized Rhineland zone in early 1936, annexing Austria in early 1938 and taking over the Sudetenland at the Munich conference in September 1938. British rearmament, particularly in the air, was proving expensive and in the winter of 1938–9 the French demanded that Britain also equip a major army as they had in the 1914–18 war or else they would seek a separate deal with Germany. Britain now faced the first stages of the crisis that was to mark its end as a world power. The British were unable to raise any loans in the United States because of their outstanding debts, yet official, and highly secret, estimates showed that their gold and foreign currency reserves were only sufficient to finance a major war for, at most, three years. Military advice suggested it would take at least that long to defeat Germany. By early 1939 the British realized that they were in an impossible situation. As a status-quo power they could only lose from another war – either they would be defeated or, in trying to secure victory, they would become dependent on the United States and possibly the Soviet Union too. Their one slim hope of remaining a major power was to win a limited, fairly quick war against Germany while Italy and Japan remained neutral. Hitler's determination to solve every problem through the use of force gave the British that slim chance. Hitler was determined to enforce his demands for the return of the Polish corridor to Gdansk (Danzig) and in late August 1939 he achieved the limited war he wanted by agreeing with the Soviet Union on the fourth partition of Poland since the mid-eighteenth century and a division of the rest of eastern Europe. Britain and France decided to fight after Germany invaded Poland.

22.10 The Second European Civil War and World War 1939–45

The impact that the dysfunctional European state system and the conflicts it generated could have on the rest of the world was demonstrated between September 1939 and December 1941. In this period what began as a very limited European war involving only Germany, Poland, France and Britain, was transformed into the first (and so far only) genuine world war. It affected every state in the world and every part of the globe. Any chance that Britain and France had of defeating Germany on their own dis-appeared with the stunning German military conquests in the early summer of 1940. After the conquest of Norway and Denmark, German forces rapidly defeated the Netherlands, Belgium and France and estab-lished domination over western, central and south-eastern Europe where the Versailles settlement was remade. The French were forced to accept an armistice, but the British were able to fight on even after Italy entered the war. However, although they could withstand a limited German aerial

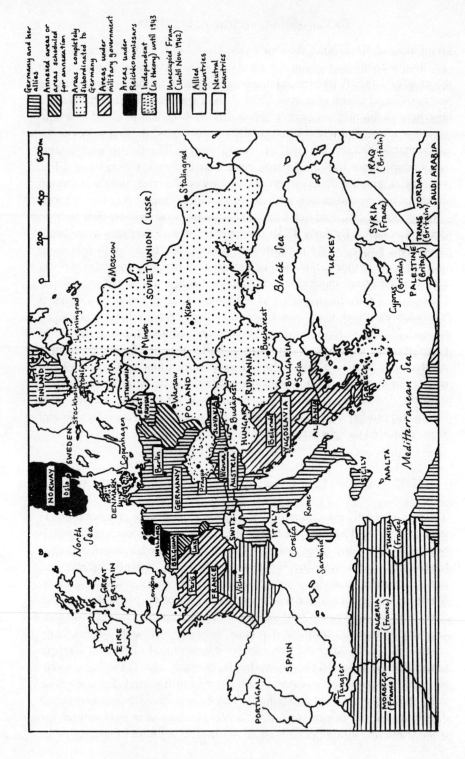

Map 76: Europe at the height of German power 1942

attack they were unable to devise a coherent strategy that would win the war with their limited resources. By the autumn of 1940 they were in an even worse state than 1917 and once again they were only rescued from a compromise peace when the United States provided free financial help, raw materials and military supplies, even though it was still neutral. In the summer of 1941 Hitler turned on his long-term ideological enemy, the Soviet Union. It provided a breathing space for the British. In Asia, Japan took advantage of the collapse of European power (in particular that of the French and Dutch) to extend its influence. However, it did not begin open aggression at what would have been the most favourable time – the summer and autumn of 1940 – when the European empires (including that of Britain) were defenceless and the United States was unwilling to help. By the time the Japanese had decided on military expansion to obtain regional predominance it was too late. A rearmed United States was prepared not only to block these demands but also to insist on Japan conforming with American security interests in the Pacific. The world war began in December 1941 following the Japanese attack on the United States and European possessions in south-east Asia and the German and Italian declarations of war on the United States.

Once the initial Japanese attack had been contained and the Germans defeated at Stalingrad and in North Africa, the balance of the war shifted rapidly in favour of the Allies. Until 1944 nearly all the equipment used in the war was based on designs either in production or development before 1939. Only in the last year or so of the war did new technologies – jet aircraft, pilotless bombs, long-range rockets and the atomic bomb – become operational and their impact on the outcome was therefore limited. As in the 1914–18 war all the combatants mobilized their economies and societies on a massive scale. It was yet another demonstration of the power of the European state (and its derivative in the United States). In the late 1930s the United States was, despite its huge economic potential (it was producing 30 per cent more steel than Germany even though two-thirds of its steel plants were idle in the depression), a sleeping giant in military terms. It spent about 1 per cent of its national wealth on defence and although it had a strong navy, its army was minute and ill-equipped and its airforce largely obsolete. Rapid rearmament increased defence spending to 11 per cent of national wealth by 1941 and this increased still further after entry into the war. In 1939 the United States built 2,100 military aircraft; in 1944 the total was 96,300. At the same time it equipped a major army to fight in both the Pacific and Europe, created the largest navy in the world and supplied much of the equipment used by its allies, in particular Britain. However, it was the Soviet Union that bore the brunt of the war effort: it lost control of 40 per cent of its population and an even higher proportion of its productive resources and arms industry when Germany conquered the western Soviet Union in 1941. This burden was increased by the mobilization of 12 million people to replace early losses. Only by an unparalleled national effort was it able to stay in the war. Germany was not fully mobilized before the spring of 1943 and although output increased phenomenally it could not match Allied production. It was the latter factor that ensured Allied victory. In total the Allies produced four times as many tanks and artillery pieces as their opponents, nine times as many mortars, seven times as many machine-guns and three times as many combat aircraft. It was a demonstration of the strategic power that came from early industrialization in the nineteenth century and the command over larger resources than one industrial state (Germany) and two semi-industrial states (Italy and Japan) could mobilize.

22.11 The Holocaust

The 1939–45 world war provided an opportunity for Germany under Hitler to demonstrate the terrible impact of the combination of state power and deep-seated European prejudices. The deliberate destruction of 6 million Jews, more than half of them in specially constructed death camps which had no other purpose than mass slaughter, was an even greater crime than the Gulag slave camps of the Soviet Union. The Holocaust could not have been carried out except by a modern state. It relied on industrialization, large-scale production and technological developments to create gas chambers and mass crematoria. It needed railways to transport the people. Most important of all it required 'rational', ordered bureaucracies which could identify, process and transport the victims, as well as order the killings without themselves being directly involved in the process.

Because of the Holocaust there has been a tendency to look back into German history to find the roots of Nazism and anti-Semitism in particular. However, German history was not very different from the rest of Europe and it did not lead inevitably to the Nazi catastrophe and the Holocaust. Anti-Semitism was nothing new in European history. Its roots went back to the centuries of deep-seated distrust and dislike between Christian and Jewish communities and the persecutions carried out by the Catholic church. Nineteenth-century European ideas such as racism, social Darwinism and eugenics simply worsened these long-standing tendencies. In the nineteenth century political liberalization across Europe saw the civic disabilities that had been imposed on Jews for centuries being slowly removed. By 1900 only a handful of states still denied full rights to Jews, and these were granted during the revolutions in Portugal (1910) and Russia (1917) and last of all (reflecting a long history of persecution) Spain in the 1920s. By the early twentieth century in Germany the Jews were highly assimilated, urban, middle class and commercial. Although some anti-Semitic feeling remained, especially among conservative groups, this was not unusual in western Europe. Probably the most anti-Semitic country in western Europe was France as the Dreyfus affair demonstrated. The most virulent anti-Semitism and widespread discrimination was found in eastern Europe, in particular Poland, Romania and Russia, where four out of five European Jews lived. They were excluded from various professions and the universities or were subject to quotas, they faced restrictions on where they could live and suffered from frequent pogroms. In Russia about 3,000 Jews were killed between 1900 and 1914 (1.3 million emigrated) and the 'white' forces in the civil war carried out their own pogroms, killing about 100,000.

Anti-Semitism became more widespread in Germany after 1918. Jews were seen as responsible for the 'stab-in-the back' which brought defeat after near triumph in early 1918 and while the army was still fighting outside Germany. They were associated with Bolshevism, which was seen as a Jewish plot because of the large proportion of Jews in the Bolshevik party. These fantasies were increased by publications such as the *Protocols of the Elders of Zion* which purported to document a worldwide plot by Jews to take over the world – it sold 120,000 copies in Germany in 1920 alone. It was an anti-modernist forgery created during the Dreyfus affair by right-wing Russians close to the tsarist secret police and disseminated by 'white' officers after 1917. The Nazis were simply one of the numerous anti-Semitic groups in Germany and although their propaganda was virulent it made little impact before they took power.

Hitler and his associates had little idea what anti-Jewish policy to adopt in 1933 apart from general discrimination and the removal of some rights. The first anti-Semitic legislation came about three months after the Nazis took power and was mainly aimed at excluding Jews from the civil service and the professions. In many ways this legislation was less discriminatory than the contemporary racial legislation in the United States and South Africa and the levels of violence in Germany were no greater. However, an important threshold had been crossed – for the first time a modern, advanced, industrial western European country deliberately discriminated against a group of its own citizens and allowed its supporters to embark on a programme of violence and boycotts (especially in the cultural sphere). For the next two years little happened and by early 1935 there was even a net inflow of Jews back into Germany. Much wider discrimination was enforced under the Nuremberg laws of 1935. For the first time a Jew was legally defined (on religious not racial grounds) and marriages between 'Aryans' and Jews were prohibited. The legislation had strong support – the Catholic archbishop of Freiburg wrote: 'The right to safeguard the purity of the race, and to devise measures necessary to that end, can be denied to no one.' There was no further legislation after 1935 and action concentrated in other areas, especially the forced takeover of Jewish businesses – by the end of 1938 hardly any were still operating. In November of that year in the *Kristallnacht* there was widespread violence against Jews and destruction of property including synagogues. Policy was still far from clear although emigration seemed to be the favoured solution to what the Nazis saw as the 'Jewish question'.

The situation was radically altered by the outbreak of war and the rapid occupation of western and central Poland where nearly 2 million Jews lived. Policy was to be very different from that adopted for the relatively small and well-integrated Jewish communities of Germany and Austria where some account had to be taken of the attitudes of the non-Jewish population. There was no attempt to go through the legal niceties of defining a Jew – anybody thought to be one, or as was often the case, denounced as such by the local population, was treated as a Jew. All 600,000 Jews living in western Poland (which was to be incorporated into Germany) were moved, leaving their property behind, to central Poland, adjacent to the Soviet-occupied area. All Jews in Poland were subject to forced labour – the councils which the Germans forced the Jewish communities to set up agreed to organize the system and provide the labour, often in brutal labour camps. The movement of hundreds of thousands of Jews into the major cities of Poland created new problems, as far as the Germans were concerned. They reverted to a long-established European anti-Semitic policy – the setting-up of ghettos. The first was in Lodz in April 1940, though the process was not completed across the country for more than a year. Here the Jews were cut off from any access to food other than what the Germans chose to provide and they always put them bottom of the priority list. By March 1942 5,000 people a month were dying in the Warsaw ghetto. Overall about 600,000 Polish Jews died in the ghettos and labour camps.

A major development in German anti-Jewish policy came with the decision to attack the Soviet Union. The army commanders enthusiastically endorsed the Nazi idea of an ideological and racial war. General von Reichenau told his troops the invasion was an attack on 'the Jewish-Bolshevik system' and that its aim was 'the complete destruction of the sources of power and the eradication of the Asiatic influence on the European cultural sphere'. The co-operation of the army was essential to allow the Einsatzgruppen (four units totalling about 20,000 men) to operate. Their task was to kill the communist leadership and as many Jews as possible as soon as areas were occupied by the army. Throughout 1941 there were sweeps across the western Soviet Union in which the Jewish populations of towns and villages were rounded up, taken to an open grave in the countryside, forced to hand over their valuables and clothing and then shot in batches. By early 1942 the Einsatzgruppen and other police units had killed about 1,400,000 people. In June 1942 a special unit was established to go over the entire occupied area, return to the sites of the massacres, dig up the graves and burn the bodies on massive funeral pyres. Extensive as these killings were, there were still millions of Jews alive in eastern Europe, Germany and occupied western Europe. In the summer and autumn of 1941 policy on the 'Jewish question' was still undecided but was to move in the direction of an even more barbaric policy. In July 1941 Göring's instructions to Heydrich to make the necessary organizational and financial preparations 'for bringing about a complete solution of the Jewish question in the German sphere of influence in Europe', probably refer to the deportation of Jews into the vast areas which seemed likely to be conquered. In the same month Hitler was still talking about sending all the Jews to Siberia or Madagascar. By the autumn, when it was clear that the war would be prolonged and that deportation would not be an option, a conference was called on 'the remaining work' on the 'final solution' of the 'Jewish question'. It eventually met at Wannsee in Berlin in January 1942 and decided on a policy unprecedented in world history.

Even before the meeting at Wannsee some killing centres where Jews were being murdered on a large scale were already operating. The construction of these centres was related to, and to some extent grew out of, an earlier German policy of killing the mentally and genetically unfit. This programme was a barbaric extension of the common European and American concern, expressed since the late nineteenth century, about eugenics and the 'fitness of the race'. In other countries such as the United States people had been forcibly sterilized to stop 'race deterioration' long before the Nazis implemented the policy, and states such as Canada and Sweden continued such policies into the 1970s. In Germany between 1934 and 1945 about 400,000 people were forcibly sterilized. A fundamental departure came after September 1939 which distinguished Germany from other European and north American countries. On Hitler's orders the policy was extended to the killing of incurable patients – about 100,000 people in mental hospitals were murdered by 1945. Many of the techniques developed in the killing of mental patients – the use of gas chambers, crematoria and the robbing of the dead for gold teeth and other useful materials – were developed on an industrial scale for use against the Jews. The final test of some of the procedures was at Auschwitz in

September 1941 when about 900 Soviet prisoners of war were killed using Zyklon B gas (hydrogen cyanide) supplied by the industrial giant, I.G. Farben. By December 1941 the first killing centre (Chelmno) was in operation and was joined in the first months of 1942 by four others – Auschwitz, Belzec, Majdanek, Sobibor – and by the last, Treblinka, in July 1942. The Germans could act on their own in Poland and the western Soviet Union and, with greater circumspection, in Germany and Austria. Elsewhere they needed the co-operation of their allies. Finland refused, as did Hungary and Italy before they were occupied. The Danes carried out a policy of mass non-cooperation which saved thousands of lives. Others such as Romania co-operated enthusiastically – the killing of 60,000 Jews when Romanian troops occupied Odessa in October 1941 was the biggest single massacre on the eastern front. The Vichy government in France also collaborated willingly and, without any prompting, they introduced their own anti-Jewish policies and helped deport Jews to the killing centres.

The victims of German policies (who also included gypsies, or Sinti and Roma) were rounded up by a series of 'selections' from the ghettos of eastern Europe and marched off to the railway station. Here they had to leave their belongings and were forced on to trains. They spent days, often weeks, in grossly overcrowded cattle trucks (usually there was no more than standing room) with little or no food and water and no sanitation. Hundreds of thousands died before they even reached the camps. Those that survived found that if they arrived at Auschwitz and Majdanek there was usually a 'selection' of those to work as slave labourers in the factories attached to the camps or they were taken for 'medical experiments'. At the other killing centres only a few hundred Jews were required to carry out the most revolting tasks – they only survived for a few days or weeks. For the rest the Germans were mainly concerned to avoid mass panic. The Jews were told they were being given baths and showers before being taken to work. All men, and women with short hair, were taken straight to the gas chambers. The remaining women and children were taken to separate rooms where Jewish barbers cut off their hair (it was used to make boots for U-boat crews). Then they were taken to the gas chambers after the first batch of people were dead. At Auschwitz the killing with Zyklon B was relatively quick, elsewhere where carbon monoxide was used it took several hours to kill everybody. The Jewish workers then entered the chambers, pulled out the dead, extracted any gold teeth and dragged the bodies to the mass graves. Chelmno operated a bone-crushing machine, but at Belzec and Sobibor the bodies were burned in open pits. Auschwitz had specially constructed crematoria capable of burning 12,000 bodies a day but this was less than the rate at which the gas chambers were killing people (often 20,000 a day). Auschwitz also had eight open pits, sixty yards long and four yards wide, where the bodies were burned. Jewish slaves had to collect the human fat which accumulated at the bottom and pour it back into the fire in order to speed up the burning process.

The killing centres operated rapidly. Chelmno was effectively closed after March 1943 and Treblinka, Sobibor and Belzec were evacuated and the facilities destroyed in the autumn of 1943. Majdanek was overrun by the Soviet army in July 1944. After this date only Auschwitz was operational but it killed hundreds of thousands of Hungarian Jews before it was evacuated in early 1945. The exact number who died at the killing centres will never be known. The most accurate estimate is about 4 million people, of whom about half were killed at Auschwitz. To this figure has to be added the roughly 600,000 who died in the Polish ghettos and the 1,400,000 killed in the mobile operations, mainly in 1941. In total therefore the Germans killed about 6 million Jews during the Holocaust.

22.12 Europe in 1945

By the time the Soviet army reached Berlin in April 1945, and the western Allies occupied western Germany, much of Europe was in ruins. The second European civil war in a generation, and the world war that grew out of it, produced the most terrible conflict in human history. Overall the death toll was four times that of the 1914–18 war. In total about 85 million people died, of whom three-quarters were Soviet citizens. About 13 million Soviet servicemen were killed but their civilian casualties were on an even higher scale as a result of deliberate German killings, deportations, slave labour and 'reprisals' – about 35 million people were killed. This was another demonstration of how war was now deliberately directed at civilians. Allied bombing of cities killed 600,000 German civilians (about twelve times the number of British civilians killed in the war) and 900,000 Japanese. At the end of the war the Japanese cities of Hiroshima and Nagasaki were the first to suffer the effects of the atomic bomb. Across the world about 25 million civilians became refugees and another 23 million were forcibly resettled or deported.

The cities and countryside in many areas of Europe lay devastated. The destruction in Germany, dreadful as it was, did not compare with that in the Soviet Union. Most of the destruction was concentrated in Ukraine and Belorussia where whole regions were destroyed and depopulated. Overall the Soviet Union lost about a quarter of its pre-war population and a third of its capital assets. The total cost of the war was equivalent to ten years of its pre-war economic output (far more if the population losses are taken into account). The other victors were almost as weak. France had suffered considerable destruction (as had the Benelux countries) and was eclipsed as a power following defeat and occupation. Britain's position was also weak, especially economically, where it was still dependent on American help for its post-war economic recovery.

After 1945 the map of Europe was only partially recast. The Versailles settlement had been destroyed between 1938 and 1941, when the main gainers had been Hungary and Bulgaria (the two powers worst affected by Versailles) and the other 'mini-empires' of Czechoslovakia and Yugoslavia were partitioned. In 1945 most of the Versailles position was restored. Romania did not regain Bessarabia and the southern Dobruja and took control of only part of northern Transylvania. Bulgaria and Hungary were larger than in 1919 but far short of their gains earlier in the war. Yugoslavia was reconstituted, as was Czechoslovakia, minus part of Ruthenia which went to the Soviet Union to provide a common frontier. The Baltic states were all incorporated into the Soviet Union – a recognition by the western Allies of what the Soviets had achieved by force in 1940. The greatest change came with the shift of Poland hundreds of miles to the west, losing most of its eastern territories to the Soviet Union (far further west than the Allies envisaged in 1919) but gaining East Prussia and Silesia up to the line of the Oder and Neisse rivers. The Soviets also took the historic German city of Königsberg on the Baltic coast. The only way this settlement could be justified was through the mass expulsion of 12 million Germans from territories that had been ethnically German for almost a thousand years. About 2 million died in this brutal process. It was the final reversal of the great German eastward expansion of 1000–1300. Overall the result was to move the Soviet frontier further west than it had ever been under the tsars.

Europe was not only internally devastated but its position in the world was changed for ever. The United States had been the largest economic power in the world since the late nineteenth century but its political and military power had not been effectively deployed until 1940. Apart from the rescue of the Allies in 1917 and the very limited military deployment by the autumn of 1918, US power had remained latent. Rapid rearmament after 1939, followed by open-ended assistance to the British after early 1941 and the increasing pressure put on the Japanese from the summer of 1941, marked the emergence of the United States as a global power. It was the European dependence on the United States, caused by its civil wars (and demonstrated in 1917 and 1940) that speeded up what would otherwise have been a long-drawn-out transition of power from Europe to the United States. It was the final collapse of the European security order in 1939–41, and its consequences across the globe, which allowed the United States to step into a power vacuum. By 1943 it was the only global power and by the end of the war it deployed 1,200 warships and 3,000 heavy bombers and had sixty-nine divisions in Europe and twenty-six in the Pacific. It was also the only state to possess the atomic bomb. In addition it was the predominant economic power in the world – it produced half the world's industrial output and held two-thirds of the world's gold. The European empires in Asia had only been restored after the devastating impact of the Japanese conquests in late 1941 and early 1942 through American power – most had not been reconquered before the final Japanese surrender.

The period of European predominance in the world which developed in the century or so after 1750 had proved to be very short-lived. The massive self-confidence that characterized Europe in the early twentieth century had been destroyed by the civil wars. Although Europe, particularly after the rapid economic recovery in the 1950s, remained a major industrialized region in the world economy, its political power disintegrated. Its influence was rapidly replaced by that of the United States which came to dominate much of the politics and economics of western Europe after 1945. Even more remarkable was the rapid end of the European empires. Within ten years of the end of the war Europe controlled only a handful of areas in Asia. Within a quarter of a century all of the empires had, apart from a few scattered territories and islands, ceased to exist.

23

The Modern World Economy

The industrialization and urbanization of the world in the nineteenth century was largely confined to western Europe and the United States. The lead that this gave them over the rest of the world meant that by the early twentieth century they had transformed the world economy. The majority of the world suffered from deindustrialization during the nineteenth century and increasingly provided food and raw materials for the industrial countries. However, as with other developments in world history these changes could not be confined to one area or set of countries. Just as China could not maintain a monopoly over the various inventions it made (silk production, cast iron, paper, printing, the compass and gunpowder) so western Europe and the United States had no more than a headstart over the rest of the world. The twentieth century was marked by the growing pace of industrialization and urbanization throughout the world as technologies spread rapidly. From a wider perspective it is clear that industrialization, greater energy consumption, urbanization and the accompanying pollution are factors that have affected almost all of the world. What was new was the pace of change. Nevertheless, the industrial countries of 1900 (the 'core states') retained their predominance and only Japan was able not only to develop to their level but overtake many of them. By the second half of the century it was also becoming clear that the increasing pace of industrialization in China was bound to have a growing effect on the rest of the world simply because of the sheer size of the Chinese economy. By the 1990s China had recovered from the disasters of the period from 1850 to 1950 and was one of the top seven industrial countries in the world.

In parallel with these developments there was another that was equally, if not more, important. Over the course of world history rulers and states had always found it difficult to control the activities of merchants and manufacturers. Industrialization, the growth of world trade, the increasing scale and complexity of the world economy and the development of massive flows of money around the world now began to have a fundamental impact on the power of the state. Largely autonomous firms, corporations and financial institutions became even more powerful and important. Indeed the scale of their operations, the resources they commanded and the wealth they controlled meant that by the end of the twentieth century they were far more powerful than the overwhelming majority of states in the world. At the same time the financial flows within the world economy expanded so that they were beyond the control of individual states and even international institutions.

23.1 People and Disease

23.1.1 Population

Despite large-scale industrialization, the balance between population and food supply, together with the impact of disease, remained fundamental factors in human history, just as they had been since the development of farming. The modern world was characterized by the most rapid population growth in human history. It took until about 1825 before the world's population reached one billion. The next billion was added in only a hundred years. The rate of growth then became even faster. A further billion (taking the total to 3 billion) was added in about thirty-five years between 1925 and 1960. The next billion was added in only fifteen years (by 1975) while the increase from 4 billion to 5 billion took about twelve years and was completed in the late 1980s. Another billion was added at the same rate bringing the total to slightly over 6 billion by the end of the twentieth century. By the last decades of the twentieth century the world had to support about 90 million extra people every year – equivalent to the total world population in 500 BCE.

The rise in population was very unevenly spread across the world. In Europe the main burst of growth came in the century and a half after 1750 when the population increased from about 140 million to just over 400 million (despite the mass emigration of the nineteenth century). Thereafter growth was fairly slow at less than half the world average. This meant that in 1900 Europe accounted for about a quarter of the world's population but by the end of the twentieth century the proportion had fallen to less than an eighth of the total. In China growth in the nineteenth century was slower than in the eighteenth century largely because of the mid-century crisis. From about 450 million in 1900 (slightly larger than the whole of Europe) it increased rapidly to over one billion in the late twentieth century. In India growth was slow in the nineteenth century – the total increase was no more than a half. The rate doubled in the first half of the twentieth century and then doubled again to reach a total of one billion by 2000. However, the most remarkable change came in Africa. Until 1900 the continent was characterized by relatively low population levels and slow growth. Between 1700 and 1900 the population did not even double (in Europe it tripled). Yet in the twentieth century the population of Africa more than quadrupled at the fastest rate ever known in human history.

What were the causes of these very different patterns? In the industrialized countries the crucial factor was an increase in life expectancy achieved by conquering childhood diseases and ending a situation where a majority of babies died before they reached the age of five. Airborne diseases such as tuberculosis, bronchitis and pneumonia were largely eliminated, as were the less virulent waterborne diseases such as cholera and dysentery. These reductions are often supposed to stem from better medical treatment, but in practice this played only a minor role. The development of vaccines against many diseases came very late in the nineteenth century (the 1890s for cholera, typhoid and diphtheria) and tuberculosis was in steep decline long before even a partially effective vaccine was available (the 1920s) or the bacillus responsible was even identified. Some other diseases also seem to have become less virulent – over four-fifths of the fall in the death rate from measles occurred before any treatment was available. (By the time immunization was available the death rate had already fallen to one in a thousand.) For pneumonia some treatment was available with the new sulphonamide drugs from the late 1930s but by then the death rate from the disease was already half that at the beginning of the century. It is clear that the fall in death rates was largely produced by environmental improvements and better diet. In nineteenth century Europe and the United States the slow construction of sewage systems and water purification plants almost eliminated water-borne intestinal diseases. Better housing, which reduced overcrowding, damp and poor ventilation, was particularly important, especially for reducing diseases such as tuberculosis. Food imports from the rest of the world and better transport systems significantly improved diets, as did slowly increasing wealth. New technologies such as the pasteurization of milk, canning and refrigeration were also important.

These improvements were largely responsible for the considerable rise in population in Europe in the nineteenth century. Yet this increase did not continue in the twentieth century, despite further large falls in infant mortality rates (child mortality rates in Sweden in the 1980s were one-fortieth of the rate in 1900). The reason was a large fall in birth rates. This was first apparent by the last couple of decades of the nineteenth century and by the 1930s they had fallen by a third and were at historically low levels. After a short 'baby boom' for a decade or so after 1945, birth rates continued to fall – by the late twentieth century the fertility rate was near or below (in some cases substantially below) the population replacement rate of just over two children per couple. Birth rates at these levels were unprecedented in human history and reflected the complex interaction of a number of factors – class, gender, community, beliefs and costs – which produced a new attitude to the number of children couples thought appropriate and the regulation of family size. Many of these decisions had been made long before easy access to the contraceptive pill from the mid-1960s made them easier to take.

Outside the core industrialized states the population pattern reflected a different sequence of events. A major increase in life expectancy did not occur until the twentieth century but was then brought about by medical advances imported from the industrialized countries rather than a general improvement in social and economic conditions. The introduction, mainly from the late 1940s, of vaccinations, antibiotics and chemical spraying of mosquito breeding grounds to control malaria, produced unprecedented reductions in death rates. In Mauritius, for example, the death rate fell by 80 per cent between the mid-1940s and the mid-1950s – a similar decline had taken more than 150 years to achieve in Europe. The incidence of some diseases was also altered fundamentally – by the 1990s smallpox had been eradicated from the world and polio had been eliminated in 145 countries. The impact of these improvements was to produce a very rapid increase in population because falls in the birth rate did not begin to occur until the mid-1960s at the earliest. The pace of reduction quickened in the late twentieth century so that by the 1990s the birth rate in some countries such as China, Thailand, Indonesia, Mauritius and Cuba was approaching those of Europe. The major exceptions to this trend were large parts of the Islamic world (especially Pakistan and Bangladesh) and nearly all of Africa. Here over three-quarters of the population was still rural and children were, as they had always been in every agricultural society, an economic asset. Very high birth rates, combined with a significant fall in child mortality, produced a huge increase in the child population. By 1990 in most countries across Africa over half the population was aged under fourteen.

23.1.2 Disease

Ever since the development of farming and the evolution of settled societies humans had had to live with a high level of infectious disease. From the mid-nineteenth century environmental improvements, better diet and medical advances produced a situation where, for the first time in human history, the impact of disease was brought under control in many parts of the world. By the late twentieth century there were an increasing number of signs that this phase of human history might be very difficult to sustain. High usage levels of the antibiotic drugs developed from the late 1930s were beginning to produce resistant disease strains. Infectious diseases were on the increase and they were spread more rapidly because of the improvement in communications. The number of malaria cases in India rose from 100,000 in 1965 to 10 million in 1977. Yellow fever deaths in

Africa rose from a few hundred a year in the 1940s to over 200,000 a year by the 1990s. Bubonic plague re-emerged in India. Cholera spread from Asia into Latin America for the first time since the nineteenth century. New infectious diseases such as ebola emerged in Africa. The worldwide outbreak of AIDS in the 1980s (yet another example of a disease spreading from animals to humans, this time from monkeys) showed the limitations of medical science when no vaccine was available. The disease was contained in the industrialized countries but by the 1990s over 40 million people were infected, mainly in Africa where one in five of the population were affected in some regions.

The conquest of childhood diseases and changes to the diet had other darker consequences, particularly in the industrialized states. A richer diet – higher fat intake, largely in the form of dairy products (not eaten by humans until the last five thousand years), more processed food, less fresh fruit and vegetables, higher sugar consumption (on average thirty times the level of the mid-eighteenth century), lack of fibre (mainly through eating white bread which was a luxury for the elite until the mid-nineteenth century) – combined with less exercise, increased levels of smoking and greater pollution, led to huge increases in the number of deaths from heart disease and cancer. Even in 1930 coronary heart disease was responsible for only 1 per cent of British deaths. By the mid-1990s this figure had risen to over 30 per cent. About a fifth of the deaths from heart disease were directly attributable to smoking, which was also a major determinant in the rise in cancer rates. In 1900 cancer affected one in twenty-seven Americans. In 1980 it affected one in three with one in four Americans dying from the disease. Although cancer rates in the industrialized countries were at least ten times those of Africa there were, by the end of the twentieth century, the first signs that heart disease and cancer rates were rising there too.

23.2 Food and Land

[Earlier European agriculture 20.3 & 21.9]
The more than seven-fold increase in the world's population after the mid-eighteenth century required an equally large rise in the world's output of food. As in the past much of this was achieved by bringing new land into cultivation. Between 1860 and 1920 about one billion acres of new land was converted to agricultural use – 40 per cent of it in the United States (mainly in the corn belt), 20 per cent on the black earth soils of Russia and another 20 per cent in Asia. (The arable area in western Europe fell in this period.) In the sixty years after 1920 about another one billion acres was

brought into production. Some of the increases were even bigger, particularly in the newly settled countries such as Argentina, Brazil and Australia where the frontier of settlement was still pushing away from the coastal areas. In Africa, as the population rose steeply in the twentieth century, peasant farmers cut down the forests. However, this extra land was not sufficient to feed all the extra people in the world. This could only be done by two further revolutions after 1850 – mechanization and the adoption of high-input farming.

Until the late nineteenth century agriculture everywhere in the world had been dependent on human labour, hand tools and limited animal power. The use of more machinery was dependent on technological developments but its introduction was speeded up by the labour shortages in the newly settled countries. Mechanical reapers were first introduced in the 1860s in the United States where they were pulled by teams of up to twenty horses because the large-scale application of steam power on farms was uneconomic. Major mechanization had to await the development of the internal combustion engine and the tractor. In the United States they were adopted quickly – by 1920 there were 250,000 tractors and ten times that number by 1945. Their use only became widespread in Europe after about 1950. At the same time new machines such as combine harvesters were in use – in the United States from the 1920s but again much later in Europe. The first electric milking machines were introduced in 1895 and almost three-quarters of the farms in New Zealand used them by 1920. In western Europe only 3 per cent of cows were machine-milked in 1950 yet within thirty years only 3 per cent were hand-milked. Greater mechanization made it possible to increase farm size, reduce the number of farms and also cut the number of people working in agriculture. In the United States the number of farms fell from 7 million in the 1930s to below 3 million in the 1980s when over half of all agricultural output came from just 5 per cent of those farms. The agricultural workforce in the United States declined from over 11 million in 1910 to just over 3 million sixty years later. The fundamental transition away from the agricultural societies that had dominated human history since about 8000 BCE was complete in the major industrialized countries.

Until the nineteenth century farms were dependent almost entirely upon manures and composts produced on the farm itself in order to maintain soil fertility. Then western Europe, and later the United States, were able to use their increasing control over the world's resources to import new fertilizers. The first guano was brought to Europe from Latin America in the 1820s. Later, phosphates were mined around the world, and some Pacific islands such as Nauru and Ocean Island were effectively destroyed in the process. New industrial processes produced new artificial fertilizers

– superphosphates in the 1840s and nitrogenous fertilizers (from the fixing of atmospheric nitrogen) in the 1920s. After about 1950 this process increased dramatically as farming became an industry – the soil was treated less as a living organism and more as a medium to hold crops in position as more and more chemicals were poured on to them. Increasing industrialized production on farms led to increasing dependence on single crops which were far more susceptible to diseases and pests. The chemical industry produced a growing range of herbicides and pesticides to spray on crops – their use in western Europe and the United States rose fifteen-fold in the quarter-century after 1950.

The agricultural history of most of the world in the nineteenth and twentieth centuries was very different from that of the industrialized world. People in these countries (the overwhelming majority of the world's population) had only very limited access to the products of the new lands settled by the Europeans. The amount of new land available in an area such as Asia was very limited because production was already intense and using the best land. Land was also very unequally distributed – in Latin America by the mid-twentieth century two-thirds of the land was owned by less than two per cent of the population. A rapidly rising population meant that the amount of arable land per head of the population began to decline almost everywhere after the late nineteenth century. In the mid-twentieth century it was hoped that the so-called 'Green Revolution', the introduction of new high-yielding varieties of wheat and rice, would transform the situation. Yields often doubled, but the social and economic impact of the new varieties was usually disastrous. They required large amounts of fertilizer and pesticide use and the cost of growing them was therefore much higher. Small peasant farmers did not have enough land and capital to make it economic to grow the new varieties and it was the large landowners who did have the resources who benefited. They therefore only accelerated trends towards greater social differentiation, larger holdings and more landless labourers.

After the mid-twentieth century there was, for the first time in world history, enough food in the world to feed everybody adequately. The problem was that it was very unequally distributed. By the late twentieth century the people of the industrialized countries of western Europe, Japan and north America ate half the world's food even though they constituted only a quarter of the world's population. Much of the problem was caused by the fact that land in Asia, Africa and south America was devoted to growing crops for export to the major industrialized countries. A large proportion of this trade was simply to provide greater variety in the diet for people who were already well fed. In the second half of the twentieth century a domestic cat in the United States ate more meat than most people living in Africa and Latin America. The world food trade increased five-fold in the thirty years after 1950. Over fifty countries which had been self-sufficient in food in the 1930s were net importers fifty years later.

Crop failure and famine largely disappeared from Europe after the severe crisis of 1816–17 caused by the amount of dust in the atmosphere following the eruption of the Tomboro volcano in Indonesia in 1815. Thereafter, apart from Ireland in the late 1840s (caused by an outbreak of potato blight), famine was only associated with the disruption caused by war and civil war – Belgium in 1914–18, Germany at the end of that war, western Russia in the civil war, Leningrad in 1941–2 and the Netherlands in the winter of 1944–5. The situation was very different in the rest of the world. Until the mid-twentieth century probably about half the world's population suffered from malnutrition. By the early 1950s this had risen to over six out of ten, and it affected about 2 billion people in 1960. From the early 1960s the situation improved so that by 1980 'only' about a quarter of the world's population suffered from malnutrition. However, because of the rise in the population the number affected was still well over 1 billion. After 1980 the situation deteriorated again – by the end of the twentieth century at least 2 billion people were affected by a grossly inadequate diet and over 40 million a year were dying from hunger and its related diseases. For these people even the most basic benefits of the adoption of agriculture some ten thousand years earlier had still to arrive. Famine also remained endemic as it had throughout human history. Before 1950 there were major famines across the Sahel in 1913–14 and again in 1931 – the French blamed them on African 'idleness', 'apathy' and 'fatalism' and they continued to requisition food. Famines occurred in Niger (1942) and Bengal (1943–4), where about 3 million people died, and in Henan province in China where another 3 million died. In the second half of the twentieth century probably the worst famine in world history occurred in China between 1958–61 when about 30 million people died – it was the direct result of the communist government's policy. Elsewhere they occurred in Bangladesh (1975), the Sahel (throughout the 1970s), Ethiopia (1984–5) and Somalia in the early 1990s. In every case (except that of China) famine resulted not from a shortage of food (in Bengal the 1943 famine followed the largest ever rice crop) but from a lack of available land, poverty and rising food prices, which left many people unable to either grow enough food to survive or earn enough money to buy it.

Rising population, the expansion of the cultivated area and the intensification of agriculture led to increasing environmental damage. In western Europe the native woodlands had mostly been cleared in the period after 900 CE. In the mid-eighteenth century, when settlements were largely confined to the eastern seaboard, forests covered about one million square miles of the United States. By 1850, as the frontier moved westwards, about 40 per cent of these ancient forests had been destroyed. By the late twentieth century about 5 per cent of the forests still survived. From the mid-twentieth century the population in tropical areas, particularly Africa, rose rapidly and led to massive forest loss. In the second half of the century about half the world's tropical forests were destroyed. About three-quarters of this loss was to provide land for agriculture, the rest for the export of timber to the industrialized countries. However, much of the land cleared, especially in Latin America, was not for peasant agriculture, or to feed the local population, but for plantations and ranches for the export of food to the industrialized countries.

Deforestation together with the cultivation of unsuitable soils has led, throughout human history, to soil erosion. Much of the huge extension of the world's cultivated area that took place after 1850 occurred in areas with marginal soils that were not well suited to intensive agriculture. The Great Plains of the central United States were originally avoided by settlers because the ploughs they had available were not capable of breaking up the tough, compacted grass. The development of the heavy steel plough, pulled by teams of up to twelve oxen made this possible in the latter part of the nineteenth century. However, the climate was semi-arid with rainfall of only about twenty inches a year and the thin topsoil was only held together by the grass. Between the 1880s and the 1920s about 45 million acres of land were ploughed up and cultivated with new drought-resistant forms of wheat. The early 1930s brought one of the periodic droughts that affect the area and the loose, fragile, dry soil was blown away by the high winds, creating huge dust storms across the region. The first major storm picked up about 350 million tons of topsoil and deposited it over the eastern United States (it was even detected on ships 300 miles out in the Atlantic). By 1938, 10 million acres of land had lost their top five inches of soil and another 13 million acres the top two-and-a-half inches. Over three million people abandoned farms in the area, Oklahoma lost a fifth of its population and in some counties almost half the people left. The 'dust bowl' returned to large areas of the Great Plains in 1952–7 and again in the 1970s. By then a third of the topsoil of the United States had been ruined or made highly marginal for cultivation.

The Soviet Union's major agricultural catastrophe came in the 1950s with the 'virgin lands' programme – the drive to open up the marginal grasslands of areas such as Kazakhstan. In total about 100 million acres were ploughed up between 1954 and 1960. Yields peaked in 1956 and then fell steadily. Practices such as deep ploughing and leaving the soil bare during fallow periods, together with a severe drought in 1963, led to major soil erosion. In just three years 40 million acres of land were lost to cultivation and very rapidly more than half the new land was abandoned. After the mid-1960s a million acres a year were being lost. The most extreme form of soil loss is desertification – the permanent loss of land to deserts. This problem became particularly apparent in the twentieth century. Between 1925 and 1975 the Sahara desert grew by about 250,000 square miles along its southern edge. By the late twentieth century over ten per cent of the world's population lived in arid and semi-arid areas of the world threatened by desertification and the permanent loss of crop and grazing land.

The intensification of food production led to a vast increase in the amount of irrigated land in the world. In 1800 about 20 million acres were irrigated and this rose to about 100 million acres by the early twentieth century. By 1980 it had risen to over 500 million acres. Although, as the earliest farming communities discovered, irrigation is a highly effective way of increasing crop yields it has two major drawbacks. First, the amount of water it uses. By the late twentieth century over three-quarters of the world's water use was for irrigation and most of it was used inefficiently: in India and China two-thirds of the water was lost through evaporation and seepage. Second is the problem that the earliest societies of Mesopotamia encountered – waterlogging of the soil which, combined with high temperatures and evaporation from the surface, leaves a crust of salt which makes it impossible to grow crops. By the 1980s over 80 per cent of the irrigated land in the Punjab was affected. Across the world, as much irrigated land was being abandoned as was being brought into cultivation. The greatest environmental disaster caused by irrigation occurred in the Soviet Union around the Aral Sea. This large inland sea was unusual in that although two of the great rivers of central Asia flowed into it, none flowed out and the lake was maintained in size by very high evaporation rates. In the early 1970s the Soviet authorities implemented a grandiose scheme to use the two rivers to irrigate over 18 million acres so cotton and rice could be grown in highly unsuitable climates and soils. Predictably this major diversion of water caused the Aral Sea to shrink rapidly. By the early 1990s two-thirds of it had dried up, exposing the seabed across an area of over 12,000 square miles. The consequences were catastrophic. Temperatures in the region rose and rainfall declined, the fishing industry collapsed, villages were abandoned, the salinity of the Aral tripled, salt-dust storms swept the area, the water table fell causing the sewerage system to collapse leading to outbreaks of typhoid and eventually bubonic plague.

23.3 Technology

[Nineteenth-century technology 20.4 & 21.2]
Technological change in the nineteenth century was concentrated in two 'waves'. The first was characterized by the use of steam power, mass production of textiles and the widespread use of iron. This was beginning to fade by the 1840s and in its turn the second wave of railway construction and the adoption of steel was fading by the end of the century. This reflected the fact that new technologies were able to create new markets and rapid growth but were followed by market saturation and slowed growth before another wave developed. World industrialization from the late nineteenth century was dominated by the 'third wave' based on the increasing use of electricity, the bringing together of a number of new technologies to create the motor vehicle industry and new processes in the chemical industry.

The widespread use of electricity in the industrialized states began in the last quarter of the nineteenth century. At first it was used to provide light rather than power, mainly in public places such as theatres, restaurants, shops and banks; less than 1 per cent of homes had electricity. Gradually, better technologies developed such as the tungsten-filament light bulb and larger and more reliable generators, as well as distribution networks at local, regional and eventually national levels. For the first time humans had available an easily distributed form of energy. Electricity then became the foundation for most other technological advances – in the twentieth century its use increased twice as fast as overall energy consumption. Factories were powered by electricity rather than steam, new industries such as aluminium production (which needed vast quantities of electricity) were established and new markets opened up, particularly in products for the home. The United States was the first country to be electrified on a major scale, in urban areas in the 1920s and a decade later in the countryside. In Europe the countryside did not generally receive electricity until the 1950s. This phasing largely determined the emergence of consumer-durable industries supplying new products, such as refrigerators and washing machines, which occurred in the United States in the 1920s, western Europe in the 1950s and Japan in the 1960s. However, the availability of electricity across the world varied greatly. By the late twentieth century in western Europe nearly all homes had electricity whereas in the Ivory Coast it was less than 1 per cent.

The key production industry for much of the twentieth century was vehicles – not just the manufacture of cars and lorries, but also the ancillary activities of vehicle maintenance, road building and fuel provision. In the 1880s and the 1890s the development of the internal combustion engine and the pneumatic tyre made possible the evolution of the first primitive cars. In 1899 just 2,500 vehicles were sold in the United States (and most of those were electric or steam-driven). By 1922 this figure had risen to 2,270,000. The number of vehicles on the road in the United States rose from about 80,000 in 1905 to over 10 million in the early 1920s and to 30 million by the late 1930s. The impact of car production on the American economy was fundamental. By the late 1930s it was taking up half of all steel production, four-fifths of rubber output, two-thirds of plate-glass production and about a third of nickel and lead output. It was not until the 1950s that western Europe experienced a similar surge in car ownership and production and in Japan it did not occur until the 1960s. By the 1990s world output of cars was about 35 million a year and world car ownership had risen from about 100,000 in 1900 to nearly 600 million.

The chemical industry had only a slightly less spectacular impact on the world economy through the production of a wide range of new materials. The first synthetic fibre, rayon, was manufactured in 1910, but the real boom came in the 1920s when it could be produced for a quarter of the price of silk. In the 1920s and 1930s world output increased seventy-fold. This was followed by a whole range of new fibres starting with nylon in 1938 – by the late twentieth century over half the world's output of textile fibres came from synthetics. This was another fundamental shift in world history from a situation where all human societies had depended on natural products. Indeed it would not have been possible to provide clothes for the greatly expanded world population of the twentieth century using natural products – there would not have been enough suitable land to grow cotton or graze sheep and it could only have been provided at the expense of land needed to grow food. The chemical industry also depended on new methods of oil refining to produce an increasingly diverse range of plastics after 1945. Thereafter world production of plastics doubled every twelve years and by the 1970s exceeded the combined production of copper, lead and zinc. This was another fundamental departure – without this invention natural products and metals would not have been sufficient to meet demand.

By the late 1960s there were signs in the major industrial economies that the impetus provided by the vehicle and chemical industries was fading. It was gradually replaced by the 'fourth wave' of technological change based on electronics and communications, a process that was still gathering momentum at the end of the century. It was the development of the electric telegraph and then cable transmission in the mid-nineteenth century that first broke the link between communication and the speed of human movement by land and sea which had characterized all earlier societies. For the first time a worldwide communication system existed. This was supplemented by the development of the telephone in the late nineteenth century and then by the development of radio in the first decades of the twentieth century. By the 1920s numerous radio stations were broadcasting programmes in all of the industrialized countries. A further series of important changes occurred between 1935 and 1950 with the invention of radar, the tape recorder and television (the first stations in Britain and Germany were broadcasting programmes by the late 1930s). Probably the most important was the invention of the transistor in 1948 – it replaced the valve and began the process of miniaturization. In communications another fundamental change came in the early 1960s with the development of geostationary satellites capable of transmitting multiple circuits. At first they were on a small scale – Intelsat I, launched in 1965, could carry 120 simultaneous telephone circuits and two TV channels. By the 1990s satellites could carry 120,000 bi-directional circuits and the cost of using them fell to a sixth of 1960s levels. On telephone circuits the telex was replaced by fax machines in the 1980s and shortly afterwards mobile telephones became common.

Even more remarkable was the speed of miniaturization in electronics. The first primitive electro-mechanical computers were developed in the early 1940s for codebreaking. The introduction of the transistor did not bring about major changes – they depended on the invention of the integrated circuit (a huge number of miniaturized transistors on a 'chip' of silicon) followed by the microprocessor (a huge number of solid-state circuits on a 'chip' the size of a fingernail – in effect a computer on a chip). A highly sophisticated industry developed to manufacture silicon chips of ever-increasing capacity, as did a software industry to create the programs to process large amounts of information. From the early 1980s computers were no longer vast machines occupying several rooms and using special cooling facilities. They were tabletop sized and could be linked together into networks capable of processing huge amounts of data and, together with other improvements in communications, made possible rapid transmission and processing on a worldwide scale. The Internet was only one aspect of this phenomenon. Computers transformed nearly all industries, especially the service industries where large numbers of clerical jobs devoted to accumulating and analysing data were eliminated and in warehousing and stock control where procedures were revolutionized. The introduction of industrial robots into the vehicle industry from the 1980s not only reduced the amount of labour needed but also enabled a multiplicity of models to be made on a single production line. (The number of industrial robots in Japan increased from 14,000 in 1981 to nearly 330,000 by the end of the decade.) New combinations of technologies produced new industries. The bringing together of micro-electronics and lasers (developed in the early 1960s) created the compact disc in the early 1980s. It was used, in conjunction with computers, to store large quantities of data and also to reproduce music for a new domestic consumer industry, largely replacing the long-playing record, which had been invented in 1948.

23.4 Production and Energy

The deepening of industrialization in the major economies of western Europe, the United States and Japan, the development of new technologies and the spread of industrialization across the globe produced a revolution in the world economy. The first phases of world industrialization between 1750 and the late nineteenth century saw world industrial output triple. In the twentieth century it rose about 35-fold. The real burst in growth occurred after 1950 when it was twice as fast as in the first half of the century. Such was the pace of change that world industrial output between 1953 and 1973 was equivalent to the *total* industrial output of the whole period between 1800 and 1950. By the 1990s the annual growth in the world economy was at such a level that every two years it added to world output the equivalent of the total world output in 1900.

Industrialization was not spread evenly across the globe. As we have seen, there was a fundamental change in the nineteenth century. From a position of rough equality in industrial output between India, China and western Europe in 1750, huge disparities had been created by the end of the nineteenth century when over nine-tenths of the world's industrial output came from western Europe and the United States. That proportion was reduced by the industrialization of the Soviet Union in the 1930s and by Japan and eastern Europe after 1945, but it was only slightly reduced by the so-called 'newly industrializing countries' of Asia. The one country that did have an impact, because of the sheer size of its economy, was China. By the 1990s three-quarters of the world's industrial output came from just seven countries – the United States, Russia, Japan, China, Germany, France and Britain. Most of the rest came from the other countries of western Europe – Sweden, Belgium, the Netherlands and Italy. The impact of the remaining countries was minimal in world terms but vitally important for their own economies and societies. Of the new industrial economies, that of Brazil was the most important though it contributed less than 2 per cent of world industrial output. For both south Korea and Taiwan the figure was less than 1 per cent. Countries in Latin America and, in particular, Africa, saw their share of world industrial output fall in the twentieth century just as it had in the nineteenth century.

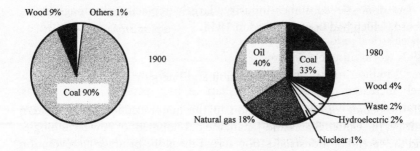

Percentage share of world energy consumption

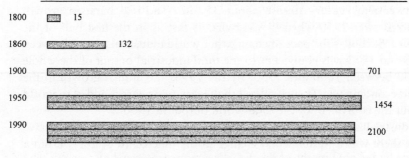

World coal consumption (millions of tons)

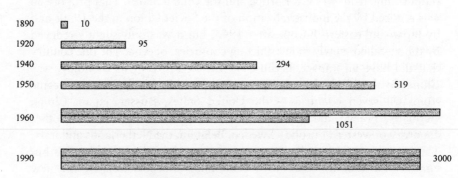

World oil consumption (millions of tons)

Chart 6: World energy consumption

The huge increases in industrial output demanded a major increase in mineral extraction. Between 1900 and 1960 more metals were mined than in all previous human history. Demand continued to grow for the rest of the twentieth century and world consumption of metals rose about sixteen-fold over the century as a whole. Some of the increases were even greater. The electrical industries and car production relied heavily on copper. In the 1890s world output was about 150,000 tons a year, a century later it was over 9 million tons a year. Production of nickel (mainly used to harden steel) increased over seventy-fold. Part of this increase in output was obtained by technological improvements which allowed lower-grade ores to be used. In the late nineteenth century the lowest workable grade of copper ore was about 3 per cent – a century later this had fallen to 0.35 per cent. However, exploiting this ore involved breaking, transporting and milling over 300 tons of rock and then removing it as waste in order to obtain a ton of copper. The amounts of energy used in these processes were immense – by the second half of the twentieth century over a fifth of US energy consumption was used to extract and process minerals.

Rapidly rising industrial production and mineral extraction, the even greater growth of electricity consumption and the huge increases in vehicle use, all depended on increases in energy consumption. During the twentieth century world energy consumption increased over thirty-fold. The nineteenth century was the age of coal and the increase in industrial production could not have been sustained without its use. In the 1890s coal provided nine-tenths of the world's energy yet a century later this had fallen to less than a third even though the total output of coal increased six-fold. The twentieth century was the age of another fossil fuel – oil. World production rose from 10 million tons a year in 1890 to over 3,000 million tons a year a century later.

Oil had been obtained by the earliest societies in Mesopotamia from places where it seeped out on to the surface and it was used mainly in the form of bitumen for caulking ships and even for medicinal purposes. It was not until the mid-nineteenth century that efforts to extract and exploit it on a commercial scale began: the world's first commercial oil came from the Drake well in Pennsylvania in 1859. The demand for oil came, at first, from two factors. First, lubricants such as whale and vegetable oils were proving inadequate for the demands of new industrial machinery. Second, whale oil was in increasingly short supply which made it more and more difficult and costly to provide domestic and industrial lighting in areas which did not have town gas derived from coal. At first over four-fifths of the world's oil was refined into kerosene to provide illuminating oil and most of the rest went to make industrial lubricants. The development of oil-burning furnaces meant that by the first decade of the twentieth century fuel oil made up about half of the industry's output. Even in 1910 only 5 per cent of the world's energy came from oil – wood was still far more important. The boost in overall demand from the vehicle industry came a little later and it was not until the 1930s that gasoline (petrol) became the main product of the oil industry.

By the late 1930s oil had replaced coal as the main source of energy in the United States as relatively cheap domestic sources in Oklahoma and Texas were discovered. The United States was the main producer in the world (it never produced less than half the world's output between 1920 and 1950), followed by Venezuela. Yet the world trade in oil was small – over half of all the oil produced was consumed in the country of production. This was partly because western Europe was still almost totally reliant on domestically produced coal – in 1950 it still provided over 90 per cent of energy needs. In the twenty years after 1950 western Europe shifted rapidly to dependence on imports of cheap oil for over two-thirds of its energy – the result was the large-scale closure of coal mines – a major reversal of the nineteenth-century pattern. At the same time the United States share of world production fell from a half to about a fifth and it too began to import oil on an extensive scale. Much of this oil came from the rapid expansion of production in Iraq, Iran, the Gulf and Saudi Arabia. In 1950 the region provided less than a tenth of the world's oil; by the early 1970s the figure was about a third and two-thirds of the world's proven reserves were in the region. After the 1970s production also moved into technically more difficult areas such as Alaska and the North Sea.

A major by-product of the exploitation of the world's oilfields was the increasing importance of natural gas as an energy source. Although it was used locally near US oilfields from the early twentieth century, its widespread use depended on improvements in pipeline technology making it possible to pump the gas under pressure over long distances. This was achieved in the United States in the 1930s but it was not until the 1960s that its use became widespread in western Europe, with the development of the Groningen field in the Netherlands and reserves in the North Sea. Later the huge fields in Siberia were developed and much of their output pumped to western Europe. By the late twentieth century natural gas accounted for over a fifth of world energy consumption.

The history of energy in the nineteenth and twentieth centuries was characterized by the ever-increasing consumption of non-renewable fossil fuels – coal, oil and natural gas. Only two other technologies contributed any real alternatives – hydroelectric and nuclear power. The use of the former grew steadily in the early twentieth century and reached a peak of importance in the late 1920s when it provided about 40 per cent of the world's electricity. Then it became steadily less important – by the end of the twentieth century it accounted for about 2 per cent of the world's energy use. The development of nuclear power in the 1950s was a spin-off from the production of the atomic bomb. Its advocates argued it was a route to very cheap electricity but it turned out to be a failure. It was dogged by safety problems and poor designs and none of the electricity generated was cheaper than that obtained from conventional sources. By the late twentieth century over fifty stations had already been closed and it provided about 1 per cent of the world's energy.

Until the early nineteenth century renewable sources of energy – human, animal, wind, water and wood – had provided nearly all of the world's energy needs. By the twentieth century the world's consumption of energy reflected an entirely different pattern from that which had prevailed in all previous human societies. Over 90 per cent of energy came from fossil fuels. By the late twentieth century the world's annual consumption of coal was 280 times greater than in 1800 and the amount of oil used every year was 300 times greater than in the late nineteenth century. Throughout the period world energy consumption was highly inequitable. As early as 1929 the average American used over seven times as much energy as the world average. By the late twentieth century the United States, which had about 5 per cent of the world's population, used a third of all the energy consumed in the world. The majority of the world's people remained dependent on organic fuels, in particular wood and cow dung – in India they still constituted 90 per cent of all the energy consumed.

23.5 Urbanization

[*Earlier urbanization 20.11.2*]
The industrialization of western Europe and the United States in the nineteenth century produced the first fully urbanized societies in world history where about three out of four people lived in cities. However, the impact of this trend on the world as a whole was still small. In 1900 just 160 million people, 10 per cent of the world's population, lived in cities. The twentieth century was marked by three major trends – the diffuse growth of cities in the industrialized world, the urbanization of the rest of the world and the growth of giant cities. By the end of the twentieth century, for the first time in world history, a majority of the world's population lived in cities.

In western Europe and the United States the proportion of the population living in cities began to decline in the mid-twentieth century. In London this was noticeable from the 1950s and within a decade the urban population in Britain as a whole was falling steadily. Paris lost over a tenth

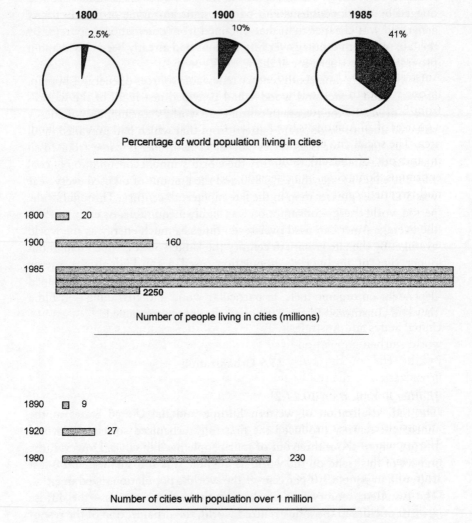

Chart 7: World urbanization

of its population between 1968 and 1975. Cities also continued to spread outwards, a trend encouraged by the building of new rail networks in cities such as Paris and Tokyo, but mainly resulting from increasing use of the car. By the 1980s the urban area of New York was over five times its extent sixty years earlier even though the population had only doubled. Further large urban sprawls developed in Tokyo (which was over fifty miles wide by the second half of the twentieth century), the Randstad in the Netherlands (a huge urban area joining Rotterdam, The Hague, Amsterdam and Utrecht, and containing a third of the Dutch population in one-twentieth of the land area) and the massive urban belt stretching from Boston to Washington on the east coast of the United States, where a quarter of all Americans lived on less than 2 per cent of the country's land area. The social and economic costs of moving all these millions of people in and out of the city centres every day by both road and rail was enormous. Some cities had effectively been taken over by the car. From the mid-twentieth century two-thirds of central Los Angeles was given over to the car in the form of streets, freeways, parking and garages. The large numbers of cars meant that traffic jams were the norm and that there was no improvement in journey times from the horse-drawn era of the late nineteenth century. In New York the average speed of traffic was just over eleven miles an hour in 1907, but this had fallen to six miles an hour by the 1980s.

In 1900 two-thirds of the world's urban population lived in Europe, the United States and Australasia. By 1975, for the first time, a majority of the world's urban population lived outside the main industrialized countries. By the end of the twentieth century over two-thirds did so. The urbanization of the rest of the world was not associated with industrialization, indeed growth rates were highest in the least industrialized countries. On average the urban population grew twice as fast as in the industrialized states in the nineteenth century, in some cases much faster. The population of Lagos in Nigeria rose from 126,000 in 1931 to 5 million fifty years later. Nairobi in Kenya increased faster still from 11,500 in 1906 to 1 million in 1982. Most of this growth came from migration from the rural areas because, unlike Europe in the nineteenth century, many facilities such as health care were far better in towns than in the countryside. Cities also tended to have, for political reasons, better food supplies (rather like Rome two thousand years earlier but without the circuses). However, conditions in the cities could be extremely harsh. In India in the 1990s 1.5 million people lived on the streets simply because they could not afford housing, even though many had jobs. The infrastructure of the cities was unable to cope with the massive influx of people and most of the new residents had to live in one of the vast illegal squatter areas. In cities such as Addis Ababa in Ethiopia and Yaounde in Cameroon, over nine out of ten of the population did so.

Across the world cities became bigger in the twentieth century. In 1890 there were only nine cities in the world with more than one million people and only London, New York and Paris had a population of over two million. By 1920 twenty-seven cities had more than one million people and five had over four million – New York (8 million), London (7.2 million), Paris (4.9 million), Tokyo and Berlin (both 4 million). By 1960 there were sixteen cities of over four million with the largest being New York (14.1 million) and Tokyo (13.5 million). By the 1980s there were 230 cities in the world with over one million people (a 25-fold increase in less than a century). Eight cities had more than ten million people and two – New York and Tokyo – had populations of more than 20 million. These giant cities were very different from the industrial cities of the past. They reflected a further change in society – the declining importance of industrial activity and the rise of tertiary activities such as finance, banking and other associated functions. They were tightly integrated into the growing world economy of trade and finance and often had more contacts with each other than with the rest of the country in which they were located.

23.6 Globalization

23.6.1 Trade and finance
One of the major trends in world history was the growing importance of trade between different societies and the development of increasingly sophisticated forms of finance and credit to support that trade. Nearly all of these developments took place beyond the control of the different states and empires in the world. The twentieth century witnessed the spectacular continuation of these trends on a previously unimaginable scale. It witnessed the emergence of truly global economic systems from the tentative structures built in previous centuries. They involved an increase in world trade, the development of a complex world financial structure, the increasing importance of transnational corporations and the linked internationalization of both production and services. Service industries became increasingly important in every society as the transition from agricultural to industrial economies was succeeded by the transition to 'post-industrial' economies. This was made possible by the huge increases in productivity in both agriculture and industry – an American factory worker in the 1990s produced six times more than his counterpart at the beginning of the century. This meant that far more people could be employed in other sectors of the economy such as finance, advertising, tourism, education and

health care. The magnitude of this transition can be judged from the fact that in the industrialized economies in 1900 about a third of overall output came from agriculture and slightly more from industry. By the end of the twentieth century, despite the large increases in agricultural output and even bigger increases in industrial production, agriculture contributed just over 3 per cent of total output, industry about 35 per cent and over 60 per cent came from services.

The development of the world economy in the twentieth century was not a continuous process. There were major discontinuities during the wars of 1914–18 and 1939–45 and during the great depression of the 1930s, which saw countries either being forced or choosing to adopt a policy of greater self-sufficiency. Until 1950 world trade grew at a little over 1 per cent a year, which was less than the overall growth in output. After 1950 world trade grew on average at over 6 per cent a year, far faster than the growth in output. By the 1990s world trade was over twelve times greater than in 1950 and it was taking up about a fifth of the world's output of goods and services. However, world trade remained dominated by the countries that had begun to industrialize in the nineteenth century (including Japan): they accounted for three-quarters of the total in 1900 and almost exactly the same proportion a century later. But the nature of that trade changed significantly. Food fell from about a quarter of the total in 1900 to less than a tenth (despite a large increase in the amount traded) and the share of manufactured goods doubled to three-quarters. In general the main industrialized countries became increasingly dependent on trade and the import of raw materials to support their massive growth in output and consumption. In 1900 they imported just 1 million tons of iron ore a year, by 1990 western Europe was a net importer of 65 million tons and Japan of 75 million tons. Until 1950 western Europe was a net exporter of energy (coal) but by 1973 was importing over 40 per cent of its energy needs. World trade became increasingly regionalized in the second half of the twentieth century. In north America the proportion of intra-regional trade rose from 25 per cent in the 1950s to nearly 40 per cent by the 1990s when a quarter of all American-manufactured exports went to just one country – Canada. The creation of the European Economic Community in the 1950s meant that the proportion of members' trade within the community rose from less than a third to over two-thirds.

As in the past, the international economy depended on a number of key mechanisms. It needed a recognized monetary unit for transactions – in the past this was normally gold and silver coins, hence the importance for western Europe of its control over the resources of the Americas which enabled trade with Asia to be financed. For much of the twentieth century this remained the case, although individual currencies, at first sterling and then the dollar, played a central role. Eventually, just as in individual economies paper money had replaced coins as assets (something pioneered by China around 1000 CE), so in the international economy intangible assets and entirely artificial units (such as 'Special Drawing Rights') replaced gold and holdings of foreign currency as methods for backing financial transactions. The international system also needed a system for dealing with trade (and therefore monetary) imbalances as some states accumulated surpluses and others deficits. In the past if exchange of products was not possible then payment had to be in hard currency – if that ran out trade was usually impossible. The system also needed to adjust to shifts in the values of national currencies – in the past debasement of the currency, if carried too far, simply meant that no one would accept it. States had to be prepared to be bound by the minimal rules of the system and adjust national economic policies as necessary – in the past they had little option, now some, in particular the United States, had greater room to manoeuvre.

In the period up to 1914 world trade was dominated by Europe, partly because the United States was almost entirely self-sufficient, and the trade in primary products (food and minerals) accounted for almost two-thirds of the total. As world trade and the communications infrastructure increased from the mid-nineteenth century a multilateral payments network developed which reduced the need for the physical movement of gold and silver. However, it covered only about a quarter of world trade and no institutional mechanism evolved to regulate the system. Neither was there a single world financial system. By the late nineteenth century most of Europe and north America had adopted a gold standard for their currencies but large parts of the world – China, Latin America and most of Africa – remained on a silver standard. The financial institutions of the City of London were at the centre of world finances, reflecting Britain's position as the largest trader, its role as the biggest single source of overseas investment and the sophistication and standing of its financial institutions. In practice gold was not used to settle international debts and finance trade – this was done through sterling bills of exchange. This mechanism depended on the free convertibility of sterling into gold – the problem was that Britain only held a fifth of the world's gold reserves and this was insufficient to back all transactions. The system continued to function for a number of fortuitous reasons. British control of the resources of India helped offset the chronic British trade deficit. The substantial British surplus on 'invisible' items such as finance, shipping and insurance was enough to create an overall surplus and this was largely recycled in the international system through overseas investment. It was just enough to keep the system afloat.

The system was wrecked by the 1914–18 war, the eleven-fold increase in the British national debt and its massive debt to the United States incurred to pay for munitions. The attempt to set up a system whereby German reparations helped the Allies to pay off their debts to Britain so that it could pay its debts to the Americans failed when it became clear in the early 1920s that reparations at a large enough level could not be enforced. By 1919 the US held nearly 45 per cent of the world's gold reserves and Britain less than 10 per cent. The United States was therefore central to any revitalized world financial system, but its increasingly high tariffs meant that the Europeans could not earn enough dollars to pay off their debts. The British attempt to remain a central financial power was doomed by its lack of reserves and made worse by the decision in 1925 to restore the pre-1914 exchange rate as symbol of a return to normality. The inevitable result was an overvalued pound, a further decline in British exports and a continued weakening of the British position.

The world financial system finally collapsed in the great depression after 1929. The US stock market crash caused the collapse of a large number of weak, poorly regulated banks. Between 1929 and 1932 gross domestic product in the United States fell by almost a third and unemployment affected a quarter of the workforce. The international financial system magnified the problems leading to more bank failures in Germany and Austria. One of the worst-affected areas was Latin America where exports fell by a third and imports by two-thirds. Nearly every country in the region defaulted on its debts. Action taken by individual states, in particular the massive US tariff increases of 1929, made matters worse and led to a breakdown of world trading and financial structures. In September 1931 Britain abandoned the gold standard and was followed by over thirty other countries by the end of 1932. The World Economic Conference collapsed almost as soon as it started in June 1933 and over thirty countries, starting with France, began imposing physical quotas on imports. This was followed by a series of regional trade agreements – the Danube group (Hungary, Romania, Yugoslavia and Bulgaria), the 1934 Rome agreement (Italy, Austria and Hungary), the Oslo group (the Nordic and Benelux countries) and, most important of all, the Ottawa agreements of 1932, which established a preferential trade system within the British empire. In some places the normal mechanisms of trade broke down altogether: in 1932 Hungary and Czechoslovakia were reduced to exchanging eggs for coal. At the same time a series of currency blocs emerged based on sterling, the dollar, the yen and in Europe two blocs – one dominated by Germany and the other a gold bloc of Belgium, France, the Netherlands and Switzerland. International trade depended on complex deals between the blocs such as the Anglo-American agreement of 1938.

In 1944–6 the victorious allies attempted, for the first time in world history, to design an international finance system. It was built around an International Monetary Fund (IMF) to manage the financial system, provide liquidity and help countries running balance of payments deficits. Not surprisingly, it reflected the interests of the United States which made over half the manufactured goods in the world and held over half the world's gold reserves. In practice it never operated as proposed and most of its aims could not be met. Until the late 1950s the IMF was almost moribund because under its rules the dollar should have been declared a 'scarce currency' as a result of the huge American trade surplus – the US provided a third of the world's exports but accounted for only a tenth of its imports. Other states should therefore have been able to impose controls over imports from the United States to correct the imbalance and this the Americans were not prepared to accept. The Europeans operated their own currency payments union and the British maintained a sterling bloc with free movement of the pound within the bloc but a single account (controlled in London) for all external payments. The world financial system operated as intended for a few years after the late 1950s when the huge American payments surplus disappeared as European exports recovered and US military spending abroad rose rapidly. Full convertibility of currencies was finally achieved between 1958 and 1961 and the dollar was pegged to an internationally agreed gold price.

Within a decade the system collapsed. The main reason was that the United States was not prepared to accept the disciplines that applied to other states. The continuing US trade deficit combined with high military spending abroad (especially after 1965 with the escalating Vietnam war) provided enough dollars to finance world trade but meant that other states accumulated large dollar reserves. By the late 1960s these exceeded the value of American gold holdings and the whole system depended on 'confidence' in the United States. However, the US preferred to print money to finance its geopolitical policies and high domestic spending. (In parallel the British found they could not sustain even their very limited role in the world system. Sterling was devalued in 1967 and its role in the international financial system ended.) The amount of gold was inadequate to fund the rapid increase in world trade and the IMF had to create an artificial unit (Special Drawing Rights). The post-war system finally collapsed in 1971. The United States ended the convertibility of the dollar into gold and imposed a surcharge on imports. The dollar was devalued again a year later and all attempts to regulate the value of the world's currencies was abandoned.

Throughout world history individual governments and rulers had always found it difficult to control the activities of merchants and bankers.

The same factors now began to operate on a global scale. From the early 1970s governments in the industrialized world gradually dropped any attempt to regulate the world's financial system. The first signs of this trend came in the early 1960s when the growing American financial deficit produced a surplus of dollars in Europe. An unregulated Eurodollar market developed centred on London – it was worth $9 billion in 1964 and $57 billion by the end of the decade. The huge flow of funds to the oil-producing countries after the quintupling of oil prices in 1973–4 created a massive expansion of the Eurodollar market because these states feared political interference if they placed their funds in the United States. By 1981 the Eurodollar market was worth $661 billion. However, the United States continued to run a huge balance of payments deficit and also, after 1980, a huge fiscal deficit of about $200 billion a year (largely accounted for by increased military spending) which was not corrected until the late 1990s. The world financial system was kept afloat by the willingness of the major creditors (Germany and Japan) to invest in the United States. American net assets abroad of $141 billion in 1982 turned into a debt of $1 trillion within a decade. This caused the Eurodollar market to more than triple to over $2,800 billion by the late 1980s, making it more than thirty times bigger than in the early 1960s. The removal of all foreign exchange controls by all the major industrialized states in the early 1980s caused a massive increase in dealings from $100 billion a day in 1979 to $1.5 trillion a day by the late 1990s. A global market in equities also emerged in the 1980s, worth about $1,000 billion. These markets depended on the development of worldwide communications systems linking computers in all the major trading cities. They were also no longer related to the world's trade in physical goods – they were primarily speculative and on a vast scale with the foreign exchange market eighty times bigger than the value of world trade. By the late 1980s the turnover of the London Eurodollar market was twenty-five times the level of world trade and foreign exchange markets were ten times bigger.

23.6.2 Transnational corporations

The huge growth in world trade and the creation of a complex global financial system were two aspects of the increasing scale and integration of the world economy. Another was the rise of the transnational corporation (TNC) – a company with a national identity but with operations and assets across the globe. Until the late nineteenth century companies were national and small-scale and many were controlled by single individuals or families. The increasing level of industrial production saw the rise of large corporations with professional managers and institutional shareholders. The rise of the TNC was a further extension of this trend. Until well into the twentieth century TNCs were almost entirely confined to the extractive industries, in particular oil, and agricultural commodities. For example, the American-owned United Fruit Company dominated the economies (and politics) of many central American states. The major exceptions were the two American car giants, Ford and General Motors. Ford opened its first overseas plant in Windsor, Ontario in 1904 and moved to Europe with the opening of the Trafford Park plant in Manchester in 1911 and a Bordeaux plant in 1913. After the 1914–18 war Ford built new plants in Berlin and Cologne and, in 1931, the massive integrated plant at Dagenham in east London. General Motors did not build its own plants, but instead bought up foreign firms, starting with the Canadian firm McLoughlin in 1918 and moving into Europe with the purchase of Vauxhall in 1926 and Opel in 1929.

Until the mid-twentieth century most TNCs followed a relatively simple corporate strategy allowing largely autonomous subsidiaries to operate in separate national markets with the profits repatriated to the parent group. Most TNCs were American (the British were second) but they only operated in a small number of countries. The one exception was the giant oil companies – the 'Seven Sisters'. They operated a highly effective cartel held together by a series of anti-competitive agreements. These involved monopoly bargaining over extraction rights in areas such as the Gulf, a totally artificial world oil price, an agreement to maintain market shares as in 1928 (expanding demand provided growing profits), and deals to equalize excess crude oil production and excess refining capacity so that no market in oil could develop. By 1949 these companies owned, outside the United States and the Soviet Union, over four-fifths of known reserves, nearly nine-tenths of crude oil production, over three-quarters of refining capacity, two-thirds of the oil tanker fleet and nearly all the pipelines.

From the early 1950s external factors induced changes in the way TNCs operated. The growing ease of travel by jet aircraft and faster communications through computers and satellites meant that greater central control and integration was possible – global marketing and production was now relatively easy. By the late 1960s the formation of overseas subsidiaries by TNCs was running at ten times the rate of the 1920s and the domination of US firms was declining as major TNCs emerged in Germany, Japan and, by the end of the century, south Korea. The main areas of TNC activity were, in order of importance, petrochemicals, cars, consumer electronics, tyres, pharmaceuticals, tobacco, soft drinks, fast food, financial consultancies and luxury hotels. Although these firms retained a distinct national ethos their operations were increasingly international. Over 40 per cent of the assets of IBM and Ford were overseas and for corporations such as Ford, Unilever, ITT and Philips over half their employment was abroad.

TNCs from smaller countries were even more international – the Swiss-Swedish corporation Asea, Brown Boveri and the Dutch group Philips made over four-fifths of their sales overseas. One consequence of the rise of TNCs and the greater integration of the world economy was the internationalization of production. In the early 1960s Ford designed and built the Cortina car in Britain for the British market. Twenty years later its replacement, the Escort, was a multinational car designed for the European market, assembled at three plants but incorporating parts made in fifteen countries. Corporations also sub-contracted operations around the world to take advantage of cheap labour or other cost savings. For example, precision drilling for 'Swiss' watches took place in Mauritius and rapid telecommunications created data-processing industries in low wage areas such as south-east Asia and the Caribbean.

The impact of TNCs on national economies was enormous and the ability of any government, even those of the industrialized states of western Europe and the United States, to exercise any control over them was very limited. By the last quarter of the twentieth century about a quarter of all industrial production in the main industrialized economies was undertaken by TNCs. In international trade their domination was far greater. The old idea that such trade was about a national firm buying or selling in an overseas market was outdated. By the 1980s a third of all world trade took place as transactions within TNCs. About a half of all American and Japanese imports and exports was trade within TNCs. The economic importance of TNCs can be judged from the fact that by the end of the twentieth century half of the 100 largest economic entities in the world were states and half were corporations. The Exxon oil company had a turnover six times bigger than Morocco's gross national product, and General Motors had a turnover twice Egypt's GNP.

23.7 Economies

After 1900 all the economies in the world were influenced by the major and unprecedented forces of population growth, technological change, increasing production, greater energy consumption, rising world trade and financial flows and the internationalization of production. However, the world economy remained dominated by the states which had industrialized in the nineteenth century – the one exception was the rise of Japan. Every state became wealthier, but the fundamental problem faced by the less industrialized states was that, although they found it relatively easy to adopt the latest technology, they could not break the grip of the industrial powers of western Europe and the United States. The huge differences in wealth in the world, which had developed between 1750 and 1900 not only remained but grew bigger.

By the last decades of the nineteenth century the United States overtook Britain as the leading industrial power in the world and maintained that position thereafter. In the 1890s it made about 30 per cent of the world's manufactured output, a proportion that grew to over 40 per cent by the late 1920s; it faltered in the 1930s but rose to nearly 50 per cent in 1950 as the European economies struggled to recover from the war. Some decline from that position was inevitable but the American position was significantly eroded in the second half of the twentieth century. By the late 1980s its share of world industrial production was back to the level a century earlier – in 1950 it made three-quarters of all the cars in the world, by the early 1990s less than a fifth. It was also losing some of its long-standing advantages. Its natural resources were suffering from heavy exploitation and costs were rising, whereas western Europe and Japan could exploit changes in bulk transportation technology (very large oil and ore carriers) to gain easy access to low-cost resources. The size of the internal American market was also no longer a unique asset – by the end of the twentieth century that of the European Union was bigger.

In the late nineteenth century the second most dynamic economy in the world was that of Germany. Despite defeat in two wars and the catastrophic inflation of the early 1920s it maintained its position as one of the top three industrial economies in the world. France was far behind Germany in the 1890s because of slow population growth and a poor endowment of coal and iron ore, the key elements of nineteenth-century industrialization. However, it was able to adapt quickly to the new twentieth-century technologies and industries, especially after 1950, to be only just behind Germany. Italy, with its markedly dual economy (industry in the north and a backward agriculture in the south), remained well behind the other major European economies until after 1950. Then it became one of the most successful in the world, growing faster than both Germany and France. The one relative failure among the major industrial economies was the first country to industrialize – Britain. Its rate of growth (always low in the nineteenth century) remained slower than that of its rivals. During the twentieth century it made the same technological transitions as all the other industrial economies but for reasons that are far from clear it remained less dynamic. After 1900 Germany was able to maintain its share of world industrial output, but Britain suffered a clear and, in the later stages, precipitous decline. In 1900 Britain made 20 per cent of the world's manufactured goods – by the end of the century it had fallen to about 2 per cent and in the early 1980s Britain became a net importer of manufactured goods for the first time since it began to industrialize in the late eighteenth century.

Undoubtedly the most successful economy in the twentieth century was that of Japan. In the late nineteenth century although industrialization was under way it remained limited – in 1900 India exported more manufactured goods than Japan and was not overtaken until the late 1920s. By the late twentieth century Japan was second only to the United States as an industrial economy. Early industrialization was based, as in Britain, on textiles. Once Japan controlled its domestic market it moved on to dominate the Chinese market and by 1935 it was exporting nearly half the world's textiles. Iron and steel production also grew and by the 1930s Japan was the third largest shipbuilder in the world. However, it still had only a semi-industrial economy – a majority of the labour force was still employed in agriculture and forestry. Even after recovery from defeat in 1945 Japan's GNP was still at one-fifteenth of the US level and 40 per cent of the workforce was still engaged in agriculture. Then, in the twenty years up to 1973, Japan achieved the fastest growth experienced by any economy in world history over a substantial period. Overall growth was about 10 per cent a year, but industrial output grew at over 14 per cent a year. By the late 1960s Japan was the largest shipbuilder in the world, the second largest car manufacturer and the biggest producer of key consumer items such as televisions, radios, cameras and sewing machines. By 1968 Japan had the second biggest GDP in the non-communist world.

The causes of such unprecedented growth were probably a mix of factors: the movement of labour from agriculture, rapid adoption of the latest technology, very high investment rates (three times that of the United States), a rigorously educated workforce, long hours of work and a highly protected domestic market. Growth slowed, as it did everywhere in the industrialized world, after 1973, but remained higher than in the other industrial economies. By the last quarter of the twentieth century the fundamental transformation of Japan's position was complete. It was the first country to overtake all the early industrializing countries of western Europe and even challenge US dominance in many areas. Its rise marked a fundamental transition in world economic power. In 1948 Japan made 1.6 per cent of the world's industrial output, by the 1990s nearly 15 per cent. Car production was just 165,000 vehicles in 1960, but within twenty years it had overtaken the United States as the biggest producer in the world. By the 1990s it was making almost 10 million vehicles a year, half of which were exported. In the last quarter of the twentieth century Japan ran the largest trading surplus of any country and was the world's largest creditor nation. Over the course of the twentieth century its GDP per head increased nearly fifteen-fold, twice as fast as that of any other state and more than three times as fast as the United States.

In the late nineteenth century Russia was probably more industrialized than Japan although it demonstrated many of the features of the economies of countries such as Argentina and Australia – large agricultural exports and foreign ownership of most important industries. In Russia the oil industry around Baku was entirely foreign-owned as was nearly all the mining industry, half the chemical industry and most railways. Nevertheless Russia was industrializing rapidly – between 1890 and 1914 industrial output rose at about 6 per cent a year. However, the overall level of industrialization was about the same as in Britain in the early nineteenth century and France in about 1860. The decision of the Soviet government to embark on forced industrialization after 1928 was successful, despite the terrible costs paid by the peasants (three-quarters of all workers) during collectivization. Investment doubled in the decade after 1928, iron and coal output quadrupled, electricity generation rose seven-fold and machine-tool output seventeen-fold. Even the most conservative estimates accept that the Soviet economy grew at about 12 per cent a year in the 1930s, producing an overall quadrupling of industrial output. However, there were problems – consumer-goods output rose only slowly and private consumption fell substantially (something which was typical of many economies in the early phases of industrialization).

After the recovery from the devastating impact of the war with Germany major economic problems began to emerge. Strong state direction of the economy, in a situation where only limited information was available, led to poor decision taking made worse by the growth of entrenched state bureaucracies. It was therefore difficult to produce a dynamic and technologically responsive economy. The economy remained excellent at producing basic industrial goods but relatively poor at making the more sophisticated products typical of the later stages of industrialization. Given its strategic situation and vast internal resources the Soviet economy tended to be autarkic with low levels of foreign trade. After 1950 the growth in industrial output slowed steadily from about 15 per cent a year to less than a quarter of that figure, although this was still as high as in many west European economies. Overall the Russian/Soviet economy grew to be the third largest in the world although its level of sophistication remained low. In the course of the twentieth century GDP per head increased by just over seven-fold, but that was no better than that of many other European countries in a similar position to Russia in the 1890s such as Spain and Portugal. However, the Soviet model of industrialization was important because it seemed to offer a different path from that found in the capitalist states. The expansion of Soviet control into eastern Europe after 1945 meant that similar policies were tried out in these economies (only Czechoslovakia had made significant steps towards industrialization before 1945). Initially the same high growth rates were achieved as in the

Soviet Union in the 1930s but these economies also ran into the same problems in trying to shift into the consumer-goods and high-technology sectors. Overall growth in eastern Europe after 1945 was no different from other similar economies such as Greece.

Elsewhere in the world many states such as Turkey, Iran, Brazil and Mexico were able to develop industrial sectors and although they remained well behind the major industrial countries they were equally far ahead of others, especially most African states. In the late nineteenth century all these states had populations which were almost entirely rural and illiterate. (In 1913 Turkey had just 269 factories using machines and they employed only 17,000 people. As late as 1948 the industrial labour force in Iran was only 40,000 strong.) Growth in Turkey remained relatively slow, partly because of the lack of major natural resources – not until the 1960s did modern industries such as synthetic-fibre production and car assembly develop. By the 1980s industrial output accounted for about a quarter of GDP. Development in Iran was even slower until the mid-1950s when increasing oil revenues were used to support a state-directed plan for industrialization. Growth rates at about 11 per cent a year were high but the social strains they produced in an increasingly unequal society were important factors in the revolution of 1979 which overthrew the Shah. Industrialization in Brazil and Mexico did not begin to take off until the 1940s – until 1943, when the first integrated steel mill was operational, the Brazilian steel industry was still reliant on melting scrap iron. In both countries state direction was important – in Mexico after the nationalization of the oil industry in the late 1930s and in Brazil under the military government after 1964 when growth rates reached 10 per cent a year.

After 1950 four states in Asia – Taiwan, south Korea, Singapore and Hong Kong – followed Japan and industrialized on a substantial scale. The last two were unique instances of economies built on trade and services from the beginning. They did not have a large rural hinterland and so did not have to face the difficult problems involved in the transition from agricultural economies. Both practised free trade because the domestic market was so small it was not worth protecting and cheap food imports were required. In manufacturing economies of scale could only come from exporting. Both Taiwan and south Korea faced far more complex problems but had authoritarian governments determined on industrial-ization for political reasons and prepared for state intervention on a major scale to direct the process. Both governments saw land reform (to improve agricultural productivity) and major education programmes as the essential foundations for industrialization. In the late 1940s about 40 per cent of the workforce in south Korea was still illiterate and in both states children, on average, spent just over three years in school. Within forty years this last figure had risen to over twelve years, near the average for the major industrialized countries. From the late 1950s both states underwent an extraordinarily compressed period of development, moving quickly into basic industries such as iron and steel, more sophisticated industries such as chemicals and car manufacture and finally into high-technology electronics. Until the 1960s Taiwan did not have a single steel mill; neither did south Korea until the early 1970s, when the state provided over $3.5 billion to create an industry. In 1986 the Koreans were advising US Steel on how to modernize its plants. South Korea built its first major ship in 1973, yet within a decade the industry's output had overtaken that of Japan. By the 1990s south Korea had its own TNCs such as Samsung and Goldstar and had begun exporting cars to western Europe. The overall impact of industrialization in these two countries was stunning. In 1975 the GDP per head in south Korea was still at the same level as Guatemala – by the 1990s it was almost the same as European countries such as Portugal and Greece. In the late nineteenth century the GDP per head of Taiwan was about the same as that of Bangladesh (then part of British India), a hundred years later it was over thirteen times higher.

What was the overall effect of all these changes? The disparities in wealth in the world which emerged with west European and American industrialization in the nineteenth century did not disappear in the twentieth century. The richest countries in 1900 were still the richest in 2000 (although there had been changes within the group) and the poorest were, by and large, still the poorest. Despite growing industrialization in the rest of the world the disparities of wealth grew greater not smaller. In 1900 on average a person living in the industrialized states of western Europe was about three times wealthier than someone living in the poorer countries of the world. By the late 1990s they were about seven times richer. Some of the differences were even greater than the broad figures suggested. By the 1990s income per head in the United States was, on average, eighty times greater than in the Congo. Many countries were in steep decline in the late twentieth century. By the mid-1990s, people living in eighty-nine countries in the world were poorer than they were in 1980 and in forty-three countries (mainly in Africa) they were poorer than in 1970 – these were absolute not relative declines.

23.8 Pollution

[Earlier pollution 20.11.3]
The huge increases in industrial production and energy use in the twentieth century produced pollution on a scale unprecedented in world history.

Unregulated industrialization in the nineteenth century led to acute environmental problems in the major cities and over wider regions such as the Ruhr in Germany, Limburg in Belgium, the Black Country of England. Many areas were turned into poisoned wastelands by industrial fumes and residues – everywhere rivers were treated as an easy way of disposing of a lethal cocktail of chemical wastes, leaving them incapable of supporting life and a danger to the human population. The spread of industrialization across the globe in the twentieth century replicated these conditions in many areas. This was particularly the case in the communist states which put a high priority on industrialization. Some of worst pollution developed in parts of east Germany, Bohemia and upper Silesia with their heavy concentration of iron and steel plants, metal industries and chemical factories all using poor-quality lignite coal. By the 1980s in the area around Most in Czechoslovakia sulphur dioxide emissions were twenty times higher than the maximum recommended by the World Health Organization (WHO) and school children often had to use portable respirators. Around Katowice in Poland two-thirds of the food produced was so contaminated that it was unfit for human consumption and three-quarters of the water could not be drunk. A third of all rivers had no life in them and the Vistula was unfit even for industrial use over two-thirds of its length because it was so corrosive. In the Baltic an area of over 100,000 square miles was biologically dead because of the poisons brought down by the rivers. In China industrialization, also using easily available poor-quality lignite coal, produced heavy pollution – sulphur dioxide levels in the major industrial cities rose to over seven times WHO-recommended levels. In Brazil the Cubatão area near São Paulo became the most polluted on earth.

From the middle of the twentieth century new industrial processes, in particular the huge increase in synthetic chemical production (US production rose 400-fold in the forty years after 1945), produced a wide range of chemicals which were toxic even in minute quantities. These included pesticides such as DDT (eventually banned in the industrialized countries because of its effects on wildlife) and the organo-phosphate compounds, and PCBs (the most carcinogenic compounds known to science) used as insulators in electrical products and additives in paint, which were not banned for forty years. When these chemicals escaped into the environment the effects could be catastrophic. At Seveso in Italy the top eight inches of soil over an area of seven square miles had to be removed after dioxin escaped from a chemical plant and at Bhopal in India methyl isocyanate killed about 10,000 people and disabled twice that number (most of them were blinded). In the 1940s the United States produced 1 million tons of hazardous waste, within forty years this had risen to over 250 million tons.

Another major source of pollution was the growing number of vehicles in cities which replaced the pollution from horses that characterized the nineteenth century. This was first noticed in the United States with its high level of car ownership. The first photochemical smog produced by car exhaust gases occurred in Los Angeles in 1943 (the valley has a natural inversion layer which traps the gases for much of the year). By the late 1980s similar conditions affected over a hundred American cities. As large-scale car ownership spread worldwide these problems were repeated. By the late 1960s severe pollution affected Tokyo, and in Mexico City (which also has a natural inversion layer) there were over 300 days of severe smog a year by the 1980s. No government was seriously prepared to limit car use or ownership, and controls, such as they were, concentrated on techno-logical fixes – phasing out lead additives in petrol and fitting catalytic converters to remove some of the harmful chemicals in exhausts. Outside the major industrialized countries few controls were introduced. Smoke pollution in urban areas was improved as coal fires were phased out and replaced by the greater use of oil, gas and electricity. The terrible condi-tions that developed in nineteenth-century London remained until the mid-twentieth century. Between 1920 and 1950 the average number of hours of sunshine in central London was a fifth less than in the outer areas less affected by smogs. It was the terrible smog of December 1952, when over 4,000 people died, that finally brought some action. Legislation in 1956 introduced controls over the type of fuel that could be burnt in cities and by 1970 the amount of smoke in the air over London had fallen by 80 per cent. Elsewhere in the world conditions remained dreadful. By the late twentieth century pollution levels were fourteen times higher in Delhi than in London and three times higher in Baghdad than Athens (the worst city in Europe).

All of these pollution problems were essentially localized: they produced appalling environmental conditions in concentrated areas, but their wider impact was usually limited. However, during the twentieth century the rapidly increasing pace of industrialization and its spread across the globe meant that environmental problems began to change, become more complex and increase in scale from a local to a regional level and then to a global phenomenon. They were yet another indicator of the growing integration of the world. Acid rain was first identified in British industrial cities in the 1850s. Until well into the twentieth century most factories and power stations had low chimneys which kept acid rain localized around the main industrial centres. But the ever-greater consumption of fossil fuels and the expansion of industrial output, together with the misguided policy of building very tall chimneys in an attempt to reduce local pollution problems by dispersing the pollutants, turned acid rain into a major regional problem. Global sulphur dioxide output (the main producer of acid rain as it turned to sulphuric acid in the atmosphere) rose from 45 million tons a year in the 1890s to 170 million tons a century later. A quarter of these emissions came from just two countries – the United States and Canada. In just ten years in the middle of the twentieth century the Sudbury copper and nickel smelter in Ontario emitted more sulphur dioxide than all the volcanoes (the main natural source) in the history of the earth. Downwind from these areas the acidity of rain rose rapidly: on many occasions it was as acid as vinegar and once in Wheeling, West Virginia, in the heart of one of the most polluted areas in the United States, it reached the level of battery acid. As the rain moved into rivers and lakes the rising acid levels caused animal life to die out. In western Sweden, which suffered from acid rain produced in Britain, the lakes were a hundred times more acidic in the 1980s than they had been fifty years earlier and a quarter of them no longer contained any life. International agreements took time to emerge because of the very different interests of the states which produced the pollution and those that suffered from it. The agreements which were reached between the mid-1980s and late 1990s were only between the main industrialized countries and were aimed at solving the problems in north America and Europe. Outside these areas almost no action was taken and sulphur dioxide emissions and consequently acid rain levels continued to increase.

Acid rain remained a regional problem. However, growing industrialization also produced two worldwide problems – ozone-layer destruction and global warming. For the first time in world history human activities threatened the complex global mechanisms that make life on earth possible. The first arose from the development of synthetic chemicals known as chlorofluorocarbons (CFCs) in the 1920s. At first they seemed a classic example of the beneficial aspects of technological progress. They were non-poisonous, did not burn and did not react with other substances. They were widely adopted as coolants in refrigerators and air-conditioning systems, to make expanded foam containers, to clean electronic circuit boards and, after 1950, as propellants in spray cans. No precautions were taken to stop them escaping into the atmosphere and emissions rose from 100 tons in 1931 to 650,000 tons a year by the mid-1980s. Nearly all CFCs were used by the major industrial states. It was only in the late twentieth century that some of the later industrializing states began to make an impact: the number of people owning fridges in Peking rose from 3 per cent of the population to 60 per cent in the ten years after 1975. In the mid-1970s it was discovered that CFCs were accumulating in the atmosphere and destroying the ozone layer which forms a protective layer around the world to absorb ultra-violet radiation, which is harmful to nearly all forms of life. Although CFCs were only present in relatively small concentrations compared with the vast size of the atmosphere they were extremely potent – one chlorine atom released from a CFC molecule can destroy up to 100,000 ozone molecules.

The first major falls in ozone levels occurred over the South Pole, where conditions in the winter were ideal for large-scale destruction. By the end of the 1980s about half the ozone over Antarctica was destroyed and the 'hole' created each spring covered an area equivalent in size to the continental United States. Early in the summer the 'hole' drifted northwards over south America, Australia and New Zealand, where ozone levels fell by a quarter. In the early 1990s a severe thinning of the ozone layer was also evident in the northern hemisphere in the spring and early summer. Despite strong scientific evidence from the early 1970s it was a long time before effective action was taken. CFCs could be removed from spray cans because alternatives were easily available, but the major chemical companies strenuously denied any link between CFCs and ozone destruction and it was not until they were able to manufacture alternatives that the governments of the industrialized world were prepared to take action. In a series of negotiations in the late 1980s and early 1990s agreement was reached on a worldwide phasing-out of CFC production by 1996 and for transferring technology from the major industrialized countries to assist the rest of the world to change over. The problem with these agreements was that the substitute chemicals HCFCs (hydrochlorofluorocarbons) also destroyed the ozone layer – their only advantage was that they were less long-lived than CFCs. Atmospheric concentrations of CFCs and HCFCs continued to rise and are not likely to return to the levels of the 1970s until the mid-twenty-first century.

Ozone-layer destruction was caused by a single synthetic chemical, wrongly thought to be benign, but able to create a global problem even though it was only emitted from a few states. The problem could be alleviated and eventually cured by the substitution of alternative chemicals, a solution which was relatively pain-free for the industrialized countries. Global warming demonstrates the problems caused by processes deeply embedded in modern world history. The problem has been caused by a combination of factors – the change to the consumption of fossil fuels from the seventeenth century, the phenomenal expansion in their use after the late eighteenth century, growing industrialization, increasing vehicle use and agricultural expansion to feed the unprecedented increase in world population. Global warming, over and above the natural processes essential to maintain life on earth, is caused by three gases (apart from CFCs). Nitrous oxides come from vehicle exhausts and the greater use of nitrate fertilizers. Methane is produced by the decaying vegetation at the bottom of paddy fields and from the guts of cattle and termites. The number of paddy fields in the world (mainly in Asia) increased by about 1 per cent a year in the twentieth century, the number of cattle in the world doubled between 1960 and 1980 alone and deforestation caused a massive increase in the number of termites feeding on the decaying wood. All these factors reflected the quadrupling of the world's population in the twentieth century. The amount of methane in the atmosphere rose by 135 per cent between 1750 and the end of the twentieth century. However, the principal gas involved in global warming is carbon dioxide which is produced every time fossil fuels are burnt whether as wood, coal, oil or gas. World coal consumption increased 280-fold in the two centuries after 1800 and world oil use increased 300-fold in the course of the twentieth century. The consequences can be traced in the accumulating levels of carbon dioxide in the atmosphere. From the mid-eighteenth century to the late twentieth century levels rose by a third from 270 parts per million to just over 360 parts per million. Until the twentieth century, reflecting the slow pace of nineteenth-century industrialization, the increases were very small. Indeed over half of the total increase between 1750 and 1990 occurred in the forty years after 1950. In that period world carbon dioxide emissions quadrupled and by the 1990s were rising at about 4 per cent a year (equivalent to a doubling every sixteen years).

The consequences of releasing large quantities of carbon dioxide into the atmosphere through the burning of fossil fuels were first set out by the Swedish scientist, Svante Arrhenius, in 1896. Carbon dioxide (and the other three gases) all trap heat in the atmosphere and therefore cause global temperatures to rise. As we have seen in chapter 2 the reasons for the natural fluctuations in the world's temperature were identified in the 1920s by the Yugoslav scientist Milutin Milankovic. These fluctuations have had a considerable effect on human societies – the general warming around 1000–1200 CE followed by the decline from 1300, which was severe in Europe from the mid-sixteenth century and led to the 'Little Ice Age' which lasted until the mid-nineteenth century. After 1850 global temperatures increased slightly for natural reasons but by the mid-1990s scientific evidence made it clear that human activities had caused a further 0.5°C rise in temperature. However, most of the gases put into the atmosphere in the last few decades of the twentieth century had still not had any effect on temperatures and a further rise of 0.5°C was therefore inevitable with a total rise of 2.5°C by the first decades of the twenty-first century almost certain if the rise in gases continues at the current projected rate. The speed of the rise in temperature would be far faster than the ability of natural ecosystems to adapt and would bring global temperatures to their highest level since the major inter-glacial period about 120,000 BCE.

By the late 1990s, despite almost continuous international negotiations, no effective action had been taken and no agreement had been reached for binding, enforceable and major reductions in the output of the gases causing global warming. The reasons for this failure lie deeply embedded in the way the modern world economy developed after 1750. Greenhouse gas emissions, especially carbon dioxide, in the period from 1750 to the late twentieth century were overwhelmingly the responsibility of the first states to industrialize in Europe and the United States. They, together with Japan, produced most of the world's industrial output, owned most of the vehicles in the world and consumed most of the world's energy. Those countries, especially the United States, were unwilling to make substantial cuts in emissions because of the effects it would have on their levels of consumption and prosperity. However, any attempt to deal with the problem of global warming by freezing greenhouse gas output at the emission levels of the 1990s would penalize the late industrializing states by restricting their future economic growth when they were some of the poorest states in the world and had not been the prime cause of the global problem. On the other hand failure to impose some controls over the industrial expansion and energy consumption of China, one of the largest economies in the world, would mean that any reductions by the main industrialized powers (if they were willing to make them) would be offset very rapidly. Prospects for dealing with the most serious environmental legacy of recent world history looked bleak by the end of the twentieth century.

24

The Changing Balance
(*c*.1900–2000)

From the mid-nineteenth century until 1940 Europe was the dominant region of the world. It ruled about half the world's population in its formal empires and dominated other areas, in particular Latin America, through its 'informal empire' of economic influence. The European power balance affected the lives of hundreds of millions of people around the globe. It was in the aftermath of the first of the great European civil wars that the Christian powers of Europe achieved what they had attempted for the previous five hundred years – the final defeat and partition of the Ottoman empire. Until 1940 the non-European powers were only of marginal importance. The United States was the largest single economy in the world but in political and strategic terms it was, apart from its brief excursion into the European conflict between 1917 and 1919, still introverted. It dominated the Caribbean and central America but it accepted the political division of the world imposed by the European powers in the last decades of the nineteenth century. Japan was an important regional power but was, until the early 1930s, also content to play a subordinate role and recognized the European spheres of influence – what the British foreign secretary Anthony Eden described as the 'white race preserves' of Asia. China was at the lowest point in its long history, partly as a result of Japanese actions. Yet even before the collapse of European power in 1940–2 (as the result of the second civil war) there were signs that European influence had already reached its apogee. In particular the revival of Turkey under Kemal Ataturk, the growing nationalist movement in Egypt and the difficulties the British faced in governing India, all indicated an increasing challenge to European predominance.

24.1 European Empires

In the first decades of the twentieth century the European powers were still engaged in warfare to control a number of areas in their colonies (the British in Somaliland, Afghanistan and Iraq were using modern techniques such as bombing and poison gas) and the last war of conquest was the Italian attack on Ethiopia in 1935–6. However, the main aim of empire was exploitation. This centred around two factors – land and labour – with the balance between the two varying according to local circumstances. In a minority of cases the local population was willing to grow crops for export. In the Dutch East Indies and elsewhere in south-east Asia peasants grew sugar, cotton, tobacco, spices and rubber, as they had for centuries (apart from rubber). In west Africa the production of palm oil and ground-nuts was almost entirely in the hands of peasants. However, attempts to force peasants to cultivate particular crops usually failed. In east Africa in 1903 the German authorities imposed cotton cultivation on highly disadvantageous terms – the local peasants received only a third of the sale price, with the rest being split between the German agent and the government. Within two years there was a major rebellion in which about 75,000 Africans died. The Portuguese also imposed cotton cultivation on Angola in the 1920s, and rice on Mozambique after 1941. The problem for the over 100,000 peasants involved was that if the crop failed they had no money and no means of subsistence. Thousands of peasants fled into neighbouring colonies to avoid the system and it was a major factor behind the nationalist revolts that began in the early 1960s.

The colonial authorities needed labour, not just to cultivate European-owned land, but also for public works. Slavery was ruled out in the twentieth century, except in the Portuguese colonies where it was not formally abolished until 1913. At that time there were still about 60,000 slaves (they could be bought for about £30 in Angola) but there were also 100,000 forced labourers on the cocoa plantations of São Tomé who, only in theory, were not slaves. After 1913 in the Portuguese and French colonies forced labour of about four months a year was the norm. Between 1922 and 1934 the French used 120,000 forced labourers to build a railway in Equatorial Africa and in the mid-1930s they extracted 2.7 million man-days a year of forced labour just from the colony of Guinea. The French did not commute the forced labour requirement to taxation until 1937 and the Portuguese did not ratify the International Labour Organization's Forced Labour Convention until 1956. In the rest of the European colonies there was a more subtle approach to obtaining the labour the colonial authorities wanted. The imposition of a hut tax or poll tax, which had to be paid in cash, was a way of forcing Africans to give up subsistence agriculture and do the work the Europeans wanted. As Pierre Ryckmans, the governor of the Belgian Congo, put it in 1934: 'What we must overcome in order to lead the Black to work is not so much his laziness as his distaste for *our* work, his indifference to *our* wage system.' The French generally imposed a poll tax on all Africans over the age of eight, which provided all the tax revenue for the colony (colonies were normally expected to be self-financing). As soon as the British took over Kenya they imposed a hut tax, but when more Africans started living in each hut this was changed to a poll tax. In 1910 forced labour of sixty days a year was added. When the handful of European settlers thought they still lacked sufficient labour the poll tax was tripled in 1920. Work was for African males, leaving the women to take on all the agricultural tasks. Wages were usually low, except in the mines, though here the migrant workers were kept in poor conditions in squalid barracks under strict disciplinary regimes.

Asia and Africa remained marginal areas for European settlement – emigrants preferred to go to the white colonies of Australasia, Canada and Latin America. In the three areas of Africa south of the Sahara which did receive significant European settlement – South Africa, southern Rhodesia and Kenya – the takeover of African land was on a massive scale. In South Africa in the early 1930s, 6 million Africans were confined to the 'native reserves' which comprised 34,000 square miles of the worst land and the less than 2 million whites were allocated 440,000 square miles, much of which was never cultivated. The situation in southern Rhodesia was similar. In Kenya the British government decided in 1905 to open the Highlands to European settlement – they were climatically suitable, had the most fertile soil and access to the only railway in the colony. Land was forcibly taken from the Africans and their cattle sold if they objected. By 1910 about 600,000 acres a year were going to the Europeans who rented farms on 999-year leases from the government at £10 a year for a 5,000-acre holding. By 1930 2,000 white settlers owned 5 million acres of Kenya, all formerly held by the Africans, although they cultivated less than an eighth of their holdings. The crops they grew were chosen by the government for imperial reasons and shifted from maize to sisal and eventually to coffee to reduce Britain's dependence on imported coffee from Brazil. While this expropriation was going on the African population fell from 4 million in 1902 to 2.5 million twenty years later. They also bore the burden of taxation. An import tax was instituted, but only on agricultural implements used by the local population – those for the Europeans were duty free. In the 1920s the rich white settlers paid in total £7,500 a year in direct taxes and the African population £558,000.

Development in the colonies, particularly in Africa, was not encouraged and industry in particular was actively discouraged so as to give domestic producers easy access to colonial markets. One major area of investment was mining, which took up two-thirds of all the capital investment in Africa before 1935. By then minerals accounted for over half the continent's exports and in some cases, such as northern Rhodesia with its extensive copper deposits, they were all but 4 per cent of the total. The communications infrastructure was usually very limited – some railways and ports were built but they were to ensure the export of the crucial raw materials the Europeans wanted. Once this had been done capital spending usually stopped. In Africa two-thirds of the continent's railways were in the mining countries of South Africa, the Rhodesias and the Belgian Congo. Little attempt was made to educate the local population. In 1921 out of a population of nearly 3 million in French Equatorial Africa, only 4,000 children attended primary school. In the late 1950s, just before the Belgian Congo became independent, there were sixteen African university graduates in the whole country and not one lawyer, engineer or doctor. In the top three grades of the administration there were 4,500 Europeans and six Africans. The main reason for this situation was that the Belgians did not provide secondary education for the African population.

By the 1930s the initial period of conquest and 'pacification' in the European empires had given way to one of consolidation and administration. All the colonial authorities believed that they were in for the long haul – no non-white colony had been given independence and only the Philippines had been promised it for 1944. In 1929 the British Colonial Office decided that self-government for black Africa could be deferred until 'the next century and possibly the next'. In 1936 the Governor-General of the Dutch East Indies remarked, 'We have ruled here for three hundred years with the whip and the club and we shall be doing it in another three hundred years.'

24.2 Rising Nationalism

There were, however, already signs that European control was not as firmly based as many in their domestic and colonial administrations liked to believe. Although the Allies defeated the Ottomans in 1918 they were ultimately unable to impose the peace they wanted. The revival of Turkey under the nationalist army commander Mustafa Kemal meant that by 1923 the new state, which controlled Anatolia and a small part of the western shore of the Bosphorus, had been established after defeating the Greeks, the French and the British. It became the first ideological one-party state anywhere in the world. Its policy of secularization and modernization seemed to be the way to meet the European challenge. Kemal was elected president in 1923 and retained the post until his death in 1938 – he was given the name Ataturk in 1934 when the law on the adoption of European-style surnames was passed. This law was only part of a major process of change. At its centre was a strict separation of religion and the state for the first time in the Islamic world. Religious courts were abolished in 1924, as were all titles, brotherhoods and orders. The Islamic calendar was replaced by the European one and the weekly day of rest moved from

Friday to Sunday. The sultanate and caliphate were formally abolished (the latter had survived since the foundation of Islam). In 1928 the government adopted Latin rather than Arabic script for Turkish. The revolution was also strongly nationalist and based on a Turkish linguistic and cultural identity rather than an Islamic one. Although it might incorporate Christians, it did not accommodate groups such as Armenians and Kurds. Government remained strongly dominated by the military and the degree of economic and social reform remained limited.

Egypt remained formally a part of the Ottoman empire until 1914 when the British, who had occupied and effectively governed the country since 1882, declared it a protectorate. Nationalist agitation increased in 1919 when the British initially refused to allow Egypt its own representation at the Versailles conference. In order to contain nationalism and retain effective control, the British recognized Egypt as formally independent in 1922, but subject to conditions giving the British the crucial powers they wanted over military and foreign policy. The main nationalist party – the Wafd – was a group of conservative, elite landowners unwilling to risk any widespread nationalist agitation that might undermine their social and economic position. In 1936, after the first moderately free elections, the Wafd formed a government and the British negotiated a new treaty. This restricted British troops to a zone along the Suez Canal in peacetime, agreed a final withdrawal in 1956, but allowed the British to re-occupy the country in the event of war. The British retained effective control and found nominal Egyptian independence no hindrance to their military operations after 1939.

Further east, Iran was nominally independent under the weak Qajar dynasty which had taken power at the end of the eighteenth century. An elitist revolution, which created the first national assembly (the Majlis) in 1906, was countered a year later by an Anglo-Russian agreement which created 'spheres of interest', with the British predominant in the south where they controlled the oilfields. In 1926 a new ruler, Reza Khan, seized power and established his own dynasty. Nominally a nationalist with aims similar to those of Kemal Ataturk, he found it much more difficult to make progress because of British control over the oil industry. However, Iran survived as an independent state and remained so despite occupation by British and Soviet forces in 1941 and the imposition of Reza Shah's son as the new Shah.

The area where the British encountered the greatest problems was in India. They needed, because of their own limited military and administrative resources, to find a group of collaborators to help run the country. The 562 princes provided this in their states and they always retained a direct interest in maintaining British rule as a way of securing their position. In the directly ruled parts of India a different solution was required. The central British aim was to divide India into as many different communities and political units as possible (especially by emphasizing the Hindu–Muslim division) so as to make it more difficult for a single movement dedicated to removing the British to emerge. When the Congress party, founded in the 1880s, became stronger after 1919, the British devoted their efforts to limiting its influence. In 1908 the British set up local councils and then in 1919 provincial governments. Both had very limited powers and were chosen by very small electorates – the aim was to provide a class of administrators to help the British and undertake those tasks such as health, education and public works which they did not regard as important. After 1919 there was a powerless parliament in New Delhi but the Viceroy retained control of finance and could promulgate legislation regardless of the wishes of the legislature. Congress refused to co-operate with these 'reforms' and campaigns of non-co-operation and civil disobedience under Gandhi were forcibly suppressed. Between 1920 and 1939 the British were able to keep Gandhi, the other Congress members, such as Nehru, and the civil disobedience movement under control.

In 1917 the British committed themselves to the 'progressive realization of responsible government' in India, but the phrase was so ambiguous that it might mean almost anything. In 1929 they promised eventual dominion status, but the timescale remained carefully undefined, as did the internal government arrangements. In 1935 the latter were settled strictly according to British priorities. Each province was given an autonomous Indian government elected by just 10 per cent of the adult population. (The British governor retained the right to declare a state of emergency and rule by decree.) The distribution of seats was far from democratic – in Bengal a few thousand Europeans controlled twenty-five seats and 17 million non-Muslim Indians controlled fifty seats. The separate racial and religious electorates (a separate Muslim electorate had been conceded in 1906) were designed to fragment India as much as possible. New provinces such as Sind and the North-west Frontier were created to provide areas with a Muslim majority. The Viceroy in Delhi retained full control of all imperial matters, but his Executive Council was carefully constructed to reflect the divisions the British wished to emphasize. It had representatives not just from the major communities but also from artificial and minute social categories – caste Hindu, Muslim, scheduled castes, Sikhs, Europeans, Christians, Parsees, landlords and businessmen. The princely states were excluded from all these arrangements. A federation of India (Burma became a separate colony) was in theory possible but in practice highly unlikely because the princes had a veto. Congress wanted to reject the deal but local politicians, attracted by power in the provinces, forced them to change their minds. After the 1937 elections Congress took control of all the provinces except Punjab and Bengal but the British were pleased that they had inveigled them into a scheme under which they would never control a united India. The scheme only lasted two years – in September 1939 the Viceroy declared war on behalf of India without bothering to consult any Indian politicians. This gave Congress the excuse to withdraw from provincial government and return to the more congenial politics of opposing the British. In return the British reverted to rule by decree. India was deadlocked.

24.3 The Vicissitudes of China

[*Earlier China* **21.14** *&* **21.18**]

The 'Boxer' movement in China in 1900 demonstrated the strength of Chinese nationalism. Imposition of harsh terms by the European states and Japan after the occupation of Peking, in particular the huge indemnity and the takeover of the Chinese customs revenues, only increased such feelings. Although the Chinese government was gravely weakened by these terms it began its own programme of reform designed to emulate the Japanese achievement after 1868. The education system was remoulded along Japanese lines and over 100,000 modern schools were opened by 1909. The old imperial army was disbanded and new units formed. New ministries of trade, police, education, war and foreign affairs were established. The first cautious steps towards a parliamentary system were taken with the establishment of provincial assemblies in 1909 (elected on a very restricted franchise) and a national consultative assembly (but not a parliament) the next year. Although these essentially conservative reforms were not sufficient to win over the more radical groups they went too far for the ultra-conservative groups in the imperial court where the child emperor was under the control of a reactionary regent. Many of the revolutionary leaders such as Sun Yat-sen were in exile and therefore not very influential. However, the United League, formed in 1905 by a fusion of the Revive China Society, the China Revival Society and the Restoration Society, did accept Sun Yat-sen's three very general principles of nationalism, democracy and socialism. In essence they boiled down to being opposed to the Manchu dynasty, advocating representative government and a land tax. There was an optimistic belief that this limited programme would bring about 'progress'.

The spark that brought an end to the imperial government of the Manchus (who had ruled China since the mid-seventeenth century) and also to the type of government which had typified China since the foundation of the Chin and Han empires around 200 BCE was, surprisingly, the decision to nationalize the railways in May 1911. This alienated the local gentry who owned many of the lines. Financing the programme with a £6 million foreign loan alienated the nationalists. During the second half of 1911 three very disparate movements came together: the gentry in the 'Railway Protection League', a series of peasant uprisings (there had been over 280 in the previous year) and a series of army mutinies. In November the Manchu dynasty was removed from power and once the revolutionaries had recognized all the treaties and loans made with the European powers by the imperial government they in their turn were recognized. Sun Yat-sen was in Denver when the revolt began, but he quickly returned and was elected president of the new Chinese republic on 1 January 1912.

The problems facing the new government were vast and centred around whether, given its dreadful inheritance, it could organize and unify China and begin the process of renewal. Most of the state's finances had been appropriated by foreigners and foreign loans were difficult to raise, and when they were obtained more Chinese assets had to be handed over as security. Sun Yat-sen proved incapable of strong leadership and resigned within six weeks, to be replaced by a very weak parliamentary system (in which most MPs belonged to more than one party). This only lasted until late 1913 when it was replaced by a military dictatorship under Yüan Shi-kai. He was supported by a consortium of foreign banks who provided the loans that enabled the government to function. Britain and Russia refused to recognize the new government until it had recognized the autonomy of Tibet and Outer Mongolia where they had established their respective spheres of influence. On the outbreak of the war in Europe in August 1914, Japan joined the allies, invaded and took over the German concessions in China. In January 1915 it presented its 'Twenty-One Demands' which would have turned China into a Japanese dependency – Japanese 'advisers' would have held all the key posts in government and only Japan would be allowed to supply China with arms. Ever since the war of 1895–6 it was clear that Japan posed the major external threat to China and these demands were clearly an attempt to exploit the European preoccupation with its own conflicts. Although, despite popular protests, the Chinese government accepted the Japanese demands, the other powers had enough diplomatic power to force their withdrawal. Between 1916 and 1919 a central state in China existed in name only after the death of Yüan Shi-kai and the emergence, as so often in the past, of regional military rulers. However, China, though extremely weak, remained independent and ultimately in charge of its own destiny.

A major turning point came on 4 May 1919 when news of the Treaty of

Versailles reached China. Although China had declared war on Germany in August 1917 and supported the Allied war effort by sending over 200,000 labourers to Europe, the treaty confirmed that the pre-war German concessions would not be restored to China, but instead would be given to Japan. Student demonstrations and strikes by workers across the country were a massive patriotic protest against both the government, which was prepared to accept the treaty, and the Japanese. It was a spontaneous series of protests led by a new generation of leaders (many of the key figures who emerged later in the Communist Party such as Mao Tse-tung and Chou En-lai began their political careers in this way). At this stage the protests were ineffective. The main beneficiary of the rising nationalist feeling was the Kuomintang (National People's Party) which had been founded in 1912 by Sun Yat-sen but forcibly dissolved a year later. It re-emerged in the early 1920s and at its congress in Canton in 1924 set out its basic policies. They were based on the establishment of a strong government able to revise the unequal treaties with the European powers and the Japanese, control the militarists, impose universal suffrage and nationalize industry. Sun Yat-sen died in March 1925, but he left a large body of writings which in 1928 the Kuomintang declared had the force of law. The Kuomintang also adopted the Leninist principle of 'democratic centralism' – strict control from the top of the party. After Sun's death there was a short period of collective leadership, but by 1926 the dominant figure in the party was Chiang Kai-shek, the commander of the army. In the two years after 1926 the Kuomintang were able to gain control over much of China, including Peking and Shanghai, and establish themselves as the government of the country.

During this period the Kuomintang was allied with the small Communist Party which was founded in 1921 at a meeting in Shanghai attended by just twelve delegates. It still had fewer than a thousand members at the end of 1925 and by 1927 this had only risen to 58,000. Both groups took aid from the Soviet Union but in April 1927, after the capture of Shanghai, Kuomintang troops turned on the communists in a vicious purge which effectively eliminated them in the urban areas. Up until this point the communists had been ideologically orthodox in basing their expected revolution on the workers in the cities. The problem was that in China this provided neither a sufficient level of support nor a suitable base for operations. After their defeat in the cities some of the communists found themselves isolated in Kiangsi province, one of the most primitive in China. The party here was a small collection of peasants and intellectuals. One of its leaders, Mao Tse-tung, visited his home province of Hunan and wrote a *Report of an Investigation into the Peasant Movement in Hunan*. It had an elegant simplicity in arguing for a revolution based on Chinese reality – the overwhelming dominance of the peasantry. The party, Mao argued, should support the poor peasants as the foundation of the revolution. As Marxist theory it was absurd and it is unclear how much Marxism Mao ever understood (in 1942 he told party intellectuals that dogma was 'less useful than excrement'). However, it was good politics and based on a very shrewd analysis of Chinese reality and the possibility of revolution in a peasant society.

Mao was disowned by the party and the Comintern in Moscow, which had little idea of what was going on in a remote mountain range in China (it did not even know Mao's correct name). Moscow-trained communists controlled the Politburo in the early 1930s and Mao spent much of the period in disgrace. However, he was one of the few revolutionaries in China with a power base, however limited. In September 1927 he went back to Hunan and led what later became known as the 'Autumn Harvest Uprising'. It was no more than an attack on the city of Changsha by a small group of peasants and it failed. Mao was captured and only escaped death by buying his release. The next month he was joined by about 10,000 men – the remnants of the communists escaping the Kuomintang armies. For three years they could do no more than try and survive, build up their strength and accumulate a few weapons. In November 1931 a Chinese Soviet Republic was declared with Mao as its president – it controlled a few areas in the upper and middle Yangtze valley. The base of the revolutionary movement had, however, shifted dramatically – of the 821 delegates at the Congress of Soviets in January 1934 just eight were urban workers. The communists were under increasing pressure from the Kuomintang and Mao decided, in October 1934, to retreat. He and his followers embarked on what became the great symbolic moment in Chinese communism and an event which established Mao as undisputed leader – the Long March. It was a year-long epic on a continental scale and involved a march of over 6,000 miles along a convoluted route across China to the remote area of northern Shanshi province in the far north-west of the country. About 100,000 people started the march, fewer than 10,000 reached its destination.

Until the late 1930s the communists remained a small group with little impact on the fate of China. That was in the hands of the Kuomintang once they had established control over most of the country by the late 1920s. On taking power they proclaimed the period of 'tutelage' by the party which had always been Sun Yat-sen's policy – there was to be no democracy because the Kuomintang were the only group who understood China's true interests. It was optimistically claimed that this period would end in 1935 – in 1931 all other political parties were banned and formal one-party rule established. In practice, almost from the beginning, the military were the basis of Kuomintang rule. The party abandoned its control of the military through commissars after 1927 and less than half the provinces even had a party committee. Kuomintang rule was exercised through a confederation of regional military regimes which accepted varying degrees of central control. In the guerrilla war with the communists extensive 'Bandit Suppression Zones' were declared in which authority was handed over to the National Military Council which developed its own administrative network which had more power than either the party or civilian state networks. By the mid-1930s most provinces were ruled by the military command based at Chunking rather than the party apparatus, which was centred on Nanking. As head of the Kuomintang military and chairman of the National Military Council, Chiang Kai-shek was the predominant influence in the government. He also developed his own network of power. In 1932 he founded (though he always denied this in public) the 'Blue Shirts' (technically the 'Restoration Society'), a quasi-fascist elite of some 10,000 men fanatically loyal to Chiang himself. By 1935 Chiang's supremacy was finally recognized when he became head of the government as well as head of the National Military Council.

Despite the political turmoil in China in the first four decades of the twentieth century there were signs of substantial economic growth in many sectors. This was particularly apparent in Manchuria. The construction of the Chinese Eastern Railway in 1901 and the South Manchurian two years later were crucial in making this vast area comparable to Canada, Australia and Argentina. New agricultural land was opened up and ports were developed for food exports, mainly to Japan. The population grew rapidly with large-scale immigration from the rest of China. In the 1920s industry developed rapidly (mainly based on foreign investment from Japan) and within a couple of decades Manchuria contained about a third of all Chinese industry and the average income was nearly twice that of the rest of the country. The other major sector of growth was in trade through the great port cities of the south of the country. Overall China's industrial output grew substantially after 1914 but, because of the turmoil of the nineteenth century and the amount of external pressure applied, it was far below the level of Japan. By the 1930s the industrial sector (which was nearly half foreign-owned) still produced less than 5 per cent of national wealth.

24.4 The Impact of Japan

[*Earlier Japan 21.17–21.18*]
The most important power in Asia in the early twentieth century was

Japan. Its actions were fundamental in bringing about major changes in China and also in ending the European empires in the region. Its earlier attempts to dominate China in 1895–6 and again in 1915 were resisted by the European powers and the United States who were determined to preserve their own interests. However, in the early 1930s Japan took over Manchuria, long within its sphere of influence, and set up a puppet government headed by the last Manchu emperor. Although the other powers (and the League of Nations established under the Versailles Treaty) condemned the action, no effective measures were taken to reverse it. Any hope that the Kuomintang might have had of leading a Chinese revival (and there were few signs of this by the mid-1930s) were ended in the summer of 1937 when the Japanese exploited a minor incident to launch a full-scale invasion. In the short term it was highly successful and led to the capture of many of the most important cities and commercial areas. But the Kuomintang government retreated westwards, continued the fight and the Japanese became bogged down in the vast distances of China and were unable to inflict a decisive defeat on the Chinese. Nevertheless the Kuomintang central government was gravely weakened and what resources it could mobilize had to be devoted to the fight against Japan. This gave considerable scope for the communists, who were also leading resistance to the Japanese, to extend their area of control.

24.4.1 The European empires

The crisis of European rule in Asia came in 1940–2. Defeat and occupation by Germany in the summer of 1940 left the French and Dutch colonies highly vulnerable. The British too were extremely weak – they had to concentrate the few military resources they had available on the defence of Britain itself. The Japanese government and the military were divided over their course of action. They agreed on the creation of a substantial sphere of Japanese influence across much of Asia but how this could be achieved was much less obvious. The military were deeply committed in China and the leadership was split over whether to attack northwards against the Soviet Union or southwards against the European empires (with the risk of dragging in the Americans too). No decisive action was taken when the Europeans were at their weakest in the summer and autumn of 1940. The Japanese restricted themselves to forcing the British to stop their assistance to the Chinese for a few months and to occupying the northern part of French Indochina.

By early 1941 the strategic balance was tilting against the Japanese. They now faced a United States increasingly willing to assert its power in the Pacific as its rearmament gathered pace. For almost a year the two sides negotiated about a possible deal but their demands were ultimately incompatible – the US was not prepared to recognize a Japanese sphere in the Pacific or China and the Japanese were not prepared to settle for being subordinate to American interests. A badly handled decision by the United States to impose an oil embargo on Japan in the summer of 1941 left the Japanese with a stark choice – either they attacked to secure their oil supplies or they accepted the American terms. After considerable agonizing they decided to attack. The Japanese attack in early December 1941 on both the American fleet at Pearl Harbor and the European empires was phenomenally successful. Within a few months they had conquered the Philippines, Hong Kong, Malaya, Singapore, the Dutch East Indies, Indochina and Burma. The carefully maintained façade of European superiority, which was so vital for colonial governments because of their military and administrative weakness, was destroyed in a few months by an Asian power. It was a blow to their prestige from which they were never to recover. Although Japan was defeated within three and a half years by overwhelming American military superiority, the European empires could not be restored.

In early 1942, as Japanese troops approached the borders of India, the British tried to negotiate a deal with the Congress party. The negotiations failed because many British politicians did not want a settlement and Congress was reluctant to take responsibility (without independence) in the middle of a disastrous war. Instead Congress shifted to a policy of 'Quit India' and civil disobedience. The British used force to keep control and arrested the leaders of Congress. However, by 1943 India could hardly be used as a military base – over a hundred British battalions were being used on internal security duties rather than fighting the Japanese. After the war the British found it impossible to find any basis either for their continued rule or for a handover of power which avoided a massive loss of face. During the war the Muslim League, which demanded a separate state of Pakistan, continued to co-operate with the British and was in a strong position by 1945. In the negotiations after 1945 Congress was deeply opposed to a partition of India, the British insistence on a weak central government and a federal system safeguarding the position of the princely states. All the negotiations failed and by early 1947 British rule was disintegrating. The only option left was to announce a date for a withdrawal (August 1947) and negotiate the best deal possible. In the end the British left precipitously having secured none of their objectives. The Muslims gained an independent Pakistan, but it was weak and physically divided by hundreds of miles of Indian territory, and hundreds of thousands of people died in the communal violence that followed the partition of Bengal and the Punjab. Congress took power over a unified but partitioned India. The British had to accept the one thing they had always struggled to avoid – the domination of Congress. The bastions of British rule, the princes, were left in the lurch to get the best deal they could from Congress. The loyal warrior group – the Sikhs – were left without even their own province let alone a separate state. Most important of all, from a British point of view, an independent India refused to play the role allocated to it of being a bulwark of British imperial and defence policy in south-east Asia. It was an ignominious end to almost two hundred years of British rule over what they always regarded as the 'jewel in the crown' of their empire.

India had avoided being occupied by the Japanese. In the other colonies, in particular, Burma, the Philippines and the Dutch East Indies, local nationalist politicians were happy to work with the Japanese (as were a number of Indian nationalists) and they gradually established strong positions in their countries. Their position was strengthened by the fact that no European colony was fully reoccupied before the Japanese surrender in August 1945. The resulting hiatus in power before some sort of colonial rule could be re-established further strengthened the hand of the nationalists. In the Philippines the United States could do no more than, as promised for more than a decade, transfer power to the local oligarchy, which had long dominated the economy and society – in return a compliant government granted the Americans the extensive military facilities which were all that they really wanted. In Burma attempts to slow down progress towards independence failed and the British were forced to deal with the man who had collaborated with the Japanese, Aung San, in order to keep even the vestiges of control during the transition. The Burmese insisted on becoming a republic and rejected any defence agreement with the British. The British had no power to impose anything different and Burma became independent in January 1948. The only area where the British faced few problems was Sri Lanka. Like the Americans in the Philippines they handed power to the local landowners in return for continued use of military bases. In Indonesia the Dutch attempted to restore colonial rule in the last months of 1945, even though the nationalists under Sukarno had already declared independence in the immediate aftermath of the Japanese surrender. There was bitter fighting as the Dutch, supported by the British, sought to gain control of Java. They tried to impose a federation, in which the outlying islands, still under Dutch influence, would counterbalance the nationalists. This failed and once Sukarno had suppressed the communists, the Americans pressurized the Dutch into a settlement. A deal agreed in August 1949, which sketched the outlines of a Dutch-Indonesian union, was enough of a fig-leaf to allow the Dutch to withdraw leaving behind a unified Indonesia. It was the end of Dutch rule in an area they had controlled for over three hundred years.

The colonies which provided the greatest problems after the Japanese surrender were in French Indochina. In the months of chaos after August 1945 the Vietminh nationalists under the communist Ho Chi Minh (who had been backed by the Americans during the war) were able to gain control of much of the north around Hanoi. The French, with British assistance, controlled the south, in particular Saigon. During 1946 the French tried to negotiate a new form of colonialism based on a federated Indochina consisting of a French-controlled southern Vietnam, monarchical Laos and Cambodia, and Vietminh control of the north. At the end of the year the French decided to pressurize the Vietminh into an agreement by bombarding Haiphong and occupying Hanoi. The result was a growing guerrilla war and Vietminh control of most of the north. By emphasizing the anti-communist rather than the colonial nature of the war, the French gained increasing American support. However, they were unable to control the guerrillas and by 1954 they were also facing units of the regular Vietminh army. An attempt to fight a large conventional battle at Dien Bien Phu was a disaster and led to the surrender of the French army in early May 1954. At this stage Britain and the United States intervened and together with the Soviet Union and China agreed a division of Indochina at the July 1954 Geneva conference. Laos and Cambodia became independent and Vietnam was split along the old wartime boundary of allied spheres of interest – the seventeenth parallel. Both sides promised to hold 'free elections' in 1956 to produce a unified Vietnam, but nobody believed this was likely. The United States took over the French role of trying to build up some sort of government in the south whilst the north was controlled by the communist Vietminh, who never accepted the division of their country.

24.4.2 China

The Japanese impact on China was equally fundamental. The long war from 1937 to 1945 saw the heaviest fighting in Asia and stretched the resources of the Kuomintang to breaking point. At first their popularity rose significantly as they led the national struggle against the invasion. However, as control was lost over the most productive parts of the country and a large proportion of the population, the maintenance of an effective military effort proved very difficult. These problems were exacerbated by divisions between the military commanders who were mainly interested in keeping as many troops as possible under their own control so as to increase their own political power. External aid was limited by lack of interest and the absence of good routes into remote areas of China. After the Japanese attack in late 1941 aid to China increased but it proved almost impossible to construct an effective fighting force – the Chinese were still losing ground as late as 1944. The main symbolic gesture made by Britain and the United States was the end of extra-territoriality in 1943. The United States treated Chiang Kai-shek as a major allied leader – he was invited to the Cairo conference in 1943 and China was given one of the permanent seats, and therefore a right of veto, on the Security Council of the new United Nations. This was partly because the United States believed China would remain subservient and support the American position.

The war with Japan created a major opportunity for the communists to extend their power. They joined a 'popular front' with the Kuomintang and they too took on the mantle of the national struggle. However, they were able to fight a largely independent war free of Kuomintang control and greatly expand their area of influence. In these areas they mobilized the peasantry and introduced land reform. By 1945 they controlled large areas of Shansi, Hopei and Shantung and about 100 million people (ten years earlier at the end of the Long March they had controlled fewer than a million people). For four years after 1945 there was full-scale civil war in China. On the Japanese surrender the Kuomintang regained control of most of the cities with American help. The Soviet Union invaded Manchuria in the last days of the war and ensured the communists took control. By 1946 there was open fighting between the People's Liberation Army and Kuomintang forces. For the first eighteen months the Kuomintang were reasonably successful but in 1948 they suffered a series of major defeats. In January 1949 communist troops entered Peking and then expanded their control southwards. After the fall of Shanghai, the Kuomintang moved to Taiwan and the People's Republic of China was formally declared at the beginning of October 1949.

In many respects, events in China in the century after 1850 bore a remarkable resemblance to a pattern that had occurred on many occasions in the past. Dynastic breakdown accompanied by large-scale peasant revolts brought instability, weak government and eventually the end of the ruling dynasty. A period of internal chaos with a strong role for the military led to the eventual success of a new ruling regime. In this case it led to the triumph of the communists who in many ways were remarkably similar to the peasant revolutionaries of the mid-fourteenth century who set up the Ming dynasty. The pattern of events was complicated on this occasion by the intervention of external powers (at first the Europeans and then Japan) seeking advantages for themselves, but also applying pressure to which the Chinese had to respond. However, the ability of the external powers to influence the outcome of events in China was very limited. The destiny of China was, as in the past, decided by the Chinese themselves. By 1949 a new strong group of rulers was established over the whole of the country. They were determined on a revitalization of the largest country in the world. It was one of the decisive moments in modern history.

24.5 The World Balance in the Mid-Twentieth Century

Within ten years of the Japanese defeat in 1945 the European empires in Asia had largely disappeared. Even those areas that were still controlled, such as Malaya and Singapore, were heading rapidly towards independence. Only a few relatively unimportant colonies remained. It was a remarkably rapid transformation and reflected the devastating blow the Japanese conquests in 1941–2 dealt to the fragile structures the Europeans had built. It was only the beginning of a further major decline in European power in the rest of the world and, even more important, within their own continent following the rapid changes brought about by the second European civil war in two decades. No longer would the disputes and rivalries between the European powers determine world politics and strategy as they had for most of the previous century. The defeat of Germany, largely through the economic and military efforts of the United States and the unparalleled military resolve of the Soviet Union, marked a fundamental transition both in Europe and the rest of the world. In Europe the west was dominated by the United States and in the east Soviet (Russian) power reached its greatest ever extent with the takeover of large parts of eastern Poland, the creation of a common border with Czechoslovakia and with Soviet troops occupying eastern Germany and Berlin. Each of the two major powers was in a position to ensure that it obtained the governments it wanted in the areas it occupied at the end of the war. Europe was rapidly divided into two parts. The major advantage of this division of the continent, and the application of external power to the divided states of Europe, was the creation of a zone of stability. Europe was, unusually, to be almost entirely free of internal and external conflict for almost fifty years.

24.5.1 The United States and the Soviet Union
From the middle of the nineteenth century many commentators had prophesied that the United States and Russia (now the Soviet Union) would become the great powers of the future, because of their vast size and therefore the resources they could command. It was the European and world war of 1939–45 that finally brought about that transformation. By accident both countries were on the same side in that war and were therefore forced to reach some tacit and actual understandings. The process began at the Teheran conference of 1943, followed by those at Yalta and

Potsdam in 1945. However, there was a vast difference in the relative power of the two states. The United States was the only world power – it had its army and navy deployed on every continent and ocean, it was the predominant economic power in the world and it was the sole possessor of the atomic bomb. It also asserted its role as a world power – as President Roosevelt reminded Churchill during the latter's visit to Moscow in October 1944 to negotiate with Stalin over the future of Europe: 'In this global war there is literally no question, political or military, in which the United States is not interested.' The United States was itself transformed by the war – it was no longer the demilitarized state it had been in the 1920s and 1930s. What later became known as 'the military-industrial' complex was created by the war and survived into peace as the United States continued to maintain and deploy forces on an unprecedented scale. By 1949 the US was spending nearly $15 billion a year on the military and had about 1.5 million people in the armed forces. A 'national security' state emerged in which new institutions such as the Central Intelligence Agency and the National Security Council, together with a far more powerful military, produced a new emphasis in decision taking. The United States had always believed in its mission to change the world and, as Woodrow Wilson put it: 'make the world safe for democracy'. It also detested communism and was driven by a rapidly increasing domestic hysteria (personified by politicians such as Richard Nixon and Senator Joe McCarthy) about subversion, communist influence and 'un-American activities'. As the major power in the world it allocated the Soviet Union a subordinate role which it believed could be enforced through pressure.

The Soviet Union had, as Russia had always had, a large army (4 million-strong in the late 1940s, though this was less than a third of the level at the end of the war). In global terms, however, the Soviet Union was weak. It was a land-based power and unable to deploy forces far beyond its borders. Its main aim was the stabilization of those borders by ensuring that there were compliant regimes in eastern Europe and that Germany remained extremely weak and under control. Both requirements were easily explained by the vast destruction wrought on the Soviet Union during the war. Its view of the outside world was one of suspicion, formed by its ideological isolation and the experience of outside intervention during the civil war after 1917. Like Germany before 1914, it was easy for the Soviet leaders to see themselves as 'encircled' by hostile states. Their foreign policy, despite its revolutionary rhetoric, was in practice cautious, though it was often carried out in a crude and clumsy manner. When the Soviets refused to accept the subordinate role allocated to them by the Americans and asserted their own interests disagreements were bound to arise. Very quickly a 'ratchet effect' operated – failure to agree, or the expression of different perceptions of a problem, simply 'proved' Soviet intransigence, increased American hostility and made future agreements even more difficult. The United States rapidly came to see the Soviet Union as an inherently aggressive, ideologically committed power with whom it was impossible to reach any agreement. The result was the so-called 'Cold War' which lasted, with varying degrees of intensity, until the late 1980s.

It was a strange and ultimately sterile confrontation with no direct fighting between the two powers. In the conventional sense they had no real issues over which to fight – they had no common frontier of any consequence (that in the Bering Strait was unimportant) and no territorial disputes. The conflict therefore became a contest for influence, with the Americans determined on a 'containment' of 'communist' influence. The problem was that the American perception of almost every problem in the world as being part of the 'Cold War' led them to make a number of serious misjudgements. The one area where the two states did confront each other on the ground – central Europe, especially along the inner German border – was the most stable. Fairly rapidly after the end of the war the two sides reached a tacit understanding that the best solution in Germany was to divide the country along the boundaries of their respective zones of occupation – all the alternatives were far too difficult and probably too dangerous to contemplate. This solution also solved the problem of how to avoid a strong and united Germany in the centre of Europe – the factor that had destabilized the continent for three-quarters of a century. By 1949 Germany was divided and after the Berlin airlift the old capital was left as an anomaly under the control of all the occupying powers.

The United States began to build a series of new alliances across the globe and to deploy military forces to defend its interests. In 1947 the Truman Doctrine provided immediate economic and military resources for Greece and Turkey, replacing a long tradition of British influence. Two years later the creation of NATO (from an existing west European alliance) established an American-led alliance which rapidly embraced the entire area from the North Cape in Norway to Turkey's borders in south-west Asia. The Rio pact confirmed American supremacy in the entire western hemisphere. In 1950 the ANZUS treaty made clear American domination of the south-west Pacific and the reliance by Australia and New Zealand on American rather than British support. In the early 1950s bilateral treaties gave the Americans military facilities in Japan, south Korea, Taiwan and Spain. In 1954 the creation of SEATO brought in Pakistan and Thailand, and after the French withdrawal the United States dominated south Vietnam too. The CENTO alliance included Turkey, Iraq, Iran and Pakistan. Elsewhere there were agreements with Israel,

Saudi Arabia and Jordan and in 1957 the Eisenhower Doctrine extended aid and the prospect of military intervention to all Arab states. By the early 1960s the United States had over one million servicemen deployed overseas in over thirty countries. It was part of four regional defence pacts, it had 'mutual defence' treaties with forty-two countries and it gave military aid to over a hundred states. In 1965 the Secretary of State, Dean Rusk, repeated Roosevelt's wartime caution to Churchill in a slightly different formulation: 'This has become a very small planet. We have to be concerned with all of it – with all of its land, waters, atmosphere and with surrounding space.' This was an unprecedented assertion of global power and of the right of the United States to interfere in any part of the world.

The Soviet Union, on the other hand, pursued a much more limited policy. It concentrated on trying to maintain control of its sphere of influence in eastern Europe. It intervened to support the communist governments of Hungary and Czechoslovakia in 1956 and 1968. Even in this area, though, it had to contend with the fiercely independent government of President Tito which emerged out of the wartime partisan movement in Yugoslavia, and with the infinitely less influential, but equally independent, Albanian government. By the mid-1960s the Soviets also had to take account of the growing rift with China which rapidly developed into a series of border clashes. In 1967 the Soviets maintained fifteen divisions along the Chinese frontier; by 1972 this figure had risen to forty-four (compared with thirty-one in eastern Europe). To the Soviet leadership this seemed like 'encirclement' on a grand scale. Not until the late 1950s did the Soviets begin even a limited extension of influence, through arms supplies to a handful of states such as Egypt and India, and later to Cuba after the 1959 revolution. In most areas its influence was minimal and even where it was successful it was rarely able to sustain its position for long against American pressure. It was expelled from Egypt in 1972 and one of its few bases outside eastern Europe, Mogadishu in Somalia, was lost in 1977. The Soviet Union used force outside its sphere of influence in eastern Europe just once, in Afghanistan in 1979. In comparison the United States either engaged in war or other military operations, deployed troops and went on nuclear alert on nearly 300 occasions in the forty-five years after 1945.

The nature of the confrontation between the United States and the Soviet Union was largely determined by military technology. After 1945 it was generally highly conservative; all the weapons used – tanks, jet aircraft, ships, submarines, rockets and guided missiles – had been used during the 1939–45 war. All that happened was that their capabilities developed and their costs rose enormously, especially as the amount of electronics used increased exponentially. They became much more difficult to make, were no longer mass-production weapons and the number that could be afforded fell drastically. The most fundamental and unprecedented problems were posed by atomic weapons which had been used against the cities of Hiroshima and Nagasaki in Japan at the end of the war. Because of their destructive power, could they simply be regarded as just another weapon to be used whenever the circumstances seemed right? Until the mid-1950s the United States seemed to take that view and nearly used the atomic bomb in the Korean war and again when the French faced defeat in Indochina. Although the United States had a complete monopoly of nuclear weapons until the first test by the Soviet Union in 1949 (and an effective one for some years thereafter), it had only a limited stock of weapons, which would have been incapable of stopping a Soviet conventional offensive. The United States developed the first H-bomb in 1952 but a weapon that could be dropped from an aircraft was not tested until 1956 and it was the late 1950s before it was deployed in any quantity. By the time that the United States did have a major nuclear arsenal, in the mid-1950s, the Soviets had the capability to inflict enough damage on the United States to deter the latter from attacking. As Soviet capabilities increased, at first with long-range bombers and then with missiles, a theory of deterrence developed but both states built the weapons that were possible and worried about the implications later. With limited intelligence about the other's capabilities there were a number of 'scares' in the United States about 'gaps' in capabilities (at first bombers and then inter-continental missiles) and each side built more and more weapons and nuclear warheads. From the mid-1960s new technologies such as multiple warheads and multiple independently targeted warheads were introduced, but neither side could establish any significant strategic advantage. By the 1980s the United States had over 30,000 nuclear warheads (the Soviet Union rather less), but most had no real military function. Use of even a small proportion of them would have destroyed most of the opponent's military, economic and social infrastructure and killed hundreds of millions of people but this could only be done at the expense of inevitable retaliation and similar destruction.

Both sides rapidly realized that nuclear weapons were unusable and found that their military and diplomatic actions in any crisis would have to ensure that the risk of use was minimized. Even before nuclear weapons were available on a large scale and long before theories of deterrence were elaborated, both powers had worked out an effective modus vivendi. Each recognized the other's sphere of influence, particularly in Europe. In 1953 the United States and its European allies did not intervene when the Soviets suppressed workers' demonstrations in East Berlin, nor did they do so during the USSR's more violent repression of the revolt in Hungary in

1956. There were only a few direct confrontations (Berlin in 1960–61 and Cuba in 1962), but these were contained and resolved. Nuclear weapons probably played only a limited role in avoiding conflict from which neither side could gain. Even without nuclear weapons, neither side could have won a war in any meaningful sense, given the geographical size and economic power of the two states.

24.5.2 The European powers

The rapid expansion of American power from the early 1940s, enshrined in the doctrine developed at the end of the decade of a global 'containment' of communism, did not come at the expense of the Soviet Union which was able to consolidate and retain control over the territories it occupied at the end of the war. The increase in American power came at the expense of its allies in western Europe, in particular the British and French. In 1945 these powers were in the paradoxical situation of being both weak and strong at the same time. They were weak because of their relative lack of military power and their economic dependence on the United States but strong because they still retained their empires and the worldwide military bases they provided. The latter were valuable to the Americans who, for some time after 1945, lacked a global network of bases. The problem for the European powers was what level of independent power they could exercise in a world dominated by the United States and the USSR, especially when they relied on the former to provide their security in Europe against the latter. Both Britain and France considered trying to use their empires as a way of remaining world powers but both rejected the option as too expensive. The outcome was that they rapidly lost the influence they had established over the previous centuries to the Americans. The latter had always run the Pacific war as their own private concern and Britain in particular was excluded in all but name from the occupation and peace settlement with Japan. The United States took over from Britain the predominant role in Greece and Turkey in 1947 and then in a wide area of the old Ottoman empire. The British abandoned their attempt to rule Palestine in the face of Zionist extremism and terrorism and the Americans became the main supporter of the new state of Israel. The US refused to support the British in Egypt, especially after the 1952 revolution which overthrew the monarchy, and British troops left in 1956. France evacuated Syria and Lebanon. Further east the British lost influence in Iran after an attempted nationalization of the oil industry in the late 1940s. Although a joint operation with the Americans organized a coup to put the Shah back on the throne in the early 1950s, it was the US that then became the main external supporter of the new regime.

The last attempt by Britain and France to use their power on a significant scale without the approval of the United States came in 1956. The Egyptian nationalization of the Suez Canal (to pay for the Aswan Dam that the United States, Britain and France would not help fund) was taken as a direct challenge to European power. The French were alienated by Egyptian support for the Algerian nationalists and the British, who saw Arab nationalism as a threat to their rapidly declining influence in the region, kept drawing wholly inappropriate parallels between Gamal Abdel Nasser, the Egyptian leader, and Adolf Hitler. Attempts at a diplomatic settlement were effectively blocked by Britain and France who preferred to collude with Israel to attack Egypt so that British and French forces could 'intervene' to 'protect' the canal. The United States was strongly opposed to this action which was condemned by the United Nations and it ended in total and humiliating failure. It was followed by a major extension of American influence in the region, especially after a military coup replaced the monarchy in Iraq. Britain was left with some influence over the minor Gulf states, Oman and in Aden until the early 1970s. Although both Britain and France developed nuclear weapons they were, at best, no more than medium-sized powers and, within a few decades, not even that. The escalating cost of military equipment meant that whole areas of capability could not be afforded. The British attempted to build an intermediate-range rocket (Blue Streak) in the late 1950s, but abandoned it and instead relied on American missiles. No attempt was ever made to build intercontinental-range missiles, satellites, submarine-launched strategic missiles and 'stealth' bombers. In 1966 even an attempt to build a major aircraft carrier was abandoned as too expensive. From the late 1960s the British strategic nuclear weapon system was almost entirely American apart from the warheads.

24.5.3 The end of the European empires

By the late 1950s the major European powers were also rethinking their attitudes to the empires they had constructed in the previous hundred years, especially in Africa – those in Asia had nearly all been lost. Within the colonies it was becoming clear that, following decades of neglect, economic development would be very expensive and it was unlikely that the colonial power would see much benefit from the huge investment required. The strategic situation had also been radically transformed. The great imperial expansion of the late nineteenth century had, to a large extent, resulted from competitive pressures within Europe – the perceived need to deny territories to rival powers. After 1945 that was no longer the case. There was no competition for colonial possessions. There was the possibility of an expansion of communist influence, but countering that threat could be left to the Americans with their larger resources. The economic rationale for colonial possessions could therefore be reassessed. The European powers had mainly been concerned about access to raw materials, but by the mid-twentieth century it was possible to obtain this without formal political control – the industrialized powers and their transnational corporations had enough economic and political power to ensure any newly independent country had little choice but to collaborate. Independence would therefore mean little more than handing over power to those groups which had always worked with the colonial power. Once this process started, with one state moving down the road to extensive decolonization, it was more difficult for others to resist and so the process snowballed.

In 1957 the Gold Coast, as Ghana, became the first African colony to become independent. A mishandled referendum in French west Africa led to the independence of Guinea in 1958 and that provided an example for others to follow. By 1960 all the French colonies in west and equatorial Africa were independent. This increased pressure on the other European powers. Belgium rushed through independence for the Congo in a little over eighteen months and because it had built no social infrastructure during its period of rule the state disintegrated – an army mutiny led to chaos and near anarchy. This concentrated the minds of the British and they too speeded up moves to independence across the whole of Africa. The most rapid was in Somaliland which moved from colonial autocracy to independence in the space of just four and a half months in early 1960. Only in a few cases where European settlers were well entrenched such as Algeria (constitutionally part of France rather than a colony) were there major problems and extensive conflict over independence. By the mid-1960s the European empires in Africa had come to an end and nearly all the remaining colonies around the world were independent by the early 1970s. The last to go were the Portuguese colonies after the revolution in 1974 and southern Rhodesia in 1980 after the ruling white minority had illegally declared independence in 1965.

The dissolution of the European empires by the late 1960s marked the end of the period of European predominance in the world that had lasted since the mid-nineteenth century. The creation of a mass of new, independent states transformed the world balance of power. It led to the emergence of a number of 'security complexes' – regional security regimes with their own dominant and subordinate powers and their own conflicts. Until the mid-1940s there were only two security complexes in the world – Europe and Asia – and the former could affect the whole world. It was not until December 1941 that the two complexes were brought together with the attack by Japan (the dominant regional power in Asia) on the United States and the European powers. In the late 1940s two new complexes developed. The first, in south Asia, was dominated by India and the Indo-Pakistan conflict, with a number of small states such as Nepal and Sri Lanka playing a minor role. The second, in what became known as the Middle East, centred around the newly independent state of Israel and the opposition to it of the Arab states, in particular Egypt, Jordan, Syria and Saudi Arabia. Later another complex emerged in the Gulf area involving Iraq, Iran and Saudi Arabia, and later the smaller states such as Bahrain, Kuwait and the Emirates. In Africa three different complexes developed after independence. The first was in the Horn of Africa and involved Ethiopia, Sudan, Somalia and later Eritrea. In the Maghreb, the second included Algeria, Morocco, Tunisia, Libya, Chad and Mauritania. The third, in southern Africa, was built around opposition to the white minority government in South Africa (and to a more limited extent that of southern Rhodesia) and included the so-called 'front-line' states that surrounded these last bastions of European rule. Although the United States in particular tried to force all of these different problems and conflicts into the procrustean bed of the 'Cold War' they all had their own origins and dynamics and continued after the 'Cold War' was over. They became even more dangerous as states such as Israel, India and Pakistan developed nuclear weapons.

Although the stand-off between the United States and the Soviet Union produced two heavily armed states, there was stability in the one area where the two sides directly confronted each other – Europe. Until the late 1980s Europe was generally peaceful, with just three conflicts. The most important was the Greek civil war from 1944 to 1949, in which about 160,000 died, followed by the Soviet interventions in Hungary (1956) and Czechoslovakia (1968) in which at most 10,000 died, nearly all of them in Hungary. Outside this zone of stability, and the generally peaceful Latin America, the world was racked by almost continuous conflict. Nearly 30 million people were killed, 24 million were refugees in their own country and another 18 million were refugees abroad. Four out of five of all the casualties were civilians; most of them in Asia, in particular during the thirty-year conflict to secure an independent and united Vietnam. It was here that the Americans learnt (as the Soviets did later in Afghanistan) that deploying 500,000 troops, together with huge air and naval operations and the use of high-technology weapons, was no guarantee of success against a lightly armed but determined opponent with substantial civilian support. In addition Asia suffered from three Indo-Pakistan wars, the Korean war and the major revolts in Kashmir and East Timor. The other major zone of conflict was the Middle East. There were six Arab-Israeli wars (1948–9, 1956, 1967, 1969–70, 1973, 1982), together with almost continuous low-level conflict involving the Palestinians, as the Israelis continued the Zionist project of expelling the original inhabitants of Palestine and taking over land beyond the frontiers of Israel recognized by international law and the United Nations. In addition there was the conflict between Iran and Iraq which lasted for most of the 1980s, the Gulf War of 1991, low-level violence involving the Kurds in both Iran and Iraq (as well as Turkey) and continued attacks on Iraq throughout the 1990s. In Africa many of the problems were internal and most states accepted their artificial colonial boundaries because any alternative was far too destabilizing for all of them. But there were conflicts between Libya and Chad, Tanzanian intervention in Uganda and intervention in Liberia and Sierra Leone. In addition there was widespread fighting for decades against Portuguese rule in Angola and Mozambique. These wars continued after independence and involved other powers, in particular South Africa. Apart from a few border disputes (such as that between Ecuador and Peru) the only major conflict in south America was between Britain and Argentina in 1982 over the Falklands/Malvinas islands. Central America was generally peaceful apart from the numerous civil conflicts and interventions by the United States including Guatemala (1954), Cuba (the 1960s), Nicaragua, El Salvador, Grenada and Panama (the 1980s) and Haiti (the 1990s).

24.6 Europe: Stability and Instability

24.6.1 Stability in western Europe

For over forty years after 1945 the international instability that had characterized Europe for centuries was replaced by stability because of the predominance of the United States and the Soviet Union. In western Europe there was also a new stability in politics. It was not until after 1945 that conservative groups finally came to accept a liberal-democratic system. They did so in conditions that were highly favourable to them – the presence of American troops and a strong anti-communist, free-market consensus. The disintegration (and to some extent discrediting) of the authoritarian, monarchical right and many of the pre-war parties left a gap in the political spectrum. It was filled by the emergence of strong Christian Democratic parties, which came to dominate post-war politics. After 1945 social democratic parties gained power occasionally in western Europe. They lacked any clear 'socialist' ideology and, as in the past, they concentrated on immediate problems. Under American pressure through the Marshall Aid programme and confronting the realities they faced in operating within a capitalist economy, social democratic parties came to accept capitalism. The most they now hoped to do was make it marginally more just socially. Many, beginning with the German SPD in 1959, specifically rejected any Marxist heritage they might have had. Only in Scandinavia did they dominate politics. The most stabilizing factor in western Europe was the long post-war boom which began in the early 1950s and lasted until 1973. During a period of relatively rapid growth, low unemployment and low inflation it was easy for governments to deal with any social discontents by spending more money. Most people were satisfied with the huge growth in consumer spending, particularly when it was compared with the generally depressed inter-war years. In these circumstances there was little demand for any alternative and the loss of European power in the world passed with hardly any domestic consequences. Even when economic conditions worsened after 1973, and the effects of an increasingly global and unregulated economy were felt more acutely, there was no rise in instability.

The greatest departure from the past was the gradual construction of a form of economic and social union, and later a loose political union, between the states of western Europe. It emerged from a mixture of motives. The relative weakness of a number of the small states such as the Benelux countries had been recognized by proposals for a customs union made during the 1939–45 war. The French, invaded three times by Germany within the previous seventy years, were determined to offset their weakness by incorporating the German economy into a wider unit. The west Germans, seeking respectability after the horrors of the Nazi period, were in little position or mood to disagree. Overall, the west European states were bound to feel crushed between the power of the United States and the Soviet Union and greater union was a way of increasing their economic and later their political power. The process came about not because of the work of a few federalist visionaries such as Jean Monet, but because the states of western Europe realized that it was in their own national interests to take part in this process as the only way of maintaining their prosperity, power and influence. The first major institution to be created was the Coal and Steel Community in the early 1950s and this led on to the negotiations that brought about the Treaty of Rome and the establishment of the European Economic Community in 1957. Although primarily a customs union, it provided a framework for the development of a deeper economic and social union through the creation of a single market and also provided an institutional structure that went far beyond that necessary for the harmonization and elimination of tariff barriers.

Originally the EEC had six members – France, Italy, the Benelux countries (Belgium, the Netherlands and Luxemburg) and west Germany. Britain, still believing that its role lay outside Europe with the Commonwealth and the United States, and not reconciled to its rapid loss of power (both strategic and economic), stood aside. However, the initial success of the EEC and the inability of Britain to exercise any influence from outside led to a rapid change of mind. British applications to join in 1963 and 1967 were rejected and membership was not obtained until 1973 (together with Ireland and Denmark). There were further increases in membership with the accession of Greece, followed by Spain and Portugal. Further expansion had to await the end of the 'Cold War' and the admission of the former neutral countries of Sweden, Finland and Austria. Progress towards economic integration was slow and a single market was not created until the early 1990s. Monetary union was even more elusive – there had been a European Payments Union in the immediate aftermath of the war but it was wound up and attempts at establishing a European Monetary System from the mid-1970s were unsuccessful. Not until the late 1990s were the outlines of a single currency created. The institutional structures of the European Union (as it was known from the mid-1980s) were also slow to develop but included a European Court, supremacy for European law, a Commission in Brussels to administer European-wide programmes, and a weak European parliament. After forty years of development a unique hybrid had emerged. The member states retained nearly all of their powers (including a veto on most issues) but, although the EU was far from being a federal state, supranational institutions and policies did exist. It was a fundamental departure in European history and seemed to have ended some of the worst aspects of the European state system as it had developed over the previous six hundred years. Greater integration had also produced the biggest single market in the world and gave western Europe the basis to challenge American economic power, even though its military and diplomatic power was almost non-existent.

24.6.2 Stability and instability in eastern Europe

Soviet domination of eastern Europe also produced general stability (though with internal discontent, particularly in Hungary, Czechoslovakia and Poland). The tensions which had dominated the region in the two decades after the Versailles treaty were suppressed by authoritarian regimes and the presence of Soviet troops. That situation lasted until the late 1980s when the collapse of the Soviet Union and the end of the Cold War brought about the greatest-ever restructuring of the map of Europe and the re-emergence of problems and divisions which had seemed to have been either resolved or forgotten. The changes profoundly altered the European balance and demonstrated once again the highly unstable nature of the European state structure.

After the death of Stalin in 1953, and particularly after the peaceful removal of Nikita Khrushchev in 1964, the Soviet Union settled into a semi-torpor with a poorly performing economy, weak leadership from an ageing political elite personified by leaders such as Leonid Brezhnev, and an institutionalized and partly corrupt party bureaucracy. It was the attempt to reform the system under Mikhail Gorbachev from the mid-1980s, under the twin policies of *perestroika* (restructuring) and *glasnost* (openness), which opened a Pandora's Box of problems. By far the most important was nationalism within the Soviet Union. The structure of the state as created in the 1920s and made more explicit in the 1936 constitution was unusual in that it was the first state in the world where different nationalities were recognized in the creation of the republics that made up the union. They were given the right to secede, although it was assumed that it would never be exercised by the members of the ruling Bolshevik party. In practice the Soviet Union was characterized by Russian dominance, chauvinism and superiority over the other nationalities (in particular the Muslims of central Asia). From the early 1960s there was growing national control of the communist parties in the constituent republics and the emergence of entrenched local elites in their governments. It was this growing nationalism, compounded by the attempt to have multi-candidate elections, that was to bring down the Soviet Union.

In the late 1980s the central government lost power and found that it was unable, except at the cost of the unacceptable use of violence, to enforce its decisions. Gradually the constituent republics became more powerful and autonomous. The process was largely peaceful (the worst problems occurred in Nagorno-Karabakh, an Armenian enclave in the neighbouring republic of Azerbaijan). In late 1989 the constitution was changed to allow a form of 'home rule' in the republics but by then the Baltic republics had declared themselves to be sovereign states and in March 1990 Lithuania proclaimed its independence. The government in Moscow was powerless to stop the process. In early 1991 a new 'federation' (not 'union') of republics was overwhelmingly accepted in a referendum but the limitations of central power were starkly apparent when the Baltic states, Armenia, Georgia and Moldova (the old Bessarabia) refused to take part. It was tacitly assumed that they would formally secede when the new federal treaty was completed. The day before that treaty was due to be signed in August 1991 an attempted coup by conservative groups in the communist party and armed forces failed. In the new political environment that followed (including the abolition of the communist party) the independence of the Baltic republics was recognized in September and that of the other three republics accepted but not recognized. By the autumn of 1991 even the 'Slav' republics demanded independence and Russia, Belorussia, Ukraine and the central Asian republics formed a Confederation of Independent States – it had no central authority and was no more than an association of sovereign states. On 25 December 1991 Gorbachev resigned as president of the Soviet Union – it was a state that no longer existed beyond the confines of his office in Moscow.

In parallel with its internal disintegration the Soviet Union lost control over its sphere of influence in eastern Europe. The problems began in Poland where, in the early 1980s, the popular workers' and intellectuals' movement 'Solidarity' had eventually been suppressed by a military coup. By the late 1980s partially open elections led to a decisive victory by Solidarity and, after tortuous negotiations, the formation of the first non-communist government in the Soviet sphere for forty years. The unwillingness of the Soviet Union to use force to preserve the communist monopoly of power was immediately noticed in the other states. Hungary refused to keep its western border closed, a flood of refugees ensued, and demonstrations across eastern Europe produced even more instability. The crucial moment came when the east German government vacillated over the future of the Berlin Wall (built in 1961) and demonstrators pulled it down. By the end of 1989 communist governments had effectively ceased to exist in eastern Europe, though many of the old guard transformed themselves into new political groupings. The end of the communist government in east Germany led to the rapid reunification of Germany through its absorption into the west German state.

The end of communist rule in eastern Europe resulted in the re-emergence of old problems that it was widely, but erroneously, believed had been resolved. It led to the disintegration of the two 'mini-empires' created at Versailles some seventy years earlier – Czechoslovakia and Yugoslavia. The first was a peaceful process; the second was extremely violent, far more so than the collapse of the Soviet Union. The establishment of communist rule in Yugoslavia under the partisan leader Tito had seemed to signify a new era in a deeply divided state. The carefully nurtured myths of the resistance and the need to defend socialism, federalism and non-alignment after Tito's break with Stalin and the rest of the Soviet bloc in the late 1940s created some sense of unity. In practice Tito, a Croat-Slovene, deliberately reduced the power of the Serbs through the creation of a separate republic of Macedonia, the establishment of autonomous provinces of Kosovo and Vojvodina, the giving of a veto at federal level to the Albanian majority in Kosovo and the creation of a separate Muslim nationality in Bosnia-Herzegovina. However, the Serbs still dominated the state, in particular the army. Tito was able to control the situation because of his strong personal rule. After his death in May 1980 the new constitution came into effect. The provision that the posts of president and party leader should rotate every year on a national basis only legitimized divisions and proved unworkable in practice.

The reassertion of the latent divisions within Yugoslavia combined with economic decline and the establishment of a multi-party system destroyed the state. The catalyst was the emergence of a strong Serbian nationalism under Slobodan Milošović after 1987, his attempt to act as protector of the Serbs in every constituent republic, and his opposition to any break-up of Yugoslavia which would reduce Serb power. The first area to secede was the relatively prosperous republic of Slovenia in 1991 – despite some skirmishes there was no real fighting. In the end Slovenia could be allowed to leave because it was ethnically homogeneous, not central to the main issues in the country and had always been closer to Austria than the rest of Yugoslavia. The Serbs, after border wars over the ethnically confused frontier areas, eventually accepted an independent Croatia (short of all-out war they had little alternative). The nationalists in Macedonia won power in the 1990 elections and gained independence after complex negotiations involving other states such as Bulgaria and Greece with traditional claims over the area. Bosnia-Herzegovina proved to be a far more difficult problem because the Muslims were the largest single group but not a majority and there were large Serb and Croat minorities. Only a federal Yugoslavia could make sense of such a divided area and it took six years of intermittent warfare, a misjudged international recognition of independence in 1992, shifting alliances, intervention by both the Serbs and Croats, and eventually weak outside intervention before a limited and fragile settlement was achieved. By the mid-1990s, after an intermittent but occasionally extremely nasty civil war, Yugoslavia had effectively ceased to exist. However, another problem remained. The Serbs revoked the autonomy of Kosovo, a site of great historic and mythic importance in Serb history, and thereby finally alienated the Albanian majority in the province (it was the western European powers which had refused to allow Kosovo to join Albania in 1912–13 and again in 1918). A terrorist movement led to international negotiations over revived autonomy. The Serb refusal to accept a proposal (which they saw, probably rightly, as leading to the eventual secession of Kosovo) led in early 1999 to massive outside intervention by NATO and the Serb expulsion of most of the population. That failed but the prospects for a lasting settlement looked remote even after international control of the province was established.

Although the Cold War had been a sterile but stable interlude in European history its end revived some of the older questions and problems that had plagued the European world for centuries. The decade after 1989 saw the greatest-ever remaking of the map of Europe and the creation of a number of features which appeared to be highly unstable. First, Russia was left weaker and with its borders further east than they had been for the previous four centuries. Not only did it lose the gains made in 1945 it also lost the Baltic states (which had been independent in the inter-war period) together with Ukraine and Belorussia which it had controlled from the first expansion of the early Russian state in the seventeenth century. In the Caucasus it lost all the areas gained in the early nineteenth century and in central Asia it similarly lost all the territories taken in the mid-nineteenth century. It was one of the most rapid and massive losses of territory and power in world history. Second, the reunification of Germany and the end of the remnants of Allied occupation, produced once again the strongest state in Europe in the centre of the continent. This had been the principal destabilizing factor in European history between 1871 and 1945. Although Germany finally accepted its radically different borders in the east (the loss of east Prussia and the Oder-Neisse line as the western border of Poland, as agreed by the Allies in 1945) and was closely integrated into the European Union, other states were left worried about the containment of German power. The third factor was the re-emergence of a multitude of independent states in central and eastern Europe. Some of these were the states created at Versailles, or which emerged in the chaos at the end of the 1914–18 war (such as the Baltic states). Others, such as Ukraine and Belorussia, had only ever been independent for a few months. The largest group – Moldova, Croatia, Slovenia, Macedonia, Bosnia-Herzegovina and Slovakia – had (like the Caucasian and central Asian republics) never been fully independent. In some places the map of eastern Europe looked more as it had done after the Treaty of Brest-Litovsk in early 1918, when Germany had imposed its war aims on a defeated Russia. In the Balkans such a multitude of states had never existed before.

24.7 The Revival of China

The hundred years between the mid-nineteenth and mid-twentieth centuries in China had been a period of civil war, revolution, outside intervention and war. It saw China slip from its position in the late eighteenth century as one of the most prosperous and stable states in the world to being a poor and weak power. This was a major reversal of one of the most persistent factors in world history – the position of China as normally the most economically developed and powerful state in the world. The re-establishment in 1949 of a strong central government committed to economic development and the rebuilding of China as a major power was, therefore, a highly significant moment in modern history. However, the full implications of the change took more than three decades to become apparent as divisions within the communist leadership about the way ahead produced shifting policies and acute internal problems.

In 1949 the communist party in China had the Soviet Union as an example of how to consolidate its power and begin full-scale industrialization. There were, however, two major differences. The base of the party in China was in the countryside whereas the Bolsheviks had almost no contact with the mass of peasants. Second, the economy was far less industrialized than that of the Soviet Union in the late 1920s. The government's initial policy was the radical land-reform programme of the early 1950s, under which land was confiscated and landlords were forced to return rents the peasants had paid. This was achieved by so-called 'struggle rallies' with party members using poor peasants to lead the movement locally. Probably about 5 million 'landlords' and 'rich peasants' were killed in the process. However, there was little improvement in agricultural output and the government decided to move to what was probably always its preferred option – collectivization; this was achieved by 1957 without the terrible outcome seen in the Soviet Union in the early 1930s. A year later the government decided on a further radical departure under the slogan of the 'Three Red Banners'. It involved a simultaneous development of agriculture and industry (the 'Great Leap Forward') and a comprehensive collectivization of life. Within three years the programme had collapsed through widespread opposition, economic chaos, starvation and a death toll of about 30 million people.

In the early 1960s the party was still arguing about the way forward in much the same way as the Soviet party in the 1920s. Nobody suggested political liberalization but some such as Teng Hsiao-ping argued for a more market-oriented, pro-peasant policy. Eventually the radicals in the People's Liberation Army under Marshal Lin Piao, backed by Mao and his wife Chiang Ch'ing as a way of maintaining their dominance within the party, gained the upper hand. In the summer of 1966 a decision was taken to initiate the 'Great Proletarian Cultural Revolution'. Education was to be combined with long periods of manual work so that 'intellectuals' experienced the reality of peasant life – the outcome would be a new proletarian ideology which would completely reject both 'western' and traditional Chinese values. It had a strong popular base with over 10 million members in the new 'Red Guard' units. However, across China there was near anarchy as the control structures of the party and state collapsed, local party groups resisted decrees from Peking, and PLA and Red Guard units disintegrated into factions and fought street battles with each other. Not until the summer of 1968 was the army able to get the situation under control when they 'helped' students back to school and university. Slowly more moderate factions gained control – Lin Piao was 'purged' in mysterious circumstances in 1971 and two years later Teng Hsiao-ping was re-elected to the Politburo. There was a further radical period in the mid-1970s after the deaths of Mao and Chou En-lai but the radical leaders ('the Gang of Four') were removed and a moderate leadership re-established.

Despite the political turmoil in China for a decade after the mid-1960s and the disastrous mistakes in economic policy made in the late 1950s, the performance of the Chinese economy matched that of any industrializing economy. Overall growth rates were as high as those of the Soviet Union in the 1930s, Brazil in the 1960s and south Korea in the 1970s and were sustained for far longer. Industrial output rose at over 10 per cent a year in the three decades from the early 1950s, doubling China's share of world industrial production. By the early 1980s China was making more iron and steel than Britain and France combined. Investment levels were also the highest in the world. The average number of years children spent in education doubled during the period. By the late 1970s the new moderate leadership had to decide how to build on this base now that basic industrialization was complete. They adopted a policy remarkably like the New Economic Policy in the Soviet Union in the 1920s – economic liberalization combined with absolute political control as the suppression of the student demonstrations in Tienanmen Square in Peking in 1989 demonstrated. The first key changes were, as the new leader Teng Hsiao-ping had always advocated, agrarian reform through the transformation of communes into 'townships' which were allowed to sell their produce on the open market. Output rose at 8 per cent a year and the real income of the peasantry doubled in the six years after the reforms were introduced in 1978. This provided the base for further industrialization and the granting of much greater freedom to factories and individuals. State planning was retained at the macro-economic level but below this a form of capitalism emerged. The import of foreign technology and production for export was based on the creation of joint enterprises with overseas corporations and the four special economic zones in southern China (for almost a thousand years the area with the greatest external contacts). From the early 1980s the economy continued to grow at about 10 per cent a year.

The strategic position of China was also changing. For about a decade after the communists took power they were close to the Soviet Union as their only ally. The United States was strongly opposed to the new government and backed Chiang Kai-shek and the Kuomintang on Taiwan who still clung to their dream of regaining power on the mainland. Direct confrontation between the two was kept under control. However, the Chinese gained little from the Soviet Union and resentment over what the Chinese saw as the continuation of the 'unequal treaties' of the nineteenth century led to a permanent break between the two in the early 1960s. In 1964 the Chinese developed their own nuclear weapons and by the end of the decade there were military clashes along the disputed border with the Soviet Union in the Amur river area. In the early 1970s the Americans finally gave up the pretence that the Kuomintang were the government of China, recognized the government in Peking and allowed it to join the United Nations and take over the seat on the Security Council. This reflected the overriding American aim to create more problems for the Soviet Union. From the Chinese point of view the end of the humiliating treaties of the nineteenth century came in 1997, when Britain handed back Hong Kong, followed in 1999 by the return of Macao from the Portuguese. Economic development was also reinforcing the scale of the Chinese recovery. Within half a century of the communist party taking over as the government in China it had, like the Ming in the late fourteenth century, restored China's formal position in world history as one of the major powers in the world.

24.8 The World Balance at the End of the Twentieth Century

The world balance at the end of the twentieth century reflected an unprecedented degree of complexity caused by overlapping economic, military and strategic trends. At a military level the situation seemed relatively simple. The end of the Cold War, the collapse of the Soviet Union and the still developing power of China meant that the United States was the sole global power. It was the only state to deploy certain types of weapon, its technological resources were unmatched and its military expenditure was greater than that of Russia, Britain, France and Germany combined. However, this military power was of limited use. It could be deployed to great effect, with the support of a number of allies, in the Gulf war in 1991, although even here it was unable to resolve the question of how to deal with the Iraqi government, but in dealing with terrorist threats and low-level conflict it had little value. The American ability to influence the different security complexes across the world was also limited.

The fundamental problem was that the security of states could no longer be defined purely in military and strategic terms. The United States was no longer the dominant economic power – its rivals among the major industrialized economies (the European Union and Japan) created a different nexus of economic power. Competition between the major economies devastated some industries – the European shipbuilding, motorcycle and television industries collapsed under Japanese competition. By the 1980s the United States found that its superiority in the production of sophisticated armaments did not protect it from the devastating consequences of Japanese competition in the car and consumer electronics industries. At the same time all states were losing power to transnational corporations. Their ability to shift production around the world according to their own priorities had major effects on national economies which governments were largely unable to control. Indeed states became competitors for the favours of these corporations and attempted to attract them by various subsidies and grants. As international financial flows and foreign exchange dealings rose exponentially their magnitude was far beyond the reserves held by a single state or even those of the major economies and international institutions put together. By the end of the twentieth century even the largest industrial states found that they had little alternative but to adapt their policies to what were seen as 'economic realities' – in practice the operation of impersonal and uncontrolled (and uncontrollable) economic forces. These were now operating on a scale previously unknown in world history.

The security of states was also affected by other developments in world history. The rapid rise in population since the eighteenth century, together with the gigantic increases in energy consumption and industrial output were creating new problems. Deforestation, desertification, pollution spreading beyond national boundaries and, worst of all, the destruction of the ozone layer and global warming, were all world dilemmas which affected the security of every state and which none could counter on its own. One of the problems in dealing with them was the balance between the different interests of the almost two hundred states in the world (in 1900 there were fewer than fifty). This situation was unprecedented and stemmed from the period of European supremacy. For most of history the world had been divided into a mix of large empires and small city-states. The history of Europe was unusual in that it produced a system with a multitude of competing states (rather like the 'Warring States' of China in the three centuries before the establishment of the Chin and Han around 200 BCE) which no single state could dominate and therefore a single empire was not created. Over the period from about 1300 the European state system turned out to be highly dysfunctional in terms of the level of conflict and destruction it produced. The expansion of European power after 1750 and, in particular, decolonization after 1945, produced an expansion of the state system to cover the rest of the world. Whether it would be equally dysfunctional on a global scale remained to be seen.

However, other developments in world history were also affecting the position of the world's states. Developments in the world economy produced a complex structure of overlapping economic and political power which did not coincide with state boundaries. Many states were far weaker and exercised much less economic and political power than non-sovereign bodies such as transnational corporations and international institutions. States were not the only institutions to wield force – something they had long claimed as their exclusive prerogative since the full development of the European state in the seventeenth century. Internally private security organizations were increasingly important and in some, such as Colombia and Russia (and, to some extent, Italy), the state was unable to control the power of large-scale criminal groups. Externally small terrorist groups were powerful and in some instances transnational corporations were hiring their own armed forces to defend their investments in some of the weaker states of the world. Many of the weaker states had little choice but to accept the policies imposed by international organizations such as the International Monetary Fund and the World Bank. In areas like western Europe, even theoretically strong governments were giving authority to supranational institutions such as NATO in military and strategic affairs and the European Union in the social and economic spheres.

As well as this diffusion and increasing complexity of economic and political power it was also clear that, by the late twentieth century, the world balance was changing significantly. Two areas were, as in the past, marginal to this process. Latin America had not been central to world history after it obtained independence in the early nineteenth century – there was little conflict between the states but they remained deeply divided and unstable internally. None had significant economic power and all remained in a position of dependency within the world economy. The situation was even worse in most of Africa. Nearly the whole of the continent (apart from the southern shore of the Mediterranean) had always been irrelevant to the main dynamics of world history. It had hardly been incorporated into the mainstream by the impact of Europe (apart from the slave trade) and the legacy of European colonialism was extremely thin. The new states inherited huge economic and social problems, partly stemming from a lack of investment in the colonial period. Because of the way the Europeans had divided up the continent many states were so small as to be hardly viable. By 1980 twenty-two out of the forty-nine independent states had populations of fewer than 5 million and nine had fewer than 1 million. To these problems were added falling commodity prices (the major source of export revenue), rising oil prices, growing debt and rampant corruption by the elite. The result was economic stagnation and in some cases actual decline.

Of greater importance was the area which had become known as the Middle East. It had been the centre of many of the major societies and empires of world history and it had also formed the core of the Islamic world – one of the two major political and cultural areas in the world in the thousand years after the early seventh century. It had found it difficult to adapt to the impact of European power in the nineteenth and early twentieth centuries and especially to the creation of artificial states after the defeat of the Ottomans in 1918. This was made worse by the major European colonial venture – Zionism – which led to the expulsion of a majority of the original inhabitants of Palestine, a takeover by Jewish immigrants and the creation of the state of Israel. Until the 1970s the region was also heavily exploited economically by the industrialized countries and the oil companies – it received very little from the production of oil which was the foundation of the great industrial expansion of the twentieth century. Even after greater control was obtained in the early 1970s, leading to huge increases in wealth, the states in the region were unable to use their power over oil as a strategic weapon. There was also an internal conflict between a belief in secularism, and the acceptance of 'western' ideas and institutions as the way to 'modernization' (exemplified by Turkey after 1923 and Iran from the early 1950s to the late 1970s), and a revival of Islamic beliefs and traditions. In the late twentieth century there were signs of a significant revival in fundamentalist Islam although this was usually opposed by the secularized elites which dominated countries such as Egypt.

The majority of the world's people always lived in Asia (in particular in China and India). It was also normally the wealthiest region of the world. The emergence of Europe after 1500 and its use of the wealth derived from the Americas and the Atlantic economy to penetrate this long-established, prosperous and stable world, marked a significant change in the world balance. However, the period of European supremacy was very short-lived. It was not until after 1750 that Europe had enough power to influence Asia and even then its impact on China and Japan was very limited. European domination lasted at best from the mid-nineteenth century until the early 1940s. By 1900 the United States was already the largest economy in the world and it was only the peculiar hiatus in military power that enabled European predominance to continue until the 1940s. Then the impact of the European civil wars on the rest of the world proved to be decisive. The United States became the only global power, it replaced European power in many parts of the world and Japan, the first country outside of Europe and the United States to industrialize, damaged the European empires beyond repair. By the last quarter of the twentieth century Europe was an important regional economic power but no longer a major world power. The American economic superiority of the early and mid-twentieth century was also lost in the second half of the century as Europe recovered from its civil wars, more countries industrialized and

Japan became just as wealthy. America's global military power had seen off the limited challenge by the Soviet Union but it provided little real gain in power in circumstances where security problems were increasingly diffuse and not susceptible to military solutions.

The most significant factor in world history in the last part of the twentieth century was the revival of Asia after its temporary eclipse in the two centuries after 1750. The first signs of this process were apparent in the late nineteenth century. The early industrialization of Japan, its emergence as a regional power capable of defeating not only China but also Russia, and its courtship by Britain as an ally, were the first illustrations of this trend. Growing nationalism and opposition to foreign rule in India, Burma and the Philippines were similar indicators. Even China, gravely weakened by the events of the mid-nineteenth century, was able to keep control of its own destiny. From the mid-twentieth century these trends accelerated rapidly. In 1949 China was reunified and began a process of national revival, rapid economic growth and industrialization which, within little more than half a century, again turned it into one of the largest economies in the world (a position it had held until about 1850). Phenomenal growth in Japan created one of the wealthiest societies in the world. Similar industrialization was also under way in south Korea, Taiwan, Thailand and the Philippines. Only India was a relative failure in the second half of the twentieth century.

The revival of Asia was reflected in the relative decline of the 'Atlantic world' and the rise of the Pacific. This too was a trend which became increasingly apparent from the mid-nineteenth century. The United States became a Pacific power with the acquisition of California in 1848, followed by the gradual extension of its possessions to Hawaii and the Philippines, and its increasing economic interests from whaling to the first mission to Japan within a decade of taking California. In the 1930s and early 1940s it was far more inclined to use its military power in the Pacific than it was in Europe. In the second half of the twentieth century the increasing economic importance of the Pacific and the increasing levels of trade between the states on its shores (California also became the most populous American state) merely reinforced these trends. This was, however, a major departure in world history. Until the development of modern communications the Pacific had acted as a barrier to interchange between the various societies that clustered around its shores.

By the end of the twentieth century it was clear that Europe had, like other societies in the past, been unable to retain a monopoly over the technological developments it had initiated. It was still a major economic power but other areas were just as dynamic and developed industrially and technologically. Europe's political domination of the world (always very far from complete) was even more short-lived. The offshoot of Europe, the United States, found too that its short-lived economic supremacy was rapidly fading. Its military power was also less and less useful in dealing with the problems it faced. Asia was rapidly recovering the position it had lost, temporarily, after 1750. Japan was an economic power of the first rank. China, always the largest state in the world, was industrializing rapidly and increasing its military and political influence. The world seemed to be returning towards its more normal balance.

Guide to Further Reading

This is not a comprehensive list of all the books and articles consulted during the research for this book. Instead it is a selection of those works, mainly written in the last two decades or so, which provide further information about some of the themes and arguments in the preceding chapters. In most cases, general histories of particular periods and areas have been excluded.

General

Barfield, T., *The Perilous Frontier: Nomadic Empires and China* (Oxford, 1989)

Bentley, J., *Old World Encounters: Cross-Cultural Contacts and Exchanges in Pre-Modern Times* (Oxford, 1993)

Blaut, J., *The Colonizer's Model of the World: Geographical Diffusionism and Eurocentric History* (New York, 1993)

Chandler, T. and Fox, G., *3000 Years of Urban Growth* (New York, 1974)

Chase-Dunn, C. and Hall, T., *Core/Periphery Relations in Precapitalist Worlds* (Boulder, 1991)

Curtin, P., *Cross-Cultural Trade in World History* (Cambridge, 1984)

Davies, N., *Europe: A History* (Oxford, 1996)

Eisenstadt, S., *The Origins and Diversity of Axial Age Civilizations* (Albany, NY, 1986)

Franck, I. and Brownstone, D., *The Silk Road: A History* (New York, 1986)

Frank, A., *The Centrality of Central Asia* (Amsterdam, 1992)

Frank, A. and Gills, B., *The World System: Five hundred years or five thousand?* (London, 1993)

Gernet, J., *A History of Chinese Civilization* (2nd edition; Cambridge, 1996)

Hall, T., 'Civilizational Change: The Role of Nomads', *Comparative Civilizations Review*, Vol. 24, 1991, pp. 34–57

Hodgson, M., *Rethinking World History: Essays on Europe, Islam and World History* (Cambridge, 1993)

Jones, E., *Growth Recurring: Economic Change in World History* (Oxford, 1988)

McEvedy, C. and Jones, R., *Atlas of World Population History* (London, 1978)

McNeill, W., *The Rise of the West: A History of the Human Community* (Chicago, 1963)

——, *Plagues and Peoples* (Oxford, 1977)

——, *The Pursuit of Power: Technology, Armed Force and Society since 1000 AD* (Oxford, 1983)

——, 'The Rise of the West After Twenty-Five Years', *Journal of World History*, Vol. 1, 1990, pp. 1–21

——, *Keeping Together in Time: Dance and Drill in Human History* (Cambridge, 1995)

McNeill, W. and Adams, R., *Human Migration: Patterns and Policies* (Bloomington, 1978)

Mann, M., *The Sources of Social Power* (2 vols; Cambridge, 1986)

Melko, M., *The Nature of Civilizations* (Boston, 1969)

Modelski, G. and Thompson, W., *Leading Sectors and World Powers: The CoEvolution of Global Politics and Economics* (Columbia, 1996)

Mokyr, J., *The Lever of Riches: Technological Creativity and Economic Progress* (Oxford, 1990)

Newman, L. (ed.), *Hunger in History: Food Shortage, Poverty and Deprivation* (Oxford, 1990)

Ponting, C., *A Green History of the World* (London, 1991)

Quigley, C., *The Evolution of Civilizations* (New York, 1961)

Rotberg, R. and Rabb, T. (eds), *Hunger and History: The Impact of Changing Food Production and Consumption Patterns on Society* (Cambridge, 1985)

Sanderson, S. (ed.), *Civilizations and World Systems: Studying World-Historical Change* (Walnut Creek, 1995)

Sinor, D., (ed.), *The Cambridge History of Early Inner Asia* (Cambridge, 1990)

Tainter, J., *The Collapse of Civilizations* (Cambridge, 1988)

Toynbee, A., *A Study of History* (12 vols; Oxford, 1934–61)

Wenke, R., *Patterns in Prehistory: Humankind's First Three Million Years* (New York, 1990)

Yoffe, N. and Cowgill, G., *The Collapse of Ancient States and Civilizations* (Tucson, 1988)

Part One: Ninety-nine Per Cent of Human History

Bahn, P. and Vertut, J., *Images of the Ice Age* (Leicester, 1988)

Covey, C., 'The Earth's Orbit and the Ice Ages', *Scientific American*, Vol.

250, 1984, pp. 42–50

Dennell, R., *European Economic Prehistory: A New Approach* (London, 1983)

Durrant, J. (ed.), *Human Origins* (Oxford, 1989)

Fagan, B., *The Journey From Eden: The Peopling of Our World* (London, 1990)

——, *People of the Earth: An Introduction to World Prehistory* (8th edition; New York, 1995)

Gamble, C., *The Palaeolithic Settlement of Europe* (Cambridge, 1992)

Grayson, D., 'Late Pleistocene Mammalian Extinctions in North America: Taxonomy, Chronology and Explanations', *Journal of World Prehistory*, Vol. 5, 1991, pp. 193–231

Harding, R. and Teleki, G., *Omnivorous Primates: Gathering and Hunting in Human Evolution* (New York, 1981)

Higgs, E., *Papers in Economic Prehistory* (Cambridge, 1972)

——, *Palaeoeconomy* (Cambridge, 1975)

Irwin, G., *The Prehistoric Exploration and Colonization of the Pacific* (Cambridge, 1992)

Lee, R. and DeVore, I., *Man the Hunter* (Chicago, 1968)

Lewin, R., *Human Evolution* (Oxford, 1989)

Martin, P. and Wright, H., *Pleistocene Extinctions: The Search for a Cause* (New Haven, 1967)

Megaw, J., *Hunters, Gatherers and the First Farmers Beyond Europe* (Leicester, 1977)

Mellars, P. and Stringer, C., *The Human Revolution: Behavioural and Biological Perspectives on the Origin of Modern Humans* (Edinburgh, 1989)

Price, T., 'The Mesolithic of Western Europe', *Journal of World Prehistory*, Vol. 1, 1987, pp. 225–305

Sahlins, M., *Stone Age Economics* (Chicago, 1972)

Shick, K. and Toth, N., *Making the Silent Stones Speak: Human Evolution and the Dawn of Technology* (London, 1993)

Soffer, O. and Gamble, C., *The World at 18,000 BP* (London, 1990)

Stringer, C. and Gamble, C., *In Search of the Neanderthals: Solving the Puzzle of Human Origins* (London, 1993)

Part Two: The Great Transition

Algaze, G., 'The Uruk Expansion: Cross-Cultural Exchange in Early Mesopotamian Civilization', *Current Anthropology*, Vol. 30, 1989, pp. 571–608

Algaze, G., 'Expansionary Dynamics of Some Early Pristine States', *American Anthropologist*, Vol. 95, 1993, pp. 304–33

Allchin, B. and Allchin, R., *The Rise of Civilization in India and Pakistan* (Cambridge, 1982)

Barnes, G., *China, Korea and Japan: The Rise of Civilization in East Asia* (London, 1993)

Berrin, K. and Pasztory, E., *Teotihuacan: Art from the City of the Gods* (London, 1993)

Blanton, R., *Monte Alban: Settlement Patterns at the Ancient Zapotec Capital* (New York, 1978)

Blanton, R. and Feinman, G., 'The Mesoamerican World System', *American Anthropologist*, Vol. 86, 1984, pp. 673–82

British Academy (various authors), *The Early History of Agriculture* (Oxford, 1976)

Brumfiel, E., 'Aztec State Making: Ecology, Structure and the Origin of the State', *American Anthropologist*, Vol. 85, 1983, pp. 261–84

Butzer, K., *Early Hydraulic Civilization in Egypt: A Study in Cultural Ecology* (Chicago, 1976)

Claessen, H. and Skalnik, P., *The Early State* (New York, 1978)

Clendinnen, I., *Aztecs: An Interpretation* (Cambridge, 1991)

Clutton-Brock, J., *The Walking Larder: Patterns of domestication, pastoralism and predation* (London, 1989)

Coe, M., *Mexico* (London, 1968)

——, *Breaking the Maya Code* (London, 1992)

Conrad, G. and Demarest, A., *Religion and Empire: The Dynamics of Aztec and Inca Expansionism* (Cambridge, 1984)

Crawford, H., *Sumer and the Sumerians* (Cambridge, 1991)

Culbert, P., *The Classic Maya Collapse* (Albuquerque, 1973)

——, *Classic Maya Political History: Hieroglyphic and Archaeological Evidence* (Cambridge, 1991)

Drennan, R., 'Long Distance Transport Costs in Pre-Hispanic Mesoamerica', *American Anthropologist*, Vol. 86, 1984, pp. 105–12

Gebauer, A. and Price, T., *Transitions to Agriculture in Prehistory* (Madison, 1992)

Gledhill, J., Bender, B. and Larsen, M., *State and Society: The Emergence and Development of Social Hierarchy and Political Centralization* (London, 1988)

Haas, J., Pozorski, S. and Pozorski, T., *The Origins and Development of the Andean State* (Cambridge, 1987)

Hammond, N., *Ancient Maya Civilization* (Cambridge, 1982)

Harris, D. and Hillman, G., *Foraging and Farming: The Evolution of Plant Exploitation* (London, 1989)

Hassan, F., 'The Predynastic of Egypt', *Journal of World Prehistory*, Vol. 2, 1988, pp. 135–85

Hassig, R., *War and Society in Ancient Mesoamerica* (Berkeley, 1992)

Henry, D., *From Foraging to Agriculture: The Levant at the End of the Ice Age* (Philadelphia, 1989)

Kemp, B., *Ancient Egypt: Anatomy of a Civilization* (London, 1989)

Kirch, P., *The Evolution of the Polynesian Chiefdoms* (Cambridge, 1984)

McAdams, R., *The Evolution of Urban Society: Early Mesopotamia and Prehispanic Mexico* (London, 1966)

McCorriston, J. and Hole, F., 'The Ecology of Seasonal Stress and the Origins of Agriculture in the Near East', *American Anthropologist*, Vol. 93, 1991, pp. 46–69

Maisels, C., *The Emergence of Civilization: From hunting and gathering to agriculture, cities and the state in the Near East* (London, 1990)

Marcus, J., *Mesoamerican Writing Systems: Propaganda, Myth and History in Four Ancient Civilizations* (Princeton, 1992)

Moorey, P., *The Origins of Civilization* (Oxford, 1979)

Ping-Ti Ho, *The Cradle of the East: An Inquiry into the Indigenous Origins of Techniques and Ideas of Neolithic and Early Historic China 5000–1000 BC* (Hong Kong, 1975)

Postgate, J., *Early Mesopotamia: Society and Economy at the Dawn of History* (London, 1992)

Rindos, D., *The Origins of Agriculture: An Evolutionary Perspective* (Orlando, 1984)

Sabloff, J. and Lamberg-Karlovsky, C., *Ancient Civilization and Trade* (Albuquerque, 1975)

Sanders, W. and Price, B., *Mesoamerica: The Evolution of a Civilization* (New York, 1968)

Smith, B., *The Emergence of Agriculture* (New York, 1995)

Trigger, B., Kemp, B., O'Connor, D. and Lloyd, A., *Ancient Egypt: A Social History* (Cambridge, 1983)

Ucko, P. and Dimbleby, G., *The Domestication and Exploitation of Plants and Animals* (London, 1969)

van de Mieroop, M., *The Ancient Mesopotamian City* (Oxford, 1997)

Wenke, R., 'The Evolution of Early Egyptian Civilization: Issues and Evidence', *Journal of World Prehistory*, Vol. 5, 1991, pp. 279–329

Zohary, D. and Hopf, M., *Domestication of Plants in the Old World: The Origin and Spread of Cultivated Plants in West Asia, Europe and the Nile Valley* (Oxford, 1988)

Part Three: The Early Empires

Adams, R., 'Anthropological Perspectives on Ancient Trade', *Current Anthropology*, Vol. 15, 1974, pp. 239–58

Aubet, M., *The Phoenicians and the West: Politics, Colonies and Trade* (Cambridge, 1993)

Bernal, J., *Black Athena: The Afro-Asiatic Roots of Classical Civilization* (2 vols; London, 1987)

Bouzek, J., *The Aegean, Anatolia and Europe: Cultural Interrelations in the Second Millennium* BC (Gothenburg [Göteborg], 1985)

Bradley, J., *Slaves and Masters in the Roman Empire: A study in social control* (Oxford, 1987)

——, *Slavery and Society at Rome* (Cambridge, 1994)

Chadwick, J., *The Mycenaean World* (Cambridge, 1976)

Chang, K-C., *Shang Civilization* (New Haven, 1980)

Cohen, M., *Health and the Rise of Civilization* (New Haven, 1989)

Coles, J. and Harding, A., *The Bronze Age in Europe: An Introduction to the Prehistory of Europe* (London, 1979)

Colledge, M., *The Parthians* (London, 1967)

Collis, J., *The European Iron Age* (London, 1984)

Craddock, P., *Early Metal Mining and Production* (Edinburgh, 1995)

Crawford, M., 'Rome and the Greek World: Economic Relationships', *Economic History Review*, Vol. 30, 1977, pp. 42–52

Crone, P., *Pre-Industrial Societies* (Oxford, 1989)

Dani, A. and Masson, V., *History of Civilizations of Central Asia*, Vol. 1; *The dawn of civilization: earliest times to 700* BC (Paris, 1992)

de Ste Croix, G., *The Class Struggle in the Ancient Greek World: From the Archaic Age to the Arab Conquests* (London, 1983)

Dickinson, O., *The Aegean Bronze Age* (Cambridge, 1994)

Drews, R., *The End of the Bronze Age: Changes in Warfare and the Catastrophe c.1200* BC (Princeton, 1993)

Duncan-Jones, R., *Structure and Scale in the Roman Economy* (Cambridge, 1990)

Ferrill, A., *The Origins of War: From the Stone Age to Alexander the Great* (London, 1985)

Finley, M., *Ancient Slavery and Modern Ideology* (London, 1980)

——, *Classical Slavery* (London, 1987)

Frank, A., 'Bronze Age World System Cycles', *Current Anthropology*, Vol. 34, 1993, pp. 383–429

Garnsey, P., 'Legal Privilege in the Roman Empire', *Past and Present*, 41, 1968, pp. 3–24

Garnsey, P., Hopkins, K. and Whittaker, C., *Trade in the Ancient*

Economy (London, 1983)

Garnsey, P. and Saller, R., *The Roman Empire: Economy, Society and Culture* (London, 1987)

Garnsey, P., *Famine and Food Supply in the Graeco-Roman World: Responses to Risk and Crisis* (Cambridge, 1988)

Gilman, A., 'The Development of Social Stratification in Bronze Age Europe', *Current Anthropology*, Vol. 22, 1981, pp. 1–23

Green, P., *Alexander to Actium: The Historical Evolution of the Hellenistic Age*, (Berkeley, 1990)

Harris, W., *War and Imperialism in Republican Rome 327–70 BC* (Oxford, 1991)

Hedeager, L., *Iron-Age Societies: From Tribe to State in Northern Europe 500 BC to AD 700* (Oxford, 1992)

Hodges, H., *Technology in the Ancient World* (New York, 1970)

Hopkins, K., *Conquerors and Slaves: Sociological Studies in Roman History*, Vol. 1, (Cambridge, 1978)

Hughes, J., *Ecology in Ancient Civilizations* (Albuquerque, 1975)

Hughes, P., *Pan's Travail: Environmental Problems of the Ancient Greeks and Romans* (Baltimore, 1994)

Hsu, C., *Han Agriculture: The Formation of the Early Chinese Agrarian Economy 206 BC–AD 220* (Seattle, 1980)

James, P., Thorpe, I., Kokkinos, N., Morkot, R. and Frankish, J., *Centuries of Darkness: A challenge to the conventional chronology of Old World archaeology* (New Brunswick, 1993)

Jones, A., *The Later Roman Empire 284–602: A Social, Economic and Administrative Survey* (2 vols; Oxford, 1964)

Kohl, P., 'The Balance of Trade in Southwestern Asia in the Mid-Third Millennium BC', *Current Anthropology*, Vol. 19, 1978, pp. 463–92

Kristiansen, K. and Jensen, J., *Europe in the First Millennium BC* (Sheffield, 1994)

Krupp, E., *Echoes of the Ancient Skies: The Astronomy of Lost Civilizations* (New York, 1983)

Kuhrt, A., *The Ancient Near East c.3000–330 BC* (2 vols; London, 1995)

Lane Fox, R., *Pagans and Christians* (London, 1986)

Larsen, M., *Power and Propaganda: A Symposium on Ancient Empires* (Copenhagen, 1979)

Lee, A., *Information and Frontiers: Roman Foreign Relations in Late Antiquity* (Cambridge, 1993)

Lewis, M., *Sanctioned Violence in Early China* (Albany, 1990)

Liu, X., *Ancient India and Ancient China: Trade and Religious Exchanges AD 1–600* (Delhi, 1988)

Loewe, M., *Crisis and Conflict in Han China 104 BC–AD 9* (London, 1974)

MacMullen, R., *The Roman Government's Response to Crisis* AD 235–337 (New Haven, 1976)
——, *Paganism in the Roman Empire* (New Haven, 1981)
——, *Christianizing the Roman Empire (AD 100–400)* (New Haven, 1984)
——, 'What Difference Did Christianity Make?', *Historia*, Vol. 35, 1986, pp. 322–43
——, *Corruption and the Decline of Rome* (New Haven, 1988)
McNeill, W., 'The Eccentricity of Wheels, or Eurasian Transportation in Historical Perspective', *American Historical Review*, Vol. 92, 1987, pp. 1111–26
Mallory, J., *In Search of the Indo-Europeans: Language, Archaeology and Myth* (London, 1989)
Muhly, J., 'Sources of Tin and the Beginning of Bronze Metallurgy', *American Journal of Archaeology*, Vol. 89, 1985, pp. 275–91
North, J., 'Democratic Politics in Republican Rome', *Past and Present*, 126, 1990, pp. 3–21
Randsborg, K., *The First Millennium* AD *in Europe and the Mediterranean: An Archaeological Essay* (Cambridge, 1991)
Renfrew, C., *Archaeology and Language: The Puzzle of Indo-European Origins* (London, 1987)
Rowlands, M., Larsen, M. and Kristiansen, K., *Centre and Periphery in the Ancient World* (Cambridge, 1987)
Runciman, W., 'Origins of States: The Case of Archaic Greece', *Comparative Studies in Society and History*, Vol. 24, 1982, pp. 351–77
Scullard, H., *The Etruscan Cities and Rome* (London, 1967)
Shaw, B., 'Bandits in the Roman Empire', *Past and Present*, 105, 1984, pp. 3–52
Shennan, S., 'Settlement and Social Change in Central Europe, 3500–1500 BC', *Journal of World Prehistory*, Vol. 7, 1993, pp. 121–61
Silver, M., *Economic Structures of the Ancient Near East* (London, 1985)
Sinclair, R., *Democracy and Participation in Athens* (Cambridge, 1988)
Sjoberg, G., *The Pre-Industrial City: Past and Present* (New York, 1960)
Storey, R., 'An Estimate of Mortality in a Pre-Columbian Urban Population', *American Anthropologist*, Vol. 87, 1985, pp. 519–35
Teggart, F., *Rome and China: A Study of Correlations in Historical Events* (Berkeley, 1939)
Thirgood, J., *Man and the Mediterranean Forest: A history of resource depletion* (London, 1981)
Turcan, R., *The Cults of the Roman Empire* (Oxford, 1996)
Wang, Z., *Han Civilization* (New Haven, 1982)
Wertime, T. and Muhly, J., *The Coming of the Age of Iron* (New Haven, 1980)

Wheatley, P., *The Pivot of the Four Quarters: A Preliminary Enquiry into the Origins and Character of the Ancient Chinese City* (Chicago, 1971)

Wood, E., *Peasant-Citizen and Slave: The Foundations of Athenian Democracy* (London, 1989)

Ying-shih Yü,*Trade and Expansion in Han China: A Study in the Structure of Sino-Barbarian Economic Relations* (Berkeley, CA, 1967)

Zagarell, A., 'Trade, Women, Class and Society in Ancient Western Asia', *Current Anthropology*, Vol. 27, 1986, pp. 415–30

Zurcher, E., *The Buddhist Conquest of China* (2 vols; Leiden, 1959)

Part Four: The Great Empires

Abu-Lughod, J., *Before European Hegemony: The World System* AD *1250–1350* (Oxford, 1989)

Allsen, T., *Mongol Imperialism: The Policies of the Grand Qan Mongke in China, Russia and the Islamic Lands 1251–1259* (Berkeley, 1987)

Ashtor, E., *A Social and Economic History of the Near East in the Middle Ages* (London, 1976)

Beckwith, C., *The Tibetan Empire in Central Asia: A History of the Struggle for Great Power among Tibetans, Turks, Arabs and Chinese During the Early Middle Ages* (Princeton, 1987)

Bloch, M., *Feudal Society* (London, 1961)

Brown, E., 'The tyranny of a construct: feudalism and historians of medieval Europe', *American Historical Review*, Vol. 79, 1974, pp. 1063–88

Bulliet, R., *The Camel and the Wheel* (Cambridge, 1975)

Chao, K., *Man and Land in Chinese History: An Economic Analysis* (Stanford, 1986)

Chaudhuri, K., *Trade and Civilization in the Indian Ocean: An Economic History from the Rise of Islam to 1750* (Cambridge, 1985)

Cipolla, C., *Before the Industrial Revolution: European Society and Economy 1000–1700* (3rd edition; London, 1993)

Cook, M., *Muhammad* (Oxford, 1983)

Crone, P., *Slaves on Horses: The Evolution of the Islamic Polity* (Cambridge, 1980)

Crosby, A., *The Measure of Reality: Quantification and Western Society 1250–1600* (Cambridge, 1997)

Dien, A., *State and Society in Early Medieval China* (Stanford, 1990)

Eberhard, W., *Conquerors and Rulers: Social Forces in Medieval China* (Leiden, 1965)

Elvin, M., *The Pattern of the Chinese Past* (London, 1973)

Fernandez-Armesto, F., *Before Columbus: Exploration and Colonization from the Mediterranean to the Atlantic 1229–1492* (London, 1987)

Gimpel, J., *The Medieval Machine: The Industrial Revolution of the Middle Ages* (London, 1977)

Golas, P., 'The Sung Economy: How Big?', *Bulletin of Sung-Yüan Studies*, 1988, pp. 90–4

Haeger, J., *Crisis and Prosperity in Sung China* (Tucson, 1975)

Hall, K., *Maritime Trade and State Development in Early South-East Asia* (Honolulu, 1985)

Hartwell, R., 'Markets, Technology and the Structure of Enterprise in the Development of the Eleventh Century Chinese Iron and Steel Industry', *Journal of Economic History*, Vol. 26, 1966, pp. 29–58

——, 'Demographic, Political and Social Transformations of China 750–1550', Harvard Journal of Asiatic Studies, Vol. 42, 1982, pp. 365–442

Harvey, A., *Economic Expansion in the Byzantine Empire 900–1200* (Cambridge, 1989)

Hassan, A. and Hill, D., *Islamic Technology* (Cambridge, 1986)

Hodges, R., *Dark Age Economics: The Origins of Towns and Trade AD600–1000* (London, 1982)

Hodgson, M., *The Venture of Islam: Conscience and History in a World Civilization* (3 vols; Chicago, 1974)

Holt, P., *The Age of the Crusades: The Near East from the eleventh century to 1517* (London, 1986)

Hucker, C., *The Ming Dynasty: Its Origins and Evolving Institutions* (Ann Arbor, 1978)

Kaegi, W., *Byzantium and the Early Islamic Conquests* (Cambridge, 1992)

Kennedy, H., *The Prophet and the Age of the Caliphates: The Islamic Near East from the sixth to the eleventh century* (London, 1986)

Kwanten, L., *Imperial Nomads: A History of Central Asia 500–1500* (Leicester, 1979)

Lapidus, I., *A History of Islamic Societies* (Cambridge, 1988)

Lewis, A., 'Maritime Skills in the Indian Ocean 1368–1500', *Journal of the Economic and Social History of the Orient*, Vol. 16, 1973, pp. 238–64

Lewis, B., *Race and Slavery in the Middle East: An Historical Enquiry* (Oxford, 1990)

Lombard, M., *The Golden Age of Islam* (Amsterdam, 1975)

Lopez, R., *The Commercial Revolution of the Middle Ages 950–1350* (Cambridge, 1976)

Manz, B., *The Rise and Rule of Tamerlane* (Cambridge, 1989)

Moore, R., *The Formation of a Persecuting Society: Power and Deviance in Western Europe 950–1250* (Oxford, 1987)

Morgan, D., *The Mongols* (Oxford, 1987)

Needham, J., *Science and Civilization in China* (7 vols; Cambridge, 1954–)

——, *The Grand Titration: Science and Society in East and West* (London, 1969)

——, *Clerks and Craftsmen: Lectures and Addresses on the History of Science and Technology* (Cambridge, 1970)

——, *Gunpowder as the Fourth Estate, East and West* (Hong Kong, 1985)

Ostrowski, D., *Muscovy and the Mongols: Cross-Cultural Influences on the Steppe Frontier 1304–1589* (Cambridge, 1998)

Perry, J. and Smith, B., *Essays on T'ang Society: The Interplay of Social, Political and Economic Forces* (Leiden, 1976)

Pipes, D., *Slave Soldiers and Islam: The Genesis of a Military System* (New Haven, 1981)

Reynolds, S., *Fiefs and Vassals: The Medieval Evidence Re-interpreted* (Oxford, 1994)

Scammell, G., *The World Encompassed: The First European Maritime Empires c.800–1650* (London, 1981)

Shiba, Y., *Commerce and Society in Sung China* (Ann Arbor, 1970)

Sinor, D., *Inner Asia and its Contacts with Medieval Europe* (London, 1977)

Treadgold, W., *A History of the Byzantine State and Society* (Stanford, 1997)

Watson, A., *Agricultural Innovation in the Early Islamic World: the diffusion of crops and farming techniques 700–1100* (Cambridge, 1983)

White, L., *Medieval Technology and Social Change* (Oxford, 1962)

Willard, A., 'Gold, Islam and Camels: The Transformative Effects of Trade and Ideology', *Comparative Civilizations Review*, Vol. 28, 1993, pp. 80–105

Yamamura, K., *The Cambridge History of Japan*, Vol. 3, *Medieval Japan* (Cambridge, 1990)

Part Five: The World Balance

Archer, L., *Slavery and Other Forms of Unfree Labour* (London, 1988)

Attman, A., *The Bullion Flow Between Europe and the East 1000–1750* (Gothenburg [Göteborg], 1981)

——, *American Bullion in European World Trade 1600–1800* (Gothenburg [Göteborg], 1986)

Atwell, W., 'International Bullion Flows and the Chinese Economy c.1530–1650', *Past and Present*, 95, 1982, pp. 68–90

——, 'Some Observations on the "Seventeenth Century Crisis" in China and Japan', *Journal of Asian Studies*, Vol. 45, 1985–6, pp. 223–44

Baechler, J., Hall, J. and Mann, M., *Europe and the Rise of Capitalism* (Oxford, 1988)

Blackburn, R., *The Making of New World Slavery: From the Baroque to the Modern 1492–1800* (London, 1997)

Braudel, F., *The Mediterranean and the Mediterranean World in the Age of Philip II* (2 vols; London, 1972)

——, *Civilization and Capitalism 1400–1800* (3 vols; London 1974–84)

Brewer, J., *The Sinews of Power: War, Money and the English State 1688–1783* (London, 1989)

Chaudhuri, K., *Asia Before Europe: Economy and Civilization of the Indian Ocean from the Rise of Islam to 1750* (Cambridge, 1990)

Crosby, A., *The Columbian Exchange: Biological and Cultural Consequences of 1492* (Westport, 1972)

——, *Ecological Imperialism: The Biological Expansion of Europe 900–1900* (Cambridge, 1986)

Curtin, P., *The Rise and Fall of the Plantation Complex: Essays in Atlantic History* (Cambridge, 1990)

Das Gupta, A. and Pearson, M., *India and the Indian Ocean 1500–1800* (Calcutta, 1987)

de Vries, J., *European Urbanization 1500–1800* (Cambridge, 1984)

Downing, B., *The Military Revolution and Political Change: Origins of Democracy and Autocracy in Early Modern Europe* (Princeton, 1992)

Eisenstein, E., *The Printing Revolution in Early Modern Europe* (Cambridge, 1983)

Elliott, J., 'A Europe of Composite Monarchies', *Past and Present*, 137, 1992, pp. 48–71

Feuerwerker, A., 'Questions About China's Early Modern Economic History I Wish I Could Answer', *Journal of Asian Studies*, Vol. 51, 1992, pp. 757–69

Fletcher, J., 'Integrative History: Parallels and Interconnections in the Early Modern Period 1500–1800', *Journal of Turkish Studies*, Vol. 9, 1985, pp. 37–58

Frank, A., *World Accumulation 1492–1789* (London 1978)

Goldstone, J., 'East and West in the Seventeenth Century: Political Crisis in Stuart England, Ottoman Turkey and Ming China', *Comparative Studies in Society and History*, Vol. 30, 1988, pp. 103–42

Hall, J., *Powers and Liberties: the Causes and Consequences of the Rise of the West* (Oxford, 1985)

Hall, J., Keiji, N. and Yamamura, K., *Japan Before Tokugawa: Political Consolidation and Economic Growth 1500–1650* (Princeton, 1981)

Inalcik, H., *The Ottoman Empire: The Classical Age 1300–1600*, (London, 1973)

Inalcik, H. and Quataert, D., *An Economic and Social History of the Ottoman Empire 1300–1914* (Cambridge, 1994)

Islamoglu-Inan, H., *The Ottoman Empire and the World Economy* (Cambridge, 1987)

Israel, J., *Dutch Primacy in World Trade 1585–1740* (Oxford, 1989)

Jones, E., *The European Miracle: Environments, Economies and Geopolitics in the History of Europe and Asia* (Cambridge, 1981)

Kallgren, J., 'Food, Famine and the Chinese State: A Symposium', *Journal of Asian Studies*, Vol. 41, 1982, pp. 685–797

Karpat, K., *The Ottoman State and its Place in World History* (Leiden, 1974)

Kennedy, P., *The Rise and Fall of the Great Powers: Economic Change and Military Conflict from 1500 to 2000* (London, 1988)

Kunt, M. and Woodhead, C., *Suleyman the Magnificent and his Age: The Ottoman Empire in the Early Modern World* (London, 1995)

Levack, B., *The Witch-Hunt in Early Modern Europe* (London, 1987)

McNeill, W., *Europe's Steppe Frontier 1500–1800* (Chicago, 1964)

Naquin, S. and Rawski, E., *Chinese Society in the Eighteenth Century* (New Haven, 1987)

North, D. and Thomas, R., *The Rise of the Western World* (Cambridge, 1973)

Parker, G., *The Military Revolution: Military Innovation and the Rise of the West 1500–1800* (Cambridge, 1988)

Parker, G. and Smith, L., *The General Crisis of the Seventeenth Century* (London, 1978)

Patterson, O., *Slavery and Social Death: A Comparative Study* (Cambridge, 1982)

Perlin, F., 'Proto-Industrialization in Pre-Colonial South Asia', *Past and Present*, 98, 1983, pp. 30–95

Qaisar, A., *The Indian Response to European Technology and Culture 1498–1707* (Delhi, 1982)

Raychaudhuri, T. and Habib, I., *The Cambridge Economic History of India*, Vol. I, *c.1200–c.1750* (Cambridge, 1982)

Richards, J., *Precious Metals in the Later Medieval and Early Modern Worlds* (Durham, 1983)

——, *The New Cambridge History of India*, Vol. I:5, *The Mughal Empire* (Cambridge, 1993)

Shennan, J., *The Origins of the Modern European State 1450–1725* (London, 1974)

Smith, T., *The Agrarian Origins of Modern Japan* (Stanford, 1959)

——, 'Pre-Modern Economic Growth: Japan and the West', *Past and Present*, 60, 1973, pp. 127–60

Solow, B. and Engerman, S., *British Capitalism and Caribbean Slavery: The Legacy of Eric Williams* (Cambridge, 1987)

Spence, J. and Wills, J., *From Ming to Ch'ing: Conquest, Region and Continuity in Seventeenth Century China* (New Haven, 1979)

Steensgaard, N., *Carracks, Caravans and Companies: The Structural Crisis in the European-Asian Trade in the Early Seventeenth Century* (Odense, 1973)

Thornton, J., *Africa and Africans in the Making of the Atlantic World 1400–1680* (Cambridge, 1992)

Thornton, R., *American Indian Holocaust and Survival: A Population History* (Norman, 1987)

Tilly, C., *The Formation of National States in Western Europe* (Princeton, 1975)

——, 'War Making and State Making as Organized Crime', in Evans, P., Rueschemeyer, D. and Skocpol, T., *Bringing the State Back In* (Cambridge, 1985)

——, *Coercion, Capital and European States AD 990–1990* (Cambridge, 1990)

Toby, R., *State and Diplomacy in Early Modern Japan: Asia in the Development of the Tokugawa Bakufu* (Princeton, 1984)

Tracy, J., *The Rise of Merchant Empires: Long-Distance Trade in the Early Modern World 1350–1750* (Cambridge, 1990)

——, *The Political Economy of Merchant Empires* (Cambridge, 1991)

van Leur, J., *Indonesian Trade and Society: Essays in Asian Social and Economic History* (The Hague, 1955)

Wallerstein, I., *The Modern World System* (3 vols; New York, 1974–89)

Walter, J. and Schofield, R., *Famine, Disease and the Social Order in Early Modern Society* (Cambridge, 1989)

Walvin, J., *Questioning Slavery* (London, 1996)

Wolf, E., *Europe and the People Without History* (Berkeley, 1982)

Part Six: The Creation of the Modern World

Acton, E., *Rethinking the Russian Revolution* (London, 1990)

Albertini, R. von, *European Colonial Rule 1880–1940: The Impact of the West on India, South-east Asia and Africa* (Oxford, 1982)

Bailey, R., 'The Slave(ry) Trade and the Development of Capitalism in the United States: The Textile Industry in New England', *Social Science History*, Vol. 14, 1990, pp. 373–414

Bairoch, P., 'International Industrialization Levels from 1750 to 1980', *Journal of European Economic History*, Vol. 11, 1982, pp. 269–333

Bayly, C., *The New Cambridge History of India*, Vol II:1, *Indian Society and the Making of the British Empire* (Cambridge, 1988)

——, *Imperial Meridian: The British Empire and the World 1780–1830* (London, 1989)

Berry, B., *Comparative Urbanization: Divergent Paths in the Twentieth Century* (London, 1981)

Blinkhorn, M., *Fascists and Conservatives: The Radical Right and the Establishment in Twentieth Century Europe* (London, 1990)

Blum, J., *The End of the Old Order in Rural Europe* (Princeton, 1978)

Cameron, R., 'A New View of European Industrialization', *Economic History Review*, Vol. 38, 1985, pp. 1–23

Castles, S. and Miller, M., *The Age of Migration: International Population Movements in the Modern World* (London, 1993)

Clark, J., *The Political Economy of World Energy: A Twentieth-Century Perspective* (London, 1990)

Clarke, J., *Oriental Enlightenment: The Encounter Between Asia and Western Thought* (London, 1997)

Dicken P., *Global Shift: The Internationalization of Economic Activity* (London, 1992)

Duplessis, R., *Transitions to Capitalism in Early Modern Europe* (Cambridge, 1997)

Eatwell, R., *Fascism: A History* (London, 1995)

Fairbank, J., *The Chinese World Order: Traditional China's Foreign Relations* (Cambridge, 1968)

Feuerwerker, A., 'State and Economy in Late Imperial China', *Theory and Society*, Vol. 13, 1984, pp. 297–326

Fieldhouse, D., *The Colonial Empires: A Comparative Survey from the Eighteenth Century* (2nd edition; London, 1982)

Fogel, R., *Without Consent or Contract: The Rise and Fall of American Slavery* (3 vols; New York, 1989)

Fores, M., 'The Myth of a British Industrial Revolution', *History*, Vol. 66, 1981, pp. 181–98

Frederikson, G., *White Supremacy: A Comparative Study in American and South African History* (New York, 1981)

Hanley, S. and Yamamura, K., *Economic and Demographic Change in Pre-Industrial Japan 1600–1868* (Princeton, 1977)

Hanley, S., 'A High Standard of Living in Nineteenth Century Japan: Fact or Fantasy?', *Journal of Economic History*, Vol. 43, 1983, pp. 183–92

Harley, C., 'Ocean Freight Rates and Productivity 1740–1913: The Primacy of Mechanical Invention Reaffirmed', *Journal of Economic History*, Vol. 48, 1988, pp. 851–76

Headrick, D., *The Tools of Empire: Technology and European Imperialism in the Nineteenth Century* (Oxford, 1981)

——, *The Tentacles of Progress: Technology Transfer in the Age of Imperialism 1850–1940* (Oxford, 1988)

Higgonet, P., Landes, D. and Rosovsky, H., *Favorites of Fortune: Technology, Growth and Economic Development since the Industrial Revolution* (Cambridge, 1991)

Hillberg, R., *The Destruction of the European Jews* (Chicago, 1961)

Hirschfeld, G., *The Policies of Genocide: Jews and Soviet Prisoners of War in Nazi Germany* (London, 1986)

Holland, R., *European Decolonization 1918–81* (London, 1985)

Howe, C., *The Origins of Japanese Trade Supremacy: Development and Technology in Asia from 1540 to the Pacific War* (London, 1996)

Hudson, P., *The Industrial Revolution* (London, 1992)

Inikori, J., 'Slavery and the Revolution in Cotton Textile Production in England', *Social Science History*, Vol. 13, 1989, pp. 343–79

Jansen, M., *The Cambridge History of Japan*, Vol. 5, *The Nineteenth Century* (Cambridge, 1989)

Kemp, T., *Industrialization in Nineteenth Century Europe* (2nd edition; London, 1985)

Kolchin, P., *American Slavery 1619–1877* (New York, 1993)

Kuper, L., *Genocide: Its Political Use in the Twentieth Century* (London, 1981)

Landes, D., *The Unbound Prometheus: Technological Change and Industrial Development in Europe from 1750 to the Present* (Cambridge, 1969)

Licht, W., *Industrializing America: The Nineteenth Century* (Baltimore, 1995)

Maddison, A., 'A Comparison of Levels of GDP Per Capita in Developed and Developing Countries 1700–1980', *Journal of Economic History*, Vol. 43, 1983, pp. 27–41

——, *The World Economy in the Twentieth Century* (Paris, 1989)

Marshall, P., *The New Cambridge History of India*, Vol II: 2, *Bengal: The British Bridgehead. Eastern India 1740–1828* (Cambridge, 1987)

Mayer, A., *The Persistence of the Old Regime: Europe to the Great War* (London, 1981)

Moulder, F., *Japan, China and the Modern World Economy: Toward a reinterpretation of East Asian development c.1600–c.1918* (Cambridge, 1977)

Mukherjee, R., 'Trade and Empire in Awadh 1765–1804', *Past and Present*, 94, 1982, pp. 85–102

Ness, G. and Stahl, W., 'Western Imperialist Armies in Asia', *Comparative Studies in Society and History*, Vol. 19, 1977, pp. 2–29

O'Brien, P., 'European Economic Development: The Contribution of the Periphery', *Economic History Review*, Vol. 35, 1982, pp. 1–18

——, *Railways and the Economic Development of Western Europe 1830–1914* (London, 1983)

——, 'Do We Have a Typology for the Study of European Industrialization in the XIXth Century?', *Journal of European Economic History*, Vol. 15, 1986, pp. 291–333

Owen, R., *The Middle East in the World Economy 1800–1914* (London, 1981)

Pearson, R., *National Minorities in Eastern Europe 1848–1945* (London, 1983)

Ponting, C., *Progress and Barbarism: The World in the Twentieth Century* (London, 1998)

Smith, T., *Native Sources of Japanese Industrialization 1750–1920* (Berkeley, 1988)

Snooks, G., *Was the Industrial Revolution Necessary?* (London, 1994)

Sugiyama, S., *Japan's Industrialization in the World Economy 1859–1899* (London, 1988)

Suny, R., *The Revenge of the Past: Nationalism, Revolution and the Collapse of the Soviet Union* (Stanford, 1993)

Sylla, R. and Toniolo, G., *Patterns of European Industrialization: The Nineteenth Century* (London, 1991)

Thomas, B., 'Escaping from Constraints: The Industrial Revolution in a Malthusian Context', *Journal of Interdisciplinary History*, Vol. 15, 1984–85, pp. 729–53

Tilly, C., *Big Structures, Large Processes, Huge Comparisons* (New York, 1984)

——, *Popular Contention in Great Britain 1758–1834* (Cambridge, 1995)

Wakeman, F. and Grant, C., *Conflict and Control in Late Imperial China* (Berkeley, 1975)

Wrigley, E., *Continuity, Chance and Change: The Character of the Industrial Revolution in England* (Cambridge, 1988)

Yapp, M., *The Making of the Modern Near East 1792–1923* (London, 1987)

Index

Abahai, Jürchen leader 591
Abaqa, Il-khan 433, 440
Abaza Hasan Pasha 600
Abbas, Shah 546, 547
Abbasid caliphate 302, 335–9, 380, 394,
  399, 400, 433; slave soldiers 337–8
Abd al-Malik, caliph 303, 308
Abd al-Rahman ibn Muawiya, caliph
  336
Abd al-Rahman III, caliph 337
Abd-es-Salaam 543
Abdera (Adra), Spain 207
Abkhazia 710
Abner 213
Aborigines, Australian 40, 43, 701
Aboukir Bay, battle of (1798) 626
Abraham 303
Abu Bakr, caliph 306
Abu Hureyra, Syria 56, 57
Abu Simbel 167
Abydos, Egypt 92, 167
Acapulco, Mexico: silver shipments 519
Achaemenid (Iranian) empire 148, 188,
  206, 214–16, 221, 222, 223, 225, 251
Aceh, Malaysia 462; Sultanate of 522,
  523
Acheulian tools 32
acid rain 668, 818–19
Acolhua confederacy 125
Acre, Israel 398, 612; battle (1799) 705
Actium, battle of (31 BCE) 248
Adadnirari I, of the Assyrians 166
Adam 303
Adams, President John 690
Addis Ababa, Ethiopia 734, 804
Aden 357, 363, 522, 532
Adonis, cult of 218
Adowa, battle of (1896) 734
Adrianople, Thrace 310, 465, 466; battle
  (378) 289
Aegean 155, 166, 171–2, 178, 184, 209,
  224
Aegytopithecus 15
Aeschylus 172
Afghanistan 214, 395, 397, 398, 401,
  463, 630, 632, 684, 823; Balkh 335,
  429; Soviet invasion 842, 847; tin

deposits 101
Africa 11, 148–9, *404*, 847; agriculture
  66, 405, 789; AIDS 788; Chinese
  explorers 453–4; colonies 732–5, *736*,
  737, 824–5; education 826; European
  explorers 480; European traders
  515–16; hominids 16, 22–4, 28, 31;
  since independence 848, 859; Islam
  405–9; manioc 496; mining 825;
  Phoenician circumnavigation 209;
  population 732–3, 785, 789; railways
  825–6; slave trade 481–2, 503–6, 507,
  510, 513–15, 516–18, 530–1, 532,
  733, 734, 739; *see* South Africa *and
  specific countries*
Afrikaners 733–4
Aghlabid dynasty 337
Agincourt, battle of (1415) 473
Agra, India 548, 549; population (1600)
  549; Taj Mahal 630
agriculture 33–4, 51–3, *54*, 55–9; and
  chemicals 789–90, 817; European
  60–1 (Neolithic), 350, 351, 354,
  638–9 (1000–1300), 362–3 (15th
  century), 554–5 (16th century), 585,
  586–8 (17th century), 637, 640–3
  (18th century), 643, 661, 700, 701–2
  (19th century), 788–90, 791 (20th
  century); and technology 99–100, 178,
  189, 195, 366, 370–1, 639, 641, 646,
  789; *see specific countries*
Aguta 380
Ahhiyawa 166
Ahiram, King 212
Ahmad, Muhammad 676
Ahmadabad, India 548
Ahmed Jezzar Pasha 612
Ahmed Shah Abdali 632
Ahuitzotl, Aztec emperor 127
Ahur (deity) 215
AIDS 788
Ain Jalat, battle of (1260) 433
Ainu people 325, 392, 722
air warfare 751, 753, 754, 772
aircraft 751
aircraft carriers 772, 845
Aisha 308

881

Index

'pit-grave' ('Kurgan') culture 177–8
Pitcairn Island 47, 136
Pithekoussai, Ischia 219
Pizarro, Francisco 491, 501
plagues 470, 598, 664, 788; *see also*
Black Death
Plassey, battle of (1757) 682
plastics, production of 795
Plataea, battle of (479 BCE) 216
Plato 217, 220, 301; *Republic* 220
Pliny the Elder 253, 257
ploughs 99, 178, 366, 370, 646
pneumonia 786
P'o-hai, kingdom of 315
Podladsie, Ukraine 570
Podolya, Russia 610
Poitiers, battle of (733) 330; (1356) 473
Poland 423, 578, 579, 610, 618, 624,
710; Christianity 414; Jews 598, 777,
778; pollution 817; and Russia 624–5,
628, 839, 850; serfdom 599; Solidarity
852; after World War I 759–60, 764;
World War II 773, 782; *see also*
Poland-Lithuania
Poland-Lithuania 475, 476, 479, 569–71,
573, 597–8, 599
pollution 667–8, 788, 817–22, 858
Polo, Marco 380, 384, 387, 437, 461,
462
Polonnaruwa, Sri Lanka 394
Poltava, battle of (1709) 624
Polynesians 45, 47, 133–7, 488; writing
136
Pomerania 414
Pompeius 246, 248
Pondicherry, India 527, 679
Pontus 190, 239, 241, 247
Poor Law (1834) 670
porcelain, Chinese 531, 534
Port Arthur (Lü-shun), China 730, 753
Portugal 412, 475, 583, 611, 738;
African colonies 515–16, 733, 734,
735, 824, 846, 848; and Brazil 498,
502, 506–7, 694–5; dictatorship 763;
Empire 739; independence 595; and
Japan 552, 553; Jews 563, 77; opium
smuggling 714; ships 647; slave trade
481–2, 508, 512, 514; trade 518–19,
520, *521*, 522–3, 527, 528–9; *see also*
Iberian peninsula
potatoes 66, 496, 791
Potosí mines, Bolivia 502, 519
pottery 59, 61, 67, 98–9, 190; Aegean
171–2; Americas 110; 'Banderkeramik'
culture 61; 'bell beakers' 179; Chinese

63; Corinth 218; Iranian 407; Jomon
48, 52; Mycenaean 176; Polynesian
133; Sumerian 76, 77, 81; Ubaid 81;
see also porcelain
Poznan, bishopric of 414
Prague 415
Pratiharas, the 401
prehistoric cave paintings 38–40
primates 15–16
Primo de Rivera, General Miguel 763
printing 10, 374–5
Proconsul africanus 15–16
professions 671–2
Prophet, the *see* Muhammad, Prophet
prostitutes 417
Protestantism 541–2, 558, 560–1, 612;
and capitalism 6; and slavery 503; *see*
Calvin, John; Luther, Martin;
Reformation
Proto-Indo-European (PIE) 162, 163–4
Protocols of the Elders of Zion 777
Provence, France 330, 473, 586, 594
Prussia 410–11, 476, 615, 618, 624–5,
626, 628, 710, 744, 746; army 616,
748; education 671; and German
unification 745; serfdom 599, 643; *see*
also Franco-Prussian War
Psammetichus, client-king of Egypt 205
Pskov, Russia 479, 571
Ptolemy, ruler of Egypt 224
Ptolemy (astronomer) 301, 365, 368, 557
Puerto Rico 500, 740
Pulakeshin II 288
pulses 55
Punic Wars 242–3
Punjab, the 238, 287, 793, 829; Sikhs
632, 684, 688
Pure Land school (Buddhism) 320, 461
Puteoli: treatment of slaves 245
Pydna, battle of (168 BCE) 243
Pylos 173, 175
Pyongyang, Korea 389
pyramids: Egyptian 93–4, 100, 170;
Maya 119; Toltec 121
Pyrenees, France 38; Treaty (1659)
566
Pyrrhus, ruler of Epirus 242
Pythagoras 274

Qadisiya, battle of (637) 306
Qafzeh cave, the Levant: hominid 22
Qajars, the 611, 612, 827
Qara-Balghasun 323, 341
Qaramani family 705
Qaraqanid state 397